UNITED KINGDOM

G.R. Hidderley, University of Central England, Birmingham

Jonathan Liebenau, London School of Economics and Political Science

UNITED STATES OF AMERICA

Kimberly Cass, Marquette University

P.C. Chu, Ohio State University, Columbus

Frank S. Davis, Jr, Bloomsburg University

William DeLone, American University

Vasant Dhar, New York University

Robert A. Fleck, Jr., Columbus College

Jeet Gupta, Ball State University

Vijay Gurbaxani, University of California, Irvine

Bart Hodge, Virginia Commonwealth University

Rob Kauffman, University of Rochester

Rob Kling, University of California, Irvine

Roger Letts, Fairleigh Dickinson University

Jane Mackay, Texas Christian University

Efrem G. Mallach, University of Lowell

Richard O. Mason, Southern Methodist University

Khris McAlister, University of Alabama, Birmingham

Sheizaf Rafaeli, University of Michigan

Brian Reithel, University of Mississippi

James Riha, Northern Illinois University

Edward M. Roche, Seton Hall University

Naveed Saleem, University of Houston, Clear Lake

Cort Schlichting, Spring Hill College

Ivan J. Singer, University of Hartford

Jill Y. Smith, University of Denver

William H. Starbuck, New York University

Kathy Stevens, Merrimack College

Dennis Strouble, Bowling Green State University

E. Burton Swanson, University of California, Los Angeles

Bernadette Szajna, Texas Christian University

Kranti Toraskar, Penn State University

Duane Truex, State University of New York, Binghamton

Patrick J. Walsh, State University of New York, Binghamton

Diane Walz, University of Texas, San Antonio

About the Authors of

Management Information Systems:
Organization and Technology

Kenneth C. Laudon is Professor of Information Systems at New York University's Stern School of Business. He holds a B.A. in Economics from Stanford and a Ph.D. from Columbia University. He has authored nine books dealing with information systems, organizations, and society. Professor Laudon has also written over forty articles concerned with the social, organizational, and management impacts of information systems, privacy, ethics, and multimedia technology.

Professor Laudon's current research is on the planning and management of large-scale information systems for the 1990s and multimedia information technology. He has received grants from the National Science Foundation to study the evolution of national information systems at the Social Security Administration, the IRS, and the FBI. A part of this research is concerned with computer-related organizational and occupational changes in large organizations, changes in management ideology, changes in public policy, and understanding productivity change in the knowledge sector. Ken Laudon is the Director of the Stern School Virtual Multimedia Facility.

Ken Laudon has testified as an expert before the United States Congress. He has been a researcher and consultant to the Office of Technology Assessment (United States Congress) since 1978, and to the Office of the President, several executive branch agencies, and Congressional Committees. Professor Laudon also acts as a consultant on systems planning and strategy to several Fortune 500 firms.

Ken Laudon's hobby is sailing.

Jane Price Laudon is a management consultant in the information systems area and the author of seven books. Her special interests include systems analysis, data management, MIS auditing, software evaluation, and teaching business professionals how to design and use information systems.

Jane received her Ph.D. from Columbia University, her M.A. from Harvard University, and her B.A. from Barnard College. She has taught at Columbia University and the New York University Graduate School of Business. She maintains a lifelong interest in Oriental languages and civilizations.

The Laudons have two daughters, Erica and Elisabeth.

Management Information Systems: Organization and Technology reflects a deep understanding of MIS research and teaching as well as practical experience designing and building real world systems.

3RD EDITION

Management Information Systems

Organization and Technology

Kenneth C. Laudon
New York University

Jane Price Laudon
Azimuth Corporation

PRENTICE HALL, Upper Saddle River, New Jersey 07458

Library of Congress Cataloging in Publication Data
Laudon, Kenneth C.
    Management information systems: organization and technology
    Kenneth C. Laudon, Jane Price Laudon. - 3rd ed.
        p.   cm.
    Includes indexes.
    ISBN 0-02-368121-7
    1. Management information systems. I. Laudon, Jane Price.
II. Title.
T58.6.L376   1994
658.4'038--dc20   93-1557
                                                             CIP

Editor: Charles E. Stewart, Jr.
Developmental Editor: Nancy Perry
Production Supervisor: John Travis
Production Manager: Paul Smolenski
Art Director: Patricia Smythe
Text Designer: A Good Thing Inc.
Cover Designer: A Good Thing Inc.
Photo Editor: Chris Migdol
Photo Researcher: Dallas Chang
Illustrations: A Good Thing Inc.

Cover illustration: Matisse, Henri. *Memory of Oceania*
[Souvenir d'Oceanie]. Nice, summer 1952-early 1953.
Gouache and crayon on cut-and-pasted paper over canvas,
9'4" x 9'4 7/8". The Museum of Modern Art, New York.
Mrs. Simon Guggenheim Fund. Photograph © 1993
The Museum of Modern Art, New York.

This book was set in Sabon by Carlisle Communications.

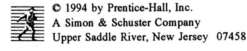

© 1994 by Prentice-Hall, Inc.
A Simon & Schuster Company
Upper Saddle River, New Jersey 07458

Printed in the United States of America
10 9 8 7 6 5 4

ISBN 0-02-368121-7

Prentice-Hall International (UK) Limited, *London*
Prentice-Hall of Australia Pty. Limited, *Sydney*
Prentice-Hall Canada Inc., *Toronto*
Prentice-Hall Hispanoamericana, S.A., *Mexico*
Prentice-Hall of India Private Limited, *New Delhi*
Prentice-Hall of Japan, Inc., *Tokyo*
Simon & Schuster Asia Pte. Ltd., *Singapore*
Editora Prentice-Hall do Brasil, Ltda., *Rio de Janeiro*

3RD EDITION

Management Information Systems

Organization and Technology

Kenneth C. Laudon
New York University

Jane Price Laudon
Azimuth Corporation

PRENTICE HALL, Upper Saddle River, New Jersey 07458

Library of Congress Cataloging in Publication Data
Laudon, Kenneth C.
   Management information systems: organization and technology
Kenneth C. Laudon, Jane Price Laudon. - 3rd ed.
    p. cm.
Includes indexes.
ISBN 0-02-368121-7
  1. Management information systems. I. Laudon, Jane Price.
II. Title.
T58.6.L376   1994
658.4'038--dc20   93-1557
                                               CIP

Editor: Charles E. Stewart, Jr.
Developmental Editor: Nancy Perry
Production Supervisor: John Travis
Production Manager: Paul Smolenski
Art Director: Patricia Smythe
Text Designer: A Good Thing Inc.
Cover Designer: A Good Thing Inc.
Photo Editor: Chris Migdol
Photo Researcher: Dallas Chang
Illustrations: A Good Thing Inc.

Cover illustration: Matisse, Henri. *Memory of Oceania*
[Souvenir d'Oceanie]. Nice, summer 1952-early 1953.
Gouache and crayon on cut-and-pasted paper over canvas,
9'4" x 9'4 7/8". The Museum of Modern Art, New York.
Mrs. Simon Guggenheim Fund. Photograph © 1993
The Museum of Modern Art, New York.

Photo credits are on pp. P1-P2, following the index, which
constitute a continuation of this copyright page.

This book was set in Sabon by Carlisle Communications.

© 1994 by Prentice-Hall, Inc.
A Simon & Schuster Company
Upper Saddle River, New Jersey 07458

Printed in the United States of America
10 9 8 7 6 5 4

ISBN 0-02-368121-7

Prentice-Hall International (UK) Limited, *London*
Prentice-Hall of Australia Pty. Limited, *Sydney*
Prentice-Hall Canada Inc., *Toronto*
Prentice-Hall Hispanoamericana, S.A., *Mexico*
Prentice-Hall of India Private Limited, *New Delhi*
Prentice-Hall of Japan, Inc., *Tokyo*
Simon & Schuster Asia Pte. Ltd., *Singapore*
Editora Prentice-Hall do Brasil, Ltda., *Rio de Janeiro*

Dedicated to *Erica and Elisabeth*

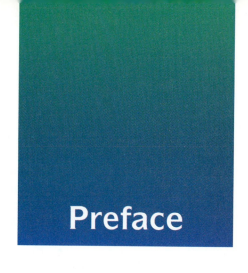

Preface

Management Information Systems: Organization and Technology (Third Edition) is based on the premise that professional managers in both the private and public sectors cannot afford to ignore information systems. In today's business environment, professional managers must learn how to use information technology to create competitive firms, manage global corporations, and provide useful products and services to customers. Information systems have become so vital to the management, organization, operation, and the products of large organizations that they are too important to be left to technicians. A few years ago, this statement was not true. Briefly, it is difficult—if not impossible—to manage a modern organization without at least some grounding in the fundamentals of what information systems are and how they affect the organization and its employees.

Accordingly, this book has been written for nontechnical undergraduate and MBA students in finance, accounting, management, and the liberal arts who will find a knowledge of information systems vital for their professional success. This book may also serve as a first course for students who subsequently major in information systems at either the undergraduate or graduate level. We have made every effort here to provide a comprehensive and current survey of research and literature on organizations and systems presented in a highly readable style.

The Contemporary Environment

The book reflects major trends in the business environment of the 1990s. Three related trends are apparent. The globalization of markets puts new emphasis on organizational design and management control. When your parts originate in Korea, your assembly occurs in Mexico, and your finance, marketing, and general counsel are in New York, then you know you face tough challenges in designing the proper organization and managing the work.

Second, the transformation of the American and other advanced industrial economies into full-fledged knowledge and information economies puts new emphasis on time-based competition, productivity of knowledge workers, short product life cycles, and employee training. When 70% of the gross national product is an output of the information sector, then the productivity of information workers is a central societal concern. When your firm's future depends on having a new product in the marketplace in nine months, then you face a difficult challenge as a manager in speeding up the work of engineers and other knowledge workers. The demand for information, for communications, has never been so great.

Third, the development of powerful microprocessors and telecommunications networks has brought forth a new information architecture based on powerful desktop computers and communications networks. We can now put what used to be called a mainframe computer on every desktop, and we can now design organizations in which every desktop and information worker can be part of the firm's information network. A few years ago this was a dream.

These changes in demand and technical capacity have brought about a change in the role and conception of information, from that of a nuisance to that of a strategic resource. The work of an organization—and its employees—depends increasingly on what its information systems are capable of doing. Increasing market share, becoming the high-quality or low-cost producer, developing new products, and increasing employee productivity, depend more and more on the kinds and quality of information systems in the organization.

One result of these trends is a change in the role of the modern manager. Today's managers are not only expected to use systems but are also expected to:

- Know how to use information technology to design competitive and efficient organizations.
- Understand the business and system requirements of a global environment.
- Use information systems to ensure quality throughout the firm.
- Participate in the design of a firm's information architecture and systems.
- Manage the procurement of a variety of information technologies.
- Choose among alternative telecommunications options.
- Manage and control the influence of systems on employees and customers.
- Allocate resources to competing system alternatives.
- Suggest new uses for systems.
- Understand the ethical dilemmas and controversies that surround the use of advanced information systems.

In essence, contemporary managers are expected to know enough about information technology to use it in the design and management of their organizations. These new management responsibilities require a deeper understanding of information technology and systems than ever before. Although this book primarily deals with private organizations, public sector managers are no less susceptible to these trends and changes in management and organization.

Features of This Text

This book makes a large stylistic departure from other texts in the field. The emphasis is always on the real world, on real business firms, and on the people who manage and work in them. We believe that students can appreciate and understand information systems concepts more easily if they see their relevance to real-world events and if systems are presented in a framework that they can immediately use in problem-solving and analysis. The following design features reflect these beliefs:

- **An integrated framework for describing and analyzing information systems.** An integrated framework portrays information systems as being composed of management, organization and technology elements. This framework is used throughout the text to describe and analyze information systems and information system problems. A special diagram accompanying each chapter-opening vignette graphically illustrates how management, organization, and technology elements work together to create an information system solution to the business challenges discussed in the vignette. The diagram can be used as a starting point to analyze any information system problem.

- **WINDOW ON Boxes:** Each chapter contains three WINDOW ON boxes (WINDOW ON MANAGEMENT, WINDOW ON ORGANIZATIONS, WINDOW ON TECHNOLOGY) that present real-world examples illustrating the management, organization, and technology issues in the chapter. Each WINDOW ON box concludes with a section called *To Think About* which consists of a question or series of questions for students to apply chapter concepts to management problem solving. The themes for each box are:

 WINDOW ON MANAGEMENT: Management problems raised by systems and their solution; management strategies and plans; careers and experiences of managers using systems.

 WINDOW ON TECHNOLOGY: Hardware, software, telecommunications, data storage, standards, and systems-building methodologies.

 WINDOW ON ORGANIZATIONS: Activities of private and public organizations using information systems; experiences of people working with systems.

- **Real-world examples:** Real-world examples drawn from business and public organizations are used throughout to illustrate text concepts and to supply material for the Window On boxes and case studies. Each chapter opens with a vignette illustrating the themes of the chapter by showing how a real-world organization meets a business challenge using information systems. More than 100 companies in the United States and over 100 organizations in Canada, Europe, Australia, and Asia are discussed (see the Organization and International Organization indexes.)

- **Management Challenges Section.** Each chapter concludes with a description of major challenges relating to the chapter topic that managers are likely to encounter. These challenges are multifaceted and sometimes pose dilemmas. They make excellent springboards for class discussion. Some of these Management Challenges are the organizational obstacles to building a database environment, determining the right level of integration between different types of systems, and building robust systems that can anticipate the organization's future information requirements.

- **Chapter Cases:** Each chapter concludes with a case study based on a real-world organization. These cases help students synthesize chapter concepts and apply this new knowledge to real-world problems and scenarios.

- **Major Case Studies:** At the end of each part, there are major case studies of well-known firms and organizations: Chrysler and General Motors, Keyport Life Insurance, First Fidelity BankCorp., EPRINET, and the Social Security Administration. These part-ending case studies integrate the major themes of each section. These cases can be used for class discussion or term projects.

- **International Case Studies:** Six cases of businesses and organizations in Europe, Canada, and Australia conclude the text. These cases have been provided by leading international experts in MIS: Andrew Boynton, International Institute for Management Development (Switzerland); Len Fertuck, University of Toronto (Canada); Helmut Krcmar and Bettina Schwarzer, Hohenheim University (Germany); Tapio Reponen, Turku School of Economics and Business Administration (Finland); Alan Underwood, Queensland University of Technology (Australia); and Peter Weill and Joel B. Barolsky, University of Melbourne (Australia).

Overview of This Book

The four parts of the book are designed to be relatively independent of each other. Each instructor may choose to emphasize different parts.

Part One is concerned with the organizational foundations of systems and their emerging strategic role. It provides an extensive introduction to real-world systems, focusing on how they are related to organizations and to management. This section is important for understanding the larger environment in which systems operate and for showing students how systems relate to organizational design, strategy, and operations.

Part Two provides the technical foundation for understanding information systems, describing hardware, software, storage, and telecommunications technologies. For students who come to class with knowledge of computer hardware and software from previous courses, Chapters 6 and 7 may be skipped. Students who are less well-prepared in database concepts and telecommunications will find the chapters on these topics helpful. Chapter 10 concludes the section by describing connectivity, standards, and the challenge of making all of the information technologies work together in a new information architecture based on enterprise-wide networks.

Part Three focuses on the process of redesigning organizations using information systems. Because information systems and organizations are so closely intertwined, we see systems analysis and design as an exercise in organizational design, one that requires great sensitivity to the right tools and techniques, quality assurance and change management. Example systems analysis and design exercises are included at the end of Chapter 13.

Part Four describes the role of information systems in capturing and distributing organizational knowledge and intelligence and in enhancing management decision-making. It shows how knowledge creation and distribution, workgroup collaboration, and individual and group decision making can be supported by knowledge work systems, decision support systems, and executive support systems. Organizational performance can also be enhanced by carefully chosen artificial intelligence applications.

Part Five concludes the text by examining the special management challenges and opportunities created by the pervasiveness and power of contemporary information systems: ensuring security and control, developing global systems, and coping with the ethical and social impact of information systems. Throughout the text emphasis is placed on using information technology to redesign the organization's products, services, procedures, jobs and management structures, with numerous examples drawn from multinational systems and global business environments.

CHAPTER OUTLINE

Each chapter contains the following:

- A detailed outline at the beginning to provide an overview.
- An opening vignette describing a real-world organization to establish the theme and importance of the chapter.
- A diagram analyzing the opening vignette in terms of the management, organization, and technology model used throughout the text.
- A list of learning objectives.
- Marginal glosses of key terms in the text.
- Management challenges.
- A chapter summary keyed to the learning objectives.
- A list of key terms that the student can use to review concepts.
- Review questions for students to test their comprehension of chapter material.

- A set of discussion questions that can be used for class discussion or for research topics.
- A group project to develop teamwork and presentation skills.
- A chapter-ending case study that illustrates important themes.
- A list of references for further research on topics.

What's New in the Third Edition?

Five years ago when the first edition was published, the predominant issues in the field were microcomputers, end-user computing, and how to manage the decentralization of information and computing power. In the second edition the predominant issues were using information technology to design competitive organizations, the business value of investment in information technology, telecommunications, networking and standards, and how to create a seamless information architecture for the firm in a global environment.

While these are still powerful themes, other issues have emerged. The growing internationalization of business and the movement toward knowledge-based economies require that managers understand how to deploy information systems internationally and how to promote productivity through knowledge work systems. Heightened concern over quality and quality-based competition call for knowledge of how information systems can promote quality throughout the firm and how to enhance the quality of information systems themselves. It is obvious that information systems have become a pervasive and powerful force in daily life. Managers in charge of these systems have a special responsibility for ensuring that they are used in an ethically and socially responsible manner. To reflect these new themes, the third edition of this book has been totally recrafted in style and substance. An extensive effort was made to incorporate new research findings, real-world examples, and many new features. These new features include:

1. **Four entirely new chapters:** Four entirely new chapters reflect these new themes: Managing International Information Systems (Chapter 19); Ethical and Social Issues in Information Systems (Chapter 20); Ensuring Quality with Information Systems (Chapter 13); and Knowledge and Information Work Systems (Chapter 15).

2. **Coverage of new leading-edge topics.** Entirely new sections have been added to ensure up-to-date coverage of the following topics:

   - Re-engineering and business process redesign (redesigning organizations with information systems)
   - Justifying the business value of information systems
   - Outsourcing
   - Multimedia
   - Object-oriented systems development
   - Object-oriented and multimedia databases
   - Fuzzy logic
   - Microeconomic and behavioral theories describing the relationship of information systems and organizations
   - Networked "task force" organizations
   - Workflow management
   - Information systems and productivity

   The third edition also expands coverage of collaborative work and groupware, group decision support systems, imaging, executive support systems, the strategic impact of information systems, and enterprise networking in a global business environment. All chapters have been thoroughly revised and updated to include the most current topics and research findings, as well as new real-world examples for WINDOW ON boxes, vignettes, and case studies.

3. **A truly international perspective:** An entire chapter is devoted to Managing International Information Systems. All of the other chapters are illustrated with real-world examples from one hundred corporations in Europe, Asia, Latin America, Australia, and the Middle East. Each chapter contains at least one WINDOW ON box, case study, or opening vignette drawn from a non-U.S. firm, and often more. The text concludes with six major international case studies contributed by leading MIS experts in Canada, Europe, and Australia.

4. **Ethics and social impacts treated throughout.** An in-depth new chapter provides a comprehensive discussion of the leading social and ethical issues which surround the use of information systems. In addition, ethical and social impact issues are treated through illustrations, WINDOW ON boxes, vignettes, and cases throughout the text.

5. **More activist pedagogy to teach management problem-solving.** This edition adds to the pedagogical strengths of earlier editions by putting more emphasis on having students actively learn and engage in management problem-solving.

    Group projects: At the end of each chapter is a group project that encourages students to develop teamwork and oral and written presentation skills. The group project exercise asks students to work in groups of three or four to research a specific topic, analyze the pros and cons of an issue, write about it, and orally present the group's findings to the class. For instance, students might be asked to work in small groups to analyze a business and to suggest appropriate strategic information systems for that particular business or to develop a corporate ethics code on privacy that considers E-mail privacy and employers' use of information systems to monitor work sites.

    To Think About questions, concluding every WINDOW ON box, require students to apply chapter concepts to real-world scenarios. These questions frequently ask students to assume the role of managers, use multiple perspectives, consider different alternatives, and think creatively. The questions can be used for class discussion or for short written projects.

    Case studies: Management problem-solving opportunities are also provided by the case studies for every chapter and part, and by the six international case studies concluding the text.

Instructional Support Materials

SOFTWARE

A series of optional management software cases called *Solve it! Management Problem Solving with PC Software* has been developed to support the text. *Solve it!* consists of 10 spreadsheet and 10 database cases drawn from real-world businesses, plus a data diskette with the files required by the cases. The cases are graduated in difficulty. The case book contains complete tutorial documentation showing how to use spreadsheet and database software to solve the problems. A new version of *Solve it!* with all new cases is published every year. *Solve it!* can be purchased directly from the supplier, Azimuth Corporation, 124 Penfield Ave., Croton-on-Hudson, New York 10520 (Telephone 914-271-6321).

MULTIMEDIA MANUAL: INSTRUCTOR'S/LECTURE MANUAL, VIDEO GUIDE, TEST BANK, TRANSPARENCY MASTERS

Written by Ken and Jane Laudon and Marshall R. Kaplan, has been fully revised and now includes lecture outlines as well as answers to review questions, discussion questions, group project exercises, case study questions, video cases, and To Think About questions. The Test Bank has been expanded to include of 25 true-false questions, 25 multiple choice questions, and 25 fill in the blank questions for each chapter. The MULTIMEDIA Manual also contains transparency masters.

VIDEO CASES

Five video cases based on the real-world corporations and organizations used in the text are available to adopters. The five video cases illustrate the concepts in each section and can be used for class discussion or written projects. The video cases are analyzed in the Instructor's Resource Manual.

INSTRUCTOR'S RESOURCE MANUAL ON DISK

The Instructor's Resource Manual is available, on disk, to any adopters wishing to put it on their computers.

COMPUTERIZED TEST BANK

All test bank questions are available in computerized form.

TRANSPARENCY ACETATES

A set of 100 full-color transparency acetates is available to illuminate key concepts.

Acknowledgments

The production of any book involves many valuable contributions from a number of persons. We would like to thank in particular our editors at Macmillan for encouragement, insight, and strong support for many years. We are grateful to Charles Stewart for his energy, enthusiasm, and insight in guiding the preparation of the third edition and earlier editions of this text. Nancy Perry directed the extensive developmental work for this edition. We deeply appreciate her dedication and tenacity. We commend Paul Smolenski, John Travis, and the Macmillan Production Department for guiding the production of the third edition under a very ambitious schedule. We thank Patricia Smythe for directing the beautiful design.

We are deeply indebted to Marshall R. Kaplan for his invaluable assistance in the writing of Chapters 13, 15, and 16 and for his work on the Instructor's Resource Manual. Rachel Bunin and Marjorie Singer Anderson provided excellent additional developmental resources.

The Stern School of Business at New York University and the Information Systems Department provided a very special learning environment, one in which we and others could rethink the MIS field. Special thanks to Vasant Dhar, Robert Kauffman, and Stephen Slade for providing critical feedback and support where deserved. Professor Norm White was especially helpful in commenting on the technical chapters in Part Two, and we thank him. Professor William H. Starbuck of the Management Department at NYU provided valuable comments and insights.

Professor Al Croker of Baruch College and NYU, Professor Kenneth Marr of Hofstra University, Professor Edward Roche of Seton Hall University, Jiri Rodovsky, and Russell Polo provided additional suggestions for improvement.

We are truly grateful to our colleagues in the MIS field who shared their expertise and comments with us. We want to thank Joel Barolsky, Andrew Boynton, Len Fertuck, Helmut Krcmar, Tapio Reponen, Bettina Schwarzer, Alan Underwood, and Peter Weill for contributing case studies. They deeply enrich the text.

One of our goals in the third edition was to continue writing a book which was comprehensive, synthesized diverse views in the MIS literature, and helped define a common academic field. A large number of leading scholars in the field were contacted and assisted us in this effort. Reviewers and consultants for the second and third editions took considerable time and care to examine individual chapters as specialists and the entire manuscript as instructors in the MIS course. Insofar as possible we have tried to incorporate their ideas in the text. We deeply appreciate their work and their suggestions for improving this text. These consultants are listed in the front endpapers of the book. It is our hope that this group endeavor contributes to a shared vision and understanding of the MIS field.

K. C. L.
J. P. L.

Brief Table of Contents

Contents

Windows On MIS

ONE

Organizational Foundations of Information Systems

Contemporary information systems are both technical and social in nature. Managers must understand the relationship between the technical components of an information system and the structure, functions, and politics of organizations. Information systems must be responsive to the objectives of management and to an organization's decision-making processes. Part One places information systems in the context of organizations and highlights their strategic role.

Chapter 1 introduces the concept of an information system and illustrates the critical role that information systems play in organizations. Information systems literacy embraces both technical and behavioral perspectives, emphasizing awareness of the managerial, organizational, and technological dimensions of information systems. Information systems pose five key challenges to today's managers: the strategic business challenge; the globalization challenge; the information architecture challenge; the information systems investment challenge; and the responsibility and control challenge.

Chapter 2 provides realistic examples of the six major types of information systems in contemporary organizations: transaction processing systems, knowledge work/office automation systems, management information systems, decision-support systems, and executive support systems. These systems serve various purposes, supporting different organizational levels and functions.

Chapter 3 highlights how businesses can use information systems to gain a competitive advantage. Strategic information systems have transformed organizations' products and services; marketing strategies; relationships with customers and suppliers; and internal operations. To use information systems strategically, organizations have to undergo both technical and social change.

Chapter 4 explores the relationship between information systems and organizations. Information systems are shaped by organizational structure, culture, political processes, and management, but information technology can influence organizations as well. The chapter uses both economic and behavioral theories to explain how information systems have affected organizations.

Chapter 5 examines how information systems can support management decision making. It describes how managers actually make decisions, and discusses the different levels, types, and stages of decision making. The chapter compares individual and organizational models of decision making and shows how information systems should be designed to support managerial decision making.

Part One Case Study: Chrysler and GM: Can Information Technology Save the U.S. Auto Industry? This case illustrates how two giant American corporations, Chrysler and General Motors, have tried to use information technology to combat foreign and domestic competitors. The case explores the relationship between each firm's management strategy, organizational characteristics, and information systems. It poses the following question: To what extent can information technology solve the problems confronting the U.S. automobile industry?

The Challenge of Information Systems

UPS Competes Globally with Information Technology

United Parcel Service, the world's largest air and ground package distribution company, started out in 1907 in a closet-sized basement office. Jim Casey and Claude Ryan—two teenagers from Seattle with two bicycles and one phone—promised the "best service and lowest rates." UPS has used this formula successfully for nearly 90 years.

UPS still lives up to that promise today, delivering close to 3 billion parcels and documents each year to any address in the United States and to more than 180 countries and territories. The company not only excels at traditional package delivery but is competing against Federal Express in the overnight delivery business as well. Critical to the firm's success has been its investment in advanced information technology. Between 1992 and 1996, UPS expects to invest $3.2 billion on information technology that will keep it a worldwide market leader. Technology has helped UPS boost customer service while streamlining its overall operations.

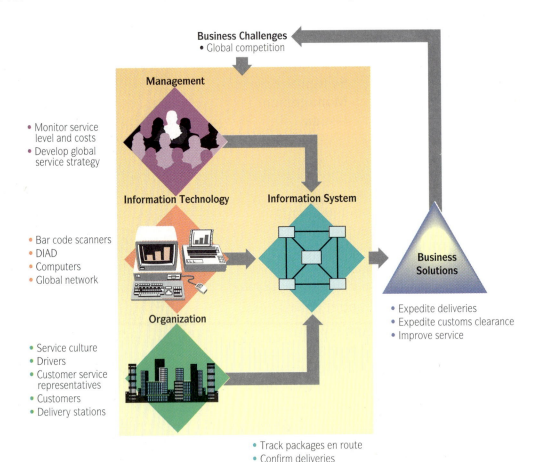

Business Challenges
- Global competition

Management
- Monitor service level and costs
- Develop global service strategy

Information Technology
- Bar code scanners
- DIAD
- Computers
- Global network

Organization
- Service culture
- Drivers
- Customer service representatives
- Customers
- Delivery stations

Information System

Business Solutions
- Expedite deliveries
- Expedite customs clearance
- Improve service

- Track packages en route
- Confirm deliveries
- Provide customs clearance documents
- Generate bills

Using a handheld Delivery Information Acquisition Device (DIAD), UPS drivers automatically capture customers' signatures along with pickup, delivery, and timecard information. The drivers then transmit this information to UPS's computer network, where it is stored in UPS's Delivery Information Automated Lookup System (DIALS). If retrieved, the information can provide proof of delivery to the customer. The system can also generate a printed response to queries for the customer.

With its Package Tracking System (PTS), UPS can monitor packages throughout the delivery process. At various points along the route from sender to receiver, a bar code device scans shipping information on the package label; the information is then fed into a central computer. Customer service representatives can check the status of any package from desktop computers linked to the central computer and are able to respond immediately to inquiries from customers.

UPS's Inventory Express, launched in 1991, warehouses customers' products and ships them overnight to any destination the customer requests. Customers using this service can transmit electronic shipping orders to UPS by 1:00 A.M. and expect delivery by 10:30 that same morning.

In 1988, UPS moved aggressively into overseas markets and set up its own global communications network, UPSnet, as the information processing pipeline for worldwide operations. UPSnet extends the system's capabilities internationally by providing access to information for billing and delivery confirmation, tracking international shipments, and expediting customs clearance. UPS uses its network to transmit documentation electronically on each shipment directly to customs officials prior to the arrival of shipments. The customs officials clear the shipment or flag it for inspection. Partly because of these advanced systems, UPS has been much more successful than its rivals in Europe.

Sources: Linda Wilson, ''Stand and Deliver,'' *InformationWEEK* (November 23, 1992) and *UPS Public Relations,* ''High Tech Advances Lead UPS into the Paperless Age'' (April 1992).

Ups's reliance on information technology to drive its business illustrates the essential role that information systems have come to play in organizations and industries. The company's successes demonstrate how information systems can help businesses compete in today's global business environment.

Like UPS, most organizations will need information systems to survive and prosper. This chapter starts our investigation of information systems and organizations by explaining what an information system is and describing its management, organization, and technology dimensions.

After completing this chapter, you will be able to:

- Define an information system.
- Explain the difference between computer literacy and information systems literacy.

- Describe the information needs of different organizational levels.
- Explain why information systems are so important today.
- Identify the major conceptual approaches to information systems.
- Identify the major management challenges to building and using information systems in organizations.

1.1 Why Information Systems?

Until the 1980s, there was little need for this textbook or course. Managers generally did not need to know much about how information was collected, processed, and distributed in their organizations, and the technology involved was minimal. Information itself was not considered an important asset for the firm. In most organizations, information was viewed as an unfortunate, costly by-product of doing business—simply "red tape." The management process was considered a face-to-face, personal art and not a far-flung, global coordination process. But today few managers can afford to ignore how information is handled by their organization.

The Competitive Business Environment of the 1990s

Two very powerful worldwide changes have altered the environment of business. The first change is the emergence and strengthening of the global economy. The second change is the transformation of industrial economies and societies into knowledge- and information-based service economies. These changes in the business environment and climate, summarized in Table 1.1, pose a number of new challenges to business firms and their management.

EMERGENCE OF THE
GLOBAL ECONOMY

A growing percentage of the American economy—and other advanced industrial economies in Europe and Asia—depends on imports and exports. Foreign trade—both exports and imports—accounts for a little over 25 percent of the goods and services produced in the United States, and even more in countries like Japan and Germany. This percentage will grow in the future. The success of firms in the 1990s depends on their ability to operate globally.

Globalization of the world's industrial economies greatly enhances the value of information to the firm and offers new opportunities to businesses. Today,

Table 1.1 THE CHANGING BUSINESS ENVIRONMENT OF THE 1990s

Globalization
- Management and control in a global marketplace
- Competition in world markets
- Global work groups
- Global delivery systems

Transformation of Industrial Economies
- Knowledge- and information-based economies
- Productivity
- New products and services
- Leadership
- Time-based competition
- Shorter product life
- Turbulent environment
- Limited employee knowledge base

information systems provide the communication and analytic power that firms need for conducting trade and managing businesses on a global scale. To provide worldwide package delivery service, for instance, companies like UPS must develop global information systems that can trace specific packages, analyze information on package flow and costs, operate 24 hours a day in different national environments, and service local as well as international management reporting needs. In short, controlling the far-flung global corporation is a major business challenge that requires powerful information system responses.

Globalization and information technology also bring new threats to domestic business firms: Because of global communication and management systems, customers now can shop in a worldwide marketplace, obtaining price and quality information reliably, 24 hours a day. This phenomenon heightens competition and forces firms to play in open, unprotected worldwide markets. To become effective and profitable participants in international markets, firms need powerful information and communication systems.

TRANSFORMATION OF INDUSTRIAL ECONOMIES

The United States—the world's largest single economy and marketplace—is going through its third economic revolution. In the first revolution, the nation had by 1890 transformed itself from a colonial backwater to an agrarian powerhouse capable of feeding large segments of the world population. In the second revolution, the United States had by 1920 transformed itself from an agrarian nineteenth-century society to a first-class industrial power. In the third revolution, now in progress, the country is transforming itself into a knowledge- and information-based service economy. Both Japan and Germany, and the other major industrial powers to varying degrees, are experiencing a similar revolution.

The knowledge and information revolution began at the turn of the twentieth century and has gradually accelerated. Figure 1.1 shows that by 1976 the number of white-collar workers employed in offices surpassed the number of farm workers, service workers, and blue-collar workers employed in manufacturing. Today, most people no longer work in farms or factories but instead are found in sales, education, health care, banks, insurance firms, and law firms; they also provide business services like copying, computer software, or deliveries. These jobs primarily involve working with, distributing, or creating new information and knowledge. In fact, knowledge and information work now account for a significant 75 percent of the American gross national product, and nearly 70 percent of the labor force.

In a knowledge- and information-based economy, information technology and systems take on great importance. For instance, information technology consti-

Figure 1.1
The growth of the information economy. Since the turn of the century, the United States has experienced a steady decline in the number of farm workers and blue-collar workers who are employed in factories. At the same time, the country is experiencing a rise in the number of white-collar workers who produce economic value using knowledge and information. By 1976 the number of white-collar workers had surpassed the number of blue-collar, service, and farm workers. *Source: Adapted from ''The Mechanization of Office Work,'' by Vincent Guiliano*, Scientific American, *September 1982. Copyright © 1982 by Scientific American, Inc. All rights reserved.*

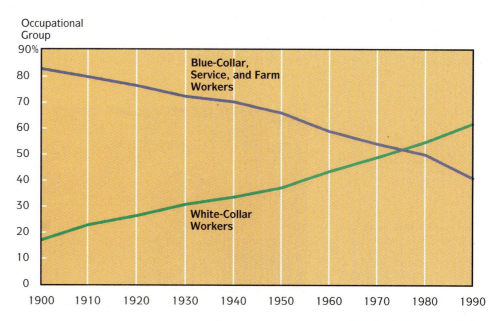

tutes more than 70 percent of the invested capital in service industries like finance, insurance, and real estate. This means that for many managers—perhaps for most—decisions about information technology will be the most common investment decisions.

Because the productivity of employees will depend on the quality of the systems serving them, management decisions about information technology are critically important to the prosperity and survival of a firm. Consider also that the growing power of information technology makes possible new services of great economic value. Credit cards, overnight package delivery, and worldwide reservation systems are examples of services that are based on new information technologies. Over the next decade, information and the technology that delivers it will become critical, strategic resources for business firms and their managers.

What Is an Information System?

Information system:
Interrelated components that collect, process, store, and disseminate information to support decision making, control, analysis, and visualization in an organization.

An **information system** can be defined technically as a set of interrelated components that collect (or retrieve), process, store, and distribute information to support decision making and control in an organization. In addition to supporting decision making, coordination, and control, information systems may also help managers and workers analyze problems, visualize complex subjects, and create new products.

Information systems may contain information about significant people, places, and things within the organization or in the environment surrounding it (see Figure 1.2).

Three activities in an information system produce the information organizations need for making decisions, controlling operations, analyzing problems, and creating new products or services. These activities are input, processing, and output. **Input** captures or collects raw data from within the organization or from its external environment. **Processing** converts this raw input into a more meaningful form. **Output** transfers the processed information to the people or activities where it will be used. Information systems also require **feedback,** which is output that is returned to appropriate members of the organization to help them evaluate or correct the input stage. In the information system used by UPS, the raw input is the data on the shipping label. The central computer processes these data into reports that become output on the computer terminals of UPS customer service representatives, who use them to check the status of packages.

Our interest in this book is in formal, organizational computer-based information systems (CBIS) like those designed and used by UPS. Formal systems rest on accepted and fixed definitions of data and procedures for collecting, storing, processing, disseminating, and using these data. The formal systems we describe in this text are structured—that is, they operate in conformity with predefined rules that are relatively fixed and not easily changed. For instance, UPS's package

Input: The capture or collection of raw data from within the organization or from its external environment for processing in an information system.

Processing: The conversion of raw input into a form that is more meaningful to humans.

Output: The distribution of processed information to the people or activities where it will be used.

Feedback: Output that is returned to the appropriate members of the organization to help them evaluate or correct input.

The sales clerk at this grocery store is able to capture the inventory control information by using a hand-held terminal and scanning gun. The clerk scans the Universal Product Codes and enters the quantity of each dairy product left on the shelf.

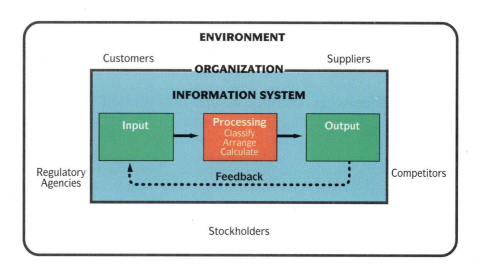

Figure 1.2
Functions of an information system. An information system contains information about an organization and its surrounding environment. Three basic activities—input, processing, and output—produce the information organizations need. Feedback is output returned to appropriate people or activities in the organization to evaluate and refine the input.

delivery system requires that all packages be identified with both the sender's and recipient's name and address.

Informal information systems (such as office gossip networks) rely, by contrast, on implicit agreements and unstated rules of behavior. There is no agreement on what is information, or on how it will be stored and processed. They are essential for the life of an organization, but an analysis of their qualities is beyond the scope of this text.

Formal information systems can be either computer-based or manual. Manual systems use paper and pencil technology. These manual systems serve important needs, but they too are not the subject of this text. **Computer-based information systems (CBIS),** in contrast, rely on computer hardware and software technology to process and disseminate information. From this point on, when we use the term *information systems* we will be referring to computer-based information systems—formal organizational systems that rely on computer technology. The

Computer-based information systems (CBIS): Information systems that rely on computer hardware and software for processing and disseminating information.

W I N D O W   O N

TECHNOLOGY

The 'Rite' Approach to Inventory Management

A shoe store's stockroom is often a jumble of shoeboxes piled loosely together. Shoe store managers consequently do not know precisely what items they have in stock and may order the wrong items. Stride Rite, the children's footwear giant that makes Keds and Sperry topsiders, has changed that situation for its customers with telecommunications and bar code technology.

About 50 representatives in Stride Rite's children's shoe and Keds divisions make sales calls using an oversized briefcase with a scanning gun, a handheld terminal and a miniature printer. The sales representatives use the scanning gun to take inventory of Stride Rite products rapidly in each retail

shoe store by scanning the shelves. The handheld terminal captures that information. Then the reps plug the terminal into a telephone line, and dial up an electronic Universal Product Code catalog on a computer in a network. The portable printer puts out a precise snapshot of the retailer's inventory.

The technology has reduced the time required to take inventory from eight hours to less than two hours and eliminates some of the guesswork in writing orders. The sales representatives can write up more "intelligent orders"—orders that identify exactly what inventory items need to be replenished. Stride Rite plans to enhance this system in the future so that it can

compare the store's stock against an inventory model specified by the retailer and can recommend what the retailer should order.

Stride Rite believes that with this system it can respond to retail stores more rapidly and accurately and that faster order turnaround gives the company an advantage over competitors.

Source: Paul Gillin, "The 'Rite' Approach," *Computerworld*, June 1, 1992.

To Think About: What are the inputs, processing, and outputs of this system? What technologies are used? What would happen if these technologies were not available?

Window on Technology describes some of the typical technologies used in contemporary computer-based information systems.

The Difference Between Computers and Information Systems

Although computer-based information systems use computer technology to process raw data into meaningful information, there is a sharp distinction between a computer and a computer program on the one hand, and an information system on the other. Electronic computers and related software programs are the technical foundation, the tools and materials, of modern information systems. Computers provide the equipment for storing and processing information. Computer programs, or software, are sets of operating instructions that direct and control computer processing. Knowing how computers and computer programs work is important in designing solutions to organizational problems, but the reason for using them comes from the information system of which computers are just a part.

Housing provides an appropriate analogy. Houses are built with hammers, nails, and wood, but these do not make a house. The architecture, design, setting, landscaping, and all of the decisions that lead to the creation of these features are part of the house and are crucial for finding a solution to the problem of putting a roof over one's head. Computers and programs are the hammer, nails, and lumber of CBIS, but alone they cannot produce the information a particular organization needs. To understand information systems, one must understand the problems they are designed to solve, their architectural and design elements, and the organizational processes that lead to these solutions. Today's managers must combine computer literacy with information system literacy.

A Business Perspective on Information Systems

From a business and management perspective, information systems are far more than just input–process–output machines operating in a vacuum. *From a business perspective, an information system is an organizational and management solution, based on information technology, to a challenge posed by the environment.* Examine this definition closely because it emphasizes the organizational and management nature of information systems: Information systems provide a major organizational solution to challenges and problems created in the business environment. To understand information systems—to be information systems literate as opposed to computer literate—a manager must understand the broader organization, management, and information technology dimensions of systems (see Figure 1.3) and their power to provide solutions to the business challenges that are described in this text.

Review the diagram at the beginning of the chapter, which reflects this expanded definition of an information system. The diagram shows how UPS's information systems provide a solution to the business challenges posed by intense global competition. The diagram also illustrates how management, technology, and organization elements work together to create these systems. We begin each chapter of the text with a diagram like this one to help you analyze the opening case. You can use this diagram as a starting point for analyzing any information system or information system problem you encounter.

To design and use information systems effectively, you must first understand the environment, structure, function, and politics of organizations, as well as the role of management and management decision making. Then you must examine the capabilities and opportunities provided by contemporary information technology to provide solutions. This text is organized to fulfill this plan.

ORGANIZATIONS   Information systems are a part of organizations. Indeed, for some companies, such as credit reporting firms, without the system there would be no business. The

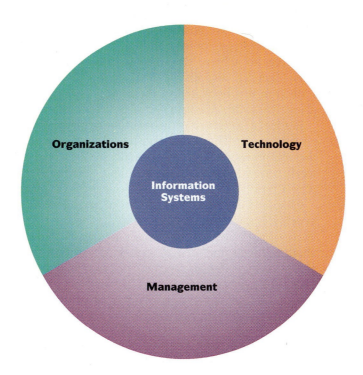

Figure 1.3
Information systems are more than computers. Using information systems effectively requires an understanding of the organization, management, and information technology shaping the systems. All information systems can be described as organizational and management solutions to challenges posed by the environment.

Standard operating procedures (SOPs): Precise, defined rules for accomplishing tasks that have been developed to cope with expected situations.

Knowledge workers: People such as engineers or architects who design products or services and create knowledge for the organization.

Data workers: People such as secretaries or bookkeepers who process and disseminate the organization's paperwork.

Production or service workers: People who actually produce the products or services of the organization.

key elements of an organization are its people, structure and operating procedures, politics, and culture. We introduce these components of organizations here and describe them in greater detail in Chapter 4.

Formal organizations are composed of different levels and specialties. Their structures reveal a clear-cut division of labor. Experts are employed and trained for different functions, including sales, manufacturing, accounting, finance, and human resources. An organization coordinates work through a structured hierarchy and formal, standard operating procedures. The hierarchy arranges people in a pyramidal structure of rising authority and responsibility. The upper levels of the hierarchy consist of managerial, professional, and technical employees, while the lower levels consist of operational personnel.

Standard operating procedures (SOPs) are precise, defined rules for accomplishing tasks that have been developed to cope with expected situations; these rules guide employees in a variety of procedures, from writing an invoice to responding to complaining customers. Most standard operating procedures are formalized and written down, but some are informal work practices. Many of a firm's SOPs are incorporated into information systems—such as how to pay a supplier or how to correct an erroneous bill.

Organizations require many different kinds of skills and people. In addition to managers, **knowledge workers** (such as engineers, architects, or scientists) design products or services, and **data workers** (such as secretaries, bookkeepers, or clerks) process the organization's paperwork. **Production** or **service workers** (such as machinists, assemblers, or packers) actually produce the products or services of the organization.

Each organization has a unique culture, or fundamental set of assumptions, values, and ways of doing things, that have been accepted by most of its members. Parts of an organization's culture can always be found embedded in its information systems. For instance, the concern with putting service to the customer first is an aspect of the organizational culture of United Parcel Service that can be found in the company's package tracking systems.

Different levels and specialties in an organization create different interests and points of view. These views often conflict. Conflict is the basis for organizational politics. Information systems come out of this cauldron of differing perspectives, conflicts, compromises, and agreements that are a natural part of all organizations. In Chapter 4 we will examine these features of organizations in greater detail.

MANAGEMENT

Managers perceive business challenges in the environment; they set the organizational strategy for responding, and they allocate the human and financial resources to achieve the strategy and coordinate the work. Throughout, they must exercise responsible leadership. The business information systems described in this book reflect the hopes, dreams, and realities of real-world managers. These are managers' conventional responsibilities.

But less understood is the fact that managers must do more than manage what already exists. They must also create new products, services, and even re-create the organization from time to time. A substantial part of management is creative work driven by new knowledge and information. Information technology can play a powerful role in re-engineering the organization.

Senior managers: People at the highest organizational level who are responsible for making long-range decisions.

Middle managers: People in the middle of the organizational hierarchy who are responsible for carrying out the plans and goals of senior management.

Operational managers: People who monitor the day-to-day activities of the organization.

Chapter 5 describes the activities of managers and management decision making in detail. It is important to note that managerial roles and decisions vary at different levels of the organization. **Senior managers** make long-range strategic decisions about products and services to produce. **Middle managers** carry out the programs and plans of senior management. **Operational managers** are responsible for monitoring the firm's daily activities. All levels of management are expected to be creative: to develop novel solutions to a broad range of problems. Each level of management has different information needs and information system requirements.

TECHNOLOGY

Information systems technology is one of many tools available to managers for coping with change. More importantly today, information technology is the glue that holds the organization together. It is the instrument through which management controls and creates, and it is an arrow in the manager's quiver. CBIS utilize computer hardware, software, storage, and telecommunications technologies.

Computer hardware: Physical equipment used for input, processing, and output work in an information system.

Computer software: Detailed, preprogrammed instructions that control and coordinate computer hardware components in an information system.

Storage technology: Physical media and software governing the storage and organization of data for use in an information system.

Telecommunications technology: Physical devices and software that link various computer hardware components and transfer data from one physical location to another.

Computer hardware is the physical equipment used for input, processing, and output activities in an information system. It consists of the following: the computer processing unit; various input, output, and storage devices; and physical media to link these devices together. Chapter 6 describes computer hardware in greater detail.

Computer software consists of the detailed preprogrammed instructions that control and coordinate the computer hardware components in an information system. Chapter 7 explains the importance of computer software in information systems.

Storage technology includes both the physical media for storing data, such as magnetic disk or tape, and the software governing the organization of data on these physical media. More detail on physical storage media can be found in Chapter 6, whereas Chapter 8 treats data organization and access methods.

Telecommunications technology, consisting of both physical devices and software, links the various pieces of hardware and transfers data from one physical location to another. Chapter 9 covers telecommunications technology and issues.

Returning to the Stride Rite system in the Window on Technology, let us identify the management, organization, and technology elements. The organization element anchors the inventory analysis system in Stride Rite's sales function. It identifies the required procedures for taking inventory, such as counting the number of boxes in each retail store and providing reports for retail store managers and for higher-level managers in Stride Rite itself. The system must also satisfy the needs of Stride Rite managers and workers. Sales representatives need to be trained in both inventory counting procedures and in how to use the system so that they can sell more effectively. Stride Rite's management perceived it was losing sales by not having an up-to-date inventory control system to drive manufacturing. Management strategy, hence, was to achieve a closer coordination between shoe production and customer demand, thereby reducing manufacturing costs and increasing sales revenues. It needed to plan shoe production based on sales patterns and inventory turnover in its retail outlets. Retail shoe store managers needed some way of controlling their inventory to make sure that they were stocking the styles and sizes that they could sell. The technology supporting this system consists of scanning guns, handheld terminals, printers,

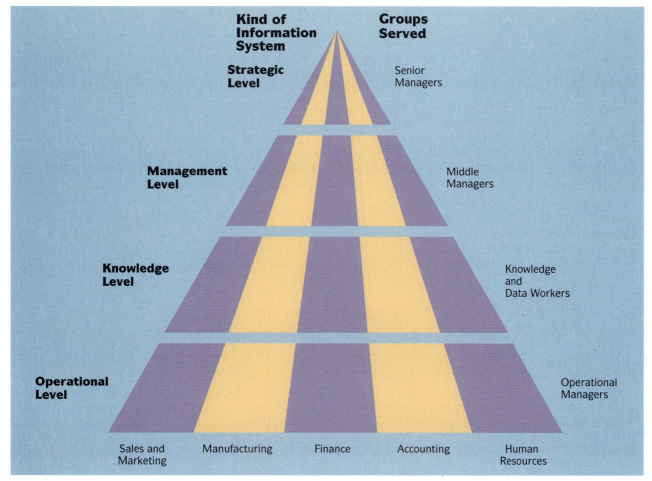

Figure 1.4

Types of information systems. Organizations and information systems can be divided into strategic, management, knowledge, and operational levels. They can be divided further into five functional areas: sales and marketing, manufacturing, finance, accounting, and human resources. Information systems serve each of these levels and functions. Strategic-level systems help senior managers with long-term planning. Management-level systems help middle managers monitor and control. Knowledge-level systems help knowledge and data workers design products, distribute information, and cope with paperwork. Operational-level systems help operational managers keep track of the firm's day-to-day activities.

telecommunications links, Stride Rite's central computer, and storage technology for the Universal Product Code catalog. The result is an information system solution to a business challenge.

Different Kinds of Systems

Because there are different interests, specialties, and levels in an organization, there are different kinds of systems. Figure 1.4 illustrates one way to depict the kinds of systems found in an organization. In the illustration, the organization is divided into strategic, management, knowledge, and operational levels and then is further divided into functional areas such as sales and marketing, manufacturing, finance, accounting, and human resources. Systems are built to serve these different organizational interests (Anthony, 1965).

Operational-level systems: Information systems that monitor the elementary activities and transactions of the organization.

Operational-level systems support operational managers by keeping track of the elementary activities and transactions of the organization, such as sales, receipts, cash deposits, payroll, credit decisions, and the flow of materials in a factory. The principal purpose of systems at this level is to answer routine questions and to track the flow of transactions through the organization. How many parts are in inventory? What happened to Mr. Williams's payment? What

ORGANIZATIONS

Computers Speed Up Product Design

Manufacturers have long tried to use teams of design engineers to speed up the development of new products. Thanks to computer-aided design (CAD) systems, it is now possible to eliminate much of the manual drafting and building of physical prototypes that slowed down the design process.

For instance, Odense Steel Shipyards, part of Denmark's huge Maersk shipping group, has developed a CAD system that can establish a three-dimensional topographic model of an entire ship with all components. Bath Iron Works Inc. in Bath, Maine, uses CAD workstations with three-dimensional solid modeling capabilities to help build naval destroyers, considered among the most complex pieces of equipment that can be manufactured. Up to 2000 design engineers collectively decide the locations for massive quantities of cables, plumbing equipment, and other structures inside the cramped confines of a destroyer. An object placed by one engineer that might interfere with one placed by another can be detected and corrected before the ship is built. Before, when design-

ers relied solely on manual drafting, engineers could not detect such problems until the ship was under construction.

Engineers at the Greenville, South Carolina North American research center for Groupe Michelin S. A.— a French-based firm that is the largest tire manufacturer in the world—created and tested hundreds of tires before building any actual prototypes and doing any road testing. The engineers dis-

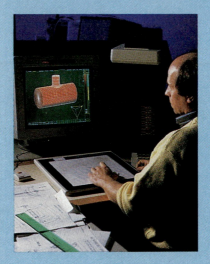

covered that tires will last longer if the tire/ground contact stresses are evenly distributed throughout the contact area. This often produces a rectangular contact area, compared to a more oval contact area frequently obtained with older tire designs. The new computer techniques allow computation of contact stresses and contact area prior to prototype fabrication. Before engineers used computerized systems to design and test tires, they would build prototypes, hire drivers to drive them for two months or more, and then change the design as needed. Developing a tire could take several years.

The prototyped designs from CAD systems can automatically feed the design specifications to many firms' computerized manufacturing systems.

Sources: *New York Times,* "Computer Tests Pump More Miles Into Tires," April 1, 1992; Paul Tate, "Maersk Spots LAN-Ho," *InformationWEEK,* January 27, 1992; and John J. Xenakis, "3-D Engineering," *InformationWEEK,* February 25, 1991.

To Think About: What problems can such systems solve?

---

is the size of the payroll this month? To answer these kinds of questions, information generally must be easily available, current, and accurate. Examples of operational-level systems include a system to record bank deposits from automatic teller machines or one that tracks the number of hours worked each day by employees on a factory floor.

Knowledge-level systems support knowledge and data workers in an organization. The Window on Organizations illustrates how knowledge-level systems can improve the productivity of engineers and designers. The purpose of knowledge-level systems is to help the business firm integrate new knowledge into the business and to help the organization control the flow of paperwork. Knowledge-level systems, especially in the form of workstations and office systems, are the fastest-growing applications in business today.

Management-level systems are designed to serve the monitoring, controlling, decision-making, and administrative activities of middle managers. The principal question addressed by such systems is: Are things working well? These systems compare the current day's output with that of a month or a year ago. Management-level systems typically provide periodic reports rather than instant information on operations. There is less need for instant information, but periodic reports are still required. An example is a relocation control system that

Knowledge-level systems:
Information systems that support knowledge and data workers in an organization.

Management-level systems:
Information systems that support the monitoring, controlling, decision-making, and administrative activities of middle managers.

reports on the total moving, house-hunting, and home financing costs for employees in all company divisions, noting wherever actual costs exceed budgets.

Some management-level systems support nonroutine decision making (Keen and Morton, 1978). They tend to focus on less structured decisions for which information requirements are not always clear. These systems often answer "what if" questions: What would be the impact on production schedules if we were to double sales in the month of December? What would happen to our return on investment if a factory schedule were delayed for six months? Answers to these questions frequently require new data from outside the organization, as well as data from inside that cannot be drawn from existing operational-level systems.

Strategic-level systems:
Information systems that support the long-range planning activities of senior management.

Strategic-level systems help senior management tackle and address strategic issues and long-term trends, both in the firm and in the external environment. Their principal concern is matching changes in the external environment with existing organizational capability. What will employment levels be in five years? What are the long-term industry cost trends, and where does our firm fit in? What products should we be making in five years?

The next chapter describes the types of information systems found at each organizational level. It also shows typical applications of each type of system.

Information systems may also be differentiated by functional specialty. Major organizational functions, such as sales and marketing, manufacturing, accounting, finance, and human resources, are each served by their own information systems. In large organizations, subfunctions of each of these major functions also have their own information systems. For example, the manufacturing function might have systems for inventory management, process control, plant maintenance, computer-aided engineering, and material requirements planning.

A typical organization has operational-, management-, knowledge-, and strategic-level systems for each functional area. For example, the sales function generally has a sales system on the operational level to record daily sales figures and to process orders. A knowledge-level system designs promotional displays for the firm's products. A management-level system tracks monthly sales figures by sales territory and reports on territories where sales exceed or fall below anticipated levels. A system to forecast sales trends over a five-year period serves the strategic level.

Finally, different organizations have different information systems for the same functional areas. Because no two organizations have exactly the same objectives, structures, or interests, information systems must be custom-made to fit the unique characteristics of each. There is no such thing as a universal information system that can fit all organizations, even in such standard areas as payroll or accounts receivable. Every organization does the job somewhat differently.

1.2 The Changing Management Process

Information systems cannot be ignored by managers because they play such a critical role in contemporary organizations. The first information systems of the 1950s were operational systems that automated such clerical processes as check processing. These were followed by management-level systems in the 1970s and strategic-level systems in the 1980s. Because early systems addressed largely technical operational issues, managers could afford to delegate authority and concern to lower-level technical workers. But because today's systems directly affect how managers decide, how senior managers plan, and in many cases what products and services are produced (and how), responsibility for information systems cannot be delegated to technical decision makers. Information systems today play a strategic role in the life of the firm.

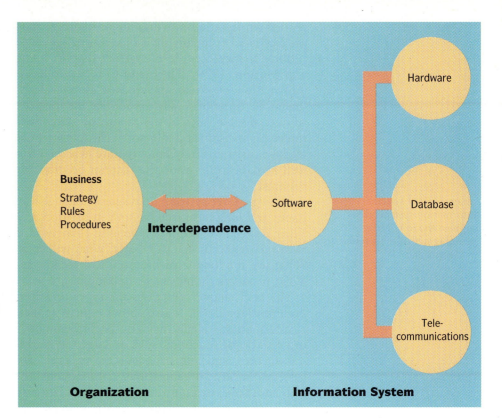

Figure 1.5
The interdependence between organizations and information systems. In contemporary systems there is a growing interdependence between organizational business strategy, rules, and procedures and the organization's information systems. Changes in strategy, rules, and procedures increasingly require changes in hardware, software, databases, and telecommunications. Existing systems can act as a constraint on organizations. Often, what the organization would like to do depends on what its systems will permit it to do.

The New Role of Information Systems in Organizations

Figure 1.5 illustrates the new relationship between organizations and information systems. There is a growing interdependence between business strategy, rules, and procedures, on the one hand, and information systems software, hardware, data, and telecommunications on the other. A change in any of these components often requires changes in other components. This relationship becomes critical when management plans for the future. What a business would like to do in five years is often dependent on what its systems will be able to do.

A second change in the relationship of information systems and organizations results from the growing complexity and scope of system projects and applications. Building systems today involves a much larger part of the organization than it did in the past (see Figure 1.6). Whereas early systems produced largely technical changes that affected few people, contemporary systems bring about managerial changes (who has what information about whom, when, and how often) and institutional "core" changes (what products and services are produced, under what conditions, and by whom).

Figure 1.6
The widening scope of information systems. Over time, information systems have come to play a larger role in the life of organizations. Early systems brought about largely technical changes that were relatively easy to accomplish. Later systems affected managerial control and behavior; ultimately systems influenced "core" institutional activities concerning products, markets, suppliers, and customers.

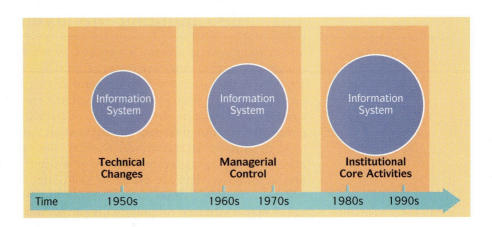

e desk top manual adding machine was early entry to the information system na providing a simple number keypad perform basic calculations.

The UNIVAC II computer represented a first step in the changing management process by automating clerical processes such as data entry and led the way for contemporary information systems.

The desk top microcomputer is the foundation of a contemporary information system.

In the 1950s, a computerized payroll system involved employees in the treasurer's office, a few part-time programmers, a single program, a single machine, and a few clerks. The change from a manual to a computer system was largely technical. The computer system simply automated an existing procedure. In contrast, today's integrated human resource system (which includes payroll processing) may involve all major corporate divisions, the human resources department, dozens of full-time programmers, a flock of external consultants, multiple machines (or remote computers linked by telecommunications networks), and perhaps hundreds of end users in the organization who use payroll data to make calculations about benefits and pensions and to answer a host of other questions. The data, instead of being located in and controlled by the treasurer's office, are now available to hundreds of employees via desktop computers, each of which is as powerful as the large computers of the 1970s. This contemporary system embodies both managerial and institutional changes.

The Changing Nature of Information Technology

One reason why systems play a larger role in organizations, and why they affect more people, is the growing power and declining cost of information technology—the computers and peripheral devices that make up the core of information systems. Although the details are covered in later chapters, here it is sufficient to note that it is now possible to put the power of a large mainframe computer—which took up nearly an entire floor of a company in the 1970s—on every desktop in an organization of the 1990s. This new hardware capability makes powerful, easy-to-use software available to complete novices. In a few hours, relatively unskilled employees can be taught word processing, project scheduling, spreadsheet preparation, and telecommunications applications on a microcomputer. The skills needed for these activities once belonged exclusively to employees who had been through extensive specialized training. Now it is conceivable that everyone in an organization may be using a computer simultaneously in some way during the work day.

In addition, it is now possible for end users to design their own applications and simple systems without the help of professional programmers. A good manager cannot afford to ignore the fact that many of his or her employees are using information technology much of the time. Is this use productive? Could it be made more productive? Where are the major bottlenecks? How can we measure the benefits of investing in the technology? When should professional help be sought, and when can end users design their own solutions?

The Changing Character of Applications

Both the changing role of systems and the new technology have brought about new kinds of systems and applications. Whereas in the past massive systems were built to provide generic information on sales, inventory, production, finance, and marketing, it is now feasible and desirable to create custom-made, specialized applications that serve just one or a few people or groups in the organization. Whether they are microcomputer-based spreadsheet applications, collaborative group computing applications, or support systems for middle management, the new kinds of applications require direct, close interaction between technical support personnel and managers who will use the system, plus senior management support. Managers need some computer understanding to maximize the benefit from such applications.

One class of new applications—called expert systems, described in Chapter 17—requires technical experts known as *knowledge engineers* to capture the knowledge of skilled workers and managers. These kinds of systems illustrate the close cooperation and understanding required of both managers and information systems specialists.

The Need to Plan the Information Architecture of an Organization

Figure 1.7
The information architecture of the firm. Today's managers must know how to arrange and coordinate the various computer technologies and business system applications to meet the information needs of each level of their organization, as well as the needs of the organization as a whole.

It is not enough for managers to be computer literate. Systems today require that a manager have an understanding of major islands or constellations of technologies: data processing systems, telecommunications, and office technologies (see the articles by McKenney and McFarlan, 1982; McFarlan et al., 1983a, 1983b). As the scope of information systems widens, these previously separate islands of technology must be closely coordinated. Managers today must know how to track, plan, and manage the many islands of technology in a way best suited to their organization. This systems knowledge is important.

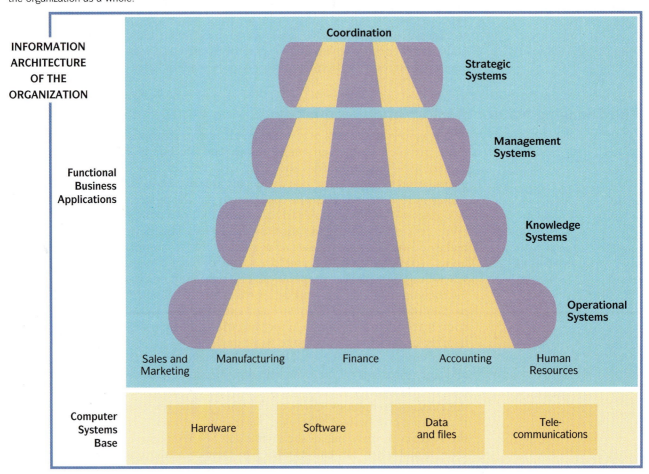

MANAGEMENT

Send an Accountant to Cure Ailing Systems

When its information systems couldn't keep up with corporate growth plans, medical products maker McGaw Inc. chose an accountant to reshape its information systems department.

Previously, McGaw had been owned by a succession of parent corporations—American Hospital Supply, Colgate-Palmolive, and then the Kendall Company. It became an independent company in 1990. McGaw's managers never gave information systems much attention, and the owners didn't understand what systems could contribute to the business's bottom line. McGaw had two choices in its search for a new head of information systems. One choice was to find an experienced information systems executive who could appreciate business and finance. The alternative was to find an experienced business and finance executive who appreciated information systems. McGaw chose the latter course, and hired Rich Hirschberg, the former controller of Metwest,

Inc., to head its information systems department.

Before hiring Hirschberg, McGaw did not take advantage of the potential in information technology. Its information systems were outdated and they slowed down operations. Systems weren't properly designed to provide the information required by the business. For instance, sales and marketing staff had trouble obtaining information on specific accounts or on the market in general. Information systems were organized along departmental lines—manufacturing, sales, and so forth; they did not address the needs of the organization as a whole.

Hirschberg brought a "business view" to information systems, working toward making information systems a competitive tool. He reorganized his information systems staff to create one generic group of information systems professionals and created the firm's first cohesive information systems plan in years.

McGaw is not alone in choosing someone with business expertise to manage information systems. A significant number of top information systems executives actually started their careers in other business departments. Most have a broad base of experience in other areas. For instance, Sid Diamond, former vice president of worldwide information services at the Black and Decker Corporation in Towson, Maryland, worked in marketing planning before moving to information systems. Al Hyland, director of worldwide systems for the Polaroid Corporation in Waltham, Massachusetts, started in research.

Sources: Jim Nash, "Just what the doctor ordered," *Computerworld*, June 1, 1992 and Katie Crane, "Take chances and diversify on your journey to upper ranks," *Computerworld*, November 4, 1991.

To Think About: Many believe the ideal manager has both information systems and business experience. Do you agree? Why or why not?

In addition, managers must know how to recognize organizational problems and find a systems solution. For this, knowledge of the organization is required. As corporations realize the need for conscious planning of the information architecture in a firm, they are placing MBAs and other generalists in charge of the information systems function. This phenomenon is illustrated by the Window on Management.

Information architecture: The particular form that information technology takes in a specific organization to achieve selected goals or functions.

Together, systems knowledge and organizational understanding shape the information architecture of the organization. **Information architecture** is the particular form that information technology takes in an organization to achieve selected goals or functions. Information architecture includes the extent to which data and processing power are centralized or distributed. Managers increasingly play the critical role in determining the information architecture of their organizations. There is no one else to do the job.

Figure 1.7 illustrates the major elements of information architecture that a student will have to understand in the 1990s if he or she is to become an effective manager. Although the computer systems base is typically operated by technical personnel, general management must decide how to allocate the resources it has assigned to hardware, software, and telecommunications. Increasingly, the top managers of systems and communications departments are also general managers. Resting upon the computer systems base are the major business application systems, or the major islands of applications. Because managers and employees directly interact with these systems, it is critical for the success of the organization that these systems meet business functional requirements now and in the future. In many service industries—such as airlines, hotels, banks, insurance firms, and brokerages—the major business applications provide unique competitive advantages. Failure to develop these systems can lead to business failure.

The following are some typical questions regarding information architecture that today's managers should be able to answer: Should the corporate sales data and function be distributed to each corporate remote site, or should it be centralized at headquarters? Should the organization purchase stand-alone microcomputers or build a more powerful centralized mainframe environment within an integrated telecommunications network? Should the organization build its own data communications utility to link remote sites or rely on external providers like the telephone company? Although there is no one right answer to these questions (see Allen and Boynton, 1991), a manager today should at least have the knowledge to deal with them.

1.3 Contemporary Approaches to Information Systems

The study of information systems is a multidisciplinary field; no single theory or perspective dominates. Figure 1.8 illustrates the major disciplines that contribute perspectives, issues and insights in the study of information systems. In general, the field can be divided into technical and behavioral approaches. Information systems are sociotechnical systems. Though they are composed of machines, devices, and "hard" physical technology, they require substantial social, organizational, and intellectual investments to make them work properly.

Technical Approach

Technical approaches to information systems dominated the field in its early years. The disciplines that contribute to the technical approach are computer science, management science, and operations research. Computer science is concerned with establishing theories of computability, methods of computation, and methods of efficient data storage and access. Management science emphasizes the development of models for decision making and management practices. Operations research focuses on mathematical techniques for optimizing selected parameters of organizations such as transportation, costs, inventory control, and transaction costs.

The technical approach to information systems emphasizes mathematically based, normative models to study information systems, as well as the physical technology and formal capabilities of these systems.

Figure 1.8
Contemporary approaches to information systems. The study of information systems deals with issues and insights contributed from technical and behavioral disciplines.

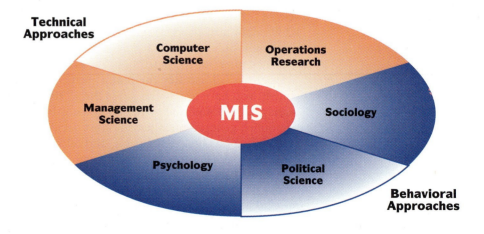

Examples of literature in these fields can be found in *Communications of the Association of Computing Machinery (CACM), Management Science,* and *Operations Research*. Articles from these three journals are excerpted and referenced throughout the text, and interested students should examine these sources to learn more about this approach to modern information systems.

Behavioral Approach

A growing part of the information systems field is concerned with behavioral problems and issues. Many behavioral problems, such as system utilization, implementation, and creative design, cannot be expressed with the normative models used in the technical approach. Other behavioral disciplines also play a role. Sociologists focus on the impact of information systems on groups, organizations, and society. Political science investigates the political impacts and uses of information systems. Psychology is concerned with individual responses to information systems and cognitive models of human reasoning. The leading journals in these areas are the *American Sociological Review, Administrative Science Quarterly, American Political Science Review,* and the *Journal of Psychology.*

The behavioral approach does not ignore technology. Indeed, information systems technology is often the stimulus for a behavioral problem or issue. But the focus of this approach is generally not on technical solutions; it concentrates rather on changes in attitudes, management and organizational policy, and behavior (Kling and Dutton, 1982).

Approach of This Text: Sociotechnical Systems

The study of management information systems (MIS) arose in the 1960s and focused exclusively on computer-based information systems aimed at managers (Davis and Olsen, 1985). The MIS discipline, and the first academic departments, emerged in business schools in the United States. MIS combines the theoretical work of computer science, management science, and operations research with a practical orientation toward building systems and applications. It also pays attention to behavioral issues. The leading journals in this field are *MIS Quarterly* and the *Journal of Management Information Systems*. Business journals such as the *Harvard Business Review* and the *Sloan Management Review* also contain articles relevant to MIS.

Our experience as academics and practitioners leads us to believe that no single perspective effectively captures the reality of information systems. Problems with systems—and their solutions—are rarely all technical or all behavioral. Our best advice to students is to understand the perspectives of all disciplines. Indeed, the challenge and excitement of the information systems field is that it requires an appreciation and tolerance of many different approaches.

A sociotechnical systems perspective helps to avoid a purely technological approach to information systems. For instance, the fact that information technology is rapidly declining in cost and growing in power does not necessarily or easily translate into productivity enhancement or bottom-line profits.

In this book, we stress the need to optimize the performance of the system as a whole. Both the technical and behavioral components need attention. This means that technology must be changed and designed in such a way as to fit organizational and individual needs. At times, the technology may have to be "de-optimized" to accomplish this fit. Organizations and individuals must also be changed through training, learning, and planned organizational change in order to allow the technology to operate and prosper (see, for example Liker et al., 1987). Figure 1.9 illustrates this process of mutual adjustment in a sociotechnical system.

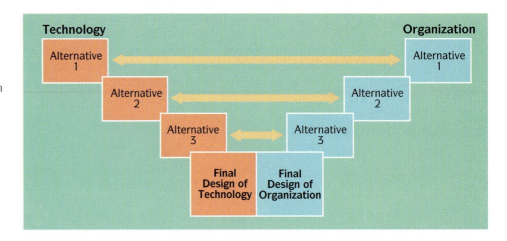

1.4 The Challenge of Information Systems: Key Management Issues

A senior executive was in charge of a $275 million software redevelopment project in the Social Security Administration; the project was three years behind schedule. The executive lamented that "senior management just did not understand the difficulty of rewriting over 10 million lines of programming code" (Laudon, 1989).

Increasingly, information systems are bringing about changes in business goals, relationships with customers and suppliers, and internal operations. Creating a new system now means much more than installing a new machine in the basement. Today, this process typically places thousands of terminals or microcomputers on the desks of employees who have little experience with them, connecting the devices to powerful communications networks, rearranging social relations in the office and work locations, changing reporting patterns and asking employees to achieve higher levels of productivity. Briefly, new systems today often require the development of a new information architecture.

One message of this text is that despite, or perhaps because of, the rapid development of computer technology, there is nothing easy or mechanical about building workable information systems. Building, operating, and maintaining information systems are challenging activities for a number of reasons. We believe there are five key challenges that managers should heed:

1. The Strategic Business Challenge: How can businesses use information technology to design organizations that are competitive and effective?

Investment in information technology amounts to over half of the annual capital expenditures of most large, service sector firms. Yet despite investing more in computers than any other country, the United States still faces a serious productivity challenge. America's productivity growth rate in the last decade of just under 2 percent per year is far below that of other industrial countries. The product life cycle for Ford's Taurus is ten years, but Toyota redesigns its cars every five years. On average, the time to bring a new manufactured product to market in the United States is twice that of Japanese industry. The productivity lag is especially pronounced in the service sector. White-collar productivity has increased at an annual rate of only .28 percent (Roach, 1991).

Technical change moves much faster than humans and organizations are changing. The power of computer hardware and software has grown much more rapidly than the ability of organizations to apply and use this technology. To stay competitive, many organizations actually need to be redesigned. They will need to use information technology to simplify communication and coordination, eliminate unnecessary work, and eliminate the inefficiencies of outmoded organizational structures. If organizations merely automate what they are doing today, they are largely missing the potential of information technology. Organizations need to rethink and redesign the way they design, produce, deliver, and maintain goods and services.

2. The Globalization Challenge: How can firms understand the business and system requirements of a global economic environment?

The rapid growth in international trade and the emergence of a global economy call for information systems that can support both producing and selling goods in many different countries. In the past, each regional office of a multinational corporation focused on solving its own unique information problems. Given language, cultural, and political differences among countries, this focus frequently resulted in chaos and the failure of central management controls. To develop integrated multinational information systems, businesses must cope with restrictive transborder dataflow legislation in more than 25 countries, and must create cross-cultural accounting and reporting structures (Roche, 1992; Buss, 1982; Carlyle, 1988).

3. The Information Architecture Challenge: How can organizations develop an information architecture that supports their business goals?

While information technology can suggest some new ways of doing business, firms still need to have a clear idea of their business goals and how these can best be supported by information systems. Many organizations cannot meet their goals because they are crippled by fragmented and incompatible computer hardware, software, telecommunications networks, and information systems. Integrating these "islands of information" into a coherent architecture is now a priority.

4. The Information Systems Investment Challenge: How can organizations determine the business value of information systems?

A major problem raised by the development of powerful inexpensive computers involves not technology but rather management and organizations. It's one thing to use information technology to design, produce, deliver and maintain new products. It's another thing to make money doing it. How can organizations obtain a sizable payoff from their investment in information systems?

Engineering massive organizational and system changes in the hope of positioning a firm strategically is complicated and expensive. Is this an investment that pays off? How can you tell? Senior management can be expected to ask these questions: Are we receiving the kind of return on investment from our systems that we should be? Do our competitors get more? While understanding the costs and benefits of building a single system are difficult enough, it is daunting to consider whether the entire systems effort is "worth it." Imagine, then, how a senior executive must think when presented with a major transformation in information architecture, a bold venture in organizational change costing tens of millions of dollars and taking many years.

5. The Responsibility and Control Challenge: How can organizations design systems that people can control and understand? How can organizations ensure that their information systems are used in an ethically and socially responsible manner?

CBIS play such a critical role in business, government, and daily life that organizations must take special steps to ensure that they are accurate, reliable, and secure. Automated or semi-automated systems that malfunction or are poorly operated can have extremely harmful consequences. A firm invites disaster if it uses systems that don't work as intended, that don't deliver information in a form that people can interpret correctly and use, or that have control rooms where controls don't work or where instruments give false signals. The potential for massive fraud, error, abuse, and destruction is enormous.

Information systems must be designed so that they function as intended and so that humans can control the process. When building and using information systems, health, safety, job security, and social well-being should be considered as carefully as meeting an organization's business goals. Managers will need to ask: Can we apply high quality assurance standards to our information systems as well as to our products and services? Can we build information systems that respect people's rights of privacy while still pursuing our organization's goals? Should information systems monitor employees? What do we do when an information system designed to increase efficiency and productivity eliminates people's jobs?

This text is designed to provide future managers with the knowledge and understanding required to deal with these challenges. To further this objective, each chapter concludes with a Management Challenges box that outlines the key issues managers should be aware of.

Summary

Define an information system.

The purpose of a CBIS is to collect, store, and disseminate information from an organization's environment and internal operations for the purpose of supporting organizational functions and decision making, communication, coordination, control, analysis, and visualization. Information systems transform raw data into useful information through three basic activities: input, processing, and output.

Explain the difference between computer literacy and information systems literacy.

Information systems literacy requires an understanding of the organizational and management dimensions of information systems as well as the technical dimensions addressed by computer literacy.

Describe the information needs of different organizational levels.

To be useful, a CBIS must faithfully reflect the organization's requirements for information. It must fit the needs of the specific organizational level and the business function that it is intended to support.

Operational-level systems keep track of the firm's day-to-day activities. Knowledge-level systems support the integration of new knowledge throughout the firm; they also exist to manage paperwork. Management-level systems support the planning, controlling, and monitoring activities of middle management. Strategic-level systems support long-term planning. Each functional specialty, such as sales, manufacturing, accounting, finance, and human resources, typically has all four types of systems.

Explain why information systems are so important today.

In general, there is a much greater need to plan for the overall information architecture of the organization. The kinds of systems built today are more important for the overall performance of the organization, especially in today's highly globalized and information-based economy; technologies have become more powerful and more difficult to implement; and new applications require intense interaction between professional technical experts and general management.

Identify the major conceptual approaches to information systems.

There are both technical and behavioral approaches to studying information systems. Both perspectives can be combined into a sociotechnical approach to systems.

Identify the major management challenges to building and using information systems in organizations.

There are five key management challenges in building and using information systems: 1) designing systems that are competitive and efficient; 2) understanding the system requirements of a global business environment; 3) creating an information architecture that supports the organization's goals; 4) determining the business value of systems; and 5) designing systems that people can control, understand, and use in a socially and ethically responsible manner.

Review Questions

1. Distinguish between a computer, a computer program, and an information system.

2. What activities convert raw data to usable information in information systems? What is their relationship to feedback?

3. What is the relationship between an information system, the organization, and the organizational environment?

4. What is information systems literacy?

5. What are the organization, management and technology dimensions of information systems?

6. Identify and describe the four levels of the organizational hierarchy. What types of information systems serve each level?

7. Why should managers study information systems?

8. What is the relationship between an organization and its information systems? How is this relationship changing over time?

9. What do we mean by the information architecture of the organization?

10. Distinguish between a behavioral and a technical approach to information systems in terms of the questions asked and the answers provided.

11. What major disciplines contribute to an understanding of information systems?

12. What are the key management challenges involved in building, operating, and maintaining information systems today?

Discussion Questions

1. Some people argue that the creation of CBIS is fundamentally a social process. Hence, a person who is an expert in information technology may not be suited to design a CBIS. Discuss and comment.

2. Most of the problems we have with information systems will disappear when computers become faster and cheaper. Discuss and comment.

Group Project

In a group with three or four classmates find a description in a computer or business magazine of an information system used by an organization. Describe the system in terms of its inputs, processes, and outputs and in terms of its management, organization, and technology features. Present your analysis to the class.

Writing the Book in the Year 2000

Publishing companies have avoided information technology in the same way that they have rejected bad manuscripts. Outside writers or artists created manuscripts. These were sent to outside designers, who designed the jackets and art work. Then the job was sent to outside typesetting shops, who set the art and manuscript into type. Finally the work went to a printer. The process took six to ten months for a book, sometimes a full two months for a brochure. Despite the time-consuming process, the book publishers have been slow to change.

In 1986, for instance, Simon & Schuster, the $1.5 billion publishing arm of Paramount Communications, didn't have a personal computer and was using decades-old filing and processing systems. Then in 1990 Simon & Schuster launched a six-year plan to incorporate information technology into all facets of the company.

Simon & Schuster hopes to become a "print/technology" company by the year 2000, converting a paper-bound publishing and distribution process into an electronic digital one. Everything from writing manuscripts to tracking royalties to warehousing and order management is being restyled with computer and telecommunications technology. Simon & Schuster has three goals for its information systems: cutting costs, speeding the delivery of products, and boosting efficiency. The firm hopes to boost its profit margins to 15 percent, well above the industry average which is typically in the single digits. According to CEO Richard Snyder, publishing is process-oriented, and the winning firm is the one that processes the best, the fastest, and the most economically.

Simon & Schuster has installed more than 3000 personal computers and workstations, providing 65 percent of its employees—from editors to production people—with desktop computers. Soon more than 90 percent will have computers on their desktops. A typical desktop system is the forecasting system that creates models for book sales and inventory management. One of the great challenges of publishing is knowing how many books to print. The system will forecast demand, control the number of books the firm warehouses, and measure book levels in retail stores.

In book publishing, cutting costs in inventory and distribution isn't enough unless costs are also minimized while the books are actually being produced. During the pre-press part of the process, publishers have to determine advances on royalties to be paid to authors; they have to make budgets for editing and research; and they need to decide how many books to print. Often they have only a 20-page book proposal as a guideline. Educational book projects are especially tricky, since big curriculum projects such as a new reading program for kindergarten through sixth grade require up-front expenditures of tens of millions of dollars.

It may never be possible always to predict correct advances or sales, but Simon & Schuster feels it can reduce production costs using Electronic Manuscript Management (EMM). The traditional method of preparing a book for publication is tediously manual, entailing hard copies of marked-up manuscripts, page proofs, and illustrations passed back and forth between authors and editors. Simon & Schuster expects EMM to reduce the production process from two years to a matter of weeks and months. Authors' manuscripts will be prepared on computer diskettes and submitted directly to typesetters. Book pages can be composed entirely electronically. Art and design images will be prepared by computer or will be digitized and then integrated into the manuscript using computerized "composition page makers."

The EMM system enhances the creative process. Before, when Simon & Schuster pasted up hard copy, even simple changes cost hundreds of dollars. Now changes can be made using personal computers in-house, rather than being sent out to freelance designers.

Simon & Schuster has also installed a new royalty tracking system and a new order management system that speeds the processing of orders placed by retail bookstores and schools. A new automated warehousing system will improve inventory management.

Savings are already apparent—approximately $500 per book on typesetting alone. This amounts to companywide savings of $275,000 per year. By installing its own private network to transmit voice and data domestically and to international facilities in Europe and Australia, Simon & Schuster cut telecommunications costs by more than 60 percent in two years. That is important because the firm determined that its investment in information systems had to compete with other investments. If the technology investments don't return a payback, the expenditures won't be made.

Simon & Schuster is also using its new information technologies to diversify its products. In March 1990 the firm acquired Computer Curriculum Corporation, which develops software for integrated learning systems and custom "on-demand" books. A Technology Group oversees Computer Curriculum and three other divisions responsible for computerized business training, educational media projects, and consumer education services. Computer-based remedial, technical, and management training programs are being tested with major corporations such as General Motors.

The firm has some concerns that its 10,000 employees won't assimilate the new technology at the pace it is being introduced. How quickly, for instance, can an employee skilled in an age-old manual hard-copy tradition take advantage of the capabilities of a state-of-the-art design workstation?

Source: Bob Violino, "Writing the Book on Technology," *InformationWEEK*, March 16, 1992.

Case Study Questions

1. How large a role do information systems play at Simon & Schuster?

2. What management, organization, and technology issues do you think Simon & Schuster addressed when it put in its new information systems?

3. Simon & Schuster's information systems are used by people in many different functions who need different kinds of information. What kinds of organizational decisions and functions do they support? You may find it helpful to organize your answers in tabular form.

   Organizational Level   Function   Decision

4. Why do you think that book publishers have not more rapidly embraced information systems technology?

5. How much advantage do Simon & Schuster's information systems provide over more traditional publishers? What problems do they solve?

6. What are the costs and effects of not embracing this technology? Are there benefits to maintaining traditional book production methods?

7. How important are information systems in solving the problems of book publishing? What are some problems that technology cannot address?

References

Alavi, Maryam, and Patricia Carlson. "A Review of MIS Research and Disciplinary Development." *Journal of Management Information Systems* 8, no. 4 (Spring 1992).

Allen, Brandt R., and Andrew C. Boynton. "Information Architecture: In Search of Efficient Flexibility." *MIS Quarterly* 15, no. 4 (December 1991).

Anthony, R. N. *Planning and Control Systems: A Framework for Analysis.* Cambridge, MA: Harvard University Press, 1965.

Buss, Martin D. J., "Managing International Information Systems," *Harvard Business Review* (September 1982).

Carlyle, Ralph Emmett, "Managing IS at Multinationals," *Datamation* (March 1, 1988).

Cash, James I., F. Warren McFarlan, James L. McKenney, and Lynda M. Applegate. *Corporate Information Systems Management*, 3rd ed. Homewood, IL: Irwin, 1992.

Clark, Thomas D. Jr., "Corporate Systems Management: An Overview and Research Perspective," *Communications of the ACM* 35, no. 2 (February 1992).

Davis, Gordon B., and Margrethe H. Olson. *Management Information Systems: Conceptual Foundations, Structure, and Development,* 2nd ed. New York: McGraw-Hill, 1985.

Gorry, G. A., and M. S. Morton. "Framework for Management Information Systems." *Sloan Management Review* 13, no. 1 (Fall 1971).

Keen, Peter G. W. *Shaping the Future: Business Design through Information Technology.* Cambridge, MA: Harvard Business School Press, 1991.

Keen, P. G. W., and M. S. Morton. *Decision Support Systems: An Organizational Perspective.* Reading, MA: Addison-Wesley, 1978.

Kling, Rob, and William H. Dutton. "The Computer Package: Dynamic Complexity," in *Computers and Politics,* edited by James Danziger, William Dutton, Rob Kling, and Kenneth Kraemer. New York: Columbia University Press, 1982.

Laudon, Kenneth C. "A General Model for Understanding the Relationship Between Information Technology and Organizations." Working paper, Center for Research on Information Systems, New York University, 1989.

Liker, Jeffrey K, David B. Roitman, and Ethel Roskies. "Changing Everything All at Once: Work Life and Technological Change." *Sloan Management Review* (Summer 1987).

McFarlan, F. Warren, James L. McKenney, and Philip Pyburn. "The Information Archipelago—Plotting a Course." *Harvard Business Review* (January–February 1983a).

McFarlan, F. Warren, James L. McKenney, and Philip Pyburn. "Governing the New World." *Harvard Business Review* (July–August 1983b).

McKenney, James L., and F. Warren McFarlan. "The Information Archipelago—Maps and Bridges." *Harvard Business Review* (September–October 1982).

Niederman, Fred, James C. Brancheau, and James C. Wetherbe. "Information Systems Management Issues for the 1990s." *MIS Quarterly* 15, no. 4 (December 1991).

Orlikowski, Wanda J., and Jack J. Baroudi. "Studying Information Technology in Organizations: Research Approaches and Assumptions." *Information Systems Research* 2, no. 1 (March 1991).

Roach, Stephen S. "Services Under Siege—The Restructuring Imperative." *Harvard Business Review* (September–October, 1991).

Roach, Stephen S. "Technology and the Services Sector: The Hidden Competitive Challenge." *Technological Forecasting and Social Change* 34 (1988).

Roche, Edward M. "Planning for Competitive Use of Information Technology in Multinational Corporations." AIB UK Region, Brighton Polytechnic, Brighton, U.K., Conference Paper, March 1992. Edward M. Roche, W. Paul Stillman School of Business, Seton Hall University.

Scott-Morton, Michael, Ed. *The Corporation in the 1990s.* New York: Oxford University Press, 1991.

Strassman, Paul. *The Information Payoff—The Transformation of Work in the Electronic Age.* New York: Free Press, 1985.

Tornatsky, Louis G., J. D. Eveland, Myles G. Boylan, W. A. Hertzner, E. C. Johnson, D. Roitman, and J. Schneider. *The Process of Technological Innovation: Reviewing the Literature.* Washington, D.C.: National Science Foundation, 1983.

Caterpillar Unearths
New Business Programs

Caterpillar, Inc. is noted worldwide for the tractors, loaders, and bulldozers it manufactures. This $11.1 million Peoria, Illinois-based firm sells nearly all of its products through dealers. Because Caterpillar's dealer organization is its main sales channel, Caterpillar is developing new business systems to buttress its 75 North American dealers.

Dealers' local computers are linked to Caterpillar's central computers so that they can exchange data. A Dealer Business System enables dealers to access product and repair data from the central computers through their own local computers. Another system called Antares lets dealers order parts and process invoices and warranties from their local computers. A Service Information System delivers the catalogs of Caterpillar's engine parts electronically to the dealers' local computers. The system is intended as a graphical diagnostic tool that dealers can use to identify and repair problems with Caterpillar machines or parts. Caterpillar's equipment commonly

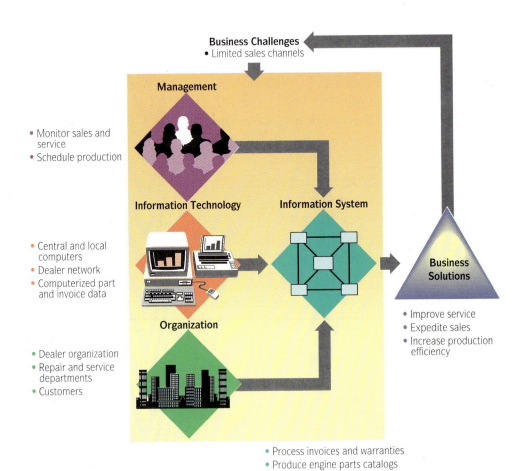

stays in use for 15 years or more, so dealers and field technicians have an ongoing need for parts data.

The systems eliminate time and paperwork because dealers don't have to call different people to obtain copies of invoices or information on customers and parts; dealers now obtain all of this informa-

tion immediately on-line. Caterpillar also manufactures many of its own parts, and the systems expedite order fulfillment by allowing the immediate transmission of part orders to Caterpillar's manufacturing and production systems. Thus, managers have an easier time scheduling production.

Source: Bob Violino, "Unearthing a New Approach," *Information WEEK*, April 13, 1992.

Caterpillar's information systems illustrate the key features of contemporary information systems:

- Single systems serving multiple business functions and levels in the firm.
- Immediate on-line access to large amounts of information.
- Heavy reliance on telecommunications technology.
- Increasing intelligence or expertise embedded into systems.
- The ability to combine data and graphics.

In this chapter we show how information systems can be classified to correspond with different organizational levels and different business functions. Sometimes an information system will support a single business level and a single business function. However, we are more likely to find systems such as those illustrated in our opening vignette that serve multiple levels of the organization and multiple users, providing data for more than one business function. Caterpillar's information systems are primarily for the sales function, but they also use engineering and design data and they provide data for systems supporting the manufacturing and production function. Caterpillar's operational level uses these systems to track orders and invoices. The firm's knowledge level uses them to distribute the information that dealers need to diagnose repair problems.

The types of information systems discussed in this chapter are presented from a functional rather than a technical standpoint. They illustrate how systems work, what kinds of information they contain, who uses the result, and various system designs.

After completing this chapter, you will be able to:

- Use vocabulary and symbols for describing information systems.
- Distinguish between batch and on-line processing.
- Identify the six types of information systems in organizations.
- Discuss the relationship among the various types of information systems.

2.1 Describing Systems: Vocabulary and Symbols

Systems are described using a special vocabulary and a special set of graphic symbols. Systems designers and other computer professionals rely on these symbols and terminology to represent system functions and design. We use them later in the chapter to describe the various types of information systems in organizations.

Rationalization of Procedures

Rationalization of procedures: Streamlining of standard operating procedures in order to maximize the advantages of computerization and make information systems more efficient.

An information system is distinct from the technology on which it operates. (We will explain the technology of systems in later chapters.) Many of the advances in information processing in the last decade have resulted from innovative and powerful systems design and rationalization of procedures, not just from better technology. **Rationalization of procedures** is the streamlining of standard operating procedures so that they can maximize the advantages of computerization and make information systems more efficient.

Note that Caterpillar's systems are effective not just because they utilize state-of-the-art computer technology but because their design allows Caterpillar to operate efficiently. The procedures of Caterpillar, or any organization, must be rationally structured to achieve this result. Before Caterpillar could automate its parts information, it had to have standard codes and descriptions for every part used by all of its dealers. It also had to have a shipping network in place, with formal rules for placing and shipping parts orders from dealers. Without a certain amount of rationalization in Caterpillar's organization, its on-line telecommunications technology would have been useless.

Symbols Used to Describe Information Systems

If an information system is represented graphically, it is often easier to understand how it works. To help you interpret system functions and design, this section introduces some of the more common symbols for representing information systems. Other symbols are introduced as they are needed in the chapters on systems analysis and design.

Figure 2.1 shows the major graphic symbols used in this text to describe systems. Five kinds of symbols are important in most system descriptions:

- Input: Keyboard input and digitizing devices
- Processing: Computers
- Storage: Magnetic tape, on-line storage, database, optical disk
- Telecommunications: links such as cable, telephone line or wireless transmission
- Output: on-line display terminal, document, printer

Figure 2.2 shows how these elements make up a system.

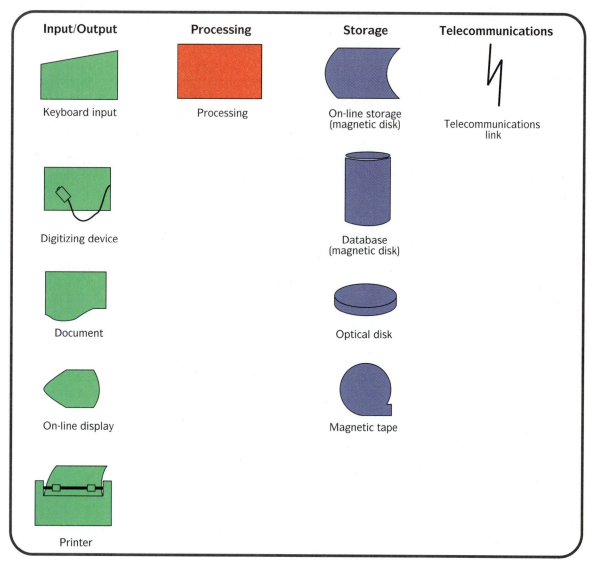

Figure 2.1
Common graphic symbols used to represent the major components of information systems.

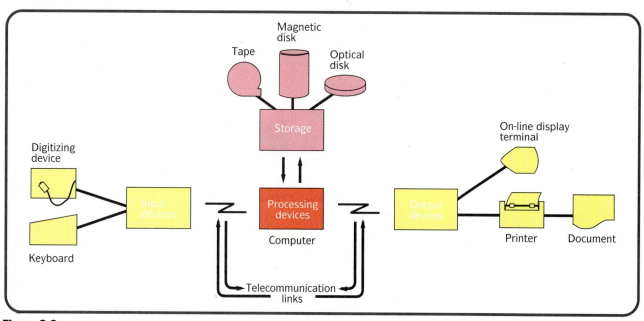

Figure 2.2
Graphic symbols displaying how these devices make up a typical information system.

In Figure 2.1, four of the symbols refer to different ways of storing information: on-line storage (usually a magnetic or optical disk), database (usually a magnetic disk), and magnetic tape. *On-line storage* refers to information that the computer and user can access immediately. An example might be a computerized file of your class list, which contains the names and identification numbers of all the members of your class and which you can access directly from a computer terminal. The computer, in other words, is directly connected to the computerized file. A *database* is simply (for now) a collection of files to which the user can gain access. The technology of these and other storage devices is described in later chapters. *Magnetic tape* stores data much like audiotape and videotape store pictures and music—namely, in sequential order using magnetic impressions on a thin film.

Batch and On-Line Processing

Batch processing: A method of processing information in which transactions are accumulated and stored until a specified time when it is convenient and/or necessary to process them as a group.

On-line processing: A method of processing information in which transactions are entered directly into the computer system and processed immediately.

The systems we discuss in the next section process information in one of two ways: through batch or through on-line processing. In **batch processing**, transactions such as orders or payroll timecards are accumulated and stored in a group or batch, until the time when, because of some reporting cycle, it is efficient or necessary to process them. This was the only method of processing until the early 1960s, and it is still used today in older systems. In **on-line processing**, which is now very common, the user enters transactions into a device that is directly connected to the computer system. The transactions are usually processed immediately.

The demands of the business determine the type of processing. If the user needs periodic or occasional reports or output, as in payroll or end-of-the-year reports, batch processing is most efficient. If the user needs immediate information and processing, as in the Caterpillar system, then the system should use on-line processing.

Figure 2.3
A comparison of batch and on-line processing. In batch processing, transactions are accumulated and stored in a group. Since batches are processed on a regular interval basis, such as daily, weekly, or monthly, information in the system will not always be up-to-date. A typical batch-processing job is payroll preparation. In on-line processing, transactions are input immediately and usually processed immediately. Information in the system is generally up-to-date. A typical on-line application is an airline reservation system.

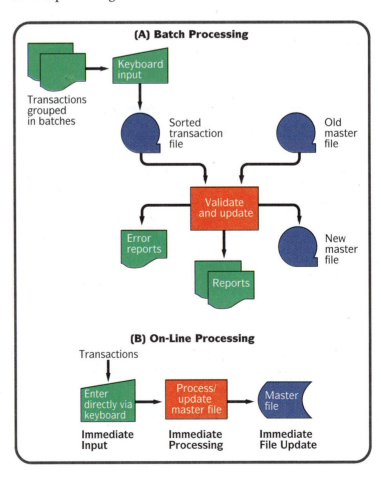

(A) Batch Processing

Keyboard input

Transactions grouped in batches

Sorted transaction file

Old master file

Validate and update

Error reports

New master file

Reports

(B) On-Line Processing

Transactions

Enter directly via keyboard

Process/ update master file

Master file

Immediate Input

Immediate Processing

Immediate File Update

Figure 2.3 compares batch and on-line processing. Batch systems often use tape as a storage medium, whereas on-line processing systems use disk storage, which permits immediate access to specific items of information. In batch systems, transactions are accumulated in a **transaction file**, which contains all the transactions for a particular time period. Periodically this file is used to update a **master file**, which contains permanent information on entities. (An example is a payroll master file with employee earnings and deductions data. It is updated with weekly timecard transactions.) Adding the transaction data to the existing master file creates a new master file. In on-line processing, transactions are entered into the system immediately and the system usually responds immediately. The master file is updated continually. In on-line processing, there is a direct connection to the computer for input and output.

These symbols and vocabulary will help us describe the major types of systems found in contemporary organizations and explain how these systems relate to one another.

> **Transaction file:** In batch systems, the file in which all transactions are accumulated to await processing.
>
> **Master file:** Contains all permanent information and is updated during processing by the transaction data.

2.2 Overview of Systems in the Organization

No single system provides all the information an organization needs. Organizations have many information systems serving different organizational levels and functions. Thus, the typical systems found in organizations are designed to assist workers or managers at each level and in the functions of sales and marketing, manufacturing, accounting, finance, and human resources. In this section we describe the specific categories of systems serving each organizational level.

Six Major Types of Systems

In Chapter 1 we explained why different types of systems are needed at different levels of the organization and by different functional specialties. Figure 2.4 shows the specific types of information systems that correspond to each organizational level. The organization has executive support systems (ESS) at the strategic level; management information systems (MIS) and decision support systems (DSS) at the management level; knowledge work systems (KWS) and office automation systems (OAS) at the knowledge level; and transaction processing systems (TPS) at the operational level. Systems at each level in turn are specialized to serve each of the major functional areas.

Transaction processing systems (TPS) serve the operational level of the organization. A transaction processing system is a computerized system that performs and records the daily routine transactions necessary to the conduct of the business. Examples are sales order entry, hotel reservation systems, client information (for public agencies), payroll, employee recordkeeping, and shipping. The Antares system that lets Caterpillar dealers order parts and process invoices and warranties is a TPS.

Tasks, resources, and goals at the organization's operational level are predefined and highly structured. The decision to grant credit to a customer, for instance, is made by a lower-level supervisor according to predefined criteria. The decision, in that sense, has been "programmed." All that must be determined is whether the customer meets the criteria.

Two features of TPS are noteworthy. First, TPS span the boundary between the organization and its environment. They connect customers to the firm's warehouse, factory, and management. If TPS do not work well, the organization fails either to receive inputs from the environment (orders) or to deliver outputs (assembled goods). Second, TPS are major producers of information for the other types of systems. Because TPS track relations with the environment, they are the only place where managers can obtain both up-to-the-minute assessments of organizational performance and long-term records of past performance. TPS

> **Transaction processing systems (TPS):** Computerized systems that perform and record the daily routine transactions necessary to the conduct of the business; they serve the operational level of the organization.

Types of Systems

	Strategic-Level Systems				
Executive Support Systems (ESS)	5-year sales trend forecasting	5-year operating plan	5-year budget forecasting	Profit planning	Manpower planning

	Management-Level Systems				
Management Information Systems (MIS)	Sales management	Inventory control	Annual budgeting	Capital investment analysis	Relocation analysis
Decision Support Systems (DSS)	Sales region analysis	Production scheduling	Cost analysis	Pricing/profitability analysis	Contract cost analysis

	Knowledge-Level Systems		
Knowledge Work Systems (KWS)	Engineering workstations	Graphics workstations	Managerial workstations
Office Automation Systems (OAS)	Word processing	Image storage	Electronic calendars

	Operational-Level Systems				
Transaction Processing Systems (TPS)	Machine control	Payroll	Auditing	Compensation
	Order tracking	Plant scheduling	Accounts payable	Tax reporting	Training & development
	Order processing	Material movement control	Accounts receivable	Cash management	Employee recordkeeping

Sales and Marketing	Manufacturing	Finance	Accounting	Human Resources

Figure 2.4

The six major types of information systems needed for the four levels of an organization. Information systems are built to serve each of the four levels of an organization. Transaction processing systems (TPS) serve the operational level of an organization. Knowledge work systems (KWS) and office automation systems (OAS) serve the knowledge level of an organization. Decision support systems (DSS) and management information systems (MIS) serve the management level of the organization. Executive support systems (ESS) serve the strategic level of an organization.

can be viewed as "organizational message processing systems" (Huber, 1982), informing managers about the status of internal operations and about the firm's relations with the external environment, and supporting other information systems that facilitate management decision making (Culnan, 1989).

It is difficult to imagine a modern organization without a transaction processing system. In the 1960s it was estimated that organizations could survive for a day without functioning computer systems. In the 1990s, TPS failure for a few hours can spell the demise of a firm and perhaps other firms linked to it. The Window on Organizations describes what happened when the computerized reservation systems of American Airlines and other carriers could not handle the upsurge in reservation transactions triggered by an air fare war.

Knowledge work systems (KWS) and **office automation systems (OAS)** serve the information needs at the knowledge level of the organization. Knowledge work systems aid knowledge workers, whereas office automation systems primarily aid data workers.

In general, knowledge workers are people who hold formal university degrees and who are often members of a recognized profession, like engineers, doctors, lawyers, and scientists. Their jobs consist primarily of creating new information and knowledge. Knowledge work systems, such as scientific or engineering design workstations, promote the creation of new knowledge and ensure that new knowledge and technical expertise are properly integrated into the business.

Data workers typically have less formal, advanced educational degrees and tend to process rather than create information. They consist primarily of secre-

Knowledge work systems (KWS): Information systems, that aid knowledge workers in the creation and integration of new knowledge in the organization.

Office automation systems (OAS): Computer systems, such as word processing, electronic mail systems, and scheduling systems, that are designed to increase the productivity of data workers in the office.

ORGANIZATIONS

Fare War Overwhelms Computerized Reservation Systems

In late May 1992, American Airlines announced it was slashing its lowest advance purchase ticket prices by 50 percent. The other airlines followed suit, triggering a deluge of calls for reservations. For instance, Delta Airlines received nearly 3 million calls in a single day; its normal daily volume is between 250,000 and 300,000.

The computerized reservation systems of American Airlines and other carriers buckled under the heavy transaction volume. American's Sabre, United Airlines' Covia and Continental Airlines' System

One computerized reservation systems were plagued by outages. Sabre had to intermittently bring down service to agencies, airlines, and ticketing offices throughout the United States to avoid a total system breakdown. At one point Sabre was handling 3,000 messages per second. Sabre repeatedly had to warn customers of impending outages, and American received many complaints.

Carlson Travel Network in Minneapolis, which has 300 Sabre sites, had offices down for up to 2½ hours at a time. Atlas Travel in

Coral Gables, Florida, which uses Sabre and System One (a rival computerized reservation system), was losing money because it could not use these systems two or three times a day for up to a half-hour at a time. Its agents were sitting around waiting to use the system and the agency would have to pay them overtime. A & S Travel in Wallingford, Connecticut, had to redo hundreds of tickets. Sabre could not print the invoices for discount credits. A & S was spending extra time and effort doing double the work.

Because of the heavy transaction volume, the computerized reservation systems had to cut back on other services as well. Sabre restricted the use of its Star Files service, which maintains records of client accounts and travel requirements until its reservation system was running smoothly again.

Sources: Bridget O'Brian and Brett Pulley, "American Airlines Slashes Its Fares Yet Again," *The Wall Street Journal*, May 28, 1992; and Bob Violino with Karen M. Carrillo, "Up, Up and Awry," *InformationWEEK*, June 8, 1992.

To Think About: Why are airline reservation transaction processing systems so important?

taries, accountants, filing clerks, or managers whose jobs are primarily to use, manipulate, or disseminate information. Office automation systems are information technology applications designed to increase the productivity of data workers in the office by supporting the coordinating and communicating activities of the typical office. Office automation systems coordinate diverse information workers, geographic units, and functional areas: the systems communicate with customers, suppliers, and other organizations outside the firm, and serve as a clearinghouse for information and knowledge flows. These activities primarily involve managing documents, communicating, and scheduling. Caterpillar's Service Information System, which delivers parts catalogs electronically to dealers, is an example of an OAS.

Typical office automation systems handle document management (through word processing, desktop publishing, digital filing), scheduling (through electronic calendars), and communication (through electronic mail, voice mail, or videoconferencing.) **Word processing** refers to the software and hardware that

Word processing: Office automation technology that facilitates the creation of documents through computerized text editing, formatting, storing, and printing.

creates, edits, formats, stores, and prints documents (see Chapters 7 and 15). Word processing systems represent the single most common application of information technology to office work, in part because producing documents is what offices are all about. **Desktop publishing** produces professional publishing-quality documents by combining output from word processing software with design elements, graphics, and special layout features.

In addition to data workers, knowledge workers who create and produce knowledge have traditionally utilized office automation technology as well. Now, however, new technologies are available to support their role in the firm. Powerful desktop computers called **workstations** with graphic, analytic, document management, and communications capabilities can pool together information from diverse perspectives and sources both inside and outside the firm. In the engineering field, knowledge work systems might use such tools to run thousands of calculations before designers are satisfied that a specific part is safe. Designers and drafting experts might want to use workstations with 3-D graphics software to visualize a model of a product more fully. (See the Window on Organizations in Chapter 1.) Lawyers, in turn, may want to scan thousands of legal findings on their desktop before recommending a strategy. More details on these powerful desktop tools can be found in Chapter 15.

The role of knowledge work and office automation systems in the firm cannot be underestimated. As the economy shifts from relying on manufactured goods to producing services, knowledge, and information, the productivity of individual firms and the entire economy will increasingly depend on knowledge-level systems. This is one reason knowledge-level systems have been the fastest-growing applications over the last decade and are likely to grow in the future. Knowledge-level systems also have become tied in more closely with the other systems in the firm.

Management information systems (MIS) and **decision support systems (DSS)** serve the management level of the organization. Management information systems provide managers with reports and, in some cases, with on-line access to the organization's current performance and historical records. MIS primarily serve the functions of planning, controlling, and decision making at the management level. Generally, they condense information obtained from TPS and present it to management in the form of routine summary and exception reports. MIS have highly limited analytical capabilities; they use very simple models to present data. Typically, they are oriented almost exclusively to internal, not environmental or external, events. An example is an accounts receivable subsystem that totals the outstanding balances overdue each month.

Some researchers use the term *MIS* to include all of the information systems that support the functional areas of the organization (Davis, 1985). However, in this book we prefer to use *computer-based information systems (CBIS)* as the umbrella term for all information systems and to consider management information systems as those that are specifically dedicated to management-level functions.

Managers use decision support systems (DSS) to assist them in making decisions that are semistructured, unique or rapidly changing, and not easily specified far in advance. DSS differ from MIS in several ways. DSS have more advanced analytical capabilities that permit the user to employ several different models to analyze information. These systems draw on internal information from TPS and MIS, and they often bring in information from external sources (e.g., current prices of financial futures supplied by another company). DSS tend to be more interactive, providing users with easy access to data and analytical models through user-friendly computer instructions. An example is a system that helps managers decide whether to lease or buy office equipment, depending on the price of the equipment and changing interest rates.

Desktop publishing: Technology that produces professional-quality documents combining output from word processors with design, graphics, and special layout features.

Workstations: Powerful desktop computers that combine high-quality graphics, analytical capabilities, and document management. Generally used in engineering and design applications.

Management information systems (MIS): Computer systems at the management level of an organization that serve the functions of planning, controlling, and decision making by providing routine summary and exception reports.

Decision support systems (DSS): Computer systems at the management level of an organization that combine data and sophisticated analytical models to support semistructured and unstructured decision making.

Executive support systems (ESS) are being used by the executives in this boardroom meeting. Video conferencing and advanced graphic software create an integrated computing and communications environment to enhance decision making.

Executive support systems (ESS): Information systems at the strategic level of an organization designed to address unstructured decision making through advanced graphics and communications.

Senior managers use a category of information systems called **executive support systems (ESS)** to make decisions. ESS serve the strategic level of the organization. ESS address unstructured decisions and create a generalized computing and communications environment rather than providing any fixed application or specific capability. ESS are designed to incorporate data about external events such as new tax laws or competitors, but they also draw summarized information from internal MIS and DSS. Although they have limited analytical capabilities, ESS employ the most advanced graphics software and can deliver graphs and data from many sources immediately to a senior executive's office or to a boardroom.

Unlike the other types of information systems, ESS are not designed primarily to solve specific problems. Instead, ESS provide a generalized computing and telecommunications capacity that can be applied to many situations. Compared to DSS, ESS tend to make less use of analytical models. Instead, ESS deliver information to managers on demand and on a highly interactive basis; ESS operate in a more open-ended manner.

Table 2.1 summarizes the features of the six types of information systems. It should be noted that each of the different kinds of systems may have components that are used by organizational levels and groups other than their main constituencies. A secretary may find information on an MIS, or a middle manager may need to extract data from a TPS.

The Strategic Role of Systems

One of the most exciting trends in information systems has been the growth of strategic information systems that give organizations a competitive advantage. These systems include those that support upper-management planning as well as those that create new products and services, open new markets, improve the delivery of services, and reduce costs. Information systems are now recognized as playing a strategic role in an organization's survival and prosperity. The strategic uses of information and information systems have become so critical to business success that the next chapter of this text is devoted entirely to this issue.

TABLE 2.1   CHARACTERISTICS OF INFORMATION PROCESSING SYSTEMS

Type of System	Information Inputs	Processing	Information Outputs	Users
ESS	Aggregate data; external, internal	Graphics; simulations; interactive	Projections; responses to queries	Senior managers
DSS	Low-volume data; analytic models	Interactive; simulations; analysis	Special reports; decision analyses; responses to queries	Professionals; staff managers
MIS	Summary transaction data; high-volume data; simple models	Routine reports; simple models; low-level analysis	Summary and exception reports	Middle managers
KWS	Design specifications; knowledge base	Modeling; simulations	Models; graphics	Professionals; technical staff
OAS	Documents; schedules	Document management; scheduling; communication	Documents; schedules; mail	Clerical workers
TPS	Transactions; events	Sorting; listing; merging; updating	Detailed reports; lists; summaries	Operations personnel; supervisors

Relationship of Systems to One Another: Integration

Figure 2.5 illustrates how the various types of systems in the organization are related to each other. TPS is typically a major source of data for other systems, whereas ESS is primarily a recipient of data from lower-level systems. (For instance, it is likely that the Caterpillar dealers' order transaction processing system provides data on orders and repairs that is probably summarized and analyzed by a MIS serving middle management.) The other types of systems may also exchange data among each other as well.

But how much can or should these systems be integrated? Should organizations have a single information system that serves the entire organization and coordinates all of the special systems previously outlined? Would it not be best to have such a single, total system to ensure that information can flow where it is needed, that it is uniform, and that all new systems are coordinated?

This total systems view, although occasionally advocated by writers in the field (along with their references to systems theory) is rapidly becoming outdated. In fact, no organization builds systems this way, and it would be foolish to try. The total systems view assumes that some specialist exists somewhere who can understand "the total information needs" of the organization (Ackoff, 1967). But the activities of a Sears, a General Motors, or even a small manufacturer are so diverse that many different specialists are needed to build different systems serving different purposes.

A more contemporary view is that systems should be integrated with one another—that is, they should provide for the systematic flow of information among different systems. This integrated approach has merits. But integration costs money, and it would be foolish to build bridges among systems simply for the sake of building bridges.

In the real world, managers provide the level of integration needed to operate the business. Connections among systems evolve over time. Most systems are built in isolation from other systems (unless some business reason suggests a different approach). Organizations do not build all systems at once; the re-

Figure 2.5
Interrelationships among systems. The various types of systems in the organization do not work independently; rather, there are interdependencies between the systems. TPS are a major producer of information that is required by the other systems which, in turn, produce information for other systems. These different types of systems are only loosely coupled in most organizations.

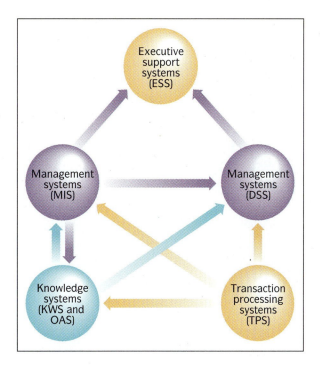

sources required to do so would be enormous, the management problems insurmountable. With the development of new hardware and software—especially database management systems and private telecommunications systems—building bridges among systems is becoming less expensive and more reliable.

Organizations pay a penalty for this evolutionary approach to systems. Systems are often not as integrated as they sometimes need to be. This situation creates bottlenecks and inefficiencies in a firm's essential business activities. Occasionally, an organization must mount a massive effort to develop new data processing and telecommunications systems that can integrate systems. General Motors purchased Electronic Data Systems (EDS), one of the largest system contractors in the United States, to replace its hodgepodge of uncoordinated computer-aided design, computer-aided manufacturing, word processing, and various other systems, plus one hundred telecommunications networks with a seamless, interconnected set of systems. GM needed to integrate its manufacturing, ordering, and delivery operations to remain globally competitive. In the case concluding Part I of this book, we discuss the pros and cons of system integration.

GM needed more integrated systems to remain competitive. But as organizations move toward centralizing, coordinating, and controlling system evolution, they create more layers of management approval for systems and more bureaucracy in the process. Eventually, centralization reaches a saturation point, and organizations start allowing their divisions or operating units to develop systems on their own. In short, decisions to integrate systems, to centralize control, are like the tides—they ebb and flow in accordance with business conditions and values. There is no "one right level" of integration or centralization (Allen and Boynton, 1991; King, 1984).

2.3 Examples of Information Systems

This section provides concrete examples of real-world systems for each category of information systems found in organizations: TPS, KWS, OAS, MIS, DSS, and ESS. The system descriptions use the graphic symbols and vocabulary that were introduced earlier in the chapter.

Type of TPS System				
	Sales/ marketing systems	Manufacturing/ production systems	Finance/ accounting systems	Human resources systems	Other types (e.g., university)
Major functions of system	Sales management	Scheduling	Budgeting	Personnel records	Admissions
	Market research	Purchasing	General ledger	Benefits	Grade records
	Promotion	Shipping/receiving	Billing	Compensation	Course records
	Pricing	Engineering	Cost accounting	Labor relations	Alumni
	New products	Operations		Training	
Major application systems	Sales order information system	Materials resource planning systems	General ledger	Payroll	Registration system
	Market research system	Purchase order control systems	Accounts receivable/payable	Employee records	Student transcript system
	Pricing system	Engineering systems	Budgeting	Benefit systems	Curriculum class control systems
		Quality control systems	Funds management systems	Career path systems	Alumni benefactor system
				Personnel planning systems	

Figure 2.6
Typical applications of TPS. There are five functional categories of TPS: Sales/Marketing, Manufacturing/Production, Finance/Accounting, Human Resources, and other types of systems specific to a particular industry. TPS support most business functions in most organizations. Within each of these major functions are subfunctions. For each of these subfunctions (e.g., sales management) there is a major application system.

Transaction Processing Systems

All organizations have five kinds of TPS, even if the systems are manual. These five kinds of TPS are sales/marketing, manufacturing/production, finance/accounting, human resources, and other types of TPS that are unique to a particular industry. Figure 2.6 identifies the major functions and typical applications of TPS.

Figures 2.7 and 2.8 depict two financial TPS: an accounts receivable system and a payroll system developed by the authors for a medium-sized consumer products distributor in New Jersey. The company has over 12,000 customers in the Northeast and a labor force of 205.

The master file in each of the systems is composed of discrete pieces of information (such as a name, address, or customer number) called data elements. Data are keyed into the system, updating the data elements. The elements on the master file are combined in different ways to make up reports of interest to management. These TPS can generate other report combinations of existing data elements.

Knowledge Work and Office Automation Systems

The ideal knowledge system supporting both knowledge work and office automation functions would allow for the seamless creation, storage, and communication of documents, voice and written messages, images, and data from any point in the organization to any other point. A more modest goal—still far away—would provide for this capability within a single division or even a single large office. The truth is that today it is still nearly impossible to create a document on a personal desktop computer, send it to a copying machine electronically for duplication or transparency creation, and then send it to other

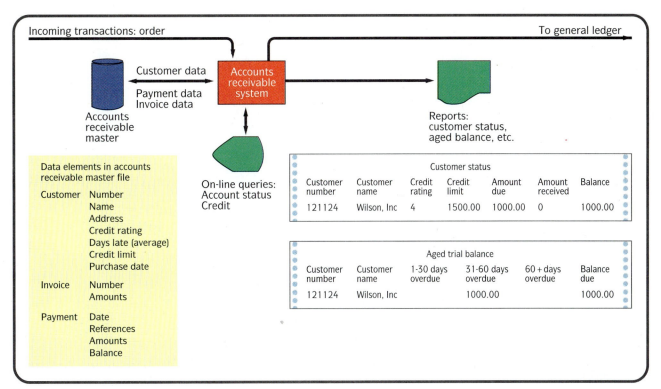

Figure 2.7
A symbolic representation for an accounts receivable TPS.

knowledge or data workers for their information. Instead of having such integrated capabilities, actual knowledge systems have many separate automated devices and limited means of connecting them.

Figure 2.8
A symbolic representation for a payroll system TPS.

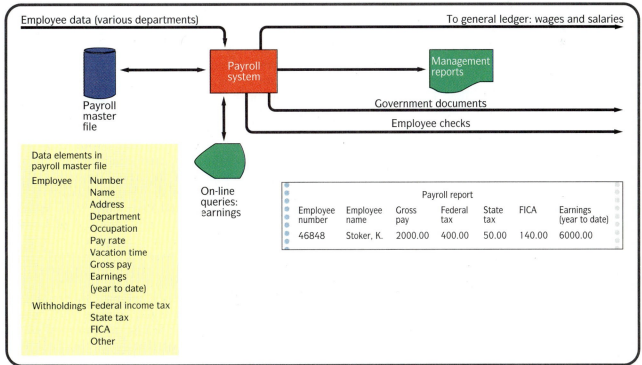

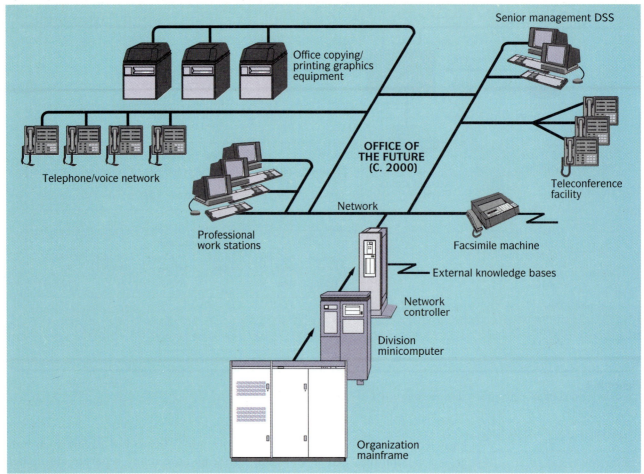

Figure 2.9
An illustration of an ideally configured knowledge level system. The office of the future will be able to coordinate the text, document, image, data, and voice needs for various groups of data and knowledge workers in a totally integrated network.

Figure 2.9 shows an ideal fully integrated knowledge level system that can coordinate the document, image, data, and voice needs of different kinds of knowledge and data workers, and tie into corporate telecommunication and data facilities. At present, however, most knowledge level systems remain isolated islands because they use devices that are not linked to one another. While the computer industry has been furiously working on connectivity technology and standards (see Chapter 10), most terminals and equipment from different manufacturers still cannot automatically be connected together. For example, an IBM Personal System/2 microcomputer workstation cannot automatically be connected to a Xerox machine or to a Macintosh microcomputer, nor are all IBM products yet interconnectable.

Most organizations have not developed single, organizationwide knowledge work or office automation systems. Nevertheless, many interesting bits and pieces of advanced knowledge applications are on the shelf. One such application is computer-aided design (CAD), introduced in Chapter 1. Chapter 15 contains a fuller discussion of office automation and knowledge work applications. Here, we examine one widely used knowledge application: **digital image processing**, the conversion of documents and images into computerized form so that they can be stored and accessed by computer systems.

Digital image processing: Technology that converts documents and graphic images into computerized form so that they can be stored, processed, and accessed by computer systems.

DIGITAL IMAGE PROCESSING

One of the largest impediments to automating offices is finding a way to digitize paper documents that must be preserved as images. For instance, many documents—from marriage licenses, to birth certificates, to contracts of all kinds—require a signature and the preservation of that signature for a long period. Moreover, many basic documents, like purchase orders, invoices, ap-

TECHNOLOGY
Conquering the Paper Mountain

The United Services Automobile Association, with 13,600 employees, provides a broad range of investment, insurance, retirement, purchasing, and travel products to 2 million military officers and their families. Based in San Antonio, USAA is the largest direct writer of property and casualty insurance in the United States. Selling directly to members via mail or telephone, it is the largest mail order firm in the United States as well. USAA receives over 100,000 letters and mails over 250,000 items daily.

USAA has developed the largest imaging system in the world, storing 1.5 billion pages. All incoming mail received each day by the policy department is scanned and stored on optical disk. The original documents are thrown away.

Six of USAA's major regional offices across the country are hooked up to its imaging network, illustrated in Figure 2.10. The net-

work consists of image scanners, optical storage units, an IBM model 4381 small mainframe computer, and a local network to link service representatives' workstations and the scanner workstations located in the firm's mailroom. Mail clerks feed documents into a scanner, which digitizes them and transmits the data into USAA's Management Folder Software for storage on optical disk. Service representatives can retrieve a client's file on-line and view documents from IBM personal computers on their desktops. About 2000 people use the network.

Users believe that the imaging system reduces the amount of time their work would take with a paper-based system by one-third, saving paper and storage costs. Before this system was introduced, 200 clerks had to search for files in a 39,000 square-foot

warehouse, a process that might take one day or up to two weeks if the files were lying on a policy reviewer's desk. Customer service has been improved because electronic documents can be accessed more rapidly. Three-week-old files can be accessed in less than one second; six-month-old letters, in 15-20 seconds; mail up to two years old, in less than two minutes.

Sources: "USAA: Insuring Progress," *InformationWEEK*, May 25, 1992; Lasher, Ives, and Jarvenpaa, December 1991; and Kathy Chin Leong, "IBM exposes image network," *Computerworld*, May 30, 1988.

To Think About: What kinds of management, organization, and technology problems can be solved by using digital image processing?

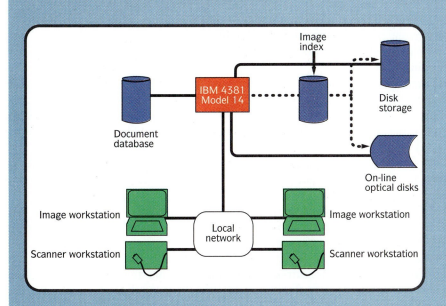

Figure 2.10
United States Automobile Association's (USAA) imaging network. Scanners enter mail received by USAA's policy department into the imaging system, which stores and distributes the digitally processed image of the document electronically. Service representatives have immediate on-line access to clients' data.

proval sheets, remittance advice, and others, are still stored manually in filing cabinets. One solution to paperwork management problems is digital image processing. This technology can be used to convert documents and graphic images into computerized form so that they can be stored, processed, and accessed by computer systems. The Window on Technology illustrates how the United Services Automobile Association solved this problem with an imaging network that eliminated paper filing systems for its policy department.

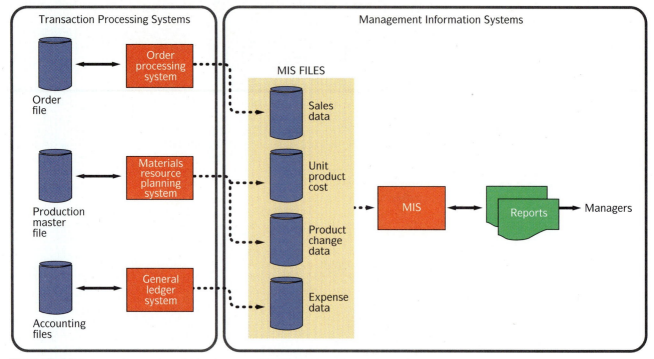

Figure 2.11

How management information systems obtain their data from the organization's TPS. In the system illustrated by this diagram, three TPS supply summarized transaction data at the end of the time period to the MIS reporting system. Managers gain access to the organizational data through the MIS, which provides them with the appropriate reports.

Management Information Systems

Management information systems (MIS) help managers monitor the organization's current performance and predict future performance, so that they can intervene when things are not going well. The systems help management control the organization.

MIS are generally dependent on underlying transaction processing systems for their data. MIS summarize and report on the basic operations of the company, often using data supplied by TPS. The basic transaction data are compressed by summarization and are usually presented in long reports. The reports are usually produced on a regular schedule; they answer structured, routine questions. Figure 2.11 shows how a typical MIS transforms transaction level data from inventory, production, and accounting into MIS files that are used to provide managers with reports. Figure 2.12 shows a sample report from this system.

The Window on Management on page 48 describes an MIS used by the Travelers Insurance Company to monitor its claims review procedures and to identify duplicate medical charges.

MIS serve managers interested in weekly, monthly, and yearly results—not day-to-day activities. MIS address structured questions that are known well in advance, are generally not flexible, and have little analytical capability. For instance, one cannot instruct an MIS to "take the monthly sales figures by zip code and correlate with the Bureau of the Census estimates of income by zip code." First, a typical MIS contains only corporate internal data, not external data like the U.S. Census figures. Second, most MIS use simple routines such as summaries and comparisons, as opposed to sophisticated mathematical models or statistical techniques. Third, data on sales by zip code would not be available on a typical MIS unless a user had informed the designer several years earlier that this arrangement of data might be useful.

Figure 2.12
A sample report that might be
produced by the MIS system in
Figure 2.11.

**Consolidated Consumer Products Corporation
Sales by Product and Sales Region: 1993**

PRODUCT CODE	PRODUCT DESCRIPTION	SALES REGION	ACTUAL SALES	PLANNED	ACTUAL VS. PLANNED
4469	Carpet Cleaner	Northeast	4,066,700	4,800,000	0.85
		South	3,778,112	3,750,000	1.01
		Midwest	4,867,001	4,600,000	1.06
		West	4,003,440	4,400,000	0.91
	TOTAL		16,715,253	17,550,000	0.95
5674	Room Freshener	Northeast	3,676,700	3,900,000	0.94
		South	5,608,112	4,700,000	1.19
		Midwest	4,711,001	4,200,000	1.12
		West	4,563,440	4,900,000	0.93
	TOTAL		18,559,253	17,700,000	1.05

Table 2.2 describes the characteristics of typical management information systems.

Newer MIS are more flexible and may include software that lets managers structure their own reports and combine data from separate files and TPS. For instance, suppose a director of sales wanted to know if prices charged to major customers this year are keeping pace with cost increases. An MIS could tell the sales director if the customer bought as much this year as last year and could compare the profit margin between this year and last. Many older MIS do not have these features.

Decision Support Systems

Any system that supports a decision is a decision support system. Nonetheless, systems support decisions in vastly different ways, and there is a class of systems that supports decisions in a unique way (at least when compared to the past).

Table 2.2   CHARACTERISTICS OF MANAGEMENT INFORMATION SYSTEMS

1. MIS support structured and semistructured decisions at the operational and management control levels. However, they are also useful for planning purposes of senior management staff.
2. MIS are generally reporting and control oriented. They are designed to report on existing operations and therefore to help provide day-to-day control of operations.
3. MIS rely on existing corporate data and data flows.
4. MIS have little analytical capability.
5. MIS generally aid in decision making using past and present data.
6. MIS are relatively inflexible.
7. MIS have an internal rather than an external orientation.
8. Information requirements are known and stable.
9. MIS require a lengthy analysis and design process (on the order of one to two years).

MANAGEMENT

Computers Combat High Health Care Costs

When a woman submits a bill for an X-ray to her medical insurer, the bill won't tell if she is a woman or if she was pregnant at the time. Pregnant women should not receive X-rays. The Travelers Insurance Company believes that helping to enforce proper standards of medical care treatment can also help reduce costs. So it built a Practice Review System both to scrutinize data on claims submitted by patients and to identify redundant charges.

Travelers already had a system to review claims for appropriate procedures and billing. But the claims were evaluated in a vacuum that did not consider the patient's history. In contrast, the Practice Review System compares bills against patient data acquired during the claims submission process. If a pregnant woman submits a bill for an X-ray, the system could determine that the patient was subjected to an improper procedure. Travelers could use this information to deny payment or to review the treatment practices of the physician who ordered the X-ray.

The system also helps Travelers more closely monitor how much health care providers charge. A physician who submits a bill for a hysterectomy that includes a charge for the total procedure along with charges for each step could be deliberately double billing or merely be confused about proper billing practices. The Practice Review System automatically reviews the bill and refuses payment for inappropriate charges. Travelers might even drop the physician from its provider network if the doctor continually submits bills with redundant charges or provides inappropriate treatment.

Figure 2.13 illustrates how the system works. Using standardized procedure codes and treatment protocols that were developed by Value Health Sciences, Inc. (an offshoot of the Rand Corporation in Santa Monica, California), each bill identifies the medical procedures performed. The system can show that most of the procedures in this particular bill are redundant because they are part of the total hysterectomy procedure.

Monitoring claims this way trims Travelers' claims administration time and costs, reduces inappropriate claims payments, and promotes quality among medical care providers. In addition to aiding insurance companies such as Travelers, computers can help lower treatment costs when they are used by the physicians themselves. Indiana University researchers studying physicians using computers to order drugs and tests for hospital patients found that charges to patients were 13 per cent lower than when doctors used paper and pen. The computer system provided comparative costs for tests and treatments and information to help doctors discard unnecessary tests. The physicians with computers could immediately see the costs of the tests and therapies they ordered for their patients and the cost of less expensive alternatives.

Sources: Ron Winslow, "Computers Helping Doctors Match Care with Costs Can Lower Bills, Study Says," *The Wall Street Journal*, January 20, 1993 and Bruce Caldwell, "Travelers' Software Cure," *InformationWEEK*, March 2, 1992.

To Think About: Is this a typical MIS? Why or why not? What benefits would managers derive from this system?

Physician's Bill

DATE	PROCEDURE CODE	PROCEDURE DESCRIPTION	FEE
01/12/94	58150	Total hysterectomy	1700
01/12/94	49000	Explore abdominal cavity	500
01/12/94	57410	Pelvic exam-anesthesia	200
01/12/94	58740	Lysis of adhesions	400
01/14/94	90260	Subsequent hospital visit	90
01/16/94	90260	Subsequent hospital visit	90
		TOTAL	$2,980

Insurer's Payment

DATE	PROCEDURE CODE	PROCEDURE DESCRIPTION	FEE
01/12/94	58150	Total hysterectomy	$1,700

Figure 2.13
The report in this figure illustrates how the Travelers Insurance Practice Review System works. The physician's bill contains additional charges with different procedure codes that were actually included as part of the entire procedure. The Practice Review System can identify these redundant charges and issue the correct payment for the procedure.

Table 2.3   CHARACTERISTICS OF DECISION SUPPORT SYSTEMS

1. DSS offer users flexibility, adaptability, and a quick response.
2. DSS allow users to initiate and control the input and output.
3. DSS operate with little or no assistance from professional programmers.
4. DSS provide support for decisions and problems whose solutions cannot be specified in advance.
5. DSS use sophisticated analysis and modeling tools.

Table 2.3 shows how contemporary decision support systems (DSS) differ from MIS and TPS systems.

DSS are quick-hit, interactive, model-oriented, and action-oriented, whereas MIS systems tend to be ponderous, batch-oriented, and data-oriented (Sprague and Carlson 1982; Keen, 1985). DSS have to be responsive enough to run several times a day in order to correspond to changing conditions. DSS have a different set of users from MIS. DSS are used by managers and also by the vast army of knowledge workers, analysts, and professionals whose primary job is handling information and making decisions.

Figure 2.14 illustrates the ideal configuration of DSS. Clearly, by design, DSS have more analytical power than other systems; they are built explicitly with a variety of models to analyze data. The database is important as well, but the emphasis is on analysis. Second, DSS are designed so that users can work with them directly; these systems explicitly include user-friendly software. This follows both from their purpose (to inform personal decision making by key actors) and from the method of design (see Chapter 16). Third, these systems are interactive; the user can change assumptions and include new data.

An interesting, small, but powerful DSS is the voyage-estimating system of a subsidiary of a large American metals company that exists primarily to carry bulk cargoes of coal, oil, ores, and finished products for its parent company. The firm owns some vessels, charters others, and bids for shipping contracts in the open market to carry general cargo. A voyage-estimating system calculates financial and technical voyage details. Financial calculations include ship/time costs (fuel, labor, capital), freight rates for various types of cargo, and port expenses. Technical details include myriad factors such as ship cargo capacity (deadweight tons, tons per inch immersion, etc.), speed, port distances, fuel and water consumption, and loading patterns (location of cargo for different ports).

Figure 2.14
A symbolic representation of an ideally configured decision support system.
Source: Sprague and Carlson, 1982.

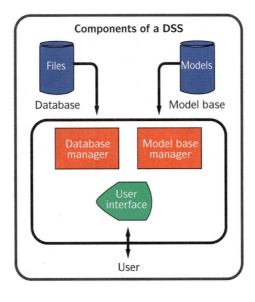

An existing system to calculate only operating costs, freight rates, and profit was run on the company mainframe computer. The reports could not be understood by the managers because of the wealth of technical details they contained; only one person in the MIS department could run the program; and it took several weeks to make changes in assumptions (cost of fuel, speed). Morever, the system could not answer questions such as the following: Given a customer delivery schedule and an offered freight rate, which vessel should be assigned at what rate to maximize profits? What is the optimum speed at which a particular vessel can optimize its profit and still meet its delivery schedule? What is the optimal loading pattern for a ship bound for the U.S. West Coast from Malaysia?

Senior and middle management wanted a more interactive system that they could control and run themselves, with as many changes in data and models as they needed and with little interference from data processing professionals. Management also needed information immediately to respond to bidding opportunities. Figure 2.15 illustrates the DSS built for this company. The system operates on a powerful desktop microcomputer, provides a system of menus that makes it easy for users to enter data or obtain information, is totally under management control, and required about 160 person-days to build.

Executive Support Systems

Unlike DSS, executive support systems (ESS) represent a generalized computing, telecommunications, and display capability that can be focused and applied to a changing array of problems. The audience is senior management. The questions ESS must assist in answering include the following: What business should we be in? What are the competitors doing? What new acquisitions would protect us from cyclical business swings? Which units should we sell to raise cash for acquisitions? What is the impact on earnings of proposed changes in the investment tax credit? (Rockart, 1982; Keen, 1985).

ESS are designed for senior managers who have little, if any, direct contact or experience with computer-based information systems. ESS combine data from

Figure 2.15
Voyage estimating decision support system. This DSS operates on a powerful microcomputer. It is used daily by managers who must develop bids on shipping contracts.

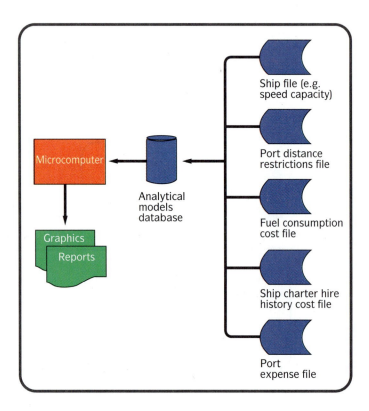

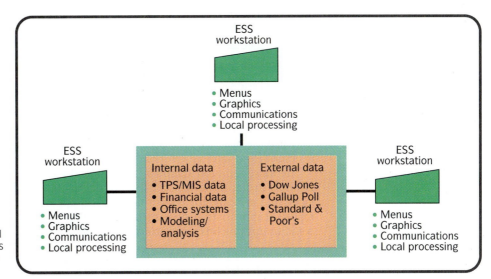

Figure 2.16
Model of a typical executive support system. This system pools data from diverse internal and external sources and makes them available to executives in an easy-to-use form.

various internal and external sources. They filter, compress, and track critical data, emphasizing the reduction of time and effort required to obtain information useful to executives. Figure 2.16 illustrates a model of an ESS. It consists of workstations with menu, interactive graphics, and communications capabilities that can access historical and competitive data from internal corporate systems and external databases such as Dow Jones News/Retrieval or the Gallup Poll.

Why were these systems not developed years ago? One reason is that senior executives associated computer terminals with clerical work. More significantly, the technology was not available. The data flows were often not established because traditional MIS departments did not think in terms of presenting data to senior managers. Equipment was expensive, especially for color graphics terminals and plotters. And, most important, user-friendly software simply did not exist before the development of microcomputers.

Senior executives have different personal styles and face radically changing environments and questions. Systems must be built that can adapt to these new conditions. ESS are one response to this challenge. More details on leading-edge applications of DSS and ESS can be found in Chapter 16.

Management Challenges

1. **Anticipating future requirements.** It is painfully difficult to build robust systems capable of handling unanticipated demands. As in the American Airlines case, a change in marketing strategy can result in a huge increase in business volume that in turn stretches the firm's information systems to the limit. However, it is prohibitively expensive to build systems so powerful that they can handle all imaginable future demands.

2. **Dependency.** Over time, firms become more and more dependent on their transaction processing systems to process virtually all cash flows. Although this situation enhances productivity and quality overall, there is a growing risk that should the TPS fail for some reason, no alternatives are in place. Usually this risk is unforeseen—hence unmanaged—and expensive to reduce.

3. **Integration.** On the one hand, it is necessary to design different systems for different levels and functions in the firm—TPS, MIS, DSS, OAS, KWS, and ESS. On the other hand, integrating the systems so they can freely exchange information can be technologically difficult, and costly. Managers need to determine what level of systems integration is required and how much it is worth in dollars.

Summary

Use vocabulary and symbols for describing information systems.

Rationalization of procedures is the streamlining of standard operating procedures so that the advantages of computerization can be maximized and so that information systems can work more smoothly. On-line storage refers to a file of information that the computer and user can access immediately. A database is a collection of files to which the user can gain access. The technology of these and other storage devices is described in later chapters.

The most common symbols for graphically representing information systems are symbols for input devices (keyboard, digitizing device); symbols for processing devices; and symbols for output devices (on-line display, printer). We can graphically represent information systems by using these symbols along with symbols for telecommunications links and storage (magnetic tape, magnetic disk, and optical disk).

Distinguish between batch and on-line processing.

In batch processing, transactions are accumulated and stored in a group until the time when it is efficient or necessary to process them. In on-line processing, the user enters transactions into a device that is directly connected to the computer system. The transactions are usually processed immediately.

Identify the six types of information systems in organizations.

There are six major types of information systems in contemporary organizations: 1) transaction processing systems (TPS) at the operational level; 2) knowledge work systems (KWS) and 3) office automation systems (OAS) at the knowledge level; 4) management information systems (MIS) and 5) decision support systems (DSS) at the management level; and 6) executive support systems (ESS) at the strategic level.

The six types of systems are designed for different purposes and different audiences: Transaction processing systems (TPS) perform and record the daily routine transactions that are necessary to conduct business. They also produce information for the other systems. Many organizations today would come to a standstill if their TPS failed for a day or even a few hours. Examples are systems for order processing, airline reservations, and payroll.

Knowledge-level systems support clerical, managerial, and professional workers. They consist of office automation systems for increasing the productivity of data workers (word processing, desktop publishing, document storage, facsimile transmission, electronic mail, videoconferencing) and knowledge work systems for enhancing the productivity of knowledge workers (professional workstations, graphics, analytical models, document preparation, and communication). Knowledge work systems are increasingly tied to other systems in the firm.

Management systems (MIS and DSS) provide the management control level with reports and access to the organization's current performance and historical records. Most MIS reports condense information from TPS and are not highly analytical. Decision support systems (DSS) support management decisions when these decisions are unique, rapidly changing, and not specified easily in advance. They have more advanced analytical models than MIS and often draw on information from external as well as internal sources.

Executive support systems (ESS) support the strategic level by providing a generalized computing and communications environment to assist senior management's decision making. They have limited analytical capabilities but can draw on sophisticated graphics software and many sources of internal and external information.

Discuss the relationship among the various types of information systems.

The various types of systems in the organization exchange data with one another. TPS are a major source of data for other systems, especially MIS and DSS. ESS is primarily a recipient of data from lower-level systems.

The different systems in an organization are only loosely integrated. There is no single total system that coordinates all the systems. In most organizations the information needs of the various functional areas and organizational levels are too specialized to be served by a single system. However, integrating information from various systems is desirable and often essential for a business. Developing links among systems is costly, but so is the lack of sufficient links.

<table>
<tr><td rowspan="7" valign="top">Key Terms</td><td>Rationalization of procedures</td><td>Word processing</td></tr>
<tr><td>Batch processing</td><td>Desktop publishing</td></tr>
<tr><td>On-line processing</td><td>Workstations</td></tr>
<tr><td>Transaction file</td><td>Management information systems (MIS)</td></tr>
<tr><td>Master file</td><td></td></tr>
<tr><td>Transaction processing systems (TPS)</td><td>Decision-support systems (DSS)</td></tr>
<tr><td>Knowledge work systems (KWS)</td><td>Executive support systems (ESS)</td></tr>
<tr><td>Office automation systems (OAS)</td><td>Digital image processing</td></tr>
</table>

Review Questions

1. What are five characteristics of contemporary information systems?
2. What do we mean by rationalization of procedures? Why is this essential for building CBIS?
3. List three devices for storing information.
4. What is the difference between batch and on-line processing? Diagram the difference.
5. List and briefly describe the major types of systems in organizations.
6. What are the five major types of TPS in business organizations? What functions do they perform? Give examples of each.
7. Describe the functions performed by knowledge work and office automation systems and the tools used for each.
8. Why has the ideal knowledge system been difficult to achieve?
9. What are the characteristics of MIS? How do MIS differ from TPS? From DSS?
10. What are the characteristics of DSS? How do they differ from ESS?
11. Why are ESS a relatively new phenomenon?
12. How are the six major types of systems in organizations related?

Discussion Questions

1. Discuss the major factors that may prevent an organization from building a totally integrated information system that combines all six major types of systems into a single design effort.
2. Review the accounts receivable and payroll TPS described in this chapter. Explain how they could be producers of data for other systems. Can you think of other reports that use data generated by these systems?
3. Most senior executives do not like to spend a lot of time learning how to use computers, and most do not spend much time looking at reports and numbers. What are the implications of this situation for ESS?

Group Project

In a group with three or four other classmates, research a business firm using annual reports or publications such as *Fortune* or *Business Week*. Describe some of the TPS, MIS, DSS, KWS, OAS, and ESS that might be found in the firm and present your group's findings to the class.

CSX Information Systems Put Service on the Right Track

CSX Transportation Inc., based in Richmond, Virginia, is the leading railroad in the United States by revenue, producing gross revenue of over $4.5 billion in 1990. Like other rail freight carriers, it has been losing business for decades to the trucking and airlines industries. To cope with the intense competition and economic slowdown during the early 1990s, the firm has been using information technology to cut its work force and to operate more cost effectively. Also, it is slowly starting to pay attention to customer service. This is important, because the railroads have acquired a reputation of being uncaring about customers. CSX diversified by acquiring and investing in oil and gas, real estate, and telecommunications ventures. It needed to focus more on its core transportation business.

In 1988, CSX launched a back-to-basics campaign, selling its other businesses to turn its attention to railway transport. The firm implemented computerized tracking and scheduling systems and it looked for innovative ways to offer customers more reliable service with fewer employees. It invested in a control and communications system that would run the railroad with as little manual input as possible. The system now tracks all freight car and train movements, handles basic accounting, and provides analysis of these functions for the firm's key decision makers. A decision-support information system provides cost and revenue data on car and train inventories.

CSX introduced radio-frequency scanners to oversee the delivery of hundreds of thousands of Chrysler Corporation automobiles carried by CSX. Before this system was installed, CSX had used a three-part paper form that was placed in each automobile. Each form had to be handled manually and was eventually entered into a computer for tracking and reconciliation. Chrysler felt hampered by the paper-based system and began placing bar-code information on each vehicle.

When cars are shipped by rail, they are off-loaded and stored until they are ready for final delivery to dealers by truck. With so many cars being transported, keeping track of where a particular make, model, and color is located becomes a gargantuan job. Obtaining this information quickly improves customer service, and benefits both CSX and Chrysler.

CSX uses the scanners to access the bar code on each vehicle and transmits the information automatically via radio equipment to a central computer. The information automatically updates the firm's inventory and tracking system. When CSX is ready to turn the car over to the dealer it can update the inventory and closely manage it for Chrysler.

When Chrysler is looking for a particular car to send to a dealer, CSX can locate the choice much faster. Chrysler benefits from the more accurate and timely information from the CSX system, while CSX cuts costs. Task time has been reduced 85 percent for a savings of 30 person-hours per week. With other carriers competing for the Chrysler account, CSX's investment in the scanners helped the firm preserve and even expand its relationship with its important client. The new system has dramatically shortened computer data entry time and reduced the time required to search and deliver a vehicle by 85 percent.

Other system applications include Mercury, which enables CSX and its customers to reduce tremendous volumes of paperwork and processing by eliminating paper-based purchase orders and bills of lading. (Bills of lading are shipping instructions from the customer to the railroad.) A total of 2000 shippers use the system; therefore, eliminating the need to key in bills of lading manually produces large savings for CSX, while electronically providing shippers with the precise locations of their shipments. The system also has electronic mail, way-bill retrieval, and railcar ordering capabilities.

Major customers' demands for railcars are complex, but these requests can now be managed electronically. Shippers transmit data about their anticipated railcar needs for a two-week period electronically to CSX's computer. Since the data goes directly into CSX's scheduling system, shippers can be queued more rapidly for railcars. CSX thus has better control over its railcar inventory.

CSX believes that it recouped the $1 million required to build the Mercury system in just one year by automating bills of lading alone. Customer service benefits from faster turnaround of status requests and investigation of billing disputes. Delays or inaccuracies caused by placing shipping instructions via telephone or mail have also been eliminated. CSX estimates that it is getting a 35 percent return on its half-billion dollar investment in information technology, much of it from driving down operating costs. The number of employees has been reduced from a peak of 80,000 in the 1980s to around 38,000 today.

CSX joined forces with the AMR Corporation, which owns American Airlines, to develop a global logistics management system called Encompass. This system links a company's suppliers, customers, shippers, carriers, freight forwarders, and consignees; they can now communicate directly with one another or monitor each other's activities. For instance, by using Encompass, Procter & Gamble detected routing delays and was able to redirect inventory from European warehouses rather than tap its safety stock locations in Japan.

Sources: Julia King, "AMR and CSX Shake Hands on Logistics Deal," *Computerworld,* August 24, 1992; "CSX Switches Tracks," *InformationWEEK,* April 13, 1992; and Jon Pepper, "Getting Service on Track," *InformationWEEK,* November 11, 1991.

Case Study Questions

1. Which characteristics of contemporary information systems are illustrated by CSX's systems?
2. Which of the major kinds of systems are described in this case?
3. Describe some of the pieces of information that might be contained in CSX's systems.
4. Diagram CSX's automobile delivery system with the system symbols introduced in this chapter. Then sketch a sample report that might be output by this system.
5. What problems did these systems solve for CSX? What problems can't they solve?
6. What management, organization, and technology changes were required by CSX's systems?
7. Can you suggest some other ways in which information systems could help CSX?

References

Ackoff, R. L. "Management Misinformation System." *Management Science* 14, no. 4 (December 1967), pp. B140–B116.

Allen, Brandt R., and Andrew C. Boynton. "Information Architecture: In Search of Efficient Flexibility," *MIS Quarterly* 15, no. 4 (December 1991).

Culnan, Mary J. "Transaction Processing Applications as Organizational Message Systems: Implications for the Intelligent Organization." Working paper no. 88-10, 22nd Hawaii International Conference on Systems Sciences (January 1989).

Davis, Gordon B., and Margrethe H. Olson. *Management Information Systems: Conceptual Foundations, Structure, and Development*, 2nd ed. New York: McGraw-Hill, 1985.

Fedorowicz, Jane, and Benn Konsynski. "Organization Support Systems: Bridging Business and Decision Processes." *Journal of Management Information Systems* 8, no. 4 (Spring 1992).

Gorry, G. A., and M. S. Scott-Morton. "A Framework for Management Information Systems." *Sloan Management Review* 13, no. 1 (1971).

Houdeshel, George, and Hugh J. Watson. "The Management Information and Decision Support (MIDS) System at Lockheed Georgia." *MIS Quarterly* 11, no. 1 (March 1987).

Huber, George P. "Organizational Information Systems: Determinants of Their Performance and Behavior." *Management Science* 28, no. 2 (1984).

Keen, Peter. "A Walk through Decision Support," *Computerworld*, January 14, 1985.

King, John. "Centralized vs. Decentralized Computing: Organizational Considerations and Management Options." *Computing Surveys* (October 1984).

Lasher, Donald R., Blake Ives, and Sirkka L. Jarvenpaa. "USAA-IBM Partnerships in Information Technology: Managing the Image Project." *MIS Quarterly* 15, no. 4 (December 1991).

Rockart, John F., and David W. DeLong. "Executive Support Systems and the Nature of Executive Work." Working paper: Management in the 1990s, Sloan School of Management, Massachusetts Institute of Technology.

Rockart, John F., and Michael E. Treacy. "The CEO Goes On-Line." *Harvard Business Review* (January–February 1982).

Sprague, Ralph H., Jr., and Eric D. Carlson. *Building Effective Decision Support Systems*. Englewood Cliffs, NJ: Prentice-Hall, 1982.

Watson, Hugh D., R. Kelly Rainer, Jr., and Chang E. Koh. "Executive Information Systems: A Framework for Development and a Survey of Current Practices." *MIS Quarterly* 15, no. 1 (March 1991).

Information Systems Keep Gillette on the Cutting Edge

In the early 1900s, when the Gillette Company introduced the first safety razor, it recognized right away that its products were vulnerable to competition. Anyone could obtain a piece of steel at a reasonable price. The way to stay ahead of the pack was to shape that same piece of steel into a sharper, sturdier blade at the lowest possible cost and to be the first to bring a superior product to market. Gillette has pursued this strategy ever since.

Gillette has 64 percent of the U.S. wet-shaving market and is a market leader in the rest of the world as well. Gillette has 70 percent of the market share in Europe and 80 percent in Latin America. This is a cutthroat market where a price difference of a few pennies can spell the difference between success and failure.

Information systems have helped Gillette stay ahead as both a low-cost, high-quality producer and

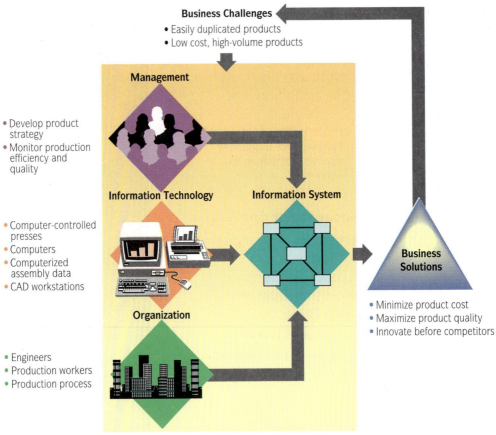

as an innovator of new shaving products. With advanced technology, Gillette can cut fractions of a cent off the cost of manufacturing a blade cartridge, yet produce a high-quality product. When you're making a billion razor blades a year, shaving a few tenths of a cent off the cost of each blade creates many millions of dollars in savings.

Virtually everything in Gillette's Boston manufacturing plant is automated. The firm's 3000 workers spend most of their time monitoring equipment, checking report printouts, or searching for bottlenecks in the production process.

With computerized process control devices, Gillette can control temperature, pressure and other machine settings more precisely while optimizing output. The result: Both blade cartridge and razor parts can be fashioned much faster and with higher quality than five or ten years ago. A ''cycle'' in the production process that used to take ten seconds is now down to seven or eight.

Gillette uses information systems to enforce scrupulous quality control standards. For instance, a high-resolution microscopic camera linked to a minicomputer examines every mounted twin blade for Gillette's Sensor razor. The minicomputer compares the images captured by the camera with the image of correctly mounted blades stored in its memory, rejecting blades that are not absolutely parallel. Since an infinitesimal change in angle will give an unsatisfactory shave, the system rejects blades that are off by a couple of microns.

Information systems help detect weak links in the production process as well. Gillette increased output of its Sensor razors by 4% by improving a small clip resembling a staple that anchors the cartridge assembly. Engineers found out that the gap in the clip was too narrow by analyzing computerized data from millions of cartridge assemblies.

Information systems have also helped Gillette capture market share with innovative new razors. Ten Gillette designers used three-dimensional computer-aided design software running on networked workstations to design the Sensor razor that uses independently suspended twin blades to deliver a closer shave. Sensor was an instant hit and became the top seller in the nondisposable razor market, with 43 percent of market share.

Sources: Lawrence Ingrassia, ''The Cutting Edge,'' *The Wall Street Journal,* April 6, 1992 and ''Gillette Holds Its Edge by Endlessly Searching for a Better Shave,'' *The Wall Street Journal,* December 10, 1992.

Gillette's use of information systems to stay ahead of the competition is one example of the strategic use of information systems. In this case, information systems enabled the firm to pursue strategies to maximize the quality and innovation of its products while minimizing costs. Information systems can be used to pursue other competitive strategies as well.

In this chapter we look at the problems firms face from competition and the ways that information systems can help businesses stay ahead of competitors.

Information systems can help businesses develop new products and services, market products more accurately, forge new relationships with suppliers and customers, and reduce internal operating costs.

After completing this chapter you will be able to:

- Explain why information is now considered a strategic resource.
- Define a strategic information system.
- Describe how the competitive forces and value chain models can be used to identify opportunities for strategic information systems.
- Describe how information systems contribute to the four competitive strategies that businesses can pursue.
- Explain why strategic information systems are difficult to build and to sustain.

3.1 Information as a Strategic Resource

In the last few decades there has been a revolution in the way that organizations treat information and information systems. Today leading companies are using information and information systems as tools for staying ahead of competitors. Organizations have developed a special category of information systems called strategic information systems for this purpose.

What Is a Strategic Information System?

Strategic information systems: Computer systems at any level of the organization that change the goals, operations, products, services, or environmental relationships to help the organization gain a competitive advantage.

Strategic information systems change the goals, operations, products, services, or environmental relationships of organizations to help them gain an edge over competitors. Systems that have these effects may even change the business of organizations. Merrill Lynch, for instance, used information systems to change from the stock brokerage business to the financial services business. State Street Bank and Trust Co. of Boston still handles traditional banking services such as customer checking and savings accounts and loans. However, its core business is now providing data processing services for securities and mutual funds. (Wilke, 1992).

Strategic information systems often change the organization as well as its products, services, and internal procedures, driving the organization into new behavior patterns. As we will see, organizations may need to change their internal operations to take advantage of the new information systems technology. Such changes often require new managers, a new work force, and a much closer relationship with customers and suppliers.

Changing Conceptions of Information and Information Systems

Behind the growing strategic uses of information systems is a changing conception of the role of information in organizations. Organizations now consider information a resource, much like capital and labor. This was not always the case.

INFORMATION AS A PAPER DRAGON

In the past, information was often considered a necessary evil associated with the bureaucracy of designing, manufacturing, and distributing a product or service. Information was a "paper dragon" that could potentially strangle the firm and prevent it from doing its real work (see Table 3.1). Information systems of the 1950s focused on reducing the cost of routine paper processing, especially in accounting. The first information systems were semi-automatic check-processing, issuing, and canceling machines—so-called electronic accounting machines (EAM). The term electronic data processing (EDP) dates from this period.

Table 3.1   CHANGING CONCEPTS OF INFORMATION SYSTEMS

Time Period	Conception of Information	Information Systems	Purpose
1950–1960	Necessary evil Bureaucratic requirement A paper dragon	Corresponding information systems of this period were called *electronic accounting machines (EAM)*	Speed accounting and paper processing
1960–1970s	General-purpose support	Management information systems (MIS) Information factory	Speed general reporting requirements
1970s–1980s	Customized management control	Decision support systems (DSS) Executive support systems (ESS)	Improve and customize decision making
1985–2000	Strategic resource Competitive advantage Strategic weapon	Strategic systems	Promote survival and prosperity of the organization

INFORMATION FOR GENERAL SUPPORT

By the 1960s, organizations started viewing information differently, recognizing that information could be used for general management support. The information systems of the 1960s and 1970s were frequently called management information systems (MIS) and were thought of as an information factory churning out reports on weekly production, monthly financial information, inventory, accounts receivable, accounts payable, and the like. To perform these tasks, organizations acquired general-purpose computing equipment that could support many functions rather than simply canceling checks.

INFORMATION FOR MANAGEMENT

In the 1970s and early 1980s information—and the systems that collected, stored, and processed it—were seen as providing fine-tuned, special-purpose, customized management control over the organization. The information systems that emerged during this period were called decision-support systems (DSS) and executive support systems (ESS). Their purpose was to improve and speed up the decision-making process of specific managers and executives in a broad range of problems.

INFORMATION AS A STRATEGIC RESOURCE

By the mid 1980s, the conception of information changed again. Information has since then been regarded as a strategic resource, a potential source of competitive advantage, or a strategic weapon to defeat and frustrate the competition. These changing conceptions of information reflect advances in strategic planning and theory (Porter, 1985). The belief that information is a resource to be managed is behind the Paperwork Reduction Act of 1980, which requires federal government agencies to develop an information resource officer. The kinds of systems being built to support this concept of information are called strategic systems, and their purpose is to ensure the survival and prosperity of the organization in the near future.

Strategic information systems should be distinguished from strategic-level systems for senior managers (discussed in Chapter 2) that focus on long-term decision-making problems. Strategic information systems can be used at all levels of the organization and are more far-reaching and deep-rooted than the other kinds of systems we have described. Strategic information systems fundamentally change the firm's goals, products, services, or internal and external relationships. Strategic information systems profoundly alter the way a firm conducts its business or the very business of the firm itself.

3.2 How Information Systems Can Be Used for Competitive Advantage

Strategic information systems can help firms overcome competition in several ways: They can help firms develop new products and services, target specific market niches, discourage customers and suppliers from switching to competitors, and provide products and services at lower cost than competitors. To identify where information systems can provide a competitive advantage, one must first understand the firm's relationship to its surrounding environment.

The Competitive Forces and Value Chain Models

In order to use information systems as competitive weapons, one must first understand where strategic opportunities for businesses are likely to be found. Two models of the firm and its environment have been used to identify areas of the business where information systems can provide advantages over competitors. These are the value chain model and the competitive forces model.

THE COMPETITIVE FORCES MODEL

Competitive forces model: Model used to describe the interaction of external threats and opportunities that affect an organization's strategy and ability to compete.

In the **competitive forces model,** which is illustrated in Figure 3.1 (Porter, 1980), a firm faces a number of external threats and opportunities: the threat of new entrants into its market; the pressure from substitute products or services; the bargaining power of buyers; the bargaining power of suppliers; and the positioning of traditional industry competitors.

Competitive advantage can be achieved by enhancing the firm's ability to deal with customers, suppliers, substitute products and services, and new entrants to its market, which in turn may change the balance of power between a firm and other competitors in the industry in the firm's favor. Businesses can use four basic competitive strategies to deal with these competitive forces:

Product differentiation: Competitive strategy for creating brand loyalty by developing new and unique products and services that are not easily duplicated by competitors.

Focused differentiation: Competitive strategy for developing new market niches where a business can compete in the target area better than its competitors.

Switching costs: The expense a customer or company incurs in lost time and resources when changing from one supplier or system to a competing supplier or system.

- **Product differentiation:** Firms can develop brand loyalty by creating unique new products and services that can easily be distinguished from those of competitors, and that existing competitors or potential new competitors can't duplicate.
- **Focused differentiation:** Businesses can create new market niches by identifying a specific target for a product or service that it can serve in a superior manner. The firm can provide a specialized product or service that serves this narrow target market better than existing competitors and that discourages potential new competitors.
- *Developing tight linkages to customers and suppliers:* Firms can create ties to customers and suppliers that "lock" customers into the firm's products and that tie suppliers into a delivery timetable and price structure shaped by the purchasing firm. This raises **switching costs** (the cost for customers to switch to competitors' products and services) and reduces customers' bargaining power and the bargaining power of suppliers.
- *Becoming the low-cost producer:* To prevent new competitors from entering their markets, businesses can produce goods and services at a lower price than competitors without sacrificing quality and level of service.

A firm may achieve competitive advantage by pursuing one of these strategies or by pursuing several strategies simultaneously. For instance, the Gillette Company described earlier is competing on quality, innovation, and cost.

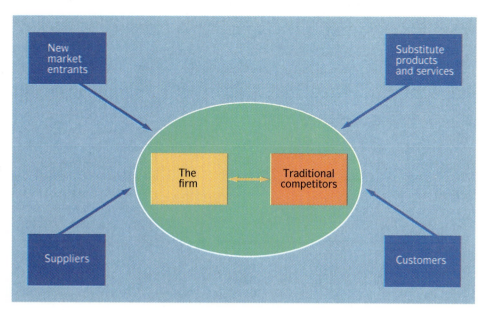

Figure 3.1
The competitive forces model. There are various forces that affect an organization's ability to compete and therefore greatly influence a firm's business strategy. There are threats from new market entrants and from substitute products and services. Customers and suppliers wield bargaining power. Traditional competitors constantly adapt their strategies to maintain their market positioning.

THE VALUE CHAIN

Value chain model: Model that highlights the activities that add a margin of value to a firm's products or services indicating where information systems can best be applied to achieve a competitive advantage.

Primary Activities: Activities most directly related to the production and distribution of a firm's products or services.

Support Activities: Activities that make the delivery of the primary activities of a firm possible.

The **value chain model** highlights specific activities in the business where competitive strategies can be best applied (Porter, 1985) and where information systems are most likely to have a strategic impact. This model views the firm as a series or "chain" of basic activities that add a margin of value to a firm's products or services. These activities can be categorized as either primary activities or support activities.

Primary activities are most directly related to the production and distribution of the firm's products and services that create value for the customer. Primary activities include inbound logistics, operations, outbound logistics, sales and marketing, and service. Inbound logistics includes receiving and storing materials for distribution to production. Operations transforms inputs into finished products. Outbound logistics entails storing and distributing products. Marketing and sales includes promoting and selling the firm's products. The service activity includes maintenance and repair of the firm's goods and services. **Support activities** make the delivery of the primary activities possible and consist of organization infrastructure (administration and management), human resources (employee recruiting, hiring, and training), technology (improving products and the production process), and procurement (purchasing input).

Organizations have competitive advantage when they provide more value to their customers or when they provide the same value to customers at a lower price. An information system could have strategic impact if it helped the firm provide products or services at a lower cost than competitors or if it provided products and services at the same cost as competitors but with greater value. The value activities that add the most value to products and services depend on the features of each particular firm. Businesses should try to develop strategic information systems for the value activities that add the most value to their particular firm. Figure 3.2 illustrates the activities of the value chain, showing examples of strategic information systems that could be developed to make each of the value activities more cost effective.

For instance, a firm could save money in the inbound logistics activity by having suppliers make daily deliveries of goods to the factory, thereby lowering the costs of warehousing and inventory. A computer-aided design system similar to those used by the Bath Iron Works, Odense Shipyards, or Group Michelin S.A.—described in the Window on Organizations in Chapter 1—might support the technology activity, helping a firm to reduce costs and perhaps to design more high-quality products than the competition produces. Gillette's computer-controlled machining supports the operations activity, reducing costs and boosting quality. Such

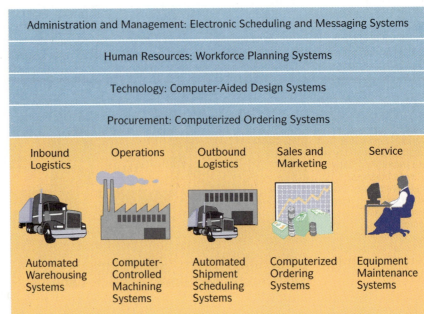

Figure 3.2
Activities of the value chain. Various examples of strategic information systems for the primary and support activities of a firm that would add a margin of value to a firm's products or services.

systems would be more likely to have strategic impact in a manufacturing firm, whereas an electronic scheduling and messaging system or office automation technology would more likely have strategic value in a law firm or consulting firm.

In the rest of this section we illustrate how businesses can use information systems to support each of the competitive strategies.

Information Systems Products and Services

Financial institutions have led the way in using information systems to create new products and services. Citibank developed automatic teller machines (ATM) and bank debit cards in 1977. Seeking to tap the largest retail depository market in the United States, Citibank installed its ATM machines throughout the New York metropolitan area, everywhere a depositor might find the time to use them

Automatic Teller Machines (ATMs) give people access to their bank accounts in remote locations at any time of day. Banks who offer ATM service have a competitive advantage over banks who don't. This woman can access her money through a Bank One ATM in a convenience store.

TECHNOLOGY

Bank Brussels Lambert Competes With Electronic House Calls

About 70 percent of all Belgian banking transactions are conducted over computer networks. With more than $71 billion in assets, Bank Brussels Lambert, one of the largest banks in Europe, has been a leader in electronic banking services. BBL is finding new ways to extend its electronic banking services to both corporate and individual customers. Customers can now tie their personal computers into the bank's electronic network to access their accounts and to make transactions. The network handles more than 500,000 customer calls per month.

Its Home Bank service permits customers to pay bills, trade securities, and transfer funds from their home PCs. A similar service, called Office Bank, lets employees at subscribing firms do their personal banking from the desktop

systems in their offices. A growing number of customers are using the Home Bank service.

Phone Bank is the latest in the series of electronic services enabling customers to link up by phone with the Bank's vocal computer for carrying out simple banking operations such as checking account balances and transferring funds from one account to another.

Besides a network of approximately 1,000 branches, BBL also has over 200 automated Self Bank branches allowing retail customers to carry out standard banking operations.

Other services offered by this bank include Telelink, which enables businesses to make direct payments to employees and suppliers, and also to consult a number of databases; and Telefin, which allows businesses

to arrange financing and obtain approval on-line for their customers. About 6000 companies worldwide use the Telelink program.

To keep its electronic services running around the clock and to ensure that no transactions are lost, BBL has added extra computer hardware and software as backups against system failure.

Sources: Sally Cusack, "Belgian Bank Performs Electronic House Calls," *Computerworld,* March 30, 1992; and John J. McCormick, "Belgian Bank Expands Services," *Information WEEK,* March 23, 1992.

**To Think About:
How can these electronic banking services help Bank Brussels Lambert maintain a strategic advantage?**

---

to deposit or withdraw money. As a leader in this area, Citibank became at one time the largest bank in the United States. Citibank ATMs were so successful that Citibank's competitors, large and small, were forced to counterstrike with a technological effort of their own called the New York Cash Exchange (NYCE). More detail on Citibank and its ATM strategy can be found in the case study concluding this chapter.

The Window on Technology illustrates how banks such as Bank Brussels Lambert are trying to extend their competitive advantage by offering new kinds of banking services.

In 1978, Merrill Lynch, the nation's largest retail brokerage firm, developed a new financial product called a Cash Management Account, which permitted customers to transfer money freely from stocks to bonds to money-market funds and to write checks against these funds cost-free. Such flexibility in a single financial product brought Merrill Lynch into the banking industry and broadened its retail market appeal. It also forced other leading brokerage firms to offer a similar service and large banking institutions such as Citibank to counterstrike with their own flexible cash management systems.

American Express Travel Related Services (TRS), one of the subsidiaries of the American Express Corporation, depends heavily on its digital imaging system to provide its "country club billing" service and aura of high status and quality. Many customers expect copies of their charge card transactions returned to them to substantiate tax deductions or business expenses. The hugh amount of paper that must be processed to include customers' receipts with their credit card bill had become prohibitively expensive and difficult to manage. In 1984, TRS adopted a digital imaging system from Technicron Financial Services that provides reduced images of the receipts on neat laser-printed pages (Connolly and Horwitt, 1988; Markoff, 1988).

These examples demonstrate the development and use of information systems to create new consumer products. In other instances, the reason for a product improvement is invisible to consumers. Variable-speed motors, numerically controlled machine tools, industrial control devices, and home burglar alarms are different from the ATMs, credit cards, cash management systems, and new payment systems previously described because they are physical products constructed with computer components and chips (see Chapter 6). The distinction between an information system and its strategic utilization, as opposed to products that incorporate computer components, is important.

Systems to Focus on Market Niche

An information system can give companies a competitive advantage by producing data to improve their sales and marketing techniques. Such systems treat existing information as a resource that can be "mined" by the organization to increase profitability and market penetration. The sophisticated merchandising systems developed by Procter & Gamble and Colgate-Palmolive, which are described in the Window on Organizations, are classic examples.

Sears, Roebuck and Company continually mines its computerized data on its 40 million retail customers—the largest retail customer base in the United States—to target groups such as appliance buyers, tool buyers, gardening enthusiasts, and mothers-to-be. For instance, when a customer buys a washer-dryer from Sears, either on credit or for cash, Sears mails a postcard advertising an annual maintenance contract. If the contract is not purchased, Sears still maintains a record of who purchased the machine, using the information the customer supplies on the written guarantee. Each year, Sears will send out an annual maintenance contract renewal form or will phone customers to keep its maintenance business humming. At the same time, Sears routinely sends out notices about special sales and products for these machines (such as soap and replacement parts). Likewise with electric hand tools: Purchasers routinely receive fliers on sales and products put out by Sears.

Sears also uses its customer information database to track the purchases made by credit customers. This information is then used to target direct mail inserts that accompany the monthly credit card bill. In addition, information obtained on the initial credit application, as well as the history of credit purchases, can be used by the Sears marketing staff to target specific subgroups such as males between the ages of 40 and 50 who have a family and live in affluent zip code areas. Sears used this information to provide sales leads to its other subsidiaries such as Allstate Insurance, brokerage house Dean Witter Reynolds, and real estate brokers Coldwell Banker when it owned these companies. Although Sears closed its mail order catalog business, it refuses to sell data on its catalog customers to other firms because this information is so valuable.

Not to be outdone, Sears's chief rival, the J C Penney Company, a retailer with a base of approximately 20 million customers, has initiated a successful technology-based counterstrike. Penney uses information gathered on its credit card applications and information purchased from the Department of Motor Vehicles of various states to target prospective insurance customers.

Linking with Customers and Suppliers

Baxter Healthcare International Inc. supplies nearly two-thirds of all products used by U.S. hospitals. It uses an information system originally developed by American Hospital Supply Corporation (which Baxter acquired in 1985) to become a full-line supplier for hospitals, a one-stop source for all hospital needs. This effort requires an inventory of more than 120,000 items. Maintaining a huge inventory is very costly. However, it is also costly *not* to have items in stock, because hospitals switch to competitors.

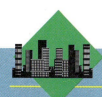

ORGANIZATIONS

Coral Lipstick? The Sales Data Say It Sells Big in Florida

Midwesterners prefer shampoo in big bottles but East Coast residents consistently buy toiletries in smaller sizes. Coral shades of lipstick sell better in Florida than in the Northeast. U.S. consumers tend to buy new toothbrushes when hundreds are in special supermarket displays.

It would have taken months and hundreds of market researchers to pinpoint these trends a decade ago. Today, businesses can identify such buying patterns in a matter of days using the data captured from portable sales systems and retailers' point-of-sale (POS) systems.

(Point-of-sale systems, which are widely used by supermarkets, department stores, and discount chains, capture data directly at the point of sale, often using bar code scanners and computerized cash registers.)

Cincinnati-based Procter & Gamble uses retail sales data to target specific consumer groups. For instance, by analyzing data captured by scanners in supermarkets and other retail outlets, P & G found out that older women were the most loyal customers of its Oil of Olay product line. The firm then launched an advertising campaign

targeted at teenagers and young women to attract new buyers. Similarly, P & G analyzed weekly retail data in relation to regional weather patterns to measure how weather affected sales of its Vick's Formula 44 and Nyquil cold products and to determine whether demand for these products was greater in cold regions of the country. Assessing the impact of the cough/cold and flu seasons on its products helped P & G develop appropriate consumer response programs such as special sales or coupon giveaways in cold regions.

The New York-based Colgate-Palmolive Corporation equips its sales force with laptop computers to transmit retail sales and merchandising information daily to corporate headquarters. The firm can then immediately activate special marketing programs for the sales trends it finds. If it finds that Mennen deodorant is selling well when an end-of-aisle display has been set up, Colgate can duplicate the displays in other stores.

Source: Julia King, ''Coral Lipstick? It Sells Big in Florida,'' *Computerworld,* May 11, 1992.

To Think About:
If you were a sales manager, what pieces of sales data would you want to collect and analyze?

Terminals tied to Baxter's own computers are installed in hospitals. When hospitals want to place an order, they do not need to call a salesperson or send a purchase order—they simply use a Baxter computer terminal on-site to order from the full Baxter supply catalog. The system generates shipping, billing, invoicing, and inventory information, and the hospital terminals provide customers with an estimated delivery date. With more than 80 distribution centers in the United States, Baxter can make daily deliveries of its products, often within hours of receiving an order.

This system is similar to the just-in-time delivery systems developed in Japan and now being used in the American automobile industry. In these systems, automobile manufacturers such as GM or Chrysler enter the quantity and delivery schedules of specific automobile components into their own information

1. Prevailing Delivery Practice

Bulk storage   Delivery   Storeroom   To the ward

Most hospitals keep a large inventory of supplies that are replenished regularly by suppliers, but require a large amount of space and staff.

2. Just-In-Time Supply Method

Bulk storage   More frequent deliveries   Storeroom   To the ward

If a hospital implements a just-in-time plan in coordination with a distributer, it can give up some of its inventory space in return for more frequent deliveries.

3. Stockless Supply Method

Bulk storage   Daily deliveries   To the ward

A stockless supply plan shifts all inventory responsibilities to the distributor. Deliveries are made daily, sometimes directly to departments that need supplies.

Figure 3.3
A comparison of traditional inventory and delivery practices to the *just-in-time supply method* and the *stockless inventory method*. Strategic systems for linking customers and suppliers have changed the way in which some companies handle the supply and inventory requirements of their businesses. The just-in-time supply method reduces inventory requirements of the customer while stockless inventory allows the customer to eliminate inventories entirely, resulting in a decided competitive advantage. Adapted from "Removing the Warehouse from Cost-Conscious Hospitals," *The New York Times*, March 3, 1991. Copyright © 1991 by The New York Times Company. Reprinted by permission.

systems. Then these requirements are automatically entered into a supplier's order entry information system. The supplier must respond with an agreement to deliver the materials at the time specified. Thus, automobile companies can reduce the cost of inventory, the space required for warehousing components or raw materials, and construction time.

Baxter has even gone one step further. Delivery personnel no longer drop off their cartons at a loading dock to be placed in a hospital storeroom. Instead, they deliver orders directly to the hospital corridors, dropping them at nursing stations, operating rooms, and stock supply closets. This has created in effect a "stockless inventory," with Baxter serving as the hospitals' warehouse. Stockless inventory substantially reduces the need for hospital storage space and personnel and lowers holding and handling costs (Caldwell, 1991).

Figure 3.3 compares stockless inventory with the just-in-time supply method and traditional inventory practices. While just-in-time inventory allows customers to reduce their inventories, stockless inventory allows them to eliminate their inventories entirely. All inventory responsibilities shift to the distributor, who manages the supply flow. The stockless inventory is a powerful instrument for binding customers, giving the supplier a decided competitive advantage.

Strategic systems aimed at suppliers, such as the automobile manufacturers' ordering systems described above, are designed to maximize the firm's purchasing power by having suppliers interact with its information system to satisfy the firm's precise business needs. These information systems also provide benefits for suppliers. Suppliers can continually monitor product requirements, factory scheduling, and commitments of their customers against their own schedule to ensure that enough inventory will be available. If suppliers are unwilling to go along with this system, they may lose business to other suppliers who can meet these demands.

Interorganizational systems:
Information systems that
automate the flow of
information across
organizational boundaries and
link a company to its
customers, distributors, or
suppliers.

Electronic market: A
marketplace that is created by
computer and communication
technologies which link many
buyers and sellers via
interorganizational systems.

The systems that link a company to its customers, distributors, or suppliers are termed **interorganizational systems** because they automate the flow of information across organizational boundaries (Barrett, 1986–1987, Johnston and Vitale, 1988). Such systems allow information or processing capabilities of one organization to improve the performance of another or to improve relationships among organizations. Interorganizational systems can tighten linkages to customers or suppliers, lower costs, and increase product differentiation.

Interorganizational systems that provide services to multiple organizations by linking together many buyers and sellers create an **electronic market.** Through computers and telecommunications, these systems function like electronic middlemen (Malone, Yates, and Benjamin, 1987).

Electronic markets are growing because computer and communication technologies can lower the costs of typical marketplace transactions such as selecting suppliers, establishing prices, ordering goods, and paying bills. For example, Charles Schwab and Company, a discount brokerage service, sells investors software for their personal computers to obtain current price quotes for stocks, bonds, and mutual funds; to access research reports from firms such as Standard & Poor's; and to execute trades themselves. Schwab customers can also place orders to trade and obtain price quotes from a touchtone telephone.

Such information systems can dominate entire industries. For instance, computerized airline reservation systems are used by airline reservation agents and also by independent travel agents (about 80 percent of all airline tickets issued in the United States are sold by travel agents using these computerized reservation systems). Although there are rival systems from other airlines, American Airlines' SABRE system and United Airlines' Apollo system control 75 percent of the computerized reservation system market.

While these systems provide unparalleled convenience to airline travelers, as well as to travel agents who must book flights (e.g., SABRE enables travel agents to serve their customers with reservations for airlines, hotels, and cars), they also confer formidable market power on the two airlines. Medium-size air carriers claimed unfair treatment by SABRE and Apollo because these reservation systems were listing American and United Airlines flights first. This example indicates how a strategic system gives a supplier a market advantage over a distributor and a customer.

Because computerized reservation systems costs tens of millions of dollars to develop, smaller carriers have been discouraged from building their own systems. The smaller carriers have their flights listed on their bigger competitors' systems but must pay a fee to the airline owning the system every time a ticket is sold through the computerized reservation system. SABRE and Apollo are major sources of revenue for their owners.

Public policy, through the courts or the legislature, has acted to set limits on the uses of information technology to preserve fairness and competition. After a Congressional investigation, the Civil Aeronautics Board in 1984 forced American Airlines to remove any bias in the display of flights on SABRE screens. Eleven other airlines joined in an antitrust suit against both United and American. Consumer advocates, competing airlines, and the U.S. Department of Transportation asked the Justice Department to block a proposed merger of American and Delta Airlines' computerized reservation systems because the combined system would control 46 percent of the market for ticket reservations.

Chapter 9 covers the technologies underlying interorganizational systems and electronic markets.

Systems to Lower Costs

The strategic systems we described change the strategic relationship between an organization and its markets, customers, and suppliers. Other strategically oriented information systems facilitate internal operations, management control, planning, and personnel. These systems are strategic because they help firms significantly lower their internal costs, allowing them to deliver products and services at a lower price than their competitors can provide. By lowering operating costs, raising profits, and making firms more efficient, such systems contribute to the survival and prosperity of the firm. The following examples describe information uses that are much more dynamic and intensive than mere management support tools.

The Wizard system developed by Avis, the car rental company, is an example of a strategic internal MIS designed to improve the firm's overall productivity. This system keeps track of the location, costs, and performance of Avis's car rental fleet. This capability, in turn, has permitted Avis to compete effectively against Hertz, National, and other car rental firms by optimizing the distribution of its car rental fleet to ensure that cars are available where there is a demand for them and that costs are kept to a minimum.

Allegheny Ludlum Corporation, a $1 billion specialty steel and metals manufacturer in Pittsburgh, Pennsylvania, has improved its fortunes steadily despite stiff foreign competition and a declining U.S. steel market. It has invested heavily in information systems aimed at coordinating personnel, manufacturing, and other sectors of the company and has one of the most sophisticated computer costing systems in the industry. The system's ability to calculate production costs per unit time has given the company a productivity edge over competitors. Ten years ago, Allegheny had twelve competitors, but today there are only four. A network links Allegheny plants in six states. A bar-coding system gathers shop floor data that are used in other business functions such as costing, technical services, quality systems, order entry, alloy test systems, and marketing. With these systems, the company can manage internal costs and market products more effectively (Emmett, 1992).

Airlines have used information systems strategically to counter competitors' discount fares. Information systems have automated a technique called yield management that allows carriers to match any discount fare that arises as efficiently and sparingly as possible. Yield management is the process of wringing the most profit out of every airline seat and determining when to drop or increase prices or offer promotions. On average, every airline seat is booked one and one-half times and canceled one and one-half times during the three months before a flight. Yield management develops a spot price for any seat at any time. For example, a Sunday-evening flight from New York to London might show 70 empty seats a week from departure. Rather than offer cut-rate fares to fill up the plane, the yield management system examines the historical pattern of that flight and determines how many seats the airline should set aside for executives willing to pay full fares at the last moment. Figure 3.4 illustrates this process.

3.3 Implications for Managers and Organizations

With these examples in mind, it should be clear that information systems can have strategic implications for the organization's internal operations and can alter critical balances with external environmental factors such as new products and services, customers, and suppliers. Together these internal and external strategic changes alter the firm's competitive advantage.

Countering Competitive Forces

The examples we have given show how firms can use strategic information systems to deal with various competitive forces. When businesses use information systems to provide products or services that cannot be easily duplicated or that serve highly specialized markets, they can raise the market entry costs for

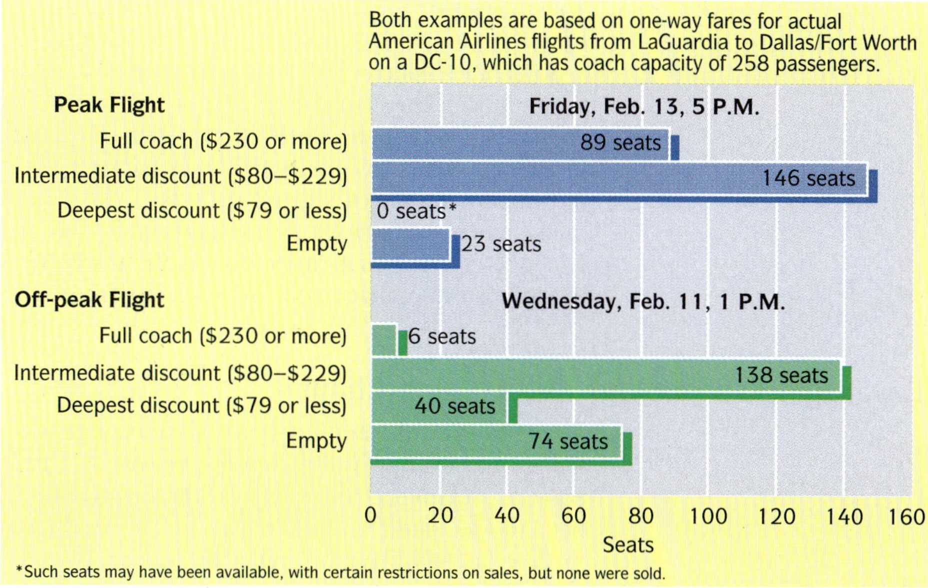

Figure 3.4
A comparison of ticket costs by type of seat sold for peak and off-peak flights. Both examples are based on one-way fares for actual American Airlines flights from LaGuardia to Dallas/Fort Worth on a DC-10 that has coach capacity of 258 passengers. Adapted from Eric Schmitt, "The Art of Devising Air Fares," *The New York Times,* March 4, 1987. Copyright © 1987 by the New York Times Company. Reprinted by permission.

Both examples are based on one-way fares for actual American Airlines flights from LaGuardia to Dallas/Fort Worth on a DC-10, which has coach capacity of 258 passengers.

Peak Flight   Friday, Feb. 13, 5 P.M.
Full coach ($230 or more) — 89 seats
Intermediate discount ($80–$229) — 146 seats
Deepest discount ($79 or less) — 0 seats*
Empty — 23 seats

Off-peak Flight   Wednesday, Feb. 11, 1 P.M.
Full coach ($230 or more) — 6 seats
Intermediate discount ($80–$229) — 138 seats
Deepest discount ($79 or less) — 40 seats
Empty — 74 seats

0 20 40 60 80 100 120 140 160
Seats

*Such seats may have been available, with certain restrictions on sales, but none were sold.

competitors. These strategic information systems can prevent the competition from responding in kind. For instance, the cost of developing airline reservation systems similar to those of American Airlines and United Airlines is so high that competitors are discouraged, especially when they can appear on the existing systems as "co-hosts" (McFarlan, 1984).

Information systems can counter competitive forces by "locking in" customers and suppliers. Strategic information systems can make the costs of switching from one product to a competing product prohibitive for customers. Electronic home banking is one example. Once customers key in all of the required digital information on their bills, department stores, checks, and so forth into a single electronic banking system, they find it very difficult to switch to another bank. The banks themselves encourage this situation by developing systems that are incompatible with each other. By making it difficult for customers to switch, the banks, in turn, can directly market to a captive audience a variety of banking services ranging from instant credit, to stocks, to cash management accounts. Baxter International's "stockless inventory" and ordering system is another information system that locks in customers. Participating hospitals become unwilling to switch to another supplier because of the system's convenience and low cost.

Strategic systems counter competitive forces by rapidly changing the basis of competition. Strategic information systems can propel a manufacturer into an unassailable position as the low-cost, high-quality producer in its field. Or, these systems can create new products or services to differentiate from competitors so that a firm no longer has to compete on the basis of cost. For instance, airlines fight to get their on-line reservation systems into travel agency offices because the systems can also offer hotel accomodations, car rentals, limousines, theater tickets, and other travel services. These features allow them to distinguish their service from that of other airlines so that they do not have to compete only on air fare prices. Airlines that can offer convenience, low prices, and quick connections tend to win out.

In general, strategic information systems provide significant, although generally temporary, market advantages, principally by raising the entry costs of competitors. If short-term advantages are repeated, however, a firm that gains an advantage for five years can utilize the time and the additional resources that leadership brings to ensure that it maintains a technological advantage for the next five years, and so on. Firms can thus build on their initial successes and can develop a stream of innovative applications if they have the staff to support their information systems and if they understand the strategic importance of information. For instance, a company can parlay a series of innovations into a valuable market image of a consistent leader at the cutting edge of technology. This image alone can help maintain the firm's market position.

Sometimes systems that first provide an exclusive advantage to one company are worth more if they are shared with others. For instance, American Airlines jealously guarded its yield management system (described earlier in this chapter). But starting in 1986, it started selling its yield management expertise to any firm that wanted to buy it. American even set up a subsidiary, AA Decision Technologies, to build yield management systems for airlines, railroads, and other companies (Hopper, 1990). Mrs. Fields Cookies is marketing its Retail Operations Intelligence system, an automated store management network, to other retail chains.

Leveraging Technology in the Value Chain

The strategic information systems that we have described leverage information system technology and technology impacts. Until recently, information systems played a relatively minor role in the production, distribution, and sale of products and services. Vast increases in the productivity of information processing made relatively little difference in the firm's productivity or bottom-line balance sheet. Now, however, as the operations of an organization have come to depend heavily on information systems, and as these systems penetrate the organization, increases in the productivity of information processing can have dramatic implications for the overall productivity of the corporation. This leveraging effect is important when we consider recommendations for management.

The value chain model can supplement the competitive forces model by identifying critical leverage points where firms can use information technology most effectively to enhance their competitive position. For instance, a strategic analysis might identify the sales and marketing activity as an area where information systems would provide the greatest productivity boost. The analysis might recommend a system similar to those used by Colgate-Palmolive or Procter & Gamble for capturing and analyzing point-of-sale data (described in this chapter's Window on Organizations) to reduce marketing costs by targeting marketing campaigns more efficiently. The system might also provide information that lets the firm develop products more finely attuned to its target market as well. Many different projects, or a series of linked systems, may be required to create a strategic advantage.

Strategic Alliances and Information Partnerships

Information partnership: Cooperative alliance formed between two corporations for the purpose of sharing information to gain strategic advantage.

Companies are increasingly using information systems for strategic advantage by entering into strategic alliances with other companies where both firms cooperate by sharing resources or services. Such alliances are often **information partnerships** in which two or more firms share data for mutual advantage (Konsynski and McFarlan, 1990). They can join forces without actually merging. American Airlines has an arrangement with Citibank to award one mile in its frequent flyer program for every dollar spent using Citibank credit cards. American benefits from increased customer loyalty, while Citibank gains new credit card subscribers and a highly credit-worthy customer base for cross-marketing. Northwest Airlines has a similar arrangement with First Bank of Minneapolis. American has also allied with MCI, awarding frequent flyer miles for each dollar of long-distance billing.

Such partnerships help firms gain access to new customers, creating new opportunities for cross-selling and targeting products. They can share investments in computer hardware and software. Sometimes traditional competitors can benefit from some of these partnerships. Baxter Healthcare International offers its customers medical supplies from competitors and office supplies through its electronic ordering channel. Even companies that were traditional competitors have found such alliances to be mutually advantageous.

The corporate alliance between MCI and American Airlines led to this marketing campaign where flyers were awarded bonus travel miles on American for using MCI to make their phone calls.

Managing Strategic Transitions

Strategic transitions: A movement from one level of sociotechnical system to another. Often required when adopting strategic systems that demand changes in the social and technical elements of an organization.

Adopting the kinds of systems described in this chapter generally requires changes in business goals, relationships with customers and suppliers, internal operations, and information architecture. These sociotechnical changes, affecting both social and technical elements of the organization, can be considered **strategic transitions**—a movement between levels of sociotechnical systems.

How much sociotechnical change occurs depends on the specific circumstances. Clearly, however, there is a connection between the strategy of an organization and its internal structure. As companies move to make information systems part of the overall corporate strategy, their internal structure must also change to reflect these new developments. The Window on Management on page 74 illustrates the kinds of organizational changes that may be required when businesses implement state-of-the-art manufacturing systems to remain competitive. Managers struggling to boost competitiveness will need to redesign various organizational processes to make effective use of leading-edge manufacturing technology.

Such changes often entail blurring of organizational boundaries, both external and internal. This is especially true of telecommunications-based strategic systems (Cash and Konsynski, 1985; Keen, 1986). Suppliers and customers must become intimately linked and may share each other's responsibilities. For instance, in Baxter International's stockless inventory system, Baxter has assumed responsibility for managing its customers' inventories (Johnston and Vitale, 1988).

Firms with successful strategic information systems have broken down organizational barriers that block the sharing of data across functions. Design, sales, and manufacturing departments must work together much more closely. Federal Express's highly publicized package-tracking system shares information among operations, customer service, and accounting functions. Firestone Tire & Rubber Company made tire design information available to quality control, production, and testing groups as well as to customers' engineers. Sundstrand Corporation halved its warehousing staff and expedited customer-order processing by improving information systems links between spare parts ordering, warehousing, and manufacturing control in the aerospace industry.

In some cases, reshaping an organization to remain competitive may necessitate an entirely new organizational structure. General Motors, in order to develop a comprehensive strategic information system strategy, had to purchase Electronic Data Systems, EDS, a consulting firm specializing in data processing and communications services. And to produce the Saturn, a new low-cost car

MANAGEMENT

Changing Manufacturing Requires Rethinking the Business

Lower inventories, streamlined operations, improved customer service: Manufacturers know they must meet these challenges to stay competitive. Companies also face new pressures to get their products to market more rapidly. While U.S. manufacturing quality has improved 7 percent annually, product lead times have grown at only half that rate. This is why Japanese automakers can get new models to market more rapidly than Detroit.

For the past two decades, businesses have used manufacturing resource planning systems to provide information on what and when to produce, how much to purchase and make, how much inventory is available, and to whom to ship products. But according to Roger Willis, factory management systems director at Andersen Con-

sulting in Chicago, it is not enough merely to automate the manufacturing processes. Management must make sure that manufacturing is part of a strategic whole that helps the company output the right products at the right time. Not only must businesses improve and link systems, but they must also rethink systems and eliminate products and processes that do not advance strategic aims. Product design, sales, and finance must be integrated with plant management.

Lee Wiley, head of manufacturing service for the Gartner Group Inc., another consulting firm, believes that meaningful gains in manufacturing cannot take place unless management sees a plant as an integral part of the overall business, instead of as an isolated island. Manufacturing systems will need to encompass not only traditional

manufacturing resource planning functions but also plant floor scheduling and execution, total quality management, maintenance, marketing forecasts, sales-order management and distribution systems, and regulatory reporting. These systems must be able to synchronize businesses with multiple manufacturing locations domestically and around the globe.

Sources: Alice Greene, "MRP II: Out with the Old," *Computerworld,* June 8, 1992 and Tony Barr, "Experts: Time to Put It Together," *Computerworld,* October 28, 1991.

To Think About: What management, organization, and technology factors must be addressed to implement state-of-the-art manufacturing technology?

competitive with Japanese models, GM also created an entirely new automotive division with a new factory, a new sales force, and a new design team to utilize the new technologies. Not all strategic information systems require such massive change, but clearly, many do.

What Managers Can Do

Managers must determine how the organization can build information systems of strategic importance. Information systems are too important to be left entirely to a small technical group in the corporation. Senior managers must initiate the search for opportunities to develop them. Although some industries are far ahead of others in their use of information technology, some of those that are far behind may be so for a good reason: The technology may not be appropriate. Other industries have simply failed to keep up with the times and thus offer considerable opportunities for vast and rapid changes. Some of the important questions managers should ask themselves are as follows:

- How is the industry currently using information and communication technology? Which organizations are the industry leaders in the application of information systems technology? What does the future look like?
- What are the direction and nature of technological change within the industry? Where are the momentum and change coming from?
- Are significant strategic opportunities to be gained by introducing information systems technology into the industry? Can information systems alter

the basis of competition, build in switching costs, generate new products, strengthen the firm's power in dealing with suppliers, or create barriers against new competitors (Cash, McFarlan, McKenney, and Applegate, 1992)?

- What kinds of systems are applicable to the industry? Does it require systems to create new products and services, supplier systems, and/or sales and marketing systems?

Once the nature of information systems technology in the industry is understood, managers should turn to their organization and ask other important questions:

- Is the organization behind or ahead of the industry in its application of information systems?
- What is the current business strategic plan, and how does that plan mesh with the current strategy for information services?
- Have the information technologies currently in use provided significant payoffs to the business? Do they largely support the business or drain its resources?
- Would a significant increase in the budget for information services result in a strategic breakthrough for the organization?

Once these issues have been considered, managers can gain a keener insight into whether their firms are ready for strategic information systems.

Studies of successful strategic systems have found that they are rarely planned but instead evolve slowly over long periods of time, and they almost always originate with practical operational problems. For instance, SABRE, the American Airlines computerized reservation system that is often cited as a classic "strategic system," originated as a straightforward inventory control and order entry system (Copeland and McKenney, 1988; Hopper, 1990). Rather than sprouting from some magical methodology, strategic systems, like most new products, come from closely observing real-world business situations. This finding may provide a clue about how to look for powerful strategic impact systems.

Management Challenges

1. **Sustainability of competitive advantage.** The competitive advantages conferred by strategic systems do not necessarily last long enough to ensure long-term profits. Competitors can retaliate and copy strategic systems. Moreover, these systems are often expensive; costs saved by some systems are expended immediately to maintain the system.

   Competitive advantage isn't always sustainable. Market conditions change. The business and economic environment changes. Technology and customers' expectations change. The classic strategic information systems—American Airlines' SABRE computerized reservation system, Citibank's ATM system, and Federal Express's package tracking system—benefited by being the first in their respective industries. But then rival systems emerged. NYCE banks blunted Citibank's ATM edge. United Parcel Service, described in the opening vignette of Chapter 1, is challenging Federal Express's domination of the overnight package market. Information systems alone cannot provide an enduring business advantage (Hopper, 1990).

   Systems originally intended to be strategic frequently become tools for survival, something every firm has in order to stay in business. Rather than conferring long-term competitive advantage, they become critical for a company just to keep abreast of the competition.

2. **Organizational barriers to strategic transitions.** Implementing strategic systems usually requires far-reaching sociotechnical changes. This goal is not easy to accomplish because organizational change is frequently resisted by

middle and even senior managers. In fact, one of the greatest obstacles to strategic transitions may be resistance to change—both the changes that are imposed on an organization and those that employees experience as their jobs are reshaped. Even the identities of employees must change. One is no longer simply a salesperson or a member of the production department. These tasks become increasingly integrated through a single information network. To be successful, strategic transitions require changes in organizational culture (see Chapter 4).

Summary

Explain why information is now considered a strategic resource.

In the past, information used to be considered a bureaucratic nuisance and a limited tool for management decision making. Today, information systems can so dramatically boost a firm's productivity and efficiency that businesses view information as a weapon against competition and a strategic resource.

Define a strategic information system.

Strategic information systems change the goals, operations, products, services, or environmental relationships of organizations to help them gain an edge over competitors.

Describe how the competitive forces and value chain models can be used to identify opportunities for strategic information systems.

The value chain and competitive forces models can help identify areas of a business where information systems can supply a strategic advantage. The competitive forces model describes a number of external threats and opportunities faced by firms that they must counter with competitive strategies. Information systems can be developed to cope with the threat of new entrants into the market, the pressure from substitute products, the bargaining power of buyers, the bargaining power of suppliers, and the positioning of traditional industry competitors.

The value chain model highlights specific activities in the business where competitive strategies can best be applied and where information systems are most likely to have a strategic impact. This model views the firm as a series or "chain" of basic activities that add a margin of value to a firm's products or services. Information systems can have strategic impact in the activities that add the most value to the firm.

Describe how information systems contribute to the four competitive strategies that businesses can pursue.

Information systems can help businesses pursue the four basic competitive strategies: Information systems can be used to develop new market niches; they can lock in customers and suppliers by raising the cost of switching; they can provide unique products and services; and they can help firms provide products and services at lower cost by reducing production and distribution costs.

Explain why strategic information systems are difficult to build and to sustain.

Not all strategic systems make a profit; they can be expensive and risky to build. Many strategic information systems are easily copied by other firms, so that strategic advantage is not always sustainable. Implementing strategic systems often requires extensive organizational change and a transition from one sociotechnical level to another. Such changes are called strategic transitions and are often difficult and painful to achieve.

Key Terms

Strategic information systems	Primary activities
Competitive forces model	Support activities
Product differentiation	Interorganizational systems
Focused differentiation	Electronic market
Switching costs	Information partnership
Value chain model	Strategic transitions

1. What is a strategic information system? What is the difference between a strategic information system and a strategic-level system?

2. Identify four different conceptions of the role of information in organizations. How have information systems changed to match these differing views of information?

3. Define and compare the value chain and competitive forces models for identifying opportunities for strategic systems.

4. What are the four basic competitive strategies? How can information systems help firms pursue each of these strategies?

5. How can a firm use information systems to create new products and services? Give an example.

6. How can information systems help firms focus on market niche? Give an example.

7. How can a firm use an information system to "lock in" customers? Give an example.

8. How can a firm use an information system to improve its bargaining power with a supplier?

9. How can a firm increase its overall operational productivity through the use of information systems?

10. Define: interorganizational systems, electronic markets, and information partnerships.

11. What is meant by leveraging technology?

12. Why are strategic information systems difficult to build?

13. What is a strategic transition?

14. How can managers find strategic applications in their firm?

1. Several information systems experts have claimed, "There is no such thing as a sustainable strategic advantage." Discuss.

2. How do the following kinds of systems give each company a strategic advantage? What competitive strategy does each support?

   a. Mazda Motors of America distributes software to its dealerships; the software compiles customer data on trade-ins and used car sales.

   b. Citibank has arranged with Federal Express to replace lost credit cards within 24 hours. Federal Express and Citibank computers networked together can track the creation and shipment of new cards to customers through the Federal Express hub in Memphis.

   c. Shell Oil Corporation in Houston introduced point-of-sale equipment for credit authorization.

   d. The Food Emporium supermarket chain is starting to use video screens attached to shopping carts. As shoppers stroll down the aisles, a sensor activates video commercials and store specials on the video screen using software attached to a computer in the store. In addition to providing information about items for sale, the video screens can give brief weather and news reports.

3. Re-examine the cases concluding Chapters 1 and 2 about Simon & Schuster and CSX Corporation in light of the value chain and competitive forces models. What forces are pressuring these companies to change? What information systems support value chain activities? Can you suggest other information systems that would make these firms more competitive?

4. Manufacturing firms in the United States and abroad are furiously adopting just-in-time delivery systems whereby firms minimize inventories by requiring suppliers to deliver just enough materials to meet the day's or week's production schedule. Does this practice convey a competitive advantage or not? Discuss.

Form a group with two or three of your classmates. Research a business using annual reports or business publications such as *Fortune, Business Week* or *The Wall Street Journal*. Analyze the business using the value chain and competitive forces models. Suggest appropriate strategic information systems for that particular business. Present your findings to the class.

CASE STUDY

What Happened to Citicorp?

During the 1970s Citicorp rose to Number 1 rank in retail banking, pioneering in information technology innovations such as ATM machines. Citi was often cited as a shining example of a company that used information systems strategically to create a competitive edge. It appeared that Citi could do no wrong.

Twenty years later, Citicorp found itself with large losses, strapped by bad loans and massive layoffs. Its status had dropped to the second tier in the global banking market. It had to cut back on innovations and consolidate some of its systems and networks. What happened?

The bank had embarked on an ambitious program to decentralize its information systems, hoping to speed up the development of new products and services by giving its business units the responsibility for developing their own systems.

Citi became crippled by non-performing Third World and commercial real estate loans made during the 1980s. These bad loans continued to mount. In the fall of 1992, 7 percent of Citicorp's loans were reported as either delinquent or so troubled that full repayment was unlikely, giving Citicorp the eighth-worst record among the 50 largest U.S. banking firms. The delinquency rate on Citicorp's mortgage loans was four times the national average.

Federal bank examiners criticized Citicorp for sloppy mortgage lending practices that did not properly identify risky loans and that overcharged many customers who relied on Citibank to keep track of monthly payments on their mortgages. Citibank was said to have incorrectly calculated the amount of customers' money accumulated in escrow accounts for real estate taxes and insurance. A total of $1.1 billion of its mortgage loans were more than 360 days delinquent but had not been identified as foreclosed.

Citi launched a $1.5 billion cost reduction campaign and tried to improve its financial position by unloading assets. It sold 50 percent of its Ambac—its municipal bond insurer—for $330 million and sold $1.25 billion of convertible preferred stock. It also had to cut costs by scaling back or cutting out pet projects such as Quotron Systems Inc. and Citicorp POS Services Inc. These projects had been designed to put Citi in the "information business."

At its height, Citicorp was jokingly described as a software company masquerading as a bank. It had over 150 computing centers, over 100 different telecommunications networks, and 4000 program developers. Many of these were cut back and consolidated to reduce costs. In 1991, Chairman John Reed announced $1.5 billion in cost reductions over the next two years, including a reduction in jobs from 95,000 to 86,000.

In the 1970s Citi had purchased Transaction Technology Inc. to develop the hardware and software for its pioneering ATM systems. These were an instant success. Citi's push into consumer banking added to Citi's revenue because more customers did more transactions with the bank. While competitors installed ATMs primarily to reduce costs, Citi used ATMs to attract more customers. An average of 75 percent of Citi's customers prefer the ATM machines to human tellers, compared to 43 percent at other banks.

As new ATM systems such as Mastercard Inc.'s Cirrus rose to compete with Citi, Citicorp refused to interconnect with them. Customers then began flocking to other banks because Cirrus and similar networks allowed them to do their banking at virtually any ATM instead of having to search for a Citibank outlet. Citi eventually joined Cirrus because it wanted global availability of customer access to ATMs for cash. But the damage was done. Citi's ATMs, which originally were leading-edge, could no longer keep up with its rivals' systems.

The early success of Citi's ATMs convinced top management of the power of business units to create their own technological innovations. Top management began to promote decentralization, believing this would encourage entrepreneurship and more strategic use of technology. It initiated Project Paradise, which showered bank managers with billions of dollars to develop the systems they wanted. No thought was given to compatibility.

But the bank was so successful that it did not recognize the systems redundancies created by Project Paradise until the mid-1980s. By then it realized that many of its systems weren't necessarily helping the customer but were merely internal bureaucratic activities.

Many consider Reed's worst strategic blunder to be Citi's 1984 purchase of Quotron for $680 million. Quotron was the market-leading computerized stock-quotation system, with 100,000 stock quotation terminals in brokerage firms. Then competing stock quotation systems started to flourish. Automatic Data Processing bought Bunker Ramo, a Quotron competitor, and expanded its computer services to brokerages. Reuters Holdings Plc. began selling quotation data on its terminals. The bulk of Quotron customers were financial services firms that did not feel comfortable buying products from Citi, which they viewed as a competitor. Quotron fell to the Number 2 position in stock quotation data, with only 60,000 terminals, while ADP grew to 70,000 terminals.

Shortly after acquiring Quotron, Citi launched Reward America, a point-of-sale business that tried to create new products and services for the retail and travel industries by capturing market data at the cash register. This project was a good idea in theory, but it turned out to be impractical. Gathering data every time the cash register rings was not practical because the data were at the individual store level. Firms such as Coca-Cola are typically not interested in one store but in the entire Boston market, for

example. Reward America was shelved in 1990, and its management was folded into Citi's card businesses. Several hundred POS employees still gather shopper data from stores for direct marketing.

Hoping to reduce costs and reassert management control, Citi is consolidating its computer centers and networks. It hopes to save $100 million annually by consolidating its 100 plus networks into a single Global Information Network. Citi does not want to eliminate local flexibility altogether. It hopes that when one of its local business units comes up with a new product, its simplified architecture will help it make "success transfers" more rapid than before. But eliminating redundancies is not easy, compared to superficial cost-cutting; it entails major cultural changes.

Source: Bruce Caldwell, "Paradise No More," *Information WEEK,* April 6, 1992; Michael Quint, "Citicorp Criticized on Mortgages that Expose It to Too Much Risk, *The New York Times,* September 3, 1992 and "Citicorp's Stock Hits 6-Month Low," *The New York Times,* October 7, 1992.

Case Study Questions

1. Use the competitive forces and value chain models to analyze Citicorp's situation. What competitive forces did Citicorp have to deal with? What kinds of strategic information systems did Citicorp use?

2. How much strategic advantage did Citicorp's information systems provide?

3. How sustainable was Citicorp's strategic advantage? Why?

4. What management, organization, and technology factors contributed to Citicorp's problems?

5. If you were a Citicorp manager, what solutions would you recommend? Would you suggest new information system applications?

References Bakos, J. Yannis. "A Strategic Analysis of Electronic Marketplaces." *MIS Quarterly* 15, no. 3 (September 1991).

Bakos, J. Yannis, and Michael E. Treacy. "Information Technology and Corporate Strategy: A Research Perspective." *MIS Quarterly* (June 1986).

Barrett, Stephanie S. "Strategic Alternatives and Interorganizational System Implementations: An Overview." *Journal of Management Information Systems* (Winter 1986–1987).

Barua, Anitesh, Charles H. Kriebel, and Tridas Mukhopadhyay. "An Economic Analysis of Strategic Information Technology Investments." *MIS Quarterly* 15, no. 5 (September 1991).

Beath, Cynthia Mathis, and Blake Ives. "Competitive Information Systems in Support of Pricing." *MIS Quarterly* (March 1986).

Betts, Mitch. "ATM Pioneers Reaped Market Share, Income." *Computerworld,* January 20, 1992.

Bower, Joseph L., and Thomas M. Hout. "Fast-Cycle Capability for Competitive Power." *Harvard Business Review* (November–December 1988).

Caldwell, Bruce. "A Cure for Hospital Woes." *InformationWEEK,* September 9, 1991.

Cash, J. I., and Benn R. Konsynski. "IS Redraws Competitive Boundaries." *Harvard Business Review* (March–April 1985).

Cash, James I., F. Warren McFarlan, James L. McKenney, and Lynda M. Applegate. *Corporate Information Systems Management,* 3rd ed. Homewood, IL: Irwin, 1992.

Cash, J. I., and P. L. McLeod. "Introducing IS Technology in Strategically Dependent Companies." *Journal of Management Information Systems* (Spring 1985).

Clemons, Eric K. "Evaluation of Strategic Investments in Information Technology." *Communications of the ACM* (January 1991).

Clemons, Eric K., and Michael Row. "McKesson Drug Co.: Case Study of a Strategic Information System." *Journal of Management Information Systems*" (Summer 1988).

Clemons, Eric K., and Michael C. Row. "Sustaining IT Advantage: The Role of Structural Differences." *MIS Quarterly* 15, no. 3 (September 1991).

Connolly, James, and Elisabeth Horwitt. "American Express Sets Own Limits." *Computerworld,* December 12, 1988.

Copeland, Duncan G., and James L. McKenney. "Airline Reservations Systems: Lessons from History." *MIS Quarterly* 12, no. 3 (September 1988).

Cushman, John H., Jr. "The High-Stakes Battle for Airline Reservations." *The New York Times,* June 18, 1989.

Emmett, Arielle. "Hot or Cold, Steel Maker Forges Ahead with IS," *Computerworld,* June 15, 1992.

Feeny, David F., and Blake Ives. "In Search of Sustainability: Reaping Long-Term Advantage from Investments in Information Technology." *Journal of Management Information Systems* (Summer 1990).

Henderson, John C., and John J. Sifonis. "The Value of Strategic IS Planning: Understanding Consistency, Validity, and IS Markets." *MIS Quarterly* 12, no. 2 (June 1988).

Hopper, Max. "Rattling SABRE—New Ways to Compete on Information." *Harvard Business Review* (May–June 1990).

Ives, Blake, and Gerald P. Learmonth. "The Information System as a Competitive Weapon." *Communications of the ACM* (December 1984).

Ives, Blake, and Michael R. Vitale. "After the Sale: Leveraging Maintenance with Information Technology." *MIS Quarterly* (March 1986).

Janulaitis, M. Victor. "Gaining Competitive Advantage." *Infosystems* (October 1984).

Johnston, H. Russell, and Shelley R. Carrico. "Developing Capabilities to Use Information Strategically." *MIS Quarterly* 12, no. 1 (March 1988).

Johnston, Russell, and Paul R. Lawrence. "Beyond Vertical Integration—The Rise of the Value-Adding Partnership." *Harvard Business Review* (July–August 1988).

Johnston, Russell, and Michael R. Vitale. "Creating Competitive Advantage with Interorganizational Information Systems." *MIS Quarterly* 12, no. 2 (June 1988).

Keen, Peter G. W. *Competing in Time: Using Telecommunications for Competitive Advantage.* Cambridge, MA: Ballinger Publishing Company, 1986.

Keen, Peter G. W. *Shaping the Future: Business Design Through Information Technology.* Cambridge, MA: Harvard Business School Press, 1991.

Konsynski, Benn R., and F. Warren McFarlan. "Information Partnerships—Shared Data, Shared Scale." *Harvard Business Review* (September–October 1990).

Lindsey, Darryl, Paul H. Cheney, George M. Kasper, and Blake Ives. "Competitive Advantage in the Cotton Industry." *MIS Quarterly* 14, no. 4 (December 1990).

Main, Thomas J., and James E. Short. "Managing the Merger: Building Partnership through IT Planning at the New Baxter." *MIS Quarterly* 13, no. 4 (December 1989).

Malone, Thomas W., JoAnne Yates, and Robert I. Benjamin. "Electronic Markets and Electronic Hierarchies." *Communications of the ACM* (June 1987).

Malone, Thomas W., JoAnne Yates, and Robert I. Benjamin. "The Logic of Electronic Markets." *Harvard Business Review* (May–June 1989).

Markoff, John. "American Express Goes High-Tech." *New York Times,* July 31, 1988.

McFarlan, F. Warren. "Information Technology Changes the Way You Compete." *Harvard Business Review* (May–June 1984).

Millar, Victor E. "Decision-Oriented Information." *Datamation* (January 1984).

Miron, Michael, John Cecil, Kevin Bradcich, and Gene Hall. "The Myths and Realities of Competitive Advantage." *Datamation* (October 1, 1988).

Pastore, Richard. "Coffee, Tea and a Sales Pitch." *Computerworld* (July 3, 1989).

Porter, Michael. *Competitive Advantage*. New York: Free Press, 1985.

Porter, Michael. *Competitive Strategy*. New York: Free Press, 1980.

Porter, Michael. "How Information Can Help You Compete." *Harvard Business Review* (August–September 1985a).

Rackoff, Nick, Charles Wiseman, and Walter A. Ullrich. "Information Systems for Competitive Advantage: Implementation of a Planning Process." *MIS Quarterly* (December 1985).

Scott Morton, Michael, Ed. *The Corporation in the 1990s*. New York: Oxford University Press, 1991.

Vitale, Michael R. "The Growing Risks of Information System Success." *MIS Quarterly* (December 1986).

Wilke, John R. "State Street Bank Is Paved with Gold of Processing Fees." *The Wall Street Journal*, June 25, 1992.

Wiseman, Charles. *Strategic Information Systems*. Homewood, IL: Richard D. Irwin, Inc., 1988.

Schneider Responds to the New Rules of the Trucking Game

Deregulation changed the whole business environment for the trucking industry overnight. Competition between trucking firms for customers heated up. Interstate truckers no longer had to follow the rules of a regulatory bureaucracy about what kinds of freight to carry and where to take them. This same regulatory red tape had also made it difficult for customers to change carriers because only certain trucking firms could meet these regulations. Large retailers and manufacturers were also trying to slash inventory costs and warehouses by installing just-in-time delivery systems. They wanted to use trucking firms that could transport their shipments right away.

To meet these new demands Schneider National, North America's biggest carrier of full-truckload cargoes, used a two-pronged strategy. First, it tried to make sweeping changes in its corporate culture. CEO Don Schneider realized he had to replace his firm's regulated-utility mentality with quick reflexes

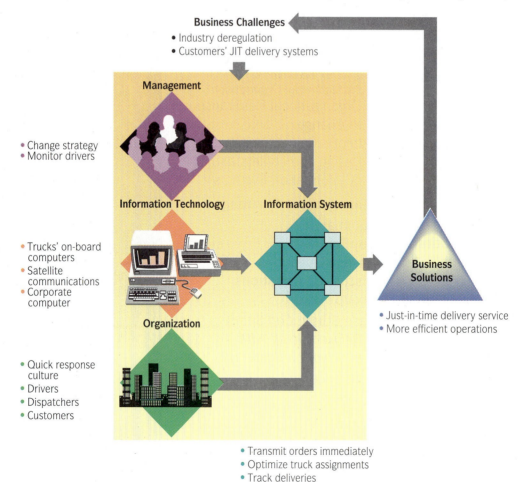

Business Challenges
- Industry deregulation
- Customers' JIT delivery systems

Management
- Change strategy
- Monitor drivers

Information Technology
- Trucks' on-board computers
- Satellite communications
- Corporate computer

Information System

Organization
- Quick response culture
- Drivers
- Dispatchers
- Customers

Business Solutions
- Just-in-time delivery service
- More efficient operations

- Transmit orders immediately
- Optimize truck assignments
- Track deliveries

and an urgency to get things done. Schneider democratized the organization by calling all employees "associates" and removing status symbols like reserved parking places. He encouraged everyone, from drivers on up, to speak out on ways to improve operations. He also instituted an extra bonus paycheck based solely on performance.

Second, Schneider deployed new information systems to support these changes. In 1988, the firm equipped each truck with a computer and a rotating antenna. A satellite tracks every rig, making sure it adheres to schedule. When an order comes into headquarters, often directly via the customer's computer to Schneider's computer, dispatchers know exactly which truck in the customer's vicinity should be assigned to the job. The dispatchers send an order directly by satellite to the driver's on-board terminal, complete with directions to the destination and instructions on what gate to use and papers to collect with the merchandise. Within 15 to 30 minutes of sending an order to Schneider's computer, customers know which trucks to expect and when.

Several other competitors responded to deregulation by merely lowering rates. They went bankrupt.

Source: Myron Magnet, "Meet the New Revolutionaries," *Fortune* (February 24, 1992).

The experience of Schneider National illustrates the interdependence of business environments, organizational culture, and the development of information systems. Schneider National developed a new information system in response to changes in competitive pressures from its surrounding environment, but it needed to make sweeping changes to its organizational culture before it could use this system successfully.

The complex relationship between organizations and information systems is explored in this chapter. Our goal is to introduce you to the salient features of organizations that you will need to know about as a manager when you envision, design, build, and operate information systems. First we will describe the features of organizations that are related to information systems—what we call the "salient" features. Then we will examine in greater detail precisely how information systems affect organizations, and just as important, how organizations affect information systems. The chapter concludes by describing some of the reasons why organizations are so difficult to change—with or without technology—and how you can use this knowledge to your advantage.

After completing this chapter you will be able to:

- Describe the salient characteristics of organizations.
- Explain the changing role of information systems within the organization.

- Compare models for describing the origins of systems in organizations.
- Identify the major theories about organizations that help us understand their relationship with information systems.
- Discuss the impact of information systems on organizational structure, culture, political processes, and management.
- Describe the organizational implications for the design and implementation of systems.

4.1 The Relationship Between Organizations and Information Systems

Can information systems "flatten" organizations by reducing their number of levels? Will information systems allow organizations to operate with fewer middle managers and clerical workers? Can information systems reduce paperwork? Can they be used to "re-engineer" organizations so they become lean, efficient, and hard hitting? Can organizations use information technology to decentralize power down to lower-level workers, thereby unleashing the creative talents of millions of employees?

These are among today's leading management questions. The issues raised by contemporary information systems—efficiency, creativity, bureaucracy, employment, quality of work life—are long-standing issues of industrial society, and they pre-date computers. Advances in information systems have heightened interest in these issues because many popular business writers claim information system technology can radically transform organizations into lean, mean machines. No one can deny that information systems have contributed to organizational efficiency and effectiveness. Yet social and behavioral scientists who have studied organizations over long periods of time argue that no such radical transformation of organizations has occurred so far, nor is it likely to occur in the future except in isolated cases. Exactly what can information systems do for organizations?

The relationship between information technology and organizations is complex, and the interpretations of this relationship are controversial. In this chapter we cannot provide a complete description of this relationship. Our goal is to present an overview of the relationship and a discussion of contemporary research so that you can understand the issues and join the debate.

The Two-Way Relationship

Let us start with a simple premise based on observation and a great deal of research: Information systems and organizations have a mutual influence on each other (see Figure 4.1). On the one hand, information systems must be aligned with the organization to provide information needed by important groups within the organization. At the same time, the organization must be aware of and must open itself to the influences of information systems to benefit from new technologies. Information systems affect organizations, and organizations necessarily affect the design of systems.

It is very convenient for journalists, scholars, and managers to think about "the impact of computers" on organizations as if it were like some ship colliding with an iceberg at sea. But the actual effect is much more complex. Figure 4.1 shows a great many mediating factors that influence the interaction between information technology and organizations. These include the organization's structure, standard operating procedures, politics, culture, surrounding environment, and management decisions. Managers, after all, decide what systems will be built, what they will do, how they will be implemented, and so forth. To a very large extent, managers and organizations choose the "computer impacts"

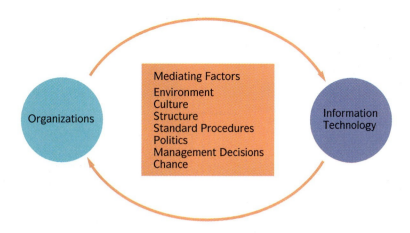

Figure 4.1
The two-way relationship between organizations and information technology. This complex two-way relationship is mediated by many factors not the least of which are the decisions made—or not made—by managers. Other factors mediating the relationship are the organizational culture, bureaucracy, politics, business fashion, and pure chance.

they want (or at least receive the impacts they deserve). Sometimes, however, the outcomes are the result of pure chance and of both good and bad luck.

Because there are many types of organizations, it stands to reason that the technology of information systems will have a different impact on different types of organizations. There is no singular effect of computers; one cannot, for example, conclude that "computers flatten hierarchies" in organizations. Instead, different organizations in different circumstances experience different effects from the same technology. Before describing how each of these mediating factors affects information systems, we must first review the salient features of organizations.

What Is an Organization?

Organization (technical definition): A stable formal social structure that takes resources from the environment and processes them to produce outputs.

An **organization** is a stable, formal social structure that takes resources from the environment and processes them to produce outputs. This technical definition focuses on three elements of an organization (see Figure 4.2). *Capital* and *labor*

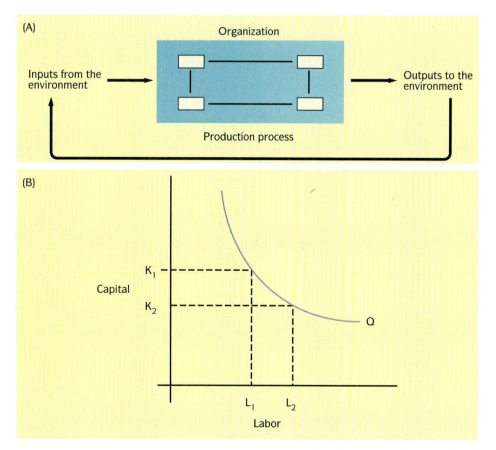

Figure 4.2
The technical microeconomic definition of the organization. In the microeconomic definition of organizations, capital and labor (the primary production factors provided by the environment) are transformed by the firm through the production process into products and services (outputs to the environment). The products and services are consumed by the environment which supplies additional capital and labor as inputs in the feedback loop.
(B) The microeconomic view is a technical model of the firm in which the firm combines capital and labor in a production function to produce a single product of the amount Q. The firm can freely substitute the capital for labor anywhere along the curve Q.

Figure 4.3
The behavioral view of organizations. The behavioral view of organizations emphasizes group relationships, values and structures.

are primary production factors provided by the environment. The organization (the firm) transforms these inputs into products and services in a *production function*—a process that transforms capital and labor into a product.[1] The products and services are *consumed by environments* in return for supply inputs.

An organization is *more stable* than an informal group in terms of longevity and routineness. Organizations are *formal* because they are legal entities and must abide by laws. They have internal rules and procedures. Organizations are *social structures* because they are a collection of social elements, much as a machine has a structure—a particular arrangement of valves, cams, shafts, and other parts.

Organizations are, in part, information-processing entities. However, it would be a mistake to view organizations or the human beings who work for them in this limited way. Organizations process and use information in order to produce outputs for an environment (e.g., products and services). Most organizations are not designed primarily for processing information. A newspaper delivers news and opinions to customers, not merely data or information. Even government agencies such as the Social Security Administration and the Internal Revenue Service, which are heavy users of information, have as their primary goal the delivery of pension and taxation services.

This definition of organizations is powerful and simple, but it is not very descriptive or even predictive of the real-world organizations that most of us belong to. A more realistic behavioral definition of an **organization** is that it is a collection of rights, privileges, obligations, and responsibilities that are delicately balanced over a period of time through conflict and conflict resolution (see Figure 4.3).

In this behavioral view of the firm, people who work in organizations develop customary ways of working; they gain attachments to existing relationships; and they make arrangements with subordinates and superiors about how work will be done, how much work will be done, and under what conditions. Most of these arrangements and feelings are not discussed in any formal rule book.

How do these definitions of organizations relate to information system technology? A technical microeconomic view of organizations encourages us to think that introducing new technology changes the way inputs are combined into outputs, like changing the spark plugs on an engine. The firm is seen as infinitely malleable, with capital and labor substituting for one another quite easily.

Organization (behavioral definition): A collection of rights, privileges, obligations, and responsibilities that are delicately balanced over a period of time through conflict and conflict resolution.

1. A typical production function is given by $Q = A* (K,L)$, where Q is the quantity of output produced by a firm; K and L are factors of production, capital, and labor. "A" represents a parameter greater than 0 reflecting the productivity of available technology—factors such as education, knowledge, and changes in technique and technology—which can alter the output Q independent of capital and labor. See any microeconomics textbook for further background. An excellent reference is Robert S. Pindyck and Daniel L. Rubinfield, *Microeconomics* (New York: Macmillan, 1992). This text has several interesting chapters on information asymmetries, although like most microeconomics texts it is limited in its coverage of technology.

But the more realistic behavioral definition of an organization suggests that building new information systems or rebuilding old ones involves much more than a technical rearrangement of machines or workers. Instead, technological change requires changes in who owns and controls information, who has the right to access and update that information, and who makes decisions about whom, when, and how. For instance, Schneider's new information system provided central managers with more information to monitor truck drivers' whereabouts. The more complex view forces us to look at the way work is designed and the procedures used to achieve outputs.

The technical and behavioral definitions of organizations are not contradictory. Indeed, they complement one another: The microeconomic definition tells us how thousands of firms in competitive markets combine capital and labor and information technology, whereas the behavioral model takes us inside the individual firm to see how, in fact, specific firms use capital and labor to produce outputs. Section 4.4 describes how theories based on each of these definitions of organizations can help explain the relationship between information systems and organizations.

Information systems can markedly alter life in the organization. Some information systems change the organizational balance of rights, privileges, obligations, responsibilities, and feelings that has been established over a long period of time. What this means is that managers cannot design new systems or understand existing systems without understanding organizations.

4.2 Salient Features of Organizations

In this section, we introduce and discuss the major features of organizations that managers should be aware of when building information systems. These organizational features are mediating factors (review Figure 4.1) that influence the relationship between organizations and information technology.

Some features of organizations are common to all organizations; others distinguish one organization from another. Let us look first at the features common to all organizations.

Why Organizations Are So Much Alike: Common Features

Bureaucracy: Formal organization with a clear-cut division of labor, abstract rules and procedures, and impartial decision making that uses technical qualifications and professionalism as a basis for promoting employees.

You might not think that Apple Computer, United Airlines, or the Aspen Colorado Police Department have much in common, but they do. In some respects, all modern organizations are alike because they share the characteristics that are listed in Table 4.1. A German sociologist, Max Weber, was the first to describe these "ideal-typical" characteristics of organizations in 1911. He called organizations **bureaucracies** that have certain "structural" features (see Table 4.1).

According to Weber, all modern bureaucracies have a clear-cut *division of labor and specialization*. Organizations employ or train individuals who possess specific talents or skills. Organizations arrange specialists in a *hierarchy* of authority in which everyone is accountable to someone and authority is limited to specific actions. Authority and action are further limited by abstract *rules or procedures* (standard operating procedures or SOPs) that are interpreted and applied to specific cases. These rules create a system of *impartial and universal-*

Table 4.1	STRUCTURAL CHARACTERISTICS OF ALL ORGANIZATIONS

Clear division of labor

Hierarchy

Explicit rules and procedures

Impartial judgments

Technical qualifications for positions

Maximum organizational efficiency

ORGANIZATIONS

Learning from Japan Takes a Long Time

Tens of thousands of manufacturing executives and production engineers have journeyed to the Toyota Motor Corporation's Georgetown, Kentucky, plant to observe how the Japanese can manufacture high-quality cars so efficiently. One reason Toyota has succeeded is by turning Henry Ford's mass-production principles on their head. Ford believed that the cheapest way to build cars was to churn out the largest number of autos by having workers repeatedly perform a simple task. By contrast, Toyota discovered that having a smaller number of workers, each capable of performing several tasks, produced cars with less inventory, less investment, and fewer mistakes.

Figure 4.4 contrasts American mass production and Japanese "lean production" methods. Standard operating procedures in classic mass production try to maximize output by running machines with as few interruptions as possible. Every worker performs only one or two tasks over and over again. The goal is to keep the machines running. Standard operating

procedures in a "lean production" environment require workers to minimize inventory and inventory costs while maintaining high quality standards. Workers have multiple jobs and responsibilities, and are allowed to stop machines often to spot defects in batches of parts or partially completed cars. When workers change the type of part each machine makes, they are encouraged to note every glitch, and, if necessary, to stop production to correct a problem.

In the Japanese auto manufacturing firms, a team of workers calculates how many seconds each task should take. Based on the speed of the assembly line, the team draws red lines to show where a car should be when work begins and where it should be when the work is completed. Workers are instructed not to start work before the car reaches the first line and to complete the job before it reaches the second line. The job is redesigned if the workers can complete the task in less time or if they cannot complete it in the time allotted.

Experts estimate that it will take years for U.S. auto makers to duplicate Toyota's efficiency. Not only must U.S. companies change the standard operating procedures on their assembly lines, but they must also find ways to involve auto workers in improving factories. This hasn't been easy, because U.S. auto companies have traditionally been hierarchical and authoritarian. Ford introduced programs ten years ago to promote worker participation. It became the most efficient U.S. auto maker during the 1980's.

Source: Doron P. Levin, "Toyota Plant in Kentucky Is Font of Ideas for U.S.," and "Detroit Is Slow to Learn from Japan," *The New York Times* (May 5, 1992).

To Think About: Why are standard operating procedures so difficult to change? What aspects of organizations must be addressed?

---

istic decision making; everyone is treated equally. Organizations try to hire and promote employees on the basis of *technical qualifications and professionalism* (not personal connections). The organization itself is devoted to the *principle of efficiency:* maximizing output using limited inputs.

Bureaucracies are so prevalent, according to Weber, because they are the most efficient form of organization. They are much more stable and powerful than mercurial charismatic groups or formal aristocracies held together by the right of birth. Other scholars supplemented Weber, identifying additional features of organizations. All organizations develop standard operating procedures, politics, and a culture.

STANDARD OPERATING PROCEDURES

All organizations, over time, stabilize to produce a given number of products and services. Over long periods of time, the organizations that survive become very efficient, producing a limited number of products and services by following standard routines. In this period of time, employees develop reasonably precise rules, procedures, and practices called **standard operating procedures** (SOPs) to cope with virtually all expected situations. Some of these rules and procedures are written down as formal procedures, but most are rules of thumb to be followed in selected situations.

Standard operating procedures (SOPs): Precise, defined rules for accomplishing tasks that have been developed to cope with expected situations.

A great deal of the efficiency that modern organizations attain has little to do with computers but a great deal to do with the development of standard oper-

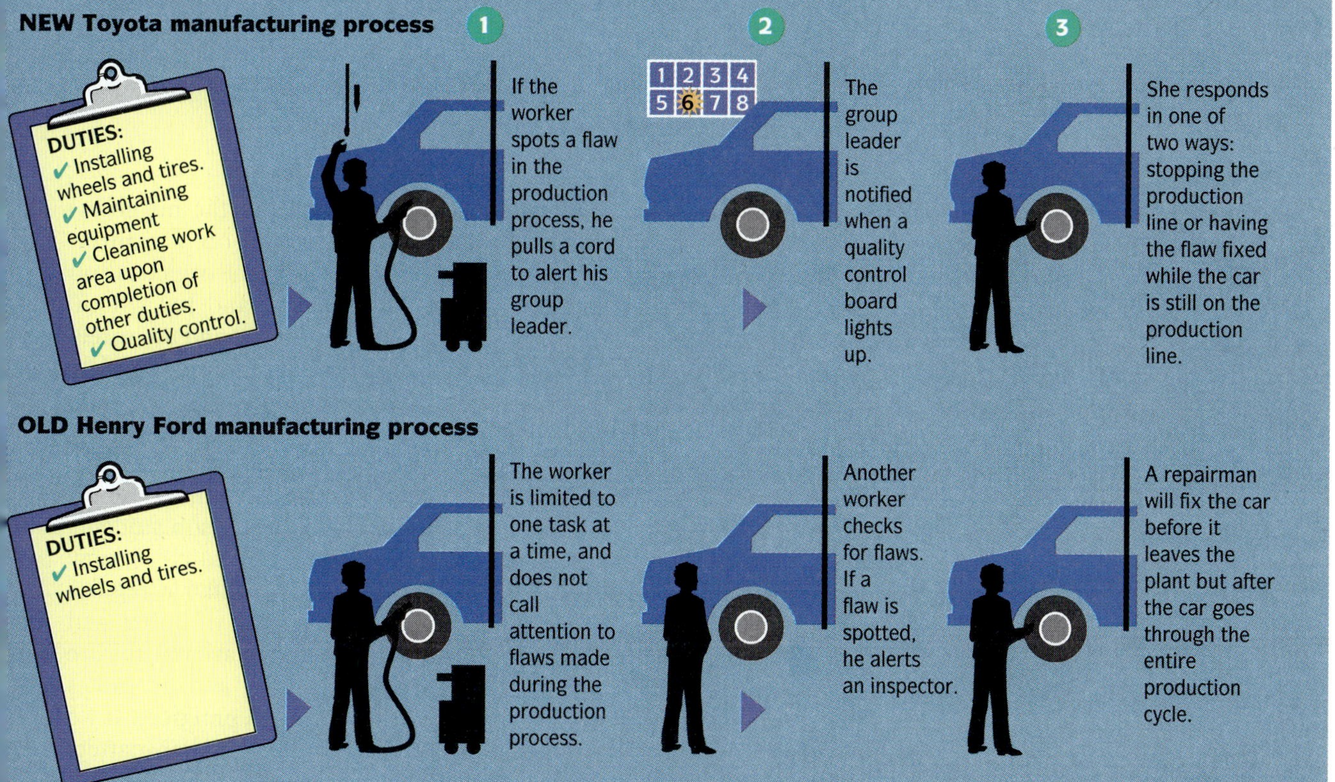

Figure 4.4
How mass production has changed. A new leaner production system asks fewer workers to perform more tasks, thereby increasing efficiency and lowering costs. Adapted from Ty Ahmed-Taylor: "How Mass Production Has Changed," *The New York Times*, May 5, 1992. Original illustration by Al Granberg. Copyright © 1992 by The New York Times Company. Reprinted by permission.

NEW Toyota manufacturing process

1

2

3

DUTIES:
✓ Installing wheels and tires.
✓ Maintaining equipment
✓ Cleaning work area upon completion of other duties.
✓ Quality control.

If the worker spots a flaw in the production process, he pulls a cord to alert his group leader.

The group leader is notified when a quality control board lights up.

She responds in one of two ways: stopping the production line or having the flaw fixed while the car is still on the production line.

OLD Henry Ford manufacturing process

DUTIES:
✓ Installing wheels and tires.

The worker is limited to one task at a time, and does not call attention to flaws made during the production process.

Another worker checks for flaws. If a flaw is spotted, he alerts an inspector.

A repairman will fix the car before it leaves the plant but after the car goes through the entire production cycle.

ating procedures. For instance, in the assembly of a car, thousands of motions and procedures must be planned and executed in a precise fashion to permit the finished product to roll off the line. If workers had to decide how each vehicle was to be built, or if managers had to decide how each day's product was to be built, efficiency would drop off dramatically. Instead, managers and workers develop a complex set of standard procedures to handle most situations. As the Window on Organizations illustrates, any change in SOPs requires an enormous organizational effort. Indeed, the organization may need to halt the entire production process, or create a new and expensive parallel system, which must then be tested exhaustively before the old SOPs can be retired. Difficulty in changing standard operating procedures is one reason Detroit auto makers have been slow to adopt Japanese mass-production methods.

ORGANIZATIONAL POLITICS

Organizations are arranged so that people occupy different positions. Because these individuals have different concerns and specialties, they naturally have differences in viewpoint, perspective, and opinion about how resources, rewards, and punishments should be distributed. These differences matter to members of organizations, both managers and employees. Because of these differences, political struggle, competition, and conflict occur in every organization. Sometimes political struggles occur when individuals or interest groups seek to exercise leadership and to gain advantages. Other times, entire groups compete, leading to clashes on a large scale. In either case, politics is a normal part of organizational life.

People use politics to gain everything worth having in a job: pay, position, job conditions, respect, prestige, and ultimately careers. Because of the stakes, players take the game very seriously. Politics, as described by the famous political scientist Harold Lasswell, is who does what to whom, where, when, and how.

One of the great difficulties of bringing about change in organizations—especially concerning the development of new information systems—is the political resistance that any important organizational change seems to bring forth. "Important" changes are those that directly affect who does what to whom, where, when, and how. Virtually all information systems that bring about significant changes in goals, procedures, productivity, and personnel are politically charged.

ORGANIZATIONAL CULTURE

Organizational culture: The set of fundamental assumptions about what products the organization should produce, how and where it should produce them, and for whom they should be produced.

All organizations have bedrock, unassailable, unquestioned (by the members) assumptions that define the goals and products of the organization. **Organizational culture** is the set of fundamental assumptions about what the organization should produce, how it should produce its products, where, and for whom. Generally, these cultural assumptions are taken totally for granted and are rarely publicly announced or spoken about. They are simply assumptions that few people, if anyone (in their right mind), would question (Schein, 1985).

Everything else—technology, values, norms, public announcements, and so on—follows from these assumptions. You can see organizational culture at work by looking around your university or college. Some bedrock assumptions of university life are that professors know more than students, the reason students attend college is to learn, the primary purpose of the university is to create new knowledge and communicate knowledge to students, classes follow a regular schedule, and libraries are repositories of knowledge in the form of books and journals. Sometimes these cultural assumptions are true. Organizational culture is a powerful unifying force, which restrains political conflict and promotes common understanding, agreement on procedures, and common practices. If we all share the same basic cultural assumptions, then agreement on other matters is more likely.

At the same time, organizational culture is a powerful restraint on change, especially technological change. Any technological change that threatens commonly held cultural assumptions will meet with a great deal of resistance. The Window on Organizations illustrates that another reason why U.S. auto makers have been slow to switch to "lean production" methods is because of long-standing assumptions that management should be very authoritarian and does not need to listen to the opinions of workers.

In general, organizational cultures are far more powerful than information technologies. Therefore, most organizations will do almost anything to avoid making changes in basic assumptions, and new technologies are almost always used at first in ways that support existing cultures.

On the other hand, there are times when the only sensible way to employ a new technology is directly opposed to an existing organizational culture. When this occurs, the technology is often stalled or delayed while the culture slowly adjusts. Organizational change requires far more time than technological change requires. On average, it takes 5 to 7 years for an industry's "best practice" to become the median practice (Klotz, 1966).[2] This statistic is derived from studies of industrial machine tools and may not apply to computer-based techniques. But is the information-systems world really any different from other forms of

2. Klotz, B. *Industry Productivity Projections: A Methodological Study.* U.S. Department of Labor, Bureau of Labor Statistics, 1966. See also T. K. Bikson and J. D. Eveland, "Integrating New Tools Into Information Work. Technology Transfer as a Framework for Understanding Success," The Rand Corporation, 1992. These estimates are for industrial-sector innovations, and no one really knows how long it takes for IT innovations to become industry median practice.

Table 4.2 A COMPARISON OF TYPES OF ORGANIZATIONS

Primary Source Author	Organizational Differences	Main Concepts	Sample Organization
Mintzberg (1979)	Have different structures	Simple structure Machine bureaucracy Professional bureaucracy Divisionalized form Adhocracy	Mom-and-Pop firm Post office Hospital Fortune 500 Research firm
Etzioni (1975)	Have different goals	Coercive, Utilitarian, Normative goals	Military Business Church
Blau and Scott (1962)	Benefit different groups	Members Clients Owners	Boy Scouts Welfare agency Business
Parsons (1960)	Perform different functions	Economic Pattern maintenance Integrative Political	Business Universities, schools Hospitals, courts Government
Gouldner (1954)	Have different leadership styles	Democratic Authoritarian Laissez-faire Technocratic Bureaucratic	Different types of leadership could occur in any organization
March and Simon (1958)	Make different decisions	Programmed Semi-programmed Unprogrammed decisions	Inventory reorder Production scheduling Selecting strategy
Blauner (1967) Woodward (1965)	Perform different tasks Use different techniques and technology	Craft Batch routine Continuous process	Woodworker Assembly line Oil refinery
Thompson (1967)	Exist in different environments	Turbulence Complexity	Rapid technology change Multiple competitors

technology? In 1992, there were about 70 million PCs in the United States. How long will it take for 50 percent of all PCs to be using a state-of-the-art operating system like Windows 3.1? Two years after its introduction in 1990, about 10 million copies of Windows 3.0 were sold, a statistic that suggests that it probably would take at least five years (until about 1995) before the median practice achieved "best practice" levels.

Why Organizations Are So Different: Unique Features

Some features vary from one organization to another. Although all organizations have some common characteristics, no two organizations are identical. Organizations have different structures, goals, constituencies, leadership styles, tasks, and surrounding environments. These differences are listed and summarized in Table 4.2, along with the main concepts, primary sources, and sample organizations that characterize these organizational differences.

DIFFERENT ORGANIZATIONAL TYPES

One important way in which organizations differ is in their structure or shape. The differences among organizational structures are characterized in many ways. Mintzberg's classification is especially useful and simple (see Figure 4.5), for it identifies five basic kinds of organizations:

Entrepreneurial structure: Young, small firm in a fast-changing environment dominated by a single entrepreneur and managed by a single chief executive officer.

Entrepreneurial structure: Organizations with simple structures tend to be young, small, entrepreneurial firms in fast-changing environments, dominated by a single entrepreneur and managed by a single chief executive officer. Information systems typically are poorly planned and significantly behind fast-breaking production developments.

Figure 4.5
Different types of organizations. Organizational types tend to be suited to specific environments: the simple entrepreneurial structure (A) and the adhocracy (E) are suited to fast changing environments. Machine (B) and divisionalized bureaucracies (D) are more suited to slowly-paced environmental changes. Professional bureaucracies (C) are suited to knowledge intensive industries where change is typically slow-paced.
Sources: Parts a-d: Henry Mintzberg, *The Structuring of Organizations,* © 1979, pp. 311, 328, 329, 382. Reprinted by permission of Prentice-Hall, Englewood Cliffs, NJ. Part e: Courtesy of the National Film Board of Canada.

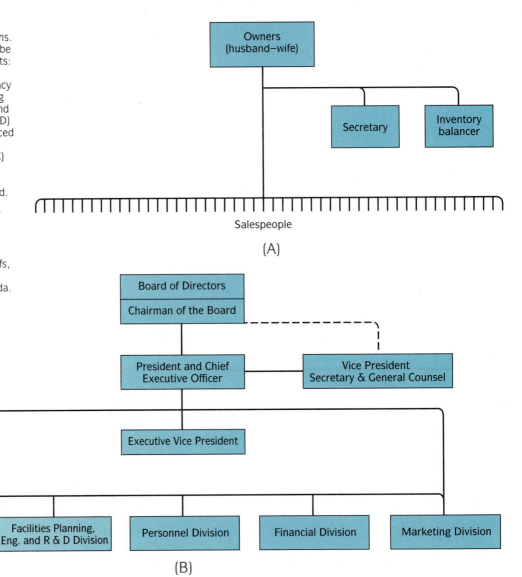

(A)

(B)

Machine bureaucracy: Large bureaucracy organized into functional divisions that centralizes decision making, produces standard products, and exists in a slow-changing environment.

Divisionalized bureaucracy: Combination of many machine bureaucracies, each producing a different product or service, under one central headquarters.

Machine bureaucracy: The large, classic bureaucracy exists in slow-changing environments, producing standardized products. It is dominated by a strategic senior management that centralizes information flow and decision authority. It is likely to be organized into functional divisions—for example, manufacturing, finance, marketing, and human resources. Information systems tend to be mainframe-based. They are well planned, but are generally limited to accounting, finance, simple planning, and administrative applications.

Divisionalized bureaucracy: This type of organization is the most common Fortune 500 form, a combination of many machine bureaucracies, each producing a different product or service, topped by a central headquarters. This type of organization is suited to slow-changing environments and standardized products, but because these kinds of organizations are divisionalized, they tend to operate in several different environments (one for each division or product line). Information systems typically are elaborate and complex so that they can support central headquarter's financial planning and reporting requirements on one hand, and the operational requirements of the divisions on the other hand. Typically there is a great deal of tension and conflict between central headquarters IS groups (who want to expand in the name of efficiency and cost control) and divisional IS groups (who want to expand in the name of more effective service to operations). Currently, the divisional IS groups have more prominent roles while central headquarters IS groups are shrinking.

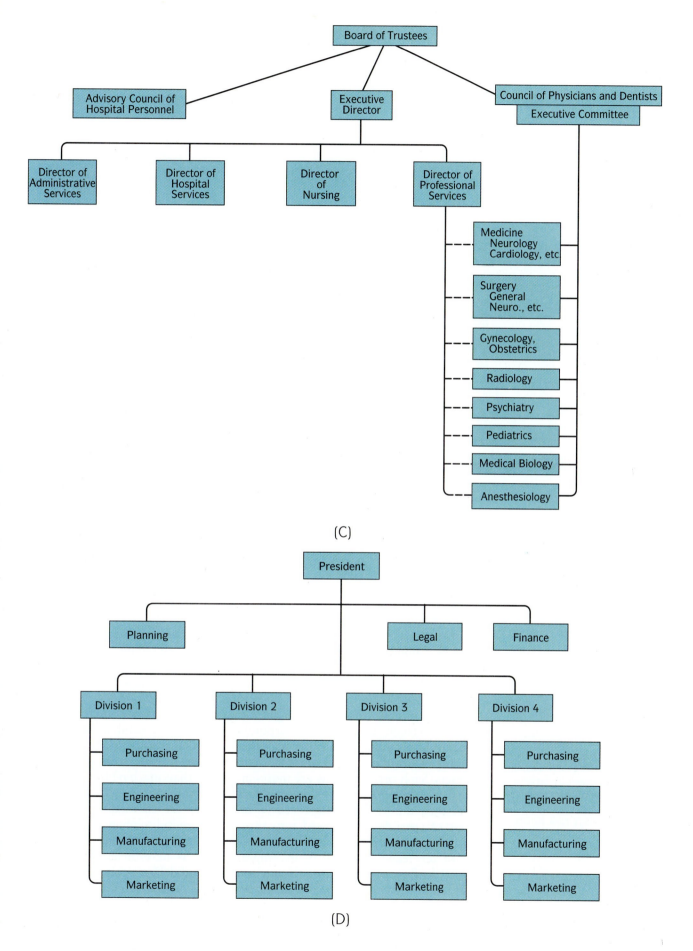

(C)

(D)

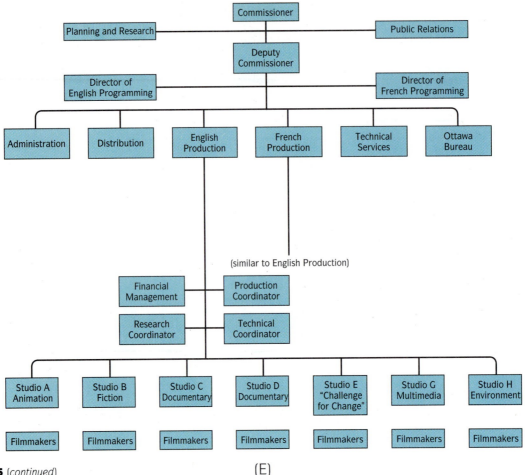

Figure 4.5 *(continued)*   (E)

Professional bureaucracy:
Knowledge-based
organization such as a law
firm or hospital that is
dominated by department
heads with weak centralized
authority; operates in a
slowly changing environment.

Professional bureaucracy: This structure is typical of law firms, school systems, accounting firms, hospitals, and other knowledge-based organizations that depend on the knowledge and expertise of professionals. Professional bureaucracies are suitable for slow-changing environments and skill sets. They are dominated by department heads and have weak centralized authority. Professional members of the organization who have considerable information and authority create the product or service. Such organizations typically have primitive central information systems for time accounting and billing for professional services, and often have very sophisticated knowledge work support systems for professionals. Knowledge work systems are described in greater detail in Chapter 15.

Adhocracy: Task force
organization, such as a
research organization,
designed to respond to a
rapidly changing environment
and characterized by large
groups of specialists organized
into short-lived
multidisciplinary task forces.

Adhocracy: This "task force" organization is typically found in research organizations (such as the Rand Corporation), aerospace companies, medical, biomedical, electronic, and other high-tech firms that must respond to rapidly changing environments and markets or that derive revenue from government contracts. Such organizations are more innovative than machine bureaucracies, more flexible than professional bureaucracies, and have more sustained, effective power than the simple entrepreneurial firm. They are characterized by large groups of specialists organized into short-lived, multidisciplinary task forces focusing on new products and by weak central management that understands little of the technical work of its employees but is nevertheless expected to manage the flow of funds from the environment and deliver products in return. Information systems are poorly developed at the central level, but are often remarkably advanced within task forces where experts build their unique systems for narrow functions.

Working task forces use their combined skills to improve on the design and manufacturing of semiconductors at this Motorola research facility.

ENVIRONMENTS
Organizations have different environments and environments exert a powerful influence on organizational structure. Generally, organizations in fast-changing environments are more like adhocracies—they are less hierarchical, with much authority delegated to subordinates. Organizations in stable environments tend to develop into machine bureaucracies.

Most people do not realize how fragile and short-lived formal organizations really are. Consider that less than 10 percent of Fortune 500 companies in 1918 survived more than fifty years; less than 4 percent of all federal government organizations ever created are still in existence; 50 percent of all new private organizations are out of business within five years; and bigness per se is only marginally protective against extinction and may only slow the decline (Laudon, 1989).

The main reasons for organizational failure are an inability to adapt to a rapidly changing environment and the lack of resources—particularly among young firms—to sustain even short periods of troubled times (Freeman et al., 1983). New technologies, new products, and changing public tastes and values (many of which result in new government regulations) put strains on any organization's culture, politics, and people.

IBM and the computer industry provide a powerful example of environmental instability brought about by rapid technological change on the one hand, and management's inability to adjust its internal culture, politics, and organizational structure on the other hand. Since 1965, with the introduction of the first microprocessor-based commercial computer, IBM dominated the mainframe market at a time when virtually all computing was done on mainframes. Unfortunately, the management of IBM failed to understand the microprocessor revolution it had begun, and the mainframe groups within IBM continued to dominate corporate decision making. When it was developing the IBM PC during the period from 1978 to 1980, IBM banished the product to an obscure development facility, lost control of the microprocessor technology to Intel Corporation, lost control of the software to Microsoft (and many other software vendors), and ultimately lost control of the PC market itself to makers of inexpensive clone products. IBM management also failed to keep pace in the UNIX workstation market which it conceded to Sun Systems, Hewlett-Packard, and Digital Equipment. By 1993, the world's largest computing firm, America's largest industrial company, was losing over $5 billion each quarter.

The airline industry provides a powerful example of environmental instability that was brought about by governmental airline deregulation and technological change in the form of powerful computer-driven airline reservation systems. The possession of these systems became a significant source of funds in the 1980s. Deregulation of airline fares and routes permitted market competition; this, in

Wang's dedicated word processors of the late 1960s and early 1970s (left) were limited to basic text creation and editing functions. Documentation was often needed to supplement a difficult user interface and desk top calculators were required for any mathematical functions. Contemporary desk top microcomputers, such as this IBM Personal System/2, (right) offer a wide array of sophisticated processing capabilities with an easy to use user interface.

turn, drove prices down. Companies that had invested heavily in airline reservations systems were much more capable of managing their passenger loads and price structure than those airlines that failed to develop such systems. Only a few airline companies survived these changes, and popular carriers like Pan American and Eastern Airlines no longer exist.

In general, most organizations do not cope well with large environmental shifts. The inertia built into an organization's standard operating procedures, the political conflict raised by potential change, and the threat to closely held cultural values typically inhibit organizations from making significant changes to cope with a changing environment. For this reason, corporate raiders and other outsiders are usually needed to save failing organizations and restructure them entirely.

From an organizational standpoint, technology is a major environmental factor that continually threatens existing arrangements. At times, technological changes occur so radically as to constitute a "technological discontinuity," a sharp break in industry practice that either enhances or destroys the competence of firms in an industry (Tushman and Anderson, 1986). When technological discontinuities happen, most organizations fail to adapt, go out of existence, and free up resources for new, younger organizations. Fast-changing technologies, like information technology, pose a particular threat to organizations. For instance, Wang Laboratories, a leading manufacturer of minicomputers and word processors, was a dominant force in the computer industry during the 1970s and early 1980s. But when powerful desktop microcomputers reduced the need for minicomputers, Wang nearly went out of business because it failed to adapt its products to the new technology.

As we see throughout this book, it is very difficult to identify precisely the impacts of computers on organizations. Much depends on the type of organization we are analyzing, the environment, management, and the underlying production technology. One cannot assume that information technologies will have the same effects on all organizations.

There are many reasons why organizations have different shapes or structures. Organizations differ in their ultimate goals and the types of power used to achieve them. Some organizations have coercive goals (e.g., prisons); other have utilitarian goals (e.g., businesses). Still others have normative goals (universities, religious groups). The kinds of power and incentives differ accordingly, as does the overall shape of the organization: A coercive organization will be very hierarchical whereas a normative organization will be less hierarchical.

Organizations serve different groups or have different constituencies. Some primarily benefit their members; others benefit clients, stockholders, or the public. The social roles or functions of organizations differ. Some organizations are primarily interested in politics (trying to change the distribution of benefits in society), while others play primarily economic roles (seeking to optimize the utilization of resources). Some organizations play integrative roles by trying to pull together diverse groups in a common enterprise; examples include hospitals devoted to the control of disease and courts devoted to the pursuit of justice. Still other organizations, such as universities, schools, and churches, work to preserve important social values (normative roles). In general, the wider the constituency that an organization serves, the less hierarchical the organization.

Clearly, the nature of leadership differs greatly from one organization to another, even in similar organizations that are devoted to the same goal. Some of the major leadership styles are democratic, authoritarian (even totalitarian), laissez-faire (leadership is absent), technocratic (according to technical criteria, formal models), or bureaucratic (strictly according to formal rules). These kinds of leadership can occur in any type of organization and seem to depend on chance and history.

Still another way organizations differ is by the tasks they perform, and the technology they use. In some cases, organizations use routine tasks that could be programmed—that is, tasks may be reduced to formal rules that require little judgment (e.g., inventory reordering). Organizations that primarily perform routine tasks are typically like machine bureaucracies—they are hierarchical and run according to standard procedures. In other cases, organizations work with highly judgmental, nonroutine tasks (e.g., a consulting company that creates strategic plans for other companies).

In summary, both the common and the unique features of organizations exert a powerful influence on precisely how information technology can be and will be used in an organization. Because organizations are so different, it is probably wrong to conclude that information systems will have certain specific impacts on all organizations: So much depends on a number of other nontechnological factors. A wise manager will attempt to take these factors into account when building or proposing new information systems. We will deal more with this issue at the end of the chapter.

Levels of Analysis

So far we have discussed the salient features of organizations that you should take into account as a manager of information systems. We now have a basis for comparing organizations, one to another, using the features we discussed above. But what about within the organization? Within organizations, there are different levels, occupations, divisions, and groups. All organizations have levels, but each organization is quite different from others in terms of what the levels are, who occupies them, and what tasks are assigned to different levels. The impact of information systems will probably be different for different levels and groups within an organization. We shall now explore some of these internal distinctions.

The term *organization* encompasses a wide range of behaviors at different organizational levels. Each level has different concerns and a different framework of analysis. This can be seen in Figure 4.6, which describes the various organizational levels and the principal concerns at each level, providing examples of information systems that are appropriate for each level.

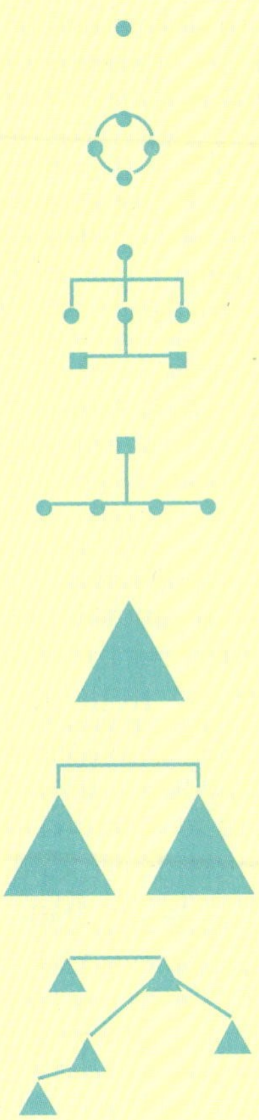

Organizational Level		Activity	Example Support System
Individual	●	Job, task	Microcomputer application; personal client database; decision-support systems
Group		Project	Product scheduling; access to mainframe data; access to external data sources; dynamic information requirements; group DSS
Department		Major function	Accounts payable; warehouse; payroll; human resources; marketing; stable information requirements; MIS; major transaction systems
Division		Major product or service	Systems to support production, marketing, administration, and personnel; access to organizational financial and planning data; MIS; major transaction systems; on-line interactive systems
Organization		Multiple products, services, and goals	Integrated financial and planning systems; MIS; on-line interactive systems; ESS
Interorganization		Alliance Competition Exchange Contact	Communication systems; intelligence, observation, and monitoring systems
Organizational network		Sector of economy: related products, services; interdependencies	Informal communication systems; industry and sector-level formal reporting systems

Figure 4.6
Organizational levels and support systems. Systems are designed to support various levels of the organization.

At the individual and small-group levels of organization, information systems apply to a particular job, task, or project. At the department and division levels, information systems deal with a particular business function, product, or service. At the organization, interorganization and organizational network levels, information systems support multiple products, services, and goals and facilitate alliances and coordination between two different organizations or groups of organizations.

Perhaps one of the most important and least heralded contributions of information systems is to support the large variety of work groups that spring up in organizations and that are not even part of the formal organization chart. While the organization chart shows the formal relationships in an organization, much of the work of an organization is done by informal task forces, interdepartmental committees, project teams, and committees. Table 4.3 presents the most important work groups and shows how systems can support them. These work groups generally have rapidly changing information needs, peak-load work schedules associated with project deadlines, and high communication requirements. Office automation systems, especially those with high-speed communication linkages, are one of the most recently developed system tools directed at work groups (see Chapter 15).

We have developed a rather long list of salient features you should know about when considering information systems in organizations (see Table 4.4). As you can see, the list of unique features of organizations is longer than the common features list. What this should suggest to you is that most organizations are quite unique. One consequence of this fact is that information systems are not completely portable from one organization to another. The impacts of systems will differ from one organization to another, and only by close analysis of a specific organization can a manager design and manage information systems.

Table 4.3 WORK GROUPS, PROBLEMS, AND SYSTEMS SUPPORT

Type of Work Group	Description	Problems	Systems Support
Hierarchical	Formal working relationship between manager and staff	Frequent meetings; dispersed work environments	Video conferencing; electronic mail (one to many)
Interdepartmental	Sequential activities; "expediters," "fixers"	Need occasional direct communication	Electronic messaging (one to one)
Project teams	Formally defined groups; close day-to-day interaction	Meeting schedules	Scheduling and communication software; meeting support tools; document interchange
Committees	Formally defined groups; occasional interaction	High peak-load; communications intermittent	Electronic bulletin boards; video conferencing; electronic mail; computer conferencing
Task force	Formally defined single-purpose group	Rapid communication; access to internal and external data	Graphics display; information utility; document interchange; meeting support tools
Peer groups/social networks	Informal groups of similar-status individuals	Intense personal communication	Telephone; electronic mail

Problems of all work groups
  Making arrangements
  Attending meetings
  Long agendas
  Cost of meetings
  Between-meeting
    activities

Table 4.4 A SUMMARY OF SALIENT FEATURES OF ORGANIZATIONS

Common Features	Unique Features
Formal structure	Organizational Type
Standard Operating Procedures (SOPs)	Environments
Politics	Goals
Culture	Power
	Constituencies
	Function
	Leadership
	Tasks
	Technology
	Levels

4.3 How Organizations Affect Information Systems

With a solid foundation in the nature of organizations, you are now ready to look more closely at the two-way relationship between information systems and organizations. We first need to explain how organizations affect technology and systems. Organizations have an impact on information systems through the decisions made by managers and employees. Managers make decisions about the design of systems; they also use information technology. Managers decide who will build and operate systems, and ultimately it is managers who provide the rationale for building systems. There are four important questions to consider in studying this issue:

- How have organizations actually used information systems?
- How has the organizational role of information systems changed?
- Who operates information systems?
- Why do organizations adopt information systems in the first place?

In this section, we answer these questions.

Decisions About the Role of Information Systems

Organizations have a direct impact on information technology by making decisions about how the technology will be used and what role it will play in the organization. Chapters 1 and 3 have described the ever-widening role of information systems in organizations. Table 4.5 shows the changing applications of information systems. Information systems have progressed from the operational-level systems of the 1950s that were designed to make elementary but vital transactions such as paying checks efficient. In the late 1960s, management systems were used for monitoring and controlling; and in the 1970s they were used for planning and simulations. By the 1980s, information systems had expanded into areas more directly related to making specific decisions: custom-built decision support systems and early strategic planning systems. In the mid 1980s, organizations were beginning to plan and manage information strategically as if it were like other resources such as capital, physical resources, and labor. In the 1990s, information systems are helping to create and disseminate knowledge and information throughout the organization through new knowledge work systems, applications providing company-wide access to data, and company-wide communications networks.

Corresponding to the changes in applications have been changes in the technical and organizational configuration of systems that have brought computing power and data much closer to the ultimate end users (see Figure 4.7).

Table 4.5 CHANGING APPLICATIONS OF INFORMATION SYSTEMS

1950s	1960s	1970s	1980s	1990s
Accounts receivable/ payable Payroll General ledger				→
	Cash flow Budgeting Personnel Manufacturing Marketing			→
		Forecasting Planning Simulation		→
			Decision support systems End-user programming Strategic planning Information resources management Information centers	→
				Information utilities ----→ Knowledge work stations Central data management

Figure 4.7
The development of information architecture of organizations. The last five decades have seen dramatic changes in the technical and organizational configurations of systems. During the 1950s organizations were dependent on computers for a few critical functions. The 1960s witnessed the development of large centralized machines. By the late 1970s and into the 1980s information architecture became complex and information systems included telecommunications links to distribute information. During the 1990s information architecture is an enterprise wide information utility.

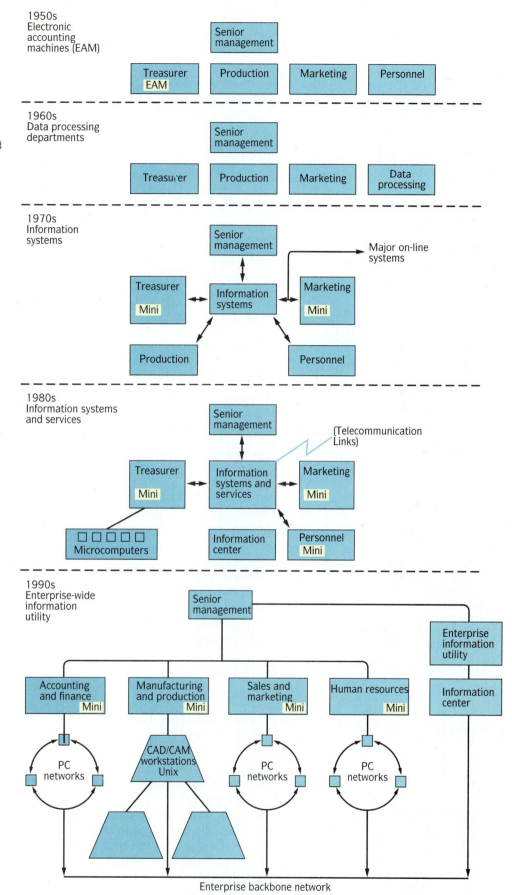

Isolated "electronic accounting machines" with limited functions in the 1950s gave way to large, centralized mainframe computers that served corporate headquarters and a few remote sites in the 1960s. In the 1970s, mid-sized minicomputers located in individual departments or divisions of the organization were networked to large centralized computers. Desktop microcomputers first were used independently and then were linked to minicomputers and large computers in the 1980s.

In the 1990s, the architecture for a fully networked organization emerged. In this new architecture, the large central mainframe computer stores information (like a library) and coordinates information flowing among desktops and perhaps among hundreds of smaller local networks. It operates much like a telephone system. Chapter 10 provides a detailed discussion of this new information architecture and the way it has reshaped the delivery of information in the firm. Instead of being an isolated "factory" making batches of information products, information systems have become integral, on-line, interactive tools deeply involved in the minute-to-minute operations and decision making of large organizations. Organizations now are critically dependent on systems and could not survive even occasional breakdowns: In most large organizations the entire cash flow is linked to information systems. System designers have begun to build in fault-tolerant and redundant capabilities to account for this new situation.

Decisions About the Computer Package: Who Delivers Information Technology Services?

A second way in which organizations affect information technology is through decisions about who will design, build, and operate the technology within the organization. Computer technology is similar to other kinds of technology, including automotive technology. In order to use automobiles, a society needs highways, mechanics, gas stations, engine designers, police, and parts manufacturers. The "automobile" is a package of services, organizations, and people. Likewise, information systems require specialized organizational subunits, information specialists, and a host of other supportive groups (Kling and Dutton, 1982). Managers (and organizations in general) make the key decisions about the computer package: These decisions determine how technology services will be delivered, and by whom, how, and when.

Information systems department: The formal organizational unit that is responsible for the information systems function in the organization.

The computer package is composed of three distinct entities (see Figure 4.8). The first is a formal organizational unit or function called an **information systems department.** The second consists of information systems specialists such as programmers, systems analysts, project leaders, and information systems managers. Also, external specialists such as hardware vendors and manufacturers, software firms, and consultants frequently participate in the day-to-day operations and long-term planning of information systems. A third element of the information systems package is the technology itself, both hardware and software.

Today the information systems group often acts as a powerful change agent in the organization, suggesting new business strategies and new information-based products and coordinating both the development of technology and the planned changes in the organization.

The size of the information systems department can vary greatly, depending on the role of information systems in the organization and on the organization's size. In most medium to large firms, the information systems group is composed of 100 to 400 people. The size of the information systems group and the total expenditures on computers and information systems are largest in service organizations (especially those that sell information products like Dow Jones News), where information systems can consume more than 40 percent of gross revenues.

Programmers: Highly trained technical specialists who write computer software instructions.

In the early years of the computer, when the role of information systems was limited, the information systems group was composed mostly of **programmers,** highly trained technical specialists who wrote the software instructions for the computer. Today, in most information systems groups, a growing proportion of staff members are systems analysts. **Systems analysts** constitute the principal

Systems analysts: Specialists who translate business problems and requirements into information requirements and systems.

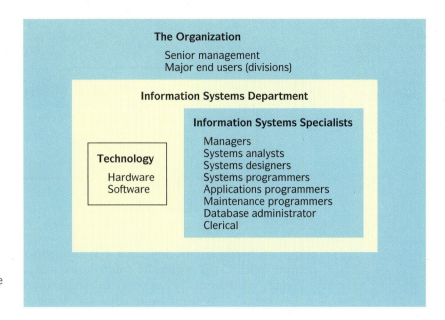

Figure 4.8
The computer package. Many groups, individuals, and organizations are involved in the design and management of information systems.

liaison between the information systems group and the rest of the organization. It is the system analyst's job to translate business problems and requirements into information requirements and systems.

Information systems managers:
Leaders of the various specialists in the information systems department.

End users: Representatives of departments outside the information systems group for whom information systems applications are developed.

Information systems managers are leaders of teams of programmers and analysts; project managers; physical facility managers; telecommunications managers; heads of office automation groups; and, finally, managers of computer operations and data entry staff.

End users are representatives of departments outside of the information systems group for which applications are developed. These users are playing an increasingly large role in the design and development of information systems.

The last element of the computer package is the technology itself, the hardware and software instructions. Chapters 6 and 7 provide detailed discussions of these topics.

Decisions About Why Information Systems Are Built

Managers provide the public and private rationales for building information systems. Managers can choose to use systems primarily to achieve economies, or to provide better service, or to provide a better workplace. The "impact" of computers in any organization depends in part on how managers make decisions.

At first glance, the answer to the question, "Why do organizations adopt information systems?" seems very simple. Obviously, organizations adopt information systems to become more efficient, to save money, and to reduce the work force. Although this response may have been generally true in the past, it no longer comprises the only or even the primary reason for adopting systems.

Systems today are, of course, built with efficiency in mind, but they have become vitally important simply for staying in business. Information systems are as vital as are capital improvements such as modern buildings or corporate headquarters. Improvements in decision making (speed, accuracy, comprehensiveness), serving ever higher customer and client expectations, coordinating dispersed groups in an organization, complying with governmental reporting regulations, and exercising tighter control over personnel and expenditures have become important reasons for building systems (Huff and Munro, 1985).

More recently, organizations have been seeking the competitive benefits of systems described in Chapter 3. It may not be more efficient for banks to gather funds using automatic teller machines (ATMs), but to stay in the retail banking business, ATM systems are required today. It may not save a company money to build an integrated financial information system to serve senior managers at

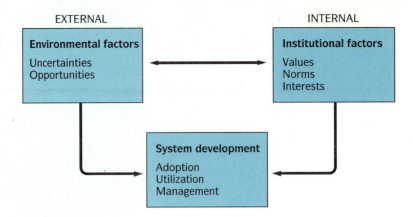

Figure 4.9
The systems development process. External environmental factors and internal institutional factors influence the types of information systems the organizations select, develop, and use.

EXTERNAL

Environmental factors

Uncertainties
Opportunities

INTERNAL

Institutional factors

Values
Norms
Interests

System development

Adoption
Utilization
Management

corporate headquarters, but such a system makes far better use of time and permits much closer corporate control of remote divisions.

Hence, what seems like an easy question to answer—*Why do organizations adopt systems?*—is really quite complex. Some organizations are simply more innovative than others. They have values that encourage any kind of innovation, regardless of its direct economic benefit to the company. In other cases, information systems are built because of the ambitions of various groups within an organization and the anticipated effect on existing organizational conflicts. And in some cases (for example, Schneider National; see the chapter vignette), changes in an organization's environment—including changes in government regulations, competitors' actions, and costs—demand a computer system response.

Figure 4.9 illustrates a model of the systems development process that includes many factors other than economic considerations. This model divides the explanations for why organizations adopt systems into two groups: *external environmental factors* and *internal institutional factors* (Laudon, 1985).

Environmental factors are factors that are external to the organization that influence the adoption and design of information systems. Some external environmental factors are rising costs of labor or other resources; the competitive actions of other organizations; and changes in government regulations. In general, these can be thought of as *environmental constraints*. At the same time, the environment also provides organizations with *opportunities:* new technologies, new sources of capital, the development of new production processes, the demise of a competitor, or a new government program that increases the demand for certain products.

Institutional factors are factors internal to the organization that influence the adoption and design of information systems. They include values, norms, and vital interests that govern matters of strategic importance to the organization. For instance, the top management of a corporation can decide that it needs to exercise much stronger control over the inventory process and therefore decides to develop an inventory information system. The resulting system is adopted, developed, and operated for purely internal, institutional reasons (for a similar model, see Kraemer et al., 1989).

Environmental factors: Factors external to the organization that influence the adoption and design of information systems.

Institutional factors: Factors internal to the organization that influence the adoption and design of information systems.

4.4 How Information Systems Affect Organizations

In the previous section, we described one side of a two-way relationship between information technology and organizations. Now we shall look at the other side, asking the following question: How do information systems affect organizations? To answer this question, we need to examine and quickly summarize a large body of research and theory. Some researchers base their work on economics, while others take a behavioral approach. In a single chart, Table 4.6

Table 4.6 THE IMPACT OF INFORMATION SYSTEMS ON ORGANIZATIONS

Theories:	(A) Economic Theories			(B) Behavioral Theories		
	Micro-Econ	Transaction Cost	Agency	Decision/Control	Social Science	Post Industrial
Unit of Analysis	The firm	Markets and the firm	The firm	The organization	The organization, sub-units, players, environments	Macro and Global society and economy
Core Concepts	Substitution of factors of production	Transactions costs Markets	Agents, principals, and contracts	Decision-making process and structure	SOPs, politics, culture, social history	Knowledge and information-intense work and products
Dynamics	Capital is substituted for labor as IT costs fall	IT reduces market transaction costs	IT reduces agency costs	IT replaces humans in the information and decision process	IT reflects bureaucratic, political, and cultural forces	IT encourages growth of information-intense occupations and goods
Impacts of IT Occupational Structure	Decline in middle managers and clericals	Decline in middle managers and clerical workers	Decline in middle managers and clerical workers	Decline in middle managers and clericals; growth in information and knowledge workers	IT has little impact per se on occupational structure; specialists try to use IT to their advantage	IT creates new occupations highly dependent on information
Organizational Structure Formal: Hierarchy Div. of Labor SOPs Authority	Reduced hierarchy Centralization	Reduced org. size Centralization of authority; decentralization of decisions; Reduction in hierarchy Less reliance on SOPs	Reduced org. size Centralization of authority, reduction in hierarchy	Authority more uniform Less specialization and less reliance on SOPs Reduction in hierarchy Formalization of information functions	Groups use IT to extend their influence, stabilize their position, and optimize performance of SOPs	IT results in more flexible, self guided work, decentralization, flattening of hierarchies, and fluid division of labor
Informal: Info. flow Decision-making Intelligence	Increased info. flow, more rapid decision making, more intelligence	Information access, timeliness, accuracy increase; decision-making units fewer and more efficient	Increased surveillance Information access, timeliness, accuracy increase; decision making units fewer and more efficient	Information access, timeliness, accuracy increase; decision making units fewer and more efficient	IT as a formal information system has little impact on informal channels of power and influence	Rigid hierarchic decision structures replaced by rich information-intense networks
Management Strategy	Employ technology to reduce labor costs	Employ IT to increase reliance on markets and reduce org. size, middle mgmt. and clericals	Senior managers employ IT to increase surveillance, reduce costs of management	Employ IT to improve decision making and restructure organization to optimize command and control technologies	Managers should understand and use IT to achieve their agendas	Managers should assist the emergence of less rigid organizations, encourage self-manager and networked organizations

*The social science reference disciplines are sociology, political science, anthropology, and social history.

Source: Azimuth Corporation, 1992

compares these theories and the hypothesized impacts of information technology on organizations. Table 4.6 is complex, and you should read the text first and then use the table for a convenient summary. In general, we have much more theory in this area than we have hard data and acceptable findings. We briefly now describe these theoretical models and the suggested information system technology impacts.

Economic Theories

Economics is the study of allocating scarce resources in markets populated by thousands of competing firms. It is also the study of national and global economies. Microeconomics focuses on individual firms and provides several models to describe the impact of information technology on organizations (see Gurbaxani and Whang, 1991).

MICROECONOMIC THEORY

Microeconomic model:
Model of the firm that views information technology as a factor of production that can be freely substituted for capital and labor.

The most widespread theory of how information technology affects thousands of firms is the **microeconomic model** portrayed in Figure 4.10. Information system technology is viewed as a factor of production that can be freely substituted for capital and labor. As the cost of information system technology falls, it is substituted for labor that historically has a rising cost. As information system technology transforms the production function—through the use of technology to automate previously manual activities or to streamline or to rethink how work is accomplished—the entire production function shifts inward. Over time, less capital and less labor are required for a given output. Moreover, the expansion trajectory of the firm is altered more towards increasing reliance on capital, and less towards reliance on labor–which historically has risen in cost (Pindyck and Rubinfield, 1992). Hence, in microeconomic theory information technology should result in a decline in the number of middle managers and clerical workers as information technology substitutes for their labor.

TRANSACTION COST THEORY

Transaction cost theory:
Economic theory that states that firms exist because they can conduct marketplace transactions internally more cheaply than they can with external firms in the marketplace.

Transaction cost theory is based on the notion that a firm incurs costs when it buys on the marketplace what it does not make itself. These costs are referred to as transaction costs. Transaction costs are the equivalent of friction in physical systems. Firms and individuals seek to economize on transaction costs (much as they do on production costs). Using markets is expensive (Williamson, 1985) because of coordination costs such as locating and communicating with distant suppliers, monitoring contract compliance, buying insurance, obtaining information on products, and so forth. Traditionally, firms sought to reduce transaction costs by getting bigger: hiring more employees; vertically integrating (as

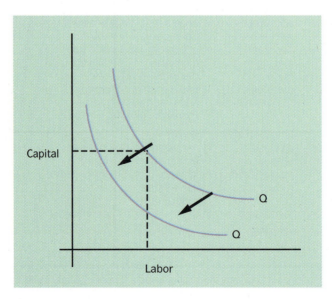

Figure 4.10
The microeconomic theory of the impact of information technology on the organization. Firms substitute IT for labor over time; when IT transforms the production function, the function shifts inward, lowering the amount of both capital and labor needed to produce level Q.

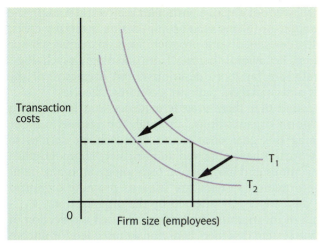

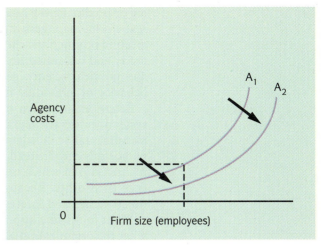

Figure 4.11
The transaction cost theory of the impact of information technology on the organization. Firms traditionally grew in size in order to reduce transaction costs. IT potentially reduces the costs for a given size, shifting the transaction cost curve inward, opening up the possibility of revenue growth without increasing size, or even revenue growth accompanied by shrinking size.

Figure 4.12
The agency cost theory of the impact of information technology on the organization. As firms grow in size and complexity, traditionally they experience rising agency costs. IT shifts the agency cost curve down and to the right allowing firms to increase size while lowering agency costs.

General Motors did—see the section-ending case on Chrysler and GM); buying their own suppliers and distributors; growing horizontally by moving into new markets; taking over smaller companies; and even developing monopolies.

Information technology could help firms lower the cost of market participation (transaction costs), making it worthwhile for firms to contract with external suppliers instead of using internal sources of supply. The size of firms (measured by the number of employees) could stay constant or contract even though they increased their revenues. As transaction costs decrease, firm size (the number of employees) should shrink because it becomes easier and cheaper for the firm to contract the purchase of goods and services in the marketplace rather than to make the product or service inside. Why hire workers, grow bigger, and suffer rising management costs when the same volume of business and profit could be obtained if the firm contracted with outside suppliers and workers in an electronic marketplace (see Figure 4.11)? These labor force reductions would probably affect middle managers and clerical workers in particular.

AGENCY THEORY

Agency theory: Economic theory that views the firm as a nexus of contracts among self-interested individuals rather than a unified, profit-maximizing entity.

In **agency theory,** the firm is viewed as a "nexus of contracts" among self-interested individuals rather than as a unified, profit-maximizing entity (Jensen and Meckling, 1976). A principal (owner) employs "agents" (employees) to perform work on his or her behalf and delegates some decision-making authority to the agent. However, agents need constant supervision and management because they otherwise will tend to pursue their own interests rather than those of the owners. This factor introduces agency costs or management costs. As firms grow in size and scope, management costs rise because owners must expend more and more effort monitoring agents, acquiring information, tracking inventory, and so on. Owners must delegate more decision-making authority to agents, who in turn may be untrustworthy.

Information technology, by reducing the costs of acquiring and analyzing information, permits organizations to reduce overall management costs, and allows them to grow in revenues while shrinking the numbers of middle management and clerical workers (see Figure 4.12).

Behavioral Theories

Although microeconomic theories try to explain how large numbers of firms act in the marketplace, most economists would agree they are quite poor at describing or predicting the actual behavior of any one particular real-world firm. In the real world, managers face unique problems such as minimizing inventory costs, meeting production schedules, devising diverse product mixes, managing a labor force, and obtaining financing. Behavioral theories from sociology, psychology, and political science generally are far more descriptive and predictive of the behavior of individual firms and managers than are economic theories.

Behavioral research has found that there is little evidence that information systems automatically transform organizations, although the systems may be instrumental in accomplishing this goal once senior management decides to pursue this end. Instead, researchers have observed an intricately choreographed relationship in which organizations and information technology mutually influence each other. Because information systems are used to promote organizational values and interests, they are deeply affected by the organization.

What looks like an impact of information technology is often a reflection of what the organization and the system designers consciously intended (or unconsciously created). In behavioral models of the firm, the influence of information systems is not as simple and direct as the economic models suggest.

DECISION AND CONTROL THEORY

Decision and control theory: Behavioral theory stating that the function of the organization is to make decisions under conditions of uncertainty and risk and that organizations centralize decision making and create a hierarchy of decision making to reduce uncertainty.

According to **decision and control theory,** the function of the organization is to make decisions under conditions of uncertainty and risk and under the constraint of bounded rationality. The theory holds that managers never have complete information and knowledge, and they can never examine all alternatives even though they would like to.[3] Organizations are decision-making structures, arranged so as to reduce uncertainty and to ensure survival. They are vitally dependent on the routine flow of information to decision makers. Because persons lower in the hierarchy do not have the information needed for making decisions, organizations must centralize decision making and create a hierarchy of decision makers. A large middle management group is necessary to gather information, analyze it, and pass it up to senior managers. In turn, senior managers require middle managers to implement policies because middle managers are in direct contact with lower-level operating units. Lower-level employees—in turn—rely on standard operating procedures designed by senior decision makers. If a situation does not fit the SOP, then senior managers must make a decision. The organization is a pyramidal structure in which authority and responsibility grow as one rises in the hierarchy.

Theoretically, information technology could change this rigid structure by lowering the costs of information acquisition and broadening the distribution of information. Information technology could bring information directly from operating units to senior managers, thereby eliminating middle managers and their clerical support workers. Information technology could permit senior managers to contact lower-level operating units directly through the use of networked telecommunications and computers, eliminating middle management intermediaries. Alternatively, information technology could distribute information to lower-level workers who could then make their own decisions based on their own knowledge and information without management intervention.

Early speculation on the impact of information systems suggested that organizations would indeed become more centralized and that middle management would tend to disappear over time because computers would give central, high-level managers all of the information they required to operate the organization without intervention from middle management (Leavitt and Whisler, 1958; Drucker, 1988; see Figure 4.13).

3. See George P. Huber, "The Nature and Design of Post-Industrial Organizations." *Management Science* 30, no. 8 (August 1984). See also the classic statement of this view in James G. March and Herbert A. Simon, *Organizations* (New York: Wiley, 1958). See also Herbert A. Simon, "Applying Information Technology to Organization Design," *Public Administration Review* (May/June, 1973).

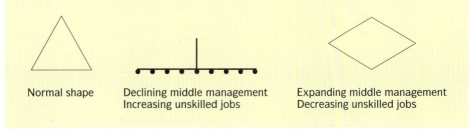

Normal shape

Declining middle management
Increasing unskilled jobs

Expanding middle management
Decreasing unskilled jobs

Figure 4.13
The impact of information systems on organizational structure. There are several hypotheses on how systems can change the structure of an organization. Three outcomes are represented here: systems can have no effect; they may reduce the number of middle managers creating an inverted "T" effect; or they may expand the capabilities and numbers of middle managers producing the diamond effect.

As Figure 4.13 illustrates, before information technology, the organization had a triangular shape with decision making concentrated at the top. After the introduction of computer systems, the organization chart would start to look like an inverted *T*. Other research suggests that computerization gives more information to middle managers, empowering them to make more important decisions than in the past and reducing the need for large numbers of lower-level workers. Over time, this results in a diamond-like structure (Shore, 1983).

SOCIOLOGICAL THEORY: OLIGARCHIES AND ROUTINES

Sociological theory:
Behavioral theory stating that organizations develop hierarchical bureaucratic structures and standard operating procedures to cope in unstable environments and that organizations can't change routines when environments change.

Sociological theory focuses on the growth of hierarchical, bureaucratic structures and standard operating procedures as primary tools for organizations trying to cope in unstable environments. Robert Michel's saying that "Whoever says organization, says oligarchy (rule by a few)" (Michels, 1962) and the phrase the "iron cage of bureaucracy" (Weber, 1947; DiMaggio and Powell, 1983) suggest that organizations inherently breed inequalities of power. Organizations hone and refine routines (SOPs) until they become extremely efficient. Unfortunately, attainment of success contains the seeds of failure. Organizations find it nearly impossible to change routines when their environment changes.

Sociologists argue that information technology has little independent power to transform organizations. Information technology is embraced by managers in various subunits of the organization insofar as it furthers their own interests or the interests of their subunit. Managers are always looking for better ways to implement existing rules and SOPs. They reject information technology if it threatens existing routines or subunits. Information technology itself becomes, over time, just another SOP, just as hard to change as any other. Information technology adds little to the survivability of firms, and given reasonable time, most organizations fail. Change comes about because new organizations form around new technologies, and they incorporate the new technologies into their SOPs. Over time, these new organizations become old, bureaucratic, and brittle, and they too pass away.

The sociological view emphasizes the power of people and organizations to control the impacts of systems. The Window on Management on page 112 illustrates that important groups in the organization determine, either consciously or unconsciously, the kinds of changes that will occur in organizational structure. Organizations adopt information technology because it suits the power interests of key subunits, divisions, and managers. Organizations can decide to centralize or decentralize power.

In recent years, many organizations have shifted authority away from central headquarters, shrinking staff and placing more power in the hands of division managers and local factory managers. Yet many organizations still consciously seek to gather more information from operating units and to develop a large central corporate staff both for planning and for operational control purposes (Leifer, 1988). Managers make these decisions in pursuit of their own interests (Kraemer et al., 1989).

MANAGEMENT

When Technology Heightens Office Tensions

The Information Age gospel preaches that network technologies have become essential for decentralizing hierarchies, empowering workers and promoting the free flow of information. Electronic mail systems and "groupware" technologies, the info-gurus insist, encourage collaboration, accelerate responsiveness and curtail internal politics.

Alas, the networks to organizational hell are wired with good intentions. In the real world, even the best designed networks can have astonishingly perverse impacts. State-of-the-art systems frequently end up producing the exact opposite of the desired results. A network intended to flatten the corporate hierarchy mutates into a medium that reinforces autocracy. In fact, the politics of corporate networks turns out to be as vicious, venal and misleading as anything you could hope to find in a presidential campaign.

Unfortunately, most companies prefer to ignore the fact that these networks don't just carry information; they also embody — for better and for worse — the values of the organization. Companies that don't understand — or kid themselves about — their core values are doomed to make painful, wasteful technology investments.

One huge multidivisional company I worked with spent tens of millions of dollars creating a superb management information network. Up-to-the-moment summaries of key sales and distribution figures became available at the touch of a button. Bidding to become a more "flexible" organization, this company also encouraged its divisions to become more autonomous. Top management insisted that it wanted to "push responsibility down into the organization" and delegate key decisions to the field.

Understandably, this excellent new information network enabled top management to retrieve data just as easily as the division managers. The technology made it possible for top management to peer over the division's shoulder as it tried to get work done: *"Saw the weekly sales figures, Tom. Apparently that promotion didn't work so well. What are you going to do?"*

As far as the divisional line managers were concerned, the network quickly became a medium for top management meddling. The network effectively became a tool that undermined trust because top management couldn't resist acting upon available information. Consequently, some of the division managers began "gaming" their numbers. Division managers now know that any initiatives they take have to be either coordinated with top management or done "off the net." So much for autonomy.

Networks don't destroy hierarchies; they reshape them. Organizations that run on power and influence do not take the "participatory management pledge" simply because they've invested a fortune in network technology. On the contrary, in most organizations I've observed, precisely because network technology blurs traditional organizational boundaries, top managers use it as a vehicle to project their personalities and impose power.

One software-savvy CEO uses an electronic thesaurus to digitally "mark" his electronic mail memos before he transmits them. Consequently, if there is an unauthorized disclosure — internal or external — he can ferret out the source. Several of his top people now follow his lead. Needless to say, this company's internal network is not a hotbed of information sharing.

Of course, this kind of network gamesmanship doesn't always

POST-INDUSTRIAL THEORY: KNOWLEDGE-INTENSIVE STRUCTURES AND SHAPES

According to theorists of post-industrial society — often sociologists and political scientists — advanced industrial countries entered a new kind of post-industrial economy and society sometime in the 1960s (Bell, 1973; Brzezinski, 1970; Masuda, 1980; Toffler, 1970; Martin, 1981). In a "post-industrial society," the service sector dominates the economy.[4] The service sector itself favors knowledge workers (scientists, engineers, and some managers) and data workers (secretaries, accountants, sales people) over service providers like chefs and custodians. In post-industrial global economies, industrial manufacturing is shifted to low-wage countries, and high-skilled, "knowledge-based" work grows rapidly in the developed, high-wage countries.

According to **post-industrial theory,** the transformation to a post-industrial society brings with it inherent changes in organizational structure: Authority should rely more on knowledge and competence, and not on mere formal po-

Post-industrial theory:
Behavioral theory stating that the transformation of advanced industrial countries into post-industrial societies creates flatter organizations dominated by knowledge workers where decision making is more decentralized.

---

4. The names for this phenomenon — of societies based primarily on knowledge and information — differ, but the underlying rationale remains the same: the "technetronic society" (Brzezinski), "telematic society" (Martin), and Toffler's Future Shock and ad-hoc organizations.

come top-down. One clever middle manager sends carefully worded electronic mail proposals to his boss for his "signature." However the boss responds, this manager electronically edits that response to make it look as if the boss had approved his plans. It is this edited version that is electronically mailed to previously recalcitrant colleagues.

These examples aren't the exceptions; they're becoming the rule. For all the promises of increased productivity, technology has a nasty way of reinforcing an organization's cultural weaknesses. In every organization I've visited, networks have become yet another battleground to play out turf wars and political vendettas.

Indeed, the most obnoxious example of network abuse I've come across is by the top manager of a large service firm who dictates daily enterprise-wide voice mail memos from his car's cellular phone as he drives in to work. These verbal missives are broadcast to 30 or 40 key people on his voice mail list.

Ignore, for the moment, the symbolic crassness of turning one's managers into a white-collar steno pool. As one unfortunate asked, "What do you do when you get

these messages?" If everybody responds, the top dog will be overwhelmed. If only a few respond, do they look like fools or do they attain special status in the boss's eyes? That you can't claim to have "misplaced" a voice mail memo further complicates matters. This is a pretty steep price to pay to avoid playing "telephone tag."

The sad truth is that many companies are making investments that empower autocrats and merely ensure that the status quo has a better information flow. Companies that want to use technology as a tool for transformation should forget about "core process engineering" and start thinking about "core value understanding."

In the current issue of Sloan Management Review, authors Thomas Davenport and Robert Eccles argue that as information becomes more important, it becomes too valuable to "give away" over a network. "If information is truly to become the most valued commodity in the business of the future," they write, "we cannot expect to acquire it without an occasional struggle."

This is absolutely true. But while politics can't be ignored, organizations must remember that infor-

mation networks—just like the television networks—change the nature and terms of the political debate. Companies must design their networks as much around their core values as around their critical information. Negotiating that relationship will be the management challenge of this decade.

Mr. Schrage explores organizational media as a visiting scholar at MIT Sloan School's Center for Coordination Science.

Source: "When Technology Heightens Office Tensions" by Michael Schrage, *The Wall Street Journal,* October 5, 1992. Reprinted with permission of *The Wall Street Journal.* Copyright © 1992 Dow Jones & Company, Inc. All rights reserved.

To Think About: Under what circumstances could a network promote decentralization and a flatter organizational hierarchy?

The advances in portable computer technology have taken the computer out of the traditional office setting and into non-traditional arenas. This car buyer is using his notebook computer to perform budgeting and cost comparison analysis at the automobile dealer prior to making his purchasing decision.

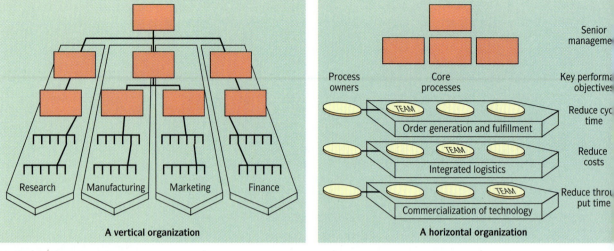

Figure 4.14
Some researchers and popular writers argue that information technology allows firms to reorganize themselves from vertical organizations to horizontal organizations where groups of people are arranged by processes. *Source:* John Pepper, "Horizontal Organization," *InformationWeek,* August 17, 1992. Copyright © 1992 by CMP Publications, Inc., 600 Community Drive, Manhasset, NY 11030. Reprinted from *InformationWeek* with permission.

sition; the shape of organizations should flatten, since professional workers tend to be self-managing; and decision making should become more decentralized as knowledge and information become more widespread throughout (Drucker, 1988).

Information technology should lead then to "task force" networked organizations in which groups of professionals come together—face-to-face or electronically—for short periods of time to accomplish a specific task (e.g., designing a new automobile); once the task is accomplished, the individuals join other task forces. Clericals are reduced because professionals maintain their own portable offices in the form of laptop and palmtop personal computers connected to powerful global networks. All organizations should look more like Mintzberg's Adhocracies depicted in Figure 4.5(E).[5]

Consultants and popular business journals have expanded on post-industrial theories by suggesting that organizations will become "flatter" and more "horizontal" not only by trimming middle managers but also by reshaping themselves around business processes instead of the traditional functional departments. Figure 4.14 shows the differences between a traditional vertical organization where groups are arranged by function and the proposed horizontal organization where teams are arranged by processes.

Business processes are sequences of logically related tasks performed to achieve a defined business outcome. Examples of processes are new product development, which turns an idea into a manufacturable prototype, or order fulfillment, which begins with the receipt of an order and ends when the customer has received and paid for the product. Processes, by nature, are generally cross-functional, transcending the boundaries between sales, marketing, manufacturing, and research and development. Processes cut across the traditional organizational structure, grouping employees from different functional specialties to complete a piece of work.

5. Post-industrial themes are echoed in Drucker's 1988 formulation of how IT affects organizations:
"The typical large business 20 years hence will have fewer than half the levels of management of its counterpart today, and no more than a third the managers. . . . the typical business will be knowledge-based, an organization composed largely of specialists, who direct and discipline their own performance through organized feedback from colleagues, customers, and headquarters. For this reason, it will be what I call an information based organization" (Drucker, 1988, p. 45).

TECHNOLOGY

Is Xerox Becoming a Post-Industrial Organization?

The Xerox Corporation is changing its corporate identity. Instead of pushing copy machines, it decided to become a "document company" that focuses on products to help office workers create, use, and share reports, memos, and data. In 1992, Xerox designed a new horizontal organization that divides its office products business into nine new businesses aimed at markets such as small businesses and individuals, office document systems, and engineering systems. Each business does its own financial reporting and is led by a team. Xerox rearranged its manufacturing so that focused factories are dedicated to specific businesses. Most of the businesses sell through a Customer Operations Group, which combines sales, shipping, installation, service, and billing.

To help empowered work groups and employees challenge its traditional bureaucracy, and distribute knowledge and accountability throughout the organization, Xerox built a massive worldwide data network. The corporation began linking its worldwide computing facilities in 1984 and now has one of the world's largest corporate networks. Xerox employees can exchange information and documents anywhere in the world within minutes. The network links 43,000 desktop devices used by 65,000 of Xerox's 110,000 employees worldwide in 18 time zones.

This enterprise-wide network facilitates independent work groups. For instance, international marketing teams can easily exchange documents without being constrained by location. With just a few keystrokes, a manager can pull in to his or her workstation data, which could be graphics, engineering drawings, text, or scanned images, from Japan, Brazil, Mexico, and California.

The next step is to tie in Xerox's mobile employees into the corporate network through the development of "virtual offices." Xerox believes its workers of the future may not always be in buildings, and it wants to accommodate these employees.

Sources: Bob Violino with Chuck Appleby, "Turning the Page at Xerox," *InformationWEEK* (March 23, 1992); and Thomas A. Stewart, "The Search for the Organization of Tomorrow," *Fortune* (May 18, 1992).

To Think About: What role did technology play in Xerox's reorganization? What features of Xerox's organization will change? How easy will it be to make these changes?

The objectives for processes are more external and linked to meeting customer and market demands than are those for the traditional functional approach. Instead of evaluating how well each functional area is performing as a discrete business function, management would evaluate how well a group executes a process. For instance, instead of measuring manufacturing independently on how well it reduces the cost to produce each unit, and shipping independently on how quickly it ships out each unit, management might look at the entire logistics process from receipt of raw material to receipt by the customer.

Information systems can help organizations achieve great efficiencies by automating parts of these processes or by helping organizations rethink and streamline these processes. Chapter 11 will treat this subject in greater detail, since it is fundamental to systems analysis and design. The Window on Technology describes how information technology is helping the Xerox Corporation redesign its organization.

Does Xerox represent the shape of the post-industrial organization of the future? Who makes sure that self-managed teams do not head off in the wrong direction? Who decides which person works on what team and for how long? How can managers judge the performance of someone who is constantly rotating from team to team? How do people know where their careers are headed when there is no clear hierarchical ladder to ascend?

No one knows the answer to these questions, and it is not clear that all modern organizations will undergo this transformation: General Motors may have many self-managed knowledge workers in certain divisions, but it still has a manufacturing division structured as a "machine bureaucracy," to use Mintzberg's category. Not all types of organizations can be "flattened." Behavioral research has found little evidence that information systems automatically transform organizational structures, although the systems may be instrumental in accomplishing this goal once senior management decides to pursue this end. No one knows if organizations designed along process lines survive longer than traditional function-based organizations.

In general, the shape of organizations historically changes with the business cycle and with the latest management fashions. When times are good and profits are high, firms hire large numbers of supervisory and nonproduction personnel. When times are tough, they let go of many of these same people (Mintzberg, 1979). In the late 1980s, times were tough: Real incomes did not expand, although profits were restored to 1980 levels by 1990. As a result, many firms, especially those in direct competition with Japanese manufacturing, shrank their middle-level management and supervisory positions. This was also a period of extensive investment in computer technology. It is not known if the shrinkage of some firms' middle management resulted from hard times or from computerization. For firms not in direct foreign competition, and for firms that experienced good business environments, employment rose throughout the 1980s even as information technology exploded. What this phenomenon suggests, then, is that the impact of information technology and systems is not limited to a simple outcome but instead will vary as a function of many behavioral factors.

CULTURAL THEORIES: IT AND FUNDAMENTAL ASSUMPTIONS

Cultural theory: Behavioral theory stating that information technology must fit into an organization's culture or the technology won't be adopted.

Cultural theory (often discussed by anthropologists) argues that information technology must fit into the organization's culture or is unlikely to be adopted. The assumption at Ford, for instance, is that the company's primary activity is to make cars (rather than to operate a credit corporation), or at IBM it is the assumption that the primary purpose of the organization is to make large mainframe computers. These assumptions are rarely challenged by members, and if members do present challenges to these assumptions, the members are ostracized (Schein, 1985).

When the assumptions no longer fit reality, members of the culture may try to deny reality, ignore reality, or reinvent reality to fit the culture. Cultures change when the organizations that support them die off, or when radical fringe groups gain control and shift cultural assumptions. This feature is usually attended by massive senior management turnover because it is the senior managers who support the old culture (indeed, they were recruited and promoted for precisely this reason).

Information technology can either threaten or support organizational culture. The emergence of microcomputer technology, for instance, threatened both the manufacturers of large mainframe computers and their customers in large corporations as well—the managers of large information system departments in Fortune 1000 corporations. Resistance, denial, and efforts to redefine the reality followed in many of these organizations. On the other hand, information technology can be supportive of organizational cultures: The insurance industry welcomed computers to reduce costs in traditional claims processing.

POLITICAL THEORIES: INFORMATION TECHNOLOGY AS A POLITICAL RESOURCE

Political theory: Behavioral theory that describes information systems as the outcome of political competition between organizational subgroups for influence over the policies, procedures, and resources of the organization.

Organizations are divided into specialized subgroups (e.g., marketing, accounting, production). These groups have different values, and they compete for resources, producing competition and conflict. **Political theory** describes information systems as the outcome of political competition between organizational subgroups for influence over the policies, procedures, and resources of the organization (Laudon, 1974; Keen, 1981; Kling, 1980; Laudon, 1986).

Information systems inevitably become bound up in the politics of organizations because they influence access to a key resource—namely, information. Information systems can affect who does what to whom, when, where, and how in an organization. For instance, a major study of the efforts of the FBI to develop a national computerized criminal history system (a single national listing of the criminal histories, arrests, and convictions of over 36 million individuals in the United States) found that the state governments strongly resisted the FBI's efforts. The states felt that this information would give the federal government,

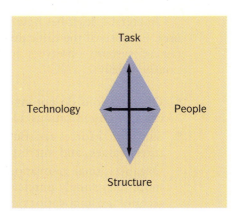

Figure 4.15
Organizational resistance and the mutually adjusting relationship between technology and the organization. Implementing information systems has consequences for task arrangements, structures, and people. According to this model, in order to implement change, all four components must be changed simultaneously. *Source:* Leavitt, 1965.

and the FBI in particular, the ability to monitor how states use criminal histories and to control the interstate dissemination of criminal history information. This was a function that the states felt they could accomplish without federal interference. The states resisted the development of this national system quite successfully (Laudon, 1986).

Table 4.6 on page 107 summarizes and compares most of the economic and behavioral theories about the impact of information systems on organizations.

Organizational Resistance to Change

Because information systems potentially change an organization's structure, culture, politics, and work, there is often considerable resistance to them when they are introduced.

There are several ways to visualize organizational resistance. Leavitt (1965) used a diamond shape to illustrate the interrelated and mutually adjusting character of technology and organization (see Figure 4.15). Here, changes in technology are absorbed, deflected, and defeated by organizational task arrangements, structures, and people. In this model, the only way to bring about change is to change the technology, tasks, structure, and people simultaneously. Other authors have spoken about the need to "unfreeze" organizations before introducing an innovation, quickly implementing it, and "re-freezing" or institutionalizing the change (Kolb, 1970; Alter and Ginzberg, 1978). (See Figure 4.16.)

Figure 4.16
Lewin/Schein and Kolb/Frohman models of change. *Source:* Keen 1981.

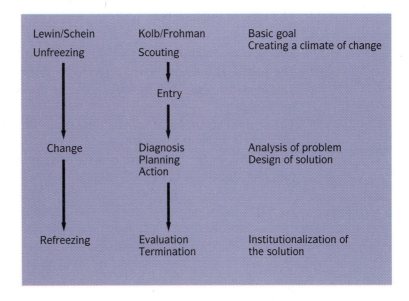

Chapter 14 describes how organizational resistance causes many systems failures. Because of the difficulties of introducing new information systems, experienced systems observers approach social change through systems very cautiously. Briefly:

- Organizations do not innovate unless there is a substantial environmental change. Organizations adopt innovations only when they must do so.
- Substantial forces resisting change are rooted in the organization's structures, values, and interest groups.
- Organizational innovation is difficult and complex to achieve. It involves more than simply purchasing technology. In order to reap the benefits of technology, innovations must be utilized and managed properly. This, in turn, requires changes in the values, norms, and interest-group alignments of the organization.
- The function of leaders is to take advantage of external circumstances to solidify their power. Leaders must use external opportunities to tilt the internal conflict in an organization in their favor and toward the successful development of their own agendas.

Implications for The Design and Understanding of Information Systems

What is the importance of these theories of organizations? How can one take these factors into account when envisioning, designing, building, or managing information systems? The primary significance of this chapter is to show you that you should not take a narrow view of organizations and their relationship to information systems. Neither should you believe that "technology will do the job" for you—whatever that job is. For the information systems to work properly, you will have to manage the process actively, adjust the technology to the situation, and accept responsibility for success as well as failure.

No formula takes these organizational factors into account. You can develop a checklist of factors to consider in your systems plans. In our experience, the central organizational factors in rough rank order of importance are these:

- The *environment* in which the organization must function.
- The *structure* of the organization: hierarchy, specialization, standard operating procedures.
- The *culture and politics* of the organization.
- The *type* of organization.
- The extent of support and understanding of *top management*.
- The *level* of organization at which the system resides.
- The principal *interest groups* affected by the system.
- The *kinds of tasks and decisions* that the information system is designed to assist.
- The *sentiments and attitudes* of workers in the organization who will be using the information system.
- The *history of the organization:* past investments in information technology, existing skills, important programs, and human resources.

1. **The difficulties of managing change.** Bringing about change through the development of information technology and information systems is slowed considerably by the natural inertia of organizations. Of course, organizations do change, and powerful leaders are often required to bring about these changes. Nevertheless, the process, as leaders eventually discover, is more complicated and much slower than is typically anticipated.

2. **Fitting technology to the organization (or vice versa).** On the one hand, it is important to align information technology to the business plan, to senior management's strategic business plans, and to standard operating procedures in the business. IT is, after all, supposed to be the servant of the organization. On the other hand, these business plans, senior managers, and SOPs may all be very outdated or incompatible with the envisioned technology. In such instances, managers will need to change the organization to fit the technology or to adjust both the organization and the technology to achieve an optimal "fit."

3. **Understanding the limits of information technology.** We often look to technology to solve what are fundamentally human and organizational problems. We often fail to realize that information technology is no better than the skills of the knowledge and information workers who use it. Ultimately, the impact of computers is decided by the intelligence of the user. Information technology is a mirror for both organizations and individuals.

Summary

Describe the salient characteristics of organizations.

All modern organizations are hierarchical, specialized, and impartial. They use explicit standard operating procedures to maximize efficiency. All organizations have their own culture and politics arising from differences in interest groups. Organizations differ in goals, groups served, social roles, leadership styles, incentives, surrounding environments, and types of tasks performed. These differences create varying types of organizational structures. Mintzberg classified organizations into five structures: the simple entrepreneurial structure, machine bureaucracy, divisionalized bureaucracy, professional bureaucracy, and adhocracy.

Explain the changing role of information systems within the organization.

Computerized information systems are supported in organizations by a "computer package" consisting of a formal organizational unit or information systems department, information systems specialists, and computer technology. The roles of information systems and the computer package in the organization have become increasingly critical to both daily operations and strategic decision making.

Compare models for describing the origins of systems in organizations.

Organizations adopt information systems for both external environmental reasons, such as to increase competition or to respond to changes in government regulations, and for internal institutional reasons, such as to promote the values or interests of top management.

Identify the major theories about organizations that help us understand their relationship with information systems.

Theories that describe the relationship between information systems and organizations can be classified as based on either economic or behavioral models of the firm. Theories based on economic models of the firm include the microeconomic model, transaction cost theory, and agency theory. Theories based on behavioral models of the firm include decision and control theory, sociological theory, post-industrial theory, cultural theories, and political theories.

Discuss the impact of information systems on organizational structure, culture, political processes, and management.

The impact of information systems on organizations is not unidirectional. Information systems and the organizations in which they are used interact with and influence each other. The introduction of a new information system will affect the organizational structure, goals, work design, values, competition between interest groups, decision making, and day-to-day behavior. At the same time, information systems must be designed to serve the needs of important organizational groups and will be shaped by the structure, tasks, goals, culture, politics, and management of the organization. The power of information systems to transform organizations radically by flattening organizational hierarchies has not yet been demonstrated for all types of organizations.

Describe the organizational implications for the design and implementation of systems.

Salient features of organizations that must be addressed by information systems include organizational levels, organizational structures, types of tasks and decisions, the nature of management support, and the sentiments and attitudes of workers who will be using the system. The organization's history and external environment must be considered as well.

Implementation of a new information system is often more difficult than anticipated because of organizational change requirements. Since information systems potentially change important organizational dimensions, including the structure, culture, power relationships, and work activities, there is often considerable resistance to new systems.

Key Terms	
Organization (technical definition)	Information systems managers
Organization (behavioral definition)	End users
Bureaucracy	Environmental factors
Standard operating procedures (SOPs)	Institutional factors
Organizational culture	Microeconomic model
Entrepreneurial structure	Transaction cost theory
Machine bureaucracy	Agency theory
Divisionalized bureaucracy	Decision and control theory
Professional bureaucracy	Sociological theory
Adhocracy	Post-industrial theory
Information systems department	Cultural theory
Programmers	Political theory
Systems analysts	

Review Questions

1. What is an organization? How do organizations use information?

2. Compare the technical definition of organizations with the behavioral definition.

3. What features do all organizations have in common?

4. In what ways can organizations diverge?

5. Describe the five basic kinds of organizational structures.

6. Name the levels of analysis for organizational behavior.

7. Name the changing applications of organizational information systems that existed from the 1950s to the 1990s. How has the role of information systems in the organization changed over this time period?

8. Name the three elements in the computer package. How has the role of each element in the organization changed over time?

9. Describe the two factors that explain why organizations adopt information systems.

10. Describe each of the three economic theories that help explain how information systems affect organizations. What are their limitations?

11. Describe each of the behavioral theories that help explain how information systems affect organizations. What are their limitations?

12. How can information systems change organizational structure?

13. What is the relationship between information systems and organizational culture?

14. What is the relationship between information systems and organizational politics?

15. Why is there considerable organizational resistance to the introduction of information systems? Describe two models that explain this resistance.

16. What aspects of organizations addressed by various theories of organizations must be considered when designing an information system?

Discussion Questions

1. It has been said that when we design an information system, we are redesigning the organization. Discuss.

2. You are an information systems designer assigned to build a new accounts receivable system for one of your corporation's divisions. What organizational factors should you consider?

3. It has been said that implementation of a new information system is always more difficult than anticipated. Discuss.

Group Project

With a group of two or three students, examine an organization such as a local drugstore or the bookstore, cafeteria, or registrar's office in your college or university. Describe some of the features of this organization, such as its standard operating procedures, culture, structure, and interest groups. Identify an information system or series of information systems that might improve the performance of this organization, and describe the changes that the organization would have to make to use information technology successfully.

CASE STUDY

Can Sears Reinvent Itself with Information Systems Technology?

On January 25, 1993, Sears Roebuck, the nation's largest retailer, announced that it was dropping its famous "big book" catalogues, closing 113 of its stores, and eliminating 50,000 jobs. Four months earlier Sears had announced plans to dispose of its Dean Witter securities business, Discover credit card, and Coldwell Banker real estate operations and to sell up to 20% of the stock in its Allstate insurance subsidiary. These moves were designed to make Sears a much smaller, leaner concern that could recapture its leadership in retailing.

During the 1980s, Sears had tried to provide middle-class consumers with almost every type of banking, investment, and real estate service in addition to selling appliances, hardware, clothes, and other goods. In recent years, Sears' financial services businesses were the healthiest parts of the company, contributing up to as much as 70 percent of its profits. What is ironic is that Sears' board of directors chose to retain its underperforming operations while it got rid of the profitable parts, and that the underperforming part represents the long-time core of the company.

The spotlight now falls on reinvigorating Sears' retail business. Will it sink or swim? Sears has steadily lost ground in retailing, moving from the Number 1 position to Number 3 behind discounters Wal-Mart Stores, Inc. and Kmart Corporation. Sears had been slow to remodel stores, trim costs, and keep pace with current trends in selling and merchan-

dising. Sears could not keep up with the discounters and with specialty retailers such as Toys R Us, Home Depot, Inc., and Circuit City Stores, Inc. that focus on a wide selection of low-price merchandise in a single category. Nor could Sears compete with trend-setting department stores.

In recent years, Sears tried to catch up. It began initiatives such as the Store of the Future, brand-name merchandise, and "everyday low pricing." None of these changes revived the flagging retail business. In 1991, retail operations contributed to 38 percent of the corporate bottom line. The rest of the merchandising group's profits came from the lucrative Sears credit card. Strategies that worked well for competitors fizzled at Sears. JC Penney successfully refocused its business to emphasize moderately priced apparel. Everyday low pricing, the pricing strategy used by Wal-Mart and other retailers, bombed at Sears because the firm's cost structure, one of the highest in the industry, did not allow for rock-bottom prices. Everyday low pricing has become "everyday fair pricing" supplemented by frequent sales.

Sears' catalogue sales also stagnated. While the Sears "big book" catalogue, founded in 1887, had the largest revenues of any mail-order business, sales had not been profitable for twenty years; the catalogue had lost ground to specialty catalogues such as those of L. L. Bean and Lands' End.

Yet Sears is heavily computerized—it spends more on information technology and networking than other noncomputer firms in the United States except the Boeing Corporation. Why hasn't this translated into competitive advantage?

One big problem is Sears' high cost of operations. Nearly 30 percent of each dollar in sales is required to cover overhead (e.g., expenses for salaries, light bills, and advertising) compared to 15 percent for Wal-Mart and about 21 per cent for Kmart. Sears now hopes to cut costs by streamlining distribution systems and by combining merchandising functions so that there are only two or three general merchandising managers instead of six. Sears also realizes that it can't compete with discounters such as Wal-Mart on price alone and hopes to build a competitive edge through superior service.

In early 1992, Sears embarked on the Store-Simplification Program, a $60 million automation project that will make Sears stores more efficient, attractive, and convenient by bringing all transactions closer to the sales floor and centralizing every store's general offices, cashiers, customer services, and credit functions. The program makes many changes in Sears' traditional retail sales efforts:

- New Point-of-Sale (POS) terminals allow sales staff to issue new charge cards, accept charge card payments, issue gift certificates, and report account information to card holders. These innovations will increase savings by reducing the size of Sears' charge card group operations while making shopping more convenient for customers.
- Some stores installed ATM machines to give customers cash advances against their Sears Discover credit cards.
- Telephone kiosks have been installed throughout the Sears retail network. Customers can use them to inquire about service, parts, and credit, check the status of their car in the tire and auto center, or call the manager.
- Customer service desks will be eliminated. Sales personnel are authorized to handle refunds and returns, eliminating the need for two separate staffs. If a customer forgets his or her charge card, he or she can obtain immediate credit by telling the cashier his or her name and address and presenting identification.

Streamlining of patterns of work in back rooms and loading docks will also trim staff and create savings. The entire simplification effort is expected to eliminate $50 million in annual back office costs, 6900 jobs, and the customer service desks at all stores. Changes will also increase the ratio of selling space to nonselling space at Sears, so that more space can be used to generate revenues.

Sears has also been trying to reduce costs by moving its 6000 suppliers to an electronic ordering system similar to that described for Baxter Health Care (see Chapter 3). By linking its computerized ordering system directly to that of each supplier, Sears plans to eliminate paper throughout the order process and hopes to expedite the flow of goods into its stores.

Sears has stopped trying to sell everything and is focusing on seven core types of merchandise—men's, women's and children's clothing, home furnishings, home improvement, automotive services and supplies, appliances, and consumer electronics. The company is rearranging its merchandise displays to resemble those of more upscale department stores.

The question is, will all these efforts make customers happier with Sears? Market research indicates that Sears continues to be the destination of choice for lawn mowers, wrenches, washing machines, and other "hard" goods. But Sears does not seem to be the place for fashionable women's clothing, which is considered the most profitable segment of Sears' merchandising. Sears has started stocking stylish women's clothes at moderate prices, hoping to appeal to middle-income women who prize both fashion and value. Can Sears break out of its "retailing no-man's land," caught between fashionable apparel retailers and big-time discounters?

According to Edward A. Weller, a retail analyst at Montgomery Securities, Sears managers and executives have been "Sears-ized." They are so indoctrinated in tales of Sears' past glories and so entrenched in a massive bureaucracy that change takes a long time. Weller believes that Sears' biggest challenge is to transform its culture radically. Another analyst likened Sears to the civil service in that "everything moves very slowly."

Sources: Stephanie Strom, "Sears Eliminating Its Catalogues and 50,000 Jobs," *The New York Times,* January 26, 1993, "Signs of Life at Sears, Roebuck," *The New York Times* (October 26, 1992), "For Sear's Stores, Do-or-Die Time," *The New York Times* (September 30, 1992), and "Further Prescriptions for the Convalescent Sears," *The New York Times* (October 1, 1992); Gregory A. Patterson and Francine Schwadel, "Sears Suddenly Undoes Years of Diversifying Beyond Retailing Field," *The Wall Street Journal* (September 30, 1992); Barnaby J. Feder, "Sears Will Return to Retailing Focus," *The New York Times* (September 30, 1992); Bruce Caldwell, "Sears Shops for Competitive Edge," *InformationWEEK* (January 13, 1992).

Case Study Questions

1. What management, organization, and technology factors were responsible for Sears' poor performance?

2. Do you believe that the Store-Simplification Program solves these problems? How successful do you think it will be? Why?

3. What management, organization, and technology factors were addressed by the Store-Simplification Program?

4. What theories about the relationship of information systems and organizations are illustrated by this case?

5. Put yourself in the place of a Sears merchandising executive. Plan five steps you would take in the next year to implement the new Sears strategy.

6. Visit a Sears store and observe sales patterns. What image or market message is being conveyed in the store? How is it implemented? How might it be improved? (You might make a comparison stop at Penney's or Wal-Mart or Kmart.)

References

Allison, Graham T. *Essence of Decision: Explaining the Cuban Missile Crisis.* Boston: Little, Brown, 1971.

Alter, Steven, and Michael Ginzberg. "Managing Uncertainty in MIS Implementation." *Sloan Management Review* 20, no. 1 (Fall 1978).

Anthony, R. N. *Planning and Control Systems: A Framework for Analysis.* Cambridge, MA: Harvard University Press, 1965.

Argyris, Chris. *Interpersonal Competence and Organizational Effectiveness.* Homewood, IL: Dorsey Press, 1962.

Barnard, Chester. *The Functions of the Executive.* Cambridge, MA: Harvard University Press, 1968.

Beer, Michael, Russell A. Eisenstat, and Bert Spector. "Why Change Programs Don't Produce Change." *Harvard Business Review* (November–December 1990).

Bell, Daniel. *The Coming of Post-Industrial Society.* New York: Basic Books, 1973.

Bikson, T. K., and J. D. Eveland. "Integrating New Tools into Information Work." The Rand Corporation, 1992. RAND/RP-106.

Blau, Peter, and W. Richard Scott. *Formal Organizations.* San Francisco: Chandler Press, 1962.

Blauner, Robert. *Alienation and Freedom.* Chicago: University of Chicago Press, 1967.

Brzezinski, Z. *Between Two Ages: America's Role in the Technetronic Era.* New York: Viking Press, 1970.

Charan, Ram. "Now Networks Reshape Organizations—For Results." *Harvard Business Review* (September–October 1991).

DiMaggio, Paul J., and Walter W. Powell. "The Iron Cage Revisited: Institutional Isomorphism and Collective Rationality in Organizational Fields." *American Sociological Review* 48 (1983).

Drucker, Peter. "The Coming of the New Organization." *Harvard Business Review* (January–February 1988).

El Sawy, Omar A. "Implementation by Cultural Infusion: An Approach for Managing the Introduction of Information Technologies." *MIS Quarterly* (June 1985).

Etzioni, Amitai. *A Comparative Analysis of Complex Organizations.* New York: Free Press, 1975.

Fayol, Henri. *Administration industrielle et generale.* Paris: Dunods, 1950 (first published in 1916).

Freeman, John, Glenn R. Carroll, and Michael T. Hannan. "The Liability of Newness: Age Dependence in Organizational Death Rates." *American Sociological Review* 48 (1983).

Gorry, G. A., and M. S. Morton. "Framework for Management Information Systems." *Sloan Management Review* 13, no. 1 (Fall 1971).

Gouldner, Alvin. *Patterns of Industrial Bureaucracy.* New York: Free Press, 1954.

Gurbaxani, V. and S. Whang, "The Impact of Information Systems on Organizations and Markets," *Communications of the ACM* 34, no. 1, Jan. 1991.

Herzberg, Frederick. *Work and the Nature of Man.* New York: Crowell, 1966.

Huber, George P. "The Nature and Design of Post-Industrial Organizations." *Management Science* 30, no. 8 (August 1984).

Huff, Sid L., and Malcolm C. Munro. "Information Technology Assessment and Adoption: A Field Study." *Management Information Systems Quarterly* (December 1985).

Jaques, Elliott. "In Praise of Hierarchy." *Harvard Business Review* (January–February 1990).

Jensen, M., and W. Mekling. "Theory of the Firm: Managerial Behavior, Agency Costs, and Ownership Structure." *Journal of Financial Economics* 3 (1976).

Keen, P. G. W. "Information Systems and Organizational Change." *Communications of the ACM* 24, no. 1 (January 1981).

Keen, P. G. W., and M. S. Morton. *Decision Support Systems: An Organizational Perspective.* Reading, MA: Addison-Wesley, 1978.

Kling, Rob. "Social Analyses of Computing: Theoretical Perspectives in Recent Empirical Research." *Computing Survey* 12, no. 1 (March 1980).

Kling, Rob, and William H. Dutton. "The Computer Package: Dynamic Complexity." In *Computers and Politics,* edited by James Danziger, William Dutton, Rob Kling, and Kenneth Kraemer. New York: Columbia University Press, 1982.

Klotz, B. *Industry Productivity Projections: A Methodological Study.* U.S. Department of Labor, Bureau of Labor Statistics, 1966.

Kolb, D. A., and A. L. Frohman. "An Organization Development Approach to Consulting." *Sloan Management Review* 12, no. 1 (Fall 1970).

Kraemer, Kenneth, John King, Debora Dunkle, and Joe Lane. *Managing Information Systems.* Los Angeles: Jossey-Bass, 1989.

Laudon, Kenneth C. *Computers and Bureaucratic Reform.* New York: Wiley, 1974.

Laudon, Kenneth C. "Environmental and Institutional Models of Systems Development." *Communications of the ACM* 28, no. 7, (July 1985).

Laudon, Kenneth C. *The Dossier Society: Value Choices in the Design of National Information Systems.* New York: Columbia University Press, 1986.

Laudon, Kenneth C. "A General Model of the Relationship Between Information Technology and Organizations." Center for Research on Information Systems, New York University. Working paper, National Science Foundation, 1989.

Lawrence, Paul, and Jay Lorsch. *Organization and Environment.* Cambridge, MA: Harvard University Press, 1969.

Leavitt, Harold J., and Thomas L. Whisler. "Management in the 1980s." *Harvard Business Review* (November–December 1958).

Leavitt, Harold J. "Applying Organizational Change in Industry: Structural, Technological and Humanistic Approaches." In *Handbook of Organizations,* edited by James G. March. Chicago: Rand McNally, 1965.

Leifer, Richard. "Matching Computer-Based Information Systems with Organizational Structures." *MIS Quarterly* 12, no. 1 (March 1988).

March, James G., and Herbert A. Simon. *Organizations.* New York: Wiley, 1958.

Martin, J. *The Telematic Society.* Englewood Cliffs, NJ: Prentice-Hall, 1981.

Masuda, Y. *The Information Society.* Bethesda, MD: World Future Society, 1980.

Mayo, Elton. *The Social Problems of an Industrial Civilization.* Cambridge, MA: Harvard University Press, 1945.

Michels, Robert. *Political Parties.* New York: Free Press, 1962. Original publication: 1915.

Millman, Zeeva, and Jon Hartwick. "The Impact of Automated Office Systems on Middle Managers and Their Work." *MIS Quarterly* 11, no. 4 (December 1987).

Mintzberg, Henry. *The Nature of Managerial Work.* New York: Harper & Row, 1973.

Mintzberg, Henry. *The Structuring of Organizations.* Englewood Cliffs, NJ: Prentice-Hall, 1979.

Parsons, Talcott. *Structure and Process in Modern Societies.* New York: Free Press, 1960.

Perrow, Charles. *Organizational Analysis.* Belmont, CA: Wadsworth, 1970.

Pindyck, Robert S., and Daniel L. Rubinfield. *Microeconomics.* New York: Macmillan, 1992.

Porat, Marc. *The Information Economy: Definition and Measurement.* Washington, D.C.: U.S. Department of Commerce, Office of Telecommunications (May 1977).

Roethlisberger, F. J., and W. J. Dickson. *Management and the Worker.* Cambridge, MA: Harvard University Press, 1947.

Schein, Edgar H. *Organizational Culture and Leadership,* San Francisco: Jossey-Bass, 1985.

Scott Morton, Michael S., ed. *The Corporation of the 1990s.* New York: Oxford University Press, 1991.

Shore, Edwin B. "Reshaping the IS Organization." *MIS Quarterly* (December 1983).

Simon, Herbert A. "Applying Information Technology to Organization Design." *Public Administration Review* (May/June 1973).

Straub, Detmar, and James C. Wetherbe. "Information Technologies for the 1990s: An Organizational Impact Perspective." *Communications of the ACM* 32, no. 11 (November 1989).

Thompson, James. *Organizations in Action.* New York: McGraw-Hill 1967.

Toffler, Alvin. *Future Shock.* New York: Random House, 1970.

Turner, Jon A. "Computer Mediated Work: The Interplay Between Technology and Structured Jobs." *Communications of the ACM* 27, no. 12 (December 1984).

Turner, Jon A., and Robert A. Karasek, Jr. "Software Ergonomics: Effects of Computer Application Design Parameters on Operator Task Performance and Health." *Ergonomics* 27, no. 6 (1984).

Tushman, Michael L., William H. Newman and Elaine Romanelli. "Convergence and Upheaval: Managing the Unsteady Pace of Organizational Evolution." *California Management Review* 29, no. 1 (1986).

Tushman, Michael L., and Philip Anderson. "Technological Discontinuities and Organizational Environments." *Administrative Science Quarterly* 31 (September 1986).

Weber, Max. *The Theory of Social and Economic Organization.* Translated by Talcott Parsons. New York: Free Press, 1947.

Williamson, Oliver E. *The Economic Institutions of Capitalism.* New York: Free Press, 1985.

Woodward, Joan. *Industrial Organization: Theory and Practice.* Oxford: Oxford University Press, 1965.

Deciding a New World Strategy for Zurich Insurance Group

Zurich Insurance Group is already one of the world's largest insurance companies, with gross annual premiums of almost $14.3 billion and all lines of life insurance and non-life insurance business in almost every insurance market in Europe and North America. But Rolf Hueppi, Zurich's president and chief executive officer, is out to change that. He believes the future of this Swiss insurance giant will be shaped by Wisconsin's meat packing plants, German retail shop floors, U.S. automobile showrooms, and Swiss dentists' offices. These are the kinds of small businesses that Zurich has identified as primary targets for growth.

Deregulation has changed the European insurance market, encouraging the formation of new integrated financial giants that engage in banking and insurance. Formerly protected national companies now compete with foreign insurers. The intensified com-

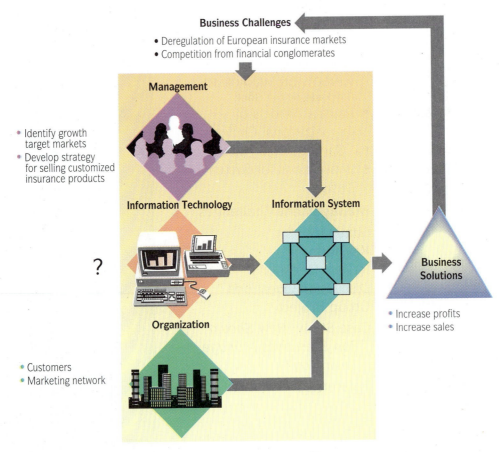

petition is driving prices relentlessly lower and forcing insurance companies to re-examine their concept of what an insurer should be doing.

Hueppi believes that companies must find ways of distinguishing themselves in a crowded market. He seeks alternatives to discounting. One way of pushing prices back up is to sell customized products and services that provide customers with greater value. More tightly focused marketing and closer customer relationships translate into higher profit margins. Companies that concentrate on specific insurance markets are usually more profitable than those that try to be all things to all customers. For instance, by concentrating on industrial steam boilers, Hartford Steam Boiler Insurance Co. has become one of the most profitable companies in the cutthroat U.S. insurance market.

Hueppi is pushing his European units to identify specific markets that Zurich can dominate. He concentrates on three criteria: geographic location, customer segments, and lines of business. In addition to independent Swiss doctors and dentists and German merchandising groups, Zurich has identified metal manufacturing and chemicals and pharmaceuticals as two other target groups for its products.

By focusing on specific markets, Zurich must pull out of others. Accordingly, it has decided to stop underwriting commercial fire risks in Germany and has cut back on Spanish car insurance sales. Zurich's lead in identifying target markets has been acknowledged by some of its European rivals, who are struggling to piece together their own international networks.

Source: Charles Fleming, "Zurich Insurance Group Is Looking for New Focus." *The Wall Street Journal* (June 26, 1992).

The decisions faced by Rolf Hueppi and his managers are typical of those facing many senior executives. In companies both large and small, managers are asking these questions: How can we enlarge market share? Where is our industry headed? Where are we strong and where are we weak? What should our strategy be? How can we design a strategy?

There are no easy answers to these questions. In some instances, managers find solutions using information systems; in other situations, computers may be of little or no use. The remainder of this text examines how information systems can be designed to support managers. In this chapter we scrutinize the role of a manager and try to identify areas where information systems can contribute to managerial effectiveness. We will also point out areas where information systems have limited value.

Decision making is a key task for managers at all levels. Many existing systems improve or enhance management decision making, but challenges remain for systems designers seeking new forms of decision support. To identify opportunities for information systems and to understand their proper role, we first look at what managers actually do. Then we examine the types of decisions managers make and the process of decision making by individuals and organizations. After completing this chapter you will be able to:

- Contrast the classical and contemporary models of managerial activities and roles.
- Describe the levels, types, and stages of decision making.
- Identify models for describing individual and organizational decision making.
- Explain how information systems can assist managers and improve managerial decision making.

5.1 What Managers Do

The responsibilities of managers might range from making decisions, to arranging birthday parties, to writing reports, to attending meetings. To determine how information systems can benefit managers, we must first examine what managers do and what information they need for decision making. We must also understand how decisions are made and what kinds of decisions can be supported by formal information systems.

Classical Descriptions of Management

Classical model of management: Traditional descriptions of management that focused on its formal functions of planning, organizing, coordinating, deciding, and controlling.

The **classical model of management,** which describes what managers do, was largely unquestioned for the more than 70 years since the 1920s. Henri Fayol and other early writers first described the five classical functions of managers as *planning, organizing, coordinating, deciding, and controlling* (see Table 5.1). This description of management activities dominated management thought for a long time, and is still popular today.

But as a description of what managers actually do, these five terms are unsatisfactory. The terms do not address what managers do when they plan. How do they actually decide things? How do managers control the work of others? What is needed in a description is a more fine-grained understanding of how managers actually behave.

Behavioral Models

Contemporary behavioral scientists have discovered from observation that managers do not behave as the classical model of management led us to believe. Kotter (1982), for example, describes the morning activities of the president of an investment management firm.

7:35 AM   Richardson arrives at work, unpacks his briefcase, gets some coffee, and begins making a list of activities for the day.

7:45 AM   Bradshaw (a subordinate) and Richardson converse about a number of topics and exchange pictures recently taken on summer vacations.

8:00 AM   They talk about a schedule of priorities for the day.

8:20 AM   Wilson (a subordinate) and Richardson talk about some personnel problems, cracking jokes in the process.

8:45 AM   Richardson's secretary arrives, and they discuss her new apartment and arrangements for a meeting later in the morning.

8:55 AM   Richardson goes to a morning meeting run by one of his subordinates. Thirty people are there, and Richardson reads during the meeting.

11:05 AM   Richardson and his subordinates return to the office and discuss a difficult problem. They try to define the problem and outline possible alterna-

Table 5.1 THE CLASSICAL MODEL OF MANAGEMENT FUNCTIONS

Planning

Organizing

Coordinating

Deciding

Controlling

Behavioral models:
Descriptions of management based on behavioral scientists' observations of what managers actually do in their jobs.

tives. He lets the discussion roam away from and back to the topic again and again. Finally, they agree on a next step.

Behavioral models state that the actual behavior of managers appears to be less systematic, more informal, less reflective, more reactive, less well-organized, and much more frivolous than students of information systems and decision making generally expect it to be. In our example, it is difficult to determine which activities constitute Richardson's planning, coordinating, and decision making.

A widely noted study of actual managerial behavior conducted by Mintzberg (1971) indicates that actual managerial behavior often contrasts with the classical description (see Table 5.2). First, modern researchers have found that the manager performs a great deal of work at an unrelenting pace and works at a high level of intensity. Some studies have found that managers engage in more than 600 different activities each day, with no break in their pace. Managers seem to have little free time. Even when they leave the office, general managers frequently take work home.

Second, managerial activities are fragmented and brief. Managers simply lack the time to get deeply involved in a wide range of issues. They shift their attention rapidly from one issue to another, with very little pattern. When a problem occurs, all other matters must be dropped until the issue is solved. Mintzberg found that most activities of general managers lasted for less than nine minutes, and only 10 percent of the activities exceeded one hour in duration.

Third, managers prefer speculation, hearsay, gossip—in brief, they enjoy current, up-to-date, although uncertain, information. They pay less attention to historical, routine information. Managers want to work on issues that are current, specific, and ad hoc.

Fourth, as noted in the previous chapter, managers maintain a diverse and complex web of contacts that acts as an informal information system. Managers converse with clients, associates, peers, secretaries, outside government officials, and so forth.

Fifth, managers prefer verbal forms of communication to written forms because verbal media provide greater flexibility, require less effort, and bring a faster response. Communication is the work of the manager, and he or she uses whatever tools are available to be an effective communicator (Olson 1981).

Despite the flood of work, the press of deadlines, and the random order of crises, Mintzberg found that successful managers appear to be able to control their own affairs. To some extent, higher-level managers are at the mercy of their subordinates, who bring to their attention crises and activities that must be

Table 5.2 THE BEHAVIORAL MODEL OF MANAGEMENT ACTIVITIES

High-volume, high-speed work

Variety, fragmentation, brevity

Issue preference current, ad hoc, specific

Complex web of interactions, contacts

Strong preference for *verbal media*

Control of the agenda

attended to immediately. Nevertheless, successful managers can control the activities that they choose to get involved in on a day-to-day basis. By developing their own long-term commitments, their own information channels, and their own networks, senior managers can control their personal agendas. Less successful managers tend to be overwhelmed by problems brought to them by subordinates.

Managerial Roles: Mintzberg

Managerial roles:
Expectations of the activities that managers should perform in an organization.

Interpersonal roles:
Mintzberg's classification for managerial roles where managers act as figureheads and leaders for the organization.

Informational roles:
Mintzberg's classification for managerial roles where managers act as the nerve centers of their organizations, receiving and disseminating critical information.

Decisional roles: Mintzberg's classification for managerial roles where managers initiate activities, handle disturbances, allocate resources, and negotiate conflicts.

Managerial roles are expectations of the activities that managers should perform in an organization. Mintzberg classified managerial activities into ten roles that fall into three categories: interpersonal, informational, and decisional. Information systems, if built properly, can support these diverse managerial roles in a number of ways (see Table 5.3).

Interpersonal roles. Managers act as figureheads for the organization when they represent their companies to the outside world and perform symbolic duties such as giving out employee awards. Managers act as leaders, attempting to motivate, counsel, and support subordinates. Lastly, managers act as a liaison between various levels of the organization; within each of these levels, they serve as a liaison among the members of the management team. Managers provide time, information, and favors, which they expect to be returned.

Informational roles. Managers act as the nerve centers of their organization, receiving the most concrete, up-to-date information and redistributing it to those who need to be aware of it. Managers are therefore disseminators and spokespersons for their organization.

Decisional roles. Managers make decisions. They act as entrepreneurs by initiating new kinds of activities; they handle disturbances arising in the organization; they allocate resources to staff members who need them; and they negotiate conflicts and mediate between conflicting groups in the organization.

Table 5.3 enables us to see where systems can help managers and where they cannot. The table shows that information systems do not as of yet contribute a great deal to many areas of management life. These areas will undoubtedly provide great opportunities for future systems and system designers.

In the area of interpersonal roles, information systems are extremely limited and currently can make only indirect contributions. The systems act largely as a

Table 5.3 MANAGERIAL ROLES AND SUPPORTING INFORMATION SYSTEMS

Role	Behavior	Support Systems
Interpersonal Roles		
Figurehead --→		None exist
Leader ----------------Interpersonal ----------→		None exist
Liaison--→		Electronic communication systems
Informational Roles		
Nerve center----------------------------------→		Management information systems
Disseminator ----------Information ----------→		Mail, office systems
Spokesman------------processing------------→		Office and professional systems Workstations
Decisional Roles		
Entrepreneur ---------------------------------→		None exist
Disturbance handler ----Decision ---------------→		None exist
Resource allocator------making----------------→		DSS systems
Negotiator-------------------------------------→		None exist

Source: Authors and Mintzberg (1971).

Table 5.4 SOME MYTHS ABOUT TOP MANAGERS

Life is less complicated at the top of the organization.

The top managers also know everything, can command whatever resources are needed, and therefore can be decisive.

The top manager's job consists of making long-range plans.

The top manager's job is to meditate about the role of the company in society.

Source: Wrapp (1984).

communications aid with some of the newer office automation and communication-oriented applications. These systems contribute more to the field of informational roles: A manager's presentation of information is significantly improved with large-scale MIS systems, office systems, and professional workstations. In the area of decision making, DSS and microcomputer-based systems have begun to make important contributions (see Chapters 10 and 16).

How Managers Get Things Done: Kotter

Kotter (1982) uses the behavioral approach to modern management to describe how managers work. Building on the work of Mintzberg, Kotter argues that effective managers are involved in three critical activities. First, general managers spend significant time establishing personal agendas and goals, both short- and long-term. These personal agendas include both vague and specific topics and usually address a broad range of financial, product-oriented, and organizational issues.

Second—and perhaps most important—effective managers spend a great deal of time building an interpersonal network composed of people at virtually all levels of the organization, from warehouse staff to clerical support personnel to other managers and senior management. These networks, like their personal agendas, are generally consistent with the formal plans and networks of an organization, but they are different and apart. General managers build these networks using a variety of face-to-face, interactive tools, both formal and informal. Managers carefully nurture professional reputations and relationships with peers.

Third, Kotter found that managers use their networks to execute personal agendas. In his findings, general managers called on peers, corporate staff, subordinates three or four levels below them, and even competitors to help accomplish goals. There was no category of people that was never used.

What Managers Decide: Wrapp

Under the classical model of management, one might expect that managers make important decisions and that the more senior the manager, the more important and profound the decisions will be. Yet in a frequently cited article about general managers, H. Edward Wrapp (1984) found that good managers do not make sweeping policy decisions but instead give the organization a general sense of direction and become skilled in developing opportunities.

Wrapp found that good managers seldom make forthright statements of policy; often get personally involved in operating decisions; and rarely try to push through total solutions or programs for particular problems. Wrapp described a number of myths about modern managers and compared them with the reality that he came to know as a member of several corporate boards (see Table 5.4).

Wrapp was able to show that contrary to popular belief, successful managers spend much time and energy getting involved in operational decisions and problems in order to stay well informed. These managers focus time and energy on

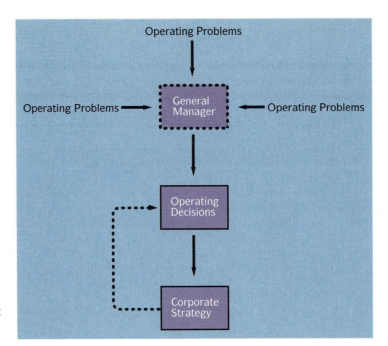

Figure 5.1
Wrapp's successful manager. According to Wrapp, successful general managers are highly involved in operating problems and decisions. Corporate strategy tends not to be systematic or comprehensive but instead is an outgrowth of day-to-day operating decisions.

a small subset of organizational problems that they can directly affect successfully; they are sensitive to the power structure of the organization because any major proposal requires the support of several organizational units and actors; and they appear imprecise in setting overall organizational goals but nevertheless provide a sense of direction. In this way, managers maintain visibility but avoid being placed in a policy straitjacket.

In contrast to the classical description, in which senior managers are thought of as making grand, sweeping decisions, Wrapp found that the contemporary manager tackles organizational decisions with a purpose, and does not seek to implement comprehensive, systematic, logical, well-programmed plans. Systematic, comprehensive plans are generally unable to exploit changes in the environment, and they are just as likely to create opposition in the organization as they are to gain support. For this reason, the manager seeks to implement plans one part at a time, without drawing attention to an explicit, comprehensive design.

Figure 5.1 illustrates Wrapp's conception of a good manager. Especially critical here is the notion of general managers becoming involved in operating problems and decisions. Corporate strategy derives from operating problems and decisions. This means that the corporate strategy is closely tied to operating problems and decisions as opposed to being an independent entity.

Implications for System Design

The classical and contemporary views of what managers do are not contradictory. Managers do, in fact, plan, organize, coordinate, decide, and control. But the contemporary view of how they manage is much more complex, more behavioral, more situational—in a word, more human—than the classical view originally suggested. What are the implications for the organization's use of information systems?

First, managers use formal information systems to plan, organize, and coordinate. However, they also use them for a variety of other less obvious (but vital) tasks such as interpersonal communication, setting and carrying out personal agendas, and establishing a network throughout the organization. This should remind information system designers that there are multiple uses for their products and that the way systems are actually used may not, in fact, reflect the original intention of the designers.

Another implication of contemporary investigations of managers is that formal information systems may be more limited in their impact on managers than was heretofore believed. As we have seen, managers appreciate verbal, current, flexible sources of information. Formal systems may have an important role to play at the operational level but are less critical at the middle and senior management levels than was previously understood. General managers may briefly glance at the output of formal information systems, but they rarely study them in great detail. Ad hoc (less formal) information systems that can be built quickly, use more current and up-to-date information, and can be adjusted to the unique situations of a specific group of managers are highly valued by the modern manager.

Finally, systems designers and builders must appreciate the importance of creating systems that can process information at the most general level; communicate with other sources of information, both inside and outside the organization; and provide an effective means of communication among managers and employees within the organization. A Hewlett-Packard Corporation study, for example, found that the firm's executives were most in need of tools for communication. These generalized computing systems, which are now technologically possible with the development of microcomputers, telecommunication networks, and related software, will have a powerful effect on the organization. Computerized meeting systems described in the Window on Technology are another promising aid for managers. These kinds of systems are discussed in detail in later chapters.

5.2 Introduction to Decision Making

The classical management theorists viewed decision making as the center of managerial activities. Although we now know that this is not exactly the case, decision making remains one of the more challenging roles of a manager. Information systems have helped managers communicate and distribute information; however, they have provided only limited assistance for management decision making. Because decision making is an area that system designers have sought most of all to affect (with mixed success), we now turn our attention to this issue. In this section we introduce the process; in the next two sections we examine models of individual and organizational decision making.

Levels of Decision Making

Differences in decision making can be classified by organizational level. Anthony (1965) grouped decision making in an organization into three categories: strategic, management control, and operational control. We include an additional category for knowledge-level decision making because Anthony did not envision the prominent role now played by knowledge work in organizations. These categories of decisions correspond to the strategic, management, knowledge, and operational levels of the organization introduced in Chapter 1.

Strategic decision making: Determining the long-term objectives, resources, and policies of an organization.

Strategic decision making determines the objectives, resources, and policies of the organization. A major problem at this level of decision making is predicting the future of the organization and its environment and matching the characteristics of the organization to the environment. This process generally involves a small group of high-level managers who deal with very complex, nonroutine problems.

Management control: Monitoring how efficiently or effectively resources are utilized and how well operational units are performing.

Decision making for **management control** is principally concerned with how efficiently and effectively resources are utilized and how well operational units are performing. Management control requires close interaction with those who are carrying out the tasks of the organization; it takes place within the context of broad policies and objectives set out by strategic decision making; and, as the

Knowledge-level decision making: Evaluating new ideas for products and services, ways to communicate new knowledge and distribute information.

Operational control: Deciding how to carry out tasks specified by upper and middle management and establishing criteria for completion and resource utilization.

behavioralists have described, it requires an intimate knowledge of operational decision making and task completion.

Knowledge-level decision making deals with evaluating new ideas for products and services, ways to communicate new knowledge, and ways to distribute information throughout the organization.

Decision making for **operational control** determines how to carry out the specific tasks set forth by strategic and middle management decision makers. Determining which units in the organization will carry out the task, establishing criteria for completion and resource utilization, and evaluating outputs: all of these tasks require decisions about operational control.

Types of Decisions: Structured vs. Unstructured

Unstructured decisions: Nonroutine decisions in which the decision maker must provide judgment,

Within each of these levels of decision making, Simon (1960) classified decisions as being either *programmed* or *nonprogrammed*. Other researchers refer to these types of decisions as *structured* and *unstructured*, as we do in this book. **Unstructured decisions** are those in which the decision maker must provide judg-

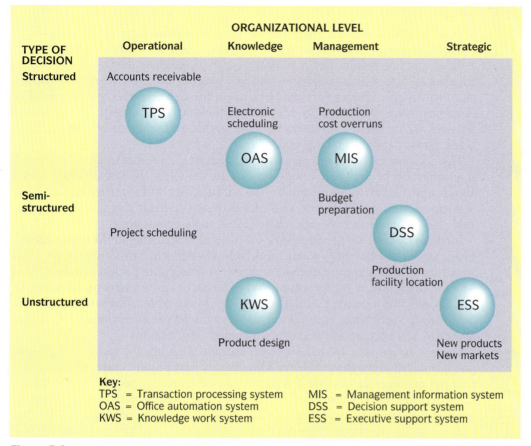

Figure 5.2

Different kinds of information systems at the various organization levels support different types of decisions. Source: Gorry and Scott-Morton (1971).

evaluation, and insights into the problem definition; there is no agreed-upon procedure for making such decisions.

Structured decisions: Decisions that are repetitive, routine, and have a definite procedure for handling them.

ment, evaluation, and insights into the problem definition. These decisions are novel, important, and nonroutine, and there is no well-understood or agreed-upon procedure for making them (Gorry and Scott-Morton, 1971). **Structured decisions,** by contrast, are repetitive, routine, and involve a definite procedure for handling them so that they do not have to be treated each time as if they were new. Some decisions are semistructured decisions; in such cases, only part of the problem has a clear-cut answer provided by an accepted procedure.

Types of Decisions and Types of Systems

Combining these two views of decision making produces the grid shown in Figure 5.2. In general, operational control personnel face fairly well-structured problems. In contrast, strategic planners tackle highly unstructured problems. Many of the problems encountered by knowledge workers are fairly unstructured as well. Nevertheless, each level of the organization contains both structured and unstructured problems.

In the past, most of the success in modern information systems came in dealing with structured, operational and management control decisions. But now most of the exciting applications are occurring in the management, knowledge, and strategic planning areas, where problems are either semistructured or are totally unstructured. Examples include general DSS; microcomputer-based decision-making systems including spreadsheets and other packages; professional design workstations; and general planning and simulation systems (discussed in later chapters).

Stages of Decision Making

Making decisions is not a single activity that takes place all at once. The process consists of several different activities that take place at different times.

Take any important decision that you as a student make—for example, whether or not to attend college—and ask yourself precisely when you decided to go to college. Chances are that you made the decision over a long period of time; you were influenced by friends, counselors, and parents; and you used different information sources to find out about each alternative. Let us try to break down decision making into its component stages.

The decision maker has to perceive and understand problems. Once perceived, solutions must be designed; once solutions are designed, choices have to be made about a particular solution; finally, the solution has to be carried out and implemented. Simon (1960) described four different stages in decision making (see Table 5.5): intelligence, design, choice, and implementation.

Intelligence: The first of Simon's four stages of decision making, when the individual collects information to identify problems occurring in the organization.

Intelligence consists of *identifying* the problems occurring in the organization. Intelligence indicates why, where, and with what effects a situation occurs. This broad set of information-gathering activities is required to inform managers how well the organization is performing and to let them know where problems exist. Traditional MIS systems that deliver a wide variety of detailed information can help identify problems, especially if the systems report exceptions (with added ability to call up text and additional detailed information).

Design: Simon's second stage of decision making, when the individual conceives of possible alternative solutions to a problem.

During **design**, the second stage of decision making, the individual *designs* possible solutions to the problems. This activity may require more intelligence so that the manager can decide if a particular solution is appropriate. The design stage may also entail more carefully specified and directed information activities. Smaller DSS systems are ideal in this stage of decision making because they operate on simple models, can be developed quickly, and can be operated with limited data.

Choice: Simon's third stage of decision making, when the individual selects among the various solution alternatives.

Choice, the third stage of decision making consists of *choosing* among alternatives. Here a manager can use information tools that can calculate and keep track of the consequences, costs, and opportunities provided by each alternative designed in the second stage. The decision maker might need a larger DSS system to develop more extensive data on a variety of alternatives and to use complex analytic models needed to account for all of the consequences.

Implementation: Simon's final stage of decision making, when the individual puts the decision into effect and reports on the progress of the solution.

The last stage in decision making is **implementation**. Here managers can use a reporting system that delivers routine reports on the progress of a specific solution. The system will also report some of the difficulties that arise, will indicate resource constraints, and will suggest possible ameliorative actions. Support systems can range from full-blown MIS systems to much smaller systems as well as project-planning software operating on microcomputers.

Table 5.5 lists the stages in decision making, the general type of information required, and specific examples of information systems corresponding to each stage.

In general, the stages of decision making do not necessarily follow a linear path from intelligence, to design, choice, and implementation. Think again

Table 5.5 STAGES IN DECISION MAKING, INFORMATION REQUIREMENT, AND SUPPORTING INFORMATION SYSTEMS

Stage of Decision Making	Information Requirement	Example System
Intelligence	Exception reporting	MIS
Design	Simulation prototype	DSS, KWS
Choice	'What-if' simulation	DSS; large models
Implementation	Graphics, charts	Microcomputer and mainframe decision aids

Source: Authors and Gorry and Scott-Morton (1971).

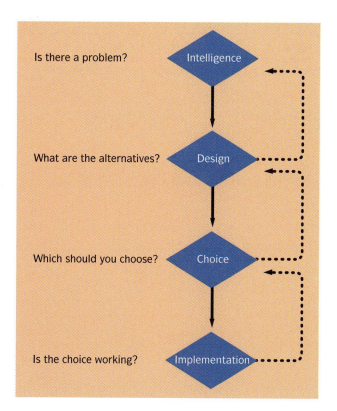

Figure 5.3
The decision-making process. Decisions are often arrived at after a series of iterations and evaluations at each stage in the process. The decision maker often must loop back through one or more of the stages before completing the process.

Figure labels: Is there a problem? — Intelligence; What are the alternatives? — Design; Which should you choose? — Choice; Is the choice working? — Implementation

about your decision to attend a *specific* college. At any point in the decision-making process, you may have to loop back to a previous stage (see Figure 5.3). For instance, one can often come up with several designs but may not be certain about whether a specific design meets the requirements for the particular problem. This situation requires additional intelligence work. Alternatively, one can be in the process of implementing a decision, only to discover that it is not working. In such a case, one is forced to repeat the design or choice stage.

Implications for System Design

From an information systems design perspective, the existence of various stages in decision making and the different requirements for each stage suggest that systems must have multiple general capabilities and must be flexible and easy to use. Up to this point, we have assumed that decision making is accomplished by rational individuals. But what does a *rational individual* mean? Do individuals always act rationally when confronted by choice?

5.3 Individual Models of Decision Making

A number of models attempt to describe how individuals make decisions (see Table 5.6). The basic assumption behind all these models is that human beings are in some sense rational.

The Rational Model

Rational model: Model of human behavior believing that people, organizations, and nations make consistent, value-maximizing calculations within certain constraints.

The **rational model** of human behavior is built on the idea that people, organizations, and nations engage in basically consistent, value-maximizing calculations or adaptations within certain constraints. Since the time of Adam Smith, this assumption has been at the heart of consumer behavior theories and microeconomics, political philosophy (which hails the individual as a free-willed value

Table 5.6 MODELS OF INDIVIDUAL DECISION MAKING

Name	Basic Concept	Inference Patterns
Rational model	Comprehensive rationality	Establish goals, examine all alternatives, and choose the best alternative.
Satisficing model	Bounded rationality	Establish goals, examine a few alternatives, and choose the first alternative that promotes the goals.
Muddling	Successive comparison	Examine alternatives to establish a mix of goals and consequences; choose policies that are marginally different from those of the past.
Psychological	Cognitive types	All decision makers choose goals, but they differ in terms of gathering and evaluating information. Systematic thinkers impose order on perceptions and evaluation; intuitive thinkers are more open to unexpected information and use multiple models and perspectives when evaluating information. Neither is more rational than the other.

maximizer), and social theory (which stresses the individual pursuit of prestige, money, and power).

The rational model works as follows: An individual has goals or objectives and has a payoff, utility, or preference function that permits him or her to rank all possible alternative actions by their contribution to his or her goals. The actor is presented with and understands alternative courses of action. Each alternative has a set of consequences. The actor chooses the alternative (and consequences) that rank highest in terms of the payoff functions (i.e., that contribute most to the ultimate goal). In a rigorous model of rational action, the actor has comprehensive rationality (i.e., he or she can accurately rank all alternatives and consequences) and can perceive all alternatives and consequences.

There are three criticisms of the rational model. First, in a human time frame, the model is computationally impossible. In a "simple" chess game there are 10^{120} moves, countermoves, and counter countermoves from start to finish, and it would take a machine 10^{95} years operating at a rate of 1 million instructions per second (MIPS) to decide the first move! Second, the model lacks realism in the sense that most individuals do not have singular goals and a consciously used payoff function, and they are not able to rank all alternatives and consequences. (To this it might be replied that realism is not required, only predictive accuracy.) Third, in real life the idea of a finite number of all alternatives and consequences makes no sense. In a maze constructed for a rat or in a game of tic-tac-toe, all alternatives and consequences can be meaningful and precise. In the real world of humans, specifying all of the alternatives and consequences is impossible.

Despite these criticisms, the rational model remains a powerful and attractive model of human decision making. It is rigorous, simple, and instructive.

Bounded Rationality and Satisficing

Satisficing: Choosing the first available alternative in order to move closer toward the ultimate goal.

In answer to the critics, March and Simon (1958) and Simon (1960) proposed a number of adjustments to the rigorous rational model. Rather than optimizing, which presumes comprehensive rationality, Simon argues that people **satisfice**— that is, choose the first available alternative that moves them toward their ulti-

Bounded rationality: Idea that people will avoid new uncertain alternatives and stick with tried-and-true rules and procedures.

mate goal. Instead of searching for all of the alternatives and consequences (unlimited rationality), Simon proposes **bounded rationality,** that people limit the search process to sequentially ordered alternatives (alternatives not radically different from the current policy). Wherever possible, people avoid new, uncertain alternatives and rely instead on tried-and-true rules, standard operating procedures, and programs. Individuals have many goals—not a single consistent set—and therefore they try to divide their goals into separate programs, avoiding interdependencies wherever possible. In this way, rationality is bounded.

"Muddling Through"

Muddling through: Method of decision making involving successive limited comparisons where the test of a good decision is whether people agree on it.

In an article on the "science of **muddling through,**" Lindblom (1959) proposed the most radical departure from the rational model. He described this method of decision making as one of "successive limited comparisons." First, individuals and organizations have conflicting goals—they want both freedom and security, rapid economic growth and minimal pollution, faster transportation and minimal disruption due to highway construction, and so forth. People have to choose among policies that contain various mixes of conflicting goals. The values themselves cannot be discussed in the abstract; they become clear only when specific policies are considered. Everyone is against crime; there is little need to discuss this issue. But many object to permitting the police to search homes without a court order (as called for in the Fourth Amendment). Hence, values are chosen at the same time as policies, and there is no easy means-end analysis (if you believe in X, then choose policy X).

Because there is no easy means-end analysis, and because people cannot agree on values, the only test of a "good" choice is whether people agree on it. Policies cannot be judged by how much of X they provide, but rather by the agreement of the people making them. Labor and management can rarely agree on values, but they can agree on specific policies.

Incremental decision making: Choosing policies most like the previous policy.

Because of the limits on human rationality, Lindblom proposes **incremental decision making,** or choosing policies most like the previous policy. Nonincremental policies are apolitical (not likely to bring agreement among important groups) and are dangerous because nobody knows what they will lead to.

Finally, choices are not "made." Instead, decision making is a continuous process in which final decisions are always being modified to accommodate changing objectives, environments, value preferences, and policy alternatives provided by decision makers.

Psychological Types and Frames of Reference

Modern psychology has provided a number of qualifications to the rational model. Psychologists have rarely challenged the basic premise that human beings are value maximizers and, in that sense, that they are rational. Instead, psychologists find that humans differ *in how they maximize their values* and in the *frames of reference* they use to interpret information and make choices.

Cognitive style: Underlying personality disposition toward the treatment of information, selection of alternatives, and evaluation of consequences.

Cognitive style describes underlying personality dispositions toward the treatment of information, the selection of alternatives, and the evaluation of consequences. McKenney and Keen (1974) described two cognitive styles that have direct relevance to information systems: systematic vs. intuitive types. **Systematic decision makers** approach a problem by structuring it in terms of some formal method. They evaluate and gather information in terms of their structured method. **Intuitive decision makers** approach a problem with multiple methods, using trial and error to find a solution, and tend not to structure information gathering or evaluation. Neither type is superior to the other, but some types of thinking are appropriate for certain tasks and roles in the organization.

Systematic decision makers: Cognitive style that describes people who approach a problem by structuring it in terms of some formal method.

Intuitive decision makers: Cognitive style that describes people who approach a problem with multiple methods in an unstructured manner, using trial and error to find a solution.

The existence of different cognitive styles does not challenge the rational model of decision making. It simply says that there are different ways of being rational.

Table 5.7 PSYCHOSOCIAL BIASES IN DECISION MAKING

1. People are more sensitive to negative consequences than to positive ones; for example, students generally refuse to flip a coin for $10 unless they have a chance to win $30.

2. People have no sensible model for dealing with improbable events and either ignore them or overestimate their likelihood; for example, one-in-a-million lotteries are popular, and people have an exaggerated fear of shark attacks.

3. People are more willing to accept a negative outcome if it is presented as a cost rather than a loss; for example, a man will continue playing tennis at an expensive club, despite a painful tennis elbow, by accepting the pain as a cost of the game rather than quit and accept the loss of an annual membership fee.

4. People given the same information will prefer alternatives with certain gains rather than alternatives with certain losses; people will gamble to avoid certain losses. For example, students and professional health workers were given the choice between alternative programs to fight a new disease that was expected to kill 600 people. When described in terms of lives saved, a large majority preferred a program that was certain to save 200 people over a program that had a possibility—but no certainty—of saving all 600. On the other hand, when presented in terms of lives lost, a large majority rejected a program that was guaranteed to lose 400 lives and preferred to gamble, against the odds, on a program that might save everyone but probably would lose everyone.

Source: Tversky and Kahneman, 1981.

More recent psychological research, such as that described in the Window on Organizations, poses strong challenges to the rational model by showing that humans have built-in biases that can distort decision making. Worse, people can be manipulated into choosing alternatives that they might otherwise reject simply by changing the *frame of reference*.

Tversky and Kahneman (1981), summarizing a decade of work on the psychology of decision making, found that humans have a deep-seated tendency to avoid risks when seeking gains but to accept risks in order to avoid losses. In other words, people are more sensitive to negative outcomes than to positive ones. College students refuse to bet $10, for instance, on a coin flip unless they stand to win at least $30. Other biases are listed in Table 5.7.

Because losses loom larger than gains, the credit card industry lobbied retailers aggressively to ensure that any price break given to cash customers would be presented publicly as a "cash discount" rather than a "credit card surcharge." Consumers would be less willing to accept a surcharge than to forgo a discount.

Implications for System Design

The research on decision making has a number of implications for information systems design and understanding. First, decision making is not a simple process even in the rigorous rational model. There are limits to human computation, foresight, and analytical powers. These limits are conceptual and are unrelated to considerations of computer size.

Second, decision situations differ from one another in terms of the clarity of goals, the types of decision makers present, the amount of agreement among them, and the frames of reference brought to a decision-making situation.

Third, an important role of information systems is not to make the decision for humans but rather to support the decision-making process. How this is done will depend on the types of decisions, decision makers, and frames of reference.

As a general rule, research on decision making indicates that information systems designers should design systems that have the following characteristics:

- They are flexible and provide many options for handling data and evaluating information.
- They are capable of supporting a variety of styles, skills, and knowledge.
- They are capable of changing as humans learn and clarify their values.

ORGANIZATIONS

Are Juries Fair?

Recent research on the behavior of juries has found that they are susceptible to influence from the moment members are selected to the time of final deliberation. The research cites stories juries tell themselves to make sense of the mounds of disconnected evidence they confront. Jurors' unspoken assumptions about human behavior have a powerful influence on verdicts.

According to Dr. Nancy Pennington, a University of Colorado psychologist, people do not listen to all the evidence and then evaluate it at the end. Instead, they process it as they go along, creating a continuing story throughout the trial so that they can make sense of what they are hearing. Jurors have little

or nothing that will enable them to tie together all the facts presented at a trial unless an attorney suggests an interpretation in an opening statement that could provide a story line for them to follow.

Dr. Pennington—along with Dr. Reid Hastie, another University of Colorado psychologist—studied people called for jury duty who were not assigned to a trial and who were asked to participate as jurors for a simulated murder trial. When Dr. Pennington interviewed jurors to find out how they reached their verdicts, 45 percent of the references they made were to events that had not been included in the courtroom testimony, including inferences abut the perpetrator and victim's motives and

psychological states, and assumptions based on jurors' personal experiences. The stories the jurors told themselves pieced together the evidence in ways that could lead to opposite verdicts.

Jurors' backgrounds played a crucial role in the assumptions they brought to their stories. Middle-class jurors were more likely to find the defendant guilty than were working-class jurors, the difference hinging mainly on how these jurors interpreted the fact that the perpetrator had a knife with him during a struggle with the victim. Working-class jurors saw nothing incriminating about a man carrying a knife for self-protection.

Other studies of jurors by psychologists have found that many tend to focus on the ability of victims to avoid being injured. Furthermore, whites trust the honesty and fairness of the police far more than blacks, and people who favor the death penalty tend to be pro-prosecution in criminal cases.

Source: Daniel Goleman, "Jurors Hear Evidence and Turn It Into Stories," *The New York Times* (May 12, 1992).

To Think About: What do these studies of juries reveal about the decision-making process?

- They are powerful in the sense of having multiple analytical and intuitive models for the evaluation of data and the ability to keep track of many alternatives and consequences.

These elements of system design form the basis for DSS discussed in Chapter 16 and the rapid growth of knowledge-intensive systems discussed in Chapter 15.

5.4 Organizational Models of Decision Making

For some purposes, it is useful to think of organizational decision making as similar to rational individual decision making. Organizations can be thought of as having singular goals, controlled by unitary rational decision makers who are completely informed, who choose among alternatives after weighing the conse-

Table 5.8 MODELS OF ORGANIZATIONAL DECISION MAKING

Name	Basic Concept	Inference Pattern
Rational actor	Comprehensive rationality	Organizations select goals, examine all alternatives and consequences, and then choose a policy that maximizes the goal or preference function.
Bureaucratic	Organizational output Standard operating procedures	Goals are determined by resource constraints and existing human and capital resources; SOPs are combined into programs, programs into repertoires; these determine what policies will be chosen. The primary purpose of the organization is to survive; uncertainty reduction is the principal goal. Policies are chosen that are incrementally different from the past.
Political	Political outcome	Organizational decisions result from political competition; key players are involved in a game of influence, bargaining, and power. Organizational outcomes are determined by the beliefs and goals of players, their skills in playing the game, the resources they bring to bear, and the limits on their attention and power.
Garbage can	Nonadaptive organizational programs	Most organizations are nonadaptive, temporary, and disappear over time. Organizational decisions result from interactions among streams of problems, potential actions, participants, and chance.

quences, and who act to maximize the goals of the organization. Thus, one can say, for instance, that General Motors "decided" to build a new type of automobile factory in order to make a profit on small cars.

But this simplified, shorthand way of talking about organizations should not conceal the fact that General Motors, and indeed any large organization, is composed of a number of specialized subgroups that are loosely coordinated, with each subgroup having a substantial life and capability of its own. What the organization ultimately does will be determined in large part by what the organizational subunits *can do*.

Organizations also are composed of a number of leaders who compete with each other for leadership. To a large extent, what the organization ultimately decides to do is the result of political competition among its leaders and staff.

Each of these perspectives reflects a different organizational model of decision making that is very different from the individual models previously described (see Table 5.8; also see Allison, 1971; Laudon, 1974; and Laudon, 1986, on which our analysis draws). **Organizational models** of decision making take into account the structural and political characteristics of an organization. Bureaucratic, political, and even "garbage can" models have been proposed to describe how decision making takes place in organizations. We shall now consider each of these models.

Organizational models: Models of decision making that take into account the structural and political characteristics of an organization.

Bureaucratic Models

Bureaucratic models: Models of decision making where decisions are shaped by the organization's standard operating procedures (SOPs).

The dominant idea of **bureaucratic models** is that whatever organizations do is the result of standard operating procedures honed over years of active use. The particular actions chosen by an organization are an output of one or several organizational subunits (e.g., marketing, production, finance, human resources).

MANAGEMENT

Blockade by the Book

In the evening of October 23, 1962, the Executive Committee of the President (EXCOM), a high-level working group of senior advisors to President John F. Kennedy, decided to impose a naval quarantine or blockade on Cuba in order to force the Soviet Union to remove its intermediate-range ballistic missiles from the island, located 90 miles south of Miami.

The naval blockade was chosen only after the Air Force reported that it could not conduct what the politicians in EXCOM called a "surgical air strike" to remove the missiles. Instead, the Air Force recommended a massive strategic air campaign against a number of ground, air, and naval Cuban targets. This was considered extreme by EXCOM, and the only other alternative seemed to be a blockade

that would give Chairman Khrushchev plenty of time to think and several face-saving alternatives.

But EXCOM was worried that the Navy might blunder when implementing the blockade and cause an incident, which in turn could lead to World War III. Secretary of Defense Robert McNamara visited the Navy's Chief of Naval Operations to make the point that the blockade was not intended to shoot Russians but to send a political message.

McNamara wanted to know the following: Which ship would make the first interception? Were Russian-speaking officers on board? How would submarines be dealt with? Would Russian ships be given the opportunity to turn back? What would the Navy do if

Russian captains refused to answer questions about their cargo?

At that point, the Chief of Naval Operations picked up the Manual of Naval Regulations, waved it at McNamara, and said "It's all in there." McNamara responded, "I don't give a damn what John Paul Jones would have done. I want to know what you are going to do tomorrow!"

The visit ended with the navy officer inviting the Secretary of Defense to go back to his office and let the Navy run the blockade.

Source: Graham T. Allison, *Essence of Decision*, 1971.

To Think About: What does this vignette tell you about decision-making at a time of national crisis? Is such decision-making rational?

The problems facing any organization are too massive and too complex to be attended to by the organization as a whole. Problems are instead divided into their components and are parceled out to specialized groups. Competing with low-priced, high-quality Asian cars, for instance, is a complex problem. There are many aspects: production, labor relations, technology, marketing, finance, and even government regulation.

Each organizational subunit has a number of standard operating procedures (SOPs)—tried and proven techniques—that it invokes to solve a problem. Organizations rarely change these standard operating procedures, because they may have to change personnel and incur risks (who knows if the new techniques work better than the old ones?).

SOPs are woven into the programs and repertoires of each subunit. Taken together, these repertoires constitute the range of effective actions that leaders of organizations can take. These repertoires are what the organization can do in the short term. As a United States president discovered in a moment of national crisis, his actions were largely constrained not by his imagination but by what his pawns, bishops, and knights were trained to do (see the Window on Management).

The organization generally perceives problems only through its specialized subunits. These specialized subunits, in turn, are concerned only with parts of the problem. They consciously ignore information not directly relevant to their part of the problem.

Although senior management and leaders are hired to coordinate and lead the organization, they are effectively trapped by parochial subunits that feed information upward and that provide standard solutions. Senior management cannot decide to act in ways that the major subunits cannot support.

Some organizations do, of course, change; they learn new ways of behaving; and they can be led. But all of these changes require a long time. Look around and you will find many organizations doing pretty much what they did ten, twenty, or even thirty years ago. Consider the steel makers, car makers, post office, universities, and hospitals. Have they changed radically in the last five or ten years? How about the last thirty years?

In general, organizations do not "choose" or "decide" in a rational sense; instead, they choose from among a very limited set of repertoires. The goals of organizations are multiple, not singular, and the most important goal is the preservation of the organization itself (e.g., the maintenance of budget, manpower, and territory). The reduction of uncertainty is another major goal. Policy tends to be incremental, only marginally different from the past, because radical policy departures involve too much uncertainty.

Political Models of Organizational Choice

Power in organizations is shared; even the lowest-level workers have some power. At the top, power is concentrated in the hands of a few. For many reasons, leaders differ in their opinions about what the organization should do. The differences matter, causing competition for leadership to ensue. Each individual in an organization, especially at the top, is a key player in the game of politics: Each is bargaining through a number of channels among players.

Political models: Models of decision making where decisions result from competition and bargaining among the organization's interest groups and key leaders.

In **political models** of decision making, what an organization does is a result of political bargains struck among key leaders and interest groups. Actions are not necessarily rational, except in a political sense, and the outcome is not what any individual necessarily wanted. Instead, policy-organizational action is a compromise, a mixture of conflicting tendencies. Organizations do not come up with "solutions" that are "chosen" to solve some "problem." They come up with compromises that reflect the conflicts, the major stake holders, the diverse interests, the unequal power, and the confusion that constitute politics.

Political models of organizations depict decision makers as having limited attention spans; participating in tens (sometimes hundreds) of games and issues; and being susceptible to misperception, extraneous influences, miscommunication, and pressures of impending deadlines. Players in the game focus almost entirely on the short-term problem: What decision must be made today? Long-term strategic thinking for the whole organization goes by the wayside as individual decision makers focus on their short-term interests and on the part of the problem they are interested in.

The United States Congress employs the political model of decision making. Governmental action reflects the compromises of all the members of Congress rather than the desires of any one member.

The Exxon Valdez oil tanker disaster in the Prince William sound in March 1989 is a classic example of the results of the "garbage can" model of decision making.

"Garbage Can" Model

All of the preceding models of organizational choice take as their starting point the basic notion that organizations try to adapt, and for the most part do so successfully, to changing environmental conditions. Presumably, over the long run, organizations develop new programs and actions in order to meet their goals of profit, survival, and so on.

In Chapter 4 we pointed out that many organizations do not survive. Indeed, 30 percent of existing corporations that are fifty years old or more can be expected to disappear (Starbuck, 1983). These findings force us to recognize that organizations are not immortal and may even be temporary. When severely challenged by a changing environment, many organizations prove to be non-adaptive, incapable of learning, and unchanging.

Garbage can model: Model of decision making that states that organizations are not rational and that decisions are solutions that become attached to problems for accidental reasons.

A relatively new theory of decision making, called the **"garbage can" model,** states that organizations are not rational. Decision making is largely accidental and is the product of a stream of solutions, problems, and situations that are randomly associated. That is, solutions become attached to problems for accidental reasons: Organizations are filled with solutions looking for problems and decision makers looking for work.

If this model is correct, it should not be surprising that the wrong solutions are applied to the wrong problems in an organization, or that, over time, a large number of organizations make critical mistakes that lead to their demise. The Exxon Corporation's delayed response to the 1989 Alaska oil spill is an example. Within an hour after the Exxon tanker *Valdez* ran aground in Alaska's Prince William Sound on March 29, 1989, workers were preparing emergency equipment; however, the aid was not dispatched. Instead of sending out emergency crews, the Alyeska Pipeline Service Company (which was responsible for initially responding to oil spill emergencies) sent the crews home. The first full emergency crew did not arrive at the spill site until at least 14 hours after the shipwreck. By the time the vessel was finally surrounded by floating oil containment booms, the oil had spread beyond effective control. Yet enough equipment and personnel had been available to respond effectively. Much of the 10 million gallons of oil fouling the Alaska shoreline in the worst tanker spill in American history could have been confined had Alyeska acted more decisively (Malcolm, 1989).

Implications for System Design

The research on organizational decision making should alert students of information systems to the fact that decision making in a business is a group and organizational process. Systems must be built to support group and organizational decision making. As we shall see in Chapter 16, the early DSS studies emphasized the individual nature of decision making by focusing on the individual choice situation and relying on psychological metaphors of decision making. While useful, these psychological approaches inherently ignore group and organizational processes. A much broader view of decision making is now appropriate; this new view consciously includes group and organizational considerations.

Systems must do more than merely promote decision making. They must also make individual managers better managers of existing routines, better players in the bureaucratic struggle for control of an organization's agenda, and better political players. Finally, for those who resist the "garbage can" tendencies in large organizations, systems should help bring a measure of power to those who can attach the right solution to the right problem.

Good information systems design must include the following:

- An understanding of group and organizational processes of decision making.
- An awareness of the bureaucratic and political requirements of systems.
- An understanding of how bureaucratic and political groups will use the information system for their own purposes.
- Attention to the "symbolism" of systems—that is, how they will be perceived by important groups.
- An understanding of compromises in system features to accommodate diverse interests.
- An awareness and appreciation of the limits of organizational change in policy and in procedure.
- Flexibility to permit changes in organizational repertoires and SOPs—that is, organizational learning and growth.
- An honest and professional awareness of the limits of information systems.

These implications form an important part of the system designer's tool kit.

Management Challenges

1. **Unstructured nature of important decisions.** Many important decisions, especially in the areas of strategic planning and knowledge, are not structured and require judgment and examination of many complex factors. Solutions cannot be provided by computerized information systems alone. System builders need to determine exactly what aspects, if any, of a solution can be computerized, and exactly how systems can support the process of arriving at a decision.

2. **Diversity of managerial roles.** Up to now, information systems have supported only a few of the roles managers play in organizations. System builders need to determine whether new technologies can create information systems to help managers in their interpersonal and decisional roles that previously were not backed up by formal systems. In addition to helping managers plan, organize, and coordinate, it is vital that systems help managers get things done through interpersonal communication, by implementing personal agendas and by establishing networks throughout the organization. Such systems require a different vision of information systems that are less formal, offer more communications capabilities, are adjustable to managers' unique situations, and utilize diverse sources of information inside and outside the firm.

3. **Complexity of decision making.** Individual decision making is not a simple rational process, and is conditioned by decision makers' goals, psychological characteristics, and frames of reference. It is challenging to build systems that genuinely support decision making because they must provide multiple options for handling data and for evaluating information; they must support different personal styles, skills, and knowledge; and they

should be easily modified as humans learn and clarify their values. Ideally, systems should not only be designed to support managers' predispositions but also to provide information supporting alternative points of view.

System builders must find new ways of building systems that support decision making in an organization as a group process, conditioned by bureaucratic struggles, political infighting, and the tendency to randomly attach solutions to problems.

Summary

Contrast the classical and contemporary models of managerial activities and roles.

Early classical models of management stressed the functions of planning, organizing, coordinating, deciding, and controlling. Contemporary research has examined the actual behavior of managers to show how managers get things done.

Mintzberg found that managers' real activities are highly fragmented, variegated, and brief in duration, with managers moving rapidly and intensely from one issue to another. Other behavioral research has found that managers spend considerable time pursuing personal agendas and goals and that contemporary managers shy away from making grand, sweeping policy decisions.

Describe the levels, types, and stages of decision making.

Decision making in an organization can be classified by organizational level: strategic, management control, knowledge and operational control.

Decisions can be either structured, semistructered, or unstructured, with structured decisions clustering at the operational level of the organization and unstructured decisions at the strategic planning level. The nature and level of decision making are important factors in building information systems for managers.

Decision making itself is a complex activity at both the individual and the organizational level. Simon described four different stages in decision making: (1) intelligence, (2) design, (3) choice, and (4) implementation.

Identify models for describing individual and organizational decision making.

Rational models of decision making assume that human beings can accurately choose alternatives and consequences based on the priority of their objectives and goals. The rigorous rational model of individual decision making has been modified by behavioral research that suggests that rationality is limited. People "satisfice," "muddle through" decisions incrementally, or select alternatives biased by their cognitive style and frame of reference.

Organizational models of decision making illustrate that real decision making in organizations takes place in arenas where many psychological, political, and bureaucratic forces are at work. Thus, organizational decision making may not necessarily be rational. The design of information systems must accommodate these realities, recognizing that decision making is never a simple process.

Explain how information systems can assist managers and improve managerial decision making.

If information systems are built properly, they can support individual and organizational decision making. Up to now, information systems have been most helpful to managers for performing informational and decisional roles; the same systems have been of very limited value for managers' interpersonal roles. Information systems that are less formal and highly flexible will be more useful than large, formal systems at higher levels of the organization.

The design of information systems must accommodate these realities. Designers must recognize that decision making is never a simple process. Information systems can best support managers and decision making if such systems are flexible, with multiple analytical and intuitive models for evaluating data and the capability of supporting a variety of styles, skills, and knowledge.

| Key | Classical model of management | Choice |
| Terms | Behavioral models of management | Implementation |

Key
Terms

Classical model of management   Choice
Behavioral models of management Implementation
Managerial roles   Rational model
Interpersonal roles   Satisficing
Informational roles   Bounded rationality
Decisional roles   Muddling through
Strategic decision making   Incremental decision making
Management control   Cognitive style
Knowledge-level decision making Systematic decision makers
Operational control   Intuitive decision makers
Unstructured decisions   Organizational models
Structured decisions   Bureaucratic models
Intelligence   Political models
Design   Garbage can model

Review Questions

1. What are the five functions of managers described in the classical model?

2. Behavioral research has identified six characteristics of the modern manager. How do these characteristics relate to the classical model?

3. What specific managerial roles can information systems support? Where are information systems particularly strong in supporting managers, and where are they weak?

4. How do managers get things done, and how can CBIS help?

5. What did Wrapp (1984) discover about the way managers make decisions? How do these findings compare with those of the classical model?

6. What are the implications of classical and contemporary views of managers for information systems design?

7. Define structured and unstructured decisions. Give three examples of each.

8. What are the four kinds of CBIS that support decisions?

9. What are the four stages of decision making described by Simon?

10. Describe each of the four individual models of decision making. What is the name, basic concept, and dominant inference pattern of each? How would the design of information systems be affected by the model of decision making employed?

11. Describe each of the four organizational choice models. How would the design of systems be affected by the choice of model employed?

Discussion Questions

1. At your college or university, identify a major decision made recently by a department, an office, or a bureau. Try to apply each of the organizational models of decision making to the decision. How was information used by the various organizational participants? What are the implications for the design of information systems?

2. Identify and describe a decision that all of you have had to make (e.g., going to college, choosing a specific college, choosing a major). Use Simon's model of stages and show how an information system might have helped or hindered you in making the decision.

Group Project

Form a group with three to four of your classmates. Observe a manager for one hour. Classify the observed behavior in two ways, using the classical model and then the behavioral model. Compare the results and discuss the difficulties of coding the behavior. Present your findings to the class.

How Should Top Executives Manage Their Day?

Should busy executives struggle to seize control of their time? Should executives avoid interruptions and deploy secretaries and assistants as "protectors" against "time robbers" who prevent them from getting their own work done? Should schedules be planned days, weeks, and months ahead of time? This is what many time management experts recommend.

The problem is that this kind of thinking has little to do with how the majority of effective executives actually handle their day. Smart executives enjoy being interrupted, and fill their days with brief, unscheduled conversations as a way of eliciting up-to-the-minute information and maintaining the vital personal ties that enable them to get things done in big organizations. If you cut yourself off from other people, do you miss out on what's happening in your company, in your industry and in the rest of the world?

Stephanie Winston, a New York City consultant who helps managers and professionals to get organized, interviewed 48 chairmen, vice chairmen, and presidents of major companies, including John Sculley (Apple Corporation), Joseph Vittoria (Avis), Katherine Graham (the *Washington Post*), and John Bryan (Sara Lee). She found that a CEO's day consists mainly of interruptions. Top executives walk into their offices in the morning with only a vague idea of what they will do that day. In contradiction to the rules of time management and efficiency, they respond largely to whatever comes next. Only two hours of a CEO's 9–10-hour working day might consist of prebooked appointments. Winston concluded that being interrupted doesn't detract from top managers' work; it *is* their work. Interruptions bring gifts of information and ties of loyalty.

Joseph Vittoria, the CEO of Avis, headquartered in Garden City, New York, blocks out two to three-hour periods or entire days for unscheduled encounters. His business requires a great deal of personal contact and he wants his staff to talk to him about what is on their minds. He believes that his responsibility is not "running the company" but communicating with the people who run the firm.

In some ways, interruptions can save time. Suzanne Rinfret Moore — president of Rinfret Associates, an economics consulting firm; Rinfret Securities, a trading operation; and co-head of Alterntrack, a firm that places Wall Street professionals in part-time and project work — feels that someone can tell her something in 30 seconds that might take 15 minutes to write up as a memo. She believes that a fluid business day fosters creativity in herself and in her staff as well.

On the other hand, Winston also found that the CEOs she interviewed did not read much, aside from their firm's internal reports and a little business journalism. Certain CEOs limited their conversations to a few close, high-level colleagues. Yet recognized leaders such as Millard S. Drexler, president of The Gap, answers his own telephone and

takes dozens of calls a week from customers. The late Sam Walton used to barnstorm the Southeast visiting his WalMart stores.

Almost every day, Linda Joy Wachner — chief executive of Warnaco, a conglomerate of women's intimate apparel brands including Warner's and Fruit of the Loom, and menswear brands such as Christian Dior, Hathaway, and Chaps by Ralph Lauren — can be found breezing through the small "stitch room" on the 12th floor of her Park Avenue headquarters in Manhattan. Eight seamstresses are turning out samples of the lingerie Warnaco will eventually manufacture in factories and sell to department and specialty stores. She picks up samples of whatever fabric, lace, or trim she finds on the women's tables.

Wachner believes she keeps her company very profitable by staying close to the customer, staying on top of the business, and watching the till. She believes even innovative marketers and product-creators must still know how to manage the cash.

In 1991, she traveled for 200 days visiting stores and plants, roaming store aisles, and chatting with salespeople to find out which products people were buying and why. Every week she pores over the sales reports from Warnaco's retail accounts. Wachner is constantly in touch with customers in the stores and with retailers. She spends hours building relationships with the merchants who stock Warnaco products to find out how she can expand her business within their stores.

Wachner uses a weekly president's letter to translate information into action. Every Friday night the seven Warnaco division heads fax her a one-page memo outlining any shipping or delivery problems that might have occurred that week. They also may explain why things went better than expected. Wachner uses this information as an overview to identify problems that must be attacked at the Monday morning meetings. For instance, a Friday fax alerted Wachner to shipping delays for special laces that were needed to complete a new piece of lingerie for the Warner's line. Wachner got right on the phone and the laces arrived on schedule. Divisions send in monthly sales projections as well.

Wachner doesn't want Warnaco's top managers waiting even 30 seconds. She insists that each carry a spiral notebook with the words DO IT NOW embossed on the cover. Executives use the notebooks to take notes about meetings or conversations with Wachner, to record business projections, or to remind them about anything requiring immediate action.

Wachner watches closely over Warnaco's cash flow and knows every single day what cash the firm received and what the total was supposed to be. If the figures are not within several dollars, Wachner calls the presidents of the companies that owe Warnaco. She lets them know that they won't receive any more shipments until they pay their bills.

CEOs may only need to read other people's reports, but what happens to the busy executives who have reports to write? Stephanie Winston advises allocating an hour or two for working alone during the part of the day when the executive works best. Often that time occurs early in the morning. The rest of the day can be left open for ad hoc meetings and conversations.

Sources: Susan Caminiti, "America's Most Successful Businesswoman." *Fortune,* June 15, 1992, and Alan Deutschman, "The CEO's Secret of Managing Time," *Fortune,* June 1, 1992.

Case Study Questions

1. Some prominent management consulting firms believe senior executives spend too much time gathering information and too little time making decisions. Do you agree?

2. Should senior executives strictly budget their time? What kinds of problems are created when they do? What kinds of problems are created when they don't?

3. What kinds of managerial roles, types of decisions, and models of decision making are illustrated here?

4. Suggest some information system applications that might help CEOs (such as Wachner, Vittoria, or Moore) manage their daily activities. Would these systems be easy to build?

References

Adams, Carl. R., and Jae Hyon Song. "Integrating Decision Technologies: Implications for Management Curriculum." *MIS Quarterly* 13, no. 2 (June 1989).

Allison, Graham T. *Essence of Decision—Explaining the Cuban Missile Crisis.* Boston: Little, Brown, 1971.

Anthony, R. N. "Planning and Control Systems: A Framework for Analysis," Harvard University Graduate School of Business Administration, 1965.

Cohen, Michael, James March, and Johan Olsen. "A Garbage Can Model of Organizational Choice." *Administrative Science Quarterly,* 17 (1972).

George, Joey. "Organizational Decision Support Systems." *Journal of Management Information Systems* 8, no. 3 (Winter 1991–1992).

Gorry, G. Anthony, and Michael S. Scott-Morton. "A Framework for Management Information Systems." *Sloan Management Review,* 13, no. 1 (Fall 1971).

Grobowski, Ron, Chris McGoff, Doug Vogel, Ben Martz, and Jay Nunamaker. "Implementing Electronic Meeting Systems at IBM: Lessons Learned and Success Factors." *MIS Quarterly* 14, no. 4 (December 1990).

Huber, George P. "Cognitive Style as a Basis for MIS and DSS Designs: Much Ado About Nothing?" *Management Science,* 29 (May 1983).

Isenberg, Daniel J. "How Senior Managers Think." *Harvard Business Review* (November–December 1984).

Ives, Blake, and Margrethe H. Olson. "Manager or Technician? The Nature of the Information Systems Manager's Job." *MIS Quarterly* (December 1981).

Jessup, Leonard M., Terry Connolly, and Jolene Galegher. "The Effects of Anonymity on GDSS Group Process with an Idea-Generating Task." *MIS Quarterly* 14, no. 3 (September 1990).

Kotter, John T. "What Effective General Managers Really Do." *Harvard Business Review* (November–December 1982).

Laudon, Kenneth C. *Computers and Bureaucratic Reform.* New York: Wiley, 1974.

Laudon, Kenneth C. *Dossier Society: Value Choices in the Design of National Information Systems.* New York: Columbia University Press, 1986.

Lindblom, C. E., "The Science of Muddling Through." *Public Administration Review* 19 (1959).

Malcolm, Andrew H. "How the Oil Spilled and Spread: Delay and Confusion Off Alaska." *The New York Times,* April 16, 1989.

March, James G., and Herbert A. Simon. *Organizations.* New York: Wiley, 1958.

Markus, M. L. "Power, Politics, and MIS Implementation." *Communications of the ACM* 26, no. 6 (June 1983).

McKenney, James L., and Peter G. W. Keen. "How Managers' Minds Work." *Harvard Business Review* (May–June 1974).

Mintzberg, Henry. "Managerial Work: Analysis from Observation." *Management Science* 18 (October 1971).

Olson, Margrethe H. "The IS Manager's Job." *MIS Quarterly* (December 1981).

Simon, H. A. *The New Science of Management Decision*. New York: Harper & Row, 1960.

Starbuck, William H. "Organizations as Action Generators." *American Sociological Review* 48 (1983).

Tversky, A., and D. Kahneman. "The Framing of Decisions and the Psychology of Choice." *Science* 211 (January 1981).

Wrapp, H. Edward. "Good Managers Don't Make Policy Decisions." *Harvard Business Review* (July–August 1984).

Chrysler and GM: Can Information Technology Save the U.S. Auto Industry?

This case illustrates how two giant American corporations, Chrysler and General Motors, have tried to use information technology to combat foreign and domestic competitors. The case explores the relationship between each firm's management strategy, organizational characteristics, and information systems. It poses the following question: To what extent can information technology solve the problems confronting the U.S. automobile industry?

On October 26, 1992, Robert C. Stempel resigned as chairman and CEO of the General Motors Corporation. Stempel was pressured to resign because he had not moved quickly enough to make the changes required to ensure the automotive giant's survival. To counter massive financial losses and plummeting market share, Stempel had announced ten months earlier that GM would have to close 21 of its North American plants and cut 74,000 of its employees over 3 years. Stempel was replaced by a more youthful and determined management team.

GM's plight reflected the depths of the decline of the once vigorous American automobile industry in the late 1980s. Year after year, as Americans came to view American-made cars as low in quality or not stylish, car buyers purchased few and fewer American cars, replacing them mostly with Japanese models.

Ironically, at about the same time, the Chrysler Corporation announced strong 1992 third-quarter earnings of $202 million. During the 1980s, Chrysler had struggled with rising costs and declining sales of mass market cars. However, demand was strong for its minivans and the hot Jeep Grand Cherokee. A stringent cost-cutting crusade eliminated $4 billion in operating costs in just 3 years. The rest of the U.S. auto industry was still in a slump from prolonged recession and losses of market share to the Japanese.

Ten years before, Chrysler had been battling bankruptcy and GM was flush with cash. Had Chrysler finally turned itself around? Was this the beginning of the end for the world's largest automobile maker? What is the role of information systems in this tale of two auto makers and in the future of the U.S. automobile industry?

GENERAL MOTORS

General Motors, the world's largest auto maker, has more than 715,000 employees in 35 countries, meets $22 billion in payrolls, and deals with 28,000 suppliers. GM's U.S. auto business accounts for about 1.5 percent of the U.S. economy, down from 5 percent in the 1950s. Its sheer size has proved to be one of GM's greatest burdens.

For 70 years, GM operated along the lines laid down by CEO Alfred Sloan, who rescued the firm from bankruptcy in the 1920s. Sloan separated the firm into five separate operating groups and divisions—Chevrolet, Pontiac, Oldsmobile, Buick, and Cadillac. Each division functioned as a semi-autonomous company with its own marketing operations. GM's management was a welter of bureaucracies.

GM covered the market with low-end Chevys and high-end Caddies. At the outset, this amalgam of top-down control and decentralized execution enabled GM to build cars at lower cost than its rivals; but it could also charge more for the quality and popularity of its models. By the 1960s, GM started having trouble building smaller cars to compete with imports and started eliminating differences among divisions. By the mid 1980s, GM had reduced differences among the divisions to the point where customers could not tell a Cadillac from a Chevrolet; the engines in low-end Chevys were also found in high-end Oldsmobiles. Its own brands started to compete with each other.

Under Roger Smith, CEO from 1981 to 1990, GM moved boldly, but often in the wrong direction. GM remained a far-flung vertically integrated corporation that at one time made up to 70 percent of its parts. Its costs were much higher than either its U.S. or Japanese competitors. Like many large manufacturing firms, its organizational culture resisted change. GM has made steady improvements in car quality, but its selection and styling have lagged behind its U.S. and Japanese rivals. GM's market share plunged from a peak of 52 percent in the early 1960s to just 35 percent today. In 1979, GM's market share was 46 percent.

In 1992, GM's labor costs were $2358 per car, compared to $1872 for Chrysler and $1563 for Ford. That makes GM 40 percent less productive than Ford. These figures do not begin to approach those of the Japanese, whose automotive productivity surpasses all U.S. corporations.

CHRYSLER

In auto-industry downturns, Chrysler was always the weakest of Detroit's Big Three auto makers (GM, Ford, and Chrysler). Founded in the 1930s by Walter P. Chrysler through a series of mergers with smaller companies like Dodge and DeSoto, Chrysler prided itself on superior engineering, especially in engines and suspensions. In the 1940s and 1950s, Chrysler grew into a small, highly centralized firm with very little vertical integration. Unlike Ford and GM, Chrysler relied on external suppliers for 70 percent of its major components and subassemblies, becoming more an auto assembler than a huge vertically integrated manufacturer like GM. Unlike its larger competitors, Chrysler did not develop a global market for its cars to cushion domestic downturns. Chrysler's centralized and smaller firm could potentially move faster and be more innovative than its larger competitors.

During the late 1980s, Chrysler lost several hundred thousand units of sales annually because it did not make improvements in engine development and in its mass market cars, the small subcompacts and large rear-wheel drive vehicles. There was no new family of midpriced, midsized cars to rival Ford's Taurus or Honda's Accord. Chrysler's key car models and brands could not be distinguished from each other. Customers migrated to other brands. Chrysler's response, the Spirit and Acclaim, brought out in 1988, were ultraconservative in styling. Yet Chrysler lavished funds on specialty niches such as coupes and convertibles. By the early 1990s, fierce price cutting had upped Chrysler's breakeven point (the number of cars the firm had to sell to start making a profit) to 1.9 million units, up from 1.4 million.

GM's INFORMATION SYSTEMS STRATEGY

Despite heavy investment in information technology, GM's information systems were virtually archaic. GM had more than 100 mainframes and 34 computer centers but had no centralized system to link computer operations or to coordinate operations from one department to another. Each division and group had its own hardware and software so that the design group could not interact with production engineers via computer.

GM adopted a "shotgun" approach, pursuing several high-technology paths simultaneously in the hope that one or all of them would pay off. GM also believed it could overwhelm competitors by outspending them. GM does spend more than its competitors on information systems. It spends 2.5 percent of sales on information systems, whereas Ford spends 1.6 percent and Chrysler 0.9 percent of sales on information systems budgets. GM also tried to use information technology to totally overhaul the way it does business.

Recognizing the continuing power of the divisions and the vast differences among them, Roger Smith, CEO of GM from 1981 to 1990, sought to integrate their manufacturing and administrative information systems by purchasing Electronic Data Systems of Houston for $2.5 billion. EDS supplies GM's data processing and communications services. EDS and its talented system designers were charged with conquering the administrative chaos in the divisions: more than 16 different electronic mail systems, 28 different word processing systems, and a jumble of factory floor systems that could not communicate with management. Even worse, most of these systems were running on completely incompatible equipment.

EDS consolidated its 5 computing centers and GM's 34 computing centers into 21 uniform information processing centers for GM and EDS work. EDS replaced the hundred different networks that served GM with the world's largest private digital telecommunications network. EDS is also starting to develop standard information systems for GM.

GM's Integrated Scheduling Project will eventually replace 30 different materials and scheduling systems with one integrated system to handle inventory, manufacturing, and financial data. Factory managers can receive orders from the car divisions for the number and type of vehicles to build and then can create an estimated 20-week manufacturing schedule for GM and suppliers. The system also sends suppliers schedules each morning on what materials need to be delivered to what docks at what hour during that manufacturing day.

Smith earmarked $40 billion for new plants and automation, but not all investments were fruitful. He spent heavily on robots to paint cars and install windshields, hoping to reduce GM's unionized work force. At first, however, the robots accidentally painted themselves and dropped windshields onto the front seats. While a number of these problems were corrected, some robots stand unused today. The highly automated equipment never did what was promised because GM did not train workers properly to use it and did not design its car models for easy robot assembly. Instead of reducing its work force, workers had to stay on the line because of frequent robotic breakdowns.

CHRYSLER'S INFORMATION SYSTEMS STRATEGY

In 1980, with $2.8 billion in debt, Chrysler seemed headed for bankruptcy. Its financial crisis galvanized its management to find new ways to cut costs, increase inventory turnover, and improve quality. Its new management team led by Lee Iacocca instituted an aggressive policy to bring its computer-based systems under management control. Chrysler didn't have the money to invest in several high-technology paths at once. It adopted a "rifle" approach to systems: Build what was absolutely essential, and build what would produce the biggest returns. Chrysler focused on building common systems—systems that would work in 6000 dealer showrooms, 25 zone offices, 22 parts depots, and all of its manufacturing plants.

Chrysler built integrated systems. When an order is captured electronically at the dealer, the same order is tied to production, schedules, invoices, parts forecasts, projections, parts and inventory management, and so forth.

Chrysler's low degree of vertical integration put the company in a better position to concentrate on only a few technologies. Because it was more of an auto assembler and distributor than a manufacturer, it had less need for leading-edge manufacturing technologies such as vision systems, programmable controllers, and robotics, all of which are far more important to GM and Ford.

Chrysler directed most of its information systems budget to corporate-wide communications systems and just-in-time inventory management. Just-in-time (JIT) inventory management is obviously critical to a company that has 70 percent of its parts made by outside suppliers. (JIT supplies needed parts to the production line on a last minute basis. This keeps factory inventory levels as low as possible and holds down production costs.) During the 1980s, Chrysler achieved a 9 percent reduction in inventory and increased average quarterly inventory turnover from 6.38 times to 13.9 times.

A single corporation-wide network connects Chrysler's large and mid-sized computers from various vendors and gives engineering workstations access to the large computers. This makes it easier to move data from one system, stage of production, or plant to another and facilitates just-in-time inventory management.

Even before the 1980s, Chrysler had decided it needed a centralized pool of computerized CAD specifications that was accessible to all stages of production. In 1981, it installed a system to provide managers in all work areas and in all nine Chrysler plants with the same current design specifications. Tooling and design can access this data concurrently, so that a last-minute change in design can be immediately conveyed to tooling and manufacturing engineers. Chrysler created centralized business files for inventory, shipping, marketing, and a host of other related activities. All of this centralized management information makes scheduling and inventory control much easier to coordinate. Chrysler's cars and trucks share many of the same parts.

Chrysler launched a satellite communication network in 1982 that provides one-way video and two-way data transmission to nearly 5000 of its dealerships and offices around the country. It will soon be expanded to sites outside the U.S.

Chrysler has set up electronic links between its computers and those of its suppliers, such as the Budd Company of Rochester, Michigan, which supplies U.S. auto companies with sheet metal parts, wheel products, and frames. Budd can extract manufacturing releases electronically through terminals installed in all of its work areas and can deliver the parts exactly when Chrysler needs them. A new enhancement verifies the accuracy of advanced shipping notices electronically transmitted by suppliers and helps Chrysler track inventory levels and payment schedules more closely.

LEARNING FROM THE JAPANESE

In the mid 1980s, MIT researchers found that the Toyota Motor Corporation's production system represented a sharp departure from Henry Ford's mass production techniques. In "lean manufacturing," Japanese auto makers focus on minimizing waste and inventory and utilizing worker's ideas (see the Window on Organizations in Chapter 4). The emphasis is on maximizing reliability and quality, and minimizing waste. The ideal

"lean" factory has parts built just as they are needed and has a level of quality so high that inspection is virtually redundant.

After studying Honda, Chrysler started to cut $1 billion a year in operating costs and began to rethink virtually everything it did, from designing engines to reporting financial results. Chrysler overhauled its top-down autocratic management structure. It replaced its traditional rigid departments, such as the engine division, with nimble Honda-like "cross-functional platform teams." The teams combined experts from diverse areas such as design, manufacturing, marketing, and purchasing together in one location and were given the power to make basic decisions ranging from styling to choice of suppliers. With this new approach, Chrysler shortened its product development cycle by 18 months and increased quality. Efficiency skyrocketed.

One team of 85 people designed the Dodge Viper sports car in just 36 months, a process that traditionally had taken Chrysler 4 ½ years. The Viper only cost $75 million to develop, compared to the $118 million Mazda Motor Corporation spent on its Miata. Chrysler's LH series of mid-sized cars went from conception to production in just 39 months, about the same time that it takes for Japanese auto makers. These newer products are considered light years ahead of the products Chrysler created in the 1980s.

Chrysler now has four separate platform teams to design its jeep, minivans, and cars. The cross-functional teams comprise about 750 people, half of the 1500 that were previously required for such projects.

Hourly workers are providing input to help Chrysler eliminate wasted steps in the assembly process. Toyota cut waste by diagramming every step of its assembly process. It moved tools closer to the workers and eliminated unnecessary motions. Chrysler is now redesigning its assembly lines to be more like those of Toyota. Ten years ago, it took 6000 workers to build 1000 cars a day. Now Chrysler can achieve the same output with half that many workers.

To support its new approach to product development, Chrysler built a new 3.5 million square-foot Chrysler Technology Center (CTC) 30 miles north of Detroit in Auburn Hills, Michigan. Chrysler leaders expect the CTC to further enhance productivity by providing the technology that will enable Chrysler to engineer things only once and not repeat them. For instance, a failed crash test in the past might have left engineers scratching their heads. Now they can compare crash data from a test with theoretical predictions, moving closer to a solution with each successive prediction cycle. Only when they need to test a solution would they actually have to crash another car. Since hand-built prototypes cost $250,000 to $400,000, avoiding a few crash tests has a large payoff. Using this approach, engineers designed the LH car so that it passed its crash test the first time out.

Every room in the CTC has 8-inch raised floors covering a total of 10,000 fiber optic cables that can transmit massive volumes of data at high speed. These cables link CTC's buildings to its main data center. The CTC itself will soon house ten mainframe computers, two supercomputers, and control systems for all the center's data and computer networks. A total of seven thousand people work there.

With a three-story atrium, the grandiose building goes far beyond functionality. It cost the cash-strapped Chrysler over $1 billion. Chrysler management claims the CTC technology makes re-engineering of the automobile design process possible, but industry experts point out that you could put platform teams in much less elaborate quarters. Hundreds of millions of the dollars spent on the CTC could have been used to bring Chrysler cars to market even sooner. Is the CTC symbolic of Chrysler's overall predicament? While Chrysler plans to spend $3 billion annually on product development through 1997, it could not find $100 million for a full-sized wind tunnel to test car designs—less money than what the monumental features of CTC added to the building's cost.

GM created an entirely new Saturn automobile with a totally new division, labor force, and production system based on the Japanese "lean production" model. Saturn workers and managers share information, authority, and decision making. The Saturn car was a market triumph. But Saturn took seven years to roll out the first model and drained $5 billion from other car projects. GM had been selling Saturn at a loss to build up market share. GM needs to find a way to bring the Saturn formula for making cars to the rest of the company. This will not be easy, because the traditional top-down management style of U.S. automaking is deeply ingrained.

GM is starting to use platform teams of engineers, designers, and marketing experts in its other divisions, and has shortened product development time. It is expected to reduce the number of chasses or platforms it uses for cars from 20 to 7 or fewer. Its models will have more common parts.

In April 1992 GM instituted a new worldwide purchasing policy to make GM's high parts costs more competitive. GM's company-owned suppliers were required to bid against outside suppliers. GM has pressured outside suppliers for immediate 20 percent price reductions and reductions of up to 50 percent in the next few years. At that time about 40 percent of GM parts were still coming from outside suppliers, whereas 70 percent of the parts in Chrysler, Ford, and Japanese firms come from the outside.

GM is also starting to roll out a satellite network for its 9700 dealerships, racing to catch up with Chrysler and Nissan Motor Corporation, who already have such networks in place.

Chrysler still needs to work on quality as well as productivity. While its cars and trucks are more reliable than they were a decade ago, they still do not match the competition. On the one hand, Detroit appears to have stopped losing ground to Japanese autos, which still represent 30 percent of the U.S. new car sales. On the other hand, Japanese car makers are continuing to improve plant efficiency. Nissan and Mazda introduced assembly lines that can make half a dozen different vehicles, whereas most Big Three plants only make one or two different cars. Will the U.S. auto industry ever catch up?

Sources: John Greenwald, "What Went Wrong?" *Time Magazine* (November 9, 1992); Leonard M. Apcar, "As G.M. Tries to Outrun Past, Critics Ask: Who's in Charge?" *The New York Times* (October 26, 1992); Alex Taylor, III, "Can GM Remodel Itself? *Fortune* (January 13, 1992); Maryann Keller, *Rude Awakening: The Rise, Fall, and Struggle for Recovery of General Motors* (New York: Harper Collins Publishers, 1990); David Woodruff with Elizabeth Lesly, "Surge at Chrysler," *Business Week* (November 9, 1992); Edward Cone, "Chrysler," *Information WEEK* (September 7, 1992); Bradley A. Stertz, "Detroit's New Strategy to Beat Back Japanese Is to Copy Their Ideas," *The Wall Street Journal* (October 1, 1992); and Doron Levin, "Chrysler's New L/H, as in Last Hope," *The New York Times* (July 12, 1992).

Case Study Questions

1. Compare the roles played by information systems at Chrysler and GM. How did they affect the structure of the automobile industry itself?

2. How much did information systems contribute to GM's and Chryslers' success or failure?

3. What management, organization, and technology issues explain the differences in the way Chrysler and GM used information systems?

4. What management, organization, and technology were responsible for Chrysler's and GM's problems?

5. How can information systems help the American automobile industry compete more effectively with the Japanese (or can they)?

6. How important are information systems in solving the problems of the American automobile industry? What are some of the problems that technology cannot address?

TWO

Technical Foundations of Information Systems

Part Two lays out the technical foundations of information systems—hardware, software, storage, and telecommunications technologies. In today's new information architecture, the computer itself is but one of many technologies that permit modern information systems to function. To build effective information systems, one must understand how all of these technologies can work together.

Chapter 6 surveys the features of computer hardware that help determine the capabilities of an information system. These features include the central processing unit, primary storage, and input and output devices. Because of the soaring power of microprocessors, the capabilities of mainframes, minicomputers, microcomputers, workstations, and supercomputers are constantly expanding. Emerging technologies include parallel processing, massively parallel processing, and multimedia.

Chapter 7 describes the role of computer software in processing information, showing its interdependence with the capabilities of computer hardware. It is through software that computer hardware becomes useful to people and organizations. There are three types of software: system software, application software, and end-user software, each with unique functions. Selection of appropriate software and programming languages requires an understanding of the organization's information needs and the capabilities of specific software products.

Chapter 8 describes how information can be organized in files and databases. Without appropriate file management techniques, organizations cannot properly access and utilize the information in their computer systems. Organizing information in databases and making effective use of database management systems can solve traditional file management problems. The chapter describes the components of a database management system and the three principal database models. Managing data as a resource requires organizational discipline as well as the appropriate data management technology.

Chapter 9 illustrates how advances in telecommunications technology have created new opportunities for information systems in organizations. Managers need to understand the components of a telecommunications system, the major types of telecommunications networks, the measurements of transmission capacity, and the costs and benefits of alternative telecommunications technologies, in order to plan for telecommunications systems and use them effectively. Telecommunications applications such as electronic data interchange (EDI), electronic mail, and videoconferencing can provide competitive advantage.

Chapter 10 describes the new information architecture of the 1990s and of the 21st century. This new architecture uses organizationwide networks to distribute computer processing power to the desktop, and it helps organizations achieve new levels of competitiveness and productivity. Implementing the new architecture has many challenges. A principal challenge is making disparate hardware, software, and communications devices work together. The chapter describes different aspects of the connectivity problem and alternative models for achieving connectivity.

Part Two Ending Case Study: *To Downsize or Not to Downsize?* This case shows what happened when several firms switched from mainframe computers to desktop processing using microcomputers and local area networks. The results were mixed. The case draws together many of the themes from this section and asks students to analyze the requirements for successful downsizing.

CHAPTER

6

Computers and Information Processing

Twin Mainframes
Keep Lufthansa Airborne

In the late 1980s, the German airline Deutsche Lufthansa AG found that its data from passenger reservations and check-ins, baggage handling, and flight scheduling was growing at a rate of 50 percent each year. Karlheinz Natt, Lufthansa's head of information technology, had to make sure that the firm's computer system could handle this torrent of data while maintaining and even improving upon a near-perfect reliability record of 99.9%.

Natt knew that the firm's 1100 series mainframe computers from the Unisys Corporation would soon not have enough computing capacity to deal with this problem. Moreover, a single mainframe computer alone could not process the huge volume of transactions Lufthansa anticipated. Natt decided to upgrade to more powerful mainframes and to cluster two mainframes so that both would process transactions from the same application together.

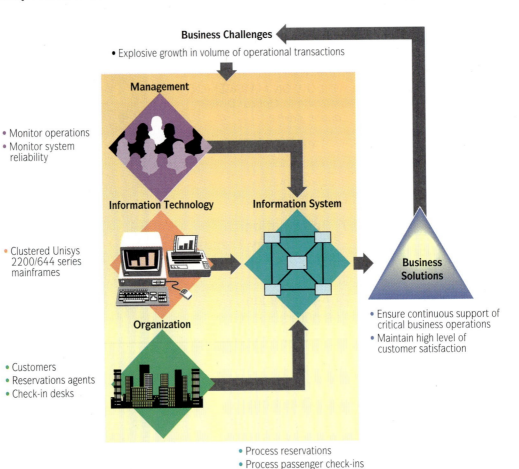

Business Challenges
- Explosive growth in volume of operational transactions

Management
- Monitor operations
- Monitor system reliability

Information Technology
- Clustered Unisys 2200/644 series mainframes

Information System

Business Solutions
- Ensure continuous support of critical business operations
- Maintain high level of customer satisfaction

Organization
- Customers
- Reservations agents
- Check-in desks

- Process reservations
- Process passenger check-ins
- Process baggage records
- Schedule flights

In February 1992, Lufthansa switched to two Unisys 2200/644 series mainframes. With four internal central processing units (CPUs), each of these machines has nearly twice the processing power of Lufthansa's old 1100 series mainframes. Using special software, the two machines are clustered together so that they function like a single powerful mainframe. The system is set up so that airline reservations or other transactions are processed alternately by each main processor.

Although Lufthansa had to modify some of its procedures and software to work with the new mainframe computers, the effort paid off. Natt claims the twin mainframes have saved money because they have the capacity to process all of Lufthansa's transactions without being overloaded. This decreases the chances for computer outage, which can be devastating in the airline business if people can't make reservations or get the seats they want at the check-in desk. Although the clustered mainframes have enough processing power to handle Lufthansa's anticipated transaction load for the next few years, Natt is already looking ahead to make sure Lufthansa's business operations won't be limited by the machine limits of its computers.

Source: Frederick V. Guterl, ''Twin Mainframes Power Lufthansa's Reservations,'' *Datamation*, October 1, 1992.

By using linked mainframe computers, Lufthansa made sure it had the right amount of computing power to drive its business operations. To implement this plan, Lufthansa's management had to understand how much computer processing capacity was required by its business and the performance criteria of various types of computers. It had to know why mainframes were more appropriate for these tasks instead of minicomputers, microcomputers or supercomputers, and it had to understand how the computer itself worked with related storage, input/output, and telecommunications technologies.

In this chapter we describe the typical hardware configuration of a computer system, explaining how a computer works and how to measure computer storage capacity and processing power. We then compare the capabilities of various types of computers and related input, output, and storage devices.

After completing this chapter you will be able to:

- Identify the hardware components in a typical computer system.
- Describe how information is represented and processed in a computer system.
- Describe the functions of the CPU and primary storage.
- Distinguish between generations of computer hardware.

- Contrast the capabilities of mainframes, minicomputers, supercomputers, microcomputers and workstations.
- Describe the various media for storing data and programs in a computer system.
- Compare the major input and output devices.
- Describe multimedia and future information technology trends.

6.1 What Is a Computer System?

In order to understand how computers process data into information, you need to understand the components of a computer system and how computers work. No matter what their size, computers represent and process data in much the same way.

System Configuration

A contemporary computer system consists of a central processor and four other hardware devices: secondary storage, input devices, output devices, and communications devices (see Figure 6.1). The central processor contains components that manipulate raw data into a more useful form and control the other parts of the computer system. Secondary storage devices (magnetic and optical disks,

Figure 6.1
Hardware components of a computer system. A contemporary computer system can be categorized into five major components. The central processor manipulates data and controls the other parts of the computer system; secondary storage feeds data and instructions into the central processor and stores data for future use; input devices convert data and instructions for processing in the computer; output devices present data in a form that people can understand; and communications devices control the passing of information between the central processor, input and output devices, and end-users.

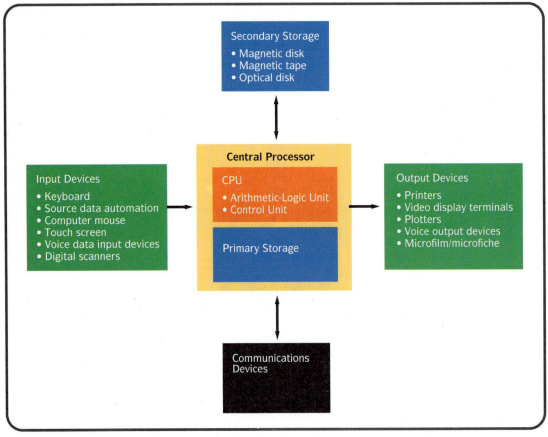

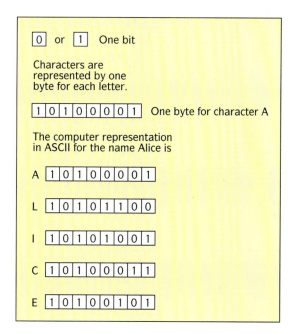

Figure 6.2
Bits and Bytes. Bits are represented by either a 0 or 1. A string of 8 bits constitutes a byte, which represents a character. The computer's representation for the word "ALICE" is a series of five bytes, where each byte represents one character (or letter) in the name.

tape) feed data and programs into the central processor and store them for later use. Input devices, such as keyboards, digital scanners, or the computer "mouse," convert data and instructions into electronic form for input into the computer. Output devices, such as printers and video display terminals, convert electronic data produced by the computer system and display it in a form that people can understand. Communications devices help control communication between the central processor, input and output devices, and end users.

Bits and Bytes: How Computers Represent Data

Bit: A binary digit representing the smallest unit of data in a computer system. It can only have one of two states, representing 0 or 1.

Byte: A string of bits, usually eight, used to represent one number or character stored in a computer system.

In order for information to flow through a computer system and be in a form suitable for processing, all symbols, pictures, or words must be reduced to a string of binary digits. A binary digit is called a **bit** and represents either a zero or a one. In the computer, the presence of an electronic or magnetic symbol means *one* and its absence signifies *zero*. Digital computers operate directly with binary digits, either singly or strung together to form bytes. A string of eight bits is called a **byte**. Each byte can be used to represent a decimal number, a symbol, or part of a picture (see Figure 6.2).

Figure 6.3 shows how decimal numbers are represented using *true binary digits*. Each position in a decimal number has a certain value. Any number in the decimal system (base 10) can be reduced to a binary number. The binary number system (base 2) can express any number as a power of the number 2. The table at the bottom of the figure shows how the translation from binary to decimal

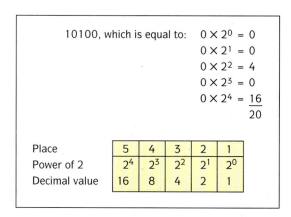

Figure 6.3
True binary digits. Each decimal number has a certain value that can be expressed as a binary number. The binary number system can express any number as a power of the number 2.

works. By using a binary number system a computer can express all numbers as groups of zeroes and ones. True binary cannot be used by a computer because, in addition to representing numbers, a computer must represent alphabetic characters and many other symbols used in natural language, like $ and &. This requirement led manufacturers of computer hardware to develop standard *binary codes*.

There are two common codes: EBCDIC and ASCII, which are illustrated in Table 6.1. The first is the **Extended Binary Coded Decimal Interchange Code** (**EBCDIC**—pronounced ib-si-dick). This binary code, developed by IBM in the 1950s, represents every number, alphabetic character, or special character with 8 bits. EBCDIC can be used to code up to 256 different characters in one byte (2 to the eighth power equals 256).

ASCII, which stands for the **American Standard Code for Information Interchange**, was developed by the American National Standards Institute (ANSI) to provide a standard code that could be used by many different manufacturers in order to make machinery compatible. ASCII was originally designed as a 7-bit code, but most computers use 8-bit versions of ASCII. EBCDIC is used in IBM and other mainframe computers, whereas ASCII is used in data transmission, microcomputers, and some larger computers.

In actual use, EBCDIC and ASCII also contain an extra ninth **parity** or check bit. Bits can be accidentally or mistakenly changed from on to off, when data are transferred from one hardware device to another or during environmental dis-

EBCDIC: Extended Binary Coded Decimal Interchange Code. Binary code representing every number, alphabetic character, or special character with 8 bits, used primarily in IBM and other mainframe computers.

ASCII: American Standard Code for Information Interchange. A 7- or 8-bit binary code used in data transmission, microcomputers, and some large computers.

Parity: An extra bit built into the EBCDIC and ASCII codes used as a check bit to ensure accuracy.

Table 6.1 EBCDIC and ASCII Codes

Character	EBCDIC Binary	Character	ASCII-8-Binary
A	1100 0001	A	1010 0001
B	1100 0010	B	1010 0010
C	1100 0011	C	1010 0011
D	1100 0100	D	1010 0100
E	1100 0101	E	1010 0101
F	1100 0110	F	1010 0110
G	1100 0111	G	1010 0111
H	1100 1000	H	1010 1000
I	1100 1001	I	1010 1001
J	1101 0001	J	1010 1010
K	1101 0010	K	1010 1011
L	1101 0011	L	1010 1100
M	1101 0100	M	1010 1101
N	1101 0101	N	1010 1110
O	1101 0110	O	1010 1111
P	1101 0111	P	1011 0000
Q	1101 1000	Q	1011 0001
R	1101 1001	R	1011 0010
S	1110 0010	S	1011 0011
T	1110 0011	T	1011 0100
U	1110 0100	U	1011 0101
V	1110 0101	V	1011 0110
W	1110 0110	W	1011 0111
X	1110 0111	X	1011 1000
Y	1110 1000	Y	1011 1001
Z	1110 1001	Z	1011 1010
0	1111 0000	0	0101 0000
1	1111 0001	1	0101 0001
2	1111 0010	2	0101 0010
3	1111 0011	3	0101 0011
4	1111 0100	4	0101 0100
5	1111 0101	5	0101 0101
6	1111 0110	6	0101 0110
7	1111 0111	7	0101 0111
8	1111 1000	8	0101 1000
9	1111 1001	9	0101 1001

Table 6.2   SIZE AND TIME IN THE COMPUTER WORLD

Time		
Second	1	Time required to find a single record on a tape
Millisecond	1/1000 second	Time needed to find a single name on a disk, 1—2 milliseconds
Microsecond	1/1,000,000 second	IBM microcomputer instruction speed, .1 microseconds per instruction
Nanosecond	1/1,000,000,000 second	Mainframe instruction speed, one instruction each 15 nanoseconds
Picosecond	1/1,000,000,000,000 second	Speed of experimental devices
Size		
Byte	String of 8 bits	1 character or number
Kilobyte	1000 bytes*	Microcomputer primary memory, 640 kilobytes
Megabyte	1,000,000 bytes	Microcomputer hard disk storage 80 megabytes; mainframe primary memory 100+ megabytes
Gigabyte	1,000,000,000 bytes	External storage disk and tape
Terabyte	1,000,000,000,000 bytes	Social security programs and records

*Actually 1024 storage positions

turbances. Parity bits are used to assist in detecting these errors. Computers are built as either *even parity* or *odd parity*. Assuming an even-parity machine, the computer expects the number of bits turned on in a byte always to be even. (If the machine were designed as an odd-parity machine, the number of bits turned on would always be odd). When the number of bits in a byte is even, the parity bit is turned off. If the number of bits in an even-parity machine in a byte is odd, the parity bit is turned on to make the total number of "on" bits even. All computer hardware contains automatic parity checking to ensure the stability of data over time.

How can a computer represent a picture? The computer stores a picture by creating a grid overlay of the picture. In this grid or matrix, the computer measures the light or color in each box or cell, called a **pixel** (picture element). The computer then stores this information on each pixel. A standard high-resolution computer terminal has a 640 × 480 VGA standard grid, creating more than 300,000 pixels. Whether pictures or text are stored, it is through this process of reduction that a modern computer is able to operate in a complex environment.

Pixel: The smallest unit of data for defining an image in the computer. The computer reduces a picture to a grid of pixels. The term *pixel* comes from *picture element*.

Time and Size in the Computer World

Table 6.2 presents some key levels of time and size that are useful in describing the speed and capacity of modern computer systems.

PROCESSING SPEED

Millisecond: One thousandth of a second.

Modern secondary storage devices generally operate at the speeds of **milliseconds** (thousandths of a second). For instance, a typical microcomputer could find your student record on a magnetic disk in about 15 milliseconds. It would take several seconds to find your name on a much slower tape system. (The

Microsecond: One millionth of a second.

Nanosecond: One billionth of a second.

reasons for this difference are discussed later in this chapter.) A middle-range microcomputer can execute approximately 10 million program instructions per second, or .1 **microseconds** per instruction. The central processing unit in contemporary mainframe computers can execute over 200 million instructions per second (200 MIPS). At this speed, the central processor is operating at speeds of **nanoseconds** (billionths of a second), or one instruction for every 15 nanoseconds.

STORAGE/MEMORY SIZE

Kilobyte: One thousand bytes (actually 1024 storage positions.) Used as a measure of microcomputer storage capacity.

Megabyte: Approximately one million bytes. Unit of computer storage capacity.

Gigabyte: Approximately one billion bytes. Unit of computer storage capacity.

Size, like speed, is an important consideration in a system. Information is stored in a computer in the form of 0s and 1s (binary digits, or bits), which are strung together to form bytes. One byte can be used to store one character, like the letter *A*. A thousand bytes (actually 1024 storage positions) are called a **kilobyte**. Small microcomputers have internal primary memories with over 600 kilobytes. A large microcomputer today can store up to 32 megabytes of information in primary memory. Each **megabyte** is approximately one million bytes. This means, theoretically, that the machine can store up to 32 million alphabetic letters or numbers. Modern secondary storage devices, such as hard disk drives in a microcomputer or disk packs in a large mainframe, store millions of bytes of information. A microcomputer may have a 80-megabyte disk, whereas a large mainframe may have many disk drives, each capable of holding 8 gigabytes. A **gigabyte** is approximately one billion bytes. Some large organizations, like the Social Security Administration or the Internal Revenue Service, have a total storage capacity adding up all their disk drive capacities measured in trillions of bytes. And if all of their records were added together, including those stored on punched cards, paper records, and tapes, the total would be at the terabyte (thousands of billions of bytes) level of information storage.

PROBLEMS OF COORDINATION IN COMPUTER HARDWARE

The vast differences in the size and speed of the major elements of computer systems introduce problems of coordination. For instance, while central processing units operate at the level of microseconds, and in some cases nanoseconds, ordinary printers operate at the level of only a few hundred to a few thousand characters per second. This means that the central processing unit can process information far faster than a printer can print it out. For this reason, additional memory and storage devices must be placed between the central processing unit and the printer so that the central processing unit is not needlessly held back from processing more information as it waits for the printer to print it out.

One of the functions of communication devices and various kinds of storage areas in the system is to stage the flow of information into and out of the machine in such a way as to maximize the utilization of the central processing unit. A major development of the last thirty years in information systems has been the creation of operating systems software (see Chapter 7) and other buffering and storage devices, all of which combine to enhance the total utilization of the central processing unit.

6.2 The CPU and Primary Storage

Central processing unit (CPU): Area of the computer system that manipulates symbols, numbers, and letters and controls the other parts of the computer system.

The **central processing unit** (CPU) is part of the central processor and is the area of the computer system where the manipulation of symbols, numbers, and letters occurs. It also controls the other parts of the computer system. The CPU consists of a control unit and an arithmetic-logic unit (see Figure 6.4). Closely connected to the CPU in the central processor is **primary storage** (sometimes called primary memory or main memory), where data and program instructions are stored temporarily during processing. The characteristics of the CPU are very important in determining the speed and capabilities of a computer.

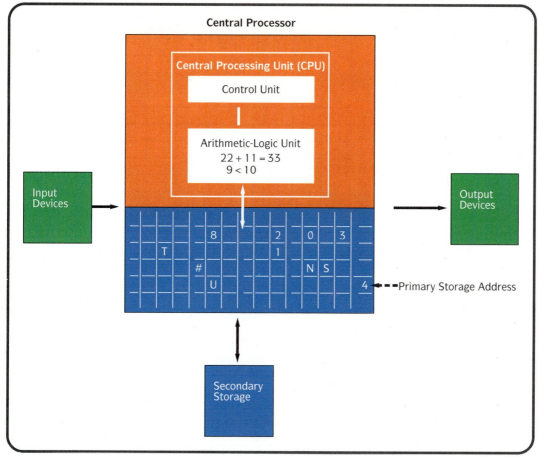

Figure 6.4
The CPU and primary storage. The CPU retrieves data and instructions from primary storage during processing. Primary storage, often called "main memory" or "random access memory," is temporary or volatile storage. Instructions and data are lost from main memory when the computer is turned off. The instructions and data are stored in specific addresses that the CPU can access during processing.

Primary Storage

Primary storage: Part of the computer that temporarily stores program instructions and data being used by the instructions for use by the CPU.

Primary storage has three functions. It stores all or part of the program that is being executed. Primary storage also stores the operating system programs that manage the operation of the computer. (These programs are discussed in Chapter 7.) Finally, the primary storage area holds data that are being used by the program. Data and programs are placed in primary storage before processing, between processing steps, and after processing has ended, prior to being returned to secondary storage or released as output.

How is it possible for an electronic device like primary storage to actually store information? How is it possible to retrieve this information from a known location in memory? Figure 6.5 illustrates primary storage in an electronic digital computer. Internal primary storage is often called **RAM**, or **random access memory.** It is called RAM because it can directly access any randomly chosen location in the same amount of time. The advantage of electronic information storage is the ability to store information in a precise known location in memory and to retrieve it from that same location.

RAM: Random access memory. Primary storage of data or program instructions that can directly access any randomly chosen location in the same amount of time.

Figure 6.5 shows that primary memory is divided into memory cells. Each cell contains a set of eight binary switches or devices, each of which can store one bit of information. The set of eight bits found in each memory cell is sufficient to store one byte, using either EBCDIC or ASCII. Therefore, in each memory cell, we could store one letter, one digit, or one special symbol (such as $). Each memory cell has an individual address indicating where it is located in RAM.

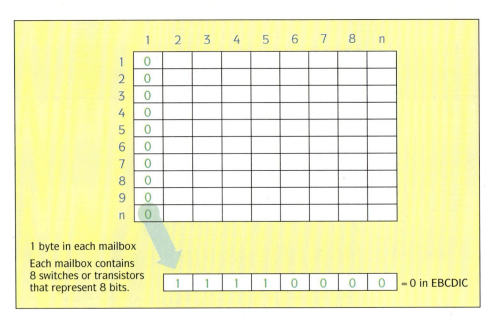

Figure 6.5
Primary storage in the computer. Primary storage can be visualized as a matrix. Each cell represents a mailbox with a unique address. In this example, mailbox [n,1] contains an 8-bit byte representing the number 0 (as coded in EBCDIC.) Each mailbox can store one byte of data or instructions.

1 byte in each mailbox

Each mailbox contains 8 switches or transistors that represent 8 bits.

| 1 | 1 | 1 | 1 | 0 | 0 | 0 | 0 | = 0 in EBCDIC |

The computer can remember where all of the data bytes are stored simply by keeping track of their addresses. Each memory location in primary storage has a specific address—similar to a mailbox. Within this mailbox, one byte of information is stored.

Most of the information used by a computer application is stored on secondary storage devices such as disks and tapes, located outside of the primary storage area. In order for the computer to do work on information, information must be transferred into primary memory for processing. Therefore, data are continually being read into and written out of the primary storage area during the execution of a program.

Types of Semiconductor Memory

Semiconductor: An integrated circuit made by printing thousands and even millions of tiny transistors on a small silicon chip.

ROM: Read-only memory. Semiconductor memory chips that contain program instructions. These chips can only be read from; they cannot be written to.

PROM: Programmable read-only memory. Subclass of ROM chip used in control devices because it can be programmed once.

EPROM: Erasable programmable read-only memory. Subclass of ROM chip that can be erased and reprogrammed many times.

Primary storage is actually composed of **semiconductors.** A semiconductor is an integrated circuit made by printing thousands and even millions of tiny transistors on a small silicon chip. There are several different kinds of semiconductor memory used in primary storage. RAM, or random access memory, is used for short-term storage of data or program instructions. RAM is volatile: Its contents will be lost when the computer's electric supply is disrupted by a power outage or when the computer is turned off. **ROM,** or **read-only memory,** can only be read from; it cannot be written to. ROM chips come from the manufacturer with programs already "burned in" or stored. ROM is used in general-purpose computers to store important or frequently used programs (such as computing routines for calculating the square roots of numbers). Other uses for ROM chips are the storage of manufacturer-specific microcodes such as the Basic Input Output System (BIOS) chip used on an IBM Personal System/2 microcomputer, which controls the handling of data within the machine.

There are two other subclasses of ROM chips: **PROM,** or **programmable read-only memory,** and **EPROM,** or **erasable programmable read-only memory.** PROM chips are used by manufacturers as control devices in their products. They can be programmed once. In this way, manufacturers avoid the expense of having a specialized chip manufactured for the control of small motors, for instance; instead, they can program into a PROM chip the specific program for their product. PROM chips, therefore, can be made universally for many manufacturers in large production runs. EPROM chips are used for device control, such as in robots, where the program may have to be changed on a routine basis. With EPROM chips, the program can be erased and reprogrammed.

Arithmetic-Logic Unit

Arithmetic-logic unit (ALU): Component of the CPU that performs the principal logical and arithmetic operations of the computer.

The **arithmetic-logic unit (ALU)** performs the principal logical and arithmetic operations of the computer. The ALU need only add and subtract numbers in order to do multiplication and division, as well as addition and subtraction. Multiplication is simply rapid addition, and division is rapid subtraction. In addition to performing these arithmetic functions, an ALU must be able to determine when one quantity is greater or less than another and when two quantities are equal. The ALU can perform logical operations on the binary codes for letters as well as numbers.

Control Unit

Control unit: Component of the CPU that controls and coordinates the other parts of the computer system.

Machine cycle: Series of operations required to process a single machine instruction.

The **control unit** coordinates and controls the other parts of the computer system. It reads a stored program, one instruction at a time, and directs other components of the computer system to perform the tasks required by the program. The series of operations required to process a single machine instruction is called the **machine cycle**. As illustrated in Figure 6.6, the machine cycle has two parts: an instruction cycle and an execution cycle.

During the instruction cycle, the control unit retrieves one program instruction from primary storage, and decodes it. It places the part of the instruction telling the ALU what to do next in a special instruction register and places the part specifying the address of the data to be used in the operation into an address register. (A register is a special temporary storage location in the ALU or control unit that acts like a high-speed staging area for program instructions or data being transferred from primary storage to the CPU for processing.)

Figure 6.6
The various steps in the machine cycle. The machine cycle has two main stages of operation: the instruction cycle (I-cycle) and the execution cycle (E-cycle.) There are several steps within each cycle required to process a single machine instruction in the CPU.

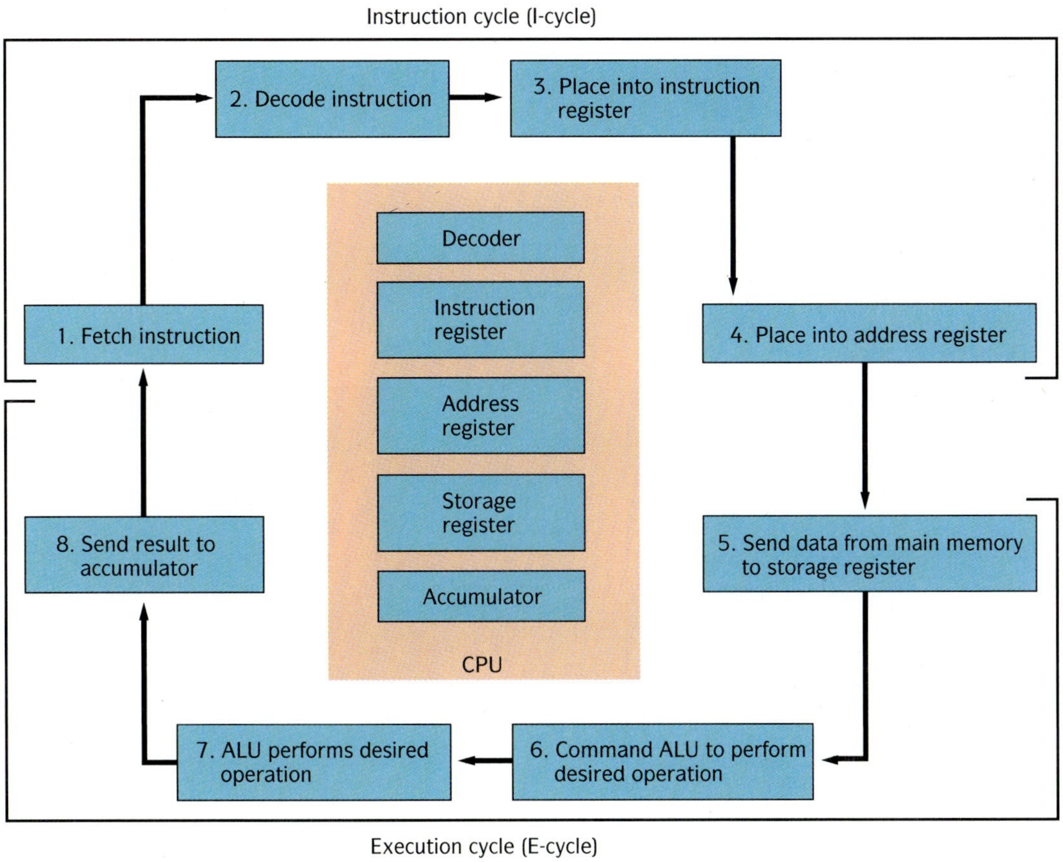

Instruction cycle (I-cycle)

2. Decode instruction

3. Place into instruction register

Decoder

Instruction register

Address register

Storage register

Accumulator

CPU

1. Fetch instruction

4. Place into address register

8. Send result to accumulator

5. Send data from main memory to storage register

7. ALU performs desired operation

6. Command ALU to perform desired operation

Execution cycle (E-cycle)

During the execution cycle, the control unit locates the required data in primary storage, places it in a storage register, instructs the ALU to perform the desired operation, temporarily stores the result of the operation in an accumulator, and finally places the result in primary memory. As the execution of each instruction is completed, the control unit advances to and reads the next instruction of the program.

6.3 The Evolution of Computer Hardware

Computer generations: Majo transitions in computer hardware; each generation is distinguished by a different technology for the components that do the processing.

There have been four major stages, or **computer generations,** in the evolution of computer hardware, each distinguished by a different technology for the components that do the computer's processing work. Each generation has dramatically expanded computer processing power and storage capabilities while simultaneously lowering costs (see Figure 6.7). For instance, the cost of performing 100,000 calculations plunged from several dollars in the 1950s to less than $0.025 in the 1980s. These generational changes in computer hardware have been accompanied by generational changes in computer software (see Chapter 7) that have made computers increasingly more powerful, inexpensive, and easy to use.

Generations of Computer Hardware

The first and second generations of computer hardware were based on vacuum tube and transistor technology, whereas the third and fourth generations were based on semiconductor technology.

FIRST GENERATION: VACUUM TUBE TECHNOLOGY, 1946–1956

The first generation of computers relied on vacuum tubes to store and process information. These tubes consumed a great deal of power, were short-lived, and generated a great deal of heat. Colossal in size, first-generation computers had extremely limited memory and processing capability and were used for very limited scientific and engineering work. The maximum main memory size was approximately 2000 bytes (2 kilobytes), with a speed of 10 kiloinstructions per

Figure 6.7
Increasing performance and falling prices of computers. MIPS: millions of instructions per second.
Adapted from "More Power for Less Money," The New York Times, *September 12, 1988.*
Copyright © 1988 by the New York Times Company. Reprinted by permission.

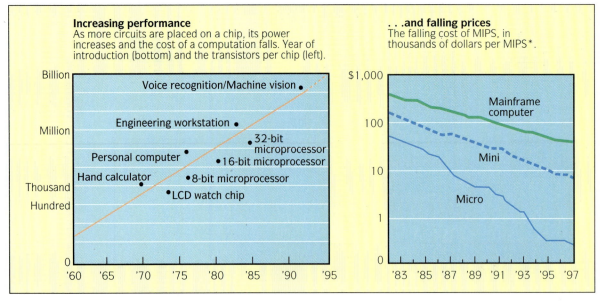

second. Rotating magnetic drums were used for internal storage and punched cards for external storage. Jobs such as running programs or printing output had to be coordinated manually.

SECOND GENERATION: TRANSISTORS, 1957–1963

In the second computer generation, transistors replaced vacuum tubes as the devices for storing and processing information. Transistors were much more stable and reliable than vacuum tubes, they generated less heat, and they consumed less power. However, each transistor had to be individually made and wired into a printed circuit board, a slow tedious process. Magnetic core memory was the primary storage technology of this period. It was composed of small magnetic doughnuts (about 1 mm. in diameter), which could be polarized in one of two directions to represent a bit of data. Wires were strung along and through these cores to both write and read data. This system had to be assembled by hand and therefore was very expensive. Second-generation computers had up to 32 kilobytes of RAM memory and speeds reaching 200,000 to 300,000 instructions per second. The enhanced processing power and memory of second-generation computers enabled them to be used more widely for scientific work and for such business tasks as automating payroll and billing.

THIRD GENERATION: INTEGRATED CIRCUITS, 1964–1979

Third-generation computers relied on integrated circuits, which were made by printing hundreds and later thousands of tiny transistors on small silicon chips. These devices were called semiconductors. Computer memories expanded to 2 megabytes of RAM memory, and speeds accelerated to 5 MIPS. This boost to processing power made it possible to develop special software called operating systems (see Chapter 7) that automated the running of programs and communications between the CPU, printers, and other devices. Third-generation computer technology introduced software that could be used by people without extensive technical training, making it possible for computers to enlarge their role in business.

FOURTH GENERATION: VERY LARGE-SCALE INTEGRATED CIRCUITS, 1980–PRESENT

The fourth generation extends from 1980 to the present. Computers in this period use very large-scale integrated circuits (VLSIC), which are packed with as many as 200,000 to over 3 million circuits per chip. Costs have fallen to the point where desktop computers are inexpensive and widely available for use in business and everyday life. The power of a computer that once took up a large room can now reside on a small desktop. Computer memory sizes have mushroomed to over one gigabyte in large commercial machines; processing speeds have exceeded 200 MIPS. In Section 6.7, we discuss the next generation of hardware trends.

VLSIC technology has fueled a growing movement toward microminiaturization—the proliferation of computers that are so small, fast, and cheap that they have become ubiquitous. For instance, many of the "intelligent" features that have made automobiles, stereos, toys, watches, cameras, and other equipment easier to use are based on microprocessors.

What Is a Microprocessor? What Is a Chip?

Microprocessor: Very large-scale integrated circuit technology that integrates the computer's memory, logic, and control on a single chip.

Very large-scale integrated circuit technology, with hundreds of thousands (or even millions) of transistors on a single chip (see Figure 6.8), integrates the computer's memory, logic, and control on a single chip; hence the name **microprocessor,** or computer on a chip. A powerful microprocessor now widely used in personal computers is the 32-bit-50-megahertz chip such as the Intel 80486.

Some popular chips are shown in Table 6.3. Chips are measured in several ways. You will often see chips labeled as 8-bit, 16-bit, or 32-bit devices. These

Figure 6.8
The latest in microprocessor technology. The Intel Corporation's 80486 microprocessor provides the computing power of a large mainframe of the mid-1980s. *Courtesy of Intel Corporation.*

Table 6.3   COMMON MICROPROCESSORS

Microprocessor Chip	Manufacturer	Word Length	Data Bus Width	Clock Speed (MHz)	Microcomputers Used in
8088	Intel	16	8	4.4–8	IBM PC and XT COMPAQ Portable
80286	Intel	16	16	8–28	IBM AT AT&T PC 6300 Plus
80386	Intel	32	32	16–40	IBM Personal System/2 COMPAQ 386
68020	Motorola	32	32	12.5–32	Macintosh II Macintosh SE
68030	Motorola	32	32	16–40	Macintosh IIx, IIcx
80486	Intel	32	32	25–66	Microcomputers and workstations
68040	Motorola	32	32	25	Mac Quadras
Pentium	Intel	32	64	60–100	High end workstations

Word length: The number of bits that can be processed at one time by a computer. The larger the word length, the greater the speed of the computer.

Megahertz: A measure of cycle speed, or the pacing of events in a computer; one megahertz equals one million cycles per second.

Data bus width: The number of bits that can be moved at one time between the CPU, primary storage, and the other devices of a computer.

Reduced instruction set computing (RISC): Technology used to enhance the speed of microprocessors by embedding only the most frequently used instructions on a chip.

labels refer to the **word length,** or the number of bits that can be processed at one time by the machine. An 8-bit chip can process 8 bits or 1 byte of information in a single machine cycle. A 32-bit chip can process 32 bits or 4 bytes in a single cycle. The larger the word length, the greater the speed of the computer.

A second factor affecting chip speed is cycle speed. Every event in a computer must be sequenced so that one step logically follows another. The control unit sets a beat to the chip. This beat is established by an internal clock and is measured in **megahertz** (abbreviated MHz, which stands for millions of cycles per second). The Intel 8088 chip, for instance, originally had a clock speed of 4.47 megahertz, whereas the Intel 80386 chip has a clock speed that ranges from 16 to 40 megahertz.

A third factor affecting speed is the **data bus width.** The data bus acts as a highway between the CPU, primary storage and other devices, determining how much data can be moved at one time. The 8088 chip used in the original IBM Personal Computer, for example, had a 16-bit word length but only an 8-bit data bus width. This meant that data were processed within the CPU chip itself in 16-bit chunks, but could only be moved 8 bits at a time between the CPU primary storage and external devices. On the other hand, the 80386 chip, used in IBM Personal System/2 machines, and the Motorola 68030 and 68040 chips used in Macintosh microcomputers, have both a 32-bit word length and a 32-bit data bus width. Obviously, in order to get a computer to execute more instructions per second and work through programs or handle users expeditiously, it is necessary to increase the word length of the processor, the data bus width, or the cycle speed—or all three. The Window on Technology on page 177 explores another way to make microprocessors more powerful, called **reduced instruction set computing (RISC).**

6.4 Mainframes, Minicomputers, Microcomputers, Workstations, and Supercomputers

Computers represent and process data the same way, but there are different classifications. We can use size and processing speed to categorize contemporary computers as mainframes, minicomputers, workstations, microcomputers, and supercomputers.

Mainframes, Minis, and Micros

Mainframe: Largest category of computer, classified as having 50 megabytes to over 1 gigabyte of RAM.

Minicomputer: Middle-range computer with about 10 to 650 megabytes of RAM.

Microcomputer: Desktop or portable computer with 640 kilobytes to 64 megabytes of RAM.

Workstation: Desktop computer with powerful graphics and mathematical capabilities and the ability to perform several tasks at once.

Supercomputer: Very sophisticated and powerful computer that can perform very complex computations extremely rapidly.

A **mainframe** is the largest computer, a powerhouse with massive memory and extremely rapid processing power. It is used for very large commercial, scientific, or military applications where a computer must handle massive amounts of data or many complicated processes. A **minicomputer** is a middle-range computer, about the size of an office desk, often used in universities, factories, or research laboratories. A **microcomputer** is one that can be placed on a desktop or carried from room to room. Microcomputers are used as personal machines as well as in business. A **workstation** also fits on a desktop but has more powerful mathematical and graphics processing capability than a microcomputer, and can perform more complicated tasks at the same time than can a microcomputer. Workstations are used for scientific, engineering, and design work that requires powerful graphics or computational capabilities. A **supercomputer** is a highly sophisticated and powerful machine that is used for tasks requiring extremely rapid and complex calculations with hundreds of thousands of variable factors. Supercomputers have traditionally been used in scientific and military work, but they are starting to be used in business as well. Representative computers in each category are listed in Table 6.4.

The problem with this classification scheme is that the capacity of the machines changes so rapidly. A microcomputer today has the computing power of a mainframe from the 1980s or the minicomputer of a few years ago. This is

Table 6.4   REPRESENTATIVE COMPUTERS

Type of Computer	Example	Memory (Megabytes)	Performance	Word Length (Bits)	Cost
Mainframe	IBM Enterprise System 9000	1000 (1 gigabyte)	240 MIPS	32	$23,000,000
Minicomputer	DEC VAX 7000 Model 600	64–2.35 gigabytes	124–508 transactions per second	32	$160,000–$650,000
Workstation	Sun SPARCstation 10 Model 330	32–512	109.5 MIPS	32	$25,000
Microcomputer	Compaq Prolinea Model 4633	4–32	10.8 MIPS	32	$1600
Supercomputer	Cray C90	256 megabytes–8 gigabytes	1–16 gigaflops	64	$3,000,000–$35,000,000

Note: Different computer manufacturers use different measures of computer performance. Many use MIPS, but some manufacturers prefer to measure performance in terms of transactions per second. Supercomputer performance is measured in flops (number of floating point operations per second).

illustrated in Figure 6.9. Powerful microcomputers have sophisticated graphics and processing capabilities similar to workstations. Microcomputers still cannot perform as many tasks at once as mainframes, minicomputers, or workstations (see the discussion of operating systems in Chapter 7); nor can they be used by as many people simultaneously as these larger machines. Still, even these distinctions will become less pronounced in the future. In another decade, desktop micros might very well have the power and processing speed of today's supercomputers.

Figure 6.9
The soaring power of microcomputer technology. The power of a mainframe computer from the mid 1980s is now available for desktop computing. The illustration shows the successive generations of microcomputers, the representative microprocessor on which each is based, the comparable minicomputer or mainframe computer, and the approximate computing power of each generation.

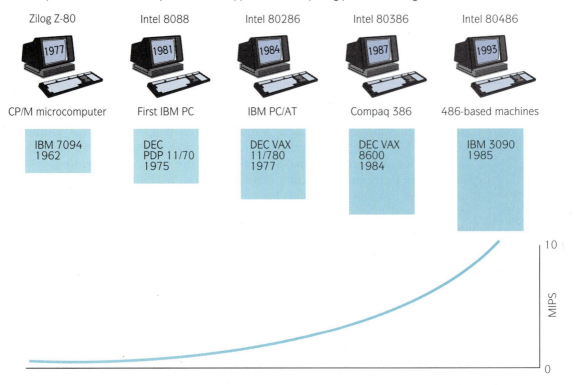

W I N D O W   O N

TECHNOLOGY
The Debate Over RISC

Conventional microprocessors have several hundred or more instructions hard-wired into their circuitry. These internal instructions can simplify software writing because some instructions are already embedded in the chip. On the other hand, these embedded instructions can create processing inefficiencies, taking several machine cycles to execute one instruction. For some applications, the full range of instructions is rarely used. Only 20 percent of these instructions are needed for 80 percent of the computer's tasks. If the little-used instructions are eliminated, the remaining instructions can execute much faster.

Reduced instruction set computing (RISC) chips only have the most frequently used instructions embedded in them. A RISC CPU can execute most of its instructions in one machine cycle, and sometimes multiple instructions at the same time. RISC is most appropriate for scientific and workstation computing where there are repetitive arithmetic and logical operations on data or when there is a need for three-dimensional rendering.

Champions of RISC claim that a computer with RISC technology, less circuitry, and simpler designs can offer the performance of minicomputers costing ten times as much. Indeed, computers and workstations using RISC technology can be incredibly fast. For in-

stance, the Digital Equipment Corporation (DEC) has developed a series of computers code-named Alpha that are powered by one or more 64-bit RISC microprocessors with speeds ranging from 50 to 200 megahertz. At 200 megahertz, the fastest of the line has roughly the same peak performance as a small supercomputer. DEC is betting its business strategy on Alpha by developing 64-bit RISC systems ranging from palmtop computers to high-performance midrange computers and supercomputers. The company hopes these advances will keep the firm competitive in the price/performance race.

Alpha designers have worked with programmers to make switching systems to Alpha RISC computers less risky. Most of the software running on DEC's earlier line of VAX computers will not need to be rewritten to run on Alpha machines, making Alpha machines appealing for business computing as well as for scientific and engineering work. However, many firms may want to make some software changes so that their programs can take advantage of Alpha's additional computing power. DEC and commercial software firms have just started to produce software that is explicitly designed to take advantage of the features of the Alpha chip.

DEC believes that even applications that were designed for its

older 32-bit computers will achieve threefold to fourfold performance gains. DEC claims Alpha should produce a 1000-fold performance improvement, to 4 billion instructions per second over the next 25 years.

Critics believe RISC increases system costs. RISC gains in processing speed may be offset by the difficulties in dropping complex instruction-set computing. Programs written for conventional processors cannot automatically be transferred to RISC machines; new software will be required. Many RISC suppliers are starting to add more instructions to appeal to more customers, and designers of conventional microprocessors are streamlining their chips. Some analysts believe that conventional 32-bit chips will soon be able to execute any instruction in just one cycle.

Sources: Elaine L. Appleton, "What's It All About, Alpha," *Datamation*, May 1, 1992; Hal Glatzer, "RISC Assessment," *Software Magazine*, June 1989; and John Markoff, "Computer Chip Starts Angry Debate," the *New York Times*, September 26, 1989.

To Think About: If you were an information systems manager, what criteria would you use in deciding whether to purchase a RISC computer?

Generally, however, mainframes can be classified as having 50 megabytes to over 1 gigabyte of RAM; minicomputers, 10 to 650 megabytes of RAM; workstations, 8 to 300 megabytes of RAM; and microcomputers, 640 kilobytes to 64 megabytes of RAM. Table 6.4 illustrates the capabilities of representative commercial computers in each of these categories today. Figure 6.10 illustrates some of the capabilities of the Sun SPARCstation, a leading-edge workstation, and of the IBM Personal System/2, a popular microcomputer.

The term *microcomputer* is sometimes used synonymously with personal computer, since micros were originally intended as primarily personal, single-user tools. However, microcomputers have become so powerful that they are no longer confined to personal information systems. Micros can operate either as individual stand-alone machines with isolated processing power or as part of a

Figure 6.10
A SunSPARCstation workstation and an IBM PS/2 microcomputer. The SunSPARCstation workstation (top) is used for sophisticated CAD/CAM applications. The IBM PS/2 (bottom) is a microcomputer capable of powerful applications processing. *Top: Tim Davis PhotoResearchers, Inc. Bottom: Courtesy of IBM.*

Distributed processing: The distribution of computer processing work among multiple computers linked by a communication network.

Centralized processing: Processing that is accomplished by one large central computer.

departmental or companywide network of intelligent devices. They may be linked to other micros, telecommunications devices, workstations, or larger computers.

In either case, microcomputers are starting to do some of the work formerly performed by larger computers in business. Chapter 9 describes how microcomputers can be linked with other micros, printers, "intelligent" copy machines, and telephones to provide processing power and to coordinate the flow of work without relying on mainframes. Micros can also be linked to minicomputers and mainframes, forming companywide information networks that share hardware, software, and data resources. The use of multiple computers linked by a communication network for processing is called **distributed processing.** In contrast with **centralized processing,** in which all processing is accomplished by one large central computer, distributed processing distributes the processing work among various microcomputers, minicomputers, and mainframes linked together.

Downsizing and Cooperative Processing

Downsizing: The process of transferring applications from large computers to smaller ones.

In some firms, microcomputers have actually replaced mainframes and minicomputers. The process of transferring applications from large computers to smaller ones is called **downsizing**. Downsizing has many advantages. The cost per MIPS on a mainframe is almost 100 times greater than on a microcomputer; a megabyte of mainframe memory costs about 10 times more than the same amount of memory on a micro. For some applications, micros may also be easier for nontechnical specialists to use and maintain. The Window on Organizations shows how installing microcomputers can help distribute processing power to organizations with branches in many different locations, even if they are in different parts of the globe. Often microcomputers are networked so that they can share data and communicate with each other. (These issues are explored in detail in Chapters 9 and 10 and in the Part II Section Ending Case.)

Cooperative processing: Type of processing that divides the processing work for transaction-based applications among mainframes and microcomputers.

Another computing pattern divides processing work for transaction-based applications among mainframes and microcomputers. Each type of computer is assigned the functions it performs best, and each shares processing (and perhaps data) over a communications link. For example, the microcomputer might be used for data entry and validation, whereas the mainframe would be responsible for file input and output. This division of labor is called **cooperative processing**. Micros are utilized because they can provide the same processing power much more economically than a mainframe or because they are superior at some tasks, such as providing screen presentations for the user interface. Figure 6.11 illustrates cooperative processing. Cooperative processing is not always easy to implement. It may require special communications and application software and an understanding of which functions are best handled by micros and which should reside with larger machines.

Figure 6.11
Cooperative processing. In cooperative processing, an application is divided into tasks that run on more than one type of computer. This example shows the tasks that a microcomputer is best at performing, the tasks that a mainframe computer is best at performing, and those tasks that each type is able to perform.

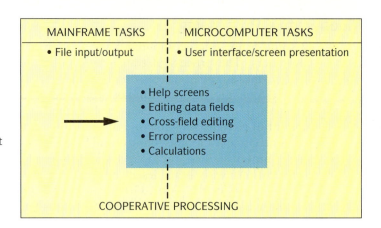

MAINFRAME TASKS	MICROCOMPUTER TASKS
• File input/output	• User interface/screen presentation

• Help screens
• Editing data fields
• Cross-field editing
• Error processing
• Calculations

COOPERATIVE PROCESSING

Microcomputers and Workstations

Since workstations are desktop machines like microcomputers, what distinguishes a microcomputer from a workstation? Workstations have more powerful graphics and mathematical processing capabilities than microcomputers, and can easily perform several tasks at the same time. They are typically used by scientists, engineers, and other knowledge workers, but are spreading to the financial industry because they have the computing power to simultaneously analyze portfolios, process securities trades, and provide financial data and news services (see Chapter 15).

Workstations are especially useful for computer-aided design (CAD) and for complex simulations and modeling. They can represent fully rendered multiple views of a physical object, such as an airplane wing, rotate the object three-dimensionally, and present design history and cost factors. Workstations can easily integrate text and graphics, displaying multiple tools, applications, and types of data simultaneously.

At present, workstations have at least 8 megabytes of RAM, 32-bit microprocessors, and the capability to perform several computing tasks at the same time (see the discussion of multitasking in Chapter 7). They come with high-resolution large-screen color monitors for detailed design work and math co-processors to speed calculations.

The distinctions between workstations and microcomputers are starting to disappear. Powerful high-end microcomputers have many of the same capabilities as low-end workstations. A low-end workstation can be purchased for around $4000–5000. As microcomputers become increasingly graphics oriented, the distinctions between the two types of computers are likely to blur further. Moreover, workstations themselves have increased in power, so that the most sophisticated workstations have some of the capabilities of earlier mainframes and supercomputers.

Supercomputers and Parallel Processing

A supercomputer is an especially sophisticated and powerful type of computer that is used primarily for extremely rapid and complex computations with hundreds or thousands of variable factors. Supercomputers have traditionally been used for classified weapons research, weather forecasting, and petroleum and engineering applications, all of which use complex mathematical models and simulations. Although extremely expensive, supercomputers are beginning to be employed in business. For instance, Northwest and other airlines use supercomputers for scheduling crews and equipment.

Supercomputers can perform complex and massive computations almost instantaneously because they can perform billions and even hundreds of billions of calculations per second—many times faster than the largest mainframes. Super-

Figure 6.12
Sequential and parallel processing. During sequential processing, each task is assigned to one CPU that processes one instruction at a time. In parallel processing, multiple tasks are assigned to multiple processing units to expedite the result.

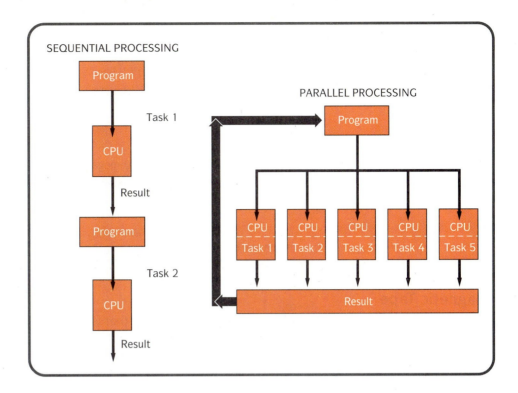

Parallel processing: Type of processing in which more than one instruction can be processed at a time by breaking down a problem into smaller parts and processing them simultaneously with multiple processors.

computers do not process one instruction at a time but instead rely on **parallel processing.** As illustrated in Figure 6.12, multiple processing units (CPUs) break down a problem into smaller parts and work on it simultaneously. Some experimental supercomputers use up to 64,000 processors. Getting a group of processors to attack the same problem at once is easier said than done. It requires rethinking of the problems and special software that can divide problems among different processors in the most efficient possible way, providing the needed data, and reassembling the many subtasks to reach an appropriate solution. Most software currently available is written for sequential processing machines.

6.5 Secondary Storage

In addition to primary storage, where information and programs are stored for immediate processing, modern computer systems use other types of storage in order to accomplish their tasks. Information systems need to store information outside of the computer in a nonvolatile state (not requiring electrical power) and to store volumes of data too large to fit into a computer of any size today (such as a large payroll or the U.S. census). The relatively long-term storage of data outside the CPU and primary storage is called **secondary storage.**

Secondary storage: Relatively long-term, nonvolatile storage of data outside the CPU and primary storage.

Register: Temporary storage location in the ALU or control unit where small amounts of data and instructions reside for thousandths of a second just before use.

Cache: High-speed storage of frequently used instructions and data.

Primary storage is where the fastest, most expensive technology is used. As shown in Table 6.5, there are actually three different kinds of primary memory: register, cache, and RAM. **Register** is the fastest and most expensive memory, where small amounts of data and instructions reside for thousandths of a second just prior to use, followed by **cache** memory (for high-speed storage of frequently used instructions and data) and RAM memory for large amounts of data. Access to information stored in primary memory is electronic and occurs almost at the speed of light. Secondary storage is nonvolatile and retains data even when the computer is turned off. There are many kinds of secondary storage; the most common are magnetic tape, magnetic disk, and optical disk. These media can transfer large bodies of data rapidly to the CPU. But since secondary storage requires mechanical movement to gain access to the data, in contrast to primary storage, it is relatively slow.

Table 6.5   DATA STORAGE DEVICES IN A MICROCOMPUTER

Type of Memory	Total Storage Capacity	Access Time
PRIMARY STORAGE		
Register	1 kilobyte	.01 microseconds
Cache	1 kilobyte	.1 microseconds
RAM	16 megabytes	.5 microseconds
SECONDARY STORAGE		
Hard disk	800 megabytes	15-20 milliseconds
High-density diskette (3.5″)	2.8 megabytes	200 milliseconds
Optical disk	660 megabytes	200–500 milliseconds
Magnetic tape (¼″ streaming tape backup)	40 megabytes	1-2 seconds

Magnetic Tape

Magnetic tape: Inexpensive and relatively stable secondary storage medium in which large volumes of information are stored sequentially by means of magnetized and nonmagnetized spots on tape.

Magnetic tape is an older device that is still important for secondary storage of large volumes of information. It is used primarily in mainframe batch applications and for archiving data. Generally, magnetic tape for large systems comes in 14-inch reels that are up to 2400 feet long and 0.5 inches wide. It is very similar to home cassette recording tape, but of higher quality. Figure 6.13 shows how information appears on magnetic tape using an EBCDIC coding scheme. Each byte of data utilizes one column across the width of the tape. Each column is composed of eight bits plus one check parity bit. Information can be stored on magnetic tape at different densities. Low density is 1600 bytes per inch (bpi), and densities of up to 6250 bpi are common. In addition to commercial-quality tape for large systems, microcomputers and some minicomputers use small tape cassettes, very similar to home audio cassettes, to store information.

The principal advantages of magnetic tape are that it is very inexpensive, that it is relatively stable, and that it can store very large volumes of information. It is a reliable technology because of several self-checking features (such as parity bits), and therefore is an ideal form of backup storage for other more volatile forms of memory. Moreover, magnetic tape can be used over and over again, although it does age with time and computer users must handle it carefully.

Figure 6.13
Magnetic tape storage. Data can be stored on nine-track magnetic tape, which is a stable and inexpensive medium. However, data are stored sequentially and therefore access and retrieval may be slow.

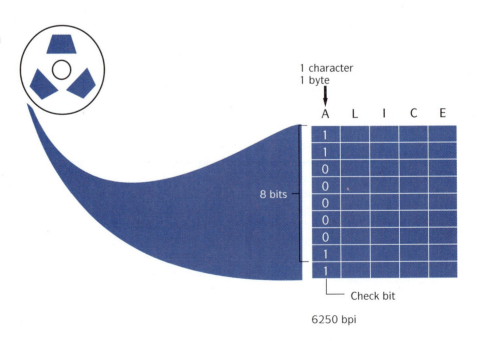

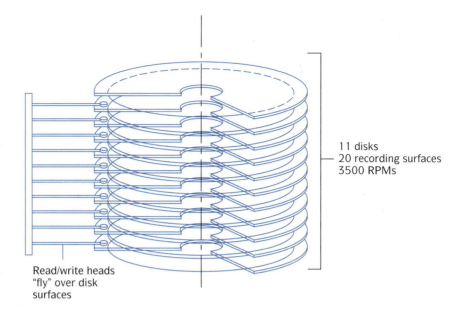

11 disks
20 recording surfaces
3500 RPMs

Read/write heads
"fly" over disk
surfaces

Figure 6.14
Disk pack storage. Large systems often rely on disk packs, which provide reliable storage for large amounts of data with quick access and retrieval. A typical removable disk-pack system contains 11 2-sided disks.

The principal disadvantages of magnetic tape are that it stores data sequentially and is relatively slow compared to the speed of other secondary storage media. In order to find an individual record stored on magnetic tape, such as your professor's employment record, the tape must be read from the beginning up to the location of the desired record. This means that the CPU must read each name from "Abelson" all the way to your professor's name before it can locate your professor's record. Hence, magnetic tape is not a good medium when it is necessary to find information rapidly (such as for an airline reservation system). Tape can also be damaged and is labor-intensive to mount and dismount. The environment in which it is stored must be carefully controlled. Since contemporary information systems call for immediate access to data, tape represents a fading technology, but it continues to exist in changing forms.

Magnetic Disk

Magnetic disk: A secondary storage medium in which data are stored by means of magnetized spots on a hard or floppy disk.

Hard disk: Magnetic disk resembling a thin steel platter with an iron oxide coating; used in large computer systems and in many microcomputers.

Cylinder: Represents circular tracks on the same vertical line within a disk pack.

Track: Concentric circle on the surface area of a disk on which data are stored as magnetized spots; each track can store thousands of bytes.

The most widely used secondary storage medium today is **magnetic disk.** There are two kinds of magnetic disks: floppy disks (used in microcomputers) and hard disks (used in commercial disk drives and microcomputers). **Hard disks** are thin steel platters with an iron oxide coating. In larger systems, multiple hard disks are mounted together on a vertical shaft. Figure 6.14 illustrates a commercial hard disk pack for a large system. It has 11 disks, each with two surfaces, top and bottom. However, although there are 11 disks, no information is recorded on the top or bottom surfaces; thus, there are only 20 recording surfaces on the disk pack. On each surface, data are stored on tracks. The disk pack is generally sealed from the environment and rotates at a speed of about 3500 rpm, creating an air-stream speed of about 50 mph at the disk surface.

Information is recorded on or read from the disk by read/write heads, which literally fly over the spinning disks. Unlike a home stereo, the heads never actually touch the disk (which would destroy the data and cause the system to "crash") but hover a few thousandths of an inch above it. A smoke particle or a human hair is sufficient to crash the head into the disk.

The read/write heads move horizontally (from left to right) to any of 200 positions called **cylinders.** At any one of these cylinders, the read/write heads can read or write information to any of 20 different concentric circles on the disk surface areas (called **tracks**). The cylinder represents the circular tracks on the same vertical line within the disk pack. Read/write heads are directed to a specific record using an address consisting of the cylinder number, the recording surface number, and the data record number.

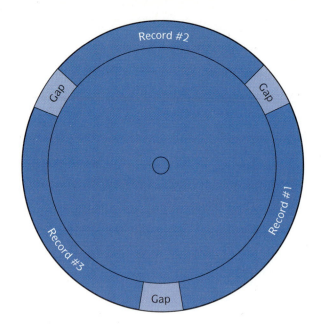

Figure 6.15
How records are stored on a single track of a disk. Each disk surface has 20 different concentric circles or tracks. The disk pack is divided into 200 cylinders, each representing a circular track on the same vertical line in the disk pack. Each track can contain several records.

The speed of access to data on a disk is a function of the rotational speed of the disk and the speed of the access arms. The read/write heads must position themselves, and the disk pack must rotate until the proper information is located. More advanced and expensive disks have access speeds of 1.5–10 milliseconds and capacities of up to 7.5 gigabytes per unit.

Figure 6.15 shows one way records can be stored on a single track of the disk. Each track, of course, contains several records. In general, 20,000 bytes of information can be stored on each track at densities of up to 12,000 bpi. If there are 20 such tracks and 200 cylinders in a disk pack, the total capacity of the illustrated disk pack is 80 megabytes. As noted previously, advanced commercial disks for large systems have much higher storage capacities over 1 billion bytes.

Microcomputers also use hard disks, which can store over 500 megabytes, but 60 to 80 megabytes are the most common size. Microcomputers also use **floppy disks,** which are flat, 5.25-inch or 3.5-inch disks of polyester film with a magnetic coating. These disks have a storage capacity ranging from 360K to 2.8 megabytes and a much slower access rate than hard disks. Floppy disks and cartridges and packs of multiple disks use a **sector** method for storing data. As illustrated in Figure 6.16, the disk surface is divided into pie-shaped pieces, the actual number depending on the disk system used. (Some disks use eight sectors, others nine). In most types of floppy disks, each sector has the same storage capacity (data are recorded more densely on the inner disk tracks). Each sector

Floppy disk: Removable magnetic disk primarily used with microcomputers. The two most common standard sizes are 3.5-inch and 5.25-inch disks that are made up of polyester film with magnetic coating.

Sector: Method of storing data on a floppy disk in which the disk is divided into pie-shaped pieces or sectors. Each sector is assigned a unique number so that data can be located using the sector number.

Figure 6.16
The sector method of storing data. Each track of a disk can be divided into sectors. Disk storage location can be identified by sector and data record number.

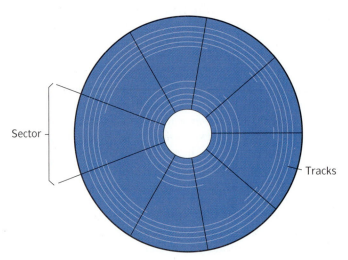

The mainframe computer room at Chrysler Corporation shows the large bank of magnetic tape drives and disk packs necessary to process and store large volumes of data for Chrysler.

is assigned a unique number. Data can be located using an address consisting of the sector number and an individual data record number.

Magnetic disks on both large and small computers have several important advantages over magnetic tape. First, they permit direct access to individual records. Each record can be given a precise physical address in terms of cylinders and tracks, and the read/write head can be directed to go to that address and access the information in about 10 to 60 milliseconds. This means that the computer system does not have to search the entire file, as in a tape file, in order to find one person's record. This creates the possibility for on-line information systems providing an immediate response, such as an airline reservation or customer information system. Disk storage is often referred to as a **direct access storage device (DASD)**.

Direct access storage device (DASD): Refers to magnetic disk technology that permits the CPU to locate a record directly, in contrast to sequential tape storage that must search the entire file.

For on-line systems requiring direct access, disk technology provides the only practical means of storage today. Records can be easily and rapidly retrieved. The cost of disks has steadily declined over the years. Moreover, as we will see in Chapter 8 in the discussion of file organization and databases, disk technology permits interrelationships among records to be built into the storage file itself. This system permits a single transaction to update or change data in a number of different files simultaneously and dramatically speeds the process of finding related records.

DASD is, however, relatively expensive compared to magnetic tape. Moreover, updating information stored on a disk destroys the old information because the old data on the disk is written over if changes are made. (In contrast, changes to data made on magnetic tape are made on a different reel of tape so that the old version of the tape can be retained and recovered.) Therefore, it becomes more difficult to back up and audit the transactions recorded on a disk. You can check this out by changing your seat selection on an airplane and then asking the clerk to tell you where you wished to sit originally. You will find that the system has no record of your previous selection because the information has been wiped off the disk.

In addition, disks can crash. The disk drives themselves are susceptible to environmental disturbances; even smoke particles can disrupt the movement of read/write heads over the disk surface. Therefore, the environment must be relatively pure and stable. That is why disk drives are sealed in a clean room.

Optical Disks

Optical disk: Secondary storage device on which data are recorded and read by laser beams rather than by magnetic means.

Optical disks, also called compact disks or laser optical disks, store data at densities many times greater than those of magnetic disks and are available for both microcomputers and large computers. Data are recorded on optical disks when a laser device burns microscopic pits in the reflective layer of a spiral track.

Binary information is encoded by the length of these pits and the space between them. Optical disks can thus store massive quantities of data, including not only text but also pictures, sound, and full-motion video, in a highly compact form. The optical disk is read by having a low-power laser beam from an optical head scan the disk.

The most common optical disk system used with microcomputers is called **CD-ROM (compact disk read-only memory)**. A 4.75-inch compact disk can store up to 660 megabytes, nearly 300 times more than a high-density floppy disk. Optical disks are most appropriate for applications where enormous quantities of unchanging data must be stored compactly for easy retrieval, or for storing graphic images and sound. CD-ROM becomes an especially attractive storage medium if a minimum of 10 megabytes of data must be stored and distributed to 100 people or more. CD-ROM is also less vulnerable than floppy disks to magnetism, dirt, or rough handling.

CD-ROM is read-only storage. No new data can be written to it; it can only be read. CD-ROM has been most widely used for reference materials with massive amounts of data, such as encyclopedias, directories, or on-line databases. There are now available on CD-ROM hundreds of databases, such as marketing, legal, and demographic databases, and financial databases from Quotron, Dun & Bradstreet, and Dow Jones.

CD-ROM is also becoming popular for image processing (review the description of the United States Automobile Association's imaging system in Chapter 2). For example, the U.S. Immigration and Naturalization Service has started to distribute an alien identification card that is keyed to the cardholder's photo-

CD-ROM: Compact disk read-only memory. Read-only optical disk storage used for imaging, reference, and database applications with massive amounts of data and for multimedia.

Figure 6.17 Using magneto-optical disks to record and read data.

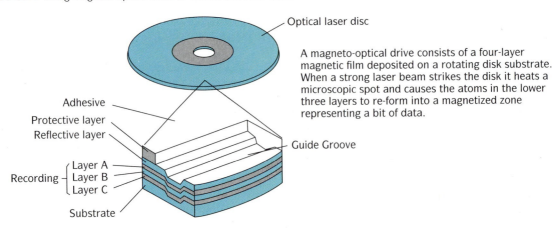

Optical laser disc

A magneto-optical drive consists of a four-layer magnetic film deposited on a rotating disk substrate. When a strong laser beam strikes the disk it heats a microscopic spot and causes the atoms in the lower three layers to re-form into a magnetized zone representing a bit of data.

Adhesive
Protective layer
Reflective layer

Guide Groove

Recording { Layer A
Layer B
Layer C

Substrate

Writing

By switching the laser beam on and off as the disk rotates, it is possible to magnetize microscopic spots in circular tracks. The size of each spot determines whether it is a 1 or 0, the binary form of data. The magnetic film can be written and erased more than 1 million times without a decline in accuracy.

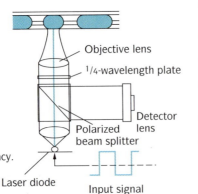

Objective lens
¼-wavelength plate
Detector lens
Polarized beam splitter
Laser diode
Input signal

Reading

To read information, a weak polarized laser scans the magnetized spots on the recording layer. This beam is reflected to a photodetector, which converts variations in spot size into binary data. Recorded areas reflect back more light than unrecorded areas

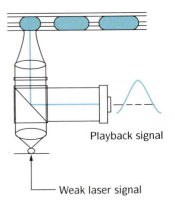

Playback signal

Weak laser signal

Adapted from: Robert Pasternak, "How the Optical Disk Drive Works," The New York Times, November 30, 1988. Copyright © 1988 by The New York Times Company. Reprinted by permission.

MANAGEMENT

Switching to Optical Disks? Caution Advised

For all the advantages of optical disks, organizations need to be careful when changing to optical-disk based systems. Conventional data can be stored optically. But if a firm is installing an imaging application, it will have to cope with people's fear of change, fear of staff reductions, and fear of new technology. Putting information on optical disk where it can be efficiently accessed and used isn't a simple matter of transferring the data.

Processing a digitized document is much more complex than processing conventional computerized data. The bit count is much higher, and one must deal with a myriad of colors, shapes, sizes, and forms. It takes an enormous amount of data to represent a graphic image in digital form. The First National Bank of Chicago found that using imaging for both check processing and commercial documents strained its computer processing resources because the digitized documents contained so much data to process. Its on-line transaction processing capability was overwhelmed when imaging was added.

Some information systems managers are troubled by the prospect of changing optical disk size in future optical disk readers. They don't want to be stuck with optical disks that can't be read by new state-of-the-art optical drives.

Another concern is the format of optical disks. As the size of commercial optical disks grows from 2 Gigabytes to 6.2 Gigabytes and upward, managers have to worry about ensuring that there is some way to back up or recover the vast amount of data housed on this medium if some disaster should occur (see Chapter 18). A way of standardizing the format of images stored on optical disk would be helpful as well.

When offered huge amounts of image storage capacity, users tend to be greedy, filling all available archival space with file cabinets and piles of documents. Many of these are not worth storing. Businesses need to think carefully about what documents are active enough to merit digitizing. If a document is over ten years old, chances are that it will never be used.

Sources: Nell Margolis, "Imaging: It's a Jungle in There," *Computerworld*, July 6, 1992; and Delphi Consulting Group, "The Document in the Year 2000," *InformationWEEK White Paper*, May 18, 1992.

To Think About: If you were a manager and wanted to convert to optical disk storage, what management, organization, and technology factors should you consider?

---

graph, signature, and fingerprint stored on optical disk. The U.S. Department of Defense has initiated a system of networks and optical imaging to reduce the mountains of paper generated by technical design information and administrative data for weapons systems. The Ford Motor Company now sends its North American dealers CD-ROM disks with technical information for servicing Ford cars; it also sends a complete parts catalog and saves significantly by not having to mail a paper version.

WORM (write once, read many) optical disk systems allow users to record data only once on an optical disk. Once written, the data cannot be erased, but can be read indefinitely. WORM has been used as an alternative to microfilm for archiving digitized document images. The disadvantages of CD-ROM and WORM optical disks are that their contents cannot easily be erased and written over, as can be done with magnetic disks, and that the access speed is slower than that of magnetic disks.

Rewritable **magneto-optical disks,** illustrated in Figure 6.17, are starting to become cost-effective for data storage. The disk surface is coated with a magnetic material that can change magnetic polarity only when heated. To record data, a high-powered laser beam heats tiny spots in the magnetic medium that allows it to accept magnetic patterns. Data can be read by shining a lower-powered laser beam at the magnetic layer and reading the reflected light. The magneto-optical disk is erasable and can be written on nearly a million times. The access speed of optical disks, while slower than that of a magnetic disk, is continuing to improve, making the optical disk a very attractive storage technology for the 1990s.

The Window on Management describes some of the factors that managers should consider when converting to optical disk storage.

WORM: Write once, read many. Optical disk system that allows users to record data only once; data cannot be erased but can be read indefinitely.

Magneto-optical disk: Optical disk system that is erasable. Data are recorded by a high-powered laser beam that heats tiny spots in the magnetic media.

6.6 Input and Output Devices

Human beings interact with computer systems largely through input and output devices. Advances in information systems rely not only on the speed and capacity of the CPU but also on the speed, capacity, and design of the input and output devices. Input/output devices are often called peripheral devices.

Input Devices

The traditional method of data entry has been by keyboarding. Keypunching belongs to an earlier era in computing. Data entry clerks used a keypunch machine to code characters on an 80-column card, designating each character with a unique punch in a specific location on the card. An electromechanical card reader sensed the holes and solid parts of the cards. A single card could store up to 80 bytes of information (80 columns). Key-to-tape or key-to-disk machines allowed data to be keyed directly onto magnetic tape or disk for later computer processing. These methods are being replaced by more efficient and direct methods of input, although some firms still use them for their older batch applications.

Today, most data are entered directly into the computer using a data entry terminal and they are processed on-line. For instance, on-line airline reservation and customer information systems have reservation clerks or salespeople enter transactions directly while dealing with the customer, and their systems are updated immediately. In this manner, a business can eliminate a separate data-entry staff and the associated costs.

THE COMPUTER MOUSE

Computer mouse: Hand-held input device whose movement on the desktop controls the position of the cursor on the computer display screen.

The "point and click" actions of the **computer mouse** have made it an increasingly popular alternative to keyboard and text-based commands. A mouse is a hand-held device that is usually connected to the computer by a cable. The computer user moves the mouse around on a desktop to control the position of the cursor on a video display screen. Once the cursor is in the desired position, the user can push a button on the mouse to select a command. The mouse can also be used to "draw" images on the screen.

Touch screen technology allows users to interface with their computer systems by simply touching menu options on the sensitized video display monitor with their fingers.

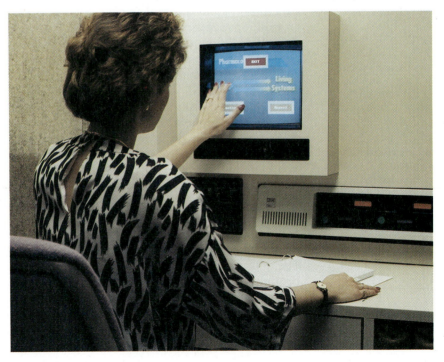

TOUCH SCREENS

Touch screen: Input technology that permits the entering or selecting of commands and data by touching the surface of sensitized video display monitor with a finger or pointer.

Touch screens are easy to use and are appealing to people who can't use traditional keyboards. Users can enter limited amounts of data by touching the surface of a sensitized video display monitor with a finger or a pointer. With colorful graphics, sound, and simple menus, touch screens allow the user to make selections by touching specified parts of the screen. Touch screens are proliferating in retail stores, restaurants, shopping malls, and even in some schools. For instance, music stores use Notestations, touch-screen equipped kiosks for selling sheet music. A customer can use the touch screen to scan more than 1000 titles, select a title, and listen to the first few bars of the score. A payment of $3.95 will print the score in any key.

SOURCE DATA AUTOMATION

Source data automation: Input technology that captures data in computer-readable form at the time and place the data are created.

Source data automation captures data in computer-readable form at the time and place it is created. Point-of-sale systems, optical bar-code scanners used in supermarkets, and other optical character recognition devices are examples of source data automation. One of the advantages of source data automation is that the many errors that occur when people use keyboards to enter data are almost eliminated. Bar code scanners make fewer than 1 error in 10,000 transactions, whereas skilled keypunchers make about 1 error for every 1000 keystrokes.

Moreover, source data automation permits information about events to be captured directly and immediately, with on-the-spot error correction. Businesses using these devices do not need a separate data entry staff. The principal source data automation technologies are magnetic ink character recognition, optical character recognition, pen-based input, digitizers, and voice input.

Magnetic ink character recognition (MICR): Input technology that translates characters written in magnetic ink into digital codes for processing.

Magnetic ink character recognition (MICR) technology is used primarily in check processing for the banking industry. The bottom portion of a typical check contains characters that are preprinted using a special ink. Characters identify the bank, checking account, and check number. A MICR reader translates the characters on checks that have been cashed and sent to the bank for processing into digital form for the computer. The amount of the check, which is written in ordinary ink, must be keyed in by hand.

Optical character recognition (OCR): Form of source data automation in which optical scanning devices read specially designed data and translate the data into digital form for the computer.

Optical character recognition (OCR) devices translate specially designed marks, characters, and codes into digital form. The most widely used optical code is the **bar code,** which is used in point-of-sale systems in supermarkets and retail stores. Bar codes are also used in hospitals, libraries, military operations, and transportation facilities. The codes can include time, date, and location data in addition to identification data; the information makes them useful for analyzing the movement of items and determining what has happened to them during production or other processes. (The discussion of the United Parcel Service in the opening to Chapter 1, and the Chapter 2 ending case on the CSX Corporation show how valuable bar codes can be for this purpose.)

Bar code: Form of OCR technology widely used in supermarkets and retail stores in which identification data are coded into a series of bars.

Handwriting-recognition devices such as pen-based "tablets," "notebooks," or "notepads," are promising new input technologies, especially for people working in the sales or service areas or for those who have traditionally shunned computer keyboards. These **pen-based input** devices usually consist of a flat-screen display tablet and a pen-like stylus.

Pen-based input: Input devices such as tablets, notebooks, and notepads consisting of a flat-screen display tablet and a pen-like stylus that digitizes handwriting.

With pen-based input, users print directly onto the tablet-sized screen. The screen is fitted with a transparent grid of fine wires that detects the presence of the special stylus, which emits a faint signal from its tip. The screen can also interpret tapping and flicking gestures made with the stylus.

Pen-based input devices transform the letters and numbers written by users on the tablet into digital form, where they can be stored or processed and analyzed. For instance, the United Parcel Service replaced its drivers' familiar clipboard with a battery-powered Delivery Information Acquisition Device (DIAD) to capture signatures (see the Chapter 1 opening vignette and photo) along with other information required for pickup and delivery. The Gillette Corporation supplied GridPad HD pen-based computers to its store merchandisers who are responsible for stocking stores and ensuring that Gillette products, such as Right

Guard, are displayed as prominently as possible. The merchandisers had never used computers before. The merchandisers enter handwritten numbers on electronic "forms" into the notebooks, and transmit the information via telephone links to Gillette. Gillette thus can receive stocking plans and information on products, pricing, and promotions immediately from the field.

This technology requires special pattern-recognition software to accept pen-based input instead of keyboard input. At present, most pen-based systems cannot recognize cursive writing. The case concluding this chapter treats this topic in more detail.

Digital scanners: Input devices that translate images such as pictures or documents into digital form for processing.

Digital scanners translate images such as pictures or documents into digital form, and are an essential component of image processing systems such as that used by the United Services Automobile Association, described in Chapter 2.

Voice input device: Technology that converts the spoken word into digital form for processing.

Voice input devices convert spoken words into digital form. Voice-recognition software (see Chapter 7) compares the electrical patterns produced by the speaker's voice to a set of prerecorded patterns. If the patterns match, the input is accepted. Most voice systems still have limited "vocabularies" of several hundred to several thousand words and can accept only very simple commands. For instance, some branches of the U.S. Postal Service are using voice recognition systems to make sorting packages and envelopes more efficient. In one application, users can speak out ZIP codes instead of keying them in, so that both hands can manipulate a package.

Output Devices

Video display terminal (VDT): A screen, also referred to as a cathode ray tube (CRT). Provides a visual image of both user input and computer output.

The major data output devices are **cathode ray tube** (CRT) terminals (sometimes called **video display terminals,** or **VDTs**) and printers.

The CRT is probably the most popular form of information output in modern computer systems. It works much like a television picture tube, with an electronic "gun" shooting a beam of electrons to illuminate the pixels on the screen. The more pixels per screen, the higher the resolution. CRT monitors can be classified as monochrome or color and by their display capabilities. Some display only text, whereas others display both text and graphics. Typical CRTs display 80 columns and 24 lines of text data. Display devices for graphics often utilize **bit mapping.** Bit

Bit mapping: The technology that allows each pixel on the screen to be addressed and manipulated by the computer.

mapping allows each pixel on the screen to be addressed and manipulated by the computer (as opposed to blocks of pixels in character addressable displays). This requires more computer memory but permits finer detail and the ability to produce any kind of image on the display screen. Special-purpose graphics terminals used in CAD/CAM and commercial art have very high resolution capabilities (1280×1024 pixels). (See Chapter 15 for further discussion.)

PRINTERS

Printer: A computer output device that provides paper "hard-copy" output in the form of text or graphics.

Printers produce a printed hard copy of information output. They include impact printers (a standard typewriter or a dot matrix) and nonimpact printers (laser, inkjet, and thermal transfer printers). Most printers print one character at a time, but some commercial printers print an entire line or page at a time. Line printers capable of printing an entire line of output in a single step can print up to 3000 lines per minute. Page printers print an entire page at a time, outputting 20,000 lines per minute. Printers working with microcomputers typically provide dot matrix print at a speed of 60 to over 400 characters per second. Much slower letter-quality printers operate in the 10 to 50 character-per-second range. In general, impact printers are slower than nonimpact printers. Laser printers for microcomputers can print four to eight pages per minute. Laser printers in large computer centers can print over 100 pages per minute.

Dot matrix printer quality is generally much lower than letter quality and is used for less important documents and spreadsheets. "Intelligence," or some processing ability, is built into many newer printers and other input and output devices to take over tasks that were formerly performed by the main computer. For example, many microcomputer printers, such as the Hewlett-Packard Laserjet 4 or the Apple LaserWriter, are programmed to store graphic elements and various type fonts, which can be used selectively by different pieces of software.

OTHER DEVICES   Microfilm and microfiche have been used to compactly store output as microscopic filmed images, and they are used mainly by insurance companies or other firms that need to output and store large numbers of documents. These media are cumbersome to search through and will be replaced by optical disk technology.

High-quality graphic documents can be created using **plotters** with multicolored pens to draw (rather than print) computer output. Plotters are much slower than printers, but are useful for outputting large-size charts, maps, or drawings.

A **voice output device** converts digital output data back into intelligible speech. Sounds are prerecorded, coded, and stored on disk, to be translated back as spoken words. For instance, when you call for information on the telephone, you may hear a computer "voice" respond with the telephone number you requested.

Voice output device: Converts digital output data into spoken words.

6.7 Information Technology Trends

Advances in materials science, manufacturing, and concepts of computing promise to maintain the historic growth pattern in hardware power. Over the last 30 years, computing costs have dropped by a factor of 10 each decade and capacity has increased by a factor of at least 100 each decade (Office of Technology Assessment, 1985). This momentum will most likely be maintained. Review Figure 6.7 again. It shows that between 1985 and 1993 the cost per MIPS on a microcomputer plummeted from about $60,000 to around $1,000. At the current rate of technological change, it should cost only $50 per microcomputer MIPS in 1995.

Today's microprocessors can put a mainframe on a desktop, and eventually into a briefcase or shirt pocket. Chapter 10 shows how the traditional mainframe is being supplanted by networks of powerful desktop machines, although the mainframe will never be eliminated. The future will see even more intelligence built into everyday devices, with mainframe and perhaps even supercomputer-like computing power packed in a pocket- or notebook-sized computer. Pen, notebook, and palmtop computers will be as pervasive as handheld calculators. Computers on a chip will help guide automobiles, military weapons, robots, and everyday household devices. Computers and related information technologies will blend data, images, and sound, sending them coursing through vast networks that can process all of them with equal ease. We can see how this might be possible through the use of multimedia, superchips, and fifth-generation computers.

Multimedia

Multimedia: Technologies that facilitate the integration of two or more types of media such as text, graphics, sound, voice, full-motion video, or animation into a computer-based application.

Multimedia is defined as the technologies that facilitate the integration of two or more types of media, such as text, graphics, sound, voice, full motion video, still video, or animation into a computer-based application. From the 1990s through the twenty-first century, multimedia will be the foundation of new consumer products and services, such as electronic books and newspapers, electronic classroom presentation technologies, full motion video conferencing, imaging, graphics design tools, and video electronic and voice mail.

By pressing a button, a person using a computer can call up a screenful of text; another button might bring up related video images. Still another might bring up related talk or music. For instance, the New York Power Authority in White Plains, New York, has multimedia training programs that enable a sales representative to press a touch screen to see a colorful video demonstration of the software he or she is learning in a corner of the computer screen while an engineer sitting nearby can use the same multimedia training system to run through mathematical formulas with graphic animations illustrating the principles involved.

Multimedia systems combine the elements of today's personal computers (a computer, printer, keyboard, and mouse) with two new elements: audio (sound) and video (pictures). Figure 6.18 illustrates some of the hardware components that would be required to create and run multimedia applications. Today's microcomputers can be converted to multimedia systems by purchasing special expansion boards. By the year 2000, computers will come with built-in multimedia capabilities.

The marriage of text, graphics, sound, and video data into a single application has been made possible by the advances in microprocessor and storage technologies described in this chapter. A simple multimedia system consists of a personal computer with a 32-bit microprocessor and a CD-ROM drive. A five-inch optical disk holding more than 600 megabytes of information can store an hour of music, several thousand full-color pictures, several minutes of video or animation, and millions of words. For instance, a single optical disk can store all 26 volumes of *Compton's MultiMedia Encyclopedia*. It includes 15,000 drawings, charts, photographs, and paintings, many in full color; 45 animated sequences; an hour of audio clips of famous speeches and music; and Webster's Intermediate Dictionary, plus about 9 million words.

The possibilities of this technology are endless, but the most promising business applications appear to be in training and presentations. For training, multimedia is appealing because it is interactive and permits two-way communication (Lambert). People can use multimedia training sessions any time of the day, at their own pace. Instructors can easily integrate words, sounds, pictures, and both live and animated video to produce lessons that capture students' imaginations. For example, students viewing "Search and Seizure," a multimedia computer lesson produced at the Harvard Law School, can press a key to stop

Figure 6.18

Multimedia applications require specially configured systems. This figure illustrates 11 components in a system used to develop a multimedia application. 1. CPU and primary storage: a minimum 80386/33 megahertz chip and 8 megabytes RAM. 2. Monitor: color monitor supporting super high resolutions from 640 × 480 to 1280 × 1024; minimum 17″ screen. 3. CD-ROM: drive with 280 millisecond access time and 150 kilobits/second data transfer rate. 4. Hard disk: minimum 300 megabytes with 15 millisecond access time. 5. Stereo speakers. 6. Microphone for voice input. 7. Mouse. 8. Video input device or video board connected to a VCR or laser video disk player. 9–11. Sound card, video card, and video compression card. Adapter cards integrate sound and video into the computer and digitally compress full-motion video.
Adapted from: J. William Semich, "Multimedia Tools for Development Pros," Datamation, August 15, 1992. Reprinted with permission from DATAMATION © 1992, Reed Publishing (USA) Inc.

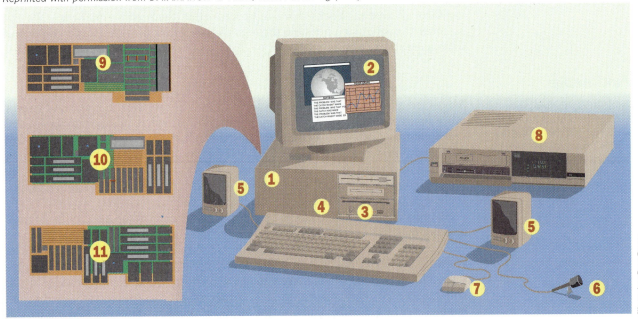

Illustration: Dave Brown

A multimedia training center provides sound and images to the trainees at this facility.

the video of a drug arrest whenever they want to question the legality of police conduct. They can bring up case citations, constitutional texts, and judicial opinions.

The multimedia training material used by the sales people at Marion Merrell Dow Pharmaceutical allows users to display an index of a video glossary by clicking a button during the presentation of a selected topic. The last term used is highlighted. The user can view the glossary clip, return to the presentation, and be quizzed by the system. Andersen Consulting Company now delivers its business practice course on three CD-ROMs with 200 minutes of digital video and interactive training and testing techniques. By replacing classroom training, this multimedia course saves the firm $10 million per year.

There will be numerous organizational applications of multimedia because multimedia is likely to be a major instrument for obtaining corporate information. When multimedia is coupled with the telecommunications technologies described in Chapters 9 and 10, desktop-to-desktop videoconferencing and file-sharing become feasible, and will likely change the way people across organizations meet and interact. People will be able to capture, store, manipulate, and transmit photos and other document images and possibly full-motion video on a network as easily as they do with text. For instance, financial service firms could index a TV news report next to a related print story about a development affecting a company. Throughout this text, we will be looking at the various ways multimedia will be used in information systems.

The most difficult element to incorporate into multimedia information systems has been full-motion video, because so much data must be brought under the digital control of the computer. While laser video disks and VCRs can deliver video images to microcomputers, this technology is limited to displaying images. The process of actually integrating video with other kinds of data requires special software or compression boards with dedicated video processing chips. The massive amounts of data in each video image must be digitally encoded, stored and manipulated electronically, using techniques that "compress" the digital data.

In 1992, Apple computers were the first to come equipped with software (called QuickTime [TM]) and some of the hardware to play back multimedia disks containing text, numbers, video and sound. Microsoft Corporation has developed multimedia standards so that personal computers based on the IBM Personal System/2 model can play back and even author multimedia presentations. By the year 2000 all computers, regardless of size, will have built-in multimedia capabilities combining existing text and numbers with music, full motion and still frame video (snapshots), animation, voice messages, telephone, and fax capabilities.

Superchips

Semiconductor researchers have continued to find means of packaging circuits more densely, so that millions of transistors can be packed onto a fingernail-sized silicon wafer. The most powerful microprocessors—such as Intel's 80486 and Pentium chips or Digital's Alpha described in the Window on Technology—package mainframe and even supercomputerlike capabilities on a single chip.

The main way microprocessors have been made to perform faster is by shrinking the distance between transistors. This process gives the electrical current less distance to travel. Figure 6.19 shows how much progress has been made. One step in fashioning microprocessors is to etch lines in silicon wafers that form the outlines of circuits. The narrower the lines forming transistors, the larger the number of transistors that can be squeezed onto a single chip, and the faster these circuits will operate. Figure 6.19 shows that line widths have shrunk from

Figure 6.19
The shrinking size and growth in number of transistors. *Courtesy of Intel Corporation.*

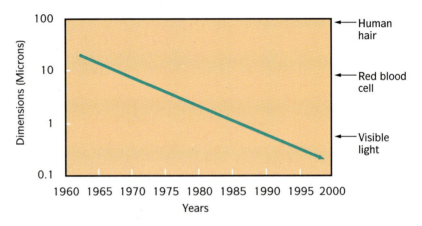

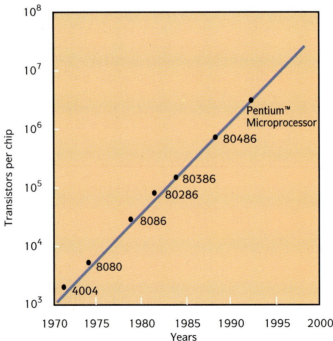

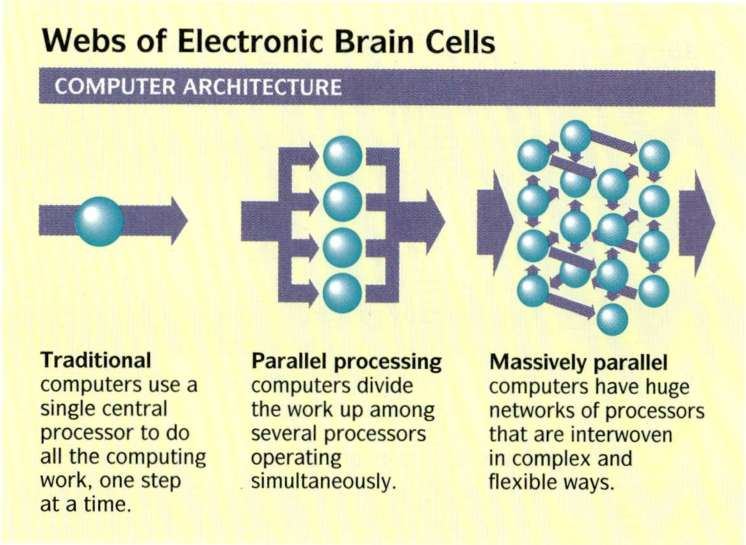

Webs of Electronic Brain Cells

COMPUTER ARCHITECTURE

Traditional computers use a single central processor to do all the computing work, one step at a time.

Parallel processing computers divide the work up among several processors operating simultaneously.

Massively parallel computers have huge networks of processors that are interwoven in complex and flexible ways.

Figure 6.20
Computer architecture. A comparison of traditional serial processing, parallel processing, and massively parallel processing. *Adapted from John Markoff, "Foray Into Mainstream for Parallel Computing," The* New York Times, *June 15, 1992. Copyright © 1992 by the New York Times Corporation. Reprinted by permission.*

the diameter of a hair to less than one micron, and should reach one-fifth of a micron by the year 2000. The lower part of the figure shows the number of transistors on some prominent microprocessors and memory chips. Since the number of transistors that can fit economically onto a single silicon chip is doubling every 18 months, between 50 and 100 million transistors could conceivably be squeezed onto a single microprocessor by the year 2000. There are physical limits to this approach that may soon be reached, but researchers are experimenting with new materials to increase microprocessor speed.

Fifth-Generation Computers

Conventional computers are based on the Von Neumann architecture, which processes information serially, one instruction at a time. In the future, more computers will use parallel processing and massively parallel processing to blend voice, images, and massive pools of data from diverse sources, using artificial intelligence and intricate mathematical models.

Massively parallel computers, illustrated in Figure 6.20, have huge networks of processor chips interwoven in complex and flexible ways. As opposed to parallel processing, where small numbers of powerful but expensive specialized chips are linked together, massively parallel machines chain hundreds or even thousands of inexpensive, commonly used chips to attack large computing problems, attaining supercomputer speeds. For instance, Wal-Mart Stores uses a massively parallel machine to sift through an inventory and sales trend database with 1.8 trillion bytes of data. Massively parallel systems are said to have cost and speed advantages over conventional parallel computers because they can take advantage of off-the-shelf chips. They may be able to accomplish processing work for one-tenth to one-twentieth the cost of traditional mainframes or supercomputers.

Today's supercomputers can perform hundreds of billions of calculations per second. Now supercomputer makers are racing to harness tens of thousands of microprocessors and memory chips together to create super-supercomputers that can perform more than a trillion mathematical calculations each second—a teraflop. The term *teraflop* comes from the Greek *teras*, which for mathematicians means one trillion, and *flop*, an acronym for floating point operations per second. (A floating point operation is a basic computer arithmetic operation, such as addition, on numbers that include a decimal point.) In the twenty-first century, teraflop machines could support projects such as mapping the surface of planets, designing new computers, or testing the aerodynamics of supersonic airplanes, where trillions of calculations would be required.

1. **Keeping abreast of technological change.** Because the technology is growing in power so rapidly and is changing basic patterns of information processing, managers must keep abreast of changes in the field. This requires time and resources. In medium to large firms, a person or small group must be assigned the task of tracking new technological developments and encouraging prototypes within the firm.

2. **Making wise purchasing decisions.** Soon after having made an investment in information technology, managers find the completed system is obsolete and too expensive given the power and lower cost of new technology. In this environment, it is very difficult to keep one's own systems up-to-date. A rather considerable amount of time must be spent anticipating and planning for technological change.

3. **Training the information systems staff and all employees.** In the transition from the mainframe computing to desktops, enormous changes in perspective and skills and attitudes are required on the part of an organization's information systems staff. Typically, they must be completely retrained every five years. All employees likewise will require extensive retraining simply to keep abreast of new ways of doing business with new information technologies.

Summary

Identify the hardware components in a typical computer system.

The modern computer system has five major components: a central processor (consisting of the CPU and primary storage), input devices, output devices, secondary storage, and communications devices.

Describe how information is represented and processed in a computer system.

Digital computers store and process information in the form of binary digits called *bits*. A string of 8 bits is called a *byte*. There are several coding schemes for arranging binary digits into characters. The most common are EBCDIC and ASCII.

Describe the functions of the CPU and primary storage.

The CPU is the center of the computer, where the manipulation of symbols, numbers, and letters occurs. The CPU has two components: an arithmetic-logic unit, and a control unit. The arithmetic-logic unit performs arithmetic and logical operations on data, while the control unit controls and coordinates the other components of the computer.

The CPU is closely tied to primary memory, or primary storage, which stores data and program instructions temporarily before and after processing.

Several different kinds of semiconductor memory chips are used with primary storage: RAM (random-access memory) is used for short-term storage of data and program instructions, while ROM (read-only memory) permanently stores important program instructions. Other memory devices include PROM (programmable read-only memory) and EPROM (erasable programmable read-only memory.)

Distinguish between generations of computer hardware.

Computer technology has gone through four generations, from vacuum tubes to transistors, integrated circuits, and very-large-scale integrated circuits, each dramatically increasing computer processing power while shrinking the size of computing hardware.

Contrast the capabilities of mainframes, minicomputers, supercomputers, microcomputers, and workstations.

Depending on their size and processing power, computers are categorized as mainframes, minicomputers, workstations, supercomputers, or microcomputers. Mainframes are the largest computers with 50 megabytes to over 1 gigabyte of RAM; minicomputers are mid-range machines with 10 to 650 megabytes of RAM; workstations are desktop machines with powerful mathematical and graphic capabilities and 8–300 megabytes of RAM; and microcomputers are desktop or laptop machines with 640 kilobytes to 64 megabytes of RAM.

The capabilities of microprocessors used in these computers can be gauged by their word length, data bus width, and cycle speed. Because of continuing advances in microprocessor technology, the distinctions between these various types of computers are constantly changing. Microcomputers are now powerful enough to perform much of the work that was formerly limited to mainframes and minicomputers.

Describe the various media for storing data and programs in a computer system.

The principal forms of secondary storage are tape, magnetic disk, and optical disk. Tape stores records in sequence, whereas disk permits direct access to specific records and is much faster than tape.

Compare the major input and output devices.

The principal input devices are keyboards, computer mice, touch screens, magnetic and optical character recognition, digital scanners, and voice input.

The principal output devices are printers, video display terminals, plotters, voice output devices, and microfilm and microfiche.

Describe multimedia and future information technology trends.

Multimedia integrates two or more types of media, such as text, graphics, sound, voice, full motion video, still video, and/or animation into a computer-based application.

The future will see steady and impressive progress toward faster chips at lower cost and microprocessors with the power of today's mainframes or supercomputers. Hardware using parallel processing will be used more widely, and computers and related information technologies will be able to blend data, images, and sound.

Key Terms

Bit
Byte
EBCDIC (Extended Binary Coded Decimal Interchange Code)
ASCII (American Standard Code for Information Interchange)
Parity
Pixel
Millisecond
Microsecond
Nanosecond
Kilobyte
Megabyte
Gigabyte
Central processing unit (CPU)
Primary Storage
RAM (random access memory)
Semiconductor
ROM (read-only memory)
PROM (programmable read-only memory)
EPROM (erasable programmable read-only memory)
Arithmetic-logic unit (ALU)
Control unit
Machine cycle
Computer generations
Microprocessor

Word length
Megahertz
Data bus width
Reduced instruction set computing (RISC)
Mainframe
Minicomputer
Microcomputer
Workstation
Supercomputer
Distributed processing
Centralized processing
Downsizing
Cooperative processing
Parallel processing
Secondary storage
Register
Cache
Magnetic tape
Magnetic disk
Hard disk
Cylinder
Track
Floppy disk
Sector
Direct access storage device (DASD)
Optical disk

CD-ROM (compact disk read only memory)
WORM (write once, read many)
Magneto-optical disk
Computer mouse
Touch screen
Source data automation
Magnetic ink character recognition (MICR)
Optical character recognition (OCR)

Bar code
Pen-based input
Digital scanners
Voice input device
Video display terminal (VDT)
Bit mapping
Printer
Voice output device
Multimedia

Review Questions

1. What are the components of a contemporary computer system?
2. Distinguish between a bit and a byte.
3. What are ASCII and EBCDIC, and why are they used? Why can true binary not be used in a computer as a machine language?
4. Name and define the principal measures of computer time and storage capacity.
5. What problems of coordination exist in a computing environment and why?
6. Name the major components of the CPU and the function of each.
7. Describe how information is stored in primary memory.
8. What are the four different types of semiconductor memory, and when are they used?
9. Describe the major generations of computers and the characteristics of each.
10. Name and describe the factors affecting the speed and performance of a microprocessor.
11. What are downsizing and cooperative processing?
12. What is the difference between primary and secondary storage?
13. List the most important secondary storage media. What are the strengths and limitations of each?
14. List and describe the major input devices.
15. List and describe the major output devices.
16. Distinguish between serial, parallel, and massively parallel processing.
17. What is multimedia? What technologies are involved?

Discussion Questions

1. What is the difference between a mainframe, a minicomputer, and a microcomputer? Between a mainframe and a supercomputer? Between a microcomputer and a work station? Why are these distinctions disappearing?
2. How are the capabilities of an information system affected by its input, output and storage devices?
3. A firm would like to introduce computers into its order entry process but feels that it should wait for a new generation of machines to be developed. After all, any machine bought now will quickly be out of date and less expensive a few years from now. Discuss.

Group Project

Form a group with three or four of your classmates. Design an ideal "student desktop workstation" using the technologies described in this chapter. What input, output, and storage technologies would you select? How much processing capacity would be required? Why? What kinds of tasks could the workstation perform? How could the workstation help students learn or complete their assignments? Present your group's description to the class.

Will Pen-Based Computers Take Over?

With 2000 claims adjusters, engineers, and premium auditors, Continental Insurance of Neptune, New Jersey, wants to move its computing power out in the field with them. Notebook computers, which are used for word processing and communications, just won't do the job because a user can't work with one using just one hand and a keyboard. Furthermore, Continental Insurance's users are not stationary long enough to sit down and type. They have had to cope by leaving their computers in a hotel room and returning to do their work at the end of the day. Their work is very data intensive. For instance, a claims adjuster must investigate thefts or accidents and file numerous forms and reports with claims offices and central headquarters. Continental thinks pen-based computers might solve this problem.

Will they? Pen-based input technology promises both familiarity and ease of use. According to Tim Bajarin, an industry analyst with Creative Strategies Research International in Santa Clara, California, pen-based systems can potentially put the computer into the hands of people who have never touched the PC. White-collar executives who traditionally have shunned keyboards or field workers who need to fill out forms are the likely targets.

There are many business settings where an electronic "notepad" would be perfect. For instance, waiters could use them to take orders and get signatures for credit card receipts. Truck drivers could use notepads filled with electronic maps and forms to plan routes, keep track of deliveries, and store customers' signatures on receipts. For executives, notepads could serve as the ultimate "little black books" that store, cross-reference, and instantly retrieve names, addresses, phone numbers, and correspondence; send memos; or review and mark up documents and contracts.

Most users of pen-based systems, which are also called notepads, notebooks, or tablets, will be in mobile occupations. Users will include insurance adjusters, financial consultants, sales representatives, police, or delivery and maintenance workers. People doing this kind of work can use pen-based systems to fill out forms, or to receive, edit, and retransmit faxes. Notepad computers can even be linked to other computers by telephone. By the mid 1990s, the most advanced notepads will incorporate cellular phone circuitry so that users will be able to obtain or transmit data, faxes, and phone calls just about anywhere.

Instead of a keyboard and mouse, pen-based computers use a stylus that looks and feels like a pen. People use the stylus to print directly on a tablet-sized screen. The writing is instantly captured and translated into digital form.

Pen input incorporates "gestures" instead of traditional commands or dragging icons. For instance, a word can be deleted by simply drawing a line through it. Users can insert a word or character by placing a caret at the desired location and tapping on the appropriate menu item. Users can move a word by circling it and drawing a line to where it belongs.

Traditional PCs require at least rudimentary keyboard skills and some training in the commands necessary to run software and keep track of stored data. The stylus combines the best attributes of both a mouse and a keyboard. You can use it not only to choose the software or document you want, but also to edit or enter text or numbers. Tapping with the stylus on the name of a document brings it up on the screen. Flicking the stylus at the bottom edge of the screen causes the computer to scroll through long documents. With the stylus, a user can write memos or reports. The notepad converts the hand-printed words into type, then formats the text into sentences and paragraphs as if they had been entered with a keyboard. In some pen-based models, users can draw pictures as easily as on paper, and the computer will straighten the wobbly lines and make circles perfectly round.

As simple as it sounds, the technology is still in its infancy. It cannot yet recognize all types of handwriting. At this point, many pen-based systems can primarily handle printed letters that are detached from one another, and even this ability to handle block printing has not been perfected. Users might find that some of the letters they entered were mistranslated and that considerable editing is required to get the desired result. There might not be a delete key if there is no keyboard.

Pen computer manufacturers have tried to get around these problems by stressing programs that permit a user to store his or her own written notes as a graphic image dubbed "ink" that can be called up later. But "ink" can't be easily indexed, searched, or manipulated in the way regular computer text can.

Clearly, this technology is not yet ready to support a general-purpose computer that would let users write entire business documents, enter a long series of figures, or perform other similar tasks that are still handled better by traditional pen and paper or keyboards. On the other hand, most computer tasks, such as requesting a report or a piece of data, require only a few numbers or words here or there.

To make sense of what is written on the screen, notepad computers contain special software that recognizes patterns. For some pen-based systems, users may have to "train" their machines to recognize their penmanship by repeatedly writing words and characters. This process takes about half an hour.

Businesses have been able to make do with pen-based notepads by equipping them with special software that consists mainly of electronic forms. The pen is used primarily to check off boxes, select from lists, or highlight built-in pictures. Freehand writing in these applications is kept to a minimum, and might require some "training" of the machine to recognize the user's scrawl.

Some firms have found that it isn't always easy to implement pen-based computer systems. Integrating potentially thousands of pen-based systems in the field with existing mainframes at company headquarters may prove challenging. For instance, the CSX Corporation, which has been described in the case concluding Chapter 2, developed a pen-based system that allows inspectors to draw a picture of an accident site and attach data to a report. The system transmits the information to the CSX mainframe, which issues instructions to dispatch a repair crew with accident information already in hand.

The pen-based system eliminated the need to rekey data, but it also raised worries about capturing too much data at the point of collection. The amount of information coming in from the field mushroomed with pen-based sys-

tems. Another project to arm rail car inspectors at each ramp in major depots with pen-based computers will place even more demands on the CSX mainframe. The inspectors will check off cargo content information using computerized forms. But with a thousand rail cars passing through each day, each pen-based computer is expected to transmit 2 megabytes of data to the mainframe, threatening to overwhelm its processing capacity. Still, the benefits cannot be ignored. CSX could use this system to give customers an hourly update on the location of their cargo.

Sources: Walter S. Mossberg, "Notepad PCs Struggle with One Small Task: Deciphering Writing," The *Wall Street Journal,* July 23, 1992; Michael Fitzgerald, "Insurer Craves Pen Technology for Its Next-Generation Portable," *Computerworld,* March 2, 1992; Bob Francis, "Pen-Based Notebooks Find Their Niche," *Datamation,* October 1, 1991; and Brenton R. Schlender, "Hot New PCs that Read Your Writing," *Fortune,* February 11, 1991.

Case Study Questions

1. What are the advantages and disadvantages of pen-based computers?

2. Are pen-based computers a solution for Continental Insurance? Why or why not? What management, organization, and technology factors should be considered to make this decision?

3. Suggest some other areas of business where pen-based input would be useful.

References

Appleby, Chuck. "Taking Note of Multimedia." *InformationWEEK,* March 16, 1992.

Bell, Gordon. "The Future of High Performance Computers in Science and Engineering." *Communications of the ACM* 32, no. 9 (September 1989).

Bell, Gordon. "Ultracomputers: A Teraflop Before Its Time." *Communications of the ACM* 35, no. 8 (August 1992).

Lambert, Craig. "The Electronic Tutor." *Harvard Magazine* (November–December 1990).

Markoff, John. "Foray into Mainstream for Parallel Computing." *The New York Times* (June 15, 1992).

Markoff, John. "Supercomputing's Speed Quest." *The New York Times* (May 31, 1991).

Mel, Bartlett W., Stephen M. Omohundro, Arch D. Robison, Steven S. Skiena, Kurt H. Thearling, Luke T. Young, and Stephen Wolfram. "Tablet: Personal Computer in the Year 2000." *Communications of the ACM* 31, no. 6 (June 1988).

National Bureau of Standards. *Forecast of Technology Trends and Implications for Management.* Mimeo. Washington, D.C.: National Bureau of Standards, 1986.

Office of Technology Assessment. *Information Technology R & D.* Washington, D.C.: Office of Technology Assessment, U.S. Congress, 1985.

Peled, Abraham. "The Next Computer Revolution." *Scientific American* 257, no. 4 (October 1987).

Press, Larry. "Compuvision or Teleputer?" *Communications of the ACM* 33, no. 3 (September 1990).

Radding, Alan. "*RISC Desktop Machines: PCs in Disguise?*" *Computerworld* (March 23, 1992).

Saffo, Paul. "Farewell PC—What's Next?" *The New York Times* (October 13, 1991).

Smarr, Larry and Charles E. Catlett. "Metacomputing." *Communications of the ACM* 35, no. 6 (June 1992).

Wetmore, Tim. "The Multimedia Challenge." *InformationWEEK* (January 13, 1992).

CHAPTER

7

Information Systems Software

Software Needed for Insight

Software Needed for Insight

The supermarket business is intensely competitive. Because retail supermarkets earn only between two and four cents on every pretax dollar, food retailers must sell food in large volumes as efficiently as possible, keeping their costs low and making sure that items move quickly off the shelves. Any information that gives them direction on items and quantities to stock will improve a skimpy bottom line. Can the sales data captured at their checkout counters be of use?

What can be learned about that can of soup that was just scanned at the supermarket checkout counter? The store can use the data to tally the day's sales and to identify items that need replenishing in inventory. But retailers and the firms that supply the cans of soup want to know more. They would like to use these data to determine the popularity of different varieties of soup, to predict sales preferences by regions or neighborhoods, or to measure sales volume over different seasons. But they can't make

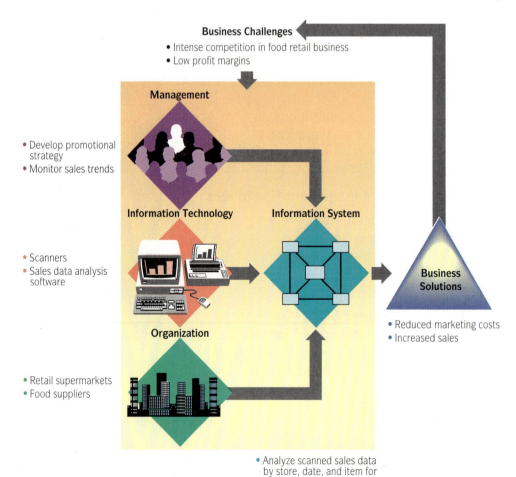

Business Challenges
- Intense competition in food retail business
- Low profit margins

Management
- Develop promotional strategy
- Monitor sales trends

Information Technology
- Scanners
- Sales data analysis software

Information System

Organization
- Retail supermarkets
- Food suppliers

- Analyze scanned sales data by store, date, and item for sales preferences
- Make analyzed data immediately available

Business Solutions
- Reduced marketing costs
- Increased sales

sense of the flood of data captured by bar-code scanners without the right software to interpret it.

Well-designed software could forecast which varieties of soup will be popular at a particular store. While sales clerks might make do by scanning one can of soup and multiplying it by the number of cans of soup purchased, the data about which kinds of soup are bought are lost.

The reams of data currently compiled and sold for long-term planning by market research firms such as A.C. Nielsen, Inc. and Information Resources Inc. won't work. This information is obtained through consumer surveys and observations of purchases. To make the most of the data already collected by computer, these research firms need to get inside the stores and warehouses. They must develop software to collect the information, to interpret it, and to make it available in a useful format to retailers and food suppliers within a few days.

One market research company, Efficient Market Services (EMS) in Deerfield, Illinois, has a software product that appears to meet these needs. The EMS software consolidates sales data from the cash registers in each store, analyzes the data, and produces completed reports 12 hours after a register has closed. Food suppliers who buy the store-specific and item-specific data collected by the EMS system can use this information to make timely deliveries of their goods, to build displays, and to assess the impact of sales promotions.

Source: Bruce Caldwell, "Scanning for Insight," *InformationWEEK* (March 30, 1992).

In the last twenty-five years, public media has paid a great deal of attention to advances in computer hardware. But without the software to utilize the expanding capabilities of the hardware, the "computer revolution" would have been still-born. The food retailers and suppliers described in the opening vignette had the data they needed and the hardware for processing these data. What prevented them from obtaining the right information to project buying trends was the lack of appropriate software.

The usefulness of computer hardware depends a great deal on available software and the ability of management to evaluate, monitor, and control the utilization of software in the organization. This chapter shows how software turns computer hardware into useful information systems, describes the major types of software, provides criteria for selecting software, and presents new approaches to software development.

After completing this chapter you will be able to:

- Describe the major types of software.
- Describe the functions of system software and compare leading microcomputer operating systems.
- Explain how software has evolved and how it will continue to develop.

- Compare strengths and limitations of the major programming languages and tools.
- Explain how to select appropriate software and programming languages.

7.1 What Is Software?

Software: The detailed instructions that control the operation of a computer system.

Software is the detailed instructions that control the operation of a computer system. Without software, computer hardware could not perform the tasks we associate with computers. The functions of software are 1) to manage the computer resources of the organization; 2) to provide tools for human beings to take advantage of these resources; and 3) to act as an intermediary between organizations and stored information.

Software Programs

Program: A series of statements or instructions to the computer.

Stored program concept: The idea that a program cannot be executed unless it is stored in a computer's primary storage along with required data.

A software **program** is a series of statements or instructions to the computer. The process of writing or coding programs is termed programming, and individuals who specialize in this task are called programmers.

The **stored program concept** means that a program must be stored in the computer's primary storage along with the required data in order to execute, or have its instructions performed by the computer. Once a program has finished executing, the computer hardware can be used for another task when a new program is loaded into memory.

Major Types of Software

System software: Generalized programs that manage the resources of the computer.

There are three major types of software: system software, application software, and end-user software. Each kind performs a different function. **System software** is a set of generalized programs that manage the resources of the computer, such

Figure 7.1
The three major types of software. The relationship between the system software, application software, and end-user software can be illustrated by a series of nested boxes. System software — consisting of operating systems, language translators, and utility programs — controls access to the hardware. Application software, such as the programming languages, must work through the system software to operate. End-user software, such as the fourth-generation languages, must work through the application software and then the system software in order to operate.

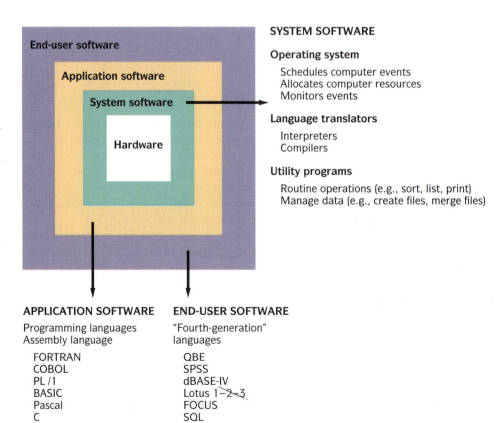

SYSTEM SOFTWARE

Operating system
Schedules computer events
Allocates computer resources
Monitors events

Language translators
Interpreters
Compilers

Utility programs
Routine operations (e.g., sort, list, print)
Manage data (e.g., create files, merge files)

APPLICATION SOFTWARE
Programming languages
Assembly language
    FORTRAN
    COBOL
    PL /1
    BASIC
    Pascal
    C

END-USER SOFTWARE
"Fourth-generation" languages
    QBE
    SPSS
    dBASE-IV
    Lotus 1-2-3
    FOCUS
    SQL

as the central processing unit, communications links, and peripheral devices. Programmers who write system software are called system programmers.

Application software describes the programs that are written for or by users to apply the computer to a specific task. Software for processing an order or generating a mailing list is application software. Programmers who write application software are called application programmers.

A special type of application software called end-user software (or fourth-generation languages) appeared in the early 1980s. **End-user software** consists of software tools that permit the development of some applications directly by end users without professional programmers. Some end-user software is used to enhance the productivity of professional programmers.

The three types of software are interrelated and can be thought of as a set of nested boxes, each of which must interact closely with the other boxes surrounding it. Figure 7.1 illustrates this relationship. The system software surrounds and controls access to the hardware. Application software must work through the system software in order to operate. Last, end-user software frequently has to work through application software and finally through system software. Each type of software must be specially designed to a specific machine in order to ensure its compatibility.

Application software: Programs written for a specific business application in order to perform functions specified by end users.

End-user software: Software tools that permit the development of applications by end users with little or no professional programmer intervention or that enhance the productivity of professional programmers.

7.2 System Software

System software coordinates the various parts of the computer system and mediates between application software and computer hardware. The system software that manages and controls the activities of the computer is called the **operating system.** Other system software consists of computer language translation programs that convert programming languages into machine language and utility programs that perform common processing tasks.

Operating system: The system software that manages and controls the activities of the computer.

Functions of the Operating System

One way to look at the operating system is as the system's chief manager. Operating system software decides which computer resources will be used, which programs will be run, and the order in which activities will take place.

An operating system performs three functions. It allocates and assigns system resources; it schedules the use of computer resources and computer jobs; and it monitors computer system activities.

ALLOCATION AND ASSIGNMENT

The operating system allocates resources to the application jobs in the execution queue. It provides locations in primary memory for data and programs and controls the input and output devices such as printers, terminals, and telecommunication links.

SCHEDULING

Thousands of pieces of work can be going on in a computer simultaneously. The operating system decides when to schedule the jobs that have been submitted and when to coordinate the scheduling in various areas of the computer so that different parts of different jobs can be worked on at the same time. For instance, while a program is executing, the operating system is scheduling the use of input and output devices. Not all jobs are performed in the order they are submitted; the operating system must schedule these jobs according to organizational priorities. On-line order processing may have priority over a job to generate mailing lists and labels.

MONITORING

The operating system monitors the activities of the computer system. It keeps track of each computer job and may also keep track of who is using the system, of what programs have been run, and of any unauthorized attempts to access the system. Information system security is discussed in detail in Chapter 18.

Figure 7.2

Single-program execution versus multiprogramming. In multiprogramming, the computer can be used much more efficiently because a number of programs can be executing concurrently. Several complete programs are loaded into memory. This memory management aspect of the operating system greatly increases throughput by better management of high-speed memory and input/output devices.

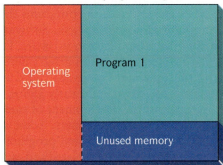

Traditional system with no multiprogramming

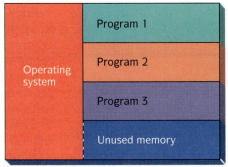

Multiprogramming environment

System residence device: The secondary storage device on which a complete operating system is stored.

Obviously, the operating system of a major mainframe computer is itself a very large program. For this reason, only parts of the operating system are actually stored in the primary storage area. Most of the operating system is stored in a copy on a disk, to which primary storage has very rapid access. Whenever parts of the operating system are required by a given application, they are transferred from the disk and loaded into primary storage. The device on which a complete operating system is stored is called the **system residence device.**

Multiprogramming, Time Sharing, Virtual Storage, and Multiprocessing

How is it possible for 1000 or more users sitting at remote terminals to use a computer information system simultaneously if, as we stated in the previous chapter, a computer can execute only one instruction from one program at a time? How can computers run thousands of programs? The answer is that the computer has a series of specialized operating system capabilities.

MULTIPROGRAMMING

Multiprogramming: A method of executing two or more programs concurrently using the same computer. The CPU only executes one program but can service the input/output needs of others at the same time.

The most important operating system capability for sharing computer resources is **multiprogramming.** Multiprogramming permits multiple programs to share a computer system's resources at any one time through concurrent use of a CPU. By concurrent use, we mean that only one program is actually using the CPU at any given moment but that the input/output needs of other programs can be serviced at the same time. Two or more programs are active at the same time, but they do not use the same computer resources simultaneously. With multiprogramming, a group of programs takes turns using the processor.

Figure 7.2 shows how three programs in a multiprogramming environment can be stored in primary storage. The first program executes until an input/output event is read in the program. The operating system then directs a channel (a small processor limited to input and output functions) to read the input and move the output to an output device. The CPU moves to the second program until an input/output statement occurs. At this point, the CPU switches to the execution of the third program, and so forth, until eventually all three programs have been executed. Notice that the interruptions in processing are caused by events that take place in the programs themselves. In this manner, many different programs can be executing at the same time, although different resources within the computer are actually being utilized.

You can observe the advantages of multiprogramming by comparing multiprogramming systems to the first operating systems, which executed only one program at a time. Before multiprogramming, whenever a program read data off a tape or disk or wrote data to a printer, the entire CPU came to a stop. This was a very inefficient way to use the computer. With multiprogramming, the CPU utilization rate is much higher.

MULTITASKING

Multitasking: The multiprogramming capability of primarily single-user operating systems such as those for microcomputers.

Multitasking refers to multiprogramming on single-user operating systems such as those in microcomputers. One person can run two or more programs concurrently on a single computer. For example, a sales representative could write a letter to prospective clients with a word processing program while simultaneously using a database program to search for all sales contacts in a particular city or geographic area. Instead of terminating his or her session with the word processing program, returning to the operating system, and then initiating a session with the database program, multitasking allows the sales representative to display both programs on the computer screen and work with them at the same time.

VIRTUAL STORAGE

Virtual storage: A way of handling programs more efficiently by the computer by dividing the programs into small fixed or variable-length portions with only a small portion stored in primary memory at one time.

Virtual storage was developed after some problems of multiprogramming became apparent. Virtual storage handles programs more efficiently because the computer divides the programs into small fixed or variable-length portions, storing only a small portion of the program in primary memory at one time. First, although two or three large programs can be read into memory, a certain part of main memory generally remains underutilized because the programs add up to less than the total amount of primary storage space available. Second, given the limited size of primary memory, only a small number of programs can reside in primary storage at any given time. For example, many business programs may require up to 200K of storage, and the computer may have only 1 megabyte of primary storage. Therefore, only a few programs can reside in memory at any given time.

Only a few statements of a program actually execute at any given moment. Virtual storage takes advantage of this feature of processing. Virtual storage breaks a program into a number of fixed-length portions called **pages** or into variable-length portions called segments. The actual breakpoint between segments can be determined either by the programmer or by the operating system. In virtual storage, each of those portions is relatively small (about 2 to 4 kilobytes). This permits a very large number of programs to reside in primary memory, inasmuch as only one page or segment of each program is actually located there (see Figure 7.3).

Page: Small fixed-length section of a program, which can be easily stored in primary storage and quickly accessed from secondary storage.

All other program pages are stored on a peripheral disk unit until they are ready for execution. Virtual storage provides a number of advantages. First, primary storage is utilized more fully. Many more programs can be in primary storage because only one page of each program actually resides there. Second, **programmers no longer have to worry about the size of the primary storage area.**

Figure 7.3
Virtual storage. Virtual storage is based on the fact that in general, only a few statements in a program can actually be utilized at any given moment. In virtual storage, programs are broken down into small sections called pages. Individual program pages are read into memory only when needed. The rest of the program is stored on disk until it is required. In this way, very large programs can be executed by small machines, or a large number of programs can be executed concurrently by a single machine.

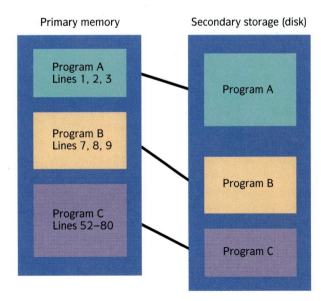

Primary memory   Secondary storage (disk)

Program A
Lines 1, 2, 3

Program A

Program B
Lines 7, 8, 9

Program B

Program C
Lines 52–80

Program C

Before virtual storage, programs could obviously be no larger than the computer's main memory that stored them. With virtual storage, programs can be of infinite length and small machines can execute a program of any size (admittedly, small machines will take longer than big machines to execute a large program). With virtual storage, there is no limit to a program's storage requirements.

TIME SHARING

Time sharing: The sharing of computer resources by many users simultaneously by having the CPU spend a fixed amount of time on each user's program before proceeding to the next.

Time sharing is an operating system capability that allows many users to share computer processing resources simultaneously. It differs from multiprogramming in that the CPU spends a fixed amount of time on one program before moving on to another. In a time-sharing environment, thousands of users are each allocated a tiny slice of computer time (2 milliseconds). In this time slot, each user is free to perform any required operations; at the end of this period, another user is given a 2-millisecond time slice of the CPU. This arrangement permits many users to be connected to a CPU simultaneously, with each receiving only a tiny amount of CPU time. But since the CPU is operating at the nanosecond level, a CPU can accomplish a great deal of work in two milliseconds.

MULTIPROCESSING

Multiprocessing: An operating system feature for executing two or more instructions simultaneously in a single computer system by using more than one central processing unit.

Multiprocessing is an operating system capability that links together two or more CPUs to work in parallel in a single computer system. The operating system can assign multiple CPUs to execute different instructions from the same program or from different programs simultaneously, dividing the work between the CPUs. While multiprogramming uses concurrent processing with one CPU, multiprocessing uses simultaneous processing with multiple CPUs.

Language Translation and Utility Software

Source code: Program instructions written in a high-level language before translation into machine language.

Compiler: Special system software that translates a higher-level language into machine language for execution by the computer.

Object code: Program instructions that have been translated into machine language so that they can be executed by the computer.

Interpreter: A special language translator that translates each source code statement into machine code and executes it one at a time.

Utility program: System software consisting of programs for routine, repetitive tasks, which can be shared by many users.

When computers execute programs written in languages such as COBOL, FORTRAN, or C, the computer must convert these "human readable" instructions into a form it can understand. Computers interpret binary ones and zeros, and the language translators found in system software make the conversion. System software includes special language translator programs that translate higher-level language programs written in programming languages such as BASIC, COBOL, and FORTRAN into machine language that the computer can execute. This type of system software is called a *compiler* or *interpreter*. The program in the high-level language before translation into machine language is called **source code.** A **compiler** translates source code into machine code called **object code.** Just before execution by the computer, the object code modules are joined together with other object code modules in a process called linkage editing. The resulting load module is what is actually executed by the computer. Figure 7.4 illustrates the language translation process.

Some programming languages, like BASIC, do not use a compiler but an **interpreter,** which translates each source code statement one at a time into machine code and executes it. Interpreter languages like BASIC provide immediate feedback to the programmer if a mistake is made, but they are very slow to execute because they are translated one statement at a time.

An assembler is similar to a compiler but is used to translate only assembly language (see Section 7.3) into machine code.

System software includes **utility programs** for routine, repetitive tasks, such as copying, clearing primary storage, computing a square root, or sorting. If you have worked on a computer and have performed such functions as setting up new files, deleting old files, or formatting diskettes, you have worked with utility programs. Utility programs are prewritten programs that are stored so that they can be shared by all users of a computer system and can be rapidly used in many different information system applications when requested.

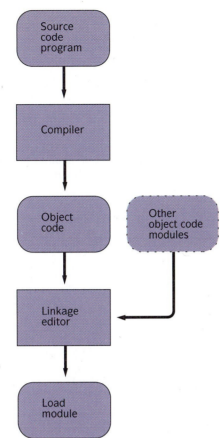

Figure 7.4
The language translation process. The source code, the program in a high-level language, is translated by the compiler into object code so that the instructions can be "understood" by the machine. These are grouped into modules. Prior to execution, the object code modules are joined together by the linkage editor to create the load module. It is the load module that is actually executed by the computer.

Microcomputer Operating Systems

Like any other software, microcomputer software is based on specific operating systems and computer hardware. A software package written for one microcomputer operating system cannot run on another. The microcomputer operating systems themselves have distinctive features—such as whether they support multitasking or graphics work—that determine the types of applications they are suited for.

Multitasking is one of the principal strengths of operating systems such as IBM's OS/2 (Operating System/2) for the IBM Personal System/2 line of microcomputers or UNIX. PC-DOS and MS-DOS, the older operating system for IBM personal computers and IBM PC clones, do not allow multitasking, although the Microsoft Corporation markets Windows software to create a multitasking environment for DOS programs.

Table 7.1 compares the leading microcomputer operating systems—OS/2, UNIX, DOS, Windows NT and the Macintosh operating system. **DOS** was the most popular operating system for 16-bit microcomputers. It is still widely used today with more powerful microcomputers based on the IBM microcomputer standard because so much available application software has been written for systems using DOS. (PC-DOS is used exclusively with IBM microcomputers. MS-DOS is used with other 16-bit microcomputers that function like the IBM microcomputer.) DOS itself does not support multitasking and limits the size of a program in memory to 640K.

OS/2 is a robust operating system that is used with new 32-bit IBM Personal System/2 microcomputer workstations. OS/2 can run faster than DOS (which can only address data in 16-bit chunks) because it can address data in 32-bit chunks. OS/2 is being used for more complex memory-intensive applications or those that require networking or multitasking. OS/2 supports multitasking, accommodates

DOS: Operating system for 16-bit microcomputers based on the IBM Personal Computer standard.

OS/2: Powerful operating system used with the 32-bit IBM/Personal System/2 microcomputer workstations that supports multitasking, networking, and more memory-intensive applications than DOS.

Table 7.1 LEADING MICROCOMPUTER OPERATING SYSTEMS

Operating System	Features
OS/2 (Operating System/2)	Operating system for the IBM Personal System/2 line of microcomputer workstations. Can take advantage of the 32-bit microprocessor. Supports multitasking and networking and can run large programs that require more than 640 K of memory.
Windows NT	32-bit operating system for microcomputers and workstations not limited to Intel microprocessors. Supports multitasking, multiprocessing and networking and can run programs that require more than 640 K of memory.
UNIX (XENIX)	Used for powerful microcomputers, workstations, and minicomputers. Supports multitasking, multi-user processing, and networking. Is portable to different models of computer hardware.
System 7	Operating system for the Macintosh computer. Supports multitasking and has powerful graphics and multimedia capabilities.
PC-DOS	Operating system for the IBM Personal Computer. Limits program use of memory to 640 K.
MS-DOS	Contains features similar to PC-DOS but is the operating system for IBM PC clones (microcomputers that function like the IBM Personal Computer).

larger applications, allows applications to be run simultaneously, supports networked applications, and is a much more protected operating system. One application that crashes is less likely to bring the whole operating system and other applications down with it. This operating system requires powerful computer hardware—a minimum 80386 microprocessor, 4 megabytes of RAM, and 60 megabyte hard disk. OS/2 provides powerful desktop computers with mainframe operating system-like capabilities, such as multitasking and supporting multiple users in networks. The CSX Corporation described in the case concluding Chapter 2 adopted OS/2 as its corporate standard because it believed OS/2 had the power to support industrial-strength applications and cooperative processing.

Windows NT is a new operating system developed by Microsoft with features that make it more appropriate for business-critical applications in networked environments than DOS or DOS with the Windows graphical user interface shell (see the following section). Windows NT uses the same graphical user interface as Windows but it has powerful multitasking and memory management capabilities. Windows NT can support existing software written for DOS and it can provide mainframe-like computing capability for new applications with massive memory and file requirements. It can address data in 32-bit chunks if required and can even support multiprocessing with multiple CPUs. Unlike OS/2, Windows NT is not tied to computer hardware based on Intel microprocessors. It can run on microcomputers and workstations using microprocessors from Mips Computer Systems Inc. or DEC's new Alpha chip (see the Window on Technology in Chapter 6). A company might choose Windows NT if it values flexibility and wants to use an operating system that can run different types of applications on a variety of computer hardware platforms using a common interface that is familiar to users. Although Windows NT can run on 80386-based microcomputers, it operates better on microcomputers or workstations with the minimum processing capacity of an 80486 microprocessor and requires 16 megabytes of RAM and a 100-megabyte hard disk.

UNIX was developed at Bell Laboratories in 1969 to help scientific researchers share data and programs while keeping other information private. It is an

Windows NT: Powerful operating system developed by Microsoft for use with 32-bit microcomputers and workstations based on Intel and other microprocessors. Supports networking, multitasking, and multiprocessing.

UNIX: Operating system for microcomputers, minicomputers, and mainframes that is machine-independent and supports multiuser processing, multitasking, and networking.

interactive, multi-user, multitasking operating system. Many people can use UNIX simultaneously to perform the same kind of task, or one user can run many tasks on UNIX concurrently. UNIX was developed to connect various machines together and is highly supportive of communications and networking.

UNIX was initially designed for minicomputers but now has versions for microcomputers and mainframes. UNIX can run on many different kinds of computers and can be easily customized. It can also store and manage a large number of files. At present, UNIX is primarily used for workstations, minicomputers, and inexpensive multi-user environments in small businesses, but its use in large businesses is growing because of its machine-independence. Application programs that run under UNIX can be ported from one computer to run on a different computer with little modification.

UNIX is accused of being unfriendly to users. It is powerful but very complex. It has a legion of commands, some of which are very cryptic and terse. A typing error on a command line can easily destroy important files. UNIX cannot respond well to problems caused by the overuse of system resources such as jobs or disk space. UNIX also poses some security problems, since multiple jobs and users can access the same file simultaneously. Finally, UNIX requires huge amounts of random access memory and disk capacity, limiting its usefulness for less powerful microcomputers.

System 7: Operating system for the Macintosh computer which supports multitasking and has powerful graphics and multimedia capabilities.

System 7, the latest version of Macintosh system software, features multitasking as well as powerful graphics capabilities, and a mouse-driven graphical user interface (illustrated in Figure 7.5). An extension of this operating system called QuickTime allows Macintosh users to integrate video clips, stereo sound, and animated sequences with conventional text and graphics software. (Recall the discussion of multimedia in Chapter 6.) System 7 has some features that make it attractive for global applications. For instance, it provides system-level support for Asian languages with large character sets.

Figure 7.5
System 7 — Macintosh system software. System 7 supports powerful graphics capabilities as well as multitasking. Users can view multiple windows and make selections by clicking on icons in pull-down menus. *Courtesy of John Greenleigh/Apple Computer, Inc.*

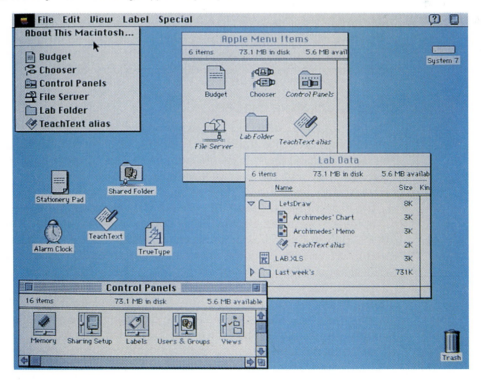

Graphical User Interfaces

Graphical user interface: The part of an operating system that users interact with that uses graphic icons and the computer mouse to issue commands and make selections.

Whenever users interact with a computer, even a microcomputer, the interaction is controlled by an operating system. The user interface is the part of an information system that users interact with. Users communicate with an operating system through the user interface of that operating system. Early microcomputer operating systems were command-driven, but the **graphical user interface,** first popularized by the Macintosh operating system, makes extensive use of icons, buttons, bars, and boxes to perform the same task. It is starting to become the dominant model for the user interface of microcomputer operating systems.

Older microcomputer operating systems, such as PC-DOS or MS-DOS, are command-driven. The user must type in commands such as *DELETE FILEB* to perform tasks such as deleting a file named FILEB. As illustrated in Figure 7.5, the Macintosh computer uses graphical symbols called icons to depict programs, files, and activities. Commands can be activated by rolling a mouse to move a cursor about the screen and clicking a button on the mouse to make selections. A file can be deleted by moving the cursor to the "Trash" icon.

Proponents of the graphical user interface claim that graphical user interfaces save learning time because computing novices do not have to learn different arcane commands for each application. Common functions such as getting help, saving files, or printing output are performed the same way. A complex series of commands can be issued simply by linking icons. Commands are standardized from one program to the next, so that using new programs is often possible without additional training or use of reference manuals. For example, the steps involved in printing a letter created by a word processing program or a financial statement generated by a spreadsheet program should be the same. Graphical user interfaces also promote superior screen and print output communicated through graphics.

Windows: A graphical user interface shell that runs in conjunction with the DOS microcomputer operating system. Supports multitasking and some forms of networking.

Microsoft **Windows** is a highly popular graphical user interface shell that runs in conjunction with the DOS operating system. Windows supports multitasking and some forms of networking but shares the memory limitations of DOS. It is not considered to run very efficiently in a multitasking environment. Early versions of Windows had some problems with application crashes when multiple programs competed for the same memory space. OS/2 has its own graphical user interface called the Workplace Shell, which resembles the graphical user interface for the Macintosh computer. It provides users with a consistent graphical user interface across applications. OS/2 supports DOS applications and can run Windows and DOS applications at the same time in its own resizable windows. The chapter-ending case explores the advantages, disadvantages, and business implications of these two graphical user interfaces and their operating systems.

Selecting a Microcomputer Operating System

How should a firm go about choosing the operating system for its microcomputer-based applications? Should the decision be made only on the basis of technical merits? Should companies look at other issues such as ease of use, training, and the cost of hardware and software that use the operating system? This brief survey suggests that there are many factors to consider.

If a firm wants an operating system for its mainstream business applications, it needs an operating system that is compatible with the software required by these applications. The operating system should be easy to use and install. The user interface features of the operating system should be easy to learn. Mission-critical applications have special operating system requirements, since businesses depend on them for their continuing operation and survival. For such applications, an operating system that provides reliable support for multitasking and memory management is essential. The operating system should be able to run multiple applications quickly without having the system crash because applications are contending for the same memory space. Mission-critical applications typically have large volumes of transactions to process and require operating systems that can handle large complex software programs and massive files.

When selecting a microcomputer operating system, some key questions to ask are:

- What application software runs on the operating system?
- What kind of computer hardware does the operating system run on?
- How quickly does the operating system run?
- How easy is the operating system to learn and use?
- Is the operating system designed for single users or for multiple users on networks?
- Does the operating system have strong multitasking capabilities?
- How reliable is the operating system?
- How much does it cost to install the operating system?
- What technical support and assistance is required to install and run the operating system? Where is this support available?

7.3 Application Software

Application software is primarily concerned with accomplishing the tasks of end users. Many different programming languages can be used to develop application software. Each has different strengths and drawbacks.

Generations of Programming Languages

Machine language:
Programming language consisting of the 1s and 0s of binary code.

To communicate with the first generation of computers, programmers had to write programs in **machine language**—the 0s and 1s of binary code. End users who wanted applications had to work with specialized programmers who could understand, think, and work directly in the machine language of a particular computer. Programming in 0s and 1s, reducing all statements such as add, subtract, and divide into a series of 0s and 1s, made early programming a slow, labor-intensive process.

As computer hardware improved and processing speed and memory size increased, computer languages changed from machine language to languages that were easier for humans to understand. Generations of programming languages developed to correspond with the generations of computer hardware. Figure 7.6 shows the development of programming languages over the last 50 years as the capabilities of hardware have increased.

Machine language was the first-generation programming language. The second generation of programming languages occurred in the early 1950s with the development of assembly language. Instead of using 0s and 1s, programmers could now substitute language-like acronyms and words such as *add, sub* (subtract), and *load* in programming statements. A language translator called a *compiler* converted the English-like statements into machine language.

When the third hardware generation was under way, programming languages entered their third generation as well. From the mid 1950s to the 1970s, the first higher-level languages emerged. These languages permitted mathematicians for the first time to work with computers through the use of languages such as FORTRAN (FORmula TRANslator program). Mathematicians were now able to define variables with statements such as $Z = A + B$. The software translated these definitions and mathematical statements into a series of 0s and 1s. COBOL (COmmon Business Oriented Language) permitted the use of English statements such as *print* and *sort* to be used by programmers, who did not have to think in terms of 0s and 1s.

High-level language:
Programming languages where each source code statement generates multiple statements at the machine-language level.

These **high-level languages** are so called because each statement in COBOL or FORTRAN generates multiple statements at the machine-language level. The use of these higher-level languages requires much faster, more efficient compilers to translate higher-level languages into machine codes.

Figure 7.6

Generations of programming languages. As the capabilities of hardware increased, programming languages developed from the first generation of machine and second generation of assembly languages of the 1950s to 1960, through the third generation high-level languages developed in the 1960s and 1970s, to the fourth-generation languages.

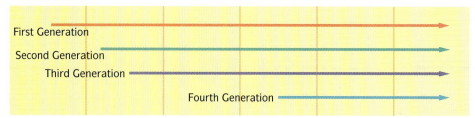

A. Generations

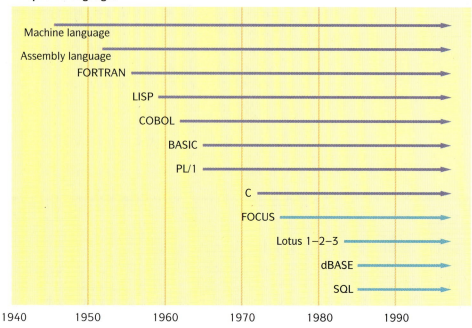

B. Specific languages

Fourth-generation computer languages emerged in the late 1970s, and their development is still in progress. These languages dramatically reduce programming time and make software tasks so easy that nontechnical computer users can develop applications without the help of professional programmers. Fourth-generation tools also include prewritten application software packages that can be used directly by end users. Using the software package LOTUS 1-2-3, for instance, users can create their own financial spreadsheets and manipulate data without programmer intervention. Such sophistication by nonspecialists using FORTRAN would have been impossible in the 1960s and 1970s.

There is, of course, a clear relationship between the increasing capacity of computer hardware and software. Each new generation of software requires more and more primary storage area, faster compilers, and larger secondary storage. Higher-level language programs require a huge amount of memory. For instance, to load the Statistical Package for the Social Sciences (SPSS), the program alone may require over 200K (200,000 bytes of primary storage). If work space is included within primary memory, up to 512K may be required.

Popular Programming Languages

Most managers need not be expert programmers, but they should understand how to evaluate software applications and to select programming languages that are appropriate for their organization's objectives. We will now briefly describe the more popular high-level and very high-level languages.

Assembly language: A programming language developed in the 1950s that resembles machine language but substitutes mnemonics for numeric codes.

Many programmers still prefer to write programs in assembly language because this language gives them close control over the hardware and very efficient execution. Like machine language, **assembly language** (Figure 7.7) is designed for a specific machine and specific microprocessors. For instance, there is a specific assembly language associated with the Intel 80386 chip used in an IBM microcomputer. In general, there is a one-to-one correspondence between machine language and assembly language. Each operation in assembly corresponds to a machine operation. On the other hand, assembly language does make use of certain mnemonics (e.g., *load, sum*) and assigns addresses and storage locations automatically. While assembly language gives programmers great control, it is costly in terms of programmer time, is difficult to read and debug, and is difficult to learn. Assembly language is used primarily today in system software.

Figure 7.7
Assembly language. This sample assembly language command adds the contents of register 3 to register 5 and stores the result in register 5.

```
AR 5, 3
```

FORTRAN (FORmula TRANslator): Programming language developed in 1956 for scientific and mathematical applications.

FORTRAN (FORmula TRANslator) (Figure 7.8) was developed in 1956 to provide an easier way of writing scientific and engineering applications. FORTRAN is especially useful in processing numeric data. Many kinds of business applications can be written in FORTRAN, it is relatively easy to learn, and contemporary versions (e.g., FORTRAN 77) provide sophisticated structures for controlling program logic. FORTRAN is not very good at providing input/output efficiency or in printing and working with lists. The syntax is very strict and keying errors are common, making the programs difficult to debug.

Figure 7.8
FORTRAN. This sample FORTRAN program code is part of a program to compute sales figures for a particular item.

```
READ (5,100) ID, QUANT, PRICE
TOTAL = QUANT * PRICE
```

COBOL (COmmon Business Oriented Language): Predominant programming language for business applications because it can process large data files with alphanumeric characters.

COBOL (COmmon Business Oriented Language) (Figure 7.9) came into use in the early 1960s. It was originally developed because the Defense Department wished to create a common administrative language for internal and external software. COBOL was designed with business administration in mind, for processing large data files with alphanumeric characters (mixed alphabetic and numeric data), and for performing repetitive tasks like payroll. Its primary data structures are records, files, tables, and lists. COBOL is easily learned by business analysts. As the most widely used programming language, it is supported by external groups, and there is an abundance of productivity aids. The weakness of COBOL is a result of its virtue. It is poor at complex mathematical calculations. There are many versions of COBOL, and not all are compatible with each other. Lengthy COBOL programs—some hundreds of thousands of lines long for major payroll programs, for example—can become so complex as to be virtually incomprehensible.

Figure 7.9
COBOL. This sample COBOL
program code is part of a
routine to compute total sales
figures for a particular item.

MULTIPLY QUANT-SOLD BY UNIT-PRICE GIVING SALES-TOTAL.

BASIC

BASIC (Beginners All-purpose Symbolic Instruction Code): General-purpose programming language used with microcomputers and for teaching programming.

BASIC (Beginners All-purpose Symbolic Instruction Code) was developed in 1964 by John Kemeny and Thomas Kurtz to teach students at Dartmouth College how to use computers. Today it is the most popular programming language on college campuses and for microcomputers. BASIC can do almost all computer processing tasks from inventory to mathematical calculations. It is easy to use, demonstrates computer capabilities well, and requires only a small interpreter. The weakness of BASIC is that it does few tasks well even though it does them all. It has no sophisticated program logic control or data structures, which makes it difficult to use in teaching good programming practices. While BASIC has only a few commands and is easily learned, subsequent versions of the language that have tried to add to the early syntax make the new versions of BASIC incompatible with the old ones. Therefore, BASIC programs often cannot be moved from one machine to another.

PL/1

PL/1 (Programming Language 1): Programming language developed by IBM in 1964 for business and scientific applications.

PL/1 (Programming Language 1) was developed by IBM in 1964. It is the most powerful general-purpose programming language because it can handle mathematical and business applications with ease, is highly efficient in input/output activities, and can handle large volumes of data.

Unfortunately, the huge volume of COBOL and FORTRAN programs written in the private sector at great cost cannot simply be jettisoned when a newer, more powerful language comes along. There are an estimated 12 billion lines of COBOL code in production in the United States. This represents an investment of over $52 trillion. PL/1 has not succeeded largely because programmers trained in COBOL could not be convinced to learn an entirely new language; and business organizations could not be convinced to spend millions of dollars rewriting their software. PL/1 is, moreover, somewhat difficult to learn in its entirety.

PASCAL

Pascal: Programming language used on microcomputers and to teach sound programming practices in computer science courses.

Named after Blaise Pascal, the seventeenth-century mathematician and philosopher, **Pascal** was developed by the Swiss computer science professor Niklaus Wirth of Zurich in the late 1960s. Pascal programs can be compiled using minimal computer memory, so they can be used on microcomputers. With sophisticated structures to control program logic and a simple, powerful set of commands, Pascal is used primarily in computer science courses to teach sound programming practices. The language is weak at file handling and input/output and is not easy for beginners to use.

ADA

Ada: Programming language that is portable across different brands of hardware; is used for both military and nonmilitary applications.

Ada was developed in 1980 to provide the United States Defense Department with a structured programming language to serve as the standard for all of its applications. This language was initially conceived for weapons systems where software is developed on a processor and then imbedded into the weapon. It was explicitly designed so that it could be uniformly executed in diverse hardware environments. The language also promotes structured software design. U.S. government experts hope Ada will produce more cost-effective software because it facilitates more clearly structured code than COBOL.

Congress passed legislation mandating Ada for all system development work for the U.S. Department of Defense, and Ada is used in nonmilitary government applications as well. The language can also be used for general business applications since it can operate on microcomputers and is portable across different brands of computer hardware. Will Ada emerge as a software standard for the business world? Many firms do not think so, for the same reasons they did not embrace PL/1. They are not convinced that it is worth the investment and risk to abandon COBOL as the business standard.

C

C: Powerful programming language with tight control and efficiency of execution; is portable across different microprocessors and is used primarily with microcomputers.

C was developed at AT&T's Bell Labs in the early 1970s and is the language in which much of the UNIX operating system is written. C combines some of the tight control and efficiency of execution features of assembly language with machine portability. In other words, it can work on a variety of computers rather than on just one. Much commercial microcomputer software has been written in C, but C is gaining support for some minicomputer and mainframe applications. C is unlikely to dislodge COBOL for mainframe business applications, but it will be used increasingly for commercial microcomputer software and for scientific and technical applications.

LISP AND PROLOG

LISP (designating LISt Processor) and Prolog are widely used in artificial intelligence. LISP was created in the late 1950s by M.I.T. mathematician John McCarthy and is oriented toward putting symbols such as operations, variables, and data values into meaningful lists. LISP is better at manipulating symbols than at ordinary number crunching.

Prolog, introduced around 1970, is also well suited to symbol manipulation and can run on general-purpose computers, whereas LISP usually runs best on machines configured especially to run LISP programs.

7.4 New Software Tools and Approaches

Fourth-generation language: A programming language that can be employed directly by end users or less skilled programmers to develop computer applications more rapidly than conventional programming languages.

Fourth-generation languages consist of a variety of software tools that enable end users to develop software applications with minimal or no technical assistance or that enhance the productivity of professional programmers. Fourth-generation languages tend to be nonprocedural or less procedural than conventional programming languages. Procedural languages require specification of the sequence of steps, or procedures, that tell the computer what to do and how to do it. Nonprocedural languages need only to specify what has to be accomplished rather than provide details about how to carry out the task. Thus, a nonprocedural language can accomplish the same task with fewer steps and lines of program code than a procedural language.

Fourth-Generation Languages

There are seven categories of fourth-generation languages: query languages, report generators, graphics languages, application generators, very-high-level programming languages, application software packages, and microcomputer tools. Figure 7.10 illustrates the spectrum of these tools and some commercially available products in each category.

QUERY LANGUAGES

Query language: A high-level computer language used to retrieve specific information from databases or files.

Query languages are high-level languages for retrieving data stored in databases or files. They are usually interactive, on-line, and capable of supporting requests for information that are not predefined. They are often tied to database management systems (see Chapter 8) and microcomputer tools (see the following discussion). Query languages can search a database or file, using simple or complex selection criteria to display information relating to multiple records. Available query language tools have different kinds of syntax and structure,

Microcomputer tools	Query languages/ report generators	Graphics languages	Application generators	Application software packages	Very high-level programming languages
Lotus 1–2–3	Easytrieve	Tell-a-Graf	FOCUS	MSA Payroll	APL
dBASE IV	Intellect	SAS Graph	DMS	Maxicalc	Nomad
WordPerfect	Query-By-Example		SAS	AVP Sales/Use Tax	
Flow Charting II+	SQL		Mapper	AMAPS	
	RPG–III		ADS/Online		
	Inquire		Ideal		
	Mark IV		Natural		
			CSP		

Figure 7.10
Fourth-generation languages. The spectrum of major categories of "fourth-generation" languages and commercially available products in each category is illustrated. Tools range from those that are simple and designated primarily for end users to complex tools designed for information systems professionals.

some being closer to natural language than others (Vassiliou, 1984–1985). Some support updating of data as well as retrieval. An example of a typical ad hoc query is "List all employees in the payroll department." Figure 7.11 illustrates how two different query languages FOCUS and Query-By-Example, express this request.

REPORT GENERATORS

Report generator: Software that creates customized reports in a wide range of formats that are not routinely produced by an information system.

Report generators are facilities for creating customized reports. They extract data from files or databases and create reports in many formats. Report generators generally provide more control over the way data are formatted, organized, and displayed than query languages. The more powerful report generators can manipulate data with complex calculations and logic before they are output. Some report generators are extensions of database or query languages. The more complex and powerful report generators may not be suitable for end users without some assistance from professional information systems specialists.

GRAPHICS LANGUAGES

Graphics language: A computer language that displays data from files or databases in graphic format.

Graphics languages retrieve data from files or databases and display them in graphic format. Users can ask for data and specify how they are to be charted. Some graphics software can perform arithmetic or logical operations on data as well. SAS, Harvard Graphics, and Graph Plan are popular graphics tools.

Figure 7.11
Query languages. This figure illustrates how the simple query, "List all employees in the Payroll department," would be handled by the two different query languages: Query-By-Example and FOCUS.

Query: "List all employees in the Payroll department."

Using Query-By-Example:

EMPLOYEE	EMPLOYEE #	NAME	DEPARTMENT
		P.	PAYROLL

Using FOCUS:

```
> > TABLE FILE EMPDEPT
> PRINT EMP_NAME IF DEPT EQ 'PAYROLL'
> END
```

APPLICATION GENERATORS

Application generator: Software that can generate entire information system applications; the user needs only to specify what needs to be done and the application generator creates the appropriate program code.

Application generators contain preprogrammed modules that can generate entire applications, greatly speeding development. A user can specify what needs to be done and the application generator will create the appropriate code for input, validation, updating, processing, and reporting. Most full-function application generators consist of a comprehensive, integrated set of development tools: a database management system, data dictionary, query language, screen painter, graphics generator, report generator, decision support/modeling tools, security facilities, and a high-level programming language. For unique requirements that cannot be met with generalized modules, most application generators contain *user exits* where custom-programmed routines can be inserted. Some application generators are interactive, enabling users sitting at a terminal to define inputs, files, processing, and reports by responding to questions on-line.

VERY-HIGH-LEVEL PROGRAMMING LANGUAGES

Very-high-level programming language: Programming language using fewer instructions than conventional languages. Used primarily as a professional programmer productivity tool.

Very-high-level programming languages are designed to generate program code with fewer instructions than conventional languages such as COBOL or FORTRAN. Programs and applications based on these languages can be developed in much shorter periods of time. Simple features of these languages can be employed by end users. However, these languages are designed primarily as productivity tools for professional programmers. APL and Nomad2 are examples of these languages.

APPLICATION SOFTWARE PACKAGES

Software package: A prewritten, precoded, commercially available set of programs that eliminates the need to write software programs for certain functions.

A **software package** is a prewritten, precoded, commercially available set of programs that eliminates the need for individuals or organizations to write their own software programs for certain functions. There are software packages for system software, but the vast majority of package software is application software.

Application software packages consist of prewritten application software that is marketed commercially. These packages are available for major business applications on mainframes, minicomputers, and microcomputers. They contain customization features so that they can be tailored somewhat to an organization's unique requirements. Although application packages for large complex systems must be installed by technical specialists, many application packages, especially those for microcomputers, are marketed directly to end users. Systems development based on application packages is discussed in Chapter 12.

MICROCOMPUTER TOOLS

Some of the most popular and productivity-promoting fourth-generation tools are the general-purpose application packages that have been developed for microcomputers, especially word processing, spreadsheet, data management, graphics, and desktop publishing software.

WORD PROCESSING SOFTWARE

Word processing software: Software that handles electronic storage, editing, formatting, and printing of documents.

Word processing software stores text data electronically as a computer file rather than on paper. The word processing software allows the user to make changes in the document electronically in memory. This eliminates the need to retype an entire page in order to incorporate corrections. The software has formatting options to make changes in line spacing, margins, character size, and column width. Microsoft Word and WordPerfect are popular word processing packages. Figure 7.12 illustrates a Microsoft Word screen for Windows displaying text and options such as printing, copying, searching, and deleting.

Most word processing software has advanced features that automate other writing tasks: spelling checkers, style checkers (to analyze grammar and punctuation), thesaurus programs, and mail merge programs (which link letters or other text documents with names and addresses in a mailing list).

Figure 7.12
Text and some of the options
available in Microsoft Word for
Windows. Word processors
provide many easy-to-use
options to create and output a
text document to meet a user's
specifications. *Courtesy of
Microsoft.*

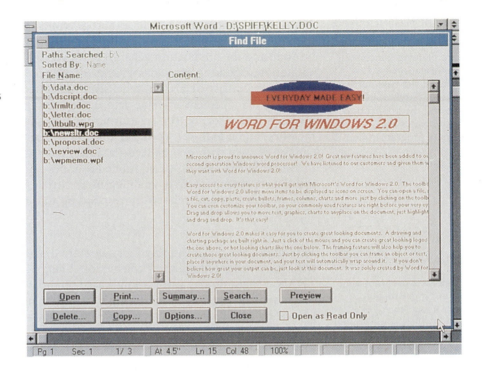

SPREADSHEETS

Spreadsheet: Software
displaying data in a grid of
columns and rows, with the
capability of easily
recalculating numerical data.

Electronic **spreadsheet** software provides computerized versions of traditional financial modeling tools such as the accountant's columnar pad, pencil, and calculator. An electronic spreadsheet is organized into a grid of columns and rows. The power of the electronic spreadsheet is evident when one changes a value or values, because all other related values on the spreadsheet will be automatically recomputed.

Spreadsheets are valuable for applications where numerous calculations with pieces of data must be related to each other. Spreadsheets are also useful for applications that require modeling and "what-if" analysis. After the user has constructed a set of mathematical relationships, the spreadsheet can be recalculated instantaneously using a different set of assumptions. A number of alternatives can easily be evaluated by changing one or two pieces of data without having to rekey in the rest of the worksheet. Many spreadsheet packages include graphics functions that can present data in the form of line graphs, bar graphs, or pie charts. The most popular spreadsheet packages are Lotus 1-2-3, Quattro, and Microsoft Excel.

Accounting and business
systems in offices at the
beginning of the twentieth
century bear little resemblance
to modern offices and
computerized information
systems.

Figure 7.13
Spreadsheet software. Spreadsheet software organizes data into columns and rows for analysis and manipulation. Contemporary spreadsheet software provides graphing abilities for clear visual representation of the data in the spreadsheets. This sample breakeven analysis is represented as numbers in a spreadsheet as well as a line graph for easy interpretation.

Total fixed cost	19,000.00
Variable cost per unit	3.00
Average sales price	17.00
Contribution margin	14.00
Breakeven point	1357

Custom Neckties Pro Forma Income Statement

Units Sold	0.00	679	1357	2036	2714
Revenue	0	11,536	23,071	34,607	46,143
Fixed Cost	19,000	19,000	19,000	19,000	19,000
Variable Cost	0	2,036	4,071	6,107	8,143
Total Cost	19,000	21,036	23,071	25,107	27,143
Profit/Loss	(19,000)	(9,500)	0	9,500	19,000

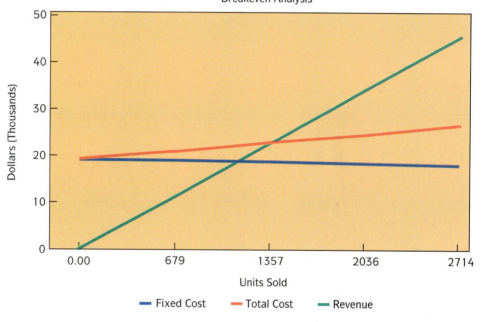

Figure 7.13 illustrates the output from a spreadsheet for a breakeven analysis and its accompanying graph.

DATA MANAGEMENT SOFTWARE

Data management software: Software used for creating and manipulating lists, creating files and databases to store data, and combining information for reports.

While spreadsheet programs are powerful tools for manipulating quantitative data, **data management software** is more suitable for creating and manipulating lists and for combining information from different files. Microcomputer database management packages have programming features and easy-to-learn menus that enable nonspecialists to build small information systems.

Data management software typically has facilities for creating files and databases and for storing, modifying, and manipulating data for reports and queries. A detailed treatment of data management software and database management systems can be found in Chapter 8. Popular database management software for the personal computer includes dBASE IV (R), dBASE III PLUS (R), Paradox, Rbase, and Foxbase. Figure 7.14 illustrates a screen from dBASE IV showing how the menu can be used to initiate creation of files, queries, reports, labels, forms, and applications.

Integrated software package: A software package that provides two or more applications, such as spreadsheets and word processing, providing for easy transfer of data between them.

Integrated software packages combine the functions of the most important microcomputer software packages, such as spreadsheets, word processing, graphics, and data management. This integration provides a more general-purpose software tool and eliminates redundant data entry and data maintenance. For example, the breakeven analysis spreadsheet illustrated in Figure 7.13 could be reformatted into a polished report with word processing software without separately keying the data into both programs. Integrated packages are a compromise. While they can do many things well, they generally do not have the same power and depth as single-purpose packages.

As Chapter 12 will discuss, these advanced tools have important limitations. They are applicable only to specific areas of application development. Nevertheless, as illustrated by the Window on Management, fourth-generation tools have provided many productivity and cost-cutting benefits for businesses.

Object-Oriented Programming

A growing backlog of software projects and the need for businesses to fashion systems that are flexible and quick to build have spawned a new approach to software development with "object-oriented" programming tools. Object-oriented concepts go back to the 1970s, but it is only recently that high-capacity hardware and iconic, graphic, windowed software (see section 7.2 on graphical user interfaces) have made them a viable alternative.

Traditional software development methods have treated data and procedures as independent components. A separate programming procedure must be written every time someone wants to take an action on a particular piece of data. The procedures act on data that the program passes to them.

W I N D O W   O N
MANAGEMENT
Can Cutting-Edge Software Pinch Pennies?

How can Merchants Distributors, Inc., a billion-dollar-a-year wholesale food distributor stay competitive in an industry known for paper-thin profit margins? One way may be to adopt a penny-pinching strategy for using information system technology.

Merchants Distributors, Inc. (MDI) is the parent organization for three companies: MDI Wholesale, a food distributor to grocery stores; Lowe's Food Stores, a 52-store retail chain in North Carolina and Virginia; and Institution Food House, Inc., a supplier to restaurants, hospitals, and other institutions. As the business grew, MDI's small IBM 4381 series mainframe began to run out of steam. Upgrading to a more technologically advanced machine required a new operating system and programming work to convert existing application software to the new environment. The total bill was estimated at about $2 million. So MDI decided in-

stead to keep its existing software and buy more powerful computer hardware—a used IBM 3081 series mainframe that could run the same operating system and application software. That cost MDI only $120,000 and bought another three years of processing.

It also freed up MDI's information systems staff to concentrate on mission-critical applications such as purchasing, billing, and order processing, rather than spending an entire year converting existing software to the new hardware environment. While staying a little technologically behind on the hardware front, MDI took a more cutting-edge tack on the software front. It decided to use fourth-generation languages and application generators in the hope that they would decrease the time the business could generate solutions.

MDI used Natural 4GL, a fourth-generation language, and Natural

Construct, an application generator from Software AG, to create a new order entry and billing system without touching existing COBOL programs for other applications. Natural Construct generates large chunks of Natural code with a few keystrokes. Using these tools, one of MDI's programmers generated a simple program at a terminal in just five minutes. About half of the source code for this new system has been generated by Natural Construct and half by Natural 4GL.

Source: Gary H. Anthes, "Cutting-Edge Software the Key to Food Distributor's Savings." *Computerworld* (February 3, 1992).

To Think About: How did software help this firm meet its goals? Was obtaining software an important management issue for MDI? Why or why not?

Figure 7.14
Data management software. This is the main menu screen from dBASE IV, a database management software package published by Borland International Inc. All rights reserved. *Reprinted by Permission. dBASE IV and dBASE III PLUS are registered trademarks of the Borland International Inc.*

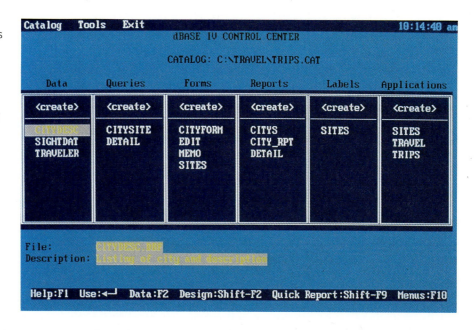

WHAT MAKES OBJECT-ORIENTED PROGRAMMING DIFFERENT?

Object-oriented programming: Approach to software development that combines data and procedures into a single object.

Object-oriented programming combines data and the specific procedures that operate on those data into one "object." The object combines data and program code. Instead of passing data to procedures, programs send a message for an object to perform a procedure that is already embedded into it. (Procedures are termed "methods" in object-oriented languages.) The same message may be sent to many different objects, but each will implement that message differently.

For example, an object-oriented financial application might have Customer objects sending debit and credit messages to Account objects. The Account objects in turn might maintain Cash-on-Hand, Accounts-Payable, and Accounts-Receivable objects.

An object's data are hidden from other parts of the program and can only be manipulated from inside the object. The method for manipulating the object's data can be changed internally without affecting other parts of the program. Programmers can focus on what they want an object to do, and the object decides how to do it.

Because an object's data are encapsulated from other parts of the system, each object is an independent software building block that can be used in many different systems without changing the program code. Thus, object-oriented programming is expected to reduce the time and cost of writing software by producing reusable program code or software "chips" that can be reused in other related systems. Future software work can draw upon a library of reusable objects, and productivity gains from object-oriented technology could be magnified if objects were stored in reusable software libraries such as those described in the Window on Organizations on page 224.

OBJECT-ORIENTED PROGRAMMING CONCEPTS

Object-oriented programming is based on the concepts of class and inheritance. Program code is not written separately for every object but for classes, or general categories of similar objects. Objects belonging to a certain class have the features of that class. Classes of objects in turn can inherit all the structures and behaviors of a more general class and then add variables and behaviors unique to each object. New classes of objects are created by choosing an existing class and specifying how the new class differs from the existing class, instead of starting from scratch each time.

ORGANIZATIONS
Libraries House Reusable Software

In July 1992 the U.S. Department of Defense (DOD) opened its center for Software Reuse Operations in Falls Church, Virginia. The Center provides access to the Pentagon's Defense Software Repository containing 2.2 million lines of Ada and COBOL code in 1531 reusable software modules. The software is primarily for financial and logistics applications.

DOD staff members and contractors can obtain the software using an automated catalog and retrieval system. According to Paul A. Strassman, director of the DOD's Corporate Information Management program, the DOD hopes to meet 50 percent of its needs from reusable components, which will help cut down on errors and reduce the effort required to maintain existing software. The Corporate Information Management (CIM) pro-

gram includes initiatives for software reuse, elimination of redundant systems, and reduction in the number of DOD data processing centers. Strassman expects software reuse to contribute half of CIM's $30 billion target reduction in annual software expenditures.

IBM and the Defense Advanced Research Projects Agency (Darpa) opened a similar library for reusable Ada software components in Morgantown, West Virginia, in December 1991. People can access the IBM-Darpa library, called the Asset Source for Software Engineering Technology, from a network, and they may browse through the catalog and request reusable modules and program codes. The library will transmit programs and supporting material back to the user.

IBM and Darpa hope to create a network of such libraries. Although the current library contains only government-owned and public domain code and information, IBM is recruiting other commercial information systems vendors to list their software in the directory.

Sources: Gary H. Anthes, "Pentagon Opens Software Reuse Center," *Computerworld* (July 27, 1992), and Robert Moran, "Checking Out Software Code," *InformationWEEK* (December 9, 1991).

To Think About: How would you decide whether to utilize a reusable software library? What management, organization and technology factors would you consider?

Class: Feature of object-oriented programming so that all objects belonging to a certain class have all of the features of that class.

Inheritance: Feature of object-oriented programming in which a specific class of objects receives the features of a more general class.

Classes are organized hierarchically into superclasses and subclasses. For example, a "car" class might have a "vehicle" class for a superclass, so that it would inherit all the methods and data previously defined for "vehicle." The design of the car class would only need to describe how cars differ from vehicles. A banking application could define a Savings-Account object that is very much like a Bank-Account object with a few minor differences. Savings-Account inherits all of the Bank-Account's state and methods and then adds a few extras.

We can see how class and **inheritance** work in Figure 7.15, which illustrates a tree of classes concerning employees and how they are paid. Employee is the common ancestor of the other four classes. Contractor and Paid weekly are subclasses of Employee, while Hourly and Salaried are subclasses of Paid weekly. The variables for the class are in the top half of the box, and the methods are in the bottom half. Shaded items in each box are inherited from some ancestor class. (For example, by following the tree upward, we can see that Name and Title in the Contractor, Paid weekly, Hourly, and Salaried subclasses are inherited from the Employee superclass [ancestor class].) Unshaded methods or class variables are unique to a specific class, and they override, or redefine, existing methods. When a subclass overrides an inherited method, its object still responds to the same message, but it executes its definition of the method rather than its ancestor's. Whereas Print is a method inherited from some superclass, the method Make_weekly_paycheck is specific to the Paid weekly class, and Make_weekly_paycheck-OVERRIDE is specific to the Hourly class. The Salaried class uses its own Print-OVERRIDE method.

Trends in Software Capabilities

A long-term view of software shows that the major trend is to increase the ease with which users can interact with the hardware and software. In the next few

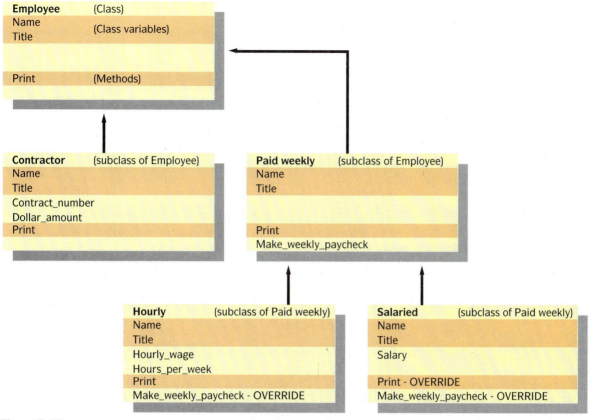

Figure 7.15
Class, subclasses, inheritance, and overriding. This figure illustrates how a message's method can come from the class itself or an ancestor class. Class variables and methods are shaded when they are inherited from above. © *Apple Computer, Inc. Used with permission.*

years, this trend is expected to accelerate. The Window on Technology on page 226 illustrates one kind of software that is being designed to ease the interaction between humans and computers; the software presents and analyzes data geographically.

Software is becoming more interactive through the use of pointer devices such as the computer mouse, the touch screen, and the graphic pad. Voice-recognition software allows people to interact with the computer by speaking. Voice recognition software converts the spoken word into a digital form that computers can recognize. The computer responds by matching the digital translation to a vocabulary database stored in its memory, consisting of phrases, words, or phonemes (units of sound). Voice-synthesis software, on the other hand, works the opposite way, converting digitized computer data back into speech. Voice-recognition and voice-synthesis systems still work with limited vocabularies. They have been used primarily for simple, routine tasks in production-line control and computer-based telemarketing but are not yet sophisticated enough for office information systems.

A second major long-term trend that is expected to accelerate throughout the decade is data access for end users. When end-user computing and microcomputers first appeared in corporations, the central information systems groups often promised that their cherished data would never be made available to nonspecialists on a daily basis. This situation has changed dramatically to the point where the only question is how well users can be brought into direct contact with corporate data.

Virtually all major mainframe database management systems (see Chapter 8) now have extraction programs that can send data to end-user networks, work-

WINDOW ON

TECHNOLOGY

Mapping Solutions with Geographic Information Software

Where are our customers and competitors? How should we organize sales territories? What are the shortest routes for deliveries? Most businesses face these questions. Now they can call on new software tools that visualize and analyze information geographically. Today's geographic information system software ties business data to points, lines, and areas on a map, with these results:

- Instead of plotting delivery routes by hand, companies can ask their information system to find the best route using a digital map of streets and delivery locations.
- With dots on a map representing customers, businesses can see where the people are located and can determine the distance and driving time from warehouses. By pointing to one of these dots, businesses can find out information such as the customer's account name, address, telephone number, sales history, and account balance.

- Businesses can identify areas where sales activity is highly concentrated and can examine the effect of competitors on the geographic distribution of customers.

These geographic systems even combine company data with data from outside sources such as a census. Johanna Dairies, based in Union, New Jersey, is saving money and improving customer service by using digital street maps and computer-aided routing and scheduling software. With routing software, the firm can use geographic locations found in customer orders downloaded from its IBM System/38 minicomputer to define delivery routes. By zooming in on different areas of a city, the firm can see which customers are on each street. This process eliminates overlaps between routes, and thereby reduces the distance trucks have to travel.

The software lets people draw a circle around a group of customers and automatically generates a route and report of the number of

cases to be delivered, their dollar value, the route times, and suggested delivery days. When a major customer changed its manner of distribution from store–door delivery to warehouse distribution, all the routes had to be reworked, and the geographic information software expedited the process.

By using geographic information software, Johanna Dairies was able to eliminate eight of its sixty routes in the New York area. One route costs $100,000 per year, including pay for the driver. Even though the firm spent $80,000 on the software and consultants, the payback started right away.

Source: David Forrest, "Seeing Data in New Ways," *Computerworld* (June 29, 1992).

To Think About: What are some other applications for geographic information software? If you were a manager, what factors would you consider to determine whether to use such software in your firm?

stations, and microcomputers. Almost all of the major microcomputer software packages are now compatible with a wide variety of telecommunications networks linking them to mainframe data.

A third trend is reflected in the marketing of software directly to individual end users. Up to the 1980s, software was marketed almost entirely by specialized software firms to specialist information systems personnel. Throughout the 1990s, we can expect to see software increasingly marketed to actual end users. This trend carries both risks and benefits. On the one hand, the marketplace will encourage the development of software that satisfies end users. On the other hand, end users are frequently incapable of making the best decisions about which software to buy. The risk of buying the wrong software will increase as individuals become bombarded with advertising claims that are difficult to evaluate.

A fourth major software trend is the development of integrated programs that support organizational needs for communication and control. Significant advances in end-user computing, as well as the advent of sophisticated on-line customer account systems like bank teller machines and brokerage firm accounts, require the development of very large, sophisticated programs to manage data for the organization as a whole, to prepare data for end users, to integrate parts of the organization, and to permit precise control and coordination of organizational decision making. (The average size of systems in 1980 was 23,000 lines of code. By 1990, it had mushroomed to 1,246,000 lines of code.

Voice recognition software converts the spoken word into digital form. This worker is using a voice recognition system to enter data into her computer system.

See Swanson et. al., 1991.) These very large systems integrate what once were separate systems (e.g., accounts receivable and order processing) operated by separate departments (e.g., accounting and sales).

7.5 How to Choose Software and Programming Languages

While managers need not become programming specialists, they should know the differences between programming languages and should be able to use clear criteria in deciding which language to use. The most important criteria will now be discussed.

Appropriateness

Some languages are general-purpose languages that can be used on a variety of problems, while others are special-purpose languages suitable for only limited tasks. Special-purpose graphics programs are excellent at creating tables but poor at routine processing of transactions. COBOL is excellent for business data processing but poor at mathematical calculations. Language selection involves identifying the use and the users.

Sophistication

High-level languages should have sophisticated control structures and data structures. Control structures shape the outcome of programs by providing clear, logical, structured programs that are easy to read and maintain. It may be impossible to create a table and then look up values in it unless the language has a table data structure capability. Languages should be selected that support many different data structures.

Organizational Considerations

In order to be effective, a language must be easily learned by the firm's programming staff, easy to maintain and change, and flexible enough so that it can grow with the organization. These organizational considerations have direct long-term cost implications.

In general, sophisticated, well-structured languages are easier to learn and much easier to maintain over the long term than less sophisticated languages.

Support

It is important to purchase software that has widespread use in other organizations and is supported by many consulting firms and services. It is often less expensive to purchase software written elsewhere, or to have a service firm write it, than to develop the software internally. In these situations, it is crucial to have software that is widely used.

A different kind of support is the availability of software editing, debugging, and development aids. Because so many organizations use COBOL, there are hundreds of contemporary software development products available to assist the programming staff. The same cannot be said of Ada, a recently developed general-purpose language.

For instance, many organizations inherit poorly written, so-called spaghetti code programs that have been patched and repaired hundreds of times. After many years, perhaps decades, few people in the organization understand how such programs work. Maintenance is difficult and expensive. Now a number of new products can take poorly written COBOL programs and transform them into sophisticated, modular, documented COBOL, which is easier to maintain.

Another option is reusable software. Only a small portion of the software written is unique, novel, and specific to individual applications. Most consist of generic functions such as edit and conversion routines for Gregorian dates and edits and validation of part, employee, and account numbers. One study found that 85 percent of all programming code written in 1983 was common to many applications and theoretically could have been developed from reusable components. Firms such as the Hartford Insurance Company and GTE Data Services have been trying to support software development by creating libraries of reusable software components.

Efficiency

Although a less important feature than in the past, the efficiency with which a language compiles and executes remains a consideration when purchasing software. Languages with slow compilers, or interpreters like BASIC, can be expensive (in terms of programmer costs) to operate and maintain. In general, fourth-generation languages are very slow and expensive in terms of machine time. As discussed in later chapters, these languages are usually inappropriate for high-speed transaction systems, which must handle thousands of transactions per second.

The digital dashboard, brakes, air bag, door locks, steering, engine, suspension, and air conditioner on luxury automobiles are controlled by software.

Some programming languages are more efficient in the use of machine time than others. PL/1, for instance, requires a large section in memory for its compiler, whereas Pascal and BASIC have much simpler interpreters that require little primary memory. In any event, efficiency should be judged in terms of both machines and personnel. As machine costs fall, personnel costs become very important in choosing a language. As machines become less expensive per unit of memory, languages that are inefficient in machine time but very efficient in programmer time will grow in importance.

Management Challenges

1. **Increasing complexity and software errors.** While much of the software of the next decade will be rapidly generated on desktops for smaller systems and applications, a great deal of what software will be asked to do remains far-reaching and sophisticated, requiring programs that are large and complex. Table 7.2 illustrates how much labor and expertise are poured into the software behind some well-known business and military applications.

   Large and complex systems tend to be error-prone, with software errors, or "bugs" that may not be revealed for years until exhaustive testing and actual use. A computerized banking system, for example, may use millions of lines of program code, written by hundreds of people, each working on small portions of the program. AT&T, for instance, found 300 errors for every 1000 lines of code in its large programs. Researchers do not know if the number of bugs grows exponentially or proportionately to the number of lines of code, nor can they tell for certain whether all segments of a complex piece of software will always work in total harmony. The process of designing and testing software that is "bug-free" is a serious quality control and management problem (see Chapter 13).

2. **The application backlog.** Advances in computer software have not kept pace with the breathtaking productivity gains in computer hardware. Developing software has become a major preoccupation for organizations. A great deal of software must be intricately crafted. Moreover, the software itself is only one component of a complete information system that must be carefully designed and coordinated with other people, as well as with organizational and hardware components. Managerial, procedural, and policy issues must be carefully researched and evaluated apart from the actual coding. The "software crisis" is actually part of a larger systems analysis, design, and implementation issue, which will be treated in detail in Part III. Despite the gains from fourth-generation languages, personal desktop software tools, and object-oriented programming, many businesses continue to face a backlog of two to three years in developing the information systems they need, or they will not be able to develop them at all.

Table 7.2 WHY SOFTWARE IS A MAJOR EFFORT

Application	Lines of Code	Labor Required (Person-Years)	Cost
Space shuttle	25,600,000	22,096	$ 1.2 billion
Citibank automatic teller machine	780,000	150	$13.2 million
Luxury automobile	83,517	35	$ 1.8 million

Source: "How to Break the Software Logjam," *Fortune* (September 25, 1989).

Summary

Describe the major types of software.

The major types of software are system, application, and end-user software. Each serves a different purpose. System software manages the computer resources and mediates between application software and computer hardware. Application software is used by application programmers and some end users to develop systems and specific business applications. End-user software usually cannot be used to develop an entire system. Instead, it is used to permit untrained end users either to use a system or to build a simple application (e.g., to create a report).

Describe the functions of system software and compare leading microcomputer operating systems.

System software coordinates the various parts of the computer system and mediates between application software and computer hardware. The system software that manages and controls the activities of the computer is called the operating system. Other system software includes computer language translation programs that convert programming languages into machine language and utility programs that perform common processing tasks.

The operating system acts as the chief manager of the information system, allocating, assigning, and scheduling system resources and monitoring the use of the computer. Multiprogramming, multitasking, multiprocessing, virtual storage, and time sharing enable system resources to be used more efficiently so that the computer can attack many problems at the same time.

Multiprogramming (multitasking in microcomputer environments) allows multiple programs to use the computer's resources concurrently. Multiprocessing is the use of two or more CPUs linked together working in tandem to perform a task. Time-sharing enables many users to share computer resources simultaneously by allocating each user a tiny slice of computing time. Virtual storage splits up programs into pages so that main memory can be utilized more efficiently.

In order to be executed by the computer, a software program must be translated into machine language via special language translation software—a compiler, an assembler, or an interpreter.

Microcomputer operating systems are starting to develop sophisticated capabilities such as multitasking and support for multiple users on networks. Leading microcomputer operating systems include OS/2, Windows NT, UNIX, DOS, and System 7. Microcomputer operating systems with graphical user interfaces are gaining popularity over command-driven operating systems. Windows is a popular graphical user interface shell for the DOS operating system.

Explain how software has evolved and how it will continue to develop.

Software has evolved along with hardware. The general trend is toward user-friendly high-level languages that both increase professional programmer productivity and make it possible for complete amateurs to use information systems. There have been four generations of software development: 1) machine language; 2) symbolic languages such as assembly language; 3) high-level languages such as FORTRAN and COBOL; and 4) fourth-generation languages, which are less procedural and closer to natural language than earlier generations of software. Software is starting to incorporate both sound and graphics and to support multimedia applications.

Compare strengths and limitations of the major programming languages and tools.

The most popular conventional programming languages are assembly language, FORTRAN, COBOL, BASIC, PL/1, Pascal, C, and Ada. Conventional programming languages make more efficient use of computer resources than fourth-generation languages and each is designed to solve specific types of problems.

Fourth-generation languages include query languages, report generators, graphics languages, application generators, very-high-level programming languages, application software packages, and personal computer tools. They are less procedural than conventional programming languages and enable end users to perform many software tasks that previously required technical specialists.

Object-oriented programming combines data and procedures into one "object," which can act as an independent software building block. Each object can be used in many different systems without changing program code.

Explain how to select appropriate software and programming languages.

Choosing the right software for a particular application requires some knowledge of the strengths and weaknesses of specific software products. Equally important is the support for software packages given by vendors, the ability of the organization to absorb new software, and the efficiency of the software in executing specific tasks.

<table>
<tr><td>Key Terms</td><td>Software</td><td>Machine language</td></tr>
<tr><td></td><td>Program</td><td>High-level language</td></tr>
<tr><td></td><td>Stored program concept</td><td>Assembly language</td></tr>
<tr><td></td><td>System software</td><td>FORTRAN (FORmula TRANslator)</td></tr>
<tr><td></td><td>Application software</td><td>COBOL (COmmon Business Oriented</td></tr>
<tr><td></td><td>End-user software</td><td>Language)</td></tr>
<tr><td></td><td>Operating system</td><td>BASIC (Beginners All-purpose Symbolic</td></tr>
<tr><td></td><td>System residence device</td><td>Instruction Code)</td></tr>
<tr><td></td><td>Multiprogramming</td><td>PL/1 (Programming Language 1)</td></tr>
<tr><td></td><td>Multitasking</td><td>Pascal</td></tr>
<tr><td></td><td>Virtual storage</td><td>Ada</td></tr>
<tr><td></td><td>Page</td><td>C</td></tr>
<tr><td></td><td>Time sharing</td><td>Fourth-generation language</td></tr>
<tr><td></td><td>Multiprocessing</td><td>Query language</td></tr>
<tr><td></td><td>Source code</td><td>Report generator</td></tr>
<tr><td></td><td>Compiler</td><td>Graphics language</td></tr>
<tr><td></td><td>Object code</td><td>Application generator</td></tr>
<tr><td></td><td>Interpreter</td><td>Very-high-level programming language</td></tr>
<tr><td></td><td>Utility program</td><td>Software package</td></tr>
<tr><td></td><td>DOS</td><td>Word processing software</td></tr>
<tr><td></td><td>OS/2</td><td>Spreadsheet</td></tr>
<tr><td></td><td>Windows NT</td><td>Data management software</td></tr>
<tr><td></td><td>UNIX</td><td>Integrated software package</td></tr>
<tr><td></td><td>System 7</td><td>Object-oriented programming</td></tr>
<tr><td></td><td>Graphical user interface</td><td>Class</td></tr>
<tr><td></td><td>Windows</td><td>Inheritance</td></tr>
</table>

Review Questions

1. What are the major types of software? How do they differ in terms of users and uses?

2. What is the operating system of a computer? What does it do?

3. Describe multiprogramming, time sharing, virtual storage, and multiprocessing. Why are they important for the operation of an information system?

4. Define multitasking.

5. What is the difference between an assembler, a compiler, and an interpreter?

6. Define graphical user interfaces.

7. Compare the major microcomputer operating systems.

8. What are the major generations of software, and approximately when were they developed?

9. What is a high-level language? Name three high-level languages. Describe their strengths and weaknesses.

10. Define fourth-generation languages and list the seven categories of fourth-generation tools.

11. What is the difference between fourth-generation languages and conventional programming languages?

12. What is the difference between an application generator and an application software package? Between a report generator and a query language?

13. Name and describe the most important microcomputer software tools.

14. What is object-oriented programming? How does it differ from conventional software development?

15. What are the four major trends in software? Can you think of more than the four described in the text?

16. What are the major factors to consider when selecting software and programming languages?

Discussion Questions

1. What factors should be considered in selecting microcomputer software?

2. Your firm wishes to develop a system that will process sales orders and update inventory. The programmers in your information systems department wish to use assembly language to write the programs for this system. Is this a good idea? Discuss.

3. Several authorities have claimed that fourth-generation languages will soon replace conventional programming languages such as COBOL for implementing the vast majority of information system applications. Discuss.

Group Project

OS/2 has been described as a "better Window than Windows and a better DOS than DOS." Your instructor will divide the class into two groups to debate this proposition, from both a technical and business standpoint. Use articles from computer magazines to help prepare your group's analysis.

CASE STUDY

OS/2 or Windows? Toronto Dominion Securities Inc. and Delta Airlines Select Operating Systems

Toronto Dominion Securities Inc. of Toronto Dominion Bank in Canada decided it was time for a change. Its business in government securities had been steadily growing, and its trade volume had doubled in two years. It moved to an amphitheater-like 11,000 square foot trading floor to give its securities traders more breathing space and a bull-pen like atmosphere for developing and discussing ideas. The new trading floor also streamlined communications that are crucial to the bank's closely related businesses. The entire project cost about $20 million Canadian.

Business heads in charge of the bank's trading operations in money market, capital market, foreign exchange, and fixed income sit in the middle of the room, surrounded by their chief traders. The proximity encourages people to

interact more frequently during the trading day. For instance, a trader in the Canadian–U.S. currency market can speak to the business head in charge of the Canadian and U.S. money market. Foreign exchange traders sit near the chief money market trader. If the chief money market trader says that rates are rising, the foreign exchange trader will use this information to purchase future contracts. Toronto believes that the trading room design has boosted revenues.

For the operating system for its new trading room floor, Toronto Dominion selected OS/2 Version 2.0, less than three months after this version of the operating system was formally released by IBM. There were both risks and rewards to installing this new version of the operating system so soon after its release. While there might be unforeseen bugs that often accompany new pieces of software, Toronto Dominion felt that this disadvantage was outweighed by OS/2's powerful multitasking capabilities and easier-to-use programs. The bank knew that it would not be easy to implement this new operating system and to get existing applications to run smoothly from the start. Some modifications to the data display software called TradeLook had to be coded and tested. To run an application on a new operating system, new versions of that application have to be created, tested, and retested.

OS/2 has a 32-bit operating system, which promises end users more power than 16-bit operating systems such as DOS. OS/2 also runs DOS and Windows-based programs. Toronto Dominion had other hardware and software options to choose from, such as UNIX-based workstations, but opted for OS/2 because it believed this system could best meet its needs. In the old trading room, the bank's traders used more than 100 DOS-based programs on mainframes and minicomputers to do, for instance, options analytics and trade analysis. The bank wanted to salvage its existing trading programs, allow its traders to run more than two applications at the same time, and let traders work with real-time data with the flick of a wrist. If systems did not work on the new version of OS/2, the bank planned to use an earlier version of OS/2.

The DOS-based programs required little or no modification to run on OS/2 and run smoothly, according to Andrew K. Annett, manager of the treasury systems integration, corporate, and investment banking group. With the new technology and trading room, traders can run a Lotus 1-2-3 spreadsheet and a profit-and-loss program simultaneously instead of wasting time jumping from one application to another. The bank feels that the OS/2 graphical user interface makes its systems easier to operate.

Because of OS/2 system glitches, Toronto Dominion found that the kernel—the part of the operating system that controls which applications run—was short on memory. Programmers had to scale back memory on computers that had less than 16 bytes of memory, and assign lower priority to background number crunching when multiple applications were run at the same time. The result—slower processing and response time. The bank is installing new kernel software and upgrading memory to 24 megabytes.

Before finalizing its decision, Toronto Dominion talked with over 10 technology vendors about hardware and software alternatives. One was to install 30 or 40 high-end UNIX-based RISC workstations in the Toronto office, where traders make markets and take positions. But the bank's other branches focus more on sales than on trading. There, that kind of technology would not be necessary and would make integration with the rest of the bank more difficult.

Toronto Dominion has planned to link all six of its corporate investment banking centers in a computer network. Its long-term strategy calls for distributing trading inventory in real-time out from its Toronto trading room to its 1000 branches and for distributing trading data to its corporate group and investment banking staff. Toronto also is thinking about providing corporate clients with the capability to execute foreign exchange transactions from their own terminals.

At about the same time Toronto Dominion selected the new version of OS/2, Delta Airlines decided to pull back from a primarily OS/2 desktop strategy to one calling for a mix of operating systems. It is replacing OS/2 with Microsoft Windows for its critical, next-generation reservation system. As the most critical airline operation, the new reservation system is mainframe-based but includes intelligent front-end workstations for reservation agents. About 900 agents will use the system initially.

In December 1991 Delta had selected OS/2 for this application as well as for another important project. Delta is not abandoning OS/2 completely, but has decided not to rely on OS/2 exclusively. The airline has changed its approach to avoid locking into a particular technical platform. It evaluates software for each information system application case by case and makes its selection based on cost and functionality. Delta, like all airlines, is suffering from tight finances, and is likely to look for the lowest cost technology solution.

Delta's corporate culture is considered to be practical and somewhat conservative. The firm tends not to make pioneering technically aggressive or risky decisions. The firm understands that the challenge of a mixed software environment is making the software all work together. Delta is finding ways to bridge the OS/2 and Windows environments. Delta plans to continue using OS/2 for its airport traffic management system and will evaluate OS/2 for future projects.

Sources: Jenna Michaels, ''Breaking in New OS/2 Technology,'' *Wall Street Computer Review,* Vol. 9, No. 12 (July 1992) and Rosemary Hamilton, ''Windows leads Delta to mixed platforms,'' *Computerworld,* July 27, 1992.

Case Study Questions

1. Why is the selection of an operating system an important business decision?
2. What are the management, technology, and organization factors that should be considered when selecting an operating system?
3. If you were in charge of selecting the operating system for Toronto Dominion and Delta, which would you have chosen for each firm? Why?

References

Abdel-Hamid, Tarek K. "The Economics of Software Quality Assurance: A Simulation-Based Case Study." *MIS Quarterly* 12, no. 3 (September 1988).

Apte, Uday, Chetan S. Sankar, Meru Thakur, and Joel E. Turner. "Reusability-Based Strategy for Development of Information Systems: Implementation Experience of a Bank." *MIS Quarterly* 14, no. 4 (December 1990).

Barnett, Jim, Kevin Knight, Inderject Man, and Elaine Rich. "Knowledge and Natural Language Processing. *Communications of the ACM* 33, no. 8 (August 1990).

Bochenski, Barbara. "GUI Builders Pay Price for User Productivity." *Software Magazine,* April 1992.

Borning, Alan. "Computer System Reliability and Nuclear War." *Communications of the ACM* 30, no. 2 (February 1987).

Fallows, James. "Crash-Worthy Speedster." *The Atlantic Monthly,* February 1993.

Freedman, David H. "Programming Without Tears." *High Technology* (April 1986).

Haavind, Robert. "Software's New Object Lesson." *Technology Review,* February/March 1992.

Jalics, Paul J. "Cobol on a PC: A New Perspective on a Language and Its Performance." *Communications of the ACM* 30, no. 2 (February 1987).

Joyce, Edward J. "Reusable Software: Passage to Productivity?" *Datamation* (September 15, 1988).

Kim, Chai, and Stu Westin. "Software Maintainability: Perceptions of EDP Professionals." *MIS Quarterly* 12, no. 2 (June 1988).

Korson, Timothy D. and Vijay K. Vaishnavi. "Managing Emerging Software Technologies: A Technology Transfer Framework." *Communications of the ACM* 35 No. 9 (September 1992).

Korson, Tim and John D. McGregor. "Understanding Object-Oriented: A Unifying Paradigm." *Communications of the ACM* 33, no. 9 (September 1990).

Lauriston, Robert. "OS/2 versus Windows NT." *PC World,* February 1993.

Layer, D. Kevin and Chris Richardson. "Lisp Systems in the 1990s," *Communications of the ACM* 34 no. 9 (September 1991.)

Littlewood, Bev and Lorenzo Strigini. "The Risks of Software." *Scientific American* 267, no. 5 (November 1992).

Monarchi, David E. and Gretchen I. Puhr. "A Research Typology for Object-Oriented Analysis and Design." *Communications of the ACM* 35 no. 9 (September 1992).

Mukhopadhyay, Tridas, Stephen S. Vicinanza, and Michael J. Prietula. "Examining the Feasibility of a Case-Based Reasoning Model for Software Effort Estimation." *MIS Quarterly* 16, no. 2 (June 1992).

Nance, Barry. "Windows NT and OS/2 Compared." *Byte,* June 1992.

Nerson, Jean-Marc. "Applying Object-Oriented Analysis and Design." *Communications of the ACM* 35, no. 9 (September 1992).

Salemi, Joe. "OS/2 2.0: Does It Fulfill the Promise?". *PC Magazine* April 28, 1992.

Schonberg, Edmond, Mark Gerhardt and Charlene Hayden. "A Technical Tour of Ada." *Communications of the ACM* 35, no. 11 (November 1992).

Swanson, Kent, Dave McComb, Jill Smith, and Don McCubbrey. "The Application Software Factory: Applying Total Quality Techniques to Systems Development." *MIS Quarterly* 15, no. 4 (December 1991.)

Vassiliou, Yannis. "On the Interactive Use of Databases: Query Languages." *Journal of Management Information Systems* 1 (Winter 1984–1985).

White, George M. " Natural Language Understanding and Speech." *Communications of the ACM* 33, no. 8 (August 1990).

Wiederhold, Gio, Peter Wegner, and Stefano Ceri. "Toward Megaprogramming." *Communications of the ACM* 35, no. 11 (November 1992).

CHAPTER

8

Managing Data Resources

Organized Information Speeds Satellite Recovery

In the 1970s, the Soviet Cosmos 954 satellite crashed in a remote section of northern Canada. On impact, it released radioactive particles from its nuclear reactor. With so many nuclear-powered satellites orbiting the globe, what can be done to prevent an incident like this, or, worse, one in which the satellite hits a heavily populated area?

Scientists have been developing recovery and disposal scenarios for nuclear-powered satellites for years. In the past, these scenarios took weeks or months to develop—far too long after a crash occurred to respond effectively. The scientists prepared these simulations manually using a complex matrix, and they had to be aware of all the various options for each recovery as they made calculations.

Now scientists can generate recovery-and-disposal scenarios in minutes by using an application called Technology Hierarchy for Orbital Recovery (THOR), developed by POD Associates in Albuquerque, New Mexico. THOR uses a relational database

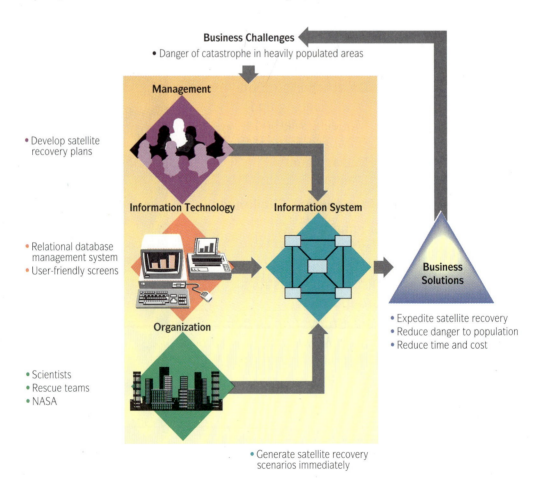

Business Challenges
• Danger of catastrophe in heavily populated areas

Management
• Develop satellite recovery plans

Information Technology
• Relational database management system
• User-friendly screens

Information System

Organization
• Scientists
• Rescue teams
• NASA

• Generate satellite recovery scenarios immediately

Business Solutions
• Expedite satellite recovery
• Reduce danger to population
• Reduce time and cost

that can store vast amounts of information collected from manufacturers and other sources on various technologies related to satellite recovery efforts. The database includes detailed data on launch sites, reactor composition, recovery vehicles, and satellite size and mass. Using menus that can be easily accessed on the computer terminal screen, scientists can input data on the type of satellite, type of reactor powering it, and whether the reactor is operational in order to design a scenario. The way the information is organized by the database software makes it easy for scientists to access and combine the information they need to generate a solution for the recovery.

THOR automatically performs the calculations the scientists need. Using the information stored in the database, scientists can present a detailed recovery scenario, including what type of recovery vehicle to use and where to launch it from. THOR is expected to save the National Aeronautic and Space Administration (NASA), the Department of Energy, and the Department of Defense a person-year's worth of work, equivalent to between $100,000 and $200,000.

Source: Christopher Lindquist, "RDBMS Helps Prevent Satellite Disaster," *Computerworld* (April 27, 1992).

T he THOR satellite recovery system illustrates how much the effective use of information depends on how data are stored, organized, and accessed. Proper delivery of information not only depends on the capabilities of computer hardware and software, but also on the organization's ability to manage data as an important resource.

This chapter examines the managerial and organizational requirements as well as the technologies for managing data as a resource. First we describe the traditional file management technologies that have been used for arranging and accessing data on physical storage media and the problems they have created for organizations. Then we describe the technology of database management systems, which can overcome many of the drawbacks of traditional file management. We end the chapter with a discussion of the managerial and organizational requirements for successful implementation of database management systems.

After completing this chapter you will be able to:

- Describe traditional file organization and management techniques.
- Explain the problems of the traditional file environment.
- Describe how a database management system organizes information.
- Identify the three principal database models.
- Explain the principles for designing a relational database.

- Discuss new database trends.
- Explain the managerial and organizational requirements for creating a database environment.

8.1 Organizing Data in a Traditional File Environment

An effective information system provides users with timely, accurate, and relevant information. This information is stored in computer files. When the files are properly arranged and maintained, users can easily access and retrieve the information they need.

You can appreciate the importance of file management if you have ever written a term paper using 3×5 index cards. No matter how efficient your storage device (a metal box or a rubber band), if you organize the cards randomly your term paper will have little or no organization. Given enough time, you could put the cards in order, but your system would be more efficient if you set up your organizational scheme early on. If your scheme is flexible enough and well documented, you can extend it to account for any changes in your viewpoint as you write your paper.

The same need for file organization applies to firms. Well-managed, carefully arranged files make it easy to obtain data for business decisions, whereas poorly managed files lead to chaos in information processing, high costs, poor performance, and little, if any, flexibility. Despite the use of excellent hardware and software, many organizations have inefficient information systems because of poor file management.

In this section we describe the traditional methods that organizations have used to arrange data in computer files. We also discuss the problems with these methods.

Figure 8.1
The data hierarchy. A computer system organizes data in a hierarchy that starts with the bit, which represents either a 0 or a 1. Bits can be grouped to form a byte to represent one character, number, or symbol. Bytes can be grouped to form a field, and related fields can be grouped to form a record. Related records can be collected to form a file and related files can be organized into a database.

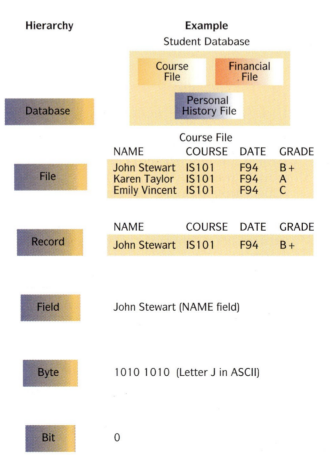

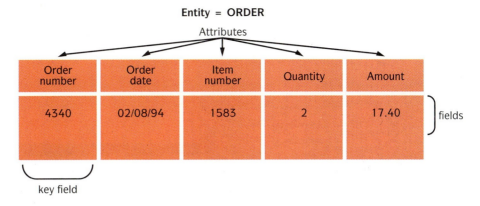

Figure 8.2
Entities and attributes. This record describes the entity called ORDER and its attributes. The specific values for order number, order date, item number, quantity, and amount for this particular order are the fields for this record. Order number is the key field because each order is assigned a unique identification number.

File Organization Terms and Concepts

Field: A grouping of characters into a word, group of words, or complete number.

Record: A group of related fields.

File: A group of records of the same type.

Entity: A person, place, or thing about which information must be kept.

Attribute: Piece of information describing a particular entity.

Key field: A field in a record that uniquely identifies instances of that record so that it can be retrieved or updated.

A computer system organizes data in a hierarchy that starts with bits and bytes and progresses to fields, records, files, and databases (see Figure 8.1).

A bit represents the smallest unit of data a computer can handle. A group of bits, called a byte, represents a single character, which can be a letter, number or other symbol. A grouping of characters into a word, group of words, or a complete number (such as a person's name or age), is called a **field.** A group of related fields, such as the student's name, the course taken, the date, and the grade make up a **record;** a group of records of the same type is called a **file.** For instance, all of the student records in Figure 8.1 could constitute a course file. A group of related files make up a database. The student course file illustrated in Figure 8.1 could be grouped with files on students' personal histories and financial backgrounds to create a student database.

A record describes an entity. An **entity** is a person, place, thing, or event on which we maintain information. An order is a typical entity in a sales order file, which maintains information on a firm's sales orders. Each characteristic or quality describing a particular entity is called an **attribute.** For example, order number, order date, order amount, item number, and item quantity would each be an attribute of the entity *order.* The specific values that these attributes can have can be found in the fields of the record describing the entity *order* (see Figure 8.2).

Every record in a file should contain at least one field that uniquely identifies that record so that the record can be retrieved, updated, or sorted. This identifier field is called a **key field.** An example of a key field is the order number for the order record illustrated in Figure 8.2 or an employee number or social security number for a personnel record (containing employee data such as the employee's name, age, address, job title, and so forth).

Accessing Records from Computer Files

Sequential file organization: A method of storing records in which records must be retrieved in the same physical sequence in which they are stored.

Direct file organization: Method of storing records so that they can be accessed in any sequence without regard to their actual physical order on storage media.

Computer systems store files on secondary storage devices. Records can be arranged in several ways on storage media, and the arrangement determines the manner in which individual records can be accessed or retrieved. One way to organize records is sequentially. In **sequential file organization,** data records must be retrieved in the same physical sequence in which they are stored. In contrast, **direct** or **random file organization** allows users to access records in any sequence they desire, without regard to actual physical order on the storage media.

Sequential file organization is the only file organization method that can be used on magnetic tape. This file organization method is no longer popular, but some organizations still use it for batch processing applications in which they access and process each record sequentially. A typical application using sequen-

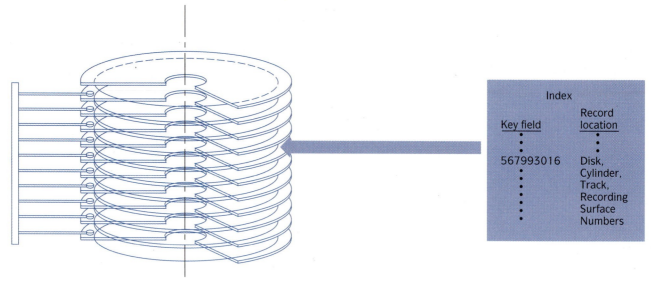

Figure 8.3
Indexed sequential access method (ISAM). ISAM allows a user to locate a record directly from a sequential file by using an index. With ISAM, records are stored on a direct access storage device (DASD) such as a disk. The index examines the unique key field of every record and finds its storage location on the disk.

tial files is payroll, where all employees in a firm must be paid one by one and issued a check. Direct or random file organization is utilized with magnetic disk technology (although records can be stored sequentially on disk if desired). Most computer applications today utilize some method of direct file organization.

THE INDEXED SEQUENTIAL ACCESS METHOD

Indexed sequential access method (ISAM): File access method to directly access records organized sequentially using an index of key fields.

Index: A table or list that relates record keys to physical locations on direct access files.

Although records may be stored sequentially on direct access storage devices, individual records can be accessed directly using the **indexed sequential access method (ISAM)**. This access method relies on an index of key fields to locate individual records. An **index** to a file is similar to the index of a book, as it lists the key field of each record and where that record is physically located in storage to expedite location of that record. Figure 8.3 shows how the index identifies the location of a specific record stored on disk. Any specific record can be located directly using its key field to find its storage address in the index. ISAM is employed in applications that require sequential processing of large numbers of records but that occasionally require direct access of individual records.

DIRECT FILE ACCESS METHOD

Direct file access method: Method of accessing records by mathematically transforming the key fields into the specific addresses for the records.

Transform algorithm: Mathematical formula used to translate a record's key field directly into the record's physical storage location.

The **direct file access method** is used with direct file organization. This method employs a key field to locate the physical address of a record. However, the process is accomplished without an index. Instead, a mathematical formula called a **transform algorithm** is used to translate the key field directly into the record's physical storage location on disk. The algorithm performs some mathematical computation on the record key, and the result of that calculation is the record's physical address. This process is illustrated in Figure 8.4.

This access method is most appropriate for applications where individual records must be located directly and rapidly for immediate processing. Only a few records in the file need to be retrieved at one time, and the required records are found in no particular sequence. An example might be an on-line hotel reservation system.

Problems with the Traditional File Environment

According to Greek legend, Gordius, King of Phrygia, tied an intricate, complex knot in a rope, of which it was said that he who untied the knot would be master of Asia. As it turned out, Alexander the Great cut the knot and went on to

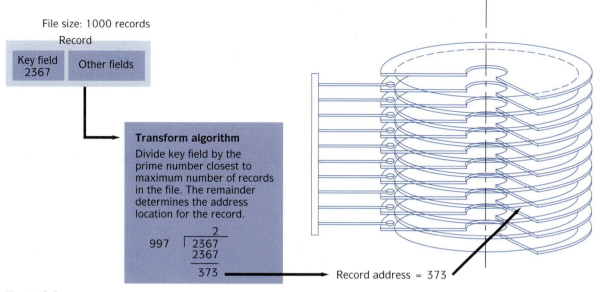

Figure 8.4
The direct file access method. Records are not stored sequentially on the disk but are arranged according to the results of some mathematical computation. Here, the transform algorithm divides the value in the key field by the prime number closest to the maximum number of records in the file (in this case, the prime number is 997). The remainder designates the storage location for that particular record.

become master of Asia. Many organizations have found that they tied themselves into an information-system Gordian knot of their own making. Here we describe the knot. In the following section, we show how to untie parts of the knot and cut through the rest.

Most organizations began information processing on a small scale, automating one application at a time. Systems tended to grow independently, and not according to some grand plan. Typically, each division of a multidivision company developed its own applications. Within each division, each functional area tended to develop systems in isolation from other functional areas. Accounting, finance, manufacturing, and marketing all developed their own systems and data files. Figure 8.5 illustrates the traditional approach to information processing.

Each application, of course, required its own files and its own computer program in order to operate. In general, the files used in an application were some version of the functional area master file. For instance, there was one very large master personnel file containing most of the basic information on all employees in the company, including current position and salary. However, over time, a number of smaller files extracted from the larger master file were spun off for processing efficiency as well as for specialized applications. Hence, the personnel master file spawned a payroll file, a medical insurance file, a pension file, a mailing list file, a list of employees who joined the company via prior acquisitions (who were paid using a different payroll program), and so forth until tens, perhaps hundreds, of files and programs existed.

In the company as a whole, this process led to multiple master files created, maintained, and operated by separate divisions or departments. Figure 8.6 shows three separate master files: customer, personnel, and sales. Creating a simple report such as that listed in this example, sales personnel by annual sales and by principal customers, required a complex "matching" program that read each of the three files, copied pertinent records, and recombined the records into an intermediate file. This intermediate file had to be sorted in the desired sequence (sales personnel ranked by highest sales) before a final report could be printed.

Of course, every data item in the various files required a set of documents to support the file and help collect information. Often the same data item, such as product code, was collected on multiple documents by different divisions and departments. In time, the file structure of the organization became so complex

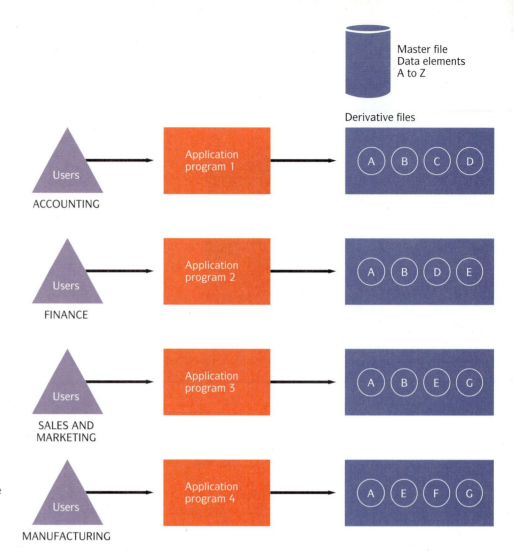

Master file
Data elements
A to Z

Derivative files

ACCOUNTING
Users
Application
program 1
(A) (B) (C) (D)

FINANCE
Users
Application
program 2
(A) (B) (D) (E)

SALES AND
MARKETING
Users
Application
program 3
(A) (B) (E) (G)

MANUFACTURING
Users
Application
program 4
(A) (E) (F) (G)

Figure 8.5
Traditional file processing. The use of a traditional approach to file processing encourages each functional area in a corporation to develop specialized applications. Each application requires a unique data file that is likely to be a subset of the master file. These subsets of the master file lead to data redundancy, processing inflexibility, and wasted storage resources.

that programmers developed specialties by focusing on subsets of files and programs. Eventually, the programs became totally dependent on a few programmers who understood the programs and files. If these programmers became ill or left the company, key applications failed.

There are names for this situation: the **traditional file environment;** the flat file organization (because most of the data are organized in flat files); and the data file approach (because the data and business logic are tied to specific files and related programs). By any name, the situation results in growing inefficiency and complexity.

As this process goes on for five or ten years, the firm becomes tied up in knots of its own creation. The organization is saddled with hundreds of programs and applications, with no one who knows what they do, what data they use, and who is using the data. There is no central listing of data files, data elements, or definitions of data. The organization is collecting the same information on far too many documents. The resulting problems are data redundancy, program-data dependence, inflexibility, poor data security, and inability to share data among applications.

Traditional file environment:
A way of collecting and maintaining data in an organization that leads to each functional area or division creating and maintaining its own data files and programs.

DATA REDUNDANCY AND CONFUSION

Data redundancy: The presence of duplicate data in multiple data files.

Data redundancy is the presence of duplicate data in multiple data files. Data redundancy occurs when different divisions, functional areas, and groups in an organization independently collect the same piece of information. For instance, within the commercial loans division of a bank, the marketing and credit information functions might collect the same customer information. Because it is

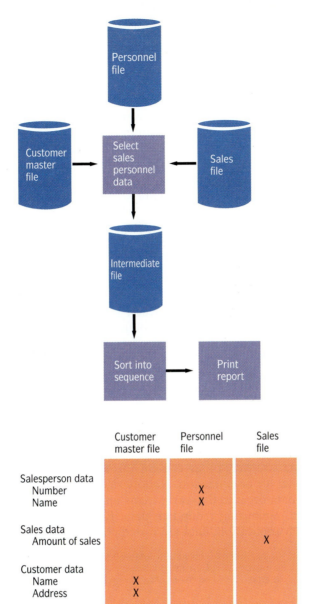

Figure 8.6
Creating a report using traditional file processing. In this example, three separate files—customer, personnel, and sales—have been created and are maintained by each respective division or department. In order to create a simple report consisting of a list of sales personnel by annual sales and principal customers, the three files had to be read, and an intermediate file had to be created. This required writing several programs. The table in the figure shows the information selected from each file.

	Customer master file	Personnel file	Sales file
Salesperson data			
Number		X	
Name		X	
Sales data			
Amount of sales			X
Customer data			
Name	X		
Address	X		

collected and maintained in so many different places, the same data item may have different meanings in different parts of the organization. Simple data items like the fiscal year, employee identification, and product code can take on different meanings as programmers and analysts work in isolation on different applications.

Program-data dependence is the tight relationship between data stored in files and the specific programs required to update and maintain those files. Every computer program has to describe the location and nature of the data with which it works. These data declarations can be longer than the substantive part of the program. In a traditional file environment, any change in data requires a change in all of the programs that access the data. Changes, for instance, in tax rates or zip code length require changes in programs. Such programming changes may cost millions of dollars to implement in each program that requires the revised data.

The development of new applications consequently takes more time and money than it would otherwise. Programmers have to write complicated programs, stripping data items from records in a variety of files to create new files. New programs require new arrangements of data. A large part of the organization's programming effort consists of updating data elements that are scattered throughout hundreds of files. In many instances, applications work with outdated data simply because of the difficulty of making updates.

LACK OF FLEXIBILITY   A traditional file system can deliver routine scheduled reports after extensive programming efforts, but it cannot deliver ad hoc reports or respond to unanticipated information requirements in a timely fashion. The information required by ad hoc requests is "somewhere in the system" but is too expensive to retrieve. Several programmers would have to work for weeks to put together the required data items in a new file. Users—in particular, senior management—begin to wonder at this point why they have computers at all.

POOR SECURITY   Because there is little control or management of data, access to and dissemination of information are virtually out of control. What limits on access exist tend to be the result of habit and tradition, as well as of the sheer difficulty of finding information.

LACK OF DATA SHARING AND AVAILABILITY   The lack of control over access to data in this confused environment does not make it easy for people to obtain information. Because pieces of information in different files and different parts of the organization cannot be related to one another, it is virtually impossible for information to be shared or accessed in a timely manner.

8.2 A Modern Database Environment

Database: Collection of data organized to service many applications at the same time by organizing data so that they appear to be in one location.

Database technology can cut through many of the problems created by traditional file organization. A more rigorous definition of a **database** is a collection of data organized to serve many applications efficiently by centralizing the data and minimizing redundant data. Rather than storing data in separate files for each application, data are stored physically to appear to users as being stored in

Figure 8.7
The contemporary database environment. A single Human Resources database serves multiple applications and also allows a corporation easily to draw together all of the information on various applications. The database management system acts as the interface between the application programs and the data.

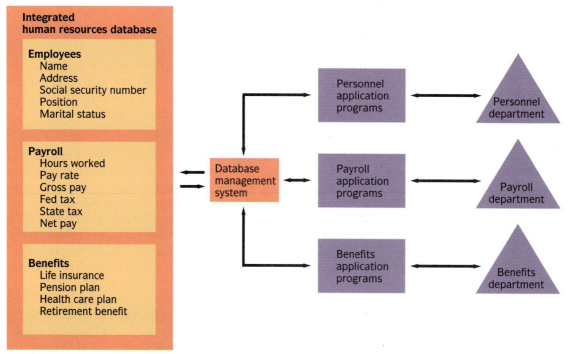

only one location. A single database services multiple applications. For example, instead of a corporation storing employee data in separate information systems and separate files for personnel, payroll, and benefits, the corporation could create a single common Human Resources database. Figure 8.7 illustrates the database concept.

Database Management Systems (DBMS)

Database management system (DBMS): Special software to create and maintain a database and enable individual business applications to extract the data they need without having to create separate files or data definitions in their computer programs.

A **database management system (DBMS)** is simply the software that permits an organization to centralize data, manage them efficiently, and provide access to the stored data by application programs. As illustrated in Figure 8.8, the DBMS acts as an interface between application programs and the physical data files. When the application program calls for a data item such as gross pay, the DBMS finds this item in the database and presents it to the application program. Using traditional data files, the programmer would have to define the data and then tell the computer where they are. A DBMS eliminates most of the data definition statements found in traditional programs.

A database management system has three components:

- a data definition language
- a data manipulation language
- a data dictionary

Data definition language: The component of a database management system that defines each data element as it appears in the database.

The **data definition language** is the formal language used by programmers to specify the content and structure of the database. The data definition language defines each data element as it appears in the database before that data element is translated into the forms required by application programs.

Data manipulation language: A language associated with a database management system that is employed by end users and programmers to manipulate data in the database.

Structured Query Language (SQL): The emerging standard data manipulation language for relational database management systems.

Most DBMS have a specialized language called a **data manipulation language** that is used in conjunction with some conventional third- or fourth-generation programming languages to manipulate the data in the database. This language contains commands that permit end users and programming specialists to extract data from the database to satisfy information requests and develop applications. The most prominent data manipulation language today is **SQL,** or **Structured Query Language.** Complex programming tasks cannot be performed efficiently with typical data manipulation languages. However, most mainframe DBMS are compatible with COBOL and FORTRAN, and other third-generation programming languages, permitting greater processing efficiency and flexibility. The Window on Management on page 246 shows how special software tools and hardware are being used for highly complex queries searching massive databases that previously could not be handled either by data manipulation languages or conventional programming languages.

Figure 8.8
Elements of a database management system. In an ideal database environment, application programs work through a database management system to obtain data from the database. This diagram illustrates a database management system with an active data dictionary that not only records definitions of the contents of the database but also allows changes in data size and format to be automatically utilized by the application programs.

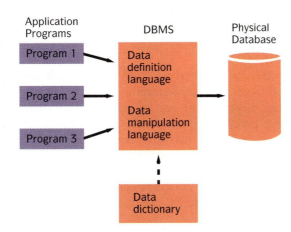

MANAGEMENT
Sifting Through Vast Pools of Data

Traders in the financial industry are always on the lookout for information that could help them make more informed trading decisions. The problem is coming up with original pieces of information, since it is hard to make money when everyone is doing the same thing. Few traders have any time to pore over charts or sift through vast pools of financial trading data.

One possible way to find unique information is to search both current and financial market historical data for new patterns and correla-

tions. Once a trader discovers a new pattern or correlation, he or she can use that information to increase the chances of making a profitable trade. Market Information Machine (MIM), created by Logical Information Machines Inc. of Chicago, provides this capability by combining an extremely fast method of searching vast databases with a powerful desktop computer.

With MIM, traders can concoct ad hoc queries with multiple variables to determine the following:

- What happened in the bond and foreign currency markets during the three days after bond prices were up 1 percent and the German mark was up 1 percent against the dollar?
- What happened to U.S. bond prices from the first hour of trading to 1 PM on days that a share of IBM stock was down more than 10 points?

Extracting answers to questions like these from conventional DBMS requires complex programming. Managers using MIM can obtain answers without using a complicated programming language.

Managers in other areas could use this technology when they need to interpret vast quantities of data in order to make decisions. For instance, a sales manager using supermarket scanner data might ask MIM to show the sales of a given product in a specific region when it is on sale on Saturday between 9 AM and noon when the competitor is not running a coupon, and when the product is in a prime display area in supermarket aisles. Insurance firms might use the system for risk analysis.

Source: Peter H. Lewis, "A Fast Way to Discover Patterns in Vast Amounts of Data," *The New York Times* (August 30, 1992).

To Think About: What are the management benefits of systems such as the Market Information Machine?

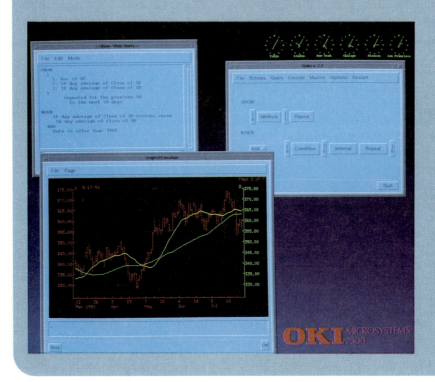

Data dictionary: An automated or manual tool for storing and organizing information about the data maintained in a database.

Data element: A field.

The third element of a DBMS is a **data dictionary.** This is an automated or manual file that stores definitions of data elements and data characteristics such as usage, physical representation, ownership (who in the organization is responsible for maintaining the data), authorization, and security. Many data dictionaries can produce lists and reports of data utilization, groupings, program locations, and so on. Figure 8.9 illustrates a sample data dictionary report that shows the size, format, meaning, and uses of a data element in a Human Resources database. A **data element** represents a field. Besides listing the standard name (AMT-PAY-BASE), the dictionary lists the names that reference this ele-

```
NAME: AMT-PAY-BASE
FOCUS NAME: BASEPLAY
PC NAME:      SALARY

DESCRIPTION: EMPLOYEE'S ANNUAL SALARY

SIZE: 9 BYTES
TYPE: N          (NUMERIC)
DATE CHANGED: 01/01/85
OWNERSHIP: COMPENSATION
UPDATE SECURITY: SITE PERSONNEL
ACCESS SECURITY: MANAGER, COMPENSATION PLANNING AND RESEARCH
                 MANAGER, JOB EVALUATION SYSTEMS
                 MANAGER, HUMAN RESOURCES PLANNING
                 MANAGER, SITE EQUAL OPPORTUNITY AFFAIRS
                 MANAGER, SITE BENEFITS
                 MANAGER, CLAIMS PAYING SYSTEMS
                 MANAGER, QUALIFIED PLANS
                 MANAGER, SITE EMPLOYMENT/EEO
BUSINESS FUNCTIONS USED BY: COMPENSATION
                            HR PLANNING
                            EMPLOYMENT
                            INSURANCE
                            PENSION
                            ISP

PROGRAMS USING: PI01000
                PI02000
                PI03000
                PI04000
                PI05000

REPORTS USING:   REPORT 124 (SALARY INCREASE TRACKING REPORT)
                 REPORT 448 (GROUP INSURANCE AUDIT REPORT)
                 REPORT 452 (SALARY REVIEW LISTING)
                 PENSION REFERENCE LISTING
```

Figure 8.9
Sample data dictionary report. The sample data dictionary report for a Human Resources database provides helpful information such as the size of the data element, which programs and reports use it, and which group in the organization is the "owner" responsible for maintaining it. The report also shows some of the other names that the organization uses for this piece of data.

ment in specific systems and identifies the individuals, business functions, programs, and reports that use this data element.

By creating an inventory of all the pieces of data contained in the database, the data dictionary serves as an important data management tool. For instance, business users could consult the dictionary to find out exactly what pieces of data are maintained for the sales or marketing function or even to determine all of the information maintained by the entire enterprise. The dictionary could supply business users with the name, format, and specifications required to access data for reports. Technical staff could use the dictionary to determine what data elements and files must be changed if a program is changed.

Most data dictionaries are entirely passive; they simply report. More advanced types are active; changes in the dictionary can be automatically utilized by related programs. For instance, to change zip codes from five to nine digits, one could simply enter the change in the dictionary without having to modify and recompile all user programs using zip codes.

In an ideal database environment, the data in the database are defined once and consistently, and used for all applications whose data reside in the database. Application programs (which are written using a combination of the data manipulation language of the DBMS and a conventional language such as COBOL) request data elements from the database. Data elements called for by the application programs are found and delivered by the DBMS. The programmer does not have to specify in detail how or where the data are to be found.

Logical and Physical Views of Data

Logical view:: Representation of data as they would appear to an application programmer or end user.

Physical view: The representation of data as they would be actually organized on physical storage media.

Schema: The logical description of an entire database, listing all the data elements in the database and the relationships among them.

Subschema: The logical description of the part of a database required by a particular function or application program.

Perhaps the greatest difference between a DBMS and traditional file organization is that the DBMS separates the logical and physical views of the data, relieving the programmer or end user from the task of understanding where and how the data are actually stored.

The database concept distinguishes between *logical* and *physical* views of data. The **logical view** presents data as they would be perceived by end users or business specialists, whereas the **physical view** shows how data are actually organized and structured on physical storage media.

The logical description of the entire database, listing all of the data items and the relationship among them, is termed the **schema.** The specific set of data from the database that is required by each application program is termed the **subschema.** For example, for the human resources database illustrated in Figure 8.7, the payroll application would have a subschema consisting of employee name, address, social security number, and would specify payroll data such as pay rate and hours worked.

Suppose, for example, that a professor of information systems wanted to know at the beginning of the semester how students performed in the prerequisite computer literacy course (Computer Literacy 101) and what their current majors are. Using a database supported by the registrar, the professor would need something like the report shown in Figure 8.10.

Ideally, for such a simple report, the professor could sit at an office terminal connected to the registrar's database and write a small application program using the data manipulation language to create this report. The professor first would create the desired logical view of the data (Figure 8.10) for the application program. The DBMS would then assemble the requested data elements, which may reside in several different files and disk locations. For instance, the student major information may be located in a file called "Student," whereas the grade data may be located in a file called "Course." Wherever they are located, the DBMS would pull these pieces of information together and present them to the professor according to the logical view requested.

The query using the data manipulation language constructed by the professor might look something like Figure 8.11. Several DBMSs working on both mainframes and microcomputers permit this kind of interactive report creation.

In the real world, there are few registration systems that permit this kind of inquiry. Many university registration systems were created in the 1960s and are of the traditional, flat-file variety. In order to produce the report shown in Figure

Sophisticated information systems are required to process the vast amount of data that is collected and organized during a typical college registration.

Student Name	ID No.	Major	Grade in Computer Literacy 101
Lind	468	Finance	A-
Pinckus	332	Marketing	B+
Williams	097	Economics	C+
Laughlin	765	Finance	A
Orlando	324	Statistics	B

Figure 8.10
The report required by the professor. The report requires data elements that may come from different files but it can easily be pulled together with a database management system if the data are organized into a database.

8.10, a COBOL programmer would have to be hired to write several hundred lines of code. The final program would require at least three or four days of work, several test runs, debugging, and so forth. The labor costs alone would be around $2,000. Several files would have to be accessed, stripped of the relevant information, and a third file would have to be created. With luck, no data inconsistencies would be found.

Imagine the cost to the university if all professors requested this or similar reports. If the university tried to meet the demand, its information processing costs would balloon rapidly. Instead, most universities simply say that the information is "in the system somewhere but is too expensive to retrieve." Only an information systems professor could understand this reply.

Advantages of Database Management Systems

The preceding discussion illustrates the advantage of a DBMS:

- Complexity of the organization's information system environment can be reduced by central management of data, access, utilization, and security.
- Data redundancy and inconsistency can be reduced by eliminating all of the isolated files in which the same data elements are repeated.
- Data confusion can be eliminated by providing central control of data creation and definitions.
- Program-data dependence can be reduced by separating the logical view of data from its physical arrangement.
- Program development and maintenance costs can be radically reduced.
- Flexibility of information systems can be greatly enhanced by permitting rapid and inexpensive ad hoc queries of very large pools of information.
- Access and availability of information can be increased.

Figure 8.11
The query used by the professor. This example shows how Structured Query Language (SQL) commands could be used to deliver the data required by the professor. These commands join two files, the student file (Student) and the course file (Course), and extract the specified pieces of information on each student from the combined file.

```
SELECT Stud_name, Stud.stud_id, Major, Grade
FROM Student, Course
WHERE Stud.stud_id = Course.stud_id
AND Course_id = "CL101"
```

The Window on Organizations illustrates the extent to which a well-organized and well-designed database can contribute to the effectiveness of a business.

Given all of these benefits of DBMS, one might expect all organizations to change immediately to a database form of information management. But it is not that easy, as we will see later.

8.3 Designing Databases

There are alternative ways of organizing data and representing relationships among data in a database. Conventional DBMSs use one of three principal logical database models for keeping track of entities, attributes, and relationships. The three principal logical database models are hierarchical, network, and relational. Each logical model has certain processing advantages and certain business advantages.

Hierarchical Data Model

Hierarchical data model: One type of logical database model that organizes data in a treelike structure. A record is subdivided into segments that are connected to each other in one-to-many parent–child relationships.

The earliest DBMS were hierarchical. The **hierarchical data model** presents data to users in a treelike structure. The most common hierarchical DBMS is IBM's IMS (Information Management System). Within each record, data elements are organized into pieces of records called segments. To the user, each record looks like an organization chart with one top-level segment called the *root*. An upper segment is connected logically to a lower segment in a parent–child relationship. A parent segment can have more than one child, but a child can only have one parent.

Figure 8.12
A hierarchical database for an airline reservation system. The hierarchical database model looks like an organizational chart or family tree. It has a single "root" segment (Origination) connected to lower-level segments (Destination). Each subordinate segment, in turn, connects to other subordinate segments. Here, Destination connects to Date; Date connects to Flight number; and Flight number connects to Passenger list. Each subordinate segment is the "child" of the segment directly above it.

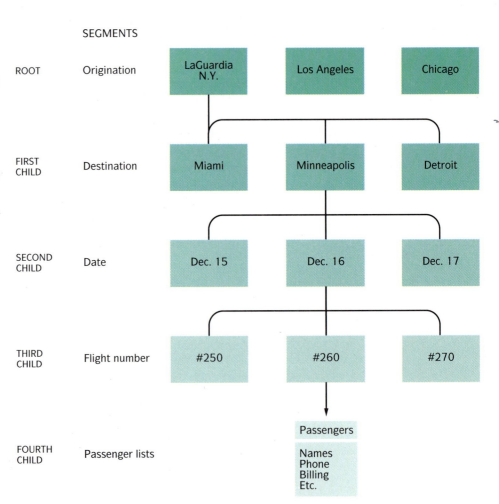

Figure 8.12 shows a hierarchical structure similar to the one used by airline reservation systems. The root segment is "Origination," which contains information about airports where flights originate. The first child is "Destination" and contains information on where flights go. The second child is "Date" (airlines generally accept reservations one year in advance). The third child is "Flight Number" because on any given day there may be multiple flights to a single destination. The fourth child is "Passenger Lists," which contain information on the passengers (e.g., name, local phone number, when the reservation was made, billing address, form of payment, and, in some cases, seat location).

Behind the logical view of data are a number of physical links and devices to tie the information together into a logical whole. In a hierarchical DBMS the data are physically linked to one another by a series of **pointers** that form chains of related data segments. Pointers are data elements attached to the ends of record segments on the disk directing the system to related records. In our example, if the route was LGA (New York's LaGuardia Airport), the end of the Origination segment would contain a series of pointers to all of the possible destinations. In turn, at the end of the Destination segment, there are pointers to the dates when the airline flies to that destination.

Because there are so many airports where flights originate, it would be convenient if the system could rapidly find the appropriate root segment, the origination airport. Rather than read each data segment (of which there are millions) one at a time until the right one (the root originating airport) is found, all originating airports can be stored in an index that lists the originating airports and their precise location on disk. Once this root segment is identified, pointers take over to guide the search of the database.

Pointer: A special type of data element attached to a record that shows the absolute or relative address of another record.

Network Data Model

Network data model: A logical database model that is useful for depicting many-to-many relationships.

The **network data model** is a variation of the hierarchical data model. Indeed, databases can be translated from hierarchical to network and vice versa in order to optimize processing speed and convenience. Whereas hierarchical structures depict one-to-many relationships, network structures depict data logically as many-to-many relationships.

A typical many-to-many relationship in which network DBMS excel in performance is the student–course relationship (see Figure 8.13). There are many courses in a university and many students, and students are usually enrolled in many courses.

The data in Figure 8.13 could be structured hierarchically. But this could result in considerable redundancy and a slowed response to certain types of information queries; the same student would be listed on the disk for each class he or she was taking instead of just once. Network structures reduce redundancy and, in certain situations (where many-to-many relationships are involved), respond more quickly. However, there is a price for this reduction in redundancy and increased speed: The number of pointers in network structures rapidly increases, making maintenance and operation more expensive.

Relational Data Model

Relational data model: A type of logical database model that treats data as if they were stored in two-dimensional tables. It can relate data stored in one table to data in another as long as the two tables share a common data element.

Tuple: A row or record in a relational database.

The **relational data model,** the most recent of these three database models, overcomes some of the limitations of the other two models. The relational model represents all data in the database as simple two-dimensional tables called relations. The tables appear similar to flat files, but the information in more than one file can be easily extracted and combined. Sometimes the tables are referred to as files.

Figure 8.14 shows a supplier table, a part table, and an order table. In each table, the rows are unique records and the columns are fields. Another term for a row or record in a relation is a **tuple.** Often a user needs information from a number of relations to produce a report. Here is the strength of the relational model: It can relate data in any one file or table to data in another file or table *as long as both tables share a common data element.*

To demonstrate, suppose we wanted to find in the relational database in Figure 8.14 the names and addresses of suppliers who could provide us with part number 137 or part number 152. We would need information from two tables: the supplier table and the part table. Note that these two files have a shared data element: SUPPLIER-NUMBER.

In a relational database, three basic operations are used to develop useful sets of data: select, project, and join. The *select* operation creates a subset consisting of all records in the file that meet stated criteria. "Select" creates, in other words,

Figure 8.13
The network data model. This illustration of a network data model showing the relationship the students in a university have to the courses they take represents an example of logical many-to-many relationships. The network model reduces the redundancy of data representation through the increased use of pointers.

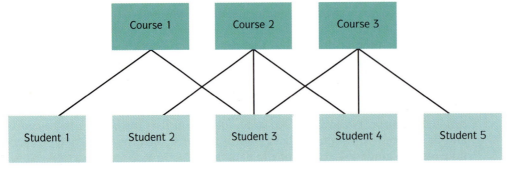

ORDER- NUMBER	ORDER- DATE	DELIVERY- DATE	PART- NUMBER	PART- AMOUNT	ORDER- TOTAL
1634	02/02/93	02/22/93	152	2	144.50
1635	02/12/93	02/29/93	137	3	79.70
1636	02/13/93	03/01/93	145	1	24.30

ORDER

Rows
(Records,
Tuples)

PART- NUMBER	PART- DESCRIPTION	UNIT- PRICE	SUPPLIER- NUMBER
137	Door latch	26.25	4058
145	Door handle	22.50	2038
152	Compressor	70.00	1125

PART

SUPPLIER- NUMBER	SUPPLIER- NAME	SUPPLIER-ADDRESS
1125	CBM Inc.	44 Winslow, Gary IN 44950
2038	Ace Inc.	Rte. 101, Essex NJ 07763
4058	Bryant Corp.	51 Elm, Rochester NY 11349

SUPPLIER

Figure 8.14
The relational data model. Each table is a *relation* and each row or record is a *tuple*. Each column corresponds to a field. These relations can easily be combined and extracted in order to access data and produce reports, provided that any two share a common data element. In this example, the ORDER file shares the data element "PART-NUMBER" with the PART file. The PART and SUPPLIER files share the data element "SUPPLIER-NUMBER."

a subset of rows that meet certain criteria. In our example, we want to select records (rows) from the part table where the part number equals 137 or 152.

The *join* operation combines relational tables to provide the user with more information than is available in individual tables. In our example, we want to join the now shortened part table (only parts numbered 137 or 152 will be presented) and the supplier table into a single new result table.

The *project* operation creates a subset consisting of columns in a table, permitting the user to create new tables that contain only the information required. In our example, we want to extract from the new result table only the following columns: PART-NUMBER, SUPPLIER-NUMBER, SUPPLIER-NAME, and SUPPLIER-ADDRESS.

Leading mainframe relational database management systems include IBM's DB2 and Oracle from the Oracle Corporation. FoxBase Plus from Fox Software Inc., and dBASE IV PLUS and Paradox from Borland International Inc. are examples of microcomputer relational database management systems.

Advantages and Disadvantages of the Three Database Models

The principal advantage of the hierarchical and network database models is processing efficiency. For instance, a hierarchical model is appropriate for airline reservation transaction processing systems, which must handle millions of structured routine requests each day for reservation information.

Hierarchical and network structures have several disadvantages. All of the access paths, directories, and indices must be specified in advance. Once specified, they are not easily changed without a major programming effort. Therefore, these designs have low flexibility. For instance, if you called an airline and said, "My parents gave me a ticket for a flight to an exciting resort, leaving from New York's LaGuardia Airport, but did not tell me exactly where or when. Where am I going?" you would discover that there is no way that the system can find the answer in a reasonable amount of time. This path through the data was not specified in advance. Or if the FBI called a major airline and asked about the movements in the last six months of a suspected terrorist traveling under a known assumed name, the airline could respond only after several months of programming effort (the records are kept for a period of five years on backup tapes).

Both hierarchical and network systems are programming-intensive, time-consuming, difficult to install, and difficult to remedy if design errors occur. They do not support ad hoc, English languagelike inquiries for information.

The strengths of relational DBMS are great flexibility in regard to ad hoc queries, power to combine information from different sources, simplicity of design and maintenance, and the ability to add new data and records without disturbing existing programs and applications. The weakness of relational DBMS are their relatively low processing efficiency. These systems are somewhat slower because they typically require many accesses to the data stored on disk to carry out the select, join, and project commands. Selecting one part number from among millions, one record at a time, can take a long time. Of course the database can be indexed and "tuned" to speed up prespecified queries. Relational systems do not have the large number of pointers carried by hierarchical systems.

Large relational databases may be designed to have some data redundancy in order to make retrieval of data more efficient. The same data element may be stored in multiple tables. Updating redundant data elements is not automatic in many relational DBMS. For example, changing the employee status field in one table will not automatically change it in all tables. Special arrangements are required to ensure that all copies of the same data element are updated together.

Hierarchical databases remain the workhorse for intensive high-volume transaction processing. Banks, insurance companies, and other high-volume users continue to use reliable hierarchical databases such as IBM's IMS, developed in 1969. It is easier to program applications in a relational environment, but many firms do not wish to spend millions of dollars converting software from a hierarchical to a relational database management system. Many organizations have converted to DB2, IBM's relational DBMS for new applications, while retaining IMS for traditional transaction processing. For example, the United Services Automobile Association described in the Window On Technology in Chapter 2 uses DB2 only for minor programming functions. Dallas-based Texas Instruments depends on IMS for its heavy processing requirements. Texas Instruments bases its complete operations, including inventory, accounting, and manufacturing, on IMS. The firm has built up a huge library of IMS applications over twenty years, and a complete conversion to DB2 would take ten more years. As relational products acquire more muscle, firms will shift away completely from hierarchical DBMS, but this will happen over a long period of time.

Table 8.1 compares the characteristics of the different database models.

Table 8.1 COMPARISON OF DATABASE ALTERNATIVES

Type of Database	Processing Efficiency	Flexibility	End-User Friendliness	Programming Complexity
Hierarchical	High	Low	Low	High
Network	Medium–high	Low–medium	Low–moderate	High
Relational	Lower but improving	High	High	Low

Creating a Database

In order to create a database, one must go through two design exercises, a conceptual design and a physical design. The conceptual design of a database is an abstract model of the database from a business perspective, whereas the physical design shows how the database is actually arranged on direct-access storage devices. Physical database design is performed by database specialists, whereas logical design requires a detailed description of the business information needs of actual end users of the database. Ideally, database design will be part of an overall organizational data planning effort (see Chapter 11).

The conceptual database design describes how the data elements in the database are to be grouped. The design process identifies relationships among data elements and the most efficient way of grouping data elements together to meet information requirements. The process also identifies redundant data elements and the groupings of data elements required for specific application programs. Groups of data are organized, refined, and streamlined until an overall logical view of the relationships among all of the data elements in the database emerges.

Entity-relationship diagram:
Methodology for documenting databases illustrating the relationship between various entities in the database.

Database designers document the conceptual data model with an **entity-relationship diagram,** illustrated in Figure 8.15. The boxes represent entities and the diamonds represent relationships. The *1* or *M* on either side of the diamond represents the relationship among entities as either one-to-one, one-to-many, or many-to-many. Figure 8.15 shows that the entity ORDER can have only one PART and a PART can only have one SUPPLIER. Many parts can be provided by the same supplier. The attributes for each entity are listed next to the entity and the key field is underlined.

In order to use a relational database model effectively, complex groupings of data must be streamlined to eliminate redundant data elements and awkward many-to-many relationships. Figures 8.16 and 8.17 illustrate this process. In the particular business modeled here, an order can have more than one part but each part is provided by only one supplier. If we had built a relation called ORDER

Figure 8.15
An Entity-Relationship diagram. This diagram shows the relationships between the entities ORDER, PART, and SUPPLIER that were used to develop the relational database illustrated in Figure 8.14.

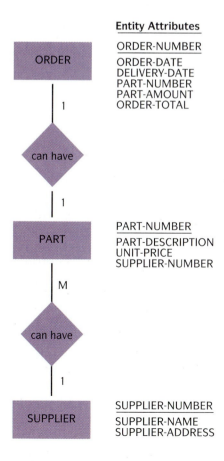

Entity Attributes

ORDER-NUMBER
ORDER-DATE
DELIVERY-DATE
PART-NUMBER
PART-AMOUNT
ORDER-TOTAL

PART-NUMBER
PART-DESCRIPTION
UNIT-PRICE
SUPPLIER-NUMBER

SUPPLIER-NUMBER
SUPPLIER-NAME
SUPPLIER-ADDRESS

ORDER										
ORDER-NUMBER	PART-AMOUNT	PART-NUMBER	PART-DESCRIPTION	UNIT-PRICE	SUPPLIER-NUMBER	SUPPLIER-NAME	SUPPLIER-ADDRESS	ORDER-DATE	DELIVERY-DATE	ORDER-TOTAL

Figure 8.16
An unnormalized relation for ORDER. In an unnormalized relation there are repeating groups. For example, there can be many parts and suppliers for each order. There is only a one-to-one correspondence between ORDER-NUMBER and ORDER-DATE, ORDER-TOTAL, and DELIVERY-DATE.

Normalization: The process of creating small stable data structures from complex groups of data when designing a relational database.

with all of the fields included here, we would have to repeat the name, description, and price of each part on the order and name and address of each part vendor. This relation contains what are called repeating groups because there can be many parts and suppliers for each order and it actually describes multiple entities—parts and suppliers as well as orders. A more efficient way to arrange the data is to break down ORDER into smaller relations, each of which describes a single entity. The process of creating small, stable data structures from complex groups of data is called **normalization.** If we go step by step and normalize the relation ORDER, we emerge with the relations illustrated in Figure 8.17.

If a database has been carefully thought out, with a clear understanding of business information needs and usage, the database model will most likely be in some normalized form. Many real-world databases are not fully normalized because this may not be the most sensible way to meet business information requirements. Note that the relational database illustrated in Figure 8.14 is not fully normalized because there could be more than one part for each order. The designers chose not to use the four relations described in Figure 8.17 because this particular business has a business rule specifying that a separate order must be placed for each part. The designers might have felt that there was no business need for maintaining four different tables.

8.4 Database Trends

Recent database trends include the growth of distributed databases and the emergence of object-oriented and hypermedia databases.

Distributed Processing and Distributed Databases

Distributed processing: The distribution of computer processing among multiple, geographically or functionally separate locations linked by a communications network.

Distributed database: A database that is stored in more than one physical location. Parts or copies of the database are physically stored in one location and other parts or copies are stored and maintained in other locations.

Beginning in the early 1970s, information processing became more distributed with the growth of powerful telecommunications networks and the decline in computer hardware costs. Instead of relying on a single centralized mainframe computer to provide service to remote terminals, organizations began to install minicomputers and microcomputers at remote sites. These distributed processors directly serve local and regional branch offices and factories and are generally linked together in networks. The dispersion and use of computers among multiple, geographically or functionally separate locations so that local computers handle local processing needs is called **distributed processing.** Chapters 9 and 10 will describe the various network arrangements for distributed processing.

It is only a short step from distributed processing to distributed databases. Although early distributed systems worked with a single centralized database, over time the smaller local systems began to store local databases as well. It soon became obvious that the central database could be entirely distributed to local processors as long as some mechanism existed to provide proper updating, integrity of data, sharing of data, and central administrative controls.

A **distributed database** is one that is stored in more than one physical location. Parts of the database are stored physically in one location and other parts are stored and maintained in other locations. There are two ways of distributing a database (see Figure 8.18). The central database (see Figure 8.18a) can be par-

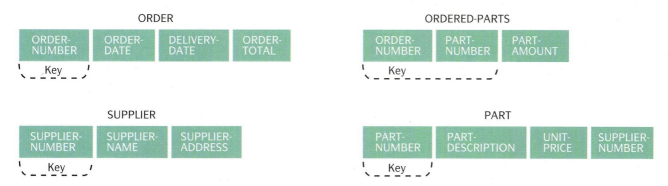

Figure 8.17

A normalized relation for ORDER. After normalization, the original relation ORDER has been broken down into four smaller relations. The relation ORDER is left with only three attributes and the relation ORDERED-PARTS has a combined, or concatenated key consisting of ORDER-NUMBER and PART-NUMBER.

titioned so that each remote processor has the necessary data on customers to serve its local area. Changes in local files can be justified with the central database on a batch basis, often at night. Another strategy is to replicate the central database (see Figure 8.18b) at all remote locations. This strategy also requires updating of the central database on off hours.

Still another possibility—one used by very large databases like the FBI's National Crime Information Center—is to maintain only a central name index and to store complete records locally (see Figure 8.18c). A query to the central name index identifies a location where the full record can be found. Here there is no central database and no updating costs. National Westminster Bank in London uses a similar approach to maintain all of its customer account information in two massive fragmented DB2 databases. Specially developed software allows each of its 22,000 users to access the data on either database with a global catalog of where the data are stored. Another variation is an ask-the-network scheme (see Figure 8.18d). There is no central index of names in this design. Instead, all remote processors are polled to find a complete record. The complete record is then transferred to whatever processor requests it (Laudon, 1986).

Both distributed processing and distributed databases have benefits and drawbacks. Distributed systems reduce the vulnerability of a single, massive central site. They permit increases in systems power by purchasing smaller, less expensive minicomputers. Finally, they increase service and responsiveness to local users. Distributed systems, however, are dependent on high-quality telecommunications lines, which themselves are vulnerable. Moreover, local databases can sometimes depart from central data standards and definitions, and pose security problems by widely distributing access to sensitive data. The economies of distribution can be lost when remote sites buy more computing power than they need.

Despite these drawbacks, distributed processing is growing rapidly. With the advent of microcomputers and powerful telecommunications systems, more and more information services will be distributed. For large national organizations working in several regions, the question is no longer whether to distribute but how to distribute in such a way as to minimize costs and improve responsiveness without sacrificing data and system integrity.

Object-Oriented and Hypermedia Databases

Conventional database management systems were designed for homogeneous data that can be easily structured into predefined data fields and records. But many applications of the 1990s will require databases that can store and retrieve not only structured numbers and characters but also drawings, images, photo-

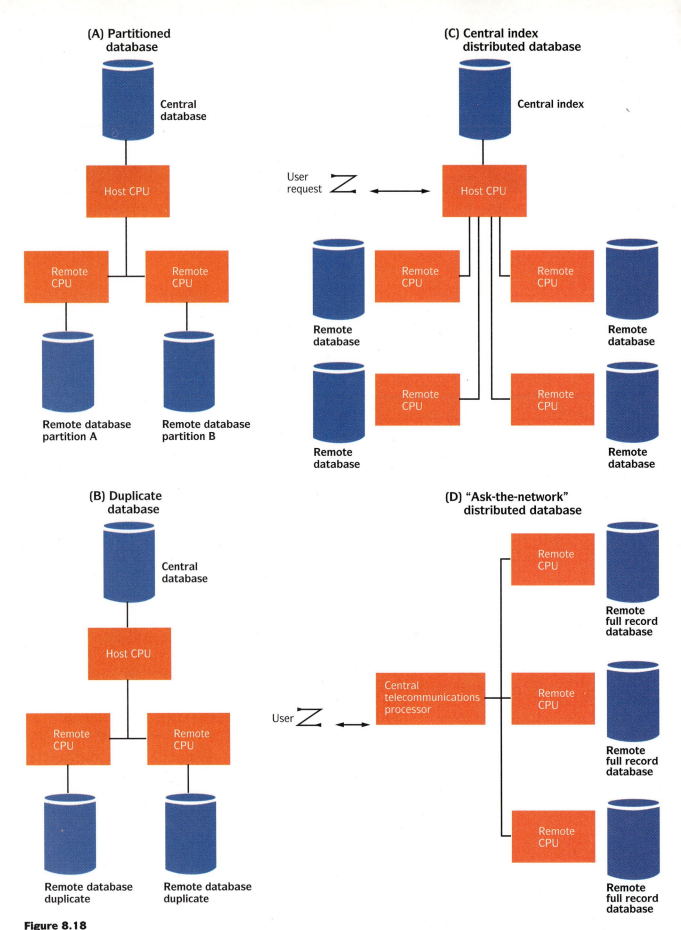

Figure 8.18
Distributed databases. There are alternative ways of distributing a database. The central database can be partitioned (A) so that each remote processor has the necessary data to serve its own local needs. The central database can also be duplicated (B) at all remote locations. In the central index distributed database (C) complete records are stored locally and can be located using a central name index. In an "ask-the-network" distributed database (D), the network polls its remote processors to locate a record and transfers the complete record to whatever processor requests it.

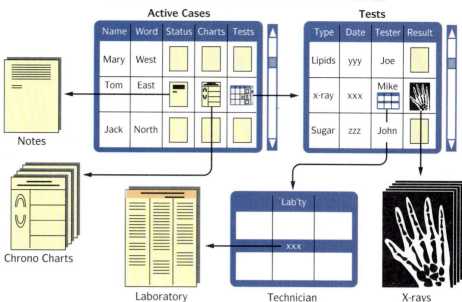

DIGITAL: BUILDING A TRUE MULTIMEDIA DATABASE

Figure 8.19
An object-oriented multimedia database. Medical data on patients in a hospital might likely be stored in a multimedia database such as this one. Doctors could access patient files including vital medical images to generate the reports and derive the information they need to deliver quality health care quickly. *Courtesy of Digital Equipment Corporation.*

Object-oriented database: Approach to data management that stores both data and the procedures acting on the data as objects that can be automatically retrieved and shared.

Hypermedia database: Approach to data management that organizes data as a network of nodes linked in any pattern established by the user.

graphs, voice, and full-motion video (see Figure 8.19). Conventional DBMS are not well-suited to handling graphics-based or multimedia applications. For instance, design data in a CAD database consist of complex relationships between many types of data. Manipulating these kinds of data in a relational system requires extensive programming to translate these complex data structures into tables and rows. An **object-oriented database,** on the other hand, stores the data and procedures as objects that can be automatically retrieved and shared. The Window on Technology on page 261 describes these new capabilities.

The **hypermedia database** approach to information management transcends some of the limitations of traditional database methods by storing chunks of information in the form of nodes connected by links established by the user (see Figure 8.20). The nodes can contain text, graphics, sound, full-motion video, or executable computer programs. Searching for information does not have to follow a predetermined organization scheme. Instead, one can branch instantly to related information in any kind of relationship established by the author. The relationship between records is less structured than in a traditional DBMS.

In most systems, each node can be displayed on a screen. The screen also displays the links between the node depicted and other nodes in the database. Figure 8.21 illustrates sample nodes from Apple Corporation's HyperCard,

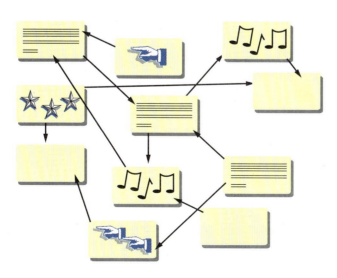

Figure 8.20
Hypermedia. In a hypermedia database, the user can choose his or her own path to move from node to node. Each node can contain text, graphics, sound, full-motion video, or executable programs.

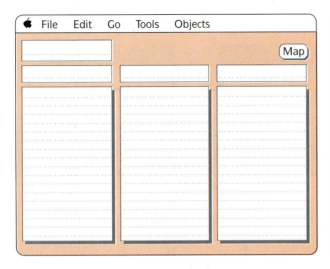

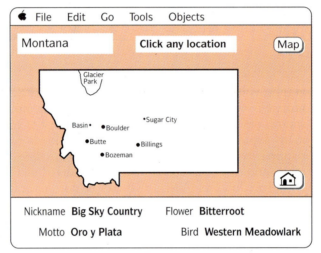

Figure 8.21
HyperCard. HyperCard programs are constructed as if they were stacks of individual cards, each of which can be linked to one or more other cards in any way the user chooses. The links do not have to follow the structured formulas of conventional databases or lists. HyperCard programs can contain digitized sound, drawings, and video images, as well as text. *Courtesy of Apple Computer, Inc.*

which is based on the hypermedia concept. The node for Sugar City, Montana is linked to a node for the state of Montana and to a node showing a map of the entire United States. The node for the state of Montana illustrated in Figure 8.21 is linked to nodes for each of the cities illustrated on the map; to a node for the map of the entire United States; and to a node to return to the Home card, the first node in the HyperCard system. HyperCard is used primarily for small, single-user applications. Massive, multi-user hypermedia databases are starting to be constructed for business and military applications (Carmel et al., 1989).

8.5 Management Requirements for Database Systems

Much more is required for the development of database systems than simply selecting a logical database model. Indeed, this selection may be among the last decisions. The database is an organizational discipline, a method, rather than a tool or technology. It requires organizational and conceptual change.

Without management support and understanding, database efforts fail. The critical elements in a database environment are 1) data administration, 2) data

AT&T Bell Laboratories in Holmdel, New Jersey, was having performance problems with its relational database management system when it ran a series of computer-aided design and manufacturing (CAD/CAM) applications that generated a great deal of graphic information. It decided to use Ontos, an object-oriented database management system from Ontos, Inc. in Burlington, Massachusetts.

CAD/CAM, which uses graphic information or images, typifies the kinds of applications that require object-oriented database management systems. Another is genetic research. Cold Spring Harbor Laboratory in Long Island City, New York wanted to rewrite some applications that examined pictures of DNA molecules and manipulated genetic research data. A relational database wouldn't do, because the laboratory wanted a database management system capable of storing images. The laboratory chose an object-oriented database management system instead. It now has three genetic research applications based on GemStone from the Servio Corporation in Alameda, California.

Firms interested in reusable code and decreased costs for maintaining existing software might be interested in object-oriented database management systems as well. Unlike relational or hierarchical database management systems, object-oriented DBMS store data as objects, which incorporate the processing rules needed to complete each database transaction. Vendors of object-oriented DBMS claim that this might boost database performance by a factor of 10 over relational DBMS. If these claims bear out, will object-oriented database management systems be the next foundation for application development just as relational DBMS are starting to displace hierarchical DBMS?

Corporations seeking to migrate to object-oriented DBMS must recognize that their staffs have been designing relational DBMS for years, with the attitude of "If it isn't broke, why try to fix it?" Training programmers to take full advantage of object-oriented techniques requires a change in mindset. Often a firm's first few object-oriented DBMS applications tend to look more like relational applications running on an object-oriented database. Corporations that have invested ten years in relational technology might not want to switch to another technology until they have obtained a significant return on their investment.

Source: Paul Korzeniowski, "Object-Oriented DBMSs Strive to Differentiate," *Software Magazine* (May 1992).

To Think About: Suggest some other applications for object-oriented DBMS. When adopting object-oriented DBMS, what management, organization, and technology factors would you consider?

planning and modeling methodology, 3) database technology and management, and 4) users. This environment is depicted in Figure 8.22 and will now be described.

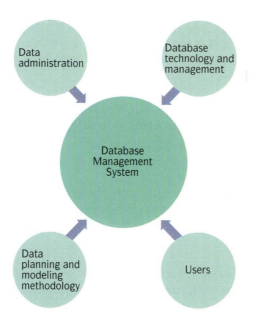

Figure 8.22
Key organizational elements in the database environment. For a database management system to flourish in any organization, data administration functions and data planning and modeling methodologies must be coordinated with database technology and management. Resources must be devoted to train end users to use databases properly.

Data Administration

Data administration: A special organizational function for managing the organization's data resources, concerned with data planning, information policy, maintenance of data dictionaries, and data quality standards.

Database systems require that the organization recognize the strategic role of information and begin actively to manage and plan for information as a corporate resource. This means that the organization must develop a **data administration** function with the power to define information requirements for the entire company and with direct access to senior management. The chief information officer (CIO) or vice president of information becomes the primary advocate in the organization for database systems.

Data administration is responsible for the specific policies and procedures through which data can be managed as an organizational resource. These responsibilities include developing information policy, planning for data, overseeing logical database design and data dictionary development, and monitoring the usage of data by information system specialists and end-user groups.

The fundamental principle of data administration is that all data are the property of the organization as a whole. Data cannot belong exclusively to any one business area or organizational unit. All data are to be made available to any group that requires them to fulfill its mission. An organization needs to formulate an **information policy** that specifies its rules for sharing, disseminating, acquiring, standardizing, classifying, and inventorying information throughout the organization. Information policy lays out specific procedures and accountabilities, specifying which organizational units share information; where information can be distributed; and who has responsibility for updating and maintaining the information.

Information policy: Formal rules governing the maintenance, distribution, and use of information in an organization.

Data Planning and Modeling Methodology

Because the organizational interests served by the DBMS are much broader than those in the traditional file environment, the organization requires enterprisewide planning for data. Enterprise analysis, which addresses the information requirements of the entire organization (as opposed to the requirements of individual applications), is needed to develop databases. The purpose of enterprise analysis is to identify the key entities, attributes, and relationships that constitute the organization's data. These techniques are described in greater detail in Chapter 11.

Database Technology and Management

Databases require new software and a new staff specially trained in DBMS techniques as well as new management structures. Most corporations develop a database design and management group within the corporate information system division that is responsible for the more technical and operational aspects of managing data. The functions it performs are called **database administration**. This group does the following:

Database administration: Refers to the more technical and operational aspects of managing data, including physical database design and maintenance.

- Defines and organizes database structure and content.
- Develops security procedures to safeguard the database.
- Develops database documentation.
- Maintains the database management software.

In close cooperation with users, the design group establishes the physical database, the logical relations among elements, and the access rules and procedures.

Users

A database serves a wider community of users than traditional systems. Relational systems with fourth-generation query languages permit employees who are not computer specialists to access large databases. In addition, users include trained computer specialists. In order to optimize access for nonspecialists, more resources must be devoted to training end users. Professional systems workers must be retrained in the DBMS language, DBMS application development procedures, and new software practices.

Hierarchical database technology first became commercially available in the early 1970s. Since then, more sophisticated database models have appeared. Nevertheless, progress in creating a true database environment in organizations has been much slower than anticipated. Why? Three challenges stand out.

1. **Organizational obstacles to a database environment.** Implementing a database requires widespread organizational change in the role of information (and information managers), the allocation of power at senior levels, the ownership and sharing of information, and patterns of organizational agreement. A DBMS challenges the existing arrangements in an organization and for that reason often generates political resistance.

   In a traditional file environment, each department constructed files and programs to fulfill its specific needs. Now, with a database, files and programs must be built that take into account the full organization's interest in data. For instance, in the past the treasurer could insulate his or her data and applications from others in the organization. Some information that once "belonged" to the treasurer is now shared through the DBMS with users in other departments. Quite naturally, the treasurer may worry that other users will not treat financial data with the same care and concern as the treasurer's personnel.

2. **Cost/benefit considerations.** The costs of moving to a database environment are tangible, up front, and large in the short term (three years). Most firms buy a commercial DBMS package and related hardware. The software alone can cost one-half million dollars for a full-function package with all options. New hardware may cost an additional $1 to 2 million annually. It soon becomes apparent to senior management that a database system is a huge investment. Although the organization has spent the money on the hardware and software for a database environment, it may not reap the benefits it should because it is unwilling to make the requisite organizational changes.

   Unfortunately, the benefits of the DBMS are often intangible, back-loaded, and long-term (five years). The systems that the DBMS seeks to replace generally work, although they are inefficient. Moreover, several million dollars have been spent over the years designing and maintaining existing systems. People in the organization understand the existing system after long periods of training and socialization. For all of these reasons, and despite the clear advantages of the DBMS, the short-term costs of developing a DBMS often appear to be nearly as great as the benefits. When the short-term political costs are added to the equation, it is convenient for senior management to defer the database investment. The obvious long-term benefits of the DBMS tend to be severely discounted by managers, especially those unfamiliar with (and perhaps unfriendly to) systems. Moreover, it may not be cost-effective to build organization-wide databases that integrate all of the organization's data (Goodhue et. al., September 1992).

3. **Organizational placement of the data management function.** Many organizations, seeking to avoid large commitments and organizational change, begin (and end) by buying a DBMS package and placing it in the hands of a low-level database group in the information systems department. Generally this leads to a piecemeal approach to database use; that is, small database systems will be developed for various divisions, functional areas, departments, and offices. Eventually this results in incompatible databases throughout the company, and fails to address the key organizational issue: What is the role of information and who will manage it for the organization as a whole? Senior management must be persuaded to implement a data administration function and data planning methodology at the highest corporate level.

Summary

Describe traditional file organization and management techniques.

In a traditional file environment, data records are organized using either a sequential file organization or a direct or random file organization. Records in a sequential file can be accessed sequentially or they can be accessed directly if the sequential file is on disk and uses an indexed sequential access method. Records on a file with direct file organization can be accessed directly without an index.

Explain the problems of the traditional file environment.

By allowing different functional areas and groups in the organization to maintain their own files independently, the traditional file environment creates problems such as data redundancy and inconsistency, program/data dependence, inflexibility, poor security, and lack of data sharing and availability.

Describe how a database management system organizes information.

Database management systems (DBMS) are the software that permits centralization of data and data management. A DBMS includes a data definition language, a data manipulation language, and a data dictionary capability.

The most important feature of the DBMS is its ability to separate the logical and physical views of data. The user works with a logical view of data. The DBMS software translates user queries into queries that can be applied to the physical view of the data. The DBMS retrieves information so that the user does not have to be concerned with its physical location. This feature separates programs from data and from the management of data.

Identify the three principal database models.

There are three principal logical database models: hierarchical, network, and relational. Each has unique advantages and disadvantages. Hierarchical systems, which support one-to-many relationships, are low in flexibility but high in processing speed and efficiency. Network systems support many-to-many relationships. Relational systems are relatively slow but are very flexible for supporting ad hoc requests for information and for combining information from different sources. The choice depends on the business requirements.

Explain the principles for designing a relational database.

Designing a database requires both a logical design and a physical design. The process of creating small stable data structures from complex groups of data when using a relational database model is termed *normalization*.

Discuss new database trends.

It is no longer necessary for data to be centralized in a single, massive database. A complete database or portions of the database can be distributed to more than one location to increase responsiveness and reduce vulnerability and costs. There are two major types of distributed databases: replicated databases and partitioned databases.

Object-oriented databases and hypermedia databases may be alternatives to traditional database structures for certain types of applications. Both can store graphics and other types of data in addition to conventional text data to support multimedia applications. Hypermedia databases allow data to be stored in nodes linked together in any pattern established by the user.

Explain the managerial and organizational requirements for creating a database environment.

Development of a database environment requires much more than selection of technology. It requires a change in the corporation's attitude toward information. The organization must develop a data administration function and a data planning methodology. The database environment has developed more slowly than was originally anticipated. There is political resistance in organizations to many key database concepts, especially to sharing of information that has been controlled exclusively by one organizational group. There are difficult cost/benefit questions in database management. Often, to avoid raising difficult questions, database use begins and ends as a small effort isolated in the Information Systems Department.

Review Questions

1. Why is file management important for overall system performance?

2. Describe how indexes and key fields enable a program to access specific records in a file.

3. Define and describe the indexed sequential access method and the direct file access method.

4. List and describe some of the problems of the traditional file environment.

5. Define a database and a database management system.

6. Name and briefly describe the three components of a DBMS.

7. What is the difference between a logical and a physical view of data?

8. List some of the benefits of a DBMS.

9. Describe the three principal database models and the advantages and disadvantages of each.

10. What is normalization? How is it related to the features of a well-designed relational database?

11. What is a distributed database, and how does it differ from distributed data processing?

12. What are object-oriented and hypermedia databases? How do they differ from a traditional database?

13. What are the four key elements of a database environment? Describe each briefly.

14. Describe and briefly comment on the major management challenges in building a database environment.

Discussion Questions

1. It has been said that you do not need database management software to have a database environment. Discuss.

2. As an information system manager, you are concerned that the percentage of your staff working on maintenance of existing programs is growing and the percentage working on new applications is declining. How could a database environment change this trend?

3. To what extent should end users be involved in the selection of a database management system and in database design?

Group
Project

Form a group with half of your classmates. Consider two strategies for building a database environment. One strategy recommends that a small group be created in the information systems department to begin exploring database applications throughout the firm. The other strategy recommends the creation of a vice president of information and subsequent development of important database applications. Debate the costs and benefits of each strategy with the other group.

CASE STUDY

Can Better Data Management Help a Regional French Bank?

The Caisse Régionale de Crédit Agricole Mutuel du Lot, a regional commercial credit division of France's largest bank, runs 70 PCs, four mainframe and minicomputers, and 500 terminals. Based in Cahors, Lot in the southwestern part of France, the operation employs 430 workers, including 40 in the data processing department.

Its parent bank, Crédit Agricole, is the seventh largest bank in the world, with assets of more than 1.4 billion francs, banking facilities in New York and Chicago, and a total of 70 million customers. Its entire workforce totals 73,700, with 530 data processing specialists. Crédit Agricole operates 91 regional banks in France, including one per French département such as Lot. (A département is similar to a state in the United States.) The bank runs more than 450 mainframe and minicomputers linking 50,000 terminals worldwide. About one-third of the French banking consumers are its clients. The bank is highly decentralized.

An extensive analysis found that Crédit Agricole du Lot needed to work with the concept of a "commercial client." It needed a database management system that could regroup and improve access to individuals maintained in the database and that could answer many different kinds of queries that were not predefined. (Banks have traditionally maintained information based on different types of accounts—checking, savings, loans, and so forth. A client may have more than one account. If files or databases are inflexible and organized around accounts, it may be impossible to draw together all the information maintained on clients.) The bank also needed tools for targeting all of its commercial operations and for facilitating multiple access queries.

The bank had been using IBM's DL/1 (Data Language/1), an extension of IBM's hierarchical DBMS, IMS. The information the bank needed was not accessible to different applications, so bank personnel had to spend a great deal of time rekeying the same information.

Competition is very tough, and the bank wanted to boost its competitive standing through quality to improve its profitability. In particular, it wanted to produce behavior studies of different categories of clients, such as individuals, organizations, companies, and self-employed persons. The bank wanted to use the results of these studies to produce quick, targeted client profiles so it could direct its marketing campaigns toward controlling risks and credits. To do this, the bank needed to update its databases easily, to access their stored information quickly, and if required, to partition the data for particular needs.

Crédit Agricole du Lot chose CA-Datacom/DB, the relational database management system from Computer Associates International in Garden City, New York, over IBM's DB2 because it could run under the bank's existing operating system, MVS/SP. At the time of selection, DB/2 required MVS/XS or MVS/ESA, newer IBM operating systems. The hardware cost of upgrading to a new operating system would have been prohibitive. The bank could continue using its older IMS database and DL/1 and share data with the new CA-Datacom/DB database, whereas comprehensive data sharing between DB2 and DL/1 was not possible. CA-Datacom/DB has SQL capabilities.

The bank took a year longer to install the new database management system than it had originally anticipated because the vendor was late delivering the DBMS capabilities it had promised to the bank and because several minor software bugs were encountered during installation.

With the improved capabilities of the relational DBMS, Crédit Agricole du Lot also hopes to introduce more self-service features into its branches. It is installing IBM Personal System/2 microcomputer workstations and distributing portable microcomputers to its commercial staff.

Source: Mike Bucken, "Relational Gives Bank Fast Access to Queries," *Software Magazine* (March 1991).

Case Study Questions

1. Was a relational database management system the best choice for Crédit Agricole du Lot? Why or why not?

2. To what extent is selecting a database management system an important business decision?

3. What are some of the data fields that would have to be maintained in the new database?

4. What management, organization and technology factors should be considered when selecting a database management system?

References   Butterworth, Paul, Allen Otis, and Jacob Stein. "The GemStone Object Database Management System." *Communications of the ACM* 34, no. 10 (October 1991).

Carmel, Erran, William K. McHenry, and Yeshayahu Cohen. "Building Large, Dynamic Hypertexts: How Do We Link *Intelligently?*" *Journal of Management Information Systems* 6, no. 2 (Fall 1989).

Date, C. J. *An Introduction to Database Systems.* 5th ed. Reading, MA: Addison-Wesley, 1990.

Date, C. J. "Twelve Rules for a Distributed Data Base." *Computerworld* (June 8, 1987).

Everest, G. C. *Database Management: Objectives, System Functions, and Administration.* New York: McGraw-Hill Book Company, 1985.

Goldstein, R. C., and J. B. McCririck. "What Do Data Administrators Really Do?" *Datamation* 26 (August 1980).

Goodhue, Dale L., Judith A. Quillard, and John F. Rockart. "Managing the Data Resource: A Contingency Perspective." *MIS Quarterly* (September 1988).

Goodhue, Dale L., Laurie J. Kirsch, Judith A. Quillard, and Michael D. Wybo. "Strategic Data Planning: Lessons from the Field." *MIS Quarterly* 16, no. 1 (March 1992).

Goodhue, Dale L., Michael D. Wybo, and Laurie J. Kirsch. "The Impact of Data Integration on the Costs and Benefits of Information Systems." *MIS Quarterly* 16, no. 3 (September 1992).

Grover, Varun, and James Teng. "How Effective Is Data Resource Management?" *Journal of Information Systems Management* (Summer 1991).

Kahn, Beverly K. "Some Realities of Data Administration." *Communications of the ACM* 26 (October 1983).

Kahn, Beverly, and Linda Garceau. "The Database Administration Function." *Journal of Management Information Systems* 1 (Spring 1985).

King, John L., and Kenneth Kraemer. "Information Resource Management Cannot Work." *Information and Management* (1988).

Kent, William. "A Simple Guide to Five Normal Forms in Relational Database Theory." *Communications of the ACM* 26, no. 2 (February 1983).

Kroenke, David. *Database Processing.* 4th ed. New York: Macmillan Publishing Company, 1992.

Laudon, Kenneth C. *Dossier Society: Value Choices in the Design of National Information Systems.* New York: Columbia University Press, 1986.

Madnick, Stuart E., and Richard Y. Wang. "Evolution towards Strategic Application of Databases through Composite Information Systems." *Journal of Management Information Systems* 5, no. 3 (Winter 1988–1989).

March, Salvatore T., and Young-Gul Kim. "Information Resource Management: A Metadata Perspective." *Journal of Management Information Systems* 5, no. 3 (Winter 1988–1989).

Martin, James. *Managing the Data-Base Environment.* Englewood Cliffs, NJ: Prentice-Hall, 1983.

Silberschatz, Avi, Michael Stonebraker, and Jeff Ullman, eds. "Database Systems: Achievements and Opportunities." *Communications of the ACM* 34, no. 10 (October 1991).

Smith, John B., and Stephen F. Weiss. "Hypertext." *Communications of the ACM* 31, no. 7 (July 1988).

Telecommuni-cations

Networks Speed Up Wal-Mart's Store-to-Supplier Orders

Wal-Mart Stores, Inc., the U.S. retail giant, is noted for its "continuous replenishment system" in which stores send orders for new merchandise directly to suppliers as soon as consumers take their purchases out the door. Wal-Mart found that to keep its operating costs below those of its competitors while providing customers with quality, "every-day low prices," and reliability it needed to fine tune its continuous replenishment system with more detailed data.

Wal-Mart used to track purchases of goods such as sweaters merely by the number sold. But it needed more detailed data about the sizes and colors of these sweaters. Such detailed information helps Wal-Mart stock its stores with exactly the products customers want. The data also minimize the amount of time that goods remain in warehouses or on store shelves. By stocking the right products and moving them quickly off the shelves, Wal-Mart achieved in 1991 an inventory-to-sales ratio of 1 to

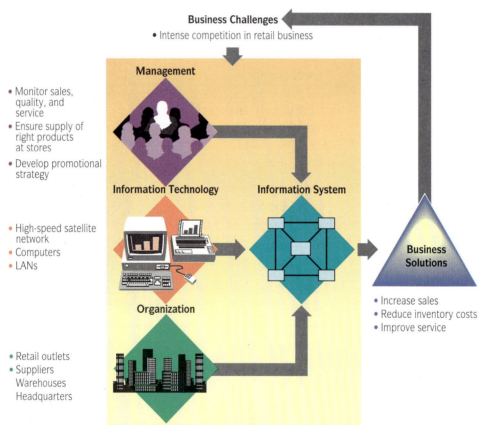

Business Challenges
• Intense competition in retail business

Management
• Monitor sales, quality, and service
• Ensure supply of right products at stores
• Develop promotional strategy

Information Technology
• High-speed satellite network
• Computers
• LANs

Organization
• Retail outlets
• Suppliers Warehouses Headquarters

Information System

Business Solutions
• Increase sales
• Reduce inventory costs
• Improve service

• Expedite orders from stores to suppliers
• Provide better data for buying decisions
• Expedite credit card verification
• Transmit store display guidelines

5.94, compared to 1 to 4.58 for its competitor Kmart.

Data at this level of detail amount to several gigabytes a day produced by each store. To transmit and analyze such massive quantities of data, Wal-Mart installed a new high-speed companywide network. The network boosts the speed of data transmitted from individual stores from 19.2 kilobits per second to hundreds of thousands of kilobits per second. Local area networks in Wal-Mart stores, warehouses, and headquarters receive data transmitted by satellites from other locations.

Wal-Mart stores order replacement items directly from their suppliers each day. Point-of-sale terminals record the bar code of each item passing the checkout counter and send the purchase transaction data to a Unix file server in a local area network located in each store. The file server sends order data via satellite to an IBM Enterprise/9000 mainframe located at Wal-Mart headquarters. The mainframe batches orders from all of the stores together and transmits the order data to suppliers. Wal-Mart vendors use the data to fulfill the orders and to see how merchandise is selling. The data help suppliers adjust their production of goods to meet customer demands.

Wal-Mart also uses its powerful network to send store managers images of how best to display merchandise items and to expedite credit card verification transactions.

Source: Elisabeth Horwitt, "Wal-Mart Spotlights Fast LANs," *Computerworld* (January 25, 1993).

W al-Mart found that it could benefit from telecommunications to respond more efficiently to customers' buying patterns and to minimize operating costs. Wal-Mart is a large company, but even small businesses and firms depend on telecommunications technology. Many of the technical advances in computing and information systems, such as on-line processing and providing direct access to data, would be impossible without telecommunications.

Telecommunications has become so essential to the conduct of business life that managers will be making telecommunications-related decisions throughout their careers. This chapter describes the components of telecommunications systems and shows how they can be arranged to create various types of telecommunications networks and network-based applications that can increase the efficiency and competitiveness of an organization.

After completing this chapter you will be able to:

- Describe the basic components of a telecommunications system.
- Measure the capacity of telecommunications channels and evaluate transmission media.

- Classify the various types of telecommunications networks.
- Describe the three basic network topologies.
- Identify telecommunications applications that can provide competitive advantages to organizations.
- Explain the criteria used in planning for telecommunications systems.

9.1 The Telecommunications Revolution

Telecommunications:
Communication of information by electronic means, usually over some distance.

Telecommunications can be defined as communication of information by electronic means, usually over some distance. We are currently in the middle of a telecommunications revolution in the United States that has two components: rapid changes in the technology of communications and equally important changes in the ownership, control, and marketing of telecommunications services. Today's managers need to understand how to use telecommunications technology and how to maximize its benefits for their organizations.

The Marriage of Computers and Communications

For most of the last 120 years since Alexander Bell invented the first "singing telegraph" in 1876, telecommunications was a monopoly either of the state or of a regulated private firm. In the United States, American Telephone and Telegraph (AT&T) was the largest regulated monopoly, providing virtually all telecommunications services. In Europe and in the rest of the world there is a state post, telephone, and telegraph authority (PTT). These monopolies have the advantage of developing nationwide, compatible, stable, and unitary systems of interconnected parts, all of which share the same standards. The disadvantage, as with any monopoly, is a lack of innovation and active efforts that prevent

Table 9.1 COMMON TASKS PERFORMED BY COMPUTER SYSTEMS REQUIRING TELECOMMUNICATIONS

Application	Example	Requirements
Business		
On-line data entry	Inventory control	Transactions occurring several times/second, direct response required
On-line text retrieval	Hospital information systems; library systems	Response required in real time; high character volumes
Inquiry/response	Point-of-sale system; airline reservation system; credit checking	Transactions several times/second; instant response within seconds
Administrative message switching	Electronic mail	Short response and delivery times (minutes to hours)
Process control	Computer-aided manufacturing (CAM); numeric control of machine tools	Continuous input transactions and on-line responses required
Intercomputer data exchange	International transfer of bank funds	Infrequent but high-volume bursts of information; transfer of large data blocks; on-line immediate response
Home		
Inquiry response	Home banking; shopping; ordering	On-line transactions collected with high frequency
Text-retrieval	Home education	High-volume, rapid transmission
Special entertainment	Sports; polling and political participation	High-capacity video and data capabilities

technical change because of the cost of the monopoly's huge, installed base of copper wires, standards, machines, and equipment. In the United States, this situation changed in 1984 when the Department of Justice forced AT&T to give up its monopoly and allow competing firms to sell telecommunications services and equipment.

The end of AT&T's monopoly widened the market for new telecommunications technologies and devices, from cheaper long distance service from new companies like SPRINT and MCI, to telephone answering equipment, to cellular car telephones, to private satellite communications systems like those owned by Boeing Aircraft, Tymnet, and other companies. AT&T itself started marketing computing services and computing equipment.

Changes in the telecommunications industry were accompanied by changes in telecommunications technology. Previously, telecommunications meant voice transmission over telephone lines. Today, much telecommunications transmission is digital data transmission, using computers to transmit data from one location to another. On-line information systems and remote access to information would be impossible without telecommunications. Table 9.1 shows some of the common tasks performed by computer systems that would be impossible without advanced telecommunications.

Deregulation and the marriage of computers and communications has also made it possible for the telephone companies to expand from traditional voice communications into new information services, such as providing transmission of news reports, stock reports, television programs, and movies. The Window on Organizations on page 275 describes how the telecommunications revolution has allowed the regional Bell telephone companies to move into the information service business.

What Managers Should Know and Why

In the 1960s, few companies had a separate telecommunications function. By the 1970s, the advent of on-line computing and time sharing had made telecommunications essential to information systems. Organizations had to start managing their own telecommunications. Entire new classes of communications technologies have emerged, so that today's managers must know the alternative technologies and systems available to their organization, the costs and benefits of each, the capabilities of various technologies, and a method for determining the organization's telecommunications requirements.

9.2 Components and Functions of a Telecommunications System

Telecommunications system: Collection of compatible hardware and software arranged to communicate information from one location to another.

A **telecommunications system** is a collection of compatible hardware and software arranged to communicate information from one location to another. Figure 9.1 illustrates the components of a typical telecommunications system. Telecommunications systems can transmit text, graphic images, voice, or video information. This section describes the major components of telecommunications systems. Subsequent sections describe how the components can be arranged into various types of networks.

Telecommunications System Components

The essential components of a telecommunications system are these:

1. Computers to process information.
2. Terminals or any input/output devices that send or receive data.

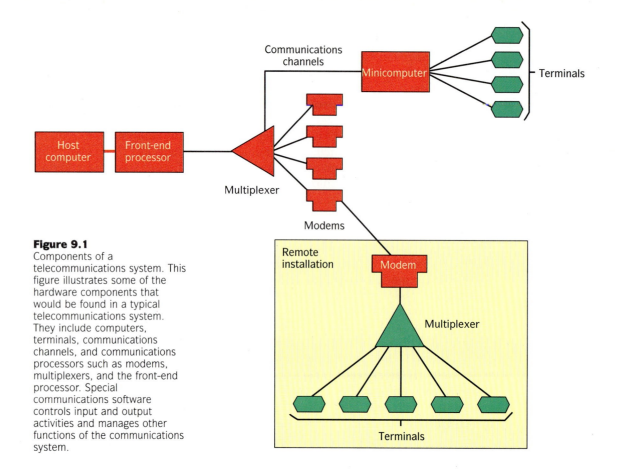

Figure 9.1
Components of a telecommunications system. This figure illustrates some of the hardware components that would be found in a typical telecommunications system. They include computers, terminals, communications channels, and communications processors such as modems, multiplexers, and the front-end processor. Special communications software controls input and output activities and manages other functions of the communications system.

3. Communications channels, the links by which data or voice are transmitted between sending and receiving devices in a network. Communications channels use various communications media, such as telephone lines, fiber optic cables, coaxial cables, and wireless transmission.

4. Communications processors, such as modems, multiplexers, and front-end processors, which provide support functions for data transmission and reception.

5. Communications software that controls input and output activities and manages other functions of the communications network.

FUNCTIONS OF TELECOMMUNICATIONS SYSTEMS

In order to send and receive information from one place to another, a telecommunications system must perform a number of separate functions. These functions are largely invisible to the people using the system. As outlined in Table 9.2, a telecommunications system transmits information, establishes the interface between the sender and the receiver, routes messages along the most efficient paths, performs elementary processing of the information to ensure that the right message gets to the right receiver, performs editorial tasks on the data (such as checking for errors and rearranging the format), and converts messages from one speed (say, the speed of a computer) into the speed of a communications line or from one format to another. Lastly, the telecommunications system controls the flow of information. Many of these tasks are accomplished by computer.

PROTOCOLS

Protocol: Set of rules and procedures that govern transmission between the components in a network.

A telecommunications network typically contains diverse hardware and software components that need to work together to transmit information. Different components in a network can communicate by adhering to a common set of rules that enable them to "talk" to each other. This set of rules and procedures governing transmission between two points in a network is called a **protocol.** Each device in a network must be able to interpret the other device's protocol.

ORGANIZATIONS

The Telephone Company Becomes an Information Service Business

In May 1993, a Federal appeals court gave the seven regional Bell telephone companies permission to provide information services such as stock quotes, sports scores, and news reports. The ruling overturned part of a previous lower court decision that lifted a long-standing ban prohibiting the regional Bell companies from owning information services. In July 1992, the Federal Communications Commission ruled that the Baby Bells could deliver movies and television to homes in the same way that they now deliver telephone calls.

The new rulings lock the Bells into a lobbying fight with newspaper publishers, cable TV, and other companies providing information services. Traditional providers of information services are pressuring Congress to create rules that would restrict the Bells from choking off competition.

The Bells have started by offering information from their own valuable databases—primarily lists of phone subscribers that make up their white- and yellow-page directories—as well as from their voice-mail services. Pacific Telesis is testing expanded directory assistance whereby operators answering 411 calls will give callers additional information on businesses.

Pacific Telesis is also developing a service for California's schools to provide access to university library data nationwide and is planning to deliver daily customized news reports. Ameritech is testing a health care network that provides information about patients to doctors, diagnostic clinics, and hospitals. Nynex is working with France's Minitel electronic information service and may introduce a home security service similar to one Minitel offers in Ireland with Telecom Eireann.

The Baby Bells are moving cautiously into videotex services, which electronically deliver information to a personal computer or television set. For instance, U.S. West has a Community Link service that gives customers with PCs or special terminals news stories, restaurant menus, theater tickets, and airline schedules. U.S. West has also embarked on a partnership with Time Warner Inc. to build a "full service network" carrying communications, entertainment and information on Time Warner's cable-TV systems.

Technology developed by Bellcore, the Baby Bells' research consortium, makes it possible to transmit high-quality video over ordinary copper telephone lines. This means that the telephone companies do not need to replace existing copper wiring with optical fiber that might cost $100 billion to $400 billion in order to transmit movies and television programs to customers at home. If shoppers at home can dial up movies or television programs over ordinary telephone lines, the Baby Bells can easily become electronic video rental stores.

Sources: Mary Lu Carnevale, "Information, Please: Battling for Business," *The Wall Street Journal* (May 18, 1992), "Cable-Phone Link Is Promising Gamble," *The Wall Street Journal,* (May 18, 1993), Edmund L. Andrews, "Ruling Backs 'Baby Bells' on Information Services," *The New York Times* (May 29, 1993) and "Court Lets 'Baby Bells' Branch Out," *The New York Times* (October 6, 1991).

To Think About: What advantages do the Bells' expanding services offer businesses? What are some of the obstacles the Bell companies face? Should telephone companies be allowed to deliver information services?

Table 9.2   FUNCTIONS OF TELECOMMUNICATIONS

Function	Definition
Transmission	Media, networks and path
Interface	Path—sender—receiver
Routing	Choosing the most efficient path
Processing	Getting the right message to the right receiver
Editorial	Checking for errors, formats, and editing
Conversion	Changing speeds and codes from one device to another
Control	Routing messages, polling receivers, providing network structure maintenance

The principal functions of protocols in a telecommunications network are to identify each device in the communication path, to secure the attention of the other device, to verify correct receipt of the transmitted message, to verify that a message requires retransmission because it cannot be correctly interpreted, and to perform recovery when errors occur.

Although business, government, and the computer industry recognize the need for common communications standards, the industry has yet to put a universal standard into effect. Chapter 10 discusses the question of telecommunications standards in greater detail.

Types of Signals: Analog and Digital

Analog signal: A continuous wave form that passes through a communications medium. Used for voice communications.

Digital signal: A discrete wave form that transmits data coded into two discrete states as 1-bits and 0-bits, which are represented as on–off electrical pulses. Used for data communications.

Modem: Device for translating digital signals into analog signals and vice-versa.

Information travels through a telecommunications system in the form of electromagnetic signals. Signals are represented in two ways: There are analog and digital signals. An **analog signal** is represented by a continuous waveform that passes through a communications medium. Analog signals are used to handle voice communications and to reflect variations in pitch.

A **digital signal** is a discrete rather than a continuous waveform. It transmits data coded into two discrete states: 1-bits and 0-bits, which are represented as on–off electrical pulses. Most computers communicate with digital signals, as do many local telephone companies and some larger networks. But if a telecommunications system, such as a traditional telephone network, is set up to process analog signals—the receivers, transmitters, amplifiers, and so forth—a digital signal cannot be processed without some alterations. All digital signals must be translated into analog signals before they can be transmitted in an analog system. The device that performs this translation is called a **modem.** (Modem is an abbreviation for (MODulation/DEmodulation.) A modem translates the digital signals of a computer into analog form for transmission over ordinary telephone lines, or it translates analog signals back into digital form for reception by a computer (see Figure 9.2).

Types of Communications Channels

Channels: The links by which data or voice are transmitted between sending and receiving devices in a network.

Communications **channels** are the means by which data are transmitted from one device in a network to another. A channel can utilize different kinds of telecommunications transmission media: twisted wire, coaxial cable, fiber optics, terrestrial microwave, satellite, and wireless transmission. Each has certain advantages and limitations. High-speed transmission media are more expensive in general, but they can handle higher volumes (which reduces the cost per bit). For instance, the cost per bit of data can be lower via satellite link than via leased telephone line if a firm uses the satellite link 100 percent of the time. There is also a wide range of speeds possible for any given medium depending on the software and hardware configuration.

TWISTED WIRE

Twisted wire consists of strands of copper wire twisted in pairs and is the oldest transmission medium. Most of the telephone system in a building relies on twisted wires installed for analog communication. Most buildings have addi-

Figure 9.2
Functions of the modem. A modem is a device that translates digital signals from a computer into analog form so that they can be transmitted over analog telephone lines. The modem is also used to translate analog signals back into digital form for the receiving computer.

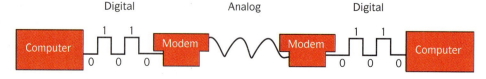

tional cables installed for future expansion, and so there are usually a number of twisted-pair cables unused in every office of every building. These unused cables can be used for digital communications. Although it is low in cost and is already in place, **twisted wire** is relatively slow for transmitting data, and high-speed transmission causes interference called *crosstalk*. On the other hand, new software and hardware have raised the capacity of existing twisted-wire cables up to 10 megabits per second, which is often adequate for connecting microcomputers and other office devices.

Twisted wire: Transmission medium consisting of pairs of twisted copper wires. Used to transmit analog phone conversations but can be used for data transmission.

COAXIAL CABLE

Coaxial cable: Transmission medium consisting of thickly insulated copper wire. Can transmit large volumes of data quickly.

Coaxial cable, like that used for cable television, consists of thickly insulated copper wire, which can transmit a larger volume of data than twisted wire can. It is often used in place of twisted wire for important links in a telecommunications network because it is a faster, more interference-free transmission medium, with speeds of up to 200 megabits per second. However, coaxial cable is thick, hard to wire in many buildings, and cannot support analog phone conversations. It must be moved when computers and other devices are moved.

FIBER OPTICS

Fiber optic cable: Fast, light, and durable transmission medium consisting of thin strands of clear glass fiber bound into cables. Data are transmitted as light pulses.

Fiber optic cable consists of thousands of strands of clear glass fiber, the thickness of a human hair, which are bound into cables. Data are transformed into pulses of light, which are sent through the fiber optic cable by a laser device at a rate of 500 kilobits to several billion bits per second. On the one hand, fiber optic cable is considerably faster, lighter, and more durable than wire media and is well suited to systems requiring transfers of large volumes of data. On the other hand, fiber optic is more difficult to work with, more expensive, and harder to install. It is best used as the backbone of a network and not for connecting isolated devices to a backbone. In most networks, fiber optic is used as the high-speed trunk line, while twisted wire and coaxial cable are used to connect the trunk line to individual devices.

WIRELESS TRANSMISSION

Microwave: High-volume, long-distance, point-to-point transmission in which high-frequency radio signals are transmitted through the atmosphere from one terrestrial transmission station to another.

Satellite: Transmission of data using orbiting satellites to serve as relay stations for transmitting microwave signals over very long distances.

Wireless transmission sends signals through air or space without any physical connection and can be accomplished using terrestrial microwave, satellites, cellular telephone, or infrared light rays.

Terrestrial **microwave** systems transmit high-frequency radio signals through the atmosphere and are widely used for high-volume, long-distance, point-to-point communication. No cabling is required. Because microwave signals follow a straight line and do not bend with the curvature of the earth, transmission stations must be positioned 25 to 30 miles apart, which adds to the expense of microwave. This problem can be solved by using microwave communication with satellites. Communication satellites are preferred because they are more cost-effective for transmitting large quantities of data over long distances.

Satellites are typically used for communications in large, geographically dispersed organizations that would be difficult to tie together through cabling media or terrestrial microwave. Satellites move in stationary orbits approximately 22,000 miles above the earth. Satellites can serve as relay stations for microwave signals transmitted from terrestrial stations.

Figure 9.3 illustrates the Omnitracs mobile communications system, which allows truckers and dispatchers to send electronic messages to each other by satellite. Each truck carries a terminal mounted on the dashboard and an antenna mounted on the roof. The driver enters short messages into the terminal and the antenna relays them to the satellite, which in turn bounces them to a central network computer at Qualcomm's San Diego processing center. From there the messages are transmitted by telephone or satellite to trucking company headquarters, where the trucking firm routes them to the appropriate dispatchers. The dispatchers can respond by sending messages back to the network computer, which passes them to the truck by satellite. The dispatchers' messages are displayed on the truckers' terminal screens. The satellite network makes it possible for trucking firms to monitor their drivers closely and schedule routes

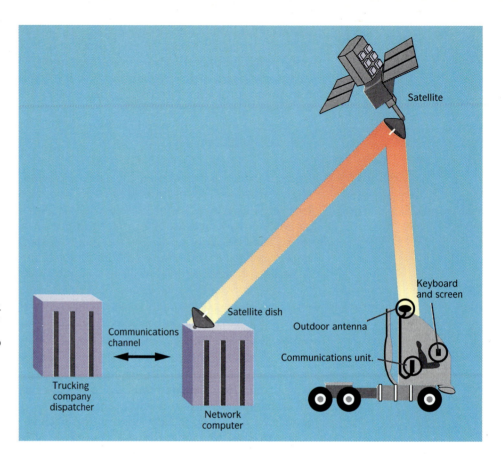

Figure 9.3:
Mobile communications systems. Satellite transmission allows geographically dispersed as well as mobile units to maintain constant communications with each other. The reliable monitoring available through satellite networks offers trucking businesses the ability to work more efficiently. *Adapted from Agis Salpukas, "Satellite System Helps Trucks Stay in Touch," The New York Times, June 5, 1991. Copyright © 1991 by The New York Times Company. Reprinted by permission.*

more efficiently because the companies always know where their drivers are (see opening vignette for Chapter 4).

Other wireless transmission technologies have recently been developed, and are being used in situations requiring mobile computing power. These technologies include high or low frequency radio or infrared light waves. In these wireless systems, a specially-equipped laptop computer or terminal can transmit data coded with the recipient's unique electronic "address" to a series of local, regional, and even national switching centers that are ultimately linked to the recipient's internal computer system.

RAM Mobile Data and Ardis are two publicly available networks that use wireless media for national two-way data transmission. Mastercard uses the RAM Mobile Data network for wireless credit-card verification terminals at county fairs or merchants' sidewalk kiosks. Otis Elevators uses the Ardis network to dispatch repair technicians around the country from a single office in Connecticut and to receive their reports.

A consortium comprising IBM and nine of the nation's largest cellular telephone companies is developing capabilities to use the country's existing analog cellular telephone network to transmit data. **Cellular telephones** (sometimes called mobile telephones) work by using radio waves to communicate with radio antennas placed within adjacent geographic areas called *cells*. As a cellular signal travels from one cell into another, a computer that monitors signals from the cells switches the conversation to a radio channel assigned to the next cell.

Cellular telephone: Device that transmits voice or data, using radio waves to communicate with radio antennas placed within adjacent geographic areas called cells.

Characteristics of Communications Channels

The characteristics of the communications channel help determine the efficiency and capabilities of a telecommunications system. These characteristics include the speed of transmission, the direction in which signals may travel, and the mode of transmission.

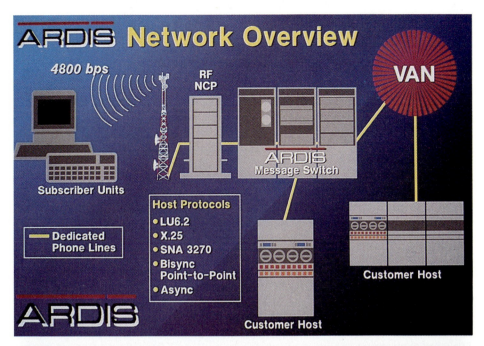

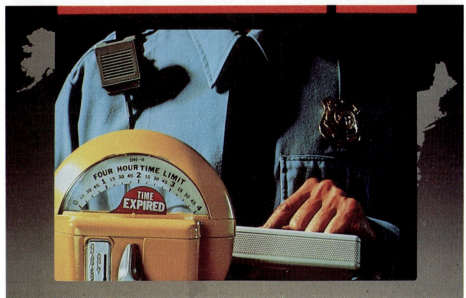

This schematic diagram (*top*) shows the network overview of the ARDIS wireless transmission system. This traffic officer (*bottom*) is using the ARDIS AGS&R communications network to record violations and enforce traffic laws.

TRANSMISSION SPEED

Baud: A change in signal from positive to negative or vice-versa that is used as a measure of transmission speed.

Bandwidth: The capacity of a communications channel as measured by the difference between the highest and lowest frequencies that can be transmitted by that channel.

The total amount of information that can be transmitted through any telecommunications channel is measured in bits per second (BPS). Sometimes this is referred to as the *baud rate*. A **baud** is a binary event representing a signal change from positive to negative or vice-versa. The baud rate is not always the same as the bit rate. At higher speeds, a single signal change can transmit more than one bit at a time, so the bit rate will generally surpass the baud rate.

Since one signal change, or cycle, is required to transmit one or several bits per second, the transmission capacity of each type of telecommunications medium is a function of its frequency, the number of cycles per second that can be sent through that medium measured in *hertz* (see Chapter 6). The range of frequencies that can be accommodated on a particular telecommunications channel is called its **bandwidth.** The bandwidth is the difference between the highest and lowest frequencies that can be accommodated on a single channel. The greater the range of frequencies, the greater the bandwidth and the greater the channel's telecommunications transmission capacity. Table 9.3 compares the transmission speed and relative costs of the major types of transmissions media.

Table 9.3 TYPICAL SPEEDS AND COST OF TELECOMMUNICATIONS TRANSMISSION MEDIA

Medium	Speed	Cost
Twisted wire	300 BPS– 10 MBPS	Low
Microwave	256 KBPS–100 MBPS	
Satellite	256 KBPS–100 MBPS	
Coaxial cable	56 KBPS–200 MBPS	
Fiber optic cable	500 KBPS– 10 GBPS	High

BPS = bits per second
KBPS = kilobits per second
MBPS = megabits per second
GBPS = gigabits per second

TRANSMISSION MODES

Asynchronous transmission: Low-speed transmission of data one character at a time.

Synchronous transmission: High-speed simultaneous transmission of large blocks of data.

There are several conventions for transmitting signals; these methods are necessary for devices to communicate when a character begins or ends. **Asynchronous transmission** (often referred to as start–stop transmission) transmits one character at a time over a line, each character framed by control bits—a start bit, one or two stop bits, and a parity bit (see Chapter 6). Asynchronous transmission is used for low-speed transmission.

Synchronous transmission transmits groups of characters simultaneously, with the beginning and ending of a block of characters determined by the timing circuitry of the sending and receiving devices. Synchronous transmission is used for transmitting large volumes of data at high speeds.

TRANSMISSION DIRECTION

Transmission must also consider the direction of data flow over a telecommunications network. In **simplex transmission,** data can only travel in one direction at all times. In **half-duplex transmission,** data can flow two ways but can travel in only one direction at a time. In **full-duplex transmission,** data can be sent in both directions simultaneously.

Communications Processors

Front-end processor: Small computer managing communications for the host computer in a network.

Concentrator: Telecommunications computer that collects and temporarily stores messages from terminals for batch transmission to the host computer.

Controller: Specialized computer that supervises communications traffic between the CPU and the peripheral devices in a telecommunications system.

Multiplexer: Device that enables a single communications channel to carry data transmissions from multiple sources simultaneously.

Communications processors, such as front-end processors, concentrators, controllers, multiplexers, and modems, support data transmission and reception in a telecommunications network.

The **front-end processor** is a small computer (often a programmable minicomputer) dedicated to communications management and is attached to the main, or host, computer in a computer system. The front-end processor performs special processing related to communications such as error control, formatting, editing, controlling, routing, and speed and signal conversion. It takes some of the load off the host computer. The front-end processor is largely responsible for collecting and processing input and output data to and from terminals and grouping characters into complete messages for submission to the CPU of the host computer.

A **concentrator** is a programmable telecommunications computer that collects and temporarily stores messages from terminals until enough messages are ready to be sent economically. The concentrator then "bursts" signals to the host computer.

A **controller,** which is often a specialized minicomputer, supervises communications traffic between the CPU and peripheral devices such as terminals and printers. The controller manages messages from these devices and communicates them to the CPU. It also routes output from the CPU to the appropriate peripheral device.

A **multiplexer** is a device that enables a single communications channel to carry data transmissions from multiple sources simultaneously. The multiplexer divides the communications channel so that it can be shared by multiple transmission devices. The multiplexer may divide a high-speed channel into multiple channels of slower speed or may assign each transmission source a very small slice of time for using the high-speed channel.

Telecommunications Software

Telecommunications software: Special software for controlling and supporting the activities of a telecommunications network.

Special **telecommunications software** is required to control and support the activities of a telecommunications network. This software resides in the host computer, front-end processor, and other processors in the network. The principal functions of telecommunications software are network control, access control, transmission control, error detection/correction, and security.

Network control software routes messages, polls network terminals, determines transmission priorities, maintains a log of network activity, and checks for errors. Access control software establishes connections between terminals and computers in the network, establishing transmission speed, mode, and direction. Transmission control software enables computers and terminals to send and receive data, programs, commands, and messages. Error-control software detects and corrects errors, then retransmits the corrected data. Security-control software monitors utilization, log-ons, passwords, and various authorization procedures to prevent unauthorized access to a network. More detail on security software can be found in Chapter 18.

9.3 Types of Telecommunications Networks

Network topology: The shape or configuration of a network.

A number of different ways exist to organize telecommunications components to form a network and hence provide multiple ways of classifying networks. Networks can be classified by their shape or **topology**. Networks can also be classified by their geographic scope and the type of services provided. Wide-area networks, for example, encompass a relatively wide geographic area, from several miles to thousands of miles, whereas local networks link local resources such as computers and terminals in the same department or building of a firm. This section will describe the various ways of looking at networks.

Network Topologies

One way of describing networks is by their shape, or topology. As illustrated in Figures 9.4–9.6, the three most common topologies are the star, bus, and ring.

THE STAR NETWORK

Star network: Network topology in which all computers and other devices are connected to a central host computer. All communications between network devices must pass through the host computer.

The **star network** (see Figure 9.4) consists of a central host computer connected to a number of smaller computers or terminals. This topology is useful for applications where some processing must be centralized and some can be performed locally. One problem with the star network is its vulnerability. All communication between points in the network must pass through the central computer. Because the central computer is the traffic controller for the other computers and terminals in the network, communication in the network will come to a standstill if the host computer stops functioning.

THE BUS NETWORK

Bus network: Network topology linking a number of computers by a single circuit with all messages broadcast to the entire network.

The **bus network** (see Figure 9.5) links a number of computers by a single circuit made of twisted wire, coaxial cable, or fiber optic cable. All of the signals are broadcast in both directions to the entire network, with special software to identify which components receive each message (there is no central host computer to control the network). If one of the computers in the network fails, none of the other components in the network is affected. This topology is commonly used for local area networks (LANs), discussed in the following section.

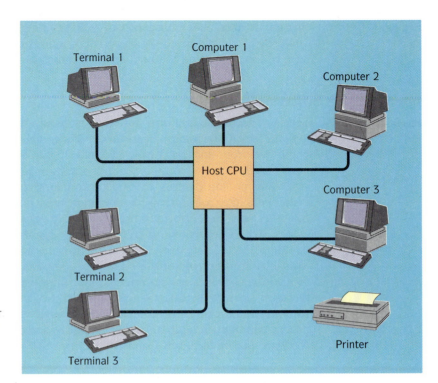

Figure 9.4
A star network topology. In a star network configuration a central host computer acts as a traffic controller for all the other components of the network. All communication between the smaller computers, terminals, and printers must first pass through the central computer.

THE RING NETWORK

Ring network: Network topology in which all computers are linked by a closed loop in a manner that passes data in one direction from one computer to another.

Like the bus network, the **ring network** (see Figure 9.6) does not rely on a central host computer and will not necessarily break down if one of the component computers malfunctions. Each computer in the network can communicate directly with any other computer, and each processes its own applications independently. However, in ring topology, the connecting wire, cable, or optical fiber forms a closed loop. Data are passed along the ring from one computer to another and always flow in one direction.

The token ring network is a variant of the ring network. In the token ring network, all of the devices on the network communicate using a signal or "to-

Figure 9.5
A bus network topology. This topology allows for all messages to be broadcast to the entire network through a single circuit. There is no central host, and messages can travel in both directions along the cable.

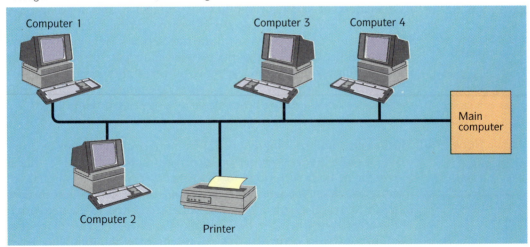

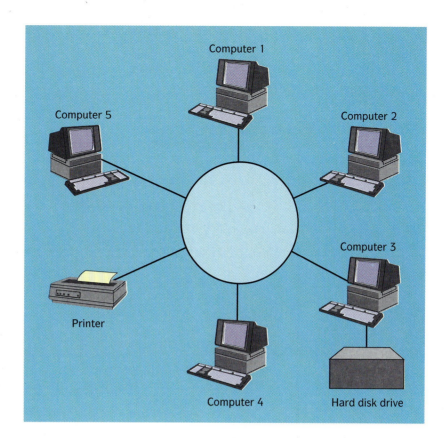

Figure 9.6
A ring network topology. In a ring network configuration, messages are transmitted from computer to computer, flowing in a single direction through a closed loop. Each computer operates independently so that if one fails, the communication through the network is not interrupted.

In the figure: Computer 1, Computer 5, Computer 2, Computer 3, Computer 4, Hard disk drive, Printer.

Node: Each of the devices in a network.

ken." Each of the devices in a network is called a **node.** The token is a predefined packet of data, which includes data indicating the sender, receiver, and whether the packet is in use. The tokens may contain a message or be empty.

A token moves from node to node, and each node examines the token as it passes by. If the token contains data and is meant for that node, the node accepts the data and marks the packet as empty. If a node wants to send a message, it finds an available token; supplies sender, receiver, and message data; loads the message onto the token; and marks it as used. If no message is pending, the token passes unchanged.

Figure 9.7 illustrates a token ring network where all of the wiring converges in one place, called the hub, and the hub contains the network ring. Message tokens move from nodes in the network through relays in the hub on to the next active node. In a token ring network, only one computer can transmit a message at a time. The token ring configuration is most useful for transmitting large volumes of data between PCs or for transmission between PCs and a larger computer.

Private Branch Exchanges and Local Area Networks

Networks may be classified by geographic scope into local networks and wide-area networks. Local networks consist of private branch exchanges and local area networks.

PRIVATE BRANCH EXCHANGES

Private branch exchange (PBX): Central switching system that handles a firm's voice and digital communications.

A **private branch exchange (PBX)** is a special-purpose computer designed for handling and switching office telephone calls at a company site. Today's PBXs can carry both voice and data to create local networks.

While the first PBXs performed limited switching functions, they can now store, transfer, hold, and redial telephone calls. PBXs can also be used to switch

Figure 9.7
A token ring network. Each token-ring node contains a network adapter card that provides power to electromechanical relays in the hub containing the network rir The energized relays connect t workstations to the ring. A message token moves from a workstation through the relay: the hub on to the next active workstation. Each device reac and relays the token. Only destination and origination nodes make changes to the token. This diagram is simplif for clarity. In actual systems, long message token can pass through several nodes at the same time. *Source: "A Toker Ring Wiring Hub," reprinted* PC Magazine, *January 30, 1990. Copyright © 1990. Zi Communications Company.*

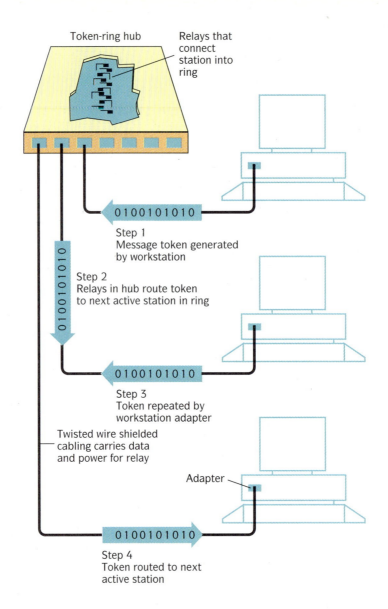

Token-ring hub

Relays that connect station into ring

0 1 0 0 1 0 1 0 1 0
Step 1
Message token generated by workstation

0 1 0 0 1 0 1 0 1 0
Step 2
Relays in hub route token to next active station in ring

0 1 0 0 1 0 1 0 1 0
Step 3
Token repeated by workstation adapter

Twisted wire shielded cabling carries data and power for relay

Adapter

0 1 0 0 1 0 1 0 1 0
Step 4
Token routed to next active station

digital information among computers and office devices. For instance, you can write a letter on a microcomputer in your office, send it to the printer, then dial up the local copying machine and have multiple copies of your letter created. All of this activity is possible with a digital PBX connecting "smart" machines in the advanced office. Figure 9.8 illustrates a PBX system.

The advantage of digital PBXs over other local networking options is that they utilize existing telephone lines and do not require special wiring. A phone jack can be found almost anywhere in the office building. Equipment can therefore be moved when necessary with little worry about having to rewire the building. A hard-wired computer terminal or microcomputer connected to a mainframe with coaxial cable must be rewired at considerable cost each time it is moved. A microcomputer connected to a network by telephone can simply be plugged or unplugged anywhere in the building, utilizing the existing telephone lines. PBXs are also supported by commercial vendors such as the local telephone company, so that the organization does not need special expertise to manage them.

The geographic scope of PBXs is limited, usually to several hundred feet, although the PBX can be connected to other PBX networks or to packet-switched networks (see the discussion of value-added networks in this section) to encompass a larger geographic area. The primary disadvantage of PBXs is that they are limited to telephone lines and that they cannot easily handle very large volumes of data.

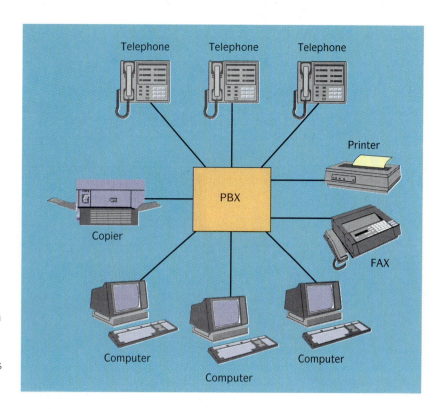

Figure 9.8
A PBX system. A PBX can switch digital information among telephones and among computers, copiers, printers, FAX machines, and other devices to create a local network based on ordinary telephone wiring.

LOCAL AREA NETWORKS

Local area network (LAN): Telecommunications network that requires its own dedicated channels and that encompasses a limited distance, usually one building or several buildings in close proximity.

A **local area network (LAN)** encompasses a limited distance, usually one building or several buildings in close proximity. Most LANs connect devices located within a 2000-foot radius and have been widely used to link microcomputers. LANs require their own communications channels.

LANs generally have higher transmission capacities than PBXs, using bus or ring topologies and a high bandwidth. A very fast PBX can have a maximum transmission capacity of over 2 megabits per second. LANs typically transmit at a rate of 256 kilobits per second to over 100 megabits per second. They are recommended for applications requiring high volumes of data and high transmission speeds. For instance, because a picture consumes so many bits of information, an organization might require a LAN for video transmissions and graphics.

LANs are totally controlled, maintained, and operated by end users. This produces the advantage of allowing user control, but it also means that the user must know a great deal about telecommunications applications and networking.

LANs allow organizations to share expensive hardware and software. For instance, several microcomputers can share a single printer by being tied together in a LAN. LANs can promote productivity because users are no longer dependent upon a centralized computer system (which can fail) or upon the availability of a single peripheral device such as a printer. Finally, there are many new applications—such as electronic mail, graphics, video teleconferencing, and on-line applications—requiring high-capacity networks.

The most common use of LANs is for linking personal computers within a building or office to share information and expensive peripheral devices such as laser printers. Another popular application of LANs is in factories, where they link computers and computer-controlled machines.

Figure 9.9 illustrates a LAN employed by the Milan division of Michelin Italia, the Italian branch of the Michelin Corporation. The corporation is noted for its tires and guides to hotels and restaurants. Michelin Italia Milan's staff uses the LAN primarily for electronic filing, word processing, and graphics applications. This LAN consists of one hundred personal computer workstations that are attached to three Compaq 386/20 file servers, each equipped with

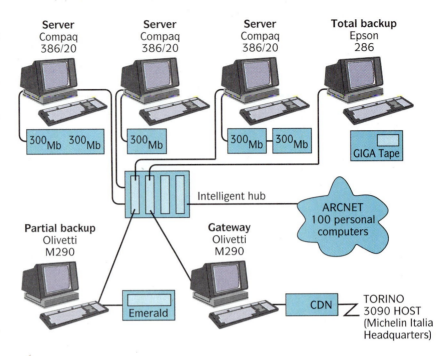

Figure 9.9
Michelin Milan's LAN. The Milan division of Michelin Italia chose ARCnet as the technology for connecting the devices in its 100-seat local area network for several reasons, including the floor plan of the Michelin building and the need for a star topology to allow upgrades to the network. *Reproduced with permission of Michelin Italy.*

File server: Computer in a network that stores various programs and data files for users of the network. Determines access and availability in the network.

Network operating system: Special software that manages the file server in a LAN and routes and manages communications on the network.

Gateway: Communications processor that connects dissimilar networks by providing the translation from one protocol to another.

Baseband: LAN channel technology that provides a single path for transmitting either text, graphics, voice, or video data at one time.

300-megabyte hard disks. The network also contains an Epson 286 PC and an Olivetti M290 PC for backup and an Olivetti M290 PC serving as a gateway. The entire network and important files are backed up every night using tapes from CigaTape and Emerald Systems Corporation of San Diego, California.

The **file server** acts as a librarian, storing various programs and data files for network users. The server determines who gets access to what and in what sequence. Servers may be powerful microcomputers with large hard disk capacity, workstations, minicomputers, or mainframes, although specialized computers are now available for this purpose. The server typically contains the LAN's **network operating system,** which manages the server and routes and manages communications on the network.

The network **gateway** connects the LAN to public networks, such as the telephone network, or to other corporate networks so that the LAN can exchange information with networks external to it. A gateway is generally a communications processor that can connect dissimilar networks by translating from one set of protocols to another. (A bridge connects two networks of the same type. A router is used to route messages through several connected LANs or to a wide area network.)

The gateway illustrated in Figure 9.9 connects Michelin Italia's Milan division to Michelin Italia's 3090 IBM mainframe host computer in its Torino headquarters. Application software, such as word processing, works with the network operating system to keep data traffic flowing smoothly.

LAN technology consists of cabling (twisted wire, coaxial, or fiber optic cable) or wireless technology that links individual computer devices, network interface cards (which are special adapters serving as interfaces to the cable), and software to control LAN activities. The LAN network interface card specifies the data transmission rate, the size of message units, the addressing information attached to each message, and network topology (Ethernet utilizes a bus topology, for example).

There are four principal LAN technologies for physically connecting devices—Ethernet, developed by Xerox, Digital Equipment Corporation, and Intel; Appletalk from Apple Computer Incorporated; token ring, developed by IBM and Texas Instruments; and ARCnet, developed by Datapoint. They employ either a baseband or a broadband channel technology. **Baseband** products provide a single path for transmitting text, graphics, voice, or video data, and only one

Broadband: LAN channel technology that provides several paths for transmitting text, graphics, voice, or video data so that different types of data can be transmitted simultaneously.

type of data at a time can be transmitted. **Broadband** products provide several paths so that different types of data can be transmitted simultaneously.

LAN capabilities are also defined by the network operating system. The network operating system can reside on every computer in the network, or it can reside on a single designated file server for all the applications on the network. Some of the leading network operating systems include Novell's Netware, Microsoft's LAN Manager, and IBM's PC LAN (Appletalk for networks of Macintosh computers combines technology for physically connecting devices with network operating system functions).

The primary disadvantages of LANs are that they are more expensive to install than PBXs and are more inflexible, requiring new wiring each time the LAN is moved. LANs require specially trained staff to manage and run them.

There are four important criteria for evaluating LANs:

1. How flexible is the system (can new users be added, and how many)?
2. What is the actual performance (as opposed to advertising claims)?
3. What is the true cost of the network, including software, implementation, rewiring, training, network management, and opportunity cost of use?
4. How reliable will the system be in the face of various sorts of disturbances?

These criteria explain why the Milan division of Michelin Italia chose a star network configuration based on ARCnet for its 100-user network. (ARCnet is one of the principal technologies for physically connecting LAN devices described earlier.) The firm wanted a LAN that was easy to install in a squared-off building built in 1949 having several floors. Michelin Italia believed that ARCnet has simple rules, few instructions, and is more reliable and economical than other alternatives. It can be wired in either twisted-pair wire or fiber optic cable and is easy to modify. While ARCnet's 2.5 megabit-per-second transmission capacity is relatively slow, Michelin Italia felt its actual performance was not much different from other alternatives. Because Michelin needed flexibility in expanding the network, it chose a star topology. When a firm cannot predict how a network will expand, the star configuration allows it to put on another node and create another point in the star.

Wide Area Networks (WANs)

Wide area network (WAN): Telecommunications network that spans a large geographical distance. May consist of a variety of cable, satellite, and microwave technologies.

Switched lines: Telephone lines that a person can access from his or her terminal to transmit data to another computer, the call being routed or switched through paths to the designated destination.

Dedicated lines: Telephone lines that are continuously available for transmission by a lessee. Typically conditioned to transmit data at high speeds for high-volume applications.

Wide area networks (WANs) span broad geographical distances, ranging from several miles to across entire continents. Common carriers (companies licensed by the government to provide communications services to the public, such as AT&T or MCI) typically determine transmission rates or interconnections between lines, but the customer is responsible for telecommunications contents and management. It is up to the individual firm to establish the most efficient routing of messages, and to handle error checking, editing, protocols, and telecommunications management.

WANs may consist of a combination of switched and dedicated lines, microwave, and satellite communications. **Switched lines** are telephone lines that a person can access from his or her terminal to transmit data to another computer, the call being routed or switched through paths to the designated destination. **Dedicated lines,** or nonswitched lines, are continuously available for transmission and the lessee typically pays a flat rate for total access to the line. The lines can be leased or purchased from common carriers or private communications media vendors. Dedicated lines are often conditioned to transmit data at higher speeds than switched lines and are more appropriate for higher-volume transmissions. Switched lines, on the other hand, are less expensive and more appropriate for low-volume applications requiring only occasional transmission.

Figure 9.10 illustrates a wide area network that links five of Europe's national telephone companies into a pan-European network. The Global European Net-

MANAGEMENT

Managing Multinationals with Virtual Private Networks

How can managers run corporations with branches in Mexico, Canada, and many other countries? Long-distance networks that can link branch offices with voice and data communications help solve the problem. Now virtual private networks provide these services at lower cost than the regular long-distance network or private networks. International telephoning and data transmission becomes faster, easier, and cheaper.

Corporations with a large volume of calls have used private networks since the 1960s to cut costs by leasing dedicated telephone circuits from the phone company. But private networks were only cost-effective for large corporations that had numerous branch offices and a high volume of calls.

For the last seven years or so, virtual private networks have offered many of the same advantages—such as abbreviated dialing—at even lower cost, with few of the technical or maintenance problems of a private network. Instead of using lines the company has leased, the call goes mainly over public lines guided by sophisticated computers. Telephone companies can create the illusion of a private network using their regular public network equipment combined with high-speed computers and sophisticated databases.

Corporations such as General Electric, Olin, United Technologies, and Xerox use virtual private networks for both voice and data communications and can send electronic mail and computer-generated blueprints quickly across the country.

Virtual private networks will be especially valuable for Mexico's business callers. Mexico's antiquated telephone system is notoriously frustrating to use. Only one of two phone calls within the country is completed successfully; the success rate for international call completion is even lower. Telmex, the recently privatized Mexican phone company, is initiating a virtual private network service that will allow businesses to connect multiple sites in Mexico as well as in the United States. Telmex is installing $8 billion in modern switching computers in some 2000 central offices serving 10,000 cities and towns.

Source: Anthony Ramirez, ''A Cheaper Way of Linking Offices,'' *The New York Times* (September 16, 1992).

To Think About: What requirements would justify a company's use of virtual private networks? What are the managerial advantages of using these networks? How will the use of virtual private networks have an impact on international business communications?

---

work (GEN) links the fiber-optic networks of five national telephone companies—Italy's Asst/Stet, the United Kingdom's British Telecom, France's Telecom, Germany's Deutsche Telekom, and Telefonica of Spain. This network provides a single point of contact for users requiring voice and data services that transcend national borders.

Individual business firms may maintain their own wide area networks. For instance, the Hewlett-Packard Corporation has a wide area network that ties together its facilities in the United States, Great Britain, France, Switzerland,

Figure 9.10
An example of a wide area network (WAN). Global European Network (GEN) links five European national telephone companies in a wide area network. Each country's operator acts as the go-between in linking users across borders. *Adapted from Joshua Greenbaum, ''Europeans Eye Joint Fiber Net,''* InformationWEEK, *July 27, 1992. Copyright © 1992 by CMP Publications, Inc., 600 Community Drive, Manhasset, NY 11030. Reprinted from* InformationWEEK *with permission.*

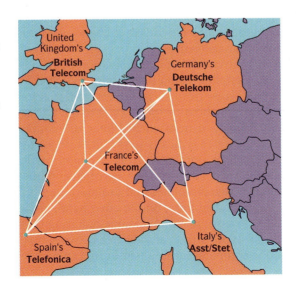

Virtual private network:
Inexpensive telecommunications over public phone lines with computers and software creating an illusion of a private network for a company.

Venezuela, Australia, Japan, India, Hong Kong, and Singapore. But private wide area networks are expensive to maintain. Virtual private networks are emerging as a less expensive alternative for linking widely dispersed corporate facilities. A **virtual private network** provides inexpensive telecommunications over public phone lines with computers and software, creating an illusion of a private network for a company. The Window on Management on page 288 describes the advantages of these virtual private networks.

Value-Added Networks

Value-added network (VAN):
Private, multipath, data-only third party managed networks that are used by multiple organizations on a subscription basis.

Value-added networks are an alternative to firms designing and managing their own networks. **Value-added networks** (VANs) are private, multipath, data-only, third-party managed networks that can provide economies in the cost of service and in network management because they are used by multiple organizations. The value-added network is set up by a firm that is in charge of managing the network. That firm sells subscriptions to other firms wishing to use the network. Subscribers pay only for the amount of data they transmit plus a subscription fee. The network may utilize twisted-pair lines, satellite links, and other communications channels leased by the value-added carrier.

The term *value added* refers to the extra "value" added to communications by the telecommunications and computing services these networks provide to clients. Customers do not have to invest in network equipment and software or perform their own error checking, editing, routing, and protocol conversion. Subscribers may achieve savings in line charges and transmission costs because the costs of using the network are shared among many users. The resulting costs may be lower than if the clients had leased their own lines or satellite services. VANs are attractive for firms such as Continental Grain because they provide special services such as electronic mail and access to foreign telecommunications systems.

Continental Grain switched from a private network to GE Information Services (GEIS)'s value-added network to link its 175 domestic locations with its 45 branch locations in South America, the Far East, and Europe. Continental found that switching to the value-added network reduced costs and reduced operational problems associated with networks. International VANs such as GEIS have representatives with language skills and knowledge of various countries' telecommunications administrations. The VANs have already leased lines from foreign telecommunications authorities or can arrange access to local networks and equipment abroad.

The leading international value-added networks, in addition to GE Information Services Company (GEIS), are Infonet, Telenet, and Tymnet. These networks provide casual or intermittent users international services on a dial-up basis and can provide a private network using dedicated circuits for customers requiring a full-time network. (Maintaining a private network may be most cost-effective for organizations with a high communications volume.)

Packet switching: Technology that breaks blocks of text into small fixed bundles of data and routes them in the most economical way through any available communications channel.

Another way value-added networks provide economies is through **packet switching.** Packet switching breaks up a lengthy block of text into small, fixed bundles of data (often 128 bytes each) called packets (see Figure 9.11). The VAN gathers information from many users, divides it into small packets, and continuously uses various communications channels to send the packets. Each packet travels independently through the network (this contrasts to one firm using a leased line, for example, for one hour and then not using it for three or four hours). Packets of data originating at one source can be routed through different paths in the network, and then may be reassembled into the original message when they reach their destination. Packet switching enables communications facilities to be utilized more fully by more users.

Frame relay: Shared network service technology that packages data into bundles for transmission but does not use error correction routines. Cheaper and faster than packet switching.

Frame relay is a faster and less expensive variant of packet switching. Frame relay is a shared network service that packages data into "frames" that are

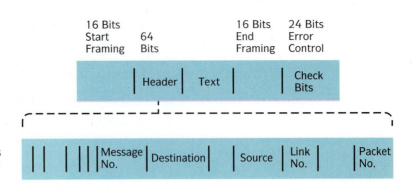

Figure 9.11
Packet switched networks and packet communications. Data are grouped into small packets, framed by identifying information, which are transmitted independently via various communication channels to maximize the potential of the paths in a network.

similar to packets. Frame relay, however, does not perform error correction. This is because so many of today's digital lines are cleaner than in the past and networks are more adept at correcting transmission problems. Frame relay can communicate at transmission speeds up to 1.544 megabits per second. Frame relay is essentially used for transmitting data. It is not recommended for any transmissions that are sensitive to varying delay, such as voice or digital video traffic, and it cannot easily control network congestion. Frame relay only works successfully over reliable lines that do not require frequent retransmission because of error.

Obviously, VANs are not for all situations. They are best at moderate-speed, high-volume, frequent long-distance communications when organizations do not need to manage their own telecommunications. They do raise security problems because company data can be mixed in with data from other companies, although very few problems have been reported.

9.4 How Organizations Use Telecommunications for Competitive Advantage

Baxter International, described in Chapter 3, realized the strategic significance of telecommunications. The company placed its own computer terminals in hospital supply rooms and provided a direct telecommunications link with its central headquarters via a VAN. Customers could dial up a local VAN node and send their orders directly to the company. Since then, many other corporations have realized the strategic potential of networked computer systems.

Telecommunications has helped eliminate barriers of geography and time, enabling organizations to accelerate the pace of production, to speed decision making, to forge new products, to move into new markets, and to create new relationships with customers. Many of the strategic applications described in Chapter 3 would not be possible without telecommunications. Firms that fail to consider telecommunications in their strategic plans will fall behind (Keen, 1986).

Facilitating Applications

Some of the leading telecommunications applications for communication, coordination, and speeding the flow of transactions and messages throughout business firms are electronic mail, voice mail, facsimile machines (FAX), teleconferencing, videoconferencing, and electronic data interchange.

ELECTRONIC MAIL

Electronic mail: The computer-to-computer exchange of messages.

Electronic mail, or E-mail, is the computer-to-computer exchange of messages. A person can use a microcomputer attached to a modem or a terminal to send notes and even lengthier documents just by typing in the name of the message's recipient. Many organizations operate their own internal electronic mail systems, but communications companies such as GTE, Telenet, MCI, and AT&T offer these services, as do on-line information services such as CompuServe and Prodigy (see Chapter 10). E-mail eliminates telephone tag and costly long-distance telephone charges, expediting communication between different parts of the organization. Nestle SA, the Swiss-based multinational food corporation, installed a new electronic mail system to connect its 60,000 employees in 80 countries. Nestle's European units can use the electronic mail system to share information about production schedules and inventory levels to ship excess products from one country to another.

VOICE MAIL

Voice mail: System for digitizing a spoken message and transmitting it over a network.

A **voice mail** system digitizes the spoken message of the sender, transmits it over a network, and stores the message on disk for later retrieval. When the recipient is ready to listen, the messages are reconverted to audio form. Various "store and forward" capabilities notify recipients that messages are waiting. Recipients have the option of saving these messages for future use, deleting them, or routing them to other parties.

FACSIMILE (FAX)

Facsimile (FAX): Machine that digitizes and transmits documents with both text and graphics over telephone lines.

Facsimile (FAX) machines can transmit documents containing both text and graphics over ordinary telephone lines. A sending FAX machine scans and digitizes the document image. The digitized document is then transmitted over a network and reproduced in hard copy form by a receiving FAX machine. The process results in a duplicate, or facsimile, of the original.

TELECONFERENCING AND VIDEOCONFERENCING

Teleconferencing: Ability to confer with a group of people simultaneously using the telephone or electronic mail group communication software.

Videoconferencing: Teleconferencing with the capability of participants to see each other over video screens.

People can meet electronically—even though they are hundreds or thousands of miles apart—by using teleconferencing or videoconferencing. **Teleconferencing** allows a group of people to "confer" simultaneously via telephone or electronic mail group communication software (see Chapter 15). Teleconferencing that has the capability to let participants see each other over video screens is termed *video teleconferencing* or **videoconferencing**. Videoconferencing usually requires special video conference rooms and videocameras, microphones, television monitors, and a computer equipped with a codec device that converts video images and analog sound waves into digital signals and compresses them for transfer over communications channels. Another codec on the receiving end reconverts the digital signals back into analog for display on the receiving monitor.

Chapter 15 will provide more detail on electronic mail and videoconferencing applications. The Window on Technology on page 292 shows how multimedia and telecommunications technology are combining to transmit sound, video, data, and graphics across networks, enhancing these telecommunications applications to create more collaborative work environments across long distances.

Electronic Data Interchange

Electronic data interchange (EDI): Direct computer-to-computer exchange between two organizations of standard business transaction documents.

Electronic data interchange (EDI) is the direct computer-to-computer exchange, between two organizations, of standard business transaction documents such as invoices, bills of lading, or purchase orders. EDI saves money and time because transactions can be transmitted from one information system to another through a telecommunications network, eliminating the printing and handling of paper at one end and the inputting of data at the other. EDI may also provide strategic benefits by helping a firm "lock in" customers, making it easier for customers or distributors to order from them rather than from competitors.

EDI differs from electronic mail in that it transmits an actual structured transaction (with distinct fields such as the transaction date, transaction amount, sender's name and recipient's name) as opposed to an unstructured text message such as a letter.

Can multimedia create a more collaborative environment across long distances? A variety of projects are examining how video, sound, and graphics can be integrated with conventional data and transmitted through networks. Researchers are studying technical requirements and people's work habits.

St. Petersburg Junior College in Florida has launched an ambitious $9 million multimedia "Project Flamingo." The college's seven sites will be tied together, partly through fiber optics. A Macintosh computer will reside on the desktop of every faculty member for the development and distribution of multimedia instruction.

The experimental Rapport System created by AT&T Bell Laboratories in Holmdel, New Jersey, presents a single uniform interface for electronic mail, voice, video, and computer communications. Users can "enter" a "virtual meeting room" on their screen and call up other people to join them. The system has a "store-and-forward" function to allow meetings to be saved or passed on. Instead of using special meeting rooms, people can participate in videoconferencing from their desktops.

Numerous hurdles remain to be solved before multimedia communications become commercial. The greatest obstacle is that multimedia require massive bandwidth (the data-carrying capacity a network needs to transmit video and other media). It is not yet clear what sorts of networks will be available to carry the new media. It is also unclear just which features of multimedia will be most valuable for people and how readily users will invest in these systems.

Companies realize that people want to share multimedia information on networks (like any other data) but this sharing cannot occur without better ways of using existing technology. Jim Long, president of the San Francisco-based Starlight Networks—a firm created to bring multimedia to networked systems—recommends having fewer users per multimedia network than on networks transmitting voice and data. Long says that a star topology is better than a ring network configuration for delivering video signals with minimal impact on other network traffic.

If multimedia networks become widespread, we will see great changes in the workplace. There may be fewer business meetings and less need to commute. It is possible that corporate sites will shrink to accommodate fewer on-site workers. But as powerful as the new multimedia tools might be, no one expects them to replace the need for human contact. There will be no substitute for establishing the rapport of meeting face-to-face.

Sources: Thomas Hoffman, "Taking Note of Multimedia," *InformationWEEK* (March 16, 1992); David Brittan, "The Promise of Multimedia Communications," *Technology Review* (May/June 1992); and Steve Polilli, "Coming to Networks Near You," *Software Magazine* (September 1992).

To Think About: Think of different areas where multimedia communications can be used in a business environment. What organizational, human, and technological factors should a manager consider in deciding whether to use multimedia communications in a firm?

Figure 9.12 illustrates how EDI operates at the Cummins Engine Company. Cummins implemented EDI to automate purchasing, shipping, and payment transactions with its customers. Cummins transmits price updates and shipping notices directly to its customers' computer system. Customers in turn transmit material releases, reports on receiving discrepancies, and payment and remittance data directly to Cummin's computer system. EDI has replaced paper for these transactions.

EDI lowers routine transaction processing costs because there is less need to transfer data from hard-copy forms into computer-ready transactions. EDI reduces transcription errors and associated costs that occur when data are entered and printed out many times. Chapter 3 has shown how EDI can also curb inventory costs by minimizing the amount of time components are in inventory. For EDI to work properly, four key requirements must be addressed:

1. *Transaction standardization:* Participating companies must agree on the form of the message to be exchanged. Transaction formats and data must be standardized. The American National Standards Institute (ANSI) has developed the X.12 data interchange protocol as a generic, flexible busi-

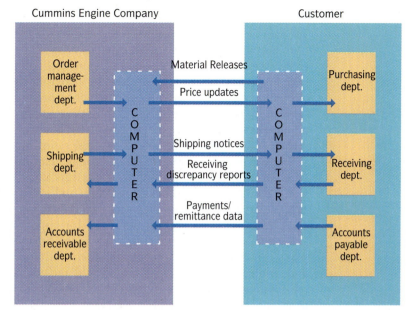

Figure 9.12
How EDI works at Cummins Engine Company. Cummins Engine Company uses EDI to automate price, shipping, receiving, and payment transactions with its customers. Cummins' price updates and shipping notices are entered by the appropriate departments directly into the Cummins' computer system which transmits them to its customers' computer systems. Customers' material releases, receiving reports, and payment data are also transmitted directly through the computer systems back to Cummins. *Source: Robert Knight, "EDI Hitting Stride in Data Entry," Software Magazine, February 1992.*

ness data interchange standard (see Chapter 10) for EDI, but specific industries have adopted multiple EDI standards. This can raise problems for interorganizational networking, since manufacturing, retail, and banking standards might collide.

2. *Translation software:* Special software must be developed to convert incoming and outgoing messages into a form comprehensible to other companies.

3. *Appropriate "mailbox" facilities:* Companies using EDI must select a third-party, value-added network with mailbox facilities that allow messages to be sent, sorted, and held until they are needed by the receiving computer. For example, the insurance field generally uses Information Network, and office systems tend to use GE Information Services.

4. *Legal restrictions:* To comply with legal requirements, certain transactions require "writing," a "signature," or the "original document" in hard copy form. (EDI messages do not, for example, deal with warranties or limitations of liability and other conditions of doing business typically contained in hard-copy business documents.) Parties must agree on the means of verifying that messages are authentic and complete according to the agreed-on protocol, the point in the transaction when the contract between the two parties goes into effect, error-checking procedures, and the level of network security to prevent unauthorized access and use of the system.

9.5 Management Issues and Decisions

The starting point for rational planning of telecommunications is to forget about the "features" of systems and instead to try to understand the requirements of one's organization. A telecommunications plan is more likely to succeed if it advances the key business goals of the company. Cutting costs and installing advanced systems for their own sake is rarely a sufficient reason to justify large telecommunications projects.

The Telecommunications Plan

Telecommunications has enormous potential for enhancing a firm's strategic position, but managers need to determine exactly how the firm's competitive position could be enhanced by telecommunications technology. Managers need to ask how telecommunications can reduce costs by increasing the *scale* and *scope* of operations without additional management costs; they need to determine if telecommunications technology can help them *differentiate* products and services; or if telecommunications technology can improve the firm's *cost structure* by eliminating intermediaries such as distributors or by accelerating business processes.

There are steps to implement a strategic telecommunications plan. First, start with an audit of the communications functions in your firm. What are your voice, data, video, equipment, staffing, and management capabilities? For each of these areas, identify and evaluate your strengths, weaknesses, exposures, and opportunities. Then identify priorities for improvement.

Second, you must know the long-range business plans of your firm. These plans can come from planning documents, interviews with senior management, and annual reports. Your plan should include an analysis of precisely how telecommunications will contribute to the specific five-year goals of the firm and to its longer-range strategies (e.g., cost reduction, distribution enhancement).

Third, identify how telecommunications support the day-to-day operations of the firm. What are the needs of the operating units and their managers? Try to identify critical areas where telecommunications currently does or can have the potential to make a large difference in performance. In insurance, these may be systems that give field representatives quick access to policy and rate information; in retailing, inventory control and market penetration; and in industrial products, rapid, efficient distribution and transportation.

Fourth, develop indicators of how well you are fulfilling your plan for enhancing telecommunications. Try to avoid technical measures (e.g., transmission rates enhanced from 300 to 1200 baud) and focus on business measures (e.g., sales force utilization of high-speed data lines increased from 10 to 40 percent).

Implementing the Plan

Once an organization has developed a business telecommunications plan, it must determine the initial scope of the telecommunications project. Deciding which telecommunications technology to adopt, and under what circumstances, can prove difficult, given the rapid rate of change in the technology and in the related costs of telecommunications.

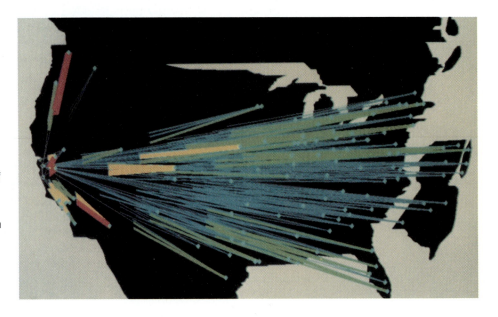

This computer-generated map of the United States was made only minutes after the October 17, 1989, earthquake in San Francisco. Phone calling into San Francisco was so heavy that circuits were quickly overwhelmed, and AT&T made the decision to block all incoming calls in favor of outgoing calls from survivors.

Managers should take eight factors into account when choosing a telecommunications network.

The first and most important factor is *distance*. If communication will be largely local and entirely internal to the organization's buildings and social networks, there is little or no need for VANs, leased lines, or long-distance communications.

Along with distance, one must consider the *range of services* the network must support, such as electronic mail, EDI, internally generated transactions, voice mail, videoconferencing, or imaging, and whether these services must be integrated in the same network.

A third factor to consider is *security*. The most secure means of long-distance communications is through lines that are owned by the organization. The next-most secure form of telecommunications is through dedicated leased lines. VANs that slice up corporate information into small packets are among the least secure modes. Finally, ordinary telephone lines, which can be tapped at several locations, are even less secure than VANs.

A fourth factor to consider is whether *multiple access* is required throughout the organization or whether it can be limited to one or two nodes within the organization. A multiple-access system requirement suggests that there will be perhaps several thousand users throughout the corporation; therefore, a commonly available technology such as installed telephone wire and the related technology of a PBX is recommended. If, however, access is restricted to fewer than 100 high-intensity users, a more advanced, higher-speed, more exotic technology like a fiber optic or broadband LAN system may be recommended.

A fifth and most difficult factor to judge is *utilization*. There are two aspects of utilization that must be considered when developing a telecommunications network: the frequency and the volume of communications. Together, these two factors determine the total load on the telecommunications system. On the one hand, high-frequency, high-volume communications suggest the need for high-speed LANs for local communication and leased lines for long-distance communication. On the other hand, low-frequency, low-volume communications suggest dial-up, voice-grade telephone circuits operating through a traditional modem.

It is important to avoid overkill by buying a state-of-the-art, high-capacity, but expensive or unreliable system. A 10-megabit-per-second data exchange rate sounds wonderful, but for many applications it simply is not necessary. In a local office where CRT displays, word processors, and microcomputers are being connected, a broadband LAN with megabit data rates is probably excessive. A PBX working in the kilobit range is totally adequate for this kind of digital communication. Telephone manufacturers have demonstrated that users can build their own inexpensive LANs by using existing telephone wires and plugging their machines into the local telephone network.

A sixth factor is *cost*. How much does each telecommunications option cost? Total costs should include costs for development, operations, maintenance, expansion, and overhead. Which cost components are fixed? Which are variable? Are there any hidden costs to anticipate? It is wise to recall the *thruway effect*. The easier it is to use a communications path, the more people will want to use it. Most telecommunications planners estimate future needs on the high side and still often underestimate the actual need. Underestimating the cost of telecommunications projects or uncontrollable telecommunications costs are principal causes of network failure (see Table 9.4).

Seventh, you must consider the difficulties of *installing* the telecommunications system. Are the organization's buildings properly constructed to install fiber optics? In some instances, buildings have inadequate wiring channels underneath the floors, which makes installation of fiber optic cable extremely difficult.

Eighth, you must consider how much *connectivity* would be required to make all of the components in a network communicate with each other or to tie

Table 9.4 THE THREE MAIN REASONS WHY NETWORKS FAIL

Reason 1: Political infighting: Networks and departments' needs to interconnect have become so important that various groups in the firm fight for network control.

Reason 2: Lax security: Networks are often used for communications outside the organization, leaving them increasingly vulnerable to hackers, computer viruses, and other security breaches. Firms don't plan for disaster recovery in the event of network crashes.

Reason 3: Hidden costs: Poor capacity planning; underestimating the cost of personnel to implement, maintain, and administer the network; and changing telecommunication tariffs undermine network projects or create uncontrollable costs.

Source: Avery Jenkins, ''Why Networks Fail,'' *Computerworld Focus on Integration,* January, 1990.

together multiple networks. There are so many different standards for hardware, software, and communication systems that it may be very difficult to get all of the components of a network to "talk" to each other or to distribute information from one network to another. Chapter 10 treats connectivity issues in greater detail. Table 9.5 summarizes these implementation factors.

Management Challenges

1. **Managing LANs.** While local area networks appear to be flexible and inexpensive ways of delivering computing power to new areas of the organization, they must be carefully administered and monitored. LANs are especially vulnerable to network disruption, loss of essential data, access by unauthorized users, and infection from computer viruses (see Chapters 10 and 18). Dealing with these problems or even installing popular applications such as spreadsheets or data management software on a network requires special technical expertise which is not normally available in end-user departments and is in very short supply.

2. **Compatibility and standards.** There is such a bewildering array of hardware, software, and network standards that managers may have trouble choosing the right telecommunications platform for the firm's information architecture. Telecommunications systems based on one standard may not be able to be linked to telecommunications based on another without additional equipment, expense, and management overhead. Networks that meet today's requirements may lack the connectivity for domestic or global expansion in the future. The compatibility and standards challenge is such a serious management challenge that an entire section of the following chapter is devoted to connectivity issues.

Table 9.5 IMPLEMENTATION FACTORS IN TELECOMMUNICATIONS SYSTEMS

Distance

Range of services

Security

Multiple access

Utilization

Cost

Installation

Connectivity

Summary

Describe the basic components of a telecommunications system.

A telecommunications system is a set of compatible devices that are used to develop a network for communication from one location to another by electronic means. The essential components of a telecommunications system are computers, terminals or other input/output devices, communications channels, communications processors (such as modems, multiplexers, controllers, and front-end processors), and telecommunications software. Different components of a telecommunications network can communicate with each other with a common set of rules termed *protocols*.

Data are transmitted throughout a telecommunications network using either analog signals or digital signals. A modem is a device that translates from analog to digital and vice versa.

Measure the capacity of telecommunications channels and evaluate transmission media.

The capacity of a telecommunications channel is determined by the range of frequencies it can accommodate. The higher the range of frequencies, called bandwidth, the higher the capacity (measured in bits per second). The principal transmission media are twisted copper telephone wire, coaxial copper cable, fiber optic cable, and wireless transmission utilizing microwave, satellite, low frequency radio, or infrared waves.

Transmission media use either synchronous or asynchronous transmission modes for determining where a character begins or ends and when data are transmitted from one computer to another. Three different transmission modes governing the direction of data flow over a transmission medium are simplex transmission, half-duplex transmission, and full-duplex transmission.

Classify the various types of telecommunications networks.

Networks can be classified by their shape or configuration or by their geographic scope and type of services provided. Local area networks (LANs) and private branch exchanges (PBXs) are used to link offices and buildings in close proximity. Wide area networks (WANs) span a broad geographical distance, ranging from several miles to entire continents and are private networks that are independently managed. Value-added networks (VANs) also encompass a wide geographic area but are managed by a third party, which sells the services of the network to other companies.

Describe the three basic network topologies.

The three common network topologies are the star network, the bus network, and the ring network. In a star network, all communications must pass through a central computer. The bus network links a number of devices to a single channel and broadcasts all of the signals to the entire network, with special software to identify which components receive each message. In a ring network, each computer in the network can communicate directly with any other computer but the channel is a closed loop. Data are passed along the ring from one computer to another.

Identify telecommunications applications that can provide competitive advantages to organizations.

Using information systems for strategic advantage increasingly depends on telecommunications technology and applications such as electronic mail, voice mail, videoconferencing, FAX, and electronic data interchange (EDI). Electronic data interchange (EDI) is the direct computer-to-computer exchange between two organizations of standard business transaction documents such as invoices, bills of lading, and purchase orders.

Explain the criteria used in planning for telecommunications systems.

Firms should develop strategic telecommunications plans to ensure that their telecommunications systems serve business objectives and operations. Important factors to consider are distance, range of services, security, access, utilization, cost, installation, and connectivity.

Telecommunications
Telecommunications system
Protocol
Analog signal
Digital signal
Modem
Channels
Twisted wire
Coaxial cable
Fiber optic cable
Microwave
Satellite
Cellular telephone
Baud
Bandwidth
Asynchronous transmission
Synchronous transmission
Front-end processor
Concentrator
Controller
Multiplexer
Telecommunications software
Network topology
Star network

Bus network
Ring network
Node
Private branch exchange (PBX)
Local area network (LAN)
File server
Network operating system
Gateway
Baseband
Broadband
Wide area network (WAN)
Switched lines
Dedicated lines
Virtual private network
Value-added network (VAN)
Packet switching
Frame relay
Electronic mail
Voice mail
Facsimile (FAX)
Teleconferencing
Videoconferencing
Electronic data interchange (EDI)

1. What is the significance of telecommunications deregulation for managers and organizations?

2. What is a telecommunications system? What are the principal functions of all telecommunications systems?

3. Name and briefly describe each of the components of a telecommunications system.

4. Distinguish between an analog and a digital signal.

5. Name the different types of telecommunications transmission media and compare them in terms of speed and cost.

6. What is the relationship between bandwidth and the transmission capacity of a channel?

7. What is the difference between synchronous and asynchronous transmission? Between half-duplex, duplex, and simplex transmission?

8. Name and briefly describe the different kinds of communications processors.

9. Name and briefly describe the three principal network topologies.

10. Distinguish between a PBX and a LAN.

11. Define a wide-area network (WAN).

12. Define the following:
    - Modem
    - Baud
    - File server
    - Value-added network (VAN)
    - Packet switching

13. Name and describe the telecommunications applications that can provide strategic benefits to businesses.

14. What are the principal factors to consider when developing a telecommunications plan?

1. Your firm has just decided to build a new headquarters building in a suburban setting. You have been assigned to work with an architect on plans for making the new building intelligent—that is, capable of supporting the computing and telecommunications needs of the business. What factors should you consider?

2. Your boss has just read in a leading business magazine that local area networks are the wave of the future. You are directed to explore how the firm can use these LANs. What words of caution and what factors should the boss consider?

3. You are an electronic parts distributor for television repair shops throughout the country. You would like to edge out regional competitors and improve service. How could you use computers and telecommunications systems to achieve these goals?

4. If a channel has capacity of 1200 bits per second, approximately how long would it take to transmit this book? (Assume that there are 250 words per page and spaces do not count as characters. Do not include graphics.)

Group Project

With a group of two or three of your fellow students, describe in detail the various ways that telecommunications technology can provide a firm with competitive advantage. Use the companies described in Chapter 3 or other chapters you have read to illustrate the points you make, or select examples of other companies using telecommunications from business or computer magazines. Present your findings to the class.

CASE STUDY

Should All Firms Move to EDI?

Is what's good for General Motors, Chrysler, and Sears good for their suppliers? All of these firms are insisting that their suppliers use electronic data interchange with them, hoping to eliminate paper and delays in the ordering process.

Sears was even willing to supply smaller vendors with limited resources with EDI translation software, training, and access to the Sears Communication Company network to speed the process. The only expense for the vendor was transportation, lodging, and the cost of an IBM-compatible PC that met specifications. The vendor had 90 days to move its purchase order, shipping notice, invoice, and functional acknowledgement transactions to EDI.

Some analysts view these highly ambitious EDI programs as unrealistic. Requiring trading partners to do EDI creates pressure and hardship, and many of the presumed benefits—such as a reduction of staff and errors—are not easy to prove. Other companies have been more lenient than GM, Chrysler, and Sears in that they use EDI with a smaller percentage of vendors.

EDI cuts down on repeated data entry and manual handling of paper transactions. Some 25 percent of the cost of processing business transactions is related to basic data entry and associated tasks. EDI can potentially reduce expenses and human error, as well as shorten transaction cycle times.

The Harper Group, a San Francisco-based freight forwarding company, found EDI especially valuable for tracking two-way movement of orders and monitoring the status of shipments. The Harper Group is a holding company that owns 12 specialized transportation businesses and employs more than 3500 people in more than 300 branches in 43 countries. Handling international shipments is very information-intensive.

EDI helped Harper to refocus its staff to take on new types of jobs. While the company doubled in its revenue between 1989–1992, its employees can spend more time servicing customers and less time on internal management. Two people on the accounting staff in San Francisco can do what fifteen used to do in a remote office, saving $400,000 annually. The initial investment was only $40,000 in software and $100,000 in hardware for the EDI system—a 10-to-1 return.

As companies move to adopt EDI, they must consider several factors if they are to achieve a meaningful implementation. EDI, more than any other technology or business strategy, requires a team approach between users from the financial area and technical systems specialists. Experts caution against adopting EDI in a piecemeal fashion. If a company still has to re-enter some of its transaction data manually, this procedure interrupts a smooth, seamless data flow.

To eliminate data entry, companies must first standardize. They must standardize the form of their purchase order transaction by examining their business documents with trading partners and establishing a set of standards to use with all of them. Once a level of standards is determined, a pilot program should be initiated to deal with customer and supplier workflow to determine the optimal point to issue a purchase order and a material release. If a company is not using standard X.12 transaction sets, the information is provided by a printout that is manually audited, edited, and finally keyed into a computer. The manual re-entering of data interrupts a smooth flow, and the translation software has to be integrated into a company's business application.

EDI requires firms to alter their company-to-company business dealings. If a single company implements EDI in isolation, it becomes an exercise in futility and a wasted investment unless a meaningful portion of its trading partners join in. Cooperation among companies, suppliers and customers is required.

Steven J. Oldon, the vice president of information services at The Harper Group, notes that EDI is not a solution by itself. It needs to be integrated with other systems in the partners' computers—finance, manufacturing, inventory, purchasing, and so on. Instead of thinking about how to send transactions back and forth, the company has to think about the entire process from both ends. Firms often underestimate the amount of money it takes to implement EDI.

Large companies and customers have accepted EDI as a way of life. The key is to get down to the smaller companies, who tend to be reactive rather than proactive in implementing EDI. There is often a lack of understanding at the management level about what EDI can do for a company and where they can go with it. Implementing EDI requires people and money resources plus management support from the top down. The information systems department has to worry about the hardware, software, and communications to integrate EDI into the business environment.

The benefits of international EDI are even greater than for using EDI domestically. There is probably three times as much paperwork involved in international shipments as in domestic, so that the efficiencies of EDI are magnified severalfold. Moving products from country to country requires that forms be filled out for customs clearance and delivery of each shipment. In many countries, EDI can move the information in advance of the goods, completing the paperwork before a plane lands.

However, using EDI for international business raises additional concerns. There is no worldwide standard for sending business transactions electronically. ANSI X.12 is the accepted U.S. standard, but Europe's dominant standard is Edifact. Most analysts say that supporting two standards is less of a problem than is solving the business issues that have to be negotiated—which transactions to receive, how often, which mailbox to send to, and deciding who is going to pay for what.

Sources: Hal Glatzer, "EDI: The information-intensive way to move cargo," *Computerworld,* September 7, 1992; Colleen Frye, "EDI Beginning to Stretch National, Business Bounds," *Software Magazine,* May 1992; and Jerry Cashin, "Business Transactions Take Electronic Route," *Software Magazine,* December 1991.

Case Study Questions

1. What management, organization, and technology factors should companies consider in assessing whether or not to adopt EDI?

2. What are the major obstacles to EDI implementation?

3. If you were a supplier for General Motors, Chrysler, or Sears, how would you feel about using their EDI system? Why?

References   Benjamin, Robert I., David W. DeLong, and Michael S. Scott Morton. "The Realities of Electronic Data Interchange: How Much Competitive Advantage?" Management in the 1990s Working Paper 88:042. Sloan School of Management, MIT, 1988.

Borenstein, Nathaniel S. "Multimedia Electronic Mail: Will the Dream Become a Reality?" *Communications of the ACM* 34, no. 4 (April 1991).

Dertouzos, Michael. "Building the Information Marketplace." *Technology Review* (January 1991).

Donovan, John J. "Beyond Chief Information Officer to Network Manager." *Harvard Business Review* (September–October 1988).

Gilder, George. "Into the Telecosm." *Harvard Business Review* (March–April 1991).

Hall, Wayne A., and Robert E. McCauley. "Planning and Managing a Corporate Network Utility." *MIS Quarterly* (December 1987).

Hammer, Michael, and Glenn Mangurian. "The Changing Value of Communications Technology." *Sloan Management Review* (Winter 1987).

Hansen, James V. and Ned C. Hill. "Control and Audit of Electronic Data Interchange." *MIS Quarterly* 13, no. 4 (December 1989).

Keen, Peter G. W. *Competing in Time*. Cambridge, MA: Ballinger Publishing Company, 1986.

Keen, Peter G. W. *Shaping the Future: Business Design Through Information Technology*. Cambridge, MA: Harvard Business School Press, 1991.

McNurlin, Barbara Canning. "The Rise of 'Cooperative' Systems." *EDP Analyzer* 25, no. 6 (June 1987).

Railing, Larry, and Tom Housel. "A Network Infrastructure to Contain Costs and Enable Fast Response." *MIS Quarterly* 14, no. 4 (December 1990).

Roche, Edward M. *Telecommunications and Business Strategy*. Chicago: The Dryden Press, 1991.

Rochester, Jack B. "Networking Management: The Key to Better Customer Service." *I/S Analyzer* 27, no. 12 (December 1989).

Rowe, Stanford H. II. *Business Telecommunications*. New York: Macmillan, 1991.

Schultz, Brad. "The Evolution of ARPANET." *Datamation* (August 1, 1988).

Torkzadeh, Gholamreza, and Weidong Xia. "Managing Telecommunications Strategy by Steering Committee." *MIS Quarterly* 16, no. 2 (June 1992).

CHAPTER

10

The New Information Architecture

British Petroleum Innovates with Networked Computers

BP Exploration, Inc., (also known as BPX), the oil exploration arm of British Petroleum America, needed to make its operation more efficient in the face of declining oil reserves and shrinking profits in the world oil industry. One way to do this was to allow its geoscientists and engineers more immediate access to the data they needed. The company decided to give more computing power to its workers in the field by replacing its larger computers with networked microcomputers and workstations.

BPX moved technical applications, such as oil field mapping and corrosion tracking, from its old Digital Equipment minicomputers and Cray supercomputers to microcomputers and workstations. BP can now do all of its seismic exploration—sending signals to the earth, recording them electronically, and processing them into two-dimensional cross-sections—on microcomputers or workstations. Workstations are used for geologic mapping, and maps can easily be sent back and forth between departments. Eventu-

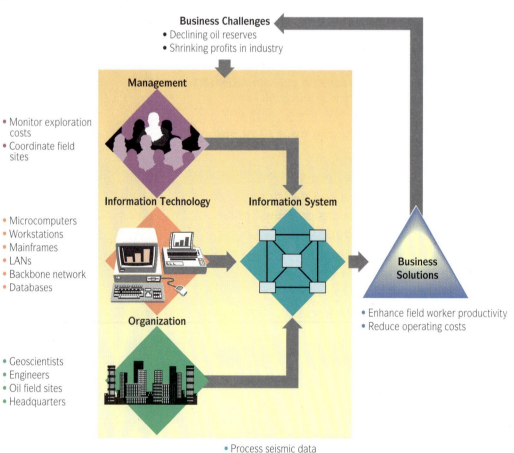

ally, administrative and personnel functions will be moved to networks as well.

BPX installed 1200 Macintosh computers in networks that use IBM RS/6000 and Sun UNIX workstations as file servers. Many of the microcomputers are linked at BPX's headquarters building in Anchorage. All of the microcomputers have access to BP databases on the file servers. Previously, mainframes processed BPX's seismic exploration data at an annual cost of $1 million. By using the new networks, desktop microcomputers, and workstations, BPX reduced the processing cost to one-fourth of that amount. The new computing arrangement is more portable too, since people can use some of the equipment while working at their hotels in remote locations.

LANs also operate at BP's Prudhoe Bay Field, 800 miles to the north. These networks are tied to the Anchorage network and to other BPX facilities using the company's worldwide backbone data network, which links North America, South America, and Europe.

BPX isn't abandoning its large computers entirely. IBM mainframes and DEC VAX minicomputers still run commercial financial systems. But BPX hopes to extend its desktop computing network throughout its operations worldwide.

Source: Bob Violino, "Exploring New Fields of IT Management," *Information WEEK* (July 6, 1992).

New information architecture: An arrangement of the organization's hardware, software, telecommunications, and data resources to put more computing power on the desktop and create a companywide network linking many smaller networks.

BPX is one of many companies in the 1990s that is rearranging its hardware, software, and communications capabilities into a new information architecture. Instead of relying on large mainframe computers for processing, BPX distributed computer power and information to powerful microcomputers and workstations on the desktop and tied its smaller networks together into a giant companywide network. We call this change in arrangement of information technology **"the new information architecture."** By putting more control of computer processing on the desktop and linking smaller networks into a companywide network, the new information architecture can help organizations achieve new levels of competitiveness and productivity. However, achieving these goals requires an understanding of how to make disparate hardware, software, and communications devices work together.

This chapter examines the components of the new information architecture and the technical, economic, and social forces that have shaped it. The key to creating networks where users can share data throughout the organization is connectivity. This chapter describes the connectivity models organizations use to link their systems and the standards that make such linkages possible. Despite the benefits of distributing computing power to the desktop and linking networks, the new information architecture has created new management problems. We describe the problems and their solutions so that organizations can maximize the benefits of the new architecture.

After completing this chapter you will be able to:

- Describe the characteristics of the new information architecture.
- Explain the difference between the client/server and X terminal implementations of the new architecture.
- Explain why connectivity is essential for the new architecture.
- Describe different models of network connectivity.
- Describe important standards used for linking hardware, software, and networks.
- Identify problems posed by the new architecture.
- Describe strategies for managing the transition to a new architecture.

10.1 What Is the New Information Architecture?

In Chapter 1 we defined information architecture as the particular form that information technology takes in an organization to achieve selected goals. An organization's information architecture consists of its computer hardware and software, telecommunications links, and data files. In the new information architecture, these components are arranged differently to place more of the organization's computing power on the desktop and to create networks that link entire enterprises.

Figure 10.1

The new information architecture at Brewer's Retail Inc. A network of Sun servers and development workstations work in tandem with over 100 PCs at Brewer's Retail Inc. Remote PCs, located in individual retail stores, are polled each night for data uploads. *Source: Lee Thé, "Downsize Your Database with UNIX," Datamation, October 15, 1992. Reproduced with permission from DATAMATION © 1992 Reed Publishing (USA) Inc.*

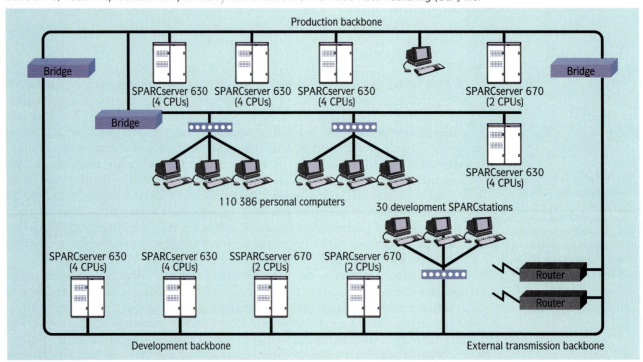

Features of the New Information Architecture

Figure 10.1 illustrates one example of this new architecture: the enterprise-wide network used by Brewers Retail, Inc., based in Mississauga, Ontario, Canada, which runs a chain of over 450 beer stores throughout Ontario. The network at company headquarters consists of nine Sun SPARCserver file servers, 30 SPARCstation workstations and 110 microcomputers with 80386 microprocessors linked in LANs. Each retail store owned by this firm has a microcomputer linked to this network. Brewers Retail polls each retail store's microcomputer every night and uploads its sales data to one of its servers. The SPARCstation workstations are used for application development. The microcomputers at corporate headquarters use the data for accounting and other applications. All of these machines use the UNIX operating system.

Figure 10.2 presents another example of the new information architecture: the network of the Microsoft Corporation, headquartered in Redmond, Washington. Microsoft is the world's leading producer of microcomputer software. Its 8400 employees operate 22,000 microcomputers worldwide. About 18,000 of these microcomputers reside in Microsoft's Redmond corporate headquarters "campus." Building 11, Microsoft's main computer center, contains two IBM AS/400 minicomputers, 9 DEC VAX minicomputers, and over 500 microcomputer-based file servers. These machines are linked to local area networks of microcomputer workstations in other Microsoft headquarters buildings using a powerful 100 megabit-per-second fiber optic backbone network. The computer center machines are also linked to the minicomputers and microcomputer workstations used by Microsoft's other 25 facilities in the United States and 30 locations overseas. The network operates around the clock.

About half of Microsoft's file servers run the UNIX operating system and are used primarily for Microsoft's massive electronic mail applications (3 million messages per month). The remaining file servers run the OS/2 operating system and hold files and databases that departments such as human resources require for their applications. The VAX minicomputers are used to process order entry and product distribution, general ledger, and other financial applications. Mi-

Figure 10.2a
The new information architecture at Microsoft Corporation. Microsoft Corporation's computer center houses two IBM AS/400 minicomputers, nine DEC VAX minicomputers, and over five hundred microcomputer-based file servers. *Adapted from Dwight B. Davis, "Clients, Servers, and the Glass House,"* Datamation, *November 1, 1991. Reproduced with permission from DATAMATION © 1992, Reed Publishing (USA) Inc.*

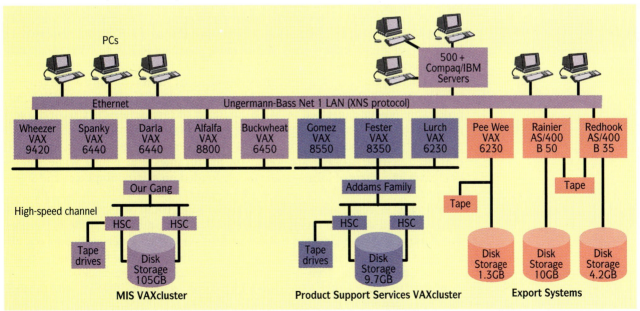

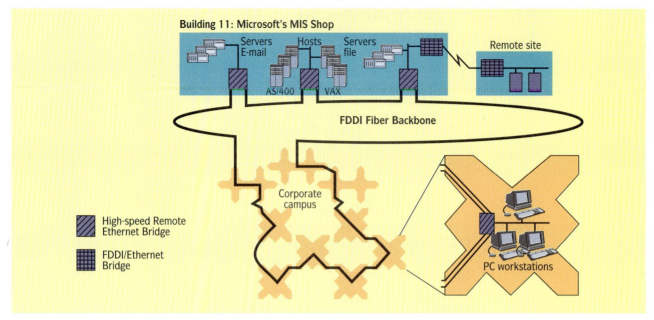

Figure 10.2b
The FDDI fiber backbone. The machines in Microsoft's computer center are linked to local area networks of microcomputer workstations in other Microsoft headquarters buildings using a fiber optic backbone network and to minicomputers and microcomputer workstations located in Microsoft's remote United States and overseas locations. *Adapted from Dwight B. Davis, "Clients, Servers, and the Glass House," Datamation, November 1, 1991. Reproduced with permission from DATAMATION © 1992, Reed Publishing (USA) Inc.*

crosoft uses the AS/400 minicomputers in Building 11 and eight AS/400s located in overseas offices for integrated financial and manufacturing applications that support its international business operations. Users with security approval can access databases that reside on the VAX or AS/400 minicomputers or the file servers for analysis and reporting. For instance, marketing specialists can download data from one VAX to follow a Microsoft product from its initial sale to the final purchase.

How do Brewers Retail and Microsoft's arrangements of machines, software, databases, and telecommunications differ from arrangements of the past? In earlier information systems, under the old architecture, mainframes and minicomputers from the same computer manufacturer were responsible for most of the firm's information processing. Microcomputers and workstations were used independently by individual users or were linked into small localized networks. By adopting a new information architecture, Brewers Retail and Microsoft now use a mixture of computer hardware consisting of workstations, microcomputers, minicomputers and mainframes supplied by different hardware vendors. Workstations and microcomputers dominate in terms of sheer numbers and processing power expressed in MIPS (millions of instructions per second), with much of the firms' computer processing taking place on the desktop. The role of the mainframes and minicomputers is diminished. Large, complex databases that need central storage are found on mainframes and minis, while smaller databases and parts of large databases are loaded on microcomputers and workstations.

Information resources considered as the sum total of the firm's software, hardware, and data are much more controlled from the desktop by the professional who uses the desktop machine. The system is a network; in fact, the system is composed of multiple networks: A high-capacity backbone network connects many local area networks and devices, and the backbone may be connected to many external networks like Bitnet, Arpanet, Internet, and through the phone system to even more networks.

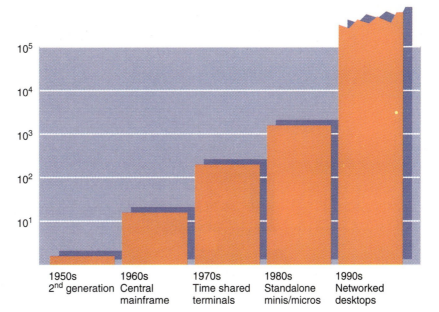

Figure 10.3
The impact of desktop computing. The number of people who can be computing simultaneously at any one site increases exponentially with the introduction of networked desktop computing. Although time-shared terminals greatly increased the number of people computing in an organization, the real expansion of computing power came from the introduction of stand-alone microcomputers and networked desktop systems.

Perhaps the most important change from the past is that, with the new architecture, just about everybody in an organization can be computing simultaneously, no matter how large the organization. Under the old architecture, a large centralized mainframe computer could accommodate up to 2000 users simultaneously. With the addition of more users, the mainframe operating system would slow down considerably, the delay in response time would increase from seconds to minutes, and major production jobs would have to be canceled because of insufficient computing power. Of course, the organization had the option to purchase a new mainframe computer for $5 to $10 million which would double or even triple the size of computing available. And, of course, it also could markedly expand its telecommunications capabilities. This very large expense may not be necessary; with microcomputers, everyone in the organization, regardless of size, can use computing facilities. Extensive use of microcomputers by large numbers of people does not slow down the system or prevent other people from computing.

Figure 10.3 compares the improvement in productivity from distributing computing power to individuals that occurs when organizations use stand-alone microcomputers and networked desktop computers. Assuming that a worker with a computer is more productive than one without a computer, the gains in overall productivity can be enormous.

Client/Server vs. X Terminal Models

In the new information architecture, there are alternative ways of delivering computing power to the desktop. Two patterns that have emerged are the client/server and the X terminal models of computing (see Figure 10.4).

In the **client/server model,** computer processing is split between "clients" on a network and "servers," with each function being assigned to the machine best suited to perform it. The client part of an application runs on the client system; the server part of the application runs on the file server. The user generally interacts only with the client portion of the application, which typically consists of the user interface, the data input process, querying a database, and obtaining reports. The server performs back-end functions not visible to users, such as

Client/server model: A model for computing that splits the processing between "clients" and "servers" on a network assigning functions to the machine most able to perform the function.

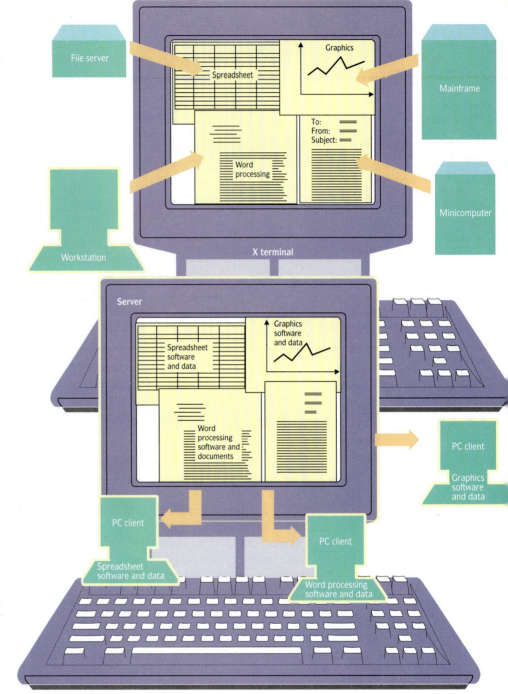

Figure 10.4
Two models of workgroup computing. In the X terminal model, illustrated at the top, the local desktop machines are not stand-alone computers but merely terminals that access the operation of several remote computers at a time. The model is inexpensive but is limited because terminals cannot be customized for specific applications. In the client/server model, illustrated at the bottom, computer processing is split between ''client'' machines and ''server'' machines, with each machine handling those tasks for which it is best suited. Users interface with the ''client'' machines. Although more expensive than the X terminal model, client/server machines afford great customization and processing power.

managing peripheral devices and controlling access to shared databases.

The exact division of tasks depends on application requirements, processing requirements, the number of users, and available resources. The client tasks may include getting user input, submitting requests to the server for programs and data, performing calculations on local data, or displaying results. The server portion may fetch or process data. The client/server model requires that application programs be written as two separate software components that run on different machines but that appear to operate as a single application. In the Brewers Retail and Microsoft networks, the clients are fully functional microcomputers and the servers are specialized workstations and microcomputers.

X terminal model: Centrally controlled inexpensive desktop terminal used on a network which can access the operations of several different remote computers simultaneously.

In the **X terminal model,** local desktop machines are not computers with individual processing capabilities, but merely terminals that can access the operations of several different remote computers at once. Using X Windows (a graphical user interface standard described in the next section), an X terminal can use a mouse, display graphics, and simultaneously run and view several different applications in separate screen windows operating on different computers. Because they have no disk drives, X terminals cost half as much as microcomputers. Because the X terminal model is so inexpensive, it is used on many networks. But it has many limitations: The X terminal model requires a UNIX operating system, and there is not as much business software available for the UNIX operating system as there is for the DOS operating system. When many terminals are being used, the responsiveness of the system declines, just as in a mainframe system of the 1970s. Additionally, the X terminal model centralizes control of desktop machines, which potentially limits software choices.

The client/server model also has limitations: It is difficult to write software that divides processing among clients and servers; the server can get bogged down quickly when too many users want service; and microcomputers with independent processing power are more difficult to coordinate and administer on a network. While the client/server model will probably dominate in the 1990s, the X terminal model will prove useful in universities and other settings—in clerical word processing, for instance, where the independent processing power of a desktop workstation will not be needed.

Forces Shaping the New Information Architecture

Businesses have adopted the new information architecture for many reasons. Improvements in hardware, software, and telecommunications capabilities; the growth of new information services; and the transformation to a knowledge-based economy are all persuading businesses to put more computing power on their workers' desktops. In this section we describe the major environmental influences that are pushing firms to shift computing capabilities to the desktop and to arrange their resources into information systems that span the entire organization.

PRICE–POWER RELATIONSHIPS

Enhanced computing power, coupled with falling prices, is an important factor promoting the new information architecture. Chapter 6 described the dramatic changes in computers' price–power relationship. The increasing capability of the hardware means that the supply of computing power has been rapidly expanding while the cost of the machinery has been falling.

These changing price–power relationships are responsible for the proliferation of microcomputers and desktop workstations, which are twin pillars of the new information architecture. Micros and workstations provide desktop computing power and can act as file servers in networks, assuming the role formerly filled by mainframes and minicomputers.

Today microcomputers can be purchased with over 32 megabytes of internal memory, hundreds of megabytes of magnetic or optical disk storage, and a sophisticated operating system that permits multiple, simultaneous uses. These machines are as powerful as the mainframe computers of the mid 1980s.

The extent of the desktop revolution is clearly visible in sales figures: Sales of microcomputers and workstations have far outpaced sales of minicomputers and mainframes, rapidly extending computing to users who had never before had contact with computers. By 1989, the total microcomputer MIPS processing power of many Fortune 500 companies exceeded that of its mainframes and minicomputers. Work that required human use of computers was increasingly performed on microcomputers and workstations and not on mainframes. This was indeed a profound change in information architecture and the organization of work.

Table 10.1   LEADING DIGITAL INFORMATION SERVICES

Provider	Type of Service
CompuServe	General interest/business information
Prodigy	General interest/business information
America Online	General interest/business information
Dow Jones News Retrieval	Business/financial information
Quotron	Financial information
Dialog	Business/scientific/technical information
Lexis	Legal research
Nexis	News/business information

END-USER SOFTWARE   The sales of microcomputers expanded rapidly in the early 1980s because internal memory became large enough to operate productivity-promoting software programs such as spreadsheets and word processing that were very easy to use (i.e., no prior computer experience was required). While the microcomputer software of the 1980s focused on accomplishing mundane office and accounting tasks, the 1990s is a decade of highly interactive audiovisual computing involving multiple media such as sound, moving pictures, and text. As desktop software for professional and clerical workers continues to expand in power and function, the desktop revolution will continue.

ELECTRONIC SERVICES   Another reason for the rapid development of the new information architecture is the emergence of powerful and far-reaching digital electronic services to support microcomputer and workstation users at their desktops. Stock prices, historical references to periodicals, industrial supplies catalogs, and travel information are just some of the electronic databases that can be accessed by desktop workstations. In the early 1980s, The Source, Prodigy, CompuServe, Dow Jones News, and other companies emerged as information utilities for owners of home and business microcomputers. Hobbyists or employees working at home can tie into information services like those listed in Table 10.1 to find information on

The Prodigy Interactive Personal Service gives subscribers access to extensive information including travel, weather, education, and financial services directly from their personal computers in their homes or offices.

airline reservations, ticket availability for popular shows in certain towns, long-range weather forecasts, stocks through the Dow Jones News Service, archival data (such as the archives of The New York Times through a service called NEXIS), and legal research through a service called LEXIS. Many of these services offer electronic mail as well, which is the most commonly requested digital service.

GROWTH OF KNOWLEDGE AND INFORMATION WORK

For much of this century, the United States, Canada, and Western Europe have been shifting from agricultural and industrial production to knowledge and information production as the basis of their wealth. In their new knowledge-based economies, more workers create or work with information than create or work with their hands. Factories are being replaced by new kinds of knowledge- and information-intensive organizations devoted entirely to the production, processing, and distribution of information. Entire new information services, such as those just described in this chapter, employ millions of people. Knowledge and information workers such as engineers, scientists, architects, accountants, or attorneys require access to desktop computing power to enhance their own productivity and effectiveness. Chapter 15 describes specific desktop applications used in knowledge work and the role of knowledge work in the organization.

TELECOMMUNICATIONS NETWORKS

The new information architecture would be impossible to sustain without improvements in telecommunications that can deliver information to desktop machines in businesses and homes. The advent of microprocessors, which made microcomputers possible, also made possible a much more rapid, dense telecommunications network in the United States and other countries.

Until the 1980s, there were technological and institutional barriers to the effective use of the existing public switched telephone network to link desktop professionals and home offices to existing databases and services in remote locations. The leading technological question was "How can you distribute access to multiple databases across a nation the size of the United States at a reasonable cost?" New easy-to-use software was needed, along with new software and hardware techniques for data transmission and delivery. The leading institutional barrier was that a federal court agreement of 1982 prohibited the owners of the largest communications network in the nation (the Bell operating companies and AT&T Long Lines) from creating and delivering services like electronic shopping, banking, news, and other database services. Since then, federal courts have ruled that phone companies could both produce and deliver computerized services of any kind. This development has created the potential for rapidly expanding the use of videotex. **Videotex** is the distribution of text and video images over telephone lines to business and home receivers, where desktop microcomputers or other devices are used to read the information. The service is two-way: Messages can be sent from a central computer to the desktop and from the desktop to the central computer. Dialog and CompuServe are leading examples of videotex services that will now have the regional Bell companies as competitors as well as providers of communications to the desktop wherever it is located.

Videotex: Multimedia delivery of information to remote terminals typically used for consumer or commercial delivery systems such as electronic shopping, banking, news, and financial database services.

In the 1990s, technology for wireless networks will expand communications capabilities even more through the use of hand-held computers and the exploitation of the cellular telephone network and underutilized FM radio bandwidths. The net result of these systems will be much faster data entry from remote locations and much tighter integration and control of mobile workers in remote locations by central offices.

Three Visions of the New Information Architecture

No single information systems architecture works for all organizations. There is more than one way to arrange hardware, software, data, and networks to implement the new information architecture. We can classify the arrangements that most firms use into three major visions: the data processing vision, the logical office vision, and the automated workplace vision. These different implementations of the new information architecture reflect the fact that not all organizations are alike; they also represent marketing strategies of the major computer vendors.

THE DATA PROCESSING VISION

Data processing vision: Vision of the new information architecture that views microcomputers and workstations as subservient to and closely integrated into the mainframe computing environment.

In the **data processing vision**, microcomputers and workstations are considered subservient to and closely integrated into the mainframe computing environment. In the final analysis, desktop computers are conceived primarily as appendages of the organization's central mainframe computer. The problem with this view has always been how to integrate microcomputers and workstations meaningfully into a mainframe environment to take advantage of the huge resources of a mainframe without destroying the personal, flexible, autonomous, and friendly characteristics of a microcomputer. The integration of mainframes (which store the vast amount of corporate data) and microcomputers (where the processing power is increasingly located) has always been problematic because mainframes and minicomputers use a data file format that is different from the file format used by microcomputers and workstations. Mainframe software itself was never intended to share processing with locally intelligent machines, and mainframe communications networks were never designed to allow communication with other computers with independent processing power.

The X terminal arrangement reflects the data processing vision. There are several ways of integrating microcomputers with independent processing power into the mainframe data processing environment. First, hardware and software can be developed so that microcomputers can emulate ordinary terminals, although terminal emulation makes little use of the micro's independent processing capability. The user is restricted to mainframe software. Second, microcomputers can also use the mainframe as a huge file server, storing data on the mainframe but performing all processing on the microcomputer. Third, microcomputers can create user-friendly interfaces for operating mainframe applications. Fourth, microcomputers can extract data from mainframes, process the data, and then upload the processed data back to the mainframe.

The data processing vision of microcomputers is promoted by large mainframe and minicomputer manufacturers who have a vested interest in making their large-scale, centralized machines a worthwhile investment. Organizations, such as banks or brokerage houses, with heavy investments in mainframes or requirements to process large volumes of transactions in one central location would support this view.

THE LOGICAL OFFICE

Logical office: Vision of the new information architecture that focuses on the ability to use portable microcomputers to work in many different physical locations outside the traditional office.

A radically different vision of the role of microcomputers in the organization arises from the new relationship between individuals and work that portable microcomputers make possible. This new relationship has been dubbed the **logical office.** As one wag put it, "A logical office is wherever your head is at when you think about business." In this view, work is done on a train, in a plane, or at the beach. Even a home office seems somewhat of an anachronism in a world of portable cellular phones, portable FAX machines, and laptop computers.

With laptop computers, people can work in many locations, and work no longer is associated with a single physical location. Proponents of this view argue that the only reason work is performed in a specified physical location is that the traditional information processing and communications technologies require central offices. People go to offices because the telephones, the secretaries, and the filing cabinets are located there. Information systems that distribute computing power to microcomputers and that connect them with high-speed telecommunications links change this picture: Work can now be distributed more evenly in space and time. There is no need for a central office or for a nine-to-five job. Vendors of laptop microcomputers and businesses with mobile workers such as sales representatives or delivery personnel are most interested in this vision of portable computing.

The logical office took this gentleman on safari in Maasal Mara (Serengeti), Kenya, with his state-of-the-art notebook computer.

THE AUTOMATED WORKPLACE

The automated workplace is a third vision of the new information architecture. Desktop microcomputers and workstations are the centerpiece of the workplace of the future (see Figure 10.5). In this view, the mainframe and the minicomputer are peripheral devices, performing storage and elementary reporting functions,

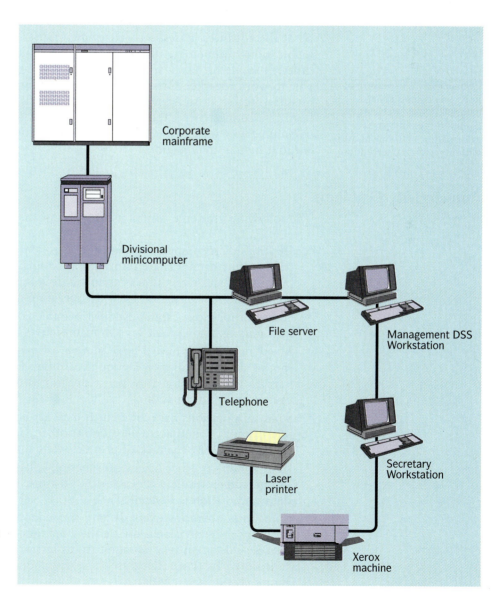

Figure 10.5
The automated workplace. In this implementation of the new information architecture, the bulk of computing and network management is performed by microcomputers and workstations at the center of the workplace. Mainframes and minicomputers are peripheral devices performing storage and elementary reporting functions.

Automated workplace: Vision of the new information architecture that makes desktop microcomputers and workstations the centerpiece of the workplace with mainframes and minicomputers at the periphery.

and the "real" computer is the one on the desktop with which the knowledge professional works and which he or she directly controls. In the **automated workplace**, the microcomputer workstation is the organization's file server and communications controller and the desktop knowledge workstation. Other digital office machinery is under the control of desktop workstations. Copying machines, printers, and telephones are linked to a single office local area network. Vendors of office automation equipment and firms specializing in knowledge work—such as publishing companies, law offices, or architectural firms—would favor this vision of the new information architecture.

Bits and pieces of each of these grand visions of the new information architecture are clearly visible in large and small corporations. Many large organizations have chosen a single path, whereas others unsure of what model is correct are experimenting with all three visions in different types of settings.

10.2 Connectivity

The ultimate goal of the new information architecture is enterprisewide networking: a vision in which digitized information can move through a seamless web of electronic networks, connecting different kinds of machines, people, sensors, databases, functional divisions, departments, and work groups. Despite all of the advances in desktop processing, user-friendly software, and telecommunications technology, this goal has been difficult to realize because many different kinds of hardware, software, and communications systems must be able to work together. Organizations trying to implement the new information architecture lose a substantial amount of productivity because they lack connectivity. **Connectivity** is the ability of computers and computer-based devices to communicate with one another and "share" information in a meaningful way without human intervention.

Connectivity: A measure of how well computers and computer-based devices communicate and share information with one another without human intervention.

Connectivity Problems

The following are some common examples of the absence of connectivity:

- Desktop microcomputers often cannot use data from the corporate mainframe, often cannot share information among different brands of microcomputers, and many times cannot share information meaningfully even among different pieces of software operating on the same microcomputer.
- Some corporations cannot establish reliable communications and information sharing among their own minicomputers and mainframes.
- Most corporations have a large number of major software programs that cannot share information among each other. For instance, some large firms have 15 to 20 pension systems written for different operating systems that cannot share information.
- Some corporations have different E-mail systems within their own firm that cannot communicate with one another. Communication among firms is complicated by the lack of products that support E-mail standards.
- IBM, as well as other hardware vendors, sells machines and software that cannot communicate with each other because of different hardware designs and operating systems.
- Companies operating overseas have tremendous difficulty building global networks that can seamlessly tie their operations together. Different countries have different telecommunications infrastructures, many owned by national PTTs, (Post, Telegraph, and Telephone monopolies), that use disparate networking standards.

There are many reasons why computers and information systems achieved such dizzying heights of incompatibility. Individual computers were designed long before computer networks were built. The focus of the first thirty years of computer development since World War II was to maximize the efficiency of large-scale individual machines. Before the 1980s, there were no standards for either hardware or software manufacturers; the buyers of equipment lacked market power to demand standards; the federal government did not impose its own standards; the technology was changing very rapidly (outdating older hardware and software); and hardware and software vendors themselves encouraged product differentiation. Bewildered management in many organizations purchased equipment on the basis of narrow considerations of project efficiency, and they lacked an enterprisewide vision.

A Garden of Buzzwords: Aspects of Connectivity

Connectivity encompasses more than just networking, and there are many different qualities that an information system with connectivity will have. Let us explore some of the terms used for describing different aspects of connectivity.

Applications portability: The ability to operate the same software on different hardware platforms.

Applications portability is the ability to operate the same piece of software on different types of computer hardware. Imagine, for instance, using Lotus 1-2-3 spreadsheet software on a microcomputer at work, saving the results in a file, removing the 1-2-3 program disk, taking it home, and using a Macintosh computer to complete the project. Imagine processing your payroll on a Hewlett Packard minicomputer, then using the same application software on an IBM mainframe at corporate headquarters.

Migration: The ability to move software from one generation of hardware to another more powerful generation.

Migration is the ability to move software from one generation of hardware to another more powerful generation. Most microcomputer software offers upward compatibility. For instance, you can run early versions of Lotus 1-2-3 on later versions of DOS (version 5.0, for example). Downward compatibility is more problematic. Much microcomputer software designed to operate under DOS 5.0 cannot operate on DOS 3.0. Migration problems occur with other operating systems as well.

Cooperative processing: Dividing computing tasks among networked mainframes, minicomputers, microcomputers, or workstations to solve a single common problem.

Cooperative processing divides computing tasks among mainframes, minicomputers, microcomputers, or workstations to solve a single common problem. Cooperative processing is a connectivity issue because different machines must be networked and programmed so that they can work together on a single application (see Chapter 6 for a more detailed description of cooperative processing).

Information portability: The sharing of computer files among different hardware platforms and software applications.

Information portability is the sharing of computer files among different types of computer hardware and different software applications. Currently, sharing of files is possible among applications such as word processing that can create a single file standard like ASCII 8 text files (see the discussion of ASCII in Chapter 6). These text files can be transferred into spreadsheet or database applications, but the transfer can take place only on the same hardware platform or machine class. Because different machines and machine classes use different coding schemes (for instance, mainframes often use EBCDIC, and some smaller machines use ASCII 7), even information portability can be difficult.

Interoperability: The ability of a software application to operate on two different machine platforms while maintaining the identical user interface and functionality.

Interoperability is the ability of a single piece of software to operate on two different kinds of computer hardware, show users an identical interface, and perform the same tasks. For instance, Microsoft Word word processing software has similar functionality and somewhat similar looks on both the Macintosh and IBM microcomputers, but different versions of the software are required to run on each type of machine.

Open systems: Software systems that can operate on different hardware platforms because they are built on public non-proprietary operating systems, user interfaces, application standards, and networking protocols.

Interoperability, as well as information and applications portability, requires open systems. **Open systems** are built upon public, nonproprietary operating systems, user interfaces, application standards, and networking protocols. In open systems, software can operate on different hardware platforms and in that sense can be "portable." It is prohibitively costly to achieve applications portability without a common shared operating system.

In the microcomputer world, most IBM-compatible microcomputers use Microsoft/IBM DOS or Microsoft Windows, an operating system shell which runs in conjunction with DOS. Their operating principles are published and they can be used by non-IBM microcomputer makers for a minimal licensing fee. DOS has no common user interface, although the graphical user interface of Microsoft Windows is a step in this direction. By contrast, most minicomputer and mainframes have proprietary operating systems that cannot be used by different classes of machines and whose operating principles are hidden from public view and vigorously defended with high licensing fees.

Perhaps the key to truly open systems is the operating system called UNIX. UNIX originated in the research labs of AT&T in the 1970s through engineers who wanted a powerful time-sharing operating system that could operate on many different kinds of computer hardware. Since then, UNIX has come to dominate the engineering market for workstations and is starting to be used by some types of microcomputers. However, there are different versions of UNIX, and no one version has been accepted as an open systems standard.

Thus, true connectivity requires a great deal more than simply wiring together different machines or providing limited access to many different computers. Connectivity requires common operating systems, common telecommunications standards, and even common user interface standards, a similar screen look and feel across different software applications.

10.3 Standards for Achieving Connectivity

Achieving connectivity requires standards for networking, operating systems, and user interfaces. To date, there are no uniform standards that ensure that information systems can achieve the attributes of connectivity described in section 10.2, but some standards do exist and others are being promoted. This section describes the most important standards that are being used today.

Who Sets Standards?

The process of setting standards is largely political and involves many powerful interest groups. Large private-sector industry associations of equipment makers have funded professional and industry groups to develop standards (see the discussion later in this section on the battle over UNIX). The federal government sets standards in two ways. As the largest purchaser of computing equipment in the world, the federal government uses its procurement policies and laws to establish what become industry standards in practice. It also sets standards through the National Institute for Standards and Technology (NIST). Professional engineering societies such as the Institute of Electrical and Electronic Engineers (IEEE) and the American National Standards Institute (ANSI) have set standards for software language definition, hardware performance, and communications protocols.

With the globalization of business, international standards are critical. The International Organization for Standardization (ISO) and the International Telephone and Telegraph Consultative Committee (CCITT) have helped legitimize one of the most powerful connectivity models, OSI, the Open Systems Interconnect reference model described in the next section.

Models of Connectivity for Networks

Reference model: A generic framework for thinking about a problem.

Because of the many interests involved in connectivity and standard setting, there are different models for achieving connectivity in telecommunications networks. A **reference model** is a generic framework for thinking about a problem. It is a logical breakdown of some activity (like communications) into a number of

Protocol: A statement that explains how a specific task will be performed.

Standard: Approved reference models and protocols as determined by standard-setting groups for building or developing products or services.

distinct steps or parts. Specific **protocols** are required in order to implement a reference model. A protocol is a statement that explains how a specific task, such as transferring data, will be performed. Reference models and protocols become **standards** when they are approved by important standard-setting groups or when industry builds or buys products that support the models and protocols.

Network connectivity can also be achieved without reference models or protocols by using gateways (see Chapter 9). Gateways are ad-hoc, single-purpose hardware and software devices that permit the translation of digital information from one protocol to another. Firms develop gateways between two disparate networks when it is impossible or too costly to integrate them by complying with reference models or standards. Gateways are expensive to build and maintain, and they can be slow and inefficient.

We now describe the most important models of network connectivity.

THE OSI MODEL

Open Systems Interconnect (OSI): International reference model for linking different types of computers and networks.

Open Systems Interconnect (OSI) is an international reference model developed by the International Standards Organization for linking different types of computers and networks. It was designed to support global networks with large volumes of transaction processing.

OSI enables a computer connected to a network to communicate with any other computer on the same network or a different network, regardless of the manufacturer. To establish this connectivity, the OSI model divides the telecommunications process into seven layers (see Figure 10.6).

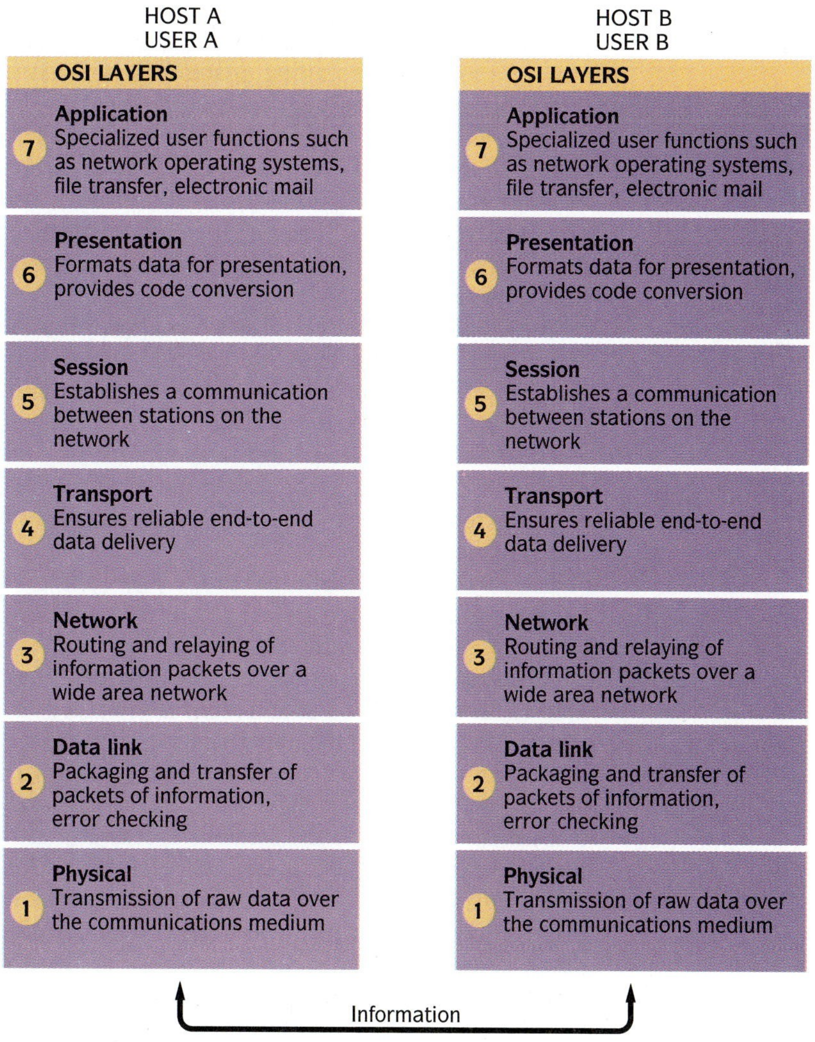

Figure 10.6
The Open Systems Interconnect (OSI) reference model. The figure illustrates the seven layers defining the communication functions—for the flow of information in an OSI network.

HOST A
USER A

OSI LAYERS

Application
7 Specialized user functions such as network operating systems, file transfer, electronic mail

Presentation
6 Formats data for presentation, provides code conversion

Session
5 Establishes a communication between stations on the network

Transport
4 Ensures reliable end-to-end data delivery

Network
3 Routing and relaying of information packets over a wide area network

Data link
2 Packaging and transfer of packets of information, error checking

Physical
1 Transmission of raw data over the communications medium

HOST B
USER B

OSI LAYERS

Application
7 Specialized user functions such as network operating systems, file transfer, electronic mail

Presentation
6 Formats data for presentation, provides code conversion

Session
5 Establishes a communication between stations on the network

Transport
4 Ensures reliable end-to-end data delivery

Network
3 Routing and relaying of information packets over a wide area network

Data link
2 Packaging and transfer of packets of information, error checking

Physical
1 Transmission of raw data over the communications medium

Information

The OSI model is a framework for defining the functions required in a telecommunications session between two or more computers. Each computer participating in an OSI network is considered to be an intelligent device, not just a terminal. Each layer in the OSI model is defined by its communications functions and deals with a specific aspect of the communications process.

Two different computers using OSI standards would each have software and hardware that correspond to each layer of the OSI model. A message sent from one computer to the other would pass downward through all seven layers. It would start with the application layer of the sending computer and pass through to the sending computer's physical layer. It would then travel over the communication channel and enter the receiving computer, rising upward through the seven layers in that machine. The process is reversed when the receiving computer responds.

The *application layer* is responsible for activities on the application level. The application layer establishes and maintains the associations between communicating application programs. It supports communications functions such as file transfer, virtual terminal message handling, transaction processing, and distributed processing.

The *presentation layer* translates the message to and from the format used in the network to a form comprehensible to the sending and receiving programs in layer 7 and vice versa. This layer negotiates, selects, and maintains the syntax of information being transferred between the applications processes.

The *session layer* establishes and controls the dialogue between the two communicating applications. In coordination with the application layer, the session layer helps select the turn of sending and receiving information, synchronization recovery, and orderly termination of the communication. It acts as the moderator of the dialogue taking place over the network, prohibiting or allowing interruptions as necessary and setting checkpoints to retain logical sequence.

The *transport layer* controls the quality of the transmission and ensures that network facilities are used effectively. This layer ensures the integrity of the entire message from its origins to its destination. If an incoming message is out of sequence, this layer will resequence it. If messages are coming in at a faster rate than the system can handle, the transport layer can establish priorities for data flow control.

The *network layer* determines the appropriate route for the data through the network. It provides the routing and switching functions that select the paths through the network, such as through circuit and packet switching and collections of internetworked resources.

The *data link layer* packages the data for transmission, unpackages data upon receipt, and handles error detection during transmission. Its chief function is error correction. It provides for the transfer of information over each leg of a transmission path.

The *physical layer* establishes the physical connection between the computer equipment and the network (i.e., the size and shape of the plug, the number of pins in a connector, and so forth).

For example, if an officer at a local bank wanted information about a particular client's checking account that was stored in the bank's central host computer, he or she would enter the instructions to retrieve the client's account records into his or her terminal under control of layer 7, the application layer. The presentation layer (layer 6) would change this input data into a format for transmission. Layer 5 (the session layer) initiates the session. Layer 4 (the transport layer) checks the quality of the information traveling from user to host node. Layers 3 and 2 (the network and data link layers) transmit the data through layer 1 (the physical layer). When the message reaches the host computer, control moves up the layers back to the user, reversing the sequence.

Essentially, the top three OSI layers are responsible for turning formatted data into a "plain vanilla" version that can travel on a generic network defined in the bottom four layers. Each layer in the OSI model has one or several associated

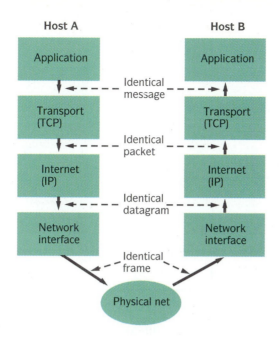

Figure 10.7
The Transmission Control Protocol/Internet Protocol (TCP/IP) reference model. This figure illustrates the five layers of the (TCP/IP) reference model for communications as set by the U.S. Department of Defense.

protocols. A multilayer protocol has the advantage of having each layer independent of the others so that it can be changed without affecting the other layers.

The OSI general model has spawned two compatible models for specific functional applications. General Motors and Boeing have developed the Manufacturing Automation Protocol (MAP) and the Technical Office Protocol (TOP), which will support manufacturing and office applications.

TCP/IP MODEL

Transmission Control Protocol/Internet Protocol (TCP/IP): U.S. Department of Defense reference model for linking different types of computers and networks.

The U.S. Department of Defense has developed its own competing reference model, called **Transmission Control Protocol/Internet Protocol (TCP/IP)**, which it launched in 1972 in conjunction with network research and development done by the Defense Advanced Research Projects Agency (DARPA) to help scientists link disparate computers. Because it is one of the oldest communications reference models, and the standard used by most commercially available products, TCP/IP is still widely used, especially in the United States (Europeans tend to favor OSI).

Figure 10.7 shows that TCP/IP has a five-layer reference model.

1. Physical net: Defines basic electrical transmission characteristic generated during communications.
2. Network interface: Handles addressing issues, usually in the operating system, as well as the interface between the initiating computer and the network.
3. Internet (IP): Handles system-to-system communication. This layer is a self-contained, connectionless datagram delivery process that does not depend on the network for message receipt acknowledgment. The datagram is a unit of information consisting of a header segment and text segment. The Internet Protocol receives datagrams from TCP and transmits them through the Internet.
4. Transmission Control Protocol (TCP): Performs transport. TCP supports program-to-program communication at the end-user level. The Transmission Control Protocol supports reliable transfer of information independent of the category of computer job at the higher layer (such as E-mail or log-on).
5. Application: Provides end-user functionality by translating the messages into the user/host software for screen presentation.

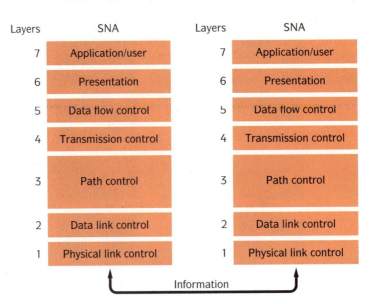

Layers	SNA		Layers	SNA
7	Application/user		7	Application/user
6	Presentation		6	Presentation
5	Data flow control		5	Data flow control
4	Transmission control		4	Transmission control
3	Path control		3	Path control
2	Data link control		2	Data link control
1	Physical link control		1	Physical link control

Information

Figure 10.8
The IBM Systems Network Architecture (SNA) reference model. This figure illustrates the seven-layer model that deals with logical units and physical units. SNA can support intelligent terminals, communication among terminals, file transfers, and on-line transaction processing. SNA is the most common communications network model for mainframes and minicomputers in use today.

Both OSI and TCP/IP will dominate multivendor systems in the next decade. Because these protocols are not totally incompatible, some communication across these different models can occur.

PROPRIETARY
APPROACHES: SNA

Systems Network Architecture (SNA): Proprietary telecommunications reference model developed by IBM.

IBM developed the first commercial computer communications model and protocol, called **Systems Network Architecture (SNA),** in 1974. Over the years, SNA evolved into a full-featured telecommunications model that could support intelligent terminals, communication among terminals, file transfers, on-line transaction processing, and some limited applications portability. SNA networks can even be configured to carry video signals in the unused portion of the bandwidth. Today there are nearly 300,000 SNA networks in the private sector worldwide, making SNA the most common communications network model for mainframes and minicomputers.

SNA is similar to OSI in that it takes a layered approach to the problem of communications among users (see Figure 10.8), but it is not entirely compatible with OSI, even though IBM has sought to make certain aspects of SNA and OSI compatible.

Like OSI, the SNA model can be seen as a seven-layer reference model. SNA divides the world into logical units (people, applications, or programs) and physical units (terminals, cluster controllers, front-end processors, and host computers). Logical units request different kinds of sessions or services from the host. Each logical unit and physical unit has its own unique network address. The goal of SNA is to separate the user from the details of telecommunications. With SNA, a complete change in the transmission technology and software will not affect the application level or users.

While SNA is a powerful communications network, it is not the total solution to connectivity problems. Despite SNA, for instance, major applications written for one IBM host computer often cannot be operated on other IBM host computers, minicomputers, or PCs. And these other machines cannot typically even gain access to the larger machines' applications or data. Moreover, mere communications is only the first step toward operating system and application portability. IBM is developing deeper strategies for assuring connectivity in the future.

Other Networking Standards

In addition to connectivity reference models, standards have been developed for transmitting digital data over public switched networks, for transmission over fiber optic cable, and for electronic mail, EDI, and packet switching.

**Integrated Services Digital
Network (ISDN):**
International standard for
transmitting voice, video, and
data to support a wide range
of service over the public
telephone lines.

Integrated Services Digital Network (ISDN) is an international standard for transmitting voice, video, and data over phone lines. It is an internationally endorsed plan to migrate the public telephone network to the standard use of digital technology. The CCITT (Consultative Committee on International Telephone and Telegraph), which is responsible for devising standards for ISDN implementation, defines ISDN as a network in general, evolving from the telephone Integrated Digital Network (IDN), that provides end-to-end digital connectivity to support a wide range of services, including voice and nonvoice services, to which users have access by a limited set of standard multipurpose customer interfaces. In the words of many industry observers, ISDN is the biggest new development in telephone communications since electronic digital switching moved into local Bell offices. In many respects, ISDN is a natural extension of digital equipment and capability from the regional Bell central office down to the desktop.

Consider the limitations of LANs and PBXs. Right now, you cannot make a telephone call on your local area network. You cannot send a FAX or video image very conveniently on your LAN. If you purchase a PBX (private branch exchanges were discussed in the previous chapter) to improve both phone service and computer connectivity in your firm, you must select and maintain the equipment, and the service ends as soon as you leave the building. Alternatively, imagine combining in one single service the following features:

- Complete voice, data, and video connection to anywhere in the world.
- Complete digital connection to any other digital device in the world, from one next door to one halfway around the world.
- Simultaneous use of voice, video, and digital devices.
- Complete freedom to move devices and people without any rewiring of buildings, or special cables, and with a single physical standard.
- User-controlled definition of video, digital, and data lines. You can use a line for digital personal service this hour, reconfigure the same phone line as an incoming 800 WATS line the next hour, and in the next hour redefine the line as a video line carrying pictures of a group videoconferencing session.

The Xerox Liveboard is an
electronic blackboard that
incorporates computer and
video technology, providing an
on-line forum for interactive
meetings throughout the world.

- Unlike with a PBX, you will be charged only for the service connect time, not the total overhead costs. The phone company assumes the costs and responsibility of installing and maintaining the equipment.

Briefly, ISDN is the everything network. The goal and promise of ISDN is to provide a more functional network to transport all kinds of digital information, regardless of its source or destination. It is a vision of the public switched-phone network turning into a vast digital super expressway.

In addition to supporting traditional services such as switched voice and private lines, ISDN also allows for new types of service such as higher transmission rates and part-time private line service. ISDN offers universal data connectivity in direct digital form. Modems are not used with ISDN except when they are needed to link up with a non-ISDN user.

ISDN uses standard twisted-pair copper wire to connect desktop devices to building-level concentrators. A central office switching device makes all connections to the outside world and controls the line characteristics. Two levels of service are offered: Basic Rate ISDN and Primary Rate ISDN.

Basic Rate ISDN serves a single desktop with three channels. Two channels are B channels with a capacity of 64 KBPS of digital data (voice, data, video). A third channel (D channel) carries control information, such as the phone number of a calling party, back and forth from the central office.

Primary Rate ISDN offers 1.5 MBPS of bandwidth. The bandwidth is divided into 23 B channels and one D channel. This service is intended to connect PBXs, central office switches, or computer systems with a need for high-speed data channels.

While these communications speeds are not noteworthy, there are plans on the drawing boards to take Basic Rate service up to 1.5 MBPS and Primary Rate service up to 50 MBPS. These speeds make ISDN fully competitive with anything offered by PBX manufacturers. With some simple technology changes, ordinary twisted copper telephone wire can be more fully utilized without expensive recabling.

Local and long-distance telephone companies are trying to stitch together isolated ISDN "islands" into a national network. Progress toward an ISDN nation will be accelerated greatly by the Federal Telephone System 2000 project, described in the Window on Technology, which is heavily based upon ISDN.

Currently ISDN faces a number of hurdles. Standards and tariffs (charges) are still undefined; ISDN is hamstrung by its current 64 KBPS B channels, which are fine for most PC applications but slow compared to 1 MBPS LANs. It is most useful in low-speed transaction oriented networks. LANs are still more appropriate for computing-intensive applications.

FIBER OPTICS TRANSMISSION STANDARD: FDDI

Fiber Distributed Data Interface (FDDI) is a standard for data transmission at 100 MBPS over fiber-optic cable in a ring configuration. FDDI LANs use the same token-passing technology as do token ring networks, but have a dual fiber optical ring configuration. Use of two rings instead of one increases reliability.

ELECTRONIC MAIL, EDI, AND PACKET-SWITCHING STANDARDS

X.400 is an IEEE and CCITT electronic mail system standard, which, if adopted, would permit E-mail systems operating on different hardware to communicate with one another. X.25 is an IEEE and CCITT packet-switching network protocol, which permits different international and national networks to communicate with one another. X.12 is a standardized transaction format for electronic data interchange in the United States (the dominant European standard is Edifact).

Software Standards

Standards are emerging for graphical user interfaces, operating systems, and tools required to build software applications.

TECHNOLOGY

FTS 2000: The New Digital Highway

The Federal Telecommunications System, used by federal employees at 1700 federal agencies, is the largest telephone system in the world. Operated by the U.S. federal government, FTS had been a relatively primitive voice-grade analog service, and was fragmented, expensive, unreliable and inefficient. So the federal government developed a powerful new telephone system called FTS 2000 (Federal Telephone System), awarding ten-year contracts to AT&T and Sprint Communications, Inc.

FTS 2000 is a new network that links 1.5 million users in 135 federal agencies in 3500 locations. The network features switched voice, data, packet-switched data, and video transmission, and dedicated high-speed, high-volume services. It can support videoconferencing, electronic mail, and high-speed data

transfer to 1.54 MBPS, and it provides emergency backup service to the public network. Initially, FTS 2000 will be able to move 70 pages of text per second from one desk to another. In essence, FTS is an ISDN standard digital network permitting each local telephone user complete access to a wide variety of services.

FTS 2000 is expected to cut the government's communications costs in half. Donald Scott, associate administrator for FTS 2000 at the General Services Agency, reported that FTS 2000 saved the federal government $500 million over three years, with prices lower than commercial rates.

FTS 2000 is the digital network for the entire U.S. government. State and local governments are expected to build similar systems in the long run. Since almost all large businesses interact with the fed-

eral government, FTS 2000 will most likely set telecommunications standards through the next century.

Sources: Gary H. Anthes, "FTS 2000 Users Anxious to Upgrade," *Computerworld* (September 21, 1992), and United States General Accounting Office, "FTS 2000: An Overview of the Federal Government's New Telecommunications System," GAO/IMTEC-90-17FS (February 1990).

To Think About: What problems can be solved by using an ISDN standard? What would happen if the federal government did not switch to an ISDN standard? If you were a manager, what factors would you consider in deciding whether to use ISDN?

GRAPHICAL USER INTERFACE STANDARD

X Windows: Standard for high-level graphics description used for standardized window management and construction of graphical user interfaces.

X Windows is a de facto standard for high-level graphics description necessary for standardized window management. X Windows can be operating-system independent, although it is currently used with the UNIX and DEC VAX/VMS operating systems. X Windows permits one to display multiple applications on the same screen and lets one application use many windows, display different fonts on the screen, and draw two-dimensional figures. The X Window system provides all of the tools necessary to build a multiwindow, icon-driven, graphical user interface.

OPERATING SYSTEMS STANDARDS: THE OPEN SYSTEMS MOVEMENT AND THE BATTLE OVER UNIX

The only nonproprietary operating system that can operate on all computers—from microcomputers to mainframes—is UNIX. However, the effort to make UNIX the operating system standard has encountered considerable opposition. UNIX is a powerful threat to existing proprietary operating systems and their attendant high-cost software. If UNIX became a standard operating system, the market for mainframe and minicomputer software would become much more competitive, prices would fall, new entrants would emerge, and old players would suffer.

The stakes are high. Briefly, standardized operating systems and communications links between computers would eliminate firms' dependence on one particular hardware vendor, such as IBM or DEC. Moreover, UNIX runs directly counter to the marketing plans of many large vendors. For instance, if UNIX becomes a standard, there is little need for Microsoft Corporation's Windows NT operating system or for IBM's OS/2. UNIX can deliver time-sharing, applications portability, seamless file transfer, and shared user interfaces. Because of the high stakes, vendors have split into two warring camps over the issue of what version of UNIX to support.

IBM and DEC teamed up with other computer companies (Apollo, Hewlett Packard, Nixdorf, Siemens AG, and Groupe Bull) in May 1988 to launch the Open Software Foundation (OSF), an open-systems standard that would take control of standardizing UNIX away from AT&T and Sun Corporation, who had formed UNIX International several years earlier. OSF operates as a non-profit organization promoting an open systems environment based on industry standards. The core of the OSF environment is a version of IBM's AIX (IBM's version of UNIX). Since 1985, the European Commission has urged Common Market members to require open-systems software for government computer bids and the use of UNIX.

THE APPLICATIONS PORTABILITY PROFILE

Applications Portability Profile (APP): Standards for operating systems, database management, data interchange, programming languages, user interfaces, and networking to be enforced by U.S. federal government procurements in order to achieve connectivity.

The National Institute for Standards and Technology (NIST) has developed an **Applications Portability Profile (APP)**, which identifies the standards to be enforced by the federal government to guide federal procurements through the 1990s. The components of the APP constitute a "toolbox" for developing and maintaining portable applications. APP includes standards for operating systems, database management, data interchange, network services, user interface, and programming languages. Figure 10.9 displays the components of the APP.

Table 10.2 summarizes all of the standards we have described. Any manager wishing to achieve some measure of connectivity in his or her organization should try to use them when designing networks, purchasing hardware and software, or developing information system applications.

10.4 Implementing the New Information Architecture

Most knowledgeable observers now believe that it will take at least a decade to fully utilize the potential of existing desktop equipment, let alone that of equipment yet to be developed. Implementing the new information architecture has created problems as well as opportunities for organizations.

Problems Posed by the New Architecture

The rapid, often unplanned, development of networks, micros, and workstations has created problems. We have already described the connectivity problems created by incompatible network components and standards. Four additional

Figure 10.9
The elements of the Applications Portability Profile. The Applications Portability Profile (APP) is a "toolbox" for developing and maintaining portable applications. It was developed by the National Institute for Standards and Technology to promote connectivity in applications for the U.S. Government. Posix is a standard interface between an application program and an operating system. Each area of the Applications Portability Profile has a precise standard that should be used.

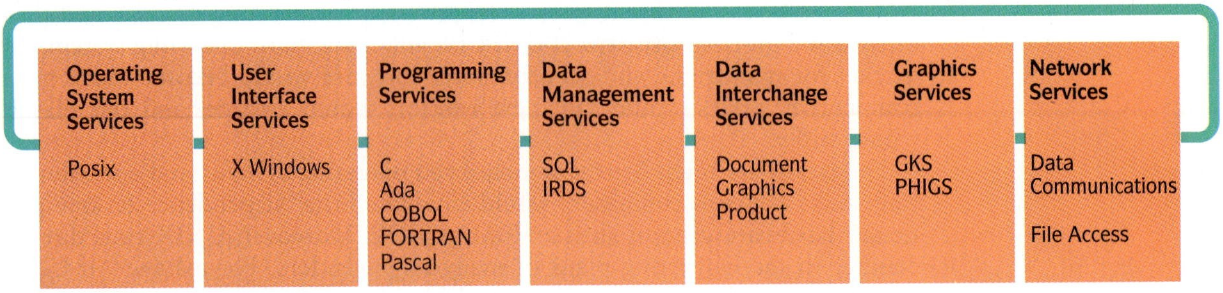

Operating System Services	User Interface Services	Programming Services	Data Management Services	Data Interchange Services	Graphics Services	Network Services
Posix	X Windows	C Ada COBOL FORTRAN Pascal	SQL IRDS	Document Graphics Product	GKS PHIGS	Data Communications File Access

IRDS = Information Resource Dictionary System
GKS = Graphical Kernel System
PHIGS = Programmer's Hierarchical Interactive Graphics System

Table 10.2 Standards for Achieving Connectivity

Area	Standard or Reference Model
Networking	OSI, TCP/IP, SNA
Fiber optic transmission	FDDI
Digital public switched network transmission	ISDN
Electronic mail	X.400
Packet switching	X.25
EDI	X.12
Graphical user interface	X Windows
Operating system	UNIX
Software application	APP

problems stand out: controlling the independence of end users; ensuring network security and reliability; loss of management control over information systems; and the hidden cost of client/server computing.

INDEPENDENCE OF END USERS

The dilemma posed by desktop computing has always been one of central management control versus end-user creativity and productivity. Permitting end users to choose hardware and software has led to complete chaos and high costs in firms. With desktop computing tools, end users can easily create their own applications and files. It becomes increasingly difficult to determine where data are located and to ensure that the same piece of information, such as a product number, is used consistently throughout the organization. User-developed applications may combine incompatible pieces of hardware and software. Yet observers worry that the data processing vision, with its emphasis on mainframe compatibility and required telecommunications links, will stifle the independence and creativity of end users and reduce their ability to define their own information needs.

ENSURING NETWORK SECURITY AND RELIABILITY

Security is of paramount importance in organizations where information systems make extensive use of networks. There are many points of access and opportunities for end users to access and modify data in networks. How can an organization rely on data if one cannot prove where the data came from and who modified them along the way?

Performance monitoring tools for client/server networks (for instance, monitoring CPU usage)—are not as well-developed or sophisticated as the tools that are available for mainframes or minis. Organizations need to establish special procedures so that users will not accidentally wipe out corporate information. "Downtime," periods of time in which the system is not operational, is much more frequent in client/server systems than in established mainframe systems and should be considered carefully before one takes essential applications off the mainframe.

LOSS OF MANAGEMENT CONTROL

The new information architecture has the potential to change the distribution of power, perquisites, advantages, and resources in organizations. Insofar as information confers power, independence, and advantage, then desktop computing changes existing power arrangements. In the 1970s, information systems were confined to a few data processing centers in the organization. By the early 1980s, some large organizations had anywhere from five to fifteen data centers, each linked to networks of minicomputers and mainframes. Nevertheless, the information processing function—that is, the information resources of the company—was confined to relatively small cells where key decisions were made slowly and were analyzed thoroughly; the data processing and human and technological resources were carefully balanced, weighed, and measured.

With desktop computing in the 1990s, however, the organization is composed not of 1, 2, 10, or 20 data centers, but of 1000, 5000, or 20,000 computing centers; conceivably, every employee in the future will become a computing center by virtue of having access to a very powerful microcomputer. Each employee will become a player in the definition of data and information and in its collection, storage, and dissemination. Since data and software are no longer confined to the mainframe under the management of the traditional information systems department, it becomes difficult to ensure that any change to business rules, such as how to verify an account number, is made to every application on every desktop system.

HIDDEN COST OF CLIENT/SERVER COMPUTING

Many companies that have moved to client/server computing have found that the savings they expected did not materialize because of unexpected costs. Hardware savings resulting from significantly lower costs of MIPs on microcomputers are often offset by the high cost of additional labor and time required for network and system management. Vendors have not yet provided tools for comprehensive, centralized management of distributed systems with heterogeneous hardware and software components tied together. People need to deal with software coordination, troubleshooting, and configuration management at every computing installation.

Changing to information systems using client/server processing typically increases training costs for both information systems specialists and end users (see the Window on Organizations). When changing to client/server computing, information systems specialists typically need more training in performance analysis, configuration management, archiving, and backup, in a network environment.

It is difficult to determine what pieces of an application should be placed on a client and which are suited to the server. It is not always evident how a new application could affect network performance.

Most mainframe or minicomputer systems have tools and guidelines to monitor system use, to partition work loads, and to help plan future hardware purchases. Capacity planning tools are not well developed for microcomputer networks. Many client/server applications and tools were developed to handle the communications of small work groups and cannot always be scaled up to work with hundreds and thousands of users.

CONNECTIVITY AND COORDINATION

The new information architecture is highly sensitive to different versions of operating systems and network management software. Some applications require specific versions of operating systems and network management software. It is difficult to make all of the components of large heterogeneous networks work together as smoothly as management envisons.

Some Solutions

Organizations can counteract problems created by the new information architecture by increasing end-user training, by asserting data administration disciplines, and by considering connectivity when planning their information architecture.

EDUCATION

Training to use desktop computers and networked applications is incomplete or entirely absent in many firms. Senior managers have not understood that it takes many hours for employees to learn how to use desktop applications and networks. They have not appreciated the ergonomic problems created by continuous use of computer terminals. (*Ergonomics* refers to the interaction of people and machines in the work environment.) A well-developed training program can help in overcoming problems resulting from the lack of corporate support and understanding (Westin et al., 1985; Bikson et al., 1985).

ORGANIZATIONS

Training Slows Texaco Down

The Scientific Systems Management (SSM) Group at Texaco, Inc. was assigned to find a way to provide users with seamless access to multiple mainframe and mini-computer-based databases containing oil exploration and production data. Texaco also wanted SSM to create a computing environment where new and existing applications could access data companywide.

SSM solved part of the problem by building a relational database running on a UNIX-based file server from Sun Microsystems, Inc. with a series of gateways. SSM's 10-person development team either developed these gateways themselves or purchased them. Users access oil exploration data and production data from 80386-based microcomputers and UNIX workstations.

The project took 18 months to complete and cost about $1.5 million, of which $1 million was spent on labor and the rest on hardware

and software. It took twice as long as originally estimated to convert the first sets of applications, which were for map generation and oil well analysis. Texaco underestimated the time and cost required to train both programmers and end users. Training took 50 percent longer and cost 300 percent more than expected.

It took nine months to separate data from applications. Texaco's programmers had been used to writing programs in FORTRAN and lacked expertise in the C programming language and in programming for a Windows graphical user interface environment. Users required additional training to use networks properly.

Hardware and software vendors were of limited help. Software vendors lacked client/server expertise and had trouble visualizing a client/server environment in an end-user setting.

Tom Peters, SSM's data group manager, observed that switching to client/server computing is more difficult than most people think. The hardware is relatively inexpensive, but it is very easy to underestimate training and implementation costs.

Many firms like Texaco have found that moving applications from mainframes to smaller systems saves as much as 50 percent in hardware costs, but such savings can be offset by the costs of setting up and running a client/server environment.

Source: Lynn Berg, "The SCOOP on Client/Server Costs," *Computerworld* (November 16, 1992).

To Think About: If you were a manager, what organization, technology, and management factors would you consider when deciding whether to switch to a client/server environment?

DATA ADMINISTRATION DISCIPLINES

Chapter 8 described the role of the data administration function in the organization. This role becomes even more important when networks link many different applications and business areas. Organizations must systematically identify where their data are located, which groups are responsible for maintaining each piece of data, and which individuals and groups are allowed to access and use that data. They need to develop specific policies and procedures to ensure that their data are accurate and available only to authorized users.

PLANNING FOR CONNECTIVITY

Workstations in a networked environment must be compatible with the other components of expensive telecommunications networks and with new mainframe software. Senior management must take a long-term view of the firm's information architecture and must make sure that its systems have the right degree of connectivity for its current and future information needs.

Most organizations do not have an idea of how much connectivity they have or how much they lack. The first step is to perform a **connectivity audit,** which examines five areas of connectivity in an organization:

Connectivity audit: A method for examining amount of connectivity an organization has by examining five areas of connectivity such as network standards, user interfaces and applications.

1. *Networks.* How many networks are there? For what class of machines? Who manufactures them? Where are they? How much did they cost?
2. *Network management and user support.* Who is in charge of the networks that have been identified? Are accurate records kept of utilization? What are the authorization procedures? How many staff members maintain and support each network and train its end users? How much does this cost?

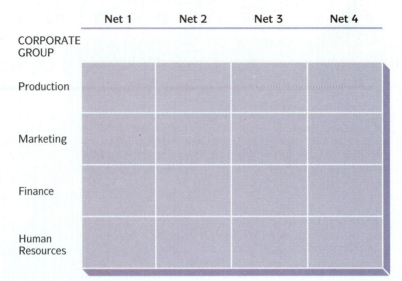

	Net 1	Net 2	Net 3	Net 4
CORPORATE GROUP				
Production				
Marketing				
Finance				
Human Resources				

Figure 10.10
A connectivity matrix. As part of a connectivity audit, the auditor can complete this connectivity matrix to identify how networks are used and by whom. The major networks are placed on the horizontal axis and the corporate user groups are placed on the vertical axis.

3. *Network services.* What services do the existing networks perform? For whom? How are the costs allocated?
4. *Applications.* What kinds of applications are supported by networks? How important are the applications to production and to information interchange?
5. *User interfaces.* What user interfaces are currently used? How do they connect or relate to one another? What applications run under various interfaces?

A connectivity matrix, composed of the major networks along the top axis and the major corporate user groups along the vertical access, can help identify how networks are used and by whom (Figure 10.10). If documented properly, the connectivity matrix should identify many areas where current networks fail to provide connectivity.

The connectivity audit period is an ideal time to interview key corporate users in order to identify problem areas and potential solutions. Clearly, complete connectivity is usually not needed in most corporations (see the Window on Management). It is far more sensible to identify classes of connectivity problems and general solutions (however, the solutions should not be so general as to require rewiring the entire company). There is a dilemma here. On one hand, it is very expensive to develop gateway solutions one at a time, solving brush fires as they flare up. On the other hand, it is usually too expensive to achieve systemic connectivity for older applications.

Managers have several connectivity strategies to consider. One strategy tries to identify a class of connectivity problems and provide a general solution. If the connectivity audit identifies large numbers of microcomputer users seeking access to mainframe data, management should try to develop a generic strategy to solve these problems. The strategy might include 1) assuring that a single microcomputer hardware model is the standard, 2) assuring that a single network vendor is chosen, and 3) developing on the mainframe side a coherent long-term strategy for integrating desktop workstations, such as implementing OSI network standards.

A longer-term strategy accepts the reality of today's incompatible systems but maintains a vision of the future, where connectivity is an important goal. Procurement strategy then should focus on new systems and follow the simple rule that, from today, systems will be developed only if 1) they support connectivity standards developed by the firm, and 2) they build upon existing networks and user applications in a seamless fashion.

MANAGEMENT

How Noranda Moved to Companywide Standards

The last year that Noranda, the $8.5 million Canadian natural resources company, owned a mainframe computer was 1985. Its 60 operating companies now use minicomputers to handle their own processing. Noranda started distributing computing in the late 1970s with multiple minicomputers. Noranda is now implementing a client/server model of the new information architecture and it is developing a single set of companywide standards.

Noranda's management believes that establishing software and communications standards will reduce software development costs. Different business units can share common applications such as process manufacturing software for mining, pulp plants, and natural gas companies. The various business units can also share the technical skills required to develop and maintain these applications.

Only a fraction of Noranda's data flows from one operating unit to another or to corporate headquarters. However, financial data such as consolidated sales figures are sent to Noranda headquarters and are processed on Hewlett Packard computers.

Noranda's information systems group developed its own comprehensive set of software standards in 1990 as part of its move to UNIX open systems and client/server computing. Task forces surveyed products in various categories and selected one standard for each, based on key criteria such as usefulness and the availability of technical support around the world. Noranda selected a single relational database management system, Ingres 6.4, and Ingres application development tools, but it is allowing some business units to keep their own database software and development tools.

Noranda uses other standards such as TCP/IP for networking, the UNIX operating system, and the Open Software Foundation's OSF/Motif and Microsoft Windows for graphical user interfaces.

Noranda is using friendly persuasion to gain support for corporate-wide standards among its operating units. It uses a coordinating committee called Noranda Enterprise Wide Systems (NEWS) group to gain compliance with its standards. NEWS has quarterly teleconferences, an annual on-site meeting, and monthly telephone calls. About

one-third of Noranda's companies send representatives to these meetings. According to NEWS chairman Murray Dunnigan, manager of information services at James Maclaren, Inc., a Noranda pulp and paper manufacturing unit in Masson, Quebec, NEWS gets the best people together, identifies the best practices in their companies, and the best technology. Noranda pays half the cost if an operating unit installs corporate standard software.

NEWS identified eight core applications that can be shared by many business units, but no single unit adopted more than two of them. Noranda does not maintain that it can standardize systems for the entire enterprise, but it has a model that can be applied to each operating unit.

Source: Jean S. Bozman, "Canadian Firm Uses Leverage to Enforce Enterprise-wide Standards," *Computerworld* (December 7, 1992).

To Think About: What kinds of standards are in place at Noranda? How successful has Noranda been in enforcing companywide standards? Why? How much connectivity is there at Noranda?

Once management has identified specific areas where connectivity is needed, it is in a position to measure how much solutions cost. Costs of networks, machines, software, and cable are usually easily measured, whereas benefits are much more difficult to determine. In terms of positions saved or reduced, productivity enhanced, and bottom-line results like more customer orders, connectivity benefits are often elusive to measure, however palpable. One possibility is to measure opportunity costs—how much extra time employees and customers must spend in order to interact with existing systems. These opportunity costs are often much easier to measure.

If we look back to the recent past and consider the promising developments of the future, we can see two lessons emerge. First, seemingly small problems in connectivity should not be solved one at a time, piecemeal, without a larger vision of how to address the connectivity and architecture problems of a business. Pursuit of a piecemeal approach seems to guarantee problems down the road. Second, it is very risky to rely on a single vendor of mainframes or minicomputers to provide connectivity solutions. To follow this approach is to lock one's firm into a particular operating system and very expensive software that can operate only on very costly machines. In the past, this strategy has resulted in enterprisewide nightmares rather than connectivity.

1. **The new information architecture requires a complete change of mindset.** Companies must consider a different organizational structure, a different support structure for information systems, and different procedures for managing employees and desktop processing functions. To implement networked computing successfully, companies must examine and perhaps redesign an entire business process rather than throw new technology at existing business practices and hope that it will stick. It is not so much the technology that impedes implementation of the new information architecture as it is the careful planning required to implement it.

2. **Connectivity and standards are very difficult to enforce, even when a firm's connectivity needs are well understood.** Firms are reluctant to abandon their existing, albeit incompatible systems because these systems represented such large investments. Corporate culture and competing interest groups within the firm often resist change. Business practices tend to favor short-term efforts over the long-term planning that is essential for creating an open systems environment.

3. **Resolving the centralization vs. decentralization debate.** Since the growth of minicomputers in the 1970s, a long-standing issue among IS managers and CEOs has been the question of centralization. Should processing power and data be distributed to departments and divisions, or should they be concentrated at a central location? The new architecture facilitates decentralization, but this may not always be in the organization's best interest. Managers need to make sure that the commitment to systems centralization or decentralization actually serves organizational objectives.

Summary

Describe the characteristics of the new information architecture.

The new information architecture has produced a mixed environment composed mostly of desktop workstations and microcomputers. Although it often contains minicomputers and mainframes, computing power tends to take place on the desktop. The organization's hardware, software, and data are much more controlled from the desktop by the professional who uses the desktop machine. The system is a network or multiple networks connecting many local area networks and devices.

There are three visions for implementing the new information architecture, each describing a different role for desktop processing in the organization. In the data processing vision, microcomputers and workstations are considered to be appendages of the mainframe data processing environment. In the logical office vision, work and processing power are portable. The automated workplace vision makes microcomputers and workstations the centerpiece of the workplace of the future, placing processing at the desktop and controlling the other components of a network.

Explain the difference between the client/server and X terminal implementations of the new architecture.

In the client/server model, computer processing is split between "clients" on a network and "servers," with each function being assigned to the machine best suited to perform it. The user generally interacts only with the client portion of the application. The exact division of tasks between client and server depends on the nature of the application.

In the X terminal model, local desktop machines are merely terminals that can access the operations of several different remote computers at once; they do not have any independent computing power.

Explain why connectivity is essential for the new architecture.

Connectivity is a measure of how well computers and computer-based devices can communicate with one another and "share" information in a meaningful way without human intervention. It is essential in the new information architecture where different hardware, software, and network components must work together to transfer information seamlessly from one part of the organization to another. Applications portability, open systems, migration, information portability, cooperative processing, and interoperability are all aspects of connectivity.

Describe different models of network connectivity.

There are several different models for achieving connectivity in networks. Public reference models like OSI and TCP/IP are recognized as important telecommunications ingredients for enhancing connectivity. Proprietary approaches like IBM's SNA offer important communications-based approaches for many firms committed to this firm's hardware.

Describe important standards used for linking hardware, software, and networks.

ISDN for digital transmission over telephone lines; FDDI for 100 megabit fiber optic transmission; X.400 for electronic mail, X.12 for EDI; and X.25 for packet switching are emerging standards used in networking. UNIX is an operating systems standard that can be used to create open systems. X Windows is a graphical interface standard. The Applications Portability Profile (APP) includes standards for operating systems, database management, data interchange, network services, user interface, and programming languages used for U.S. federal government procurements.

Identify problems posed by the new architecture.

Implementing the desktop revolution in a coherent way is no small task. There are problems in connecting mainframes to PCs; users become highly independent; much higher levels of support and training are required; and security of data weakens. Managers often face shifts in the distribution of power and a loss of control over computing; they must also rethink how information and processing power should be distributed.

Describe strategies for managing the transition to a new architecture.

As organizations develop integrated architecture plans, these organizations will naturally come to exercise more influence over desktop computing. The growth of enterprisewide networks in particular demands central planning and management of the desktop. The desktop eventually becomes part of normal management procedures. However, policy does not emerge by accident. The desktop may be the most strategic application of computing, and senior management must carefully consider how desktop computing can be integrated into the overall corporate information architecture.

While many corporations have assumed complete connectivity as a strategic goal, a more reasonable strategy would move incrementally toward greater connectivity while not giving up the vision of connectivity. The first step is to perform a connectivity audit to identify existing capabilities and future needs. From here a strategy can be developed that will lead the firm toward an amount of connectivity that is suitable for the industry and the nature of the business.

Key Terms

New information architecture	Open systems
Client/server model	Reference model
X terminal model	Protocol
Videotex	Standard
Data processing vision	Open Systems Interconnect (OSI)
Logical office	Transmission Control Protocol/Internet
Automated workplace	Protocol (TCP/IP)
Connectivity	Systems Network Architecture (SNA)
Applications portability	Integrated Services Digital Network
Migration	(ISDN)
Cooperative processing	X Windows
Information portability	Applications Portability Profile (APP)
Interoperability	Connectivity audit

1. List five characteristics of the new information architecture.

2. What is the difference between the client/server model and an X terminal model of the new information architecture?

3. What changes in technology and economic conditions have contributed to the desktop revolution?

4. What are the three different visions of the new information architecture? Why do these differences exist?

5. What is connectivity? Why is it a goal for the new information architecture?

6. Give five examples of connectivity problems involving both hardware and software.

7. What are the major causes of connectivity problems? How are these causal factors changing?

8. Make a list and be able to discuss the meaning of the six different aspects of connectivity.

9. Compare OSI, TCP/IP, and SNA. Why are these limited solutions to network connectivity problems?

10. Describe ISDN and explain why it is important.

11. Why is UNIX important to connectivity?

12. What are FDDI, X.25, X.400, and X Windows?

13. Give four examples of problems in implementing the new information architecture.

14. What are some solutions to the problems raised in the previous question?

15. What are the five ingredients of a connectivity audit?

1. Is there too much power being put on the desktops of business firms?

2. If we can work out of our homes, vans, and vacation spots, then why should we go to work at all?

3. If computing increasingly moves to the desktop, what new kinds of skills will be required of entry-level employees and management trainees? Is there any point in maintaining an information systems department when most of the computing power of the corporation resides on a desktop?

4. What problems result from choosing a single vendor's hardware and software to attain long-term connectivity?

5. Your employer has just announced a new strategic program to achieve complete connectivity of your firm's information systems in five years. What are some of the difficulties and potential dangers of such a policy?

Form a group with three or four of your classmates. Perform a connectivity audit of the information systems used by your university, using the guidelines provided in this chapter. Complete a connectivity matrix. How much connectivity exists at your university? Is this sufficient? If not, recommend a strategy for the university to achieve higher levels of connectivity in the next five years. Present your findings to the class.

CASE STUDY

Unilever Tries to Unify World Operations

The sun never sets on the worldwide holdings of Unilever, one of the world's largest multinational corporations. The sprawling conglomerate has over 350,000 employees in more than 500 companies located in 75 countries. Its holdings include T.J. Lipton, Calvin Klein Cosmetics, and Lever Brothers. Unilever's largest core business is food products. Since the 1980s, Unilever has bought more than 100 businesses and sold nearly twice as many. Nevertheless, its cost-conscious management has made sure it has a rich supply of available cash and relatively little debt.

Unilever maintains a measure of centralized control but allows decentralized operating units to meet the needs of local markets in different countries. The firm tries to "Unileverize" its managers with a common organizational culture that transcends national boundaries. Managers are trained at Unilever's international management training college near London and are assigned job positions in various countries throughout their careers.

The senior management of this London- and Rotterdam-based firm believed that with so many companies under one roof, Unilever was "drowning in technology." Unilever had many redundant systems as well as many systems that were poorly conceived and poorly implemented. Management handed Michael Johnson, Unilever's head of information technology, the responsibility of standardizing the behemoth's multitudinous hardware and software systems around an open systems architecture and bringing them together in a global network.

Unilever's old laissez-faire approach toward information systems had left it with a polyglot mix of hardware and software. Despite the official corporate policy of only using IBM, Hewlett Packard or DEC hardware, the firm had drastic incompatibility problems. The systems of various operating units had mushroomed out of control. To make his plan work, Johnson had to convince his three designated hardware vendors to cooperate on a cross-vendor software architecture.

According to Norman Weizer, a senior consultant with Big Six accounting firm Arthur D. Little, the challenge for global firms is to provide companywide information in a consistent, common format while allowing local units to perform effectively. Unilever wanted to pursue this goal by providing a common foundation for disparate far-flung operations without hamstringing its businesses.

Johnson moved quickly. In June 1990 he started focusing on applications portability. He told Unilever's three primary hardware suppliers—IBM, DEC, and Hewlett Packard—that he wanted to be able to build an application and port it anywhere in the world within ten days. He especially wanted to build "competitive-edge applications" in one place, send them to other Unilever companies, and install them instantly as if the recipients had developed them themselves.

Johnson enlisted Unilever's key hardware and software vendors to agree upon an open systems architecture for the firm that could serve as the foundation for a global network. Unilever chose the suite of standards built around the Open Software Foundation's Applications Environment Specification (AES) for systems and software throughout the corporation. AES is a massive suite of standards that includes elements of the OSF/1 operating system, the Motif graphical user interface, OSF's Distributed Computing Environment, SQL (Structured Query Language), and Posix (Posix establishes a standard interface between an applications program and an operating system rather than requiring a specific operating system).

With this base environment, Johnson added important software and database standards. Unilever chose Oracle and Sybase Inc.'s database management systems, Lotus 1-2-3 spreadsheet software, and WordPerfect word processing software. Oracle's SQL Forms and Unify Corporation's Uniface applications environments were selected as front-end software development standards.

Johnson and his team decided to use AES's distributed client/server capabilities as the foundation for Unilever's global data network. Unilever chose Sprint International to manage its pan-European data network. Eventually Unilever hopes its software tools and global network will provide the technology to manage group projects around the world.

Unilever believes its move to open systems has not stifled local technology innovation. For instance, Quest International, a Unilever food ingredients and fragrance company based in England and the Netherlands, is using AES standards to develop its critical applications. Quest is relatively small (its 1991 revenue was $842 million) and it could move quickly to new standards.

While Johnson has taken a strong position about standards and open systems, he does not want to disrupt the company's operations during implementation. He realizes that he will not be able to make all of Unilever's operations switch to open systems overnight. Unilever inherited hundreds of proprietary applications that Johnson wants to leave in place until his staff figures out how to make them communicate among computers. While Unilever's companywide open systems model excludes proprietary systems such as those using IBM's AS/400 minicomputer environment, it is too costly to shut down these machines right away. Johnson is letting companies with AS/400 computers delay the changeover while mandating that all new software purchased or developed for the AS/400 computers must be portable to RISC (reduced instruction set computing) machines that are compatible with AES standards.

Sources: Joshua Greenbaum, "Unilever's Unifying Theme," *InformationWEEK* (March 2, 1992), and Floris A. Maljers, "Inside Unilever:" The Evolving Transnational Company," *Harvard Business Review* (September–October 1992).

Case Study Questions

1. How serious were Unilever's connectivity problems? What management, technology and organization factors were responsible for these problems?

2. How would you characterize Unilever's strategy for dealing with connectivity problems? Do you agree with this strategy?

3. How much connectivity should there be at a firm like Unilever? Would you recommend a five-year systems plan for Unilever to achieve a higher level of connectivity? If so, describe your plan.

References

Apple Desktop Communications Solutions Reference Guide, Apple Computer, Inc., 1989.

Auditore, Stephen, "The Joy of X . . . Terminals." *Computerworld* (July 6, 1992).

Berg, Lynn. "The SCOOP on Client/Server Costs." *Computerworld* (November 16, 1992).

Bikson, Tora K., J. D. Eveland, and Barbara A. Gutek. "Flexible Interactive Technologies for Multi-Person Tasks: Current Problems and Future Prospects." Rand Corporation (December 1988).

Bikson, Tora K., Cathleen Stasz, and Donald A. Mankin. "Computer-Mediated Work: Individual and Organizational Impact on One Corporate Headquarters." Rand Corporation (1985).

Bochenski, Barbara, "Enterprise Developers Work to Tap the Internet." *Software Magazine* (February 1992).

Cashin, Jerry. " 'APP' Offers Guidelines for Federal Purchasing." *Software Magazine* (August 1991).

De Pompa, Barbara. "More Power at Your Fingertips." *InformationWEEK*, (December 30, 1991).

Dion, William R. "Client/Server Computing." *Personal Workstation* (May 1990).

Fisher, Sharon. "TCP/IP." *Computerworld* (October 7, 1991).

Guimaraes, Tom. "Personal Computing Trends and Problems: An Empirical Study." *MIS Quarterly* (June 1986).

Hof, Robert D. "Computer Confusion." *Business Week* (June 10, 1991).

Huff, Sid, Malcolm C. Munro, and Barbara H. Martin. "Growth Stages of End User Computing." *Communications of the ACM* (May 1988).

Johnson, Jim. "A Survival Guide for Administrators." *Software Magazine* (December 1992).

Laudon, Kenneth C. "From PCs to Managerial Workstations." In Matthias Jarke, *Managers, Micros, and Mainframes*. New York: John Wiley, 1986.

Lee, Denis M. "Usage Pattern and Sources of Assistance for Personal Computer Users." *MIS Quarterly* (December 1986).

Lee, Sunro and Richard P. Leifer. "A Framework for Linking the Structure of Information Systems with Organizational Requirements for Information Sharing." *Journal of Management Information Systems* 8, no. 4 (Spring 1992).

"Plans and Policies for Client/Server Technology." *I/S Analyzer* 30, no. 4 (April 1992).

Pyburn, Philip J. "Managing Personal Computer Use: The Role of Corporate Management Information Systems." *Journal of Management Information Systems* (Winter 1986–87).

Rash, Wayne, Jr. "Corporate Connections." *Byte* (September 1991).

Richardson, Gary L., Brad M. Jackson, and Gary W. Dickson. "A Principles-Based Enterprise Architecture: Lessons from Texaco and Star Enterprise." *MIS Quarterly* 14, no. 4 (December 1990).

Sinha, Alok. "Client-Server Computing." *Communications of the ACM* 35 no. 7 (July 1992).

Smarr, Larry, and Charles E. Catlett. "Metacomputing." *Communications of the ACM* 35, no. 6 (June 1992).

Tash, Jeffrey B., and Paul Korzeniowski. "Theory Meets Reality for New Breed of APPs." *Software Magazine* (May 1992).

United States General Accounting Office. "FTS 2000: An Overview of the Federal Government's New Telecommunications System." *GAO/IMTEC-90-17FS* (February 1990).

Westin, Alan F., Heather A. Schwader, Michael A. Baker, and Sheila Lehman. *The Changing Workplace*. New York: Knowledge Industries, 1985.

To Downsize or Not to Downsize?

Recently, the CEO at a major transportation company called the vice president of information systems into his office and chewed him out because the firm still depended heavily on mainframe computers. A member of the board of directors had told the CEO that his own company was moving successfully off the mainframe to microcomputer-based client/server networks. The CEO wanted to know why millions of dollars were being wasted on mainframe software and processing power in his company if smaller computers and networks could do the same work at a fraction of the cost.

Many other firms are asking these questions, too. The movement to downsize to smaller computers has mushroomed over the past several years. Some firms have moved portions of their processing from mainframes to minicomputers or microcomputer-based networks. Some even have managed to eliminate mainframes altogether.

Taylor Medical, Inc., a health care equipment supplier in Beaumont, Texas, was founded in 1987. Within four years it was serving 16,000 accounts nationwide and was registering annual sales of $100 million. With growth like that it is no wonder that Chief Information Officer (CIO) Jim Hayes found that his computer system had become inadequate. Hayes knew he had a problem when the cash application system response time was so slow that he told one of his employees in the cash applications department to "bring in your needlepoint" to reduce her frustration while waiting for the computer to finish processing.

Hayes was running six IBM System 36 minicomputers at four sites. More than 150 Taylor employees used the system for order entry, inventory control, and accounts receivable. These applications were written in RPG III, a programming language designed specifically to run on IBM minicomputers. To speed up the system Hayes first considered adding yet another System 36 or upgrading to a more powerful IBM AS/400 minicomputer. Instead, he chose to downsize, installing a multi-user system based on six Compaq 486/33L file servers to run a Novell NetWare local area network. For the network operating system he selected Citrix's Multiuser, a multiuser version of OS/2. Many of the applications were ported over to California Software Products' Baby/4XX, an RPG emulator that Hayes purchased to save his investment in existing RPG systems. (Baby/4XX gives applications originally written in RPG to run on a System 36 minicomputer the ability to run on microcomputers.) To hook up users to the network, he simply installed terminal cards in the employees' existing microcomputers. Taylor continued to use its System 36 minicomputers, which are linked to terminals and the networked microcomputers, but it plans eventually to phase them out.

Hayes felt that merely adding another IBM System 36 minicomputer would not satisfy Taylor's needs for in-creased processing speed and disk storage capacity. Taylor's downsizing project was gradual—the company continued to use its minicomputers, just adding networked microcomputers to the configuration. Hayes did not select UNIX, even though it is designed as a multiuser operating system and as such has been the system of choice for many who are downsizing and combining hardware and software elements from multiple vendors. Connecting microcomputers running Citrix Multiuser to a Novell NetWare LAN is considered easier to accomplish than connecting micros to LANs using UNIX. Terminal users can access shared printers, modems, and other peripherals on the LAN, although it is difficult to send E-mail in this environment. The equipment Hayes put on desktops was not particularly "high tech" and did not require providing each user with a full-function microcomputer. With Citrix Multiuser, Taylor can support 30 or 40 employees on terminals connected to only 6 file servers. Hayes initially had 100 users running Taylor Medical's accounting applications on the new system, with the intention of adding other applications as the system matured. The system is set up so that Taylor can add more terminals and workstations when required. Most of Taylor's employees use the network for simplified repetitive applications such as order entry, because these workers are not microcomputer-literate.

The project appears to have been an unqualified success. Hayes has about 200 users connected to the system. Because of the increased power, the applications run much faster—for example, an accounts receivable run timed at eight hours on the System 36 now takes about 30 minutes. Moreover, the system has a great deal of room for expansion. Taylor can add another 30 to 40 users on the current configuration and can expand the number of Compaq servers should it need to. Finally, all of this was accomplished with fewer dollars than would have been necessary had Hayes chosen to increase Taylor's minicomputer capacity.

By its own admission, Harley-Davidson was less successful with its downsizing project. At one time, this only remaining U.S.-based manufacturer of motorcycles was all but declared dead by the stock market. Since the early 1990s, it has come roaring back and has been very profitable and is growing. In 1989, to cut costs, the company decided to downsize, moving from a highly centralized mainframe architecture to an environment of PCs networked with IBM AS/400 minicomputers. According to Jeffrey Bleustein, senior vice-president at Harley-Davidson, the company took this step to save money. Bleustein estimated that Harley-Davidson "would save a lot [by downsizing] versus upgrading our mainframe." They estimated that the original savings "would be 50 percent for downsizing rather than upgrading. Bleustein then expected to save an additional 35 percent every year in operating costs.

However, in 1992 Bleustein indicated that the company has not been able to achieve the expected savings. He labeled the projected savings as a "theoretical exercise." Harley-Davidson's MIS director, Richard Kilbe, indicated that much of the problem lies with the support and skills of the employees. One of the problems they faced was with the users who were quite comfortable with the mainframe environment. Harley found that the move to a network has been a traumatic experience for the end users, resulting in the need for a great deal of retraining. MIS also experienced major difficulties, requiring a significant retraining effort. Kilbe claims the change is forcing ". . . both MIS and end users to reexamine the way they do business." Bleustein summed up the situation by saying that the move from one architecture to another has left them stuck in a transition of between two to three years, facing "the worst of both worlds."

Millpore Corporation in Bedford, Massachusetts, which manufactures technical separation equipment, started to downsize and to consolidate three computer centers in the United States in 1989. It wanted to switch from IBM, Data General, and Hewlett Packard host computers to two file servers from Sequent Computer Systems Inc. that would run software from the Oracle Corporation on a Transmission Control Protocol/Internet Protocol (TCP/IP) network. Millpore initially believed that the new setup would require one-third fewer information systems staff members to support it and budgeted accordingly. Millpore invested in networks, user workstations, hardware, software, and training, and it hired consultants to supplement its internal information systems staff during the early phases of conversion to the network. Actual spending turned out to be higher than initial projections, although Millpore believes the company will end up with much heftier computing resources and lower long-term costs.

Keyport Life Insurance Company in Boston moved its insurance policy administration and other applications from two mainframe computers to local area networks and found that the network file server based on a microcomputer with an 80386 microprocessor wasn't large enough to manage the company's policy load. Keyport maintained 180,000 policies on the database. The firm had to find a more powerful file server and switched to a NetFrame 450 superserver from Net Frame Systems Inc. of Milpitas, California, running on an Ethernet LAN. Keyport also found that running backups of the system over a local area network with a microcomputer is painfully slow, taking five hours nightly or ten hours for a full backup. Keyport did report savings of $1.3 million from its annual $5 million information systems budget.

Calspan, the research and development division of Arvin Industries, Inc., a diversified manufacturer in Buffalo, New York, began a three-year downsizing program in 1987. When Calspan replaced a centralized IBM mainframe system with a network based on two VAX 8200 computers, the division's 120 engineering-oriented users took off in every direction. One group of users set up a TCP/IP network and purchased a terminal server for UNIX terminals. But the terminal server they purchased couldn't work with TCP/IP and the VAX terminal network protocol. Other users put Macintosh microcomputers on their desks without making any provisions to handle backup. Today Calspan runs a mix of 40 to 50 assorted UNIX workstations, 40 to 50 Macintosh microcomputers, a dozen or so IBM Personal System/2 microcomputers, a VAX 8550 minicomputer, a Micro VAX 3100 Model 30 minicomputer, and various terminals connected more or less to the VAX network backbone. James Campobello, VAX systems manager, fears that much of the cost savings of the downsized systems are being eaten up by continual maintenance and cumbersome multistep conversions.

Breuners Home Furniture of Pleasant Hill, California, started its downsizing project in 1990, giving itself over two years to complete the project. While we do not yet know how successful the project has been, its approach raises interesting issues.

Breuners is a chain of 20 furniture stores in three west coast states with an annual revenue (1990) of $120 million. It had been in COBOL mainframe environment for 15 years, using an IBM 4341 when the project began. The new architecture is a PC-based network using two small, Hewlett Packard file servers. The new software environment consists of C, BASIC, UNIX and object-oriented programming. All the mainframe applications are being downsized and rewritten for this new environment. The IBM 4341 is being eliminated.

Breuners has indicated several reasons for downsizing. According to Stephen Wong, president of the company, "The old mainframe system became dysfunctional over time . . . fifteen years after it was installed, the system was determining how the business was run, rather than the other way around." In addition, John Longridge, vice president of MIS, is expecting a dramatic reduction in software maintenance costs. According to Longridge, "For the amount we spend in one month for IBM software rental, we can have a year's worth of maintenance on the HP-UX operating system and the databases." He also expects that moving to a smaller, more flexible system will reduce data entry errors, which, when the downsizing project began, were as high as 15 percent at outdated point-of-sale terminals.

Longridge viewed his 47 member MIS department as the key to the success of the project. He first focused on persuading his staff that this move would be good for them and for their careers, a sizable task given that they would be abandoning the technical world on which their careers had been based. Longridge estimates that he spent an average of $1,000 to $2,000 in training costs per programmer. While his staff was eventually reduced to 32 (a loss of one-third of his staff), most of the reduction was from staff who found jobs using the new technology after they had taken the training Breuners offered.

To rewrite the applications, Longridge established several projects headed by project managers from the user departments. Breuners' senior management was very pleased by this heavy user involvement. Longridge also believed that one key to the success of this project would be the managing of senior management's expectations regarding the time frame of the project.

Sources: Alan Radding, ''Dirty Downsizing,'' *Computerworld* (August 10, 1992); Jean S. Bozman, ''Giving Downsizing the Hard Sell,'' *Computerworld* (March 23, 1992); Bob Francis, ''Downsizing With Multiuser PCs,'' *Datamation* (November 15, 1991); Carol Hildebrand, ''Taylor Medical Overcomes Gridlock,'' *Computerworld* (March 9, 1992); John P McPartlin, Bob Violino, and Peter Krass, ''The Hidden Costs of Downsizing,'' *Information Week* (November 18, 1992); Bob Violino and Thomas Hoffman, ''From Big Iron to Scrap Metal,'' *Information Week* (February 10, 1992).

Case Study Questions

1. Why do you think Taylor Medical was successful in downsizing while Harley-Davidson, Millpore, Keyport, and Calspan encountered problems? What lessons do you draw from this comparison that you would apply to other kinds of high tech projects?

2. After two years at Taylor Medical, followed by a one-year stint at Harley-Davidson, you have just been hired by Breuners' John Longridge to work on the downsizing project. Your first assignment? Critique the Breuners' downsizing project for him. Your critique should answer such obvious questions as: Do you think the Breuners project will be successful? Why? What would you do differently if you were in charge of the project?

3. A key impetus for downsizing is lower costs, specifically the significantly reduced cost of MIPs. Can or should downsizing be justified on a cost savings basis? Join with several classmates to set up a small team to study downsizing costs. Using these six cases and any other information you can bring to the issue, list and describe all the potential costs, direct and indirect, over the first three years after the launching of a downsizing project.

4. You are the head of information systems of a growing corporation. If you find that downsizing cannot be justified on a three-year cost savings, why might you want to proceed with the project anyway? How would you justify this project to your CEO and executive committee? What risks would you specify in the downsizing proposal you submit to the firm's senior management?

6. For an information systems executive, perhaps the greatest nightmare in undertaking a downsizing project is the potential loss of control over data. Why is this a problem? Devise the elements of a downsizing strategy needed to overcome the problem as fully as possible. Include in that policy a statement of the risks and of the negative side effects of implementing the approach you are recommending.

7. Another concern information systems management has in downsizing is the loss of control over end users. In what ways is this concern legitimate? How might downsizing lead to a loss of control that can be harmful to the company? In what ways might downsizing contribute to IS management gaining some appropriate control? Devise those elements of a downsizing project that would increase management control in important ways without seriously affecting end-user creativity and productivity.

THREE

Building Information Systems: Contemporary Approaches

A new information system represents an opportunity for organizational problem-solving and planned organizational change. Alternative approaches for building systems have been devised to minimize the risks in this process. Building an effective information system is both a skill and an art, requiring sensitivity to both technical and organizational concerns. Ensuring information systems quality and managing the implementation process are essential.

Chapter 11 is an overview of systems development, showing how building a new information system can redesign and reshape an organization. It describes the basic activities required to design and build any information system. Systems analysis and design combine technical and organizational responsibilities and require participation from both end users and technical specialists. Plans for new information systems should carefully assess their business value and ensure that they support organizational goals.

Chapter 12 describes the major alternative approaches for building information systems: the traditional systems life cycle, prototyping, software packages, end-user development, and outsourcing. Each approach has its own strengths and limitations and is suitable for a particular class of problems. Management issues posed by each approach are carefully analyzed.

Chapter 13 shows the various ways that information systems can contribute to total quality management in the firm and highlights the principal problems with assuring information systems quality: software reliability and maintainability. It presents the principal methods used for software quality assurance, including analysis and design methodologies, metrics, and quality tools. An entire section analyzes the role that Computer-Aided Software

Engineering (CASE) can play in the quality assurance process.

Chapter 14 looks at the factors responsible for the success and failure of information systems, which are largely organizational in nature. To better understand these factors, one must examine the entire process of implementation and organizational change, with special attention to the role of end users; the level of management support; the dimensions of project risk; and the role of the systems builder as a change agent. While not all aspects of implementation can be controlled, a contingency approach to project management and efforts to secure management and end user support can minimize risks and problems.

Part Three Case Study: *Anatomy of an Outsourcing Deal.* First Fidelity Bancorporation of Newark, New Jersey decided to outsource its information systems development in 1990 in order to deal with problems created by an aggressive acquisitions strategy. The outsourcing arrangement solved some of these problems but introduced others. The case provides students with the opportunity to evaluate outsourcing as an alternative to other system-building approaches.

Redesigning the Organization with Information Systems

New Zealand Designs for Paperless Tax Returns

Beset by constant changes in New Zealand's tax collection management, the New Zealand Inland Revenue Department could only turn to an inflexible 20-year-old mainframe-oriented system. So in 1990 it decided to build a new $300 million information system that would automate tax filing for the country's citizens. The system's objectives were to improve efficiency, generate additional revenue, and reduce the Revenue Department's staff requirements.

The new system, dubbed Future Inland Revenue Systems and Technology (FIRST), allows taxpayers either to mail their income tax forms to a regional tax office or to transmit them electronically to the Revenue Department's computer. Tax forms that previously took three or four months to process by hand can be completed in 14 days. Such service improvements enabled the Revenue Department to cut its staff from 7000 to 5200. By 1997, the revenue de-

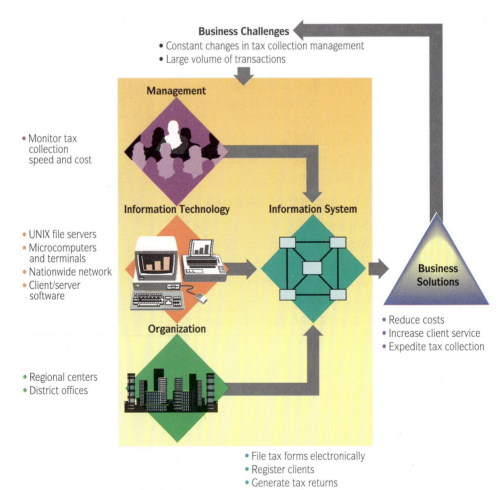

partment hopes to eliminate paper tax forms, queries, and correspondence altogether.

The systems analysis process identified redundant and paper-intensive office functions. Each of the district offices of the Revenue Department was a mirror of the other. The new system design eliminated superfluous tasks. The system building team developed new client/server software programs for functions such as client registration and tax return generation. The Revenue Department decided to implement the new system slowly to leave time for user training and to minimize organizational disruptions.

After a 12-month study, the Revenue Department's Information Technology Group began building the new system. It installed a nationwide network of UNIX file servers, microcomputers, and terminals and developed client/server applications for 40 district offices and 4 regional centers. Individual transactions would be processed on microcomputers or by using terminals in the district offices, while larger applications, such as corporate management systems, remained on the agency's two mainframes.

Although the total cost of FIRST is expected to exceed $300 million, its efficiencies have already produced savings to offset more than 90 percent of this amount.

Source: John McMullen, "Taxation without Vexation," *InformationWEEK* (March 22, 1993).

New Zealand's automated tax filing system illustrates the many factors at work in the development of a new information system. Building the new system entailed analyzing the agency's problems with existing information systems, assessing people's information needs, selecting appropriate technology, and streamlining procedures and jobs. Management had to monitor the system-building effort and evaluate its benefits and costs. The new information system represented a process of organizational change.

This chapter describes how new information systems are conceived, built, and installed. It describes systems analysis and design and other core activities that must be performed to build any information system. The chapter explains how to establish the business value of information systems and how to ensure that new systems are linked to the organization's business plan.

After completing this chapter, you will be able to:

- Understand why building new systems is a process of organizational change.
- Identify the groups who are involved in building systems.

- Identify the core activities in the systems development process.
- Describe various models for determining the business value of information systems.
- Explain how the organization can develop information systems that fit its business plan.

11.1 Systems as Planned Organizational Change

This text has emphasized that an information system is a sociotechnical entity, an arrangement of both technical and social elements. The introduction of a new information system involves much more than new hardware and software. It also includes changes in jobs, skills, management, and organization. In the sociotechnical philosophy, one cannot install new technology without considering the people who must work with it (Bostrom and Heinen, 1977). When we design a new information system, we are redesigning the organization.

One of the most important things to know about building a new information system is that this process is one kind of planned organizational change. Frequently, new systems mean new ways of doing business and working together. The nature of tasks, the speed with which they must be completed, the nature of supervision (its frequency and intensity), and who has what information about whom will all be decided in the process of building an information system. This is especially true in contemporary systems, which deeply affect many parts of the organization.

The sociotechnical perspective means that system builders have general organizational as well as technical responsibilities. There are four organizational areas in which systems builders are held accountable by senior management. First, builders are responsible for the technical quality of the information system; they ensure that the processes that are automated are timely, efficient, and highly accurate. The computerized system must provide for the proper filtering of data to avoid overloading workers and managers with too much information.

Second, builders of systems are responsible for the user interface. The user interface is the part of an information system that often untrained clerical, managerial, and supervisory workers have to interact with directly. The user interface must be designed in a flexible manner to permit change over time. The interface must encompass considerable education and retraining of the work force, take into account the human factors involved in working with the system, and include the development of understandable software and mechanisms for error correction. User skills, user tasks, and cognitive styles must be considered (Gerlach and Kuo, 1991).

A third area of responsibility for systems builders is to consider the overall impact on the organization. Builders must take into account how the system will affect the organization as a whole, focusing particularly on organizational conflict and changes in the locus of decision making. Builders must also consider how the nature of work groups will change under the impact of the new system. Builders determine how much change is needed.

Finally, builders of information systems have overall managerial responsibility for the process of design and implementation. Systems can be technical successes but organizational failures because of a failure in the social and political process of building the system. Analysts and designers are responsible for ensuring that key members of the organization participate in the design process and are permitted to influence the ultimate shape of the system. This activity must be carefully orchestrated by information system builders (see Chapter 14).

Redesigning the Business Processes

New information systems can be powerful instruments for organizational change. Not only have they helped rationalize organizational procedures and workflows, but they can actually be used to reshape how the organization carries out its business or even the nature of the business itself. For instance, Baxter International's stockless inventory system described in Chapter 3 transformed Baxter into a working partner with hospitals and into a manager of its customers' supplies.

Chapter 4 has described some of the ways in which information systems have helped organizations achieve great efficiencies by helping them rethink and streamline their business processes. A **business process** is a set of logically related tasks performed to achieve a defined business outcome. Some examples of business processes are developing a new product, ordering goods from a supplier, or processing and paying an insurance claim.

A new information system can radically redesign business processes to improve speed, service, and quality. If the business process is first redesigned before computing power is applied, organizations can obtain large payoffs from their investments in information technology. Business process redesign serves to reorganize work flows, combining steps to cut waste and eliminating repetitive, paper-intensive tasks (sometimes the new design eliminates jobs as well). Another term for business process redesign is business re-engineering.

Figure 11.1 illustrates how business process redesign worked at Banc One Mortgage, an Indianapolis-based subsidiary of Banc One Corporation in Columbus, Ohio. Banc One, the twelfth-largest bank in the United States, has expanded by aggressively pursuing acquisitions. In 1992, the company expected to move from handling 33,000 loans per year to 300,000 loans per year. To forestall a blizzard of paperwork, Banc One redesigned the mortgage application process so that it required fewer steps and paper forms to complete and reduced the time to process a mortgage to only two days.

> **Business process:** A set of logically related tasks performed to achieve a defined business outcome.

Figure 11.1
Redesigning mortgage processing at Banc One. By redesigning their mortgage processing system and the mortgage application process, Banc One will be able to handle the increased paperwork as they move from processing 33,000 loans per year to processing 300,000 loans per year.
Adapted from: Mitch Betts, "Banc One Mortgage Melts Paper Blizzard." Computerworld, December 14, 1992. Copyright 1992 by CW Publishing, Inc., Framingham, MA 01701. Reprinted from Computerworld.

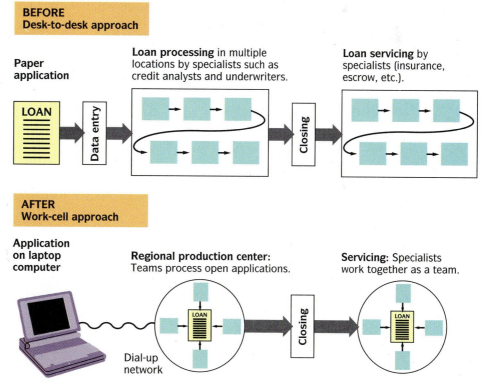

Shifting from a traditional approach helped BANC ONE Mortgage slash processing time from 17 days to two

BEFORE
Desk-to-desk approach

Paper application → Data entry → **Loan processing** in multiple locations by specialists such as credit analysts and underwriters. → Closing → **Loan servicing** by specialists (insurance, escrow, etc.).

AFTER
Work-cell approach

Application on laptop computer → Dial-up network → **Regional production center:** Teams process open applications. → Closing → **Servicing:** Specialists work together as a team.

In the past, a mortgage applicant filled out a paper loan application. The bank entered the application transaction into its computer system. Specialists such as credit analysts and underwriters from eight different departments accessed and evaluated the application individually. If the loan application was approved, the closing was scheduled. After the closing, bank specialists dealing with insurance or funds in escrow serviced the loan. This "desk to desk" assembly-line approach took 17 days.

Banc One Mortgage replaced the sequential desk-to-desk approach with a speedier "work cell" or team approach. Now, loan originators in the field enter the mortgage application directly into laptop computers. Software checks the application transaction to make sure that all of the information is correct and complete. The loan originators transmit the loan applications using a dial-up network to regional production centers. Instead of working on the application individually, the credit analysts, loan underwriters, and other specialists convene electronically, working as a team to approve the mortgage. After closing, another team of specialists sets up the loan for servicing. The entire loan application process takes only two days. Loan information is also easier to access than before, when the loan application could be in eight or nine different departments. Loan originators can also dial into the bank's network to obtain information on mortgage loan costs or to check the status of a loan for the customer.

By redesigning its entire approach to mortgage processing, Banc One achieved remarkable efficiencies. Instead of automating the way it had always done mortgage processing, it completely rethought the entire mortgage application process. Not all organizations have been as effective as Banc One in redesigning their business processes; organizational change cannot always be engineered to management's liking. But even if businesses cannot fully reshape their processes, new information systems provide opportunities for change.

Who Is Involved in Building Systems?

Because of the organizationwide impact of contemporary systems, a number of groups, both inside and outside the information systems area, are involved in building systems. The two major groups involved are the organizational and information systems groups, shown in Table 11.1.

Table 11.1   GROUPS INVOLVED IN BUILDING SYSTEMS

Groups	Role
Organizational Groups	
Senior management	Provides funding and support
Professional experts	Provide legal, procurement, and organizational expertise
Middle management	Provides entry and support
Supervisory management	Provides entry and critical insights
Factory and/or clerical workers	Provide information, job, and task details
Information Systems	
Senior information systems management	Coordinates system development and planning
Project management	Manages a specific project
Senior analysts	Coordinate systems analysts, designers, and procurement personnel
Systems analysts	Determine new system requirements, concepts, and procedures
Programmers	Responsible for technical realization of the new system

Senior management is an important actor in the development of large systems. Senior management provides overall strategic direction (making sure that systems are coordinated with strategic plans) and, equally important, provides funding and strong support. The lack of senior management involvement or senior management's inability to tie information systems to strategic business plans are probably among the most common causes of long-range strategic systems failure in organizations.

A number of professional experts participate in developing systems. Systems require contracts with outside vendors and sometimes involve securing copyright permissions; therefore, legal professionals may be required. Contracts call into play procurement specialists within the organization, and both of these groups are key players in the systems building process. They lend their organizational and legal expertise to the systems effort.

Two intermediate management groups are important to systems building: middle management and supervisory management. Typically, systems are built at the office or division level. This necessarily involves middle managers, who are crucial in providing analysts and designers with access and support during the design effort. Middle managers who are responsible for specific organizational divisions must be willing to reveal their decision-making process to information systems analysts. They must be frank and forthcoming with data and insights into the nature of their business before effective systems can be built.

On the factory floor or in the local office, supervisory management plays a critically important role in providing insights as to how the business works now and how it might be enhanced. This group also provides entry and information to the system builders.

Last, if information systems are to be used by factory and clerical workers, these workers must be interviewed and interacted with during the building of a system. This ensures that the system will help them to do their jobs better and will provide them with information.

In the information systems area, five major groups are involved in the building of systems. Senior information systems management coordinates the overall organizational systems development and planning effort. It is their responsibility to establish system priorities in cooperation with the organization's non-information systems senior management and to ensure adequate budgeting and management in order to deliver projects on time.

Project managers have the most direct responsibility for any given systems effort because it is they who manage projects. They must ensure that adequate resources are available to build the system, that personnel are hired and retained to fulfill the promises of the system, and that the target dates for completing the new system are properly met and within budget.

Three technical groups are involved in building systems: senior analysts, systems analysts, and programmers. Senior analysts are systems analysts with many years of experience who coordinate the efforts of systems analysts in building large systems. Beneath them are systems analysts, who are primarily responsible for the development of new system requirements and for the actual design or technical realization of the system. Programmers, in turn, are technical personnel who are ultimately responsible for writing software code and connecting the technical elements of the system to render it fully operational.

How Is Systems Development Managed?

There are many more ideas for systems improvement and development than there are resources. The organization must develop a technique for ensuring that the most important systems are attended to first, that unnecessary systems are not built, and that end users have a full and meaningful role in determining which new systems will be built and how.

Figure 11.2 shows the elements of a management structure for developing new systems. At the apex of this structure is the corporate strategic planning group and the information system steering committee.

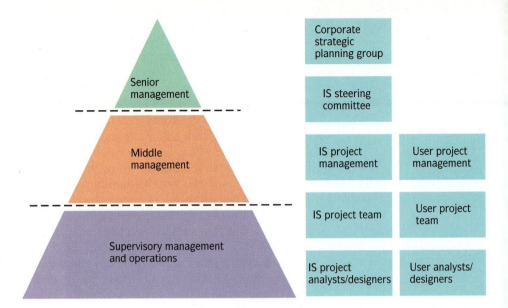

Figure 11.2
Management control of systems development. The management structure for developing and managing new systems ensures that each level of management in the hierarchy is responsible for specific aspects of development, and that the most important systems for the organization are given highest priority.

The *corporate strategic planning group* is responsible for developing the strategic organization plan. This plan may require the development of new systems. An important function of this committee, then, is to give overall strategic direction to the information systems area. A second less obvious function is to educate senior management about the systems area so that they understand how dependent the organization is on systems.

The *information systems steering committee* is the senior management group with direct responsibility for systems development and operation. It is composed of division directors from the end-user and information systems areas. The steering committee reviews and approves plans for systems in all divisions; seeks to develop common systems that can be shared; seeks to coordinate and integrate systems; sometimes becomes involved in selecting specific project alternatives; and approves training for new systems. Increasingly, the information systems steering committee is becoming a powerful gatekeeper of systems development.

The next level of management, the *project management team*, is concerned with the management of specific projects. Generally, this is a small group of senior IS managers and end-user managers with responsibility for a single project.

This project team of professionals is using the latest in portable computing in conjunction with printed documents to support their analysis and decision making.

The *project team* is composed of the systems professionals (analysts and programmers) who are directly responsible for building the system. As previously indicated, ultimate end users (e.g., the human resources department) frequently have their own systems professionals who participate directly in the project. Indeed, many large organizations have created a new job title, "business systems analyst," to identify, recruit, and reward systems personnel who work directly for user departments. This is quite a departure from the past, where the data processing department was the sole source of systems professionals.

A typical project team consists of systems analysts, functional analysts (specialists from relevant business areas), application programmers, and perhaps database specialists. This team is responsible for most of the development activities. For certain applications, legal staff representatives and behavioral specialists may be consulted. Discussions with managers from both user areas and information systems will take place at key decision points.

The mix of skills and the size of the project team vary from one application to another. Obviously, complex, far-reaching applications, such as a general ledger system or an accounts receivable system integrating corporate headquarters with a number of semi-autonomous operating units will require a much larger project team than a small system to computerize automobile insurance records for one operating unit's cars. Sometimes two or three teams operating simultaneously will be needed for large projects.

However, there is a limit to the number of people who can work effectively on a project at any one time. A project that would take fifty man-years cannot be completed by fifty people working for one year. There are too many task dependencies (tasks that cannot be started until others are completed) and inefficiencies caused by coordinating the work of so many people. For each application, there is a project team of optimal size. Up to a certain point, people can be added to a project team to raise its overall productivity, but beyond that point, every additional member successively *decreases* productivity.

Clearly, not all systems must be approved by all levels of project development management. In a large human resource database project, this effort would probably be initiated by the human resources department and proposed first by the information systems steering committee. Managers from other departments would have to approve the project (recognizing that their own projects might have to wait until this one is completed). Next, the corporate planning group would be informed of the desire to build a new system: Given the size of the project, its approval would also be required. A project management team composed of human resources and information systems management would be formed. This group would pick a project team composed of project managers, systems analysts, and programmers.

Where Do Ideas for Systems Come From?

Systems originate at different points in the organization. Generally, there are three sources: end users, the information systems department, and senior management.

End-user demands are the source of most system projects. One of the most common situations occurs when operational personnel sense that something is wrong with an existing transaction system. The system may break down frequently, fail to record new transactions properly, or fail to meet new expectations. Alternatively, middle management in an end-user area, such as human resources, may find an existing MIS inadequate to meet new demands for pensions and benefits, for example.

A second source of new systems is the information systems department. New technologies may present the organization with additional opportunities to reduce costs or pursue new lines of business. One responsibility of the information systems department is to track information technology and introduce appropriate technologies into the firm. This might be thought of as a technological push.

A third source of new systems is senior management. In developing strategic plans for the organization, senior management may conclude that new kinds of information systems will be required to support new business activities. Or it may be apparent that competitors have taken strategic advantage of new information technology, threatening the organization. A technological response of similar dimensions is often required. These kinds of systems can be thought of as the result of strategic pull.

Systems differ in terms of their size, technological complexity, and in terms of the organizational problems they are meant to solve. Chapter 4 has described the many ways in which organizations can differ. Because there are different kinds of systems and situations in which each is conceived or built, a number of methods have been developed to build systems. Chapter 12 is devoted to describing these various methods. In the next section, we focus on the core systems development activities that are common to all of them.

11.2 Overview of Systems Development

Wherever their origin, new information systems are an outgrowth of a process of organizational problem solving. A new information system is built as a solution to some type of problem or set of problems the organization perceives it is facing. The problem may be one where managers and employees realize that the organization is not performing as well as expected, or it may come from the realization that the organization should take advantage of new opportunities to perform more successfully.

Review the diagrams at the beginning of each chapter of this text. They show an information system that is a solution to a particular set of business challenges or problems. The resulting information system is an outgrowth of a series of events called systems development. **Systems development** refers to all the activities that go into producing an information systems solution to an organizational problem or opportunity. Systems development is a structured kind of problem solving with distinct activities. These activities consist of systems analysis, systems design, programming, testing, conversion, and production and maintenance.

Systems development: The activities that go into producing an information systems solution to an organizational problem or opportunity.

Figure 11.3 illustrates the systems development process. The systems development activities depicted here usually take place in sequential order. But some of the activities may need to be repeated or some may be taking place simultaneously, depending on the approach to system building that is being employed (see Chapter 12). Note also that each activity involves interaction with the organization. Members of the organization participate in these activities and the systems development process creates organizational changes. Chapter 14 describes the challenge of managing these organizational changes surrounding system building.

Systems Analysis

Systems analysis: The analysis of a problem that the organization will try to solve with an information system.

Systems analysis is the analysis of the problem that the organization will try to solve with an information system. It consists of defining the problem, identifying its causes, specifying the solution, and identifying the information requirements that must be met by a system solution.

The key to building any large information system is a thorough understanding of the existing organization and system. Thus, the systems analyst creates a road map of the existing organization and systems, identifying the primary owners and users of data in the organization. These stakeholders have a direct interest in the information affected by the new system. In addition to these organiza-

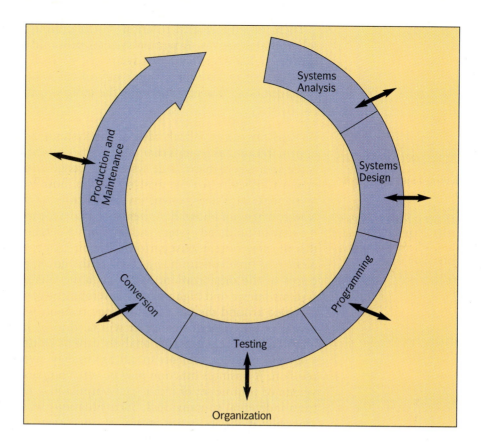

Figure 11.3
The systems development process. Each of the core systems development activities entails interaction with the organization.

tional aspects, the analyst also briefly describes the existing hardware and software that serve the organization.

From this organizational analysis, the systems analyst details the problems of existing systems. By examining documents, work papers, and procedures, observing system operations, and interviewing key users of the systems, the analyst can identify the problem areas and objectives to be achieved by a solution. Often the solution requires building a new information system or improving an existing one.

FEASIBILITY

Feasibility study: A way to determine whether a solution is achievable, given the organization's resources and constraints.

Technical feasibility: Determines whether a proposed solution can be implemented with the available hardware, software, and technical resources.

Economic feasibility: Determines whether the benefits of a proposed solution outweigh the costs.

Operational feasibility: Determines whether a proposed solution is desirable within the existing managerial and organizational framework.

In addition to suggesting a solution, systems analysis involves a **feasibility study** to determine whether that solution is feasible, or achievable, given the organization's resources and constraints. Three major areas of feasibility must be addressed:

1. **Technical feasibility:** whether the proposed solution can be implemented with the available hardware, software, and technical resources.
2. **Economic feasibility:** whether the benefits of the proposed solution outweigh the costs. We explore this topic in greater detail in section 11.3, Understanding the Business Value of Information Systems.
3. **Operational feasibility:** whether the proposed solution is desirable within the existing managerial and organizational framework.

Normally the systems analysis process will identify several alternative solutions that can be pursued by the organization. The process will then assess the feasibility of each. Three basic solution alternatives exist for every systems problem:

1. To do nothing, leaving the existing situation unchanged.
2. To modify or enhance existing systems.
3. To develop a new system.

There may be several solution design options within the second and third solution alternatives. A written systems proposal report will describe the costs, benefits, advantages and disadvantages of each alternative. It is then up to management to determine which mix of costs, benefits, technical features, and organizational impacts represents the most desirable alternative.

ESTABLISHING
INFORMATION
REQUIREMENTS

Information requirements: A detailed statement of the information needs that a new system must satisfy; identifies who needs what information, and when, where, and how the information is needed.

Perhaps the most difficult task of the systems analyst is to define the specific information requirements that must be met by the system solution selected. This is the area where many large system efforts go wrong and the one that poses the greatest difficulty for the analyst. At the most basic level, the **information requirements** of a new system involve identifying who needs what information, where, when, and how. Requirements analysis carefully defines the objectives of the new or modified system and develops a detailed description of the functions that the new system must perform. Requirements must consider economic, technical, and time constraints, as well as the goals, procedures, and decision processes of the organization. Faulty requirements analysis is a leading cause of systems failure and high systems development costs (see Chapter 14). A system designed around the wrong set of requirements will either have to be discarded because of poor performance or will need to be heavily revised. Therefore, the importance of requirements analysis cannot be underestimated.

Developing requirements specifications may involve considerable research and revision. A business function may be very complex or poorly defined. A manual system or routine set of inputs and outputs may not exist. Procedures may vary from individual to individual. Such situations will be more difficult to analyze, especially if the users are unsure of what they want or need (this problem is extremely common). To derive information systems requirements, analysts may be forced to work and rework requirements statements in cooperation with users. Although this process is laborious, it is far superior to and less costly than redoing and undoing an entire system. There are also alternative approaches to eliciting requirements that help minimize these problems (see Chapter 12.)

In many instances, business procedures are unclear or users disagree about how things are done and should be done. Systems analysis often makes an unintended contribution to the organization by clarifying procedures and building organizational consensus about how things should be done. In many instances, building a new system creates an opportunity to redefine how the organization conducts its daily business.

Some problems do not require an information system solution, but instead need an adjustment in management, additional training, or refinement of existing organizational procedures. If the problem is information-related, systems analysis may still be required to diagnose the problem and arrive at the proper solution.

Systems Design

Systems design: Details how a system will meet the information requirements as determined by the systems analysis.

While systems analysis describes what a system should do to meet information requirements, **systems design** shows how the system will fulfill this objective. The design of an information system is the overall plan or model for that system. Like the blueprint of a building or house, it consists of all the specifications that give the system its form and structure. Information systems design is an exacting and creative task demanding imagination, sensitivity to detail, and expert skills.

Systems design has three objectives. First, the systems designer is responsible for considering alternative technology configurations for carrying out and developing the system as described by the analyst. This may involve analyses of the performance of different pieces of hardware and software, security capabilities of systems, network alternatives, and the portability or changeability of systems

TECHNOLOGY

ATM Cards Go to College

One day in 1984, as Bernard W. Gleason, Jr., Boston College's executive director of information technology, stood in line in front of an ATM machine in San Francisco, he had a startling idea. If he could access money from his bank in Boston 3000 miles away, why couldn't ATM cards do the same thing for systems on campus?

Four years later, Gleason's idea materialized as the College's User Information System (UIS). UIS is a campus-based system that enables 15,000 students, 850 faculty members, and thousands of full and part-time staff members to

use ATM-like cards to check out library books, register for courses, check on grades, or pay dining hall tabs. The system can also be used to access student accounts and student records. Users can access the network from six on-campus ATM-like kiosks or from desktop microcomputers with graphical user interfaces in computer laboratories, or via dial-up from off campus or from dormitory rooms. For student course registrations, even a Touch-Tone telephone will do the job.

All of the applications in the system employ a standard user inter-

face. In the late 1970s, the college had adopted an information systems strategy—called Project Glasnost—which was designed to provide users with direct access to the university's administrative computing systems. The strategy specified that all the college's application systems would be viewed as one system and that the system should be accessible through a consistent user interface. Over the years, the college's information systems department developed consistent screens and menus for all applications. The information systems strategy also called for a consistent format for user names and identification codes. By having this policy in place, Boston College could easily link expanding numbers of IBM PC and Macintosh users into different LANs and create a single network directory of all users.

Source: Julia King, "The Secret of Their Success," *Computerworld* (March 29, 1993).

To Think About: Describe the kinds of technology decisions that Boston College made. How did those decisions affect the kinds of information systems that could be developed at Boston College?

hardware. The Window on Technology illustrates the importance of appropriate technology selection in system design.

Second, designers are responsible for the management and control of the technical realization of systems. Detailed programming specifications, coding of data, documentation, testing, and training are all the responsibility of the design staff. In addition, designers are responsible for the actual procurement of the hardware, consultants, and software needed by the system.

Third, the systems designer details the system specifications that will deliver the functions identified during systems analysis. These specifications should address all of the managerial, organizational, and technological components of the system solution. Table 11.2 lists the types of specifications that would be produced during systems design.

Table 11.2 DESIGN SPECIFICATIONS

Output
  Medium
  Content
  Timing

Input
  Origins
  Flow
  Data entry

User interface
  Simplicity
  Efficiency
  Logic
  Feedback
  Errors

Database design
  Logical data relations
  Volume and speed requirements
  File organization and design
  Record specifications

Processing
  Computations
  Program modules
  Required reports
  Timing of outputs

Manual procedures
  What activities
  Who performs them
  When
  How
  Where

Controls
  Input controls (characters, limit, reasonableness)
  Processing controls (consistency, record counts)
  Output controls (totals, samples of output)
  Procedural controls (passwords, special forms)

Security
  Access controls
  Catastrophe plans
  Audit trails

Documentation
  Operations documentation
  Systems documents
  User documentation

Conversion
  Transfer files
  Initiate new procedures
  Select testing method
  Cut over to new system

Training
  Select training techniques
  Develop training modules
  Identify training facilities

Organizational changes
  Task redesign
  Job design
  Office and organization structure design
  Reporting relationships

LOGICAL AND PHYSICAL DESIGN

Logical design: Lays out the components of the information system and their relationship to each other as they would appear to users.

Physical design: The process of translating the abstract logical model into the specific technical design for the new system.

The design for an information system can be broken down into logical and physical design specifications. **Logical design** lays out the components of the system and their relationship to each other as they would appear to users. It shows what the system solution will do as opposed to how it is actually implemented physically. It describes inputs and outputs, processing functions to be performed, business procedures, data models, and controls. (Controls specify standards for acceptable performance and methods for measuring actual performance in relation to these standards. They are described in detail in Chapter 18.)

Physical design is the process of translating the abstract logical model into the specific technical design for the new system. It produces the actual specifications for hardware, software, physical databases, input/output media, manual procedures, and specific controls. Physical design provides the remaining specifications that transform the abstract logical design plan into a functioning system of people and machines.

DESIGN ALTERNATIVES

Like houses or buildings, information systems may have many possible designs. They may be centralized or distributed, on-line or batch, partially manual, or heavily automated. Each design represents a unique blend of all of the technical and organizational factors that shape an information system. What makes one design superior to others is the ease and efficiency with which it fulfills user requirements within a specific set of technical, organizational, financial, and time constraints.

Before the design of an information system is finalized, analysts will evaluate various design alternatives. Based on the requirements definition and system analysis, analysts construct high-level logical design models. They then examine the costs, benefits, strengths, and weaknesses of each alternative.

Figures 11.4A and 11.4B illustrate design alternatives for a corporate cost system, which maintains data on the costs of various products produced by the corporation's operating units in various locations. The first alternative is a batch system that maximizes the efficiency and economy of computer processing but requires extensive manual preparation of data. The batch system requires the following steps:

1. Operating units prepare cost sheets with product cost data by plant. Sheets are mailed to Corporate Cost Accounting at corporate headquarters.
2. Corporate Cost Accounting reviews cost sheets and prepares transaction forms, which are entered into the system.
3. The corporate product database is updated twice weekly via batch processing. The database maintains standard product cost data by plant and links local product numbers to corporate product numbers. The update also produces standard cost sheets.
4. Copies of the standard cost sheets are mailed back to the operating units.

There is also a time lag between the preparation of operating unit cost sheets and the point when this information is reflected on the product database.

The second design alternative is an on-line system featuring more timely information and reduced manual effort, but at greater cost for computer processing, software, and security and recovery procedures required to maintain the integrity of the product database. The steps for the on-line system are as follows:

1. Operating units enter their own product cost data on-line via local CRT terminals with telecommunications links to the central corporate mainframe.

Figure 11.4A
First conceptual design alternative for the corporate cost system. This design entails relatively inexpensive and efficient computer processing but extensive manual preparation of data. There is also a time lag between the preparation of operating unit cost sheets and the point when this information is reflected on the product database.

Figure 11.4B
Second conceptual design alternative for the corporate cost system. This design is relatively expensive in terms of hardware and software, as well as the security and recovery procedures required to maintain the integrity of the database. On-line processing is also more expensive than batch processing. However, the design considerably streamlines manual activities and provides up-to-the-minute information to both corporate cost accounting and the operating units.

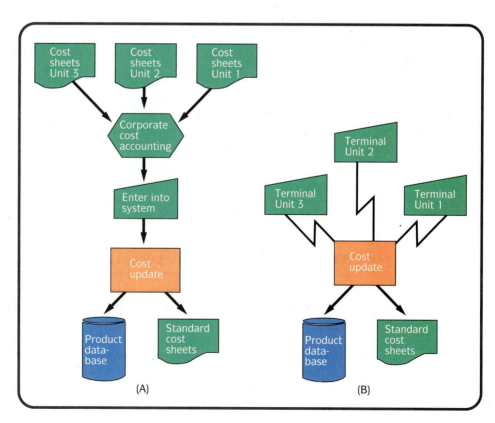

2. Through extensive on-line editing, the operating unit product data are edited. Errors are corrected and the data immediately update the corporate product database.

3. Up-to-date product cost information is available immediately after update. The system produces hard-copy standard cost sheets or allows the operating units to perform on-line inquiries about product cost information.

This alternative reduces manual activities and provides up-to-the-minute information both to corporate cost accounting and to the operating units.

THE ROLE OF END USERS

Information system design cannot be directed by technical specialists alone. It demands a very high level of participation and control by end users. User information requirements drive the entire system-building effort. Users must have sufficient control over the design process to ensure that the system reflects their business priorities and information needs, not the biases of the technical staff.

Working on design increases users' understanding and acceptance of the system, reducing problems caused by power transfers, intergroup conflict, and unfamiliarity with new system functions and procedures. As Chapter 14 points out, insufficient user involvement in the design effort is a major cause of system failure.

Some MIS researchers have suggested that design should be "user led" (Lucas, 1974). However, other researchers point out that systems development is not an entirely rational process. Users leading design activities have used their position to further private interests and gain power rather than to enhance organizational objectives. Users controlling design can sabotage or seriously impede the systems-building effort (Franz and Robey, 1984).

The nature and level of user participation in design vary from system to system. There is less need for user involvement in systems with simple or straightforward requirements than in those with requirements that are elaborate, complex, or vaguely defined. Transaction processing or operational control systems have traditionally required less user involvement than strategic planning, information reporting, and decision-support systems. Less structured systems need more user participation to define requirements and may necessitate many versions of design before specifications can be finalized.

Different levels of user involvement in design are reflected in different systems development methods. Chapter 12 describes how user involvement varies with each development approach.

Completing the Systems Development Process

The remaining steps in the systems development process translate the solution specifications established during systems analysis and design into a fully operational information system. These concluding steps consist of programming, testing, conversion, and production and maintenance.

PROGRAMMING

Programming: The process of translating the system specifications prepared during the design stage into program code.

The process of translating design specifications into software for the computer constitutes a smaller portion of the systems development cycle than design and perhaps the testing activities. But it is here, in providing the actual instructions for the machine, that the heart of the system takes shape. During the **programming** stage, system specifications that were prepared during the design stage are translated into program code. On the basis of detailed design documents for files, transaction and report layouts, and other design details, specifications for each program in the system are prepared.

Some systems development projects assign programming tasks to specialists whose work consists exclusively of coding programs. Other projects prefer programmer/analysts who both design and program functions. Since large systems entail many programs with thousands—even hundreds of thousands—of lines of code, programming teams are frequently used. Moreover, even if an entire system can be programmed by a single individual, the quality of the software will be higher if it is subject to group review (see Chapter 13).

TESTING

Testing: The exhaustive and thorough process that determines whether the system produces the desired results under known conditions.

Exhaustive and thorough **testing** must be conducted to ascertain whether the system produces the right results. Testing answers the question, "Will the system produce the desired results under known conditions?"

The amount of time needed to answer this question has been traditionally underrated in systems project planning (see Chapter 13). As much as 50 percent of the entire software development budget can be expended in testing. Testing is also time-consuming: Test data must be carefully prepared, results reviewed, and corrections made in the system. In some instances, parts of the system may have to be redesigned. Yet the risks of glossing over this step are enormous.

Testing an information system can be broken down into three types of activities:

Unit testing: The process of testing each program separately in the system. Sometimes called program testing.

Unit testing, or program testing, consists of testing each program separately in the system. While it is widely believed that the purpose of such testing is to guarantee that programs are error free, this goal is realistically impossible. Testing should be viewed instead as a means of locating errors in programs, focusing on finding all the ways to make a program fail. Once pinpointed, problems can be corrected.

System testing: Tests the functioning of the information system as a whole in order to determine if discrete modules will function together as planned.

System testing tests the functioning of the information system as a whole. It tries to determine if discrete modules will function together as planned and whether discrepancies exist between the way the system actually works and the way it was conceived. Among the areas examined are performance time, capacity for file storage and handling peak loads, recovery and restart capabilities, and manual procedures.

Acceptance testing: Provides the final certification that the system is ready to be used in a production setting.

Acceptance testing provides the final certification that the system is ready to be used in a production setting. Systems tests are evaluated by users and reviewed by management. When all parties are satisfied that the new system meets their standards, the system is formally accepted for installation.

It is essential that all aspects of testing be carefully thought out and that they be as comprehensive as possible. To ensure this, the development team works with users to devise a systematic test plan. The **test plan** includes all of the preparations for the series of tests previously described.

Test plan: Prepared by the development team in conjunction with the users; it includes all of the preparations for the series of tests to be performed on the system.

Figure 11.5 shows an example of a test plan. The general condition being tested here is a record change. The documentation consists of a series of test-plan screens maintained on a database (perhaps a microcomputer database) that is ideally suited to this kind of application.

Users play a critical role in the testing process. They understand the full range of data and processing conditions that might occur within their system. Moreover, programmers tend to be aware only of the conditions treated in their programs; the test data they devise are usually too limited. Therefore, input from other team members and users will help ensure that the range of conditions included in the test data is complete. Users can identify frequent and less common transactions, unusual conditions to anticipate, and most of the common types of errors that might occur when the system is in use. User input is also decisive in verifying the manual procedures for the system.

CONVERSION

Conversion: The process of changing from the old system to the new system.

Conversion is the process of changing from the old system to the new system. It answers the question, "Will the new system work under real conditions?" Four main conversion strategies can be employed: the parallel strategy, the direct cutover strategy, the pilot study strategy, and the phased approach strategy.

Procedure	Address and Maintenance "Record Change Series"		Test Series 2			
	Prepared By:		Date:	Version:		
Test Ref.	Condition Tested	Special Requirements	Expected Results	Output On	Next Screen	
2	Change records					
2.1	Change existing record	Key field	Not allowed			
2.2	Change nonexistent record	Other fields	"Invalid key" message			
2.3	Change deleted record	Deleted record must be available	"Deleted" message			
2.4	Make second record	Change 2.1 above	OK if valid	Transaction file	V45	
2.5	Insert record		OK if valid	Transaction file	V45	
2.6	Abort during change	Abort 2.5	No change	Transaction file	V45	

Parallel strategy: Conservative conversion approach where both the old system and its replacement are run together until everyone is assured that the new one functions correctly.

Direct cutover: A risky conversion approach where the new system completely replaces the old one on an appointed day.

Pilot study: A strategy to introduce the new system to a limited area of the organization until it is proven to be fully functional.

Phased approach: Introduces the new system in stages either by functions or by organizational units.

Conversion plan: Provides a schedule of all activities required to install a new system.

Documentation: Descriptions of how an information system works from either a technical or end-user standpoint.

In a **parallel strategy,** both the old system and its potential replacement are run together for a time until everyone is assured that the new one functions correctly. This is the safest conversion approach because, in the event of errors or processing disruptions, the old system can still be used as a backup. However, this approach is very expensive, and additional staff or resources may be required to run the extra system.

The **direct cutover** strategy replaces the old system entirely with the new system on an appointed day. At first glance, this strategy seems less costly than parallel conversion strategy. However, it is a very risky approach that can potentially be more costly than parallel activities if serious problems with the new system are found. There is no other system to fall back on. Dislocations, disruptions, and the cost of corrections may be enormous.

The **pilot study** strategy introduces the new system to only to a limited area of the organization, such as a single department or operating unit. When this pilot version is complete and working smoothly, it is installed throughout the rest of the organization, either simultaneously or in stages.

The **phased approach** strategy introduces the new system in stages, either by functions or by organizational units. If, for example, the system is introduced by functions, a new payroll system might begin with hourly workers who are paid weekly, followed six months later by adding salaried employees who are paid monthly to the system. If the system is introduced by organizational units, corporate headquarters might be converted first, followed by outlying operating units four months later.

A formal **conversion plan** provides a schedule of all the activities required to install the new system. The most time-consuming activity is usually the conversion of data. Data from the old system must be transferred to the new system, either manually or through special conversion software programs (see the Window on Organizations). The converted data then must be carefully verified for accuracy and completeness.

Moving from an old system to a new one requires that end users be trained to use the new system. Detailed **documentation** showing how the system works from both a technical and end-user standpoint is finalized during conversion time for use in training and everyday operations. Lack of proper training and

ORGANIZATIONS

Conversion: Harder Than You Think!

When two companies join, what does it take for them to live happily ever after? Some say the real marriage takes place in their information systems. The merged company Outokumpu American Brass Inc. of Buffalo, New York, recently found this out. When American Brass was purchased by Outokumpu Oy of Finland, it had to split into two corporations, one based in Buffalo, and one in Kenosha, Wisconsin. Furthermore, it had to convert to the Human Resources system specified by its parent company.

American Brass' existing human resources system, based on a software package from Software 2000 Inc. of Hyannis, Massachusetts, simply wasn't designed to handle this problem. Most human resources software packages do not use standardized codes in the systems they sell. To convert to another human resources system, information systems specialists have to use a mixture of in-house and vendor-written conversion programs. The MIS department of

American Brass wrote its own conversion software.

So did Multifoods Corporation, a century-old food distributor operating in the United States, Canada, and Venezuela. Multifoods had to add new groups of employees through mergers to its Cyborg's Solution Series Human Resources payroll system so many times that its information systems staff wrote their own COBOL conversion programs and modified them as needed. The staff developed a series of programs to convert general ledger, state and local tax, exemption, deduction, health care, and salary data from other human resources systems such as those run by Automatic Data Processing (ADP), Control Data Corporation (CDC), and some homegrown systems. But data for job descriptions and benefits plan enrollments all had to be keyed in manually.

Codes mean different things in different organizations. System builders have to analyze these differ-

ences and find a way to have them mean the same thing to everybody or no one will understand what the data mean. What one system terms *salary,* others call *pay rate, pay per period,* or *annual salary divided out.* No wonder a sizable chunk of companies merely fixes the problem the ''old way'' by rekeying in all of the data. Without standards on field length, data names, and descriptions, there will be no easy way to perform conversions (see Chapter 8.)

Source: Bill Sharp, ''Managing a Merger: HR Systems Migration,'' *Datamation,* February 15, 1993.

To Think About: Is conversion merely a technology issue? How helpful is conversion software? It has been said that the significance of conversion in systems development has been underestimated. Do you agree? If you were in charge of a systems development project, how would you plan for the conversion stage?

documentation contributes to system failure (see Chapter 14), so this portion of the systems development process is very important.

<table>
<tr><td>

PRODUCTION AND MAINTENANCE

Production: The stage after the new system is installed and the conversion is complete; during this time the system is reviewed by users and technical specialists to determine how well it has met its original goals.

Maintenance: Changes in hardware, software, documentation, or procedures to a production system to correct errors, meet new requirements, or improve processing efficiency.

</td><td>

After the new system is installed and conversion is complete, the system is said to be in **production.** During this stage, the system will be reviewed by both users and technical specialists to determine how well it has met its original objectives and to decide whether any revisions or modifications are in order. Changes in hardware, software, documentation, or procedures to a production system to correct errors, meet new requirements, or improve processing efficiency are termed **maintenance.**

Studies of maintenance have examined the amount of time required for various maintenance tasks (Lientz and Swanson, 1980). Approximately 20 percent of the time is devoted to debugging or correcting emergency production problems; another 20 percent is concerned with changes in data, files, reports, hardware, or system software. But 60 percent of all maintenance work consists of making user enhancements, improving documentation, and recoding system components for greater processing efficiency. The amount of work in the third category of maintenance problems could be reduced significantly through better system analysis and design practices. Table 11.3 summarizes the systems development activities.

</td></tr>
</table>

Table 11.3 SYSTEMS DEVELOPMENT

Core Activity	Description
Systems analysis	Identify problem(s) Specify solution Establish information requirements
Systems design	Create logical design specifications Create physical design specifications Manage technical realization of system
Programming	Translate design specifications into program code
Testing	Unit test Systems test Acceptance test
Conversion	Plan conversion Prepare documentation Train users and technical staff
Production and Maintenance	Operate the system Evaluate the system Modify the system

11.3 Understanding the Business Value of Information Systems

Information systems can have several different values for business firms. As we have pointed out in earlier chapters, information systems can provide a temporary competitive advantage to firms. A consistently strong information technology infrastructure can, over the longer term, play an important strategic role in the life of the firm. Looked at less grandly, information systems can permit firms simply to survive. In many cases, survival even at a mediocre level will dictate investment in systems. In addition, government regulations may require these investments.

Strategy cannot be pursued when a firm is financially unsound. The worth of systems from a financial perspective essentially revolves around the question of return on invested capital. The value of systems from a financial view comes down to one question: Does a particular IS investment produce sufficient returns to justify its costs? There are many problems with this approach, not the least of which is how to estimate benefits and count the costs.

Capital Budgeting Models

Capital budgeting: The process of analyzing and selecting various proposals for capital expenditures.

Capital budgeting models are one of several techniques used to measure the value of investing in long-term capital investment projects. The process of analyzing and selecting various proposals for capital expenditures is called **capital budgeting.** Firms invest in capital projects in order to expand production to meet anticipated demand, or to modernize production equipment in order to reduce costs. Firms also invest in capital projects for many noneconomic reasons, such as to install pollution control equipment, or to convert to a human resources database in order to meet some government regulations or to satisfy nonmarket public demands. Information systems are considered long-term capital investment projects.

Six capital budgeting models are used to evaluate capital projects:

- the payback method
- the accounting rate of return on investment (ROI)

- the cost/benefit ratio
- the net present value
- the profitability index
- the internal rate of return (IRR)

CASH FLOWS

All capital budgeting methods rely on measures of cash flows into and out of the firm. Capital projects generate cash flows into and out of the firm. The investment cost is an immediate cash outflow caused by the purchase of the capital equipment. In subsequent years, the investment may cause additional cash outflows that will be balanced by cash inflows resulting from the investment. Cash inflows take the form of increased sales of more products (for reasons including new products, higher quality, or increasing market share), or reduction in costs of production and operation. The difference between cash outflows and cash inflows is used for calculating the financial worth of an investment. Once the cash flows have been established, several alternative methods are available to compare different projects with one another, and to make a decision about the investment.

LIMITATIONS OF FINANCIAL MODELS

Tangible benefits: Benefits that can be quantified and assigned monetary value; they include lower operational costs and increased cash flows.

Intangible benefits: Benefits that are not easily quantified; they include more efficient customer service or enhanced decision making.

Financial models are used in many situations: to justify new systems, explain old systems post hoc, and to develop quantitative support for a political position. Political decisions made for organizational reasons have nothing to do with the cost and benefits of a system.

Financial models assume that all relevant alternatives have been examined, that all costs and benefits are known, and that these costs and benefits can be expressed in a common metric, specifically, money. When one has to choose among many complex alternatives, these assumptions are rarely met in the real world, although they may be approximated. Table 11.4 lists some of the more common costs and benefits of systems. **Tangible benefits** can be quantified and assigned a monetary value. **Intangible benefits,** such as more efficient customer

Table 11.4   COSTS AND BENEFITS OF INFORMATION SYSTEMS

Costs	Benefits
Hardware	**Tangible**
Telecommunications	Cost savings
Software	Increased productivity
Services	Low operational costs
Personnel	Reduced work force
	Lower computer expenses
	Lower outside vendor costs
	Lower clerical and professional costs
	Reduced rate of growth in expenses
	Reduced facility costs
	Intangible
	Improved asset utilization
	Improved resource control
	Improved organizational planning
	Increased organizational flexibility
	More timely information
	More information
	Increased organizational learning
	Legal requirements attained
	Enhanced employee goodwill
	Increased job satisfaction
	Improved decision making
	Improved operations
	Higher client satisfaction
	Better corporate image

service or enhanced decision making, cannot be immediately quantified but may lead to quantifiable gains in the long run.

INFORMATION SYSTEMS AS A CAPITAL PROJECT

Many well-known problems emerge when financial analysis is applied to information systems (Dos Santos, 1991). Financial models may not express the risks and uncertainty of their own cost and benefit estimates. Costs and benefits do not occur in the same time frame—costs tend to be up front and tangible, while some benefits may be back-loaded and intangible. Inflation may affect costs and benefits differently. Technology—especially information technology—can change during the course of the project, causing estimates to vary greatly. Intangible benefits are difficult to quantify. These factors affect financial models.

The difficulties of measuring intangible benefits give financial models an "application bias": Transaction and clerical systems that displace labor and save space always produce more measurable, tangible benefits than management information systems, decision-support systems, or computer-supported collaborative work systems (see Chapter 15).

There is some reason to believe that investment in information technology requires special consideration in financial modeling. Capital budgeting historically concerned itself with manufacturing equipment and other very long-term investments like electrical generating facilities, telephone networks, and the like. These investments had expected lives of more than one year and up to twenty-five years. Computer-based information systems are similar to other capital investments in that they produce an immediate investment cost, and are expected to produce cash benefits over a term greater than one year.

Information systems differ from manufacturing systems in that their expected life is shorter. The very high rate of technological change in computer-based information systems means that most systems are seriously out of date in five to eight years. Although parts of old systems survive as code segments in large programs—some programs have code that is fifteen years old—most large-scale systems after five years require significant investment to redesign or rebuild them.

The high rate of technological obsolescence in budgeting for systems means simply that the payback period must be shorter, and the rates of return higher, than typical capital projects with much longer useful lives.

The bottom line with financial models is to use them cautiously and to put the results into a broader context of business analysis. Let us look at an example to see how these problems arise and can be worked out. The following case study is based on a real-world scenario, but the names have been changed.

Case Example: Primrose, Mendel, and Hansen

Primrose, Mendel, and Hansen is a 250-person law partnership on Manhattan's West Side. Founded in 1923, Primrose has excelled in corporate, taxation, environmental, and health law. Its litigation department is also well known.

THE PROBLEM

Spread out over three floors of a new building, each of the hundred partners has a secretary. Many partners have a DOS 386 PC on their desktops, but rarely use them except to read the E-mail (which is, in fact, usually done by the secretary and then typed up for the partner to read). Virtually all business is conducted face-to-face in the office, or when partners meet directly with clients on the clients' premises. Most of the law business involves marking up (editing), creating, filing, storing, and sending documents. In addition, the tax, pension, and real estate groups do a considerable amount of spreadsheet work.

With overall business off 30 percent since 1987, the chairman, Edward W. Hansen III, is hoping to use information systems to cut costs, enhance service to clients, and bring partner profits back up.

These attorneys access legal files through a sophisticated information system to expedite their research and recording processes.

First, the firm's income depends on billable hours, and every lawyer is supposed to keep a diary of his or her work for specific clients in 30-minute intervals. Generally, senior lawyers at this firm charge about $500 an hour for their time. Unfortunately, lawyers are not good record keepers, often forget what they have been working on, and must go back to reconstruct their time diaries. The firm hopes that there will be some automated way of tracking billable hours.

Second, a great deal of time is spent communicating with clients around the world, with other law firms both in the United States and overseas, and especially with Primrose's branches in Los Angeles, Tokyo, London, and Paris. The FAX has become the communication medium of choice, generating huge bills and developing lengthy queues.

Third, Primrose has no client database! A law firm is a collection of fiefdoms—each lawyer has his or her own clients, and keeps the information about them private. This, however, makes it impossible for management to find out who is a client of the firm, who is working on a deal with whom, and so forth. The firm maintains a billing system, but the information is too difficult to search. What Primrose needs is an integrated client management system that would take care of billing, hourly charges, and make client information available to others in the firm. Even overseas offices want to have information on who is taking care of a particular client in the United States.

Fourth, there is no system to track costs. The head of the firm and the department heads who compose the executive committee cannot identify what the costs are, where the money is being spent, who is spending it, and how the firm's resources are being allocated. Perhaps, for instance, health law is declining and the firm should trim associates (nonpartnered lawyers). A decent accounting system that could identify the cash flows and the costs a bit more clearly than the existing journal does would be a big help.

THE SOLUTION

There are many problems at Primrose; information systems could obviously have some value and perhaps could grant a strategic advantage to Primrose if a system were correctly built and implemented. We will not go through a detailed systems analysis and design here. Instead, we will sketch the solution that in fact was adopted, showing the detailed costs and estimated benefits. These will prove useful for estimating the overall business value of the new system—both financial and nonfinancial.

The technical solution adopted was to create a local area network composed of 100 fully configured 486SX microcomputers, three OS/2 file servers, and an Ethernet 10 MBS (megabit per second) local area network using coaxial cable.

This network connects most of the lawyers and their secretaries into a single integrated system, yet permits each lawyer to configure his or her desktop with specialized software and hardware. The older 386 machines were passed down to the secretaries.

All machines were configured with DOS running Windows as the basic operating system, while the file servers ran OS/2. A networked relational database was installed, running under network software. Lotus Notes for Windows was chosen as the internal mail system because it provided an easy-to-use interface, and good links to external telecommunications networks and mail systems. It could be used to develop simple client management and billing applications. Notes can also incorporate spreadsheets. The Primrose network is linked to external networks so that the firm can obtain information on-line from Lexis (a legal database) and several financial database services.

The new system required Primrose to hire a Director of Systems—a new position for most law firms. Four systems personnel were required to operate the system and train lawyers. Outside trainers were hired for a short period.

Figure 11.6 shows the estimated costs and benefits of the system. The system had an actual investment cost of $1,170,700 in the first year (Year 0) and total

Figure 11.6
Costs and Benefits of the Intellex Legal Information System (ILIS). This spreadsheet analyzes the costs and the benefits of implementing an information system for the law firm. The costs for hardware, telecommunications, software, services, and personnel are analyzed over a six-year period.

Primrose, Mendelson, and Hansen
Intellex Legal Information System (ILIS)
Estimated Costs and Benefits 1993–1998

Costs	Year:		0 1993	1 1994	2 1995	3 1996	4 1997	5 1998	
Hardware									
	File Servers	3@50000	$150,000	$10,000	$10,000	$10,000	$10,000	$10,000	
	PCs	100@3000	$300,000	$10,000	$10,000	$10,000	$10,000	$10,000	
	Network cds	100@500	$50,000	$0	$0	$0	$0	$0	
	Scanners	6@1200	$7,200	$1,200	$1,200	$1,200	$1,200	$1,200	
	Fax Boards	100@250	$25,000	$0	$0	$0	$0	$0	
Telecommunications									
	Gateways	2@8000	$16,000	$400	$400	$400	$400	$400	
	Cabling	100000	$100,000	$0	$0	$0	$0	$0	
Software									
	Database	10000	$10,000	$10,000	$10,000	$10,000	$10,000	$10,000	
	Network	10000	$10,000	$2,500	$2,500	$2,500	$2,500	$2,500	
	Groupware	100@500	$50,000	$1,000	$1,000	$1,000	$1,000	$1,000	
	Windows	100@125	$12,500	$5,000	$5,000	$5,000	$5,000	$5,000	
Services									
	Nexis/Lexis	50000	$50,000	$50,000	$50,000	$50,000	$50,000	$50,000	
	Training	300@200	$30,000	$30,000	$30,000	$30,000	$30,000	$30,000	
Personnel									
	Director	100000	$100,000	$110,000	$121,000	$133,100	$146,410	$161,051	
	Systems Pers	4@50000	$200,000	$216,000	$233,280	$251,942	$272,098	$293,866	
	Trainer	2@30000	$60,000	$63,600	$67,416	$71,461	$75,749	$80,294	
Total			$1,170,700	$509,700	$541,796	$576,603	$614,356	$655,310	$4,068,466
Benefits									
1. Billing enhancements			$300,000	$400,000	$500,000	$600,000	$600,000	$600,000	
2. Reduced paralegals			$25,000	$25,000	$25,000	$25,000	$25,000	$25,000	
3. Reduced clerical			$25,000	$25,000	$25,000	$25,000	$25,000	$25,000	
4. Reduced messenger			$0	$0	$0	$0	$0	$0	
5. Reduced telecommunications			$10,000	$10,000	$10,000	$10,000	$10,000	$10,000	
6. Lawyer efficiencies			$120,000	$240,000	$360,000	$480,000	$600,000	$600,000	
Total Benefits			$480,000	$700,000	$920,000	$1,140,000	$1,260,000	$1,260,000	$5,760,000

cost over six years of $4,068,466. The estimated benefits total to $5,760,000 after six years. Was the investment worth it? If so, in what sense was it worth it? There are financial and nonfinancial answers to this question. Let us look at the financial models first. They are depicted in Figure 11.7.

THE PAYBACK METHOD

Payback method: A measure of the time required to pay back the initial investment of a project.

The **payback method** is quite simple: It is a measure of time required to pay back the initial investment of a project. The payback period is computed as

$$\frac{\text{Original investment}}{\text{Annual net cash inflow}} = \text{Number of years to pay back}$$

In the case of Primrose, it will take 5.06 years to pay back the initial investment. On the surface, this seems like a moderate time to return the investment—not too long and not very short either. The payback method is a popular method because of its simplicity and power as an initial screening method. It is especially good for high-risk projects where the useful life is difficult to know. If a project pays for itself in two years, then it matters less how long after two years the system lasts.

The weakness of this measure are its virtues: The method ignores the time value of money, the amount of cash flow after the payback period, the disposal value (usually zero with computer systems), and the profitability of the investment.

ACCOUNTING RATE OF RETURN ON INVESTMENT (ROI)

Accounting rate of return on investment (ROI): Calculation of the rate of return from an investment by adjusting cash inflows produced by the investment for depreciation. Approximates the accounting income earned by the investment.

Firms make capital investments in order to earn a satisfactory rate of return. Determining a satisfactory rate of return depends on the cost of borrowing money, but other factors can enter into the equation. Such factors include the historic rates of return expected by the firm. In the long run, the desired rate of return must equal or exceed the cost of capital in the marketplace. Otherwise, no one will lend the firm money.

The **accounting rate of return** (**ROI**) calculates the rate of return from an investment by adjusting the cash inflows produced by the investment for depreciation. It gives an approximation of the accounting income earned by the project.

To find the ROI, one first calculates the average net benefit. The formula for the average net benefit is as follows:

$$\frac{(\text{Total benefits} - \text{Total cost} - \text{Depreciation})}{\text{Useful Life}} = \text{Net benefit}$$

This net benefit is divided by the total initial investment to arrive at ROI (Rate of Return on Investment). The formula is

$$\frac{\text{Net benefit}}{\text{Total initial investment}} = \text{ROI}$$

In the case of Primrose, the average rate of return on the investment is 24 percent. The cost of capital (the prime rate) has been hovering around 6 to 8 percent, and returns on invested capital in corporate bonds are at about 10 percent. On the surface, this investment returns more than other financial investments.

The weakness of ROI is that it can ignore the time value of money. Future savings are simply not worth as much in today's dollars as are current savings. On the other hand, ROI can be modified (and usually is) so that future benefits and costs are calculated in today's dollars. (The present value function on most spreadsheets will perform this conversion.)

NET PRESENT VALUE

Evaluating a capital project requires that the cost of an investment (a cash outflow usually in year 0) be compared with the net cash inflows that occur many years later. But these two kinds of inflows are not directly comparable

Year:	0	1	2	3	4	5
Net Cash Flow	($690,700)	$190,300	$378,204	$563,397	$645,644	$604,690

(1) Payback Period = 5.06 years

With uneven cash flows, sum inflows until
they equal the initial investment (1,170,700)

Year 2 = 190,300	$190,300
Year 3 = 378,204	$568,504
Year 3 = 122,196	$690,700
Year 4 = 563,397	$1,131,901

(2) Accounting Rate of Return (ROI)

Year 5 = 38,799

$$\frac{\text{(Total Benefits-Total Costs-Depreciation)} / \text{Useful Life}}{\text{Total initial investment}} = \frac{(5,760,000-2,897,766-1,170,700) / 6}{1,170,700} = \frac{281,922}{1,170,700} = 24\%$$

With uneven cash flows, use total benefits
less total depreciation, divided by useful life
to establish the numerator

(3) Cost-Benefit Ratio

$$\frac{\text{Total Benefits}}{\text{Total Costs}} = \frac{5,760,000}{4,068,466} = 1.42$$

(4) Net Present Value @NPV(.05,D50..I50) = $1,262,120-1,170,700 = $91,420

(5) Profitability Index NPV/Investment $1,262,120/1,170,700 1.07

(6) Internal rate of return (IRR) @IRR(.05,D50..I50) = 48%

Figure 11.7
Financial models. In order to determine the financial basis for a project, a series of
financial models help determine the return on invested capital. These calculations
include the Payback Period, the Accounting Rate of Return (ROI), the Cost/Benefit Ratio,
the Net Present Value, the Profitability Index, and the Internal Rate of Return (IRR).

because of the time value of money. Money you have been promised to receive 3, 4, and 5 years from now is not worth as much as money received today. Money received in the future has to be discounted by some appropriate percentage rate—usually the prevailing interest rate, or sometimes the cost of capital. **Present value** is the value in current dollars of a payment or stream of payments to be received in the future. It can be calculated by using the formula

Present value: The value, in current dollars, of a payment or stream of payments to be received in the future.

$$\text{Payment} \times \frac{1-(1+\text{interest})^{-n}}{\text{Interest}} = \text{Present value}$$

Thus, in order to compare the investment (made in today's dollars) with future savings or earnings, you need to discount the earnings to their present value and then calculate the net present value of the investment. The **net present value** is the amount of money an investment is worth, taking into account its cost, earnings, and the time value of money. The formula for net present value is

Net present value: The amount of money an investment is worth, taking into account its cost, earnings, and the time value of money.

Present value of expected cash flows − Initial investment cost = Net present value

In the case of Primrose, the present value of the benefits is $1,262,120 and the cost (in today's dollars) is $1,170,700, giving a net present value of $91,420. In other words, the net present value of the investment is $91,420 over a six-year period.

COST-BENEFIT RATIO A simple method for calculating the returns from a capital expenditure is to calculate the **cost-benefit ratio,** which is the ratio of benefits to costs. The formula is

Cost-benefit ratio: A method for calculating the returns from a capital expenditure by dividing the total benefits by total costs.

$$\frac{\text{Total Benefits}}{\text{Total Costs}} = \text{cost-benefit ratio}$$

In the case of Primrose, the cost-benefit ratio is 1.42, meaning that the benefits are 1.42 times greater than the costs. The cost-benefit ratio can be used to rank several projects for comparison. Some firms establish a minimum cost-benefit ratio that must be attained by capital projects. The cost-benefit ratio can of course be calculated using present values to account for the time value of money.

PROFITABILITY INDEX

Profitability index: Used to compare the profitability of alternative investments; it is calculated by dividing the present value of the total cash inflow from an investment by the initial cost of the investment.

If a firm needs to compare several different potential investments, one simple solution is provided by the profitability index. The **profitability index** is calculated by dividing the present value of the total cash inflow from an investment by the initial cost of the investment. The result can be used to compare the profitability of alternative investments.

$$\frac{\text{Present Value of Cash Inflows}}{\text{Investment}} = \text{Profitability Index}$$

In the case of Primrose, the Profitability Index is equal to 1.07. The project barely returns more than its cost. Projects can be rank ordered on this index, permitting firms to focus only on the most profitable projects.

INTERNAL RATE OF RETURN (IRR)

Internal rate of return (IRR): The rate of return or profit that an investment is expected to earn.

Internal rate of return (IRR) is a variation of the net present value method. It takes into account the time value of money. **Internal rate of return (IRR)** is defined as the rate of return or profit that an investment is expected to earn. IRR is the discount (interest) rate that will equate the present value of the project's future cash flows to the initial cost of the project (defined here as a negative cash flow in year 0 of $690,700). In other words, the value of R (discount rate) is such that Present Value − Initial Cost = 0. In the case of Primrose, the IRR is 48 percent. This seems to be a healthy rate of return.

RESULTS OF THE CAPITAL BUDGETING ANALYSIS

Using methods that take into account the time value of money, the Primrose project is cash-flow positive over the time period, and does return more benefits than it cost. However, the returns are not stellar. Against this analysis, one might ask what other investments would be better from an efficiency and effectiveness point of view. Also, one must ask if all the benefits have been calculated. It may be that this investment is necessary for the survival of the firm, or necessary to provide a level of service demanded by its clients. What are other competitors doing? In other words, there may be other intangible and strategic business factors to take into account (see the Window on Management on page 370). Let's look at these other intangible possibilities.

Nonfinancial and Strategic Considerations

Other methods of selecting and evaluating information system investments involve nonfinancial and strategic considerations. When the firm has several alternative investments to select from, it can employ portfolio analysis and scoring models. Several of these methods can be used in combination.

PORTFOLIO ANALYSIS

Rather than using capital budgeting, a second way of selecting among alternative projects is to consider the firm as having a portfolio of potential applications. Each application carries risks and benefits. The portfolio can be described as having a certain profile of risk and benefit to the firm (see Figure 11.8). While there is no ideal profile for all firms, information-intensive industries (e.g., finance) should have a few high-risk–high-benefit projects to ensure that they stay current with technology. Firms in non-information-intensive industries should focus on high-benefit–low-risk projects.

Justifying Information Systems Investments in the Distribution Industry: Do They Improve Business Basics?

In the distribution industry, speed, efficiency and customer service separate the winners from the losers. Managers of distribution companies or of the distribution function for retailers and manufacturers look at whether their information systems investments make distribution faster, easier, and more customer-oriented. Will a new information system shorten delivery cycles, streamline the ordering process, or make better inventory information available to customers? If so, the investment is justified.

Nissan Motor Corporation, U.S.A., in Carson, California, evaluates information systems in terms of their ability to support customer service. It used to be that Japanese cars sold themselves. Tough competition from U.S. automakers ended all that. Now customers want to order much more specifically. They are no longer willing to buy what is sitting in dealers' lots or to accept long delays in ordering the features they want. Nissan hopes to win them over by shortening delivery cycles, with dealers ordering exactly the cars they want instead of having the orders placed by regional managers.

To improve customer service, Nissan decided to build a Dealer Or-

der Entry and Management System that links individual dealers, regional managers, corporate headquarters, and factories in Japan, Mexico and Tennessee. Dealers can enter their orders directly into this system. Plant production managers can use the system to track the changing mix of cars ordered and adjust production to demand each day. With the new system, Nissan's Smyrna, Tennessee and Japanese plants can respond to customer color changes as late as 10 days prior to the date of manufacture.

When the Dealer Order Entry System was under consideration, all management wanted to know was how much money it would take to build the system and when the system would be completed. The key measurement of information success was hitting the delivery date.

At the Port of Los Angeles, information systems are funded if they relate to some customer benefit. The port wants to win new customers but is committed to keeping its old ones. It wants to use information systems to shrink the time needed to find a customer complaint and to turn it around. The port also invested in a system to enable representatives in its overseas marketing offices to simulate

different cargo unloading configurations for potential foreign shipping customers. The port's overseas marketing representatives can sit down in Taiwan or Hong Kong and offer different options, transmit them back, and get a cost estimate very quickly. To justify information systems investments and tie them more closely to the business, Stan Johnson, the port's MIS director, formed an Information Systems policy committee consisting of high-level executives from the port's divisions, including administration, finance, personnel, and maritime affairs. Johnson and the policy committee rank each information systems project before going before the port's board of commissioners for funding.

Source: Clinton Wilder, "Value Judgment," *Computerworld* (March 2, 1992).

To Think About: Some say that business managers who demand traditional financial analysis to justify an information systems investment might miss out on valuable business opportunities. Do you agree? Should systems investments be made without any regard for financial considerations?

The general risks are as follows:

- Benefits may not be obtained.
- Costs of implementation may exceed budgets.
- Implementation time frames are exceeded.
- Technical performance is less than expected.
- The system is incompatible with existing software/hardware.

Portfolio analysis: An analysis of the portfolio of potential applications within a firm to determine the risks and benefits and select among alternatives for information systems.

Risks are not necessarily bad. They are tolerable as long as the benefits are commensurate. In general, there are three factors that increase the risks of a project: project size, organizational experience, and project task complexity (Ein-dor and Segev, 1978; McFarlan, 1981; Laudon, 1989). These are described in Chapter 14.

Once strategic analyses have determined the overall direction of system development, a **portfolio analysis** can be used to select alternatives. Obviously, one can begin by focusing on systems of high benefit and low risk. These promise

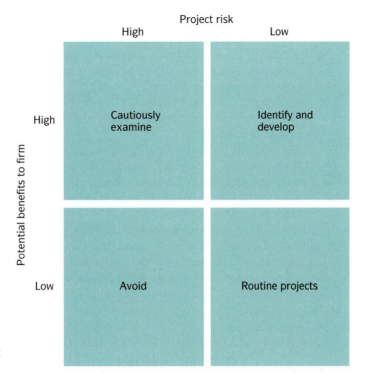

Project risk

High — Low

High

| Cautiously examine | Identify and develop |

Potential benefits to firm

Low

| Avoid | Routine projects |

Figure 11.8
A system portfolio. Companies should examine their portfolio of projects in terms of potential benefits and likely risks. Certain kinds of projects should be avoided altogether and others developed rapidly. There is no ideal mix. Companies in different industries have different profiles.

early returns and low risks. Second, high-benefit–high-risk systems should be examined. Low-benefit–high-risk systems should be totally avoided, and low-benefit–low-risk systems should be re-examined for the possibility of rebuilding and replacing them with more desirable systems having higher benefits.

SCORING MODELS

Scoring models: A quick method for deciding among alternative systems based on a system of ratings for selected objectives.

A quick, and sometimes compelling, method for arriving at a decision on alternative systems is a **scoring model**. Scoring models give alternative systems a single score based on the extent to which they meet selected objectives (the method is similar to the *objective attained* model) (Matlin, 1979; Buss, 1983).

In Table 11.5 the firm must decide among three alternative office automation systems (a mainframe system, a minicomputer system, and a microcomputer-based system). Column 1 lists the criteria that decision makers may apply to the systems. These criteria are usually the result of lengthy discussions among the decision-making group. Often the most important outcome of a scoring model is not the score but simply agreement on the criteria used to judge a system (Ginzberg, 1979; Nolan, 1982).

Table 11.5

SCORING MODEL USED TO CHOOSE AMONG ALTERNATIVE OFFICE AUTOMATION SYSTEMS*

Criterion	Weight	Central Mainframe		Department Minicomputer		Individual PCs	
Percentage of user needs met	0.40	2	0.8	3	1.2	4	1.6
Cost of the initial purchase	0.20	1	0.2	3	0.6	4	0.8
Financing	0.10	1	0.1	3	0.3	4	0.4
Ease of maintenance	0.10	2	0.2	3	0.3	4	0.4
Chances of success	0.20	3	0.6	4	0.8	4	0.8
Final score			1.9		3.2		4.0

Scale: 1 = low. 5 = high.
*One of the major uses of scoring models is in identifying the criteria of selection and their relative weights. In this instance, an office automation system based on PCs appears preferable.

Column 2 lists the weights that decision makers attach to the decision criterion. The scoring model helps to bring about agreement among participants concerning the rank of the criteria.

Columns 3 to 5 use a 1-to-5 scale (lowest to highest) to express the judgments of participants on the *relative* merits of each system. For example, concerning the percentage of user needs that each system meets, a score of 1 for a system argues that this system when compared to others being considered will be low in meeting user needs.

As with all "objective" techniques, there are many qualitative judgments involved in using the scoring model. This model requires experts who understand the issues and the technology. It is appropriate to cycle through the scoring model several times, changing the criteria and weights, to see how sensitive the outcome is to reasonable changes in criteria. Scoring models are used most commonly to confirm, to rationalize, and to support decisions, rather than being the final arbiters of system selection.

If Primrose had other alternative systems projects to select from, it could have used the portfolio and scoring models as well as financial models to establish the business value of its systems solution.

11.4 Linking Information Systems to the Business Plan

Throughout this text, we have described the critical role that systems can play in organizations. Therefore, deciding what new systems to build should be an essential component of the organizational planning process. Organizations need to develop an information systems plan that supports their overall business plan.

The Information Systems Plan

Information systems plan: A road map indicating the direction of systems development, the rationale, the current situation, the management strategy, the implementation plan, and the budget.

Once specific projects have been selected within the overall context of a strategic plan for the business and the systems area, an **information systems plan** can be developed. The plan serves as a road map indicating the direction of systems development, the rationale, the current situation, the management strategy, the implementation plan, and the budget (see Table 11.6).

The plan contains a statement of corporate goals and specifies how information technology supports the attainment of those goals. The report shows how general goals will be achieved by specific systems projects. It lays out specific target dates and milestones that can be used later to judge the progress of the plan in terms of how many objectives were actually attained in the time frame specified in the plan. An important part of the plan is the management strategy for moving from the current situation to the future. Generally, this will indicate the key decisions made by managers concerning hardware acquisition; telecommunications; centralization/decentralization of authority, data, and hardware; and required organizational change.

The implementation plan generally outlines stages in the development of the plan, defining milestones and specifying dates. In this section, organizational changes are usually described, including management and employee training requirements; recruiting efforts; and changes in authority, structure, or management practice.

Establishing Organizational Information Requirements

In order to develop an effective information systems plan, the organization must have a clear understanding of both its long- and short-term information requirements. Two principal methodologies for establishing the essential information requirements of the organization as a whole are enterprise analysis and critical success factors.

Table 11.6   INFORMATION SYSTEMS PLAN

1. Purpose of the Plan
   Overview of plan contents
   Changes in firm's current situation
   Firm's strategic plan
   Current business organization
   Management strategy

2. Strategic Business Plan
   Current situation
   Current business organization
   Changing environments
   Major goals of the business plan

3. Current Systems
   Major systems supporting business functions
   Major current capabilities
      Hardware
      Software
      Database
      Telecommunications
   Difficulties meeting business requirements
   Anticipated future demands

4. New Developments
   New system projects
      Project descriptions
      Business rationale
   New capabilities required
      Hardware
      Software
      Database
      Telecommunications

5. Management Strategy
   Acquisition plans
   Milestones and timing
   Organizational realignment
   Internal reorganization
   Management controls
   Major training initiatives
   Personnel strategy

6. Implementation Plan
   Detailed implementation plan
   Anticipated difficulties in implementation
   Progress reports

7. Budget Requirements
   Requirements
   Potential savings
   Financing
   Acquisition cycle

ENTERPRISE ANALYSIS (BUSINESS SYSTEMS PLANNING)

Enterprise analysis: An analysis of organization-wide information requirements by looking at the entire organization in terms of organizational units, functions, processes, and data elements; helps identify the key entities and attributes in the organization's data.

Enterprise analysis (also called business systems planning) argues that the information requirements of a firm can only be understood by looking at the entire organization in terms of organizational units, functions, processes, and data elements. Enterprise analysis can help identify the key entities and attributes of the organization's data. This method starts with the notion that the information requirements of a firm or a division can be specified only with a thorough understanding of the entire organization. This method was developed by IBM in the 1960s explicitly for establishing the relationship among large system development projects (Zachman, 1982).

The central method used in the enterprise analysis approach is to take a large sample of managers and ask them how they use information, where they get the information, what their environment is like, what their objectives are, how they make decisions, and what their data needs are.

The results of this large survey of managers are aggregated into subunits, functions, processes, and data matrices (see Figure 11.9). Figure 11.9 shows parts of two matrices developed at the Social Security Administration as part of a very-large-scale systems redevelopment effort called the Systems Modernization Plan, which began in 1982.

Figure 11.9(A) shows a process/organization matrix identifying those persons in the organization who participate in specific processes, such as planning. Figure 11.9(B) shows a process/data class matrix depicting what information is required to support a particular process, which process creates the data, and which uses it. (C in an intersection stands for "creators of data"; U stands for "users of data").

	PROCESS/ ORGANIZATION MATRIX — PROCESSES / ORGANIZATIONS	Commissioner	DC programs and policy	–AC disability insurance	–AC retirement and survivors ins.	–AC supp. security income	–AC governmental affairs	–AC policy	–O actuary	–O hearings and appeals	DC management and assessment	–AC assessment	––O field assessment	–O human resources	–O material resources	–O financial resources	–O training	DC systems	–AC system integration	–AC system requirements	–AC system operations	DC operations	–AC field operations	––Region	––––District/branch	––––Teleservice center	–AC Central operations	––O Program service center	––––Process center	––––––Module	––––D International opers.	––––––Module	––O Disability opers.	––––––Module	––Central records	––––––Module (cert. and coverage)	––––Data operations centers	Disability determination service
PLANNING	Develop agency plans	M	M	M	M	M		M	M	M	M	S	S	S	S	S	S	M	M	M	M	M	M	S			M	S					S		S			
	Administer agency budget	M	M	M	S	S	S	S	M	M	M	M	S	M	M	M	M	M	S	S	S	M	M	S	S		M	M	M		M		M		M		S	M
	Formulate program policies	M	M	M	M	M		M		M	M	S	S			S	S	M	S	M	S	M	M	M			M	M	S				M		S			
	Formulate admin. policies	M	M								M			M	M	M	M	M				M																
	Design work processes		M	M	M	M	S	S		M	M	M	S	S	S		S	M	M	M	M	M	M	M	M	S	M	M	M	M	S	M	M	M	M	M	M	M
GENERAL MANAGEMENT	Manage public affairs	M	M	M	S	M	M	S		S	S	S	S		S		S	S	M	M	M	S	S	M	M	M	S	M	S		M	S	M	S		M	S	M
	Manage intergovernmental affairs	M	M	M	M	M	M	M		M	M	M	S	M	M	S	S	S	M	M	M	S		M	S	S	S	S	S		M	S	M	S		S		M
	Exchange data		M	M	M	M	M	M	M	S	M	M	S	M	S	S	S	M	M	M	M	S	M	M	M	S	M	S		M	M	M		M		M		
	Maintain administrative accounts			M	S	S	S	S	S	S	M				M	M			S		S			M					S		S						S	S
	Maintain programmatic accounts		M			M					M					M					S						M		M		M		M			S		
	Conduct audits										M	S	S			S							M	S			M	S	S		S		S		S			
	Establish organizations		M	M	M	M	M	M	M	M	M	M	M	M	M	M	M	M	M	M	M	M	M	M	M	M	M	M	M	M	M	M	M	M	M	M	M	M
	Manage human resources		M	M	M	M	M	M	M	M	M	S	M	M	M	M	M	M	M	M	M	M	M	M	M	M	M	M	M	M	M	M	M	M	M	M	M	M
	Provide security									S	M				M			M	M	M	M	M	S	S	S	S	S	S	S	S	S	S	S	S	S	S	S	S
	Manage equipment		S				M			M	M	S	S		M		M	M	M		M	S	M	M	M	M	M	M	S	S	S	S	M	S	M	S	M	
	Manage facilities			S						S	M	S	S		M		M	M	S		M	S	M	M	M	M	M	M	M		S		M		M		M	
	Manage supplies		S	S	S	S	S	S	S	M	M	S	S		M		M	M	S		M	S	M	S	M	M	M	M	S	S	S	M	M	S	M	S	M	
	Manage data		M	M	M	M		M										M	M	M	M	S	S	S	S	S	S	S	S	S	S	S	S	S	S	S	S	S
	Manage workloads	M	M	M	M	M	M	M	M	M	M	M	M	M	M	M	M	M	M	M	M	M	M	M	M	M	M	M	M	M	M	M	M	M	M	M	M	M
PROGRAM ADMIN.	Issue social security numbers											S			S						S				M	M						M					S	
	Maintain earnings		S								S				S						S				M	M				S		S		S	M	M	M	
	Collect claims information																				S				M	M				M		M		M	M	S		
	Determine eligibility/entitlement		M	M	M	M		S		M		M	M								S				M	S			M	M		M	M	M	M	M	S	M
	Compute payments																				S				M	S	M			M		M		M	M			
	Administer debt management		S					S			M					M					S	M		M	M	S	M	M	M	M	M	M	M	M				
SUPPORT	Generate notices																				S				M	M				M		M		M		M		
	Respond to programmatic inquiries		M	M	M	M	M	M	M	M	M	M	S								S	M	S	M	M	M	S	M	S	M	M	M	M	M	M	M	S	M
	Provide quality assessment	M									M	M	M																									

KEY
M = major involvement
S = some involvement
DC = deputy commissioner
AC = associate commissioner
O = office

Figure 11.9A
Process/organization matrix. This chart indicates who in the organization participates in specific processes and the nature of their involvement.

The shaded boxes in Figure 11.9(B) indicate a *logical application group*—a group of data elements that supports a related set of organizational processes. In this case, actuarial estimates, agency plans, and budget data are created in the planning process. The planning process, in turn, is performed by the Commissioner's office, along with Deputy Commissioners and Assistant Commissioners.

This suggests, then, that an information system focused on actuarial, agency plan, and budget data elements should be built for the commissioners in order to support planning.

One strength of enterprise analysis is that it gives a comprehensive view of the organization and of systems/data uses and gaps.

Enterprise analysis is especially suitable for start-up or massive change situations. For instance, it is one of the methods used by the Social Security Administration to bring about a long-term strategic change in its information processing activities. This organization had never before performed a comprehensive

Logical application groups	Processes	Actuarial estimates	Agency plans	Budget	Program regs./policy	Admin. regs./policy	Labor agreements	Data standards	Procedures	Automated systems documentation	Educational media	Public agreements	Intergovernmental agreements	Grants	External	Exchange control	Administrative accounts	Program expenditures	Audit reports	Organization/position	Employee identification	Recruitment/placement	Complaints/grievances	Training resources	Security	Equipment utilization	Space utilization	Supplies utilization	Workload schedules	Work measurement	Enumeration I.D.	Enumeration control	Earnings	Employer I.D.	Earnings control	Claims characteristics	Claims control	Decisions	Payment	Collection/waiver	Notice	Inquiries control	Quality appraisal
PLANNING	Develop agency plans	C	C	C	U	U									U																												
PLANNING	Administer agency budget	C	C	C	U	U						U	U	U		U	U	U		U	U					U	U	U		U		U			U		U			U		U	U
PLANNING	Formulate program policies	U	U		C				U						U				U				U															U					U
PLANNING	Formulate admin. policies		U		U	C	C		U						U				U	U			U																				
PLANNING	Formulate data policies		U	U		U		C	U	U															U	U	U	U															
PLANNING	Design work processes		U		U	U			C	C		U	U						U																			U					U
GENERAL MANAGEMENT	Manage public affairs		U		U	U			U		C	C	C																														
GENERAL MANAGEMENT	Manage intrgovt. affairs	U	U		U	U			U		U		C	C	C															U	U		U	U		U			U				
GENERAL MANAGEMENT	Exchange data				U				U			U	U	U	U	C	U	U												U													
GENERAL MANAGEMENT	Maintain admin. accounts			U		U			U			U	U				C				U					U	U	U								U			U				
GENERAL MANAGEMENT	Maintain prog. accounts			U	U				U			U	U					C														U			U		U	U	U	U		U	
GENERAL MANAGEMENT	Conduct audits				U	U			U	U							U	U	C		U								U														
GENERAL MANAGEMENT	Establish organizations			U		U			U											C	U								U	U													U
GENERAL MANAGEMENT	Manage human resources			U		U	U		U											C	C	C	C	C																			
GENERAL MANAGEMENT	Provide security				U	U		U	U	U															C	C	C	C		U													
GENERAL MANAGEMENT	Manage equipment			U		U		U	U	U															C	C	C	C															
GENERAL MANAGEMENT	Manage facilities			U		U			U																U	U	C																
GENERAL MANAGEMENT	Manage supplies			U		U			U																C	U	U	C															
GENERAL MANAGEMENT	Manage workloads	U		U	U	U			U							U										U	U	U	C	C		U			U		U					U	U
PROGRAM ADMIN.	Issue social security nos.								U				U		U																C	C											
PROGRAM ADMIN.	Maintain earnings								U				U	U	U																U		C	C	C	U							
PROGRAM ADMIN.	Collect claims information				U	U			U						U																U	U				C	C	U	U	U			
PROGRAM ADMIN.	Determine elig/entlmt.								U																						U	U	U			U		C	U	U			
PROGRAM ADMIN.	Compute payments				U				U									U													U		U			U		U	C	C			
PROGRAM ADMIN.	Administer debt mgmt.				U				U									U																					U	C			
SUPPORT	Generate notices								U						U																U		U			U		U	U	U	C		
SUPPORT	Respond to prog. inquiries				U				U		U																				U		U	U		U		U	U	U	U	C	
SUPPORT	Provide quality assessment				U	U			U	U																					U		U			U		U			U		C

KEY
C = creators of data U = users of data

Figure 11.9B
Process/data class matrix. This chart depicts what data classes are required to support particular organizational processes and which processes are the creators and users of data.

analysis of its information requirements. Instead, it had relied on a bottom-up method of responding to whatever users requested, as well as on by-product approaches where most emphasis was placed on simply performing elementary transaction processing. Enterprise analysis was used to develop a comprehensive view of how the Social Security Administration currently uses information.

Another strength of enterprise analysis is that it helps to produce an organizational consensus by involving a large number of managers and users of data. It helps the organization find out what it should be doing in terms of information processing simply by requiring many managers to think about information (Doll, 1985).

The weakness of enterprise analysis is that it produces an enormous amount of data that is expensive to collect and difficult to analyze. It is a very expensive technique with a bias toward top management and data processing. Most of the interviews are conducted with senior or middle managers, with little effort to collect information from clerical workers and supervisory managers. Moreover, the questions frequently focus not on the critical objectives of management and where information is needed, but rather on what *existing* information is used. The result is a tendency to automate whatever exists. In this manner, manual systems are automated. But in many instances, entirely new approaches to how business is conducted are needed, and these needs are not addressed.

Critical success factors (CSFs): A small number of easily identifiable operational goals shaped by the industry, the firm, the manager, and the broader environment that are believed to assure the success of an organization. Used to determine the information requirements of an organization.

The strategic analysis or critical success factor approach argues that the information requirements of an organization are determined by a small number of **critical success factors (CSFs)** of managers. CSFs are operational goals. If these goals can be attained, the success of the firm or organization is assured (Rockart, 1979; Rockart and Treacy, 1982).

CSFs are shaped by the industry, the firm, the manager, and the broader environment. This broader focus, in comparison to that of other methods, accounts for the description of this technique as "strategic." An important premise of the strategic analysis approach is that there is a small number of objectives that managers can easily identify and information systems can focus on.

The principal method used in CSF analysis is personal interviews—three or four—with a number of top managers to identify their goals and the resulting CSFs. These personal CSFs are aggregated to develop a picture of the firm's CSFs. Then systems are built to deliver information on these CSFs. (See Table 11.7 for an example of CSFs. For the method of developing CSFs in an organization, see Figure 11.10.)

The strength of the CSF method is that it produces a smaller data set to analyze than enterprise analysis. Only top managers are interviewed, and the questions focus on a small number of CSFs rather than a broad inquiry into what information is used or needed. This method can be tailored to the structure of each industry, with different competitive strategies producing different information systems. The CSF method also depends on the industry position and even the geographical location. Therefore, this method produces systems that are more custom-tailored to an organization.

A unique strength of the CSF method is that it takes into account the changing environment with which organizations and managers must deal. This method explicitly asks managers to look at the environment and consider how their analysis of it shapes their information needs. It is especially suitable for top management and for the development of DSS and ESS. Last, the method produces a consensus among top managers about what is important to measure in order to gauge the organization's success. Like enterprise analysis, the CSF method focuses organizational attention on how information should be handled.

The weakness of this method is that the aggregation process and the analysis of the data are art forms. There is no particularly rigorous way in which individual CSFs can be aggregated into a clear company pattern. Second, there is

Table 11.7 CRITICAL SUCCESS FACTORS AND ORGANIZATIONAL GOALS

Example	Goals	CSF
Profit concern	Earnings/share Return on investment Market share New product	Automotive industry Styling Quality dealer system Cost control Energy standards
Nonprofit	Excellent health care Meeting government regulations Future health needs	Regional integration with other hospitals Efficient use of resources Improved monitoring of regulations

Source: Rockart (1979).

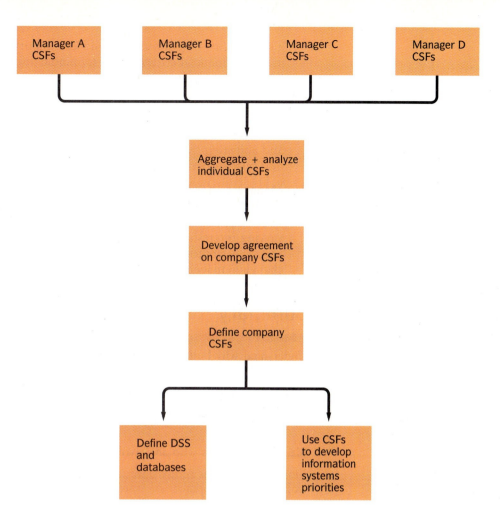

Figure 11.10
Using CSFs to develop systems. The CSF approach relies on interviews with key managers to identify their CSFs. Individual CSFs are aggregated to develop CSFs for the entire firm. Systems can then be built to deliver information on these CSFs.

often confusion among interviewees (and interviewers) between *individual* and *organizational* CSFs. They are not necessarily the same. What can be critical to a manager may not be important for the organization. Moreover, this method is clearly biased toward top managers because they are the ones (generally the only ones) interviewed. Indeed, the method seems to apply only to management reporting systems, DSS, and ESS. It assumes that successful TPSs already exist. Last, it should be noted that this method does not necessarily overcome the impact of a changing environment or changes in managers. Environments and managers change rapidly, and information systems must adjust accordingly. The use of CSFs to develop a system does not mitigate these factors.

Management Challenges

1. **Major risks and uncertainties in systems development.** Information systems development has major risks and uncertainties that make it difficult for the systems to achieve their goals. Sometimes, the cost of achieving them is too high. One problem is the difficulty of establishing information requirements, both for individual end users and for the organization as a whole. The requirements may be too complex or subject to change. Another problem is that the time and cost factors to develop an information system are very difficult to analyze, especially in large projects. Chapters 12 and 14 describe some ways of dealing with these risks and uncertainties, but the issues remain major management challenges.

2. **Determining benefits of a system when they are largely intangible.** As the sophistication of systems grows, they produce fewer tangible and more intangible benefits. By definition, there is no solid method for pricing intan-

gible benefits. Organizations could lose important opportunities if they only use strict financial criteria for determining information systems benefits. On the other hand, organizations could make very poor investment decisions if they overestimate intangible benefits.

3. **Developing an effective information systems plan.** The greatest difficulty with plans in general is choosing the right plan, implementing it effectively, and adjusting the plan as conditions merit. Simply developing an information systems plan and a strategic plan is no guarantee of success or survival.

4. **Managing change.** Although building a new information system is a process of planned organizational change, this does not mean that change can always be planned or controlled. Individuals and groups in organizations have varying interests, and may resist changes in procedures, job relationships, and technologies. Chapter 14, on implementation, describes the problems of change management in greater detail.

Summary

Understand why building new systems is a process of organizational change.

Building a new information system is a form of planned organizational change that involves many different people in the organization. Because information systems are sociotechnical entities, a change in information systems involves changes in work, management, and the organization.

Identify the groups who are involved in building systems.

Most organizations today have a well-established management structure for controlling the development of systems. All medium-sized and large systems involve senior, middle, and supervisory management, along with information systems professionals. Large and medium-sized organizations usually have a corporate information system steering committee to allocate resources to system projects. The project team is directly responsible for building the system.

Identify the core activities in the systems development process.

The core activities in systems development are systems analysis, systems design, programming, testing, conversion, and production and maintenance. Systems analysis is the study and analysis of problems of existing systems and the identification of requirements for their solution. Systems design provides the specifications for an information system solution, showing how its technical and organizational components fit together.

Describe various models for determining the business value of information systems.

Capital budgeting models such as the payback method, accounting rate of return on investment (ROI), cost–benefit ratio, net present value, profitability index, and internal rate of return (IRR), are the primary financial models for determining the business value of information systems. Portfolio analysis and scoring models include nonfinancial considerations and can be used to evaluate alternative information systems projects.

Explain how the organization can develop information systems that fit its business plan.

Organizations should develop an information systems plan that describes how information technology supports the attainment of their goals. The plan indicates the direction of systems development, the rationale, implementation strategy, and budget. Enterprise analysis and critical success factors (CSFs) can be used to elicit organizationwide information requirements that must be addressed by the plan.

Review Questions

1. Why can a new information system be considered planned organizational change?

2. What are the four organizational areas of responsibility for information system builders?

3. What is business process redesign? How does it differ from traditional rationalization of procedures?

4. Name the major organizational groups involved in building information systems. What is the role of each?

5. Name the groups responsible for the management of systems development. What are the responsibilities of each?

6. List three sources of ideas for new systems.

7. What is the difference between systems analysis and systems design?

8. What is feasibility? Name and describe each of the three major areas of feasibility for information systems.

9. What are information requirements? Why are they difficult to determine correctly?

10. What is the difference between the logical design and the physical design of an information system?

11. Why is the testing stage of systems development so important? Name and describe the three stages of testing for an information system.

12. What is conversion? Why is it important to have a detailed conversion plan?

13. What role do programming, production and maintenance play in systems development?

14. Name and describe the capital budgeting methods used to evaluate information systems projects.

15. What are the limitations of financial models for establishing the value of information systems?

16. Describe how portfolio analysis and scoring models can be used to establish the worth of systems.

17. What are the major categories of an information systems plan?

18. How can enterprise analysis and critical success factors be used to establish organization-wide information system requirements?

1. It has been said that information systems design cannot be directed by technical specialists alone. Discuss.

2. Information systems often have to be redesigned after testing. Discuss.

3. Which conversion strategy would you use for the following? Why?
   - A system to track stock purchase and sale transactions.
   - A process control system at a chemical plant.
   - A system to record student attendance at a 2000-student high school.
   - A corporate accounting system that will consolidate general ledger data from ten different operating units.

4. Discuss the roles of users and information processing specialists in the following systems development activities:
   - Systems analysis
   - Determination of information requirements
   - Assessment of feasibility
   - Design
   - Testing
   - Conversion

5. The only way to understand what information is needed by the organization is to do a comprehensive study of how various organizational groups actually use information. Discuss.

Group Project

With three or four of your classmates, read a description of another system in this text or in a business or computer magazine. Prepare a report describing (on the basis of the information provided) some of the design specifications that might be appropriate for the system you select. Present your findings to the class.

CASE STUDY

Curing Chaos

During the 1970s, Methodist Hospital, a large teaching hospital in Indianapolis, purchased a mainframe-based turnkey billing and patient records system from TDS Healthcare Systems Corporation of Atlanta. A turnkey system is delivered to a customer as a complete hardware and software configuration. The client simply has to "turn the key" to begin the system. Since then, the hospital's information systems department has spent most of their time maintaining the old system and working on a five- to seven-year application backlog. User departments such as the hospital laboratory and emergency room became frustrated because their computing needs could not be satisfied. So they bought their own systems, none of which communicated with the others.

When Walter Zerrenner took over as Methodist Hospital's chief information officer in 1989, he found three strategic information systems plans sitting on a shelf. There was never any time to implement them. The plans were developed without any user input, so no one outside the information systems department was committed to them.

Zerrenner brought in a team from Andersen Consulting in Chicago to assess the state of the hospital's information systems department as well as user attitudes toward the department. The assessment turned up 3 incompatible wide area networks, more than 20 incompatible local area networks and more than 100 different information systems throughout the hospital.

Information systems in different departments in Methodist Hospital used different identification codes for the same patients. Patients had to register separately in each department, often answering the same questions over and over again. The TDS system showed that lab tests were scheduled but did not display the results. The results of the tests were stored on a separate departmental system in the lab. The only place to find complete information on a patient was in a paper file.

Physicians complained that they could not use microcomputers in their offices to dial into the TDS system for patient information. The TDS system only kept information on patients who were formally admitted to the hospital. Even that information was only available on-line for five days after a patient's discharge. The TDS system did not handle outpatients or people who merely came in for tests. Yet most users liked the way the TDS system worked. Dr. Chris Steffy, a resident in internal medicine, believed it was more efficient and rich in functions than other systems he had used.

Zerrenner formed a 25-member information systems planning committee with representatives from all of the hospital's major departments, including a contingent of physicians and nurses. Zerrenner and the planning committee identified three options for an improved patient information system: 1) scrap the existing systems; 2) try to make all of the existing systems communicate with each other; and 3) establish a centralized database for the data collected by individual departments.

The first solution meant walking away from the hospital's enormous investment in existing systems, which did work well for individual departments. The second solution appeared to be a logistical nightmare, because the information systems department would have had to create a separate interface for every departmental system. Physicians would have had to sit at terminals and sign on and off each individual system. The third solution seemed the only reasonable choice. The database could obtain information from each departmental system and make it commonly available.

Zerrenner built a working model of the new system, called the Information Exchange Platform, for users to evaluate. People were encouraged to sit down at a workstation, sign on with a password, and use a mouse to move around sample windows, viewing patient data, graphing the results, or sending the data via E-mail to another physician for consultation. The system uses the Sybase relational database management system running on an IBM RS/6000 file server.

The Information Exchange Platform was never designed to capture all of the data from individual departments. A second committee, a broad-based information systems steering committee formed by Zerrenner, is determining what information is needed by multiple departments. The project has adopted an 80/20 rule, focusing on the most important information that is used 80 percent of the time. Most of that information consists of lab, radiology, patient demographics, and electrocardiagram interpretations.

Source: Scott D. Palmer, "A Plan That Cured Chaos," *Datamation* (January 1, 1993).

Case Study Questions

1. Prepare a report analyzing the problems with Methodist Hospital's systems. Describe the problems and their causes. What management, organization and technology factors were responsible?

2. If you were the systems analyst for this project, list five questions you would ask during interviews to elicit the information needed for your systems analysis report.

3. Do you agree that the Information Exchange Platform was the best solution for Methodist Hospital? Why or why not? What would you recommend?

4. Why could it be said that the Information Exchange Platform is only one part of the solution for Methodist Hospital?

5. Describe the role of end users and technical specialists in analyzing the problem and in developing the solution.

6. What conversion strategy would you use when the Information Exchange Platform is completed?

References   Ahituv, Niv, and Seev Neumann. "A Flexible Approach to Information System Development," *MIS Quarterly* (June 1984).

Alter, Steven, and Michael Ginzberg. "Managing Uncertainty in MIS Implementation." *Sloan Management Review* 20 (Fall 1978).

Bacon, C. James. "The Uses of Decision Criteria in Selecting Information Systems/Technology Investments." *MIS Quarterly* 16, no. 3 (September 1992).

Bostrum, R. P., and J. S. Heinen. "MIS Problems and Failures: A Socio-Technical Perspective; Part I: The Causes." *MIS Quarterly* 1 (September 1977); "Part II: The Application of Socio-Technical Theory." *MIS Quarterly* 1 (December 1977).

Bullen, Christine, and John F. Rockart. "A Primer on Critical Success Factors." Cambridge, MA: Center for Information Systems Research, Sloan School of Management, 1981.

Buss, Martin D. J. "How to Rank Computer Projects." *Harvard Business Review* (January 1983).

Cerveny, Robert P., Edward J. Garrity, and G. Lawrence Sanders. "A Problem-Solving Perspective on Systems Development." *Journal of Management Information* Systems 6, no. 4 (Spring 1990).

Davenport, Thomas H., and James E. Short. "The New Industrial Engineering: Information Technology and Business Process Redesign." *Sloan Management Review* 31, no. 4 (Summer 1990).

Davis, Gordon B. "Determining Management Information Needs: A Comparison of Methods." *MIS Quarterly* 1 (June 1977).

Davis, Gordon B. "Information Analysis for Information System Development." *Systems Analysis and Design: A Foundation for the 1980's.* Ed. W. W. Cotterman, J. D. Cougar, N. L. Enger, and F. Harold. New York: Wiley, 1981.

Davis, Gordon B. "Strategies for Information Requirements Determination." *IBM Systems Journal* 1 (1982).

Doll, William J. "Avenues for Top Management Involvement in Successful MIS Development." *MIS Quarterly* (March 1985).

Dos Santos, Brian. "Justifying Investments in New Information Technologies." *Journal of Management Information Systems* 7, no. 4 (Spring 1991).

Ein-Dor, Philip, and Eli Segev. "Strategic Planning for Management Information Systems." *Management Science* 24, no. 15 (1978).

El Sawy, Omar, and Burt Nanus. "Toward the Design of Robust Information Systems." *Journal of Management Information Systems* 5, no. 4 (Spring 1989).

Emery, James C. "Cost/Benefit Analysis of Information Systems." Chicago: Society for Management Information Systems Workshop Report No. 1, 1971.

Flatten, Per O., Donald J. McCubbrey, P. Declan O'Riordan, and Keith Burgess. *Foundations of Business Systems,* 2nd ed. Fort Worth, TX: The Dryden Press, 1992.

Franz, Charles, and Daniel Robey. "An Investigation of User-Led System Design: Rational and Political Perspectives." *Communications of the ACM* 27 (December 1984).

Gerlach, James H. and Feng-Yang Kuo. "Understanding Human-Computer Interaction for Information Systems Design." *MIS Quarterly* 15, no. 4 (December 1991).

Ginzberg, Michael J., "Improving MIS Project Selection." *Omega, Internal Journal of Management Science* 6, no. 1 (1979).

Ginzberg, Michael J. "The Impact of Organizational Characteristics on MIS Design and Implementation." Working paper CRIS 10, GBA 80-110. New York University Center for Research on Information Systems, Computer Applications and Information Systems Area, 1980.

Goodhue, Dale L., Laurie J. Kirsch, Judith A. Quillard, and Michael D. Wybo. "Strategic Data Planning: Lessons from the Field." *MIS Quarterly* 16, no. 1 (March 1992).

Gould, John D., and Clayton Lewis. "Designing for Usability: Key Principles and What Designers Think." *Communications of the ACM* 28 (March 1985).

Grudnitski, Gary. "Eliciting Decision Makers' Information Requirements." *Journal of Management Information Systems* (Summer 1984).

Hammer, Michael. "Reengineering Work: Don't Automate, Obliterate." *Harvard Business Review* (July–August 1990).

Kendall, Kenneth E., and Julie E. Kendall. *Systems Analysis and Design.* 2/e. Englewood Cliffs, NJ: Prentice-Hall, 1991.

Kim, Chai, and Stu Westin. "Software Maintainability: Perceptions of EDP Professionals." *MIS Quarterly* (June 1988).

King, William R. "Alternative Designs in Information System Development." *MIS Quarterly* (December 1982).

Konsynski, Benn R. "Advances in Information System Design." *Journal of Management Information Systems* 1 (Winter 1984–1985).

Laudon, Kenneth C. "CIOs Beware: Very Large Scale Systems." New York: Center for Research on Information Systems, New York University Stern School of Business, working paper, 1989.

Lientz, Bennett P., and E. Burton Swanson. *Software Maintenance Management.* Reading, MA: Addison-Wesley, 1980.

Lucas, Henry C., Jr. *Toward Creative Systems Design.* New York: Columbia University Press, 1974.

Matlin, Gerald. "What Is the Value of Investment in Information Systems?" *MIS Quarterly* 13, no. 3 (September 1989).

McFarlan, F. Warren. "Portfolio Approach to Information Systems." *Harvard Business Review* (September–October 1981).

Nolan, Richard L. "Managing Information Systems by Committee." *Harvard Business Review* (July–August 1982).

Parker, M. M. "Enterprise Information Analysis: Cost-Benefit Analysis and the Data-Managed System." *IBM Systems Journal* 21 (1982), pp. 108–123.

Rockart, John F. "Chief Executives Define Their Own Data Needs." *Harvard Business Review* (March–April 1979).

Rockart, John F., and Michael E. Treacy. "The CEO Goes on Line." *Harvard Business Review* (January–February 1982).

Shank, Michael E., Andrew C. Boynton, and Robert W. Zmud. "Critical Success Factor Analysis as a Methodology for MIS Planning." *MIS Quarterly* (June 1985).

Vitalari, Nicholas P. "Knowledge as a Basis for Expertise in Systems Analysis: Empirical Study." *MIS Quarterly* (September 1985).

Wetherbe, James. "Executive Information Requirements: Getting It Right." *MIS Quarterly,* 15, no. 1 (March 1991).

Zachman, J.A. "Business Systems Planning and Business Information Control Study: A Comparison." *IBM Systems Journal* 21 (1982).

Alternative Systems-Building Methods

Brookstone Shifts Its Systems-Building Strategy

Brookstone Tools, the Peterborough, New Hampshire specialty mail-order and retail firm, found that its primary focus was shifting from mail-order to retail sales. Most of its sales transactions took place during a narrow three-month period. Brookstone needed information systems that could support both retail as well as mail-order sales and handle high volumes of sales transactions during this peak period. Unfortunately, the mainframe-based systems that it had originally developed to support mail-order operations were not able to handle these functions and were in danger of imminent collapse. This arrangement was also very costly: Brookstone was spending 1.2 percent of its sales revenue on information systems, whereas the industry average was only 0.8 percent of sales. To solve both problems, in 1989 Brookstone moved to totally reorganize the way it developed its information systems.

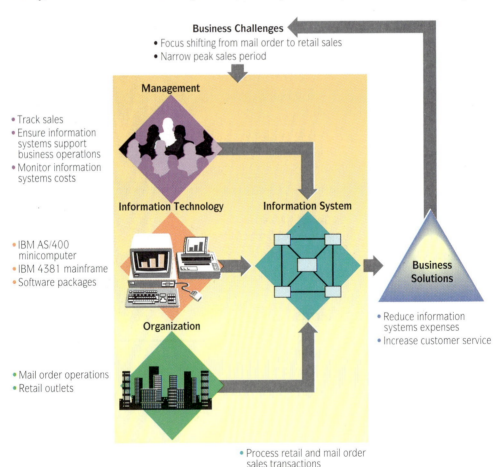

Brookstone decided to let its small IBM 4381 mainframe run only its mail-order sales systems and to use an IBM AS/400 minicomputer to run new systems for retail sales and other aspects of its retail operations. Instead of developing its own software for these new systems, Brookstone decided to use off-the-shelf software packages exclusively.

Until the new retail systems were built, Brookstone took advantage of software packages to create new applications based on its existing systems and databases. It used IBM's Data Interpretation System, a graphical front end to its DB2 database management system, and Comshare Inc.'s Arthur Planning, a merchandising planning and retail executive information system that could provide access to the large amounts of detailed data used in retail operations.

By using software packages as the foundation for new information systems, Brookstone redirected the energies of its information systems department. Instead of spending most of their effort in the costly and time-consuming development of new systems, using software packages freed them up to focus on business issues such as how to increase the timeliness and service of Brookstone's order processing during its peak selling period.

By pursuing alternative methods of building its systems, Brookstone also expected to save more than $1 million annually in reduced personnel and support expenses for information systems. As early as 1992, it was able to cut its programming staff in half.

Source: Christopher Lindquist, "Changing the Game at Brookstone," *Computerworld* (January 27, 1992).

Like Brookstone Tools, many organizations are examining alternative methods of building new information systems. While they are designing and building some applications entirely on their own, they are also turning to software packages and other strategies to reduce time, cost, and inefficiency. This chapter examines the use of prototyping, application software packages, end-user development, and outsourcing as systems-building alternatives to the traditional systems life cycle method of building an entire information system from scratch.

There is no one approach that can be used for all situations and types of systems. Each of these approaches has advantages and disadvantages, and each provides managers with a range of choices. This chapter describes and compares the various approaches so that managers know how to choose among them.

After completing this chapter you will be able to do the following:

- Distinguish between the various system-building alternatives: the traditional systems life cycle, prototyping, application software packages, end-user development, and outsourcing.

- Understand the strengths and limitations of each approach.
- Describe the types of problems for which each approach is best suited.
- Describe the solutions to the management problems created by these approaches.

12.1 The Traditional Systems Life Cycle

Systems life cycle: Traditional methodology for developing an information system that partitions the systems development process into six formal stages that must be completed sequentially with a very formal division of labor between end-users and information systems specialists.

The **systems life cycle** is the oldest method for building information systems and is still used today for medium or large complex systems projects. This methodology assumes that an information system has a life cycle similar to that of any living organism, with a beginning, middle, and end. The life cycle for an information system has six stages: project definition, systems study, design, programming, installation, and post-implementation. Figure 12.1 illustrates these stages. Each stage consists of basic activities that must be performed before the next stage can begin.

The life cycle methodology is a very formal approach to building systems. It partitions the systems development process into distinct stages and develops an information system sequentially, stage by stage. The life cycle methodology also has a very formal division of labor between end users and information systems

Figure 12.1
The life cycle methodology for system development. The life cycle methodology divides system development into 6 formal stages with specifics for milestones and end products at each stage. A typical medium-sized development project requires 2 years to deliver and has an expected life span of 3 to 8 years.

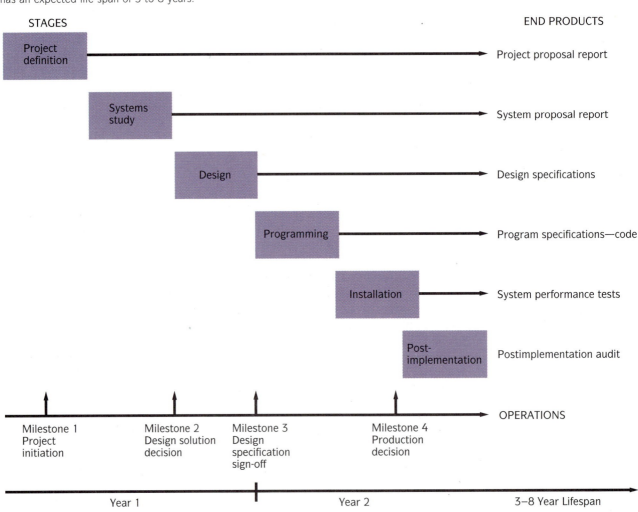

specialists. Technical specialists such as systems analysts and programmers are responsible for much of the systems analysis, design, and implementation work; end users are limited to providing information requirements and reviewing the work of the technical staff. Formal sign-offs or agreements between end users and technical specialists are required as each stage is completed.

Figure 12.1 also shows the product or output of each stage of the life cycle that is the basis for such sign-offs. The project definition stage results in a proposal for the development of a new system. The system study stage provides a detailed systems proposal report outlining alternative solutions and establishing the feasibility of proposed solutions. The design stage results in a report on the design specifications for the system solution that is selected. The programming stage results in actual software code for the system. The installation stage outputs the results of tests to assess the performance of the system. The post-implementation stage concludes with a post-implementation audit to measure the extent to which the new system has met its original objectives. We now describe the stages of the life cycle in detail.

Stages of the Systems Life Cycle

Project definition: Stage in the systems life cycle that determines whether or not the organization has a problem and whether or not the problem can be solved by launching a system project.

The **project definition** stage tries to answer the questions, "Why do we need a new system project?" and "What do we want to accomplish?" This stage determines whether the organization has a problem and whether that problem can be solved by building a new information system or by modifying an existing one. If a system project is called for, this stage identifies its general objectives, specifies the scope of the project, and develops a project plan that can be shown to management.

Systems study: Stage in the systems life cycle that analyzes the problems of existing systems, defines the objectives to be attained by a solution, and evaluates various solution alternatives.

The **systems study** stage analyzes the problems of existing systems (manual or automated) in detail, identifies objectives to be attained by a solution to these problems, and describes alternative solutions. The systems study stage examines the feasibility of each solution alternative for review by management. This stage tries to answer the questions, "What do the existing systems do?" "What are their strengths, weaknesses, trouble spots, and problems?" "What should a new or modified system do to solve these problems?" "What user information requirements must be met by the solution?" "What alternative solution options are feasible?" "What are their costs and benefits?"

Answering these questions requires extensive information gathering and research; sifting through documents, reports and work papers produced by existing systems; observing how these systems work; polling users with questionnaires; and conducting interviews. All of the information gathered during the systems study phase will be used to determine information system requirements. Finally, the systems study stage describes in detail the remaining life cycle activities and the tasks for each phase.

Design: Stage in the systems life cycle that produces the logical and physical design specifications for the systems solution.

The **design** stage produces the logical and physical design specifications for the solution. Because the life cycle emphasizes formal specifications and paperwork, many of the design and documentation tools described in Chapter 13, such as data flow diagrams, program structure charts, system flowcharts, decision tables, or decision trees, are likely to be utilized.

Programming: Stage in the systems life cycle that translates the design specifications produced during the design stage into software program code.

The **programming** stage translates the design specifications produced during the design stage into software program code. Systems analysts work with programmers to prepare specifications for each program in the system. These program specifications describe what each program will do, the type of programming language to be used, inputs and outputs, processing logic, processing schedules, and control statements such as those for sequencing input data. Programmers write customized program code typically using a conventional third-generation programming language such as COBOL or FORTRAN or a high-productivity fourth-generation language. Since large systems have many programs with hundreds of thousands of lines of program code, entire teams of programmers may be required.

Installation: Systems life cycle stage consisting of testing, training, and conversion; the final steps required to put a system into operation.

Post implementation: The final stage of the systems life cycle in which the system is used and evaluated while in production and is modified to make improvements or meet new requirements.

The **installation** stage consists of the final steps to put the new or modified system into operation: testing, training, and conversion. The software is tested to make sure it performs properly from both a technical and a functional business standpoint. (More detail on testing can be found in Chapter 13.) Business and technical specialists are trained to use the new system. A formal conversion plan provides a detailed schedule of all of the activities required to install the new system, and the old system is converted to the new one.

The **post-implementation** stage consists of using and evaluating the system after it is installed and is in production. It also includes updating the system to make improvements. Users and technical specialists will go through a formal post-implementation audit that determines how well the new system has met its original objectives and whether any revisions or modifications are required. After the system has been fine-tuned it will need to be maintained while it is in production to correct errors, meet requirements, or improve processing efficiency. Over time, the system may require so much maintenance to remain efficient and meet user objectives that it will come to the end of its useful lifespan. Once the system's life cycle comes to an end, a completely new system is called for and the cycle may begin again.

Limitations of the Life Cycle Approach

The systems life cycle is still used for building large transaction processing systems (TPS) and management information systems (MIS) where requirements are highly structured and well-defined. It will also remain appropriate for complex technical systems such as space launches, air traffic control, and refinery operations. Such applications need a rigorous and formal requirements analysis, predefined specifications, and tight controls over the systems building process. However, the systems life cycle methodology has serious limitations and is not well suited for most of the small desktop systems that will predominate during the 1990s and the twenty-first century.

The life cycle approach is very costly and time-consuming. A tremendous amount of time must be spent gathering information and preparing voluminous specification and sign-off documents. It may take years before a system is finally installed. If development time is too prolonged, the information requirements may change before the system is operational. The system that takes many years and dollars to build may be obsolete while it is still on the drawing board.

The life cycle approach is inflexible and discourages change. The life cycle approach does allow for revisions to the system to ensure that requirements are met. Whenever requirements are incorrect or an error is encountered, the sequence of life cycle activities can be repeated. But new volumes of documents must be generated, substantially increasing development time and costs. Because of the time and cost to repeat the sequence of life cycle activities, the methodology encourages freezing of specifications early in the development process. This means that changes cannot be made. Once users approve specification documents, the specifications are frozen. However, users traditionally have had trouble visualizing a final system from specification documents. In reality, they may need to see or use a system to make sure they know what it is they need or want. Because this is not possible with the life cycle approach, it is common for users to sign off on specification documents without fully comprehending their contents, only to learn during programming and testing that the specifications are incomplete or not what they had in mind. Proper specifications cannot always be captured the first time around, early enough in the life cycle when they are easy to change.

The life cycle method is ill-suited to decision-oriented applications. Decision making can be rather unstructured and fluid. Requirements constantly change or decisions may have no well-defined models or procedures. Decision makers often cannot specify their information needs in advance. They may need to experiment with concrete systems to clarify the kinds of decisions they wish to make. This high level of uncertainty cannot be easily accommodated by the life cycle aproach.

Some of these problems can be solved by the alternative strategies for building systems that are described in the remainder of this chapter.

12.2 Prototyping

Prototyping consists of building an experimental system rapidly and inexpensively for end users to evaluate. By interacting with the prototype, users can get a better idea of their information requirements. The prototype endorsed by the users can be used as a template to create the final system.

The **prototype** is a working version of an information system or part of the system, but it is meant to be only a preliminary model. Once operational, the prototype will be further refined until it conforms precisely to users' requirements. For many applications, a prototype will be extended and enhanced over and over again before a final design is accepted. Once the design has been finalized, the prototype can be converted to a polished production system.

The process of building a preliminary design, trying it out, refining it, and trying again has been called an **iterative** process of systems development because the steps required to build a system can be repeated over and over again. We noted earlier that the traditional life cycle approach involved some measure of reworking and refinement. However, prototyping is more explicitly iterative than the conventional life cycle, and it actively promotes system design changes. It has been said that prototyping replaces unplanned rework with planned iteration, with each version more accurately reflecting users' requirements.

The prototype version will not have all the final touches of the complete system. Reports, sections of files, and input transactions may not be complete; processing may not be very efficient, but a working version of the system or part of the system will be available for users to evaluate. They can start interacting with the system, deciding what they like and dislike, what they want or do not want. Since most users cannot describe their requirements fully on paper, prototyping allows them to work with a system in order to determine exactly what they need. The methodology anticipates that they will change their minds; these changes can be incorporated easily and inexpensively during an early stage of development.

Prototyping is less formal than the life cycle method. Instead of generating detailed specifications and sign-off documents, prototyping quickly generates a working model of a system. Requirements are determined dynamically as the prototype is constructed. Systems analysis, design, and implementation all take place at the same time.

> **Prototyping:** Process of building an experimental system quickly and inexpensively for demonstration and evaluation so that users can better determine information requirements.
>
> **Prototype:** Preliminary working version of an information system for demonstration and evaluation purposes.
>
> **Iterative:** Process of repeating the steps to build a system over and over again.

Steps in Prototyping

Figure 12.2 shows a four-step model of the prototyping process. The steps consist of the following:

STEP 1. *Identify the user's basic requirements.* The system designer (usually an information systems specialist) works with the user only long enough to capture his or her basic information needs.

STEP 2. *Develop an initial prototype.* The system designer creates a working prototype quickly, most likely using the fourth-generation software tools described in Chapter 7 that speed application development. (Some features of computer-aided software engineering [CASE] tools described in Chapter 13 can also be used for prototyping.) The prototype may only perform the most important functions of the proposed system, or it may consist of the entire system with a restricted file.

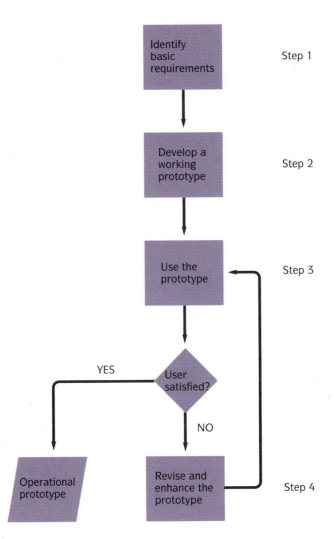

Figure 12.2
The prototyping process. The process of developing a prototype can be broken down into 4 steps. Because a prototype can be developed quickly and inexpensively, the developers can go through several iterations, repeating steps 3 and 4, in order to refine and enhance the prototype before arriving at the final operational one.

STEP 3. *Use the prototype.* The user is encouraged to work with the system in order to determine how well the prototype meets his or her needs and to make suggestions for improving the prototype.

STEP 4. *Revise and enhance the prototype.* The system builder notes all changes requested by the user and refines the prototype accordingly. After the prototype has been revised, the cycle returns to step 3. Steps 3 and 4 are repeated until the user is satisfied.

When no more iterations are required, the approved prototype then becomes an operational prototype that furnishes the final specifications for the application. Sometimes the prototype itself is adopted as the production version of the system. Prototyping is more rapid, iterative, and informal than the systems life cycle method has proven to be.

Advantages and Disadvantages of Prototyping

Certain types of information systems can be developed more efficiently and effectively using prototyping than using the traditional systems life cycle. For instance, when the Du Pont Company used prototyping along with heavy user involvement to build its systems, it produced more than 400 new programs with no failures and reduced maintenance by 70 to 90 percent (Arthur, 1992).

Prototyping is most useful when there is some uncertainty about requirements or design solutions. Requirements may be difficult to specify in advance or they may change substantially as implementation progresses. This is particularly true

TECHNOLOGY

Prototyping Graphical User Interfaces: New Tools to the Rescue

UNIX is a very flexible, powerful, and portable operating system, but it can present a forbidding or ugly interface to end users. Users of UNIX applications want graphical user interfaces (GUIs) that are attractive and easy to use like Microsoft Windows or the Macintosh graphical user interface. But generating these interfaces for the users is not easy because of the inordinate amount of time required to code a graphical user interface from scratch.

Now special GUI-building tools can help out. While the tools do not generate the entire interface, they can save about 80 percent of the work time, freeing programmers to spend more time on the underlying components of the applications and to take advantage of UNIX's strengths. Two types of tools are especially helpful: interface development tools and user interface management systems.

Interface development tools, such as Builder Xcessory from Integrated Computer Solutions (ICS) in Cambridge, Massachusetts or UIM/X from Visual Edge Software Ltd. in St. Laurent, Quebec, handle the prototyping of user interfaces and generate program code for the part of the interface that

the user would see. To use these tools, information systems specialists must be skilled in the C programming language. Most interface development tools adhere to established GUI standards, supplementing the GUI toolkit for Motif, the GUI standard used with UNIX. This feature appealed to the foreign exchange department of the Chemical Bank in New York City. The department used ICS's Builder Xcessory when it developed a trading system for Motif. Chemical Bank needed a tool for developing an interface that was both easy to use and that used the standard set of Motif graphic elements for windows, scrollbars, pop-up windows, and so forth.

User interface management systems, such as X.desktop from IXI Corporation of San Ramon, California or Looking Glass Professional from Visix Software Inc. of Reston, Virginia, are less powerful than interface development tools, but are easier to use. Most allow developers to generate user interface prototypes quickly using a mouse and a series of pull-down menus. However, few can generate complete applications by themselves. They automate generation of interface code. The remaining

code must be written in C or a fourth-generation language. So interface management systems are often used to develop prototypes for the user interface before the underlying program logic is created. Since the GUI can be developed separately from the application, the tool can be used concurrently to construct more than one GUI for the same application. For instance, one GUI might be developed for novices and another for more sophisticated professionals. Some interface management systems use proprietary toolkits that may lead to compatibility problems with future versions of Motif. In the future, these products could be producing non-standard interfaces.

Source: Bob Francis, "GUI Builders Take on UNIX," *Datamation* (July 1, 1992).

To Think About: What would be the impact on the systems development process if tools like these were unavailable? What are the advantages and disadvantages of each of these tools? What management, organization, and technology factors would you consider in deciding whether to use one of these tools?

---

of decision-oriented applications, where requirements tend to be very vague. Management realizes that better information is needed but is unsure of what this entails. For example, a major securities firm requests consolidated information to analyze the performance of its account executives. But what should the measures of performance be? Can the information be extracted from the personnel system alone, or must data from client billings be incorporated as well? What items should be compared on reports? Will intermediate processing based on some form of statistical analysis be involved? For many decision-support applications such as this one, it is unlikely that requirements can be fully captured on the initial written specifications. The final system cannot be clearly visualized because managers cannot foresee how the system will work.

Prototyping is especially valuable for the design of the **end-user interface** of an information system (the part of the system that end-users interact with, such as on-line display and data-entry screens or reports [see the Window on Technology]). User needs and behavior are not entirely predictable (Gould, 1985) and

End-user interface: The part of an information system through which the end user interacts with the system, such as on-line screens and commands.

are strongly dependent on the context of the situation. The prototype enables users to react immediately to the parts of the system they will be dealing with. Figure 12.3 illustrates the prototyping process for an on-line calendar for retail securities brokers. The first version of the screen was built according to user-supplied specifications for a calendar to track appointments and activities. But when users actually worked with the calendar screen, they suggested adding labels for month and year to the screen and a box to indicate whether the appointment had been met or an activity completed. The brokers also found that they wanted to access information that was maintained in the system about clients with whom they had appointments. The system designer added a link enabling brokers to move directly from the calendar screen to the client's records.

Figure 12.3
Prototyping a portfolio management application. This figure illustrates the process of prototyping one screen for the Financial Manager, a client and portfolio management application for securities brokers. Figure 12.3A shows an early version of the on-line appointment screen. Based on the special needs of a client, Figure 12.3B has two enhancements: a "done" indicator to show whether the task has been completed and a "link" to reference information maintained by the system on the client with whom the broker has an appointment.

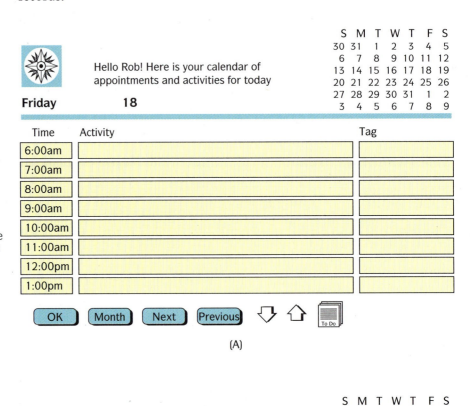

(A)

(B)

In other instances, end-user requirements may be clear enough, but systems builders may be unsure of certain technical features of the design solution. For example, a major supermarket chain contemplates revamping its inventory control system. It wants easy on-line access to its master files from multiple locations. The application will require numerous screens for on-line data entry and for retrieval of key pieces of information. But the systems team is unsure of how the screens should flow from one to the other on-line and needs to fine-tune screen formats as well. So the team decides to prototype many of the screens, using a tool for generating interactive applications. The screens are quickly developed, showing users how they will flow and how they will appear on-line.

Prototyping has been widely hailed as a panacea for the problems inherent in traditional systems development process. It encourages intense end-user involvement throughout the systems development life cycle. Users interact with a working system much earlier in the design process. As they react to and refine each version of the prototype, users become more intimately involved in the design effort (Cerveny et al., 1986). Prototyping is more likely to produce systems that fulfill user requirements, especially when it is used for decision-support applications. It promises to eliminate excess development costs and design flaws that occur when requirements are not fully captured the first time around. User satisfaction and morale are usually heightened because users can be presented with an actual working system, preliminary though it may be, in a very short period of time.

However, prototyping may not be appropriate for all applications. It should neither substitute for careful requirements analysis, structured design methodology, or thorough documentation, nor can it totally replace traditional development methods and tools. Both the method and the development tools currently used for prototyping have very real limitations.

Applications that are oriented to simple data manipulation and records management are considered good candidates for prototyping. However, systems that are based on batch processing or that rely on heavy calculations and complex procedural logic are generally unsuitable for the prototyping process. Prototyping is better suited for smaller applications. Large systems must be subdivided so that prototypes can be built one part at a time (Alavi, 1984). Subdividing a large system may not be possible without a thorough requirements analysis using the conventional approach, since it may be hard to see at the outset how the different parts will affect each other.

Rapid prototyping can gloss over essential steps in systems development. Basic systems analysis and requirements analysis cannot be short-circuited. The appeal of an easily and rapidly developed prototype may encourage the development team to move too quickly toward a working model without capturing even a basic set of requirements. This may be especially problematic when a large system is under development. It may not be clear how prototypes can be created for a big system or parts of the system unless prototyping is preceded by a comprehensive and thorough requirements analysis.

The final steps to convert the prototype into a polished production system may not be carried out. Once finished, the prototype often becomes part of the final production system. If the prototype works reasonably well, management may not see the need for reprogramming and redesign. Some of these hastily constructed systems may be difficult to maintain and support in a regular production environment. Since prototypes are not carefully constructed, their technical performance may be very inefficient. They may not easily accommodate large quantities of data or a large number of users in a production environment.

Prototyped systems still need to be fully documented and tested, but often these steps are shortchanged. Because prototypes are constructed so effortlessly, managers may assume that testing can be handled by users on their own; any oversights in testing can be corrected later. Because the system is so easily changed, documentation may not be kept up to date.

12.3 Developing Systems with Application Software Packages

Application software package: Set of prewritten, precoded application software programs that are commercially available for sale or lease.

Another alternative strategy is to develop an information system by purchasing an application software package. As introduced in Chapter 7, an **application software package** is a set of prewritten, precoded application software programs that are commercially available for sale or lease. Application software packages may range from a simple task (e.g., printing address labels from a database on a microcomputer) to over 400 program modules with 500,000 lines of code for a complex mainframe system. When an appropriate software package is available, it eliminates the need for writing software programs when an information system is developed and reduces the amount of design, testing, installation, and maintenance work as well. Table 12.1 provides examples of applications for which packages are commercially available.

Packages have flourished because there are many applications that are common to all business organizations—for example, payroll, accounts receivable, general ledger, or inventory control. For such universal functions with standard accounting practices, a generalized system will fulfill the requirements of many organizations. Therefore, it is not necessary for a company to write its own programs; the prewritten, predesigned, pretested software package can fulfill the requirements and can be substituted instead. Since the package vendor has already done most of the design, programming, and testing, the time frame and costs for developing a new system should be considerably reduced.

Table 12.1 EXAMPLES OF APPLICATIONS FOR WHICH APPLICATION PACKAGES ARE AVAILABLE

Accounts payable	Installment loans
Accounts receivable	Inventory control
Architectural design	
	Job accounting
Banking systems	Job costing
Bond and stock management	
	Library systems
Check processing	Life insurance
Computer-aided design	
Construction costing	Mailing labels
	Mathematical/statistical modeling
Data management systems	
Document imaging	Order entry
Electrical engineering	Payroll
Education	Performance measurement
E-mail	Process control
Financial control	Real estate management
Forecasting and modeling	Route scheduling
Forms design	
	Sales and distribution
General ledger	Savings systems
Graphics	Stock management
Government purchasing	
	Tax accounting
Health care	
Health insurance	Utilities control
Hotel management	
Human resources	Word processing
	Work scheduling

Packages are likely to be chosen as a development strategy under the following circumstances:

1. *Where functions are common to many companies.* For example, every company has a payroll system. Payroll systems typically perform the same functions: They calculate gross pay, net pay, deductions, and taxes. They also print paychecks and reports. Consequently, application software packages have been widely used for developing payroll systems.

2. *Where information systems resources for in-house development are in short supply.* With trained and experienced systems professionals in limited supply, many companies do not have staff that is either available or qualified to undertake extensive in-house development projects. Under such circumstances, packages may be the only way to enable a new system to be developed. Most companies also lack the budget to develop all of their systems in-house. Consequently, the most cost-effective development strategy is likely to involve an application software package.

3. *When desktop microcomputer applications are being developed for end users.* Numerous easy-to-use application packages have been developed for microcomputers and are the primary source of applications for desktop systems.

Advantages and Disadvantages of Software Packages

It is tempting to view software packages as the long-awaited antidote to escalating software and development costs. Application software packages can facilitate system design, testing, installation, maintenance support, and organizational acceptance of a new system. Packages also have serious limitations.

ADVANTAGES OF PACKAGES Design activities may easily consume up to 50 percent or more of the development effort. Since design specifications, file structure, processing relationships, transactions, and reports have already been worked out by the package vendor, most of the design work has been accomplished in advance. Software package programs are extensively pretested before they are marketed so that major technical problems have been eliminated. Testing the installed package can be accomplished in a relatively shorter period. Many vendors supply sample test data and assist with the testing effort. Vendors also supply tools and assistance in installing major mainframe or minicomputer systems and provide much of the ongoing maintenance and support for the system. For systems such as human resources or payroll, the vendor is responsible for making changes to keep the system in compliance with changing government regulations. The vendor supplies periodic enhancements or updates; these are relatively easy for the client's in-house staff to apply.

Fewer internal information systems resources are necessary to support a package-based system. Since 50 to 80 percent of information systems budgets can be consumed by maintenance costs, the package solution is one way to cut these costs and free up internal staff for other applications. The package vendor maintains a permanent support staff with expert knowledge of the specific application package. If a client's information systems personnel terminate or change jobs, the vendor remains a permanent source of expertise and help. System and user documentation are prewritten and are kept up-to-date by the vendor.

An added benefit of packages is the way they can reduce some of the organizational bottlenecks in the systems development process. The need to work and rework design specifications is reduced because the package specifications are already fixed; users must accept them as is. External design work is often perceived as being superior to an in-house effort. The package offers a fresh start by a third party who is in a stronger position to take advantage of other companies' experiences and state-of-the-art technology. Management can be more easily convinced to support a new information system based on packaged software because major software costs appear to be fixed. Problems with the system can be attributed to the limitations of the package rather than to internal sources. Thus, the major contribution of packages may be their capacity to end major sources of organizational resistance to the systems development effort.

DISADVANTAGES OF PACKAGES

Rarely noted are the disadvantages of packages, which can be considerable, and even overwhelming, for a complex system. Commercial software has not yet achieved the level of sophistication and technical quality needed to produce multipurpose packages that can do everything well that users want in a specific application. It is much easier to design and code software that performs one function very well than to create a system with numerous complex processing functions. For example, many human resources package vendors had to develop specialized packages for processing employee retirement benefits or applicant tracking because these functions were not handled well by the more comprehensive, multipurpose human resources packages.

In some circumstances, packages may actually hamper the development effort by raising conversion costs. Although package vendors often provide conversion software and consulting help, a package may actually prolong the conversion process, especially if conversion to the package is from a sophisticated automated system. In such cases, conversion costs have been known to be so astronomical as to render the entire development effort unfeasible. Conversion to a package is easiest from simple manual applications or from automated applications that are not very sophisticated.

Packages may not meet all of an organization's requirements. To maximize market appeal, packages are geared to the most common requirements of all organizations. But what happens if an organization has unique requirements that the package does not address? To varying degrees, package software developers anticipate this problem by providing features for customization that do not alter the basic software. **Customization** features allow a software package to be modified to meet an organization's unique requirements without destroying the integrity of the package software. For instance, the package may allocate parts of its files or databases to maintain an organization's own unique pieces of data. Some packages have a modular design that allows clients to select only the software functions with the processing they need from an array of options. Packages can also be customized with user exits, places in the package program code where clients can exit from the processing performed by package programs to call software modules they write themselves for their own unique processing functions.

It is standard policy among vendors to refuse to support their products if changes have been made that altered the package's source code. Some packages

Customization: The modification of a software package to meet an organization's unique requirements without destroying the integrity of the package software.

This screen shows a customized application for a client using the CA-Clipper software package from Computer Associates. The package is creating an interactive database from the scanned files of a technical book.

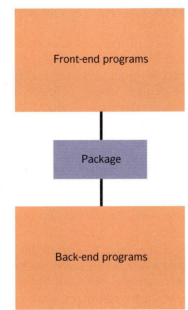

Figure 12.4
A substantially customized package. To customize some packages to meet the specific requirements of an organization may require so much modification that large front-end and back-end programs must be written to handle processing requirements not met by the original package. If extensive customization is required, the extra programs often are more elaborate than the package and the features of the original package are practically lost in the final system.

have been so heavily modified with user source code changes that they are virtually unrecognizable and unmaintainable. In addition to making maximum use of the package's customization tools, one way to prevent this situation is to add front or back end programs that run before or after the package and do not interfere with the package software. These front or back ends may be much more extensive than the package software itself. For example, one corporation we observed developed its payroll system using a leading mainframe payroll package. The package left so many important requirements unmet that the company had to use its own programmers to write huge front- and back-end programs to supplement the package. The final structure of the system with front and back ends added looked like Figure 12.4.

So much modification and additional programming may be required to customize a package that implementation is seriously prolonged. Customization that is allowed within the package framework may be so expensive and time-consuming that it eliminates many advantages of the package. Figure 12.5 shows

Figure 12.5
The effects of customizing a package on total implementation costs. Installing a package always requires some modifications. But as the modifications rise, so does the cost of implementing the package. Sometimes the savings promised by the package are whittled away by excessive changes. As the number of lines of code changed approaches 5 percent of the total lines in the package, the costs of implementation rise fivefold.

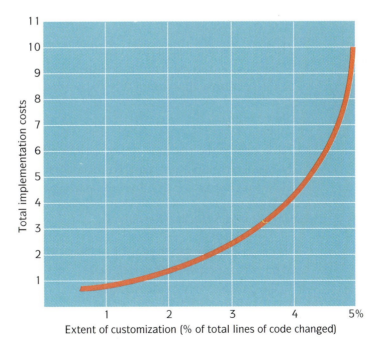

how package costs in relation to total implementation costs rise with the degree of customization.

The initial purchase price of the package can be deceptive because of these hidden implementation costs. An internal study by one company of the cost and time required to install six major application packages (including manufacturing resources planning, the general ledger, accounts receivable, and fixed assets) showed that total implementation costs ranged from 1.5 to 11 times the purchase price of the package. The ratio was highest for packages with many interfaces to other systems. The same study showed that management and support costs for the first year following installation averaged twice the original package purchase price.

Selecting Software Packages

Request for Proposal (RFP):
Detailed list of questions submitted to vendors of packaged software or other computer services to determine if the vendor's product can meet the organization's specific requirements.

Application software packages must be thoroughly evaluated before they can be used as the foundation of a new information system. The most important evaluation criteria are the functions provided by the package, flexibility, user-friendliness, hardware, software resources, database requirements, installation and maintenance effort, documentation, vendor quality, and cost. The package evaluation process is often based on a **Request for Proposal (RFP)**, which is a detailed list of questions submitted to vendors of packaged software. The RFP is likely to include questions such as the following.

PACKAGE EVALUATION CRITERIA

Functions Included
The functions included vary by application. But for the specific application, the following considerations are important:

- How many of the functional requirements will the package meet?
- How many of these functions are standard?
- Which functions can be supported only by modifying the package code?
- How extensive are the modifications required?
- Which functions cannot be supported at all by the package?
- How well will the package support future as well as current needs?

Flexibility

- How easy is the package to modify?
- What customization features are included (user exits, user data areas)?
- Is the vendor willing to modify the software for the client?

User Friendliness

- How easy is the package to use from a nontechnical standpoint?
- How much training is required to understand the package system?
- How much user control does the package allow?

Hardware and Software Resources

- What model computer can the package run on?
- What operating system is required?
- Is the package release dependent?
- How much input/output and core resources does the software take up?
- What are the package's disk storage and tape drive requirements?
- How much computer time is needed to run the package?

- Can the package run in the client's current operating environment (computer model, operating system, database management system, etc.)?

Database Characteristics

- What kind of database/file structure does the package use?
- Do the standard fields in the package file correspond to the data elements specified by the application requirements?
- Does the database or file design support the client's processing and retrieval requirements?
- Are there provisions to add customized user fields for data elements that are not standard with the package?

Installation Effort

- How much change in procedures would the package necessitate?
- How difficult would it be to convert from the current system to the package system?

Maintenance

- Does the vendor supply updates or enhancements to the system?
- How easy are these changes to apply?
- What is the minimum internal staff necessary for ongoing maintenance and support (applications programmers, analysts, database specialists)?
- Is the source code clear, structured, and easy to maintain?

Documentation

- What kind of documentation (system and user) is provided with the package?
- Is it easy to understand and use?
- Is the documentation complete, or must the client write additional instructions in order to use the package?

Vendor Quality

- Is the vendor experienced in this application area?
- Does the vendor have a strong sales and financial record?
- Will the vendor continue to remain in business and support the package?
- What kinds of support facilities does the vendor provide for installation and maintenance (support staff, hotlines, training facilities, research and development staff)?
- Is the vendor responsive to clients' suggestions for improvements?
- Does the vendor have an active user group that meets regularly to exchange information on experiences with the package?

Cost

- What is the purchase or lease price of the basic software?
- What does the purchase price include (add-on modules; on-line, retrieval, or screen generator facilities; consulting time; training; installation support)?
- Is there a yearly maintenance fee and contract?
- What are the annual operating costs for the estimated volume of processing expected from the package?
- How much would it cost to tailor the package to the user's requirements and install it?

Packages and the Systems Development Process

Table 12.2 illustrates how the use of an application software package affects the systems development process. Systems analysis will include a package evaluation effort that is usually accomplished by sending out requests for proposals (RFPs) to various package vendors. The responses to the RFP will be compared to the system requirements generated during this phase, and the software package that best meets these requirements will be selected. Design activities will focus on matching requirements to package features. Instead of tailoring the system design specifications directly to user requirements, the design effort will consist of trying to mold user requirements to conform to the features of the package.

One of the principal themes of this book has been the need to design systems that fit well with the organizations they serve. But when a package solution is selected, such a fit may be much harder to attain. The organization no longer has total control over the system design process. Even with the most flexible and easily customized package, there are limits to the amount of tailoring allowed. Firms that are experienced in using packaged software for major business applications have noted that even the best packages cannot be expected to meet more than 70 percent of most organizations' requirements. But what about the remaining 30 percent? They will have to go unmet by the package or be satisfied by other means. If the package cannot adapt to the organization, the organization will have to adapt to the package and change its procedures. One of the most far-reaching impacts of software packages is their potential impact on organizational procedures. The kind of information a company can store for an application such as accounts receivable, for example, and the way in which the company organizes, classifies, inputs, and retrieves this information can be largely determined by the package it is using.

Table 12.2   APPLICATION PACKAGE DEVELOPMENT CYCLE

Systems Analysis

Identify problem

Identify user requirements

Identify solution alternatives

Identify package vendors

Evaluate package vs. in-house development

Evaluate packages

Select package

Systems Design

Tailor user requirements to package features

Train technical staff on package

Prepare physical design

Customize package design

Redesign organizational procedures

Programming, Testing and Conversion

Install package

Implement package modifications

Design program interfaces

Produce documentation

Convert to package system

Test the system

Train users on package

Production and Maintenance

Correct problems

Install updates or enhancements to package

12.4   End-User Development

End-user development: The development of information systems by end users with little or no formal assistance from technical specialists.

In many organizations, end users are developing a growing percentage of information systems with little or no formal assistance from technical specialists. This phenomenon is called **end-user development.** End-user development has been made possible by the special fourth-generation software tools introduced in Chapter 7. Even though these tools are less computer-efficient than conventional programming languages, decreasing hardware costs have made them technically and economically feasible. With fourth-generation languages, graphics languages, and microcomputer tools, end users can access data, create reports, and develop entire information systems on their own, without professional systems analysts or programmers. Alternatively, end users may rely on information systems specialists for technical support but may perform many systems development activities themselves that had previously been undertaken by the information systems department. Many of these end-user developed systems can be created much more rapidly than with the traditional systems life cycle. Figure 12.6 illustrates the concept of end-user development.

End-User Computing Tools: Strengths and Limitations

End-user computing tools have increased the speed and ease with which certain kinds of applications can be created. Many fourth-generation tools have application design knowledge built in. For instance, when fourth-generation languages are linked to a database, the database has already been organized and defined. Many fourth-generation tools can easily access data, produce reports or graphics, or even generate simple data-entry transactions.

Many organizations have reported appreciable gains in application development productivity by using fourth-generation tools. Productivity enhancements based on conventional programming languages, such as structured programming (see Chapter 13), have only resulted in a maximum productivity improvement of 25 percent (Jones, 1979). In contrast, some studies of organizations developing applications with fourth-generation tools have reported productivity

Figure 12.6
End-user versus systems life cycle development. End users can access computerized information directly or develop information systems with minimal or no formal technical assistance. On the whole, end-user developed systems can be completed more rapidly than those developed through the conventional systems life cycle. *Source: Adapted from James Martin,* Applications Development Without Programmers, © *1982, p. 119. Adapted by permission of Prentice-Hall, Englewood Cliffs, NJ.*

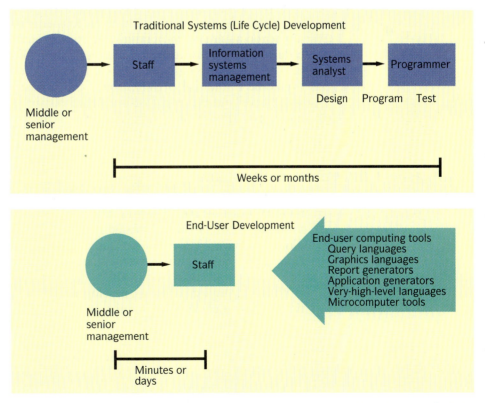

Traditional Systems (Life Cycle) Development

Middle or senior management → Staff → Information systems management → Systems analyst → Programmer

Design   Program   Test

Weeks or months

End-User Development

Middle or senior management → Staff

End-user computing tools
Query languages
Graphics languages
Report generators
Application generators
Very-high-level languages
Microcomputer tools

Minutes or days

gains of 300 to 500 percent (Green, 1984–85; Harel, 1985). While these gains are not on the order of the magnitude of ten times initially claimed for fourth-generation methods, they are still very impressive.

Finally, fourth-generation tools have new capabilities, such as graphics, spreadsheets, modeling, and ad-hoc information retrieval, that meet important business needs.

Unfortunately, fourth-generation tools still cannot replace conventional tools for some business applications because their capabilities remain limited. Most of these tools were designed for simple systems manipulating small files. Fourth-generation processing is relatively inefficient, and the languages consume large amounts of computer resources. Most fourth-generation languages process individual transactions too slowly and at too high a cost to make these systems suitable for large transaction processing systems. Slow response time and computer performance degradation often result when large files are used. For instance, the New Jersey State Division of Motor Vehicles had a backlog of 1.4 million vehicle registration and ownership records that could not be processed quickly because the department had built its new vehicle registration system using Ideal, a fourth-generation tool. Part of the system had to be reprogrammed in COBOL to accommodate the high transaction volume.

Most fourth-generation tools are more nonprocedural than conventional programming languages. They thus cannot easily handle applications with extensive procedural logic and updating requirements. For example, applications such as those used for the design of nuclear reactors, optimal production scheduling, or tracking daily trades of stocks, bonds, and other securities require complex processing and often the matching of multiple files. Procedural logic must be used to specify processing functions, utility functions, error-handling conditions, specialized interfaces, and highly customized reporting. The logic for such functions is more easily expressed and controlled by conventional procedural code. The specification of procedural logic with fourth-generation languages is slow compared to the specification of nonprocedural functions, such as the generation of screens, reports, or graphics. For applications based on a large amount of specialized procedural logic, the overall productivity advantage of fourth-generation tools may be lost (Martin, 1982).

Fourth-generation tools make their greatest contribution to the programming and detail design aspects of the systems development process but have little impact on other system-building activities. Productivity in systems analysis, procedural changes, conversion, and other aspects of design are largely independent of the choice of programming tool. Fourth-generation languages alone cannot overcome traditional organizational and infrastructural problems such as the lack of well-defined and well-integrated databases, standardized data management techniques, and integrated communications networks that typically hamper information system implementations (Grant, 1985).

Management Benefits and Problems

Since end users can create many applications entirely on their own or with minimal assistance from information systems specialists, end-user-developed information systems can be created much more rapidly and informally than traditional systems. This situation has created both benefits and problems for organizations because these systems are outside the constraints of the formal information systems environment.

Without question, end-user development provides many benefits to organizations. These include the following:

- *Improved requirements determination.* With users developing their own systems, there is less need to rely on information systems specialists for requirements analysis and less chance that user requirements will be misinterpreted by technical specialists.

- *User involvement and satisfaction.* Users are more likely to use and approve of systems they design and develop themselves.
- *Control of the systems development process by users.* Fourth-generation tools enable end users to take a more active role in the systems development process. Users can create entire applications themselves or with minimal assistance from information systems professionals. The tools often support prototyping, allowing end users to create experimental systems that can be revised quickly and inexpensively to meet changing requirements. With end users playing a much larger role in application creation, fourth-generation tools have helped break down the barrier between users and programmers that has hampered conventional systems development.
- *Reduced application backlog.* User-developed systems can help relieve the application backlog by transferring the responsibility for development from the information systems staff to end users. The productivity of professional information systems specialists can also be boosted by the use of fourth-generation languages.

At the same time, end-user computing poses organizational risks because it occurs outside of traditional mechanisms for information system management and control. Most organizations have not yet developed strategies to ensure that end-user-developed applications meet organizational objectives or meet quality assurance standards appropriate to their function. The most critical challenges posed by end-user computing are the following:

- *Insufficient review and analysis when user and analyst functions are no longer separate.* Without formal information systems analysts, user-developed applications have no independent outside review. There are no independent sources of problem analysis or alternative solutions. It may also be difficult for users to specify complete and comprehensive requirements.
- *Lack of proper quality assurance standards and controls.* User-developed systems are often created rapidly, without a formal development methodology. While there are productivity and design advantages to be gained by avoiding conventional development methodologies, user-developed systems often lack appropriate standards, controls, and quality assurance procedures. There may not be adequate disciplines for testing and documentation. User-developed systems may lack controls for the completeness and validity of input and updating, audit trails, operating controls, project controls, and standards for stable interfaces among subsystems (Chapter 18 provides more detail on these controls).
- *Uncontrolled data.* With end-user computing tools, end-user groups outside the traditional information systems department can easily create their own applications and files. Many of these end-user created files will contain the identical pieces of information, but each user application may update and define these data in a different way. Without formal data administration disciplines, it will become increasingly difficult to determine where data are located and to ensure that the same piece of information (such as product number or annual earnings) is used consistently throughout the organization (more details on the problem of uncontrolled data can be found in Chapters 8 and 10).
- *Proliferation of "private" information systems.* Users can use fourth-generation tools to create their own "private" information systems that are hidden from the rest of the organization. Such systems can conceal information from other groups. An undocumented private system cannot be easily turned over to another individual when the creator of that system leaves his or her job (Davis and Olson, 1985).

Managing End-User Development

How can organizations maximize the benefits of end-user applications development while keeping it under management control? A number of strategies have been suggested. Some, such as the use of data administration disciplines, have already been described in Chapter 10. Other measures include using information centers and other training and support facilities for end-user development, establishing application development priorities, and establishing well-defined controls for end-user developed applications.

INFORMATION CENTERS

Information center: A special facility within an organization that provides training and support for end-user computing.

One way both to facilitate and to manage end-user application development is to set up an information center. The **information center** is a special facility that provides training and support for end-user computing. Information centers feature hardware, software, and technical specialists that supply end users with tools, training, and expert advice so that they can create information system applications on their own. With information center tools, users can create their own computer reports, spreadsheets or graphics, or extract data for decision making and analysis with minimal technical assistance. Information-center consultants are available to instruct users and to assist in the development of more complex applications.

Information center staff members combine expert knowledge of the hardware, software, and databases for end-user applications with strong interpersonal communications skills. They function primarily as teachers and consultants to users, but they may also take part in the analysis, design, and programming of more complex applications. Typical services provided by information center staff include the following:

- Training in high-level languages and development tools.
- Assistance in accessing data.
- Assistance in debugging programs.
- Assistance with applications, queries, and reports requiring high-level programming languages.
- Consultation on appropriate tools and methodologies for developing applications.

Employees of this corporation are taking a computer class in their corporation-sponsored information center.

- Generation and modification of prototypes.
- Providing reference materials on information center resources.
- Providing liaison with other information processing groups (such as database specialists) that support information center resources.
- Maintaining a catalogue of existing applications and databases.
- Evaluating new hardware and software.

Information center hardware may consist of mainframes, minicomputers, microcomputers, workstations, or a combination of these machines. Typical software tools in information centers include word processing software, modeling or planning software, desktop database software, graphics software, report generators, user-friendly fourth-generation languages for queries or simple applications, and high-level programming languages for fourth-generation applications development.

Information centers provide many management benefits:

- They can help end users find tools and applications that will make them more productive.
- They prevent the creation of redundant applications.
- They promote data sharing and minimize integrity problems (see Chapter 8).
- They ensure that the applications developed by end users meet audit, data quality, and security standards.

Another important benefit of information centers is that they can help establish and enforce standards for hardware and software so that end users do not introduce many disparate and incompatible technologies into the firm (Fuller and Swanson, 1992; see Chapter 10). The information center generally works with the firm's information systems department to establish standards and guidelines for hardware and software acquisition. The information center will only assist users with hardware and software that have been approved by management.

POLICIES AND PROCEDURES TO MANAGE END-USER COMPUTING

In addition to using information centers, managers can pursue other strategies to ensure that end-user computing serves larger organizational goals (see Alavi, Nelson, and Weiss, 1987–88; Rockart and Flannery, 1983).

Managers can supplement central information centers with smaller distributed centers that provide training and computing tools tailored to the needs of different operating units and business functional areas. Managers can also make sure that the support provided is tuned to the needs of different types of end-user application developers. For instance, end users who only use high-level commands or simple query languages to access data will require different training and tools than end users who can actually write software programs and applications using fourth-generation tools (Rockart and Flannery, 1983). Training and support should also consider individual users' attitudes toward computers, educational levels, cognitive styles, and receptiveness to change (Harrison and Rainer, 1992).

Management should not allow end-user applications to be developed randomly. The organization should incorporate end-user systems into its strategic systems plans. The methodologies for establishing organizationwide information requirements that were described in Chapter 11 can help identify end-user applications with organizationwide benefits.

Management should also develop controls on end-user computing. These could include the following:

- Cost justification of end-user information system projects.
- Hardware and software standards for user-developed applications.

MANAGEMENT

What Should End Users Be Allowed to Do?

End-user computing tools have given users more access to corporate data. But what happens to security, data integrity, and network responsibility when users can freely update data that are essential to the company? A simple mistake could bring down a mission-critical set of applications. What if an end user enters incorrect information that prevents an order from being processed? Yet that user may need essential production data for analysis. What should the company do? As questions about data responsibility become more common, organizations are defining new boundaries between their information systems and end-user business departments.

One option is for the information systems department to establish restrictions on the types of hardware and software available to end users. While the information systems department may see the value in mandating which tools end users can work with, users may have already selected products and may resent interference from the information systems department.

Users may view standards and controls imposed by the information systems department as unnecessary meddling. In 1989, local staff at the Arco Corporation refinery plant in Carson, California, began to develop applications so that engineers, operations managers, and maintenance workers could track information about defective pipes. The plant hired its own consultants to build the applications and selected SQLBase, a

fourth-generation tool from Gupta Technologies in Menlo Park, California, as the foundation for the applications. The plant also selected Superbase, a desktop database management system from Precision Software Ltd. to supplement SQL-Base so that users could build applications to track job-related data.

When Arco's central MIS department examined these applications in the summer of 1991, it objected to Superbase as an application development tool because it was not compatible with IBM's Information Warehouse architecture. But by then, refinery plant employees were storing data in more than 750 different Superbase databases, which would have been difficult to replace.

Some information systems departments have found a middle ground between dictating to end users and granting them total freedom. The most common solution is to make an "extract," a copy of actual production data for end users to manipulate and use for reports. The production database itself remains on-line to support business applications and is controlled by the information systems department. The copy is extracted nightly, weekly, or monthly, depending on the immediacy of users' data needs.

The Hunt Valley, Maryland, offices of Texas Instruments Inc. provides managers with weekly extracts of budgeting data. The managers can review this data to identify mistakes or problems with items such as travel expenditures using Light-

Ship, an EIS package from Pilot Software, Inc. Since this data deals with corporate accounts that need checks and balances, the firm never considered giving these managers updating capabilities.

Another option is to use data security features found in many database management systems to provide end users with "read-only" access. This means that end users can only read data from a database but cannot write to or change that data. For instance, the Furnas Electric Company in Batavia, Illinois, provides end users with read-only access to sales and marketing data using CA-Datacom/DB as its mainframe database management system, CA-Datacom/PC, a microcomputer DBMS, and CA-QbyX, an end-user query tool. Users requiring on-line access to up-to-date information such as order entry or inventory data can use CA-QbyX queries to obtain the information from "live" production databases, but they cannot change any of that information.

Source: Paul Korzeniowski, "Shifting Access to Users," *Software Magazine* (September 1992).

To Think About: Some experts have said that giving end users access to the company's data "opens up a huge can of worms." Do you agree? How would you evaluate each of the options described here? Which would you choose?

- Companywide standards for microcomputers, word processing software, database management systems, graphics software, and query and reporting tools.
- Quality assurance reviews, specifying whether only individual end users or whether specialists from the information systems or internal audit departments should review end-user developed information systems.
- Controls for end-user developed applications covering testing, documentation, accuracy and completeness of input and update, backup, recovery, and supervision.

These controls are described in detail in Chapter 18. The control process should flag critical applications that supply data to other important systems. Such systems warrant more rigorous standards. For instance, Northwest Airlines, Inc., established policies and guidelines for end-user development that ask users to classify the applications they develop according to critical nature so that the firm can take special steps to ensure data integrity and security (McMullen, 1992).

End users may resent the standards and controls imposed by the information systems department. The Window on Management describes various options that management can pursue to deal with this problem.

12.5 Outsourcing Information Systems

If a firm does not want to use its own internal resources to build and operate information systems, it can hire an external organization that specializes in providing these services to do the work. The process of turning over an organization's computer center operations, telecommunications networks, or applications development to external vendors of these services is called **outsourcing**.

Outsourcing: The practice of contracting computer center operations, telecommunications networks, or applications development to external vendors.

Because information systems play such a large role in contemporary organizations, information technology now accounts for about half of most large firms' capital expenditures. In firms where the cost of information systems function has risen rapidly, managers are seeking ways to control those costs and are treating information technology as a capital investment instead of an operating cost of the firm. One option for controlling these costs is to outsource.

Advantages and Disadvantages of Outsourcing

Outsourcing is becoming popular because some organizations perceive it as being more cost-effective than it would be to maintain their own computer center and information systems staff. The provider of outsourcing services can benefit from economies of scale (the same knowledge, skills, and capacity can be shared with many different customers) and is likely to charge competitive prices for information systems services. Outsourcing allows a company with fluctuating needs for computer processing to pay for only what it uses rather than to build its own computer center to stand underutilized when there is no peak load. Some firms outsource because their internal information systems staff cannot keep pace with technological change. But not all organizations benefit from outsourcing, and the disadvantages of outsourcing can create serious problems for organizations if they are not well understood and managed.

ADVANTAGES OF OUTSOURCING

The most popular explanations for outsourcing are the following:

Economy. Outsourcing vendors are specialists in the information systems services and technologies they provide. Through specialization and economies of scale, they can deliver the same service and value for less money than the cost of an internal organization. For instance, American Standard reported saving $2 million annually from outsourcing its financial and payroll operations. Wabco and American Ultramar slashed annual information system processing costs approximately in half. While some outsourcing vendors have promised annual reductions of 50 percent in information technology costs, savings of 15 percent to 30 percent are more common (Loh and Venkatraman, 1992).

Service quality. Because outsourcing vendors will lose their clients if the service is unsatisfactory, companies often have more leverage over external vendors than over their own employees. The firm that outsources may be able to obtain a higher level of service from vendors for the same or lower costs.

Predictability. An outsourcing contract with a fixed price for a specified level of service reduces uncertainty of costs.

Flexibility. Business growth can be accommodated without making major changes in the organization's information systems infrastructure. As information technology permeates the entire value chain of a business, outsourcing may provide superior control of the business because its costs and capabilities can be adjusted to meet changing needs (Loh and Venkatraman, 1992).

Making fixed costs variable. Some outsourcing agreements, such as running payroll, are based on the price per unit of work done (such as the cost to process each check). Many outsourcers will take into account variations in transaction processing volumes likely to occur during the year or over the course of the outsourcing agreement. Clients only need to pay for the amount of services they consume, as opposed to paying a fixed cost to maintain internal systems that are not fully utilized.

Freeing up human resources for other projects. Scarce and costly talent within an organization can refocus on activities with higher value and payback than they would find in running a technology factory.

Freeing up financial capital. Some agreements with outsourcers include the sale for cash of the outsourced firm's technology capital assets to the vendor. For instance, when Blue Cross and Blue Shield of Massachusetts outsourced its computer operations and systems development to Electronic Data Systems (EDS), EDS paid Blue Cross with cash and a promissory note for its computer center and other computer equipment (Caldwell, 1992).

DISADVANTAGES OF OUTSOURCING
Not all organizations obtain these benefits from outsourcing. There are dangers in placing the information systems functions outside the organization. Outsourcing can create serious problems such as loss of control, vulnerability of strategic information, and dependence on the fortunes of an external firm.

Loss of control: When a firm farms out the responsibility for developing and operating its information systems to another organization, it can lose control over its information systems function. Outsourcing places the vendor in an advantageous position where the client has to accept whatever the vendor does and whatever fees the vendors charge. If a vendor becomes the firm's only alternative for running and developing its information systems, the client must accept whatever technologies the vendor provides. This dependency could eventually result in higher costs or loss of control over technological direction.

Vulnerability of strategic information: Trade secrets or proprietary information may leak out to competitors because a firm's information systems are being run or developed by outsiders. This could be especially harmful if a firm allows an outsourcer to develop or to operate applications that give it some type of competitive advantage.

Dependency: The firm becomes dependent on the viability of the vendor. A vendor with financial problems or deteriorating services may create severe problems for its clients.

When to Use Outsourcing

Since outsourcing has both benefits and liabilities, and is not meant for all organizations or all situations, managers should assess the role of information systems in their organization before making an outsourcing decision. There are a number of circumstances under which outsourcing makes a great deal of sense:

- *When there is limited opportunity for the firm to distinguish itself competitively through a particular information systems application or series of applications.* For instance, both the development and operation of payroll systems are frequently outsourced to free the information systems staff to concentrate on activities with a higher potential payoff, such as customer

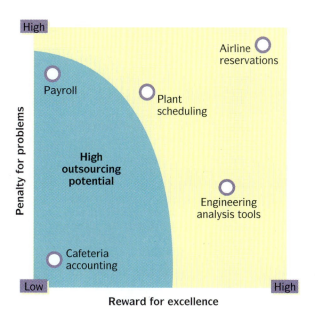

Figure 12.7
Rewards and penalties of outsourcing. This reward/penalty matrix shows that those applications with low reward for excellence and low penalty for problems are good candidates for outsourcing. *Source: Paul Clermont, "Outsourcing Without Guilt," Computerworld, (September 9, 1991). Copyright 1991 by CW Publishing, Inc., Framingham, MA 01701. Reprinted from Computerworld.*

service or manufacturing systems. Figure 12.7 illustrates a matrix that could help firms determine appropriate applications for outsourcing. Applications such as payroll or cafeteria accounting, for which the firm obtains little competitive advantage from excellence, are strong candidates for outsourcing. If carefully developed, applications such as airline reservations or plant scheduling could provide a firm with a distinct advantage over competitors. The firm could lose profits, customers, or market share if such systems have problems. Applications where the rewards for excellence are high and where the penalties for failure are high should probably be developed and operated internally.

Companies may also continue to develop applications internally while outsourcing their computer center operations when they do not need to distinguish themselves competitively by performing their computer processing on-site. For instance, the Eastman Kodak Co., which was a pioneer in outsourcing, initially farmed out its information system operations—including mainframe processing, telecommunications, and personal computer support to IBM and DEC. It kept application development and support in-house because it felt that these activities had competitive value (Clermont 1991).

- *When the predictability of uninterrupted information systems service is not very important.* For instance, airline reservations or catalog shopping systems are too "critical" to be trusted outside. If these systems failed to operate for a few days or even a few hours, they could close down the business (see Chapter 2). On the other hand, a system to process employee insurance claims could be more easily outsourced because uninterrupted processing of claims is not critical to the survival of the firm.

- *When outsourcing does not strip the company of the technical know-how required for future information systems innovation.* If a firm outsources some of its systems but maintains its own internal information systems staff, it should ensure that its staff remains technically up-to-date and has the expertise to develop future applications.

- *When the firm's existing information system capabilities are limited, ineffective, or technically inferior.* Some organizations use outsourcers as an easy way to revamp their information systems technology. For instance, they might use an outsourcer to help them make the transition from traditional mainframe-based computing to a new information architecture–distributed computing environment.

ORGANIZATIONS

Canadian Oil Firms Make a Slick Outsourcing Move

In Calgary, the heart of Canada's oil country, six major oil and gas companies decided to form a consortium to establish a common production accounting center. The center would provide both oil field accounting services and the information systems processing for these services. A team of outside contractors, consisting of a provider of computer services and an accounting firm, would manage the center.

The members of the consortium—Mobil Oil Canada, Esso Resources, Gulf Canada Resources, Ltd., Pan-Canadian Petroleum, Ltd., Petro-Canada, and Shell Canada Ltd.—originally banded together in early 1991 to persuade a vendor to make enhancements to the software they were all using. They then found that they could work together to solve other common problems too. These oil companies were duplicating many efforts. Oil wells are owned by numerous partners, each of whom is required to perform the same kind of accounting for functions such as royalty payments. The oil companies found that a combined information systems processing and accounting center run by an external consultant could meet up to 75 percent of each company's production accounting requirements and 10 percent of each company's total information sys-

tems operations if it was used as a common shared resource.

Consortium members contributed $1 to $2 million and a staff of 50 to develop a coordinated suite of 20 different accounting applications that they can share. They are examining IBM and Electronic Data Systems (EDS) Corporations as potential contractors.

Consortium members believe that this outsourcing arrangement will cut information systems processing costs and trim payrolls by thousands of jobs. It will also open up a new source of revenue, because the combined information processing and accounting center can offer its services to other companies in the region.

The Canadian oil company consortium's plans illustrate how information systems outsourcing is being combined with business functions. Management is realizing that if information systems can be outsourced, other organizational functions can be taken over by outsiders as well.

The closest comparison to the Canadian consortium is the combined data processing and accounting center operated by Andersen Consulting in Aberdeen, Scotland, for British Petroleum Exploration's North Sea oil fields. The outsourcing contract transferred 250 former members of

British Petroleum's accounting and information systems staff to Andersen.

Andersen Consulting provides its customers with high-level strategic planning as well as application management, systems development, and other products and services. It helps the organization place its information systems strategy in the context of how to remain competitive, examining whether the customer should be in certain businesses or not and evaluating user departments, policies, and procedures to determine if the company is organized properly.

Sources: Bruce Caldwell, "Slick Moves in the Back Office," *InformationWEEK* (January 27, 1992), and Dennis Livingston, "Outsourcing: Look Beyond the Price Tag" *Datamation* (November 15, 1992).

To Think About: Do you think that outsourcing was the right decision for this Canadian consortium? Why or why not? What organizational changes can be set about by outsourcing? If you were a manager, what management, technology, and organization factors would you use to decide on whether to outsource your business functions along with your information systems functions?

If systems development and the information systems function is well managed and productive, there may not be much immediate benefit that can be provided by an external vendor.

Managing Outsourcing

To obtain value from outsourcing, organizations need to make sure the process is properly managed. With sound business analysis and an understanding of outsourcing's strengths and limitations, managers can identify the most appropriate applications to outsource and develop a workable outsourcing plan.

Segmenting the firm's range of information systems activities into pieces that potentially can be outsourced makes the problem more manageable and also helps companies match an outsourcer with the appropriate job. Noncritical applications are usually the most appropriate candidates for outsourcing. Firms should identify mission-critical applications and mission-critical human resources required to develop and manage these applications. This would allow the firm to retain its most highly skilled people and focus all of its efforts on the most mission-critical applications development (Roche, 1992).

The Window on Organizations shows that sometimes it makes sense for firms to outsource not only specific information system applications but the entire business functional area supported by those applications as well.

Setting technology strategy is one area that companies should not abdicate to outsourcers. The strategic task is best kept in-house.

Ideally, the firm should have a trusting working relationship with an outsourcing vendor. The vendor should understand the client's business and work with the client as a partner, adapting agreements to meet the client's changing needs. For instance, defense contractor General Dynamics Corporation in Falls Church, Virginia, chose Computer Sciences Corporation (CSC) of El Segundo, California, to take over its data center management, network operations, applications development, and other information services. General Dynamics signed a 10-year contract worth $3 billion with CSC because CSC knew the defense business.

Table 12.3 COMPARISON OF SYSTEMS DEVELOPMENT APPROACHES

Approach	Features	Advantages	Disadvantages
Systems life cycle	Sequential step-by-step formal process Written specifications and approvals Limited role of users	Necessary for large complex systems and projects	Slow and expensive Discourages changes Massive paperwork to manage
Prototyping	Requirements specified dynamically with experimental system Rapid, informal and iterative process Users continually interact with the prototype	Rapid and inexpensive Useful when requirements uncertain or when end-user interface is important Promotes user participation	Inappropriate for large complex systems Can gloss over important steps in analysis, documentation, and testing
Application software package	Commercial software eliminates need for internally developed software programs	Design, programming, installation and maintenance work reduced Can save time and cost when developing common business applications Reduces need for internal information systems resources	May not meet organization's unique requirements May not perform many business functions well Extensive customization raises development costs
End-user development	Systems created by end users using fourth-generation software tools Rapid and informal Minimal role of information systems specialists	Users control systems building Saves development time and cost Reduces application backlog	Can lead to proliferation of uncontrolled information systems Systems do not always meet quality assurance standards
Outsourcing	Systems built and sometimes operated by external vendor	Can reduce or control costs Can produce systems when internal resources not available or technically deficient	Loss of control over the information systems function Dependence on the technical direction and prosperity of external vendors

It understood the regulations and the critical success factors for the industry. General Dynamics would have had to teach other contractors the rules of the defense environment before they could do the work (Livingston, 1992).

Firms should clearly understand the advantages provided by the vendor and what they will have to give up to obtain these advantages. For lower operating costs, can the client live with a 5-second response time during peak hours or next-day repair of microcomputers in remote offices?

Organizations should not abdicate management responsibility by outsourcing. They need to manage the outsourcer as they would manage their own internal information systems department by setting priorities, ensuring that the right people are brought in, and guaranteeing that information systems are running smoothly. They should establish criteria for evaluating the outsourcing vendor that include performance expectations and measurement methods for response time, transaction volumes, security, disaster recovery, backup in the event of a catastrophe (see Chapter 18), processing requirements of new applications, and distributed processing on microcomputers, workstations, and LANs.

Firms should design outsourcing contracts carefully so that the outsourcing services can be adjusted if the nature of the business changes. For instance, Meritor Savings Bank in Philadelphia was a $12 billion colossus when it signed a one-year outsourcing contract with Electronic Data Services. Three years later, Meritor had closed two-thirds of its branches and shrunk to $4 billion in assets. Its slimmed down state of affairs required far fewer processing services. Meritor fortunately had placed a provision into the original contract so that EDS services could be adjusted to the size of the bank (Schatz, 1993).

Table 12.3 compares the advantages and disadvantages of each of the system-building alternatives described in this chapter.

Management Challenges

1. **Determining the right systems development strategy to use.** Sometimes organizations encounter problems that cannot be addressed by any of the systems development strategies described in this chapter. For instance, a large complex system may have some unstructured features. The ultimate configuration of the system cannot be decided beforehand because information requirements or the appropriate technology are uncertain. Alternatively, a proposed system calls for major organizational as well as technical changes. In such instances, a firm may need to pursue a strategy of phased commitment in which systems projects are broken down into smaller portions and developed piece-by-piece in phases, or a firm may need to postpone the project altogether.

2. **Controlling information systems development outside the information systems department.** There may not be a way to establish standards and controls for end-user development that are appropriate. Standards and controls that are too restrictive may not only generate user resistance but may also stifle end-user innovation. If controls are too weak, the firm may encounter serious problems with data integrity and connectivity. It is not always possible to find the right balance.

3. **Selecting a systems development strategy that fits into the firm's information architecture and strategic plan.** End-user development, application software packages, or outsourcing may be appropriate short-term solutions, but they may not be in the best long-term interests of the firm. These solutions may result in disparate applications that cannot be easily integrated into the firm's overall information architecture. Organizations need to evaluate carefully the long-term impact of their applications development strategies.

Summary

Distinguish between the various system-building alternatives: the traditional systems life cycle, prototyping, application software packages, end-user development, and outsourcing.

The traditional systems life cycle—the oldest method for building systems—breaks the development of an information system into six formal stages: project definition, systems study, design, programming, installation, and post-implementation. The stages must proceed sequentially, have defined outputs, and require formal approval before the next stage can commence.

Prototyping consists of building an experimental system rapidly and inexpensively for end users to interact with and evaluate. The prototype is refined and enhanced until users are satisfied that it captures all of their requirements and can be used as a template to create the final system.

Developing an information system using an application software package eliminates the need for writing software programs when developing an information system. Using a software package cuts down on the amount of design, testing, installation, and maintenance work required to build a system.

End-user development is the development of information systems by end users, either alone or with minimal assistance from information systems specialists. End-user developed systems can be created rapidly and informally using fourth-generation software tools.

Outsourcing consists of using an external vendor to build (or operate) a firm's information systems. The system may be custom-built or may use a software package. In either case, the work is done by the vendor rather than by the organization's internal information systems staff.

Understand the strengths and limitations of each approach.

The traditional system life cycle is still useful for large projects that need formal specifications and tight management control over each stage of system building. However, the traditional method is very rigid and costly for developing a system, and is not well-suited for unstructured, decision-oriented applications where requirements cannot be immediately visualized.

Prototyping encourages end-user involvement in systems development and iteration of design until specifications are captured accurately. The rapid creation of prototypes can result in systems that have not been completely tested or documented or that are technically inadequate for a production environment.

Application software packages are helpful if a firm does not have the internal information systems staff or financial resources to custom-develop a system. To meet an organization's unique requirements, packages may require extensive modifications that can substantially raise development costs. A package may not be a feasible solution if implementation necessitates extensive customization and changes in the organization's procedures.

The primary benefits of end-user development are improved requirements determination, reduced application backlog, and increased end-user participation in and control of the systems development process. However, end-user development, in conjunction with distributed computing, has introduced new organizational risks by propagating information systems and data resources that do not necessarily meet quality assurance standards and that are not easily controlled by traditional means.

Outsourcing can save application development costs or allow firms to develop applications without an internal information systems staff, but it can also make firms lose control over their information systems and make them too dependent on external vendors.

Describe the types of problems for which each approach is best suited.

The traditional systems life cycle is appropriate for large transaction processing systems (TPS) and management information systems (MIS) with complex processing and requirements that need rigorous and formal analyses, predefined specifications, and tight controls over the systems building process.

Prototyping is useful for simple applications where requirements are vague or unstructured or for designing the end-user interface portions of large complex systems. Prototyping is not suitable for designing all aspects of large systems that require batch processing or complex processing logic.

Software packages are best suited for applications with requirements common to many organizations and a limited number of functions that can be supported by commercial software.

The best candidates for end-user development are applications with relatively simple processing logic and small files that can be developed easily with fourth-generation tools.

Outsourcing is appropriate for applications that are not sources of competitive advantage or that require technical expertise not provided by the firm.

Describe the solutions to the management problems created by these approaches.

Organizations can overcome some of the limitations of using software packages by performing a thorough requirements analysis and using rigorous package selection procedures to determine the extent to which a package will satisfy its requirements. The organization can customize the package or modify its procedures to ensure a better fit with the package.

Information centers help promote and control end-user development. They provide end users with appropriate hardware, software, and technical expertise to create their own applications and encourage adherence to application development standards. Organizations can also develop new policies and procedures concerning system development standards, training, data administration, and controls to manage end-user computing effectively.

Organizations can benefit from outsourcing by only outsourcing part of their information systems, by thoroughly understanding what information systems functions are appropriate to outsource, by designing outsourcing contracts carefully, and by trying to build a working partnership with the outsourcing vendor.

Key Terms		
Systems life cycle	Iterative
Project definition	End-user interface
Systems study	Application software package
Design	Customization
Programming	Request for Proposal (RFP)
Installation	End-user development
Postimplementation	Information center
Prototyping	Outsourcing
Prototype	

Review Questions

1. What is the traditional systems life cycle? What are its characteristics?

2. Describe each of the steps in the systems life cycle.

3. What are the advantages and disadvantages of building an information system using the traditional systems life cycle?

4. What do we mean by information system prototyping?

5. Under what conditions is prototyping a useful systems development approach? What kinds of problems can it help solve?

6. Describe five ways in which prototyping differs from the traditional systems life cycle.

7. List and describe the steps in the prototyping process.

8. List and describe four limitations of prototyping.

9. What is an application software package? Under what circumstances should packages be used to build information systems?

10. What are the principal advantages of using application software packages to develop an information system? Why do packages have a strong appeal to management?

11. List and describe several disadvantages of software packages.

12. What is package customization? Under what circumstances can it become a problem when implementing an application software package?

13. List the main criteria for evaluating an application software package.

14. How is the system development process altered when an application software package is being considered and selected?

15. What do we mean by end-user development?

16. What are the advantages and disadvantages of end-user development? What kinds of problems is it suited for?

17. What is an information center? How can information centers solve some of the management problems created by end-user development?

18. Name some policies and procedures for managing end-user development.

19. What is outsourcing? Under what circumstances should it be used for building information systems?

20. What are the advantages and disadvantages of outsourcing?

21. Describe some solutions to the management problems created by outsourcing.

Discussion Questions

1. A widely cited research report found that prototyping facilitated communication between users and information system designers but that designers who used prototyping had difficulty controlling and managing the design process. Discuss.

2. It has been observed that successful prototyping depends less on the selection of software tools than on the corporate culture. Discuss.

3. Some have said that the best way to avoid using professional programmers is to install an application software package. Discuss.

4. One information systems publication stated that, at best, in-house development of a system that is already available in package form is apt to cost fifteen times as much as the package version and take three to four times as long to recover the out-of-pocket investment. Discuss.

5. What theories describing the impact of information systems on organizations could be applied to describe outsourcing?

Group Project

With a group of your classmates, obtain product information or attend a demonstration for a microcomputer application software package such as DacEasy Accounting/Payroll, Quicken, Managing Your Money, or Microsoft Profit for Windows. Write an analysis of the strengths and limitations of the package you select. Present your findings to the class.

CASE STUDY

Can a German Software Giant Conquer North America?

SAP A.G., based in Walldorf, Germany, is Europe's largest vendor of software running on IBM mainframe computers and is an emerging leader in software packages for client/server environments. It has been aggressively pursuing corporations in North America because so many of the world's most important firms are located there. Among its clients are the Amoco Chemical Company, Dow Chemical Company, E.I. du Pont de Nemours & Company, Chevron Corporation and the Exxon Corporation.

SAP sells integrated software applications for a wide range of business functions, including human resources, plant management, and manufacturing. The software modules are integrated, so that they can automatically share data between them and they have their own common database management system. The programs come in nine foreign languages used in major Western countries. Specific versions are tailored to accommodate different currencies, tax laws, and accounting practices. Managers

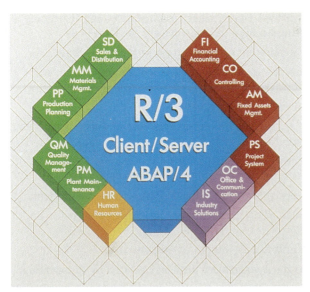

A schematic showing the R/3 software modules from SAP A. G. The modules are integrated and designed for a client/server environment.

can generate reports in their own local languages and currencies yet have the same reports generated in the language and currency that are used as the corporate standard by top management. SAP's R/2 System runs on IBM-compatible mainframes and its R/3 system runs in a client/server environment.

Businesses appreciate the multinational flavor of the software, especially its ability to overcome language and currency barriers fluently and to connect divisions and operating units spread around the world. Marion Merrel Dow Inc. is using SAP software for its financial and sales-and-service departments because it believes that no other available packages can handle its global business needs. More than 1800 firms use the R/2 system.

Despite being a standard software package, SAP software can be customized by approximately 10 percent. The software can be customized to multinational currencies and accounting practices. SAP makes this flexibility one of its key selling points. SAP has also benefited from two strategic moves. It developed R/3 to take advantage of open systems with client/server architecture and it began promoting the package as a platform for business re-engineering.

R/3 is an integrated, client/server, distributed system with a graphical user interface that runs on smaller and cheaper hardware than R/2. The back-end server and front-end client portions of R/3 can run on a number of different operating systems, including five variations of UNIX, Digital Equipment Corporation's VAX/VMS operating system, and Hewlett-Packard's MPE operating system. Versions for OS/2 and other operating systems are being developed as well. R/3 offers a number of options for its graphical user interface: Presentation Manager under OS/2, Motif under UNIX, and Microsoft Windows under DOS.

The R/3 package includes integrated financial accounting, production planning, sales and distribution, cost-center accounting, order-costing, materials management, human resources, quality assurance, fixed assets management,

plant maintenance, and project planning applications. Users do not have to shut down one application to move to another; they can just click on a menu choice. R/3 also provides word processing, filing systems, E-mail, and other office support functions.

R/3 can be configured to run on a single hardware platform, or it can be partitioned to run on separate machines in whatever combination users choose in order to minimize network traffic and place data where users need it the most. For instance, a firm could put the data used most frequently by its accounting department on a file server located close to the accounting department to minimize network traffic. A central data dictionary keeps track of data and its location to maintain the integrity of distributed data. SAP will sell clients a blueprint of R/3's information, data, and function models and software tools to facilitate custom development and integration of existing applications into R/3.

Royal LePage Real Estate Service Ltd., a $450 million commercial and residential real estate services company headquartered in Toronto, with branch offices across Canada, selected R/3 in 1991. It initially used R/3 to run a general ledger application on its IBM RS/6000 UNIX workstation. The general ledger application had to tie into an existing mainframe financial application that used a package from Dun & Bradstreet Software, a rival vendor. Royal LePage then started using R/3 for fixed assets and accounts payable applications and is adding accounts receivable, purchasing, payroll, and human resources components to the R/3 system.

Royal LePage liked R/3 because it supported the company's goal of creating a distributed computing environment that gives each branch more data and processing power and integrates its applications and branches to a greater extent than before. Don Logan, the vice president and controller, believes R/3 initially saved the firm over $2 million in systems development and support costs and perhaps $1 million more over time. Over half the savings came from reducing programming time through the use of R/3.

Klaus Besier, head of SAP America, Inc. (the Lester, Pennsylvania, subsidiary of SAP A.G.), thinks that the most important feature of R3 may be the way it helps organizations automate their business processes. By adopting the system design offered by the package, companies can evaluate and streamline their business processes. The promise of re-engineering was what initially attracted the Eastman Kodak Company to SAP software. Kodak launched a pilot project in 1991 that installed SAP programs to redefine the job of order taking. The SAP package lets order takers make immediate decisions about granting customers credit and lets them access production data on-line so that they can tell customers exactly when their orders will be available for shipment. The project resulted in a 70 percent reduction in the amount of time it took to deliver products; response time to customers was also cut in half. These results prompted Kodak to use SAP software as the global architecture for all of its core systems.

The intricate and sophisticated features of SAP software deeply affect the infrastructure of a corporation. Installing two or more SAP modules with all the business alterations that are required can easily take from one to three years. Unfortunately, SAP has lagged in product support.

SAP has a large internal staff to support its software packages, but it also uses legions of consultants from consulting firms such as Price Waterhouse, Andersen Consulting, EDS Corporation, and Coopers & Lybrand. These external consultants work with SAP clients to install the SAP packages. According to John Van de Graaf, a securities analyst at the New York-based Deutsche Bank Capital Corporation, the investment banking arm of the German Deutsche Bank, there is a worldwide shortage of SAP experts.

Louis Dingerdissen, vice president of MIS for Kodak's health group, observed that experts in SAP software are in short supply, and that it can take 16 weeks of training to get end users up to speed on SAP software — far too long. With SAP quickly signing up new clients, the support situation could worsen before it gets better, or SAP may have to slow down its growth a bit.

One reason for the shortage of SAP consultants is that it can take years for even experienced technologists to understand all of the complexities and methodologies of SAP software. SAP vice chairman and co-founder Hasso Plattner admits that it takes about three years, or two or three installations of the package, before a consultant becomes an expert in the software. SAP pairs one or more of its seasoned eight- to ten-year German veterans with less

experienced U.S. consultants at each installation. But according to Greg Staszko, a partner at the Cincinnati branch of Deloitte & Touche (a leading accounting and consulting firm), the SAP experts tend to be troubleshooters or product experts, rather than business consultants, so clients do not necessarily get the best advice on how to integrate the software into their business operations most efficiently and painlessly. The perception remains among some U.S. companies that even an on-site SAP expert who knows the financial accounting module cannot correct a bug in the sales and distribution module.

To augment the ranks of qualified consultants, SAP built a world training headquarters in Walldorf, costing an estimated $50 to $60 million. It recruited more consultants by signing agreements with new consulting firms such as Cap Gemini America and Coopers & Lybrand, and de-emphasized its relationships with firms such as Computer Sciences Corporation and KPMG Peat Marwick, which it felt have not worked out well.

Jim Bensman, the former president of SAP America Inc. (SAP's U.S. subsidiary) said that the arrangement with KPMG Peat Marwick in the United States floundered because he believed they did not train consultants sufficiently. SAP continues to work with Peat Marwick in Europe, however. Sources reported that Computer Sciences Corporation spent a lot of money on training but did not bring any clients to SAP.

Sources: Doug Bartholomew, ''An American Beachhead,'' *InformationWEEK* (March 9, 1992), and Mike Ricciuti and J. William Semich, ''SAP's Client/Server Battle Plan,'' *Datamation* (March 15, 1993).

Case Study Questions:

1. SAP's management has set goals of doubling its sales every year. Do you think it will succeed in meeting these goals? Why or why not?

2. What advantages and disadvantages of application software packages are illustrated by SAP?

3. Analyze the specific strengths and weaknesses of SAP software packages.

4. If you were the manager of a U.S. corporation looking for new business application software, would you choose SAP? Would you choose another package? Why or why not? What management, organization, and technology factors would you consider?

References

Alavi, Maryam. "An Assessment of the Prototyping Approach to Information System Development." *Communications of the ACM* 27 (June 1984).

Alavi, Maryam, R. Ryan Nelson, and Ira R. Weiss. "Strategies for End-User Computing: An Integrative Framework." *Journal of Management Information Systems* 4, no. 3 (Winter 1987–88).

Anderson, Evan A. "Choice Models for the Evaluation and Selection of Software Packages." *Journal of Management Information Systems* 6, no. 4 (Spring 1990).

Arthur, Lowell Jay. "Quick and Dirty." *Computerworld* (December 14, 1992).

Caldwell, Bruce. "Blue Cross, in Intensive Care, Beeps EDS." *InformationWEEK* (January 27, 1992).

Carr, Houston H. "Information Centers: The IBM Model vs. Practice." *MIS Quarterly* (September 1987).

Cerveny, Robert P., Edward J. Garrity, and G. Lawrence Sanders. "The Application of Prototyping to Systems Development: A Rationale and Model." *Journal of Management Information Systems* 3 (Fall 1986).

Christoff, Kurt A. "Building a Fourth Generation Environment." *Datamation* (September 1985).

Clermont, Paul. "Outsourcing Without Guilt." *Computerworld* (September 9, 1991).

Cotterman, William W., and Kuldeep Kumar. "User Cube: A Taxonomy of End Users." *Communications of the ACM* 32, no. 11 (November 1989).

Davis, Gordon B., and Margrethe H. Olson. "Support Systems for Knowledge Work." In *Management Information Systems,* 2nd ed. New York: McGraw-Hill, 1985.

Davis, Sid A., and Robert P. Bostrum. "Training End Users: An Experimental Investigation of the Role of the Computer Interface and Training Methods." *MIS Quarterly* 17, no. 1 (March 1993).

Fuller, Mary K., and E. Burton Swanson. "Information Centers as Organizational Innovation." *Journal of Management Information Systems* 9, no. 1 (Summer 1992).

Gould, John D., and Clayton Lewis. "Designing for Usability: Key Principles and What Designers Think." *Communications of the ACM* 28 (March 1985).

Grant, F. J. "The Downside of 4GLs." *Datamation* (July 1985).

Green, Jesse. "Productivity in the Fourth Generation." *Journal of Management Information Systems* 1 (Winter 1984–1985).

Harel, Elie C., and Ephraim R. McLean. "The Effects of Using a Nonprocedural Computer Language on Programmer Productivity." *MIS Quarterly* (June 1985).

Harrison, Allison W., and R. Kelly Rainer, Jr. "The Influence of Individual Differences on Skill in End-User Computing." *Journal of Management Information Systems* 9, no. 1 (Summer 1992).

Huff, Sid L., Malcolm C. Munro, and Barbara H. Martin. "Growth Stages of End User Computing." *Communications of the ACM* 31, no. 5 (May 1988).

Janson, Marius, and L. Douglas Smith. "Prototyping for Systems Development: A Critical Appraisal." *MIS Quarterly* 9 (December 1985).

Jenkins, A. Milton. "Prototyping: A Methodology for the Design and Development of Application Systems." *Spectrum* 2 (April 1985).

Johnson, Richard T. "The Infocenter Experience." *Datamation* (January 1984).

Jones, T. C. "The Limits of Programming Productivity." Guide and Share Application Development Symposium, Proceedings. New York: Share 1979.

Kozar, Kenneth A., and John M. Mahlum. "A User-Generated Information System: An Innovative Development Approach." *MIS Quarterly* (June 1987).

Kraushaar, James M., and Larry E. Shirland. "A Prototyping Method for Applications Development by End Users and Information Systems Specialists." *MIS Quarterly* (September 1985).

Livingston, Dennis. "Outsourcing: Look Beyond the Price Tag." *Datamation* (November 15, 1992).

Loh, Lawrence, and N. Venkatraman. "Determinants of Information Technology Outsourcing." *Journal of Management Information Systems* 9, no. 1 (Summer 1992).

Loh, Lawrence, and N. Venkatraman. "Diffusion of Information Technology Outsourcing: Influence Sources and the Kodak Effect." *Information Systems Research* 3, no. 4 (December 1992).

Livingston, Dennis. "Outsourcing: Look Beyond the Price Tag." *Datamation* (November 15, 1992).

Lucas, Henry C., Eric J. Walton, and Michael J. Ginzberg. "Implementing Packaged Software." *MIS Quarterly* (December 1988).

Martin, James. *Application Development without Programmers.* Englewood Cliffs, NJ: Prentice-Hall, 1982.

Martin, J., and C. McClure. "Buying Software Off the Rack." *Harvard Business Review* (November–December 1983).

Mason, R. E. A., and T. T. Carey. "Prototyping Interactive Information Systems." *Communications of the ACM* 26 (May 1983).

Matos, Victor M, and Paul J. Jalics. "An Experimental Analysis of the Performance of Fourth-Generation Tools on PCs." *Communications of the ACM* 32, no. 11 (November 1989).

McMullen, John. "Developing a Role for End Users." *InformationWEEK* (June 15, 1992).

Rivard, Suzanne, and Sid L. Huff. "Factors of Success for End-User Computing." *Communications of the ACM* 31, no. 5 (May 1988).

Roche, Edward M. *Managing Information Technology in Multinational Corporations*. New York: Macmillan Publishing Company, 1992.

Rockart, John F., and Lauren S. Flannery. "The Management of End-User Computing." *Communications of the ACM* 26, no. 10 (October 1983).

Rowe, Lawrence A. "Tools for Developing OLTP Applications." *Datamation* (August 1985).

Schatz, Willie. "Bailoutsourcing." *Computerworld* (January 25, 1993).

Timmreck, Eric M. "Performance Measurement: Vendor Specifications and Benchmarks." In *The Information Systems Handbook,* ed. F. Warren McFarlan and Richard C. Nolan. Homewood, IL: Dow-Jones-Richard D. Irwin, 1975.

Trauth, Eileen M., and Elliot Cole. "The Organizational Interface: A Method for Supporting End Users of Packaged Software." *MIS Quarterly* 16, no. 1 (March 1992).

White, Clinton E., and David P. Christy. "The Information Center Concept: A Normative Model and a Study of Six Installations." *MIS Quarterly* (December 1987).

Wilder, C. "Outsourcing: From Fad to Respectability." *Computerworld* (June 11, 1990).

CHAPTER

13

Ensuring Quality with Information Systems

Carrier and Rockwell Become Quality Champions

Five years ago the Carrier Corporation could hardly be called a hotbed of quality. The Syracuse, New York-based manufacturing giant faced eroding market share and believed it was not communicating effectively with customers. One reason: a manual order entry system that was designed to match customers and products had a 70 percent error rate. Yet this system was allowed to handle one of Carrier's best-selling products, a commercial air conditioning unit.

The system required so many steps to process an order that mistakes were all but inevitable. Errors sometimes went undetected until the end of the manufacturing line, where workers would discover a wrong coil or similar problem. Even worse, big mistakes occasionally affected customers.

In 1988, the company finally put its foot down and instituted a total quality management program (TQM) in which information technology played a large role. Carrier now coordinates everything from

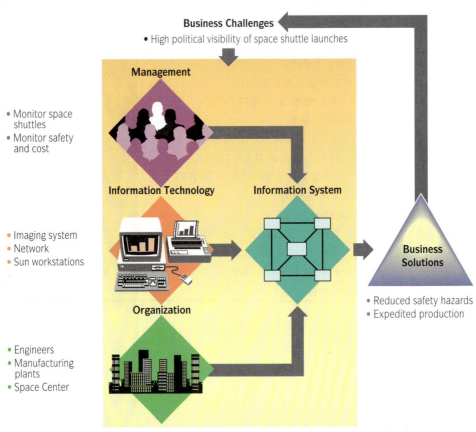

sales to manufacturing by using an expert system. The results are fewer errors, lower manufacturing costs, and happier customers. Due to this success, Carrier is looking for other ways its information systems can promote quality.

By continuously examining, documenting, and analyzing the firm's business processes, the information systems department at Rockwell International, a leading defense contractor, detected and solved a major problem in the design process of the space shuttle. It found that Rockwell's engineering depart-

ment in Downey, California, had to mail its new and updated designs to the company's manufacturing plant in Palmdale, California, and to the Kennedy Space Center in Florida. The Kennedy Space Center prepares the shuttle for its next launch. The delay constituted a possible safety hazard, so the information systems department responded by installing an automated imaging system. Now the engineering department can transmit design changes over networks to other sites, where Rockwell employees can view them on Sun workstations.

Sources: Alan Radding, "Quality is Job #1," *Datamation* (October 1, 1992) and Alice LaPlante, "For IS, Quality is 'Job None'," *Computerworld* (January 6, 1992).

The experiences of Carrier and Rockwell illustrate some of the ways in which information systems and the information systems function can be used to improve quality throughout the firm. Yet very few organizations have used information systems in this manner, and information systems have special quality problems of their own.

We have tried to explore various facets of quality in information systems throughout this text, but quality is the special focus of this chapter. Here we will examine the ways in which information systems can contribute to improving quality throughout the organization. We will then outline the quality problems peculiar to information systems, focusing on the need for quality assurance in the development of software. Finally we will describe traditional and new methodologies and tools for improving software quality and overall system effectiveness.

After completing this chapter you will be able to do the following:

- Describe how information systems can contribute to total quality management in an organization.
- Explain why information systems must pay special attention to software quality assurance.
- Identify the principal solutions to information systems quality problems.
- Describe the traditional tools and methodologies for promoting information systems quality.
- Describe new approaches for promoting information systems quality.

13.1 What Is Information Systems Quality?

Total quality management (TQM) is a concept that makes quality a responsibility to be shared by all people in an organization, with the achievement of quality control to be considered as an end in itself. Everyone is expected to contribute to the overall improvement of quality—the engineer who avoids design errors, the production worker who spots defects, the sales representative who presents the product properly, and even the secretary who avoids typing mistakes. Total quality management encompasses all of the functions of the organization.

Total quality management was popularized by the Japanese, who gave the responsibility for quality consistency to the workers who actually make the product or service, as opposed to a quality control department. Japanese management adopted the goal of zero defects, focusing on improving their product or service prior to delivery rather than correcting them after delivery. Studies have repeatedly shown that the earlier in the business cycle a problem is detected, the less it costs for the company to eliminate it. Thus the Japanese quality approach brought not only a shift in focus to the workers and an increased respect for product and service quality, but also lowered costs.

As this quality movement has spread to Europe and the United States, both quality within information systems departments and the role of information systems in the corporatewide quality programs have come under intense scrutiny. How can information systems contribute to overall quality in the organization? How can quality be promoted in information systems themselves?

How Information Systems Contribute to Total Quality Management

Quality programs differ greatly from company to company. Some are merely generalized "sales" campaigns intended to sensitize employees to strive for more quality in their daily work. At the opposite extreme, other quality programs can result in fundamental changes in the way a company does its business. The more a company tries to achieve with its program, the more information systems can contribute to the success of companywide programs.

Information systems can fill a special role in corporate quality programs because the systems are deeply involved with the daily work of other departments throughout the organization. For example, IS analysts usually have taken a leading role in designing such varied departmental systems as corporate payrolls, patent research systems, chemical process control systems, and sales support systems. IS professionals then maintain their knowledge of these departments through both their ongoing support of departmental systems and their participation in departmental information planning. In addition, IS personnel are keys to the sharing of data between departments; these employees have unique knowledge of the relationships between various departments. Often, only IS personnel know where certain data originate, how other departments use and store them, and which other functions would benefit from having access to them. With this broad understanding of the functional integration of the corporation, IS personnel can be valuable members of any quality project team.

The staff in good information systems departments have three skills that are critical to the success of a quality program. First, information systems analysts are supposed to be specialists in analyzing and redesigning business processes. That, after all, is their job. For instance, quality programs usually have a "fewer-is-better" philosophy—the fewer steps in a process, the less opportunity for an error to occur. The description of Carrier Corporation's quality program in the chapter opening vignette showed that mistakes in order entry were rampant because of the many steps in the process. When IS professionals were able to reduce the number of steps, the number of errors dropped dramatically. Good systems analysts are trained and are experienced in simplifying and redesigning business systems.

Second, many IS technicians are experienced in measuring and quantifying procedures and critical activities in any process. Typically, IS departments have long been involved with measurements of their own service. For example, they commonly measure mainframe and network downtime, the number of calls for help they receive from each department, and the amount of time their staff devotes to the maintenance of specific production systems (a key indicator of the quality of a system).

Third, IS project managers are skilled in managing tasks and projects. Project manager training has long been a staple of better IS departments; such training includes the use of project management software. These skills can contribute a great deal to any serious quality program, which should be organized as a project and will usually be heavily task-oriented.

Any study of quality programs shows that information is a top concern to those involved. To improve production or sales, for example, management needs data to determine both what is being done right and what is being done wrong. IS is usually the key to making that information available in a timely fashion and in a format useful to those who need it for quality purposes. For example, manufacturing data have traditionally been supplied to management in summary form at the end of the manufacturing process. In effect they represent historical data that at best can be used to reduce future problems. Real-time data are needed to correct problems as they occur, as the quality team at General Tire & Rubber Co., in Charlotte, North Carolina, realized. They installed a local area network that gives plant floor operators real-time data on raw materials as the materials arrive at the plant. In this way, bad raw material batches are discovered very quickly, before the plant produces any bad tires.

The information systems staff is the source of ideas on the application of technology to quality issues; often they are also the people who can make that technology available to the quality project. For example, with the help of IS departments, statistical analysis software is becoming more widely used in the drive for quality. Goodmark Foods, Inc., the leading U.S. producer of snack meats, received support from its information systems group to apply such software to their manufacturing. The software helps workers see when and by how

This quality assurance technician at the General Tire and Rubber Company in Charlotte, NC, is gathering real-time data on materials for manufacturing and production processing.

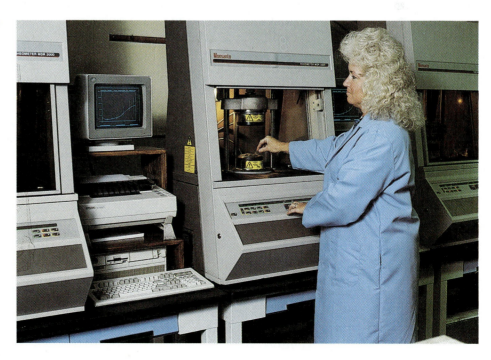

much each piece of snack meat deviates from the specified weight (Mandell, 1992).

The positive effects of a quality information systems project will be seen and felt throughout the organization. Such a project can be a stimulus to other departments to undertake their own quality project, and it often can be a model for other departments as they initiate their own projects, thus helping the whole quality process within the organization to move forward.

Yet the information systems role in corporate quality programs has provoked a great deal of controversy. IS has been criticized for a reluctance to become involved in organizationwide quality programs. Often IS will focus exclusively upon improving its own production of software applications while not reaching out to aid the rest of the company in the ways described above. Even while working to improve the quality of their own products, IS departments often fail to conceive of other departments as their customers, thereby isolating themselves from the needs of those departments. On the other hand, non-IS departments often fail to consider contributions the IS staff might make to their quality project and so do not reach out to involve them. It is not uncommon for IS to be viewed only as technical support with little to contribute to the planning or content of the quality program.

Much of information systems work is very technical, leading to another problem—information systems professionals can too easily look to technology as the answer to all quality problems. While technology has much to contribute, quality usually means shifting focus from technological to business issues. Many people, both in and out of IS departments, view technological improvement as the actual goal of the project, an approach that will almost certainly prevent a quality program from achieving success. Technology, after all, is only a tool or set of tools that, if used correctly, support the business goals of the department or company. The Window on Organizations is an example of a successful IS quality program that was possible only because of a focus on business goals and organizational needs.

A widely expressed final concern is that in some organizations IS ends up leading a companywide project by default. The rest of the company looks to the information systems department for leadership rather than just for inspiration and support. However, as we have already seen, successful quality projects must be focused on business goals and the redesign of business processes. Experience has repeatedly proven that successful projects are led by the top of the organization—the business leadership—rather than by one department.

The Need for Software Quality Assurance

Although the information systems function has a valuable role to play in total quality management, information systems departments have been criticized for not paying as much attention to quality as they should. Vaughan Merlyn, a partner at the Ernst & Young Center for Information Technology in Boston and a longtime leader in the IS quality movement, estimated in early 1992 that less than 5 percent of information systems organizations in the United States had established quality programs, despite the increased attention such programs were getting throughout the country (Radding, 1992). The underlying quality issue for information systems departments is software quality assurance.

Producing software of high quality is critical to most large organizations because of the central function that software has in so many departments—payroll, accounts receivable, manufacturing, sales, research, management. An undiscovered error in a company's credit software or process control software can result in millions of dollars of losses. For more and more companies, software has even become an integral part of the products sold. Computer software is now part of automobile fuel consumption systems, dishwasher and VCR controls, and FAX machines. Several years ago, a hidden software problem in

ORGANIZATIONS

Information Systems Help Nashua Meet Quality Goals

Even within information systems departments, quality may not be an issue of technology. Tim Gallagher, MIS director of Nashua Corporation, a $590 million manufacturer of office supplies and computer products in Nashua, New Hampshire, focused on organizational change to improve the quality of his department and of the whole corporation.

In the late 1970s, when William Conway, CEO of Nashua Corporation, brought in quality guru W. Edwards Deming to help his company improve the quality of its processes and customer service, the information systems department did not even participate in the program. Deming worked with Nashua Corporation for ten years before Gallagher joined the program. Why was there a turnaround? The answer is that Nashua faced a serious problem, and Gallagher saw the solution.

Nashua is a diverse company with nine fairly independent divisions. Like so many other companies, computer support developed at the center in the 1970s. In 1987, Gallagher realized that this centralized information systems function was a serious barrier to quality relations with customers. According to Gallagher, "It used to take us two days to process a telephone order." When a customer called in an order, the divisional order clerk had to dial into a central computer system to do a credit check on the

customer—customer and credit information were centralized. Next, the clerk would log on to a local computer to obtain pricing information, then onto a centralized computer for inventory data. Other steps followed, normally consuming two days. Such customer service had become unacceptable by the late 1980s.

The solution? Gallagher launched a five-year strategic plan to decentralize much of the information systems function. Decentralization not only addressed the customer service issue, but it also fit in with the company's overall philosophy of flattening the organization and pushing decision making down into the divisions. At each plant, small teams of users and information systems professionals were established and given real decision-making power. Each division developed its own systems, resulting in Nashua going from one computer center to nine. Nashua is working on replacing its centralized IBM 4381 (small mainframe) with smaller divisional computers ranging from DEC VAX clusters, to an IBM System/6000, four IBM System/400s and a Wang VS8360. Companywide, the information systems staff size remained constant but the IS organization was flattened from five levels to three.

The result on sales servicing has been dramatic. Clerks can now quote prices and produce orders in a matter of minutes. Gallagher

points out that the MIS budget has nearly doubled for the company, with the extra money being spent to equip the divisional computer centers. He believes Nashua has better systems in place at the functional level, and that the company is handling the unique requirements of each division. Nashua didn't get the best cost; instead, it got the best fit.

Quality improvement at Nashua did require new technology to allow the needed changes to occur. However, even though the change originated with the head of a technology department (information systems), the key was not technology. It was organizational change, made possible by the decentralization of the IS function. The result was a dramatic improvement in customer service throughout the whole company.

Source: Catherine Marenghi, "Nashua Keeps Quality Flame Burning in Customer Service," *Computerworld* (January 6, 1992).

To Think About: How did technology promote quality at the Nashua Corporation? Could technology alone have solved Nashua's quality problems? To make the quality improvements described here, what management, organization, and technology issues had to be addressed?

AT&T's long distance system brought down that system, bringing the New York-based financial exchanges to a halt and interfering with billions of dollars of business around the country for a number of hours. Modern passenger and commercial vehicles are increasingly dependent upon computer programs for critical functions. A hidden software defect in a braking system could result in the loss of lives.

Like other types of production, software production is unique and presents its own set of problems. One special characteristic of software development is that its usual goal is to build only one copy of the final product (except for companies developing software for public sale). For most manufactured products—aircraft, automobiles, paper clips, socks—once development begins, hundreds, thousands or even millions of copies of the product are manufactured. With software, quality problems must be solved the first time; the design must be of high quality on the first try.

Meeting user needs can be difficult in a process where the end user commits to the product before that product has been built. In effect, the final system is "purchased" in advance, bought "sight unseen." Defining user needs and judging the quality of the completed system have proven to be major challenges. Most systems development projects begin by defining user information requirements and specifications in the form of systems analysis and design documents.

The problem is that meeting specifications does not necessarily guarantee quality. The completed system may in fact meet the specifications but not satisfy the user's needs. This occurs because of inaccurate, incomplete, or improperly detailed specifications, omitting functions in the specifications, or changing user needs during the development period. Often quality is not quantified in the specifications so that judgments about system quality become subjective. This type of situation can easily deteriorate into finger pointing between IS and the user community, each attacking the other while not addressing system quality.

Specifications often fail to consider the system from the perspective of the users. While designers will concentrate on functionality, they frequently overlook ease of learning and use, unquestioned accuracy and reliability, or speed of response. All of these factors are important to the success of a system.

System response time is a common example of a detailed specification that is omitted or inadequately defined. A customer service representative, who is the end user in a customer service function, may need a query response time of no more than five seconds, but the specifications may contain no reference to response time. If at delivery the response time were ten seconds, the system would meet specifications but would not meet user needs. Perhaps a five-second response time was specified and was achieved during testing with one or two simultaneous users. Would the system satisfy this specification if response time deteriorates to 20 seconds when 100 users are on the system simultaneously? Does such a system serve user needs? If the system does respond within five seconds 80 percent of the time when 100 people are on the system, has the system met its specifications when it fails to meet that specification 20 percent of the time? Can a system be expected to meet such a requirement 100 percent of the time? The lack of agreed-upon measurable standards in specifications leads to dissatisfied users and systems that do not meet user needs.

User expectations also cannot be equated with quality. Users will create their own mental model of a "perfect" system. These types of unspecified expectations will affect the way a system is perceived and judged. A simple illustration should make the problem clear: Two people purchasing the same shirt may have

Table 13.1 THE MAINTENANCE PROBLEM

Annual personnel hours	
Maintain and enhance current systems	48.0%
Develop new systems	46.1%
Other	5.9%
20% of the survey allocated 85% of its efforts to maintenance and enhancements	
Frequency of activity	
Errors — emergency	17.4%
Change — data, inputs, files, hardware	18.2%
Improve — user enhancements, efficiency, documentation, etc.	60.3%
Other	4.1%

Sources: Bennett P. Lientz and E. Burton Swanson, *Software Maintenance Management.* © 1980 Addison-Wesley Publishing Company. Reprinted by permission.

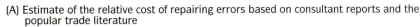

(A) Estimate of the relative cost of repairing errors based on consultant reports and the popular trade literature

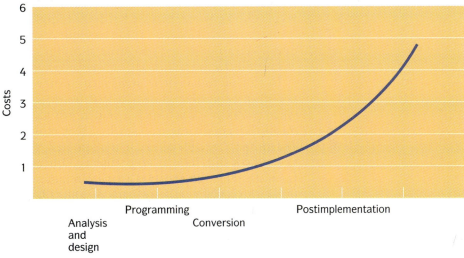

Figure 13.1
The cost of errors over the systems development cycle. The most common, most severe, and most expensive system errors develop in the early design stages. They involve faulty requirements analysis. Errors in program logic or syntax are much less common, less severe, and less costly to repair than design errors. (*Source: Alberts, 1976.*)

(B) Origin, frequency, and severity of errors in large national defense and space programs

Error Type	% of Total Errors	Relative Severity	% of Total Cost of Errors
Design	66%	2.5	83 + %
Logic	17%	1.0	8 + %
Syntax	17%	1.0	8 + %

very different expectations. If one purchaser sees the shirt as expensive, he may expect that it will hold its color through many washes, last a long time, and not need ironing. The other person may view the same item as a medium- or low-priced shirt and therefore have lower expectations. Both purchasers receive the same shirt at the same price, but the first purchaser is much more likely to be disappointed with the shirt over time. Systems, too, are judged in such subjective ways, making it difficult to determine if the system actually meets the users' needs. We treat the issue of user satisfaction again in Chapter 14.

THE MAINTENANCE NIGHTMARE

Computer software has traditionally been a nightmare to maintain. Maintenance, the process of modifying a system in production use, is the most expensive phase of the systems development process. Table 13.1 indicates the size of the maintenance problem. In one-fifth of information systems departments, 85 percent of personnel hours are allocated to maintenance, leaving little time for new systems development. In most shops, nearly half of professional personnel time is spent in the maintenance of existing systems.

Why are maintenance costs so high? One major reason is organizational change. The firm may experience large internal changes in structure or leadership, or change may come from its surrounding environment. These organizational changes affect information requirements. But an equally common cause of long-term maintenance problems is faulty systems analysis and design, especially information requirements analysis. Some studies of large TPS systems by TRW, Inc., have found that a majority of system errors—64 percent—result from early analysis errors (Mazzucchelli, 1985).

Figure 13.1 illustrates the cost of correcting errors. Part (A) is based on the experience of consultants reported in the literature. Part (B) shows the results of a quality assurance study of large national defense software projects.

If errors are detected early, during analysis and design, the cost to the systems development effort is small. But if they are not discovered until after programming, testing, or conversion has been completed, the costs can soar astronomically. A minor logic error, for example, that could take one hour to correct during the analysis and design stage could take 10, 40, and 90 times as long to correct during programming, conversion, and postimplementation, respectively.

To be able to handle maintenance quickly and inexpensively, a software system must be flexible. A flexible system can more quickly and easily be repaired when problems occur. Such a system can also be modified as business requirements change over the years—which they most certainly will. For example a sales system must be able to accommodate new products, new sales staff, and even new offices with little or no problems. Otherwise, a system that may be successful in the short run becomes a long run failure. Inflexibility is an all too common problem, partially because many designers do not consider the aspect of change as they design new systems. However, even if they do design a flexible system, flexibility can seem to be expensive and time-consuming. Its benefits are not always understood or appreciated by the users. Target dates and cost limitations often force developers to sacrifice flexibility in order to complete a project as promised or as wanted. Unfortunately, the corporation may pay a much heavier price at a later time.

BUGS AND DEFECTS

Bugs: Program code defects or errors.

A major problem with software is the presence of hidden **bugs** or program code defects. Studies have shown that it is virtually impossible to eliminate all bugs from large programs. The main source of bugs is the complexity of decision-making code. Even a relatively small program of several hundred lines will contain tens of decisions leading to hundreds or even thousands of different paths. Important programs within most corporations are usually much larger, containing tens of thousands or even millions of lines of code, each with many times the choices and paths of the smaller programs. Such complexity is difficult to document and design—designers document some reactions wrongly or fail to consider some possibilities. Studies show that about 60 percent of errors discovered during testing are a result of specifications in the design documentation that were missing, ambiguous, in error, or in conflict.

Zero defects, a goal of the total quality management movement, cannot be achieved in larger programs. Complete testing is simply not possible. Fully testing programs that contain thousands of choices and millions of paths would require thousands of years (see Figure 13.2 for a study of bug removal efforts in one system). The size of the problem can be inferred from U.S. Aviation Administration Agency regulations. Circular 25.1309-1A sets a very high standard for civil aviation. It says that aircraft problems that can lead to "catastrophic failure" must be "so unlikely that they are not anticipated to occur during the entire operational life of all airplanes of one type." Yet although software too can cause a catastrophic failure, it is specifically exempted from this regulation, "because it is not feasible to assess the number or kinds of software errors, if any, that may remain after the completion of system design, development, and testing" (Littlewood and Strigini, 1992). The message? We cannot eliminate all bugs, and we cannot even know with any certainty the seriousness of the bugs that do remain.

Even when bugs are found, they are difficult to remove. Experience has shown that bug fixes often do not work. In many cases, the effort to fix a bug will introduce an entirely new bug or series of bugs. Studies by the Predictably Dependable Computing Systems research project have shown that once a bug has been "repaired," there is only a 50–50 chance that the program will function without failure as long as it did before the attempt to fix the bug (Littlewood and Strigini, 1992).

Yet the presence of bugs can have expensive and even tragic results. One wrong number in a very large program can cause a space probe to miss its target by billions of miles. A failure in an air traffic control system at a critical moment

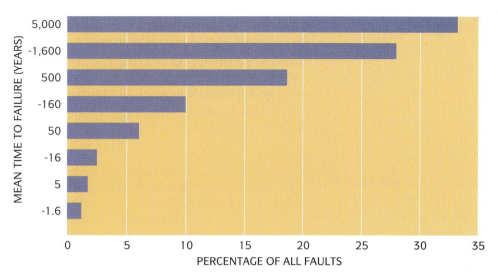

Figure 13.2
Eliminating software bugs as an exercise in diminishing returns. Residual errors persist even in programs that have been carefully debugged. The top portion of the figure shows that bugs that remained in a system after debugging were primarily "5000-year" bugs that would produce a failure only once in 5000 years. The bottom portion of the figure shows that the time needed to remove such residual bugs outpaces the resulting improvement in reliability, measured by the estimated achieved mean time to failure. *Illustration by Johnny Johnson from "The Risks of Software," by Bev Littlewood and Lorenz String,* Scientific American, *November 1992. Copyright © 1992 by Scientific American, Inc. All rights reserved.*

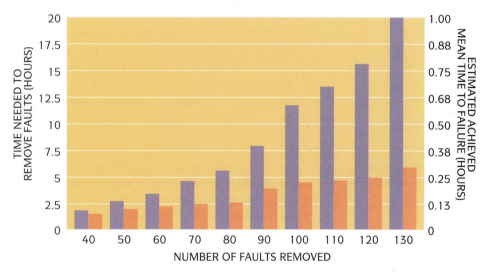

can hinder the controller from preventing the collision of two passenger planes, resulting in hundreds of deaths (see Chapters 18 and 20).

To achieve quality in software development, an organization must first reach agreement as to what quality is. Some developers view quality as the absence of programming defects. Clearly the presence of too many bugs will lower the quality of a system, but we have just learned that while zero defects may be an appropriate goal, such a situation can never be achieved in software development. Even if a system had no bugs, if it were slow, difficult to use, missing critical functions or inflexible, it certainly would not be a quality system. Any definition of quality must be viewed from the user perspective. It must be broad in scope and specific enough to encompass the satisfaction of user needs. A quality system must do the following:

- Achieve the business goals articulated by the user department
- Operate at an acceptable cost, commensurate with the value produced for the firm
- Meet carefully defined performance standards (such as response time and system availability)
- Produce accurate, reliable output
- Be easy to learn and use
- Be flexible.

Some Solutions to Information System Quality Problems

Information systems are complex, and solutions to quality problems are equally complex. We cannot examine them in depth here but will present an overview of some of the more critical areas that developers must focus upon. They include using an appropriate systems development methodology; proper resource allocation during systems development; the use of metrics; attention to testing; and the use of quality tools.

THE ROLE OF METHODOLOGIES

To limit problems and increase quality when building systems, developers must begin with a disciplined methodology that sets standards for all phases of the project. Good systems development methodologies (historically often referred to as structured development methodologies) will normally include the following:

- Proven methods for determining and documenting both system specifications and system design
- Programming standards that result in understandable, maintainable code that is not overly complex
- Guidelines for developing quality measurements to be agreed upon by all interested parties prior to development
- Standards and methods for testing the system
- Software tools to be used at every phase to standardize the work in the project and to improve the quality of the output
- Project control methods, including numerous project milestones at which user approval will be required (see Chapter 14).

Development methodology: A collection of methods, one or more for every activity within every phase of a development project.

A **development methodology** is actually just a collection of methods, one or more for every activity within every phase of a development project. The user of a methodology seldom uses every method within it because most projects do not require every possible activity. Numerous useful development methodologies exist, some suited to specific technologies, others reflecting differing development philosophies. Information systems departments, in conjunction with management of other departments, select the methodology they believe best fits the needs of their company. Larger corporations, employing multiple technologies, may select multiple methodologies to be used with differing technologies. However, the key to quality development is to select an appropriate methodology and then enforce its use. We will discuss several specific methodologies in sections 13.2 and 13.3.

As we have indicated, a quality system must achieve the business goals set by the user whom the system will serve. Therefore, system quality begins with requirements or specifications. Specifications must be approved by the users. They must be complete, detailed and accurate, and they must be documented in a format the user community can understand. Some methodologies stress flowcharts and diagrams, others the use of verbal descriptions. One popular method, prototyping, is discussed in Chapter 12. Specifications must also include agreed upon measures of system quality so that the system can be evaluated objectively while it is being developed and once it is completed. We cannot overemphasize that quality specifications—clear, precise representations of user needs—are critical to the development of a quality system.

Traditionally, specifications have focused upon the processing—how the data are transformed. Today, however, corporate management has come to understand that the most valuable portion of information systems is the data. The same data will be used differently by many different departments. For example, production quality data will be used by the production department, research labs, marketing and sales staffs, corporate management, and even customers. In addition, processing needs change—the research labs and corporate management will continually change the way they analyze the production quality data, while various customers use that data differently. The constant is the structure of the data. Therefore, good projects usually emphasize data, often using data modeling, which we have discussed in Chapter 8.

RESOURCE ALLOCATION DURING SYSTEMS DEVELOPMENT

Resource allocation: Determination of how costs time, and personnel are assigned to different activities of a systems development project.

Views on **resource allocation** during systems development have changed significantly over the years. Resource allocation determines the way the costs, time, and personnel are assigned to different phases of the project. In earlier times, developers focused on programming, with only about 1 percent of the time and costs of a project being devoted to systems analysis (determining specifications). As the information systems professionals have moved closer to a business or user perspective on quality, they have come to understand the central role of specifications. Moreover, technology that is now being used for systems development forces expenditures in analysis and design work to expand. Consequently, project resources are being shifted to earlier in the project cycle. More time is being spent in specifications and systems analysis, decreasing the proportion of programming time and reducing the need for so much maintenance time. Figure 13.3 demonstrates the shift, although the ideal allocation of time represented in the figure is now considered to be outdated. Current literature suggests that about one-quarter of a project's time and cost should be expended in specifications and analysis, with perhaps 50 percent of its resources being allocated to design and programming. Installation and postimplementation ideally should require only one-quarter of the project's resources.

SOFTWARE METRICS

Software metrics: Objective assessments of the software used in a system in the form of quantified measurements.

Software metrics can play a vital role in increasing the quality of a project. **Software metrics** are objective assessments of the system in the form of quantified measurements. Ongoing use of metrics allows the IS department and the user jointly to measure the performance of the system and identify problems as

Figure 13.3
Ideal and actual software development costs. Ideally, relatively balanced amounts of time are allowed for analysis, design, programming, and installation. About 8% of costs are allocated ideally to analysis and design, 60% to programming and installation, and 32% to long-term maintenance. Actually, however, the early stages of analysis and design receive far less resources than is desirable. Programming and installation (including all important testing) also receive less time and fewer resources than is desirable, reflecting pressure to deliver a workable system as soon as possible. As a result, systems maintenance is far more expensive than is desirable—about 50% of the total software costs over the expected life span of the system. (*Source: Alberts, 1976*).

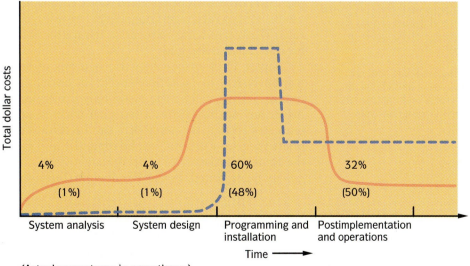

they occur. Software metrics include input metrics, output metrics, capacity metrics, performance/quality metrics, and value metrics.

The educational and experience level of system developers is an example of an input metric. The number of transactions that can be processed in a specified unit of time is an example of a capacity metric. Response time is a performance metric in an on-line system. The number of checks printed per hour is a system output metric for a payroll system. One metric for programming quality is the number of bugs per hundred lines of code. The business value of a transaction is an example of a value metric.

A widely used output metric is function points, which can help measure the productivity of software developers and the efficiency of the software itself regardless of the programming language employed. **Function point analysis** measures the number of inputs, outputs, inquiries, files, and external interfaces to other software used in an application. The results can be used to calculate the cost per function point of writing a piece of software and the number of function points written per programmer in a specified unit of time.

Function point analysis: Software output metric that measures the number of inputs, outputs, inquiries, files, and external interfaces used in an application. Used to assess developer productivity and software efficiency.

Unfortunately, many manifestations of quality are not so easy to define in metric terms. In those cases the developers must find indirect measurements. For example, an objective measurement of the ease of use of a newly developed system might be the average amount of time operators take to learn it. Throughout the life of the system, ease of use might be measured by the number of calls for help the IS staff receives per month from system operators. For metrics to be successful, they must be carefully designed, formal and objective. They must measure significant aspects of the system. One warning, however: Software metrics will only be effective in judging the quality of the system if the users agree to the measurements in advance. Finally, metrics are of no value unless they are used consistently. Few IS departments make wide use of formal, objective metrics today even though studies show they can significantly improve quality.

TESTING

Early, regular, and thorough testing will contribute significantly to system quality. In general, software testing is often misunderstood. Many view testing as a way to prove the correctness of work they have done. In fact, we know that all sizable software is riddled with errors. The reason we test must be to uncover these errors. Any other motivation will result in a less than thorough testing process.

Testing begins at the design phase. Because no coding yet exists, the test normally used is a **walkthrough**—a review of a specification or design document by a small group of people carefully selected based on the skills needed for the particular objectives being tested. Once coding begins, coding walkthroughs also can be used to review program code. However, code must be tested by computer runs. When errors are discovered, the source is found and eliminated through a process called **debugging.**

Walkthrough: A review of a specification or design document by a small group of people carefully selected based on the skills needed for the particular objectives being tested.

Debugging: The process of discovering and eliminating the errors and defects—the bugs—in program code.

Chapter 11 describes the various stages of testing required to put an information system in operation—program testing, system testing, and acceptance testing. Testing will be successful only if planned properly. Early in the project, before any testing begins, a test plan must be prepared. The plan must include test cases so that the developers can be certain that they have tested an appropriate range of valid and invalid input. Invalid input must be tested to be certain the system handles errors appropriately. Tests must also be tailored to the technology being tested, as the Window on Technology describes.

QUALITY TOOLS

Finally, system quality can be significantly enhanced by the use of quality tools. For years, the computer industry was compared to the fabled barefoot shoemaker's children. Information systems had been developed to support almost every aspect of the business except the IS function itself. IS did everything the slow, mistake-prone, manual way. This began to change in the 1980s with the development of a range of tools. Today, many tools have been developed to address every aspect of the systems development process. Information systems

Everyone loves graphical user interfaces (GUIs). Witness the sale of over 9 million copies of Windows 3.0 for desktop computers during its first two years on the market. In that same time period, over 5000 Windows applications were released. GUIs have become quite popular for custom-developed systems also, with many users refusing to accept new systems that do not use a GUI-type interface. However, software testing authorities agree that only about 5 to 10 percent of the programs developed in-house are rigorously tested. The problem is the lack of new testing methods and tools; these are not available because the technology being tested is new.

Testing a GUI interface presents special problems. One key test of DOS command interfaces is to compare one screen with another, a relatively easy test to carry out. Tools have long been available to automate this testing. But GUI screens cannot be tested this way. One of the reasons GUIs are so popular is that users can tailor the screen to their own preferences, specifying window size and shape, location, color, and background. Any screen-to-screen comparison will almost certainly turn up differences that are perfectly appropriate and so do not represent a software defect.

GUI interfaces present a memory management problem that did not exist with DOS command systems. Graphics uses a great deal of system memory (as explained in Chapter 6). Microcomputers normally do not have adequate memory to allow graphical interfaces to take control of and retain the max-imum memory they may need for the duration of the session. Therefore, GUI programming always involves memory management—allocating memory to the interface only when needed, releasing it the moment it is no longer needed. Memory that is no longer being used but that has not been released by the program is sometimes known as "garbage," and garbage collection is a serious problem. Every byte of memory that holds garbage is one byte less that is available for other uses. As garbage collects, it is like a time bomb. When too much garbage has accumulated (resulting in too little usable memory), an action or application will fail. A failure, at minimum, is a frustrating and time-consuming nuisance. Worse, it can cause the loss of a significant amount of important work. Applications that fail for lack of memory are of low quality and will be rejected by users.

Because memory allocation is hidden, the programmer has no direct way of knowing if garbage is collecting. The end result is that a GUI tester must have a testing tool that keeps track of memory allocation. Moreover, program failure rarely occurs because of a single action. Rather, failures usually happen only after a large number of individual actions have taken place. Hence, testing must include stress testing, pushing the system as far as you can.

New tools have been slow to develop, possibly because the Windows market virtually exploded, creating a large demand long before anyone predicted it. Nonetheless, some tools are available and the selection is growing. These tools perform a range of functions, including testing keystrokes and mouse clicks. Some tools systematically test applications by entering application variables, including combinations of user-configurations.

A number of products keep track of memory allocation, a complex and very data-intensive function. Locating the source of memory garbage requires that the testing software keep track of the amount of free memory available before an action occurs, the amount of memory allocated, and the amount of memory released when the action is completed. At times, such a large amount of data is required to debug a garbage memory problem. One thing is very clear: Good products are appearing. The evidence? Microsoft has released its own testing software known as Microsoft Test for Windows. Microsoft proved its quality to its own satisfaction before ever offering it for sale by using it to test its own top-selling Windows 3.1.

Sources: Lee The, "Stress Tests for GUI Programs," *Datamation* (September 1, 1992); and Dennis Hamilton, "Windows Test Tools Catching Up," *Software Magazine* (May, 1992).

To Think About: Why do you imagine so few internally developed GUI applications are properly tested before release? If you were appointed manager of development of GUI applications within a large corporation and found only a little testing of new applications, what, if anything, would you do about it? Why?

professionals are using project management software to manage their projects. Products exist to document specifications and system design in text and graphic forms. Programming tools include data dictionaries, libraries to manage program modules, and tools that actually produce program code (see Chapters 7, 8, and 12). Many types of tools exist to aid in the debugging process. The most recent set of tools automates much of the preparation for comprehensive testing. Tool technology is still relatively new and in many cases the value is still unproven. Nonetheless, tools are having a significant impact on system quality and on development costs. We will discuss various types of tools in sections 13.2 and 13.3.

13.2 Traditional Tools and Methodologies

Spaghetti code: Unstructured, confusing program code with tangled logic that metaphorically resembles a pot of cooked spaghetti.

Structured: Refers to the fact that techniques are instructions that are carefully drawn up, often step-by-step, with each step building upon a previous one.

Top-down: An approach that progresses from the highest most abstract level to the lowest level of detail.

In the early days of programming, few methodologies existed. User specifications were gathered in informal conversations that were written up in hard-to-follow narratives. Programming was an art. Programs were unstructured, written in complex and confusing code. When such code was so undecipherable that the logic flow appeared to be as entangled as a cooked pot of spaghetti it was referred to as **spaghetti code.** Systems were inflexible, maintenance all but impossible.

In reaction to these early problems, new methodologies emerged in the 1970s. These methodologies incorporated a range of methods or techniques to carry out the major functions of a development project. The methodologies, and the methods they included, usually are described by the terms *structured* and *top-down*. **Structured** refers to the fact that the techniques are instructions that are carefully drawn up, often step-by-step, with each step building upon the previous step. **Top-down** refers to an approach that progresses from the highest, most abstract level to the lowest level of detail—from the general to the specific. For example, the highest level of a top-down depiction of a human resources system would show the main human resources functions, such as personnel, benefits, employment, and Equal Economic Opportunity (EEO). Each of these would then be exploded or decomposed down to the next layer. Benefits, for example, might include pension, employee savings, health care, and insurance. Each path is broken down, layer by layer, until the material at the lowest level is easily grasped and documented. Top-down is used for analysis, design, and programming. See the discussion below of leveled data-flow diagrams for an example of top-down.

The traditional structured methodologies are process-oriented rather than data-oriented. While data descriptions are part of the methods, the methodologies focus on how the data are transformed rather than on the data themselves. These methodologies are largely linear—each phase must be completed before the next one can begin. Top-down, structured methodologies have been used to develop large numbers of systems for two decades, so that a great many existing systems have been developed in this way. Despite growing interest in other methodologies, they remain the dominant methodological approach today.

The methodologies discussed in this section include structured analysis, structured design, structured programming, decision tables, decision trees, pseudocode, and flowcharts. Using these methodologies promotes quality by improving communication, reducing errors caused by faulty program logic or unclear specifications, and creating software that is easier to understand and to maintain.

Structured Analysis

Structured analysis: Method for defining system inputs, processes, and outputs and for partitioning systems into subsystems or modules that show a logical graphic model of information flow.

Structured analysis is a widely used method for defining system inputs, processes, and outputs and for breaking systems down into subsystems. It offers a logical graphic model of information flow, partitioning a system into modules that show manageable levels of detail. The structured approach accomplishes the following:

- Views a system from the top down.
- Specifies the interfaces that exist between modules.
- Rigorously specifies the processes or transformations that occur within each module.

Structured analysis can be applied to systems analysis, requirements specification, and design. It even serves as the starting point for structured software design, described below.

Data flow diagram (DFD):
Primary tool in structured analysis that graphically illustrates the system's component processes and the flow of data between them.

Structured analysis is highly graphic, relying mainly on diagrams rather than on narrative text. Its primary tool is the **data flow diagram (DFD)**, a graphic representation of a system's component processes and the interfaces between them. DFDs show how data flow to, from, and within an information system and the processes that transform the data. DFDs also show where the data are stored.

Data flow diagrams are constructed using four basic symbols, illustrated in Figure 13.4. These symbols consist of the following:

1. The data flow symbol, an arrow showing the flow of data.
2. The process symbol, rounded boxes or bubbles depicting processes that transform the data.
3. The data store symbol, an open rectangle indicating where data are stored.
4. The external entity symbol, either a rectangle or a square indicating the sources or destinations of data.

Data flows: The movement of data between processes, external entities, and data stores in a data flow diagram.

Data flows show the movement of data between processes, external entities, and data stores. They always contain packets of data, with the name or content of each data flow listed beside the arrow. The flows are of known composition and represent data that are manual or automated. Data flows consist of documents, reports, data from a computer file, or data from a telecommunications transmission. These can be either inputs or outputs.

Processes: Portray the transformation of input data flows to output data flows in a data flow diagram.

Processes portray the transformation of input data flows to output data flows. An example is a process that transforms a sales order into an invoice or that calculates an employee's gross pay from his or her time card. The convention for naming a process consists of combining a strong verb with an object. For example, we could call the process that calculates gross pay Calculate gross pay. Each process has a unique reference number (such as 1.0, 2.0, etc.) so that it can be easily distinguished from other processes in the data flow diagram.

Data stores: Manual or automated inventories of data.

Data stores are either manual or automated inventories of data. They consist of computer files or databases, file cabinets, card files, microfiche, or a binder of paper reports. The name of the data store is written inside the data store symbol.

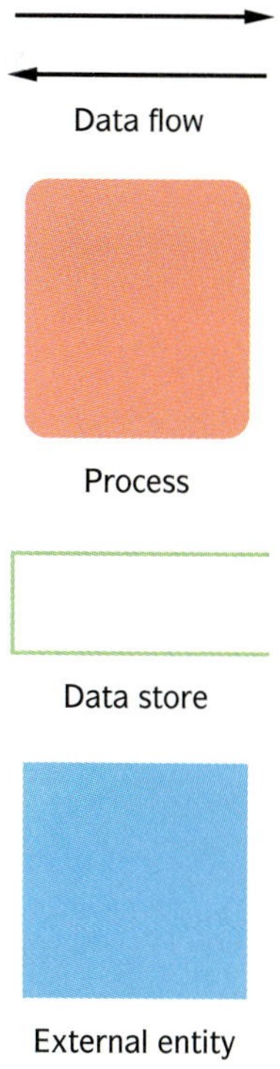

Data flow

Process

Data store

External entity

Figure 13.4
Data flow diagram symbols. Data flow diagrams can be constructed by using four symbols: *Arrows* represent the flow of data; *Processes* transform input data flows into output data flows; *Data stores* represent collections of data used or maintained by the system; and *External entities* represent sources or destinations of data and help to define the boundary of a system.

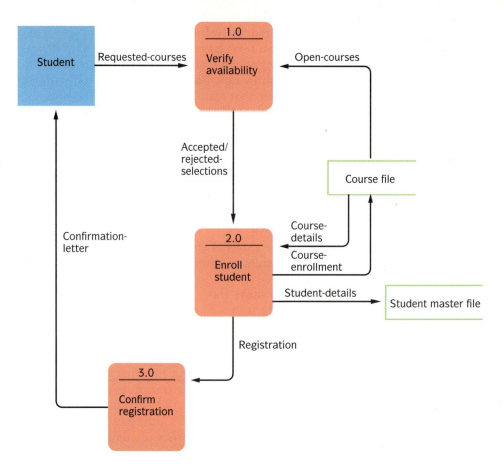

Figure 13.5
Data flow diagram for mail-in university registration system. The system has three processes: Verify availability (1.0), Enroll student (2.0), and Confirm registration (3.0). The name and content of each of the data flows appear adjacent to each arrow. There is one external entity in this system, the student. There are two data stores: the student master file and the course file.

External entities: Originators or receivers of information outside the scope of the system portrayed in the data flow diagram. Sometimes called *outside interfaces.*

External entities are originators or receivers of information. They consist of customers, suppliers, or government agencies external to the organization, or employees or departments within the organization. External entities are sometimes called outside interfaces because they are outside the boundary or scope of the system treated by the data flow diagram.

Figure 13.5 shows a simple data flow diagram for a mail-in university course registration system. Students submit registration forms with their name, identification number, and the numbers of the courses they wish to take. In process 1.0, the system verifies that each course selected is still open by referencing the university's course file. The file distinguishes courses that are still open from those that have been canceled or filled. Process 1.0 then determines which of the student's selections can be accepted or rejected. Process 2.0 enrolls the student in the courses for which he or she has been accepted. It updates the university's course file with the student's name and identification number and recalculates the class size. If maximum enrollment has been reached, the course number is flagged as closed. Process 2.0 also updates the university's student master file with information about new students or changes in address. Process 3.0 then sends each student applicant a confirmation-of-registration letter listing the courses for which he or she is registered and noting the course selections that could not be fulfilled.

The diagrams can be used to depict higher-level processes as well as lower-level details. Through leveled data flow diagrams, a complex process can be broken down into successive levels of detail. An entire system can be divided into subsystems with a high-level data flow diagram. Each subsystem, in turn, can be divided into additional subsystems with lower-level data flow diagrams, and the lower-level subsystems can be broken down again until the lowest level of detail has been reached.

Figures 13.6(A), 13.6(B), and 13.6(C) show leveled data flow diagrams for a pension recordkeeping and accounting system. Figure 13.6(A) is the most gen-

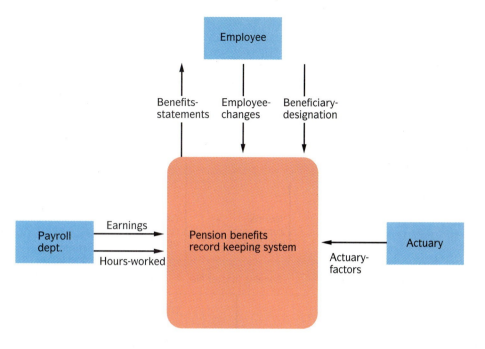

Figure 13.6A
Context diagram for a pension benefits recordkeeping and accounting system. This diagram provides an overview of the entire pension benefits recordkeeping and accounting system, showing its major inputs and outputs. The context diagram depicts the entire system as a single process that can be exploded into more detailed data flow diagrams at lower levels. Data flow to and from this pension benefits recordkeeping and accounting system. The external entities are the payroll department, the actuary, and the employee.

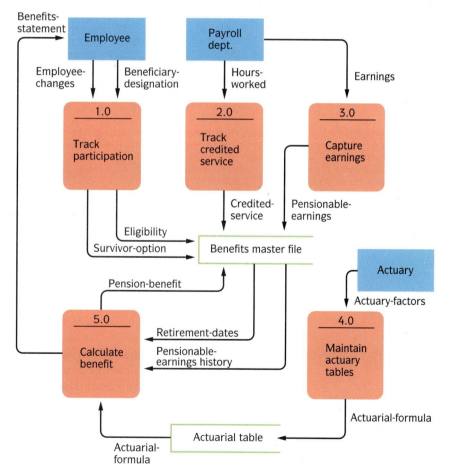

Figure 13.6B
Zero-level data flow diagram for a pension benefits recordkeeping and accounting system. This data flow diagram explodes the context diagram into a more detailed picture of the pension benefits recordkeeping and accounting system. It shows that the system consists of five major processes that can, in turn, be broken down into more detailed data flow diagrams.

Context diagram: Overview data flow diagram depicting an entire system as a single process with its major inputs and outputs.

eral picture of the system. It is called a context diagram. The **context diagram** always depicts an entire system as a single process with its major inputs and outputs. Subsequent diagrams can then break the system down into greater levels of detail.

The next level of detail, Figure 13.6(B), shows that the system is comprised of five major processes: tracking participation in the pension plan (1.0); tracking

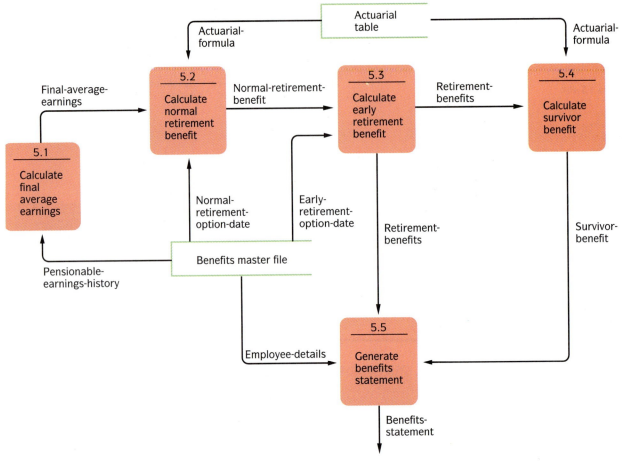

Figure 13.6C
First-level data flow diagram for a pension benefits record keeping and accounting system.
This data flow diagram breaks down the process *Calculate benefit* (5.0) into further detail.
It illustrates that calculating pension benefits entails processes to calculate final average
earnings (5.1), normal retirement benefit (5.2), early retirement benefit (5.3), survivor
benefit (5.4), and a process to generate a benefits statement (5.5).

service that can be credited to pension benefits (2.0); capturing employee earnings data (3.0); maintaining actuarial tables (4.0); and calculating pension benefits (5.0). Figure 13.6(C) explodes process 5.0, Calculate benefit, into greater detail. It shows that this process can be further decomposed into processes to calculate final average earnings (5.1); the normal retirement benefit (5.2); the early retirement benefit (5.3); the survivor's benefit (5.4); and a process to generate benefits statements (5.5).

OTHER STRUCTURED
ANALYSIS TOOLS

Other tools for structured analysis include a data dictionary, which we first described in Chapter 8. In structured analysis, the data dictionary contains information about individual pieces of data and data groupings within a system. The data dictionary defines the contents of data flows and data stores so that system builders understand exactly what pieces of data they contain. For example, a data dictionary entry for the data flow "Retirement-Benefits" in Figure 13.6(C) might look like this:

Retirement-Benefits = Normal-Retirement-Benefit-Amount
+ Normal-Retirement-Date
+ Early-Retirement-Benefit
+ Early-Retirement-Date
+ Survivor-Option

This means that the data flow called "Retirement-Benefits" consists of the data items Normal-Retirement-Benefit-Amount, Normal-Retirement-Date, Early-Retirement-Benefit, Early-Retirement-Date and Survivor-Option. The dictionary also provides information on the meaning and format of each data item and the data flows and data stores where it is used. Sometimes the dictionary also includes information about frequency, volume, values, users, security, and processes.

The data dictionary used in structured analysis can be expanded and used throughout the systems development process to help system builders keep track of all the details about data, functions, and processes that accumulate for every system.

Process specifications:
Describes the logic of the processes occurring within the lowest-level bubbles of the data flow diagrams.

Process specifications describe the transformations occurring within the lowest-level bubbles of the data flow diagrams. They express the logic for each process using one of three methods for documenting decision rules described in the following section:

- Pseudocode or structured English.
- Decision tables.
- Decision trees.

The output of structured analysis is a structured specification document that includes data flow diagrams for system functions, data dictionary descriptions of data flows and data stores, process specifications, and input and output documents, plus security, control, conversion, and performance requirements.

Documenting Decision Rules

Several sets of tools are used for documenting decisions rules and for defining processing logic in the design phase. The documentation will then be used as specifications for computer programs. These tools are decision tables, decision trees, and pseudocode.

DECISION TABLES

Decision tables: A graphic in the form of a table that portrays the conditions affecting a decision; used for documenting situations in which the decision process is highly structured.

Decision tables are considered very useful for documenting situations in which the decision process is highly structured and clearly understood. Decisions are portrayed graphically in a table expressing a series of conditions. When certain conditions are met (yes, no), decisions are made according to specified rules. The table must specify all possible conditions that affect the decision.

Figure 13.7 illustrates the most widely used decision table format. It consists of the following:

1. A header identifying the table.
2. Condition stubs with entries for each possible condition.

Figure 13.7
Decision table for monthly money market account statements. The decision table in this figure documents the processing logic for sending the monthly statements. It portrays the conditions—the account balance and the level of activity in the account—that determine whether or not the money market fund sends monthly statements of account balances with warnings to the investors.

	HEADER Send monthly statement	RULES 1	2	3	
CONDITION STUB	1. Balance > = $500	Y	N	N	CONDITION ENTRIES
	Account activity 2. during past month	–	Y	N	
	Send monthly statement 3. only	X	X		
ACTION STATEMENTS	Send monthly statement 4. with warning			X	ACTION ENTRIES

3. Action statements with entries for each possible action that could be taken. Such actions will be determined by the conditions present and the decision rules governing the decision process. The figure illustrates the following logic for sending money market account statements:

The money market fund will send monthly statements of account balances to all investors, whether those accounts have had activity or not. However, investors with account balances less than $500 will be sent warning notices of low balances along with their monthly statements unless their accounts have had activity during the past month.

DECISION TREES

Decision trees: Sequential tree-like diagrams that present the conditions affecting a decision and the actions that can be taken. The branches represent the paths that may be taken in the decision-making process.

Decision trees provide another graphical method of documenting decision rules. They present conditions and actions sequentially, showing decision paths that may be taken. The diagram resembles the branches of a tree. Different alternatives branch out from an initial decision point.

The initial decision is the root of the tree. Branches proceed from left to right. The nodes of the tree show conditions. The next path to follow depends on the outcome of a determination about which condition exists. On the right side of the tree are the actions that can be taken, depending on the sequence of conditions and alternatives that are followed. How the branches develop depends on the nature of the decision being made—the conditions and alternatives. Figure 13.8 illustrates a decision tree for the same decision rules for money market statements documented as a decision table in Figure 13.7.

Some authorities consider decision trees easier to understand than decision tables. They are especially useful for highlighting decision paths and the sequence of decisions rather than the criteria for selecting a given path. However, if a system is highly complex, with many sequences of steps and combinations of conditions, decision trees may cloud the analysis. Documentation of too many branches and paths becomes unwieldy. In such instances, decision tables are preferred.

PSEUDOCODE

Pseudocode: Method for expressing program logic that uses plain English statements rather than graphic symbols, trees, tables, or programming languages to describe a procedure.

Pseudocode is a method of expressing program logic using plain English statements rather than a programming language. It uses narrative statements rather than graphic symbols such as trees or tables to describe a procedure. An advantage of pseudocode is that system builders can concentrate on developing processing logic independent of the syntax guidelines (rules for formulating instructions) of any programming language. If the logic is sound, pseudocode can be easily translated into a programming language. Structured English is similar to pseudocode in that it uses the logical constructs of pseudocode (discussed below) but its terminology is more easily understood by end users than pseudocode.

Pseudocode uses the same logic patterns as the basic control structures of structured programming (described in further detail in the next section). These are

Figure 13.8
Decision tree for monthly money market account statements. The decision tree in this figure documents the processing logic for sending the monthly statements. It illustrates the same processing logic for the monthly money market account statements as shown in the decision table in Figure 13.7.

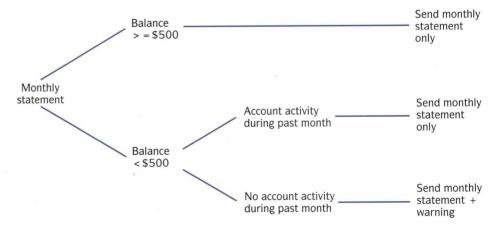

Sequence structure: The sequential single steps or actions in the logic of a program that do not depend on the existence of any condition.

Selection structure: The logic pattern in programming where a stated condition determines which of two or more actions can be taken depending on which satisfies the stated condition.

Iteration structure: The logic pattern in programming where certain actions are repeated while a specified condition occurs or until a certain condition is met.

1. The **sequence structure,** single steps or actions that follow one another without interruption. The series of actions does not depend on the existence of any condition.

   The pseudocode for the sequence structure is

   Do Action 1

   Do Action 2.

   For example:

   Read customer bill

   Print customer bill.

2. The **selection structure,** where two or more actions can be taken, depending on which one satisfies a stated condition.
   The pseudocode format for the selection structure is

   IF (condition 1 is true)

      Do X

   ELSE

      Do Y

   ENDIF.

   For example:

   IF (transaction key = master file key)

      Update Master File

   ELSE

      Reject Transaction

   ENDIF.

3. The **iteration structure,** where certain actions are repeated over and over while a specified condition occurs or until a condition occurs. The pseudocode format for the iteration structure is

   DO WHILE (condition 2 is true)

      Action Z

   ENDDO.

   For example:

   DO WHILE (End of file switch is off)

      Read each student record

      Add 1 to student record counter

   ENDDO.

Figure 13.9 shows how the same decision rules for money market fund monthly statements illustrated in the Figure 13.7 decision table and the Figure 13.8 decision tree would be expressed in pseudocode.

Figure 13.9
Pseudocode for money market
fund monthly statement. This
figure shows how pseudocode
would express the same
processing logic used in Figures
13.7 and 13.8.

> Money Market Fund Monthly Statement:
>
> IF investor's balance is greater than or equal to $500
>   Send monthly balance statement only
>   ELSE
>   IF account fund has had activity
>   Send monthly balance statement only
>   ELSE
>   Send monthly balance statement + warning notice
>
> ENDIF.

Structured Design

Structured design: Software
design discipline,
encompassing a set of design
rules and techniques for
designing a system from the
top down in a hierarchical
fashion.

Structured design is primarily a software design discipline, but it is often associated with structured analysis and other structured approaches. **Structured design** encompasses a set of design rules and techniques that promotes program clarity and simplicity, thereby reducing the time and effort required for coding, debugging, and maintenance. Sometimes structured design is also referred to as top-down design or composite design. The main principle of structured design is that a system should be designed from the top down in hierarchical fashion and refined to greater levels of detail. The design should first consider the main function of a program or system, then break this function into subfunctions and decompose each subfunction until the lowest level of detail has been reached. In this manner, all high-level logic and the design model are developed before detailed program code is written. If structured analysis has been performed, the structured specification document can serve as input to the design process.

Structure chart: System
documentation showing each
level of design, the
relationship among the levels,
and the overall place in the
design structure; can
document one program, one
system, or part of one
program.

As the design is formulated, it is documented in a structure chart. The **structure chart** is a top-down chart, showing each level of design, its relationship to other levels, and its place in the overall design structure. Figure 13.10 shows a structure chart that can be used for a payroll system. If a design has too many levels to fit onto one structure chart, it can be broken down further on more detailed structure charts. For example, details for processing gross pay on the structure chart of Figure 13.10 are treated in the detailed structure chart in Figure 13.11. A structure chart may document one program, one system (a set of programs), or part of one program.

Figure 13.10
High-level structure chart for a payroll system. This structure chart shows the highest or most abstract level of design for a payroll system, providing an overview of the entire system.

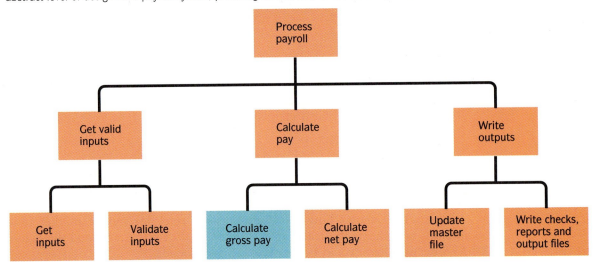

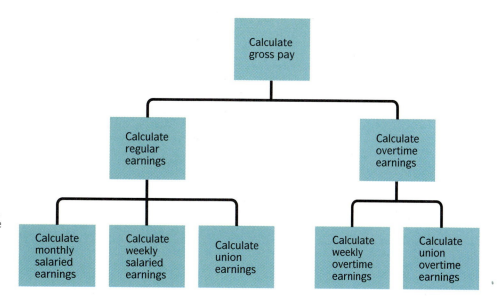

Figure 13.11
Detailed structure chart for a payroll system. This detailed structure chart shows functions required in the calculation of gross pay for the payroll system. This chart shows an intermediate level of design. A more detailed structure chart would still be required to show the lowest levels of design for calculating gross pay.

Structure chart boxes:
- Calculate gross pay
  - Calculate regular earnings
    - Calculate monthly salaried earnings
    - Calculate weekly salaried earnings
    - Calculate union earnings
  - Calculate overtime earnings
    - Calculate weekly overtime earnings
    - Calculate union overtime earnings

Structured Programming

Structured programming:
Discipline for organizing and coding programs that simplifies the control paths so that the programs can be easily understood and modified. Uses the basic control structures and modules that have only one entry point and one exit point.

Module: A logical unit of a program that performs one or a small number of functions.

Structured programming extends the principles governing structured design to the writing of programs. It also is based upon the principle of modularization, which follows from top-down development.

Structured programming is a method of organizing and coding programs that simplifies control paths so that the programs can be easily understood and modified. Structured programming reduces the complexity created when program instructions jump forward and backward to other parts of the program, obscuring the logic and flow of the program.

Each of the boxes in the structure chart represents a component **module.** Programs can be partitioned into modules, each of which constitutes a logical unit that performs one or a small number of functions. Ideally, modules should be independent of each other. They should be interconnected so that they have only one entry to and exit from their parent modules. They should share data with as few other modules as possible.

There should be no obscure connections with other modules that would create a "ripple effect," whereby a change to module A creates unanticipated changes in modules B, D, and F. Minimizing connections among modules, or coupling, minimizes paths by which errors can be spread to other parts of the system.

Each module should also be kept to a manageable size. An individual should be able to read the program code for the module and easily keep track of its functions. Within each module, program instructions should not wander and should be executed in top-down fashion.

Proponents of structured programming have shown that any program can be written using the three basic control constructs, or instruction patterns, introduced in the discussion of pseudocode: 1) simple sequence, 2) selection, and 3) iteration. These control constructs are illustrated in Figure 13.12.

The sequence construct executes statements in the order in which they appear, with control passing unconditionally from one statement to the next. The program will execute statement A and then statement B.

The selection construct tests a condition and executes one of the two alternative instructions based on the results of the test. Condition R is tested. If R is true, statement C is executed. If R is false, statement D is executed. Control then passes to the next statement.

The iteration construct repeats a segment of code as long as a conditional test remains true. Condition S is tested. If S is true, statement E is executed and

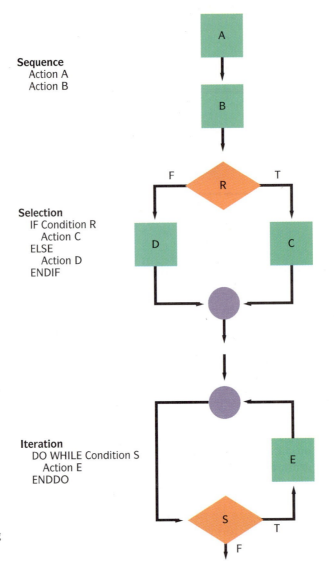

Sequence
    Action A
    Action B

Selection
    IF Condition R
        Action C
    ELSE
        Action D
    ENDIF

Iteration
    DO WHILE Condition S
        Action E
    ENDDO

Figure 13.12
Basic control constructs. The three basic control constructs used in structured programming are Sequence, Selection, and Iteration.

control returns to the test of S. If S is false, E is skipped and control passes to the next statement.

Any one or any combination of these control structures can accommodate any kind of processing logic required by a program. There is a single entry and exit point for each structure. The control structures can be strung one after the other or nested, as shown in Figure 13.13. Structured programming control structures can be used in any programming language.

Flowcharts

Flowcharting is an old design tool that is still in use. System flowcharts detail the flow of data throughout an entire information system. Program flowcharts describe the processes taking place within an individual program in the system and the sequence in which they must be executed. Flowcharting is no longer recommended for program design because it does not provide top-down modular structure as effectively as other techniques. However, system flowcharts may still be used to document physical design specifications because they can show all inputs, major files, processing, and outputs for a system and they can document manual procedures.

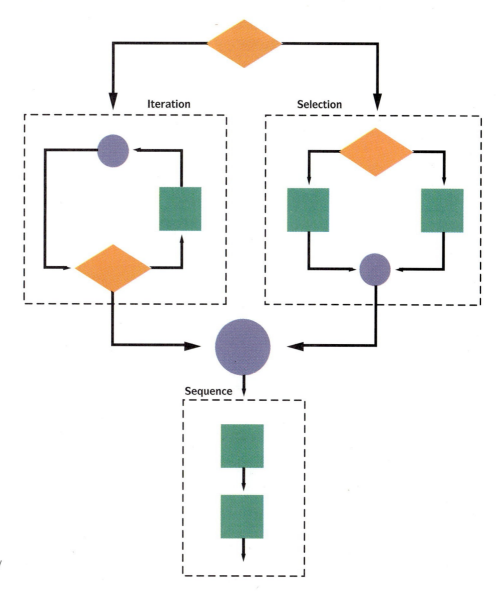

Figure 13.13
Nested control constructs. The control structures can be nested, but they will still have only one point of entry and only one point of exit.

SYSTEM FLOWCHARTS

System flowchart: Graphic design tool that depicts the physical media and sequence of processing steps used in an entire information system.

The **system flowchart** is a graphic way of depicting all of the procedures that take input data and convert them to their final output form. Using specialized symbols and flow lines, the system flowchart shows all of the processes taking place; the data acted on in each step; and the relationships between the processes. The system flowchart

- Shows the overall structure of the system.
- Traces the flow of information and work.
- Shows the physical media on which data are input, output and stored.
- Highlights key processing and decision points.

Figure 13.14 contains the basic symbols for system flowcharting. We have already introduced some of these symbols in Chapter 2. The plain rectangle is a general symbol for a major computer processing function. Flow lines show the sequence of steps and the direction of information flow. Arrows are employed to show direction if it is not apparent in the diagram.

System flowcharts can encompass different levels of detail. Figure 13.15 illustrates a high-level overview flowchart of a payroll system. Figure 13.16 on page 452

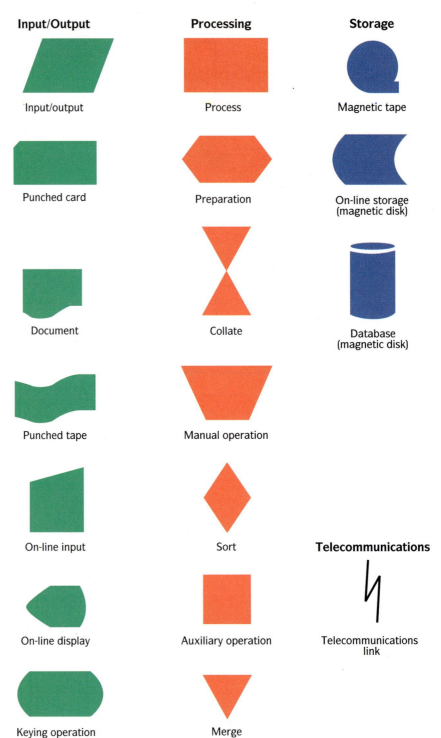

Figure 13.14
Basic system flowchart symbols. Use these symbols and interconnecting lines to show the sequence of processing taking place within a system and the physical media used in each step.

Input/Output

Input/output

Punched card

Document

Punched tape

On-line input

On-line display

Keying operation

Processing

Process

Preparation

Collate

Manual operation

Sort

Auxiliary operation

Merge

Storage

Magnetic tape

On-line storage (magnetic disk)

Database (magnetic disk)

Telecommunications

Telecommunications link

is a detailed flowchart for one portion of the payroll system, transaction editing and validation.

Limitations of Traditional Methods

The traditional structured approach has served the information systems professionals and their user communities well. Nonetheless, it has its shortcomings. Most critics consider structured methodologies to be slow and unresponsive to the fast-changing business world of the 1990s. The process is very linear. Com-

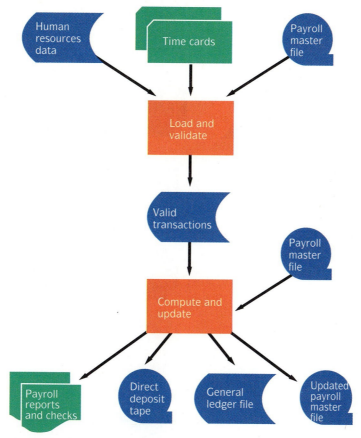

Figure 13.15
System flowchart for a payroll system. This is a high-level system flowchart for a batch payroll system. Only the most important processes and files are illustrated. Data are input from two sources: timecards and payroll-related data (such as salary increases) passed from the human resources system. The data are first edited and validated against the existing payroll master file before the payroll master is updated. The update process produces an updated payroll master file, various payroll reports (such as the payroll register and hours register), checks, a direct deposit tape, and a file of payment data that must be passed to the organization's general ledger system. The direct deposit tape is sent to the automated clearing house that serves the banks offering direct deposit services to employees.

pletion of structured analysis is required before structured design can begin, and structured programming must await the completed deliverables from structured design. Ways have been found to speed these processes up and to cut a few corners, but essentially the linear nature of structured methodologies cannot be avoided. The slowness also translates into increased cost at a time when cost cutting is very much in the spotlight.

A linear approach also makes structured methodologies rather inflexible. A large system development project will last one to two years. Specifications drawn up at the beginning are bound to change as business needs change. However, a change in specifications requires that the analysis documents and then the design documents must be modified before the programs can be changed to reflect the new requirement. A tug-of-war often develops, with IS project management trying to freeze requirements until after the project has been completed, and users finding this apparent inflexibility unacceptable.

Structured methodologies are function oriented. They focus on the processes that transform the data. The storage of the data is described as an appendage to those processes. Yet, as we explained in section 13.1, business management has come to view most information systems as data oriented. Data generated by one department may be used by many other departments, each of which will process them differently. In addition, for most systems even the department that gener-

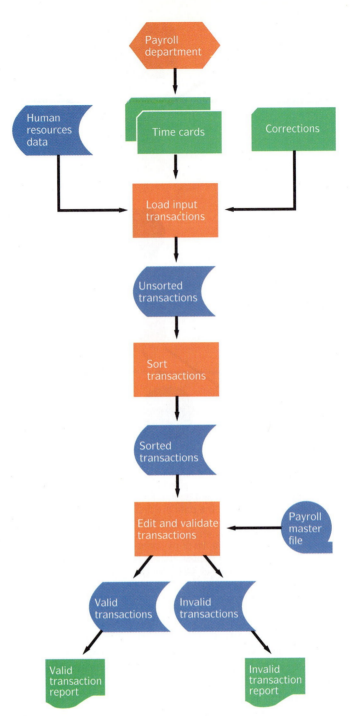

Figure 13.16
Detail payroll system flowchart. This flowchart is a detailed view of the portion of the payroll system in Figure 13.15 that is concerned with transaction editing and validation. Transactions are loaded from input, sorted, edited, and validated against the payroll master file. Separate files are created to separate invalid from valid transactions. Valid transactions are passed on for further processing. Invalid transactions are corrected and resubmitted. Reports listing both valid and invalid transactions are produced.

ates the data will use them in many ways and will continually change the ways the data are used. It has become clear that the data are more permanent than the processes that use or transform them. Systems that focus on processes are often large and inflexible. Systems that focus on data can be smaller and far more flexible, making them easier to modify and more responsive to changing business needs.

The IS profession has long wanted to find ways to re-use code as a way to reduce costs. Despite the fact that specific groups of data are usually processed the same way in different programs, a separate programming procedure must be written every time someone wants to take an action on a particular piece of data. Why take the time and pay the cost to rewrite the code each time a tax calculation needs to be done or a specific chemical needs to be analyzed? Hopes that program modularization would solve this problem of re-usability have not been fulfilled. Critics believe we must look beyond structured approaches to find solutions to this critical productivity issue.

A final major criticism is that, because the techniques used require a great deal of training and experience, structured methodologies rely too heavily on information systems professionals. The information systems industry has been undergoing a major shift as users look for ways to take more control of their own systems. User communities are very concerned about what they see as the lack of understanding of IS professionals of their business and the slow response of the IS departments to changing needs.

New structured techniques have been developed to address many of these problems. For example, **joint application design (JAD)** is a design method that brings users and IS professionals into a room together for an interactive design of the system. Properly prepared and facilitated, JAD sessions can significantly speed up the design phase while involving users in the design at a level previously not possible. Prototyping (discussed in Chapter 12) also speeds up design while involving users more and increases the flexibility of the whole process. Nonetheless, the IS profession has been trying to develop other methodologies in an attempt to replace structured methodologies.

Joint application design (JAD): A design method which brings users and IS professionals into a room together for an interactive design of the system.

13.3 New Approaches to Quality

In addition to the traditional methodologies and tools, system builders are turning to object-oriented development, computer-aided software engineering (CASE) and software re-engineering to help cope with information system quality problems.

Object-Oriented Software Development

We have already introduced object-oriented programming in Chapter 7. Object-oriented programming is part of a larger approach to systems development called object-oriented software development. **Object-oriented software development** differs from traditional methodologies in the way it handles the issue of process versus data. Traditional structured analysis and design put procedures first. They first view a system in terms of what it is intended to *do* and then develop models of procedures and data. Object-oriented software development de-emphasizes procedures. The focus shifts from modeling business processes and data to combining data and procedures that create objects. The system is viewed as a collection of objects and relationships among objects. The objects are defined, programmed, documented, and saved for use with future applications.

Object-oriented software development: Approach to software development that de-emphasizes procedures and shifts the focus from modeling business processes and data to combining data and procedures that create objects.

The objects model the way users actually work. For example, accounts receivable personnel tend to think at the level of customers, credit limits and invoices—the same level at which objects are built. Object-oriented analysis (OOA) and object-oriented design (OOD) are based upon these objects and so more closely model the real world than previous methods. Only more experience will tell if this is an improvement.

BENEFITS OF AN OBJECT-ORIENTED APPROACH

Because objects are reusable, object-oriented software development directly addresses the issue of reusability and is expected to reduce the time and cost of writing software. Of course, no organization will see savings from reusability until it builds up a library of classes and objects to draw upon. Object-oriented software development experience is still very limited, so it is too early to evaluate the approach. Nonetheless, early studies have been promising. Experience has shown that programming productivity gains of better than 10:1 are possible. Electronic Data Systems Corp. (EDS) studied the benefits by building a maintenance management system twice, once using structured techniques and once using object-oriented programming. EDS equalized the skill level of the two project teams and had them work from the same specifications. They found a productivity improvement of 14:1 using object-oriented programming (IDC White Paper, 1992). Maintenance costs are also lowered by reducing multiple maintenance changes. For example, when the U.S. postal system changed the zip code from five to nine digits, each program within a company had to be changed. If a company's programs were object-oriented, the programmer would only have had to modify the code within the object, and the change would be reflected in all the programs using that object.

Object-oriented software development is leading to other changes in methods. Once a library of objects exists, design and programming often can begin without waiting for analysis documents. Rather, in theory, design and programming can be carried out together, beginning as soon as requirements are completed. Developers—users and IS professionals—use iterations of rapid prototyping to design the system. The prototype, when completed, will encompass a great deal of the programming needed for the completion of the system.

Object-oriented methods should increase the involvement of users. As we have already indicated, users may find objects easier to understand and more natural to work with than structured tools such as design charts and pseudocode. In addition, iterative prototyping relies heavily on users, placing them at the center of design and even of programming.

OBSTACLES TO USING OBJECT-ORIENTED TECHNIQUES

Although the demand for training in object-oriented techniques and programming tools is exploding, object-oriented software development is still in its infancy and is too unproven for most companies to adopt it. No agreed-upon object-oriented methodology yet exists, although several have been proposed. Moreover, many companies are hesitant to try it because it requires extensive staff training and a major methodological reorientation. Management is also aware that a complete switch to object-oriented development will take a long time. Most companies have a major investment in existing, structured systems that would have to be maintained until the time came that they needed replacement. Until then, the IS departments would have to retain expertise in both structured and object-oriented methods.

New technology needs to be developed for the use of object-oriented methods. Data dictionaries for storing structured data definitions and program code are not appropriate for object-oriented programming. New object-oriented data dictionaries need to be developed. CASE tools (discussed below) have been developed to support structured methodologies and need to be redesigned for use with object-oriented development. Even new metrics need to be developed, as many of the metrics now used to evaluate system quality cannot be applied to object-oriented coding.

One underlying obstacle, not related to object-oriented development, is that most IS departments are not currently measuring their productivity. Without proper evidence, IS managements are not in a position to convince senior management that a major investment in new technology (whatever the technology) will in fact benefit the company.

Computer-Aided Software Engineering (CASE)

Computer-aided software engineering (CASE): The automation of step-by-step methodologies for software and systems development to reduce the amount of repetitive work the developer needs to do.

Computer-aided software engineering (CASE)—sometimes called computer-aided systems engineering—is the automation of step-by-step methodologies for software and systems development to reduce the amount of repetitive work the developer needs to do. Its adoption can free the developer for more creative problem-solving tasks. CASE tools also facilitate creation of clear documentation and coordination of team development efforts. Team members can share their work more easily by accessing each other's files to review or modify what has been done. Systems developed with CASE and the newer methodologies have been found to be more reliable and require repairs less often (Dekleva, 1992). Many CASE tools are microcomputer based, with powerful graphical capabilities.

CASE tools provide automated graphics facilities for producing charts and diagrams, screen and report generators, data dictionaries, extensive reporting facilities, analysis and checking tools, code generators, and documentation generators. Most CASE tools are based on one or more of the popular structured methodologies. Some are starting to support object-oriented development. In general, CASE tools try to increase productivity and quality by doing the following:

- Enforcing a standard development methodology and design discipline. Large teams and software projects can be coordinated more effectively. The design and overall development effort will have more integrity.
- Improving communication between users and technical specialists.
- Organizing and correlating design components and providing rapid access to them via a design repository.
- Automating tedious and error-prone portions of analysis and design.
- Automating testing and controlling rollout.

Key elements of CASE are described in Table 13.2.

EXAMPLES OF CASE TOOLS CASE tools have been classified in terms of whether they support activities at the front end or the back end of the systems development process. Front-end CASE tools focus on capturing analysis and design information in the early stages of systems development. They automate the process of creating data flow diagrams, structure charts, entity-relationship diagrams, and other specifications so that they can be easily revised to improve design before coding begins. They also require adherence to structured methodologies. Table 13.3 describes the strengths and limitations of CASE tools.

Back-end CASE tools address coding, testing, and maintenance activities and include text editors, formatters, syntax checkers, compilers, cross-reference generators, linkers, symbolic debuggers, execution profilers, code generators, and

Table 13.2 KEY ELEMENTS OF CASE

Diagramming tools: Graphics tools for drawing symbols for data flow diagrams, structure charts, entity-relationship diagrams, or other types of diagrams associated with a particular methodology.

Syntax verifier: Verifies the accuracy and completeness of information entered into a system in conformance with the rules of a particular structured methodology.

Prototyping tools: Screen, report, and menu generators allow the analyst to paint desired screen and report layouts or menu paths through a system without complex formatting specifications or programming.

Information repository: A central information database which serves as a mechanism for storing all types of software assets—screen and report layouts, diagrams, data definitions, program code, project schedules, and other documentation. The repository coordinates, integrates, and standardizes the different pieces of information so they can be easily accessed, shared by analysts, and reused in future software work.

Code generators: These can generate modules of executable code from higher-level specifications. Some CASE tools use icons to indicate various program functions and translate these symbols into programs.

Development methodology: Some CASE products contain checklists or narratives detailing an entire development methodology that helps monitor and control the entire systems development project.

Project management tools: Some CASE tools integrate their components with popular stand-alone tools for project scheduling and resource estimation, while others incorporate project management software into the CASE tool kit.

Table 13.3   WHAT CASE TOOLS CAN AND CANNOT DO

CASE Tools Can:

1. Automate many manual tasks of systems development.

2. Promote standardization based on a single methodology.

3. Promote greater consistency and coordination during a development project.

4. Generate a large portion of the documentation for a system, such as data flow diagrams, data models, structure charts, or other specifications.

CASE Tools Cannot:

1. Automatically provide a functional, relevant system. It is just as easy to produce a bad system as to produce a good system using CASE tools.

2. Interface easily with databases and fourth-generation languages.

3. Automatically force analysts to use a prescribed methodology or create a methodology when one does not exist.

4. Radically transform the systems analysis and design process.

---

application generators. Back-end tools help convert specifications automatically into program code.

CASE products such as Andersen Consulting's Foundation and Knowledge Ware's Application Development Workbench represent more fully integrated tools that are starting to support the entire systems development process, including project management and automatic generation of program code.

Analysts use CASE tools to help capture requirements and specifications by storing the information in a CASE database, where it can be easily retrieved and revised. The CASE tools facilitate up-front design and analysis work, so that there are fewer errors to correct later on. CASE text and graphics editors help the analyst create technically correct diagrams, process descriptions, and data dictionary entries. The analyst can draw diagrams by choosing from a set of standard symbols and positioning the symbols on the screen. Text information can be added to the diagram or used to describe processes and data flows using the

The Construction Workstation GUI supports the development and generation of cooperative and client/server applications with such GUI elements as windows, dialogs, graphics, hot spots, and on-line help text.

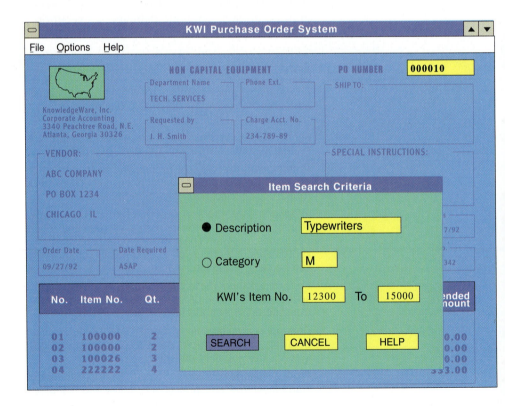

MANAGEMENT
Looking to the Future with CASE

Good management has the ability to anticipate the need for change and to take action before serious problems develop. Such management became evident at Washington, D.C.'s National Association of Securities Dealers, Inc. (NASD) when in 1991 it launched a project to install new software development methods and techniques. NASD is the parent of NASDAQ, the over-the-counter stock quotation system that has evolved into the second-largest stock market in the United States and third largest in the world. Quality systems are the life blood of NASDAQ—its basic product is instantaneous, reliable, accurate stock market information, delivered through computer systems.

In the midst of a long period of expanding success, Bill Synnott, the director of information technology at NASD, came to the conclusion that change was needed. "Our technologies were not supporting our ability to meet our business needs," he said. NASD had to come up with an approach to get its technologies in line with these needs. NASD originally planned a bottom-up project, expecting to use reverse engineering tools to give them a structured picture of what their current systems do. Unfortunately, a large portion of its systems were written in assembly language, and no appropriate re-engineering tools existed for these languages. Therefore, they shifted

to a top-down, data-driven approach. Synnott wanted a disciplined approach, which meant using a methodology that could be enforced by a CASE tool. They chose the CASE tool IE:Expert from Information Engineering.

NASD set general project targets of a 20 percent reduction in information systems operating costs. It also aimed to produce new applications in 20 percent less time. It also wanted to reduce response time (the heart of their product). Synnott set a general goal of helping NASD to "keep our competitive edge."

NASD first used IE:Expert to build a high-level strategic model, followed by a tactical model and then more specific operational models. They plan to map current systems to the operational models. This mapping will allow them to evaluate the health of their existing systems and to make appropriate changes. However, the project encompasses more than software. IS is reviewing hardware also and has issued requests for proposals (RFPs). The staff has even found another use for IE:Expert, evaluation of third-party software being considered for purchase. For example, before purchasing a new human resources information system, they used IE:Expert to build a model of the proposed system. They are evaluating packages against that model.

IS management has been far-sighted in another critical area, personnel. They recognized early that technical staff will likely be nervous about a switch to a top-down approach. Synnott says the traditional programmers are distrustful. They don't see how you can build a substantial portion of the system from a model. One approach they have followed is helping their staff connect the changes within IS to their own careers. Pam Sweet, an assistant director of IS, put it this way: "Most of the people who are becoming involved, see this as a great opportunity to broaden their scope as DP professionals." NASD hopes to have its first pilot application in production before the end of 1993.

Source: John Desmond, "Mapping the Ideal, Comparing to Real," *Software Magazine* (January 1992).

To Think About:
1. What are the management benefits of using CASE? How does CASE promote quality?
2. As the head of IS for NASD, why might you want to launch a project to map systems from the top down, even though the systems you have in production seem to be working very well? How would you sell your project to the corporate management of NASD?

CASE tool's text editor. The Window on Management illustrates how one company used a CASE tool primarily for planning, analysis, and design work.

CASE tools automatically tie data elements to the processes where they are used. If a data flow diagram is changed from one process to another, the elements in the data dictionary would be altered automatically to reflect the change in the diagram (see Figure 13.18). CASE tools also contain features for validating design; included in these features are automatic balancing of data flow diagrams and checking diagrams and specifications for completeness and consistency. Some tool kits contain prototyping features such as screen and report painters, which allow analysts to draw screen or report formats for users to review. CASE tools thus support iterative design by automating revisions and changes and providing prototyping facilities.

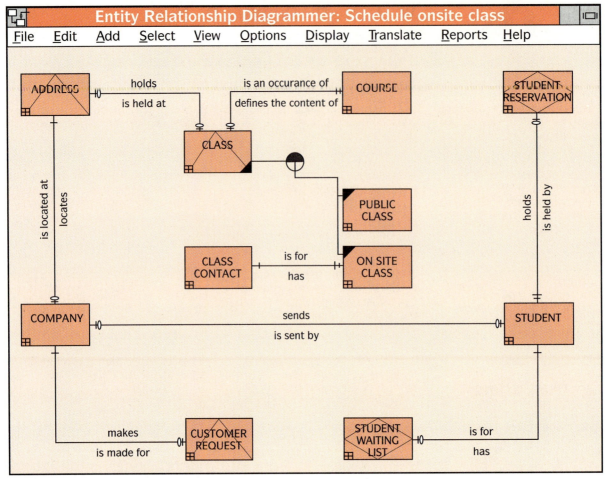

Figure 13.17
The entity-relationship diagrammer in Knowledge Ware's Application Development Workbench helps systems designers build a logical data model by documenting the types of entities found in an organization and how they relate. This CASE tool can display an entity-relationship diagram for the entire entity model or for a context-sensitive view. This figure, for example, displays only the entities and relationships relevant to the process of scheduling a class. *Diagram provided courtesy of KnowledgeWare Inc., Atlanta GA.*

A central element in the CASE tool kit is the information repository, which stores all the information defined by the analysts during the project. The repository includes data flow diagrams, structure charts, entity-relationship diagrams (see Figure 13.17), data definitions, process specifications, screen and report formats, notes and comments, test results and evaluations, source code, status and audit information, and time and cost estimates. The CASE database can be shared by members of a project team and contains features to restrict changes to only specified analysts.

THE CHALLENGE OF
USING CASE

To be used effectively, CASE tools require more organizational discipline than the manual approach. Every member of a development project must adhere to a common set of naming conventions, standards, and development methodology. Without this discipline, analysts and designers will cling to their old ways of developing systems and will attempt to incorporate the CASE tool in the process. This can actually be counterproductive because of the incompatibility between the old approach and new tools. The best CASE tools enforce common methods and standards, which may discourage their use in situations where organizational discipline is lacking.

Actual productivity gains from CASE remain difficult to define. A few firms have reported tangible cost savings from using CASE, while others note more rapid generation of systems or higher-quality software once developers have learned to use CASE tools (Banker, Kauffman and Kumar, 1991–92). The issue remains clouded because productivity gains in software development have traditionally been difficult to measure and to quantify.

While it facilitates some aspects of systems development, CASE is not a magic cure-all. It can accelerate analysis and design and promote iterative design, but it does not enable systems to be designed automatically or ensure that business requirements are met. Systems designers still have to understand what a firm's business needs are and how the business works. Systems analysis and design are still dependent upon the analytical skills of the analyst/designer. Some of the productivity gains attributed to CASE may actually be the result of system developers improving communication, coordination, and software integrity by agreeing on a standard methodology rather than from the use of automated CASE tools themselves.

CASE provides a set of labor-saving tools that automate software development work. But the actual software development process to be automated is defined by a methodology. If a firm lacks a methodology, CASE tools may be used to automate disparate, and often incompatible, practices rather than integrating or standardizing a firm's systems development approach.

Figure 13.18
The data flow diagrammer in Knowledge Ware's Application Development Workbench can produce a multi-level process model that ensures that the movement of data is consistent from one level to the next. This CASE tool ensures that the data flows entering or leaving a process are included in the level below. *Diagram provided courtesy of KnowledgeWare, Inc., Atlanta GA.*

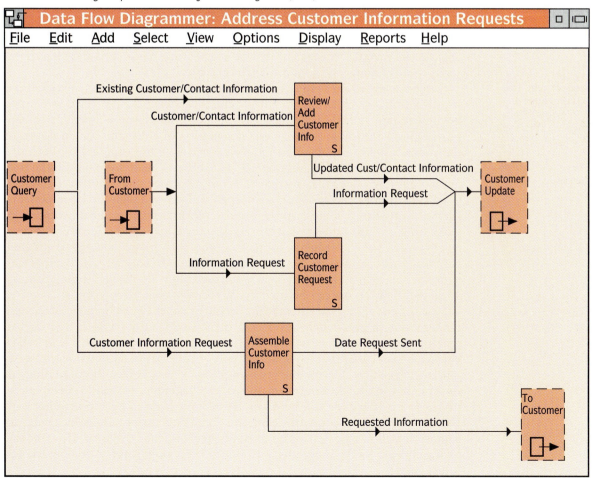

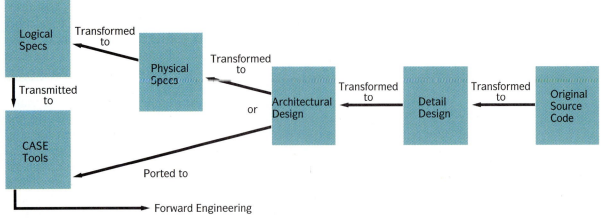

Figure 13.19
Steps in the reverse engineering process. The primary function of reverse engineering is to capture the functional capabilities—the process logic—of the existing system in a simplified form that can be revised and updated for the basis of the new replacement system. *Source: Thomas J. McCabe and Eldonna S. Williamson, "Tips on Reengineering Redundant Software," Datamation, April 15, 1992. Reproduced with permission from DATAMATION© 1992, Reed Publishing (USA) Inc.*

Software Re-Engineering

Software re-engineering: Methodology that addresses the problem of aging software by salvaging and upgrading it so that the users can avoid a long and expensive replacement project.

Reverse engineering: The process of taking existing programs, file and database descriptions and converting them into corresponding design-level components that can then be used to create new applications.

Forward engineering: The final step in re-engineering when the revised specifications are used to generate new, structured program code for a structured and maintainable system.

Software re-engineering is a methodology that addresses the problem of aging software. A great deal of the software that organizations use was written without the benefit of structured analysis, design, and programming. Such software is difficult to maintain or update. Often, however, the software serves the organization well enough to continue to be used, if only it could be more easily maintained. The purpose of re-engineering is to salvage such software by upgrading it so that the users can avoid a long and expensive replacement project. In essence, developers use re-engineering to extract intelligence from existing systems, thereby creating new systems without starting from scratch. Re-engineering involves three steps: reverse engineering, revision of design and program specifications, and forward engineering.

Reverse engineering entails extracting the underlying business specifications from existing systems. Older, nonstructured systems do not have structured documentation to clarify the business functions the system is intended to support. Nor do they have adequate documentation of either the system design or the programs. Reverse engineering tools, such as those supplied by Bachman Information Systems of Cambridge, Massachusetts, read and analyze the program's existing code, file, and database descriptions and produce structured documentation of the system. The output will show design-level components, such as entities, attributes, and processes. With structured documentation to work from, the project team can then revise the design and specifications to meet current business requirements. In the final step, **forward engineering**, the revised specifications are used to generate new, structured code for a structured and maintainable system. In Figure 13.19, you can follow the re-engineering process. Note that CASE tools can be used in the forward engineering step.

Re-engineering can have significant benefits. It allows a company to develop a modern system at a much lower cost than would be the case if they had to develop an entirely new system. The newly re-engineered system will reflect current business requirements, and it will be able to be modified as those requirements change. During the revision phase of the project, the technology of the system can also be upgraded, so that, for example, the new system can be networked or the code can be generated using relational database technology. Finally, unstructured programs contain a large amount of redundant code. Re-engineering allows the developers to eliminate redundancy, thus reducing the size and complexity of the programs, resulting in fewer opportunities for current and future bugs.

1. **Applying quality assurance standards in large system projects.** We have explained why the goal of zero defects in large, complex pieces of software is impossible to achieve. If the seriousness of remaining bugs cannot be ascertained, what constitutes an acceptable if not perfect performance? And even if meticulous design and exhaustive testing could eliminate all defects, software projects have time and budget constraints that often prevent management from devoting as much time to thorough testing as it should. Under these circumstances it will be difficult for managers either to define a standard for software quality or to enforce it.

2. **Enforcing a standard methodology.** Although structured methodologies have been available for twenty-five years, very few organizations have been able to enforce them. One survey found that only 15 to 20 percent of all organizations it studied used structured analysis and design in a consistent manner. It is impossible to use CASE or newer object-oriented methods effectively unless all participants in system building adopt a common development methodology as well as common development tools. Methodologies are organizational disciplines.

3. **Agreeing on what constitutes quality in information systems.** Many information systems professionals tend to view system problems as primarily technical issues. Yet many quality problems related to information systems, including software quality assurance, are not merely technical issues. Information systems specialists need to work in partnership with other areas of the organization to develop a shared sense of quality linked to larger business goals.

Summary

Describe how information systems can contribute to total quality management in an organization.

Information systems can contribute to total quality management by helping other business functions perform their work more effectively, by helping to analyze and redesign business processes, by suggesting new ways to apply technology to enhance quality, and by sharing their experience in quantifying and measuring procedures with other areas of the organization.

Explain why information systems must pay special attention to software quality assurance.

Software plays a central role in most organizations and is an integral part of daily operations, products, and services. However, it presents quality problems because of the difficulty in developing software that captures user specifications accurately, because software bugs may be impossible to eliminate, and because of the high costs of maintaining software and correcting errors.

Identify the principal solutions to information systems quality problems.

Information systems quality problems can be minimized by using structured systems development methodologies, software metrics, quality tools, thorough testing procedures, and by reallocating resources to put more emphasis on the early stages of the systems development cycle.

Describe the traditional tools and methodologies for promoting information systems quality.

Structured analysis highlights the flow of data and the processes through which data are transformed. Its principal tool is the data flow diagram. Structured design and programming are software design disciplines that produce reliable, well-documented software with a simple, clear structure that is easy for others to understand and maintain. Decision tables, decision trees, and pseudocode describe processing logic in tabular, graphic, and narrative form, respectively. System flowcharts are useful for documenting the physical aspects of system design.

Describe new approaches for promoting information systems quality.

Computer-aided software engineering (CASE) automates methodologies for systems development. It promotes standards and improves coordination and consistency during systems development. CASE tools help system builders build a better model of a system and facilitate revision of design specifications to correct errors. Object-oriented software development is expected to reduce the time and cost of writing software and of making maintenance changes because it models a system as a series of reusable objects that combine both data and procedures. Software re-engineering helps system builders reconfigure aging software to conform to structured design principles, making it easier to maintain.

Key Terms

Total quality management (TQM)	Decision tables
Bugs	Decision trees
Development methodology	Pseudocode
Resource allocation	Sequence structure
Software metrics	Selection structure
Function point analysis	Iteration structure
Walkthrough	Structured design
Debugging	Structure chart
Spaghetti code	Structured programming
Structured	Module
Top-down	System flowchart
Structured analysis	Joint application design (JAD)
Data flow diagram (DFD)	Object-oriented software development
Data flows	Computer-aided software engineering
Processes	(CASE)
Data stores	Software re-engineering
External entities	Reverse engineering
Context diagram	Forward engineering
Process specifications	

Review Questions

1. What is total quality management? How can information systems contribute to it?

2. Why can software become such an important quality problem for information systems?

3. Describe two software quality problems.

4. Name and describe four solutions to software quality problems.

5. What is structured analysis? What is the role of the following in structured analysis: data flow diagrams, data dictionaries, process specifications?

6. What are the three techniques for documenting decision rules? Compare the features of each.

7. What are the principles of structured design? How can it promote software quality?

8. What is the relationship of structured programming to structured design?

9. Describe the use of system flowcharts.

10. What is the difference between object-oriented software development and traditional structured methodologies?

11. What is CASE? How can it promote quality in information systems?

12. What are some of the key elements of CASE tools?

13. What are software re-engineering and reverse engineering? How can they promote quality in information systems?

1. If it is impossible to eliminate all of the errors in a complex piece of software, how much time should be spent in testing?

2. How can information system quality benefit from using some of the system-building approaches described in Chapter 12 (systems life cycle, prototyping, software packages, fourth-generation development, outsourcing)? What quality problems are created by each of these approaches?

1. Illustrate the decision rules for the following in a decision tree, decision table, and pseudocode:
   The university provides scholarships to students under the following conditions: Freshmen must have a grade point average of at least 3.3. Upperclassmen must have a grade point average of at least 3.5.

2. Illustrate the decision rules for the following in a decision tree, decision table, and pseudocode:
   Customers may purchase heating oil from the Warm and Toasty Heating Oil Company under different arrangements. Customers who pay cash immediately upon delivery or send in checks for payment within 10 days of delivery will pay five cents less per gallon than customers who pay after 10 days. Customers will be charged an 18 percent annual interest rate for bills that have not been paid within 30 days of the billing date.

3. Illustrate the decision rules for the following in a decision tree, decision table, and pseudocode:
   Authors' royalties are computed on the basis of sales volume. Royalties are 7.5 percent of a book's retail price for sales of up to 10,000 books; 10% for sales of 10,000–15,000; and 12 percent of all sales above 15,000. No royalty can be paid to the author until royalty earnings have paid back the author's prepublication advance.

4. Develop a data flow diagram for the following:
   Realty Rentals maintains a rental roll for the residential apartment complexes it owns. Whenever the rent is changed, the rental control clerk completes a rental change form showing the apartment number and the new rent. The clerk enters this information into the company's microcomputer, which maintains files on all of Realty Rental's units. The microcomputer updates the files with the new rental changes and prints out a report showing the apartments, their rental change, total number of units with rental changes, and total amount of rentals.

5. Develop a data flow diagram for the following:
   Sales orders are received by the sales order clerk and batched. The total value of the orders and the total number of orders are written on a batch header slip. The orders and header figures are keyed into CRT terminals to produce a transaction file. The sales orders and header slip are returned to the sales department and filed by date. Computer programs edit and validate the transaction file, producing a report showing the total value of orders and total number of orders. The sales department reviews this report and rejects the batch if the totals do not agree with the manual totals on the batch header.

6. Develop a context diagram and zero-level data flow diagram for the following:
   The accounts payable system is responsible for tracking and paying the money that a business owes its suppliers. The system maintains a master file for all suppliers with whom the company deals. It contains data about suppliers (name, address, payment terms) and details about outstanding transactions, invoice history, payment history, and account balances. After reviewing and approving suppliers' invoices and credit memos, the accounts payable department inputs data from these documents to update the accounts payable master file. It produces checks to pay authorized invoices, a cash disbursement report of all checks written, and an accounts payable transaction register. The system summarizes the total value of the transactions for posting to the general ledger system. The accounts payable system also summarizes items or balances, producing lists of balances and exception reports (such as debit balances) for management review. The system accommodates adjustments to correct erroneous postings or invoice amounts. It also summarizes data and reports on adjustments.

7. Draw a system flowchart to document the following system:

Order processing is an accounting application that records and screens customer orders and assists with inventory control. Purchase orders from customers are input on-line through point-of-sale terminals at various locations throughout the company's sales territory. Computer processing references a customer master file with data on each customer such as name, address, discounts, and credit standing. The computer also references an inventory master file to determine if particular goods are on hand prior to producing shipping orders. Items not on hand are placed on back order and the inventory master file is updated to reflect goods that are shipped. Back orders must be maintained on the current order file to initiate a shipping order when goods become available. The system outputs shipping orders and management reports such as "Orders Processed" and "Back Orders."

Group Project: Systems Analysis and Design Project: *Healthlite Yogurt Company*

Healthlite Yogurt Company is a market leader in the expanding U.S. market for yogurt and related health products. Healthlite is experiencing some sharp growing pains. With the growing interest in low-fat, low-cholesterol health foods, spurred on by the aging of the baby boomers, Healthlite's sales have tripled over the past five years. At the same time, however, new local competitors, offering fast delivery from local production centers and lower prices, are challenging Healthlite for retail shelf space with a bevy of new products. Without shelf space, products cannot be retailed in the United States, and new products are needed to expand shelf space. Healthlite needs to justify its share of shelf space to grocers and is seeking additional shelf space for its new yogurt-based products such as frozen desserts and low-fat salad dressings.

Healthlite's biggest challenge, however, has not been competitors, but the sweep of the second hand. Yogurt is a very short shelf-life commodity. With a shelf life measured in days, yogurt must be moved very quickly.

Healthlite maintains its U.S. corporate headquarters in Danbury, Connecticut. Corporate headquarters has a central mainframe computer that maintains most of the major business databases. All production takes place in local processing plants, which are located in New Jersey, Massachusetts, Tennessee, Illinois, Colorado, Washington, and California. Each processing plant has its own minicomputer, which is connected to the corporate mainframe. Customer credit verification is maintained at the central corporate site where customer master files are maintained and order verification or rejection is determined. Once processed centrally, order data are then fed to the appropriate local processing plant minicomputer.

Healthlite has 20 sales regions, each with approximately 30 sales representatives and a regional sales manager. Healthlite has a 12-person marketing group in corporate headquarters and a corporate director of sales and marketing. Each salesperson is able to store and retrieve data for assigned customer accounts using a terminal in each regional office linked to the corporate mainframe. Reports for individual salespeople (printouts of orders, rejection notices, customer account inquiries) and for sales offices are printed in the regional offices and mailed to them.

Sometimes, the only way to obtain up-to-date sales data is for managers to make telephone calls to subordinates and then piece the information together. Data about sales and advertising expenses and customer shelf space devoted to Healthlite products is maintained manually at the regional offices. Each regional office maintains its own manual records of customer shelf space and promotional campaigns. The central computer only contains consolidated, companywide files for customer account data and order and billing data.

The existing order processing system requires sales representatives to write up hard copy tickets to place orders through the mail. Approximately 100 workers at Healthlite corporate headquarters open, sort, keypunch, and process 100,000 order tickets per week. This order information is transmitted each evening from the mainframe to a minicomputer at each of Healthlite's processing sites. This daily order specifies the total yogurt and yogurt product demand for each processing center. Each processing center then produces the amount and type of yogurt and yogurt-related products ordered and then ships the orders out. Shipping managers at the processing centers assign the shipments to various transportation carriers.

Rapid growth, fueled by Healthlite's "health" image and by branching into new yogurt-based products, has put pressures on Healthlite's existing information systems. By mid-1992, growth in new products and sales had reached a point where Healthlite was printing new tickets for the sales force every week. The firm was choking on paper. For each order, a salesperson filled out at least two forms per account. Some sales representatives have more than 80 customers.

As it became bogged down in paper, Healthlite saw increased delays in the processing of its orders. Since yogurt is a fresh food product, it could not be held long in inventory. Yet Healthlite had trouble shipping the right goods to the right places in time. It was taking between four days and two weeks to process and ship out an order, depending on mail delivery rates. Healthlite also found accounting discrepancies of $1.5 million annually between the sales force and headquarters.

Communication between sales managers and the sales representatives has been primarily through the mail or by telephone. For example, regional sales managers have to send representatives letters with announcements of promotional campaigns or pricing discounts. Sales representatives have to write up their monthly reports of sales calls and then mail this information to regional headquarters.

Healthlite is considering new information system solutions. First of all, the firm would like a system that expedites order processing. Management would also like to make better use of information systems to support sales and marketing activities and to take advantage of leading-edge information technology.

Sales and Marketing Information Systems: Background

Sales and marketing are vital to the operation of any business. Orders must be processed and related to production and inventory. Sales of products in existing markets must be monitored and new products must be developed for new markets. The firm must be able to respond to rapidly changing market demands, proliferation of new products and competing firms, shortened product life spans, changing consumer tastes, and new government regulations.

Firms need sales and marketing information for product planning, pricing decisions, devising advertising and other promotional campaigns, forecasting market potential for new and existing products, and determining channels of distribution. They must also monitor the efficiency and effectiveness of the distribution of their products and services.

The sales function of a typical business captures and processes customer orders and produces invoices for customers and data for inventory and production. A typical invoice is illustrated here.

Customer

Highview Supermarket
223 Highland Boulevard
Ossining, NY 10562

Customer Number 00395

Order Number 598422
Order Date: 03/07/94

QTY ITEM NO.	DESCRIPTION	UNIT PRICE	AMOUNT
100 V3392	8 oz. Vanilla	$.44	$44.00
50 S4456	8 oz. Strawberry	$.44	$22.00
65 L4492	8 oz. Lemon	$.44	$28.60

SHIPPING: $6.50

TOTAL INVOICE: $101.10

Data from order entry is also used by a firm's accounts receivable system and by the firm's inventory and production systems. The production planning system, for instance, builds its daily production plans based on the prior day's sales. The number and type of product sold will determine how many units to produce and when.

Sales managers need information to plan and monitor the performance of the sales force. Management also needs information on the performance of specific products, product lines, or brands. Price, revenue, cost, and growth information can be used for pricing decisions, for evaluating the performance of current products, and for predicting the performance of future products.

From basic sales and invoice data, a firm can produce a variety of reports with valuable information to guide sales and marketing work. For weekly, monthly, or annual time periods, information can be gathered on which outlets order the most, on the average order amount, on which products move slowest and fastest, on which salespersons sell the most and least, on which geographic areas purchase the most of a given product, and on how current sales of a product compare to last year's product.

With a group of three or four of your classmates design a new system for Healthlite. Prepare a systems analysis and design report and present your results to the class. In your report you should do the following:

- Describe Healthlite's problems and their relationship to existing systems.
- List the principal goals and objectives of the system.
- Consider what pieces of information the new system or systems should contain, how this information should be organized and stored, and how it should be captured.
- Consider what new business procedures must be designed and how you will implement them without alienating major constituencies.
- Consider the human interface issues, if new software is envisioned.

Your systems design report should contain the following:

1. Management summary—relation to corporate strategy, benefits and implementation schedule.
2. Data flow diagram or system flowchart for the system.
3. Sample data entry screen design.
4. Description of the functions of the system.
5. Report specifications.
6. File design.
7. Conversion procedures.
8. Quality assurance measures.

It is important to establish the scope of the system. It should be limited to order processing and related sales and marketing activities. You do not have to redesign Healthlite's manufacturing, accounts receivable, distribution, or inventory control systems for this exercise.

CASE STUDY

A Swiss-Swedish Software Developer Becomes an Early CASE User

In 1988, ABB Network Control faced a serious product management problem that was not only costly but that also threatened to undermine the quality of their products. ABB, jointly owned by Asea of Sweden and Brown Boveri of Switzerland, is a giant European business that is headquartered in Zurich. Its Network Control division provides systems to power industry customers all over the

world (the division's principal offices are in Sweden, Germany and the United States). With systems that monitor the electrical networks run by utility companies, ABB is an international leader in its field. ABB's customers vary in size from large utilities supplying whole countries with power, to small plants serving only isolated communities. The company develops its systems on Digital Equipment

Corp. (DEC) VAX minicomputers and targets the code for either DEC VAXes or DEC's UNIX-based machines.

ABB's business approach is first to develop a generic software package and then to customize that package for each of its hundreds of customers. The generic version of each of their systems (products) contains hundreds of program modules. After producing customized copies of a generic system for each of its customers, ABB must manage tens of thousands of program modules for just that one product, an immense and costly job. When they develop an upgrade to the generic software, it must be applied to each of the customized versions. When a customer finds a software problem that turns out to be part of the generic system, all versions must be fixed. If the problem is part of a customization, ABB must not only fix it for that customer but also determine whether that particular customization is part of any other customers' systems, and if so, fix their systems also. Management logistics for all of this have been a nightmare.

Fixes and upgrades have always meant a great deal of repetitive coding to keep all versions up to date. In time, ABB's 300 software engineers began to find that they were spending too much time coding. They also realized that often they did not know which modules had actually been delivered to which customers. ABB rejected a possible partial solution of keeping a full copy of each system delivered to a customer. Making and storing so many copies was more than the company could handle. They realized they had to find a new answer.

The solution they adopted relied upon a CASE tool, CDD/Repository from Digital Equipment Corp. of Maynard, Massachusetts. The first repository tool ABB installed was the change control system. Change control protects files and keeps records of all changes to each file. A robust change control system will enforce security so that only individuals with proper authorization will be able to access and change files. It will automatically archive older versions of a file when changes are made, preserving as many back versions as desired, thus creating a history of changes for use if needed. A change control system will record the date and time of all changes and the name of the individual making the changes. It will even prevent two people from trying to make changes to the same software simultaneously. These change control features help ABB to manage many versions of a module and manage all the modules of a specific product.

CDD/Repository has object-oriented features that help ABB to keep track of data used to customize different customer systems. "It allows us to track the status and dependencies of our source modules, and of the tools and methods attached to different modules," says Stig Eklund, manager of quality and methods at ABB's Vasteras, Sweden, offices. "We can now tell much more easily which programs or modules are going to be affected by any planned change to the code."

One serious problem Eklund has noted is that performance-response time can be 20 or 30 seconds each time someone starts up a new function. In a system of this size, slow response time can be expensive and frustrating. Eklund has discussed this problem with DEC. They responded that their engineers are giving this problem a high priority and promise steady improvement.

One reason DEC's CASE tool was selected is that ABB develops its products on DEC VAXes and sells them for use on VAXes or DEC UNIX systems. CDD/Repository is a strategic product for DEC because it is central to Network Application Support (NAS), DEC's overall software strategy. One aim of NAS is to address the problem of getting various software tools to work together, a major industry problem. DEC promises to deliver links to other CASE tools, such as Foundation from Arthur Andersen Consulting and IEF from Texas Instruments. DEC's relationship with these and other independent software vendors remains unclear, however, because DEC is also a competitor of theirs.

DEC claims it has sold about 10,000 licenses for CDD/Repository, although industry watchers believe very few purchasers are actually using it fully. ABB was one of the first to use the product, having become a field test site for DEC. As of this writing, the repository has not been installed in either Germany or the United States because DEC has not yet released the distributed features of the product. Now that the change control system is in use, ABB is awaiting the release of other repository tools they plan to install—they expect to begin with a configuration management system. After some experience with DEC's repository, ABB believes the product has given them much greater facility to reuse code and to keep track of modifications.

Source: George Black, "Early User Building Repository Repertoire," *Software Magazine* (July 1992).

Case Study Questions

1. As manager of IS for ABB Network Control, would you have recommended the use of CDD/Repository? Why? Develop the pros and cons of the issue.

2. What problems do you think this tool will solve for ABB? What problems will it not address? Will it create any new problems for them?

3. "Vaporware" is the term the information systems industry uses for software promised but not yet available. How much of ABB's commitment to the DEC repository was based on promises and vaporware? What are the risks of ABB's commitment under these circumstances? In your answer, address the question of the significance of this product to ABB Network Control's future. Is it a risk you believe ABB should have taken? Why?

4. Still in your role as manager of ABB Network Control's IS, under what circumstances would you be willing to purchase a product while it was still being

tested? How would you present this issue to your management? Why do you think ABB was willing to go this route?

5. Assume the product had been tested to DEC's satisfaction and had been released for public sale. Would you be willing to be one of the first major users of the system? Why? What are the risks? What are some of the ways you might reduce the risk?

6. ABB Network Control uses DEC hardware and software for its product development and targets their products for use on DEC equipment. What are the problems that this approach to development and marketing creates for ABB? For its customers?

References

Abdel-Hamid, Tarek K. "The Economics of Software Quality Assurance: A Simulation-Based Case Study." *MIS Quarterly* (September 1988).

Alberts, David S. "The Economics of Software Quality Assurance." Washington D.C.: National Computer Conference, 1976 Proceedings.

Banker, Rajiv D., Robert J. Kaufmann, and Rachna Kumar. "An Empirical Test of Object-Based Output Measurement Metrics in a Computer-Aided Software Engineering (CASE) Environment." *Journal of Management Information Systems* 8, no. 3 (Winter 1991–92).

Banker, Rajiv D., and Chris F. Kemerer. "Performance Evaluation Metrics in Information Systems Development: A Principal-Agent Model." *Information Systems Research* 3, no. 4 (December 1992).

Boehm, Barry W. "Understanding and Controlling Software Costs." *IEEE Transactions on Software Engineering* 14, no. 10 (October 1988).

Booch, Grady. *Object Oriented Design with Applications*. Redwood City, California: Benjamin Cummings, 1991.

Bouldin, Barbara M. "What Are You Measuring? Why Are You Measuring It?" *Software Magazine* (August 1989).

Coad, Peter, with Edward Yourdon. *Object-Oriented Analysis*. Englewood Cliffs, NJ: Prentice-Hall, 1989.

Dekleva, Sasa M. "The Influence of Information Systems Development Approach on Maintenance." *MIS Quarterly* 16, no. 3 (September 1992).

DeMarco, Tom. *Structured Analysis and System Specification*. New York: Yourdon Press, 1978.

Dijkstra, E. "Structured Programming," in *Classics in Software Engineering*, ed. Edward Nash Yourdon. New York: Yourdon Press, 1979.

Flatten, Per O., Donald J. McCubbrey, P. Declan O'Riordan, and Keith Burgess. *Foundations of Business Systems*, 2nd ed. Fort Worth, TX: The Dryden Press, 1992.

Gane, Chris, and Trish Sarson. *Structured Systems Analysis: Tools and Techniques*. Englewood Cliffs, NJ: Prentice-Hall, 1979.

Henderson-Sellers, Brian, and Julian M. Edwards. "The Object-Oriented Systems Life Cycle." *Communications of the ACM* 33, no. 9 (September 1990).

International Data Corporation, "Object Technology: A Key Software Technology for the '90s." *Computerworld*, May 11, 1992.

Keyes, Jessica. "New Metrics Needed for New Generation." *Software Magazine* (May 1992).

Korson, Tim, and McGregor, John D. "Understanding Object Oriented: A Unifying Paradigm." *Communications of the ACM* 33, no. 9 (September 1990).

LaPlante, Alice. "For IS, Quality is 'Job None'." *Computerworld* (January 6, 1992).

Lientz, Bennett P., and E. Burton Swanson. *Software Maintenance Management*. Reading, MA: Addison-Wesley, 1980.

Littlewood, Bev and Lorenzo Strigini. "The Risks of Software." *Scientific American* (November 1992).

Maletz, Mark C. "KBS Circles: A Technology Transfer Initiative that Leverages Xerox's Leadership through Quality Program." *MIS Quarterly* 14, no. 3 (September 1990).

Mandell, Mel. "Statistical Software Rings in Quality." *Computerworld* (January 6, 1992).

Martin, James, and Carma McClure. *Structured Techniques: The Basis of CASE.* Englewood Cliffs, NJ: Prentice-Hall, 1988.

Mazzucchelli, Louis. "Structured Analysis Can Streamline Software Design." *Computerworld* (December 9, 1985).

Moran, Robert. "The Case against CASE." *InformationWEEK* (February 17, 1992).

McIntyre, Scott C., and Higgins, Lexis F. "Object-Oriented Analysis and Design: Methodology and Application." *Journal of Management Information Systems* 5, no. 1 (Summer 1988).

Norman, Ronald J., and Jay F. Nunamaker, Jr., "CASE Productivity Perceptions of Software Engineering Professionals." *Communications of the ACM* 32, no. 9 (September 1989).

Putnam, L. H., and A. Fitzsimmons. "Estimating Software Costs." *Datamation* (September 1979, October 1979, and November 1979).

Radding, Alan. "Quality is Job #1." *Datamation* (October 1, 1992).

Rettig, Marc. "Software Teams." *Communications of the ACM* 33, no. 10 (October 1990).

Swanson, Kent, Dave McComb, Jill Smith, and Don McCubbrey. "The Application Software Factory: Applying Total Quality Techniques to Systems Development." *MIS Quarterly* 15, no. 4 (December 1991).

Yourdon, Edward, and L. L. Constantine, *Structured Design.* New York: Yourdon Press, 1978.

Bank Combats
Runaway Systems

Westpac Banking Corporation, the banking giant of Sydney, Australia, had high hopes for its proposed new Core System 90. Core System 90 (CS90) was supposed to create a showcase of decentralized data systems that would allow bank branch managers to create new financial products rapidly, using expert systems and easy-to-use software for designing new applications. Ultimately CS90 was supposed to redefine the role of information technology at the bank by shrinking its cumbersome information sys-

tems department and creating a more streamlined, customer-responsive organization.

These hopes were dashed. More than three years after Westpac started to develop CS90, it admitted that the project was out of control. Westpac had spent nearly $150 million on the new system but had virtually nothing to show for the effort. The system's scheduled 1993 completion date was a pipe dream. Westpac decided to cut its losses by dropping IBM as the lead software developer for the

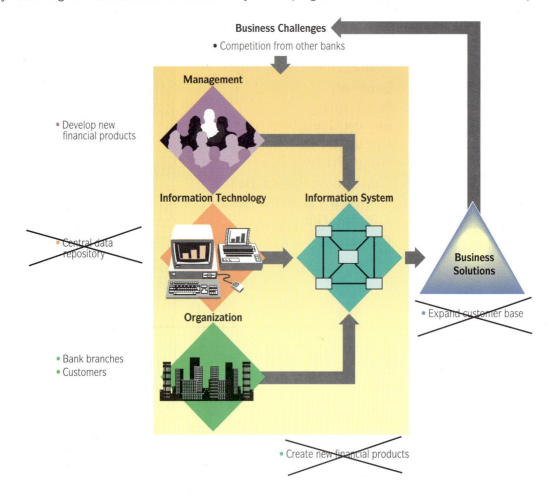

project and hiring Andersen Consulting to recommend steps to save the effort.

According to industry consultants familiar with both Westpac and IBM, CS90 was doomed to fail because it combined an ambitious business agenda with technology that didn't exist. IBM could not deliver the critical technologies it had promised for creating a central data repository that could be used throughout application development.

This system boondoggle came at exactly the wrong time for Westpac. Although the bank had $84.7 million in assets, its loan portfolio and asset management programs were performing poorly. But Westpac is not alone. CS90 is but one of a long list of over-budget and behind-schedule computer projects. A recent Peat Marwick survey showed that about 35 percent of all major information systems projects are "runaways" like Westpac's. Millions of dollars have been spent over budget, and projects are months or even years behind schedule.

Source: Mark Mehler, "Reining In Runaway Systems," *InformationWEEK*, December 16, 1991.

In nearly every organization, information systems projects take much more time and money to implement than originally anticipated, or the completed system does not work properly. Because so many information systems are trouble-ridden, designers, builders, and users of information systems should understand how and why they succeed or fail.

Problems with information system technology are only one reason why information systems succeed or fail. Managerial and organizational factors also play a powerful role in system outcome because implementing an information system is a process of organizational change. This chapter explores the managerial, organizational, and technological factors responsible for information system success and failure and examines the process of implementation.

After completing this chapter you will be able to:

- Identify major problem areas in information systems.
- Determine whether a system is successful.
- Describe the principal causes of information system failure.
- Describe the relationship between the implementation process and system outcome.
- Describe appropriate strategies to manage the implementation process.

14.1 Information System Failure

As many as 75 percent of all large systems may be considered to be operating failures. Although these systems are in production, they take so much extra time and money to implement or are so functionally deficient that businesses can't reap the expected benefits. Studies of federal government projects have found that a large number were poorly designed, full of inaccurate or incomplete data, delivered but not used, delivered late and over budget, reworked, or abandoned (Anthes, 1992).

Many information **system "failures"** are not necessarily falling apart, but they clearly are either not used in the way that they were intended, or they are not used at all. Users have to develop parallel manual procedures to make these systems work properly. For example, the employee benefits department of a multi-unit manufacturing concern continues to maintain all of the benefits data for the company's 20,000 employees manually, despite the presence of an automated, on-line system for pension and life insurance benefits. Users complain that the data in the system are unreliable because they do not capture the prior benefits plan data for employees from acquisitions and because payroll earnings figures are out of date. All pension calculations, preretirement estimates, and benefits analysis must be handled manually.

In some systems, nearly all of the reports put out for management are never read. They are considered useless and full of figures of no consequence for decision making or analysis (Lucas, 1981). For instance, managers in a prominent commercial bank with branches throughout the United States and Europe find its batch loan account system virtually useless. Pages of reports are filled with zeros, making it practically impossible to assess the status of a client's loan. The amount of the loan, the outstanding balance, and the repayment schedule must be tracked manually. The bank is also highly dissatisfied with its on-line client reporting system. Although the bank maintains files on all areas for client accounts (loans, savings, Individual Retirement Accounts, checking), only checking and savings account data are available on-line. Therefore, managers and analysts cannot obtain complete client profiles when they need them.

Other automated systems go untouched because they are either too difficult to use or because their data cannot be trusted. Users continue to maintain their records manually. For instance, a nationally known executive recruiting firm found that essential reports on search activity are routinely three months out of date. The firm has to develop statistics manually on the number of executive

A well-designed computer information system would eliminate much of this office worker's disorganization and offer him a more productive working environment.

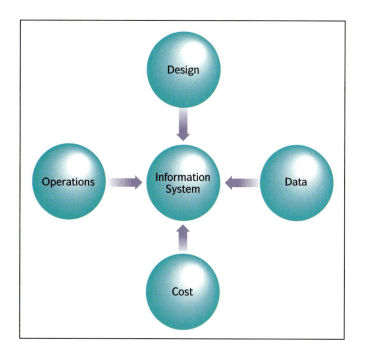

Figure 14.1
Information system problem areas. Problems with an information system's design, data, cost, or operations can be evidence of a system failure.

searches initiated in a given month. Recruiters have no way of tracking and coordinating searches among the company's branch offices in New York, Chicago, Houston, and Los Angeles.

Still other systems founder because of processing delays, excessive operational costs, or chronic production problems. For instance, the batch accounts receivable system of a medium-sized consumer products manufacturer is constantly breaking down. Production runs have been aborting several times a month, and major month-end runs have been close to three weeks behind schedule. Because of excessive reruns, schedule delays, and time devoted to fixing antiquated programs, the information systems staff has no time to work out long-term solutions or convert to an on-line system.

In all of these cases, the information systems in question must be judged failures. Why do system failures occur?

Information System Problem Areas

The problems causing information system failure fall into multiple categories, as illustrated by Figure 14.1. The major problem areas are design, data, cost, and operations. These problems can be attributed not only to technical features of information systems but to nontechnical sources as well. In fact, most of these problems stem from organizational factors.

DESIGN   The actual design of the system fails to capture essential business requirements. Information may not be provided quickly enough to be helpful; it may be in a format that is impossible to digest and use; or it may represent the wrong pieces of data.

User interface: The part of the information system through which the end user interacts with the system; type of hardware and the series of on-screen commands and responses required for a user to work with the system.

The way in which nontechnical business users must interact with the system may be excessively complicated and discouraging. A system may be designed with a poor **user interface**. The user interface is the part of the system that end users interact with. For example, an input form or on-line screen may be so poorly arranged that no one wants to submit data. Or the procedures to request on-line information retrieval may be so unintelligible that users are too frustrated to make requests. As a result, a system may go unused and eventually may have to be discontinued. The Window on Organizations illustrates some of these user interface problems.

An information system will be judged a failure if its design is not compatible with the structure, culture, and goals of the organization. As pointed out in Chapter 4, management and organization theorists have viewed information system technology as closely interrelated with all of the other components of organizations—tasks, structure, people, and culture. Since all of these components are interdependent, a change in one will affect all of the others. Therefore, the organization's tasks, participants, structure, and culture are bound to be affected when an information system is changed. Designing a system redesigns the organization.

Historically, information system design has been preoccupied with technical issues at the expense of organizational concerns. The result has been information systems that are often incompatible with their organization's structure, culture, and goals. Without a close organizational fit, such systems have created tensions, instability, and conflict.

DATA   The data in the system have a high level of inaccuracy or inconsistency. The information in certain fields may be erroneous or ambiguous; or it may not be broken out properly for business purposes. Information required for a specific business function may be inaccessible because the data are incomplete.

COST   Some systems operate quite smoothly, but their cost to implement and run on a production basis is way over budget. These excessive expenditures cannot be justified by the demonstrated business value of the information they provide. The experience of Westpac Banking Corporation in the opening vignette is typical.

OPERATIONS   The system does not run well. Information is not provided in a timely and efficient manner because the computer operations that handle information processing break down. Jobs that abort too often lead to excessive reruns and delayed or missed schedules for delivery of information. An on-line system may be operationally inadequate because the response time is too long.

Measuring System Success

How can we tell whether a system is successful or not? This is not always an easy question to answer. Not everyone may agree about the value or effectiveness of a particular information system. Individuals with different decision-making styles or ways of approaching a problem may have totally different opinions about the same system. A system valued highly by an analytical, quantitatively oriented user may be totally dismissed by an intuitive thinker who is more concerned with feelings and overall impressions. Likewise, a junior sales manager with a new MBA in marketing may be more appreciative of information system reports on the demographic characteristics of his territory than a veteran representative who has worked the same territory for 15 years and knows it thoroughly. The perception and use of information systems can be heavily conditioned by personal and situational variables (Lucas, 1981).

Nevertheless, MIS researchers have looked for a formal set of measures for rating systems. Various criteria have been developed, but the following measures of system success, illustrated in Figure 14.2, are considered the most important.

1. *High levels of system use,* as measured by polling users, employing questionnaires, or monitoring parameters such as the volume of on-line transactions.
2. *User satisfaction with the system,* as measured by questionnaires or interviews. This might include users' opinions on the accuracy, timeliness, and relevance of information; on the quality of service; and perhaps on the

ORGANIZATIONS
Programmers Need to Keep It Simple

Programmers speak in software code, but the people yelling at them speak in what the computer industry calls "natural language." Who will translate? At first, almost nobody did. Then programmers started writing manuals in English but their language wasn't plain enough. So they started developing interfaces that used pictures called icons and making computer screens that gave users lists of choices called "pull-down menus." Some users still couldn't understand what was required of them.

Using methods borrowed from consumer products companies, a few big software firms recently instructed their programmers to watch "non-techies" actually working with computers. They built rooms where programmers could observe users from behind one-way mirrors and where video cameras could record people trying out a piece of software for the first time. The software firms called these rooms "usability labs."

The usability studies showed that many people can't understand programmers even when the programmers try to write in a natural language. The programmers would wonder why the user didn't understand what seemingly simple technical terms such as "pop out DOS" meant. When the programmer saw a person struggling with a program, the programmer would conclude that this person wasn't the "target user" and would wonder where the usability testers found so many dumb users. The programmer's mentality appeared to be that if software was hard to write, it should be hard for other people to use.

The difference between the right word and the almost-right word can be critical. Microsoft found that when the term "preferences" flashed on the screen for its Excel spreadsheet program, more than half the users didn't know what to do. However, when the word was changed to "options" almost everyone understood. Usability Sciences Corporation, a Dallas-based firm that does testing for various software developers, found that an on-screen calculator for doing arithmetic in one tax software program baffled users. Users could not understand that they had to use the commands "get" and "put" to incorporate the results into a tax form. The problem was solved by changing the commands to "cut" and "paste" (which are recognizable by most users because they are standard terms in the Windows and Macintosh graphical user interfaces).

Icons can be as difficult to understand as words. Programmers commonly design witty icons only to discover that users find them incomprehensible. One programmer created a piggy-bank icon to designate the SAVE command. Users had no idea what it meant. It is useful to remember that sometimes words are better than pictures. When Microsoft programmers designed Publisher, a desktop publishing program, they used a flashing cursor with arrows pointing in four different directions to designate that users had the option of moving a box around. Users were baffled until the programmers added a truck with the word "move" on it.

Source: William Bulkeley, "Programmers Attempt to Keep It Simple," *The Wall Street Journal*, June 30, 1992.

To Think About: To what extent can usability labs solve these user interface problems? Who would be the best people to use as testers in usability studies? What kinds of design problems can't be solved this way? If you were a manager, what steps would you take to eliminate user interface problems?

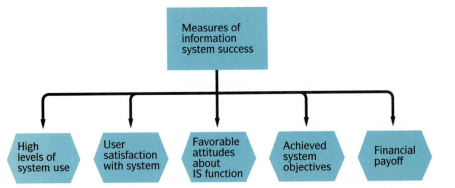

Figure 14.2
Measures of information system success. MIS researchers have different criteria for measuring the success of an information system. They consider the five measures in the figure to be the most important.

schedule of operations. Especially critical are managers' attitudes on how well their information needs were satisfied (Ives et al., 1983; Wescott, 1985) and users' opinions about how well the system enhanced their job performance (Davis, 1989).

3. *Favorable attitudes* of users about information systems and the information systems staff.

4. *Achieved objectives*, the extent to which the system meets its specified goals, as reflected by the quality of decision making resulting from use of the system.

5. *Financial payoff* to the organization, either by reducing costs or by increasing sales or profits.

The fifth measure is considered to be of limited value even though cost/benefit analysis may have figured heavily in the decision to build a particular system. The benefits of an information system may not be totally quantifiable. Moreover, tangible benefits cannot be easily demonstrated for the more advanced decision-support system applications. And even though cost/benefit methodology has been rigorously pursued, the history of many systems development projects has shown that realistic estimates have always been difficult to formulate. MIS researchers have preferred to concentrate instead on the human and organizational measures of system success such as information quality, system quality, and the impact of systems on organizational performance. (Lucas, 1981; DeLone and McLean, 1992).

14.2 Causes of Information System Success and Failure

As described in Chapter 4, systems are developed in the first place because of powerful external environmental forces and equally powerful internal or institutional forces. Many systems fail because of the opposition of either the environment or the internal setting.

As many MIS researchers have pointed out, the introduction or alteration of an information system has a powerful behavioral and organizational impact. It transforms the way various individuals and groups perform and interact. Changes in the way information is defined, accessed, and used to manage the resources of the organization often lead to new distributions of authority and power (Lucas, 1975). This internal organizational change breeds resistance and opposition and can lead to the demise of an otherwise good system. An important characteristic of most information systems is that individuals are asked or required to change their behavior in order to make the system function.

But there are other reasons why a system may fail. Several studies have found that in organizations with similar environments and institutional features, the same innovation will be successful in some organizations but fail in others. Why? One explanation focuses on different patterns of implementation.

APPROACHES	IMPLEMENTATION STAGES		
	Adoption	Management	Routinization
Actors' roles	XXXX	XXXX	
Strategy		XXXX	
Organizational factors		XXXX	XXXX

Figure 14.3
Approaches and implementation stages in the implementation literature. The Xs indicate the stages of implementation on which the different approaches tend to focus. For instance, literature that uses an actor/role approach to implementation tends to focus on the early stages of adoption and management.

The Concept of Implementation

Implementation: All of the organizational activities working toward the adoption, management, and routinization of an innovation.

Implementation refers to all of the organizational activities working toward the adoption, management, and routinization of an innovation. Figure 14.3 illustrates the major stages of implementation described in research literature and the major approaches to the subject (see also Tornatsky et al., 1983).

Some of the implementation research focuses on actors and roles. The belief is that organizations should select actors with appropriate social characteristics and systematically develop organizational roles, such as "product champions," in order to innovate successfully (see Figure 14.4). Generally, this literature focuses on early adoption and management of innovations.

A second school of thought in the implementation literature focuses on strategies of innovation. The two extremes are top-down innovation and grass-roots innovation. There are many examples of organizations in which the absence of senior management support for innovation dooms the project from the start. At the same time, without strong grass-roots, end-user participation, information system projects can also fail.

Figure 14.4
Actors in the innovation process. During implementation, the roles of actors include being product champions, bureaucratic entrepreneurs, and gatekeepers. In order to be successful in their roles as innovators and sponsors of change, actors should have certain demographic characteristics including social status in the organization, higher education, and social, technical, and organizational sophistication.

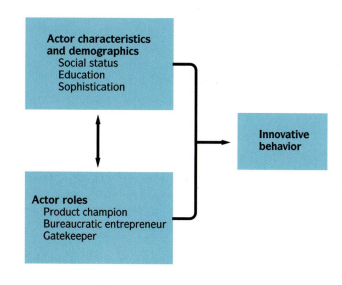

Table 14.1 ACTIONS AND INDICATORS FOR SUCCESSFUL SYSTEM IMPLEMENTATION

Support by local funds
New organizational arrangements
Stable supply and maintenance
New personnel classifications
Changes in organizational authority
Internalization of the training program
Continual updating of the system
Promotion of key personnel
Survival of the system after turnover of its originators
Attainment of widespread use

Source: Yin (1981).

A third approach to implementation focuses on general organizational change factors as being decisive to the long-term routinization of innovations. Table 14.1 illustrates some of the key organizational actions required for long-term, successful implementation, and indicators of success. (Yin, 1981).

Change agent: In the context of implementation, the individual acting as the catalyst during the change process to ensure successful organizational adaptation to a new system or innovation.

In the context of implementation, the systems analyst is a **change agent.** The analyst not only develops technical solutions but redefines the configurations, interactions, job activities, and power relationships of various organizational groups. The analyst is the catalyst for the entire change process and is responsible for ensuring that the changes created by a new system are accepted by all parties involved. The change agent communicates with users, mediates between competing interest groups, and ensures that the organizational adjustment to such changes is complete.

One model of the implementation process is the Kolb/Frohman model of organizational change. This model divides the process of organizational change into a seven-stage relationship between an organizational *consultant* and his or her *client*. (The consultant corresponds to the information system designer and the client to the user.) The success of the change effort is determined by how well the consultant and client deal with the key issues at each stage (Kolb and Frohman, 1970). Other models of implementation describe the relationship as one between designers, clients, and decision makers, who are responsible for managing the implementation effort to bridge the gap between design and utilization (Swanson, 1988).

Studies of the implementation process have examined the relationship between information system designers and users at different stages of systems development. Studies have focused on issues such as the following:

- Conflicts between the technical or machine orientation of information systems specialists and the organizational or business orientation of users.
- The impact of information systems on organizational structures, work groups, and behavior.
- The planning and management of systems development activities.
- The degree of user participation in the design and development process.

Causes of Implementation Success and Failure

Implementation research to date has found no single explanation for system success or failure. Nor does it suggest a single formula for system success. However, it has found that implementation outcome can be largely determined by the following factors:

- The role of users in the implementation process.
- The degree of management support for the implementation effort.

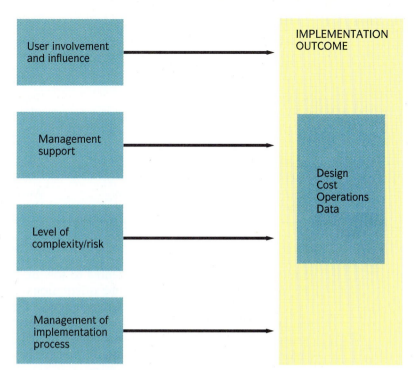

Figure 14.5
Factors in information system success or failure. The implementation outcome can be largely determined by the role of users; the degree of management support; the level of risk and complexity in the implementation project; and the quality of management of the implementation process. Evidence of success or failure can be found in the areas of design, cost, operations, or data of the information system.

- The level of risk and complexity of the implementation project.
- The quality of management of the implementation process.

These are largely behavioral and organizational issues and are illustrated in Figure 14.5.

USER INVOLVEMENT AND INFLUENCE

User involvement in the design and operation of information systems has several positive results. First, if users are heavily involved in systems design, they have more opportunities to mold the system according to their priorities and business requirements. Second, they are more likely to react positively to the system because they have been active participants in the change process. Their participation in implementation fosters favorable attitudes toward the system and the changes it engenders (Lucas, 1974).

Experiments and field studies have shown that participation inspires favorable attitudes for the following reasons:

- The participation process is challenging and ego enhancing.
- Participation usually fosters more commitment to change.
- Participants in the process become more knowledgeable about the change itself and develop more skills and opportunities to control it.

Incorporating the user's knowledge and expertise also leads to better solutions.

THE USER–DESIGNER COMMUNICATIONS GAP

User-designer communications gap: The differences in backgrounds, interests, and priorities that impede communication and problem-solving among end users and information systems specialists.

The relationship between consultant and client has traditionally been a problem area for information system implementation efforts. Users and information system specialists tend to have different backgrounds, interests, and priorities. This is referred to as the **user-designer communications gap.** These differences lead to divergent organizational loyalties, approaches to problem solving, and vocabularies. Information system specialists, for example, often have a highly technical or machine orientation to problem solving. They look for elegant and sophisticated technical solutions in which hardware and software efficiency is optimized at the expense of ease of use or organizational effectiveness. Users, on the other

Table 14.2 THE USER–DESIGNER COMMUNICATIONS GAP

User Concerns	Designer Concerns
Will the system deliver the information I need for my work?	How much disk storage space will the master file consume?
How quickly can I access the data?	How many lines of program code will it take to perform this function?
How easily can I retrieve the data?	How can we cut down on CPU time when we run the system?
How much clerical support will I need to enter data into the system?	What is the most efficient way of storing this piece of data?
How will the operation of the system fit into my daily business schedule?	What database management system should we use?

hand, prefer systems that are oriented to solving business problems or facilitating organizational tasks. Often the orientations of both groups are so at odds that they appear to speak in different tongues. These differences are illustrated in Table 14.2, which depicts the typical concerns of end users and technical specialists (information system designers) regarding the development of a new information system. Communication problems between end users and designers are a major reason why user requirements are not properly incorporated into information systems and why users are driven out of the implementation process.

Systems development projects run a very high risk of failure when there is a pronounced gap between users and technicians and when these groups continue to pursue different goals. Under such conditions, users are often driven out of the implementation process. Participation in the implementation effort is extremely time-consuming and takes them away from their daily activities and responsibilities. Since they cannot comprehend what the technicians are saying, the entire project is best left in the hands of the information system specialists alone. With so many implementation efforts guided by purely technical considerations, it is no wonder that many systems fail to serve organizational needs.

MANAGEMENT SUPPORT   If an information systems project has the backing and approval of management at various levels, it is more likely to be perceived positively by both users and the technical information services staff. Both groups will feel that their participation in the development process will receive higher-level attention and priority. They will be recognized and rewarded for the time and effort they devote to implementation. Management backing also ensures that a systems project will receive sufficient funding and resources to be successful. Furthermore, all of the changes in work habits and procedures and any organizational realignments associated with a new system depend on management backing to be enforced effectively. If a manager considers a new system to be a priority, the system will more likely be treated that way by his or her subordinates (Doll, 1985; Ein-Dor et al., 1978).

LEVEL OF COMPLEXITY   Systems differ dramatically in their size, scope, level of complexity, and organi-
AND RISK   zational and technical components. Some systems development projects, such as the Confirm project described in the Window on Technology, are more likely to fail because they carry a much higher level of risk than others.

Researchers have identified three key dimensions that influence the level of project risk (McFarlan, 1981).

Project Size. The larger the project—as indicated by the dollars spent, the size of the implementation staff, the time allocated to implementation, and the number of organizational units affected—the greater the risk. Therefore, a $5 million

TECHNOLOGY

Do Mega-Projects Have Mega-Problems?

In March 1988, the Hilton Hotels Corporation, Marriott Corporation, Budget Rent-A-Car Corporation, and AMR, the parent company of American Airlines, joined forces to develop Confirm, the first system to fully integrate hotel, rental car, and airline reservations. The system was supposed to be completed in June 1992 at a cost of $125 million. Five hundred technical personnel worked on the project. But after more than three years of work, it was delayed another 18 months. The International Reservations and Information Consortium (Intrico) overseeing the project discovered major problems when the system was tested on site by the Hilton Hotels Corporation. Hilton users found that the system's user interface, mainframe transaction processing, and mainframe database did not adequately communicate with each other.

Confirm runs on two IBM 3090 mainframes. One houses the central reservations system, which runs under Transaction Processing Facility (a special operating system environment for processing heavy volumes of transactions). The other mainframe houses a DB2 relational database in a MVS (an IBM mainframe operating system)

environment. The database contains decision support information such as customer histories and pricing data. The system requires application-to-application bridging between the two CPUs for some sixty applications. When processing the internal transactions, the operating systems and application software on both computers must be closely coordinated.

Intrico used Information Engineering Facility (IEF), Texas Instrument's CASE product to automatically generate the software code that ran on the MVS operating system. However, IEF could not generate the right code to make the software that allows the two machines to communicate with the outside world work properly. This software front end, called Transaction Management Function, served as a gateway to the various airline, hotel, and rental car airport reservation systems and would direct incoming data from each center to the appropriate mainframe. The software running on the mainframe using Transaction Processing Facility was written in the C programming language.

When it came time to connect the two separately developed system

modules, Intrico found that they did not communicate very well. The program sending information from one processor could not coordinate with the program receiving information in the other processor. In the event of a system crash, Confirm's DB2 database could be recovered only in pieces, not in its entirety. The problems were not insurmountable, but they would require another two years to fix. In September 1992, AMR sued the other three Confirm partners for breach of contract. Marriott countersued two days later.

Sources: John P. McPartlin, "The Collapse of Confirm," *InformationWEEK,* October 19, 1992; and Clinton Wilder, "Travel System Delayed til 93," Computerworld, May 11, 1992.

To Think About: Evaluate the level of complexity and risk in this project. What management, organization, and technology issues had to be addressed by the Confirm system? What problems did the project encounter? Why do you think the project had these problems? How might they have been avoided?

project lasting for four years and affecting five departments in twenty operating units and 120 users will be much riskier than a $30,000 project for two users that can be completed in two months. Another risk factor is the company's experience with projects of given sizes. If a company is accustomed to implementing large, costly systems, the risk of implementing the $5 million project will be lowered. The risk may even be lower than that of another concern attempting a $200,000 project when the firm's average project cost has been around $50,000.

Project Structure. Some projects are more highly structured than others. Their requirements are clear and straightforward, so that the outputs and processes can be easily defined. Users know exactly what they want and what the system should do; there is almost no possibility of their changing their minds. Such projects run a much lower risk than those whose requirements are relatively undefined, fluid, and constantly changing, where outputs cannot be easily fixed because they are subject to users' changing ideas or because users cannot agree on what they want.

Experience with Technology. The project risk will rise if the project team and the information system staff lack the required technical expertise. If the team is

Table 14.3 DIMENSIONS OF PROJECT RISK

Project Structure	Project Technology Level	Project Size	Degree of Risk
High	Low	Large	Low
High	Low	Small	Very low
High	High	Large	Medium
High	High	Small	Medium-low
Low	Low	Large	Low
Low	Low	Small	Very low
Low	High	Large	Very high
Low	High	Small	High

unfamiliar with the hardware, system software, application software, or database management system proposed for the project, it is highly likely that one or all of the following will occur:

- Unanticipated time slippage because of the need to master new skills.
- A variety of technical problems if tools have not been thoroughly mastered.
- Excessive expenditures and extra time because of inexperience with the undocumented idiosyncracies of each new piece of hardware or software.

These dimensions of project risk will be present in different combinations for each implementation effort. Table 14.3 shows that eight different combinations are possible, each with a different degree of risk. The higher the level of risk, the more likely it is that the implementation effort will fail.

MANAGEMENT OF THE IMPLEMENTATION PROCESS

The development of a new system must be carefully managed and orchestrated. Each project involves research and development. Requirements are hard to define at the level of detail for automation. The same piece of information may be interpreted and defined differently by different individuals. Multiple users have different sets of requirements and needs. Costs, benefits, and project schedules must be assessed. The final design may not be easy to visualize. Since complex information systems involve so many interest groups, actors, and details, it is sometimes uncertain whether the initial plans for a system are truly feasible.

Often basic elements of success are forgotten. Training to ensure that end users are comfortable with the new system and fully understand its potential uses is often sacrificed or forgotten in system development projects. In part this is because the budget is strained toward the end of a project, and at the very point of startup there are insufficient funds for training (Bikson et al., 1985).

The conflicts and uncertainties inherent in any implementation effort will be magnified when an implementation project is poorly managed and organized. As illustrated in Figure 14.6, a systems development project without proper management will most likely suffer these consequences:

- Cost overruns that vastly exceed budgets.
- Time slippage that is much greater than expected.
- Technical shortfalls resulting in performance that is significantly below the estimated level.
- Failure to obtain anticipated benefits.

Figure 14.6
Consequences of poor project management. Without proper management, a systems development project will take longer to complete and most often will exceed the budgeted cost. The resulting information system will most likely be technically inferior and may not be able to demonstrate any benefits to the organization.

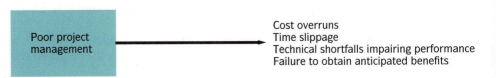

Poor project management → Cost overruns
Time slippage
Technical shortfalls impairing performance
Failure to obtain anticipated benefits

How badly are projects managed? On average, private-sector projects are underestimated by one-half in terms of budget and time required to deliver the complete system promised in the system plan. A very large number of projects are delivered with missing functionality (promised for delivery in later versions). Government projects suffer about the same failure level, perhaps worse (Laudon, 1989; Helms and Weiss, 1986).

Why are projects managed so poorly and what can be done about it? Here we discuss some possibilities.

IGNORANCE AND OPTIMISM

The techniques for estimating the length of time required to analyze and design systems are poorly developed. There are no standards; there is little sharing of data within and across organizations; and most applications are "first time" (i.e., there is no prior experience in the application area). Academics generally do not study large-scale commercial systems, but instead focus on small-scale, easily taught or learned software projects. The larger the scale of systems, the greater the role of ignorance and optimism. Very large scale systems (VLSS)—sometimes called Grand Design systems—suffer extraordinary rates of failure (Laudon, 1989; United States General Services Administration, 1988). The net result of all these factors is that estimates tend to be optimistic, "best case," and wrong. It is assumed that all will go well when in fact it rarely does.

THE MYTHICAL MAN-MONTH

Man-month: The traditional unit of measurement used by systems designers to estimate the length of time to complete a project. Refers to the amount of work a person can be expected to complete in a month.

The traditional unit of measurement used by systems designers to project costs is the **man-month.** Projects are estimated in terms of how many man-months will be required. However, while costs may vary as a product of people and months, the progress of the project does not, as pointed out by Frederick P. Brooks (Brooks, 1974). As it turns out, people and months are not interchangeable in the short run on systems projects. (They may be interchangeable in the long run, but we live in the short run.) In other words, adding more workers to projects does not necessarily reduce the time needed to complete a systems project.

Unlike cotton picking, where tasks can be rigidly partitioned, communication between participants is not required, and training is unnecessary, systems analysis and design involves *tasks that are sequentially linked, cannot be performed in isolation, and require extensive communications and training.* Software development is inherently a group effort, and hence communication costs rise exponentially as the number of participants increases. Moreover, when personnel turnover approaches 20 to 30 percent, many of the participants in software projects require a great deal of learning and communication.

Given these characteristics, adding labor to projects can often slow down delivery, as the communication, learning, and coordination costs rise very fast and detract from the output of participants. For comparison, imagine what would happen if five amateur spectators were added to one team in a championship professional basketball game. Chances are quite good that the team composed of five professional basketball players would do much better in the short run than the team with five professionals and five amateurs.

FALLING BEHIND: BAD NEWS TRAVELS SLOWLY UPWARD

Slippage in projects, failure, and doubts are often not reported to senior management until it is too late. To some extent, this is characteristic of projects in all fields. The crash of the space shuttle Challenger in January 1986 exemplifies this problem.

The information that O-ring seals on the space shuttle might not perform well in the cold January weather and that engineers strongly objected to launching the shuttle in cold weather did not reach the top National Aeronautics and Space Administration (NASA) management team, which ultimately decided to launch. The reasons, while not entirely clear, in part involve the well-understood principle that bearers of bad news are often not appreciated and that senior management wants schedules to be met.

Organizational hierarchy has a pathological and deadly side: Senior management is often kept in the dark (see Chapters 4 and 5). For systems projects, this seems to be especially true. Systems workers know that management has promised a delivery date to important user groups, that millions of dollars have been spent, and that careers depend on timely delivery of the whole system. As the project falls behind, one day at a time, no one wants to bother senior management with minor slippage details. Eventually, days add up to months and then to years. By then it is too late to save the project, no matter how many people are added to the team.

The Implementation Process: What Can Go Wrong

The following problems are considered typical for each stage of systems development when the implementation process is poorly managed.

ANALYSIS

- Time, money, and resources have not been allocated to researching the problem. The problem remains poorly defined. Objectives of the implementation project will be vague and ambiguous; benefits will be difficult to measure.

- Little or no time is spent in preliminary planning. There are no standards to use in estimating preliminary costs or the duration of the project.

- The project team is not properly staffed. Personnel are assigned on an as-available basis and cannot dedicate themselves to the project. User groups to be served by the system are not represented on the team.

- The information services staff promises results that are impossible to deliver.

- Requirements are derived from inadequate documentation of existing systems or incomplete findings from systems study activities.

- Users refuse to spend any time helping the project team gather the requisite information.
- Project analysts cannot interview users properly. They do not know how to ask the right questions. They cannot carry on an extended conversation with users because they lack good communications skills.

DESIGN
- Users have no responsibility for or input to design activities. The design, therefore, reflects the biases of the technical staff. It does not mesh well with the structure, activities, and culture of the organization or the priorities of management.
- The system is designed only to serve current needs. No flexibility has been built in to anticipate the future needs of the organization.
- Drastic changes in clerical procedures or staffing are planned without any organizational impact analysis.
- Functional specifications are inadequately documented.

PROGRAMMING
- The amount of time and money required for software development is underestimated.
- Programmers are supplied with incomplete specifications.
- Not enough time is devoted to the development of program logic; too much time is wasted on writing code.
- Programmers do not take full advantage of structured design or object-oriented techniques. They write programs that are difficult to modify and maintain.
- Programs are not adequately documented.
- Requisite resources (such as computer time) are not scheduled.

TESTING
- The amount of time and money required for proper testing is underestimated.
- The project team does not develop an organized test plan.
- Users are not sufficiently involved in testing. They do not help to create sample test data or review test results. They refuse to devote much time to the testing effort.
- The implementation team does not develop appropriate acceptance tests for management review. Management does not review and sign off on test results.

CONVERSION
- Insufficient time and money are budgeted for conversion activities, especially for data conversion.
- Not all of the individuals who will use the system are involved until conversion begins. Training begins only when the system is about to be installed.
- The system is made operational before it is fully ready to compensate for cost overruns and delays.
- System and user documentation is inadequate.
- Performance evaluations are not conducted. No performance standards are established, and the results of the system are not weighed against the original objectives.
- Provisions for system maintenance are inadequate. Insufficient information systems personnel are trained to support the system and to make maintenance changes.

14.3 Managing Implementation

Not all aspects of the implementation process can be easily controlled or planned (Alter and Ginzberg, 1978). However, the chances for system success can be increased by anticipating potential implementation problems and applying appropriate corrective strategies. Various project management, requirements gathering, and planning methodologies have been developed for specific categories of problems. Strategies have also been devised for ensuring that users play an appropriate role throughout the implementation period and for managing the organizational change process.

Controlling Risk Factors

One way implementation can be improved is by adjusting the project management strategy to the level of risk inherent in each project. If a systems development project is placed in the proper risk category, levels of risk can be predicted in advance and strategies developed to counteract high-risk factors (McFarlan, 1981).

Implementers must adopt a contingency approach to project management, handling each project with the tools, project management methodologies, and organizational linkages geared to its level of risk. There are four basic project management techniques:

1. External integration tools link the work of the implementation team to that of users at all organizational levels.
2. Internal integration tools ensure that the implementation team operates as a cohesive unit.

Table 14.4 STRATEGIES TO MANAGE PROJECTS BY CONTROLLING RISKS

Project Structure	Project Technology Level	Project Size	Degree of Risk	Project Management Tool
1. High	Low	Large	Low	High use of formal planning High use of formal control
2. High	Low	Small	Very low	High use of formal control Medium use of formal planning
3. High	High	Large	Medium	Medium use of formal control Medium use of formal planning
4. High	High	Small	Medium-low	High internal integration
5. Low	Low	Large	Low	High external integration High use of formal planning High use of formal control
6. Low	Low	Small	Very low	High external integration High use of formal control
7. Low	High	Large	Very high	High external integration High internal integration
8. Low	High	Small	High	High external integration High internal integration

3. Formal planning tools structure and sequence tasks, providing advance estimates of the time, money, and technical resources required to execute them.
4. Formal control tools help monitor the progress toward goals.

The risk profile of each project will determine the appropriate project management technique to apply, as illustrated in Table 14.4.

EXTERNAL INTEGRATION TOOLS

External integration tools: Project management technique that links the work of the implementation team to that of users at all organizational levels.

Projects with relatively *little structure* must involve users fully at all stages. Users must be mobilized to support one of many possible design options and to remain committed to a single design. Therefore, **external integration tools** must be applied.

- Users can be selected as project leaders or as the second-in-command on a project team.
- User steering committees can be created to evaluate the system's design.
- Users can become active members of the project team.
- The project can require formal user review and approval of specifications.
- Minutes of all key design meetings can be distributed widely among users.
- Users can prepare the status reports for higher management.
- Users can be put in charge of training and installation.
- Users can be responsible for change control, putting a brake on all nonessential changes to the system once final design specifications have been completed.

INTERNAL INTEGRATION TOOLS

Internal integration tools: Project management technique that ensures that the implementation team operates as a cohesive unit.

Projects with *high levels of technology* benefit from **internal integration tools.** The success of such projects depends on how well their technical complexity can be managed. Project leaders need both heavy technical and administrative experience. They must be able to anticipate problems and develop smooth working relationships among a predominantly technical team.

- Team members should be highly experienced.
- The team should be under the leadership of a manager with a strong technical and project management background.
- Team meetings should take place frequently, with routine distribution of meeting minutes concerning key design decisions.
- The team should hold regular technical status reviews.
- A high percentage of the team should have a history of good working relationships with each other.
- Team members should participate in setting goals and establishing target dates.
- Essential technical skills or expertise not available internally should be secured from outside the organization.

FORMAL PLANNING AND CONTROL TOOLS

Formal planning tools: Project management technique that structures and sequences tasks; budgeting time, money, and technical resources required to complete the tasks.

Projects with *high structure* and *low technology* present the lowest risk. The design is fixed and stable and the project does not pose any technical challenges. If such projects are large, they can be successfully managed by **formal planning and control tools.** With project management techniques such as PERT (Program Evaluation and Review Technique) or Gantt charts, a detailed plan can be developed. (PERT lists the specific activities that make up a project, their duration, and the activities that must be completed before a specific activity can start. A

Gantt chart such as that illustrated in Figure 14.7 visually represents the sequence and timing of different tasks in a development project, as well as their resource requirements.) Tasks can be defined and resources budgeted. These project management techniques can help managers identify bottlenecks and determine the impact problems will have on project completion times.

- Milestone phases can be selected.
- Specifications can be developed from the feasibility study.
- Specification standards can be established.
- Processes for project approval can be developed.

Standard control techniques will successfully chart the progress of the project against budgets and target dates, so that the implementation team can make adjustments to meet their original schedule.

Figure 14.7

Formal planning and control tools help to manage information systems projects successfully. The Gantt chart in this figure was produced by a commercially available project management software package. It shows the task, man-days, and initials of each responsible person, as well as the start and finish dates for each task. The resource summary provides a good manager with the total man-days for each month and for each person working on the project to successfully manage the project. The project described here is a data administration project.

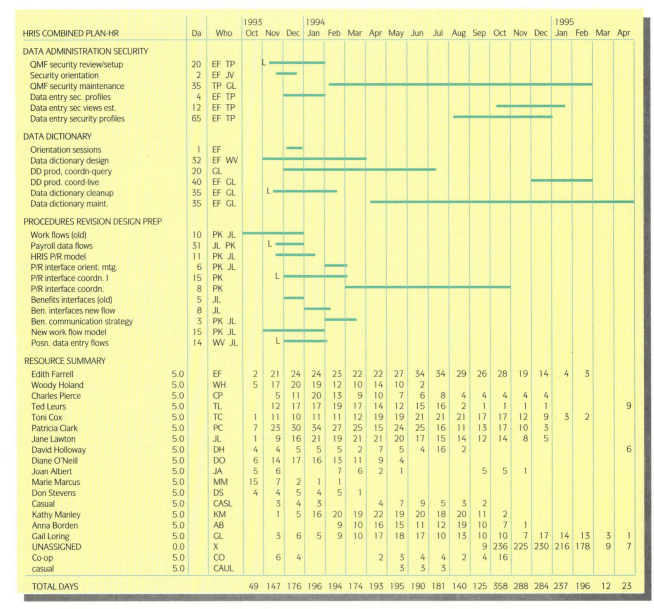

HRIS COMBINED PLAN-HR

Task	Da	Who
DATA ADMINISTRATION SECURITY		
QMF security review/setup	20	EF TP
Security orientation	2	EF JV
QMF security maintenance	35	TP GL
Data entry sec. profiles	4	EF TP
Data entry sec views est.	12	EF TP
Data entry security profiles	65	EF TP
DATA DICTIONARY		
Orientation sessions	1	EF
Data dictionary design	32	EF WV
DD prod, coordn-query	20	GL
DD prod. coord-live	40	EF GL
Data dictionary cleanup	35	EF GL
Data dictionary maint.	35	EF GL
PROCEDURES REVISION DESIGN PREP		
Work flows (old)	10	PK JL
Payroll data flows	31	JL PK
HRIS P/R model	11	PK JL
P/R interface orient. mtg.	6	PK JL
P/R interface coordn. I	15	PK
P/R interface coordn.	8	PK
Benefits interfaces (old)	5	JL
Ben. interfaces new flow	8	JL
Ben. communication strategy	3	PK JL
New work flow model	15	PK JL
Posn. data entry flows	14	WV JL

RESOURCE SUMMARY

Name		Who	Oct 93	Nov	Dec	Jan 94	Feb	Mar	Apr	May	Jun	Jul	Aug	Sep	Oct	Nov	Dec	Jan 95	Feb	Mar	Apr
Edith Farrell	5.0	EF	2	21	24	24	23	22	22	27	34	34	29	26	28	19	14	4	3		
Woody Holand	5.0	WH	5	17	20	19	12	10	14	10	2										
Charles Pierce	5.0	CP		5	11	20	13	9	10	7	6	8	4	4	4	4	4				
Ted Leurs	5.0	TL		12	17	17	19	17	14	12	15	16	2	1	1	1	1				9
Toni Cox	5.0	TC	1	11	10	11	11	12	19	19	21	21	21	17	17	12	9	3	2		
Patricia Clark	5.0	PC	7	23	30	34	27	25	15	24	25	16	11	13	17	10	3				
Jane Lawton	5.0	JL	1	9	16	21	19	21	21	20	17	15	14	12	14	8	5				
David Holloway	5.0	DH	4	4	5	5	5	2	7	5	4	16	2								6
Diane O'Neill	5.0	DO	6	14	17	16	13	11	9	4											
Joan Albert	5.0	JA	5	6			7	6	2	1					5	5	1				
Marie Marcus	5.0	MM	15	7	2	1	1														
Don Stevens	5.0	DS	4	4	5	4	5	1													
Casual	5.0	CASL		3	4	3			4	7	9	5	3	2							
Kathy Manley	5.0	KM		1	5	16	20	19	22	19	20	18	20	11	2						
Anna Borden	5.0	AB					9	10	16	15	11	12	19	10	7	1					
Gail Loring	5.0	GL		3	6	5	9	10	17	18	17	10	13	10	10	7	17	14	13	3	1
UNASSIGNED	0.0	X												9	236	225	230	216	178	9	7
Co-op	5.0	CO		6	4				2	3	4	4	2	4	16						
casual	5.0	CAUL								3	3	3									
TOTAL DAYS			49	147	176	196	194	174	193	195	190	181	140	125	358	288	284	237	196	12	23

Albert Lederer, Professor of MIS at Oakland University in Rochester, Michigan, and Jayesh Prasad, Assistant Professor of MIS at the University of Dayton, in Dayton, Ohio, studied information systems projects at 115 organizations, including manufacturing, insurance, and banking firms, and government organizations. They found that 63 percent of these organizations had major information systems projects that were "significantly" over budget. More than three-fourths of the respondents had mistakenly estimated the cost of their projects.

Why is this problem so pervasive? Why do managers have such problems estimating information system development costs? Lederer and Prasad suggested five top reasons: 1. Users frequently request changes. 2. Tasks required by the project are overlooked. 3. Users do not understand their own information requirements. 4. The problem that the new information system is supposed to solve is poorly defined. 5. Users and technical specialists cannot communicate with and understand each other.

Everyone wants to know how to develop accurate cost estimates.

Lederer and Prasad developed the following guidelines, based on what their survey respondents said they did right and what they did wrong.

1. Assign the initial task of estimating cost to the people who will be developing the system, and review the estimates both with information systems management and with business management. Lederer and Prasad found that companies with high cost overruns used different systems analysts to estimate costs and to design and program the system. Having both technical and business managers involved increases the chances of a solid estimate.

2. Try to anticipate the frequency and extent of user changes and keep them under control. The 115 companies studied rated user changes as the factor most responsible for inaccurate cost estimates. System developers need to understand the business functions of users to establish as many user requirements up front as possible, but the developers should also anticipate users requesting some changes as the project goes on. Some firms try to discourage unnecessary user changes to keep

their projects on target. For instance, Dayton Power requires executive approval before changes to a project can be made.

3. Base estimates on documented facts, standards and mathematical formulas rather than guesses, intuition, and personal memory.

4. Use a formal monitoring process to monitor the progress of the project.

Source: Albert L. Lederer and Jayesh Prasad, "Putting Estimates on Track," *Computerworld*, August 24, 1992.

To Think About: Which of the four project management techniques are reflected in these recommendations? To what extent can these recommendations produce accurate cost estimates for information system projects? What management, organization, and technology issues in implementation do these recommendations address?

- Disciplines to control or freeze the design can be maintained.
- Deviations from the plan can be spotted.
- Periodic formal status reports against the plan will show the extent of progress.

The Window on Management describes some recommendations for managers who hope to control information system project costs that reflect these project management strategies.

OVERCOMING USER
RESISTANCE

In addition to fine-tuning project management strategies, implementation risks can be reduced by securing management and user support of the implementation effort. Section 14.2 has shown how user participation in the design process builds commitment to the system. The final product is more likely to reflect users' requirements. Users are more likely to feel that they control and own the system. Users are also more likely to feel satisfied with an information system if they have been trained to use it properly (Cronan and Douglas, 1990).

However, MIS researchers have also noted that systems development is not an entirely rational process. Users leading design activities have used their position to further private interests and to gain power rather than to promote organizational objectives (Franz and Robey, 1984).

Participation in implementation activities may not be enough to overcome the problem of user resistance. The implementation process demands organizational change. Such change may be resisted because different users may be affected by the system in different ways. While some users may welcome a new system because it brings changes they perceive as beneficial to them, others may resist these changes because they believe the shifts are detrimental to their interests (Joshi, 1991).

If the use of a system is voluntary, users may choose to avoid it; if use is mandatory, resistance will take the form of increased error rates, disruptions, turnover, and even sabotage. Therefore, the implementation strategy must not only encourage user participation and involvement; it must also address the issue of counterimplementation (Keen, 1981). **Counterimplementation** is a deliberate strategy to thwart the implementation of an information system or an innovation in an organization.

Researchers have explained user resistance with one of three theories (Markus, 1983; Davis and Olson, 1985):

1. **People-oriented theory.** Factors internal to users as individuals or as a group produce resistance. For instance, users may resist a new system or any change at all because they are lazy and do not wish to learn new ways of doing things.

2. **System-oriented theory.** Factors inherent in the design create user resistance to a system. For instance, users may resist a system because its user interface is confusing and they have trouble learning how to make the system work.

3. **Interaction theory.** Resistance is caused by the interaction of people and systems factors. For instance, the system may be well designed and welcomed by some users but resisted by others who fear it will take away some of their power or stature in the organization.

Strategies have been suggested to overcome each form of user resistance:

People-oriented: User education (training)
                                       Coercion (edicts, policies)
                                       Persuasion
                                       User participation (to elicit commitment)

System-oriented: User education
                                       Improved human factors (user/system interface)
                                       User participation (for improved design)
                                       Package modification to conform to organizational procedures

Interaction: Solve organizational problems before introducing new systems
                                       Restructure incentives for users
                                       Restructure the user–designer relationship
                                       Promote user participation when appropriate

Strategies appropriate for the interaction theory incorporate elements of people-oriented and system-oriented strategies. There may be situations in which user participation is not appropriate. For example, some users may react negatively to a new design even though its overall benefits outweigh its drawbacks. Some individuals may stand to lose power as a result of design decisions (Robey and Markus, 1984). In this instance, participation in design may actually exacerbate resentment and resistance.

Counterimplementation: A deliberate strategy to thwart the implementation of an information system or an innovation in an organization.

People-oriented theory: User-resistance theory focusing on factors internal to users.

System-oriented theory: User-resistance theory focusing on factors inherent in the design of the system.

Interaction theory: User-resistance theory stating that resistance is caused by the interaction of people and systems factors.

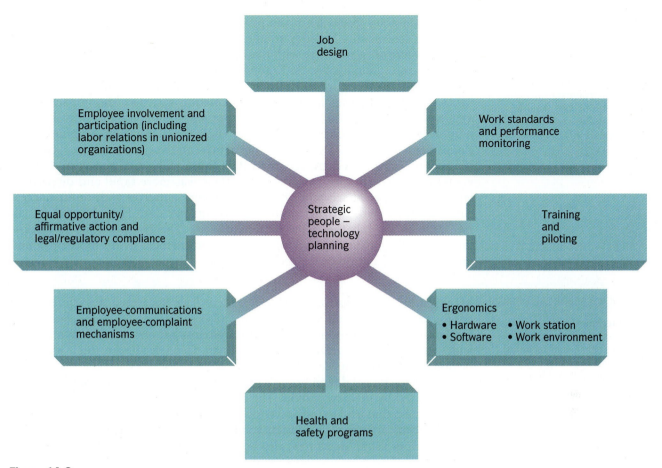

Figure 14.8
Key human organizational factors for office automation planning and implementation.
For successful implementation, the planner must consider ergonomics, training, employee
communications, employee participation, and legal/regulatory factors. *Reprinted with permission of
G. K. Hall & Co., an imprint of Macmillan Publishing Company, from* The Changing Workplace *by
Alan F. Westin et al. Copyright © 1985 by G. K. Hall & Co.*

Designing for the Organization

The entire systems development process can be viewed as planned organizational
change, since the purpose of a new system is to improve the organization's
performance. Therefore, the development process must explicitly address the
ways in which the organization will change when the new system is installed. In
addition to procedural changes, transformations in job functions, organizational
structure, power relationships, and behavior will all have to be carefully planned.
For example, Figure 14.8 illustrates the organizational dimensions that would
need to be addressed for planning and implementing office automation systems.

Although systems analysis and design activities are supposed to include an
organizational impact analysis, this area has traditionally been neglected. An
organizational impact analysis explains how a proposed system will affect organizational structure, attitudes, decision making, and operations. To integrate
information systems successfully with the organization, thorough and fully documented organizational impact assessments must be given more attention in the
development effort.

**Organizational impact
analysis:** Study of the way a
proposed system will affect
organizational structure,
attitudes, decision making,
and operations.

ALLOWING FOR THE
HUMAN FACTOR

The quality of information systems should be evaluated in terms of user criteria
rather than the criteria of the information systems staff. In addition to targets
such as memory size, access rates, and calculation times, systems objectives
should include standards for user performance. For example, an objective might

be that data entry clerks learn the procedures and codes for four new on-line data entry screens in a half-day training session.

Areas where users interface with the system should be carefully designed, with sensitivity to ergonomic issues. **Ergonomics** refers to the interaction of people and machines in the work environment. It considers the design of jobs, health issues, and the end-user interface of information systems. The impact of the application system on the work environment and job dimensions must be carefully assessed. One noteworthy study of 620 Social Security Administration claims representatives showed that the representatives with on-line access to claims data experienced greater stress than those with serial access to the data via teletype. Even though the on-line interface was more rapid and direct than teletype, it created much more frustration. Representatives with on-line access could interface with a larger number of clients per day. This changed the dimensions of the job for claims representatives. The restructuring of work—involving tasks, quality of working life, and performance—had a more profound impact than the nature of the technology itself (Turner, 1984).

Ergonomics: The interaction of people and machines in the work environment, including the design of jobs, health issues, and the end-user interface of information systems.

SOCIOTECHNICAL DESIGN

Sociotechnical design: Design to produce information systems that blend technical efficiency with sensitivity to organizational and human needs.

Management and organizational researchers have suggested a *sociotechnical* approach to information system design and organizational change. **Sociotechnical design** aims to produce information systems that blend technical efficiency with sensitivity to organizational and human needs, leading to high job satisfaction (Mumford and Weir, 1979).

The sociotechnical design process emphasizes participation by the individuals most affected by the new system. The design plan establishes human objectives for the system that lead to increased job satisfaction. Designers set forth separate sets of technical and social design solutions. The social design plans explore different work group structures, allocation of tasks, and the design of individual jobs.

The proposed technical solutions are compared with the proposed social solutions. Social and technical solutions that can be combined are proposed as sociotechnical solutions. The alternative that best meets both social and technical objectives is selected for the final design. Systems with compatible technical and organizational elements are expected to raise productivity without sacrificing human and social goals.

Management Challenges

1. **Organizational inertia.** In the absence of an organizational crisis, it is difficult to focus organizational attention and resources on developing new systems because organizations are so resistant to change. Much large-scale system development is initiated in periods of organizational crisis, and is not planned. These periods are not well-suited to rational planning and implementation.

2. **Dealing with the complexity of large-scale systems projects.** Large-scale systems that affect large numbers of organizational units and staff members and that have extensive information requirements are difficult to oversee, coordinate, and plan for. Implementing such systems, which have multi-year development periods, is especially problem-ridden because the systems are so complex.

3. **Estimating the time and cost to implement a successful large information system.** There are few reliable techniques for estimating the time and cost to develop medium- to large-scale information systems. Few projects take into account the long-term maintenance costs of systems. Guidelines presented in this chapter are helpful but cannot guarantee that a large information system project can be precisely planned and given a projected budget.

Summary

Identify major problem areas in information systems.

A high percentage of systems are considered failures because they are not used in the way they were intended. Some are not used at all. System failure is evidenced by problems with design, data, operations, or costs. The sources of system success or failure are primarily behavioral and organizational.

Determine whether a system is successful.

Criteria for evaluating the success of an information system include 1) level of system use, 2) user satisfaction, 3) favorable user attitudes about the information systems staff, 4) achieved objectives, and 5) financial payoff to the organization.

Describe the principal causes of information system failure.

The principal causes of information system failure are 1) insufficient or improper user participation in the systems development process, 2) lack of management support, 3) poor management of the implementation process, and 4) high levels of complexity and risk in systems development projects.

Describe the relationship between the implementation process and system outcome.

Implementation is the entire process of organizational change surrounding the introduction of a new information system. One can better understand system success and failure by examining different patterns of implementation. Especially important is the relationship between participants in the implementation process, notably the interactions between system designers and users. Conflicts between the technical orientation of system designers and the business orientation of end users must be resolved. The success of organizational change can be determined by how well information systems specialists, end users, and decision makers deal with key issues at various stages in implementation.

Describe appropriate strategies to manage the implementation process.

Management support and control of the implementation process are essential, as are mechanisms for dealing with the level of risk in each new systems project. Some companies experience organizational resistance to change. Project risk factors can be brought under some control by a contingency approach to project management. The level of risk in a systems development project is determined by three key dimensions: 1) project size, 2) project structure, and 3) experience with technology. The risk level of each project will determine the appropriate mix of external integration tools, internal integration tools, formal planning tools, and formal control tools to be applied.

Appropriate strategies can be applied to ensure the correct level of user participation in the systems development process and to minimize user resistance. Information system design and the entire implementation process should be managed as planned organizational change. Sociotechnical design emphasizes the participation of the individuals most affected by a new system and aims for an optimal blend of social and technical design solutions.

Key Terms

System failure	Formal control tools
User interface	Counterimplementation
Implementation	People-oriented theory
Change agent	System-oriented theory
User-designer communications gap	Interaction theory
Man-month	Organizational impact analysis
External integration tools	Ergonomics
Internal integration tools	Sociotechnical design
Formal planning tools	

1. What do we mean by information system failure?

2. What kinds of problems are evidence of information system failure?

3. How can we measure system success? Which measures of system success are the most important?

4. Define implementation. What are the major approaches to implementation?

5. Why is it necessary to understand the concept of implementation when examining system success and failure?

6. What are the major causes of implementation success or failure?

7. What is the user–designer communications gap? What kinds of implementation problems can it create?

8. List some of the implementation problems that might occur at each stage of the systems development process.

9. What dimensions influence the level of risk in each systems development project?

10. What project management techniques can be used to control project risk?

11. What strategies can be used to overcome user resistance to systems development projects?

12. What organizational considerations should be addressed by information system design?

1. You are a member of your corporation's management committee, which oversees and approves systems development projects. What criteria would you consider in evaluating new project proposals? What would you look for to determine whether the project was proceeding successfully?

2. A prominent MIS researcher has observed that "The reason most information systems have failed is that we have ignored organizational behavior problems in the design and operation of computer-based information systems" (Lucas, 1974). Discuss.

Form a group with two or three other students. Write a description of the implementation problems you might expect to encounter for the information system you designed for your systems analysis and design project. Write an analysis of the steps you would take to solve or prevent these problems. Alternatively, you could describe the implementation problems that might be expected for one of the systems described in the Window on boxes or chapter-ending cases in this text. Present your findings to the class.

CASE STUDY

Federal Bailout Agency's Systems Need Bailing Out

When the Resolution Trust Corporation was established in 1989, it was supposed to help the federal government recover many billions of dollars spent trying to bail out failing savings and loan institutions. But federal investigators reported that RTC became a fiscal nightmare in its own right. Inept information systems could cost the U.S. taxpayer a sizable portion of what RTC was intended to save.

In February 1992 the General Accounting Office, the Congressional audit agency, testified before the House Committee on Banking, Finance and Urban Affairs that RTC did not have adequate systems in place to support its critical mission of managing and selling assets. It described RTC's information systems as "plagued with fundamental problems" including inaccurate and incomplete data, poor response times and non-user friendly software. A source within the House Banking Committee admitted that there is no system in Washington that lets RTC know what assets they have and what should be done. These matters should have been planned before RTC was opened. RTC appeared to have done no information systems planning.

GAO found specific problems with all of RTC's major

systems—real estate, loan inventory, asset management, and contract oversight systems—to the point where it believed RTC could not get any real benefit out of its systems. For instance, in 1990 a man wanted to buy property that RTC had listed for sale in Maryland for $3 million. He tried for over a year to contact RTC to make a purchase offer but was unable to contact anyone familiar with the property. In RTC's files, no one could even locate the land he was interested in. Then, in 1991, at a RTC auction the same man successfully bid on the property for only $700,000, more than $2 million less than what he had been willing to pay a year earlier.

While the RTC's national sales office was selling properties in 1991 to Patriot American Investors, a group of American and Canadian investors, RTC's regional sales offices were still competing with each other to sell properties from the same pool. Some packaged properties were not deleted from the RTC database of assets. RTC found itself selling land that had already been sold.

Another system intended to oversee contracts was unable to indicate whether the services or goods in question had arrived on schedule, how much they had cost, or whether they had been delivered at all.

The General Accounting Office believes that RTC's real estate systems are only 60 percent accurate. RTC staff members probably felt the same way because they developed their own systems or performed some functions manually. The systems they did develop were incapable of sharing data with RTC headquarters. In both cases, important information was not reported to RTC's central databases.

One instance may have cost taxpayers $7 billion. RTC initiated a Western Region Asset Stratification and Reconciliation project to counteract faulty recordkeeping at its regional site in Denver. The goal of the project was to clean up discrepancies between field ledgers and the RTC's regional ledger in Denver. According to the GAO, record-keeping at the site was haphazard, with little effort made to update the general ledger with changes originating at local thrifts. This left records $7 billion out of balance. The money is largely unaccounted for.

RTC reported to both the board of the FDIC (Federal Deposit Insurance Corporation) and to the Thrift Depositor Protection Oversight Board headed by the Secretary of the Treasury. This may have created the feeling that no one was in charge.

Albert V. Casey, the former chairman of AMR, the parent corporation of American Airlines, was appointed president and CEO of RTC in February 1992. Casey felt that RTC was unable to develop and implement major information systems successfully. To remedy the situation, Casey planned to improve communication between staffers and system developers, to set higher standards of accountability for systems development, to guarantee data quality and integrity, and to institute streamlined approval procedures for new or developing systems projects. In January 1992, Casey transferred the majority of systems development to RTC's operation area to encourage a strong relationship between system users and computer experts. Casey appointed Ed Mahany, the director of office systems development, to take charge of software operations, replacing G. Brooks Dickerson, who still remains in charge of hardware and telecommunications. Critics of RTC claim that Mahany has very little experience managing software projects and that Dickerson may be a scapegoat for problems that existed before he joined RTC.

After the GAO's troubling testimony, Congress awarded RTC another $25 billion, bringing the total to $105 billion that RTC had been awarded as of February 1992. By the time the savings and loan cleanup is completed, the final bill for the bailout could go as high as $500 billion.

Resolution Trust Corporation is not alone. The GAO produces an average of one report per week criticizing various federal agencies for their handling of information systems.

Sources: John P. McPartlin, "S & L Crisis: Federal Bailout Agency Digs the Hole Deeper," *InformationWEEK*, March 2, 1992 and Gary H. Anthes, "Why Uncle Sam Can't Compute," *Computerworld*, May 18, 1992.

Case Study Questions

1. Describe the problems with the Resolution Trust Corporation's information systems. Classify these problems using the categories of information system problems described in this chapter.

2. What management, organization, and technology factors caused these problems?

3. Evaluate the solutions proposed to solve RTC's information system problems. Are they adequate? What would you recommend?

References   Alter, Steven, and Michael Ginzberg. "Managing Uncertainty in MIS Implementation." *Sloan Management Review* vol. 20 (Fall 1978).

Anthes, Gary H. "Why Uncle Sam Can't Compute." *Computerworld* (May 18, 1992).

Barki, Henri, and Jon Hartwick. "Rethinking the Concept of User Involvement." *MIS Quarterly* 13, no. 1 (March 1989).

Baroudi, Jack, Margrethe H. Olsen, and Blake Ives. "An Empirical Study of the Impact of User Involvement on System Usage and Information Satisfaction." *Communications of the ACM* 29, no. 3 (March 1986).

Baroudi, Jack, and Wanda Orlikowski. "A Short Form Measure of User Information Satisfaction: A Psychometric Evaluation and Notes on Use." *Journal of Management Information Systems* 4, no. 4 (Spring 1988).

Batiste, John L. "The Application Profile." *MIS Quarterly* (September 1986).

Best, James D. "The MIS Executive as Change Agent." *Journal of Information Systems Management* (Fall 1985).

Bikson, Tora K., Cathleen Stasz, and D. A. Mankin. "Computer Mediated Work. Individual and Organizational Impact in One Corporate Headquarters." Santa Monica, CA: Rand Corporation, 1985.

Brooks, Frederick P. "The Mythical Man-Month." *Datamation* (December 1974).

Cooper, Randolph B., and Zmud, Robert W. "Information Technology Implementation Research: A Technological Diffusion Approach." *Management Science* 36, no. 2 (February 1990).

Corbato, Fernando J. "On Building Systems that Will Fail." *Communications of the ACM* 34 No. 9 (September 1991).

Cronan, Timothy Paul, and David E. Douglas. "End-user Training and Computing Effectiveness in Public Agencies: An Empirical Study." *Journal of Management Information Systems* 6, no. 4 (Spring 1990).

Davis, Fred R., "Perceived Usefulness, Ease of Use, and User Acceptance of Information Technology." *MIS Quarterly* 13, no. 3 (September 1989).

Davis, Gordon B., and Margrethe H. Olson. "Developing and Implementing Application Systems." *Management Information Systems,* 2nd ed. New York: McGraw-Hill, 1985.

DeLone, William H, and Ephraim R. McLean. "Information System Success: The Quest for the Dependent Variable." *Information Systems Research* 3, no. 1 (March 1992).

Delong, William H. "Determinants of Success for Computer Usage in Small Business." *MIS Quarterly* 12, no. 1 (March 1988).

Doll, William J. "Avenues for Top Management Involvement in Successful MIS Development." *MIS Quarterly* (March 1985).

Ein-Dor, Philip, and Eli Segev. "Organizational Context and the Success of Management Information Systems." *Management Science* 24 (June 1978).

Franz, Charles, and Daniel Robey. "An Investigation of User-Led System Design: Rational and Political Perspectives." *Communications of the ACM* 27 (December 1984).

Ginzberg, M. J. "The Impact of Organizational Characteristics on MIS Design and Implementation." Working paper CRIS 10, GBA 80-110. New York University Center for Research on Information Systems, Computer Applications and Information Systems Area, 1980.

Ginzberg, Michael J. "Early Diagnosis of MIS Implementation Failure: Promising Results and Unanswered Questions." *Management Science* 27 (April 1981).

Gould, John D., and Clayton Lewis. "Designing for Usability: Key Principles and What Designers Think." *Communications of the ACM* 28 (March 1985).

Gullo, Karen. "Stopping Runaways in Their Tracks." *InformationWEEK* (November 13, 1989).

Helms, Glenn L., and Ira R. Weiss. "The Cost of Internally Developed Applications: Analysis of Problems and Cost Control Methods." *Journal of Management Information Systems* (Fall 1986).

Hirscheim, R. A. "User Experience with and Assessment of Participative Systems Design." *MIS Quarterly* (December 1985).

Ives, Blake, Margrethe H. Olson, and Jack J. Baroudi. "The Measurement of User Information Satisfaction." *Communications of the ACM* 26 (October 1983).

Joshi, Kailash. "A Model of Users' Perspective on Change: The Case of Information Systems Technology Implementation." *MIS Quarterly* 15, no. 2 (June 1991).

Keen, Peter W. "Information Systems and Organizational Change." *Communications of the ACM* 24 (January 1981).

Kolb, D. A., and A. L. Frohman. "An Organization Development Approach to Consulting." *Sloan Management Review* 12 (Fall 1970).

Laudon, Kenneth C. "CIOs Beware: Very Large Scale Systems," Center for Research on Information Systems, New York University Stern School of Business, working paper, 1989.

Lederer, Albert L., Rajesh Mirani, Boon Siong Neo, Carol Pollard, Jayesh Prasad, and K. Ramamurthy. "Information System Cost Estimating: A Management Perspective." *MIS Quarterly* 14, no. 2 (June 1990).

Lederer, Albert and Jayesh Prasad. "Nine Management Guidelines for Better Cost Estimating." *Communications of the ACM* 35, no. 2 (February 1992).

Lucas, Henry C., Jr. *Implementation: The Key to Successful Information Systems.* New York: Columbia University Press, 1981.

Lucas, Henry C., Jr. *Toward Creative Systems Design.* New York: Columbia University Press, 1974.

Lucas, Henry C., Jr. *Why Information Systems Fail.* New York: Columbia University Press, 1975.

Markus, M. L. "Power, Politics and MIS Implementation." *Communications of the ACM* 26 (June 1983).

McFarlan, F. Warren. "Portfolio Approach to Information Systems." *Harvard Business Review* (September–October 1981).

McPartlin, John P. "Uncle Sam Calls in the Reserves." *InformationWEEK* (April 27, 1992).

Moore, Gary C., and Izak Benbasat. "Development of an Instrument to Measure the Perceptions of Adopting an Information Technology Innovation." *Information Systems Research* 2, no. 3 (September 1991).

Mumford, Enid, and Mary Weir. *Computer Systems in Work Design: The ETHICS Method.* New York: Wiley, 1979.

Raymond, Louis. "Organizational Context and Information System Success: A Contingency Approach." *Journal of Management Information Systems* 6, no. 4 (Spring 1990).

Robey, Daniel, and M. Lynne Markus. "Rituals in Information System Design." *MIS Quarterly* (March 1984).

Singleton, John P., Ephraim R. McLean, and Edward N. Altman. "Measuring Information Systems Performance." *MIS Quarterly* 12, no. 2 (June 1988).

Swanson, E. Burton. *Information System Implementation.* Homewood, IL: Richard D. Irwin Inc., 1988.

Tait, Peter, and Iris Vessey. "The Effect of User Involvement on System Success: A Contingency Approach." *MIS Quarterly* 12, no. 1 (March 1988).

Tornatsky, Louis G., J. D. Eveland, M. G. Boylan, W. A. Hetzner, E. C. Johnson, D. Roitman, and J. Schneider. *The Process of Technological Innovation: Reviewing the Literature.* Washington, DC: National Science Foundation, 1983.

Turner, Jon A. "Computer Mediated Work: The Interplay Between Technology and Structured Jobs." *Communications of the ACM* 27 (December 1984).

United States General Services Administration. "An Evaluation of the Grand Design Approach to Developing Computer-Based Application Systems." Washington, DC: General Services Administration, September 1988.

Westcott, Russ. "Client Satisfaction: The Yardstick for Measuring MIS Success." *Journal of Information Systems Management* (Fall 1985).

Westin, Alan F., Heather A. Schweder, Michael A. Baker, and Sheila Lehman. *The Changing Workplace.* White Plains, NY, and London: Knowledge Industry Publications, Inc., 1985.

White, Kathy Brittain, and Richard Leifer. "Information Systems Development Success: Perspectives from Project Team Participants." *MIS Quarterly* (September 1986).

Yin, Robert K. "Life Histories of Innovations: How New Practices Become Routinized." *Public Administration Review* (January/February 1981).

Anatomy of an Outsourcing Deal

In early 1990, First Fidelity Bancorporation (FFB) of Newark, New Jersey, ranked 44th in operating efficiency among the 50 largest banks in the United States. The United States was in the midst of a credit crunch, as was FFB. Real estate values were falling as a result of the worsening economy. Federal bank regulators were questioning the value of many banks' assets, First Fidelity's amongst them. The federal government was taking over large numbers of failing banks and selling them off at bargain prices to prevent their total collapse. While FFB's management did not fear imminent failure, they saw it as a future possibility. In the shorter run (one to two years down the road), they feared a hostile takeover, a forced merger where FFB would lose its identity.

FFB had expanded over the previous two decades through mergers and acquisitions, combining with or buying twenty-one different banks. Although most of the banks had been assimilated, by 1990 FFB was still left with eight partially independent banking systems run by eight different top executives. Each of the eight bank groups had its own separate information system executives and information system applications. Each bank group offered its own products, competing with the other bank groups for the same customers. Each group had its own procedures for processing loans and checks. The banks' various information systems groups maintained a total of approximately 260 different applications.

FFB had back office operations in 48 locations throughout New Jersey and Pennsylvania. Checks were encoded at 18 different sites. The bank itself lacked unity, and the operation was slow and expensive. Had the bank decided to offer a new systemwide product, it would have had to develop eight different information systems, requiring eight separate development projects. Information systems costs were $112 million in 1989 and were projected to rise by nearly 10 percent in 1990 (against an industrywide increase of just 6 percent).

To deal with these problems, in February 1990 the board of directors brought in Tony Terracciano as the new chairman and chief executive officer. Terracciano, the former president of Pittsburgh's Mellon Bank NA, quickly hired Donald Parcells as executive vice president for operations and systems. The new leadership immediately took dramatic action, cutting 1990 expenses by $85 million, and laying off 1600 employees. To avoid being taken over themselves, they decided that FFB had to grow, and grow quickly. The only way the bank could do that in a weak economy was through additional acquisitions, buying some of the weakened banks the government was taking over. Given their current unintegrated operating environment, however, they knew that further acquisitions would only make their problems worse. FFB needed first to consolidate its operations, starting with its information systems. In June 1990, Terracciano gave Parcells 18 months to install a common infrastructure and to convert all the banks to it. IS faced an impossible task, but knew they had to find a way.

FFB's management wanted all FFB banking units to work with a single standard set of core banking applications. Parcells estimated that converting FFB's hodgepodge of existing systems to this new set of standard applications would take three and a half years with FFB's internal staff. He had neither the time nor the funding to bring in enough people to do the job. Consequently, he decided that his only alternative was outsourcing. Negotiations for an outsourcing contract ate up two of the eighteen months. FFB had some very tough demands:

- Completion within the time frame (16 months once the contract was signed)
- A cap on conversion costs
- A provision that any FFB IS workers laid off because of the conversion were to be guaranteed jobs at comparable salary and benefits at the outsourcing company that was awarded the contract
- A provision that FFB must be able to keep its 250 systems developers on the bank's payroll after the conversion project was completed (in order to protect the bank's independence)
- A provision that FFB's computer center was to remain on FFB property (again to protect the bank's independence)

First Fidelity eventually signed the contract with Electronic Data Systems Corp. (EDS) of Dallas, Texas. The final contract gave FFB what it wanted. The costs were fixed by setting a cap for each of the conversions to be done (the average cap per conversion was $2 to $3 million). FFB retained ultimate control over its own systems developers, although during the life of the conversion project, those developers reported to EDS, who had full authority to hire, fire, and promote.

Such a contract was not profitable for EDS (or any of its competitors) by itself, so to entice them to sign, FFB offered to outsource its computer center operations for ten years. The computer center did remain on FFB property. However, EDS moved about 300 FFB employees onto its own staff, most of them from the computer center itself. The contract was valued at about $450 million over the ten years, with 95 percent of that amount attributed to computer center outsourcing.

Before any conversions could begin, the project team first had to develop a common infrastructure. For three weeks, the EDS–FFB team examined the 260 current applications running in the banks. Most of these applications were based on software packages. The team selected 52 of them as the new common core applications that all FFB banks would use. They all had to run on IBM mainframes under IBM's MVS/XA operating system. The applications selected were considered the best currently in use at the banks. By selecting from among existing applications, the project team avoided the expense and time of developing or buying new packages. Because the applications were selected from different bank groupings within FFB, they did not all work with each other. The second phase of the project, therefore, was the development of interfaces that allowed these applications to pass data back and forth. For example, they built interfaces between the application that records checks and the system that manages auto and mortgage loans. The team developed an integrated environment they called the Common Application System (CAS). Interfaces were well tested, including user acceptance testing. The team then began training back office staff in the use of the new applications.

The next step was to work out a conversion process that would not interrupt the daily operations of the banks. The team decided to convert one bank at a time, starting on a Friday morning and finishing in time for the bank to reopen the following Monday. To accomplish this so quickly, the developers needed to automate the process. For each conversion, they had to develop software to convert the data from the format of the old application to that of the new one. Conversion procedures called for employees responsible for accounting to come in early Saturday morning and stay as long as necessary while they checked and signed off on the converted data. The final step was to build the bank's general ledger system from the newly converted data.

The process needed strict controls. The team developed formal checklists and set a series of deadlines for each step during the weekend conversion. They also established conflict resolution centers at each bank to enable them to solve problems rapidly. While these procedures and methods were set in place partially to guarantee the accuracy of the data and the proper functioning of the software, they also had another purpose in mind. FFB did not want to arrive Monday morning with the bank not ready to open. The tight schedule with checklists allowed them to abort the conversion early enough to reopen on Monday using the old systems if necessary.

According to Louis Ivey, chief of EDS operations, the early conversions encountered problems because workers were trained too far ahead of the conversions. EDS had to delay conversions for two months to add new features required by government regulations or to support existing bank products. By the time FFB's employees actually needed to use their new systems, many had forgotten how.

EDS and FFB did not properly estimate the load the banks would place on system resources. Overnight batch processing jobs took too long and interfered with on-line systems the next morning.

The first conversion began in early 1991. Two years later, conversions are continuing, but not because the team fell behind the schedule. Terracciano did not wait until the end of the conversions to pursue his policy of growth. During the first half of 1991, FFB acquired two banks with 101 branches. The second half of 1991 brought three banks with 68 branches. By the end of 1991 (the original 18-month deadline), the number of bank conversions needed had risen from eight to thirteen. Of course all newly acquired banks had to be converted also in order to integrate them fully into the new infrastructure. In 1992, two more banks with numerous branches were acquired. In early 1993, only two conversions had not been completed, one of which was for another bank that was acquired in January 1993. The project had not fallen behind schedule, and to date no conversion had been aborted.

The project has had gratifying results. A few key measures help to tell the tale:

- Assets have grown from $29 to $32 billion, mostly through acquisitions.
- FFB's efficiency ranking rose from 44th to 6th amongst the largest 50 U.S. banks.
- The company's stock value has risen from $11 per share in 1990 to $40 per share in 1993.
- Third quarter 1992 earnings were projected to be $112 million versus $86 million for the same quarter in 1990.
- Check encoding sites have been reduced from 18 to 6.

Once again the systems development staff is reporting to FFB, so that new conversions (and development) are now under the bank's control. Parcells estimates that a conversion now takes the bank two or three months, allowing the bank to acquire and integrate other banks speedily and inexpensively. The EDS outsourcing agreement has brought FFB another benefit—they are able to hire EDS developers on an "as needed" basis without having to increase their own fixed charges. As Parcells put it, "I don't have to keep them on the payroll forever. I pay a premium for those resources for a finite period of time, and then they leave."

How have FFB's internal employees reacted to the outsourcing deal? Eugene T. Jones, a former FFB employee claims that the obvious message is that the new bank management had little respect for the bank's IS staff. He maintains that the new information systems plan did not improve productivity. Once the outstanding deal was in place, Parcells instituted longer work days: 8:30 A.M. to 5:00 P.M. for low-level employees, 7:30 A.M. to 6:00 P.M. for senior vice presidents. During the conversions, FFB employees were asked to work up to seven months at a stretch with no days off. The long hours and lack of time off required during the conversions made the staff feel like they were victims of a hostile takeover. Parcells agrees that the working conditions were difficult. But, he says, "We had a choice. The choice is, if we don't do this, we're going to lose 50 percent of the jobs." The loss of jobs would come, of course, as a result of a takeover by another organization, a threat that has been avoided.

Source: Jeff Moad, "Inside An Outsourcing Deal," *Datamation* (February 15, 1993).

Part Three Case Study Questions:

1. Who (or what) do you think were responsible for FBB's problems when Terracciano and Parcells took over? One former FFB employee claimed that management's view of IS "was uniformly bad." Given the condition of the bank when the new management took over, do you think such a view is justified? What role did the information systems group play in creating the problems within the bank?

2. Define the central goals of the project from Terracciano's perspective. Define them from Parcells' perspective, and then from the perspective of an FFB information system manager assigned to the project.

3. The conversion project seems to have been a success from the perspective of FFB's management. What factors do you think were critical to that success? Do you agree that it was a success? Why? Were there any risks to FFB's rapid conversion?

4. What alternatives to outsourcing existed? Why do you think FFB's management decided to outsource? Do you agree with the decision? Why?

5. From the description of the project, do you think FFB paid adequate attention to quality? What did they do to assure the quality of the new systems? What else do you think they should have done?

FOUR

Management and Organizational Support Systems

Today's information economy requires special attention to the management of information in the organization. Capturing and distributing intelligence and knowledge, leadership, collaboration, and group decision making have become vital to organizational innovation and survival. This section describes how information systems can foster these objectives and support new kinds of management decision making by individuals and groups.

Chapter 15 examines the principal types of information systems supporting knowledge and information work in the organization. Technologies for document management, collaborative work, and project management facilitate communication, collaboration and coordination among groups in the organization. Knowledge work systems are explicitly customized to meet the unique information requirements of skilled professionals and knowledge workers.

Chapter 16 focuses on decision support systems (DSS), group decision support systems (GDSS) and executive support systems (ESS). These systems are more helpful to managers faced with unstructured and semi-structured decisions than traditional information systems. Examples of individual, group, and organizational decision support systems and of leading-edge executive support applications show how these systems enhance the management decision-making process.

Chapter 17 traces developments in artificial intelligence and shows how they can create information systems that capture knowledge and intelligence for organizations. Businesses can benefit from expert systems, which automate selected aspects of the decision-making process and from neural network applications, which imitate the thought processes of the biological brain. Numerous examples of expert systems, neural networks, and other intelligent techniques illuminate the capabilities and limitations of artificial intelligence applications in business.

Part Four Case Study: *EPRINET: A Strategic Network for the Utility Industry.* This case illustrates how information technology was used to enhance the effectiveness of the Electronic Power Research Institute EPRI, an organization whose principal product was new knowledge. It illustrates some of the benefits and problems of implementing ambitious knowledge work systems. EPRINET was part of a larger strategic transition that EPRI had to undergo.

504

The Virtual Research Institute

Unlike many leading medical schools, Harvard Medical School does not have its own teaching hospital. Instead, it uses a series of affiliated institutions in the greater Boston area, staffed by more than 10,000 physicians and medical workers. Among all of these institutions is a huge pool of expertise and knowledge that faculty and researchers and the medical school want to tap. But until recently, the setup was so huge and dispersed geographically that the vast expertise that was available was practically unreachable and unlocatable.

Jim Fitchett, the chief information officer at Harvard Medical School, decided to change this situation. He implemented the Longwood Medical Area Network (LMA Net), which now ties Harvard Medical School and eight affiliated institutions together into a virtual research institute. He linked ten additional institutions with an electronic mail system and shared

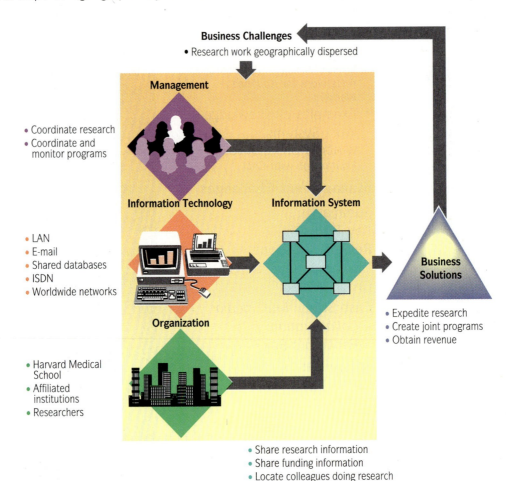

databases. This network supports wide-scale information sharing and also gives users access to Internet (a worldwide collection of networks linking academic researchers) and to a growing list of libraries and databases.

The network makes collaboration instantaneous. For instance, Dr. Lawrence C. Madoff, a bacterial vaccine researcher at Brigham and Women's Hospital, uses the network to access genetic database servers at Massachusetts General Hospital and to locate colleagues doing similar research. He plans to use Internet to participate in a national multicenter study on Group B streptococcus. LMA Net also permitted the medical school to create joint programs in neonatology, nuclear medicine, and alcohol and substance abuse disciplines. Fitchett cabled the medical school campus with fiber optics and installed an Integrated Services Digital Network (ISDN).

SIMON, a medical research community database introduced in the fall of 1992, allows researchers to obtain information more rapidly and serves as a matchmaker between research projects and sources of funding. The database contains information about the research interests of all of the medical school professors and their willingness to use students to do research in labs. When Harvard Medical School receives notices of funding opportunities, it uses SIMON to track down who is doing the kind of research that the sources are willing to fund. When SIMON was tapped during a recent funding cycle for pediatric AIDS, it turned up 14 potential candidates for funding. Four applied for grants. In addition to furthering research, SIMON can help speed up medical advances by making research information immediately available to companies interested in developing new drugs and products.

While they are erudite in other areas, many physicians and medical researchers are reluctant to use computers. According to Audrey Bernfield, Harvard Medical School's director of enrichment programs, people feel that since they can pick up their telephones and call colleagues to ask who is doing cellular biology research, they do not need computers and databases.

Fitchett found that the truly pressing need of these professionals is communication. Information is the lifeblood of medical research, especially information about what research is being conducted where and by whom and about possible sources of funding. When Fitchett installed Lotus Development Corporation's CC: Mail electronic mail system, researchers found that queries that might have gone unanswered for days were being answered in four hours. People who had questions in the middle of the night could get answers. E-mail vastly expanded the span of control researchers had over their work.

Source: Nell Margolis, "Strong Medicine," *Computerworld* (March 8, 1993).

Collaborating and communicating with other experts and sharing ideas and information are essential requirements not only for academic institutions such as Harvard Medical School, but for businesses today as well. Advanced industrial societies have shifted from manufacturing to an information economy in which the basis of wealth is the production of information and knowledge. The shift calls for new kinds of information systems to help organizations create, coordinate and distribute information to achieve their goals. Such systems are called information and knowledge work systems, and they are the focus of this chapter.

This chapter describes the emergence of information and knowledge work and the unique information requirements of information and knowledge workers. Because offices play such a pivotal role in contemporary organizations, information systems designed to support major office activities and to promote collaborative work have become increasingly critical. We describe the major types of information systems used for disseminating and coordinating the flow of information in the organization and for supporting the activities of highly skilled knowledge workers and professionals.

After completing this chapter you will be able to:

* Define information work and the information economy.
* Describe the roles of knowledge workers and data workers in the organization.
* Describe the roles and principal activities of the office in contemporary business.
* Explain the contributions of the principal types of office automation technologies.
* Understand unique requirements of knowledge work systems.
* Describe the major types of knowledge work systems.

15.1 Knowledge and Information Work

Chapter 1 introduced the emergence of information economy as one of the key challenges of information systems today. The shift to an economy where the major source of wealth and prosperity is the production and distribution of information and knowledge has profound implications for the kinds of information systems found in contemporary organizations and the way they are used.

Transformation of the Economy

Since the turn of the century, the United States, Canada, and Western Europe have been moving toward a service and information economy and away from an agricultural and manufacturing economy. Figure 1.1 in Chapter 1 shows that the percentage of people who work in offices using information to produce economic value has been rising and the percentage of workers who work with their hands in factories or on farms has been declining. (In the United States, the percentage of jobs in manufacturing has fallen from 27 percent in 1920 to 17 percent today and is expected to be 12 percent by 2005.) Among white-collar workers, the fastest growing occupations have been clerical, professional, and technical workers, and managers and administrators (see Figure 15.1).

Four factors are involved in this shift. First, there has been a worldwide shift in the production of manufactured goods in which third-world and developing societies have become centers of manufacturing. At the same time, the so-called advanced societies have shifted toward services. Textile products and steel ingots are more economically produced in Asian countries, while North American and European countries are the primary sources for bioengineering services and products or computer software.

Knowledge- and information-intense products: Products that require a great deal of learning and knowledge to produce.

Second, there has been a rapid growth in knowledge and information-intense products and services. **Knowledge- and information-intense products** are products that require a great deal of learning and knowledge to produce. Intensification of knowledge utilization in the production of traditional products has increased as well. This trend is readily seen throughout the automobile industry where both design and production now rely heavily upon knowledge-intensive

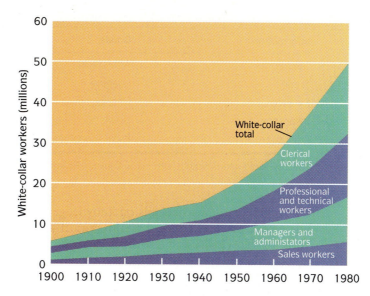

Figure 15.1
Changes in the nature of work during the 20th century. Both the number and proportion of white-collar jobs in the U. S. labor force have grown considerably over the last 90 years, with the fastest growth occurring among clerical, professional and technical, and managerial and administrative occupations. *Adapted from "The Mechanization of Office Work" by Vincent Guiliano,* Scientific American, *September 1982. Copyright © 1982, by Scientific American, Inc. All rights reserved.*

information technology. Over the past decade, the automobile producers have sharply increased their hiring of computer specialists, engineers, and designers while reducing the number of blue-collar production workers. Entire new information services have sprung up, such as Compuserve, Dow Jones News Service and Lexis. These fields are now employing millions of people.

Third, there has been a substitution of knowledge and information workers for manual production workers within the goods sectors. Machine tool operators, for instance, have often been replaced by technicians who monitor computer-controlled machine tools. Fourth, new kinds of knowledge- and information-intense organizations have emerged that are devoted entirely to the production, processing, and distribution of information. For instance, environmental engineering firms, which specialize in preparing environmental impact statements for municipalities and private contractors, simply did not exist prior to the 1960s. These new kinds of organizations also employ millions of people.

With these changes, there were conservatively 63 million information workers in the U.S. economy (around 52 percent of the labor force) by 1980. As early as 1976, the value of information-sector products and services had already exceeded that of the manufacturing or goods sector (see Figure 15.2). By 1990, the information sector (including services) accounted for $3 out of every $4 of GNP in the United States. The shift toward information work and workers has had profound implications for the kinds of information technologies and systems found at the heart of business enterprises. Because so much of the U.S. and other

Figure 15.2:
Emergence of the information economy. The value of the information sector in the U.S. economy began to exceed the value of the manufacturing or goods sector by 1976 and has continued to surpass it into the 1990s. *Reprinted by permission of the publisher from "Technology and the Service Sector." by Stephen S. Roach,* Technological Forecasting and Social Change, *Vol. 34, No. 4, December 1988. Copyright 1988 by Elsevier Science Publishing Co., Inc.*

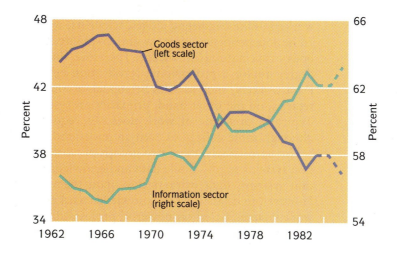

Table 15.1 EXAMPLES OF INFORMATION, SERVICE, AND GOODS INDUSTRIES

Information	Goods	Service
Telephone	Agriculture	Hotels
Trade	Logging	Business service
Finance	Chemicals	Auto repair
Insurance	Steel	Medical service
Education	Farm machines	Amusements

Sources: Wolff and Baumol, 1987; U.S. Census 1980.

advanced economies depends on knowledge and information work, any overall advance in productivity and wealth critically depends on increasing the productivity of knowledge and information workers.

What Is Knowledge and Information Work?

To describe how information systems can increase the productivity of information and knowledge workers, we need to understand what kinds of jobs these workers perform. First, we have to establish some basic definitions. Table 15.1 gives some examples of information, service, and goods industries.

DISTINGUISHING KNOWLEDGE AND DATA WORKERS

Information workers: People in the labor force who primarily create, work with, or disseminate information.

Information work: Work that primarily consists of creating or processing information.

Knowledge workers: People such as engineers, scientists, or architects who design products or services or create new knowledge for the organization.

Data workers: People such as secretaries or bookkeepers who primarily process and disseminate the organization's paperwork.

The U.S Department of Labor defines as **information workers** all those people in the labor force who primarily create, work with, or disseminate information. **Information work** is work that consists primarily of creating or processing information. There are two commonly accepted types of information workers: **knowledge workers** (those who primarily create new information and knowledge) and **data workers** (who primarily use, process, or disseminate information). Thus, knowledge work refers to work that primarily creates new information or knowledge. Data work is work that involves the use, manipulation, or dissemination of information.

In contrast, service workers are those people who primarily deliver a service, and goods workers are those who primarily work with physical objects or transform physical materials. Examples of each of these four kinds of workers are given in Table 15.2.

These distinctions are not always easy to apply, and some occupations like managers both create new information and distribute data. Scholars handle this ambiguity by classifying half the managers as knowledge workers and half as data workers.

Knowledge and data workers can be distinguished by the amount of formal education required for them to be qualified to work in the field. Knowledge workers—like engineers, judges, scientists, writers, and architects—all must exercise independent judgment and creativity based on their mastery of a large body of specialized knowledge. Therefore, they usually must obtain an advanced degree and/or a professional certification before beginning their work careers. Data workers, such as sales personnel, accountants, real estate agents, and secretaries, on the other hand, primarily process information and do not create it. Typically, this type of work does not require advanced educational degrees, although some college or even an undergraduate degree is often required.

Not surprisingly, these two groups of workers tend to have different information systems needs. While data and knowledge workers both use office automation systems, data workers rely upon them as their primary or only system. However, to do their work, knowledge workers often require specific knowledge work systems based on powerful professional workstations and highly specialized software.

Table 15.2   EXAMPLES OF OCCUPATIONS FOR KNOWLEDGE, DATA, SERVICE, AND GOODS WORKERS

Knowledge	Data	Service	Goods
Architect	Salesperson	Waiter	Teamster
Engineer	Accountant	Sanitary engineer	Welder
Judge	Lawyer	Cook	Machine operator
Scientist	Pharmacist	Nurse	Lumberman
Reporter	R.R. conductor	Hairdresser	Fisherman
Researcher	Foreman	Child care worker	Farmer
Writer	Draftsman	Gardener	Construction worker
Actuary	Real estate salesperson	Cleaner	Miner
Programmer	Secretary	Barber	Glazier
Manager*	Manager	Clergy*	Factory operative

Source: Wolff and Baumol, 1987; Porat, 1977.

*Many occupations—like managers and clergy—cannot be easily classified. Managers, for instance, sometimes create new knowledge and information when they write reports and hence often act like knowledge workers. At other times, they read and disseminate reports like data workers. Scholars handle this situation by classifying half of the managers as knowledge workers and half as data workers. A similar situation exists with clergy: They both provide a service and disseminate information. In the future we will need better data on specific occupations.

Where are knowledge and data workers concentrated? All information workers work in offices (even if that office is at home or the work is being done on a plane) or rely directly on offices for support (such as salespeople or laboratory researchers). However, knowledge workers and data workers are distributed differently in the economy. Knowledge workers are rather equitably distributed across all industries, whereas data workers are concentrated in service industries, finance, government, and trade (see Figure 15.3). This stands to reason; data workers are predominantly the clerical and sales workers, who dominate in the service sector.

Figure 15.3
The distribution of knowledge and data workers in the U.S. economy. Where are the knowledge and data workers? Knowledge workers are distributed equally across all industries whereas data workers are concentrated in service industries, finance, government, and trade. Source: Wolff and Baumol, 1987.

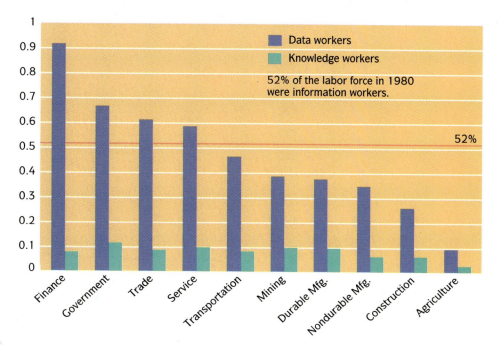

Information Work and Productivity

Over the past several years business has become intensely aware of competition from other industrialized economies. The United States has led the world in productivity throughout most of the twentieth century. While the United States still maintains its productivity lead, the size of that lead is shrinking as the growth of U.S. productivity declines relative to that of Germany, Japan, and many other industrialized countries.

As we have indicated, knowledge- and information-intense industries have become the fastest growing industries in the United States, while the fastest growing segment of the American labor force is the information workers. The country has also experienced a dramatic shift in capital investment patterns in recent years—in the early 1980s, for the first time, capital investment per information worker began to surpass capital investment per factory worker. In 1989, over 70 percent of all capital investment was in the area of information technology, with most of that 70 percent going directly into offices.

Thus, clearly if the United States is to increase its international competitiveness, American business must address the issue of the productivity of its information workers. The extent to which computers have enhanced the productivity of information workers is the subject of considerable debate. Some studies show that investment in information technology has not led to any appreciable growth in productivity among office workers. While productivity did rise, Morgan Stanley senior economist Stephen Roach estimates that the average white-collar productivity gain from 1980 to 1990 has only been 0.28 percent annually (Roach, 1988). Service sector productivity grew nearly 3% annually in 1991–92 but it is still too early to tell whether these gains are short-term or whether they represent an end to the stagnation of the past decade (Roach, 1993). Figure 15.4 shows that the amount of gross national product (the total value of goods and services produced per employee) in the finance, insurance, and real estate industries remained stag-

Figure 15.4

Productivity in three knowledge and information-intense industries—finance, insurance, and real estate. This chart compares employment levels, investment in information technology, gross national product, and the amount of gross national product per employee in the finance, insurance, and real estate sectors of the U. S. economy. It shows that the amount of gross national product produced per employee in this sector remained stagnant and even slightly declined between 1970 and 1989 while the capital investment in information technology increased tenfold. Employment levels and the amount of GNP produced by this sector only rose slightly during this period. (The amounts are in 1982 dollars.) *Source: Azimuth Corporation, 1993. Copyright 1993 by Azimuth Corporation. Reprinted by permission.*

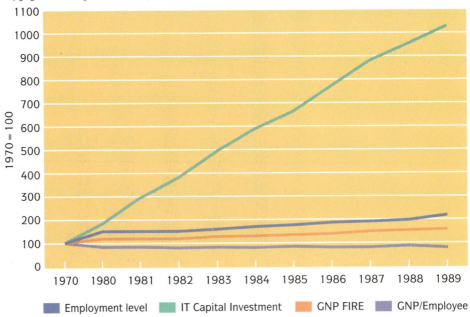

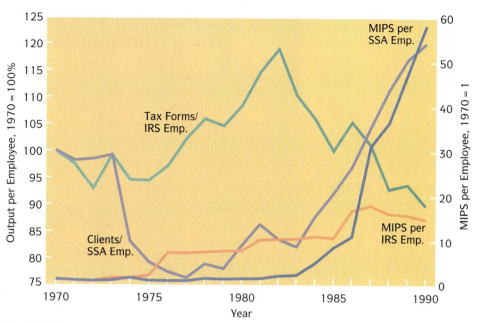

Figure 15.5

Productivity and investment in information technology in the U.S. Internal Revenue Service (IRS) and the Social Security Administration (SSA). Between 1970 and 1990 both organizations invested heavily in information technology. The amount of investment in information technology is indicated by MIPS per employee. IRS productivity is measured by the number of forms completed per employee, and SSA productivity is measured by the number of clients handled per employee. The left and right axes are indexes. The chart shows that between 1970 and 1990 the number of tax forms completed per IRS employee at first rose but then declined 10%, while the number of MIPS per employee rose fifteen-fold. During the same period the number of clients handled per SSA employee increased 20% with a sixty-fold increase in MIPS per employee. These findings suggest that investing in information technology does not necessarily increase productivity.

nant and even declined slightly between 1970 and 1989, while the capital investment in information technology increased tenfold.

On the other hand, productivity changes among information workers are difficult to measure because of the problems of identifying suitable units of output for information work (Panko, 1991). How does one measure the output of a law office? Should one measure productivity by examining the number of forms completed per employee (a measure of physical unit productivity), or by examining the amount of revenue produced per employee (a measure of financial unit productivity) in an information- and knowledge-intense industry?

Even if one agrees on a suitable measure of productivity, different organizations can produce different results. Figure 15.5 compares the productivity of two major U.S. government agencies, the Internal Revenue Service (IRS) and the Social Security Administration (SSA). Both were early users of computers and both invested heavily in new information system technology between 1970 and 1990. If we measure IRS productivity by looking at the number of forms completed per employee, and SSA productivity by the number of clients handled per employee, the productivity of the Internal Revenue Service remained stagnant between 1970 and 1990, while Social Security Administration productivity grew during the same period. The reasons for these differences are not only technological. During the 1980s, Congress demanded that SSA cut its work force by one third in exchange for providing $1 billion in new information system technology. The Social Security Administration had to make procedural and job design changes to accommodate a growing number of clients with fewer staff members. These organizational changes were enhanced by new information systems technology, but without these changes, gains in SSA productivity would probably not have been possible. Introduction of information technology alone does not necessarily guarantee productivity.

15.2 Information Work and Office Automation

Information work is concentrated in offices, and office automation systems have been developed to facilitate the processing, distribution, and coordination of information in the firm. Here we describe the role of offices in contemporary organizations and show how this role can be supported by various types of office automation technologies.

Three Roles of the Office Within the Organization

No longer a mundane clerical typing pool or simply a "bureaucratic nightmare," by the 1980s, scholars and computer vendors alike came to see the office as one of the most important work sites for professional knowledge and data workers. Offices today involve an incredibly diverse array of professional, managerial, sales, and clerical employees. Offices are groups composed of people who work together toward shared goals. In this sense, office work is complex and cooperative, and yet highly individualistic. It represents not a factory of collaborating workers so much as an orchestra of highly trained individuals. Offices perform three critical organizational roles (see Figure 15.6):

- They coordinate and manage the work of local professional and information workers within the organization.
- They link the work being performed across all levels and functions throughout the organization.
- They couple the organization to the external environment, including to its clients and suppliers; when you call an organization, you call an office.

Major Office Activities

Office activities: The principal activities performed at offices; these include managing documents, scheduling and communicating with people, managing data, and managing projects.

To fulfill the roles that we have described, offices usually perform the five major **office activities** illustrated in Table 15.3: managing documents, scheduling individuals and groups, communicating with individuals and groups, managing data on individuals and groups, and managing projects. Table 15.3 also contains the authors' estimate, on average, of percentage of effort (capital investment and time) the office invests in each activity. For example, we estimate that document management characteristically consumes about 40 percent of the total office effort in time expended and capital investment. Information technology which

Figure 15.6
The three major roles of offices. Offices perform three major roles. [1] They coordinate the work of local professionals and information workers. [2] They couple the organization to the external environment. [3] They coordinate work in the organization across levels and functions.

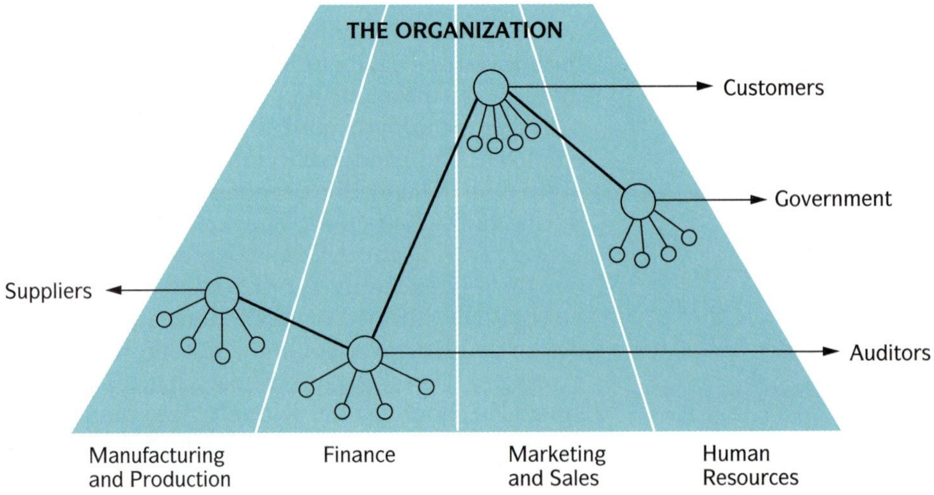

THE ORGANIZATION

Customers

Government

Auditors

Suppliers

Manufacturing and Production

Finance

Marketing and Sales

Human Resources

Table 15.3 OFFICE AUTOMATION: ROLES, ACTIVITIES, AND SYSTEMS IN THE MODERN OFFICE

General Roles of Offices	Activities in an Office	Percentage of Effort	Information Technology Assistance
1. Coordination and management of people and work	1. Managing documents Creating, storing/retrieving, and communicating image (analog) and digital documents	40%	Document management Word processing hardware and software Desktop publishing Digital image processing
2. Linking organizational units and projects	2. Scheduling individuals and groups Creating, managing, and communicating documents, plans, and calendars	10%	Digital calendars Electronic calendars and schedules Electronic mail Groupware
3. Coupling the organization to outside groups and people	3. Communicating with individuals and groups Initiating, receiving, and managing voice and digital communications with diverse groups and individuals	30%	Communications PBX and digital phone equipment Voice mail Groupware
	4. Managing data on individuals and groups Entering and managing data to track external customers, clients, and vendors and internal individuals and groups	10%	Data management Desktop database for client/customer tracking, project tracking, and calendar information (personal information manager)
	5. Managing projects Planning, initiating, evaluating, monitoring projects Resource allocation Personnel decisions	10%	Project management Desktop project management tools CPM and PERT methods

Source: © 1990 Azimuth Corporation

has been developed to support each of these activities, is listed in the far right column of the table. Some of these technologies, such as groupware, actually support more than one of these activities.

The Office Automation Movement

Office automation systems (OAS): Computer systems, such as word processing, voice-mail systems, and video conferencing systems, that are designed to increase the productivity of information workers in the office.

Office automation systems (OAS) can be defined as any application of information technology that intends to increase productivity of information workers in the office. Office automation has a long history. We could trace its beginnings back to the year 1460, when Johannes Gutenberg first used movable type to publish books. The nineteenth century saw major developments with the invention of mechanical calculators (1840), typewriters (1860), and electrical innovations such as the teletype, telephones, adding machines, duplicators, and small offset presses. In the early decades of the twentieth century, progress in office automation consisted of motorizing the existing equipment and developing machines such as the electric typewriter. During the 1920s, for example, such large organizations as the Internal Revenue Service motorized their huge tubs of manual files—when the file clerk typed a three-letter combination into a register box, the tub would spin to the indicated files. In the 1950s, when computers first came into use, they were too large, expensive, and centralized to be applied to office work.

However, the development of transistors and integrated circuits in the 1960s made available technology that could dramatically change the office automation movement. During the mid-1970s, computerized office automation tools appeared. IBM developed a number of mainframe-based tools, such as PROFS (Professional Office System). Minicomputer vendors like Wang developed dedicated word processing systems.

In the 1980s, expensive mainframe and minicomputer systems began to lose out in the marketplace to much more powerful and less expensive desktop microcomputers and workstations. Only big companies with large mainframe installations continued to rely on the mini- and mainframe computers for office automation. Today office automation software tends to reside on stand-alone or networked desktop 80386- and 80486-based microcomputers and on the Apple Macintosh. Even small companies and individuals can now afford office automation.

Office automation functionality also increased dramatically. Fifteen years ago, office automation meant only the creation, processing, and management of documents. Today, although professional knowledge and information work remains highly document-centered, office work requires a great deal more from its office automation systems. Digital image processing—word and document—is also at the core of today's systems, as are high speed digital communications services. Because office work involves many people jointly engaged in projects, contemporary office automation systems have powerful project management tools and group assistance tools like networked digital calendars. An ideal contemporary office automation system would involve a seamless network of digital machines linking professional, clerical, and managerial work groups and running a variety of types of software (see, again, Table 15.3).

Office Activities and Technologies

While the first wave of office automation systems established technologies designed to support such obvious office clerical activities as word processing and simple task coordination, in the 1990s new office applications are based on emerging technologies: document management technologies, technologies for collaborative work, desktop data management technologies, and project management technologies (see Table 15.4).

Table 15.4 EMERGING OFFICE TECHNOLOGIES OF THE 1990S

Office Activity	Emerging Technology
Managing documents	Document imaging/workflow management
Collaborative work	Groupware, E-mail, electronic calendars
Managing information	Desktop data management (personal information managers)
Managing projects	Desktop project managers

MANAGING DOCUMENTS

Technologies that are used to create, process, and manage documents are known as document management technologies. These technologies include word processing, desktop publishing, document imaging, and workflow management.

WORD PROCESSING AND DESKTOP PUBLISHING

Word processing: Office automation technology that facilitates the creation of documents through computerized text editing, formatting, storing, and printing.

Word processing technology is used to create, format, edit, store, manage, and print documents. Word processing is the most widely used technology in today's offices. Its popularity is a result of the dramatic increase in productivity it has brought to all information workers—clerks, managers, and knowledge workers alike. Because the text is stored electronically rather than on paper, changes and corrections can be made in a moment without requiring the user to retype the document. The software allows an almost unlimited combination of formatting options—top, bottom, and side margins; line spacing; tabs; columns; font (character) selections and character (point) sizes; and even such formatting features as automated footnoting.

A word processing system must contain both the hardware and software to input, process, store, and output the data. For each of these functions a range of technology exists, as shown in Figure 15.7.

Frequently, word processing software packages include such advanced features as a dictionary for spell checking, a thesaurus, a style checker (which analyzes both grammar and punctuation), and mail merge facilities (typically used to link documents to separately stored mailing list names and addresses). They often allow the user to insert graphic images into the document. In addition, these packages permit the user to produce hard copy easily when desired on most popular printers.

Desktop publishing: Technology that produces professional-quality documents combining output from word processors with design, graphics, and special layout features.

Desktop publishing technology goes a step beyond word processing, allowing the user to produce professional publishing-quality output using documents created with word processing software. A skilled user of a desktop publisher can produce brochures, newsletters, and reports that approach the quality of a pro-

Figure 15.7
Components of a word processing system. A word processing system includes hardware, software, and storage components for creating, editing, storing, printing, and distributing documents. This diagram lists the devices that are most commonly used for input, processing, output, and storage in word processing systems.

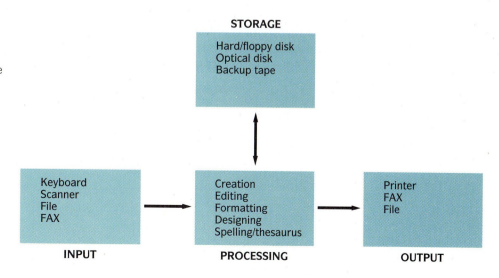

fessional typesetter and graphics designer. Desktop publishing packages, such as PageMaker by Aldus, surpass the options available in word processing software; these packages offer enhanced text handling and page layout capabilities. They allow the user to resize, rotate, and modify graphics images. This technology also includes a computer language, often Adobe System's Postscript, to define the page, type fonts, and graphics for high-quality laser printers and other output devices. Desktop publishing truly lives up to its name by bringing professional publishing to the desktop computer.

DOCUMENT IMAGING AND WORKFLOW SYSTEMS

While word processing and desktop publishing address the creation and presentation of documents, they only exacerbate the existing paper avalanche problem. Hundreds of billions of pieces of paper are produced by businesses each year (see Figure 15.8). Several examples may help us to visualize the extent of the problem. The U.S. banking industry handled 50 billion checks in 1990 at an average handling cost of five cents, or a total handling cost of $2.5 billion. Ultramar Oil, a Long Beach, California, oil refinery, maintains about 20,000 material safety data sheets in huge notebooks; if an emergency chemical spill occurs, employees must manually search these notebooks for the appropriate sheet or sheets that contain the life-saving and damage control information they urgently need.

The issue concerns far more than sheer quantity, however. Workflow problems arising from paper handling are enormous. For instance, a large American health insurance company processes more than 80,000 claims per day; the mail room staff sorts the claims by type and category, and in the process 8 percent (about 6,500) are lost or missorted, costing the company an extra $4 million per year. According to International Data Corporation (IDC 1990), an insurance application submitted on paper would typically require about eleven clerical and six professional steps, and could take 33 days. Customer calls often require the customer service staff to locate paper documents and then call the customer back; a major New York bank estimated that if it eliminated the return calls, it could save millions of dollars every year just in the phone bill (not to mention staff time costs and customer relations problems).

Chapter 2 introduced the concept of digital image processing, whereby documents and images are converted into digitized form so that they can be stored and accessed by the computer. **Document imaging systems** are systems that employ digital image processing to store, retrieve, and manipulate a digitized image of a document, allowing the document itself to be discarded. The system must contain a scanner that converts the document image into a bit-mapped image, storing that image as a graphic. This technology is different from optical character recognition (OCR) which "reads" a printed optical character, identifies the character by determining its pattern, and then stores it in the computer in its digital form. With OCR, a document is character-based and can be edited like any document created in a word processor. However, with imaging systems, a picture of the document is stored. With imaging systems, the document will originally be stored on a magnetic disk, where it can be retrieved instantly. When it ceases to be active, it will be transferred to an optical disk where it will be

Document imaging systems: Systems that employ digital image processing to store, retrieve, and manipulate a digitized image of a document, allowing the document itself to be discarded.

Figure 15.8
The number of documents stored by U.S. businesses. U.S. businesses store hundreds of billions of documents annually. Image management systems can manage the avalanche of paper and streamline workflow. *Source: "Image Management Systems," IDC White Paper,* Computerworld, *September 24, 1990. Copyright 1990 by CW Publishing, Inc., Framingham, MA 01701. Reprinted from* Computerworld.

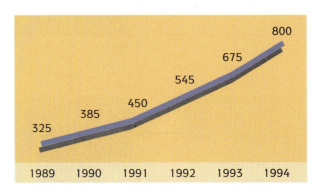

Paper system insurance application

11 clerical steps   6 professional steps   = 33 Days

Imaging system insurance application

3 clerical steps   4 professional steps   = 5 Days

Figure 15.9
Insurance underwriting application enhanced by imaging and workflow automation. The improved efficiency and reduced workflow justify the expense of an image management system. The application requiring 33 days in a paper system would take only 5 days with image management and workflow redesign, resulting in tremendous savings to the insurance company. *Source: "Image Management Systems," IDC White Paper,* Computerworld, *September 24, 1990. Copyright 1990 by CW Publishing, Inc., Framingham, MA 01701. Reprinted from* Computerworld.

Jukebox: A device for storing and retrieving many optical disks.

Index server: In imaging systems, a device that stores the indexes that allow a user to identify and retrieve a specific document.

stored for as many months or years as is needed. Optical disks, kept on-line in a **jukebox** (a device for storing and retrieving many optical disks) require up to a minute to retrieve the document automatically. A typical large jukebox will store over 10,000,000 pages (an 8 1/2″ by 11″ document usually requires about 50 kilobytes of storage after data compression).

An imaging system also requires an **index server** to contain the indexes that will allow users to identify and retrieve the document when needed. Once the document has been scanned, index data are entered so that the document can be retrieved in a variety of ways, depending upon the application. For example, the index may contain the document scan date, the customer name and number, the document type, and some subject information. Finally, the system must include retrieval equipment, primarily workstations capable of handling graphics, although printers are usually included.

To achieve the large productivity gains promised by imaging technology, organizations must redesign their workflow. In the past, the existence of only one copy of the document largely shaped workflow. Work had to be performed serially; two people could not work on the same document at the same time. Documents needed to be protected so they would not be lost or destroyed. Documents containing confidential data had to be locked up. Significant staff time had to be devoted to filing and retrieving documents. Critical analytical work could not be done because files could not be found—either because they were out (in use) or because they were not filed according to the kind of data the individual needs to analyze (an insurance company cannot study breast cancer claim costs if the documents are filed by the name of the insured rather than by the type of illness).

Workflow management: The process of streamlining business procedures so that documents can be moved easily and efficiently from one location to another.

Once a document has been stored electronically, workflow management can change the traditional methods of working with documents. **Workflow management** is the process of streamlining business procedures so that documents can be moved more easily and efficiently from one location to another. Imaging technology automates processes such as routing documents to different locations, securing approvals, scheduling, and generating reports. Document integrity—protection against loss, destruction or prying eyes—can be handled through data backup, and through terminal and/or login ID security, just as with other computer data. Two or more people can work simultaneously on the same document, allowing a much quicker completion date. Work need not ever be delayed because a file is "out" or a document is "in transit." And with a properly designed indexing system, users will be able to retrieve files in many different ways, based upon the content of the document. Figure 15.9 illustrates the efficiency and productivity gains that could result from using imaging and workflow automation in an insurance underwriting application.

Let us look at two actual success stories. The San Jose Medical Center is a 315-bed community trauma facility in San Jose, California. In the fall of 1991, it began installing an imaging system based upon a Banyan Systems, Vines network, and 21 Wang and IBM-compatible 80386 workstations. The system cost about $450,000. The center expects full payback in less than 18 months ($380,000 payback the first year), partially through staff reductions and partially through elimination of the estimated $13 cost for retrieving each file manually. In addition, the center will use the system to generate an additional $150,000 annual income through making document copies. In the past, it met requests for copies by sending the documents to a copying service, with the copy-requester paying the copying service. The hospital estimates it did 70 percent of the copying work without any compensation. Now it will be paid for the service without an accompanying increase in work. Most important to the mission of the center, document retrieval time is reduced from about 20 minutes to almost instantaneously, a critical improvement when a medical emergency occurs (Nash, 1992).

Iowa's Central Life Assurance Co. (CLA) in Des Moines turned to imaging in an attempt to achieve a paperless workflow. CLA handles more than $18 billion in individual life insurance (operating in 44 states) and was being overwhelmed by paper. Its problems were typical: misfilings, lost documents, outdated documents mixed in with current documents, expensive floor space given over to armies of file cabinets. The company decided to try imaging technology, starting with policy applications only. It purchased Metaview, a desktop system from Metafile Information Systems, Inc. (see Figure 15.10). The images are stored

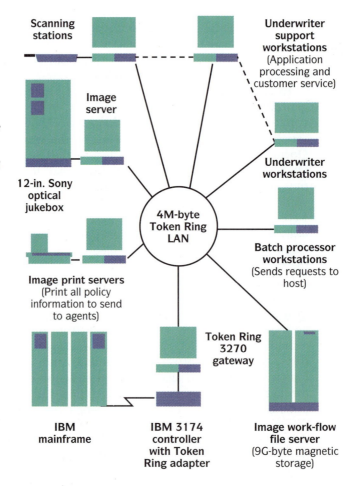

Figure 15.10
Central Life Assurance's document imaging system. A token ring LAN provides the network support to link the data entry, underwriting and policy preparation for document management at the Central Life Assurance Company. *Source: James Daly, "Insurer sees Future in Imagining Strategy,"* Computerworld, *January 6, 1992, p. 41. Copyright 1992 by CW Publishing, Inc., Framingham, MA 01701. Reprinted from* Computerworld.

Scanning stations

Underwriter support workstations (Application processing and customer service)

Image server

Underwriter workstations

12-in. Sony optical jukebox

4M-byte Token Ring LAN

Batch processor workstations (Sends requests to host)

Image print servers (Print all policy information to send to agents)

Token Ring 3270 gateway

IBM mainframe

IBM 3174 controller with Token Ring adapter

Image work-flow file server (9G-byte magnetic storage)

magnetically for the period when the document is active, after which they are copied to a 12-inch optical disk in a Sony Corp. 50-disk jukebox. Daily, the mail room scans approximately 700 pages of applications as they are received. The mail room staff then enters the index data, checks the image for quality, and electronically routes the document to the appropriate work queue. CLA's staff uses about 60 80386 IBM PS/2s to access the applications through a fiber-optic Netframe NF 400 network. The electronic file will be updated as processing continues. Ultimately, each application file will contain all required information—application, financial reports, medical information, even photographs. Once the file is complete, the underwriters review the application and approve or deny it (Daly, 1992).

Imaging systems, combined with workflow management, can bring many benefits to an organization:

- *Cost savings, as we have documented, can be significant.* According to the International Data Corporation, such corporations as American Express, Citicorp, and Federal Express believe they are realizing annual savings of 20 percent.
- *Paper reduction is clear.* Most people will be working from electronic copies, not paper copies.
- *Linked closely to paper reduction is floor space.* One major U.S. law firm estimates that turning to document imaging freed up 80 percent of its office space.
- *Time saving is another benefit.* The same law firm claims a 50 percent reduction in time spent filing, copying, storing, and retrieving documents. This benefit can be very significant for organizations that currently archive paper documents and then require two or more days to locate these documents.
- *Work management is enhanced.* One bank mortgage department has automated the work queues so that no mortgage operator has more than five mortgages in his or her queue at a time.
- *Customer service can be dramatically improved.* Customer service staff can answer questions instantly. Customers are not placed on hold while the staff member searches for the file. Customers do not have to be called back because the file is not available. Customer satisfaction can be enhanced by a company's ability to complete its work more quickly; for example, a company can respond to a medical claim in days instead of weeks.

Image technology is also a source of genuine competitive advantage. American Express card holders know that their monthly bill contains an image of each transaction because of the company's commitment to image technology (see Chapter 3). By using imaging in creative ways, American Express claims to have reduced its billing costs by 25 percent while offering its customers a new and important service at least two years before its competition.

However, installing new, far-reaching technology is usually expensive and risky. Imaging technology is no exception:

- *Imaging can be very expensive.* The average significant imaging project starts out in the $1 million to $2 million range. To succeed, the project must commence after careful planning, including a thorough up-front feasibility study.
- *Hardware and software compatibility is a major stumbling block.* While every vendor professes to have open systems, many imaging systems have connectivity problems. Even if a firm purchases a complete system from one vendor so that all parts work well together, the system may not work with the firm's existing technology. It is not uncommon for a purchaser to discover that its new imaging system is not compatible with the network

already in use throughout the company. To avoid this problem, the purchaser should demand on-site testing of all components before signing an agreement with the vendor.

- *Power demands for an imaging system can be very large.* The firm should include power usage costs and any upgrading costs in its plan and estimates.
- *Major benefits will not accrue if the imaging system is installed only to increase automation of the current workflow.* Organizations must use the opportunity to make workflow changes that will provide the large productivity gains this technology promises.
- *Major workflow changes can result in organizational disruption and worker distress.* Because jobs and patterns of work are affected by imaging technology and workflow redesign, organizations should plan carefully to include a great deal of training in their imaging projects.

Reports of major productivity gains have come from both businesses and the government. However, such gains will come only if the application is chosen carefully. The following areas are considered very promising for imaging:

- *Banks*—check processing, loan (including mortgage) processing, credit cards, international funds transfer, finance, trust and stock ownership transfer.
- *Insurance companies*—underwriting, claims processing, investment management.
- *Pharmaceutical industry*—applications, regulatory affairs, medical libraries.

Groupware: New Technology for Collaborative Work

Groupware: Software that recognizes the significance of groups in offices by providing functions and services that support the collaborative activities of work groups.

Almost all office automation software has been designed for the individual who is working alone. Yet our definition of an office (earlier in this chapter) states that offices are work groups composed of people who work together toward shared goals. **Groupware** is a new kind of software that recognizes the significance of groups in offices by providing functions and services that support the collaborative activities of work groups. The goal of groupware is to improve the effectiveness of the work group by providing electronic links between its members.

What happens in groups? Members of the group perform the following activities:

- schedule meetings
- hold meetings
- communicate with each other
- collaborate to develop ideas
- share the preparation of documents
- share knowledge
- share information on the work each member is doing.

Groupware is a growing field of software meant to support all of these activities. No precise definition of groupware has emerged, but terms like *cooperative* and *collaborative* are commonly used when discussing it. Groupware usually includes such functions as information sharing, electronic meetings, scheduling, and E-mail. This technology requires the use of a network to connect the members of the group as they work on their own desktop computers, often in widely scattered locations. The groupware definition of groups is fluid, allowing users to define the work groups, with multiple group definitions allowed. For example, a manager may define a group of only those people who work for him. A group may be established for all employees dealing with a specific customer. A com-

Electronic calendaring: Software that tracks appointments and schedules in an office.

Electronic mail (E-mail): Software that allows the electronic exchange of messages between users in remote locations.

Electronic meeting software: Software designed to enhance the productivity of face-to-face meetings or of meetings among participants in scattered locations.

panywide group may be established. Of course, an individual will belong to as many of those groups as is appropriate.

Electronic calendaring is a broadly accepted technology. Although its software has been typically used to keep track of appointments for individuals, groupware calendaring software adds a focus on group schedules, allowing individuals to view the calendars of other members of their own group. One popular function is the ability of the software automatically to search the calendars of members of the group for an acceptable meeting time and then to schedule that meeting for each individual in the group.

Electronic mail (E-mail) is software that allows the electronic exchange of messages. Electronic mail can enhance productivity by speeding up information flow and lessening the need for placing telephone calls or paper-based messaging systems. E-mail thus reduces group coordination costs. It also creates new patterns of social interaction so that people can share new data and ideas (Sproull and Kiesler, 1991). Some E-mail systems are limited to message exchanges between users of a single computer. More commonly, however, E-mail systems also pass messages from computer to computer, sometimes within the same location, sometimes halfway round the world. Many UNIX systems accomplish this by a dial-up telephone link. However, in recent years E-mail has come more and more to reside on networks. Because groupware, by definition, must connect workers on separate computers, groupware software often includes an E-mail function, even though many purchasers of groupware already have one or more E-mail systems installed. For E-mail to be fully effective within an organization that uses multiple E-mail systems, that organization must make those systems "talk" to each other so that an individual on one system can communicate with someone on a different E-mail system.

Electronic meeting software packages are designed to increase the productivity of a face-to-face group meeting or to make possible a meeting of participants in scattered locations. Some such software will do both, and some electronic meeting software utilizes videoconferencing (see the chapter-ending case study). We discuss the way in which this software enhances the decision-support function in Chapter 16.

We will discuss the remainder of the workgroup functions together, as they all involve shared messages and documents. Groupware enhances collaboration by allowing the exchange of ideas (in the form of electronic messages) on a given topic. All the messages on that topic will be saved in a group, stamped with the date, time, and author. Any group member can review the ideas of others at any time and add ideas of his or her own. Similarly, individuals can post a document for other members of the group to comment upon and/or edit. Members of a group can post requests for help from the group, and any member of the group can respond and can view the responses of other members of the group. Finally, if a group so chooses, the members of that group can store their work notes on the groupware so that all others in the group can see what progress is being made, what problems occur, what activities are planned.

LOTUS NOTES

Groupware products such as Higgins, The Coordinator, and Microsoft's Windows for Workgroups are all commercially available, but the leading groupware software is Lotus Notes from Lotus Software, in Cambridge, Massachusetts. To illustrate the power and value of groupware, we will describe the functions contained in Lotus Notes and also discuss several of its actual applications.

Lotus Notes is essentially a way to share a database over a network to create information-sharing applications. The databases are collections of documents stored in a group and can contain free-form text, graphics, file attachments, and—with additional software and hardware—sound, image, and video data.

A technological overview should help us to understand its capabilities. Lotus Notes can operate on IBM-compatible microcomputer workstations running OS/2 or Windows, Macintosh computers, or workstations running UNIX. The

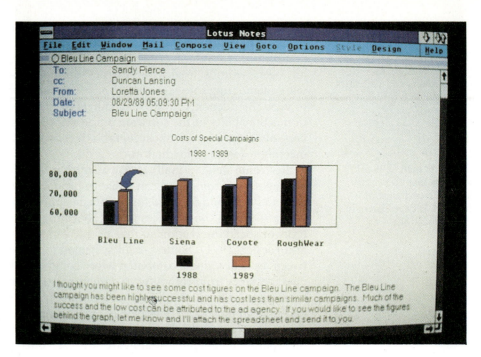

Figure 15.11
Compound document on Lotus Notes. Lotus Notes groupware provides an organization-wide forum to discuss issues and brainstorm solutions. In this example, the author is discussing the cost of a special campaign using a compound document that incorporates spreadsheet charts and a report. *Courtesy of Lotus Development Corporation.*

Compound document:
Electronic document that consists of differing types of information acquired from separate sources such as graphics, database, spreadsheet, and text-based programs.

data are stored in a distributed database, with servers at key locations wherever needed. Lotus Notes runs on both LANs and WANs, using several popular network operating systems, such as Novell, Banyan and IBM. The user interface is Windows-like and icon-based.

The software supports **compound documents,** which are documents that consist of differing types of information from separate sources; for example, a single document combining graphics, spreadsheet data, and character-based text is a compound document. Figure 15.11 illustrates a compound document displayed through Lotus Notes. In Notes the whole document—graphics, spreadsheet data and text—is stored as a single record, whereas with normal office software the various elements are stored as separate files that are combined at print time.

Figure 15.12
Lotus Notes desktop. Each icon represents a different Notes application. By clicking on the icon, this user can work with people all over the world, including the sales team, and senior management. *Courtesy of Lotus Development Corporation.*

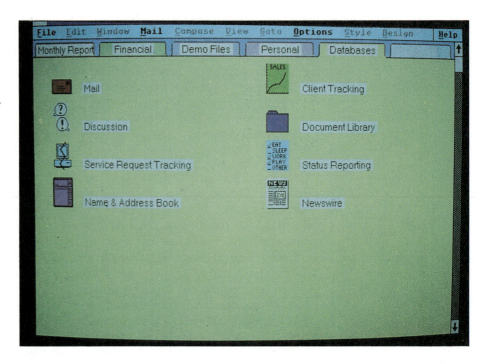

Lotus Notes is compatible with a wide range of popular desktop word processors, spreadsheets, and graphics packages.

In Notes, each application is a separate database. The system is delivered with predefined, template applications that can be used as is or modified. The user can also create customized applications from scratch. Each application has its own icon on the main menu (see Figure 15.12). To enter data into a database, one uses a Form (Lotus Notes comes with predefined forms, but the users can easily create their own). The Form will contain a date-time stamp, the originator of the data, any indexing keys, and a field that contains the document. Retrieving data requires a View, again usually defined by the users. Views are actually selections of documents based upon key fields in the records, sorted in a specified order.

Each Notes database logs all pertinent communications among members of a workgroup so that the notes can be kept for future reference and shared. Members of the team can access each member's contribution and comment on it, or they can use Notes to distribute reference information to other team members. Figure 15.13 and Figure 15.11 show how Notes was used to distribute information and to pool ideas in a sales discussion database. Members of the entire organization involved in sales and marketing could access documents, comment on them, or add new information. Figure 15.13 shows a sales activity report that includes related business and customer issues.

The Emergency Operations Center of Pacific Gas and Electric (PG&E) uses Lotus Notes to receive damage reports and repair requests from 150 offices throughout the 93,000 square miles in Northern California. While management in San Francisco may use the database to view a chronological list of outages, the local offices will use it to produce a listing of outages that still need repairing. When the San Francisco earthquake hit in October 1989, PG&E found the system to be quite effective in facilitating the management of the many repairs urgently needed. The database was also the source for information supplied to the press on the types of outages that had occurred (Lotus Notes Application Profile).

Harmon Contract W.S.A., Inc., is a Minneapolis-based construction company that focuses on skyscraper shell construction all over the world. With annual sales totaling well over $200 million, sales is a key function. Recently, manage-

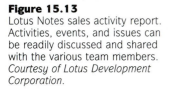

Figure 15.13
Lotus Notes sales activity report. Activities, events, and issues can be readily discussed and shared with the various team members. *Courtesy of Lotus Development Corporation.*

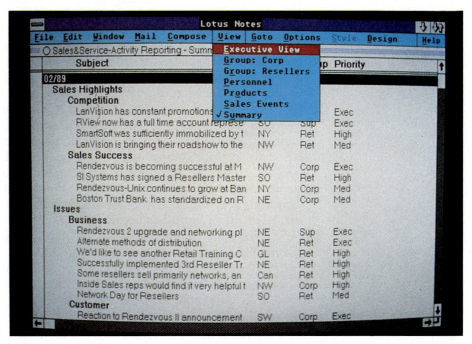

ment became concerned that Harmon did not have an effective method of passing sales skills and information from the top sales persons to the newer staff. Over a four-week period, using Lotus Notes, the firm developed an oral history database. All sales documents, including graphics documents, relevant to a specific project are now entered into the database, making the data available to management and to other sales staff. The database is used both to facilitate current sales projects and to give the less experienced sales staff access to the methods and approaches of the senior sales personnel (Bermant, 1992).

Manufacturers Hanover Trust (MHT), one of the ten largest banks in the United States, also turned to Notes originally to improve the effectiveness of its sales operation. MHT found itself with vast quantities of data that were neither well integrated nor easily accessible. Using Lotus Notes, the account officers and corporate trust sales staff now can maintain their records in a way that is organized and widely accessible. They set up a company profiles database that centralizes client and prospect information. The communications profiles database is used to keep track of day-to-day communications between the MHT staff and its customers. As MIS Vice President Rich Luciano put it, "Selling involves knowing as much about your customer as you can." Account officers can bring up a one-page summary of information on the customer, view contacts for a specific product, or examine all contacts for the past six months. MHT's staff is now able to be far more knowledgeable as it deals with customers—from knowing the nickname of the client or contact to knowing which banks that customer uses in Norway. Before Notes, sharing of information was time-consuming and was not successful if one did not know whom to ask, or if that person was on vacation. Of course, in the past when a staff member left MHT, he or she took valuable information. Now all of that information is stored on Notes and is easily retrieved when needed, using a range of flexible views. The applications also help managers track staff activities, analyze the effectiveness of their time use, and plan future work (Lotus Notes Application Profile).

Groupware has not been well accepted wherever it has been installed. The Window on Organizations provides insight into the serious controversies that groupware has engendered in a number of companies.

Other problems are emerging. One concern is that groupware allows too much data to be collected. When this occurs, it becomes easy for the trivial to flood out the significant. Chase Manhattan Bank, NA, found its Lotus Notes forum so flooded with messages that it appointed expert editors to delete insignificant, inaccurate, or misleading entries. Electronic scheduling can have the same result. Metropolitan Life Insurance Co. found that meetings that used to take hours to arrange took only 30 seconds when scheduled electronically. People found that it was so easy to schedule meetings that they started scheduling unnecessary meetings. E-mail can also swamp staff with an overabundance of information (Sheng et al., 1989/90). Heavy users of multiple E-mail facilities might have to check Microsoft Mail, Vax Notes, CompuServe, and MCI Mail for messages. The list could go on and on. Groupware alone is not able to promote information-sharing if team members do not feel it is in their interest to share, especially in organizations that encourage competition among employees. For instance, a sales representative might hesitate to share prospect information in a common database if it helps another person win the customer. One study of a consulting firm found that junior staff members did not want to use Notes to share valuable information because the firm had an up-or-out promotion policy and junior staff were expected to bill directly all of their time. Time spent communicating with other workers could not be billed to clients. Staff were evaluated in terms of both the quality of their work and the number of hours billed. Yet such information-intensive organizations stood to benefit substantially if people shared their expertise (Orlikowski, 1992; Press, 1992b; "Lotus Notes," 1992).

Nonetheless, it seems clear from our examples (and many others) that the use of this technology can enhance the work of a group if the applications are

ORGANIZATIONS
The Groupware Controversy

Groupware focuses on technology needed to support small groups as they work together. As a result, it incorporates a broad range of office functions—the creation, editing, storage and management of documents, electronic mail, calendaring, and even electronic videoconferencing. Individual employees, who have been accustomed to working independently, are now experiencing both the benefits and the problems of working more closely as a team. The shift in work methods, made possible by groupware, has engendered a surprising amount of contention.

Many find that groupware brings productivity gains by shortening meeting times or reducing the frequency of meetings. For example, Fred Bonner, director of computer systems for the Discovery Channel, believes that meeting room vacancies have risen by 40 percent since his company has begun using groupware. Similarly, Barry Barron, who is manager of information systems for the Port of Oakland (California), states that "We hold fewer meetings now, and those that we do hold involve fewer people." He attributes the reduction in numbers of meetings to the ability of groupware to keep each department informed about other departments' activities.

Some of the controversy arises from the functions and controls built into the software. For example, Action Technologies, Inc.'s Coordinator Workgroup Productivity System includes "voucher routing" in its groupware. To circulate a memo electronically, the software requires that the memo be classified prior to being sent. The user classifies the memo (request, consultation, order, etc.) and establishes action deadlines. The software updates the schedules of both the recipients and their groups, which includes the recipients' managers. The recipient need not have been consulted about these deadlines.

Ray Howell, who is assistant vice-president for information management in NCR's commercial insurance division, believes that many employees "might be afraid of a product that automatically schedules people, puts priorities on things, and possibly sends messages to management when they fail." He says that employees "might feel Big Brother is watching."

Christine Bullen (who studied groupware at MIT's Sloan School of Management), has found that some features in groupware software have aroused a great deal of hostility. She has heard groupware labeled as "a power tool for authoritarians," and has heard the system called "fascist existentialism." She reports that many users seek out ways to short circuit some of the objectionable functions, particularly the requirement that a memo be classified in advance.

Group editing of documents has also generated controversy. Using Instant Update from On Technology, Inc., in Cambridge, Massachusetts, an author can use the network to make a document available to a selected list of employees for updating. Matthew Ghourdjian, IS director of Hennigan & Mercer (a Los Angeles law firm) finds that this function allows his firm to create needed legal documents rapidly. However, Greg O'Hara, a system supervisor at Wright-Patterson Air Force Base, believes that software that allows someone other than the author to update a document threatens the integrity of that document. Moreover, groupware often does not manage document update timing adequately. If two people are simultaneously editing the same document, the changes made and saved by the first person might be wiped out when the second person saves later changes.

Groupware E-mail raises additional problems. Employees comfortable with their E-mail systems may actively resist joining group discussions. The privacy of traditional E-mail systems has a different "look and feel" from the much more public space of workgroup computing.

In most large organizations, E-mail was installed by local business units, resulting in numerous, noncompatible systems being installed. A typical example is US West Communications of Denver, which has about 38,000 employees in 15 states running 14 different E-mail systems—DEC's All-In-1, IBM's PROFS, Wang's WangOffice, and a number of UNIX-based local area network systems. Most of these systems do not "talk" with each other, effectively preventing most employees from communicating through E-mail. Groupware does not solve this problem. Rather, it can only contribute to the confusion and further restrict communications by bringing in yet another E-mail system. Obviously, what many corporations need is either standardization on a single corporatewide E-mail system, or at least a limited, approved list of systems that can communicate with each other.

Sources: Emma Zevik, "Getting a Grip on Groupware," *Computerworld* (March 30, 1992); John J. Xenakis, "Documents by Committee," *InformationWEEK* (December 9, 1991) and "Shared Interests," *InformationWEEK* (December 30, 1991); and Mark Dowie, "Friend or Big Brother?" *InformationWEEK* (July 23, 1990).

To Think About: Assume your manager has asked you to make a recommendation as to whether or not your work group should install groupware. From what you know about groupware, would you recommend this technology? Why or why not? What management, organization and technology factors would you consider in making your recommendation? What steps would you take to reduce the problems and maximize the value of the software?

properly designed to fit the organization's needs and work practices. Groupware today may be compared to the situation surrounding spreadsheets ten years ago—its use is new and we can only dimly see its long-range value.

Managing Information: Desktop Databases

Personal information manager: Packaged database tool designed to support specific office data management tasks for an information worker.

Desktop microcomputers provide many office workers with the opportunity to develop their own individual client tracking systems, customer lists, and supplier and vendor databases. However, most office workers do not create these databases on their own because microcomputer database languages are still too difficult for nonprogrammers to use. Instead, a new kind of software that is customized for specific data management needs of salespersons, managers, real estate agents, stockbrokers, and the like is now beginning to appear. This new software is often called **personal information managers;** it consists of packaged database tools designed to support specific office data management tasks.

One example of a personal information manager is The Financial Manager (Azimuth Corporation), designed to serve the desktop information needs of account executives and portfolio managers in the financial services industry. Financial managers typically have from 500 to 1000 clients; each client has one or more accounts or portfolios of investments. Financial managers also have a full calendar of events, activities, and planned actions. In addition, each manager has several routine projects; these include sending letters to clients, telephoning clients, and prospecting for business. The Financial Manager keeps track of a manager's clients, portfolios, calendars, appointments, and projects.

Figure 15.14 illustrates two on-line screens for this system. The first screen lists the user's appointments for the day. The second screen is for client data. This particular screen indicates that data are about a prospect—someone who is not yet a client. Additional screens with more detailed information follow this screen. With The Financial Manager, a stockbroker can select any subgroup of clients, call them on the phone, or send them a special letter describing recent stock market developments.

Managing Projects: Desktop Project Managers

Project management software: Software that facilitates the development, scheduling, and management of a project by breaking the complex project into simpler subtasks, each with its own completion time and resource requirements.

Offices are the organization's control points that coordinate the flow of resources to projects and evaluate results. **Project management software** breaks a complex project down into simpler subtasks, each with its own completion time and resource requirements. Once a user knows what is needed by each subtask, delivery schedules can be written and resources allocated. Two traditional project management techniques (see Chapter 14) are CPM (Critical Path Method) and PERT (Program Evaluation and Review Technique).

Contemporary project managers in the 1990s have begun to use graphical user interfaces, permitting managers to operate the programs with a mouse. Project managers also have access to high-quality presentation graphics, permitting photographic slide and overhead transparency output. Whereas project management software initially focused on a single user, contemporary packages can be accessed by many members of a work group.

15.3   Knowledge Work Systems

Because knowledge work and data work are both information work, both use many of the same information systems (particularly office automation systems). However, knowledge work is also specialized; thus it requires specialized information systems. This section describes the features of knowledge work that can be supported by specific knowledge work systems.

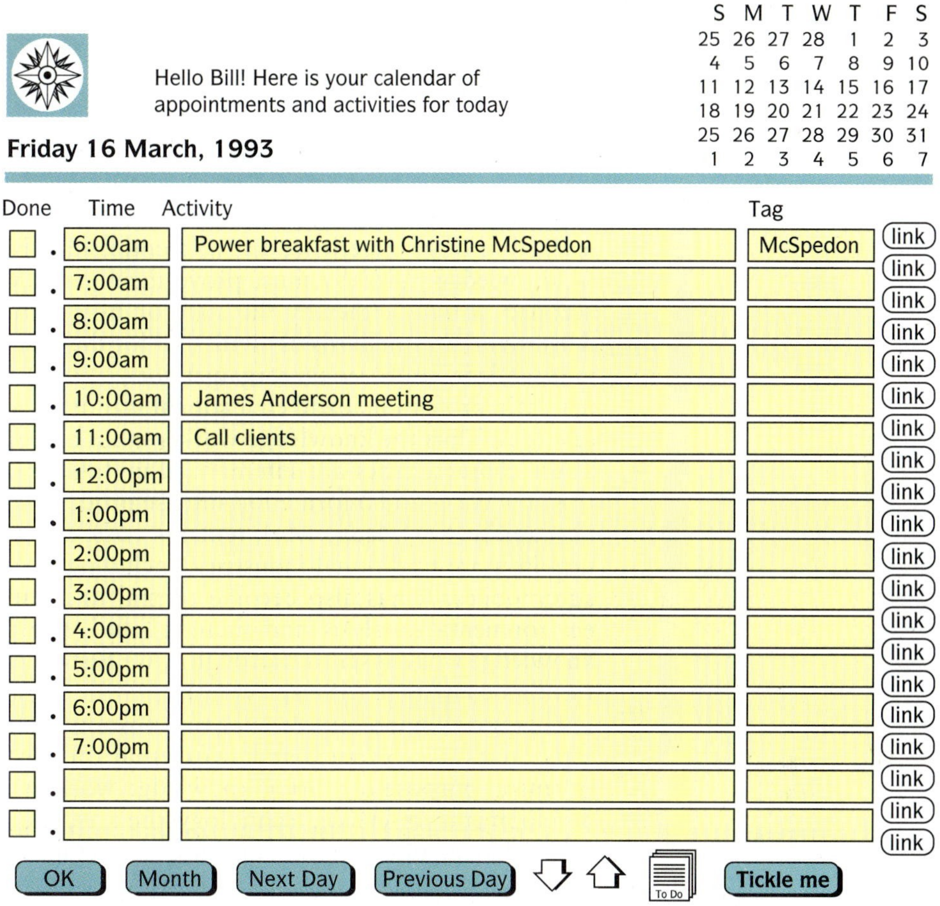

S M T W T F S
25 26 27 28 1 2 3
4 5 6 7 8 9 10
11 12 13 14 15 16 17
18 19 20 21 22 23 24
25 26 27 28 29 30 31
1 2 3 4 5 6 7

Hello Bill! Here is your calendar of
appointments and activities for today

Friday 16 March, 1993

Done	Time	Activity	Tag	
☐ .	6:00am	Power breakfast with Christine McSpedon	McSpedon	link
☐ .	7:00am			link
☐ .	8:00am			link
☐ .	9:00am			link
☐ .	10:00am	James Anderson meeting		link
☐ .	11:00am	Call clients		link
☐ .	12:00pm			link
☐ .	1:00pm			link
☐ .	2:00pm			link
☐ .	3:00pm			link
☐ .	4:00pm			link
☐ .	5:00pm			link
☐ .	6:00pm			link
☐ .	7:00pm			link
☐ .				link
☐ .				link

[OK] [Month] [Next Day] [Previous Day] ⇩ ⇧ [To Do] [Tickle me]

(A)

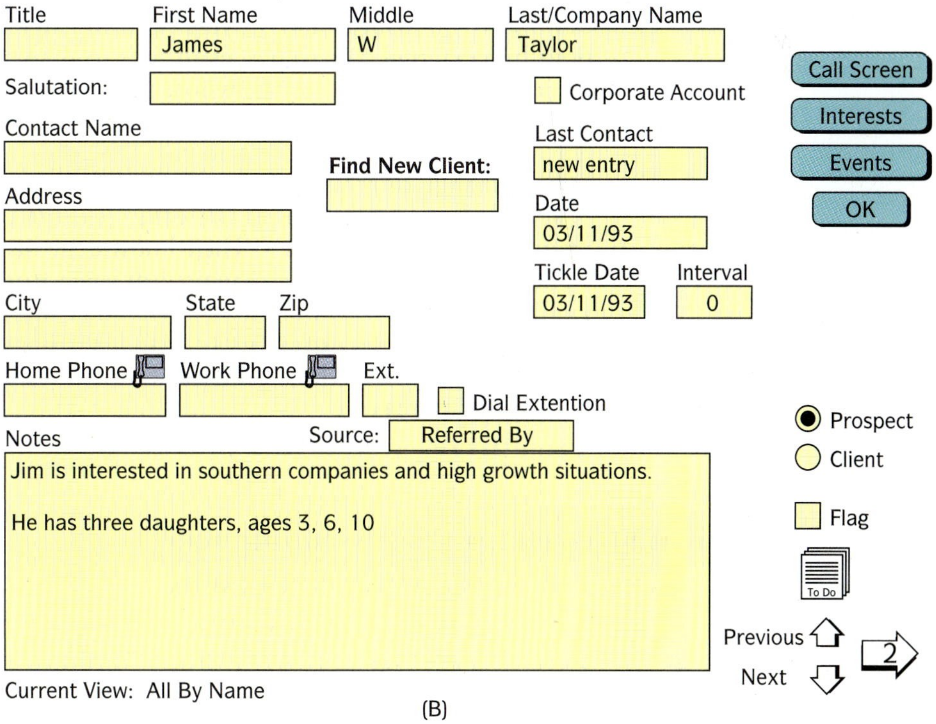

Title	First Name	Middle	Last/Company Name
	James	W	Taylor

[Call Screen]

Salutation: _____   ☐ Corporate Account

[Interests]

Contact Name _____   Last Contact: new entry

[Events]

Find New Client: _____   Date: 03/11/93

[OK]

Address _____

Tickle Date: 03/11/93   Interval: 0

City _____ State _____ Zip _____

Home Phone 🖀 _____ Work Phone 🖀 _____ Ext. _____ ☐ Dial Extention

Notes _____ Source: Referred By

Jim is interested in southern companies and high growth situations.

He has three daughters, ages 3, 6, 10

◉ Prospect
○ Client

☐ Flag

[To Do]

Previous ⇧   2⇨
Next ⇩

Current View: All By Name

(B)

Figure 15.14a and 15.14b
Personal information manager:
The Financial Manager. Figure
15.14A shows the opening
screen from the Financial
Manager, a personal information
manager. The opening screen
greets the manager each day
the program is run with a
schedule of the day's events.
Figure 15.14B shows the client
screen. Each client has a record
in the database which contains
relevant background information
and investment objectives.
*Source: Azimuth Corporation,
1993. Copyright © 1993
Azimuth Corporation. Reprinted
by permission.*

The Role of Knowledge Work in the Organization

The Bureau of Labor Statistics defines knowledge work as having four characteristics. This definition has generally been accepted by sociologists and economists as well. First, knowledge work is supported by a codified body of knowledge that is generally and widely accepted as valid. The body of knowledge is usually found in books stored in a library. Second, this body of knowledge must be capable of being taught at universities. It differs from a skill that can only be learned through experience and apprenticeship. Third, practitioners of the body of knowledge normally must prove their mastery of that knowledge by being certified, usually either by the state or by a university. Fourth, the profession must maintain standards of admission for the practitioner through regulation by independent professional organizations. The professional bodies must also maintain professional and educational standards and guidelines and a statement of ethics. Thus the knowledge worker must have more than technique and skill. These characteristics are summarized in Table 15.5.

Knowledge- and information-intense products and services have been expanding rapidly. Knowledge work remains critical to the development of new products in more traditional industries, including pharmaceuticals, electronics, and automobiles. It has also become central to a range of newer services such as environmental analysis and financial and investment advice. To understand knowledge work systems thoroughly, we first must explore the ways knowledge workers contribute to business firms.

Three roles stand out. Perhaps the most distinctive role of knowledge workers is to interpret the ever expanding external knowledge bases for the organization. A central purpose for hiring knowledge workers is to keep the firm abreast of developments in science, technology, the arts, and social thought. Developments in these areas often contain business opportunities or risks. As more and more value in the economy depends on knowledge and information products, the only way a firm can keep up is to invest heavily in knowledge workers. Indeed, the fastest-growing industries are those that produce information- and knowledge-intensive products.

A second role that knowledge workers are uniquely qualified to perform is as internal consultants to their firms. They can advise managers about changes in technology and science, and can bring formal models to bear on problems. They can also write reports, and provide professional expertise. While most corporations hire external consultants from time to time to supplement their work, it is the internal knowledge worker who is the main source of consulting information.

Third, knowledge workers are organizational change agents. Based on external developments in science and the arts, they are expected to evaluate and initiate change projects and to promote them.

Knowledge workers exhibit two other relevant characteristics that are unique among information workers. Their knowledge base and their understanding of what to do with that knowledge prevent them from being subjected to the same kind of supervision and authority that other information workers will be subjected to. They often know more than their boss. Therefore, they are usually autonomous. In addition, knowledge workers often are physically segregated into research areas.

Table 15.5 CHARACTERISTICS OF KNOWLEDGE WORK

1. Based on codified body of knowledge
2. Body of knowledge taught at schools or universities
3. Practitioners usually require certification by the state or school
4. Practitioners regulated by independent professional organizations

These unique roles and conditions of knowledge workers produce special requirements for the information systems they use and provide the rationale for the development of those systems. **Knowledge work systems** are specifically designed to promote the creation of new knowledge and ensure that new knowledge and technical expertise are properly integrated into the business.

Requirements of Knowledge Work Systems

Knowledge workers are focused on the expanding knowledge base external to their work group and to the organization that employs them. They need easy access to electronically stored external knowledge bases. The knowledge they must access might be in journal articles stored in libraries or in collections of scientific research or legal findings. They usually need mail links to other professionals working in universities or in other businesses. They also often need mail links to other knowledge workers working within their own organization, whether at another site within the country or abroad. Consequently, one characteristic of knowledge work systems is that they incorporate more links to external data and information than is customary with other corporate systems. The Window on Management shows the management benefits of using a network such as the Internet to provide knowledge workers with these external data. On page 513 Figure 15.5 summarizes the requirement of knowledge work systems.

A second characteristic of knowledge work systems is the software they require. Typically their software contains far more powerful graphic, analytic, document management, and communications capabilities than other corporate systems.

Third, knowledge work systems require considerably more computing power than is true for other information work. Engineers may need to run thousands of complex calculations to determine the strength and safety of a specific part they are designing. Lawyers may need to scan through thousands of documents and legal findings before recommending a strategy. Graphics applications are particularly greedy for computing power. To understand the greater power needs of graphics, remember that a one-page document stored in character format (an ordinary word processing document) requires perhaps 8K of disk space to store, while that document stored in a bit-mapped graphic format requires about 50K, a ratio of maybe 6:1. The computer requires a commensurate increase in power to manipulate the larger, bit-mapped file rather than the smaller character-based file. Graphic simulations have become common and even necessary to much of the work of knowledge workers, from architects to pharmaceutical research chemists. Designers and draftsmen, using computer-aided design (CAD) systems to design such products as automobile bodies, need three-dimensional graphics software to visualize and model the product on screen before producing a physical model. Even more intensive simulations, called virtual reality, can be so large as to require very large and fast supercomputers.

A user-friendly interface is very important to a knowledge worker's system. User friendly interfaces save a lot of time by allowing the user to perform the needed tasks and get to the required information without having to spend a lot of time learning how to use the computer. While saving time is important to any worker, it is more important for knowledge workers than for most other employees because a knowledge worker's time is so costly—wasting a knowledge worker's time is simply too expensive.

Finally, knowledge work systems usually require the use of workstations. As described in Chapter 6, a **workstation** is a desktop computer that is far more powerful than a conventional microcomputer. The workstation has powerful graphics, analytic, document management, and communications capabilities and the ability to perform several complicated tasks at one time. Knowledge workstations are often designed and optimized for the specific tasks to be performed so that a design engineer will require a different workstation than a lawyer. Figure 15.15 summarizes these requirements of knowledge work systems.

MANAGEMENT

A Network for Knowledge Workers

Because modern economies have become information economies, access to knowledge is critical to the success of many companies. Yet new knowledge is expanding so swiftly that keeping up is an immense task that requires management's attention. The Internet system may help with this problem. Established in the 1970s by the U.S. Pentagon to allow academic and corporate researchers and government officials to share data using E-mail and remote computers, the Internet has become the world's largest network, with about 800,000 computers and 4 million users in 107 countries.

The Internet, in fact, is a network of networks—over 21,000 at last count. Member networks share software standards so that messages flow without technical restrictions. The most popular Internet function is E-mail. Many users prefer it to other public networks and even to their own corporate systems. Its E-mail is very fast, delivering in seconds or minutes a message that might take hours or days with other networks. At the same time, the technology it uses keeps the cost relatively low. Another advantage is that its E-mail system allows messages to include fax, video, and desktop print files. Cygnus Support Inc., a Mountain View, California, software company, uses the Internet E-mail to maintain contact with its Cambridge, Massachusetts, office, while SRI International, a Menlo Park, California, consulting firm, uses it to link to its London office. Salespeople all over the world find it easy to keep in contact with customers and with their offices using the Internet and laptop computers. Tom Stone, a senior editor at Addison-Wesley in Reading, Mas-

sachusetts, claims that correspondence with an author that used to take a week can now be completed in a day. He now handles proposal submissions through the Internet and even allows text submission via the Internet so that he can copyedit without ever handling paper. Newspapers such as *The New York Times* and *The Economist* use the network to gather information on their readers' interests, using the E-mail system's facility to define large mailing lists. Many businesses try to be on selected mailing lists so that they can more easily keep abreast of developments in their industries. These mailing lists cover many topics worldwide, including, for example, an oil and gas industry list.

With blinding speed, the Internet can link a lone researcher sitting at a computer screen to mountains of data otherwise too expensive to tap; to large electronic meetings, work sessions, and bulletin boards; and to numerous electronic journals.

Several hundred library catalogues are on-line through the Internet, including those of such giants as the Library of Congress, the University of California, and Harvard University. General Motors claims that Internet library research is vital to its product development. In addition, users are able to search over 400 databases containing information such as the Central Intelligence Agency's world almanac, the latest satellite weather photos (updated hourly), science fiction reviews, and a molecular biology library. The network is also the source of a great deal of high-quality, free software. General Electric research physicist Dick St. Peters says his group has used "hundreds or thousands" of software packages off the net-

work. In return his group has made available to medical research and development sites a package it has written for medical imaging; they even use the Internet to "remotely log in and help" the users of this program if the users report having problems.

Problems with the Internet include its current lack of tight security and the overwhelming amount of information available on it. So many people are putting so much material on the network that fears are mounting about data overload and psychological burnout. (Some Internet users report receiving 500 messages a day.) Human editors and software to filter data and to pinpoint desired information are emerging Internet aids. The question facing corporate management is, "Do we make use of this network and if so, how?"

Sources: John S. Quarterman, "What Can Businesses Get Out of Internet," *Computerworld* (February 22, 1993); John Markoff, "A Web of Networks, an Abundance of Services," *The New York Times* (February 28, 1993); and Gary H. Anthes, "Internet Tapped for Global Virtual Publishing Enterprise," *Computerworld* (March 23, 1992).

To Think About: As a member of the management team of a high-tech company, what advantages would the Internet offer you? What problems do you see with relying upon the Internet for E-mail, for research, and for a source of software? Do you think you would support or oppose using the Internet and why? What other elements would be needed in a cost-effective policy to support knowledge worker access to public information worldwide?

Examples of Knowledge Work Systems

Knowledge work systems will vary greatly, depending upon the profession and the specific application being supported. Design engineers need graphics with enough power to handle three-dimensional computer-aided design (CAD) systems. On the other hand, financial analysts are more interested in having access

Figure 15.15
Requirements of knowledge
work systems. Knowledge work
systems require strong links to
external knowledge bases in
addition to specialized hardware
and software.

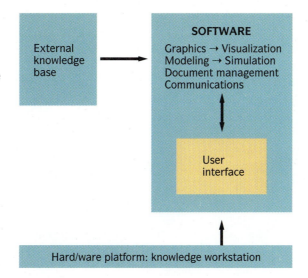

to a myriad of external databases and in optical disk technology so that they can access massive amounts of financial data very quickly. In this text we cannot describe all the knowledge work systems or even all of the many types of knowledge work systems. What we have done, instead, is to select three very different types of such systems as examples that will help you to understand the breadth and power of knowledge work systems. We now examine a conventional computer-aided design system, "virtual reality" systems for simulation and modeling, and a financial workstation.

COMPUTER-AIDED DESIGN: DEVELOPING A NEW PRODUCT

Computer-aided design (CAD): Information system that automates the creation and revision of designs using sophisticated graphics software.

Tires have been much the same for 100 years. They consist of rubber and composition using air pressure as a spring. Alan R. Burns, a mining engineer from Perth, Australia, had an innovative idea, and using computer-aided design software (CAD), he turned that idea into reality. **Computer-aided design (CAD)** automates the creation and revision of designs, using computers and sophisticated graphics software. Mr. Burns knew that off-road vehicle tires take a terrible beating because of the many hazards they are subjected to. The result is frequent tire replacement and repeated, costly job downtime. His idea was a modular tire made of independent tread segments that could be replaced individually. The segments are not pneumatic and so are not subject to punctures. If one segment needs to be replaced, the job can be quickly done by the operator, who does not need to remove the wheel from the vehicle. The segments are bolted around the circumference of a steel wheel hub.

To turn his idea into an actual usable and saleable tire, Burns turned to computer modeling. But before he could begin the actual design, he needed to understand market requirements. He decided to start his venture by focusing on one market segment, and for market reasons he settled on tires for loaders used in such sectors as construction, mining, and waste dumps. Usage parameters like speed, load, temperature, and surface characteristics were turned into targets for traction, wear life, and ride performance. He then used a CAD workstation to develop a visual representation of the segment, and he modified thickness, tread shape, and other factors until an acceptable design was achieved. He also entered the usage parameter data into the software, as well as characteristics of the rubber compound being used. Utilizing CAD software, he was able to simulate operational characteristics for each visual model and to calculate the tire's stresses and strains under specified loading and usage conditions. The results were evaluated in terms of user-perceived qualities of traction, wear, and ride.

Once Burns approved a design, the same software used the same model data to design the mold tooling for the manufacture of the tire segment. The program

With the assistance of computer-aided design, Alan R. Burns was able to design and develop, and Airboss is able to manufacture and market, this revolutionary segmented tire. The tires are ideally suited for heavy equipment applications such as these earth movers because of their superior handling traction and maneuverability.

could perform flow analysis and also could locate potential problems such as uneven cooling or shrinkage. The output of this phase became the instructions for the milling machines that cut the actual shape into tool steel.

The benefits of CAD systems are clear. The designer is able to produce a more sophisticated and functional design than he or she could possibly have done manually. The design is done right before production begins, significantly reducing both design time and expensive engineering changes once production has begun. Equally large savings come during the modeling function. Using a more traditional design methodology, each new design modification requires a mold to be made and a prototype to be physically tested. That process has to be repeated many times over, which is a very expensive and time-consuming process. Using a CAD workstation, the designer only needs to make a prototype toward the end of the design process. The ability of the CAD software to design the tooling and the manufacturing process also saves a great deal of time and money while producing a manufacturing process with far fewer problems.

Airboss, the Australian company Burns founded to manufacture his invention, is already an apparent success. Its tires do not need some of the complicated manufacturing processes required for competitive pneumatic tires. The result has been lower capital equipment investment costs. Because the tires are not pneumatic, Burns is able to use a simpler composition that is more environmentally sound. The tires he designed have better handling traction and maneuverability than the tractor belts loaders traditionally use, resulting in faster task completion and less equipment stress. All in all, it is no surprise that demand has already outstripped supply, with orders coming in from American and European as well as Australian equipment makers. Burns says he is planning to expand into tires for other applications such as earth-moving equipment (Shapiro, February 28, 1993).

CAD workstations are starting to be used in many areas. For example, the development of new automobiles, from idea to the first delivery, traditionally required about five years. Using CAD software, Japanese auto makers have taken

TECHNOLOGY

Flying High with CAD

Hong Kong's Kai Tak airport is the fifth busiest international airport in the world, and it will reach its absolute capacity in 1994. It cannot be enlarged because it sits in the middle of densely populated Kowloon, the section of Hong Kong on the Kowloon Peninsula. A new airport will be built at a cost of $16 billion on land that will be reclaimed on a nearby island. It is being designed to meet predicted traffic through the year 2040. The airport will be connected to Hong Kong by a 1500-yard bridge, the second largest suspension bridge in the world. It will include both a highway and a rail link. Finally, a complete town for 20,000 employees will be built, including housing, shopping and commercial centers, recreation facilities, and sewage and refuse systems.

The design of the airport is a massive undertaking involving a number of design firms and an astonishing array of computer-aided design (CAD) software packages and other sophisticated technology. It also involves sophisticated, creative ways to link the designers and their designs.

A consortium called Greiner-Maunsell created the basic design. The runway design had to take into account local topology, the urban surroundings, prevalent wind patterns, and criteria from the International Civil Aviation Authority. The designers had to assume the airport would be able to accommodate 900-passenger jets that are now only on the drawing boards. CAD software from Intergraph Corp. integrates "protection surfaces" into the design—

complex 3-D pictures of heights and patterns that airplanes will be able to fly. All the data had to be related to the basic Hong Kong survey grid maps so that the output could be used by other disciplines designing more detailed plans of portions of the airport. The final master plan was produced using a CAD package called AutoCAD, which allows a user to overlay the basic plan without having to combine plans.

The Mott Consortium, comprising three companies, is using a CAD network to design the 3/4-mile long, 60-dock terminal building. The client, Hong Kong's Provisional Airport Authority, requires that all 10,000 design and construction drawings be produced using CAD software. To integrate all the work, Mott networked 11 Intergraph workstations and about 21 486-PCs. The network allows any designer to easily call up his or her own work at any workstation or PC. The software being used includes Intergraph's Microstation for consistent interfacing, and its Modelview for visualization and perspective. CADDET from Mott MacDonald offers concrete detailing and analysis. To visualize the terminal from the view of the passenger by simulating walkthroughs, they are using Intergraph's Design Review. This software is also useful for obtaining client approval on details. The roof design is being done by Ove Arup & Partners, who are using a structural analysis package, Oasys, on a PC-LAN. Numerous other packages are being used for design of terminal details.

Other facets of the project, including land reclamation, the bridge, the highway, the railway systems, and an analysis of the town and its infrastructure, are being designed by other companies. All are using a wide array of specialized CAD programs. Each team is very dependent upon the output of work by other teams. To integrate the work, the Mott Consortium uses an optical jukebox holding 54 read-only optical disks of 650M each. Finished drawings are archived to the optical disks, where they are immediately available to all via a network. Each drawing has a version number so that it can be updated later if needed. When updates do occur that might affect the work of other teams, earlier versions of the same document are marked with a warning.

The airport project is the largest such project in the history of Hong Kong. It is difficult to imagine how this project could take place without the technology the designers have available.

Source: Ross Milburn, "Flying High," *Computer Graphics World,* February, 1993.

To Think About: Do you think this project could be attempted without CAD technology? Why or why not? How would the lack of CAD technology affect the cost and timing of such a project? What benefits to the clients might have caused them to require the designers to produce all documents on CAD software?

---

about a year out of that cycle, and American manufacturers are now rapidly moving to achieve similar results. Faster development not only lowers the cost significantly, but also allows the producer to respond more quickly to changing market demands.

The new Hong Kong airport is being designed with CAD software. The Window on Technology describes this project, illustrating the wide range of specialized CAD systems that exist.

Figure 15.16:
Virtual reality for Wall Street traders. This data distribution and display system uses virtual reality technology to let traders grasp otherwise unmanageable amounts of complex information. Individual instruments are presented as three-dimensional objects. *Courtesy of Maxus Systems International.*

VIRTUAL REALITY: IMMERSION IN FANTASY

Virtual reality systems:
Interactive graphics software and hardware that create computer-generated simulations that provide sensations that emulate real-world activities.

Virtual reality systems have visualization, rendering, and simulation capabilities that go far beyond those of conventional CAD systems. They use interactive graphics software to create computer-generated simulations that are so close to reality that users believe they are participating in a "real" world situation. Virtual reality is such a new technology that few commercial applications have been developed. While its approach may appear to be fantasy to many, its benefits may turn out to be very real.

Virtual reality is interactive in such a way that the user actually feels immersed in the "world" the computer creates. Imagine, for example, a computer version of an architectural design for a house. The house will be built for you, but for now it is still only a design in a computer. Now imagine that with the aid of the computer, you walk through that house, checking out its features and making changes on the spot until you are satisfied with the design. Perhaps the door to the bathroom opens the wrong way, or the living room is too narrow and its north window is not high enough for its width, or the light switch in the front hall is on the wrong side, or you want the linen closet in the kitchen instead of in the hallway. Once construction began, these changes would be very expensive. Even worse, you might not even realize you wanted these changes until after the house is complete and you move in. At the design stage, however, such changes are quick and inexpensive to make. This is the very real fantasy world of virtual reality—software of this type actually exists and is being used today.

How does it work? The virtual world is an implicit world, one that exists only in the computer. To enter that world, the user dons special clothing, headgear, and equipment, depending upon the application. The clothing contains sensors that record the user's movements and immediately transmit that information back to the computer. For instance, to walk through the house, you will need garb that monitors the movement of your feet, hands, and head. You will also need goggles that contain video screens and sometimes audio attachments and feeling gloves so that you can be immersed in the computer feedback. As you walk straight ahead through the house, the images in front of you come closer. If you turn to the right (or turn your head to the right), the image will shift to your left. If you open the door, you will see the door opening and the next room will appear through the doorway. Walk through that doorway and look around, and you will find you are in the next room. Turn around and you can see the previous room through the doorway (unless you already closed the door behind you).

As you might imagine, this is new and very expensive technology. It may take years for the price to come down. For that reason, it may also take many years for large numbers of applications to be developed. In the meantime, however, some commercial applications have been developed and are in use. For instance, virtual reality applications are starting to be developed for the financial industry (see Figure 15.16).

Matsushita Electric Works in Japan has put virtual reality to work in its department stores; it has developed an application very similar to the house example we used above. The stores sell kitchen appliances and cabinets. To promote these products Matsushita has created an application it calls Virtual Kitchen. The prospective buyers bring their kitchen layouts to the department store where trained staff enters a copy of the design into the computer. The customers then don the appropriate equipment and suddenly find themselves in their own kitchen. Now they can try out the appliances in various sizes, colors, and locations. They can test new cabinets, opening and closing the cabinet doors and drawers. They can place their existing table and chairs into the picture so the scene will be very realistic. They can walk around and discover the feel and ambiance of the new kitchen. With this technology, the customer is able to buy with a great deal more confidence. Matsushita is able to make many more on-the-spot sales.

Other architectural applications have been developed. Hewlett-Packard is designing a new European office using virtual reality equipment from VPL Research of Redwood City, California. The city of Berlin, Germany, is using the same equipment to design a new subway system to link the formerly separated East and West sections of the city. The University of North Carolina at Chapel Hill has its own virtual reality system that it is using to design its new computer sciences building, Sitterson Hall (Newquist, March 30, 1992).

Many major pharmaceutical firms have research centers in the Chapel Hill area. Using the University of North Carolina's virtual reality system, they create computer-generated molecular worlds. In recent years they have been using a mouse and CAD software to move structures around as they search for workable compounds. However, using Chapel Hill's virtual reality system, they simply reach in, seize the structures, and break them, move them, or bind them as they wish.

At General Electric's Research and Development Center in Schenectady, New York, GE scientists are working with a group of surgeons from Boston's Brigham and Women's Hospital to develop a virtual reality system to be used in surgery. One of their stated goals is to be able to superimpose a 3-D image of the patient onto the patient and then to operate on the image and the patient at the same time. Further in the future, they want to be able to create an image of the patient and then "walk through" that image, moving between various organs. They hope they will then be able to perform surgery on the image, surgery with such precision that no damage to surrounding tissue will occur. The surgeon's actions on the large virtual image would be duplicated by computer-controlled instruments on the patient.

While these are futuristic hopes, the GE research team is making progress. Currently, for example, they are able to use a magnetic resonance imaging machine (MRI) to make two-dimensional slice pictures of a volunteer's brain. Using virtual reality goggles, and with those MRI images as input, they are able to view the virtual brain with superb, three-dimensional reality. They not only are able to rotate the brain, but are also able to peel off layers of the image to reveal the parts below. They have used these images to put a special cap on a volunteer, project the image of his own brain on that cap, and then sketch onto the cap the surgical pathway through the brain's furrows to a spot where they might need to perform surgery. While the process of operating on the image itself is still a long way away, the team does hope that within the next several years they will be able to create a "virtual" image that surgeons can have beside the operating table so that they can consult it during the operation (Naj, March 3, 1993).

INVESTMENT
WORKSTATIONS:
LEVERAGING KNOWLEDGE
WORKERS IN THE
FINANCIAL INDUSTRY

The key assets of knowledge workers are their knowledge and their time. While some knowledge workers use workstations that are on the cutting edge of technologies, others use more established technologies to leverage those two key assets. New York-based Chancellor Capital Management, Inc., developed its own investment workstations to help it manage $25 billion in assets for 300 clients. The workstations integrate the wide range of data required by portfolio managers from the firm's investment management systems and its portfolio accounting systems and make them available with the touch of a button. By providing one-stop information faster and with fewer errors, the workstations streamline Chancellor's entire investment process, from stock selection to updating accounting records.

The workstations were developed in-house; the computers are Intel-based microcomputers built within Chancellor. The software was either written within Chancellor or purchased by them to integrate into software they had written. Their goals? First, they wanted to eliminate much of the drudgery that goes with computers to give their traders and asset managers more time to concentrate on making decisions and developing strategies. Second, they wanted to integrate their front and back offices so that data integrity issues would disappear and all systems would report identical data. Third, they wanted a more open, flexible system environment, one that could be tailored to an individual's needs while also being able to integrate new software when needed.

Previously Chancellor's data were stored separately in its accounting, trading, research and analytical systems. That not only meant a loss of data integrity, but also an increase in the difficulty the professional staff had in locating and accessing data. The professional staff had to use separate systems to access data on differing areas of investment.

Chancellor built software bridges between these systems with one feeding the other, thus reducing data integrity problems while making access easy. It installed a new user interface so that users have one very friendly screen with a number of windows on it. Different users have different windows, depending upon their own needs. The user can move from one window to another with ease, noting a market trend in one window, checking a second window to determine the state of his or her assets, then to a third window to check analysts' reports on stocks he or she is interested in, and finally moving to a fourth window to execute the trades he or she has decided upon. In the past, each of these moves would have required the user to log off one system and on to another, a process that is not only time-wasting but frustrating as well. These windows represent a tremendous enhancement in speed and efficiency.

Integrating the software used in the front office and the back office enabled trading within the firm to become paperless. Moreover, Chancellor was able to automate its share allocation function. In the past, when it had an order to buy 100,000 shares of x, y or z stock, Chancellor had to figure out manually what percentage was allocated to each account. The process was very time-consuming. Aside from the time saved and the errors reduced, this change brought another benefit: Chancellor can now handle any trade volume it needs to. For example, in September 1992 Chancellor officially turned bullish on stocks. In a few days they went from a significant cash position down to near zero, executing 1200 to 1500 trades per day—double or triple their normal volume. No problems were encountered.

Next Chancellor added electronic mail to its workstation network. Then the firm began to add electronic interfaces to its brokers so that even the orders to the brokers and the trade-execution confirmations became electronic. To keep the system open and give Chancellor the freedom to change brokers, if desired,

Chancellor's staff wrote these interfaces themselves, formatting the data to meet the specific broker's needs. Chancellor also finds that because of its open systems environment, new programs can be integrated with little problem. For example, at the time of this writing, the users of Telerate, one of Chancellor's fixed income services, must access the software through dedicated terminals supplied by Telerate's vendors. With its new, open system, however, Chancellor is planning to distribute Telerate through its own workstation network, making it as easy to access as other Chancellor systems (Michaels, February 1993).

Management Challenges

1. **Increased demands for employee learning and change.** Because the knowledge base and the technologies used in information and knowledge work change rapidly, people are under a great deal of pressure to continue learning and training to maintain their jobs and may need to learn new and different jobs in a short time. Organizations must identify and recruit employees who have the capacity and desire to learn, and they must devote more resources to training. If retraining fails, they may need to retire older workers earlier than in the past. This may both raise costs and create an ethical dilemma for the firm (see Chapter 20).

2. **Integration of knowledge work into the organization.** It is difficult to integrate knowledge workers into a traditional, hierarchical organization. Knowledge workers tend to be very self-directed and autonomous and are somewhat set off from the rest of the organization. They cannot be told what to do. Changes in authority structure and work arrangements are necessary if companies are to utilize their talents without alienating them.

3. **Designing information systems that truly enhance the productivity of knowledge workers.** Information systems that truly enhance the productivity of knowledge workers may be difficult to build because the manner in which information technology can enhance higher-level tasks such as those performed by managers and professionals (i.e., scientists or engineers) is not always clearly understood (Sheng et al. 1989/90). High-level knowledge workers may resist the introduction of any new technology, or they may resist knowledge work systems because such systems diminish personal control and creativity. For instance, some architects may resist using computer-aided architectural rendering systems because they fear the computer-generated representations of buildings cannot convey the individual artistry and imagination of hand-drawn renderings.

Summary

Define information work and the information economy.

Advanced economies in the United States, Canada, and Western Europe have been transformed from industrial economies where most wealth came from manufacturing to information economies where most wealth originates in information and knowledge production. Today, the majority of workers perform information work. Information work is work that consists primarily of creating or processing information.

Describe the roles of knowledge workers and data workers in the organization.

There are two kinds of information workers. Knowledge workers are employees such as engineers, architects, scientists, or attorneys, whose primary job is to create new information for the organization. Knowledge workers interpret the external knowledge base for the organization, advise management, and act as change agents to bring new knowledge into the firm. Data workers are employees such as secretaries, accountants, or salespersons, whose primary job is to process, use, or disseminate information for the organization. Managers perform both knowledge and data work.

Describe the roles and principal activities of the office in contemporary business.

Offices coordinate information work in the organization, link the work of diverse groups in the organization, and couple the organization to its external environment. Offices and office work are therefore central to the success of any contemporary organization. The major office activities are document management, communications, scheduling, data management, and project management.

Explain the contributions of the principal types of office automation technologies.

Word processing, desktop publishing, and digital imaging systems support the document management activities of the office. Electronic mail systems and groupware support its communications activities. Electronic calendar and groupware systems support scheduling activities. Desktop data management systems and customized personal information managers support data management activities. Project management systems break down complex projects into simpler subtasks, producing delivery schedules, allocating resources, and supporting the project management activities of the office.

Understand unique requirements of knowledge work systems.

Knowledge work systems require easy access to an external knowledge base; powerful computer hardware than can support software with intensive graphics, analysis, document management, and communications capabilities; and a friendly user interface. Knowledge work systems often run on workstations.

Describe the major types of knowledge work systems.

Knowledge work systems must be customized for the particular type of knowledge work being performed. Computer-aided design systems and virtual reality systems that create interactive simulations that behave like the real world require graphics and powerful modeling capabilities. Knowledge work systems for financial professionals provide access to external databases and the ability to access massive amounts of financial data very quickly.

Key Terms

Knowledge- and information-intense products	Workflow management
Information workers	Groupware
Information work	Electronic calendaring
Knowledge workers	Electronic mail (E-mail)
Data workers	Electronic meeting software
Office activities	Compound document
Office automation systems (OAS)	Personal information manager
Word processing	Project management software
Desktop publishing	Knowledge work systems (KWS)
Document imaging systems	Workstation
Jukebox	Computer-aided design (CAD)
Index server	Virtual reality systems

Review Questions

1. What are the characteristics of an information economy?

2. Describe the differences between information workers, knowledge workers, data workers, and service workers.

3. What is the relationship between information work and productivity in contemporary organizations?

4. Describe the roles of the office in organizations.

5. What are the five major activities that take place in offices?

6. What is office automation? How has it changed over time?

7. What are the principal types of information systems technology that support the roles and activities of the office? Relate each technology to the role(s) they support.

8. List and describe the uses for document imaging systems in the modern office.

9. What is groupware? How does it support information work? Describe its capabilities.

10. What are the four distinguishing characteristics of knowledge work?

11. What role do knowledge workers play in the organization?

12. What are the generic requirements of knowledge work systems? Why?

13. What is CAD? Describe its role and significance in business today.

14. What is virtual reality? How does it differ from CAD?

Discussion Questions

1. Knowledge workers tend to be treated differently than other workers within businesses today. Define the nontechnical problems these differences might create within the organization. Do you think the problems are significant? Discuss how you would deal with these problems.

2. Perhaps the largest challenge corporate management faces today is finding ways to keep up with the explosion of new information. In what ways is this critical to the future of a knowledge-intensive high-tech company? What long-range strategies do you think such companies need to institute to meet this challenge? Discuss them, their cost, their potential effectiveness.

Group Project

With three or four of your classmates, investigate a high-tech business nearby and observe the role played by knowledge workers in this business. Describe the kinds of knowledge work systems that would be valuable for that business. Define the hardware, software, data, and procedural components for each system, and design a knowledge workstation for one of these systems. Your workstation description could consist of a written report, a diagram, or both. Present your findings to the class. Alternatively, your group could select a professional occupation such as a scientist, engineer, architect, or attorney, and design a professional workstation for that occupation.

CASE STUDY

Multimedia Collaboration: A Pandora's Box?

Pandora, in Greek mythology, was created by Zeus (the principal god and ruler of all gods and humans), and was endowed with great curiosity. She was also given a box but was warned not to open it. Her curiosity won out: She opened the box and all the troubles and diseases of the world escaped before she could close it.

Olivetti Research Laboratory chose the name Pandora for its research project on multimedia systems. The research is being done at Olivetti's research lab in Cambridge, England. The team works in a science fiction environment where their office doors unlock and open as they approach, their workstation turns on, and the work they left yesterday appears almost magically on their screens. When they check their E-mail, they see video messages left by their coworkers. A staff member can scan the other members' offices through his or her workstation to see if they are in and busy. If he or she wishes (and the others are amenable), he or she can, with no effort, start a video conference with several other staff members, again through his or her (and their) workstation. If, while he or she is in someone else's office, and receives a call, it is automatically forwarded to the office being visited without the visitor having taken any action.

The magic of the doors, the automatic turning on of the computer, and the automatic phone forwarding is done through a system called Active Badge, a small badge all team members wear that emits the wearer's infrared identification every 15 seconds. Monitors throughout the site

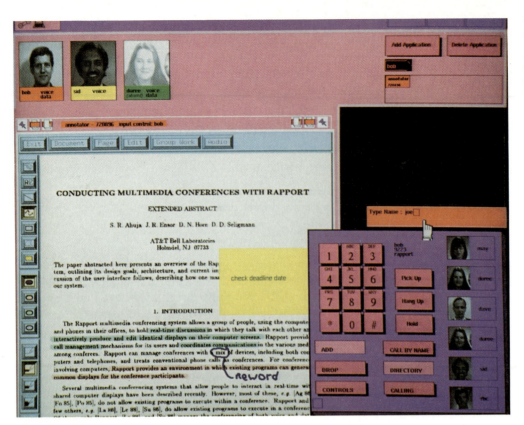

Bell Labs' Rapport system lets co-workers jointly edit computer files as they discuss them. Participants may communicate through voice and data only, as they are doing in the illustration, or add full-motion video.

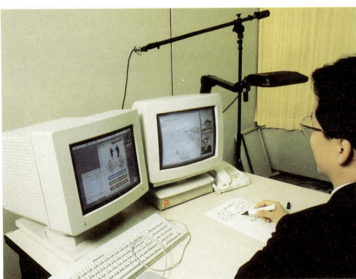

With NTT's TeamWorkStation, users can transfer work from their individual screen (left) to a "shared workspace" (right) for collaboration. Tiny cameras mounted on the black boom and on the lamp send images of the user's face and desktop to the shared screen.

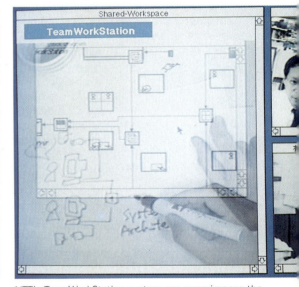

NTT's TeamWorkStation system can superimpose the image of a hand pointing and making corrections onto that of a document lying on a co-worker's desktop.

pick up the signal and keep track of who and where the wearer is and trigger action wherever appropriate, such as unlocking and opening a door.

The multimedia communications portion of Pandora — video messages and video conferencing — however, is the heart of the system. The technology is relatively simple, consisting of networked, UNIX-based workstations each with a video camera, microphone, and loudspeaker attached, plus a special interface to the network to handle the audio and video. The system includes cut-and-paste facilities for editing videos and for creating text-video composite recordings. The cameras are on, pointed toward the face of the staff member when he or she is at his computer; anyone can simply scan the other offices to see who is there and if they are working. An individual can leave another a video mail message with great ease because the function is built into the system. Video conferencing is equally easy. To set the conference up, the initiator merely invites the others to join. The participants see a series of windows on their computer screens during the conference, a window showing the face of each participant plus one or more windows of documents or whatever the individuals want to share. Obviously, those in the Olivetti Research Center could just walk down the hall (and often do), but in the real world the people we want to talk with often work in different buildings, different cities, even different countries, so electronic communications is clearly here to stay, The question the researchers ask is how to make those communications more human, more flexible, and ultimately more effective.

Answering that question raises other questions on how people actually work. How lifelike does a system have to be? How important is it that we recreate the conditions of the intimate office and the face-to-face meeting? Social scientists do not agree on answers, and the differences have spawned a number of very different multimedia communications research projects.

Rapport, a project of AT&T Bell Laboratories in Holmdel, New Jersey, focuses on a uniform interface for E-mail, voice, video and computer communications. The head of the Rapport project, Sudhir Ahuja, describes that interface as a "virtual meeting room" that users "enter" on their screens. To set up a meeting, an individual calls others through the system and asks them to join in. As with Pandora, each participant sees the faces of other participants plus any document being worked on. Each can watch as one of the participants makes changes to the document (one person at a time). The cursor arrow displays the name of the person who has control of changes at that moment. Individuals can switch freely from one conference to another. A virtual meeting can remain around for days, awaiting the next activity by the participants. One interesting aspect of the Rapport approach is that Ahuja does not believe that eye contact is all that important. "Even in a regular meeting," he says, "you don't look at the person all the time – you look at

the blackboard, you write, you look for information. You make eye contact occasionally, just to test whether the person is paying attention."

The Human Interface Laboratories of Japan's NTT, emphasizes the hand and natural marks on paper. Each work station uses a Macintosh computer with two screens (one for the individual and one for the shared work), a speaker phone, and two video cameras (one for the face and one mounted to show the desktop and the user's hand gestures). An individual can draw a diagram, by hand, on the document being discussed and all others will see it, including the writing hand. Hiroshi Ishii, the project designer, believes that this is a more natural method of collaboration.

Multimedia is still a technology of the future One immediate problem is the enormous bandwidth required to carry video messages; this makes the technology very expensive. A conference between two people requires four channels (assuming one camera at each desk) – one for sound and one for video in each direction. Add others and bandwidth requirements climb geometrically – 12 channels for three participants, 24 channels for four, and so on. At this time, the expense is prohibitive, given current bandwidth costs. It is expected that technology will overcome this question in time. A second matter is the issue of how we work, how necessary the technology is, and will it improve our productivity and our creativity? If so, which are the useful approaches, and which are dead ends? The third and largest question returns us to Pandora's box – the "dark side" of the technology. How will staff members feel about having a camera pointed at them all day long? Is this technology an invasion of privacy? Will management use this facility to monitor and even "spy upon" their workers? Can these problems be handled by giving each employee a lens cap and the right to cover the lens whenever he or she wishes?

Sources: David Brittan, "The Promise of Multimedia Communications," *Technology Review* (May/June 1992); Andy Hopper, "The Walk-and-Wear Office," *Computerworld* (April 20, 1992).

Case Study Questions

1. How important are the traditional ad hoc office collaborations and working groups for productivity?
2. What management, organization, and technology challenges need to be overcome to install multimedia communication systems successfully?
3. What are the benefits of multimedia collaboration? Do you think the multimedia technology described in this article will contribute to improved productivity? What features and functions do you think are critical for this technology to succeed?

4. Why do you think that the Pandora project does or does not deserve the name it was given? What personnel concerns would you have if you were the head of a department and were ordered to install one of these multimedia systems? What restrictions might you require? How would you prepare your staff for the installation?

References Amaravadi, Chandra S., Olivia R. Liu Sheng, Joey F. George, and Jay F. Nunamaker, Jr. "AEI: A Knowledge-Based Approach to Integrated Office Systems." *Journal of Management Information Systems* 9, no. 1 (Summer 1992).

Applegate, Linda. "Technology Support for Cooperative Work: A Framework for Studying Introduction and Assimilation in Organizations." *Journal of Organizational Computing* 1, no. 1 (January–March 1991).

Bair, James H. "A Layered Model of Organizations: Communication Processes and Performance." *Journal of Organizational Computing* 1, no. 2 (April–June 1991).

Bermant, Charles. "Notes Records 'Fables'." *Computerworld* (April 6, 1992).

Berst, Jesse. "Deciphering Lotus' Notes." *Computerworld* (May 18, 1992).

Bikson, Tora K., J. D. Eveland, and Barbara A. Gutek. "Flexible Interactive Technologies for Multi-Person Tasks: Current Problems and Future Prospects." Rand Corporation (December 1988).

Busch, Elizabeth, Matti Hamalainen, Clyde W. Holsapple, Yongmoo Suh, and Andrew B. Whinston. "Issues and Obstacles in the Development of Team Support Systems." *Journal of Organizational Computing* 1, no. 2 (April–June 1991).

Daly, James. "Insurer Sees Future in Imaging Strategy." *Computerworld* (January 6, 1992).

Edelstein, Herbert A. "Imaging Shifts Emphasis To Workflow Management." *Software Magazine* (November 1991).

Giuliao, Vincent E. "The Mechanization of Office Work." *Scientific American* (September 1982).

Horton, Marjorie, Priscilla Rogers, Laurel Austin, and Michael McCormick. "Exploring the Impact of Face-to-Face Collaborative Technology on Group Writing." *Journal of Management Information Systems* 8, no. 3 (Winter 1991–1992).

International Data Corporation White Paper. "Image Management Systems." *Computerworld*, September 20, 1990.

International Data Corporation White Paper. "Workgroup Technology: Tying Technology to Business Objectives."

Johansen, Robert. "Groupware: Future Directions and Wild Cards." *Journal of Organizational Computing* 1, no. 2 (April–June 1991).

Kling, Rob, and Charles Dunlop. "Controversies about Computerization and the Character of White Collar Worklife." *The Information Society* 9, no. 1 (January–March 1993).

Korzeniowski, Paul. "Building New APPS on E-mail." *Software Magazine* (March 1992).

Kusekoski, Gene. "Corporate Videotex: A Strategic Business Information System." *MIS Quarterly* 13, no. 4 (December 1989).

LaPlante, Alice. "Group(ware) Therapy." *Computerworld* (July 27, 1992).

Lee, Soonchul. "The Impact of Office Information Systems on Power and Influence." *Journal of Management Information Systems* 8, no. 2 (Fall 1991).

Liker, Jeffrey K., Mitchell Fleischer, Mitsuo Nagamachi, and Michael S. Zonnevylle. "Designers & Their Machines: CAD Use and Support in the U.S. and Japan." *Communications of the ACM* 35, no. 2 (February 1992).

Lotus Development Corporation. "Lotus Notes Application Profile" (1991).

Mann, Marina M., Richard L. Rudman, Thomas A. Jenckes, and Barbara C. McNurlin. "EPRINET: Leveraging Knowledge in the Electronic Industry." *MIS Quarterly* 15, no. 3 (September 1991).

Margolis, Nell. "Imaging: It's a Jungle in There." *Computerworld* (July 6, 1992).

Michaels, Jenna. "Managing Technology." *Wall Street & Technology* (February 1993).

Naj, Amal Kumar. " 'Virtual Reality' Isn't a Fantasy for Surgeons." *Wall Street Journal* (March 3, 1993).

Nash, Jim. "Imaging Heals Hospital's Sick File System." *Computerworld* (March 2, 1992).

Newquist, Harvey P. "Virtual Reality's Commercial Reality," *Computerworld* (March 30, 1992).

Olson, Gary M. and Judith S. "User-Centered Design of Collaboration Technology." *Journal of Organizational Computing* 1, no. 1 (January–March 1991).

Orlikowski, Wanda J. "Learning from Notes: Organizational Issues in Groupware Implementation." Sloan Working Paper no. 3428, Cambridge, MA: Sloan School of Management, Massachusetts Institute of Technology.

Panko, Raymond R. "Is Office Productivity Stagnant?" *MIS Quarterly* 15, no. 2 (June 1991).

Porat, Marc. *The Information Economy: Definition and Measurement.* Washington, D.C.: U.S. Department of Commerce, Office of Telecommunications (May 1977).

Press, Lawrence. "Systems for Finding People." *Journal of Organizational Computing* 2, no. 3 and 4 (1992a).

Press, Lawrence. "Lotus Notes (Groupware) in Context." *Journal of Organizational Computing* 2, no. 3 and 4 (1992b).

Ramanathan, Srinivas, P. Venkat Rangan, and Harrick M. Vin. "Designing Communication Architectures for Inter-Organizational Multimedia Collaboration." *Journal of Organizational Computing* 2, no. 3 and 4 (1992).

Roach, Stephen S. "Industrialization of the Information Economy." New York: Morgan Stanley and Co., 1984.

Roach, Stephen S. "Making Technology Work." New York: Morgan Stanley and Co., 1993.

Roach, Stephen S. "Services Under Siege — The Restructuring Imperative." *Harvard Business Review,* September–October 1991.

Roach, Stephen S. "Technology and the Service Sector." *Technological Forecasting and Social Change* 34, no. 4 (December 1988).

Ruhleder, Karen, and John Leslie King. "Computer Support for Work Across Space, Time, and Social Worlds." *Journal of Organizational Computing* 1, no. 4 (1991).

Schatz, Bruce R. "Building an Electronic Community System." *Journal of Management Information Systems* 8, no. 3 (Winter 1991–1992).

Shapiro, Joshua. "From the Rugged Outback, a Quick-Fix Modular Tire." *The New York Times* (February 28, 1993).

Sheng, Olivia R. Liu, Luvai F. Motiwalla, Jay F. Nunamaker, Jr., and Douglas R. Vogel. "A Framework to Support Managerial Activities Using Office Information Systems." *Journal of Management Information Systems* 6, no. 3 (Winter 1989/90).

Smarr, Larry, and Charles E. Catlett. "Metacomputing." *Communications of the ACM* 35, no. 6 (June 1992).

Sproull, Lee, and Sara Kiesler. "A Two-Level Perspective on Electronic Mail in Organizations." *Journal of Organizational Computing* 1, no. 2 (April–June 1991).

Sproull, Lee, and Sara Kiesler. *Connections: New Ways of Working in the Networked Organization.* Cambridge, MA: MIT Press, 1992.

Starbuck, William H. "Learning by Knowledge-Intensive Firms." *Journal of Management Studies* 29, no. 6 (November 1992).

Sterling, Theodor D., and James J. Weinkam. "Sharing Scientific Data." *Communications of the ACM* 33, no. 8 (August 1990).

Westin, Alan F., Heather A. Schwader, Michael A. Baker, and Sheila Lehman. *The Changing Workplace.* New York: Knowledge Industries, 1985.

Wolff, Edward N., and William J. Baumol. "Sources of Postwar Growth of Information Activity in the U.S." C.V. Starr Center for Applied Economics, New York University, no. 87-14 (June 1987).

Enhancing Management Decision Making

The Ideal Investment Portfolio: What Does the System Say?

Redstone Advisors is a $550-million money management firm specializing in taxable and tax-exempt fixed income investments. It must track and analyze complex financial instruments under rapidly changing market conditions. Redstone has monthly policy meetings to determine how its investment portfolios will be constructed. The meetings establish general guidelines for the portfolios, such as the percentage of cash, the weight of each sector, and the average duration of the portfolios (that is, the average num-

ber of years for the underlying bonds to reach maturity). The firm then makes trades to bring its portfolios into line with the established guidelines.

To help its traders make buy and sell decisions, Redstone uses a LAN-based portfolio management system called PORTIA supplied by Thomson Financial Services in Boston and London. Redstone analysts enter proposed trades into PORTIA. The system has a ''what-if'' capability; when they enter the proposed trades it tells them what the portfolio will look

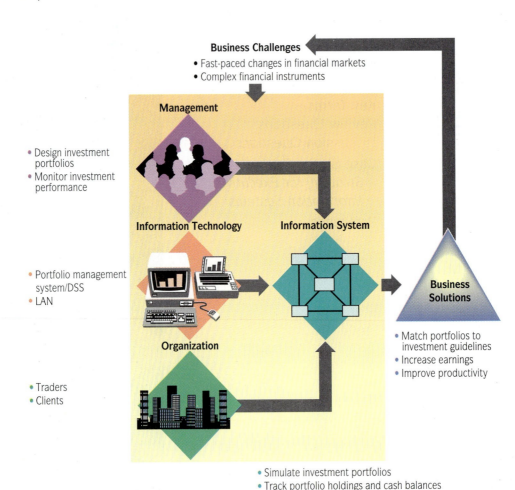

like. The traders can keep experimenting with different trades until the simulated portfolio matches the investment guidelines. With this information, they then make the trades. Once the actual trades have been entered into PORTIA the change is instantly reflected in a portfolio's cash balances and holdings. According to Marc Vincent, Redstone's management director, the ability to perform what-if analysis and to know exact portfolio holdings and cash balances improves productivity and decision making.

Source: "Fixed Income Money Manager Boosts Efficiency with Flexible, Comprehensive System," *Wall Street and Technology* 10, no. 9 (April 1993).

With the ability to perform complex calculations and to create "what-if" scenarios, Redstone's portfolio management system is a classic example of a decision-support system. Decision-support systems (DSS) provide powerful analytic capabilities for supporting managers during the process of arriving at a decision.

Most of the information systems described throughout this text help people make decisions in one way or another, but DSS are part of a special category of information systems that are explicitly designed to enhance managerial decision making. Other systems in this category are group decision-support systems (GDSS), which support decision making in groups, and executive support systems (ESS), which provide information for making strategic-level decisions. This chapter describes the characteristics of each of these types of information systems and shows how each actually enhances the managerial decision-making process.

After completing this chapter, you will be able to:

- Define a decision-support system (DSS) and a group decision-support system (GDSS).
- Describe the components of decision-support systems and group decision-support systems.
- Explain how decision-support systems and group decision-support systems can enhance decision making.
- Describe the capabilities of executive support systems (ESS).
- Describe the benefits of executive support systems.

16.1 Decision-Support Systems (DSS)

In the 1970s, a number of companies began developing information systems that were quite different from traditional MIS systems. These new systems were smaller (in terms of labor and cost). They were interactive (unusual at the time), and were designed to help end users utilize data and models to discuss and decide (not solve) semistructured and unstructured problems (Henderson and Schilling, 1985). By the late 1980s, these early efforts to assist individual decision making were extended to groups and entire organizations.

What Are Decision-Support Systems (DSS)?

Decision-support systems (DSS): Computer systems at the management level of an organization that combine data and sophisticated analytical models to support semistructured and unstructured decision making.

These systems are called decision-support systems (DSS). As we noted in Chapter 2, **decision-support systems (DSS)** assist management decision making by combining data, sophisticated analytical models, and user-friendly software into a single powerful system that can support semistructured or unstructured decision making. The DSS is under user control from early inception to final implementation and daily use. Figure 16.1 is a schematic diagram of a DSS.

In Figure 16.1, the relationships between DSS and the organization's existing TPS, KWS, and MIS are left deliberately vague. In some cases, DSS are linked closely to existing corporate information flows (see Chapter 2). Often, however, DSS are isolated from major organizational information systems. DSS tend to be stand-alone systems, developed by end-user divisions or groups not under central IS control, although it is obviously better if they are integrated into organizational systems when this is a functional requirement (Hogue, 1985).

DSS AS A PHILOSOPHY

Schematic diagrams of DSS fail to convey their purpose. Stated simply, the philosophy of DSS is to give users the tools necessary to analyze important blocks of data, using easily controlled sophisticated models in a flexible manner. DSS are designed to deliver capabilities, not simply to respond to information needs (Keen and Morton, 1982; Sprague and Carlson, 1982).

DSS are more targeted than MIS systems. MIS systems provide managers with routine flows of data and assist in the general control of the organization. In contrast, DSS are tightly focused on a specific decision or classes of decisions such as routing, queueing, evaluating, and so forth. Table 16.1 summarizes the differences between MIS and DSS. In philosophy, DSS promises end-user control of data, tools, and sessions. MIS is still largely dominated by professionals: Users receive information from a professional staff of analysts, designers, and programmers. In terms of objectives, MIS focuses on structured information flows to middle managers. DSS is aimed at top managers and middle managers, with emphasis on change, flexibility, and a quick response; with DSS there is less of an effort to link users to structured information flows and a correspondingly greater emphasis on models, assumptions, and display graphics. Both DSS and MIS rely on professional analysis and design. However, whereas MIS usually

Table 16.1   DIFFERENCE BETWEEN DSS AND MIS

Dimension	DSS	MIS
Philosophy	Provide integrated tools, data, models, and language to users	Provide structured information to end users
Systems Analysis	Establish what tools are used in the decision process	Identify information requirements
Design	Iterative process	Deliver system based on frozen requirements

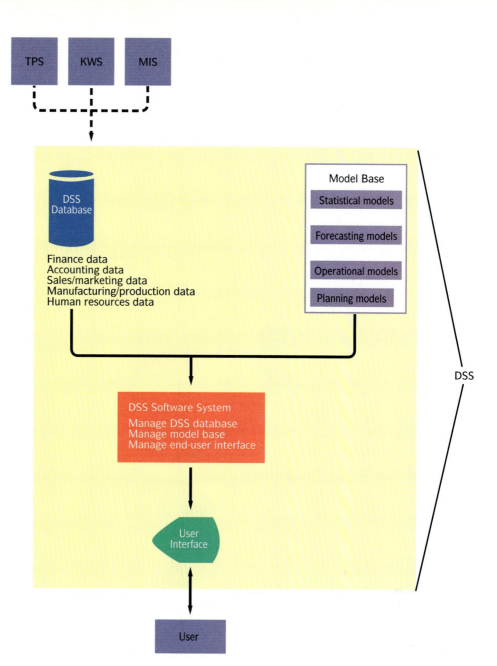

Figure 16.1
Overview of a decision support system (DSS). The DSS is often isolated from the corporation's transaction processing systems (TPS), knowledge work systems (KWS), and management information systems (MIS). The main components of the DSS are the model base, the DSS database, and the DSS software system and user interface.

follows a traditional systems development methodology, freezing information requirements before design and throughout the life cycle, DSS systems are consciously iterative, are never frozen, and in a sense are never finished.

The best way to understand the difference between DDS and a more traditional approach to systems support of decision making is to consider the analysis of a stock investment decision as both a DSS and an MIS. The investment advisor reviews portfolios, individual company research data, and stock data (the databases). In general, the advisor reviews individual portfolios by comparing each stock to its industry performance. If the stock is performing well for its industry, it is kept; if it is performing poorly, it is sold. If it is sold, a new stock is purchased to replace it. This calls for an examination of institutional analyses of companies and stock performance. On the basis of a promising report and good price performance, the stock is added to the portfolio.

Figure 16.2 illustrates this decision process. If the MIS is built along these lines, the decision-making pattern is frozen and built into the system. Indeed, the systems analyst might very well draw Figure 16.2, and submit it for review to investment advisors. Once they accept and sign off on the design because they

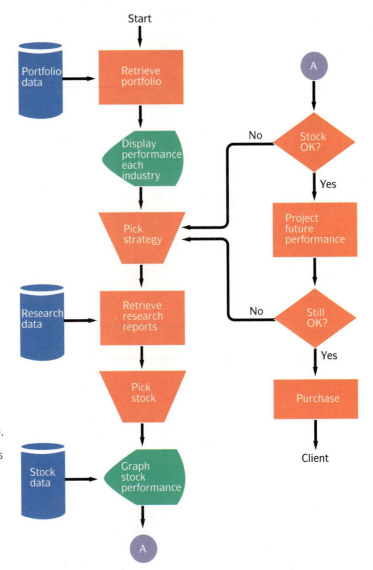

Start

Portfolio data → Retrieve portfolio

Display performance each industry

Pick strategy

Research data → Retrieve research reports

Pick stock

Stock data → Graph stock performance

A

A

Stock OK? — No → Pick strategy

Yes

Project future performance

Still OK? — No → Retrieve research reports

Yes

Purchase

Client

Figure 16.2
Traditional MIS approach to an investment decision. In a traditional approach and system, the analyst seeks to obtain a consensus view of how decisions are reached. This consensus view is frozen and is difficult to change as the system is developed. *Source: Adapted from Sprague, R. H., and E.D Carlson,* Building Effective Decision Support Systems, *Englewood Cliffs, NJ: Prentice-Hall, 1982.*

Representations: In DSS, conceptualization of information in the form of graphs, charts, lists, reports, and symbols to control operations.

Operations: In DSS, logical and mathematical manipulations of data.

Memory aids: In DSS, capabilities to update and refresh memory, including databases, views of data, work spaces, and libraries.

Control aids: Capabilities that allow the user to control the activities and functions of the DSS.

accept this as a good representation of what the system should do, the system is frozen. If new advisors come along who have different decision processes, the whole system will have to be changed or the new advisors will have to change their decision-making process to be able to use the MIS system.

Figure 16.3 shows a different way of building a system to support the same—and many other—decision processes. In this figure, a DSS is portrayed as a set of capabilities that would be useful in a number of decision processes used in making investment decisions. Four capabilities are portrayed in Figure 16.3, and all DSS can be characterized in this manner (Sprague and Carlson, 1982):

- **Representations:** Conceptualizations of information used in making decisions, such as graphs, charts, lists, reports, and symbols to control operations.
- **Operations:** Logical and mathematical manipulations of data, such as gathering information, generating lists, preparing reports, assigning risks and values, generating statistics, and simulating alternatives.
- **Memory aids:** Databases, views of data, work spaces, libraries, links among work spaces and libraries, and other capabilities to refresh and update memory.
- **Control aids:** Capabilities that allow the user to control the activities of the DSS. They include a software language permitting user control of rep-

resentations, operations, and memory which features menus, function keys, conventions, training, "help" commands, and tutorials.

In essence, a DSS is a decision-making scratch pad, backed up by databases, that decision makers can use to support many decision-making processes. This approach to DSS as a set of core capabilities goes to the heart of the DSS philosophy and provides a benchmark against which we can compare and critique any DSS in the marketplace.

CHARACTERISTICS OF DSS: WHAT IT MEANS TO SUPPORT DECISIONS

With this understanding of the components and philosophy of DSS, it is possible to discuss more precisely what is meant by decision support. (Here it may be helpful to review Chapter 5, which discusses management decision making from several perspectives.) Chapter 5 introduces the distinction between structured, semistructured, and unstructured decisions. Structured problems are repetitive and routine, for which known algorithms provide solutions. Unstructured problems are novel and nonroutine, for which there are no algorithms for solution. One can discuss, decide, and ruminate about unstructured problems, but they are not solved in the sense that one finds an answer to an equation (Henderson and Schilling, 1985). Semistructured problems fall between structured and unstructured problems. DSS are designed to support semistructured and unstructured problem analysis.

Chapter 5 also introduces Simon's description of decision making, which consists of four stages: intelligence, design, choice, and implementation. Traditionally, TPS and MIS have provided managers with information on day-to-day operations, whereas operations research (OR) has provided management with models for making choices. DSS is designed to incorporate the data of TPS/MIS and the models of OR. It is intended to help design and evaluate alternatives and monitor the adoption or implementation process.

While many early DSS were aimed at senior management, many users of DSS are now found at middle-management levels. There are many reasons for this, but experience indicates that a well-designed DSS can be used at many levels of the organization. Senior management can use a financial DSS to forecast the availability of corporate funds for investment by division. Middle managers within divisions can use these estimates and the same system and data to make decisions about allocating division funds to projects. Capital project managers within divisions, in turn, can use this system to begin their projects, reporting to the system (and ultimately to senior managers) on a regular basis about how much money has been spent.

Figure 16.3
DSS approach to investment decisions. In a DSS approach to systems, the emphasis is on providing capabilities to answer questions and reach decisions. The four core capabilities are representations, operations, memory aids, and control aids. *Source: Adapted from Sprague, R. H., and E. D Carlson,* Building Effective Decision Support Systems, *Englewood Cliffs, NJ: Prentice-Hall, 1982.*

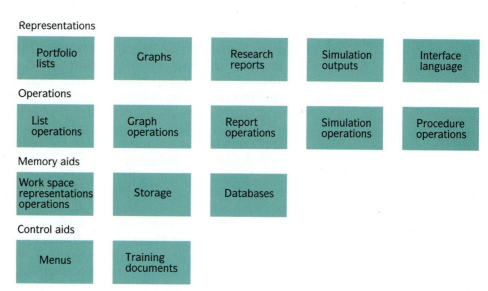

Representations

| Portfolio lists | Graphs | Research reports | Simulation outputs | Interface language |

Operations

| List operations | Graph operations | Report operations | Simulation operations | Procedure operations |

Memory aids

| Work space representations operations | Storage | Databases |

Control aids

| Menus | Training documents |

Table 16.2 EXAMPLES OF DSS SYSTEMS

American Airlines	Price and route selection
Champlin Petroleum	Corporate planning and forecasting
Equico Capital Corporation	Investment evaluation
Frito-Lay, Inc.	Price, advertising, and promotion section
General Dynamics	Price evaluation
Juniper Lumber	Production optimization
Kmart	Price evaluation
National Gypsum	Corporate planning and forecasting
Southern Railway	Train dispatching and routing
Texas Oil and Gas Corporation	Evaluation of potential drilling sites
United Airlines	Flight scheduling
U.S. Department of Defense	Defense contract analysis

As noted in Chapter 5, it is a mistake to think that decisions are only made by individuals in large organizations. In fact, most decisions are made collectively. Chapter 5 describes the rational, bureaucratic, political, and "garbage-can" models of organizational decision making. Frequently, decisions must be coordinated with several groups before being finalized. In large organizations, decision making is inherently a group process, and DSS can be designed to facilitate group decision making. The next section of this chapter deals with this issue.

Finally, DSS should provide session control for end users. That is, end users should be able to find relevant data, choose and operate relevant models, and control operations without professional intervention. Professionals are, of course, needed to build the databases, model bases, and control language. Experts should be available for consultation, training, advice, and support, but sessions should be end-user driven.

Examples of DSS Applications

There are many ways in which DSS can be used to support decision making. Table 16.2 lists examples of DSS in well-known American organizations. To illustrate the range of capabilities of DSS, we will now describe some recent DSS applications.

THE ADVANCED PLANNING SYSTEM—A MANUFACTURING DSS

To support most kinds of manufacturing, companies use a type of software known as Manufacturing Resources Planning (MRPII). The typical MRPII system includes such applications as master production scheduling, purchasing, material requirements planning, and even general ledger. Many thousands of these packages have been installed around the world. While they are useful as far as they go, these packages usually run on a mainframe so that they can process massive amounts of data. As a result, they are too large and slow to be used for "what-if" simulations and too procedural to be modified into decision-support software. A Canadian company, Carp Systems International of Kanata, Ontario, sells the Advanced Planning System (APS) to give the user DSS functionality using the data from existing MRPII systems.

APS allows a range of "what-if" processing by pulling the relevant data from the manufacturing software and performing calculations based upon user-defined variables. After Hurricane Andrew hit south Florida in 1992, Trane's Unitary Productions division in Fort Smith, Arkansas, was asked to quickly ship 114 five-ton air-conditioning systems to small businesses in the affected area. Using APS, within minutes Trane's could determine not only how long it would take to build the units but also how the added production would affect their existing customer commitments. They found that they were able to fit the added production in without disrupting existing orders. They delivered the units weeks before their competition.

Another user of APS, Compaq Computer of Houston, Texas, received an order for 10,000 of one of its personal computer models in 1990, just as it was phasing the model out. Cal Monteith, Compaq's manager of master scheduling and production control, knew the firm lacked the parts. He had the task of determining both part availability and plant capacity for the added production. The Carp software allowed him quickly to break the units down to their component parts right down to the piece level. It told him precisely how many of which parts he needed and when he would need them. Armed with this information, Compaq was able to send off orders immediately for the right parts. In the end, Compaq manufactured and sold 30,000 more PC units on time, adding $6 million to the bottom line in net revenues.

Pitney Bowes, the $3.3 billion business equipment manufacturer, uses the software to simulate supply changes. Pitney Bowes carries enough manufacturing inventory to satisfy demand for 30 days. Using APS, the firm asked to see the impact if it would reduce the inventory to 15 days. APS responded with an answer within five minutes, including an estimate of what Pitney Bowes would save. Similarly, Sikorsky Aircraft of Stratford, Connecticut, claims that over a three-year period, the company has been able to use this software to help halve their inventory even while they doubled their sales.

APS is a complex piece of software costing from $150,000 to $1 million and requiring intensive computing power. It runs on an IBM RS/6000 workstation. As with any other software, users caution that APS (and similar packages) are only as good as the data. If the data are out of date or wrong, APS only allows the user to do wrong things more quickly (Rifkin, 1992).

ATLAS CRIME ANALYSIS – MAPPING CRIMINAL ACTIVITY

In the early 1970s, IBM developed an interactive system called Geodata Analysis and Display System (GADS) to enable noncomputer people to access, display, and analyze data that have geographic content and meaning. Users can load different maps, data, and analysis routines to solve many different problems. Seventeen specific applications were developed from GADS in the areas of police, school, urban planning, fire, even bus route planning. Police used the software in a number of ways, including to help a city allocate its police to the beat patrols. GADS cost several hundred thousand dollars less than solutions developed by manual methods, and yet it provided a solution that was acceptable to the police officers.

More recently, the San Bernardino, California, Sheriff's Department has begun using a newly developed DSS to aid in a range of police-related tasks. The software package, Atlas Crime Analysis, was developed by Strategic Mapping, Inc. of Santa Clara, California. The San Bernardino Sheriff's Department stores its crime data on a Digital Equipment Corporation VAX minicomputer. Atlas Crime Analysis downloads the needed crime data from the VAX onto Intel 486-based microcomputers at 15 police stations. The software on the microcomputers matches the crime data with computerized street maps to produce the information needed, based upon the request. The software is considered very user friendly, as it relies on menus and plain English. For example, to show all burglaries on a map being displayed, the user simply selects "Burglaries" from a menu.

The county covers 20,000 square miles, a large area to map manually. The Sheriff's Department uses the Atlas software to determine the best places to patrol by having it generate maps showing criminal activity in a specific area. Alternatively, it displays geographic patterns for only certain types of crimes, such as armed robbery (see Figure 16.4 for a sample output). The county has used the software to support a court case by showing that a series of rapes

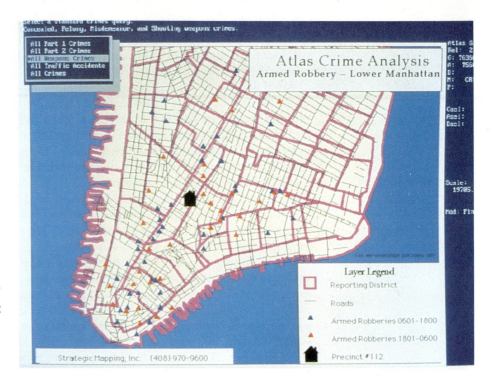

Figure 16.4
The Atlas Crime Analysis system. Atlas Crime Analysis plots crime locations on computerized street maps to help police track crime sprees, analyze crime patterns, and compile evidence to bring suspects to court. *Courtesy of Strategic Mapping, Inc.*

occurred on the suspect's route between home and work. The Sheriff's Department has used it to plot crimes in a specific area before and after a recent parolee moved into the neighborhood. It has even used it to track a spree of shootings from an automobile. One planned use, once the software is enhanced, is to have the system automatically generate alert reports when certain crime thresholds are reached. For example, if a neighborhood normally has four to five crimes per month, the user may want a report automatically generated if the number of crimes in a month exceeds six in that neighborhood.

THE EGYPTIAN CABINET DSS

The Egyptian Cabinet is composed of the Prime Minister, thirty-two other ministers, and four ministerial-level committees with their staffs. Decision making here is, by its very nature, strategic because it involves questions of survival: balance of payments, deficit management, public-sector performance, economic growth, and national defense.

Decision making at these high levels of governments, or corporations, is often portrayed as a rational decision process. But in fact, decision making involves managing issues that are forced on decision makers with varying and shifting priorities. Issues circulate continuously; they enter and exit through participants and are resolved in the sense that they dissolve or go away or are overtaken by other issues. The issues are themselves complex, poorly defined, interdependent, and related to many features of society. Information is voluminous but unreliable and qualitative.

In 1985, the Egyptian Cabinet developed a three-person Information and Decision Support Center (IDSC) to assist its own decision-making process (Figure 16.5). Today, 150 people work full time providing DSS services to the Cabinet on critical issues. The IDSC system is based upon a network of 110 microcomputers connected to a mainframe. Software includes standard desktop packages such as dBASE III for database management, Lotus 1–2–3 spreadsheet software, and FOCUS, a fourth-generation language and application generator, all of which have been fully converted to Arabic form. The electronic mail system is bilingual (Arabic/English).

One of the first uses of IDSC was to develop a new tariff structure to replace an inconsistent and complex structure that was thought to be impeding economic growth. The goal of the policy set forth by the Cabinet was to create a consistent, simple tariff structure; increase revenues to the treasury; and promote economic growth without harming poor citizens. A microcomputer-based DSS model was built of the proposed new tariff structure, using a prototyping methodology.

The new policy activated many opposing groups. The Ministry of Industry, hoping to increase local production of auto parts, supported new tariffs on imported auto parts. This was supported as well by the Ministry of Economy, which supported local production. But the policy was opposed by the Ministry of Finance because it would reduce customs revenue.

The DSS was walked around, back and forth, from one ministry to another, making adjustments to the proposed tariffs, playing "what-if" games to see the impact of tariff changes on revenue and local employment. After one month of intensive effort, agreement was reached on the new tariff policy. Builders of the DSS felt the system reduced conflict by clarifying the tradeoffs and potential impacts of tariff changes. While early estimates of higher tariffs claimed $250 million in increased revenues would result, the DSS predicted $25 million. By 1987, the actual increased revenue was $28 million (El Sherif and El Sawy, 1988).

The Egyptian Cabinet's DSS illustrates the idea that a DSS is not just an application, but a generalized capability for addressing decision makers' needs. Unlike an MIS system, DSS do not simply involve a routine, steady flow of data, but instead can be flexibly responsive to new situations by using data and analytic models (even spreadsheets) to work through the consequences of decisions and assumptions.

Figure 16.5
The cabinet decision-making process with IDSC. *Source: Figure 2. The Cabinet Decision-Making Process After IDSC (El Sherif and El Sawy. Reprinted with permission from MIS Quarterly, Volume 12, Number 4, December 1988).*

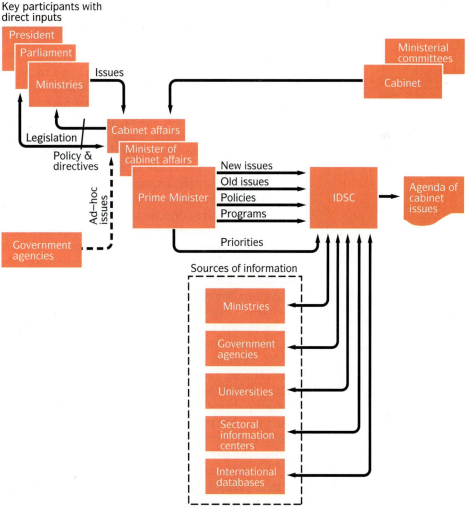

Components of DSS

DSS database: A collection of current or historical data from a number of applications or groups.

Review Figure 16.1 again. It shows that a decision-support system has three basic components—a database, a model base, and the DSS software system. The **DSS database** is a collection of current or historical data from a number of applications or groups, organized for easy access by a range of applications. The DSS database management system protects the integrity of the data while controlling the processing that keeps the data current; it also saves historical data. DSS do not create or update data, for that is not their purpose. Rather, they use live organizational data (from such systems as production and sales) so that individuals and groups are able to make decisions based upon actual conditions.

Most DSS do not have direct access to organizational data for two reasons. First, the organization will want to protect the data from accidental or inappropriate changes. In addition, it is a slow and expensive process for the DSS to search through large corporate databases. The process affects not only the performance of the DSS but also all the other systems using the database. Instead, DSS usually use data that have been extracted from relevant databases (internal and external) and stored specifically for use by the DSS.

Model base: A collection of mathematical and analytical models that can easily be made accessible to the DSS user.

Model: An abstract representation that illustrates the components or relationships of a phenomenon.

A **model base** is a collection of mathematical and analytical models that easily can be made accessible to the DSS user. A **model** is an abstract representation that illustrates the components or relationships of a phenomenon. A model can be a physical model (such as a model airplane), a mathematical model (such as an equation), or a verbal model (such as a description of a procedure to write up an order). Each decision support system is built for a specific set of purposes and will make different collections of models available depending upon those purposes.

Perhaps the most common models available in model bases are libraries of statistical models. Such libraries usually contain the full range of expected statistical functions including means, medians, deviations, and scatter plots. The software has the ability to project future outcomes by analyzing a series of data. Statistical modeling software can be used to help establish relationships, such as relating product sales to differences in age, income or other factors between communities. Optimization models, often using linear programming, determine optimal resource allocation to maximize or minimize specified variables such as cost or time. The Advanced Planning System (discussed above) uses such software to determine the effect that filling a new order will have upon meeting target dates for existing orders. A classic use of optimization models is to determine the proper mix of products within a given market to maximize profits.

Forecasting models are often used to forecast sales. The user of this type of model might supply a range of historical data to project future conditions and the sales that might result from those conditions. The decision maker could then vary those future conditions (entering, for example, a rise in raw materials costs or the entry of a new, low-priced competitor in the market) to determine how these new conditions might affect sales. Companies often use this software to attempt to predict the actions of competitors. Model libraries exist for specific functions, such as financial and risk analysis models.

Sensitivity analysis: Models that ask "what-if" questions repeatedly to determine the impact of changes in one or more factors on outcomes.

Among the most widely used models are **sensitivity analysis** models that ask "what-if" questions repeatedly to determine the impact of changes in one or more factors on outcomes. "What-if" analysis—working forward from known or assumed conditions—allows the user to vary certain values to test results in order to better predict outcomes if changes occur in those values. "What happens if" we raise the price by 5 percent or increase the advertising budget by $100,000? What happens if we keep the price and advertising budget the same? Desktop spreadsheet software, such as Lotus 1−2−3 or Microsoft Excel, is often used for this purpose. Backwards sensitivity analysis software is used for goal seeking: If I want to sell one million product units next year, how much must I reduce the price of the product?

DSS software system: DSS component that permits easy interaction between the users of the system and the DSS database and model base.

The third component of DSS is the **DSS software system.** The DSS software system permits easy interaction between users of the system and the DSS database and model base. The DSS software system manages the creation, storage, and retrieval of models in the model base and integrates them with the data in the DSS database. The DSS software system also provides a graphic, easy to use, flexible user interface that supports the dialogue between the user and the DSS. DSS users are usually corporate executives or managers, persons with well-developed working styles and individual preferences. Often they have little or no computer experience and no patience for learning to use a complex tool, so the interface must be relatively intuitive. In addition, what works for one may not work for another. Many executives, offered only one way of working (a way not to their liking) will simply not use the system. In order to mimic a typical way of working, a good user interface should allow the manager to move back and forth between activities at will.

Building DSS

Building a DSS is different from building a TPS or MIS system. DSS generally use smaller amounts of data, do not need on-line transaction data, involve a smaller number of important users, and tend to employ more sophisticated analytic models than other systems. Because DSS are customized to specific users and specific classes of decisions, they require much greater user participation to develop. In addition, they must be flexible and must evolve as the sophistication of users grows. In this section, we describe how to build such systems.

ANALYSIS The purpose of systems analysis in MIS is to deliver a system in response to a specific set of information needs. The purpose of systems analysis in DSS construction is to identify a problem and a set of capabilities that users consider helpful in arriving at decisions about that problem. The project will deliver capabilities independent of processes. We described these capabilities earlier in this chapter as representations, operations, memory aids, and control mechanisms.

How can one identify a problem susceptible to DSS techniques?

- First, problems should be identified by users.
- Second, there must be a body of data to work with and analyze.
- Third, the problem must be one for which no simple formula provides a solution.
- Fourth, there must be some systematic way of thinking about the problem (graphs, lists, charts, operations, etc.) that a DSS can automate or assist.
- Fifth, the problem must be important enough to engage the time and energy of management groups ranging from first-line supervisors to senior management.

DESIGN Unlike the traditional systems life cycle, in DSS there is no list of information requirements, and initially the user does not know what the final system will look like. All the vital features of the system that are decided up front in the traditional life-cycle methodology are decided at the end in DSS design. DSS must therefore use a changing, evolving method that is iterative. Iterative design utilizing prototyping is recommended (see Chapter 12).

IMPLEMENTATION A DSS differs from traditional MIS systems in that there is no separate implementation stage. Rather, the system is continually growing, and the users see it develop before their eyes. Nevertheless, DSS developers must address several issues that are part of a formal implementation phase. They must document the application to ensure transportability, maintainability, and user independence. Most end users will be computer literate, but most will need training in the specific

DSS syntax, operations, controls, and representations. This is also an ideal opportunity to educate users about the role of DSS and to search for new DSS applications. Finally, implementation often involves a process of system evaluation and tracking. The DSS development group must find ways to evaluate the system just developed and continually to clarify the group's contribution to the firm, allowing it to identify problems in its internal operations and personnel.

FACTORS IN DSS SUCCESS AND FAILURE

As experience with DSS has grown, a number of factors have been identified as important to their success and failure. The success factors are not very different from those of MIS and other systems. These factors are described in detail in Chapter 14. Several studies have noted that user training, involvement, and experience; top management's support; length of use; and novelty of the application were the most important factors in DSS success. Success is defined as perceived improvements in decision making and overall satisfaction with the DSS (Alavi and Joachimsthaler, 1992; Sanders and Courtney, 1985).

A smaller study of 34 DSS found that DSS orientation toward top management (assistance with making important decisions) and return on investment are the most important factors in the approval process for DSS (Meador and Keen, 1984; King, 1983). This is an important finding because it highlights what organizations are looking for when they develop DSS. Organizations need support for upper management decision making, which requires custom-built, flexible, and easy-to-use systems that address important organizational problems.

16.2 Group Decision-Support Systems (GDSS)

The early work in DSS focused largely on supporting individual decision making. However, because so much work is accomplished in groups within organizations, during the late 1980s system developers and scholars began to focus on how computers can support group and organizational decision making. This work followed even earlier efforts to develop electronic aids to community and societal decision making in the 1970s, based largely on mainframes (see Laudon, 1977). As a result of the focus on computer support of group decision making, a new category of systems developed, known as group decision-support systems (GDSS).

What Is a GDSS?

Group decision-support system (GDSS): An interactive computer-based system to facilitate the solution to unstructured problems by a set of decision makers working together as a group.

A group decision-support system (GDSS) is an interactive computer-based system to facilitate the solution of unstructured problems by a set of decision makers working together as a group (DeSanctis and Gallupe, 1987). GDSS were developed in response to growing concern over the quality and effectiveness of meetings. The underlying problems in group decision making have been the explosion of decision-maker meetings, the growing length of those meetings, and the increased number of attendees. Estimates on the amount of a manager's time spent in meetings range from 35 to 70 percent.

Meeting facilitators, organizational development professionals, and information systems scholars have been focusing on this issue and have identified a number of discrete meeting elements that need to be addressed (Grobowski et al., 1990; Kraemer and King, 1988; Nunamaker et al., 1991). Among these elements are the following:

1. *Improved pre-planning* to make meetings more effective and efficient.

2. *Increased participation* so that all attendees will be able to contribute fully even if the number of attendees is large. Free riding (attending the meeting but not contributing) must also be addressed.

3. *Open, collaborative meeting atmosphere* in which attendees from various organizational levels feel able to contribute freely. The lower-level attendees must be able to participate without fear of being judged by their management; higher-status participants must be able to participate without having their presence or ideas dominate the meeting and result in unwanted conformity.

4. *Criticism-free idea generation,* enabling attendees to contribute without undue fear of feeling personally criticized.

5. *Evaluation objectivity,* creating an atmosphere where an idea will be evaluated on its merits rather than on the basis of the source of the idea.

6. *Idea organization and evaluation,* which require keeping the focus on the meeting objectives, finding efficient ways to organize the many ideas that can be generated in a brainstorming session, and evaluating those ideas not only on their merits but also within appropriate time constraints.

7. *Setting priorities and making decisions,* which require finding ways to encompass the thinking of all the attendees in making these judgments.

8. *Documentation of meetings* so that attendees will have as complete and organized a record of the meeting as may be needed to continue the work of the project.

9. *Access to external information,* which will allow significant, factual disagreements to be settled in a timely fashion, thus enabling the meeting to continue and be productive.

10. *Preservation of "organizational memory"* so that those who do not attend the meeting can also work on the project. Often a project will include teams at different locations who will need to understand the content of a meeting at only one of the affected sites.

One response to the problems of group decision making has been the adoption of new methods of organizing and running meetings. Techniques such as facilitated meetings, brainstorming, and criticism-free idea generation have become popular and are now accepted as standard. Another response has been the application of technology to the problems resulting in the emergence of group decision-support systems.

Characteristics of GDSS

How can information technology help groups to arrive at decisions? Scholars have identified at least three basic elements of GDSS: hardware, software, and people. *Hardware* refers first to the conference facility itself, including the room, the tables and chairs. Such a facility must be physically laid out in a manner that supports group collaboration. It must also include some electronic hardware, such as electronic display boards, as well as audiovisual and computer equipment. The Window on Organizations on page 562 examines one important aspect to the physical setup—the ergonomics of the meeting room design.

A wide range of *software tools,* including tools for organizing ideas, gathering information, ranking and setting priorities, and other aspects of collaborative work are now being used to support decision-making meetings. We describe these tools below. *People* refers not only to the participants, but also to a trained facilitator and often to a staff that supports the hardware and software. Together these elements have led to the creation of a range of different kinds of GDSS, from simple electronic boardrooms to elaborate collaboration laboratories. See

ORGANIZATIONS

The Hohenheim CATeam Room

How does the physical environment of a group decision-support system meeting room affect the work of a GDSS-supported group? How do ergonomics affect the decision-making process? These are some of the questions that were explored by information systems researchers at the University of Hohenheim, in Stuttgart, Germany. Their methodology? Do the research and design their own GDSS room—the Computer Aided Team Room, known as the CATeam Room.

The information systems specialists worked with interior and furniture design architects from the State Academy of the Arts in Stuttgart. Realizing that people's sense of privacy and their social interactions can be affected by their level of physical comfort and the design of their meeting environment, the team looked into alternative designs for meeting rooms. In their quest for a meeting room design that would enhance group work, the team consulted specialists in psychology and ergonomics and visited GDSS research laboratories in the United States.

One of the principal questions addressed by the project was the relationship of seating arrangements in the GDSS meeting room to meeting interactions. The team started with a set of basic rules that demanded a maximum of 12 participants in a meeting (a limitation set because of the small size of the room they had available). The table they endorsed at the end included built-in computer equipment that could automatically be

stored inside the table at the push of a button so that the room could be used for traditional non-GDSS meetings. The table also is modular, allowing flexibility. For example, the room could be rearranged into a U-shape for a teaching situation. The team also wanted seating arrangements that would create a friendly teamwork atmosphere. While their principles did not include a specification for participant equality, that proved, in the end, to be the deciding factor for the table set-up. This issue is particularly important because meeting attendees often come from a range of different organizational levels, creating an initial atmosphere of inequality.

The final decision for table shape called for a round table called a Roundabout (see Figure 16.6). With a round table, everyone is equal, and the arrangement is democratic. Face-to-face contact is equally possible with anyone at the table. A GDSS requires a computer projection screen so that all can view the common screens together (as well as independently on their own PCs). To support the Roundabout solution, the CATeam project decided to use two common screens opposite each other. That way everyone would be able to view a screen easily and comfortably without attendees having to turn around or otherwise disturb the symmetry of the arrangement.

The placement of the computer equipment within the table also contributed to an environment of equality. When in use, the computer screen is placed slightly below table level (Figure 16.6). The team saw two advantages to this arrangement. First, no computer equipment would interfere with the attendees' eye-to-eye contact with other attendees. Second, an attendee's monitor can only be viewed by the closest neighbor, if at all. They believe that privacy, and therefore anonymity, are protected.

The Roundabout design was selected for display by the jury of the 1989 "Anno 2000 Office Design Competition" in Milan.

Sources: Henrik Lewe and Helmut Krcmar, "The Design Process for a Computer-Supported Cooperative Work Research Laboratory: The Hohenheim CATeam Room," *Journal of Management Information Systems,* Winter 1991–92. Helmut Krcmar, Henrik Lewe, and Gerhard Schwabe: *Empirical CATeam Research of Meetings.* Working Paper no. 38 of the Information Systems Department, University of Hohenheim, Germany, 1993.

To Think About:
1. This chapter listed ten specific meeting elements that need to be addressed to improve decision-making meetings. Which of these elements are addressed by the CATeam ergonomic design, and in what ways might the design improve meetings?
2. Do you believe that the physical placement of the computer is adequate for guaranteeing the privacy of an attendee's work? Can you think of ways that privacy could be further protected?

Figure 16.7 for an illustration of an actual GDSS collaborative meeting room. In a collaboration laboratory, individuals work on their own desktop microcomputers. Their input is integrated on a file server and is viewable on a common screen at the front of the room; in most systems the integrated input is also viewable on the individual participant's screen.

One can appreciate the potential value of GDSS by examining their software tools. We describe the functions of several types of tools central to a full-blown collaboration laboratory. We then give an overview of a GDSS meeting so that you can understand its potential to support collaborative meetings. Finally, we

Figure 16.6
The Roundabout Table Model. The system that the CATeam researchers at the University of Hohenheim settled upon as the final design for a GDSS room table was the Roundabout table. With this design, everybody is equal, and face-to-face contact is equally possible with all participants at the table. *Courtesy of Dollinger & Partner.*

examine how GDSS affect the problems we have described, and their power to enhance group decision making.

GDSS Software Tools

Some of the features of the groupware tools for collaborative work described in Chapter 15 can be used to support group decision making. But GDSS are considered more explicitly decision-oriented and task-oriented than groupware, as they focus on helping a group solve a problem or reach a decision (Dennis et al.,

1988). Groupware is considered more communication-oriented. Specific GDSS software tools include the following:

- *Electronic questionnaires* aid the organizers in pre-meeting planning by identifying issues of concern and by helping to insure that key planning information is not overlooked.
- *Electronic brainstorming tools* allow individuals simultaneously and anonymously to contribute ideas on the topics of the meeting.
- *Idea organizers* facilitate the organized integration and synthesis of ideas generated during brainstorming.
- *Questionnaire tools* support the facilitators and group leaders as they gather information before and during the process of setting priorities.
- *Tools for voting or setting priorities* make available a range of methods from simple voting, to ranking in order, to a range of weighted techniques for setting priorities or voting.
- *Stakeholder identification and analysis tools* use structured approaches to evaluate the impact of an emerging proposal upon the organization, and

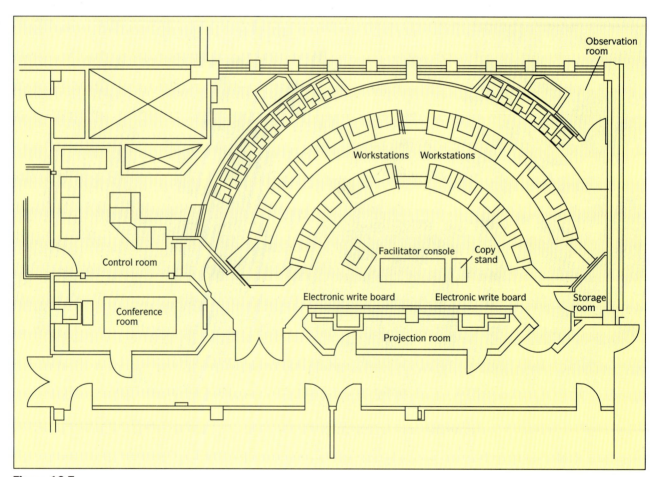

Figure 16.7
Illustration of PLEXSYS decision room. The large group room was opened in 1987, with twenty-four IBM PS/2 workstations. A gallery holds eighteen observers. The room has thirty-eight audio pick-up microphones and six video cameras with stereo audio. Two large-screen electronic displays and projectors permit playing of videotapes, discs, 35 MM slides, and computer graphics presentations. *Source: Figure 2b. Decision Room for Larger Groups (Dennis, George, Jessup, Nunamaker, and Vogel. Reprinted with permission from the* MIS Quarterly, *Volume 12, Number 4, December 1988).*

to identify stakeholders and evaluate the potential impact of those stakeholders upon the proposed project.

- *Policy formation tools* provide structured support for developing agreement on the wording of policy statements.
- *Group dictionaries* document group agreement on definitions of words and terms central to the project.

Additional tools are available, such as group outlining and writing tools, software that stores and reads project files, and software that allows the attendees to view internal operational data stored by the organization's production computer systems.

OVERVIEW OF A GDSS MEETING

Electronic meeting system (EMS): Collaborative GDSS that uses information technology to make group meetings more productive by facilitating communication as well as decision making. Supports meetings at the same place and time or in different places and times.

An **electronic meeting system (EMS)** is a type of collaborative GDSS that uses information technology to make group meetings more productive by facilitating communication as well as decision making. It supports any activity where people come together, whether at the same place at the same time or in different places at different times (Dennis et al., 1988; Nunamaker et al., 1990/1991). IBM has a number of EMS installed at various sites, one of which is pictured in Figure 16.8. Each attendee has a workstation. The workstations are networked and are connected to the facilitator's console that serves as both the facilitator's workstation and control panel and the meeting's file server. All data that the attendees forward from their workstations to the group are collected and saved on the file server. The facilitator is able to project computer images onto the projection screen at the front center of the room. The facilitator also has an overhead projector available. Whiteboards are visible on either side of the projection screen. Many electronic meeting rooms are arranged in a semicircle and are tiered in legislative style to accommodate a larger number of attendees.

The facilitator controls the use of tools during the meeting, often selecting from a large tool box that is part of the organization's GDSS. Tool selection is part of the pre-meeting planning process. Which tools are selected depends upon the subject matter, the goals of the meeting, and the facilitation methodology the facilitator will use.

Each attendee has full control over his or her own microcomputer. An attendee is able to view the agenda (and other planning documents), look at the

Figure 16.9
Group system tools. The sequence of activities and collaborative support tools used in an electronic meeting system (EMS) facilitates communication among attendees and generates a full record of the meeting. *Adapted from "Electronic Meeting Systems to Support Group Work," by Nunamaker, Dennis, Valacich, Vogel, and George, printed in* Communications of the ACM, July 1991.

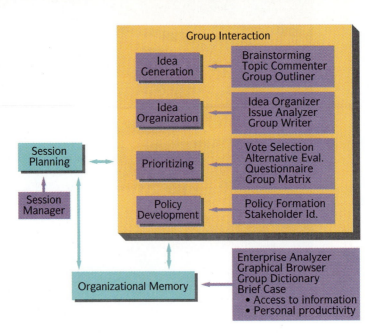

integrated screen (or screens as the session moves on), use ordinary desktop microcomputer tools (such as a word processor or a spreadsheet), tap into production data that have been made available, or work on the screen associated with the current meeting step and tool (such as a brainstorming screen). However, no one can view anyone else's screens so that an individual's work is confidential until he or she releases it to the file server for integration with the work of others. All input to the file server is anonymous—at each step everyone's input to the file server (brainstorming ideas, idea evaluation and criticism, comments, voting, etc.) can be seen by all attendees on the integrated screens, but no information is available to identify the source of specific inputs. Attendees enter their data simultaneously rather than in round-robin fashion as is done in meetings that have little or no electronic systems support.

Figure 16.9 shows the sequence of activities at a typical EMS meeting. For each activity it also indicates the type of tools used and the output of those tools. During the meeting all input to the integrated screens is saved on the file server. As a result, when the meeting is completed, a full record of the meeting (both raw material and resultant output) is available to the attendees and can be made available to anyone else with a need for access.

How GDSS Can Enhance Group Decision Making

GDSS are still relatively new, so firm conclusions are not yet possible. Nonetheless, scholars and business specialists have studied these systems, and the systems are now being used more widely, so that we are able at least to understand their potential benefits and even evaluate some of the tools. We look again at how GDSS affect the ten group meeting issues raised earlier.

1. *Improved pre-planning.* Electronic questionnaires, supplemented by word processors, outlining software, and other desktop PC software, can structure planning, thereby improving it. The availability of the planning information at the actual meeting also can serve to enhance the quality of the meeting. Experts seem to feel that these tools add significance and emphasis to meeting pre-planning.

2. *Increased participation.* Studies show that in traditional decision making meetings without GDSS support the optimal meeting size is three to five attendees. Beyond that size, the meeting process begins to break down. Using GDSS

software, studies show the meeting size can increase while productivity also increases. One reason for this is that attendees contribute simultaneously rather than one at a time, and can thus make more efficient use of the meeting time. Free riding is apparently decreased too, perhaps because the one or two individuals who are not working will stand out when everyone else in the room is busy at workstations. Interviews of GDSS meeting attendees indicate that the quality of participation is higher than in traditional meetings.

3. *Open, collaborative meeting atmosphere.* GDSS contribute to a more collaborative atmosphere in several ways. First, anonymity of input is essentially guaranteed. An individual need not be afraid of being judged by his or her boss for contributing a possibly off-beat idea. Anonymity also reduces or eliminates the deadening effect that often occurs when high-status individuals contribute. Even the numbing pressures of social cues are reduced or eliminated. Attendees find that GDSS meetings are often more open and freewheeling.

4. *Criticism-free idea generation.* Anonymity ensures that attendees can contribute without fear of personally being criticized or of having their ideas rejected because of the identity of the contributor. Several studies show that interactive GDSS meetings generate more ideas and more satisfaction with those ideas than verbally interactive meetings (Nunamaker et al., 1991).

5. *Evaluation objectivity.* Anonymity prevents criticism of the source of the ideas, thus supporting an atmosphere in which attendees focus on evaluating the ideas themselves. The same anonymity allows participants to detach themselves from their own ideas and so are able to view them from a critical perspective. Evidence suggests that evaluation in an anonymous atmosphere increases the free flow of critical feedback and even stimulates the generation of new ideas during the evaluation process.

6. *Idea organization and evaluation.* GDSS software tools used for this purpose are structured and are based on methodology. They usually allow individuals each to organize and then submit their results to the group (still anonymously). The group then iteratively modifies and develops the organized ideas until a document is completed. Attendees have generally viewed this approach as productive.

7. *Setting priorities and making decisions.* Anonymity helps lower-level participants have their positions taken into consideration along with the higher-level attendees.

8. *Documentation of meetings.* Evidence at IBM indicates that post-meeting use of the data is crucial. Attendees use the data to continue their dialogues after the meetings, to discuss the ideas with those who did not attend, and even to make presentations (Grobowski et al., 1990). Some tools even enable the user to zoom in to more detail on specific information.

9. *Access to external information.* Often a great deal of meeting time is devoted to factual disagreements. More experience with GDSS will indicate whether or not GDSS technology reduces this problem.

10. *Preservation of "organizational memory."* Specific tools have been developed to facilitate access to the data generated during a GDSS meeting, allowing nonattendees to locate needed information after the meeting. The documentation of a meeting by one group at one site has also successfully been used as input to another meeting on the same project at another site.

Experience to date suggests that GDSS meetings can be more productive, make more efficient use of time, and produce the desired results in fewer meetings. One problem with understanding the value of GDSS is their complexity. A GDSS can be configured in an almost infinite variety of ways. In addition, the effectiveness of the tools will partially depend upon the effectiveness of the facilitator, the quality of the planning, the cooperation of the attendees, and the appropriateness of tools for different types of meetings. These systems are also rather expensive, so that much of the usage to date has been by corporations holding meetings at university GDSS research facilities. Because of their high

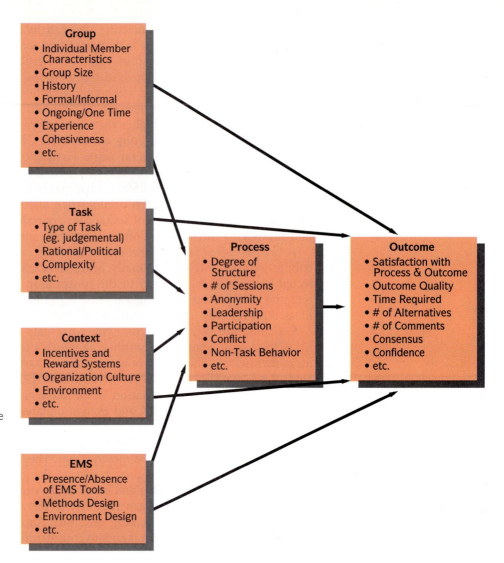

Figure 16.10
The research model for electronic meetings, For effective group meetings, include the nature of the group, the task to be accomplished, and the context of the meeting in the design of the EMS. *Source: Figure 3. A Research Model (Dennis, George, Jessup, Nunamaker, and Vogel. Reprinted with permission from the* MIS Quarterly, *Volume 12, Number 4, December 1988).*

price, GDSS integration into daily corporate life must await further evidence of their effectiveness.

Researchers have noted that the design of an electronic meeting system is only one of a number of contingencies that affect the outcome of group meetings. Other factors, including the nature of the group, the task, and the context also affect the process of group meetings and meeting outcomes (Dennis et al., 1988; Nunamaker et al., 1991). Figure 16.10 graphically illustrates these relationships.

16.3 Executive Support Systems (ESS)

Executive support systems (ESS): Information systems at the strategic level of an organization designed to address unstructured decision making through advanced graphics and communications.

We have described how DSS and GDSS help managers make unstructured and semistructured decisions. **Executive support systems (ESS)** also help managers with unstructured problems, focusing on the information needs of senior management. Combining data from both internal and external sources, ESS create a generalized computing and communications environment that can be applied to a changing array of problems. ESS help senior executives spot problems, identify opportunities, and forecast trends.

The Changing Role of ESS

Executive information systems (EIS): Early ESS that provide senior executives information without the capabilities of ESS for broad-based electronic communications, data analysis, scheduling, and organizing.

Briefing books: On-line data in the form of fixed-format reports for executives; part of early EIS.

Drill down: The ability to move from summary data down to lower and lower levels of detail.

Executive support systems were originally called **executive information systems (EIS).** That name is still in common usage for these systems, although ESS are considered to have a broader set of capabilities than traditional EIS. Executive information systems (EIS) primarily provide information, whereas ESS provide not only information but also capabilities for electronic communications, data analysis, scheduling, and organizing (Watson et al., 1991).

Prior to EIS it was common for executives to receive numerous fixed-format reports, often hundreds of pages every month (or even every week). The first systems developed specifically for executives in the early 1980s were mainframe systems designed to replace that paper, delivering the same data to the executive in days rather than in weeks. Executives had access to the same data, only it was on-line in the form of reports. Such systems were known as senior management **briefing books.** Using a briefing book, executives usually could **drill down** (move from a piece of summary data down to lower and lower levels of detail). Briefing books did not spread widely through the executive suites, although many lessons were learned. Several key problems became apparent.

Early EIS were tailored to the demands of a specific executive, but this approach had two shortcomings. First, executives found that their staffs did not have the same data they did. In fact, in many cases the data used by the executives and that used by their staffs came from two different sources and did not agree. Their staffs could not answer their questions. Doubts about the integrity of the organizational data resulted. In addition, briefing books were inflexible—they were essentially reports on screens. While the interests of an executive changed very rapidly with the changing business conditions, briefing books remained frozen in their design format. They did not change along with the shifting of the executives' interests.

The inflexibility of traditional EIS presented another problem as well. Executives use data in a range of ways, looking at them this way today and analyzing them that way tomorrow. Traditional systems were not responsive to executives' needs.

While the understanding of these problems was growing, technology was also developing. Networks and new approaches to storing and accessing data matured, allowing sharing of data and the development of desktop systems. Microcomputers and workstations developed the computing power to analyze the data rapidly and do so even in easy-to-understand graphic formats. The computer mouse, graphical user interfaces, and even touch screens made intuitive use without much training a reality. We will discuss the technology of ESS below.

By the late 1980s, briefing books—preformatted, static data—gave way to an emphasis on flexibility and analysis. Ways were found to bring together data from throughout the organization and allow the manager to select, access, and tailor them easily as needed. Today, an ESS is apt to include a range of easy-to-use desktop analytical tools. Use of the systems has migrated down several organizational levels so that the executive and his or her subordinates are able to look at the same data in the same way.

Today's systems try to avoid the problem of data overload so common in paper reports because the data can be filtered or viewed in graphic format (if the user so chooses). Systems have maintained the ability to drill down (even starting from a graph). However, with access to so much critical data, designers must be certain that any ESS protects against altered data finding their way back to the originating system.

One limitation in ESS is that they use data from systems designed for very different purposes. Often data that are critical to the executive are simply not there. For example, sales data coming from an order entry transaction processing system are not linked to marketing information, a linkage the executive would find useful. External data are now much more available in many ESS systems. Executives need a wide range of external data, from current stock market news to competitor information, industry trends, and even projected legislative action. Through their ESS, many managers have access to news services, financial market databases, economic information, and whatever other public data they may require.

ESS today include more tools for modeling and analysis. For example, many ESS use Lotus 1–2–3, Excel, or other spreadsheets as the heart of their analytical tool base (see the Window on Technology). With only a minimum of experience, most managers find they can use these common software packages to create graphic comparisons of data by time, region, product, price range, and so on. Costlier systems include more sophisticated specialty analytical software.

ESS are increasingly being used by employees several levels below the senior executives. This has solved the problem of members of executives' staffs working from different data than the executive, and this is one of the reasons use of these systems is spreading. Middle management will use the same data in a somewhat different manner, focusing on their own area of responsibility and emphasizing plan-versus-actual analysis (variances between forecasts and actual results).

Developing ESS

ESS are executive systems, and executives create special development problems (we introduced this topic in section 16.1). Because executives' needs change so rapidly, most executive support systems are developed through prototyping. A major difficulty for developers is that high-level executives expect success the first time. Developers must be certain that the system will work before they demonstrate it to the user. In addition, the initial system prototype must be one that the executive can learn very rapidly. Finally, if the executive finds that the ESS offers no added value, he or she will reject it.

One area that merits special attention is the determination of executive information requirements. ESS need to have some facility for environmental scanning. A key information requirement of managers at the strategic level is the capability to detect signals of problems in the organizational environment that indicate strategic threats and opportunities (Walls et al., 1992). The ESS needs to be designed so that both external and internal sources of information can be used for environmental scanning purposes. The Critical Success Factor methodology for determining information requirements (see Chapter 11) is recommended for this purpose. Table 16.3 suggests steps for eliciting such requirements.

Development must occur, of course, but executives are not known to sit patiently while developers build a system. The IS department must be prepared to roll out the first prototype very quickly once the project begins. Often this means selecting and learning a third-party ESS software package in advance of working with the executive. The system is usually converted into production in a staged manner. Experience has shown that when an ESS is introduced into a company, the number of users should be kept very small at first, perhaps to only two or three users. That way, the needs of those few (who are upper management, after all) can truly be met and the project will gain their support. Many information

Table 16.3	STEPS FOR DETERMINING ESS REQUIREMENTS

1. Identify a set of issue generating critical events.
2. Elicit from the executive his assessment of the impact of the critical events on his goals and derive a set of critical issues.
3. Elicit from the executive three to five indicators which can be used to track each critical issue.
4. Elicit from the executive a list of potential information sources for the indicators.
5. Elicit from the executive exception heuristics for each indicator.

Reprinted by permission of Joseph G. Walls, George R. Widmeyer, and Omar A. El Sawy, "Building Information System Design Theory for Vigilant EIS," *Information Systems Research*: Vol. 3, No. 1 (March 1992), p. 56, The Institute of Management Sciences.

TECHNOLOGY
Spreadsheets Team Up with ESS

Executive support systems are usually high-priced custom programs running on mainframes that simplify and present complex data for top management. So what are ESS doing with spreadsheets? The answer is, providing new views of data that were not available before.

Early ESS plucked data from mainframe financial systems and simplified them, graphically illustrating key performance indicators and highlighting variances between forecasts and actual results. An ESS might provide an overview of a company's financial and business condition, using performance indicators such as the firm's profit margin or the average number of minutes customers wait on the telephone for customer service. The system might use arrows near the numbers to indicate whether the performance measures are improving, staying the same, or declining, and it might color-code the numbers to indicate whether the situation has reached a state of alarm.

But today's ESS can do much more. They have capabilities to let executives examine areas that warrant further attention, or go through the process of drilling down. For instance, a manager might drill down to find sales and operating expense amounts separately and drill even further to see the dollar figures for individual sales regions. The level of detail conceivably could enfold all the way down to individual invoices and inventory items.

Contemporary ESS can attach snapshots of Lotus 1–2–3 spreadsheets to various reports; they can compile disparate data and let users work through multiple levels of detail to find the information; or they can use spread-

sheets as a front end to examine vast quantities of business data. In many instances, systems allowing high-level executives access to spreadsheets let them see the underlying formulas and the assumptions that were used to calculate the numbers. For instance, they could see that a forecast was based on a 6 percent interest rate and either say "I believe that" or not. Senior executives can see information that they were not seeing in hard copy reports.

An executive who wants to get a high-level picture of business activities may need data from a number of disparate spreadsheets, a daunting task if done manually. Boston Edison Co., a Massachusetts-based electric utility, addresses this problem using Clipper, a database package from Nantucket Corp. Clipper includes a module that allows the creators of their 1–2–3 spreadsheets to upload the spreadsheets into Clipper for storage. Users of the Boston Edison Co.'s ESS can then retrieve them with just a click on an icon, using their ESS menu.

The Boston Edison approach has a major problem, however—the spreadsheets are static, and data cannot be further massaged. Material Service Corp., a division of General Dynamics, is addressing that deficiency through a product called DrillDown from Specialized Systems & Software. According to Iris Sherman, Material Service's manager of personal information systems, DrillDown can group and total records (rolling up, the opposite of drilling down). For example, if their company stores sales invoices on 1–2–3, DrillDown will create aggregate sales figures that can then be given to management. Executives can then use DrillDown to look at the totals or to drill

down to the details as they wish. For example, they might look at sales by region, by product within that region, and even by salesperson. DrillDown includes one very handy feature: As executives search through the data, DrillDown will create a template of the search that can be saved to enable the same drilling in the future even without training in the product.

As their analytic and graphic power has grown, spreadsheets have become the presentation tool of choice for many. Using Microsoft Windows, data stored in dedicated databases can now easily be loaded into a spreadsheet (through Microsoft's Dynamic Data Exchange). As a result, some corporations are now using spreadsheets as front ends to their ESS. Not surprisingly, one of these companies is Lotus Development Corp. Their spreadsheet of choice? Their own 1–2–3! Lotus' home-grown ESS, the Lotus Information System (LIS) is used by about 100 executives, including Chairman Jim Manzi. Key data are stored in SQL Server, a database manager. Users access the system through a graphic, icon-based dialogue. The data can be analyzed using the full power of 1–2–3. In addition, LIS provides 17 pre-developed views, from sales figures to daily stock prices.

Source: Don Steinberg, "EIS Meets 1–2–3," *Lotus,* September, 1992.

To Think About: From management, organization, and technology standpoints, what are the advantages of off-the-shelf spreadsheet software like Lotus 1–2–3 in developing an ESS? What are the disadvantages of using such software?

systems departments assign several staff members to support their new ESS, even when it has less than half a dozen users. This level of support enables IS to respond rapidly enough to keep the executives satisfied until the wrinkles are ironed out, thus preventing the failure of the project. In addition, a larger staff will be able to continue to develop the system, prototyping another function.

Because ESS could potentially give top executives the capability of examining other managers' work without their knowledge, there may be some resistance to ESS at lower levels of the organization. Implementation of ESS should be carefully managed to neutralize such opposition (see Chapter 14).

What do ESS systems cost? They can be installed from well under $100,000 to well over $2 million. The differences are in the technology used and the functionality of the delivered system. One 1991 study placed the average cost at a little more than $200,000 (Watson et al., 1991).

Cost justification presents a different type of problem with ESS. Since much of an executive's work is unstructured, how does one quantify benefits for a system that primarily supports such unstructured work? An ESS is often justified in advance by the intuitive feeling that it will pay for itself (Watson et al., 1991). If ESS benefits can ever be quantified, it is only after the system is operational.

Benefits of ESS

How do executive support systems benefit managers? As we stated earlier, it is difficult at best to cost-justify an executive support system. Nonetheless, interest in these systems is growing, so it is essential to examine some of the potential benefits scholars have identified.

Much of the value of ESS is found in their flexibility. These systems put data and tools in the hands of executives without addressing specific problems or imposing solutions. Executives are free to shape the problems as they need, using the system as an extension of their own thinking processes. These are not decision-making systems; they are tools to aid executives in making decisions.

The most visible benefit of ESS is their ability to analyze, compare, and highlight trends. The easy use of graphics allows the user to look at more data in less time with greater clarity and insight than paper-based systems can provide. In the past, executives obtained the same information by taking up days and weeks of their staffs' valuable time. By using ESS, those staffs and the executives themselves are freed up for the more creative analysis and decision making in their jobs.

Executives are using ESS to monitor performance more successfully in their own areas of responsibility. Some are also using these systems to monitor key performance indicators. The timeliness and availability of the data result in needed actions being identified and taken earlier. Problems can be handled before they become too damaging; opportunities can also be identified earlier as well.

ESS can and do change the workings of organizations. Immediate access to so much data allows executives to better monitor activities of lower units reporting to them. That very monitoring ability often allows decision making to be decentralized and to take place at lower operating levels. Executives are often willing to push decision making further down into the organization as long as they can be assured that all is going well. ESS can enable them to get that assurance. A well-designed ESS could dramatically improve management performance and increase upper management's span of control.

The Window on Management on page 574 looks at some effects of an ESS at Fidelity Investments, one of the largest investment firms in the world.

We will close our examination of ESS by looking at actual examples of ESS systems in use.

Examples of ESS

To illustrate the various ways in which ESS can enhance management decision making, we now describe two executive support systems, one for private industry and one for the public sector. These systems were developed for very different reasons and serve their organizations in different ways.

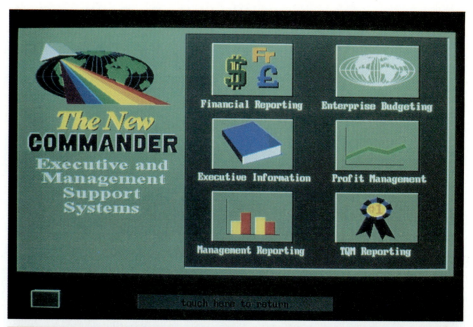

An executive can use the various graphing and financial analysis tools available through the menus of Commander EIS to create a graphic image of the overall quality measures for the corporation.

PRATT & WHITNEY

Pratt & Whitney is a multibillion dollar corporation located in East Hartford, Connecticut, whose Commercial Engine Business (CEB) produces jet engines. The firm's executives view customer service and product performance as the heart of their business and therefore the heart of their strategic plan to expand their market share. Walt Dempsey, a member of the company's Business Management and Planning department, launched a study to assess the information needs that would support their strategic plan. The study led to their purchase of Commander EIS, a leading ESS package from Comshare. Commander EIS features colorful presentations and a pictorial menu that can be learned intuitively, with variances and exceptions highlighted in color. Users can access data with a touch screen, mouse, or keyboard and they can zoom in for deeper levels of detail by either navigating on their own or by following predefined paths.

Implementation began with a prototype built for the president of CEB, Selwyn Berson. Commander EIS allows Berson to track key quality and reliability measures for each jet engine model by customer. The data are shown from existing production systems and provide information on reliability, spare engine and

MANAGEMENT

Fidelity Brings Financial Data to Executives' Fingertips

Privately held Fidelity Investments, Inc. of Boston manages more than $200 billion through its famous array of Fidelity Funds. In 1990, Fidelity commissioned Coopers & Lybrand to conduct a 12-week efficiency study. The study concluded that management could not obtain important day-to-day operational information as easily as it needed to do so. Control of the data was too centralized.

One sign of this problem was management's weekly 45-page report on Fidelity's financial health. The report had three problems: The data came only weekly; management could not easily analyze the data because they were paper-bound; and the preparation of the report required 10 employees to spend several days a week gathering the data from diverse business units.

To eliminate the extra footwork, Fidelity replaced the 45-page financial health report with an ESS called the Financial and Management Information System (FAMIS). FAMIS is a client/server-based system that uses Microsoft's Excel for Windows spreadsheet as a front end to bring relevant data to financial executives with a few keystrokes. The system collects the data from Fidelity's various business units and stores it in a Sybase database. Users click on a Windows icon that brings up the data in an Excel spreadsheet format. Users can manipulate the data using any of the many Excel spreadsheet analytical and graphics tools. They can also extract the data for use with a Windows-based modeling tool. Instead of pasting together a report from diverse spreadsheets and databases, analysts and managers can access the data on-line, saving the weekly report preparation time of ten employees. Windows ad hoc query and reporting capabilities have also been added. Users can extract data, and store the data on LANs for sharing with work groups. Bill Niemi, director of distributed systems development at Fidelity, believes that when fully developed, the system will eliminate the need for one or two full-time financial analysts.

FAMIS was initially rolled out to 100 users, but the goal is to have it sit on over 350 desks, mostly those of chief financial officers and financial analysts. Fidelity would like FAMIS to provide financial managers with the ability to extract such data as the number of new accounts sold for the Magellan fund. In the past, it might have taken the information systems department a week to produce that data, or the data might not have been available at all. Niemi believes the system will be a long-run success because it will give the financial managers the ability to access the latest data in a timely way.

Source: Anita Amirrezvani, "Fidelity Investments Builds EIS to Simplify Access to Financial Data," *Computerworld,* April 6, 1992.

To Think About: What were the management benefits of FAMIS? What management, organization and technology factors had to be addressed in building FAMIS?

parts availability, and deliveries. Using this system, CEB is able to answer customers' questions regarding repair status and can project how long repairs will take. Berson and others are able to drill down to determine reasons for repairs on specific engines. They also are capable of drilling down to specific data on service to an individual customer. Thus, CEB executives are able to determine where quality improvements need to be made in terms of both customer service and engine quality. CEB's ESS is helping them to meet their strategic plan objectives. The system was originally used by about 25 senior executives, although Pratt & Whitney expects the number of users to grow to over 200 (I/S Analyzer, January 1992).

NEW YORK STATE OFFICE OF
GENERAL SERVICES

The New York State Office of General Services (OGS) is responsible for servicing other state agencies throughout New York. Its services include (but are not limited to) design and construction, maintenance of state buildings, food and laundry services to both correctional facilities and health-related institutions, statewide vehicle management, and centralized printing. With this diversity of services, an annual budget well over $500 million, and more than 4000 employees, executive oversight was a nightmare. Until 1986, OGS automatically received annual budget increases in line with inflation rates. Budget deficits were made up through supplemental allocations by the legislature. OGS felt no pressures to improve efficiency or stay within its budget. That changed in 1986 when a new administrative head of the agency was appointed. He decided that the organization had to operate in a more efficient, effective, and responsive manner.

He also wanted to avoid year-end deficits. These objectives required better management at the top.

The first module of a new OGS ESS was implemented in 1988. The system allows the executives to monitor status by program, comparing budget to actual expenditures and showing estimated expenditures through the remainder of the fiscal year. Management can drill down to see specific details in any category. The system contains only raw data, allowing the users great flexibility in aggregating and analyzing it to meet their needs. For example, users are able to view a single expense category by month across organizations, or view several months of expenses for a given unit. Because the raw data are there, the executives can drill down to the source. The system includes exception reporting so that budget problems are highlighted and detected early. Executives are also using the system to compare budgetary control by units to spot personnel performance problems.

Since the system was developed for a government agency, the cost was of more than normal concern—the system had to be built inexpensively. The system uses ordinary microcomputers networked with the agency's mainframe and off-the-shelf, standard, inexpensive software tools. The total cost was less than $100,000. The system is menu-driven and very easy to use. New users are trained through a 30-minute demonstration, and experience has shown that this is all that they need. No user manual is available.

One interesting by-product of the system has been the need to develop productivity measures. Future development will focus on the area of performance analysis, attempting to answer such questions as how many people are required to work in specific units. The ESS called for OGS to measure something that it had never measured before. The work of developing these measures should in itself contribute to the drive for more efficiency (Mohan et al., 1990). This ESS is helping the Office of General Services enhance management control.

Management Challenges

1. **Building information systems that can actually fulfill executive information requirements.** Even with the use of Critical Success Factors and other information requirements determination methods, it may still be difficult to establish information requirements for ESS and DSS serving senior management. Chapter 5 has already described why certain aspects of senior management decision making cannot be supported by information systems because the decisions are too unstructured and fluid. Even if a problem can be addressed by an information system, senior management may not understand their true information needs. For instance, senior managers may not agree on the firm's critical success factors, or the critical success factors they describe may be inappropriate or outdated if the firm is confronting a crisis requiring a major strategic change.

2. **Integrating DSS and ESS with existing systems in the business.** Even if system builders do know the information requirements for DSS or ESS, it may not be possible to fulfill them using data from the firm's existing information systems. Various MIS or TPS may define important pieces of data, such as the time period covered by fiscal year, in different ways. It may not be possible to reconcile data from incompatible internal systems for analysis by managers. A significant amount of organizational change may be required before the firm can build and install effective DSS and ESS.

Summary

Define a decision-support system (DSS) and a group decision-support system (GDSS).

A decision-support system (DSS) is an interactive system under user control that combines data, sophisticated analytical models, and user-friendly software into a single powerful system that can support semistructured or unstructured decision making. A group decision-support system (GDSS) is an interactive computer-based system to facilitate the solution of unstructured problems by a set of decision makers working together as a group rather than individually.

Describe the components of decision-support systems and group decision-support systems.

The components of a DSS are the DSS database, the model base, and the DSS software system. The DSS database is a collection of current or historical data from a number of applications or groups that can be used for analysis. The model base is a collection of mathematical and analytical models that are used for analyzing the data in the database. The DSS software system allows users to interact with the DSS database and model base directly.

Group decision-support systems (GDSS) have hardware, software, and people components. Hardware components consist of the conference room facilities, including seating arrangements and computer and other electronic hardware. Software components include tools for organizing ideas, gathering information, ranking and setting priorities, and documenting meeting sessions. People components include participants, a trained facilitator, and staff to support the hardware and software.

Explain how decision-support systems and group decision-support systems can enhance decision making.

Both DSS and GDSS support steps in the process of arriving at decisions. DSS provide results of model-based analysis that help managers design and evaluate alternatives and monitor the progress of the solution that was adopted. GDSS help decision makers meeting together to arrive at a decision more efficiently and are especially useful for increasing the productivity of meetings larger than four or five people. However, the effectiveness of GDSS is contingent upon the nature of the group, the task, and the context of the meeting.

Describe the capabilities of executive support systems (ESS).

Executive support systems (ESS) help managers with unstructured problems that occur at the strategic level of management. ESS provide data from both internal and external sources and provide a generalized computing and communications environment that can be focused and applied to a changing array of problems. ESS help senior executives spot problems, identify opportunities, and forecast trends. They can filter out extraneous details for high-level overviews or they can drill down to provide senior managers with detailed transaction data if required.

Describe the benefits of executive support systems.

ESS help senior managers analyze, compare, and highlight trends so that they more easily may monitor organizational performance or identify strategic problems and opportunities. ESS may increase the span of control of senior management and allow decision making to be decentralized and to take place at lower operating levels.

Key Terms

Decision-support systems (DSS)	Sensitivity analysis
Representations	DSS software system
Operations	Group decision-support system (GDSS)
Memory aids	Electronic meeting system (EMS)
Control aids	Executive support systems (ESS)
DSS database	Executive information systems (EIS)
Model base	Briefing books
Model	Drill down

Review Questions

1. What is a decision-support system (DSS)? How does it differ from a management information system (MIS)?

2. What are the four capabilities of a DSS?

3. How can DSS support unstructured or semistructured decision making?

4. What are the three basic components of a DSS? Briefly describe each.

5. In what ways is building decision-support systems different from building traditional MIS systems?

6. What is a group decision-support system (GDSS)? How does it differ from a DSS?

7. What are the three underlying problems in group decision making that have led to the development of GDSS?

8. Describe the three elements of a GDSS.

9. Name five GDSS software tools.

10. What is an electronic meeting system (EMS)?

11. For each of the three underlying problems in group decision making referred to in question 7, describe one or two ways GDSS can contribute to a solution.

12. What is the difference between an executive support system (ESS) and an executive information system (EIS)?

13. Define *briefing books*. List and explain at least three reasons why they were not adequate to support executive decision making.

14. List four types of technological changes in the 1980s that allowed more effective ESS to be developed. How did each of these changes contribute to solving the earlier problems of ESS?

15. In what ways is building executive support systems different from building traditional MIS systems?

16. What are the benefits of ESS? How do they enhance managerial decision making?

Discussion Questions

1. Some have argued that all information systems support decision making. The argument holds that conceptually, a DSS is just a good MIS. Discuss.

2. What kinds of skills must you, as an end user of systems, have in order to participate in the design and use of a DSS?

3. Identify an organization with which you are familiar. Identify specific areas where DSS could help decision making and describe the DSS you would recommend.

Group Project

With three or four of your classmates, identify several groups in your university that could benefit from a GDSS. Design a GDSS for one of those groups, describing its hardware, software, and people elements. Present your findings to the class.

CASE STUDY

Setting a Strategy for Executive Information Systems

This case is based on a real-world company with a real-world dilemma, although the names have been changed to enable the circumstances to be made public. The names and positions of the experts whose recommendations we will examine are real. These four experts bring four different perspectives to the case.

The company, Thor Industries, is a U.S.-based aerospace/defense company operating in a highly competitive and cost-conscious government market. Thor recently went through a major reorganization that has left the IS department severely overburdened. The company has a high-

level ESS Planning Committee made up of the vice presidents of information systems, production, finance, engineering and sales/marketing. That committee has just launched its first ESS project.

The ESS Planning Committee informed David Saunders, Vice President of MIS, that it wants an ESS to span several Thor operating groups, using data from a number of current mainframe, midrange and server-based databases and applications. The purpose of the ESS is to facilitate joint development of budgets, schedules, and measures of progress and to monitor the ongoing performance of major projects. The ESS has to be easy to use. The system will be based on a network of desktop equipment and will heavily emphasize graphics.

Saunders sees the project as a real opportunity for his staff to become more closely involved with the company while they build their own skills and reputations. But he has a number of concerns. First, the project has high profile inside the company because it is beamed toward senior management—*he* must succeed. Second, the chairman of the ESS Planning Committee, Howard Leaderman, has informed Saunders that there will be a budget large enough to allow software and hardware purchases but that IS will be "evaluated on its ability to manage costs over the long term." Third, Saunders' senior staff is apprehensive because they do not know desktop technology and are concerned that they will lose their value to the company. They also fear that the project will result in their being moved into line units as ongoing support where, they believe, their careers will be damaged. Some of the lower-level staff are also concerned because their experience is primarily with technology that could now become out-of-date. Saunders does have one advantage in his staff—some of his lower-level employees have gained extensive experience at Thor over the past several years installing desktop systems. Saunders has also already prepared some of his management for the coming changes in IS technology—for example, Leaderman has just attended a client/server conference on Saunders' recommendation.

What follows are the recommendations to Saunders made by four people with real experience in planning such projects.

Phil Carpenter, Marketing Manager of Mozart Systems, proposes a strategy that preserves Thor's investment in its current systems. He recommends that the system be built on top of the existing mainframe, midrange and server-based data, leaving that data and the systems that produce it in place. Thor should develop a graphical microcomputer-based executive information system that will act as a bridge to data stored in disparate locations. The system would provide an easy, intuitive way to view and manipulate data from multiple sources without changing the software code of the company's underlying business applications.

To do so requires a careful selection of a development tool. The tool not only must create an easy-to-use graphical interface (which many tools do), but it must also have some capabilities for accessing databases using SQL (Structured Query Language) and for linking up to mainframes and minicomputer systems (which few tools do).

Advantages of this approach are many. Investment in current systems will indeed be protected—they will not be touched. Staff fears should be allayed because the company will continue to need the same staff as before. Little additional training will be needed, so costs will be kept down. Costs will be minimized in another way also. The approach will require the purchase of only a modest amount of hardware and software, and will mainly use Thor's existing stock. Development time will also be minimal, with the use of the appropriate, user-friendly tool (he does not recommend a specific tool).

Saj-Nicole A. Joni, Regional Practice Manager for Microsoft Consulting, also sees leaving current production systems in place for now. She would build a client/server based ESS on top of the existing systems. However, she raises a whole set of different issues, most of which are nontechnical.

Successful executive information systems require a strong sense of ownership and support from top management. Joni wonders if the project has the necessary charter to go forward and to make the key decisions that will affect the involved divisions. She wants to know where the clear executive project ownership is that must exist if the project is to avoid failure. Thor's executives appear enthusiastic, but the specifications for the ESS do not answer questions such as the following: What are the critical short-term business issues to be addressed by the system? What are the long-term issues? Who will use the system and how will they use it? How will this ESS actually improve the way Thor's executives manage the business?

This project will result in a major change in how critical data are used at high levels and how the data are shared. Thor's management needs to define the information that will be used, and it needs to ensure that the ESS will provide a fair and consistent view of that information across divisions. The system designers should develop a clear data model based on the executives' information needs for meeting business objectives. Joni does not believe that modifying Thor's existing applications will provide the unified information that top management needs on its desktop.

Joni wonders if the project is addressing such major information systems issues as restructuring the department, reducing headcount, or retraining workers. She believes that with such a high visibility and high impact project, IS should form a special project team made up of smart, eager volunteers. The team should be supplemented by outside expertise in building GUI-based ESS client/server systems.

Joni believes that client/server technology is the direction of the future. Thor does not yet have a centralized client/server infrastructure. She suggests that Thor start to construct such an infrastructure with an open architecture using appropriate standards. She recommends that the graphical user interface for the ESS be built with off-the-shelf tools to standardize application interfaces and to provide flexibility for the future.

Ronald Sella is Manager of Emerging Technology Services for Information Builders, Inc. Sella believes that the most difficult issues for Thor are the human ones—retraining Saunders' staff and redefining job descriptions. He recommends that Saunders solve his problem by purchasing a third-party, 4GL-based ESS package.

Sella sees several "human factor" advantages to using a purchased ESS package. First, the IS staff would remain in their traditional positions, thus eliminating their fears over their future. They would, however, have to provide some technical support to the project and its resulting system. Second, training is minimal and easy. The ESS software vendor will train Thor's staff to use the software and will provide technical support for that software. System development using the 4GL software will, he believes, be relatively easy; for this reason he suggests purchasing such a package.

Sella also recommends that Saunders base the new system on client/server technology, suggesting that the database software be SQL-based and relational to facilitate multivendor cross-platform connectivity. The software used by the new ESS system must support access to a wide variety of databases so that it can access Thor's current data. Costs would be limited because Thor would have to purchase little new software or hardware and would avoid large training or reorganization costs.

Jim Powell, Distributed Information Services manager for Texas Instruments, brings a focus on changing technology to the discussion. He believes that the emergence of client/server technology has been an information systems watershed, bringing changes as significant as the development of microcomputers did in the beginning of the 1980s. Powell concludes that Thor must pursue the change to client/server technology—the risks of doing so are less than in staying with technology that is becoming outdated.

A technology transition of such fundamental importance cannot simply happen. Powell recommends that Saunders make a reformulation of Thor IS strategy his first priority. He then urges the setting of very clear architectural standards to push new development towards the emerging

environment. He also warns Saunders not to "manually hard code each [client/server] application." He believes that Thor will be developing hundreds of such applications over the coming five to ten years. Such a large amount of work must be done in a standardized way, using a software development tool.

Powell raises yet another issue, one he believes Saunders has not addressed. The growth of microcomputers and now the change to client/server technology means that data will no longer be centralized. They will be "spread out across thousands of workstations and hundreds of servers." Controlling and even just keeping track of data is a massive problem that Saunders must address.

Finally, Powell believes the staff issues are also critical—but he has a very different slant. He notes that IS professionals keep close track of changes in their industry. Regardless of what they are saying, Powell asserts, Saunders' IS staff will ultimately be more troubled by working in a company where technology is falling behind than by working in one that is moving to leading-edge technology. To help the staff make the transition, he emphasizes the need for an organized training program to teach new skills. He also urges the company to map out new career paths for the staff. As he says, "It will not happen by osmosis."

Which strategy for building ESS should Saunders follow?

Source: Damian Rinaldi and John Desmond, "Preserve Investment or Move On?" *Software Magazine,* March, 1992.

Case Study Questions:

1. If you were in David Saunders' position, what would you recommend? Why? Develop the pros and cons of your decision. What management, organization, and technology issues would you consider?

2. None of the four consultants lay out the risks of their recommendations. Add a paragraph to each description delineating those risks.

3. Joni raises the issue of effective executive sponsorship. Why do you think she stresses this issue? Why will this particular project need such strong, high-level leadership?

4. All the recommendations dealt with staff issues, with several of them stressing these issues above all

others. From what you know, do you believe the staff problem will be as significant as they indicate? Why? How would you handle the staff issue? Why?

5. Two of the experts (Joni and Powell) urge that Saunders use this project to make a transition to client/server technology, indicating this as a fundamental shift in IS strategic direction. Assuming they are correct about the direction of technology, do you think Saunders should make this technology shift? Why? What are the risks of making that shift through the ESS high-visibility project? Would you accept Joni and Powell's client/server recommendations? Why?

References   Alavi, Maryam, and Erich A. Joachimsthaler. "Revisiting DSS Implementation Research: A Meta-Analysis of the Literature and Suggestions for Researchers." *MIS Quarterly* 16, no. 1 (March 1992).

Betts, Mitch. "Computer Maps Help Cops Catch Crooks." *Computerworld* (February 15, 1993).

Bonzcek, R. H., C. W. Holsapple, and A. B. Whinston. "Representing Modeling Knowledge with First Order Predicate Calculus." *Operations Research* 1 (1982).

Chidambaram, Laku, Robert P. Bostrom, and Bayard E. Wynne. "A Longitudinal Study of the Impact of Group Decision Support Systems on Group Development." *Journal of Management Information Systems* 7, no. 3 (Winter 1990/1991).

Dennis, Alan R., Jay F. Nunamaker, Jr., and Douglas R. Vogel. "A Comparison of Laboratory and Field Research in the Study of Electronic Meeting Systems." *Journal of Management Information Systems* 7, no. 3 (Winter 1990/1991).

Dennis, Alan R., Joey F. George, Len M. Jessup, Jay F. Nunamaker, and Douglas R. Vogel. "Information Technology to Support Electronic Meetings." *MIS Quarterly* 12, no. 4 (December 1988).

DeSanctis, Geraldine, Marshall Scott Poole, Howard Lewis, and George Desharnias. "Computing in Quality Team Meetings." *Journal of Management Information Systems* 8, no. 3 (Winter 1991–92).

DeSanctis, Geraldine and R. Brent Gallupe. "A Foundation for the Study of Group Decision Support Systems." *Management Science* 33, no. 5 (May 1987).

Easton, George K., Joey F. George, Jay F. Nunamaker, Jr., and Mark O. Pendergast. "Two Different Electronic Meeting Systems." *Journal of Management Information Systems* 7, no. 3 (Winter 1990/1991).

El Sawy, Omar. "Personal Information Systems for Strategic Scanning in Turbulent Environments." *MIS Quarterly* 9, no. 1 (March 1985).

El Sherif, Hisham, and Omar A. El Sawy. "Issue-Based Decision Support Systems for the Egyptian Cabinet." *MIS Quarterly* 12, no. 4 (December 1988).

Gallupe, R. Brent, Geraldine DeSanctis, and Gary W. Dickson. "Computer-Based Support for Group Problem-Finding: An Experimental Investigation." *MIS Quarterly* 12, no. 2 (June 1988).

Ginzberg, Michael J., W. R. Reitman, and E. A. Stohr (ed). *Decision Support Systems.* New York: North Holland Publishing Co., 1982.

Gopal, Abhijit, Robert P. Bostrum, and Wynne W. Chin. "Applying Adaptive Structuration Theory to Investigate the Process of Group Support Systems Use." *Journal of Management Information Systems* 9, no. 3 (Winter 1992–93).

Grobowski, Ron, Chris McGoff, Doug Vogel, Ben Martz, and Jay Nunamaker. "Implementing Electronic Meeting Systems at IBM: Lessons Learned and Success Factors." *MIS Quarterly* 14, no. 4 (December 1990).

Henderson, John C., and David A. Schilling. "Design and Implementation of Decision Support Systems in the Public Sector." *MIS Quarterly* (June 1985).

Hiltz, Starr Roxanne, Kenneth Johnson, and Murray Turoff. "Group Decision Support: Designated Human Leaders and Statistical Feedback. *Journal of Management Information Systems* 8, no. 2 (Fall 1991).

Ho, T. H., and K. S. Raman. "The Effect of GDSS on Small Group Meetings." *Journal of Management Information Systems* 8, no. 2 (Fall 1991).

Hogue, Jack T. "Decision Support Systems and the Traditional Computer Information System Function: An Examination of Relationships During DSS Application Development." *Journal of Management Information Systems* (Summer 1985).

Hogue, Jack T. "A Framework for the Examination of Management Involvement in Decision Support Systems." *Journal of Management Information Systems* 4, no. 1 (Summer 1987).

Houdeshel, George, and Hugh J. Watson. "The Management Information and Decision Support (MIDS) System at Lockheed, Georgia." *MIS Quarterly* 11, no. 2 (March 1987).

Jessup, Leonard M., Terry Connolly, and Jolene Galegher. "The Effects of Anonymity on GDSS Group Process with an Idea-Generating Task." *MIS Quarterly* 14, no. 3 (September 1990).

Keen, Peter G. W., and M. S. Scott Morton. *Decision Support Systems: An Organizational Perspective.* Reading, MA: Addison-Wesley, 1982.

King, John. "Successful Implementation of Large Scale Decision Support Systems: Computerized Models in U.S. Economic Policy Making." *Systems Objectives Solutions* (November 1983).

Kraemer, Kenneth L., and John Leslie King. "Computer-Based Systems for Cooperative Work and Group Decision Making." *ACM Computing Surveys* 20, no. 2 (June 1988).

Laudon, Kenneth C. *Communications Technology and Democratic Participation.* New York: Praeger, 1977.

Le Blanc, Louis A., and Kenneth A. Kozar. "An Empirical Investigation of the Relationship Between DSS Usage and System Performance." *MIS Quarterly* 14, no. 3 (September 1990).

Lewe, Henrik, and Helmut Krcmar. "A Computer-Supported Cooperative Work Research Laboratory." *Journal of Management Information Systems* 8, no. 3 (Winter 1991–92).

McLeod, Poppy Lauretta, and Jeffry R. Liker. "Electronic Meeting Systems: Evidence from a Low Structure Environment." *Information Systems Research* 3, no. 3 (September 1992).

Meador, Charles L., and Peter G. W. Keen. "Setting Priorities for DSS Development." *MIS Quarterly* (June 1984).

Mohan, Lakshmi, William K. Holstein, and Robert B. Adams. "EIS: It Can Work in the Public Sector." *MIS Quarterly* 14, no. 4 (December 1990).

Nunamaker, J. F., Alan R. Dennis, Joseph S. Valacich, Douglas R. Vogel, and Joey F. George. "Electronic Meeting Systems to Support Group Work." *Communications of the ACM* 34, no. 7 (July 1991).

Panko, Raymond R. "Managerial Communication Patterns." *Journal of Organizational Computing* 2, no. 1 (1992).

Post, Brad Quinn. "A Business Case Framework for Group Support Technology." *Journal of Management Information Systems* 9, no. 3 (Winter 1992–93).

Rifkin, Glenn. " 'What-If' Software for Manufacturers." *The New York Times* (October 18, 1992).

Rockart, John F., and David W. DeLong. "Executive Support Systems and the Nature of Work." Working Paper: Management in the 1990s, Sloan School of Management (April 1986).

Rockart, John F., and David W. DeLong, *Executive Support Systems: The Emergence of Top Management Computer Use.* Homewood, IL: Dow-Jones Irwin, 1988.

Sambamurthy, V., and Marshall Scott Poole. "The Effects of Variations in Capabilities of GDSS Designs on Management of Cognitive Conflict in Groups." *Information Systems Research* 3, no. 3 (September 1992).

Sanders, G. Lawrence, and James F. Courtney. "A Field Study of Organizational Factors Influencing DSS Success." *MIS Quarterly* (March 1985).

Silver, Mark S. "Decision Support Systems: Directed and Nondirected Change." *Information Systems Research* 1, no. 1 (March 1990).

Sprague, R. H., and E. D. Carlson. *Building Effective Decision Support Systems.* Englewood Cliffs, NJ: Prentice-Hall, 1982.

Stefik, Mark, Gregg Foster, Daniel C. Bobrow, Kenneth Kahn, Stan Lanning, and Luch Suchman. "Beyond the Chalkboard: Computer Support for Collaboration and Problem Solving in Meetings." *Communications of the ACM* (January 1987).

"The New Role for 'Executive Information Systems'." *I/S Analyzer* (January 1992).

Turban, Efraim. *Decision Support and Expert Systems,* 2nd ed. New York: Macmillan, 1990.

Turoff, Murray. "Computer-Mediated Communication Requirements for Group Support." *Journal of Organizational Computing* 1, no. 1 (January–March 1991).

Tyran, Craig K., Alan R. Dennis, Douglas R. Vogel, and J. F. Nunamaker, Jr. "The Application of Electronic Meeting Technology to Support Senior Management." *MIS Quarterly,* 16, no. 3 (September 1992).

Vogel, Douglas R., Jay F. Nunamaker, William Benjamin Martz, Jr., Ronald Grobowski, and Christopher McGoff. "Electronic Meeting System Experience at IBM." *Journal of Management Information Systems* 6, no. 3 (Winter 1989/90).

Volonino, Linda, and Hugh J. Watson. "The Strategic Business Objectives Method for EIS Development." *Journal of Management Information Systems* 7, no. 3 (Winter 1990/1991).

Walls, Joseph G., George R. Widmeyer, and Omar A. El Sawy. "Building an Information System Design Theory for Vigilant EIS." *Information Systems Research* 3 no. 1 (March 1992).

Watson, Hugh J., Astrid Lipp, Pamela Z. Jackson, Abdelhafid Dahmani, and William B. Fredenberger. "Organizational Support for Decision Support Systems." *Journal of Management Information Systems* 5, no. 4 (Spring 1989).

Watson, Hugh J., R. Kelly Rainer, Jr., and Chang E. Koh. "Executive Information Systems: A Framework for Development and a Survey of Current Practices." *MIS Quarterly* 15, no. 1 (March 1991).

Watson, Richard T., Geraldine DeSanctis, and Marshall Scott Poole. "Using a GDSS to Facilitate Group Consensus: Some Intended and Unintended Consequences." *MIS Quarterly* 12, no. 3 (September 1988).

Singapore Money Managers Use Machines to Pick Stocks

What makes international stock markets tick? There is no exact science to provide the answer because not all factors that influence financial data are known and their interrelationship is highly complex. Nevertheless, Singapore-based Koeneman Capital Managers is trying to come closer to the answer by using artificial intelligence software. Its goal is to uncover the economic factors that drive global stock performance in the world's 11 major equity markets and the emerging Asian markets in Hong Kong, Thailand, Indonesia, Korea, and Taiwan.

KCM manages over $400 million in total assets, half of which comes from Australian pension and other funds. The firm uses a contrarian investment strategy, trying to sell in a rising stock market and to buy when the market is falling. KCM's base in Singapore gives it both a front-row view of emerging Asian equity markets and access to advanced infor-

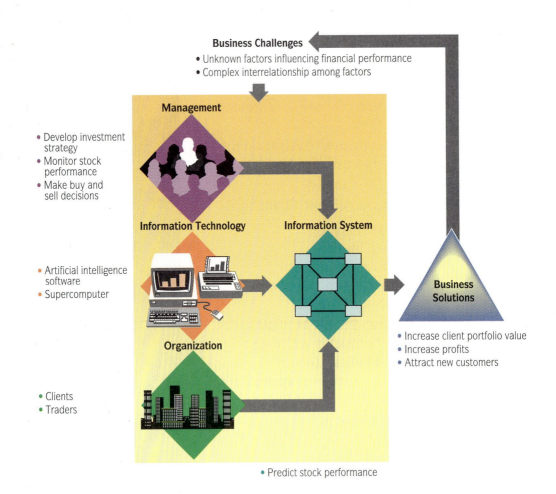

Business Challenges
- Unknown factors influencing financial performance
- Complex interrelationship among factors

Management
- Develop investment strategy
- Monitor stock performance
- Make buy and sell decisions

Information Technology
- Artificial intelligence software
- Supercomputer

Information System

Business Solutions
- Increase client portfolio value
- Increase profits
- Attract new customers

Organization
- Clients
- Traders

- Predict stock performance

mation system technology that can help make the strategy work.

KCM rents time on a NEC SX-1A supercomputer at Singapore Technologies, a government-affiliated technology center, to run special artificial intelligence software that builds predictive models for selecting international stocks. The software can sift through vast streams of data about economic conditions, stock prices, interest rates, and currency exchange rates, to find subtle cause-and-effect patterns that would be impossible for humans to discern. KCM uses the findings to build models that predict how stocks will perform under a wide range of variable factors in each of the major equity markets. The models attempt to determine what factors drive asset returns by testing out millions of combinations. After creating and testing the models, KCM tailors them to conditions specific to each country.

The models provide information to help KCM make buy-and-sell decisions, but they do not make the decisions themselves. According to Geoffrey Wang, KCM's director of investment technology, KCM makes stock trading decisions using qualitative judgment along with the output of its quantitative tools. The models for evaluating equity performance may be totally automated, but humans are still needed to determine whether the models make financial and economic sense.

Have KCM's models paid off? In the world of finance, any information that provides a company with the slightest advantage over competitors can produce millions in extra profits. John K. Koeneman, KCM's founder, believes that the firm's use of superior information system technology has created that advantage. While most international money management firms with Far East portfolios were slaughtered by the 65 percent decline in share price in Japanese stocks, just before the beginning of the Persian Gulf War in January 1991, KCM's country valuation models had warned it to exit the Japanese market. In 1992, KCM was the top performing money management firm in the Pacific region.

Source: Ivy Schmerken, "Research Reaches New Heights," *Wall Street & Technology* (November 1992).

By using artificial intelligence techniques, Koeneman Capital Managers was able to develop sophisticated models to predict the behavior of stocks. Other artificial intelligence applications capture the knowledge of recognized experts and make that knowledge available to other workers in the organization. Organizations can benefit from a variety of software and hardware techniques for acquiring, retaining, and leveraging knowledge, provided they understand both the potential and pitfalls.

This chapter explains what artificial intelligence is and what artificial intelligence systems can and cannot do. It shows how expert systems, neural networks, and other artificial intelligence techniques capture knowledge and intelligence while pointing out their limitations. The chapter then describes how these techniques can create information systems that capture knowledge and intelligence for organizations; the chapter also identifies the requirements of successful artificial intelligence applications.

After completing this chapter you will be able to:

- Define artificial intelligence.
- Describe how artificial intelligent techniques evolved.
- Define an expert system and explain how it is built.
- Define neural networks and show how they are used in business.
- Identify other intelligent techniques.

17.1   What Is Artificial Intelligence?

The effort to use computers to understand or imitate aspects of human intelligence began in the 1950s. In 1956, Marvin Minsky (now at MIT), Claude Shannon of Bell Laboratories, and other innovators in the early study of computers and intelligence met at a conference at Dartmouth College. John McCarthy, then an assistant professor of mathematics at Dartmouth, coined the term *artificial intelligence* for the theme of the conference. The conference's high point was the unveiling of what some people thought was the first expert system, Logic Theorist. The system processed nonnumerical symbols instead of crunching numbers, and it proved several theorems in the *Principia Mathematica* of Alfred North Whitehead and Bertrand Russell. No magazine would publish the proof of the theorems because the results had been produced by a machine. This was the first software to claim properties of artificial intelligence. Ever since that time, skeptics, pundits, journalists, and serious scholars have argued over what artificial intelligence means.

What Artificial Intelligence Is and Is Not

Artificial intelligence: The effort to develop computer-based systems that can behave like humans, with the ability to learn languages, accomplish physical tasks, use a perceptual apparatus, and emulate human expertise and decision making.

Artificial intelligence is commonly defined as the effort to develop computer-based systems (both hardware and software) that behave as humans. Such systems would be able to learn natural languages, accomplish coordinated physical tasks (robotics), utilize a perceptual apparatus that informs their physical behavior and language (visual and oral perception systems), and emulate human expertise and decision making (expert systems). Such systems would also exhibit logic, reasoning, intuition, and the just plain common-sense qualities that we associate with human beings. Figure 17.1 illustrates the elements of the artificial intelligence family. Another important element here is "intelligent" machines, the physical hardware that performs these tasks.

No existing system comes close to possessing any of these human qualities, but what has been developed is nevertheless of profound interest. Artificial intelligence has become, without doubt, the most controversial subject in computer science and information systems circles, as well as in the broader community of scholars and decision makers. Since the Renaissance, men and women in their physical form and mental accomplishments have been at the center of the cultural universe, the measure of all things. Now to be joined by a lowly machine, an artificial, inanimate object, represents a challenging cultural revolution that most people resist. Critics of the study of artificial intelligence argue that it is a waste of time and resources, a study dotted with significant failures and few accomplishments that succeeds only insofar as it denigrates the power and elegance of human thought processes. The most militant critics argue that artificial intelligence insults the very nature and role of human beings.

Moreover, critics point out, the current media fascination with machines that think obscures the fact that leading artificial intelligence thinkers have been wrong in the past. More than thirty-five years ago, Herbert Simon and Alan

Figure 17.1
The artificial intelligence family.
The field of AI currently includes
many initiatives: natural
language, robotics, perceptive
systems, expert systems, and
intelligent machines.

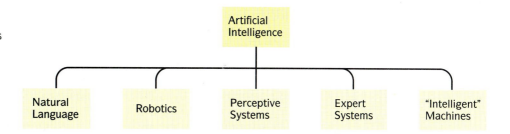

Newell (1958) claimed: "There are now in the world machines that think, that learn, and that create. Moreover, their ability to do these things is going to increase rapidly until—in the visible future—the range of problems they can handle will be coextensive with the range to which the human mind has been applied." Not even the most ardent supporters of artificial intelligence today believe that such machines are now available or that they are likely to be in the foreseeable future.

Supporters of the study of artificial intelligence point to the noble goal of using it as a way of understanding human intelligence and as a vehicle for distributing expertise. Artificial intelligence systems, if they could be developed, might lead to a quantum leap in social wealth and well-being. It has been claimed that several successful artificial intelligence systems have been developed that work in the real world. These successes support the further commitment of resources. The new technology, supporters argue, will increase individual and social potential by distributing knowledge more widely. Supporters dismiss the critics as Luddites standing in the way of science and technology, which they see as supporting the rapid exploitation of artificial intelligence. History, they argue, is propelling artificial intelligence forward.

In this chapter, we will try to avoid making judgments about whether artificial intelligence is a worthwhile pursuit. Instead, we will give the views of both critics and supporters, as well as some real-world examples. You can decide for yourself whether artificial intelligence is a worthwhile pursuit with potential real-world benefits.

Human and Artificial Intelligence

Before describing artificial intelligence, it is worthwhile to distinguish more fully between *artificial* and human intelligence. Much of the controversy that surrounds artificial intelligence results from the poor choice of words used to describe the activity. The term *artificial intelligence* is flamboyant and provocative. If the term *advanced programming* had been used in 1956 by John McCarthy to describe the Logic Theorist, much of the controversy might never have occurred. However, most of the public interest and funding might also have disappeared.

Successful artificial intelligence systems are neither artificial nor intelligent. This raises the question: What would a truly *artificial intelligent* system look like? A thermostat and an autopilot are the best examples of systems that solve problems in a goal-oriented, machinelike, artificial way. Yet no one calls thermostats or autopilots intelligent.

All successful artificial intelligence systems are based on human expertise, knowledge, and selected reasoning patterns (syllogisms, rules of thumb, etc.). Successful artificial intelligence systems are, if anything, "naturally" intelligent. They act like textbooks and other human artifacts of intelligence. Indeed, you will learn in this chapter that most artificial intelligence systems can be developed only when human knowledge can be effectively expressed in simple textbook form (e.g., "if *x*, then *y*"). Successful artificial intelligence systems—like textbooks—cannot learn without being rewritten. Existing artificial intelligence systems do not come up with new and novel solutions to problems. Existing, practical artificial intelligence systems that try to reproduce the expertise of humans do not behave like human experts at all, but rather are limited to mundane yet important tasks. Existing systems extend the powers of experts, but in no way substitute for them or "capture" much of their intelligence. Briefly, existing systems lack the common sense and generality of naturally intelligent machines like human beings, a feature that was understood by the early founders of artificial intelligence but that was lost by later exponents.

For instance, John McCarthy, one of the early founders of the study of artificial intelligence, noted in 1987 that "no one knows how to make a general database of common-sense knowledge that could be used by any program that needed the knowledge. Along with other information, such a database would contain what a robot would need to know about the effects of moving objects around, what a person can be expected to know about his family, and the facts about buying and selling. This does not depend on whether the knowledge is to be expressed in a logical language or in some other formalism. When we take the logic approach to AI, lack of generality shows up in that the axioms we devise to express common-sense knowledge are too restricted in their applicability for a general common-sense database." McCarthy believed that "getting a language for expressing general common sense knowledge for inclusion in a general database is the key problem of generality in AI," (McCarthy, 1987) although he expected intelligent computer programs to eventually be developed.

Now let us examine *human* intelligence. As it turns out, human intelligence is vastly complex and much broader than computer or information systems. Philosophers, psychologists, and other students of human cognition have all recog-

Figure 17.2
The evolution of artificial intelligence. The parallel development of the top-down and bottom-up approaches can be traced through the various milestones supporting each approach.

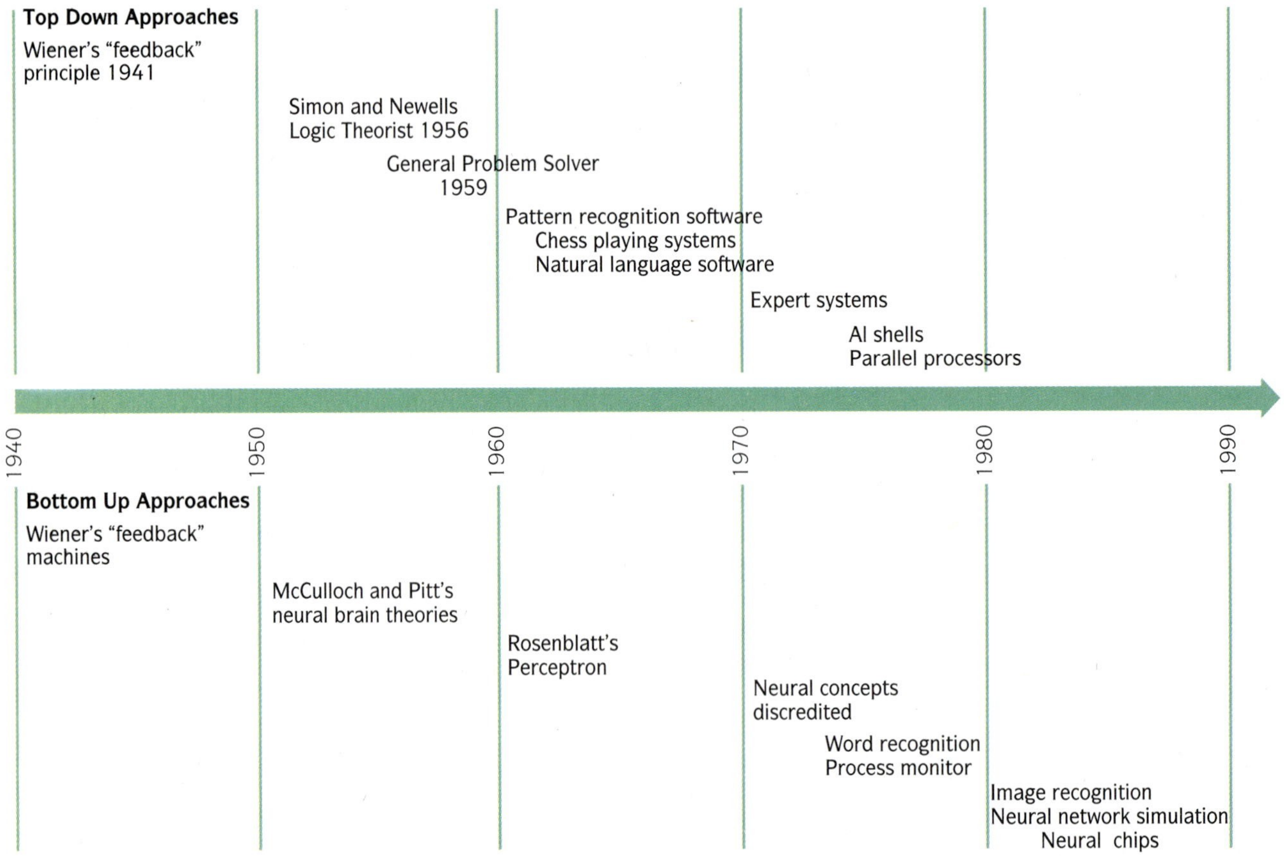

Top Down Approaches

Wiener's "feedback" principle 1941

Simon and Newells Logic Theorist 1956

General Problem Solver 1959

Pattern recognition software
Chess playing systems
Natural language software

Expert systems

AI shells
Parallel processors

1940   1950   1960   1970   1980   1990

Bottom Up Approaches

Wiener's "feedback" machines

McCulloch and Pitt's neural brain theories

Rosenblatt's Perceptron

Neural concepts discredited

Word recognition
Process monitor

Image recognition
Neural network simulation
Neural chips

nized that key aspects of human intelligence are beyond description and therefore are not easily imitated by a consciously designed machine. If a problem cannot be described, it cannot be programmed.

At least four important capabilities are involved in human intelligence: reasoning, behavior, the use of metaphor and analogy, and the creation and use of concepts.

- *Human intelligence is a way of reasoning.* One part of human intelligence can be described as the application of rules based on human experience and genetics. (Whether this rule-governed behavior takes the form "if *x*, then *y*" is not known.) These rules, although not always consciously invoked, are an important part of the knowledge carried by all human beings as an inheritance from the broader culture and the human gene pool.
- *Human intelligence is a way of behaving.* Even if humans do not actually invoke rules, they are obligated to act as if they did by a culture and a society that values reasonable, intelligent behavior. Human intelligence, at the very least, consists of acting in a way that can be described as intelligent.
- *Human intelligence includes the development and use of metaphors and analogies.* What distinguishes human beings from other animals is their ability to develop associations and to use metaphors and analogies such as "like" and "as." Using metaphor and analogy, humans create new rules, apply old rules to new situations, and at times act intuitively and/or instinctively without rules. Much of what we call "common sense" or "generality" in humans resides in the ability to create metaphor and analogy.
- *Human intelligence includes the creation and use of concepts.* It has long been recognized that humans have a unique ability to impose a conceptual apparatus on the world around them. Meta-concepts such as cause and effect and time, and concepts of a lower order such as breakfast, dinner, and lunch, are all imposed by human beings on the world around them. Thinking in terms of these concepts and acting on them are central characteristics of intelligent human behavior.

Artificial intelligence, then, refers to an effort to develop machines that can reason, behave, compare, and conceptualize, as just described. While this may be a noble effort, clearly none of the successful systems described in this chapter comes close to achieving this form of human intelligence. What has been developed is of interest and is starting to provide some benefits to organizations. Moreover, there is no evidence that systems capable of exhibiting some kinds of intelligent behavior could not be developed in the future.

The Development of Artificial Intelligence

Bottom-up approach: In the history of artificial intelligence, the effort to build a physical analog to the human brain.

The story of artificial intelligence, or AI, is really two stories.[1] (See Figure 17.2.) One is the history of efforts to develop physical machines that mimic what people at the time think is the way an animal or human physical brain works. This is called the **bottom-up approach,** the effort to build a physical analog to

[1]Actually, the story of AI is much deeper and more controversial than can be presented here in such a brief introduction. Involved in this larger debate are questions about the nature of human beings and knowledge, the proper relationship between responsible human beings and machines, and the difference between promise and reality. For a positive view of AI, see Edward A. Feigenbaum and Pamela McCorduck, *The Fifth Generation: Artificial Intelligence and Japan's Computer Challenge to the World*, Reading, MA.: Addison-Wesley, 1985 and Paul M. Churchland and Patricia Smith Churchland, "Could A Machine Think?" *Scientific American*, January 1990. For a counter view of AI, see Hubert L. Dreyfus and Stuart E. Dreyfus, *Mind Over Machine: The Power of Human Intuition and Expertise in the Era of the Computer*, New York: The Free Press, 1986 and John R. Searle "Is the Brain's Mind a Computer Program?" *Scientific American*, January 1990.

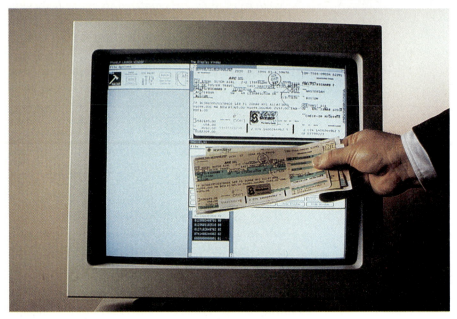

NorthWest Airlines Inc. uses an AI-based expert auditing system, which is responsible for ensuring that airline passenger tickets are properly priced and that the correct travel agency commission is applied.

Top-down approach: In the history of artificial intelligence, the effort to develop a logical analog to how the brain works.

the human brain. A second story focuses on the effort to develop a logical analog to how the brain works. This approach is called the **top-down approach.**

The effort to develop intelligent machines is hardly new. In fact, the earliest inventor of a mechanical calculator, Charles Babbage, called his proposed calculating machine of 1834 an "analytical engine," or thinking machine, which he felt could play chess at some point. This was perhaps the first top-down intelligent device.

THE BOTTOM-UP APPROACH

But the beginnings of contemporary AI started in World War II with the concept of "feedback." Norbert Wiener, a scientist and mathematician at MIT in the 1940s, developed a method of radar control of anti-aircraft guns for the U.S. army that required calculating the expected location of an aircraft based on new information—"feedback"—from radar. Wiener went on to propose in several books that feedback could explain how humans think. He believed that the principle could be applied to make machines think like humans.

This early period of self-correcting artillery machines started the physical or bottom-up approach to artificial intelligence. Warren McCulloch, a biologist interested in brain function, and Walter Pitts, a mathematician, used Wiener's idea of feedback to develop a theory of how brains work. In their theory, a brain was composed of millions of neuron cells, which processed binary numbers (they were either "on" or "off") that were connected into a network that took in feedback or information from the environment. Learning was simply a matter of teaching the neurons in a brain how to respond to the environment. These ideas were taken further by Frank Rosenblatt, a Cornell psychologist and scientist, who in 1960 demonstrated a machine he called a Perceptron. This machine was composed of 400 photoelectric cells that could perceive letters or shapes and 512 neuron-like relays that conveyed information from the photoelectric cells to response units. The machine could recognize letters (as long as they were all the same size and type) and could be taught: Operators would increase or decrease voltages in certain areas of the machine when mistakes were made.

In 1969, the top-down logical school, led by Marvin Minsky and Seymour Papert, both at MIT, published a book called *Perceptrons,* which "proved" mathematically that such devices could never come anywhere near the intelligence of even lowly animals. This book ended serious research in the bottom-up school for many years, until the 1980s when work began on word, pattern, and image recognition and on neural networks machines that attempt to emulate the physical thought processes of the human brain (Section 17.4 describes neural networks in greater detail). Since then, Minsky has withdrawn his critique and now supports research on neural networks.

THE TOP-DOWN APPROACH

The logical theorists were hard at work in the late 1950s even though the bottom-up school received most of the press. The logical or top-down school of AI has gone through three stages. In its earliest stage, the goal was to develop a general model of human intelligence. This was followed by a period in which the extraordinary power of third-generation computers—the machines of the 1960s—was applied to more limited problems like playing chess games or to special areas like machine tool control. Last, beginning in the 1970s, expert systems emerged in which the goals of AI were more limited to understanding knowledge in specific and highly limited areas.

One of the first top-down efforts was the Logic Theorist, introduced in 1956 at the Dartmouth Summer Research Project on Artificial Intelligence. Its developers, Herbert Simon (a Carnegie-Mellon psychologist and scientist) and Alan Newell (a RAND corporation scientist), used software that was based on mimicking deductive logic: selecting the correct rules and postulates so as to create a coherent logical chain from premises to conclusion.

The Logic Theorist, unfortunately, could not be easily adapted to other areas of life where deductive reasoning was used. The problem with this approach of following chains of "if x then y" statements is that hundreds of thousands, or millions, of such rules are required for even simple real-world problems.

In the 1960s, the newly developed third-generation computers made it possible to consider thousands of computations per second. Attention turned to pure "power" approaches: using the new machines to test out millions of rules, one at a time. But even a simple game like chess contained 10^{120} possible moves, and ways had to be found to pare down the search tree in order to avoid a **combinatorial explosion.** A combinatorial explosion arises when a problem requires a computer to test more rules than it has the capacity to examine in order to reach a solution. An exhaustive search through all possibilities on a chessboard would quickly swamp all the computers known to exist in the 1980s. Newell and Simon responded by developing a model of human problem solving, called the *General Problem Solver.* The objective was to use simple rules to pare down the search tree. But this solution did not work either because no one could come up with sensible general rules of problem solving that were useful in all situations. However, in restricted domains—like chess—and with sufficient processing power, a number of strategies can be pursued and processed with some success.

From these developments emerged expert systems, which consist of rules limited to a very specific and limited domain of human expertise (such as chess). In order to avoid a combinatorial explosion, some rules of thumb or heuristics are needed. Figure 17.3 shows several decision trees and some possible search strategies (random, exhaustive, and rule-guided).

Combinatorial explosion: In computer processing, the overload that results when trying to test more rules to reach a solution than the computer is capable of handling.

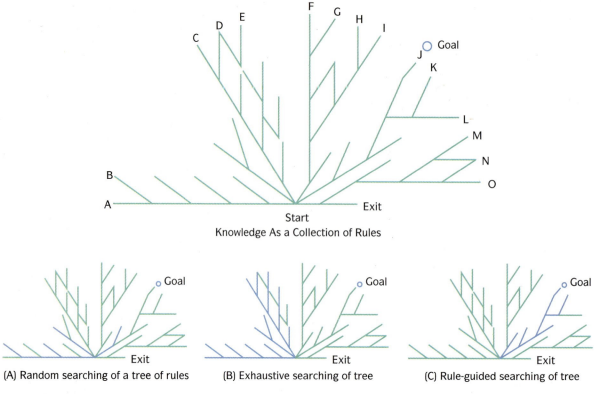

Figure 17.3
Decision making in AI systems. Some kinds of knowledge can be represented as a decision tree, a collection of paths from an origin to a goal. The various techniques for searching from the origin to the goal illustrated are: (A) random searching that will repeat errors and attain the goal only by chance; (B) exhaustive searching that will record all searches and not take the same path twice, eventually reaching the goal; and (C) rule-guided searching that evaluates the paths and takes the first path to reduce the distance between the origin and the goal until the goal is reached.

Figure 17.3 illustrates the search strategies that could be used to solve a simple problem: finding the goal at *J*. One possibility (*A*) is to search the tree randomly until the goal at *J* is found. Without recording failed paths, a random search will repeat errors and attain the goal only by chance. Another possibility (*B*) is exhaustive searching of the tree, recording all choices and not taking the same path twice. A simple set of rules is to start always on the far left, take every path to its end, retrace one, two, or three steps if you do not attain the goal, and try again. Eventually you will find the goal at *J*. A much more economical method is a rule-guided search (*C*). Here the rule is to evaluate all paths and to take the first path that reduces the distance between the origin and the goal. If the distance to the goal is not reduced, backtrack one step and try again.

A major effort of AI systems is to develop simple rules that can pare down the search tree and make searching efficient. In limited areas of expertise, from diagnosing a car's ignition system, to classifying biological specimens, the rules of thumb used by real-world experts can be understood, codified, and placed in a machine. In the next section we explain what expert systems are and how they work.

17.2 Knowledge-Based Expert Systems

While manufacturing companies have traditionally focused on artificial intelligence for robots and vision systems to assist assembly, management and service industries, in particular, are more interested in expert systems. Expert systems automate part, and in some cases all, of the decision-making process.

What Is an Expert System?

Expert system:
Knowledge-intensive computer program that captures the expertise of a human in limited domains of knowledge.

An **expert system** is a knowledge-intensive program that solves a problem by capturing the expertise of a human in limited domains of knowledge and experience. An expert system can assist decision making by asking relevant questions and explaining the reasons for adopting certain actions.

Some of the common characteristics of expert systems are the following:

- They perform some of the problem-solving work of humans.
- They use knowledge in the form of rules or frames.
- They interact with humans.
- They can consider multiple hypotheses simultaneously.

Expert systems are therefore different from thermostats and autopilots insofar as they attempt to base their actions on human knowledge rather than on physical principles.

It should also be clear what expert systems are not. Today, expert systems are quite narrow, shallow, and brittle. They lack the breadth of knowledge and the understanding of fundamental principles of a human expert. Expert systems today do not "think" as a human being does. A human being perceives significance, works with abstract models of causality, and can jump to conclusions. Expert systems do not resort to reasoning from first principles, do not draw analogies, and lack common sense.

Above all, expert systems are not a generalized expert or problem solver. They typically perform very limited tasks, such as scanning, tracking, interpreting, and diagnosing, that can be performed by professionals in a few minutes or hours. Problems that cannot be solved by human experts in the same short period of time are far too difficult for an expert system. As it turns out, cloning a human expert is impossible with today's tools, although parts of human expertise can be captured by computer programs, including expert system languages.

The Different Roles of Expert Systems

The most common role for an expert system is that of an *assistant*. This system helps a decision maker by doing the routine analysis and pointing out those portions of the work where human expertise is required. The **assistant expert system,** like a robot, does the tedious work while the human thinks.

Assistant expert system: In the role of an assistant, an expert system that helps a decision maker by doing the routine analysis and tedious work and pointing out the portions of the work where human expertise is required.

General Electric's SCISOR system fits this pattern. SCISOR (System for Conceptual Information, Summarization, Organization, and Retrieval) is an information retrieval system that automatically scans real-time text messages such as news articles. Instead of using keywords to search databases, SCISOR actually diagrams sentences and develops a primitive but useful "understanding" of each sentence in an article (Jacobs and Rau, 1990). The system buzzes through the Dow Jones wire services and identifies articles and messages about impending corporate takeovers.

Colleague expert system: In the role of a colleague, an expert system that permits a decision maker to engage in a discussion of the problem, add information, or even bypass the system entirely, until a joint decision is reached.

A second-level system is that of a colleague. With a **colleague expert system,** the user discusses the problem until a joint decision is reached. When the system reaches a wrong conclusion, the user adds more information to get it back on track. Sometimes the user pulls the plug if the results are not commonsensical. One system that falls into this category is American Express's Authorizer's Assistant, described in the Window on Management later in this chapter. Authorizer's Assistant provides screens that guide human credit authorizers through detailed telephone conversations with retail merchants. The system will recommend approval or disapproval of credit card charges.

Complete expert automaton: An expert system that operates remotely by making decisions without the additional input of human experts or human intervention.

A third-level system is a **complete expert automaton** that makes the decisions for users without question, operating remotely beyond human intervention. Despite many popular discussions, there are no practical areas today in which decision making has been completely given over to an expert system.

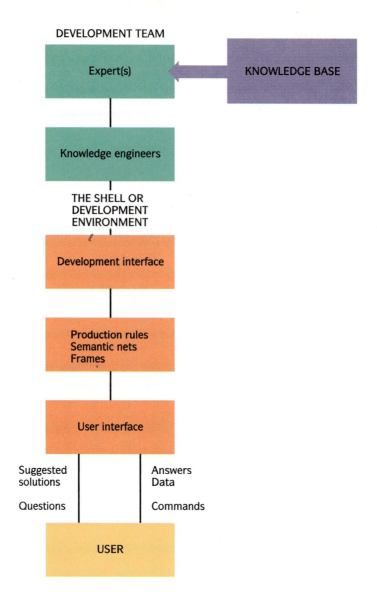

DEVELOPMENT TEAM

Expert(s)

KNOWLEDGE BASE

Knowledge engineers

THE SHELL OR
DEVELOPMENT
ENVIRONMENT

Development interface

Production rules
Semantic nets
Frames

User interface

Suggested
solutions

Answers
Data

Questions

Commands

USER

Figure 17.4
Components of an expert
system. The four basic elements
of an expert system are the
knowledge base, the
development team, the AI shell,
and the user.

How Expert Systems Work

Four major elements compose an expert system: the knowledge domain or base, the development team, the AI shell, and the user (see Figure 17.4). Subsequently, we will describe each of these parts.

THE KNOWLEDGE BASE

Knowledge base: Model of
human knowledge that is used
by expert systems.

What is human knowledge? AI developers sidestep this thorny issue by asking a slightly different question: How can human knowledge be modeled or represented in a way that a computer can deal with it? This model of human knowledge used by expert systems is called the **knowledge base.** Three ways have been devised to represent human knowledge and expertise: rules, semantic nets, and frames.

A standard structured programming construct (see Chapter 13) is the IF–THEN construct, in which a *condition* is evaluated. If the condition is true, an *action* is taken. For instance:

IF
    INCOME > $45,000 (condition)
    PRINT NAME AND ADDRESS (action)

A series of these rules can be used to represent a knowledge base. Indeed, as any reader who has written computer programs knows, virtually all traditional computer programs contain IF–THEN statements, and one can argue that these programs are intelligent. *What then is the difference between an AI system and a traditional program?*

The difference between a traditional program and a **rule-based expert system** program is one of degree and magnitude. AI programs can easily have 200 to 10,000 rules, far more than traditional programs, which may have 50 to 100 IF–THEN statements. Moreover, in an AI program the rules tend to be interconnected and nested to a far larger degree than in traditional programs, as shown in Figure 17.5. Hence the complexity of the rules is considerable.

In Figure 17.5, the order in which the rules are searched depends in part on what information the system is given. Multiple paths lead to the same result, and the rules themselves can be interconnected. The system is not necessarily sequential: You can get a $10,000 line of credit in several ways.

Could you represent the knowledge in the *Encyclopedia Britannica* this way? Probably not, because the **rule base** would be too large, and not all the knowledge in the encyclopedia can be represented in the form of IF–THEN rules. In general, expert systems can be efficiently used only in those situations where the domain of knowledge is highly restricted (such as in granting credit) and involves only a few thousand rules.

Semantic nets can be used to represent knowledge when the knowledge base is composed of easily identified chunks or objects of interrelated characteristics. Semantic nets can be much more efficient than rules. Figure 17.6 shows a semantic net that is used to classify kinds of automobiles. Semantic nets use the property of inheritance to organize and classify objects and a condition like "IS

Rule-based expert system: An AI program that has a large number of interconnected and nested IF–THEN statements or "rules" that are the basis for the knowledge in the system.

Rule base: The collection of knowledge in an AI system that is represented in the form of IF–THEN rules.

Semantic nets: Expert systems that use the property of inheritance to organize and classify knowledge when the knowledge base is composed of easily identifiable chunks or objects of interrelated characteristics.

Figure 17.5
Rules in an AI program. An expert system contains a number of rules to be followed when utilized. The rules themselves are interconnected; the number of outcomes is known in advance and is limited; there are multiple paths to the same outcome; and the system can consider multiple rules at a single time. The rules illustrated are for simple credit-granting expert systems.

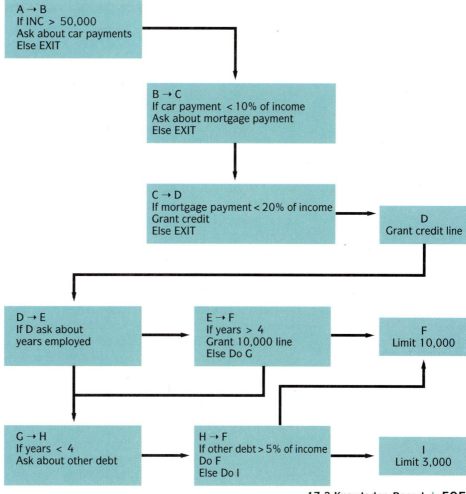

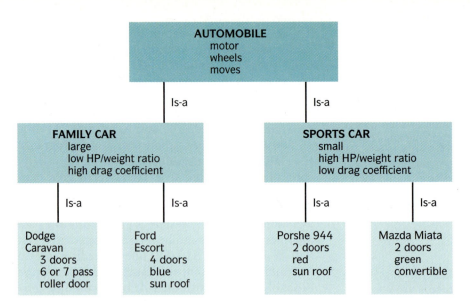

Figure 17.6
Semantic nets to model knowledge. Knowledge can be organized into semantic nets with inheritance. All lower levels inherit the characteristics of those objects above. For example, a Dodge Caravan inherits the characteristics of "family car" as well as "automobile." The link among levels is crucial; in this case, the link is "is-a." In other instances it could be "produces," "looks like," and so forth.

A" to tie objects together. "IS A" is a pointer to all objects of a specific class. For instance, all specific automobiles in the lower part of the diagram inherit characteristics of the general categories of the automobiles above them. Insurance companies, for instance, can use a semantic net to classify cars into rating classes. A clerical worker merely types into a terminal the name and model of a car, and the system can properly classify the car and decide on a rate.

Frames: Method of organizing expert system knowledge into chunks, but the relationships are based on shared characteristics determined by the user rather than a hierarchy.

Knowledge **frames** are similar to semantic nets in that knowledge is organized into chunks, but the relationships between chunks is less hierarchical and is based instead on shared characteristics. This approach is based on the belief that humans use "frames" or concepts to narrow the range of possibilities when scanning incoming information in order to make rapid sense out of perceptions. For instance, when a person is told to "look for a tank and shoot when you see one," experts believe humans invoke a concept or frame of what a tank should look like. Anything that does not fit this concept of a tank is ignored. In a similar fashion, AI researchers can organize a vast array of information into frames. The computer is then instructed to search the database of frames and list connections to other frames of interest. The user can then follow the various pathways pointed to by the system.

Figure 17.7 shows a part of a knowledge base organized by frames. A "CAR" is defined by characteristics or slots in a frame as a vehicle, with four wheels, a gas or diesel motor, and an action like rolling or moving. This frame could be related to just about any other object in the database that shares any of these characteristics, such as the tank frame. The manner in which the frames are connected can be user-determined. Frame-based AI systems bear some similarity to a Hypercard database organized into cards where each object is described on a card (see Chapter 8).

THE DEVELOPMENT TEAM

Knowledge engineer: Specialist who elicits information and expertise from other professionals and translates it into a set of rules, frames, or semantic nets for an expert system.

An AI development team is composed of one or several "experts" who have a thorough command over the knowledge base and one or more **knowledge engineers** who can translate the knowledge (as described by the expert) into a set of rules, frames, or semantic nets. A knowledge engineer is similar to a traditional systems analyst, but has special expertise in eliciting information and expertise from other professionals.

THE SHELL

AI shell: The programming environment of an expert system.

The **AI shell** is the programming environment of an expert system. AI systems can be developed in just about any programming language, such as BASIC, C, or Pascal. In the early years of expert systems, computer specialists developed specialized software languages that could process lists of rules efficiently. One lan-

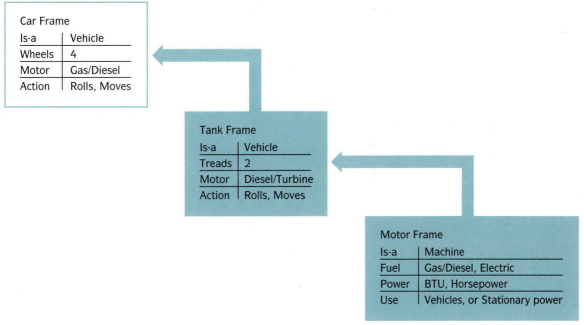

Figure 17.7
Frames to model knowledge. Knowledge and information can be organized into frames in a manner similar to semantic nets. Frames capture the relevant characteristics of the objects of interest. This approach is based on the belief that humans use "frames" or concepts to narrow the range of possibilities when scanning incoming information in order to make rapid sense out of perceptions.

Inference engine: The strategy used to search through the rule base in an expert system: can be forward or backward chaining.

Forward chaining: Strategy for searching the rule base in an expert system that begins with the information entered by the user and searches the rule base to arrive at a conclusion.

Backward chaining: Strategy for searching the rule base in an expert system that acts like a problem solver by beginning with a hypothesis and seeking out more information until the hypothesis is either proved or disproved.

guage is LISP, and a second specialized language is called PROLOG (see Chapter 7). However, while efficient, these languages have proved difficult to standardize and even more difficult to integrate both into traditional business environments and into the data structures commonly found in business environments. Hence, a growing number of expert systems today use either the C language or, more commonly, AI shells that are user-friendly development environments. AI shells can quickly generate user interface screens, capture the knowledge base, and manage the strategies for searching the rule base. The best of these AI shells generate C code, which can then be integrated into existing programs or tied into existing data streams and databases.

One of the most interesting parts of expert systems is the **inference engine.** The inference engine is simply the strategy used to search through the rule base. Two strategies are commonly used: forward chaining and backward chaining (see Figure 17.8).

In **forward chaining,** the inference engine begins with the information entered by the user and searches the rule base to arrive at a conclusion. The strategy is to "fire," or carry out, the action of the rule when a condition is true. In Figure 17.8, if the user enters a client with income greater than $100,000, the engine will fire all rules in sequence from left to right. If the user then enters information indicating that the same client owns real estate, another pass of the rule base will occur and more rules will fire. The rule base can be searched each time the user enters new information. Processing continues until no more rules can be fired.

In **backward chaining,** an expert system acts more like a problem solver who begins with a question and seeks out more information to evaluate the question. The strategy for searching the rule base starts with a hypothesis and proceeds by asking the user questions about selected facts until the hypothesis is either confirmed or disproved. In our example in Figure 17.8, ask the question, "Should we add this person to the prospect database?" Begin on the right of the diagram and work toward the left. You can see that the person should be added to the database if a sales rep is sent, term insurance is granted, or a financial advisor will be sent to visit the client. But will these events take place? Yes, if life insurance is recommended, and so forth until enough information is gathered.

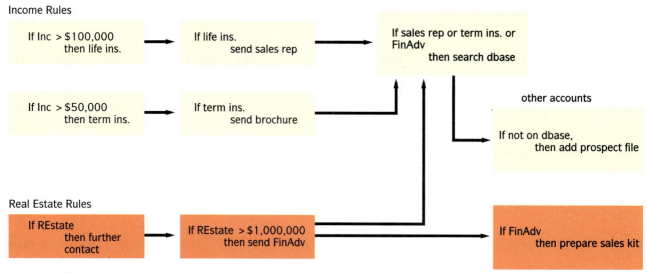

Income Rules

| If Inc > $100,000 then life ins. | → | If life ins. send sales rep | → | If sales rep or term ins. or FinAdv then search dbase |

| If Inc > $50,000 then term ins. | → | If term ins. send brochure |

other accounts

If not on dbase, then add prospect file

Real Estate Rules

| If REstate then further contact | → | If REstate > $1,000,000 then send FinAdv |

If FinAdv then prepare sales kit

Figure 17.8

Inference engines in expert systems. An inference engine works by searching through the rules and "firing" those rules that are triggered by facts gathered and entered by the user. Basically, a collection of rules is similar to a series of nested "IF" statements in a traditional software program; however, the magnitude of the statements and degree of nesting are much greater in an expert system.

THE USER   The role of the user is both to pose questions of the system and to enter relevant data to guide the system along. The user may employ the expert system in any of three roles: the assistant, the colleague, or the automaton.

Examples of Successful Expert Systems

There are many successful expert systems, such as the CLUES loan underwriting system described in the Window on Organizations. However, there is no accepted definition of *successful*. What is successful to an academic ("It works!") may not be successful to a corporation ("It cost a million dollars!"). While some of the better-known expert systems are quite large and cost millions of dollars, others are less expensive and tackle interesting but smaller problems. Some of the most celebrated systems are not used to facilitate routine decision making. Finding out which successful systems are used on a daily basis is difficult because corporations regard this information as proprietary. Nevertheless, we can briefly describe some of the better-known commercial success stories.

Whirlpool uses the *Consumer Appliance Diagnostic System* (CADS) to help its customer service representatives handle its 3 million annual telephone inquiries. The system expedites customer service by directing customers to a single source of help without delay. Previously, customers who had a problem or question about Whirlpool products might have to be put on hold or directed to two or three different representatives before their questions could be answered. Whirlpool developed CADS using Aion's Development System for OS/2 as its expert system shell. Two knowledge engineers worked with one programmer and three of the company's customer service experts to capture 1000 rules for 12 product lines. CADS runs on 300 IBM PS/2 Model 57 microcomputers linked by 8 Token Ring networks in Whirlpool's corporate headquarters in Benton Harbor, Michigan, and in Knoxville, Tennessee, and is linked to Whirlpool's mainframe computer with a DB/2 database containing raw product information. By 1999, Whirlpool expects to use CADS to respond to 9 million calls annually.

The National Aeronautic and Space Administration (NASA) developed MARVEL, its Multimission Automation for Real-Time Verification of Spacecraft Engineering Link to monitor its Voyager missions without burning out analyst after analyst. Spacecraft flights on long missions generate voluminous and critical

ORGANIZATIONS

Will You Get the Loan? Ask the System

It is axiomatic to say that we live in a world of big businesses. Yet large size creates problems that organizations must solve if they are to survive and prosper. How can critical policies be carried out at large and small sites scattered throughout the country (or world)? How can management know that the staff is working efficiently? In some growing companies, expert systems have been one of the tools used to address these problems.

Countrywide Funding Corp. in Pasadena, California, is one such company. They are loan underwriters with about 400 underwriters in 150 offices around the country. The company has seen rapid, continuing growth. In planning for that growth, Countrywide's chief underwriting officer, Ralph Mozilo, asked the key question, "How do you get consistent and high-quality [loan] decisions across the country with a work force that large?" His answer was CLUES (Countrywide's Loan Underwriting Expert System), a microcomputer-based expert system designed to make preliminary creditworthiness decisions on loan requests.

Development of CLUES began in 1991. By the fall of 1992, CLUES was being tested in six offices around the country. The system has about 400 rules. As part of the test, every loan application handled by a human underwriter was fed to CLUES. Mozilo's standards required that to be successful the system had to agree with the underwriter in 95 percent of the cases. However, Countrywide will not rely on CLUES to reject loans because the expert system cannot be programmed to handle exceptional situations such as those involving a self-employed person or complex financial schemes. An underwriter will review all rejected loans and will make the final decision.

As a result of this system, Mozilo can be comfortable that his underwriters at offices all over the country will apply uniform standards in handling loans. Rapid expansion should not threaten his ability to maintain appropriate organizational controls. In addition, CLUES offers productivity benefits. Traditionally an underwriter could handle six or seven applications a day. Using CLUES, the same underwriter can evaluate at least sixteen per day. The productivity gain comes because CLUES can review the pile of forms filled out by each loan applicant and can issue a preliminary decision in eight seconds; the underwriter will usually need about forty-five minutes to do the same work. Countrywide expects CLUES to pay back its $1.5 million development cost within the first year and hopes that it will win Countrywide more business.

Mozilo indicates that the system has other benefits as well. Companies that issue loans are legally restrained by equal opportunity laws. Therefore, management needs to know that its underwriters are not racially discriminating in their lending practices. Mozilo points out that CLUES "is color blind." CLUES, he said, "is another step in making sure irrelevant factors are ignored in lending."

In the process of developing CLUES, Mozilo was surprised at what was found out about the loan decision-making process. When he and his staff sat down and wrote loans in front of the knowledge engineers, they found out that there were about 50 decision-making questions asked in making a determination about a loan. Mozilo hence discovered that his approach to loan writing was very intuitive.

Source: Jim Nash, "State of the Market, Art, Union, and Technology," *AI Expert* (January 1993).

To Think About: What are four rules that might be included in the CLUES system? Is loan underwriting an appropriate application for an expert system? Why or why not? What management, organization, and technology factors would you want to consider before implementing such a system? If you were denied a loan and knew that CLUES was utilized to make that decision, how would you feel?

information that must be carefully analyzed. MARVEL monitors NASA's computer-command subsystem, which receives and executes commands from the ground and also analyzes power, propulsion flight-data subsystems and telecommunications functions. NASA developed MARVEL with the assistance of the equivalent of 1.5 full-time computer scientists and two mission experts. MARVEL is based on Software Architecture and Engineering's Knowledge Engineering System expert system shell and runs on Sun workstations.

MSE—*Market Surveillance Expert*—is used by the American Stock Exchange to assist analysts investigating cases of insider trading. The system was built using a shell from Exsys Inc., which uses Lotus 1-2-3 spreadsheets as the knowledge base and a set of built-in rules to guide the inference engine.

TradeCenter is used by Merrill Lynch and several other Wall Street firms to act as an assistant to traders by watching price movements reported by real-time price feeds. Block and institutional traders trade huge blocks of stocks at a single time, often based on momentary price movements in several different markets. Traders often have to keep track of a dozen different screens, with each screen divided into several different windows. There is simply too much information for any human to monitor in real time properly. TradeCenter keeps track of the information a trader wants to follow and reports price movements accordingly. The service displays, for instance, forty-day price tick charts, money-flow analysis, commodity prices, synthetic instrument and basket analysis, and a real-time ticker at the bottom of the screen showing prices on major markets.

The Securities and Exchange Commission (SEC) requires that all publicly held companies submit detailed financial statements to the SEC on a monthly and a quarterly basis. These statements are utilized to investigate possible violations of security laws, but the financial information is of enormous utility to competitors and other persons interested in the financial health of firms. The Arthur Andersen Company developed an expert system to read corporate proxy statements with a sophistication unmatched by the average human investigator. When the system is asked to identify, for instance, companies that have taken actions in the past year to dodge a leveraged buy-out attempt, it searches for concepts rather than specific words, just as a knowledgeable investor would.

XCON configures VAX computers on a daily basis for the Digital Equipment Corporation (DEC). DEC and Carnegie Mellon University first developed this system in the late 1970s (see the case at the end of the chapter).

Table 17.1 describes other well-known expert systems in terms of their size and programming languages. As can be seen, these systems generally have a minimum of several hundred rules. XCON, for instance, started out with 250 rules but has expanded to about 10,000.

17.3 Building Expert Systems

Expert systems can be built in several different ways. Each approach has risks and benefits.

Three Different Approaches to Expert Systems

There are three general approaches to expert systems: purchase of fully developed, off-the-shelf systems; purchase of artificial intelligence shells; and development of custom systems that have been fully developed for a specific application.

OFF THE SHELF One well-known, fully developed, off-the-shelf system is the Financial Advisor system, produced by Palladian Software, Inc., of Cambridge, Massachusetts. Financial Advisor helps executives analyze a proposed investment in a new plant, warehouse, or product or examine the acquisition of another company. The system has captured the expertise of financial analysts in many corporations and made this knowledge base (set of rules) available to other corporations. The system runs on a Texas Instruments Explorer or Symbolics 3600 and uses data from an IBM or DEC mainframe.

Here is how the system works. Assume that a company is thinking about marketing a new product. When it is first released, the product will have no direct competition. If it is successful, however, competitors can be expected to bring out similar products in a short time. To analyze this situation, the first step is to build a business case for the product. The system helps managers and staff to create this business case by asking for data to be entered: Data include the equipment that will be used to produce the product, the capital cost, the plants that will be used, how many people will be needed, the useful life of the equipment, the discount rate, and so forth.

Table 17.1 SOME WELL-KNOWN EXPERT SYSTEMS

Name of System or Project	Brief System Description	Method of Verification	Number of Rules	Programming Language
Authorizer's Assistant (American Express)	Authorize credit transactions	Field test	850	ART
Hub Slaashing (American Airlines)	Recommend flight schedule changes when airports disrupted	Field test	39	C
CLUES (Countrywide Funding Corp.)	Authorize loans	Field test	400	Inference Corp. ART–IM (AI shell)
Robot (Ford Motor)	Diagnose sick robots	Field test	200	Texas Instruments Personal Consultant
Mail Prospector (R.R. Donnelly)	Test mailing lists	Field test	NA	More/2
Heuristic Dendral	Identify organic compounds by analysis of mass spectrograms	Field use	400	Interlisp
MYCIN	Diagnose certain infectious diseases and recommend appropriate drugs	Scientific (BV)	400	Interlisp
Prospector	Aid geologists in evaluating mineral sites for potential deposits	Field use	Largest knowledge base, 212 assertions and 133 inference rules	DEC 10
XCON (DEC)	Configure VAX computer systems	Field use	10,000	OPS4 (implemented in MACLISP)

NA = Not available

Compare this approach to that of an ordinary spreadsheet. With a spreadsheet, the user has to know all the factors to be included in the business plan, but with an expert system such as Financial Advisor, the many factors that should be considered in any investment are included by the system. Some of the intelligence thus lies in the system, not in the user. On the other hand, if the user does not want to consider a factor or wants to enter new, nonstandard factors, the system can be adjusted.

When the business case is built, the analysis starts. The year-by-year net cash flow is computed and displayed graphically. The discounted cash flow is also computed. At this point, the user begins to interact with the system by changing some of the variables. If a discounted cash flow tends toward zero or even goes negative, the human analyst can make some changes. Perhaps less expensive equipment can be used. The cheaper equipment will have a shorter useful life, and the system will ask for the new useful life. The cheaper equipment will require earlier replacement, and the system will automatically factor this information into its calculation of cash flow. The system will also ask about various competitive responses and then compute the critical values. This process can be repeated at higher levels of management and by different managers individually as they probe the effects of changes in the assumptions on the final outcome.

Financial Advisor provides an excellent example of an intelligent decision support system (DSS). It also demonstrates how close DSS as a concept is to expert systems. Unlike the interaction with a DSS, users of an expert system are systematically led through a set of assumptions and exposed to a body of knowledge that is much broader than their own. Nevertheless, the difference between a DSS and an expert system is one of degree, not concept.

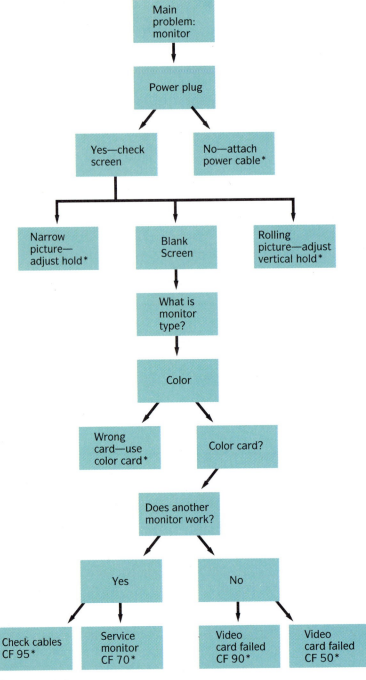

Figure 17.9
How an expert system shell works. This diagram illustrates how the M.1 expert system diagnoses a problem with a microcomputer monitor.

AI SHELLS

A second approach to expert systems is to build a new one using an artificial intelligence shell. A shell is a piece of software that uses a predetermined strategy and a limited, reasonably user-friendly language to develop small expert systems. With artificial intelligence shells, the user has to supply the knowledge to the system. This is very different from buying a packaged expert system.

A good example of an expert system shell is M.1, manufactured by Teknowledge, Inc., of Palo Alto, California. This system operates on large microcomputers and is priced considerably less than the $100,000 to multi-million dollar systems that operate on mainframes.

M.1, according to the manufacturer, is best suited to structured selection applications. Teknowledge defines such problems as those that a human expert can solve in less than 30 minutes, that do not involve extensive calculations, that can be solved through a telephone discussion with an expert, and that have only a few dozen conclusions to choose from.

In general, M.1 can be used to create "intelligent manuals" that clients can consult in a question-and-answer fashion. The demonstration disk of M.1's capabilities includes a wine advisor (which recommends what type of wine to serve with meals), a bank services advisor (which matches banking requirements with bank services), and a photography advisor (which uses information about environmental conditions to recommend which shutter speed and film type to use). Figure 17.9 illustrates how M.1 was used to diagnose a problem with a microcomputer monitor.

CUSTOM BUILT SYSTEMS

A third approach is to have a knowledge engineer custom build an expert system. The knowledge engineer interviews the expert (or experts), develops the decision rules and knowledge frames, and builds the expert system. Of necessity, knowledge engineers are specialists in getting information from experts, prototyping a system, and working with the experts to improve the system until a useful system has been created. This suggests a highly interactive and evolutionary approach to systems.

In building the system, the knowledge engineer may use a development tool such as an artificial intelligence shell. More commonly, however, a programming language such as LISP, Prolog, C, or some other language will be employed because it is useful in representing the knowledge. Expert systems may be built in traditional languages like C because of their compatibility with existing systems and their transportability to different platforms, from microcomputers to UNIX machines. Generally, these projects require one or a few knowledge engineers and a few experts. Only the largest corporations attempt to build extensive custom-developed systems.

An Expert System Life Cycle

A suggested six-phase life cycle for developing expert systems is illustrated in Figure 17.10. This cycle is not fixed. Because experts often have trouble explaining their solutions, problems may have to be broken down into subproblems

Figure 17.10
The life cycle of an expert system. The development of an expert system can be broken down into a six-phase cycle. Each phase may be repeated as needed prior to moving on through the next phase.

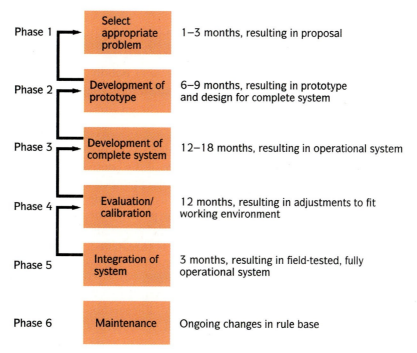

Phase 1 — Select appropriate problem — 1–3 months, resulting in proposal

Phase 2 — Development of prototype — 6–9 months, resulting in prototype and design for complete system

Phase 3 — Development of complete system — 12–18 months, resulting in operational system

Phase 4 — Evaluation/ calibration — 12 months, resulting in adjustments to fit working environment

Phase 5 — Integration of system — 3 months, resulting in field-tested, fully operational system

Phase 6 — Maintenance — Ongoing changes in rule base

before solutions can be defined (Weitzel and Kerschberg, 1989). Each phase may require several iterations before a full system is developed. These phases will now be described.

PHASE 1: SELECTION OF AN APPROPRIATE PROBLEM

Phase 1 consists of finding an appropriate problem for an expert system, identifying an expert to contribute the expertise, establishing a preliminary approach, analyzing the costs and benefits, and finally preparing a development plan.

Most expert systems focus on a narrow specialty. It is important to avoid problems that involve the following:

- Understanding English.
- Complicated geometric or spatial models.
- Complex causal or temporal models.
- Understanding human intentions.
- A knowledge of organizational history.
- Common sense or background knowledge.

The important point in the early design stage is to avoid complex problems that are beyond the provable expertise of the designers.

Generally, finding an appropriate problem will put the knowledge engineer in touch with experts throughout the company who would like to develop systems based on their knowledge. Obviously, expert systems require an expert who can and will explain how he or she works. A tentative approach to a problem can then be formulated.

Once a task has been identified, the potential savings produced by such a system must be balanced against the cost. Table 17.2 shows an estimate of tentative costs related to system size. As expert-system software becomes more efficient, it should become less expensive. Currently, expert systems of any magnitude are 10 to 25 percent more expensive than ordinary system projects.

PHASE 2: DEVELOPMENT OF A PROTOTYPE SYSTEM

A prototype system is a small version of an expert system designed to test assumptions about how to encode the facts, the relationships, and the knowledge of experts. The prototype permits the knowledge engineer to gain the experts' commitment and to develop a deeper understanding of the field of expertise. Other subtasks in this phase include the following:

- Learning about the domain and the task.
- Specifying performance criteria.
- Selecting an expert-system building tool.
- Developing an implementation plan.
- Developing a detailed design for a complete system.

PHASE 3: DEVELOPMENT OF A COMPLETE SYSTEM

The development of a full-scale system is probably the most complex stage of the effort. The core structure of the complete system has to be identified; that is, the knowledge base has to be expanded to the full knowledge base appropriate to the real world, and the user interface has to be developed.

The main work in this phase is the addition of a very large number of rules. The complexity of the entire system grows with the number of rules, and the integrity of the system is threatened. A fundamental conflict develops in this period between faithfulness to the complexity of the real world and the comprehensibility of the system.

Generally, during this stage the system is pruned to make it more realistic and suitable to the real world. Eliminating rules and achieving simplicity and power are important aspects of developing a complete system.

Table 17.2 RESOURCES REQUIRED TO DEVELOP AN EXPERT SYSTEM

Resources	Type of System		
	Small	Large	Very Large
Rules	50–450	500–3000	3000–10,000
Person-years needed for development	0.25–0.50	1–3	3–25
Project cost (including design and development staff, knowledge engineers, computing, and overhead).	$50,000–$80,000	$300,000–$1.5 million	$2–30 million

PHASE 4: EVALUATION OF THE SYSTEM

When the expert and the knowledge engineer are satisfied that the system is complete, it can be tested against the performance criteria established in earlier stages. It is also time to unveil the system to the organization and to invite other experts to test the system and to present it with new cases.

PHASE 5: INTEGRATION OF THE SYSTEM

Once built, the expert system has to be integrated into the data flow and work patterns of the organization. New procedures usually have to be developed, along with new forms, new subunits in the organization, and new training procedures. In this stage, the expert system has to be interfaced with other databases, instruments, and hardware. The speed and friendliness of the system usually must be improved.

PHASE 6: MAINTENANCE OF THE SYSTEM

As with any system, the environment in which an expert system operates is continually changing. This means that the expert system must also continually change. For example, the DEC XCON system (described previously and in the case study at the end of the chapter), which configures new VAX computer installations, must continually change as DEC adds new lines of computer equipment. A group of DEC experts constantly changes the rules of the system as new computer systems and equipment are manufactured. The highly modularized nature of the rule-based system makes modification feasible and ensures that the system is always current.

Very little is known about the long-term maintenance costs of expert systems, and even less is published. Some expert systems, especially large ones, are so complex that in a few years the maintenance costs will equal the development costs. In the case of XCON, about 30 to 50 percent of the rules are changed each year.

In addition to a knowledge engineer, skillful project managers and outside consultants are generally required by expert system projects of any size. Few knowledge engineers today have enough experience to determine what problems a company should address. Much political work is needed in an organization to provide the funding for large-scale projects. The money and time required to develop expert systems are generally far greater than predicted by early advocates of expert systems. The Window on Management on page 606 shows that successful implementation of artificial intelligence applications requires the continued participation of top management.

Problems with Expert Systems

A thorough understanding of expert systems also requires awareness of their current limitations and problems.

MANAGEMENT

Venturing into the Brave New World of Artificial Intelligence

Introduction of new technology is a complex issue for corporate management. Risks can be high, and costs can be great. Management must have a vision and a tolerance for those risks if it wants its company to be a leader. Management also must have effective strategies that will offer significant benefits while handling the problems and limiting the losses.

American Express originally ventured into artificial intelligence in 1984. It was one of the earliest companies to do so. The first project was an attempt to develop an expert system to aid in managing foreign exchange rates, a function that goes to the heart of their business. When the project was declared a failure and abandoned before completion, the company could easily have stopped. But they did not. Instead, they began to build a system to support the work of their credit authorizers. That project succeeded.

Today that system, titled Authorizer's Assistant, has saved American Express tens of millions of dollars by doing the work of 700 credit authorizers. The credit authorizers sit at terminals and decide whether to approve a charge. Since American Express has no credit limits on its cards, credit authorization is a crucial function to reduce the use of stolen cards and the accumulation of high charge card bills by people who cannot afford to pay. At the same time, credit authorizers do not want to deny credit to legitimate cardholders, which may result in losing business. Early tests showed that the system was accurate 95.5 percent of the time, compared to a human average of 85 percent.

Before Authorizer's Assistant, a credit authorizer would look at as many as 16 screens of data per customer, a cumbersome process that resulted in too many wrong authorization decisions. Authorizer's Assistant distills the knowledge of AmEx's best authorizers

into an 850-rule expert system that assists and works with human authorizers. The system requires only two screens and recommends credit approval, disapproval, or further search.

Spurred on by this success, AmEx then went on to build Credit Assistant that helps its staff review accounts for credit risk and for fraud. The company estimates that this system saves $1.4 million annually while ensuring consistent credit policies worldwide.

Why did these projects succeed? A number of factors are obvious. American Express grasped the potential *significance* of the technology to its core business, as is clear from the pivotal nature of the functions it selected to address in its first development projects. The early date of these initial projects reveals management's willingness to take a *risk*. Management's cancellation of the project before its completion indicates that it *understood* both the risk and the necessity of limiting it. Finally management's *commitment* can be seen by its willingness to proceed on to other projects.

Perhaps most important, American Express management had *vision*. In the 1980s, most other companies were avoiding long-term spending commitments because of the emphasis the financial markets placed on short-term profit and immediate payback. At American Express, management knew how critical new technology was to the long-term health of their company. In 1984, Louis Gerstner, then CEO of American Express's Travel Related Services division, set up a corporate technology research fund, meant to give 100 percent funding to cutting-edge technology application projects. He quickly received proposals for all kinds of projects from a range of business units.

In reviewing the proposals, Gerstner quickly realized that the projects had a problem—Gerstner could be

sure neither of the commitment of the proposing units nor of the long-term benefits. Gerstner realized that the source of the problem was his own offer to have American Express's corporate group fully fund the projects. The proposing units risked nothing, so they needed neither commitment nor careful evaluation of a project to make a proposal. Such projects are designed for failure. Gerstner quickly revised the offer. His fund would supply only 40 percent of the cost of a project. A further 40 percent would have to come from the proposing business unit itself, all but guaranteeing commitment and a careful evaluation of that project's long-term contribution. In addition, Gerstner was interested in benefits that could be shared by other business units as well. Therefore, he required that the final 20 percent had to come from a second business unit.

This fund spawned Authorizer's Assistant and other projects in expert systems and artificial intelligence. The careful design of the funding process gave American Express management the *confidence* they needed to continue funding, despite the early failure. Today, American Express has justifiably earned its reputation as a leader in the field of AI. They have also demonstrated one effective way to manage technological change for success.

Source: Harvey P. Newquist III, "AI at Amex," *AI Expert* (January 1993).

To Think About: Can you suggest other ways in which the corporate technology fund benefited American Express? What problems do you see with that fund? What do you think would have been the advantages and disadvantages to American Express if its management had waited five to seven years before attempting to develop systems using AI (as most companies did)?

EXPERT SYSTEMS ARE LIMITED TO CERTAIN PROBLEMS

In answer to the question, "Why do some expert systems work?" critics point out that virtually all successful expert systems deal with problems of classification in which there are relatively few alternative outcomes and in which these possible outcomes are all known in advance. Contrary to early promises, expert systems do best in automating lower-level clerical functions. Even in these comparatively simple situations, however, expert systems require large, lengthy, and expensive development efforts. For these kinds of problems, hiring or training more experts may be less expensive than building an expert system. Some firms that were early investors in large expert systems have found them to be of dubious value.

IMPORTANT THEORETICAL PROBLEMS EXIST

There are significant theoretical problems in knowledge representation. "IF–THEN" knowledge exists primarily in textbooks. There are no adequate representations for deep causal models or temporal trends. No expert system, for instance, can adequately employ deep causal models of interesting phenomena. No expert system can write a textbook on information systems or engage in other creative activities not explicitly foreseen by system designers. Many experts cannot express their knowledge using an "IF–THEN" format. Sometimes expert knowledge is intuitive, based on analogy, on a "sense of things" that expert systems cannot yet replicate.

There is little substantiation for the claim that expert systems' methods or tools are well suited to the emulation or support of human expertise in decision making. At best, this is a hypothesis. Labeling oneself a knowledge engineer does not necessarily confer any special skills in eliciting the human intelligence of an expert. Many claim that the new profession of knowledge engineering is just another case of glamorizing the familiar with pretentious new terminology. There is no credible evidence, critics argue, that knowledge engineers have advanced our understanding or mastery of the problems of knowledge acquisition, representation, or use.

EXPERT SYSTEMS ARE NOT APPLICABLE TO MANAGERIAL PROBLEMS

The applicability of expert systems to managerial problems is currently highly limited. Managerial problems generally involve drawing facts and interpretations from divergent sources, evaluating the facts, and comparing one interpretation of the facts with another, and do not involve analysis or simple classification. Expert systems based on the prior knowledge of a few known alternatives are unsuitable to the problems managers face on a daily basis.

EXPERTISE IS COLLECTIVE

For many problems there are no single experts. Expertise may be distributed throughout an organization. Coordinating this expertise to formulate policies and actions is a key focus of management efforts. Expert systems cannot help here because they cannot synthesize knowledge from several different experts any better than ordinary systems analysis and design can.

EXPERT SYSTEMS ARE EXPENSIVE TO TEACH

The knowledge base of expert systems is fragile and brittle; they cannot learn or change over time. In fast-moving fields like medicine or the computer sciences, keeping the knowledge base up to date is a critical problem.

For applications of even modest complexity, expert systems code is generally hard to understand, debug, and maintain. For example, adding new rules to a large rule-based program nearly always requires revision of the control variables and conditions of earlier rules. Which of these entities must be changed to make the new rule work is often far from obvious.

A MORE LIMITED ROLE FOR EXPERT SYSTEMS

Even the critics point out, however, that research on artificial intelligence and expert systems is useful. It may be entirely appropriate that artificial intelligence researchers based in university laboratories continue contemplating toy problems and simplistic models of cognition to highlight certain themes and issues.

Moreover, expert systems may be used as electronic checklists for lower-level employees in service bureaucracies like banking, insurance, sales, and welfare agencies. There is clearly a market for software products that includes artificial intelligence, or just smart programming. The market for these kinds of applications may be substantial.

When it comes to more complex problems, many critics point out that it is a very long step from the classroom to the factory floor, to the battlefield, or to the corporate boardroom.

17.4 Other Intelligent Techniques

Clearly the pursuit of artificial intelligence will remain a persistent theme of the 1990s. While some considerable progress will be made in expert systems, the development of parallel processing at the hardware level—the idea of breaking up a problem into many small components and then processing each component simultaneously using hundreds or even thousands of computers operating in parallel—is likely to unleash a host of new possibilities. Subsequently, we review briefly the development of three intelligent computing techniques that stand the best chance in the 1990s of developing into major fields of business applications.

Neural Networks

There has been an exciting resurgence of interest in bottom-up approaches to artificial intelligence in which machines are designed to imitate the physical thought process of the biological brain. Figure 17.11 shows two neurons from a leech's brain. The soma or nerve cell is at the center, and it acts like a switch, stimulating other neurons and being stimulated in turn. Emanating from the neuron is an axon, which is an electrically active link to the dendrites of other neurons. Axons and dendrites are the "wires" that electrically connect neurons to one another. The junction of the two is called a synapse. This simple biolog-

Figure 17.11
Biological neurons of a leech. Simple biological models, like the neurons of a leech, have influenced the development of artificial or computational neural networks in which the biological cells are replaced by transistors, or entire processors. *Source: Defense Advance Research Projects Agency (DARPA), 1988. Unclassified. Hereinafter "DARPA, 1988."*

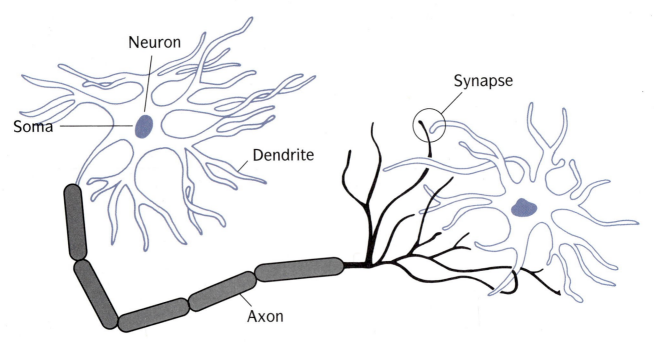

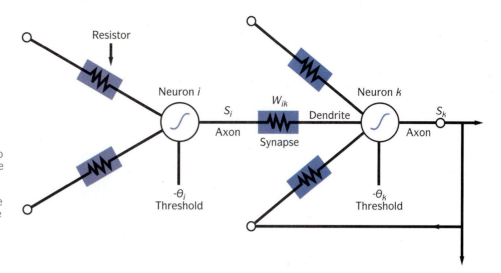

Figure 17.12
Artificial neural network with two neurons. In artificial neurons, the biological neurons become processing elements (switches), the axons and dendrites become wires, and the synapses become variable resistors that carry weighted inputs (currents) that represent data. Source: DARPA, 1988.

Neural network: Hardware or software that attempts to emulate the processing patterns of the biological brain.

ical model is the metaphor for the development of neural networks. **Neural networks** consist of hardware or software that attempts to emulate the processing patterns of the biological brain.

The human brain has about 100 billion (10^{11}) neurons, each having about 1000 dendrites, which form 100,000 billion (10^{14}) synapses. The brain operates at about 100 hertz (each neuron can fire off a pulse 100 times per second)—very slow by computer standards where, for example, an Intel 80486 chip operates at up to 66 megahertz, or millions of cycles per second, executing one instruction at a time. But the brain's neurons operate in parallel, and the human brain can accomplish about 10^{16} or ten million billion interconnections per second. This far exceeds the capacity of any known machine, or any machine now planned or ever likely to be built with current technology. The human brain weighs three pounds and occupies about .15 square meters. You can think of the brain as several score supercomputers on your shoulder and then some.

No technology known now can come close to these capabilities. But elementary neuron circuits can be built and studied, and far more complex networks of neurons have been simulated on computers. Figure 17.12 shows an artificial neural network with two neurons. The resistors in the circuits are variable and can be used to "teach" the network. When the network makes a mistake (i.e., chooses the wrong pathway through the network and arrives at a false conclusion), resistance can be raised on some circuits, forcing other neurons to fire. If this learning process continues for thousands of cycles, the machine "learns" the correct response.

One feature that distinguishes neural networks from digital computers is the inherent parallelism: The simple neurons or switches are highly interconnected and operate in parallel. Instead of a single personal computer executing a single instruction at a time, imagine 64,000 personal computers all connected to one another and all working simultaneously on parts of the same problem.

A neural network computer can be defined, then, as an interconnected set of parallel switches or processors for which the network can be controlled by intervention. Neural networks are very different from expert systems, where human expertise has to be modeled with rules and frames. In neural networks, the physical machine emulates a human brain and can be taught from experience.

THE DIFFERENCE BETWEEN NEURAL NETWORKS AND EXPERT SYSTEMS

What is different about neural networks? Several answers can now be given. First, expert systems, like most traditional systems, seek to emulate or model a human expert's way of solving a set of problems. The knowledge engineer observes humans, builds a model of their expertise, and then writes a computer program or algorithm that implements the model. The resulting expert system is optimized to perform a single task for which it was designed.

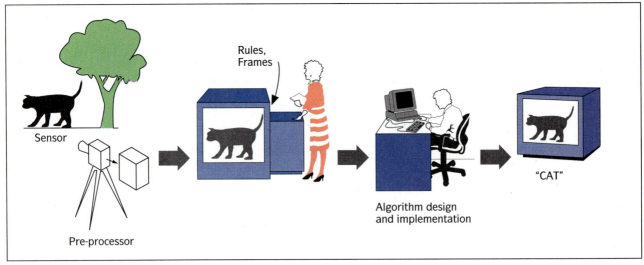

Figure 17.13A
An expert system approach. The expert system would rely upon a large set of rules or frames as the knowledge base for identifying a cat. Using the rules, the system would analyze the information gathered or data supplied by a television camera scanning signals to determine the classification of the scanned image.

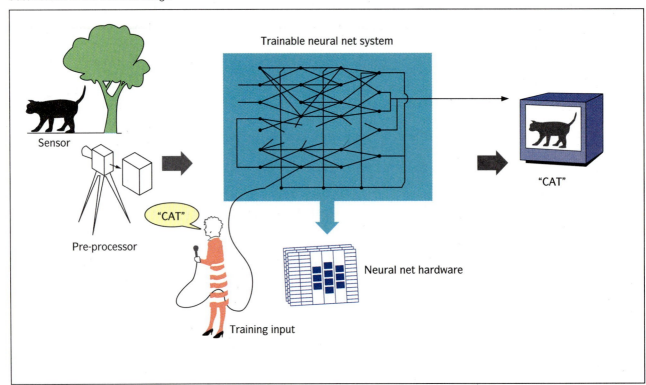

Figure 17.13B
A neural network approach. Without an established rule base to rely on, the trainable neural network will start out on the process of learning based on the scanned images provided. Interconnections are adjusted when the images are correctly perceived, resulting in a ''learning process.''

Neural networks, so their builders claim, do not model human intelligence, do not program solutions, do not use knowledge engineers, and do not aim to solve specific problems per se. Instead of putting intelligence into programs, neural network designers seek to put the intelligence into the hardware in the form of a generalized capability to learn. The idea is to build machines that solve entire classes of problems.

Take a simple problem like identifying a cat. An expert system approach (Figure 17.13A) would interview hundreds of people to understand how humans recognize cats. This would result in a large set of rules, or frames, programmed into an expert system. A television camera connected to the system would scan shapes in the environment, and the system would analyze the signals against the rule base of the system. After scanning a few thousand rules, one at a time, the system would label each perceived object as either a cat or not a cat.

In contrast, a trainable neural network (Figure 17.13B) would be brought to the test site, connected to the television, and started out on the process of learning. Every time a cat was not correctly perceived, the system's interconnections would be adjusted. When cats were correctly perceived, the system would be left alone and another object scanned.

Whereas the expert system is highly specific to a given problem and cannot be easily retrained, the neural network could be more easily modified and taught to recognize automobiles or animals, or to solve other visual pattern recognition problems.

Briefly, neural networks promise a substantial saving in development cost and time. They promise greater generality and more closely approximate what we think of as "intelligent."

BUILDING NEURAL NETWORKS

While neural networks now promise a great deal, the available tools are quite primitive by biological standards. Basically, there are two approaches to building neural networks. In one approach, specialized machines are hardwired in the form of neural network computing machines. The resulting systems are expensive, experimental, and largely confined to laboratories, although some are just now appearing commercially. A second and much less expensive approach is to simulate a neural network on a traditional computer. While a traditional computer will not have a parallel machine capability, and processing will be slower, to some extent this can be compensated for by using high-speed machines.

The power of neural network machines is measured differently from standard machines, where storage is measured in bytes of RAM memory and speed is measured in MIPS (millions of instructions per second). In neural machines, storage is measured in terms of capacity, which is measured in terms of the total number of interconnects between neurons. Speed is measured in terms of the total number of interconnects that can take place per second. Figure 17.14 compares the power of some available neural network simulators to the power of common biological brains.

There remains a considerable gap between available machine power and, say, the processing capabilities of higher-order animals like dogs and cats, or even

Figure 17.14
Computational capabilities of neural and biological networks. The shaded area shows the range of speeds and storage capacities of neural networks in relation to those of biological networks. Neural networks, although powerful, only have the computational power of a fly's brain.

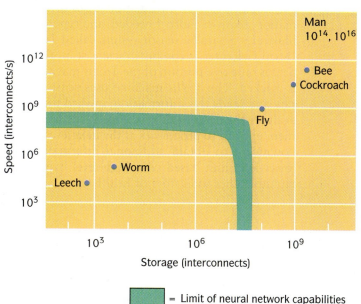

= Limit of neural network capabilities

humans. Special-purpose neural network chips specifically designed to operate as neural nets (as opposed to simulating neural nets with software) will rapidly advance the state of the art.

Despite these advances, the most powerful dedicated neural network machines today equal the thinking ability of a fly or at best a cockroach. Several orders of magnitude of enhancements in neural network technology are required to produce high levels of intelligence. Nevertheless, even at this level, as illustrated by the Window on Technology, the pattern-recognition power of neural networks is starting to be harnessed by medicine, science, and business.

As illustrated by the chapter-opening vignette, neural network applications are starting to be used by the financial industry to discern patterns in vast pools of data that might help investment firms predict the performance of equities, corporate bond ratings, or corporate bankruptcies (Lin, 1993). Mellon Bank in Pittsburgh, Pennsylvania, is using a neural network to help detect credit card fraud. The network was taught to recognize irregular patterns in charge card purchases and to evaluate potentially fraudulent transactions. California-based Sears Savings Bank is experimenting with a neural net application to help its mortgage underwriters evaluate loan applications. After being fed extensive historical data on mortgages, the neural net was trained to recognize patterns for successful and unsuccessful loans.

Because of the way neural nets "learn," they can identify relationships and patterns, and are appropriate for making classifications, generalizations, or decisions in cases where less than 100 percent accuracy can be tolerated. However, neural nets cannot always guarantee a completely certain solution, arrive at the same solution again with the same input data, or always guarantee the "best" solution (Trippi and Turban, 1989–1990). Both the chapter-opening vignette and these examples suggest that in most current applications, neural networks are best used as aids to human decision makers instead of substitutes for them.

Parallel Sensor Systems

Suppose a hospital wanted to watch and monitor all of its patients at once, or wished to closely monitor all the indicators on a single patient simultaneously to alert nurses in case something is wrong or to continually analyze the patient's health status? Could a computer, or collection of computers, keep track of all this information?[2]

Parallel sensor system: A machine consisting of many nodes that each act as a processor feeding information to a hierarchy of higher-level nodes.

One solution is to use a **parallel sensor system,** which is a machine consisting of a series of nodes. Each node functions like a processor or computer that continually receives information from lower-level sensors, evaluates the information, requests more if needed, and reports to higher-level nodes. Figure 17.15 illustrates a parallel sensor system called Trellis machine by one of its inventors, David Gelernter, a computer scientist at Yale University. The machine depicted here is only one portion of the Trellis machine, showing how raw blood pressure is tracked. The Trellis machine uses sensors to track blood pressure and heart rate and sends this information upward through the "trellis" to processors that evaluate the data. Each processor in the hierarchy evaluates the data and directs them upward to processors at the next level. Higher-level units may send queries downward to obtain additional information or to change the behavior of a lower-level unit based on a high-level hypothesis. Other parts of the machine monitor other indicators of health.

[2]This section benefits from an article by David Gelernter, "The Metamorphosis of Information Management," *Scientific American* (August 1989). This article outlines a number of possibilities for extending computing through parallel processing to areas heretofore impossible.

TECHNOLOGY

Computers That See and Learn

By combining the ability of neural networks to *learn* with technology that allows computers to *see,* important and exciting applications involving pattern recognition are now being developed.

Pap smear tests, used to detect cervical cancer, have until recently relied solely on a visual examination of every smear to find abnormal cells. The technician uses a microscope to search each smear for the telltale abnormal cells that indicate cancer or a precancerous condition. Most smears will be negative (contain only healthy cells), indicating the absence of cancer. However, each smear might contain up to 500,000 cells, and only a tiny percentage of the cells might be abnormal, making it very difficult to locate them. Manually searching the cells is a slow, tedious, and inexact process. Estimates are that 30 to 50 percent of all positive smears (those containing abnormal cells) are falsely rated negative — that the cancerous condition is not identified and treated in 30 to 50 percent of the cases.

Neural network technology has been used to develop a system that reduces the error rate to about 3 percent. Papnet by Neuromedical Systems Inc. of Suffern, New York, examines all the cells in the smear and selects the 128 most abnormal cells for display on the monitor. However, the computer is not able to make the final decision — that takes human judgment. The technician will review the selected cells and have the software mark and record any that are deemed to be truly abnormal. Using this system, the technician requires less than one-fifth the time to examine a smear while achieving perhaps ten times the accuracy of the existing manual methods.

Papnet had to learn to distinguish between normal and abnormal cells. It was *shown* thousands of both normal and abnormal cells. The cells were in many different positions, even touching and overlapping, as they would be in real life. Many different color stains were used. When Papnet improperly identified a cell, the system

was corrected, and in this way it slowly *learned* to distinguish between normal and abnormal. Papnet's accuracy has been verified through studies done at Montefiore Medical Center in the Bronx, New York.

Neural networks have also been used to aid in the reading of the magnetic ink numbers at the bottom of paper checks. Conventional check readers have trouble with checks because the numbers are often blurred, off center or incomplete. Onyx, developed by Verifone of Redwood City, California, uses shape recognition to identify most numbers, even when the numbers have the same printing problems. This unusual product is a point-of-sale (POS) system, used to verify a check at a retail store much as the salesclerk would verify a credit card. With widespread use, the system should allow more retail outlets to accept checks without risk.

Sources: Kay Keppler, "Neural Nets Clarify Pap Smears," *AI Expert* (January 1993); Hal Glatzer, "Neural Networks Take on Real-World Problems," *Computerworld* (August 10, 1992).

To Think About: Neural networks still involve a new technology, not yet widely used or well proven. As a middle-level manager, under what conditions would you recommend this new technology? What are the risks of being the first to introduce such technology in your company? How would you handle these risks?

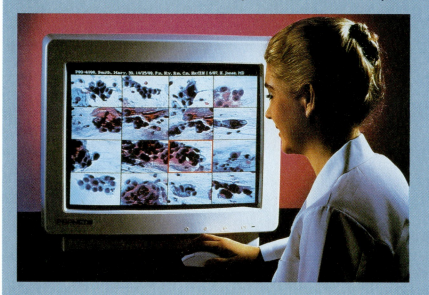

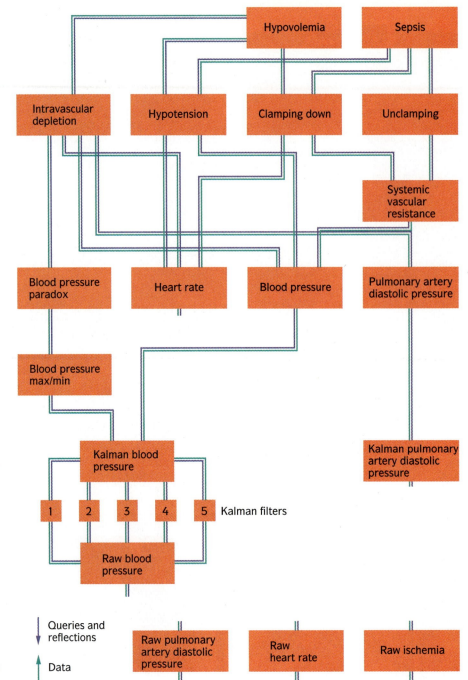

Figure 17.15
Parallel sensor machines. A Trellis machine for monitoring patients has sensors at the bottom that send information up the hierarchy to units that consider ever more complex hypotheses about the patient's status (arrows indicate connections between units). Higher-level units may send queries and comments down the trellis to elicit additional information or to change the behavior of a lower-level unit based on a high-level hypothesis. *Source: David Gelernter, "The metamorphosis of Information Management,"* Scientific American, *August 1989. Copyright © 1989 by Scientific American, Inc. All rights reserved.*

Intelligent Database Search Machines

Intelligent database search machine: A master machine that can direct the search of a massive database by giving a target pattern to subordinate machines that search the database simultaneously.

Imagine that you had to search the Library of Congress (50 million volumes) for all articles or book chapters having to do with computer security. One possibility is, of course, to have a massively large computer go through each volume, one by one, looking for articles that match the descriptions you have given. Another possibility is to use an intelligent database search machine. An **intelligent database search machine** is a "master" machine that can direct a search of a massive database by giving the target pattern to many subordinate machines called workers that search the database simultaneously. When a machine finds a possible match, it sends it to the master machine, which makes the final assessment.

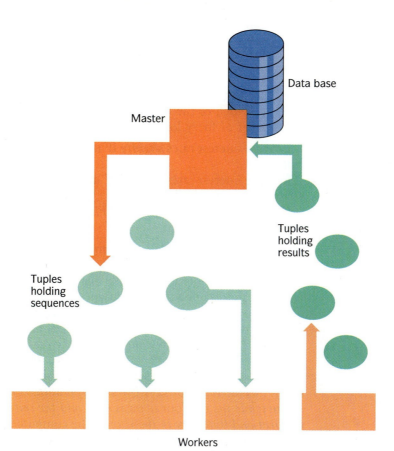

Figure 17.16

An intelligent database search machine. This mass search machine matches an unknown DNA sequence against known sequences in the database. The master module creates tuples containing the known sequences; worker modules compare them with the target sequence and generate tuples containing the results of the comparisons. The master module then collects the tuples to determine which cataloged sequence the target most closely resembles. *Source: David Gelernter, "The Metamorphosis of Information Management."* Scientific American, *August 1989, p. 71. Copyright 1989 by*

Figure 17.16 illustrates an intelligent database search machine that has been asked to match a particular DNA sequence against a massively large database of all known sequences. The master machine creates tuples containing the known sequences. Worker modules search the database simultaneously and compare what they have located with the target sequence. The workers then generate tuples containing the results of the comparisons. The master then collects the tuples to determine which sequences most closely resemble the target. In a test of the concept, sixty-four 80386 Intel processors wired in parallel completed the job in four minutes.

Fuzzy Logic

Traditional computer programs require precision—on/off, yes/no, right/wrong. However, we human beings do not experience the world this way. We might all agree that 120° is hot, and −40° is cold, but is 75° hot, warm, comfortable, or cool? The answer depends on many factors—the wind, the humidity, the individual experiencing the temperature, one's clothing, one's expectations. Many of our activities are also inexact. Tractor-trailer drivers would find it nearly impossible to back their rig into a space precisely specified to less than an inch on all sides. Fuzzy logic, a relatively new, rule-based development in AI, tolerates imprecision and even uses it to solve problems we could not have solved before. **Fuzzy logic** consists of a variety of concepts and techniques for representing and inferring knowledge that is imprecise, uncertain, or unreliable. Fuzzy logic can create rules that use approximate or subjective values and incomplete or ambiguous data. By expressing logic with some carefully defined imprecision, fuzzy logic is closer to the way people actually think than traditional IF–THEN rules.

Ford Motor Co. has developed a fuzzy logic application that backs a simulated tractor-trailer into a parking space. The application uses the following three rules:

Fuzzy logic: Rule-based AI that tolerates imprecision by using nonspecific terms called membership functions to solve problems.

IF the truck is *near* jackknifing, THEN *reduce* the steering angle;

IF the truck is *far away* from the dock, THEN steer *towards* the dock;

IF the truck is *near* the dock, THEN point the trailer *directly at* the dock.

The following set of fuzzy logic rules control interest rates; they were developed by Lofti Zadeh of the University of California at Berkeley (widely regarded as the founder of fuzzy logic programming):

Increase interest rates *slightly* IF unemployment is *low* AND inflation is *moderate;*

Increase interest rates *sharply* IF unemployment is *low* AND inflation is *moderate* BUT rising *sharply;*

Decrease interest rates *slightly* IF unemployment is *low* BUT increasing AND inflation rate is *low* and *stable.*

This logic makes sense to us as human beings, for it represents how we think as we back that truck into its berth or make economic decisions.

How does the computer make sense of this programming? The answer is relatively simple. The terms (known as *membership functions*) are imprecisely defined so that, for example, in Figure 17.17 *cool* is between 50° and 70°, although the temperature is most clearly cool between about 60° and 67°. Note that cool is overlapped by *cold* or *norm.* To control the room environment using this logic, the programmer would develop similarly imprecise definitions for humidity and other factors such as outdoor wind and temperature. The rules might include one that says *If the temperature is cool or cold and the humidity is low while the outdoor wind is high and the outdoor temperature is low, raise the heat and humidity in the room.* The computer would combine the membership function readings in a weighted manner and, using all the rules, raise and lower the temperature and humidity.

Fuzzy logic is widely used in Japan and is gaining popularity in the United States. Its popularity has occurred partially because managers find they can use it to reduce costs and shorten development time. Fuzzy logic code requires few IF–THEN rules, making it simpler than traditional code. The rules required in the trucking example above, plus its term definitions, might require hundreds of IF–THEN statements to implement in traditional logic. Rockwell International uses fuzzy logic to control motor idling because they are able to reduce system implementation time by a factor of ten. Compact code requires less computer capacity, allowing Sanyo Fisher USA to implement camcorder controls without adding expensive memory to their product.

Figure 17.17

Implementing fuzzy logic rules in hardware. The membership functions for the input called temperature are in the logic of the thermostat to control the room temperature. Membership functions help translate linguistic expressions such as "warm" into numbers that can be manipulated by the computer. *Source: James M. Sibigtroth, "Implementing Fuzzy Expert Rules in Hardware," AI Expert, April 1992. © 1992 Miller Freeman, Inc.*

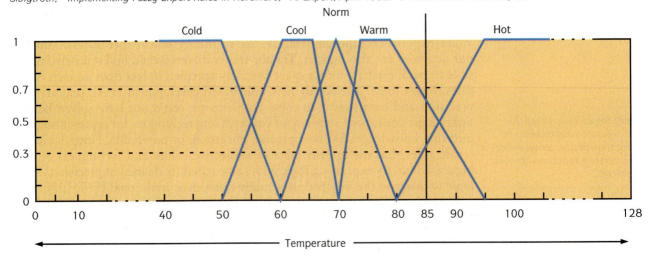

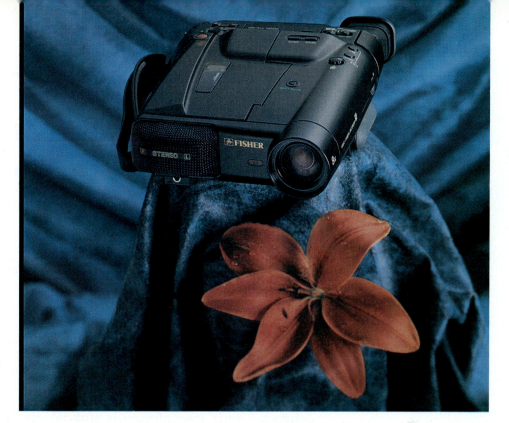

The Smart AF system in this Fisher FVC990 8mm camcorder employs a focus algorithm using fuzzy logic. The camera examines three focus points and then uses fuzzy logic to determine the one spot that has the highest probability of being the main subject.

Fuzzy logic also allows us to solve problems not previously solvable, thus improving product quality. In Japan Sendai's subway system uses fuzzy logic controls to accelerate so smoothly that standing passengers need not hold on. Mitsubishi Heavy Industries in Tokyo has been able to reduce the power consumption of its air conditioners by 20 percent through implementing control programs in fuzzy logic. The auto-focus device in our cameras is only possible because of fuzzy logic.

Management has also found it useful for decision making and organizational control. A Wall Street firm had a system developed that selects companies for potential acquisition, using the language stock traders understand. Recently a system has been developed to detect possible fraud in medical claims submitted by health care providers anywhere in the United States. Fuzzy logic technology is rapidly becoming a major factor in the AI field.

Why Are These Machines Intelligent?

Assessing the intelligence of machines is no different than assessing the intelligence of people. Intelligence is in the eye of the beholder and reflects the culture and *Zeitgeist,* or spirit, of every age. Machines like the Trellis and the mass database search machines exhibit such power, in the sense of mastery over an environment, that they assume in the eyes of many the quality of "intelligence," a quality normally reserved for humans.

But we must remember always that we use this word *intelligence* only metaphorically. These machines are not human. There is a difference between a "model" of human knowledge and human knowledge itself. Economists who "model" the economy never claim that their models "are" the economy. While the human brain is "just a machine" and potentially understandable, as is any machine, the human brain nevertheless is a very special kind of machine, and not much progress has been made in understanding it.

In this light, artificial intelligence applications are programmed reflections of human intelligence, artifacts of humans, presumably under our control. And it is well to remember their limitations.

Why Business Should Be Interested in Artificial Intelligence

Given the experimental nature and high costs of artificial intelligence systems, why should businesses be interested in them at this point? The most important reasons are the following:

- To preserve expertise that might be lost through the retirement, resignation, or death of an acknowledged expert.
- To store information in an active form—to create an organizational knowledge base—that many employees can examine, much like an electronic textbook or manual, so that others may learn rules of thumb not found in textbooks.
- To create a mechanism that is not subject to human feelings like fatigue and worry. This may be especially useful when jobs may be environmentally, physically, or mentally dangerous to humans. These systems may also be useful advisors in times of crisis.
- To eliminate routine and unsatisfying jobs that are currently held by human beings.
- To maintain the strategic position of a company in an industry. Expert systems, like other systems, can be used as a marketing device, to reduce the cost of production or to improve existing product lines.

All of these contributions of artificial intelligence have potential strategic importance. Clearly, most progress in artificial intelligence of direct relevance to general business has been made in expert systems, but neural systems are rapidly developing more powerful applications than expert systems.

Management Challenges

1. **Creating robust expert systems.** Expert systems must be changed every time there is a change in the organizational environment. Every time there is a change in the rules used by experts, they have to be reprogrammed. It is difficult to provide expert systems with the flexibility of human experts.

2. **Creating cost-effective expert systems.** Many thousands of businesses have undertaken experimental projects in expert systems, but only a small percentage have created expert systems that are actually used on a production basis. We have already described the problems of building and maintaining expert systems and the limitations of expert system applications. In many cases, expert systems that would be genuinely useful in business settings cannot be cost-justified.

3. **Determining appropriate applications for artificial intelligence.** Finding suitable applications for artificial intelligence techniques is not so easy. Some parts of business processes are rule based, others based on patterns, and still others based on exhaustive searching of manual files for the "needle in the haystack." Identifying the business process, identifying the right technique, and determining how to build the system requires a focused effort.

Summary

Define artificial intelligence.

Artificial intelligence is the development of computer-based systems that behave like humans. There are five members of the artificial intelligence family tree: natural language, robotics, perceptive systems, expert systems, and "intelligent" machines. The field of artificial intelligence is controversial because of disagreements about theory, practical worth, and social consequences.

Describe how artificial intelligent techniques evolved.

Artificial intelligence has two main thrusts. The bottom-up approach attempts to mimic the physical human brain at the machine level. Norbert Weiner's "feedback" machines, Frank Rosenblatt's Perceptron, and contemporary neural network computers are based on this approach. The top-down approach attempts to represent human knowledge through logic. Newell and Simon's Logic Theorist and General Problem Solver and contemporary expert systems are the leading examples of this school of thought.

Define an expert system and explain how it is built.

Expert systems are knowledge-intensive computer programs that solve problems that heretofore required human expertise. The systems embody human knowledge using rules, frames, or concepts. Expert systems have four components: the knowledge base, the development team, the AI shell, and the user. The knowledge base can be represented using rules, semantic nets, or frames. The strategy to search through the knowledge base, called the inference engine, can use either forward or backward chaining. Development of expert systems requires the use of prototyping and special knowledge engineers to elicit knowledge from the organization's experts.

Define neural networks and show how they are used in business.

Neural networks consist of hardware and software that attempts to mimic the thought processes of the human physical brain. Neural networks are notable for their ability to "learn" without programming and to recognize patterns that cannot be easily described by humans. They are being used in science, medicine, and business primarily to discriminate patterns in massive amounts of data.

Identify other intelligent techniques.

Other examples of machine intelligence are parallel sensor machines, intelligent database search machines, and fuzzy logic. Fuzzy logic is a software technology that expresses logic with some carefully defined imprecision so that it is closer to the way people actually think than traditional IF–THEN rules. Fuzzy logic has been used for controlling physical devices and is starting to be used for limited decision-making applications.

Key Terms	
Artificial intelligence	Semantic nets
Bottom-up approach	Frames
Top-down approach	Knowledge engineer
Combinatorial explosion	AI shell
Expert system	Inference engine
Assistant expert system	Forward chaining
Colleague expert system	Backward chaining
Complete expert automaton	Neural network
Knowledge base	Parallel sensor system
Rule-based expert system	Intelligent database search machine
Rule base	Fuzzy logic

Review Questions

1. What is artificial intelligence?

2. What are the five elements of artificial intelligence research?

3. What is the difference between artificial intelligence and natural or human intelligence? What devices use truly artificial intelligence?

4. Name four attributes of human intelligence. Can you think of four more?

5. What are the two major lines of development in artificial intelligence research? Describe the key aspects of each.

6. State a good working definition of an expert system.

7. Describe three different roles for expert systems in their interactions with humans.

8. What is the difference between a rule-based system and a frame-based system?

9. What is meant by forward- and backward-chaining expert systems?

10. Cite three examples of successful expert systems. How many rules does each possess?

11. List important criteria used to gauge the success of expert systems.

12. Describe three approaches to the development of expert systems.

13. What is the difference between knowledge engineering and conventional systems analysis?

14. Describe the six stages of the expert system life cycle.

15. Describe five tasks (or jobs) that are suitable for an expert system and five tasks that are not.

16. Describe a neural network.

17. What kinds of tasks would a neural network be good at?

18. Define and describe each of the following: parallel sensor systems, intelligent database search machines, fuzzy logic.

19. State four reasons why business should be interested in artificial intelligence.

Discussion Questions

1. A famous person has declared that artificial intelligence will lead to a fundamental redistribution of knowledge because all persons will be able to have their own knowledge-based system, giving them access to knowledge that heretofore only experts have possessed. Discuss.

2. The CEO, in an effort to cut middle-management costs, has just announced a major effort to use artificial intelligence and expert systems to assist managers and if possible, through attrition, to reduce the total cost of management. Discuss.

3. Describe some information system applications that would benefit from using fuzzy logic.

Group Project

With a group of your classmates, find a task in an organization (near your college or university) that requires some intelligence to perform and that might be suitable for an expert system. Describe as many of the rules required to perform this task as possible. Interview and observe the person performing this task. Consider changing the task in order to simplify the system. Report your findings to the class.

CASE STUDY

Technology for Survival in a Growing Market—Digital Equipment Corporation's XCON

In the 1970s and 1980s, Digital Equipment Corporation (DEC) was the second-largest computer manufacturer in the United States. Digital's culture is highly focused on engineering, and the company has a history of innovation. Its corporate strategy was based partly on well-engineered products that offered a superior price/performance ratio. A second critical element of its strategy, the subject of this case study, was flexibility—flexibility that enabled DEC to configure a computer system to meet very precisely the customer's needs. In 1975, DEC offered 50 types of central processors with 400 core options. The estimated possible number of configurations at that time was already in the millions. DEC's flexibility worked so well that equipment sales revenue grew 29 percent per year compounded from 1972 to 1985.

System configuration was the key process in DEC's flexibility strategy, for it converted a customer's order into a fully configured system that was designed, checked and ready for delivery. This process involved three separate reviews of each order. The first two steps relied upon highly skilled and talented technical editors (TEs) who learned their craft through a long apprenticeship. The final review was FA&T (fast assembly and test)—an actual assembly of the system prior to delivery. In 1975, DEC maintained a 13-acre, $15 to $20 million facility to carry out these test assemblies. Elapsed time from signed order to delivery was ten to fifteen weeks, extending at times even up to six months. Growth projections indicated that DEC would need three more FA&T facilities over the next ten years, an enormous expense just to maintain the already slow delivery time. In addition, estimates were that the configuration expert staff of 50 to 60 would have to increase to perhaps 200. To make matters worse, computers were growing more complex, increasing even further the number of configuration options. DEC had to find a new way to configure its orders, and so XCON, DEC's configuration system, was born.

DIGITAL'S XCON: LEARNING BY DOING

XCON was one of the first expert systems in daily production use in industry. The project was established in 1979 with a staff of two and an expert rule base of 250 rules. The project, which was called CSDG (the Configuration System Development Group), was originally a research effort composed largely of engineers and technologists. Today the rule base has expanded to over 10,000 rules. CSDG has grown to maintain a staff of over 60. The system continues to function and has grown in strategic significance for the company. Several related expert systems have spun off the original XCON: XSEL, XFL, XCLUSTER, XNET, and SIZER.

Before XCON, DEC's technical editors (TEs) were critical to configuration, which means they were critical to sales, field service, and manufacturing. The position required a great deal of technical knowledge and skill. DEC maintained a permanent apprenticeship program to develop the essential skill pool. The TE staff had to be large enough to handle orders during peak periods. TEs were dispersed and in daily contact with sales, field service, and manufacturing personnel.

Today the crucial knowledge base that had resided within the TEs has migrated to CSDG, a centralized and somewhat isolated organization of programmers. TEs still exist in DEC but the position has become more clerical; activities tend to concern reviewing rather than decision making. They are consulted much less than in the past and no longer have the authority to block an order pending the solution of technical problems.

Manufacturing, sales, and other operating units were strongly supportive of efforts to solve the configuration problems and to use results from configuration systems to solve other problems. Development of XCON did not involve major turf battles within DEC.

As XCON grew in power, informal contacts with business planners and leaders who strongly supported the project were the primary means of linking the programmers to the business. Later the Configuration Systems Steering Committee (CSSC) was formed, made up of strategically focused managers representing XCON's major business constituencies.

WHAT THE XCON SYSTEMS CAN DO

XCON is used to configure customer orders and to guide the assembly of these orders at the customer site. Using the customer order as input, it provides the following functionality:

- Configures CPUs, memory, cabinets, power supplies, disks, tapes, printers, and so on.

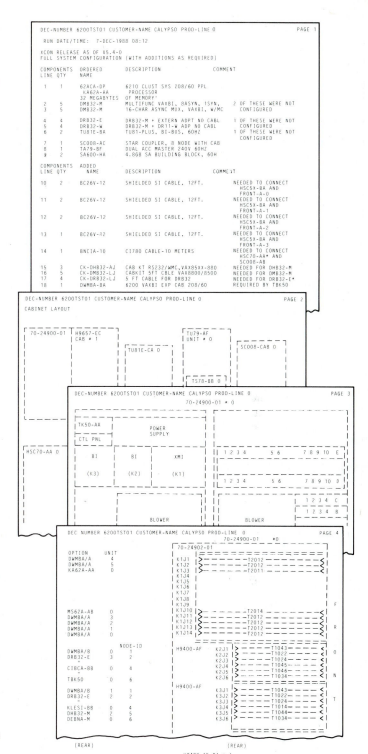

Figure 17.18

Sample output from XCON. The information provided by XCON will assist a broad set of users from sales, manufacturing, and field service by configuring a customer's order. *Adapted from: Virginia E. Barker and Dennis E. O'Connors "Expert Systems for Configuration at Digital: XCON and Beyond."* Communications of the ACM, *March 1989. Copyright 1989, Association for Computing Machinery, Inc. Reprinted by permission.*

- Diagrams complete system configuration (See overlay samples of XCON output, Figure 17.18).
- Determines and lists cabling information.
- Lists components ordered with configuration-related comments.

- Generates warning messages on issues affecting technical validity.

XSEL, which relies on XCON's data, is used interactively to assist in the selection of saleable parts that make up a customer order. Begun in 1981, it provides the following functionality:

- Allows interactive selection by generic component name, and by partial or full model number.
- Performs completeness checking, while adding and suggesting required parts.
- Checks software compatibility, prerequisites, license and media completeness.
- Provides computer room environmental data and requirements.

XFL, begun in 1986, is used to diagram a computer-room floor layout for the configuration(s) under consideration. XCLUSTER is used to assist in configuring computer clusters.

Besides these four systems currently in production use, two other configuration systems are under development. XNET is used to design local area networks, to select appropriate components for such networks, and to validate the technical correctness of the resultant network configu-

rations. SIZER assists in sizing computing resources required for any of a wide variety of uses in various types of organizations. See Figure 17.19 for system architecture supporting peripherals and software.

SCOPE OF XCON AND RELATED SYSTEMS

The configuration systems provide full product coverage for Digital's current product set. In 1990, this product set consisted of 42 different families of central processor types and their supporting peripherals and software. To be useful business tools, released versions of the CSDG systems must include configuration knowledge of Digital's newest products at the time of the product announcement. In practice, this means that CSDG provides major releases of its systems once each quarter, with at least one interim upgrade to ensure adherence to the time-of-announcement requirement.

The configuration systems are used worldwide, throughout the corporation. The user profile of the configuration systems has expanded dramatically (see Table 17.3). The initial purpose of XCON was to assist manufacturing plant personnel in validating the technical correctness of system orders about to be filled. It is now used by a broad set of

Figure 17.19
XSEL/XCON architecture. *Adapted from Virginia E. Barker and Dennis E. O'Connor, ''Expert Systems for Configuration at Digital: XCON and Beyond.''* Communications of the ACM, *March 1989. Copyright 1989, Association for Computing Machinery, Inc. Reprinted by permission.*

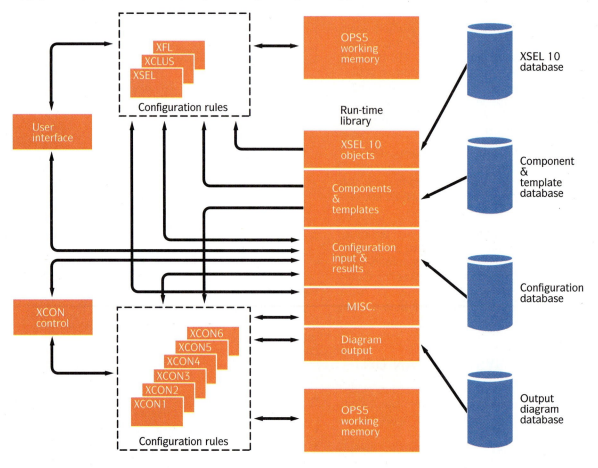

Table 17.3 DIGITAL CONFIGURATION SYSTEMS TIMELINE.

	1979	1980	1981	1982	1983	1984	1985	1986	1987	1988	1989
STAGE OF LIFE											
XCON	Proof of Concept	→ Useable prototype	→ Evolving production system						Rewritten using RIME methodology	→ Evolving production system	
		Limited field test									
XSEL				Proof of Concept	→ Limited field test	→ Evolving production system			XCLUS developed	XSEL/XCLUS Evolving production systems	
XFL								developed			
XCLUS									developed →		
XNET									Proof of Concept →	Multiple useable prototypes	
SIZER										Proof of Concept →	Field Test
SCOPE AND SIZE											
Configuration Task Definition	Single CPU system						→ Clusters of CPUs	→ Network of CPUs clusters	→ Software/Hardware interdependency		
					New buses → FCC regulation, new enclosures, marketing strategies, etc. →						
CPU family coverage #	1		2		3	10	14	18	23	32	42
Component data coverage (# parts in database)	100	500	800			5,100	8,600	10,600	14,800	25,100	31,100
Number of rules (total all systems)	250	750→500	850		2,200	4,900	7,200	9,100	10,700	14,600	17,500
MANAGEMENT											
Development process	Frequent, irregular releases				Monthly → releases	Quarterly releases		Quarterly releases w/ interim upgrades			
Development Group Size	2 → 4	11		21	22		25		33	45	59

Aapted from Virginia E. Barker and Dennis E. O'Connor, "Expert Systems for Configuration at Digital: Xcon and Beyond," *Communications of the ACM* (March 1989). Copyright 1989, Association for Computing Machinery, Inc., Reprinted by permission.

users across the company's major functions: sales and marketing, manufacturing and production, field service, and engineering. The users of these systems perform functions that span Digital's complete order flow and manufacturing cycle; thus they are involved with many different business processes. This is a large and varied constituency to support—each has different needs and takes a different perspective on the configuration information provided.

- *Sales* uses the configuration systems as an integral part of the automated process to generate quotations for customers and to ensure that every order is technically valid.
- *Manufacturing* uses the information to verify buildability of all incoming orders, to understand physical partitioning of an order into various subassemblies, to determine which plants should build which segments of an order, to guide the assembly of all orders, and to determine the optimal set of diagnostics to run on each order.
- *Field service* has the perspective of assembling the order in the customer's unique environment, possibly consolidating it with existing equipment already installed.
- *Manufacturing and engineering* benefit from the configuration systems' focus on system integration, as analysis of product knowledge for inclusion in the configuration systems, and can identify potential problems in system-level design and manufacturability.

XSEL was originally designed for use by sales representatives and is now used by Original Equipment Manufacturer (OEM) customers as well. Implementation of XNET will add specialized field support personnel to the user list in the near future. There are additional "indirect" users of these systems through automated linkages to other software systems (both traditional and expert systems) that depend on the configuration information supplied.

Overall, the CSDG configuration systems support over 50 production installation sites as well as traditional and expert systems that depend on their data.

BENEFITS

XCON plays a strategic role for DEC, permitting DEC to deliver to customers, in a timely fashion, precisely what they require. Using XCON, DEC was able to eliminate FA&T and to reduce average shipping time to three or four weeks, sometimes even to only two or three days. As the computer market changed in the 1980s, rapid turnaround of orders became a requirement for survival. Because of XCON, DEC was ready. These systems allowed DEC to remain competitive and even to thrive in the 1980s as DEC's sales mushroomed and the market demanded shorter response time.

DEC is highly dependent on its configuration systems. It considers them to be a solid success for the company by contributing to customer satisfaction, lower costs, and higher productivity. They are viewed as absolutely critical to the strategy of customizing applications for customers. Specific benefits include the following:

- Only complete and consistent orders are shipped.

- Systems are optimized for the customer and confusion is minimized.
- A single source of configuration information for the company aids in the introduction of new products by showing how they fit into the whole DEC product line.
- Flexible manufacturing is aided by the precise knowledge of which parts are needed in inventory.
- Flexible distribution is aided by allowing system field experts rapidly to assemble parts originating from different factories. There is no need for independent assembly, test, and disassembly before shipping to the customer.

DEC has never conducted a formal study of the benefits of XCON and its related systems, and although the costs might be known, they are not published. Officials estimate that the configuration systems save $40 million per year net of all costs.

OTHER CHALLENGES

Massive technological change creates many and sometimes severe challenges. Along with some of those raised already, DEC found itself facing a number of other issues, some of which are described here.

Tools

Expert system tools today are highly limited. They tend not to produce efficient systems. Often they are hard to maintain, and are not easily connected to existing business system data flows or databases. XCON was originally written in a proprietary language called OPS5, which is very good at situation recognition but poor at algorithmic controls. To extend the power of OPS5, over 350 programs and 50,000 lines of code were written in traditional languages like BASIC and C.

When XCON first started, there was no architectural concept, everything was experimental, and there was no systems development methodology. After ten years of development, the entire system was redeveloped using a more explicit and efficient methodology called RIME. RIME has simplified the rule base and made it easier for people to learn and understand the system.

Size

Today XCON is large and complex by any standard. XCON alone has over 10,000 rules, and the related systems have another 8000 rules. But these numbers do not portray the representational complexity of the rule base (see Table 17.4). Consider, for instance, that

- The average number of condition elements per rule (the "if" portion) is 6.
- The average number of attributes per condition (tests, patterns, etc.) is 5.
- The average number of action elements per rule (the "then" portion) is 4.

Thus, the average number of tests that each rule must make on each cycle to determine whether it is applicable is $6 \times 5 = 30$.

Table 17.4 SAMPLE RULES FROM XCON.

Rule Name: R1a-unmounted-ubx-options	Comments

IF

C1 The current step in the configuration process involves mounting options in containers;

This condition is used to distinguish the group of rules that can potentially activate.

C2 and the system being configured is not a vax11/780, vax11/782, vax11/785, vax8650, or vax8600;

This rule is not applicable to those types of hardware systems.

C3 and there is no unconfigured disk which sits on the idc bus;

This condition ensures that the rule will not activate before all disks on an idc bus have been configured. ("Disk" actually means "disk drive.")

C4 and there is an unconfigured r102-type disk which needs to mount inside a cabinet and whose pre-assigned controller sits on a unibus and it is the first disk assigned;

This identifies the properties required of an appropriate disk to be configured by this rule.

C5 and there is no unconfigured r102-type disk assigned to a controller that is placed closer to the cpu than the controller assigned to the aforementioned disk;

Disks assigned to controllers that are closest to the cpu need to be placed first, in case there is insufficient capacity for all of them.

C6 and there is a requirement to cable the disk to be configured to a controller;

Part of the activity of this rule is to determine that cabling. There may be several possibilities.

C7 and there has been no connection made between the disk to be configured and anything else;

This indicates that some of the activities that this rule will perform have not yet occurred.

C8 and there is a controller to which the disk to be configured has been pre-assigned and which sits on a unibus;

This identifies the appropriate controller.

C9 and there is a requirement to cable the controller to a disk whose type and quantity of cable match one of the possibilities specified for the disk;

This identifies the type and quantity of cable needed for this particular disk/controller combination.

C10 and there has been no connection created yet to this controller from any disk;

Another indication that the activities to be performed by this rule have not occurred.

C11 and there are no unused disk spaces in any unibus cabinet;

This ensures that any spaces appropriate for disks in this type of cabinet will be filled before the rule can activate.

C12 and there is a description for the capacity of a disk cabinet, whose name is not "h9643";

This identifies a special type of cabinet that can only contain disks. An "h9643" is one variation of a cabinet to which the rule does not apply.

C13 and there is an unconfigured disk cabinet;

This identifies an appropriate cabinet in which the disk to be configured will be placed by the rule.

C14 and the top space available for disk placement is unused;

This identifies a location in the aforementioned cabinet where the disk to be configured can be placed. It needs to be on the top because of the removable medium.

THEN

A1 mark the disk configured;

A2 and update the top space in the cabinet to be used;

The location needs to be marked so that nothing else will be placed there.

A3 and create a connection relationship between the disk and its controller, fully specifying the identifying information for the disk, controller, cabinet, and the type and quantity of the cable to be used for the connection;

This establishes the connection between the disk and its controller. Other rules will determine the length and choose the exact cable(s).

A4 and create a containing relationship between the disk and the cabinet, specifying the identifying information for the disk and cabinet as well as the location of the placement;

This establishes the placement of the disk in the cabinet.

A5 and create labels for the output diagram showing the disk within the cabinet for both the skyline view of the cabinet layout and the detailed view of the particular cabinet.

This ensures that the output diagram will display this information correctly.

Adapted from Judith Bacharat and Elliot Soloway, "The Engineering of Econ" In Virginia E. Barker and Dennis E. O'Connor, "Expert Systems for Configuration at Digital: Xcon and Beyond," *Communications of the ACM (March 1989). Copyright 1989, Association for Computing Machinery, Inc.; Reprinted by permission.*

In 1989 there were 5 databases in XCON containing information on 30,000 parts, with 25 to 125 fields per part. The databases are so large that they are compiled, compressed, and kept memory resident, with multiple indices to speed processing.

Maintenance

Maintainability is a critical issue. Each year about 40 percent of the 18,000 rules change because of changes in marketing, manufacturing, and engineering. Major and minor new products are always being introduced. As computer architectures move away from the single computer and toward clusters of machines and networks of components, the configuration options have exploded. The learning curve for new developers is about 12 months. The system is so complex that even experienced software engineers require a long training period.

Testing

Testing poses difficult issues in expert systems. Can you evaluate XCON as if it were a human? As the system improves over time, you have to readjust tests. What is correctness? Can we differentiate between optimal solutions and workable solutions? What about where experts disagree? What about the situation where the system comes up with the right answer for the wrong reasons?

Expansion

The uses and users of XCON have changed over the years, and new demands are being placed on the system. New types of users with new perspectives generate new requirements that were not foreseen. For instance, when plant technicians began using XCON configuration diagrams as the official document from which to construct a computer system, a whole new set of requirements was generated. The original "working diagram" had to be more carefully constructed, new code for diagram creation had to be written, and a whole new database defined.

Human Resource and Organizational Challenges

Over the years, CSDG has learned to appreciate the many different kinds of roles involved in building a complex system like XCON. Some of the key roles are as follows:

- *Champion:* Executives with strategic vision and a knowledge of what the technology can do. They must have strong connections with sponsors.
- *Sponsor:* Business people who want to solve problems and can get things done, deliver the budget and protect from enemies.
- *Program manager:* An integration role, filled by a person with a keen sense of the business rather than a technical focus.
- *Technical team:* Composed of knowledge engineers, who develop the knowledge base, and software systems integration engineers who develop the overall software and hardware foundation.
- *Experts and users:* People who provide domain knowledge and insight into the business problem.

Development Tasks

The development of these expert systems has spanned over ten years. In this time, CSDG has gained considerable understanding of all phases of the life cycle of production quality expert systems. The XCON team developed a general model of expert systems development based on four major tasks. These tasks are the following:

- Defining and redefining the system.
- Extending and refining the system.
- Delivering the system.
- Evaluating the system.

The team has found that delivering expert systems resembles traditional systems development. The only exception is that the technology is less settled, reliable, and predictable. The business problems are not often well understood when compared to, say, an accounting system. And the business being served will itself often change greatly as a result of the expert system, sometimes in unpredictable ways. However, DEC's experience indicates that once the managerial and technical problems are solved or at least addressed, it is possible to develop systems capable of saving millions of dollars and providing a strategic platform for the corporation.

Sources: Virginia E. Barker and Dennis E. O'Connor, "Expert Systems for Configuration at Digital XCON and Beyond," *Communications of the ACM* (March 1989); John J. Sviokla, "An Examination of the Impact of Expert Systems on the Firm: The Case of XCON," *MIS Quarterly* 14, no. 5 (June 1990).

Case Study Questions

1. Why do major technology projects like XCON result in such significant, unforeseen organizational changes? If you were the corporate sponsor of a project of this type at its beginning, how would you prepare for and anticipate this problem? With your project team (use several of your classmates), define your goals for this aspect of the project.

2. Before a system like XCON can help a company, management must first determine that the problem to be solved is appropriate and that the risk (including cost) is worth it. As well as you can, define and quantify the risk DEC was taking when it began this project. If you were the CEO at that time, how would you evaluate the risk against the size of the problem and against the projected benefits? Remember, you are making this evaluation in 1979 and so you cannot know that the market will change or that the 29 percent annualized growth will continue.

3. Organizationally, DEC was changed by XCON. Describe the organizational and staffing problems created when the configuration expertise migrated from the TEs to CSDG. From the description in the case study, do you think that DEC handled these problems well? What issues did they seem to miss? How might you have improved their handling of this change?

4. Major technological change often requires a concurrent change in technology architecture to control the growth in size and complexity of the new technology. Describe the problems of this type that emerged from the XCON project. Knowing what you know now, devise an approach to the next massive technological change that might lessen the negative impact of that change.

5. In what ways might other new technology complicate or simplify management of XCON? Identify some major technological trends and explore how they might increase demands on XCON as well as how they might be used to manage and expand XCON.

References

Barker, Virginia E., and Dennis E. O'Connor. "Expert Systems for Configuration at Digital: XCON and Beyond." *Communications of the ACM* (March 1989).

Basu, Amit, and Alan R. Heyner. "Embedded Knowledge-based Systems and Box Structure Methods." *Journal of Management Information Systems* 8 no. 4 (Spring 1992).

Blanning, Robert W., David R. King, James R. Marsden, and Ann C. Seror. "Intelligent Models of Human Organizations: The State of the Art." *Journal of Organizational Computing* 2, no. 2 (1992).

Bobrow, D. G., S. Mittal, and M. J. Stefik. "Expert Systems: Perils and Promise." *Communications of the ACM* 29 (September 1986).

Braden, Barbara, Jerome Kanter, and David Kopcso. "Developing an Expert Systems Strategy." *MIS Quarterly* 13, no. 4 (December 1989).

Brody, Herb. "The Neural Computer." *Technology Review* (August/September 1990).

Byrd, Terry Anthony. "Implementation and Use of Expert Systems in Organizations: Perceptions of Knowledge Engineers." *Journal of Management Information Systems* 8, no. 4 (Spring 1992).

Carlson, David A., and Sudha Ram. "A Knowledge Representation for Modeling Organizational Productivity." *Journal of Organizational Computing* 2, no. 2 (1992).

Churchland, Paul M., and Patricia Smith Churchland. "Could a Machine Think?" *Scientific American* (January 1990).

Clifford, James, Henry C. Lucas, Jr. and Rajan Srikanth. "Integrating Mathematical and Symbolic Models through AESOP: An Expert for Stock Options Pricing." *Information Systems Research* 3, no. 4 (December 1992).

Cox, Earl. "Applications of Fuzzy System Models." *AI Expert* (October 1992).

Cox, Earl. "Solving Problems with Fuzzy Logic." *AI Expert* (March 1992).

Creecy, Robert H., Brij M. Masand, Sephten J. Smith, and Davis L. Waltz. "Trading MIPS and Memory for Knowledge Engineering." *Communications of the ACM* 35, no. 8 (August 1992).

Dhar, Vasant. "Plausibility and Scope of Expert Systems in Management." *Journal of Management Information Systems* (Summer 1987).

Feigenbaum, Edward A. "The Art of Artificial Intelligence: Themes and Case Studies in Knowledge Engineering." *Proceedings of the IJCAI* 5 (1977).

Feigenbaum, Edward A., and J. A. Feigenbaum (eds.). *Computers and Thought.* New York: McGraw-Hill, 1963.

Feigenbaum, Edward A., and Pamela McCorduck. *The Fifth Generation: Artificial Intelligence and Japan's Computer Challenge to the World.* Reading, MA.: Addison-Wesley, 1985.

Gelernter, David. "The Metamorphosis of Information Management." *Scientific American* (August 1989).

Griggs, Kenneth. "Visual Aids that Model Organizations." *Journal of Organizational Computing* 2, no. 2 (1992).

Hayes-Roth, Frederick. "Knowledge-Based Expert Systems." *Spectrum IEEE* (October 1987).

Hinton, Gregory. "How Neural Networks Learn from Experience." *Scientific American* (September 1992).

Jacobs, Paul S., and Lisa F. Rau. "SCISOR: Extracting Information from On-line News." *Communications of the ACM* 33, no. 11 (November 1990).

Leonard-Barton, Dorothy, and John J. Sviokla. "Putting Expert Systems to Work." *Harvard Business Review* (March–April 1988).

Lin, Frank C., and Mei Lin. "Neural Networks in the Financial Industry." *AI Expert* (February 1993).

Marsden, James R., David E. Pingry, and Ming-Chian Ken Wang. "Intelligent Information and Organization Structures: An Integrated Design Approach." *Journal of Organizational Computing* 2, no. 2 (1992).

McCarthy, John. "Generality in Artificial Intelligence." *Communications of the ACM* (December 1987).

Meador, C. Lawrence, and Ed G. Mahler. "Choosing an Expert System Game Plan." *Datamation* (August 1, 1990).

Meyer, Marc H. and Kathleen Foley Curley. "An Applied Framework for Classifying the Complexity of Knowledge-Based Systems." *MIS Quarterly* 15, no. 4 (December 1991).

"M.1 Makes a Direct Hit." *PC Magazine* (April 16, 1985).

Michaelson, Robert, and Donald Michie. "Expert Systems in Business." *Datamation* (November 1983).

Motiwalla, Luvai and Jay F. Nunamaker, Jr. "Mail-Man: A Knowledge-Based MAIL Assistant for Managers." *Journal of Organizational Computing* 2, no. 2 (1992).

Mykytyn, Kathleen, Peter P. Mykytyn, Jr., and Craig W. Stinkman. "Expert Systems: A Question of Liability." *MIS Quarterly* 14, no. 1 (March 1990).

Nash, Jim. "Expert Systems: A New Partnership." *AI Expert* (December 1992).

Rich, Elaine. *Artificial Intelligence*. New York: McGraw-Hill, 1983.

Searle, John R. "Is the Brain's Mind a Computer Program?" *Scientific American* (January 1990).

Self, Kevin. "Designing with Fuzzy Logic." *Spectrum IEEE* (November 1990).

Sibigtroth, James M. "Implementing Fuzzy Expert Rules in Hardware." *AI Expert* (April 1992).

Simon, H. A., and A. Newell. "Heuristic Problem Solving: The Next Advance in Operations Research." *Operations Research* 6 (January–February 1958).

Stein, Eric W. "A Method to Identify Candidates for Knowledge Acquisition." *Journal of Management Information Systems* 9, no. 2 (Fall 1992).

Storey, Veda C., and Robert C. Goldstein, "Knowledge-Based Approaches to Database Design," *MIS Quarterly*, 17, no. 1 (March 1993).

Stylianou, Anthony C., Gregory R. Madey and Robert D. Smith. "Selection Criteria for Expert System Shells: A Socio-Technical Framework." *Communications of the ACM* 35, no. 10 (October 1992).

Sviokla, John J. "Expert Systems and Their Impact on the Firm: The Effects of PlanPower Use on the Information Processing Capacity of the Financial Collaborative." *Journal of Management Information Systems* 6, no. 3 (Winter 1989–90).

Sviokla, John J. "An Examination of the Impact of Expert Systems on the Firm: The Case of XCON." *MIS Quarterly* 14, no. 5 (June 1990).

Tam, Kar Yan. "Automated Construction of Knowledge-Bases from Examples." *Information Systems Research* 1, no. 2 (June 1990).

Tank, David W., and John J. Hopfield. "Collective Computation in Neuronlike Circuits." *Scientific American* (October 1987).

Trippi, Robert, and Efraim Turban. "The Impact of Parallel and Neural Computing on Managerial Decision Making."*Journal of Management Information Systems* 6, no. 3 (Winter 1989–1990).

Turban, Efraim, and Paul R. Watkins. "Integrating Expert Systems and Decision Support Systems." *MIS Quarterly* (June 1986).

Wallich, Paul. "Silicon Babies." *Scientific American* (December 1991).

Waltz, David L. "Artificial Intelligence." *Scientific American* (December 1982).

Weitzel, John R., and Kenneth R. Andrews. "A Company/University Joint Venture to Build a Knowledge-Based System." *MIS Quarterly* 12, no. 1 (March 1988).

Weitzel, John R., and Larry Kerschberg. "Developing Knowledge Based Systems: Reorganizing the System Development Life Cycle." *Communications of the ACM* (April 1989).

Weizenbaum, Joseph. *Computer Power and Human Reason—From Judgment to Calculation*. San Francisco: Freeman, 1976.

Weizenbaum, Joseph. "ELIZA—A Computer Program for the Study of Natural Language Communication Between Man and Machine." *Communications of the ACM* (January 1983).

White, George M. "Natural Language Understanding and Speech Recognition." *Communications of the ACM* 33, no. 8 (August 1990).

Zadeh, Lotfi A. "The Calculus of Fuzzy If/Then Rules." *AI Expert* (March 1992).

EPRINET: A Strategic Network for the Utility Industry

The Electric Power Research Institute (EPRI) is the research and development consortium for the U.S. electric utility industry. It is one of the largest private research firms in the United States, with headquarters in Palo Alto, California and search sites around the country. EPRI has six technical research divisions: Generation and Storage, Nuclear Power, Environment, Electrical Systems, Customer Systems, and Exploratory Research. EPRI's business is information and its product is knowledge. EPRI contracts with energy experts in 36 countries to research subjects of interest to its members.

EPRI is funded by its member firms and since its founding in 1972 has invested $4.3 billion in various research projects. The funds for these projects have come from the contributions of 700 member electrical utilities, representing 70% of total electricity sales in the United States. EPRI recently added its first international affiliate, the British utility PowerGen.

EPRI's internal research and development staff of 450 scientists and engineers manage 1600 projects, which are conducted by over 400 utility, university, commercial, government, and other R & D contractors in 36 countries. The projects span many technologies, from electricity generation at the power station to electricity use in the home. Many of the issues they deal with are global, such as the greenhouse effect, acid rain, and superconductivity.

EPRI is a very information-intensive organization. Spanning 19 years of research, EPRI's databases contain over eight gigabytes of information, equivalent to 2.7 million pages of technical documents with diagrams and formulas. Each year EPRI distributes millions of copies of reports, report summaries, and software. Each year EPRI also holds several hundred seminars and workshops and handles over 13,000 hotline telephone inquiries.

Originally EPRI's mission extended only to the management of its research and development program. This changed after 1978. Because of deregulation, the electric utility industry experienced intense change. In the past, federal regulations defined and protected individual utility service territories. Since deregulation, electric utilities compete for large customers against gas utilities, independent power producers, other utilities, and sometimes the large customers themselves. They must also contend with rising public pressure to protect the environment. For instance, Pacific Gas & Electric (PG&E) is working with the environmental groups on renewable energy sources.

Competitive pressures in the utility industry required EPRI to find more efficient ways to deliver the results of its research and expertise to its clients. EPRI and its members wanted to compress the "information float," the time from the findings of R&D to the analysis of their results to the application of those results in industry. The sheer volume and complexity of its scientific information made it difficult to distribute this information. Research results were unavailable for one to 24 months while detailed reports were being produced. When the technical reports finally made it out the door, members were expected to wade through massive volumes of documents to find the nuggets of documents they needed.

EPRI tried to solve these problems in 1984 by launching the development of a state-of-the-art electronic information and communications network called EPRINET. EPRINET provides four anchor services and various specialty services. The anchor services are electronic mail, natural language retrieval system, electronic directories and catalogues, and videoconferencing.

The natural language retrieval system allows users to retrieve information from EPRI's databases by entering a few keywords in English. Users can use this facility to search on-line directories, abstracts, catalogues, and papers.

EPRINET's principal directory describes its technical staff, listing their names, positions, relevant publications, and recent projects by area of expertise. The directory also catalogues EPRI research work, including status reports, papers, articles, videotapes, and speeches. EPRI wants to put Technical Interest Profiles on-line. The profiles identify the kind of information members want to obtain from EPRI.

EPRI introduced videoconferencing in April 1991. Some members prefer to videoconference rather than to scan research papers on a specific topic. They can use EPRINET to identify the EPRI experts and arrange a videoconference with those experts. The network posts an announcement telling members the date and time of the videoconference.

The specialty services are special products and services that help people deal with information overload and locate colleagues with similar interests. These services are tailored to a particular use. An example might be an on-line forum that allows engineers to discuss and evaluate various options for keeping biological organisms out of hydropower plant machinery. Each forum can have its own news briefs, announcements, report database, software models, and directory of participants. The specialty services even provide up-to-date industry news, electronic bulletin boards, and an "ask the EPRI expert" facility for answering questions on-line. If a requestor does not know the name of the appropriate expert, the system will route the request to be reviewed by an EPRI staff member, who forwards it to the appropriate expert.

EPRIGEMS are interactive expert system modules that use expert system technology to capture EPRI research findings and the knowledge of EPRI staff. Each module works on a particular utility problem, such as boiler maintenance or nuclear plant life extension. Some EPRIGEMS provide users with appropriate experts whom they can contact through EPRINET's electronic mail system.

ElectriGuide is a research catalog on CD-ROM that contains three major databases, with abstracts of 7000 EPRI technical reports, plus descriptions of 1000 EPRI products and 23,000 research projects. It contains color slide presentations for selected topics such as end-user forecasting. After using the CD-ROM catalog, users can order published and audiovisual items on-line through EPRINET.

EPRI's management launched EPRINET by initiating a period of intense automation from 1984 to 1987. EPRI's information technology division focused on raising the level of computer literacy of EPRI staff members, establishing connectivity among EPRI's internal computer environments and to external computer networks, and building a core of strategic databases. Management realized that some of EPRI's suppliers and customers might become their competitors unless EPRI retained its position as the hub of research in the industry.

EPRI installed microcomputers on virtually every desk in 1985 and established a lending library of laptop microcomputers. A series of user-friendly programs was written to help project managers use computers to administer research projects. EPRINET's E-mail facility was introduced in 1985, but persuading staff to use it required active use by EPRI's president, senior executives, and project managers. EPRI installed a telephone help line and software lending library and began training its members in the most commonly used software programs. EPRI developed a facility to transfer documents in revisable format between IBM mainframes, IBM PCs and clones, Macintosh microcomputers, and NBI word processors, using PROFS and a translation program among word processing packages. Management selected the IBM Information Network, supplemented by Tymnet for high-speed global transmission of data (About 40% of U.S. electric utilities use that network) and customized PROFS to send and receive messages from two other international networks, BITNET and MCI Mail.

EPRI established an EPRINET Utility Advisory Group (UAG) to involve its member utilities from the start in its information technology planning. UAG represented the full range of utility responsibilities, including technology transfer, power plant operations, R & D engineering, and design. One of UAG's first assignments was to describe the utility engineer of the future and what information technologies the engineer would need.

The first production version of EPRINET was released in May 1990. Soon after management began a marketing campaign to promote use of the network internally among EPRI project and program managers and externally among member utilities and research contractors. Since that time the number of EPRINET users has climbed steadily. By April 1991 virtually every EPRINET employee was connected.

Management originally believed that the implementation of EPRINET and cultural changes associated with the organization's strategic transition could be undertaken separately. The average age of the EPRI scientific staff was over 45 years and the staff was unaccustomed to working with computers. EPRI's new mission required that staff members change their roles and accept responsibility for delivering the results of their research to EPRI's members. They had to learn to travel with laptop computers, retrieve information electronically, and use electronic mail to "talk" with colleagues and contractors instead of the telephone. EPRI won some immediate converts but many staff members changed reluctantly. Some instability resulted from trying to undertake intense automation without readying the organization for new ways of working. EPRI's management could not resolve these problems all at once.

The EPRINET project needed a top-level executive from outside the information systems department to serve as its sponsor to the rest of the organization. Initially, it could not find a corporate champion from the R & D staff because the organization was in such transition. The project "sponsor" wound up being a coalition of three executives. Although not ideal, the coalition worked.

At first the EPRINET project team avoided corporate naysayers, who worried about licensing agreements, information overload, and whether money to sustain the new databases would be taken away from advanced research projects. The project team feared they would undermine the project. As time went on, the team realized that these opponents identified some real problems and that they made valuable suggestions, so the teams started drawing them out. The team tried to win over opponents by demonstrating EPRINET's value in saving staff and member time to communicate research findings, experimenting with pilot systems, and launching a program to orient member utilities to EPRINET's services and benefits.

How successful is EPRINET? Heavy users of the system believe EPRINET provides a collaborative environment where people feel more informed and task forces and businesses can operate more efficiently. A number of users have reported finding in minutes pieces of information that might have taken several weeks in the past. Member utilities have reported that EPRINET allows them to make better use of EPRI's knowledge, saving time, developing new products, and increasing revenue. For instance, Commonwealth Edison estimated that the market-targeting capabilities of EPRI's industrial market information system software helped it make new sales in the industrial sector that increased its revenues by $2 million a year. EPRI is continuing to refine the network and incorporate new technologies.

Source: Marina M. Mann, Richard L. Rudman, Thomas A. Jenckes, and Barbara C. McNurlin, "EPRINET: Leveraging Knowledge in the Electric Utility Industry," MIS Quarterly, 15, no. 3 (September 1991).

Case Study Questions

1. What is EPRI's goal as an organization? Why did that goal change?
2. What are the strategic implications of EPRINET for EPRI and for its subscribing members?
3. What are EPRI's critical success factors? How well did EPRINET address those factors?
4. What kinds of problems did EPRI encounter during implementation of EPRINET? What management, organization and technology factors were responsible for those problems? Would you have managed the EPRINET project differently?
5. How important is EPRINET for solving the problems faced by the electric utility industry? What are some of the problems it cannot address?
6. Can you suggest some other information system applications that would benefit EPRI?

FIVE

Managing Contemporary Information Systems

The pervasiveness and power of contemporary information systems have brought three key management problems to the fore. They are security and control, developing global systems, and using information systems in an ethically and socially responsible manner. Part Five concludes the text by examining the management challenges posed by these problems.

Chapter 18 demonstrates why management must take special measures to ensure that information systems are secure and effectively controlled. Without proper safeguards, information systems are highly vulnerable to destruction, abuse, error, and loss. Both general and application-specific controls can be applied to ensure that information systems are accurate, reliable, and secure. An appropriate control structure for information systems will consider costs and benefits. This chapter highlights the importance of information system security and auditing.

Chapter 19 analyzes the principal challenges confronting organizations that want to use information systems on an international scale. Organizations need to design appropriate business strategies and information systems infrastructures for this purpose and they need to overcome significant management, organization, and technology obstacles to systems that transcend national boundaries.

Chapter 20 describes the ethical dimensions of information systems in contemporary society. The widespread use of information systems has created new ethical and social problems. The issues of information rights (including privacy), intellectual property rights, accountability, liability, system quality, and quality of life must be carefully examined in light of the new power of information technology.

Part Five Case Study: *Is the Social Security Administration Ready for the Twenty-First Century?* In the early 1980s, the Social Security Administration found that its information systems were totally inadequate for its mission and operational needs. To forestall collapse, SSA launched the Systems Modernization Plan, one of the largest information system projects in history. The story of this project and of subsequent efforts to streamline SSA illustrates not only themes from this section but also from the entire text: using information systems to raise productivity in information-intense organizations, planning for systems, using systems to redesign organizations, the need for management control and oversight, management of large-scale information systems projects, and organizational obstacles to "strategic transitions."

Controlling Information Systems

Flood Brings Chicago's Systems to a Standstill

On April 13, 1992, a construction crew driving pilings into the Chicago River accidentally caused a leak in a network of coal delivery tunnels that had been built at the turn of the century. Within hours, more than 250 million gallons of water poured into the tunnels below Chicago's business district. The ensuing flood caused power failures and water damage that forced Chicago's businesses to a standstill.

Electrical cables supplying power to these businesses were shielded, but their electrical systems were not. Commonwealth Edison cut power to 200 buildings, and 200,000 people had to be evacuated immediately. The flood hit the headquarters of the Chicago Board of Trade (CBOT) which contains the computers that run Chicago's commodity trading systems and offices of 80 member brokerages. (The

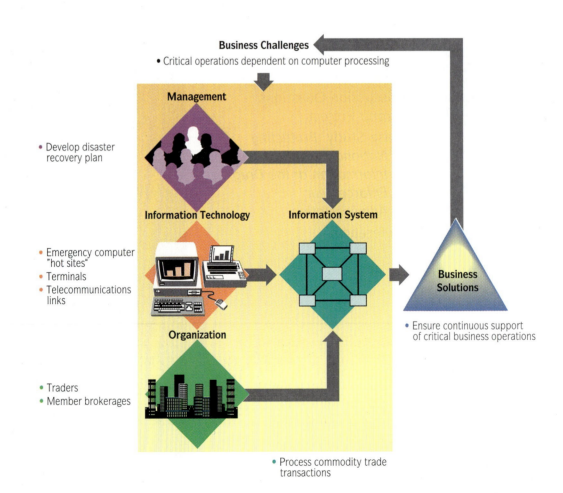

Business Challenges
• Critical operations dependent on computer processing

Management

• Develop disaster recovery plan

Information Technology

• Emergency computer "hot sites"
• Terminals
• Telecommunications links

Information System

Business Solutions

• Ensure continuous support of critical business operations

Organization

• Traders
• Member brokerages

• Process commodity trade transactions

Chicago Board of Trade processes between 500,000 and 600,000 commodity futures transactions daily.) All trading stopped. Major banks, retail stores, and government centers were crippled. Billions of dollars reportedly were lost.

For most firms the problem was not flood water but power and telecommunications outages. Flood waters gushed into the sub-basement of the building occupied by Arthur Andersen, SC, a leading information systems consulting firm. The flood battered down the walls of an electrical vault, wiping out a packet-switched network that Andersen used to deliver its North American payroll. The network also carried time reports used for billing clients. A simultaneous power failure at another building brought down Andersen's mainframe.

Some firms, including the Chicago Board of Trade, had contingency plans for such disasters. Half of CBOT's 140-member staff packed backup tapes and traveled 35 miles to a Northbrook, Illinois, "hot site" run by Sungard Recovery Services to provide emergency computing facilities to subscribing businesses. Just six hours after the disaster, CBOT resumed processing trading transactions at its temporary computer headquarters. It arranged for brokers to use 30 terminals at the Chicago Mercantile Exchange, about five blocks away from its crippled headquarters, and terminals at 35 other firms. The terminals were linked by modem to CBOT's temporary mainframe facilities at Sungard. CBOT had daily reports required by traders flown by helicopter from the Sungard computer center to Chicago. The exchange was able to fully open trading.

Firms like CBOT that had disaster recovery plans also switched their information system operations to other computer centers. About eighteen companies used the facilities of Comdisco Disaster Recovery Services. Other firms armed small groups of workers with laptop computers, cellular phones, fax and copy machines, and had them work in local hotel rooms outside the evacuated downtown district.

Sources: "Down and Out in Chicago," *InformationWEEK* (April 20, 1992); Julia King, "Traders Wheel, Deal, Soar to Keep Chicago Commodities Exchange Humming in Flood," *Computerworld* (June 29, 1992); and Ellis Booker and Jim Nash, "Great Chicago Flood of '92: IS Groups Stay High and Dry," *Computerworld* (April 20, 1992).

Vulnerability to floods and other natural disasters is but one of many problems that organizations relying on computer-based information systems may face. Hardware and software failures, employee errors, and use by unauthorized people may prevent information systems from running properly or running at all.

Computer systems play such a critical role in business, government, and daily life that organizations must take special steps to protect their information systems and ensure that they are accurate and reliable. The Chicago Board of Trade and other Chicago firms with disaster recovery plans took these steps; others did not. This chapter describes how information systems can be *controlled* so that they serve the purposes for which they are intended.

After completing this chapter you will be able to:

- Show why automated information systems are so vulnerable to destruction, error, and abuse.
- Describe the role of controls in safeguarding information systems.
- Distinguish between general controls and application controls.
- Describe the most important techniques for controlling information systems.
- Identify the factors that must be considered when developing the controls for information systems.
- Explain the importance of auditing information systems.

18.1 System Vulnerability and Abuse

Before computer automation, data about individuals or organizations were maintained and secured as paper records dispersed in separate business or organizational units. Information systems concentrate data in computer files that can potentially be accessed more easily by large numbers of people and by groups outside the organization. Consequently, automated data are more susceptible to destruction, fraud, error, and misuse.

When computer systems fail to run or work as required, firms that depend heavily on computers experience a serious loss of business function. Figure 18.1

Figure 18.1
Downtime's Downside. The study, commissioned by Stratus Computer Inc. and conducted by New York research firm Find/SVP, surveyed 450 IS executives at Fortune 1000 firms. It found that unplanned system downtime occurs nine times per year, on average; systems stay down an average four hours; and customer dissatisfaction and lost productivity are the two most negative effects of the crashes. *Adapted from John P. McPartlin, "The True Cost of Downtime," InformationWEEK (August 3, 1992). Reprinted by permission of InformationWeek and Stratus Computer, Inc.*

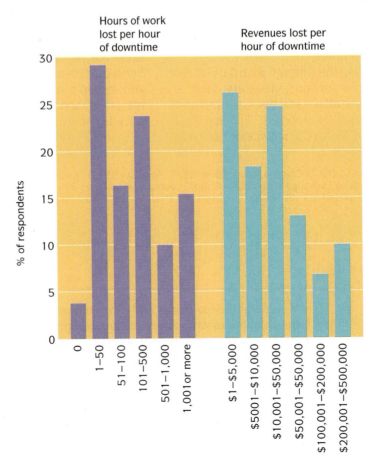

shows the results of one survey of 450 Fortune 1000 firms: Disruptions in computer service cost U.S. businesses $4 billion a year and result in at least 37 million hours of lost worker productivity. The longer computer systems are "down," the more serious the consequences for the firm. Some firms relying on computers to process their critical business transactions might experience a total loss of business function if they lose computer capability for more than a few days.

Why Systems Are Vulnerable

There are many advantages to information systems that are properly safeguarded. But when large amounts of data are stored in electronic form they are vulnerable to many more kinds of threats than when they exist in manual form. For example, an organization's entire recordkeeping system can be destroyed by a computer hardware malfunction. Table 18.1 lists the most common threats against computerized information. They can stem from technical, organizational, and environmental factors compounded by poor management decisions.

Computerized systems are especially vulnerable to such threats for the following reasons:

- A complex information system cannot be replicated manually. Most information cannot be printed or is too voluminous to be handled manually.
- There is usually no visible trace of changes in computerized systems because computer records can be read only by the computer.
- Computerized procedures appear to be invisible and are not easily understood or audited.
- Changes in automated systems are more costly and often more complex than changes in manual systems.
- The development and operation of automated systems require specialized technical expertise, which cannot be easily communicated to end users. Systems are open to abuse by highly technical staff members who are not well integrated into the organization. (Programmers and computer operators can make unauthorized changes in software while information is being processed or can use computer facilities for unauthorized purposes. Employees may make unauthorized copies of data files for illegal purposes.)
- Although the chances of disaster in automated systems are no greater than in manual systems, the effect of a disaster can be much more extensive. In some cases, all of the system's records can be destroyed and lost forever.
- There are fewer hard-copy documents to process and review when systems are automated. Less manual scrutiny is possible.
- Most automated systems are accessible by many individuals. Information is easier to gather but more difficult to control.
- Data in computer systems undergo many more processing steps than in manual systems, each of which is open to errors or abuse. Each of these functions—data origination, recording, transmission for processing, processing, storage, retrieval, and dissemination—requires a separate set of physical, administrative, and technical controls.

Table 18.1   THREATS TO COMPUTERIZED INFORMATION SYSTEMS

Hardware failure	Fire
Software failure	Electrical problems
Personnel actions	User errors
Terminal access penetration	Program changes
Theft of data, services, equipment	Telecommunications problems

• On-line information systems are even more difficult to control because data files can be accessed immediately and directly through computer terminals. Legitimate users may gain easy access to computer data that were previously not available to them. They may be able to scan records or entire files that they are not authorized to view. By obtaining valid users' logons and passwords, unauthorized individuals can also gain access to such systems. The chances of unauthorized access to or manipulation of data in on-line systems are considerably higher than in the batch environment. Figure 18.2 illustrates the vulnerabilities of on-line systems.

New Vulnerabilities

Advances in telecommunications and computer software have magnified these vulnerabilities. Through telecommunications networks, information systems in different locations can be interconnected. The potential for unauthorized access, abuse, or fraud is not limited to a single location but can occur at any access point in the network.

Additionally, more complex and diverse hardware, software, organizational, and personnel arrangements are required for telecommunications networks, creating new areas and opportunities for penetration and manipulation. Wireless networks using radio-based technology are even more vulnerable to penetration because radio frequency bands are easy to scan. The vulnerabilities of telecommunications networks are illustrated in Figure 18.3. Developing a workable system of controls for telecommunications networks is a complex and troubling problem.

Hacker: A person who gains unauthorized access to a computer network for profit, criminal mischief, or personal pleasure.

The efforts of "hackers" to penetrate computer networks have been widely publicized. A **hacker** is a person who gains unauthorized access to a computer network for profit, criminal mischief, or personal pleasure. The potential damage from intruders is frightening. In July 1992, a Federal grand jury in Manhattan indicted five computer hackers who belonged to a group called the Masters

Figure 18.2
Vulnerabilities of on-line systems. This figure illustrates that error, unauthorized access, and data destruction can occur at any point in the hardware and software of an on-line system. The areas of vulnerability include manual procedures, computer terminal hardware, line concentrators, front-end control processors, system software and applications programs, system and application files on disk, and tape files.

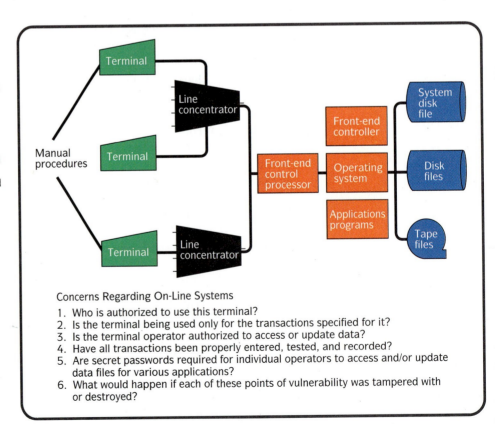

Concerns Regarding On-Line Systems

1. Who is authorized to use this terminal?
2. Is the terminal being used only for the transactions specified for it?
3. Is the terminal operator authorized to access or update data?
4. Have all transactions been properly entered, tested, and recorded?
5. Are secret passwords required for individual operators to access and/or update data files for various applications?
6. What would happen if each of these points of vulnerability was tampered with or destroyed?

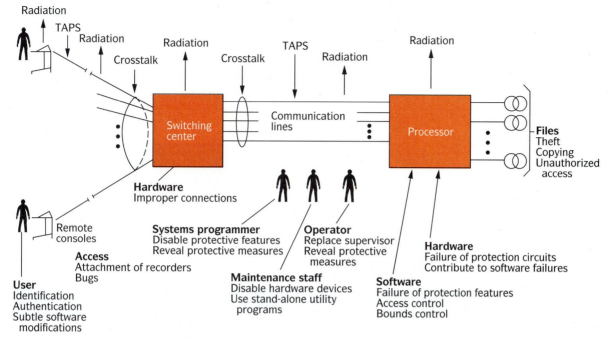

Figure 18.3

Telecommunication network vulnerabilities. Telecommunications networks are highly vulnerable to natural failure of hardware and software and to misuse by programmers, computer operators, maintenance staff, and end users. It is possible to "tap" communications lines and illegally intercept data. High-speed transmission over twisted wire communications channels causes interference called crosstalk. Radiation can disrupt a network at various points as well.

Computer virus: Rogue software programs that are difficult to detect and spread rapidly through computer systems, destroying data or disrupting processing and memory systems.

of Deception. They were charged with breaking into the information systems of three regional telephone companies, numerous credit bureaus, and BankAmerica Corporation, stealing telephone service and selling information on how to obtain credit reports.

Most recently, alarm has risen over hackers propagating **computer viruses,** rogue software programs that spread rampantly from system to system, clogging computer memory or destroying programs or data. The most notorious virus outbreak occurred in November 1988, when Robert Morris, a brilliant computer science student, introduced a program through a Cornell University terminal that spread uncontrollably throughout the Internet network, which ties together numerous other networks, including National Science Foundation Network [NSF Net] which links universities, research labs, and other institutions. Morris intended his program to reside quietly on Internet computers, but it echoed throughout the network in minutes, tying up computer memory and storage space as it copied and recopied itself hundreds of thousands of times.

The virus was quickly detected, but hundreds of computer centers in research institutions, universities, and military bases had to shut down. Estimates of the number of systems actually infected ranged from 6,000 to 250,000. A virus that was not intended to harm caused upwards of $100 million in lost machine time, lost access, and direct labor costs for recovery and cleanup.

In addition to spreading via computer networks, viruses can invade computerized information systems from "infected" diskettes from an outside source or through infected machines. The potential for massive damage and loss from future computer viruses remains. Figure 18.4 illustrates four stages of viral infection, each progressively more difficult and expensive to recover from.

Fears mounted about predictions of a Michelangelo virus that was scheduled to erupt on March 6, 1992 to destroy computer data on hard disks around the globe. The virus was so-named because its creator programmed it to come alive on Michelangelo's 517th birthday. Alarmists worried that hundreds of thousands of systems could be affected. Fortunately, when the dreaded day arrived,

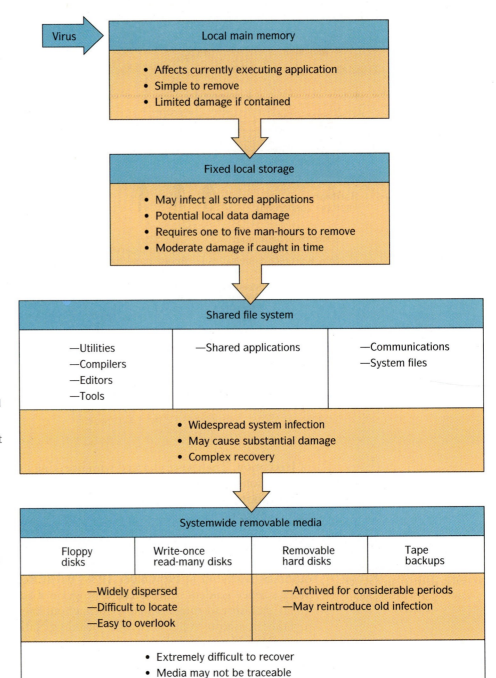

Figure 18.4

How bad is it? Four stages of viral infection. The degree of damage to a computer system can be assessed by the level of penetration of the virus. At the first stage, the virus is contained in local main memory; it then moves to the second stage, residing in fixed local storage. At this point the virus is still localized and damage would be moderate if the virus were detected and eradicated at this time. Once the virus self-replicates and infects the shared file system, complex recovery is required to restore any damage and to remove the virus. The fourth stage, infection of the systemwide removable media, is extremely difficult to recover and the probability of reinfection is very high. *Source: Computer Virus Industry Association. Adapted from John D. McAfee, "Managing the Virus Threat,"* Computerworld, *February 13, 1989. Copyright 1989 by CW Publishing Inc. Framingham, MA. 01701. Reprinted from* Computerworld.

Antivirus software: Software designed to detect and often eliminate computer viruses from an information system.

only a few hundred systems reported damage. Organizations were able to use antivirus software and screening procedures to reduce the chances of infection. **Antivirus software** is special software designed to check computer systems and disks for the presence of various computer viruses. Often the software can eliminate the virus from the infected area.

Advances in computer software have also increased the chances of information system misuse and abuse. Using fourth-generation languages, discussed in Chapter 7, end users can now perform programming functions that were formerly reserved for technical specialists. They can produce programs that inadvertently create errors, and they can manipulate the organization's data for illegitimate purposes. Chapter 20 contains a detailed discussion of computer crime and abuse.

The growth of database systems, where data are shared by multiple application areas, has also created new vulnerabilities. All data are stored in one common location, but many users may have the right to access and modify them. It may not be easy to identify who is using or possibly misusing the data in such circumstances. Since the data are used by more than one organizational unit, the effect of an error may reverberate throughout the organization. There may also be less chance of discovering errors. Each functional unit has less individual control over the data and has fewer grounds for knowing whether the computer is right.

Concerns for System Builders and Users

The heightened vulnerability of automated data has created special concerns for the builders and users of information systems. These concerns include disaster, security, and administrative error.

DISASTER   Computer hardware, programs, data files, and other equipment can be destroyed by fires, power failures, or other disasters. Such disasters can disrupt normal operations and even bring an entire organization to a standstill. It may take many years and millions of dollars to reconstruct destroyed data files and computer programs. If an organization needs them to function on a day-to-day basis, it will no longer be able to operate. This is why Visa USA Inc., for example, employs elaborate emergency backup facilities.

Visa USA Inc. has duplicate mainframes, duplicate network pathways, duplicate terminals, and duplicate power supplies. Visa even uses a duplicate data center in McLean, Virginia, to handle half of its transactions and to serve as an emergency backup to its primary data center in San Mateo, California.

Fault-tolerant computer systems contain extra hardware, software, and power supply components that can back the system up and keep it running to prevent system failure. Fault-tolerant computers contain extra memory chips, processors, and disk storage devices. (See the Window on Technology on page 644.) They can use special software routines or self-checking logic built into their circuitry to detect hardware failures and automatically switch to a backup device. Parts from these computers can be removed and repaired without disruption to the computer system.

Fault-tolerant technology is used by firms for critical applications with heavy on-line transaction processing requirements. In **on-line transaction processing,** transactions entered on-line are immediately processed by the computer. Multitudinous changes to databases, reporting, or requests for information occur each instant.

Rather than build their own backup facilities, many firms contract with disaster recovery firms, such as Comdisco Disaster Recovery Services in Rosemont, Illinois, and Sungard Recovery Services headquartered in Wayne, Pennsylvania. The chapter opening vignette showed how these disaster recovery firms provide "hot sites" housing spare computers at various locations around the country where subscribing firms can run their critical applications in an emergency. Disaster recovery firms also offer "cold sites," special buildings designed to house computer equipment; they do not contain computers, but they can be made operational in one week.

SECURITY   Security refers to the policies, procedures, and technical measures used to prevent unauthorized access or alteration, theft, and physical damage to record systems. Security can be promoted with an array of techniques and tools to safeguard computer hardware, software, communications networks, and data.

Fault-tolerant computer systems: Systems that contain extra hardware, software and power supply components that can back the system up and keep it running to prevent system failure.

On-line transaction processing: Transaction processing mode in which transactions entered on-line are immediately processed by the computer.

If the European Community is a unified economic area, it makes sense to have it use a single currency and a central bank. Anticipating a single European Currency Unit (ECU) and European Central Bank, European banks have selected fault-tolerant computer systems from Stratus Computer Inc. to run clearing systems for cross-border ECU transactions. Fault-tolerant computers contain one or more duplicates of every part and guarantee maximum downtime of no more than a few minutes a year.

The ECU, which derives its value from a basket of European currencies, was initially symbolic but is expected to be adopted by all members of the European Community. Banks need to ensure that payments in that currency can be cleared in the best way possible.

Any clearing system for a single European currency must be extremely efficient and reliable. Foreign exchange systems must be linked. The European Central Bank must be able to perform open market operations similar to the U.S. Federal Reserve System. In 1992, the ECU Banking Association, which represents 90 European banks, processed 40 billion ECUs a day. The clearing system cannot afford failure. There are

critical points in the day, especially toward the end of the day's trading cycle, when it needs to provide information back to other banks.

The Stratus systems, which are widely used in European trading rooms (more than 80 percent of London's stock market uses Stratus equipment), can support greatly increased transaction flows in critical on-line transaction processing environments. Stratus's fault-tolerant design is especially well-suited to financial number crunching. The machines are designed to keep working even when they break.

One director of a London investment bank observed that the Stratus hardware is very reliable, as is the vendor's customer assistance center. Stratus machines automatically interface with its customer assistance center so that there are diagnostics and alarms when things go wrong. Most of the components are backed up with duplicates. The system is modular, so that failure of one component will not spell disaster. If a unit fails, it does not take other modules down too. Faulty components are easily replaced. Built-in battery packs can support the system even during power failures. Stratus computers offer the high-risk financial

community an unmatched level of reliability.

Securities dealers use Stratus systems to alert the marketplace to prices and to process buy and sell orders. The system updates itself in real-time as trades are made, and it reports deals immediately to the London Stock Exchange. The system even calculates profit and relays details for back-office settlement in real time.

However, some dealers question Stratus's staying power as a major computer hardware vendor and the compatibility of new Stratus models with various versions of UNIX.

Source: Bob O'Connor, "Stratus Adopts European Accent," *InformationWEEK* (August 17, 1992).

To Think About: Why are fault-tolerant computers an appropriate technology for currency clearing systems? Can you suggest other applications that would benefit from fault-tolerant technology? What are the disadvantages of using the Stratus fault-tolerant computers for European currency clearing?

MANAGEMENT

Managing Network Security: The Enemy Within

Desktop data and LANs represent the weak link in many corporate security chains. As corporations move critical data from mainframes to distributed networked environments, LANs have become a major cost drain. Various estimates put losses from networked data abuse at close to $2 billion each year. The original security measures companies designed for their centralized mainframe computer systems may no longer fit. Securing networks has become a major management problem.

It is widely agreed that users, rather than new technology, pose the biggest threat to network security. Managers need to find ways to teach users sound security procedures and to ensure that users adhere to them. Most managers are more concerned about security breaches created by employees inside the firm than about penetration of networks by outsiders.

Jack Skalon, network administrator for University Hospital Consortium in Oak Brook, Illinois, combines commonsense policies with the security features built into the NetWare network operating system to monitor network users in

order to keep security tight among the organization's 115 users on 10 Novell file servers. Skalon scans the network four or five times a week to make sure all software is licensed and certified virus-free. The hospital keeps the computer room locked and off-limits to all but a few selected supervisors.

United Parcel Service scans its network drives for viruses each day and ties an information system audit into an annual accounting audit at all UPS sites. The firm checks to see that its security procedures are being followed at the same time it is measuring costs.

Hypobank in New York disables access to the floppy disk drive for all microcomputers throughout the bank. If a user tries to insert a disk into the off-limits drive, a product called Watchdog Director made by Fisher International Systems Corporation in Naples, Florida, flashes a warning message and creates an audit trail to identify who has been trying to load disks.

The trick is to be effective without costly overkill. Not every site or application requires bulletproof security unless it houses mission-

critical data. DHL Airways uses this enough-but-not-too-much approach to manage its LAN security. It sorts key financial data on a secure mainframe but is moving to distributed networked IBM RISC System/6000 workstations and plans to run a new accounting system on a networked IBM AS/400 minicomputer. IBM assured Michael Lanier, DHL's chief information officer, that it had security capabilities for such networks.

According to Robert Courtney, head of a LAN security consulting firm in Port Ewen, New York, the issue is accountability. If managers cannot hold people accountable for their actions, no amount of technology will help.

Sources: Joseph Maglitta and John P. Mello, Jr., "The Enemy Within," *Computerworld* (December 7, 1992), and Jon Pepper, "The Bigger the Network, the Scarier," *InformationWEEK* (September 7, 1992).

To Think About: One manager has said that information protection is technology and psychology? Do you agree? Why?

Security: Policies, procedures, and technical measures used to prevent unauthorized access, alteration, theft, or physical damage to information systems.

We have already discussed disaster protection measures. The Window on Management shows how management policies and procedures can make networks more secure. Other tools and techniques for promoting **security** will be described in subsequent sections.

ERRORS

Computers can also serve as instruments of error, severely disrupting or destroying an organization's recordkeeping and operations. Errors in automated systems can occur at many points in the processing cycle: through data entry, program error, computer operations, and hardware. Figure 18.5 illustrates all of the points in a typical processing cycle where errors can occur. Even minor mistakes in automated systems can have disastrous financial or operational repercussions. For instance, on February 25, 1991, during Operation Desert Storm, a Patriot missile defense system operating at Dharan, Saudi Arabia, failed to track and intercept an incoming Scud missile launched by Iraq. The failure was traced to a software error in the system's weapons control computer. The Scud hit an Army barracks, killing 28 Americans.

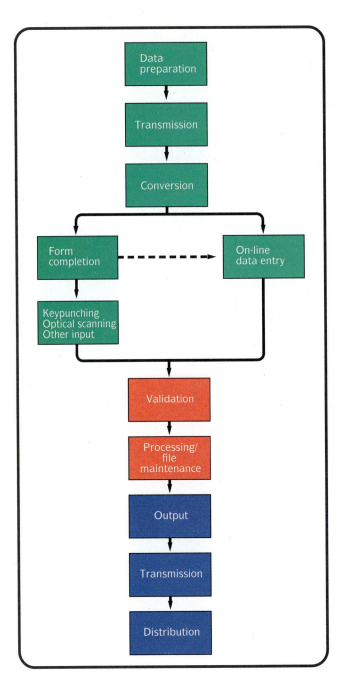

Figure 18.5
Points in the processing cycle where errors can occur. Each of the points illustrated in this figure represents a control point where special automated and/or manual procedures should be established to reduce the risk of errors during processing.

18.2 Controls

Controls: All of the methods, policies, and procedures that ensure protection of the organization's assets, accuracy and reliability of its records, and operational adherence to management standards.

To minimize errors, disaster, computer crime, and breaches of security, special policies and procedures must be incorporated into the design and implementation of information systems. The combination of manual and automated measures that safeguard information systems and ensure that they perform according to management standards is termed controls. **Controls** consist of all the methods, policies, and organizational procedures that ensure the safety of the organization's assets, the accuracy and reliability of its accounting records, and operational adherence to management standards.

In the past, the control of information systems was treated as an afterthought, addressed only toward the end of implementation, just before the system was installed. Today, however, organizations are so critically dependent on information systems that vulnerabilities and control issues must be identified as early as possible. The control of an information system must be an integral part of its design. Users and builders of systems must pay close attention to controls throughout the system's life span.

Computer systems are controlled by a combination of general controls and application controls.

General controls are those that control the design, security, and use of computer programs and the security of data files in general throughout the organization. On the whole, general controls apply to all computerized applications and consist of a combination of system software and manual procedures that create an overall control environment.

Application controls are specific controls unique to each computerized application, such as payroll, accounts receivable, and order processing. They consist of both controls applied from the user functional area of a particular system and from programmed procedures.

General controls: Overall controls that establish a framework for controlling the design, security, and use of computer systems throughout an organization.

Application controls: Specific controls unique to each computerized application.

General Controls

General controls are overall controls that ensure the effective operation of programmed procedures. They apply to all application areas. General controls include the following:

- Controls over the system implementation process.
- Software controls.
- Physical hardware controls.
- Computer operations controls.
- Data security controls.
- Administrative disciplines, standards, and procedures.

Table 18.2 ESSENTIAL USER AND TECHNICAL DOCUMENTATION FOR AN INFORMATION SYSTEM

Technical Documentation	User Documentation
System flowchart	Sample reports/output layouts
File layouts	Sample input forms/screens
Record layouts	Data preparation instructions
List of programs/modules	Data input instructions
Program structure charts	Instructions for using reports
Narrative program/module descriptions	Security profiles
Source program listings	Functional description of system
Module cross references	Work flows
Error conditions/actions	Error correction procedures
Abnormal termination	Accountabilities
Job setup requirements	Processing procedure narrative
Job run schedules	List/description of controls
Report/output distribution	Responsible user contact
Responsible programmer contact	
Job control language listings	
Backup/recovery procedures	
Run control procedures	
File access procedures	
Hardware/operating system requirements	

IMPLEMENTATION CONTROLS

Implementation controls: Audit of the systems development process at various points to make sure that it is properly controlled and managed.

Implementation controls audit the system development process at various points to ensure that it is properly controlled and managed. The system development audit should look for the presence of formal review points at various stages of development that enable users and management to approve or disapprove the implementation. (Examples of such review points are user and management sign-offs on the initial systems proposal, design specifications, conversion, testing, and the postimplementation audit described in Chapter 12.)

The system development audit should also examine the level of user involvement at each stage of implementation and check for the use of a formal cost/benefit methodology in establishing system feasibility. The audit should also look for the use of controls and quality assurance techniques for program development, conversion, and testing. (These issues are discussed in Chapters 11–13).

An important though frequently neglected requirement of systems building is appropriate documentation. Without good documentation that shows how a system operates from both a technical and a user standpoint, an information system may be difficult, if not impossible, to operate, maintain, or use. Table 18.2 lists the various pieces of documentation that are normally required to run and maintain an information system. The system development audit should look for system, user, and operations documentation that conforms to formal standards.

SOFTWARE CONTROLS

Software controls: Controls to ensure the security and reliability of software.

Controls are essential for the various categories of software used in computer systems. **Software controls** monitor the use of system software and prevent unauthorized access of software programs, system software, and computer programs.

System software controls govern the software for the operating system, which regulates and manages computer resources to facilitate execution of application programs. System software controls are also used for compilers, utility programs, reporting of operations, file setup and handling, and library recordkeeping. System software is an important control area because it performs overall control functions for the programs that directly process data and data files. **Program security controls** are designed to prevent unauthorized changes to programs in systems that are already in production.

Program security controls: Controls designed to prevent unauthorized changes to programs in systems that are already in production.

HARDWARE CONTROLS

Hardware controls: Controls to ensure the physical security and correct performance of computer hardware.

Hardware controls ensure that computer hardware is physically secure and check for equipment malfunction. Computer hardware should be physically secured so that it can be accessed only by authorized individuals. Access to rooms where computers operate should be restricted to computer operations personnel. Computer terminals in other areas or microcomputers can be kept in locked rooms. Computer equipment should be specially protected against fires and extremes of temperature and humidity. Organizations that are critically dependent on their computers must also make provisions for emergency backup in case of power failure.

Many kinds of computer hardware also contain mechanisms that check for equipment malfunction. Parity checks detect equipment malfunctions responsible for altering bits within bytes during processing. Validity checks monitor the structure of on-off bits within bytes to make sure that it is valid for the character set of a particular computer machine. Echo checks verify that a hardware device is performance ready. Chapter 6 discusses computer hardware in detail.

COMPUTER OPERATIONS CONTROLS

Computer operations controls: Procedures to ensure that programmed procedures are consistently and correctly applied to data storage and processing.

Computer operations controls apply to the work of the computer department and help ensure that programmed procedures are consistently and correctly applied to the storage and processing of data. They include controls over the setup of computer processing jobs, operations software and computer operations, and backup and recovery procedures for processing that ends abnormally.

Instructions for running computer jobs should be fully documented, reviewed, and approved by a responsible official. Controls over operations software in-

Sophisticated computer operations controls monitor the computer operations across the nation for this corporation.

clude manual procedures designed to both prevent and detect error. These include specified operating instructions for system software, restart and recovery procedures, procedures for the labeling and disposition of input and output magnetic tapes, and procedures for specific applications.

Human-operator errors at a computer system at the Shell Pipeline Corporation caused the firm to ship 93,000 barrels of crude oil to the wrong trader. This one error cost Shell $2 million. A computer operator at Exxon Corporation headquarters inadvertently erased valuable records about the 1989 grounding of the Exxon *Valdez* and the Alaskan oil spill that were stored on magnetic tape. Such errors could have been avoided had the companies incorporated tighter operational safeguards.

System software can maintain a system log detailing all activity during processing. This log can be printed for review so that hardware malfunction, abnormal endings, and operator actions can be investigated. Specific instructions for backup and recovery can be developed so that in the event of a hardware or software failure, the recovery process for production programs, system software, and data files does not create erroneous changes in the system.

DATA SECURITY CONTROLS

Data security controls:
Controls to ensure that data files on either disk or tape are not subject to unauthorized access, change, or destruction.

Data security controls ensure that data files on either disk or tape are not subject to unauthorized access, change, or destruction. Such controls are required for data files when they are in use and when they are being held for storage. It is easier to control data files in batch systems, since access is limited to operators who run the batch jobs. However, on-line and real-time systems are vulnerable at several points. They can be accessed through terminals as well as by operators during production runs.

When data can be input on-line through a terminal, entry of unauthorized input must be prevented. For example, a credit note could be altered to match a sales invoice on file. In such situations, security can be developed on several levels:

- Terminals can be physically restricted so that they are available only to authorized individuals.
- System software can include the use of passwords assigned only to authorized individuals. No one can log on to the system without a valid password.
- Additional sets of passwords and security restrictions can be developed for specific systems and applications. For example, data security software can

Figure 18.6
Security profiles for a personnel system. These two examples represent two security profiles or data security patterns that might be found in a personnel system. Depending upon the security profile, a user would have certain restrictions on access to various systems, locations, or data in an organization.

limit access to specific files, such as the files for the accounts receivable system. It can restrict the type of access so that only individuals authorized to update these specific files will have the ability to do so. All others will only be able to read the files or will be denied access altogether.

Systems that allow on-line inquiry and reporting must have data files secured. Figure 18.6 illustrates the security allowed for two sets of users of an on-line personnel database with sensitive information such as employees' salaries, benefits, and medical histories. One set of users consists of all employees who perform clerical functions such as inputting employee data into the system. All individuals with this type of profile can update the system but can neither read nor update sensitive fields such as salary, medical history, or earnings data. Another profile applies to a divisional manager, who cannot update the system but who can read all employee data fields for his or her division, including medical history and salary. These profiles would be established and maintained by a data security system. A multilayered data security system is essential for ensuring that this information can be accessed only by authorized persons. The data security system illustrated in Figure 18.6 provides very fine-grained security restrictions, such as allowing authorized personnel users to inquire about all employee information except in confidential fields such as salary or medical history.

Although the security risk of files maintained off-line is smaller, such data files on disk or tape can be removed for unauthorized purposes. These can be secured in lockable storage areas, with tight procedures so that they are released only for authorized processing. Usage logs and library records can be maintained for each removable storage device if it is labeled and assigned a unique identity number.

Administrative controls are formalized standards, rules, procedures, and control disciplines to ensure that the organization's controls are properly executed and enforced. The most important administrative controls are 1) segregation of functions, 2) written policies and procedures, and 3) supervision.

Segregation of functions is a fundamental principle of internal control in any organization. In essence, it means that job functions should be designed to minimize the risk of errors or fraudulent manipulation of the organization's assets. The individuals responsible for operating systems should not be the same ones who can initiate transactions that change the assets held in these systems. Responsibilities for input, processing, and output are usually divided among different people to restrict what each one can do with the system. For example, the individuals who operate the system should not have the authority to initiate payments or to sign checks. A typical arrangement is to have the organization's information systems department responsible for data and program files and end users responsible for initiating input transactions or correcting errors. Within the information systems department, the duties of programmers and analysts are segregated from those of computer equipment operators. (The organization of the information systems department is discussed in Chapter 4.)

Written policies and procedures establish formal standards for controlling information system operations. Procedures must be formalized in writing and authorized by the appropriate level of management. Accountabilities and responsibilities must be clearly specified.

Supervision of personnel involved in control procedures ensures that the controls for an information system are performing as intended. With supervision, weaknesses can be spotted, errors corrected, and deviations from standard procedures identified. Without adequate supervision, the best-designed set of controls may be bypassed, short-circuited, or neglected.

Weakness in each of these general controls can have a widespread effect on programmed procedures and data throughout the organization. Table 18.3 summarizes the effect of weaknesses in major general control areas.

Table 18.3 EFFECT OF WEAKNESS IN GENERAL CONTROLS

Weakness	Impact
Implementation controls	New systems or systems that have been modified will have errors or fail to function as required.
Software controls (program security)	Unauthorized changes can be made in processing. The organization may not be sure of which programs or systems have been changed.
Software controls (system software)	These controls may not have a direct effect on individual applications. Since other general controls depend heavily on system software, a weakness in this area impairs the other general controls.
Physical hardware controls	Hardware may have serious malfunctions or may break down altogether, introducing numerous errors or destroying computerized records.
Computer operations controls	Random errors may occur in a system. (Most processing will be correct, but occasionally it may not be.)
Data file security controls	Unauthorized changes can be made in data stored in computer systems or unauthorized individuals can access sensitive information.
Administrative controls	All of the other controls may not be properly executed or enforced.

Application Controls

Application controls are specific controls within each separate computer application, such as payroll or order processing. They include both automated and manual procedures that ensure that only authorized data are completely and accurately processed by that application. The controls for each application should take account of the whole sequence of processing, manual and computer, from the first steps taken to prepare transactions to the production and use of final output.

Not all of the application controls discussed here are used in every information system. Some systems require more of these controls than others, depending on the importance of the data and the nature of the application.

Application controls focus on the following objectives:

1. *Completeness of input and update.* All current transactions must reach the computer and be recorded on computer files.
2. *Accuracy of input and update.* Data must be accurately captured by the computer and correctly recorded on computer files.
3. *Validity.* Data must be authorized or otherwise checked with regard to the appropriateness of the transaction. (In other words, the transaction must reflect the right event in the external world. The validity of an address change, for example, refers to whether a transaction actually captured the right address for a specific individual.)
4. *Maintenance.* Data on computer files must continue to remain correct and current.

Application controls can be classified as 1) input controls, 2) processing controls, and 3) output controls.

INPUT CONTROLS

Input controls: Procedures to check data for accuracy and completeness when they enter the system, including input authorization, batch control totals, and edits.

Input authorization: Proper authorization, recording, and monitoring of source documents as they enter the computer system.

Data conversion: Process of properly transcribing data from one form into another form for computer transactions.

Batch control totals: A type of input control that requires counting transactions or any quantity field in a batch of transactions prior to processing for comparison and reconciliation after processing.

Input controls check data for accuracy and completeness when they enter the system. There are specific input controls for input authorization, data conversion, data editing, and error handling.

Input authorization. Input must be properly authorized, recorded, and monitored as source documents flow to the computer. For example, formal procedures can be set up to authorize only selected members of the sales department to prepare sales transactions for an order entry system. Sales input forms might be serially numbered, grouped into *batches,* and logged so that they can be tracked as they pass from sales units to the unit responsible for inputting them into the computer. The batches may require authorization signatures before they can be entered into the computer.

Data conversion. Input must be properly converted into computer transactions, with no errors as it is transcribed from one form to another. Transcription errors can be eliminated or reduced by keying input transactions directly into computer terminals from their source documents. (Point of sale systems can capture sales and inventory transactions directly by scanning product bar codes.)

Batch control totals are an extremely valuable technique in this area. They can be established beforehand for transactions grouped in batches. These totals can range from a simple document count to totals for quantity fields such as total sales amount (for the batch). Some applications write batch control totals on a separate batch control record. Computer programs then count the batch totals from transactions input and either compare them with the batch control record or print the totals. (If the totals are printed, they can be reconciled manually with the original batch totals.) Batches that do not balance are rejected. Figure 18.7 illustrates batch totaling.

On-line, real-time systems can also utilize batch controls by creating control totals to reconcile with hard copy documents that feed input or by assigning batch numbers to each on-line transaction that can be used for totaling automatically.

Batch totaling by computer. Transactions are manually grouped into batches, and a control total is established over each batch. The batch total can be a total document count, item count, or dollar amount. The batch total is calculated before processing and recorded on a special batch control record, which is input in addition to all of the transactions for that particular batch. The computer accumulates the batch total itself and compares it to the total input with the batch. If the totals do not agree, the computer rejects the batch and prints the details on the Out-of-Balance-Batches Report. If the totals agree, the batch is accepted for further processing and is recorded in the Batches-in-Balance-Report. Since the out-of-balance batches are held again in a separate file, they can be corrected and input again.

Edit checks: Routines performed to verify input data and correct errors prior to processing.

Edit checks. Various routines can be performed to edit input data for errors before they are processed. Transactions that do not meet edit criteria will be rejected. The edit routines can produce lists of errors to be corrected later. The most important types of edit techniques are summarized in Table 18.4.

An advantage of on-line, real-time systems is that editing can be performed up front. As each transaction is input and entered it can be edited, and the terminal operator can be notified immediately if an error is found. Alternatively, the operator may fail to correct the error on purpose or by accident. The system can be designed to reject additional input until the error is corrected or to print a hard-copy error list that can be reviewed by others.

PROCESSING CONTROLS

Processing controls: Routines for establishing that data are complete and accurate during processing.

Run control totals: Procedures for controlling completeness of computer updating by generating control totals that reconcile totals before and after processing.

Computer matching: Processing control that matches input data to information held on master files.

Processing controls establish that data are complete and accurate during updating. The major processing controls are run control totals, computer matching, and programmed edit checks.

Run control totals reconcile the input control totals with the totals of items that have updated the file. Updating can be controlled by generating control totals during processing. The totals, such as total transactions processed or totals for critical quantities, can be compared manually or by computer. Discrepancies are noted for investigation.

Computer matching matches the input data with information held on master or suspense files, with unmatched items noted for investigation. Most matching occurs during input, but under some circumstances it may be required to ensure completeness of updating. For example, a matching program might match employee time cards with a payroll master file and report missing or duplicate time cards.

Edit checks verify reasonableness or consistency of data. Most edit checking occurs at the time data are input. However, certain applications require some type of reasonableness or dependency check during updating as well. For example, consistency checks might be utilized by a utility company to compare a customer's electric bill with previous bills. If the bill was 500 percent higher this month compared to last month, the bill would not be processed until the meter was rechecked.

Table 18.4 IMPORTANT EDIT TECHNIQUES

Edit Technique	Description	Example
Reasonableness check	To be accepted, data must fall within certain limits set in advance, or they will be rejected.	If an order transaction is for 20,000 units and the largest order on record was 50 units, the transaction will be rejected.
Format checks	Characteristics of the contents (letter/digit), length, and sign of individual data fields are checked by the system.	A nine-position Social Security number should not contain any alphabetic characters.
Existence checks	The computer compares input reference data to tables or master files to make sure that valid codes are being used.	An employee can have a Fair Labor Standards Act code of only 1, 2, 3, 4, or 5. All other values for this field will be rejected.
Dependency checks	The computer checks whether a *logical* relationship is maintained between data for the *same* transaction. When it is not, the transaction is rejected.	A car loan initiation transaction should show a logical relationship between the size of the loan, the number of loan repayments, and the size of each installment.
Check digit	An extra reference number called a *check digit* follows an identification code and bears a mathematical relationship to the other digits. This extra digit is input with the data, recomputed by the computer, and the result compared with the one input.	See the check digit in Figure 18.8 for a product code using the Modulus 11 check digit system.

Figure 18.8
Check digit for a product code. This is a product code with the last position as a check digit, as developed by the Modulus 11 check digit system, the most common check digit method. The check digit is 7 and is derived by the steps listed in this figure. Errors in the transcription or transposition of this product code can be detected by a computer program that replicates the same procedure for deriving the check digit. If a data-entry person mistakenly keys in the product number as 29753, the program will read the first five digits and carry out the Modulus 11 process. It will derive a check digit of 4. When this is compared to the original check digit on the last position of the product code, the program will find that the check digits do not match and that an error has occurred.

Product Code:	2 9 7 4 3
Weight:	6 5 4 3 2
Multiply each product code number by weight:	12 45 28 12 6
Sum results:	12 + 45 + 28 + 12 + 6 = 103
Divide the sum by modulus:	103/11 = 9 with remainder of 4
Subtract remainder from modulus number to obtain check digit:	11 − 4 = 7
Add check digit to original product code to obtain new code:	297437

Output controls: Ensure that the results of computer processing are accurate, complete, and properly distributed.

Output controls ensure that the results of computer processing are accurate, complete, and properly distributed. Typical output controls include the following:

- Balancing output totals with input and processing totals.
- Reviews of the computer processing logs to determine that all of the correct computer jobs executed properly for processing.
- Audits of output reports to make sure that totals, formats, and critical details are correct and reconcilable with input.
- Formal procedures and documentation specifying authorized recipients of output reports, checks, or other critical documents.

Developing a Control Structure: Costs and Benefits

Information systems can make exhaustive use of all of the control mechanisms previously discussed. But they may be so expensive to build and so complicated to use that the system is economically or operationally unfeasible. Some cost/benefit analysis must be performed to determine which control mechanisms provide the most effective safeguards without sacrificing operational efficiency or cost.

One of the criteria that determine how much control is built into a system is the *importance of its data.* Major financial and accounting systems, for example, such as a payroll system or one that tracks purchases and sales on the stock exchange, must have higher standards of controls than a system to inventory employee training and skills or a "tickler" system to track dental patients and remind them that their six-month checkup is due.

Standing data: Data that are permanent and affect transactions flowing into and out of a system.

Standing data, the data that are permanent and that affect transactions flowing into and out of a system (e.g., codes for existing products or cost centers) require closer monitoring than individual transactions. A single error in transaction data will affect only that transaction, while a standing data error may affect many or all transactions each time the file is processed.

The cost effectiveness of controls will also be influenced by the efficiency, complexity, and expense of each control technique. For example, complete one-for-one checking may be time-consuming and operationally impossible for a system that processes hundreds of thousands of utilities payments daily. But it might be possible to use this technique to verify only critical data such as dollar amounts and account numbers, while ignoring names and addresses.

Risk assessment: Determining the potential frequency of occurrence of a problem and the potential damage if the problem were to occur. Used to determine the cost/benefit of a control.

A third consideration is the *level of risk* if a specific activity or process is not properly controlled. System builders can undertake a **risk assessment,** determining the likely frequency of a problem and the potential damage if it were to occur. For example, if an event is likely to occur no more than once a year, with a maximum of a $1000 loss to the organization, it would not be feasible to spend $20,000 on the design and maintenance of a control to protect against that event. However, if that same event could occur at least once a day, with a potential loss of over $300,000 a year, $100,000 spent on a control might be entirely appropriate.

Table 18.5 illustrates sample results of a risk assessment for an on-line order processing system that processes 30,000 orders per day. The probability of a power failure occurring in a one-year period is 30 percent. Loss of order transactions while power is down could range from $5000 to $200,000 for each occurrence, depending on how long processing was halted. The probability of embezzlement occurring over a yearly period is about 5 percent, with potential losses ranging from $1000 to $50,000 for each occurrence. User errors have a 98 percent chance of occurring over a yearly period, with losses ranging from $200 to $40,000 for each occurrence. The average loss for each event can be weighted by multiplying it by the probability of its occurrence annually to determine the expected annual loss. Once the risks have been assessed, system builders can

Table 18.5 ON-LINE ORDER PROCESSING RISK ASSESSMENT.

Exposure	Prob. of Occurr. (%)	Loss Range/ Average ($)	Expected Annual Loss ($)
Power failure	30	5000–200,000 (102,500)	30,750
Embezzlement	5	1000–50,000 (25,500)	1,275
User error	98	200–40,000 (20,100)	19,698

This chart shows the results of a risk assessment of three selected areas of an on-line order processing system. The likelihood of each exposure occurring over a 1-year period is expressed as a percentage. The next column shows the highest and lowest possible loss that could be expected each time the exposure occurred and an "average" loss calculated by adding the highest and lowest figures together and dividing by 2. The expected annual loss for each exposure can be determined by multiplying the "average" loss by its probability of occurrence.

concentrate on the control points with the greatest vulnerability and potential loss. In this case, controls should focus on ways to minimize the risk of power failures and user errors.

In some situations, organizations may not know the precise probability of threats occurring to their information systems, and they may not be able to quantify the impact of events that disrupt their information systems. In these instances, management may choose to describe risks and their likely impact in a qualitative manner (Rainer, Snyder, and Carr, 1991).

To decide which controls to use, information system builders must examine various control techniques in relation to each other and to their relative cost effectiveness. A control weakness at one point may be offset by a strong control at another. It may not be cost effective to build tight controls at every point in the processing cycle if the areas of greatest risk are secure or if compensating controls exist elsewhere. The combination of all of the controls developed for a particular application will determine its overall control structure.

18.3 Auditing Information Systems

Once controls have been established for an information system, how do we know that they are effective? To answer this question, organizations must conduct comprehensive and systematic *audits*. Large organizations have their own internal auditing group that is charged with this responsibility.

The Role of Auditing in the Control Process

MIS audit: Identifies all the controls that govern individual information systems and assesses their effectiveness.

An **MIS audit** identifies all of the controls that govern individual information systems and assesses their effectiveness. To accomplish this, the auditor must acquire a thorough understanding of operations, physical facilities, telecommunications, control systems, data security objectives, organizational structure, personnel, manual procedures, and individual applications.

The auditor should collect and analyze all of the material about a specific information system, such as user and system documentation, sample inputs and outputs, and relevant documentation about integrity controls. The auditor usually interviews key individuals who use and operate the system concerning their activities and procedures. Application controls, overall integrity controls, and control disciplines are examined. The auditor should trace the flow of sample transactions through the system and perform tests, using, if appropriate, automated audit software.

Function: Personal Loans _____
Location: Peoria, Ill. _____

Prepared by: _____ J. Ericson _____
Preparation date: __ June 16, 1993 _____

Received by: _____ T. Barrow _____
Review date: _____ June 28, 1993 _____

Nature of Weakness and Impact	Chance for Substantial Error		Effect on Audit Procedures	Notification to Management	
	Yes/ No	Justification	Required Amendment	Date of Report	Mangement Response
Loan repayment records are not reconciled to borrower's records during processing.	Yes	Without a detection control, errors in individual client balances may remain undetected.	Confirm a sample of loans.	5/10/93	Interest Rate Compare Report provides this control.
There are no regular audits of computer-generated data (interest charges).	Yes	Without a regular audit or reasonableness check, widespread miscalculations could result before errors are detected.		5/10/93	Periodic audits of loans will be instituted.
Programs can be put into production libraries to meet target deadlines without final approval from the Standards and Controls group.	No	All programs require management authorization. The Standards and Controls group controls access to all production systems, and assigns such cases to a temporary production status.			

Figure 18.9
Sample auditor's list of control weaknesses. This chart is a sample page from a list of control weaknesses that an auditor might find in a loan system in a local commercial bank. This form helps auditors record and evaluate control weaknesses and shows the result of discussing those weaknesses with management, as well as any corrective actions taken by management.

The audit lists and ranks all control weaknesses and estimates the probability of their occurrence. It then assesses the financial and organizational impact of each threat. Figure 18.9 is a sample auditor's listing of control weaknesses for a loan system. It includes a section for notifying management of such weaknesses and for management's response. Management is expected to devise a plan for countering significant weaknesses in controls.

Data Quality Audits

Data quality audit: Survey of files and samples of files for accuracy and completeness of data in an information system.

An important aspect of information system auditing is an analysis of data quality. **Data quality audits** are accomplished by the following methods:

* Surveying end users for their perceptions of data quality.
* Surveying entire data files.
* Surveying samples from data files.

This data quality auditor is analyzing the quality of data for a client by conducting a survey of the data files for accuracy in the information system.

ORGANIZATIONS
Bad Data Make Bad Business

Data that are inaccurate, untimely, or inconsistent with other sources of information create trouble for many organizations in a broad range of industries. Although several vendors offer data-quality tools for a variety of computers, most organizations do not fix the root causes of corrupted data. The same errors occur over and over again. When bad data go unnoticed, they can lead to bad decisions, product recalls, and even financial losses. Bad data make bad business.

The risk of bad data doing harm is compounded when the organization moves from a series of isolated databases to massive, distributed databases that all employees can access. The responsibility for maintaining the accuracy of the data becomes diffused. Poor quality data also surfaces when organizations update or replace older applications.

Data errors were common at Charles E. Smith Co., a property development and management company in Arlington, Virginia. But no one did anything about them until an audit showed that nearly every report issued by the company contradicted another internal report. For instance, entries in general ledger reports didn't match corresponding items in accounts receivable summary reports. No one could explain the discrepancies.

To make matters worse, Smith used incompatible systems, including a Digital Equipment Cor-

poration VAX minicomputer-based system, several outside service bureaus, and manual systems. It took information systems employees weeks to straighten out the mess. Smith finally made the necessary changes to keep its data clean. All departments now share a single integrated database that is stored on an IBM AS/400 minicomputer. Users access the data through local area networks. But Smith executives worry that inaccurate data will return because users control their own data with a PC network and because Smith is still trying to figure out how the errors occurred in the first place.

Geer DuBois, a New York advertising agency, lost a $25 million a year account after the agency's billing system failed to credit the client for a six-figure payment. Even though Geer DuBois repaid the client with interest, the client decided to use another advertising firm. A total of 21,000 bondholders of Prudential Securities unknowingly paid too much tax in 1989 and 1990 because Prudential's system miscalculated the amount they owed on their bonds. First Financial Management Corporation of Atlanta had to restate its earnings for the first nine months of the year because a subsidiary had lost track of some records after changing its accounting system.

Even though data errors are common, few organizations are addressing the problem because it is hard to pin down the costs of bad

data. Without cost figures, it is difficult to persuade top management to devote resources to correct data errors. Most firms have their employees manually inspect data and correct obvious errors, but that procedure does not correct whatever business process is the cause of bad data in the first place.

Trump's Casino needs up-to-date reliable mailing lists because it uses direct mail to keep in touch with its customers. The casino's marketing campaign also depends on an accurate summary of how much each customer spends playing each game. The casino used to have only two clerks process 50 customers an hour, an average of 800 to 900 customers per day. All of the customers were waited on in person. About 80 percent of the customer list was inaccurate. Trump then redesigned all of its customer screens on its IBM AS/400 customer billing system, to make the addition of new customers to its master customer database occur much faster and more accurately.

Source: Linda Wilson, "Devil in Your Data," *InformationWEEK* (August 31, 1992).

To Think About: Why is bad data such a problem for businesses? What organization, management, and technology factors are responsible for bad data? How can the problems described here be solved?

Unless regular data quality audits are undertaken, organizations have no way of knowing to what extent their information systems contain inaccurate, incomplete, or ambiguous information. Some organizations, such as the Social Security Administration, have established data quality audit procedures. These procedures control payment and process quality by auditing a 20,000-case sample of beneficiary records each month. The FBI, on the other hand, did not conduct a comprehensive audit of its record systems until 1984. With few data quality controls, the FBI criminal record systems were found to have serious problems.

Table 18.6 shows the kinds of record quality problems uncovered in a recent study of the FBI's computerized criminal record systems. A total of 54.1 percent of the records in the National Crime Information Center System were found to

Table 18.6

	NCIC-CCH	Ident Criminal-History Records
Arrests in sample	400	400
Positive verification	256	235
Response rate	64.0%	58.5%
Arrests not verifiable because		
Pending or sealed	6	19
No record locatable*	54	37
No prosecution of arrest	10	7
Fugitive	1	1
No arrest data	24	—
	95(37.1%)	64(27.2%)
Total arrest cases verified	161	171
Characteristics of verified arrest case		
1. No disposition reported	27.9%(45)	40.9%(70)
2. Incomplete record	0.6%(1)	2.3%(4)
3. Inaccurate record	16.8%(27)	10.5%(18)
4. Ambiguous record	2.5%(4)	6.4%(11)
5. Combined problems	6.2%(10)	14.1%(24)
Complete, accurate, and unambiguous	45.9%(74)	25.7%(44)
Total	100.0%(161)	100.0%(171)

*In situations of "no record locatable," this generally reflected a police disposition of the arrest; for example, the person was released prior to presenting to a district attorney. This was removed from further analysis even though it might have been included as a "no disposition recorded"; hence, estimates of record characteristics are conservative.

1. If *no disposition* was reported ("record blank"), the data analysis exempted the record from further consideration even though it might have other problems of accuracy and ambiguity. Estimates of these features are therefore conservative.
2. A record was *incomplete* if it failed to record conviction or correctional data.
3. A record was *inaccurate* if it incorrectly reflected the court records of disposition, charges, or sentence.
4. A record was *ambiguous* if it indicated more charges than dispositions, but did not specify charges of conviction; or if a record indicated more dispositions than charges; *or* if for a number of reasons the record was not interpretable (see text).
5. A record had *combined problems* if it indicated more than one of the four logically possible permutations of incompleteness, inaccuracy or ambiguity.

Source: Laudon, 1986a.

be inaccurate, ambiguous, or incomplete, and 74.3 percent of the records in the FBI's semi-automated Identification Division system exhibited significant quality problems. A summary analysis of the FBI's automated Wanted-Persons File also found that 11.2 percent of the warrants were invalid. A study by the FBI itself found that 6 percent of the warrants in state files were invalid and that 12,000 invalid warrants are sent out nationally each day.

The low levels of data quality in these systems have disturbing implications.

- More than 14,000 persons are at risk of being falsely detained and perhaps arrested because of invalid warrants.
- In addition to their use in law enforcement, computerized criminal history records are increasingly being used to screen employees in both the public and private sectors. This is the fastest growing use of these records in some states. Many of these records are incomplete and show arrests but no court disposition; that is, they show charges without proof of conviction or guilt. Many individuals may be denied employment unjustifiably because these records overstate their criminality.

These criminal record systems are not limited to violent felons. They contain the records of 36 million people, about one-third of the labor force. Inaccurate and potentially damaging information is being maintained on many law-abiding citizens.

The level of data quality in these systems threatens citizens' constitutional right to due process and impairs the efficiency and effectiveness of any law enforcement programs in which these records are used (Laudon, 1986a).

The Window on Organizations on page 658 describes how poor data quality can create serious operational and financial problems for businesses.

Management Challenges

1. **Controlling large distributed multi-user networks.** No system is totally secure, but large distributed multi-user networks are especially difficult to secure. Security becomes more problematic when networks are no longer confined to individual departments or groups or to centralized mainframe systems. It is very difficult to assert companywide control over networks using heterogeneous hardware, software, and communications components when thousands of workers can access networks from many remote locations.

2. **Subjectivity of risk analysis.** Risk analysis depends on assumptions. For instance, the flawed Patriot missile system described earlier in this chapter was originally designed to work under a much less stringent environment than that in which it was actually used during Operation Desert Storm. Subsequent analyses of its effectiveness were downgraded from 95 percent to 13 percent (Neumann, 1993). Since risks are only potential events, not certainties, they are often either overestimated or underestimated. Measures to avoid risk can also be used to stifle innovation or change.

3. **Designing systems that are neither overcontrolled nor undercontrolled.** The biggest threat to information systems is posed by authorized users, not outside intruders. Most security breaches and damage to information systems come from organizational insiders. If there are too many passwords and authorizations required to access an information system, the system will go unused. Controls that are effective but that do not prevent authorized individuals from using a system are difficult to design.

Summary

Show why automated information systems are so vulnerable to destruction, error, and abuse.

Organizations have become so dependent on computerized information systems that they must take special measures to ensure that these systems are properly controlled. With data easily concentrated into electronic form and many procedures invisible through automation, systems are vulnerable to destruction, misuse, error, fraud, and hardware or software failures. The effect of disaster in a computerized system can be greater than in manual systems because all of the records for a particular function or organization can be destroyed or lost. On-line systems and those utilizing telecommunications are especially vulnerable because data and files can be immediately and directly accessed through computer terminals or at many points in the telecommunications network. Computer "viruses" can spread rampantly from system to system, clogging computer memory or destroying programs and data.

Describe the role of controls in safeguarding information systems.

Controls consist of all the methods, policies, and organizational procedures that ensure the safety of the organization's assets, the accuracy and reliability of its accounting records, and adherence to management standards. For computerized information systems, controls consist of both manual and programmed procedures. Controls that safeguard information system security are especially important in today's on-line networked environment.

Distinguish between general controls and application controls.

There are two main categories of controls: general controls and application controls. General controls control the overall design, security, and use of computer programs and files for the organization as a whole. They include physical hardware controls; system software controls; data file security controls; computer operations controls; controls over the system implementation process; and administrative disciplines.

Application controls are controls unique to specific computerized applications. They focus on the completeness and accuracy of input, updating and maintenance, and the validity of the information in the system. Application controls consist of 1) input controls, 2) processing controls, and 3) output controls.

Describe the most important techniques for controlling information systems.

Some of the principal application control techniques are programmed routines to edit data before they are input or updated; run control totals; and reconcile input source documents with output reports.

Identify the factors that must be considered when developing the controls for information systems.

To determine what controls are required, designers and users of systems must identify all of the control points and control weaknesses and perform risk assessment. They must also perform a cost/benefit analysis of controls and design controls that can effectively safeguard systems without making them unusable.

Explain the importance of auditing information systems.

Comprehensive and systematic MIS auditing can help organizations to determine the effectiveness of the controls in their information systems. Regular data quality audits should be conducted to help organizations ensure a high level of completeness and accuracy of the data stored in their systems.

Key Terms

Hacker	Administrative controls
Computer virus	Segregation of functions
Antivirus software	Input controls
Fault-tolerant computer systems	Input authorization
On-line transaction processing	Data conversion
Security	Batch control totals
Controls	Edit checks
General controls	Processing controls
Application controls	Run control totals
Implementation controls	Computer matching
Software controls	Output controls
Program security controls	Standing data
Hardware controls	Risk assessment
Computer operations controls	MIS audit
Data security controls	Data quality audit

Review Questions

1. Why are computer systems more vulnerable than manual systems to destruction, fraud, error, and misuse? Name some of the key areas where systems are most vulnerable.

2. Name some features of on-line information systems that make them difficult to control.

3. What are fault-tolerant computer systems? When should they be used?

4. What are controls? What distinguishes controls in computerized systems from controls in manual systems?

5. What is the difference between general controls and application controls?

6. Name and describe the principal general controls for computerized systems.

7. Describe how each of the following serve as application controls: batching, edits, computer matching, run control totals.

8. What kinds of edit techniques can be built into computer programs?

9. How does MIS auditing enhance the control process?

10. What is the function of risk assessment?

11. Why are data quality audits essential?

12. What is security? List and describe controls that promote security for computer hardware, computer networks, computer software, and computerized data.

Discussion Questions

1. It has been said that controls and security should be one of the first areas to be addressed by information system designers. Discuss.

2. The Young Professional Quarterly magazine publishing company receives thousands of subscription orders by mail each day. A document is created for each order. The order documents are batched in groups of thirty to fifty, and a header form is completed showing the total number of documents per batch. The documents are then keyed and verified by separate data entry clerks and processed each night. An edit/validation program rechecks the number of units in each batch. It prints valid and invalid batch reports and posts valid batches to a valid transaction file. The valid transaction file is fed to a series of programs that update Young Professional Quarterly's inventory, produce sales invoices, and feed the accounts receivable system. The Valid Batch Report is reconciled to the totals on the batch headers. Batches listed in the Invalid Batch Report are reviewed, corrected, and resubmitted.

   List and discuss the control weaknesses in this system and their impact. What corrective measures would you suggest?

3. Suppose you were asked to help design the controls for an information system. What pieces of information would you need?

4. Many organizations, such as Visa USA, cited earlier in this chapter, take elaborate precautions for backing up their computer systems. Why is this essential? What considerations must be addressed by a backup plan?

Group Project

Form a group with two or three other students. Write a description of the general and application controls that should be used for the information system you designed for your systems analysis and design project in Chapter 13. What are the most important controls for these systems? Alternatively you could describe the controls that might be used for one of the systems described in the Window on boxes or chapter-ending cases in this text (the Stride Rite system in Chapter 1, the Travellers claims review and CSX systems in Chapter 2, or the Credit Agricole system in Chapter 8 could be analyzed). Present your findings to the class.

CASE STUDY

Protecting National Security Information at the Drug Enforcement Administration

The Drug Enforcement Administration was established in 1973 under the Department of Justice to enforce laws and regulations relating to the use and distribution of legal and illegal drugs. The agency consists of 7000 agents and other employees with domestic and foreign offices located worldwide. DEA uses information systems to process highly sensitive and national security information collected from a variety of sources. Such information includes detailed data on known or suspected drug violators and informants and data on domestic and international drug operations.

The DEA maintains some of this data on paper and some in computerized form. It is putting less emphasis on improving arrest and seizure statistics and more on systematically analyzing drug trafficking organizations to pinpoint efforts more effectively. It replaced outdated equipment in its 19 divisions with 2000 high-speed Unisys workstations, linking all its divisions to a central database.

Executive Order 12356, dated April 2, 1982, requires federal agencies to establish controls to ensure that classified information is protected and guarded from unauthorized access. Justice Department policy requires its component agencies, including DEA, to ensure that adequate security safeguards are in place for its computer systems and to identify those systems that process classified data.

In February 1991, DEA informed the Justice Department that it had an inventory of computers that process classified information. The inventory was based on a survey conducted by the Office of Security Programs. The General Accounting Office found that this inventory did not include computers that DEA headquarters and its Division B use to process classified data because headquarters offices were never surveyed and Division B did not respond to requests for this information. DEA's Division A did not report any classified computer systems either in response to the Office of Security Programs survey. The GAO also found Division A personnel using computers to process classified information.

In accordance with federal guidelines, Justice Department policy requires that computer systems processing classified information be approved by the Department Security Officer and have the necessary security safeguards in place, including security safeguards for protecting classified data transmitted on networks. GAO observed many instances where DEA headquarters and division personnel were using DEA's Office Automation system routinely to process classified data. This system had not been approved for processing national security information and DEA had not completed a risk analysis of the system.

DEA began installing the Office Automation system in 1987. DEA's Office Automation workstations were operated in open, unshielded work areas and used fixed-disk storage devices. Federal guidelines discourage the use of this equipment because information may be inadvertently stored on the computer's fixed disk and be vulnerable to retrieval by unauthorized persons. The guidelines recommend computer equipment with removable storage media only for processing classified information in open areas. (The U.S. Attorney's Office in Lexington, Kentucky, made headlines when it sold surplus Department of Justice computer equipment containing sensitive grand jury material and information on confidential informants in 1991.)

The equipment was not TEMPEST-protected. TEMPEST is a technology that shields computer equipment to keep electromagnetic emissions from being intercepted and deciphered by eavesdroppers. The workstations were connected by data communications lines that were not encrypted. The Office Automation network allowed individuals working on workstations in one office to access data stored in workstations located elsewhere and used by others. Any DEA employee could use the system to obtain classified data stored in another employee's workstation without that employee's knowledge. Employees of the original equipment vendor had access to Office Automation workstations because the vendor-issued system passwords had never been changed.

GAO studied DEA's procedures for controlling access to areas where computer equipment is used. Table 18.7 summarizes the results of GAO's analysis of physical security at DEA.

Another problem was found at headquarters and the two division offices. There, contract cleaning and maintenance personnel (who do not have national security clearances) were allowed to work unescorted in areas where computers process national security information. Janitorial staff were permitted to work alone in these areas before and after regular business hours. Computers in each of these offices were often left signed on and unattended. Electric card-key devices on doors to areas that contain national security information are turned off during normal working hours. The doors are left open. Division security staff were

Table 18.7 PHYSICAL SECURITY WEAKNESSES AT DEA HEADQUARTERS AND DIVISIONS

	DEA Headquarters	Division A	Division B
Inadequately controlled access to sensitive areas	X	X	X
Individuals without national security clearances working unescorted in sensitive areas	X	X	X
Unattended computers left signed on[a]	X	X	X
Computer-generated materials left unattended and unsecured		X	X
Documents left unattended and unsecured	X	X	X
Safes left open and unattended	X	X	

[a]A computer operational state allowing a user to access data files and retrieve information.

not reviewing card-key access logs to see who was entering these areas after normal working hours. The GAO found that one card-key that was reported lost was still active. Individual card-keys with the same access codes had been issued to groups of individuals, including non-DEA employees. DEA employees did not wear security badges.

The GAO found that Division B had not changed the locks to its division offices since their installation in 1985. DEA and task force employees reported 17 instances in which their keys were either lost or stolen, including master keys to all areas where computers process national security information and where employees regularly collect, analyze, and store this information. An employee reported the loss of office keys on a key chain marked with the initials DEA. The Division Security Office informed GAO that the locks were being rekeyed and that Division B is being relocated to a new space that has a card-key system.

At both DEA divisions the GAO found that floppy diskettes labeled as containing classified information were routinely left unattended in open and unprotected mail trays. Anyone could access these trays. The GAO observed several instances at DEA headquarters where documents labeled as classified were left unsecured in areas where cleaning personnel were working. In one, documents marked classified were left out on a desk next to a window on the first floor. After notifying a DEA employee that the documents were classified, GAO investigators returned five minutes later and found that the documents were still unattended. In another instance, GAO investigators found a classified document lying unattended in the machine tray of a facsimile machine located in an open mail room where non-DEA personnel work regularly. GAO investigators found many instances at DEA headquarters and division offices where documents labeled classified were left unattended in open cubicles and unlocked offices. They observed open and unattended safes that DEA personnel said contained national security information.

Examining another major DEA field location, a Department of Justice review team found that 1) DEA personnel were processing and storing national security information on unapproved and unprotected computer equipment; 2) communications lines connecting remote workstations were not safeguarded to meet national security requirements; 3) individuals with access to sensitive areas did not have proper security clearances; and 4) access to the Sensitive Compartmented Information Facility that houses highly classified information was not properly controlled.

DEA officials said they knew of no instance where classified information was compromised.

Sources: United States General Accounting Office, ''Computer Security: DEA Is Not Adequately Protecting National Security Information,'' GAO/IMTEC-92-31 (February 1992), and Jason Forsythe, ''New Weapons in Drug Wars,'' *InformationWEEK* (July 16, 1990).

Case Study Questions

1. Write an analysis of the control weaknesses in DEA systems.
2. What are the possible consequences of these control weaknesses?
3. What management, organization and technology factors were responsible for these weaknesses?
4. What recommendations would you make to correct these weaknesses?

References Borning, Alan. "Computer System Reliability and Nuclear War." *Communications of the ACM* 30, no. 2 (February 1987).

Boockholdt, J. L. "Implementing Security and Integrity in Micro-Mainframe Networks." *MIS Quarterly* 13, no. 2 (June 1989).

Buss, Martin D. J., and Lynn M. Salerno. "Common Sense and Computer Security." *Harvard Business Review* (March–April 1984).

Charette, Ron, "Inside RISKS: Risks with Risk Analysis." *Communications of the ACM* 34, no. 5 (June 1991).

Chaum, David. "Security Without Identification: Transaction Systems to Make Big Brother Obsolete." *Communications of the ACM* 28 (October 1985).

Halper, Stanley D., Glenn C. Davis, Jarlath P. O'Neill-Dunne, and Pamela R. Pfau. *Handbook of EDP Auditing*. Boston: Warren, Gorham and Lamont, 1985.

Hoffman, Lance. *Rogue Programs*. New York: Van Nostrand Reinhold, 1990.

"Information Security and Privacy." *EDP Analyzer* (February 1986).

Kahane, Yehuda, Seev Neumann, and Charles S. Tapiero. "Computer Backup Pools, Disaster Recovery, and Default Risk." *Communications of the ACM* 31, no. 1 (January 1988).

King, Julia. "It's C.Y.A. Time." *Computerworld* (March 30, 1992).

Laudon, Kenneth C. "Data Quality and Due Process in Large Interorganizational Record Systems." *Communications of the ACM* 29 (January 1986a).

Laudon, Kenneth C. *Dossier Society: Value Choices in the Design of National Information Systems.* New York: Columbia University Press, 1986b.

Littlewood, Bev and Lorenzo Strigini, "The Risks of Software." *Scientific American,* 267, no. 5 (November 1992).

Loch, Karen D., Houston H. Carr, and Merrill E. Warkentin. "Threats to Information Systems: Today's Reality, Yesterday's Understanding." *MIS Quarterly* 16, no. 2 (June 1992).

Maglitta, Joe, and John P. Mello, Jr. "The Enemy Within." *Computerworld* (December 7, 1992).

Neumann, Peter G., "Risks Considered Global(ly)." *Communications of the ACM* 35, no. 1 (January 1993).

Perrow, Charles. *Normal Accidents.* New York: Basic Books, 1984.

Rainer, Rex Kelley, Jr., Charles A. Snyder, and Houston H. Carr. "Risk Analysis for Information Technology." *Journal of Management Information Systems* 8, no. 1 (Summer 1991).

Post, Gerald V., and J. David Diltz. "A Stochastic Dominance Approach to Risk Analysis of Computer Systems." *MIS Quarterly* (December 1986).

Straub, Detmar W. "Controlling Computer Abuse: An Empirical Study of Effective Security Countermeasures." Curtis L. Carlson School of Management, University of Minnesota (July 20, 1987).

Tate, Paul. "Risk! The Third Factor." *Datamation* (April 15, 1988).

Thyfault, Mary E., and Stephanie Stahl. "Weak Links." *InformationWEEK* (August 10, 1992).

United States General Accounting Office. "Computer Security: DEA Is Not Adequately Protecting National Security Information." *GAO/IMTEC-92-31* (February 1992).

United States General Accounting Office. "Computer Security: Virus Highlights Need for Improved Internet Management." *GAO/IMTEC-89-57* (June 1989).

United States General Accounting Office. "Patriot Missile Defense: Software Problem Led to System Failure at Dharan, Saudi Arabia." *GAO/IMTEC-92-26* (February 1992).

Weber, Ron. *EDP Auditing: Conceptual Foundations and Practice.* 2nd ed. New York: McGraw-Hill, 1988.

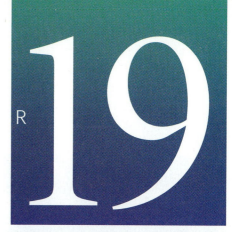

CHAPTER

19

Managing International Information Systems

DuPont's New Chemistry for International Business

In 1903, E. I. DuPont de Nemours & Co., shook up the business world when it launched an innovative approach to centralized management. Now, in order to remain globally competitive, it is shaking up its organizational chemistry again.

DuPont is a $40 billion conglomerate with five principal business segments producing chemicals, fibers, gasoline, polymers, and specialties such as agricultural and electronics products. More than 40 percent of DuPont's sales come from the oil company, Conoco. DuPont is under serious challenge from competitors overseas. For instance, former buyers of DuPont nylon in China are now likely to produce the nylon themselves. DuPont is responding by shedding businesses and products that are either unprofitable or that do not fit well with its strategic mix. It is also restructuring its organization, moving toward a nonhierarchical team-based management style that it believes is more appropriate for a far-flung global company.

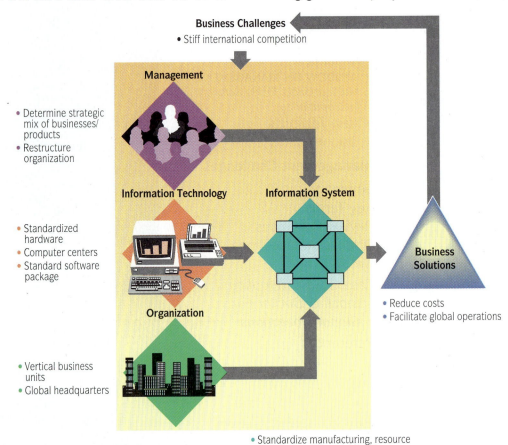

Part of this restructuring consists of converting Du-Pont's global information systems to a set of common standards, hardware and software platforms, and vendors. DuPont cut down on redundant systems, seeing no competitive advantage in having separate information systems for entering an order, managing inventory, or paying a bill in each of its vertical business units. It reduced the number of computer centers housing Digital Equipment Corporation VAX minicomputers from 150 to 75. These computer centers help control plant production and operate distribution centers. DuPont also cut its hardware vendors from 100 to a dozen, making DEC, IBM, and Apple Computer Corporation its primary suppliers.

DuPont installed an application software package from SAP America, the U.S. unit of SAP A.G., the German software firm, to provide standard software for manufacturing resource planning and financial applications that could be used by its various business units. The software can accommodate differences in language, currency, and accounting practices. DuPont believes that all of these measures not only reduce costs but support its global operations.

Source: Chuck Appleby, "The Teflon Company," *InformationWEEK* (December 21, 1992).

DuPont is one of many business firms that are moving toward global forms of organization that transcend national boundaries. But DuPont could not make this move unless it restructured itself and reorganized its information systems. DuPont switched to a less centralized organizational structure, consolidated its computer centers, streamlined its computer hardware, and standardized some of its information systems so that the same system could be used by disparate business units in different countries.

The changes DuPont made are some of the changes in international information infrastructures—the basic systems needed to coordinate worldwide trade and other activities—that organizations need to consider if they want to operate across the globe. Information technology is both a powerful driver of the movement toward international business, and a powerful servant. This chapter explores how to organize, manage, and control the development of international information systems.

After completing this chapter you will be able to:

- Identify the major factors behind the growing internationalization of business.
- Choose among several global strategies for developing business.
- Understand how information systems support different global strategies.

- Manage the development of international systems.
- Understand the main technical alternatives in developing global systems.

19.1 The Growth of International Information Systems

We have already described two powerful worldwide changes driven by advances in information technology that have transformed the business environment and posed new challenges for management. One is the transformation of industrial economies and societies into knowledge- and information-based economies. The other is the emergence of a global economy and global world order.

The precise outlines of the new global world order are unclear but the general dimensions and features are unmistakable. The goal from the American point of view is to become the world's leading supplier of sophisticated products, high valued-added services, and new useful knowledge, designs, and ideas. In this pursuit, the United States is in direct competition with Western Europe and Japan, to be joined by China, and a resurgent middle Europe in the middle of the twenty-first century. The new world order will sweep away national corporations, national industries, and national economies controlled by domestic politicians. Many of the Fortune 500, the 500 largest U.S. corporations, will disappear in the next 50 years, mirroring past behavior of large firms since 1900. Except for a few nimble survivors, most of these dinosaurs will be replaced by fast-moving net-worked corporations that transcend national boundaries. It is vital that you as

Figure 19.1
International information systems infrastructure. The major dimensions for developing an international information systems infrastructure are the global environment, the corporate global strategies, the structure of the organization, the management and business procedures, and the technology platform.

Global Environment:
Business Drivers & Challenges

Corporate Global Strategies

Organization Structure

Management & Business Procedures

Technology Platform

International Information Systems Infrastructure

future managers understand the forces moving us toward this new world order, and learn how to control this new empire.

In 1970 only 5 percent of the manufactured goods sold in the United States were imported and 30 percent of the labor force worked in manufacturing. Today, about 21 percent of the manufactured goods sold in the country are imported and only about 17 percent of the labor force works in manufacturing.[1] A similar story can be told about Europe and Japan: The growth of international trade has radically altered domestic economies around the globe. About $1 trillion worth of goods, services, and financial instruments—one fifth of the annual U.S. Gross National Product—changes hands each day in global trade.

Consider the laptop computer as an example. The CPU is likely to have been designed and built in the United States; the DRAM (or dynamic random access memory, which makes up the majority of primary storage in a computer) was designed in the United States but built in Malaysia; the screen was designed and assembled in Japan using American patents, the keyboard is from Taiwan, and finally assembly was in Japan where the case was also made. Management of the project was located in Silicon Valley along with marketing, sales, and finance that coordinated all the myriad activities from financing and production to shipping and sales efforts. None of this would be possible without powerful international information and telecommunication systems, an international information systems infrastructure.

For today's manager this means that in order to compete effectively you will need a global perspective on business and the support systems needed to conduct business on an international scale.

Developing the International Information Systems Infrastructure

International information systems infrastructure: The basic information systems required by organizations to coordinate worldwide trade and other activities.

This chapter describes how to go about building an international information systems infrastructure suitable for your international strategy. An infrastructure is the constellation of facilities and services, such as highways or telecommunications networks, required for organizations to function and prosper. An **international information systems infrastructure** consists of the basic information systems required by organizations to coordinate worldwide trade and other activities. As we noted in Chapter 1, a firm will not be able to achieve its goals and strategies without appropriate information systems. Figure 19.1 illustrates the reasoning we will follow throughout the chapter, and depicts the major dimensions of an international information systems infrastructure.

Business driver: A force in the environment to which businesses must respond and that influences the direction of business.

The basic strategy to follow when building an international system is first to understand the global environment in which your firm is operating. This means understanding the overall market forces or *business drivers* that are pushing your industry toward a global competition. A **business driver** is a force in the environment to which businesses must respond and that influences the direction of the business. Likewise, examine carefully the inhibitors or negative factors that create *management challenges*—factors that could scuttle the development of a global business. Once you have examined the global environment, you will need to consider a *corporate strategy for competing in that environment.* How will your firm respond? You could ignore the global market and focus on domestic competition only, sell to the globe from a domestic base, or organize production and distribution around the globe. There are many in-between choices.

Once you have developed a strategy, it is time to consider *how to structure your organization* so it can pursue the strategy. How will you accomplish a division of labor across a global environment? Where will production, administration, accounting, marketing and human resource functions be located? Who will handle the systems function?

[1]See *Statistical Abstract of the United States,* Tables No. 1409 and 1301.

Once you have designed an international organization, you will have to consider the management issues in implementing your strategy and making the organization design come alive. Key here will be the design of business procedures. How can you discover and manage user requirements? How can you induce change in local units to conform to international requirements? How can you re-engineer on a global scale, and how can you coordinate systems development?

The last issue to consider is the technology platform. Although changing technology is a key driving factor leading toward global markets, you need to have a corporate strategy and structure before you can rationally choose the right technology.

Once you have completed this process of reasoning you will be well on your way toward an appropriate international information infrastructure capable of achieving your corporate goals. Let us begin by looking at the overall global environment.

The Global Environment: Business Drivers and Challenges

Table 19.1 illustrates the business drivers in the global environment that are leading all industries toward global markets and competition.

The global business drivers can be divided into two groups: general cultural factors and specific business factors. There are five easily recognized general cultural factors driving internationalization since World War II. Information, communication, and transportation technologies have created a *global village* in which communication (by telephone, television, radio, or computer network) around the globe is no more difficult and not much more expensive than communication down the block. Moving goods and services to and from geographically dispersed locations has fallen dramatically in cost.

Global culture: The development of common expectations, shared artifacts, and social norms among different cultures and peoples.

The development of global communications has created a global village in a second sense: there is now a **global culture** created by television and other globally shared media like movies which permits different cultures and peoples to develop common expectations about right and wrong, desirable and undesirable, heroic and cowardly. A shared culture, with shared cultural artifacts like news programs and movies permits the emergence of shared *societal norms* concerning proper attire, proper consumption, good and bad government. These cultural and societal sentiments are bolstered by a prolonged period of *political stability* on a global scale not seen in the modern age. The collapse of the Eastern bloc has speeded up enormously the growth of a world culture, increased support for capitalism and business, and reduced the level of cultural conflict considerably.

A last factor to consider is the growth of a *global knowledge base*. At the end of World War II, knowledge, education, science, and industrial skills were highly

Table 19.1	THE GLOBAL BUSINESS DRIVERS

General Cultural Factors

Global communication and transportation technologies

Development of "global culture"

Emergence of global social norms

Political stability

Global knowledge base

Specific Business Factors

Global markets

Global production and operations

Global coordination

Global economies of scale

The universally recognizable McDonald's menu offers Russian diners a full selection of burgers, fries, and drinks. McDonald's patrons in Japan will find the same choices available to them in Japanese. The golden arches translate across all languages and cultures.

concentrated in North America, Europe, and Japan, with the rest of the world euphemistically called the "Third World." This is no longer true. Latin America, China, Southern Asia, and Eastern Europe have developed powerful educational, industrial, and scientific centers, resulting in a much more democratically and widely dispersed knowledge base.

These general cultural factors leading toward internationalization result in four specific business globalization factors that affect most industries. The growth of powerful communications technologies and the emergence of world cultures creates the condition for *global markets*—global consumers interested in consuming similar products that are "culturally" approved. Coca-Cola, American tennis shoes (made in Korea but designed in Los Angeles), and Dallas (a TV show) can now all be sold in Latin America, Africa, and Asia.

Responding to this demand, *global production and operation* has emerged with precise on-line coordination between far-flung production facilities and central headquarters thousands of miles away. At Sealand Transportation, a major global shipping company based in Newark, New Jersey, shipping managers in Newark can watch the loading of ships in Rotterdam on-line, check trim and ballast, and trace packages to specific ship locations as the activity proceeds. This is all possible through an international satellite link.

The new global markets and pressure toward global production and operation have called forth whole new capabilities for *global coordination* of all factors of production. Not just production, but also accounting, marketing and sales, human resources, and systems development (all the major business functions) can now be coordinated on a global scale. Frito Lay, for instance, can develop a marketing sales force automation system in the United States, and once provided, may try the same techniques and technologies in Spain. Micro marketing—marketing to very small geographic and social units—no longer means marketing to neighborhoods in the United States, but to neighborhoods throughout the world! In our laptop computer example above, design has become internationalized and coordinated through shared culture (defining what is good design) and dense communications networks. These new levels of global coordination permit for the first time in history the location of business activity according to comparative advantage. Design should be located where it is best accomplished, as should marketing, production, and finance.

Finally, global markets, production, and administration create the conditions for powerful, *sustained global economies of scale*. Production driven by world-wide global demand can be concentrated where it can be best accomplished, fixed resources can be allocated over larger production runs, and production runs in larger plants can be scheduled more efficiently and precisely estimated. Lower cost factors of production can be exploited wherever they emerge. The result is a powerful strategic advantage to firms that can organize globally.

These general and specific business drivers have greatly enlarged world trade and commerce. Figure 19.2A shows that world trade is growing faster than the world gross domestic product (GDP). Figure 19.2B shows that in the United States, world trade is growing faster than the economy as a whole.

Not all industries are similarly affected by these trends. Clearly, manufacturing has been much more affected than services that still tend to be domestic—and highly inefficient. However, the localism of services is breaking down in telecommunications, entertainment, transportation, financial services, and general business services, including law. Clearly those firms within an industry who can understand the internationalization of their industry and respond appropriately will reap enormous gains in productivity and stability.

BUSINESS CHALLENGES

While the possibilities of globalization for business success are enormous, it would be a mistake to think the path toward a truly global economy is free of fundamental obstacles, or that your company can simply coast to international glory. Far from it. Fundamental forces are operating to inhibit a global economy and to disrupt international business. Table 19.2 lists the most common and powerful challenges to the development of global systems.

At a cultural level, **particularism**, making judgments and taking action on the basis of narrow or personal characteristics, in all its forms (religious, nationalistic, ethnic, regionalism, geopolitical position) rejects the very concept of a shared global culture, and rejects the penetration of domestic markets by "foreign" goods and services. Differences among cultures produce differences in social expectations, politics, and ultimately legal rules. In certain countries, like the United States, consumers expect "domestic" name brand products to be built

Particularism: Making judgments and taking actions on the basis of narrow or personal characteristics.

Figure 19.2a
The growth of world trade compared to the growth of the world gross domestic product (GDP) (1950–1990). As can be seen from this graph, world trade is growing faster than world gross domestic product (GDP.) *Source: U.S. Department of State, Bureau of Intelligence and Research, Report No. IRR 220, 1991.*

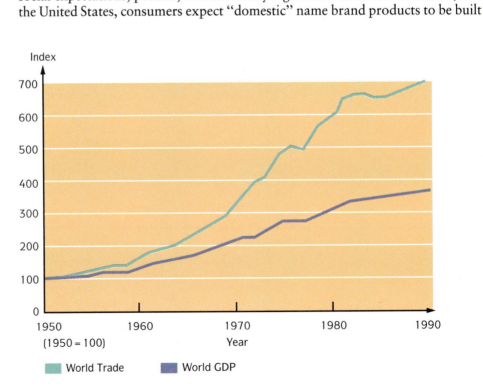

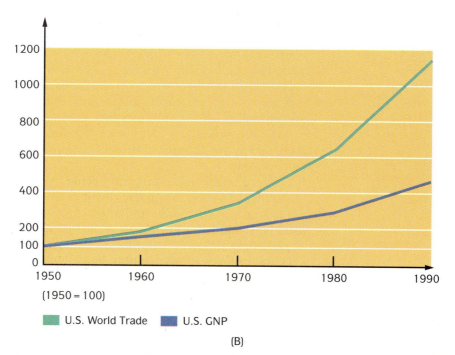

Figure 19.2b
The growth of U.S. world trade compared to the growth of the U.S. gross national product (GNP) (1950–1990.) As can be seen from this graph, U.S. world trade is growing faster than the domestic economy.

(B)

domestically, and are disappointed to learn that much of what they thought of as domestically produced is in fact foreign made.

Different cultures produce different political regimes. Among the many different countries of the world there are different laws governing the movement of information, information privacy of citizens, origins of software and hardware in systems, and radio and satellite telecommunications. Even the hours of business, and the terms of business trade vary greatly across political cultures. These different legal regimes complicate global business and must be taken into account when building global systems.

Transborder data flow: The movement of information across international boundaries in any form.

For instance, European countries have very strict laws concerning transborder data flow and privacy. **Transborder data flow** is defined as the movement of information across international boundaries in any form. Some European countries prohibit the processing of financial information outside their boundaries or the movement of employee information to foreign countries. The European Commission (the highest planning body for the integration of Europe) is considering a Digital Services Data Protection Directive that would restrict the flow of information to countries (like the United States) that do not meet strict European information laws on personal information. That means, for instance, that a French marketing manager may not be able to use his or her credit card in New York because the credit information cannot be forwarded to the United

Table 19.2   CHALLENGES AND OBSTACLES TO GLOBAL BUSINESS SYSTEMS

General

Cultural particularism: Regionalism, nationalism.

Social expectations: ''Brand name'' expectations; work hours

Political laws: Transborder data and privacy laws.

Specific

Standards: Different EDI, E-Mail, telecommunications standards

Reliability: Phone networks not reliable

Speed: Data transfer speeds differ, slower than U.S.

Personnel: Shortages of skilled consultants

States given its privacy laws. In response, most multinational firms develop information systems within each European country to avoid the cost and uncertainty of moving information across national boundaries.

Cultural and political differences profoundly affect organizations' standard operating procedures. A host of specific barriers arise from the general cultural differences, everything from different reliability of phone networks to the shortage of skilled consultants (see Steinbart and Nath, 1992). The Window on Organizations illustrates how such differences have shaped accounting procedures in various countries, seriously complicating the process of international management.

Language remains a significant barrier. Although English has become a kind of standard business language, this is truer at higher levels of companies and not throughout the middle and lower ranks. Software may have to be built with local language interfaces before a new information system can be successfully implemented.

Currency fluctuations can play havoc with planning models and projections. Although a great deal of progress has been made in developing a common currency for the European Economic Community, occasionally this regime breaks down, evidenced by the British pound fluctuation in 1992 and 1993, or the American dollar fluctuating from 1990 to 1993 against the Japanese yen and stronger European currencies. In the absence of world currency, or a world bank, currency fluctuations remain a major source of business uncertainty.

These inhibiting factors must be taken into account when you are designing and building an international infrastructure for your business.

State of the Art

Where do firms now have international applications and where do they plan expansion in the future? Figure 19.3 indicates the state of the art in terms of current applications and likely future growth areas of international systems infrastructure.

One might think, given the opportunities for achieving competitive advantages outlined above, and the interest in future applications, that most international companies have rationally developed marvelous international systems architec-

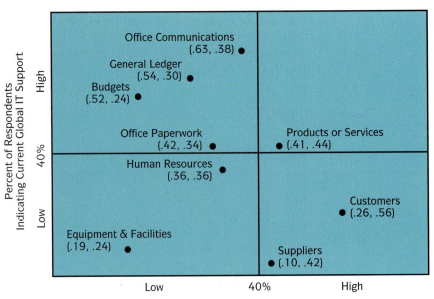

Figure 19.3
Frequency and type of business entities supported by global systems and databases. Most current IT applications are relatively simple office systems involving budgeting, communications, and general ledger financial coordination. Most corporations have local human resource and equipment/facilities systems. In the future, global firms plan to expand product support, customer service, and supplier systems to global stature. *Source: Adapted from Blake Ives and Sirkka Jarvenpaa, "Wiring the Stateless Corporation: Empowering the Drivers and Overcoming the Barriers," SIM Network, September/October 1991, p. 4C. Reprinted courtesy of Society for Information Management.*

ORGANIZATIONS

Snarled by Accounting Rules

Suppose you are the CEO of a global chemical company with 100 plants organized in 32 divisions and 25 national subsidiaries. How do you get consistent data to figure out how the entire organization is performing? It's not easy, and might be virtually impossible.

Accounting practices diverge sharply from one country to another. Although the European Community and European Free Trade Association are creating a vast "single market" spanning 19 countries, there is no agreement on a single set of accounting standards. Accountants have radically different ideas of the proper way to value assets and total up profits and losses, reflecting their national laws and traditions.

For instance, German companies generally do not recognize profit from a project until it is completed and they have been paid. British firms, in contrast, start posting a profit before completion when they are reasonably certain they will get the money. Many companies on the European continent do not report per-share earnings, which is considered vital among

U.S. and British firms. Complicating matters further, European companies have myriad ways of defining net profit, shareholders' equity, and extraordinary items.

Each country's accounting practices are intertwined with its legal system, tax code, and business philosophy. Britain, the United States and the Netherlands share a primarily Anglo-Saxon business tradition that separates tax calculations from reports to shareholders and which uses more flexible accounting rules. Accountants focus on presenting a "true and fair view" of the company as opposed to adhering to rigid rules with the objective of showing shareholders how fast profit is growing. The accounting goals of most continental countries, on the other hand, emphasize compliance with strict rules and holding down tax liabilities. These countries are less interested in impressing investors. Many Germans are even appalled by the lack of precise rules in Anglo-Saxon accounting. Since Anglo-Saxon and German accounting do not even share the same basic goals, it is hard to imagine a single accounting system that could serve both sides.

These diverging accounting practices inhibit cross-border business in a number of ways. Investors may be deterred from buying shares abroad because they cannot understand foreign accounting statements even when the language is translated. Investment analysts generally cannot make meaningful comparisons such as which European country has the cheapest food company shares. Companies have trouble identifying healthy companies for cross-border acquisitions or cooperation. Multinational firms must present the same accounting reports in different formats.

Source: Bob Hagerty, "Differing Accounting Rules Snarl Europe," *The Wall Street Journal* (September 14, 1992).

To Think About: Why are changes in SOPs an enormous organizational effort? How easily could information systems deal with the problems described here? If you were a manager of a multinational firm, how easy would it be to create a management reporting system? Why?

tures. Nothing could be further from the truth. Most companies have inherited patchwork international systems from the distant past, often based on concepts of information processing developed in the 1960s—batch-oriented reporting from independent foreign divisions to corporate headquarters, with little on-line control and communication. At some point, corporations in this situation will face powerful competitive challenges in the market place from firms who have rationally designed truly international systems. Still other companies have recently built technology platforms for an international infrastructure, but have nowhere to go with it because they lack global strategy. For instance, one survey of 100 global firms found that 52 percent never or rarely considered information systems when devising global strategies (Cox, 1991).

As it turns out, there are significant difficulties in building appropriate international infrastructures. The difficulties involve planning a system appropriate to the firm's global strategy, structuring the organization of systems and business units, solving implementation issues, and choosing the right technical platform. Let us examine these problems in greater detail.

Table 19.3   GLOBAL BUSINESS STRATEGY AND STRUCTURE

	STRATEGY			
BUSINESS FUNCTION	Domestic Exporter	Multinational	Franchiser	Transnational
Production	Centralized	Dispersed	Coordinated	Coordinated
Finance/Accounting	Centralized	Centralized	Centralized	Coordinated
Sales/Marketing	Mixed	Dispersed	Coordinated	Coordinated
Human Resources	Centralized	Centralized	Coordinated	Coordinated
Strategic Management	Centralized	Centralized	Centralized	Coordinated

19.2 Organizing International Information Systems

There are three organizational issues facing corporations seeking a global position: choosing a strategy, organizing the business, and organizing the systems management area. The first two are closely connected, so we will discuss them together.

Global Strategies and Business Organization

There are four main global strategies that form the basis for global firms' organizational structure. These four strategies are domestic exporter, multinational, franchiser, and transnational. Each of these strategies is associated with a specific business organizational structure (see Table 19.3). For simplicity, we describe three kinds of organizational structure or governance: centralized (in the home country), decentralized (dispersed to local foreign units), and coordinated (all units participate as equals). There are other types of governance patterns observed in specific companies (e.g., authoritarian dominance by one unit, a confederacy of equals, a federal structure balancing power among strategic units, and so forth; see Keen, 1991).

Domestic exporter: Global strategy characterized by heavy centralization of corporate activities in the home country of origin.

The **domestic exporter** strategy is characterized by heavy centralization of corporate activities in the home country of origin. Nearly all international companies begin this way, and some move on to other forms. Production, finance/accounting, sales/marketing, human resources, and strategic management are set up to optimize resources in the home country. International sales are sometimes dispersed using agency agreements or subsidiaries, but even here foreign marketing is totally reliant on the domestic home base for marketing themes and strategies. Caterpillar Corporation and other heavy capital equipment manufacturers fall into this category of firm.

Multinational: Global strategy that concentrates financial management and control out of a central home base while decentralizing production, sales, and marketing operations to units in other countries.

The **multinational** strategy often concentrates financial management and control out of a central home base while decentralizing production, sales, and marketing operations to units in other countries. The products and services on sale in different countries are adapted to suit local market conditions. The organization becomes a far-flung confederation of production and marketing facilities in different countries. Many financial service firms, along with a host of manufacturers like General Motors, Chrysler, and Intel fit this pattern.

Franchiser: Firm where the product is created, designed, financed, and initially produced in the home country, but must rely heavily on foreign personnel for further production, marketing, and human resources.

Franchisers are an interesting mix of old and new. On the one hand the product is created, designed, financed and initially produced in the home country, but for product-specific reasons must rely heavily on foreign personnel for further production, marketing, and human resources. Food franchisers like McDonald's, Mrs. Fields' Cookies, and Kentucky Fried Chicken fit this pattern. McDonald's created a new form of fast-food chain in the United States, and continues to rely largely on the United States for inspiration of new products, strategic management, and financing. Nevertheless, because the product must be produced locally—it is perishable—extensive coordination and dispersal of production, local marketing, and local recruitment of personnel are required. Generally, foreign franchisees are clones of the mother country units, yet fully coordinated worldwide production that could optimize factors of production is not possible. For instance, potatoes and beef can generally not be bought where they are cheapest on world markets but must be produced reasonably close to the area of consumption.

Transnational firms are the stateless, truly globally managed firms which may represent a larger part of international business in the future. Transnational firms have no single national headquarters but instead have many regional headquarters and perhaps a world headquarters. In a **transnational** strategy, nearly all of the value-adding activities are managed from a global perspective, without reference to national borders, optimizing sources of supply and demand wherever they appear, and taking advantage of any local comparative advantages. Transnational firms take the globe as their management frame of reference, not the home country. The governance of these firms has been likened to a federal structure in which there is a strong central management core of decision making, but considerable dispersal of power and financial muscle throughout the global divisions. Few companies have actually attained transnational status but Citicorp, Sony, Ford, and others are attempting this transition.

Information technology and improvements in global telecommunications are giving international firms more flexibility to shape their global strategies. Protectionism and a need to serve local markets encourage companies to disperse production facilities and at least become multinational. At the same time, the drive to achieve economies of scale and take advantage of short-term local advantages forces transnationals toward a global management perspective and a concentration of power and authority. Hence, there are forces of decentralization and dispersal, as well as forces of centralization and global coordination. (Ives and Jarvenpaa, 1991).

Transnational: Truly globally managed firms which have no national headquarters; value-added activities are managed from a global perspective without reference to national borders, optimizing sources of supply and demand and taking advantage of any local competitive advantage.

The Colonel greets diners in this Kentucky Fried Chicken restaurant in South Korea. Diners will find that the food available in this KFC is similar to the food served in any KFC in the United States.

SYSTEM CONFIGURATION	STRATEGY			
	Domestic Exporter	Multi National	Franchiser	Transnational
Centralized	X			
Duplicated			X	
Decentralized	x	X	x	
Networked		x		X

Figure 19.4
Global strategy and systems configurations. The large Xs show the dominant pattern, and the small xs show the emerging patterns. For instance, domestic exporters rely predominantly on centralized systems but there is continual pressure and some development of decentralized systems in local marketing regions.

Global Systems to Fit the Strategy

The configuration, management, and development of systems tend to follow the global strategy chosen (Roche, 1992; Ives and Jarvenpaa, 1991). Figure 19.4 depicts one view of typical arrangements, recognizing that some firms' systems may not fit the pattern precisely. By "systems" we mean the full range of activities involved in building information systems: conception and alignment with the strategic business plan, systems development, and ongoing operation. For the sake of simplicity, we consider four types of systems configuration. *Centralized systems* are those where systems development and operation occurs totally at the domestic home base. *Duplicated systems* are those where development occurs totally at the home base, but operations are handed over to autonomous units in foreign locations. *Decentralized systems* are those where each foreign unit designs its own, totally unique solutions and systems. Last, *networked* systems are those in which system development and operations occur in an integrated and coordinated fashion across all units. As can be seen in Figure 19.4, domestic exporters tend to have highly centralized systems in which a single domestic systems development staff develops worldwide applications. Multinationals offer a direct and striking contrast: Here foreign units often devise their own systems solutions based on local needs with few if any applications in common with headquarters (the exception being financial reporting and some telecommunications applications). Franchisers have the simplest systems structure: like the products they sell, franchisers develop a single system usually at the home base and then replicate it around the world. Each unit—no matter where it is located—has the same identical applications. Last, the most ambitious form of system development is found in the transnational: Networked systems are those in which there is a solid, singular global environment for developing and operating systems. This usually presupposes a powerful telecommunications backbone, a culture of shared applications development, and a shared management culture that crosses cultural barriers. The networked systems structure is most visible in financial services where the homogeneity of the product, money, and money instruments, seems to overcome cultural barriers.

Reorganizing the Business

How should a firm organize itself for doing business on an international scale? Developing a global company and an information systems support structure requires following these principles:

1. Organize value-adding activities along lines of comparative advantage. For instance, marketing/sales functions should be located where they can best be performed, for least cost and maximum impact; likewise with production, finance, human resources, and information systems.

2. Develop and operate systems units at each level of corporate activity— national, regional, and international. In order to serve local needs, there should be *host country systems units* of some magnitude. *Regional systems* units should handle telecommunications and systems development across national boundaries that take place within major geographic regions (European, Asian, American). *Transnational systems units* should be established to create the linkages across major regional areas and coordinate the development and operation of international telecommunications and systems development (Roche, 1991).

3. Establish at world headquarters a single office responsible for development of international systems, a global Chief Information Officer (CIO) position.

Many successful companies have devised organizational systems structures along these principles. The success of these companies relies not just on proper organization. A key ingredient is a management team that can understand the risks and benefits of international systems, and that can devise strategies for overcoming the risks. We turn to these management topics next.

19.3 Managing Global Systems

The survey of 100 large global corporations referenced earlier found that CIOs believed the development and implementation of international systems were their most difficult problems. Table 19.4 lists what these CIOs believed were the principal management problems posed by developing international systems.

It is interesting to note that these problems are the chief difficulties managers experience in developing ordinary domestic systems as well! But these are enormously complicated in the international environment.

A Typical Scenario: Disorganization on a Global Scale

Let us look at a common scenario. A traditional multinational consumer goods company based in the United States and operating in Europe would like to expand into Asian markets and knows that it must develop a transnational strategy and a supportive information systems structure. Like most multinationals it has dispersed production and marketing to regional and national centers while maintaining a world headquarters and strategic management in the United States. Historically, it has allowed each of the subsidiary foreign divisions to develop its own system. The only centrally coordinated system is financial controls and reporting. The central systems group in the United States focuses only on domestic functions and production. The result is a hodgepodge of hardware,

Table 19.4 MANAGEMENT ISSUES IN DEVELOPING INTERNATIONAL SYSTEMS

Agreeing on common user requirements	88%
Inducing procedural business changes	79%
Coordinating applications development	77%
Coordinating software releases	69%
Encouraging local users to take on ownership	58%

Source: Adapted from Butler Cox, *Globalization: The IT Challenge*. Amdahl Executive Institute (Sunnyvale, California, 1991).

software, and telecommunications. The mail systems between Europe and the United States are incompatible. Each production facility uses a different manufacturing resources planning system (or different version with local variations), and different marketing, sales, and human resource systems. The technology platforms are wildly different: Europe is using mostly UNIX-based file servers and PC clones on desktops. Communications between different sites are poor given the high cost and low quality of European intercountry communications. The U.S. group is moving from an IBM mainframe environment centralized at headquarters to a highly distributed network architecture based on a national value-added network, with local sites developing their own local area networks. The central systems group at headquarters was recently dispersed to the U.S. local sites in the hope of serving local needs better and reducing costs.

What do you recommend to the senior management leaders of this company who now want to pursue a transnational strategy and develop an information systems infrastructure to support a highly coordinated global systems environment? Consider the problems you face by re-examining Table 19.4. The foreign divisions will resist efforts to agree on common user requirements—they have never thought about much other than their own units' needs. The systems groups in American local sites, which have been recently enlarged and told to focus on local needs, will not easily accept guidance from anyone recommending a transnational strategy. It will be difficult to convince local managers anywhere in the world that they should change their business procedures to align with other units in the world, especially if this might interfere with their local performance. After all, local managers are rewarded in this company for meeting local objectives of their division or plant. Finally, it will be difficult to coordinate development of projects around the world in the absence of a powerful telecommunications network, and difficult to encourage local users to take on ownership in the systems developed. What should you recommend given these typical obstacles?

Strategy: Divide, Conquer, Appease

Core systems: Systems that support functions that are absolutely critical to the organization.

Figure 19.5 lays out the main dimensions of a solution. First, consider that not all systems should be coordinated on a transnational basis—only some "core" systems are truly worth sharing from a cost and feasibility point of view. **Core systems** are systems that support functions that are absolutely critical to the organization. Other systems should only be partially coordinated because they share key elements, but they do not have to be totally common across national boundaries. For such systems, a good deal of local variation is possible and desirable. A last group of systems are peripheral and truly provincial, and are needed to suit local requirements only.

DEFINE CORE BUSINESS PROCESSES

Business processes: Sets of logically related tasks performed to achieve a defined business outcome; each business process typically involves many functional areas working together.

How do you identify "core systems?" The first step is to define a short list of truly critical core business processes. Business processes have been defined before in Chapter 11, which you should review. Briefly, **business processes** are sets of logically related tasks performed to achieve a defined business outcome, such as shipping out correct orders to customers or delivering innovative products to the market. Each business process typically involves many functional areas working together, effectively communicating and coordinating.

The way to identify these core business processes is to conduct a workflow analysis. How are customer orders taken, what happens to them once they are taken, who fills the order, how is it shipped to the customer? What about suppliers? Do they have access to manufacturing resource planning systems so supply is automatic? You should be able to identify and set priorities in a short list of ten business processes that are absolutely critical for the firm.

Next, can you identify centers of excellence for these processes? Is the customer order fulfillment superior in the United States, manufacturing process control superior in Germany, and human resources superior in Asia? You should

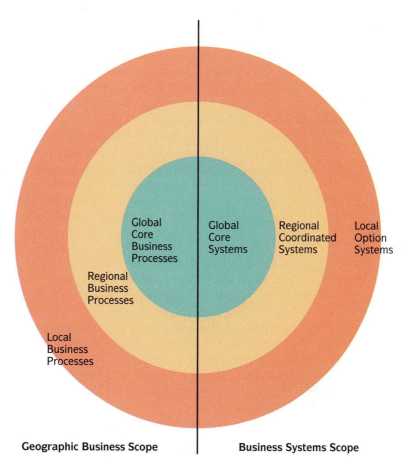

Figure 19.5
Agency and other coordination costs increase as the firm moves from local option systems toward regional and global systems. On the other hand, transaction costs of participating in global markets probably decrease as firms develop global systems. A sensible strategy is to reduce agency costs by developing only a few "core" global systems which are vital for global operations, leaving other systems in the hands of regional and local units. *Adapted from Edward M. Roche,* Managing Information Technology in Multinational Corporations. *New York: Macmillan, 1992.*

Global
Core
Business
Processes

Global
Core
Systems

Regional
Coordinated
Systems

Local
Option
Systems

Regional
Business
Processes

Local
Business
Processes

Geographic Business Scope

Business Systems Scope

be able to identify some areas of the company, for some lines of business, where a unit stands out in the performance of one or more business functions.

When you understand the business processes of a firm, you can rank order them. You can then decide which processes should be core applications, centrally coordinated, designed, and implemented around the globe, and which should be regional and local. At the same time, by identifying the critical business processes, the really important ones, you have gone a long way to defining a vision of the future that you should be working towards.

IDENTIFY CORE SYSTEMS TO COORDINATE CENTRALLY

By identifying the critical core business processes, you begin to see opportunities for transnational systems. The second strategic step is to conquer the core systems and define these systems as truly transnational. The financial and political costs of defining and implementing transnational systems are extremely high. Therefore, keep the list to an absolute minimum, letting experience be the guide, and erring on the side of minimalism. If building a transnational system appears too daunting, it may be useful to identify the data elements required for global decision-making and build bridges between different systems to deliver this firm-wide data (Roche, 1992). By dividing off a small group of systems as absolutely critical, you divide opposition to a transnational strategy. At the same time, you can appease those who oppose the central worldwide coordination implied by transnational systems by permitting peripheral systems development to go on unabated, with the exception of some technical platform requirements.

CHOOSE AN APPROACH: INCREMENTAL, GRAND DESIGN, EVOLUTIONARY

A third step is to choose an approach. Avoid piecemeal approaches. These will surely fail for lack of visibility, opposition from all who stand to lose from transnational development, and lack of power to convince senior management that the transnational systems are worth it. Likewise, avoid *grand design* approaches that try to do everything at once. These also tend to fail because they fail to focus resources. Nothing gets done properly, and opposition to organizational change is needlessly strengthened because the effort requires huge resources. An alternative approach is to evolve transnational applications from existing applications with a precise and clear vision of the transnational capabilities the organization should have in five years.

MAKE THE BENEFITS CLEAR

What is in it for the company? One of the worst situations to avoid is to build global systems for the sake of building global systems. From the beginning, it is crucial that senior management at headquarters and foreign division managers clearly understand the benefits that will come to the company as well as to individual units. While each system offers unique benefits to a particular budget, the overall contribution of global systems lies in four areas.

Global systems—truly integrated, distributed, and transnational systems—contribute to superior management and coordination. A simple price tag cannot be put on the value of this contribution, and the benefit will not show up in any capital budgeting model. It is the ability to switch suppliers on a moment's notice from one region to another in a crisis, the ability to move production in response to natural disasters, and the ability to use excess capacity in one region to meet raging demand in another.

A second major contribution is vast improvement in production, operation, and supply and distribution. Imagine a global value chain, with global suppliers and a global distribution network. For the first time, senior managers can locate value-adding activities in regions where they are most economically performed.

Third, global systems mean global customers and global marketing. Fixed costs around the world can now be amortised over a much larger customer base. This will unleash new economies of scale at production facilities.

Last, global systems mean the ability to optimize the use of corporate funds over a much larger capital base. This means, for instance, that capital in a surplus region can be moved efficiently to expand production of capital-starved regions; that cash can be managed more effectively within the company and put to use more effectively.

These strategies will not by themselves create global systems. You will have to implement what you strategize and this is a whole new challenge.

Implementation Tactics: Cooptation

Cooptation: Bringing the opposition into the process of designing and implementing the solution without giving up control over the direction and nature of the change.

The overall tactic for dealing with resistant local units in a transnational company is cooptation. **Cooptation** is defined as bringing the opposition into the process of designing and implementing the solution without giving up control over the direction and nature of the change. As much as possible, raw power should be avoided. Minimally, however, local units must agree on a short list of transnational systems and raw power may be required to solidify the idea that transnational systems of some sort are truly required.

How should cooptation proceed? Several alternatives are possible. One alternative is to permit each country unit the opportunity to develop one transnational application first in its home territory, and then throughout the world. In this manner, each major country systems group is given a piece of the action in developing a transnational system, and local units feel a sense of ownership in the transnational effort. On the down side, this assumes the ability to develop high quality systems is widely distributed, and that, say, the German team, can successfully implement systems in France and Italy. This will not always be the case. Also, the transnational effort will have low visibility.

A second tactic is to develop new transnational centers of excellence, or a single center of excellence. There may be several centers around the globe that focus on specific business processes. These centers draw heavily from local national units, are based on multinational teams, and must report to worldwide management—their first line of responsibility is to the core applications. Centers of excellence perform the initial identification and specification of the business process, define the information requirements, perform the business and systems analysis, and accomplish all design and testing. Implementation, however, and pilot testing, occur in World Pilot Regions where new applications are installed and tested first. Later, they are rolled out to other parts of the globe. This phased roll-out strategy is precisely how national applications are successfully developed.

Wrapping Up: The Management Solution

We can now reconsider how to handle the most vexing problems facing managers developing the transnational information system infrastructures that were described in Table 19.4.

- *Agreeing on common user requirements:* Establishing a short list of the core business processes and core support systems will begin a process of rational comparison across the many divisions of the company, develop a common language for discussing the business, and naturally lead to an understanding of common elements (as well as the unique qualities that must remain local).

- *Inducing procedural business changes:* Your success as a change agent will depend on your legitimacy, your actual raw power, and your ability to involve users in the change design process. **Legitimacy** is defined as the extent to which your authority is accepted on grounds of competence, vision, or other qualities. The selection of a viable change strategy, which we have defined as evolutionary but with a vision, should assist you in convincing others that change is feasible and desirable. Involving people in change, convincing them that change is in the best interests of the company and their local units is a key tactic.

- *Coordinating applications development:* Choice of change strategy is critical for this problem. At the global level there is simply far too much complexity to attempt a grand design strategy of change. It is far easier to coordinate change by making small incremental steps toward a larger vision. Imagine a five-year plan of action rather than a two-year plan of action, and reduce the set of transnational systems to a bare minimum in order to reduce coordination costs.

- *Coordinating software releases:* Firms can institute procedures to ensure that all operating units convert to new software updates at the same time so that everyone's software is compatible.

- *Encouraging local users to take on ownership:* The key to this problem is to involve users in the creation of the design without giving up control over the development of the project to parochial interests. Recruiting a wide range of local individuals to transnational centers of excellence helps send the message that all significant groups are involved in the design and will have an influence.

Even with the proper organizational structure and appropriate management choices, it is still possible to stumble over technological issues. Choices of technology, platforms, networks, hardware, and software are the final elements in building transnational information system infrastructures.

Legitimacy: The extent to which one's authority is accepted on grounds of competence, vision, or other qualities.

19.4 Technology Issues and Opportunities

Information technology is itself a powerful business driver encouraging the development of global systems, but it creates significant challenges for managers. Global systems presuppose that business firms develop a solid technical foundation and are willing to continually up-grade facilities.

The Main Technical Issues

Hardware, software, and telecommunications pose special technical challenges in an international setting. The major hardware challenge is finding some way to standardize the firm's computer hardware platform when there is so much variation from operating unit to operating unit and from country to country. Managers will need to think carefully about where to locate the firm's computer centers and about how to select hardware suppliers. The major global software challenge is finding applications that are user friendly and that truly enhance the productivity of international work teams. The major telecommunications challenge is making data flow seamlessly across networks shaped by disparate national standards. Overcoming these challenges requires systems integration and connectivity on a global basis.

HARDWARE AND SYSTEMS INTEGRATION

The development of transnational information system infrastructures based on the concept of "core" systems raises questions about how the new core systems will fit in with the existing suite of applications developed around the globe by different divisions, different people, and for different kinds of computing hardware. The goal is to develop global, distributed, and integrated systems. Briefly, these are the same problems faced by any large domestic systems development effort. However, the problems are more complex because of the international environment. For instance, in the United States, IBM hardware and IBM operating systems have played the predominant role in building core systems for large organizations, whereas in Europe UNIX has been much more commonly used for large systems. How can the two be integrated in a common transnational system?

There are two choices to solve integration problems: Remain with a proprietary architecture (generally IBM), or move new core systems to an open architecture. Generally, an open architecture means a UNIX foundation, a client/server architecture, and reliance on PC DOS/Windows machines or UNIX machines on the desktop.

The correct choice will often depend on the history of the company's systems, and the extent of commitment to proprietary systems. For instance, finance and insurance firms typically relied almost exclusively on IBM proprietary equipment and architectures in the 1980s and it would be extremely difficult and cost-ineffective to abandon that equipment and software. Newer firms and manufacturing firms generally find it much easier to adopt open UNIX systems for international systems. As we pointed out in previous chapters, open UNIX-based systems are far more cost-effective in the long run, provide more power at a cheaper price, and preserve options for future expansion.

Once a hardware platform is chosen, the question of standards has to be addressed. Just because all sites use the same hardware does not guarantee common, integrated systems. Some central authority in the firm has to establish data, as well as other technical standards, for sites to comply with. For instance, technical accounting terms must be standardized (e.g., the beginning and end of the fiscal year—review the Window on Organizations), as well as the acceptable interfaces between systems, communications speeds and architectures, and network software.

CONNECTIVITY

The heart of the international systems problem is telecommunications—linking together the systems and people of a global firm into a single integrated network just like the phone system but capable of voice, data, and image transmissions. The Window on Technology explains why an integrated global network is extremely difficult to create.

Firms have two basic options for providing international connectivity: Build their own international private network, or rely on a network service based on the public switched networks throughout the world.

TECHNOLOGY

Global Networks: A Colossal Headache

If you are a multinational corporation looking to meld your organization into a global entity unfettered by geographic boundaries and time zones, what you want is a global network that seamlessly provides the data to tie your operations together. The problem is, you won't be able to find it.

Many countries cannot even fulfill basic business telecommunications needs such as obtaining reliable circuits, coordinating among different carriers and the regional telecommunications authority, obtaining bills in a common currency standard, and obtaining standard agreements for the level of telecommunications service provided. Many firms find themselves grappling with inconsistent telecommunications service, unreliable costs, and tariff and regulatory problems. Figure 19.6 illustrates the range of these problems.

Europe, for instance, is a hodgepodge of disparate national technical standards and service levels. The problem is especially critical for banks or airlines which must move massive volumes of data around the world. Although most circuits leased by multinational corporations are fault-free more than 99.8 percent of the time, line quality and service vary widely from the north to the south of Europe. Network service is much more unreliable in southern Europe.

European firms realized some time ago the need for developing connectivity standards. The European Economic Community has endorsed EDIfact as the European electronic data interchange (EDI) standard, but the existing European standards for networking and EDI are very industry-specific and country-specific. Most European banks use the SWIFT (Society for Worldwide Interbank Finan-

cial Telecommunications) protocol for international funds transfer, while automobile companies and food producers often use industry-specific or country-specific versions of standard protocols for EDI. Complicating matters further, the United States standard for EDI is ANSI (American National Standards Institute) X.12. Although the Open Standards Interconnect (OSI) reference model for linking networks is more popular in Europe than it is in the United States, it is not universally accepted. Various industry groups have standardized on other networking architectures, such as Transmission Control Protocol/Internet Protocol (TCP/IP); IBM's proprietary Systems Network Architecture (SNA); and Digital Equipment's proprietary network architecture, Decnet. Even standards such as ISDN (Integrated Services Digital Network) vary from country to country.

Sources: Stephanie Stahl, "Global Networks: The Headache Continues," *InformationWEEK* (October 12, 1992); Richard L. Hudson, "Multinational Companies in Europe Demand Improvement in Phone Lines," *The Wall Street Journal* (August 3, 1992); and Elisabeth Horwitt, "Systems without Borders," *Computerworld* (August 12, 1991).

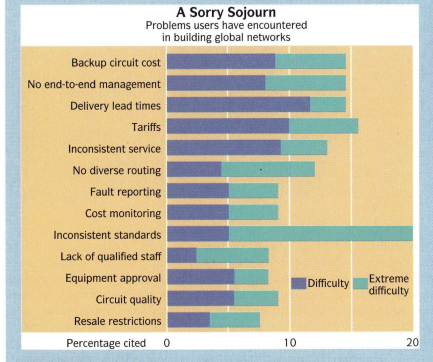

A Sorry Sojourn
Problems users have encountered
in building global networks

	Difficulty	Extreme difficulty

Percentage cited 0   10   20

To Think About: What are the managerial, organizational, and technological implications of these international connectivity problems? If you were the head of information systems for a multinational company, how would you deal with these problems?

Figure 19.6
Problems users have encountered in building global networks. *Adapted from Stephanie Stahl, "Global Networks: The Headache Continues,"* InformationWEEK *(October 12, 1992). Copyright © 1992 by CMP Publications, Inc., 600 Community Drive, Manhasset, NY 11030. Reprinted from InformationWEEK with permission.*

If you are the Chief Information Officer (CIO) of a global chemical company with 300 plants in 43 divisions and 30 national subsidiaries, how do you get consistent data to run your worldwide organization? Chances are, you can't.

Multinationals are likely to have at least five or six different hardware platforms—some IBM, some Digital Equipment, some Hewlett-Packard, some Fujitsu, some Siemens Nixdorf. Each division is likely to have its own systems, shaped by national characteristics. Language differences, such as writing from right to left, also get in the way, as do national disparities in accounting and taxation methods. Painless global software compatibility is virtually impossible.

One solution is to standardize on application software packages. Courtaulds Plc., a London-based conglomerate that makes everything from tea bags to synthetic fiber clothing and bottle tops, has to manage more than 100 business units in 37 countries around the world. Each of these units developed software programs that are woefully incompatible with each other. Bill Stubbins, a group information technology executive in Courtauld's London home office, decided to look for a common enterprisewide software package for manufacturing resource planning that could be used throughout the company and all of its units.

According to Stubbins, it did not make sense to have each division and business unit shop for themselves. He believed that if Courtauld's corporate information systems group did a thorough analysis of commercially available software packages, all of its businesses would benefit. The corporate information systems department wanted individual MIS departments to focus on applying software packages to their businesses rather than creating the software themselves.

Assisted by the Manchester, England, branch of Andersen Consulting, Stubbins and his staff polled twelve vice presidents of manufacturing at twelve major business units, six in the United Kingdom, five in the United States, and one in Germany. They started with a list of fifty-two manufacturing resource planning software packages and eventually pared it down to five. Stubbins finally chose two, MFG Probe, a software package from QAD, a software vendor near Ventura, California, and Gemms, a fourth-generation relational database product from Datalogix. The two packages have eighteen modules between them, covering everything from sales order processing, inventory control, quality management, manufacturing scheduling, purchase ledgers, and distribution requirements planning.

Stubbins believes that standardizing on a package reduces the risk of

implementation failure. The more effort the information systems department puts into the same system, the more it can reassure users that it can do it right. Another advantage is cost leveraging. The central information systems department can purchase software at a discount because it purchases packages as a group rather than for each individual unit.

A major hurdle is convincing Courtauld's business units that they won't have to change their business strategies to use the software packages. Eleven business units have installed the package. Stubbins claimed he would be pleased if 85 percent of the business units sign up for one of the two standard packages.

Dell Computer Corporation of Austin, Texas, with 20 international business units and 1,777 of its 6,100 employees working outside the United States, found its international business was growing faster than its domestic side. Dell is developing consistent and focused strategies for its European business and requires a unified sales and marketing function shared by its major subsidiaries in these countries. The new strategy, for instance, might outline an innovative way of marketing account development mailings. Without standardized systems, Dell would not be able to install the account mailing upgrades, and a standard

One possibility is for the firm to put together its own private network based on leased lines from each country's PTT (Post, Telegraph, and Telephone authorities). Each country, however, has different restrictions on data exchange, technical standards, and acceptable vendors of equipment. These problems magnify in certain parts of the world. In Europe and the United States, reliance on PTTs makes more sense while these public networks expand services to compete with private providers.

The second major alternative to building one's own network is to use one of several expanding network services. With deregulation of telecommunications around the globe, private providers have sprung up to service business customers' data needs, along with some voice and image communications.

Although common in the United States, IVANs (International Value-Added Network Services) are expanding in both Europe and Asia. These private firms

But in the United States, accounts are allocated on a location-by-location basis. A global sales and marketing system has to be flexible enough to accommodate these different national sales structures. Convincing sales representatives that a new standardized sales system will actually benefit them and not just accumulate data at some central office is critical.

A significant advantage of standardization is reduced training costs. The cost of training people to use a new system and then paying them to operate it can easily exceed hardware and software expenditures. When people change jobs or divisions within a company, standardized software offers large productivity savings.

Source: Jason Forsythe, "The Global Data Dilemma," *InformationWEEK* (April 27, 1992).

system that was truly integrated could pass the strategy along from the marketing and operations group to the subsidiaries on-line. Dell is exploring the use of a standardized sales and marketing software package.

Standardizing sales procedures across national boundaries can present challenges. In the United Kingdom, sales accounts are traditionally assigned at the company level, with one sales representative handling an entire company.

To Think About: What are the management benefits of using a standard software package in a multinational corporation? What problems can software packages solve for multinational corporations? What problems do they create?

offer value-added telecommunications capacity usually rented from local PTTs or international satellite authorities, and then resell it to corporate users. IVANs add value by providing protocol conversion, operating mailboxes and mail systems, and offering integrated billing that permits a firm to track its data communication costs. Currently these systems are limited to data transmissions, but in the future they will expand to voice and image.

SOFTWARE Compatible hardware and communications provide a platform but not the total solution. Also critical to global core infrastructure is software (see the Window on Management). The development of core systems poses unique challenges for software: How will the old systems interface with the new? Entirely new interfaces must be built and tested if old systems are kept in local areas (which is

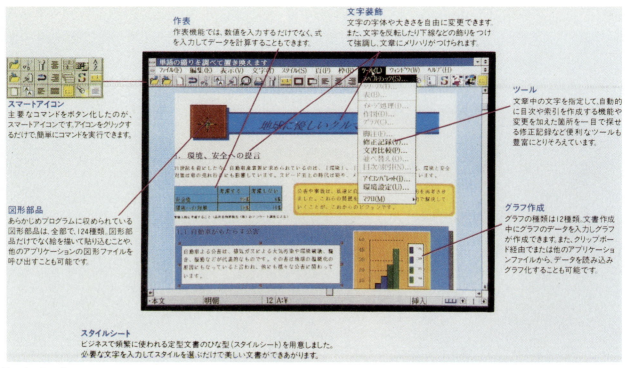

The AmiPro GUI is easily recognizable to users of this Lotus Development Corporation word processor with SmartIcons and pull down menus. All text screens and menu options in the user interface have been translated into Japanese to accommodate end users in Eastern Asia.

common). These interfaces can be costly and messy to build. If new software must be created, another challenge is to build software that can be realistically used by multiple business units from different countries when these business units are accustomed to their unique procedures and definitions of data.

Aside from integrating the new with the old systems, there are problems of human interface design and functionality of systems. For instance, in order to be truly useful for enhancing productivity of a global workforce, software interfaces must be easily understood and mastered quickly. Graphical user interfaces are ideal for this but presuppose a common language—often English. When international systems involve knowledge workers only, English may be the assumed international standard. But as international systems penetrate deeper into management and clerical groups, a common language may not be assumed and human interfaces must be built to accommodate different languages and even conventions.

What are the most important software applications? While most international systems focus on basic transaction and MIS systems, there is an increasing emphasis on international collaborative work groups. *EDI*—electronic data interchange—is a common global transaction processing application used by manufacturing and distribution firms to connect units of the same company, as well as customers and suppliers on a global basis. *Groupware systems* like electronic mail, videoconferencing, Lotus Notes, and other products supporting shared data files, notes, and electronic mail are much more important to knowledge- and data-based firms like advertising firms, research-based firms in medicine and engineering, and graphics and publishing firms.

New Technical Opportunities

Virtual private networks: The ability to custom-configure a network using a portion of the public switched network to create the illusion of a private network for a company.

There are four major technical advances that should fall in price and gain in power over the next few years that have importance to global networking and systems. After many years of stagnant development, PTTs in Europe and local Bell operating companies in the United States are finally moving ISDN (Integrated Services Digital Network) into the marketplace. Chapter 10 has described the benefits of using ISDN as an international standard for transmitting voice, images, and data over the public telephone network. ISDN will make networking services of all kinds as readily available as a phone jack in the wall. International ISDN services are just now becoming available as the United States and other countries extend their geographic coverage.

Virtual private networks (see Chapter 9) add features to the basic public telephone system that are usually only available to private networks. The basic idea of these services is that the local phone company provides each corporate user the ability to custom configure a network and use whatever portion of the public switched net is needed to do the job while charging only for services used. In a sense, the phone company becomes a digital network company, providing many features of a private network for firms operating internationally. This is an improvement over leasing entire lines, or capabilities as in a VAN when you may not need them.

Finally, a variety of satellite systems are being developed that will revolutionize communications because they bypass existing ground-based systems. Motorola in partnership with others, for instance, is developing a worldwide 40-satellite system that will permit hand-held mobile units carried by sales personnel to communicate with headquarters via voice or computer anywhere in the world at any time. Thus, a sales person in China could send an order confirmation request to the home office in London effortlessly and expect a reply instantly. The evolution of digital cellular phone technology will greatly increase the number of cellular communications units, and cellular networks, which in turn may use Motorola's systems to connect subscribers into a new worldwide network. Much of the 1990s will be spent building these kinds of communicate and compute anytime, anywhere networks.

Management Challenges

1. **The social and political role of "stateless" firms.** It is one thing to talk about a stateless transnational firm, but the people who work in these firms do have states, cultures, and loyalties; the operating divisions of these firms do in fact reside in various nation states with their own laws, politics, and cultures. It is unclear precisely how these stateless firms fit into the national cultures that they must serve. In reality, so-called stateless firms have had to be very careful to show local populations that they in fact do serve the interests of the state and broader culture.

2. **The difficulties of managing change in a multicultural firm.** While engineering change in a single corporation in a single nation can be difficult, costly, and long-term, bringing about significant change in very large scale global corporations can be daunting. Agreeing on "core business processes" in a transnational context, and then deciding on common systems either requires extraordinary insight, a lengthy process of consensus building, or the exercise of sheer power.

3. **Lines of business and global strategy.** Firms will have to decide whether some or all of their lines of business should be managed on a global basis. There are some lines of business in which local variations are slight, and the possibility exists to reap large rewards by organizing globally. Microcomputers and power tools may fit this pattern, as well as industrial raw mate-

rials. Other consumer goods may be quite different by country or region. It is likely that firms with many lines of business will have to maintain a very mixed organizational structure.

Summary

Identify the major factors behind the growing internationalization of business.

There are both general cultural factors as well as specific business factors to consider. The growth of cheap international communication and transportation has created a "global culture" with stable expectations or norms. Political stability and a growing global knowledge base that is widely shared contribute also to the global culture. These general factors create the conditions for global markets, global production, coordination, distribution, and global economies of scale.

Choose among several global strategies for developing business.

There are four basic international strategies: domestic exporter, multinational, franchiser, and transnational. The trend is toward a transnational strategy in which all factors of production are coordinated on a global scale. However, the choice of strategy is a function of the type of business and product.

Understand how information systems support different global strategies.

There is a connection between firm strategy and information system design. Transnational firms must develop networked system configurations and permit considerable decentralization of development and operations. Franchisers almost always duplicate systems across many countries and use centralized financial controls. Multinationals typically rely on decentralized independence among foreign units with some movement toward development of networks. Domestic exporters are typically centralized in domestic headquarters with some decentralized operations permitted.

Manage the development of international systems.

Implementing a global system requires an implementation strategy. Typically, global systems have evolved without conscious plan. The remedy is to define a small subset of core business processes and focus on building systems which could support these processes. Tactically, you will have to coopt widely dispersed foreign units to participate in the development and operation of these systems, being careful not to lose overall control.

Understand the main technical alternatives in developing global systems.

The main hardware and telecommunications issues are systems integration and connectivity. The choices for integration are either to go with a proprietary architecture or with an open systems technology like UNIX. Global networks are extremely difficult to build and operate. Some measure of connectivity may be achieved either by relying on local PTT authorities to provide connections, building a system oneself, or relying on private providers to supply communications capacity. The trend appears towards growing reliance on private providers, although public authorities and PTTs are moving forward rapidly with ISDN and other digital services to compete with private companies. The main software issue concerns building interfaces to existing systems and providing much-needed group support software.

Key Terms

International information systems infrastructure
Business driver
Global culture
Particularism
Transborder data flow
Domestic exporter
Multinational

Franchiser
Transnational
Core systems
Business processes
Cooptation
Legitimacy
Virtual private networks

Review Questions

1. What are the five major factors to consider when building an international information system infrastructure?

2. Describe the five general cultural factors leading toward growth in global business and the four specific business factors. Describe the interconnection among these factors.

3. What is meant by a global culture?

4. What are the major challenges to the development of global systems?

5. Why have firms not planned for the development of international systems?

6. Describe the four main strategies for global business and organizational structure.

7. Describe the four different system configurations that can be used to support different global strategies.

8. What are the major management issues in developing international systems?

9. What are three principles to follow when organizing the firm for global business?

10. What are three steps of a management strategy for developing and implementing global systems?

11. What is meant by cooptation, and how can it be used to build global systems?

12. Describe the main technical issues facing global systems.

13. Describe three new technologies that can help firms develop global systems.

Discussion Questions

1. As a member of your company's global information systems group that oversees development of global core systems, what criteria would you use to determine if an application should be developed as a global application or as a peripheral local application?

2. As the CEO of a domestic exporter with large production facilities in the U.S., you are considering moving toward a multinational model by creating production facilities in Europe and Asia. What strategy would you follow in building an international information infrastructure; what applications would you recommend be shared and global or common; and how would you implement the strategy?

Group Project

With a group of students, identify an area of emerging information technology and explore how this technology might be useful for supporting global business strategies. For instance, you might choose an area like digital telecommunications (e.g., electronic mail, wireless communications, value added networks), or collaborative work group software, or new standards in operating systems, or EDI. It will be helpful to choose a business scenario to discuss the technology. You might choose, for instance, an automobile parts franchiser, or a clothing franchise like the Limited Express as example businesses. What applications would you make global, what core business processes would you choose, and how would the technology be helpful?

CASE STUDY

Retooling Black & Decker For Global Operations

Black & Decker had worked its way out of a market share slump and decline in the early 1980s to become the world's largest manufacturer and distributor of power tools for the do-it-yourself market in the 1990s. After losing market share for both professional and home use tools in the early 1980's, CEO Nolan Archibald, who joined Black & Decker in 1985, instituted a "cut and build" strategy: cut expenses to the bone and plow the savings

back into new products. Then, in 1989, Black & Decker acquired Emhart Corporation (a diversified company known for its home improvement products such as Kwiket locks and Price Pfister faucets, commercial/industrial products, and information systems and services.) With the acquisition, Black & Decker doubled sales from $2.2 billion to $4.8 billion in 1991. Approximately fifty percent of Black & Decker's product sales come from overseas. One way Black & Decker plans to retain its worldwide leadership is through the development of global information systems. According to CEO Archibald, IS was one area where progress was not being made toward a global operational capability. "We couldn't get information into the hands of managers to run things as well as we'd like to," explained Archibald.

Black & Decker applied the "cut and build" strategy to IS with a new twist: "push and pull." Since 1988 the company has tried to push development resources and computing power down as close to the end user as possible while at the same time pulling together computer hardware and software resources on a global basis. Here are some of their specific accomplishments:

- Linked acquired business operations via standard financial reporting systems.
- Implemented EDI and bar coding selectively at major retailers in the United States and initiated pilot projects in Europe.
- Initiated development of a strategic IS plan to support global business operations.
- Shifted some IS development to business units.
- Consolidated multiple mainframe data centers and initiated migrations from mainframes to PCs, LANs and midrange platforms, and consolidated telecommunications networks.
- Implemented a total quality process in IS.

The point of global systems, according to Black & Decker, is to "improve management of information flow on a worldwide basis, but still have the feel that things are local and are getting done on a timely basis." In Europe Black & Decker has run into difficulties trying to consolidate data centers and introduce common systems. Data definition is a real problem because Black & Decker operates in 15 European countries. In the United States it was much more centralized, but in Europe, Black & Decker, like most multinationals, was organized on a country basis with each country running its own show. This meant that there was no standard coding structure for products, customers, spare parts, invoices, or bills of lading. In short, the entire paper processing enterprise was for local needs. Business has certain inherent inefficiencies if each country produces its own parts manuals, each with different numbers. On the other hand, a company cannot force common systems or data definitions that are contrary to local practices. You have to be flexible, allowing for different languages, accounting methods, products, and retail markets.

Black & Decker's European MIS Director started the long process toward common systems by focusing on those countries where Black & Decker has large manufacturing facilities (Italy, Germany, and the United Kingdom). From 1986 to 1989, Black & Decker standardized the manufacturing countries on IBM mainframes and adopted the same CAD/CAM software standards for engineering and design as used in the United States.

Common worldwide financial systems were developed. It used to take several weeks to roll up the year-end figures from 40 different financial reports produced by 120 Black & Decker offices around the world. The reports used to be delivered by courier, fax, and E-mail, causing cumbersome administration.

The solution was a common financial software package. Black & Decker's U.S. businesses converted to a PC-based software package. In 1993 the Micro Control system was rolled out to all offices throughout the globe. Budgets are produced on Micro Control templates and then reported automatically to corporate headquarters. Now, year-end results are available in a couple of days (not weeks). Monthly budgets can be done in days.

Even with common software, some problems remain. The most significant is data architecture, and behind this problem, the question of what's best: global or regional definitions and systems, and business. For instance, it may be best to develop regional suppliers, closer to the factories, and closer to ultimate customers. If this is true, it may be best to develop regional data definitions rather than imposing some grand worldwide standard that does not satisfy anyone in Europe, the United States or Asia. If regional is better, this means parts, customer numbers, and vendors should be defined regionally. Currently, Black & Decker is building repositories for key corporate data in both North America and Europe.

Sales support systems offer an interesting insight into these kinds of issues. Black & Decker has several experiments in the United States and Europe with EDI. In the United States there is a common set of standards for EDI, but in Europe EDI has made progress mostly in the United Kingdom and Sweden, with other countries trailing behind and with slightly different standards in each country.

Source: Bruce Caldwell, "Black & Decker Retools," *InformationWeek* (September 23, 1991).

Case Study Questions

1. What kind of a global business strategy do you think Black & Decker is pursuing? Are they pursuing the right kind of systems appropriate for their business strategy?
2. How should Black & Decker decide on whether to develop global, regional, and local systems?
3. Is there a contradiction between "global information management" and the feeling that things are being done locally in a timely manner?
4. What should Black & Decker managers do about the different EDI standards in Europe? How can they convince retailers or vendors to adopt common standards? Which ones should they adopt—U.S. or European?

References   Cash, James I., F. Warren McFarlan, James L. McKenney, and Lynda M. Applegate. *Corporate Information Systems Management.* 3rd edition. Homewood, IL: Irwin, 1992.

Chismar, William G. and Laku Chidambaram. "Telecommunications and the Structuring of U.S. Multinational Corporations." *International Information Systems* 1, no. 4 (October 1992).

Cox, Butler. *Globalization: The IT Challenge.* Sunnyvale, CA: Amdahl Executive Institute, 1991.

Deans, Candace P. and Michael J. Kane. *International Dimensions of Information Systems.* Boston, MA: PWS-Kent, 1992.

Deans, Candace P., Kirk R. Karwan, Martin D. Goslar, David A. Ricks, and Brian Toyne. "Key International Issues in U.S.-Based Multinational Corporations." *Journal of Management Information Systems* 7, no. 4 (Spring 1991).

Dutta, Amitava. "Telecommunications Infrastructure in Developing Nations." *International Information Systems* 1, no. 3 (July 1992).

Holland, Christopher, Geoff Lockett, and Ian Blackman. "Electronic Data Interchange Implementation: A Comparison of U.S. and European Cases." *International Information Systems* 1, no. 4 (October 1992).

Ives, Blake, and Jarvenpaa, Sirkka. "Applications of Global Information Technology: Key Issues for Management." *MIS Quarterly* 15, no. 1 (March 1991).

Ives, Blake, and Jarvenpaa, Sirkka. "Global Information Technology: Some Lessons from Practice." *International Information Systems* (July 1992).

Karin, Jahangir and Benn R. Konsynski. "Globalization and Information Management Systems." *Journal of Management Information Systems* 7, no. 4 (Spring 1991).

Keen, Peter. *Shaping the Future.* Cambridge, MA: Harvard Business School Press, 1991.

King, William R., and Vikram Sethi. "An Analysis of International Information Regimes." *International Information Systems* 1, no. 1 (January 1992).

Mannheim, Marvin L. "Global Information Technology: Issues and Strategic Opportunities." *International Information Systems* 1, no. 1 (January 1992).

Nelson, R. Ryan, Ira R. Weiss, and Kazumi Yamazaki. "Information Resource Management within Multinational Corporations: A Cross-Cultural Comparison of the U.S. and Japan." *International Information Systems* 1, no. 4 (October 1992).

Neumann, Seev. "Issues and Opportunities in International Information Systems." *International Information Systems* 1, no. 4 (October 1992).

Palvia, Shailendra, Prashant Palvia, and Ronald Zigli, eds. *The Global Issues of Information Technology Management.* Harrisburg, PA: Idea Group Publishing, 1992.

Roche, Edward M. *Managing Information Technology in Multinational Corporations.* New York: Macmillan, 1992.

Steinbart, Paul John, and Ravinder Nath. "Problems and Issues in the Management of International Data Networks." *MIS Quarterly* 16, no. 1 (March 1992).

CHAPTER 20

Ethical and Social Issues in Information Systems

Should Automation Stamp Out Jobs?

The United States Post Office has been under intense public pressure to provide better service while keeping its rates down. To combat a rising tide of red ink, it embarked on a six-year $3.5 billion automation project. The Post Office started to mechanize mail handling down to the carrier level. It began using optical character recognition (OCR) technology to expedite letter sorting and handling by zip code. In cases where OCR could not determine the ZIP code, the Post Office planned to use an imaging system to put the address on a terminal screen so that operators could key in the ZIP code for remote printing of the bar code on the envelope. The Post Office planned to have all letters and eventually other classes of parcel post bar coded by 1995.

But when Postmaster General Marvin Runyon took office in May, 1992, he put the automation project on hold for a close review. Congress and organized labor were protesting the job reductions that directly resulted from the automation. The Post Office

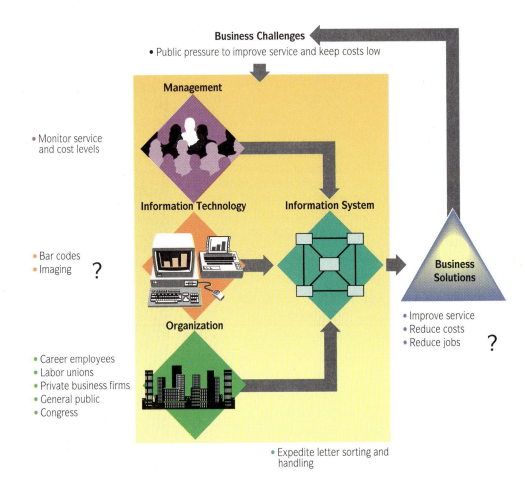

Business Challenges
• Public pressure to improve service and keep costs low

Management

• Monitor service and cost levels

Information Technology

Information System

• Bar codes
• Imaging   ?

Business Solutions

• Improve service
• Reduce costs
• Reduce jobs   ?

Organization

• Career employees
• Labor unions
• Private business firms
• General public
• Congress

• Expedite letter sorting and handling

planned to eliminate 40,000 positions through early retirement.

Although less than one-third of the automated equipment has been installed, what was put in place enabled the Post Office to cut more than 39,000 jobs through attrition over three years, reducing the number of career employees to 748,961. In September 1992, Representative Frank McCloskey of Indiana reported a "feeling of gloom and hysteria" among postal employees at a House subcommittee meeting. Job cuts appeared to be accelerating. The Post Office expected to eliminate another 19,000 career employee positions by the end of that year.

The General Accounting Office pointed out that automation was not a magic bullet that could reverse the trend toward rising postal expenses, noting that wage and benefit increases amounted to four times the amount saved by cutting labor costs in 1991. The GAO found that the Post Office had not been able to manage the work force to realize the full potential of automation. However, business analysts have applauded the Post Office's efforts to reduce inefficiencies and to respond to customers. For instance, the bar-code technology that was installed has cut the postage bills for some of the Post Office's largest customers, such as CoreStates Financial Corporation in Philadelphia, who receive hefty discounts for doing their own bar coding.

Runyon has been in a tight spot. He made a commitment to hold postal rates steady through 1994.

Source: Paula Klein, "Stamping Out Jobs," *InformationWEEK,* September 28, 1992.

The Post Office automation plan promised savings for both private industry and the general public but it also threated to eliminate the jobs of many valuable employees. Faced with these alternatives, what should the Post Office do? The plight of the Post Office is an example of an ethical dilemma created by information systems, one that is shared by many organizations today.

Balancing the need for efficiency with responsibility toward employees is one of many ethical and social issues faced by organizations using information systems. Others include establishing information rights, including the right to privacy; protecting intellectual property rights; establishing accountability for the consequences of information systems; setting standards to safeguard system quality that protect the safety of individuals and society; and preserving values and institutions considered essential to the quality of life in an information society. This chapter describes these issues and suggests guidelines for dealing with these questions.

After completing this chapter you will be able to:

- Understand the relationship among ethical, social, and political issues raised by information systems.
- Identify the main moral dimensions of an information society and apply them to specific situations.
- Apply an ethical analysis to difficult situations.
- Understand specific ethical principles for conduct.
- Develop corporate policies for ethical conduct.

20.1 Understanding Ethical and Social Issues Related to Systems

In Chapter 1 we identified one of the key management challenges facing you as the ethical and socially responsible use of information systems. Now it is time to put some flesh on that call.

Ethics refers to the principles of right and wrong that can be used by individuals acting as free moral agents to make choices to guide their behavior. Information technology and information systems pose unique problems for both individuals and societies because they create opportunities for social change. It is sometimes possible to create social change in a "socially responsible manner," one that takes into account the delicate balances among groups arrived at in the past. With new information technology it will also be possible for you—but not necessary—to decentralize power in an organization, invade the privacy of your employees while you improve service to customers, reach markets served by your global competitors and cause widespread unemployment, engage in new kinds of criminal activity as your company seeks to protect itself from information disclosures, and create new kinds of products which eliminate older products and the employment of people who make those products.

Information technology is certainly not the first technology to offer these potentials for radical social change. Steam engines, electricity, internal combustion engines, telephone and radio—each in their day offered new opportunities for social change and for individual action. At the same time, these new technologies threatened existing distributions of power, money, rights, and obligations—in short, the things considered worth having. Likewise with information technology: The development of IT will produce losers and winners, will produce benefits for many, and costs for others. In this situation, what is the ethical and socially responsible course of action?

Societies do not stand naked before technological change, swept along before the tide. Historically, societies have reacted to technological change by mitigating its influence, civilizing the change, compensating injured individuals, and attempting to restore balances struck over centuries. For instance, in response to vast advances in productivity brought about by modern technology, most industrial societies were able to reduce the work week from over 60 hours in 1900 to less than 40 hours in 1990. Technology, in other words, does not stand "outside" of society, acting upon it. Instead, technology—its manufacturers, benefactors, users—is a social phenomenon itself subject to all the constraints of other social actors. Among these constraints is the notion of social responsibility: you can and will be held accountable for your actions.

Ethics: Principles of right and wrong that can be used by individuals acting as free moral agents to make choices to guide their behavior.

A Model for Thinking about Ethical, Social and Political Issues

Ethical, social and political issues are of course tightly coupled together. The ethical dilemma you may face as a manager of information systems typically is reflected in social and political debate. One way to think about these relationships is given in Figure 20.1.

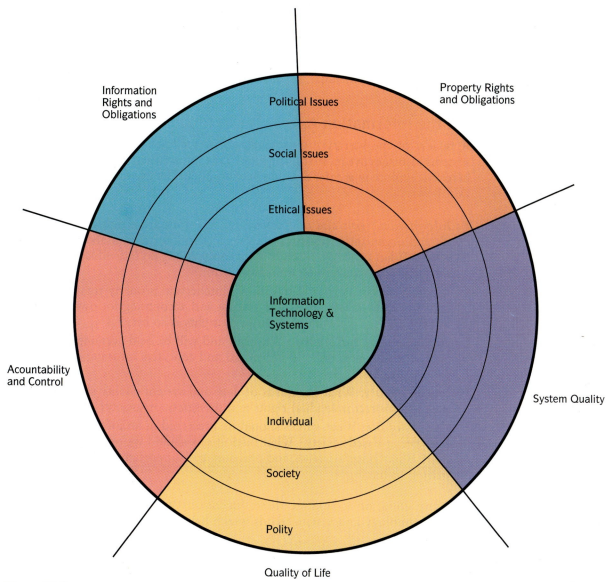

Figure 20.1
The relationship between ethical, social and political issues in an information society. The
introduction of new information technology has a ripple effect, raising new ethical, social and
political issues that must be dealt with on the individual, social, and political levels. These
issues have five moral dimensions: information rights and obligations, property rights
and obligations, system quality, quality of life, and accountability and control.

Imagine society as a more or less calm pond on a summer day, a delicate
ecosystem in partial equilibrium with individuals and with social and political
institutions. Individuals know how to act in this pond because social institutions
(family, education, organizations) have developed well-honed rules of behavior,
and these are backed up by laws developed in the political sector that prescribe
behavior and promise sanctions for violations. Now toss a rock into the center
of the pond. But imagine instead of a rock that the disturbing force is a powerful
shock of new information technology and systems hitting a society more or less
at rest. What happens? Ripples, of course.

Suddenly individual actors are confronted with new situations often not covered by the old rules. Social institutions cannot respond overnight to these
ripples—it may take years to develop etiquette, expectations, "socially responsible," "politically correct" attitudes, or approved rules. Political institutions
also require time before developing new laws and often require the demonstration of real harm before they act. In the meantime, you may have to act. You may
be forced to act in a legal "gray area."

We can use this model as a first approximation to the dynamics which connect ethical, social, and political issues. This model is also useful for identifying the main moral dimensions of the "information society" which cut across various levels of action—individual, social, and political.

Five Moral Dimensions of the Information Age

A review of the literature on ethical, social and political issues surrounding systems identifies five moral dimensions of the information age that we introduce here and explore in greater detail in Section 20.3. The five moral dimensions are as follows:

Information rights: The rights that individuals and organizations have with respect to information that pertains to themselves.

- *Information rights and obligations:* What **information rights** do individuals and organizations possess with respect to information about themselves? What can they protect? What obligations do individuals and organizations have concerning this information?
- *Property rights:* How will traditional intellectual property rights be protected in a digital society where tracing and accounting for ownership is difficult, where ignoring such property rights is so easy?
- *Accountability and control:* Who can and will be held accountable and liable for the harm done to individual and collective information and property rights?
- *System quality:* What standards of data and system quality should we demand to protect individual rights and the safety of society?
- *Quality of life:* What values should be preserved in an information- and knowledge-based society? What institutions should we protect from violation? What cultural values and practices are supported by the new information technology?

Before going on to analyze these dimensions we should briefly review the major technology and system trends which have heightened concern about the issues above.

Key Technology Trends Which Raise Ethical Issues

In what ways have information technology and systems created the ethical issues described above? In fact, these ethical issues long preceded information technology—they are the abiding concerns of free societies everywhere. Nevertheless, information technology has heightened ethical concerns, put stress on existing social arrangements, and made existing laws obsolete or severely crippled. There are four key technological trends responsible for these ethical stresses.

The doubling of computing power every 18 months since the early 1980s has made it possible for most organizations to utilize information systems for their core production processes. As a result, our dependence on systems and our vulnerability to system errors and poor data quality have increased. Occasional system failures heighten public concern over our growing dependence on some critical systems. Social rules and laws have not yet adjusted to this dependence. Standards for ensuring the accuracy and reliability of information systems (see Chapters 13 and 18) are not universally accepted or enforced.

Advances in data storage techniques and rapidly declining storage costs have been responsible for the multiplying databases on individuals—employees, customers, and potential customers—maintained by private and public organizations. These advances in data storage have made the routine violation of individual privacy both cheap and effective. For example, EMASS Storage Systems of Dallas advertises its new mass storage system as one capable of holding 6 terabytes of data in a 27 square foot space, at a media cost of $2 a gigabyte, a

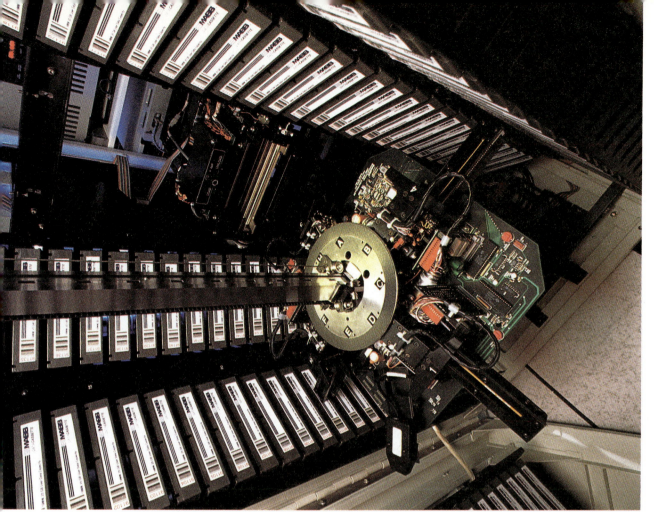

The EMASS data tower provides state of the art mass data storage and retrieval facilities for its clients.

data transfer rate of 15 megabytes per second, and a record access time of a few seconds (Datamation, 1992). This is a bit slow for on-line transaction processing, and slower than even a 600 megabyte CD-ROM with record access times of 150 milliseconds. Still, it is pretty impressive when you consider that the Social Security Master Beneficiary File requiring about one terabyte could be put on the EMASS system and take up only one sixth of the space! Already huge terabyte size storage systems are cheap enough for regional and even local retailing firms to use in identifying customers.

Advances in data mining techniques for large data bases are a third technological trend that heightens ethical concerns. For instance, cheap parallel supercomputers are used by Hallmark Cards, Kmart, Wal-mart Stores Inc., American Express, and others to very rapidly identify buying patterns of customers and suggest appropriate responses. One retailer examined customer "buying trips" as the unit of analysis. They discovered that if someone in the Midwest buys disposable diapers at 5 P.M., the most common thing next purchased is a six-pack of beer. The retailer decided, therefore, to put beer and snacks next to the diapers rack (*The Wall Street Journal,* December 23, 1992). These data mining techniques further shrink the penumbra of privacy created by older less powerful technologies.

But the impact of widely distributed supercomputing also has equity implications for society. As with mainframes of the past, supercomputing capacity will largely be dominated by elite groups in society—large business and government organizations, and the dominant professional and business classes running these institutions. In turn, these large groups may grow to become far more powerful vis-à-vis individuals and small groups than is now the case. What can be done to preserve equity, to encourage widely dispersed access to data and computing power?

Last, *advances in telecommunications infrastructure* like ISDN (Integrated Services Digital Network) and proposed national telecommunications networks like the National Research Education Network (NREN)—see the Window on Technology—promise to reduce greatly the cost of moving large data sets, and open the possibility of mining large data sets remotely using smaller desktop machines. Local Bell operating companies (BOCs) have been slow to adopt ISDN for lack of regulatory incentives. But more and more regulators are moving to allow the BOCs to distribute a wide range of data services (e.g., news, sports, movies, and data along with voice, and even to own the contents of what they distribute) over the strong opposition of the Newspaper Association and the Cable Television Industry Association.

By the year 2000 it is conceivable that many homes and business offices will have communication lines with up to 100 megabits per second capacity. This capability will radically reduce the cost of mining huge terabyte size databases, permitting the invasion of privacy on a scale and precision unimaginable to us now. Even the Census Bureau would lose its shelter: With commonly available census data on blocks, along with other data, we could easily pick out information about individuals with great regularity.

The development of national digital superhighway communication networks widely available to individuals and businesses poses many ethical and social concerns. Who will account for the flow of information over these networks? Will you be able to trace information collected about you? What will these networks do to the traditional relationships between family, work, and leisure? How will traditional job designs be altered when millions of "employees" become subcontractors using mobile offices that they themselves must pay for?

In the next section we will consider some ethical principles and analytical techniques for dealing with these kinds of ethical and social concerns.

20.2 Ethics in an Information Society

Ethics is a concern of humans who have freedom of choice. Ethics is about individual choice: When faced with alternative courses of action, what is the correct moral choice? When freedom of choice is restricted or impaired for whatever reason—reasoning ability, situational factors, or forced choice—then ethical analysis is less appropriate. What are the main features of "ethical choice?"

Basic Concepts: Responsibility, Accountability, and Liability

Responsibility: Accepting the potential costs, duties, and obligations of one's decisions.

Accountability: The mechanisms for assessing responsibility for decisions made and actions taken.

Liability: The existence of laws that permit individuals to recover the damages done to them by other actors, systems, or organizations.

Ethical choices are decisions made by individuals who are responsible for the consequences of their actions. Responsibility is a feature of individuals and is a key element of ethical action. **Responsibility** means that you accept the potential costs, duties, and obligations for the decisions you make. **Accountability** is a feature of systems and social institutions: it means that mechanisms are in place to determine who took responsible action. Systems and institutions where it is impossible to find out who took what action are inherently incapable of ethical analysis or ethical action. Liability extends the concept of responsibility further to the area of laws. **Liability** is a feature of political systems in which a body of law is in place which permits individuals to recover the damages done to them by other actors, systems, or organizations. Due process is a related feature of law-governed societies: it means a process in which laws are known and understood and there is an ability to appeal to higher authorities to ensure that the laws were applied correctly.

MANAGEMENT

Procter & Gamble Looks For a Leak

On June 10 and June 11, 1991, Alecia Swasy, a Pittsburgh-based reporter for *The Wall Street Journal* reported in the *Journal* that, according to inside sources at the Procter & Gamble Company, a senior executive was under pressure to resign and that the company might sell several unprofitable divisions. Based in Cincinnati, Ohio, Procter & Gamble is one of the world's largest consumer products companies with such brand names as Tide detergent, Crest toothpaste, and many other products.

In response to the articles, senior executives of Procter & Gamble, and corporate security officer Jim Jessee, asked the Cincinnati police to determine if any current or former employees were leaking confidential corporate information to *The Wall Street Journal*. In response to the complaints from the company, the Hamilton County Prosecutor subpoenaed Cincinnati Bell Telephone Company to identify all 513 area code numbers that had dialed Ms. Swasy's home or office telephones in Pittsburgh during an eight-week period that started on March 1, 1991. Cincinnati Bell serves 655,297 customers in the 513 area code, which also includes localities in Kentucky and Pennsylvania. About 13 million calls are placed each month in the 513 area code.

Cincinnati Bell refused comment on what it actually turned over to the prosecutor, but said that it routinely complies with subpoenas. A phone company spokesman said that under normal procedures the company's computers would have automatically searched its customer list and printed out the originating numbers, but not the names or addresses, of calls to Ms. Swasy's telephones.

Ohio has several statutes that prohibit the unauthorized disclosure of trade secrets or transmission of any confidential information, or formulas, customer lists, or other tangible pieces of information that would be valuable to a company and its competitors.

Civil liberties experts argued that Procter & Gamble's actions, and those of the prosecutor, may have violated the privacy rights of thousands of people, not to mention their First Amendment and Fourth Amendment guarantees of freedom of speech, and protections against unreasonable search and seizure. Much depends on how the investigation was actually carried out. If Procter & Gamble turned over its records of current and former employees and the police matched their list against the records from the phone company, then the rights of uninvolved parties may not have been violated. But if police learned the names of people unaffiliated with Procter & Gamble who called the *Journal*, or if they turned over an entire list of numbers of people who called the *Journal* to Procter & Gamble, then Fourth Amendment protections were violated.

One privacy expert argued that technological capacity has gone over the line of reasonable search and seizure when a computer system permits you to scan millions of calls made by hundreds of thousands of customers in order to identify who called a person based on the suspicion that a crime may have been committed.

Source: Randall Rothenberg, ''Search for News Leak Spurs Ohio Phone Sweep,'' *The New York Times* (August 16, 1991).

To Think About: If instead of phone records the records involved were letters sent and received through the post office, do you think the prosecutor should have or would have been able to subpoena all mail correspondence between Swasy and citizens in the (513) area code? Why are telephone records different from mailed letters? What do you think the public reaction to Procter & Gamble's actions was? What is your reaction? Who should be held responsible for the large scale sweep of telephone calls if it is determined this action violated the First and Fourth Amendments? Procter & Gamble management, the security officer, the phone company, or the prosecutor?

These basic concepts form the underpinning of an ethical analysis of information systems and those who manage them. First, as we discussed in Chapter 4 (Information Systems and Organizations), information technologies are filtered through social institutions, organizations, and individuals. Systems do not have "impacts" all by themselves. Whatever information system impacts exist are a product of institutional, organizational, and individual actions and behaviors. Second, responsibility for the consequences of technology falls clearly on the institutions, organizations, and individual managers who choose to use the technology. Using information technology in a "socially responsible" manner means that you can and will be held accountable for the consequences of your actions. Third, in an ethical political society, individuals and others can recover damages done them through a set of laws characterized by due process. The example of Procter & Gamble's efforts to detect an information leak among its employees is an instructive illustration of the difficulties of applying these principles.

Ethical Analysis

When confronted with a situation that seems to present ethical issues, how should you analyze and reason about the situation? Here's a five-step process that should help:

1. *Identify and describe clearly the facts.* Find out who did what to whom, and where, when, and how. You will be surprised in many instances how wrong the initially reported facts typically are, and often you will find that simply getting the facts straight helps define the solution. It also helps to get the opposing parties involved in an ethical dilemma to agree on the facts.

2. *Define the conflict or dilemma and identify the higher order values involved.* Ethical, social and political issues always reference higher values. The parties to a dispute all claim to be pursuing higher values (e.g., freedom, privacy, protection of property, and the free enterprise system).

   Typically, an ethical issue involves a dilemma: two diametrically opposed courses of action that support worthwhile values. In the Procter & Gamble case, you have two competing and opposing values: the right of a company to protect its internal information processes, and the rights of individuals to be free from unreasonable search and seizure, as well as to speak their minds.

3. *Identify the stakeholders.* Every ethical, social, and political issue has stakeholders: players in the game who have an interest in the outcome, who have invested in the situation, and usually who have vocal opinions. Find out who these groups are and what they want. This will be useful later when designing a solution.

4. *Identify the options that you can reasonably take.* You may find that none of the options satisfy all the interests involved, but that some options do a better job than others. Sometimes arriving at a "good" or ethical solution may not always be a "balancing" of consequences to stakeholders.

5. *Identify the potential consequences of your options.* Some options may be ethically correct, but disastrous from other points of view. Other options may work in this one instance, but not be generalizable to other similar instances. Always ask yourself, "What if I choose this option consistently over time?"

Once your analysis is completed, what ethical principles or rules should you use to make a decision? What higher-order values should inform your judgement?

Candidate Ethical Principles

While you are the only one who can decide which among many ethical principles you will follow, and how you will give priority to them, it is helpful to consider some ethical principles with deep roots in many cultures that have survived throughout recorded history.

Immanuel Kant's Categorial Imperative: A principle that states that if an action is not right for everyone to take it is not right for anyone.

Descartes' rule of change: A principle that states that if an action cannot be taken repeatedly, then it is not right to be taken at any time.

1. Do unto others as you would have them do unto you (the Golden Rule). Putting yourself into the situation of others, and thinking of yourself as the object of the decision, can help you think about "fairness" in decision making.

2. If an action is not right for everyone to take, then it is not right for anyone (**Immanuel Kant's Categorical Imperative**). Ask yourself, "If everyone did this, could the organization, or society, survive?"

3. If an action cannot be taken repeatedly, then it is not right to be taken at any time (**Descartes' rule of change**). This is the slippery-slope rule: An action may bring about a small change now that is acceptable, but if re-

peated would bring unacceptable changes in the long run. In the vernacular, it might be stated as "once started down a slippery path you may not be able to stop."

Utilitarian Principle: Principle that one should take the action that achieves the higher or greater value.

4. Take the action that achieves the higher or greater value (the **Utilitarian Principle**). This rule assumes you can prioritize values in a rank order, and understand the consequences of various courses of action.

Risk Aversion Principle: Principle that one should take the action that produces the least harm or incurs the least cost.

5. Take the action that produces the least harm, or the least potential cost (**Risk Aversion Principle**). Some actions have extremely high failure costs of very low probability (e.g., building a nuclear generating facility in an urban area), or extremely high failure costs of moderate probability (speeding and automobile accidents). Avoid these high failure cost actions, with greater attention obviously to high failure cost potential of moderate to high probability.

Ethical no free lunch rule: Assumption that all tangible and intangible objects are owned by someone else unless there is a specific declaration otherwise and that the creator wants compensation for this work.

6. Assume that virtually all tangible and intangible objects are owned by someone unless there is a specific declaration otherwise. (This is the ethical "no free lunch" rule.) If something created by someone else is useful to you, it has value and you should assume the creator wants compensation for his or her work.

None of these ethical rules can survive the detailed analytical mind of a contemporary philosopher or critical pundit. They have too many logical and substantive exceptions to be absolute guides to action. Nevertheless, actions that do not easily pass these rules deserve some very close attention and a great deal of caution if only because the appearance of unethical behavior may do as much harm to you and your company as actual unethical behavior.

Professional Codes of Conduct

When groups of people claim to be professionals, they take on special rights and obligations. They do not cease to be moral agents—all of their actions must be justified by moral reasoning as outlined above. As professionals, they enter into even more constraining relationships with employers, customers, and society given their special claims to knowledge, wisdom, and respect. Professional codes of conduct are promulgated by associations of professionals like the American Medical Association (AMA), the American Bar Association (ABA), and the American Society of Mechanical Engineers (ASME). These professional groups take responsibility for the partial regulation of their professions by determining entrance qualifications and competence. Codes of ethics are promises by the profession to regulate themselves in the general interest of society. In return, professionals seek to raise both the pay and the respect given their profession (See Table 20.1).

Table 20.1	ASSOCIATION OF COMPUTING MACHINERY CODE OF PROFESSIONAL CONDUCT

Recognition of professional status by the public depends not only on skill and dedication but also on adherence to a recognized code of professional conduct.

General Moral Imperatives

Contribute to society and human well being.

Avoid harm to others.

Be honest and trustworthy.

Honor property rights including copyrights and patents.

Give proper credit for intellectual property.

Access computing resources only when authorized.

Respect the privacy of others.

Source: The Association of Computing Machinery, New York, New York, 1993.

The largest association of computer professionals in the United States is the Association of Computing Machinery (ACM). The ACM has developed a professional code of conduct with moral imperatives.

These General Moral Imperatives are more fully detailed in a related and longer set of professional responsibilities and organizational imperatives. These extensions state for instance that ACM professions should consider the health, privacy, and general welfare of the public in the performance of their work and that professionals should express their professional opinion to their employer regarding any adverse consequences to the public.

Some Real-World Ethical Dilemmas

There are no "typical" ethical dilemmas involving information systems or the professionals who work in such systems. The recent ethical problems described below illustrate a wide range of issues. Some of these issues are obvious ethical dilemmas. Others represent some type of breach of ethics. In either instance, there are rarely any easy solutions.

Continental Can: Based in Norwalk, Connecticut, Continental Can Co. developed a human resources database with files on all of its employees. Besides the typical employee data, the system included the capability to "red flag" employees nearing retirement or approaching the age at which a pension would be vested in the individual. Throughout the 1980s, when the red flag went up, management would fire the person even after decades of loyal service. In 1991 a federal district court in Newark, New Jersey, awarded ex-employees $445 million for wrongful dismissal (McPartlin, June 22, 1992).

Computer Sciences Corporation at the EPA: In 1990 the Environmental Protection Agency (EPA) signed a $347 million outsourcing contract with Computer Sciences Corporation (CSC), which essentially gave CSC the entire responsibility for running the agency's computers and information systems. Investigations by the House Subcommittee on Oversight and Investigation, and the agency's own inspector general, in 1992 claimed that CSC overcharged and double charged the agency by $13 million, engaged in wholesale fraud, and had taken over the most sensitive information at the agency including databases on bids of competitors and the systems that processed orders for its own contract. According to the inspector general, CSC practically took over the agency and in the process hired more than 1400 of its own workers working on 200 separate projects. CSC denied these allegations and claimed that it was only EPA's administrative details that needed cleaning up, not CSC's practices (McPartlin, March 9, 1992).

Software bomb at Revlon: In 1988 Revlon Inc., one of the world's largest cosmetics firms, contracted with a small software firm called Logisticon Inc. to develop inventory control software for the sum of $600,000. In October 1990, the Revlon vice president for systems development, Nathan Amitai, sought to terminate the contract, claiming the work had not been "up to expectations." At that point, Revlon owed Logisticon $180,000 but refused to pay this amount until work for the first phase of the project was completed. Logisticon President Donald Gallagher blamed any performance faults on bugs in Revlon's systems, and demanded payment. Revlon refused.

At 2:30 A.M. on October 16, 1990, Revlon systems personnel reported systemwide breakdowns in Logisticon software. Logisticon faxed a letter to Revlon the next day, stating, "Logisticon disabled the operation of its Dispatcher System software last night but took great care to do it in an orderly fashion and not violate or corrupt your data. If you use or attempt to use Logisticon proprietary software to restart the Dispatcher System application package, we believe there is a real possibility that you could corrupt your data, and we will not be responsible. When and if agreement is reached on outstanding payments, systems can be restored in a few hours."

During the next three days, sales from the two affected distribution facilities "were brought to a standstill," resulting in the loss of millions of dollars of orders, and temporary layoffs of hundreds of workers. The systems were restored by Logisticon by October 19. On October 22, Revlon filed suit against Logisticon, charging intentional interference with contractual relations, trespass, conversion, misappropriation of trade secrets, and breach of contract and warranty. One of Revlon's complaints was that Logisticon did not mention in the contract with Revlon that a "drop dead" or software bomb device had been implanted in the software. Had this been a part of the contract, Revlon would have acted differently (Caldwell, 1990).

Technological Threats at AT&T: In March 1992, four months before entering into contract negotiations with the Communications Workers of America (CWA) and the International Brotherhood of Electrical Workers (IBEW), AT&T announced that it was introducing technology that would replace one-third of its 18,000 long-distance operators by 1994. The unions quickly branded the announcement as an "intimidation tactic" designed to soften up the unions' demands for higher wages and better working conditions.

AT&T plans to use voice recognition software to reduce the need for human operators by allowing computers to recognize a customer's responses to a series of computerized questions. New algorithms called "word spotting" allow the computer to recognize speech that is halting, stuttering, paused, or ungrammatical.

AT&T claims the new technology will permit it to eliminate 3000 to 6000 operator jobs nationwide, and 200 to 400 management positions. It will also be able to close 31 offices in 21 states. Long-distance operators earn anywhere from $10,300 to $27,100 a year, with benefits adding another third of the cost. AT&T claims not all workers will be dismissed and that many will be retrained for other positions.

Communications Workers of America officials expressed outrage at AT&T's announcement at the time, especially the announcement that entire offices will be closed. AT&T now claims it made the announcement because of leaks from the union officials and that managers only wanted to inform workers before the news spread further (Ramirez, March 4, 1992).

E-mail privacy at EPSON: In March 1990, E-mail administrator Alana Shoars filed a suit in Los Angeles Superior Court alleging wrongful termination, defamation, and invasion of privacy by her former employer, Epson America Inc. of Torrance, California. She sought $1 million in damages. In July 1990, Shoars filed a class suit seeking $75 million for 700 Epson employees and approximately 1800 outsiders whose E-mail may have been monitored. Shoars contends that she was fired because she questioned the company's policy of monitoring and printing employees' E-mail messages. Epson claims that Shoars was fired because she opened an MCI:Mail account without permission. Many firms claim that they have every right to monitor the electronic mail of their employees because they own the facilities, intend their use to be for business purposes only, and create the facility for a business purpose (Rifkin, 1991).

In each instance, you can find competing values at work, with groups lined up on either side of a debate. A close analysis of the facts can sometimes produce compromised solutions that give each side "half a loaf." Try to apply some of the principles of ethical analysis described above to each of these cases. What is the right thing to do?

20.3 The Moral Dimensions of Information Systems

In this section, we take a closer look at the five moral dimensions of information systems first described in Figure 20.1. In each dimension we identify the ethical, social, and political levels of analysis and illustrate with real-world examples the values involved, the stakeholders, and the options chosen.

Information Rights: Privacy and Freedom in an Information Society

Privacy: The claim of individuals to be left alone, free from surveillance or interference from other individuals, organizations, or the state.

Privacy is the claim of individuals to be left alone, free from surveillance or interference from other individuals or organizations, including the state. Claims to privacy are also involved at the workplace: millions of employees are subject to electronic and other forms of hi-tech surveillance. Information technology and systems threaten individual claims to privacy by making the invasion of privacy cheap, profitable, and effective.

The claim to privacy is protected in the U.S., Canadian, and German constitutions in a variety of different ways, and in other countries through various statutes. In the United States, the claim to privacy is protected primarily by the First Amendment guarantees of freedom of speech and association, the Fourth Amendment protections against unreasonable search and seizure of one's personal documents or home, and the guarantee of due process.

Due process has become a key concept in defining privacy where absolutist claims to be left alone are not tenable. Due process requires that a set of rules or laws exist which clearly define how information about individuals will be treated, and what appeal mechanisms are available. Perhaps the best statement of the due process in record keeping is given by the Fair Information Practices doctrine developed in the early 1970s.

Fair Information Practices (FIP): A set of principles originally set forth in 1973 that governs the collection and use of information about individuals and forms the basis of most U.S. and European privacy law.

Most American and European privacy law is based on a regime called Fair Information Practices (FIP) first set forth in a report written in 1973 by a federal government advisory committee (U.S. Department of Health, Education, and Welfare, 1973). **Fair Information Practices** (FIP) is a set of principles governing the collection and use of information about individuals. The five fair information practices principles are shown in Table 20.2.

FIP principles are based on the notion of a "mutuality of interest" between the record holder and the individual. The individual has an interest in engaging in a transaction, and the recordkeeper—usually a business or government agency—requires information about the individual to support the transaction. Once gathered, the individual maintains an interest in the record, and the record may not be used to support other activities without the individual's consent.

Fair Information Practices form the basis of 13 federal statutes listed in Table 20.3 that set forth the conditions for handling information about individuals in such areas as credit reporting, education, financial records, newspaper records, cable communications, electronic communications, and even video rentals.

In the United States, privacy law is enforced by individuals who must sue agencies or companies in court in order to recover damages. European countries and Canada define privacy in a similar manner to that in the United States, but they have chosen to enforce their privacy laws by creating Privacy Commissions or Data Protection Agencies to pursue complaints brought by citizens.

Despite this legislation, most Americans feel there is less privacy today than ever. Public opinion polls show that when it comes to information privacy, most Americans are bewildered, fearful, confused, and increasingly distrustful about

---

Table 20.2   FAIR INFORMATION PRACTICES PRINCIPLES

1. There should be no personal record systems whose existence is secret.
2. Individuals have rights of access, inspection, review, and amendment to systems that contain information about them.
3. There must be no use of personal information for purposes other than those for which it was gathered without prior consent.
4. Managers of systems are responsible and can be held accountable, and liable for the damage done by systems, for their reliability and security.
5. Governments have the right to intervene in the information relationships among private parties.

Table 20.3 FEDERAL PRIVACY LAWS IN THE U.S.

(1) General Federal Privacy Laws

Freedom of Information Act, 1968 as Amended (5 USC 552)

Privacy Act of 1974 as Amended (5 USC 552a)

Electronic Communications Privacy Act of 1986

Computer Matching and Privacy Protection Act of 1988

Computer Security Act of 1987

Federal Managers Financial Integrity Act of 1982

(2) Privacy Laws Affecting Private Institutions

Fair Credit Reporting Act, 1970

Family Educational Rights and Privacy Act of 1978

Right to Financial Privacy Act of 1978

Privacy Protection Act of 1980

Cable Communications Policy Act of 1984

Electronic Communications Privacy Act of 1986

Video Privacy Protection Act of 1988

public policy in this area. According to a recent Harris poll, 76 percent of Americans believe they have lost all control over personal information, and 67 percent believe that computers must be restricted in the future to preserve privacy (Equifax, 1992). There are several causes of this erosion of public confidence: distrust of all institutions, the rapid growth of computer transactions not protected by any privacy legislation, and the loss of control over personal information which individuals, in fact, experience in a highly computerized transaction-oriented society. The development of law is clearly lagging far behind the reality of computer-based information.

ETHICAL ISSUES   The ethical privacy issue in this information age is as follows: Under what conditions should I (you) invade the privacy of others? What legitimates intruding into others' lives through unobtrusive surveillance, through market research, or by whatever means? Do we have to inform people we are eavesdropping? Do we have to inform people that we are using credit history information for employment screening purposes?

SOCIAL ISSUES   The social issue of privacy concerns the development of "expectations of privacy" or privacy norms, as well as public attitudes. In what areas of life should we as a society encourage people to think they are "in private territory" as opposed to public view? For instance, should we as a society encourage people to develop expectations of privacy when using electronic mail, cellular telephones, bulletin boards, the postal system, the workplace, the street? Should expectations of privacy be extended to criminal conspirators?

POLITICAL ISSUES   The political issue of privacy concerns the development of statutes which govern the relations between record keepers and individuals. Should we permit the FBI to prevent the commercial development of encrypted telephone transmissions so they can eavesdrop at will? Should a law be passed to require direct marketing firms to obtain the consent of individuals before using their names in mass marketing (a consensus database). Should E-mail privacy—regardless of who owns the equipment—be protected in law? In general, large organizations of all kinds—public and private—are reluctant to give up the advantages which come from the unfettered flow of information on individuals. Civil liberties and other private groups have been the strongest voices supporting restraints on large organization information gathering activities.

Property Rights: Intellectual Property

Contemporary information systems have severely challenged existing law and social practice which protects private intellectual property. In so doing, information systems have resulted in the loss of billions of dollars in software sales due to outright theft or piracy, and retarded the growth of the software industry by reducing its profitability. At the same time, the existence of so much stolen "free" software, the ease of creating perfect copies, has greatly expanded the use of software and hardware.

Intellectual property is considered to be intangible property created by individuals or corporations and is subject to a variety of protections under three different legal traditions: trade secret, copyright, and patent law. Each provides different kinds of protections for software (Graham, 1984).

Intellectual property: Intangible property created by individuals or corporations which is subject to protections under trade secret, copyright, and patent law.

TRADE SECRETS

Trade secret: Any intellectual work product used for a business purpose that can be classified as belonging to that business provided it is not based on information in the public domain.

Any intellectual work product—a formula, device, pattern, or compilation of data—used for a business purpose can be classified as a **trade secret,** provided it is not based on information in the public domain. Trade secrets have their basis in state law, not federal law, and protections vary from state to state. In general, trade secret laws grant a monopoly on the ideas behind a work product, but it can be a very tenuous monopoly.

Software which contains novel or unique elements, procedures, or compilations can be included as a trade secret. Trade secret law protects the actual ideas in a work product and not just their manifestation. In order to make this claim, the creator or owner must take care to bind employees and customers with nondisclosure agreements and to prevent the secret from falling into the public domain.

Here is the limitation of trade secret protection: While virtually all software programs of any complexity contain unique elements of some sort, it is difficult to prevent the ideas in the work from falling into the public domain when the software is widely distributed. For instance, the idea of highlighting text and then copying that text to a separate storage area called the Clipboard was an idea that quickly fell into the public domain and could not receive protection as a trade secret. However, the manner in which a proprietary direct marketing software program searches a huge national database to identify prospects can be protected as a trade secret provided the creator can show the process relies on novel or unique elements, or even that it simply provides a competitive business advantage using less well-known techniques. The key is to avoid having ideas fall into public domain.

COPYRIGHT

Copyright: A statutory grant which protects creators of intellectual property against copying by others for any purpose for a period of 28 years.

Copyright is a statutory grant which protects creators of intellectual property against copying by others for any purpose for a period of 28 years. Since the first Federal Copyright Act of 1790, and the creation of the Copyright Office to register copyrights and enforce copyright law, Congress has extended copyright protection to books, periodicals, lectures, dramas, musical compositions, maps, drawings, artwork of any kind, and motion pictures. Since the earliest days, the Congressional intent behind copyright laws has been to encourage creativity and authorship by ensuring that creative people receive the financial and other benefits of their work. Copyright provides a limited monopoly on the commercial use of a work, but does not protect the ideas behind a work. Most industrial nations have their own copyright laws, and there are several international conventions and bilateral agreements through which nations coordinate and enforce their laws.

In the mid 1960's the Copyright Office began registering software programs, and in 1980 Congress passed the Computer Software Copyright Act, which clearly provides protection for source and object code, for copies of the original sold in commerce, and sets forth the rights of the purchaser to use the software while the creator retains legal title. This follows a pattern in which Congress will periodically update copyright laws to take into account new forms of expression. For instance, Congress acted at the turn of the century to protect mass market sheet music, and later to protect musical works against misappropriation by radio and television, through a series of acts which ensured authors receive payments anytime their sheet music is sold or their recordings are played on radios or other media.

Copyright protection is explicit and clear-cut: it protects against copying of entire programs or their parts. Damages and relief are readily obtained for infringement. The drawback to copyright protection is that the underlying ideas are not protected, only their manifestation in a work. A competitor can use your software, understand how it works, and build his or her own software that follows the same concepts without enfringing on a copyright.

"Look and feel" copyright infringement law suits are precisely about the distinction between an idea and its expression. For instance, in the early 1990s Apple Computer sued Microsoft Corporation and Hewlett-Packard Inc. for infringement of the expression of Apple's Macintosh interface. Among other claims, Apple claimed that the defendants copied the expression of overlapping windows. The defendants counterclaimed that the idea of overlapping windows can only be expressed in a single way, and therefore was not protectable under the "merger" doctrine of copyright law. When ideas and their expression merge, the expression cannot be copyrighted. In general, courts appear to be following the reasoning of a 1989 case—Brown Bag Software v. Symantec Corp.—in which the court dissected the elements of software alleged to be enfringing. The court found that neither similar concept, function, general functional features (e.g., drop-down menus) or colors are protectable by copyright law (Brown Bag v. Symantec Corp., 1992).

PATENTS

Patent: A legal document that grants the owner an exclusive monopoly on the ideas behind an invention for 17 years; designed to ensure that inventors of new machines or methods are rewarded for their labor while making widespread use of their inventions.

The first patent was granted by Congress in 1790, and the Patent Office was established in 1836. A **patent** grants the owner an exclusive monopoly on the ideas behind an invention for 17 years. The Congressional intent behind patent law was to ensure that inventors of new machines, devices, or methods receive the full financial and other rewards of their labor and yet still make widespread use of the invention possible by providing detailed diagrams for those wishing to use the idea under license from the owner of the patent. The granting of a patent is determined by the Patent Office and relies on court rulings.

The key concepts in patent law are originality, novelty, invention. The Patent Office did not accept applications for software patents routinely until a 1981 Supreme Court decision which held that computer programs could be a part of a patentable process. Since then hundreds of patents have been granted and thousands await consideration.

The strength of patent protection is that it grants a monopoly on the underlying concepts and ideas of software. The difficulty is passing stringent criteria of nonobviousness (e.g., the work must reflect some special understanding and contribution), originality, and novelty, as well as years of waiting to receive protection.

Contemporary information technologies, especially software, pose a severe challenge to existing intellectual property regimes, and therefore create significant ethical, social, and political issues. Digital media differ from books, periodicals, and other media in terms of ease of replication, ease of transmission, ease of alteration, difficulty classifying a software work as a program, book, or even music, compactness—making theft easy, and difficulties in establishing uniqueness. Does a hypertext document where concepts are linked via software links become unique from the original document? (See Samuelson, October 1991.)

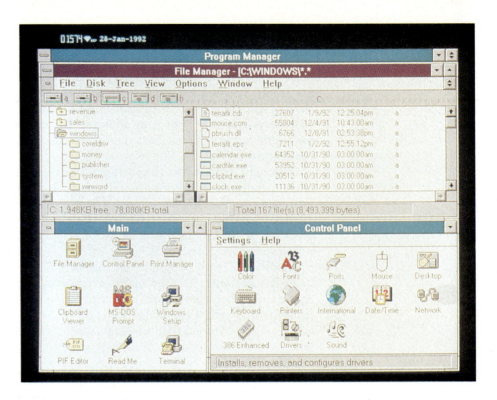

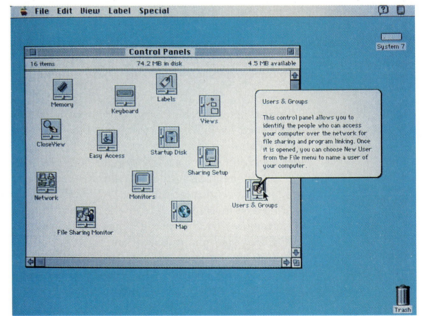

The look and feel of the Microsoft Windows Program Manager's control panel is similar to the Control Panel for a Macintosh System 7. Both systems use windows, scroll bars, icons, and pull down menus to interface with the users.

ETHICAL ISSUES   The central ethical issue posed to individuals concerns copying software: Should I (you) copy for our own use a piece of software protected by trade secret, copyright, and/or patent law? In the information age, it is so easy to obtain perfect, functional copies of software, that the software companies themselves have abandoned software protection schemes to increase market penetration, and enforcement of the law is so rare. However, if everyone copied software, very little new software would be produced because creators could not benefit from the results of their work.

SOCIAL ISSUES

There are several property-related social issues raised by new information technology. Most experts agree that the current intellectual property laws are breaking down in the information age. The vast majority of Americans report in surveys that they routinely violate some minor laws—everything from speeding, to taking paper clips from work, to copying software. The ease with which software can be copied contributes to making us a society of lawbreakers. In 1990, the Software Publishers Association (SPA) estimated it lost $2.4 billion or half the total of $5.7 billion in software sales. Copied software is routinely found in both personal and business settings (Markoff, July 27, 1992). These routine thefts threaten significantly to reduce the speed with which new information technologies can be and will be introduced, and thereby threaten further advances in productivity and social well-being.

POLITICAL ISSUES

The main property-related political issue concerns the creation of new property protection measures to protect investments made by creators of new software. Apple, Microsoft, and 900 other hardware and software firms formed the Software Publishers Association (SPA) to lobby for new protection laws and enforce existing laws. SPA has distributed more than 30,000 copies of SPAaudit—a software inventory management tool used by corporations to establish control over software used on individual PCs; established a toll free antipiracy hotline (1-800-388-7478) for employees to report on their corporations; completed 75 surprise audits or raids; sent 560 cease and desist letters; and filed more than 100 lawsuits since its inception (80 percent against corporations, 20 percent against bulletin board operators, training facilities, schools and universities). The SPA has developed a model Software Code of Ethics, described in the following Window on Organizations.

Allied against SPA are a host of groups and millions of individuals who resist efforts to strengthen antipiracy laws, and instead encourage situations where software can be copied. These groups believe that software should be free, that antipiracy laws cannot in any event be enforced in the digital age, or that software should be paid for on a voluntary basis (shareware software). According to these groups, the greater social benefit results from the free distribution of software and the "benefits" of software should accrue to the creators in the form of greater prestige perhaps but not in the form of profits.

Accountability, Liability and Control

Along with privacy and property laws, new information technologies are challenging existing liability law and social practices for holding individuals and institutions accountable. If a person is injured by a machine controlled in part by software, who should be held accountable and therefore held liable? Should a public bulletin board or an electronic service like Prodigy or CompuServe permit the transmission of pornographic or offensive material (as broadcasters), or should they be held harmless against any liability for what users transmit (as is true of common carriers like the telephone system)? Is Prodigy a common carrier? If you outsource your information processing, can you hold the external vendor liable for injuries done to your customers? Try some real-world examples.

SOME RECENT LIABILITY PROBLEMS

In February 1992, hackers penetrated the computer network of Equifax, Inc. in Atlanta, Georgia, one of the world's largest credit reporting bureaus that sells 450 million reports annually. Consumer files, credit card numbers and other confidential information were accessed. The company is working with police and reviewing all files to catch the criminals. When finished, it will notify all affected customers. Who is liable for any damages done to individuals (King, 1992)?

On March 13, 1993, a blizzard hit the East Coast of the United States, knocking out an EDS (Electronic Data Systems Inc.) computer center in Clifton,

ORGANIZATIONS
A Corporate Software Code of Ethics

This code of ethics states our organization's policy concerning software duplication. All employees shall use software only in accordance with its license agreement. Unless otherwise provided in the license, any duplication of copyrighted software, except for backup and archival purposes, is a violation of the law. Any unauthorized duplication of copyrighted computer software violates the law and is contrary to the organization's standards of conduct. The following points are to be followed to comply with software license agreements:

1. We will use all software in accordance with their license agreements.

2. Legitimate software will promptly be provided to all employees who need it. No company employee will make any unauthorized copies of any software under any circumstances. Anyone found copying software other than for backup purposes is subject to termination.

3. We will not tolerate the use of any unauthorized copies of software in our company. Any person illegally reproducing software can be subject to civil and criminal penalties including fines and imprisonment. We do not condone illegal copying of software under any circumstances and anyone who makes, uses, or otherwise acquires unauthorized software shall be appropriately disciplined.

4. No employee shall give software to any outsiders including clients, customers and others.

5. Any employee who determines that there may be a misuse of software within the company shall notify their department manager or legal counsel.

6. All software used by the organization on company computers will be properly purchased through appropriate procedures.

I have read the company's software code of ethics. I am fully aware of our software policies and agree to abide by those policies.

Source: *Software Management Guide: A Guide for Software Asset Management,* version 1.0. Courtesy of Software Publishers Association, 1992.

To Think About: Try to find out your university's policy regarding software. Is there a software code of ethics on campus? If an employee finds routine copying of software in a firm, should he or she a) call the firm's legal counsel, or b) call SPA on the antipiracy hotline? Are there any circumstances in which software copying should be allowed?

New Jersey. The center operated 5200 ATM machines in 12 different networks across the country involving more than one million card holders. In the two weeks required to recover operations, EDS informed its customers to use alternative ATM networks operated by other banks or computer centers, and offered to cover more than $50 million in cash withdrawals. Because the alternative networks did not have access to the actual customer account balances, EDS is at substantial risk of fraud. Cash withdrawals were limited to $100 per day per

On March 13, 1993, a winter storm devastated this Electronic Data Systems facility in Clifton, New Jersey. The building's collapse not only disabled the resident computer systems but knocked out the 12 different networks across the nation operating more than 5,000 ATM machines.

customer to reduce the exposure. Most service was restored by March 26. Although EDS had a disaster recovery plan, it did not have a dedicated backup facility. Who is liable for any economic harm caused individuals or businesses who could not access their full account balances in this period (Joes, 1993)?

In April 1990, a computer system at Shell Pipeline Corporation failed to detect a human operator error. As a result, 93,000 barrels of crude oil were shipped to the wrong trader. The error cost $2 million because the trader sold oil that should not have been delivered to him. A court ruled later that Shell Pipeline was liable for the loss of the oil because the error was due to a human operator who entered erroneous information into the system. Shell was held liable for not developing a system that would prevent the possibility of misdeliveries (King, 1992). Who would you have held liable—Shell Pipeline? The trader for not being more careful about deliveries? The human operator who made the error?

CATEGORIES OF LIABILITY

These cases point out the difficulties faced by IS executives who ultimately are responsible for the harm done by systems developed by their staffs. Traditionally, there are three categories of liability that courts use to deal with claims that products or services have caused physical or economic injury to consumers: breach of warranty, negligence, and strict liability in tort.

In general, insofar as computer software is part of a machine, and the machine injures someone physically or economically, the producer of the software and the operator can be held liable for damages. Insofar as the software acts more like a book, storing and displaying information, courts have been reluctant to hold authors, publishers and booksellers liable for contents (the exception being instances of fraud or defamation), and hence courts have been wary of holding software authors liable for "book-like" software.

The distinction between software as machine versus software as book permeates all three kinds of liability. A **warranty** can be expressly stated by the seller of goods, or implied by simply being sold on the marketplace where it is assumed by courts that the merchant is making an implied representation that the goods are of fair or average quality and fit for consumption. In either case, if software is part of a machine, it will be treated as a machine and warranty promises are enforceable. If the software is a service, warranty law does not apply unless the software author makes some specific warranties in contract about the performance of the software. If the software is a book, or an information service, then it is very unlikely warranties will apply.

Negligence also applies only to products and not, so far, to services. **Negligence** occurs when a product causes physical or economic harm to individuals, when the injury could have and should have been prevented, and when the producer has a "duty to care" about the consumer of the product. Negligence requires fault. Mere information providers have rarely been held liable no matter what media they use (the exception being professional advice of doctors or scientists and engineers). Producers of software have been found liable only in those cases where the software is part of a machine.

Strict liability in tort is a separate class of liability that arises whenever a defective product causes injury. In these cases, individuals can bring suits against the manufacturer independent of the question of fault, warranty, or duty to care. In other words, a manufacturer of a defective product that injures people can be held strictly liable regardless of whether or not he could have, or should have, prevented the defect. In software cases, as before, it is only when software acts as part of a defective product (rather than a service) that strict liability obtains.

From this brief assessment, you should conclude that in general it is very difficult (if not impossible) to hold software producers liable for their software products when those products are considered like books, regardless of the physical or economic harm which results. Historically, print publishers, books, or periodicals have not been held liable because of fears that liability claims would interfere with First Amendment rights guaranteeing freedom of expression.

What about "software as service"? ATM machines are a service provided to bank customers. Should this service fail, customers will be inconvenienced and perhaps harmed economically if they cannot access their funds in a timely manner. Should liability protections be extended to software publishers and operators of defective financial, accounting, simulation, financial, or marketing systems?

Warranty: A representation expressed by the seller of goods that the goods are fit for purchase and use.

Negligence: Finding of fault when a product causes physical or economic harm to individuals that could and should have been prevented.

Strict liability in tort: Class of liability whenever a defective product causes injury and the manufacturer can be held liable regardless of whether or not the defect could have or should have been prevented.

Table 20.4 REGULATORY REGIMES FOR VARIOUS INFORMATION PROVIDERS IN THE U.S.

Provider	Regulatory Regime
Book Publisher	None
Newspaper	None
Bookstore	None
Television Broadcaster	Federal Communications Commission (FCC), Courts, Congress
Radio Broadcaster	FCC, Courts, Congress
AT&T Long Lines	FCC, Courts, Congress
Local Bells (BOC)	States, Legislatures, Commissions
Cable Television Operator	Congress, States, Localities
Computer Bulletin Boards	Undecided
Public E-mail	Undecided
National Computer Networks	Undecided

ORGANIZATIONS:

Liability on the Prodigy Network

Medphone Corporation is a New Jersey manufacturer of transtelephonic defibrillators, devices that allow doctors to transmit computer signals remotely via a telephone system to heart patients undergoing shock therapy. The firm sued a disgruntled investor, Mr. DeNigris of Babylon, New York, for posting statements on Prodigy—the electronic information service run by IBM and Sears. The suit alleges that DeNigris violated securities laws when he posted a notice that said "The bottom line is that insiders are waiting to unload big amounts of the stock before the company collapses," and "No cash, no sales, no profits, and terrible management." Medphone claims these statements are not true and violate securities laws against stock price manipulation through spreading of false information.

DeNigris is a $47,000 a year government worker who lost $9,000 on Medphone stock. He said that if he had any idea that the Prodigy bulletin board would subject him to a libel suit and allegations of security fraud, he never would have bought a personal computer in the first place. DeNigris complained:

"If this is what a bulletin board is all about, my goodness."

Prodigy receives 60 million messages a year, and according to George Perry, Prodigy's general counsel, is in no position to do the kind of fact checking and analysis that is performed by a newspaper to protect against libel claims. However, Prodigy does monitor messages posted to bulletin boards to maintain a "family environment."

In the only other similar case to date, CompuServe was sued for posting libelous statements. In this case (Cubby v. CompuServe), the court ruled that CompuServe acted more like a bookstore and would not be held responsible for libelous messages posted to its bulletin boards. Some lawyers claim that Prodigy is liable for messages posted on its system because it failed to screen them and did not exercise due care. Other lawyers claim it is best if Prodigy—like CompuServe—does not screen any messages, thereby insulating itself from liability. Screening implies censorship and this would interfere with First Amendment rights of free speech, and perhaps increase the risk of liability (what if a false defaming message somehow were missed by the Prodigy censor?). According to some lawyers, if bulletin boards and networks are held liable for the messages posted on their systems or sent through their systems, most providers would get out of the business.

In a chilling afternote, Prodigy has complied with subpoenas from the Medphone attorneys seeking the names of people who read DeNigris' Prodigy message, or who communicated with him over Prodigy. This means the Prodigy network records can be used to trace communication patterns among users, perhaps further chilling the atmosphere for the free exchange of ideas.

Source: Arthur S. Hayes, "Computer Message Prompts Libel Suit," *The Wall Street Journal* (March 26, 1993).

To Think About: What are the implications of a monitored computer bulletin board? Of one that has no restrictions? What measures would you take to prevent bulletin boards from being used for posting libelous statements?

Software is very different from books. Software users may develop expectations of infallibility about software; software is less easily inspected than a book, and more difficult to compare to other software products for quality; and software claims actually to perform a task rather than describe a task like a book; people come to depend on services essentially based on software. Given the centrality of software to everyday life, the chances are excellent that liability law will extend its reach to include software even when it merely provides an information service.

Liability and accountability are also at the heart of debates over the responsibility and freedoms of computer bulletin boards and networks. Table 20.4 illustrates the different regulatory regimes of various information providers in the United States. The Window on Organizations describes a recent lawsuit seeking to establish the liability of a Bulletin Board user.

There are virtually no liabilities imposed on book publishers, bookstores, or newspapers (outside of outright defamation and certain local restrictions on pornographic materials). This is because of the historic roles these media have played in the evolution of First Amendment rights. Telephone systems are regulated "common carrier" monopolies. Corporations are granted a monopoly on telephone service with no liability for content of messages transmitted. In return they must provide access to all, at reasonable rates, and achieve acceptable reliability. Broadcasters are granted monopolies by the Federal Communications Commission, which allocates frequency spectrum according to the 1934 Communications Act and subsequent amendments. In return, broadcasters are subject to a wide variety of federal and local constraints on content and facilities. Cable television systems are directly regulated by Congress, as well as by states and localities. They too are liable for content of messages and are subject to many local regulations on content and community service.

ETHICAL ISSUES The central liability-related ethical issue raised by new information technologies is whether or not individuals and organizations who create, produce, and sell systems (both hardware and software) are morally responsible for the consequences of their use. If so, under what conditions? What liabilities (and responsibilities) should the user assume, and what should the provider assume?

SOCIAL ISSUES The central liability-related social issue concerns the expectations that society should allow to develop around service-providing information systems. Should individuals (and organizations) be encouraged to develop their own backup devices to cover likely or easily anticipated system failures, or should organizations be held strictly liable for system services they provide? If organizations are held strictly liable, what impact will this have on the development of new system services? Can society permit networks and bulletin boards to post libelous, inaccurate, and misleading information that will harm many persons? Or should information service companies become self-regulating, self-censoring?

POLITICAL ISSUES The leading liability related political issue is the debate between information providers of all kinds (from software developers to network service providers) who want to be relieved of liability insofar as possible (thereby maximizing their profits), and service users—individuals, organizations, communities—who want organizations to be held responsible for providing high quality system services (thereby maximizing the quality of service). Service providers argue they will withdraw from the marketplace if they are held liable, while service users argue that only by holding providers liable can we guarantee a high level of service and compensate injured parties. Should legislation impose liability or restrict liability on service providers? This fundamental cleavage is at the heart of numerous political and judicial conflicts.

System Quality: Data Quality and System Errors

The debate over liability and accountability for unintentional consequences of system use raises a related but independent moral dimension: What is an acceptable, technologically feasible level of system quality (see Chapter 13)? At what point should system managers say, "Stop testing, we've done all we can to perfect this software. Ship it!" Obviously, individuals and organizations cannot be held responsible or liable for "acts of God" or technologically unavoidable errors. They may be held responsible for avoidable consequences, foreseeable consequences, which they have a duty to perceive and correct. And there is a gray area: some system errors are foreseeable and correctable only at very great expense, an expense so great that pursuing this level of perfection is not feasible economically—no one could afford the product. What if the product was not offered on the marketplace, would social welfare as a whole not advance and perhaps even decline? Carrying this further, just what is the responsibility of a producer of computer services—should it withdraw the product that can never be perfect, warn the user, or forget about the risk (caveat emptor—let the buyer beware)?

As we have discussed in Chapters 13, 14, and 18, three principal sources of poor system performance are software bugs and errors, hardware or facility failures due to natural or other causes, and poor input data quality. Chapter 13 established that zero defects in software code of any complexity cannot be achieved and the seriousness of remaining bugs cannot be estimated. Hence, there is a technological barrier to perfect software and users must be aware of the potential for catastrophic failure. Nevertheless, there are industry standard test routines which if followed can produce software of acceptable but not perfect performance. For life-dependent applications additional protection is possible by independently building redundant software modules and checking their results against one another.

System hardware and facility failures are much better documented and more easily managed. Redundancy of processors in mission critical applications can reduce the probabilities of failure by known amounts; and even weather system patterns routinely used by civil engineers in designing buildings and bridges can be used as a rationale (by responsible system developers) to build emergency backup facilities for mission critical and life dependent applications.

Perhaps the single largest cause of system failure is seemingly trivial: poor input data quality. A survey of 50 large business CIOs found that half of the executives believed their corporate data were less than 95 percent accurate (Bulkeley, 1992). Some of the glitches are reported in Table 20.5.

While software bugs and facility catastrophe are likely to be widely reported in the press, by far the most common source of business system failure is data quality. A total of 70 percent of IS executives in a recent survey reported data corruption as a source of business delay, 69 percent said their corporate data accuracy was unacceptable, and 44 percent said no systems were in place to check database information quality (Wilson, 1992).

ETHICAL ISSUES   The central quality-related ethical issue raised by information systems is at what point should I (or you) release software or services for consumption by others? At what point can you conclude that your software or service achieves an economically and technologically adequate level of quality? What are you obliged to know about the quality of your software, its procedures for testing, and its operational characteristics?

Table 20.5   ILLUSTRATIVE REPORTED DATA QUALITY PROBLEMS

- An airline inadvertently corrupted its database of passenger reservations while installing new software and for months planes took off with half loads.

- A manufacturer attempted to reorganize its customer files by customer number only to discover the sales staff had been entering a new customer number for each sale because of special incentives for opening new accounts. One customer was entered 7000 times. The company scrapped the software project after spending $1 million.

- J. P. Morgan, a New York bank, discovered that 40 percent of the data in its credit-risk management database was incomplete, necessitating doublechecking by users.

- Several studies have established that 5—12 percent of bar code sales at retail grocery and merchandise chains are erroneous and that the ratio of overcharges to undercharges runs as high as 5:1, with 4:1 as a norm. The problem tends to be human error in keeping shelf prices accurate, and corporate policy which fails to allocate sufficient resources to price checking, auditing, and development of error-free policies. The cause of the high overcharge has not yet been determined but the pattern is disturbing, suggesting intentional behavior.

Sources: Bulkeley, op. cit., and Doug Bartholomew, ''The Price is Wrong,'' InformationWEEK (September 14, 1992).

SOCIAL ISSUES   The leading quality-related social issue once again deals with expectations: do we want as a society to encourage people to believe that systems are infallible, that data errors are impossible? Or do we instead want a society where people are openly skeptical and questioning of the output of machines, where people are at least informed of the risk? By heightening awareness of system failure, do we inhibit the development of all systems which in the end contribute to social well-being?

POLITICAL ISSUES   The leading quality-related political issue concerns the laws of responsibility and accountability. Should Congress establish or direct the National Institute of Science and Technology (NIST) to develop quality standards (software, hardware, data quality) and impose those standards on industry? Or should industry associations be encouraged to develop industry-wide standards of quality? Or should Congress wait for the marketplace to punish poor system quality, recognizing that in some instances this will not work (e.g., if all retail grocers maintain poor quality systems, then customers have no alternatives)?

Quality of Life: Equity, Access, Boundaries

Not all sins are crimes. The negative social costs of introducing information technologies and systems are beginning to mount as the power of the technology bounds upwards. Many of these negative social consequences are not violations of individual rights defended in the Constitution or statute, nor are they property crimes. Nevertheless, these negative consequences can be extremely harmful to individuals, societies, and political institutions. Computers and information technologies potentially can destroy valuable elements of our culture and society even while they bring us benefits. If there is a balance of good and bad consequences to the use of information systems, who do we hold responsible for the bad consequences? Below, we briefly examine just some of the negative social consequences of systems, considering individual, social, and political responses.

BALANCING POWER: One of the earliest fears of the computer age was that huge centralized mainframe
CENTER VS. PERIPHERY   computers would centralize power at corporate headquarters and in the nation's capital, resulting in a "Big Brother" society suggested in George Orwell's novel *1984*. The shift towards highly decentralized computing in the 1990s, coupled with an ideology of "empowerment" of thousands of workers, and the decentralization of decision making to lower organizational levels, have reduced fears of power centralization in institutions. Yet much of the "empowerment" and devolution described in popular business magazines is trivial. Lower-level employees may be empowered to make minor decisions about their work pace, and they may be able in some cases to stop the production line on observing defects, but the key policy decisions may be as centralized as in the past. Many of the participatory mechanisms dreamed up by consultants to tap into the profitable ideas of the workforce bring unclear and inequitable rewards to employees.

RAPIDITY OF CHANGE: Information systems have helped to create much more efficient national and
REDUCED RESPONSE TIME   international markets. The now more efficient global marketplace has reduced
TO COMPETITION   the normal social buffers which permitted businesses many years to adjust to competition. "Time-based competition" has an ugly side: The business you work for may not have enough time to respond to global competitors and may be wiped out in a year, along with your job. We stand the risk of developing a "just-in-time society" with "just-in-time jobs" and "just-in-time" workplaces, families, and vacations.

The film adaptation of George Orwell's novel *1984* portrayed a frightening vision of the future. "Big Brother" kept a constant surveillance over every aspect of the daily lives of all citizens.

MAINTAINING BOUNDARIES: FAMILY, WORK, LEISURE

Parts of this book were produced on trains, planes, as well as on family "vacations," and what otherwise might have been "family" time. The danger to ubiquitous computing, telecommuting, nomad computing, and the "do anything anywhere" computing environment is that it might actually come true. If so, the traditional boundaries that separate work from family and just plain leisure will be weakened. While authors have traditionally worked just about anywhere (typewriters have been portable for nearly a century), the advent of information systems, coupled with the growth of knowledge work occupations, means that more and more people will be working when traditionally they would have been playing or communicating with family and friends. The "work umbrella" now extends far beyond the eight-hour day.

Weakening these institutions poses clear-cut risks. Family and friends historically have provided powerful support mechanisms for individuals, and they act as balance points in a society by preserving "private life," providing a place for one to collect one's thoughts, to think in ways contrary to one's employer, and to dream.

DEPENDENCE AND VULNERABILITY

Our businesses, governments, schools and private associations like churches are incredibly dependent now on information systems and therefore highly vulnerable. With systems now as ubiquitous as the telephone system, it is startling to remember that there are no regulatory or standard setting forces in place similar to telephone, electrical, radio, television, or other public utility technologies. Information systems are unprecedented as a technology for their lack of societal oversight. This reflects the differences in technology—information systems are not utilities. There are multiple providers, no natural monopolies, and a free market with many alternatives. Information systems are not as systemic as telephone systems, and their failure (when it occurs) is therefore isolated to local nodes. The evolution of a national computer network in the 1990s in the United

The massive crater underneath the World Trade Center was the result of the terrorist attack on February 26, 1993. The blast killed 5 people, injured more than 300 people, and knocked out the communications, electrical, fire, safety and computer systems that supported the Towers.

States will result in a highly decentralized network, so that no single node failure can affect the nation. Nevertheless, the absence of standards and the criticality of some system applications will probably call forth demands for national standards, perhaps regulatory oversight.

Consider, for instance, that on any given business day more than $1 trillion worth of electronic transactions occur in New York City, and that a recent mayoral task force discovered that 90 percent of the large businesses in the city had no disaster contingency plan (Office of the Mayor, 1991). Table 20.6 lists the biggest system disasters culled from a list of more than 300 begun in 1987.

While distributed networks are seemingly more resistant to disaster than centralized mainframe installations, the terrorist attack on the World Trade Center—business home to more than 50,000 workers and hundreds of LANs—on February 26, 1993 demonstrated that it may be far easier to protect and backup a 20,000 square foot centralized data center than it is to achieve similar results for over one million square feet of office space.

COMPUTER CRIME AND ABUSE

Computer crime: The commission of illegal acts through the use of a computer or against a computer system.

Computer abuse: The commission of acts involving a computer that may not be illegal but are considered unethical.

Computer crime can be defined as the commission of illegal acts through the use of a computer or against a computer system. Computers or computer systems can be the object of the crime (destroying a company's computer center or a company's computer files) as well as the instrument of a crime (stealing computer lists by illegally gaining access to a computer system using a home microcomputer). Simply accessing a computer system without authorization, or intent to do harm, even by accident, is now a federal crime. **Computer abuse** is the commission of acts involving a computer which may not be illegal but are considered unethical.

No one knows the magnitude of the computer crime problem—how many systems are invaded, how many people engage in the practice, or what is the total economic damage. Many companies are reluctant to report computer crimes because they may involve employees. The most economically damaging kinds of computer crime are introducing viruses, theft of services, disruption of computer systems, and theft of telecommunications services. Computer crime has been estimated to cost over $1 billion in the United States, and an additional billion dollars if corporate and cellular phone theft is included. "Hackers" is the pejorative term for persons who use computers in illegal ways. Federal law enforcement officials have estimated that 50,000 computer users "hack" at some time or another, while others put the number at a more modest 5,000 (Sterling, 1992).

Computer viruses have grown exponentially since 1987: More than 1,000 viruses have been documented. The average corporate loss for a bad virus outbreak is $250,000, and the probability of a large corporation experiencing a significant computer virus infection in a single year is 50 percent according to

Table 20.6 THE LARGEST INFORMATION SYSTEM CATASTROPHES

Date	Event	Location	Number of Data Centers Downed
8/14/87	Rain storm	Chicago	5
10/1/87	Earthquake	Whittier, Calif.	3
5/8/88	Network outage	Hinsdale, Ill.	3
8/15/89	Hurricane Hugo	Charleston, S.C.	5
10/17/89	Earthquake	San Francisco	18
8/13/90	Power outage	New York	28
12/27/90	Utility vault fire	New York	2
8/19/91	Hurricane Bob	Northeast	3
4/10/92	Terrorist bomb	London	7
4/13/92	Flood	Chicago	33
5/1/92	Riot	Los Angeles	2
8/24/92	Hurricane Andrew	Southeast	39
12/11/92	Nor'easter	New York	7
2/26/93	Bombing	New York	21

Note: Incidents selected from 333 hot site recoveries since 1982

Source: "The Largest System Catastrophes," *InformationWEEK*, March 8, 1993. Copyright © 1993 by CMP Publications, Inc., Manhasset, NY 11030. Reprinted from InformationWEEK with permission.

some experts. However, examination of large-scale empirical data by IBM suggests a much lower rate of infection, on the order of 38 incidents per 100,000 PC machines, largely because most PCs are stand-alone machines or are tied into local networks that inherently limit the spread of viruses (Markoff, November 1, 1992). In a population like that of the United States, with more than 50 million microcomputers, this would suggest a total of 19,000 infections annually. This is no doubt an underestimate. While many firms now use antivirus software, the sale of more than 400,000 computer networks in the United States in 1992 will surely increase the probability of infections.

Many new technologies in the industrial era have created new opportunities for committing crime. Technologies create new valuable things to steal, new ways to steal them, and new ways to harm others. Automobiles, and the state highway system, gave a whole new twist to bank robbery in the 1930s in the United States, leading to stiff new laws adding penalties for interstate movement to avoid prosecution. Society responds historically to these challenges by extending existing legislation to cover new circumstances, and inventing new names for old crimes and whole new classes of crime. (Robbery becomes bank robbery, and crossing state lines to avoid prosecution while you are fleeing a bank robbery becomes a federal crime.)

Below we describe some illustrative computer crimes:

- "Hacker" Robert T. Morris, a computer science student at Cornell University, unleashed a computer virus over the Internet Network on November 2, 1988, jamming thousands of machines in tens of networks throughout the system. He was convicted under the Computer Fraud and Abuse Act, given three years probation, a $10,000 fine, and 400 hours of community service.
- In July 1992, a Federal grand jury indicted five members of a group of hackers calling themselves MOD—Masters of Deception. Theirs was one of the largest thefts of computer information and services in history. The hackers were charged with computer tampering, computer fraud, wire fraud, illegal wiretapping, and conspiracy. The group broke

into over 25 of the largest corporate computer systems in the United States, including TRW. Information Services (a prominent credit reporting firm), Southwestern Bell Corporation, New York Telephone, and Pacific Bell. The group stole and resold credit reports, credit card numbers, and other personal information. Federal investigators used court-ordered wiretaps to monitor the calls of members. The firms blamed their own lax security and a philosophy of "openness" for not detecting the hackers themselves. All the hackers involved were under 22 years of age (Tabor, 1992).

- At AT&T's British headquarters in London, three technicians set up their own company in 1992, assigned it a 900 number, and then programmed AT&T computers to dial the number often. The loss amounted to just under $500,000 before the fraud was accidentally detected.

- In 1991, at General Dynamics corporation, Michael Lauffenburg, a disgruntled employee, created a duplicate of an inventory control program used for the Atlas missile. The duplicate was a time bomb program designed to go off just before Lauffenburg quit the company. The duplicate program would erase the original program, disrupt building the missile, then erase itself to avoid detection. Lauffenburg felt underpaid and hoped to rejoin the company as a highly paid consultant to rebuild the original inventory program.

- In 1990, the Pinkerton Detective Agency discovered that employee Marita Juse had been siphoning off more than $1 million since 1988. Juse had been given a computer code to access Pinkerton bank accounts. She had discovered a second code that was required to provide payment authorization. The authorization code was given to her by her boss who told her to cancel it. Instead, she used it for two years without detection (Carley, 1992).

In general, it is employees—insiders—who have inflicted the most injurious computer crimes because they have the knowledge, access, and frequently a job-related motive to commit such crimes.

Congress responded to the threat of computer crime in 1984 with the Computer Fraud and Abuse Act (enacted in 1984 and amended in 1986). This act makes it illegal to access a computer system without authorization. Most of the states have similar laws, and nations in Europe have similar legislation. Other existing legislation covering wire tapping, fraud, conspiracy by any means, regardless of technology employed, is adequate to cover computer crimes committed so far.

EMPLOYMENT: TRICKLE-DOWN TECHNOLOGY AND RE-ENGINEERING JOB LOSS

Re-engineering work (see Chapter 11) is typically hailed in the information systems community as a major benefit of new information technology. Much less frequently noted is that redesigning business processes could potentially cause millions of middle level managers and clerical workers to lose their jobs. Worse, if re-engineering actually worked as claimed, these workers could not find similar employment in the society because of an actual decline in demand for their skills. One economist has raised the possibility that we will create a society run by a small "high tech elite of corporate professionals . . . in a nation of the permanently unemployed" (Rifkin, 1993). Some have estimated that if re-engineering were seriously undertaken by the Fortune 1000 companies, about 25 percent of the U.S. labor force could be displaced. But re-engineering is being seriously used at only 15 percent of American service and manufacturing companies, and the average reduction in employment in downsizing companies is 10 percent in a year. Several surveys have documented re-engineering failure rates at from 50 to 90 percent (Cafasso, 1993). While re-engineering projects can produce 50 percent declines in employment, this is rare and likely to happen in companies facing declining demand.

Economists are much more sanguine about the potential job losses. They believe relieving bright educated workers from re-engineered jobs will result in these workers moving to better jobs in fast-growth industries. Left out of this equation are blue-collar workers, and older, less well-educated middle managers.

It is not clear that these groups are infinitely malleable or can be retrained easily for high-quality (high-paid) jobs. Fortunately, demographers point out, the economy tends to generate jobs to accommodate whatever the existing labor is. In the period from 1960 to 1990, the labor force doubled because of the entrance of women and minorities. In the period from 1990 to 2010, the labor force is expected to be stagnant or even decline in size. Re-engineering may be necessary to accommodate a no-growth labor force. Alternatively, careful planning and sensitivity to employee needs can help companies redesign work to minimize job losses.

EQUITY AND ACCESS: INCREASING RACIAL AND SOCIAL CLASS CLEAVAGES

Does everyone have an equal opportunity to participate in the digital age? Will the social, economic, and cultural gaps which exist in American and other societies be reduced by information systems technology? Or will the cleavages be increased, permitting the "better off" to become still better off? When and if computing becomes ubiquitous, does this include the poor as well as the rich?

The answers to these questions are clearly not known, the differential impact of systems technology on various groups in society is not well studied. What is known is that information and knowledge, and access to these resources through educational institutions and public libraries, are inequitably distributed (see Table 20.7). Access to computers is distributed inequitably along racial and social class lines as are many other information resources. Left uncorrected, we could end up creating a society of information haves, computer literate and skilled versus a large group of information have-nots, computer illiterate and unskilled.

Poor children attending poor school districts are less likely to use computers at school. Children from wealthy homes are five times as likely to use PCs for school work than poor children. Whites are three times more likely to use computers at home for school work than Afro-Americans. Schools and other institutions make up for some of the social disparities in access in computing, but not all. Potentially we could create a society of information haves and information have-nots.

HEALTH RISKS: RSI, CVS, AND TECHNOSTRESS

Repetitive stress injury (RSI): Occupational disease that occurs when muscle groups are forced through the same, repetitive actions with high impact loads or thousands of repetitions with low impact loads.

Carpal tunnel syndrome (CTS): Type of RSI in which pressure on the median nerve through the wrist's bony carpal tunnel structure produces pain.

In 1980, at the beginning of the microcomputer revolution, no one thought that by 1992 business would be paying $20 billion a year to compensate and treat victims of the most important occupational disease today: **repetitive stress injury (RSI)**. RSI occurs when muscle groups are forced through the same, repetitive actions often with high impact loads (like tennis) or tens of thousands of repetitions under low impact loads (like working at a computer keyboard.)

The single largest source of RSI is computer keyboards. Forty-six million Americans use computers at work, and 185,000 cases of RSI are reported each year according to the National Center for Health Statistics. The most common kind of computer-related RSI is **carpal tunnel syndrome (CTS)** in which pressure on the median nerve through the wrist's bony structure called a "carpal tunnel" produces pain. The pressure is caused by constant repetition of keystrokes: in a single shift a word processor may perform 23,000 keystrokes. Symptoms of carpal tunnel syndrome include numbness, shooting pain, inability to grasp objects, and tingling. So far, 1.89 million workers have been diagnosed with carpal tunnel syndrome.

Treating RSI is expensive; on average, $29,000 per case. Affected workers generally cannot sue a company for exposing them to poorly constructed keyboards because of state workmen compensation laws that remove liability from companies and pay workers directly for lost income. However, there are more than one hundred lawsuits outstanding against keyboard and computer manufacturers (Feder, 1992).

RSI is avoidable. Designing workstations for a neutral wrist position (using a wrist rest to support the wrist), proper monitor stands, and footrests all contribute to proper posture and reduced RSI. New ergonomically correct key-

Characteristic	Percent
PERCENT USING COMPUTERS AT SCHOOL	
Sex: Male	43.5
Female	41.9
Race: White[1]	45.7
Black[1]	32.5
Hispanic	42.5
Other[1]	35.0
Household income: Under $5,000	36.7
$5,000 to $9,999	36.1
$10,000 to $14,999	38.4
$15,000 to $19,999	41.5
$20,000 to $24,999	42.4
$25,000 to $29,999	46.1
$30,000 to $34,999	44.2
$35,000 to $39,999	45.2
$40,000 to $49,999	44.7
$50,000 to $59,999	48.4
$60,000 to $74,999	45.3
$74,999 or more	51.2
Control of school: Public	43.3
Private	38.9
PERCENT USING COMPUTERS AT HOME	
Sex: Male	20.7
Female	17.0
Race: White[1]	22.6
Black[1]	7.3
Hispanic	19.0
Other[1]	7.4
Household income: Under $5,000	8.4
$5,000 to $9,999	5.4
$10,000 to $14,999	7.2
$15,000 to $19,999	11.3
$20,000 to $24,999	12.9
$25,000 to $29,999	17.0
$30,000 to $34,999	17.7
$35,000 to $39,999	21.4
$40,000 to $49,999	25.7
$50,000 to $59,999	31.1
$60,000 to $74,999	32.2
$74,999 or more	43.8
Control of school: Public	17.9
Private	24.4

Table 20.7 (continued)

Characteristic	Percent
PERCENT USING COMPUTERS AT HOME FOR SCHOOL WORK	
Sex: Male	9.5
Female	8.3
Race: White[1]	10.7
Black[1]	3.4
Hispanic	9.1
Other[1]	3.6
Household income: Under $5,000	5.0
$5,000 to $9,999	3.2
$10,000 to $14,999	3.5
$15,000 to $19,999	4.5
$20,000 to $24,999	5.7
$25,000 to $29,999	6.4
$30,000 to $34,999	8.0
$35,000 to $39,999	10.5
$40,000 to $49,999	11.9
$50,000 to $59,999	15.7
$60,000 to $74,999	14.6
$74,999 or more	22.0

[1] Non-Hispanic.

Source: U.S. National Center for Education Statistics, *Digest of Education Statistics,* 1990. Based on Current Population Survey and subject to sampling error.

boards are also an option. These measures should be backed up by frequent rest breaks, rotation of employees to different jobs, and moving towards voice or scanner data entry.

In 1991, San Francisco passed legislation requiring companies with 15 or more workers to grant 15-minute rest periods every two hours, and to provide workers with ergonomically designed equipment. Many other localities have passed or are considering similar legislation. The law was struck down by a Superior Court judge on the grounds that only the state can regulate safety in the workplace. The legal challenge was brought by two small local firms but was backed financially by several large computer manufacturers (Pollack, 1992).

RSI is not the only occupational illness caused by computers: back and neck pain, leg stress, and foot pain also result from poor ergonomic designs of workstations (see Table 20.8).

Computer vision syndrome (CVS) refers to any eye strain condition related to cathode ray tube (CRT) use. Its symptoms are headaches, blurred vision, and dry and irritated eyes. The symptoms are usually temporary (Furger, 1993).

Computer vision syndrome (CVS): Eye strain condition related to cathode ray tube (CRT) use, with symptoms including headaches, blurred vision, and dry, irritated eyes.

Table 20.8 COMPUTER-RELATED DISEASES

Disease/Risk	Incidence
RSI	185,000 new cases a year
Other joint diseases	Unknown
Computer Vision Syndrome	10 million cases a year
Miscarriage	Unknown. Related to manufacturing chemicals
Technostress	5–10 million cases
VDT Radiation	Unknown impacts

Apple Computer Corporation offers an ergonomically designed keyboard and mouse. The adjustable keyboard and desktop bus mouse can be positioned to meet the needs of any user.

Technostress: Stress induced by computer use whose symptoms include aggravation, hostility toward humans, impatience, and enervation.

The newest computer-related malady is **technostress,** defined as a computer-use induced stress and whose symptoms are aggravation, hostility towards humans, impatience, and enervation. According to the National Council on Compensation Insurance, occupational disease claims for stress doubled in 1980 (from 5 percent to 10 percent of claims), and in California stress claims for compensation have increased 500 percent since 1980. The California Workers Compensation Institute has concluded that exposure to computer-intense environments is a major factor in stress disease (McPartlin, 1990; Brod, 1982). The problem according to experts is that humans working continuously with computers come to expect other humans and human institutions to behave like computers, providing instant response and attentiveness, with an absence of emotion. Computer-intense workers are aggravated when put on hold during a phone call, tend to yell or mutter at ATM machines that are slow, become incensed or alarmed when their PCs take a few seconds longer to perform a task, lack empathy for humans, and seek out friends who mirror the characteristics of their machines. Technostress is thought to be related to high levels of job turnover in the computer industry, high levels of early retirement from computer-intense occupations, and elevated levels of drug and alcohol abuse.

The incidence of technostress is not known but is thought to be in the millions in the United States and growing rapidly. Although frequently denied as a problem by management, computer-related jobs now top the list of stressful occupations based on health statistics in several industrialized countries. The costs worldwide of stress are put at $200 billion. In the United Kingdom, 10 percent of the gross national product is eaten up by the effects of stress, not all of it computer related (McPartlin, 1993).

To date the role of CRT radiation in occupational disease has not been proven. Video display terminals (VDTs) emit nonionizing electric and magnetic fields at low frequencies. These rays enter the body and have unknown effects on enzymes, molecules, chromosomes, and cell membranes. Early studies suggesting a link between low level EMFs (electromagnetic fields) and miscarriages have been contradicted by one later, superior study published in 1991 (Schnorr, 1991; Stevens, 1991). Longer-term studies are investigating low-level EMFs and birth defects, stress, low birth weight, and other diseases. All manufacturers have

TECHNOLOGY:

The Coming of a National Digital Superhighway Raises Many Ethical and Social Issues

In 1989, Congress passed the High Performance Computing Act that provided $3 billion in seed money to spur the development of supercomputer centers in the United States and a very high capacity network called the National Research Education Network (NREN) to connect universities and research centers. The bill was spearheaded by then-Senator Albert Gore, who went on to become Vice President of the United States in 1992. Gore and President Bill Clinton began building on the High Performance Computing Act by suggesting a much larger-scale national computing network to connect individuals, businesses, libraries, research centers, and universities. According to one pundit, the proposed national computing network would be the "mother of all networks," a network of networks like Internet. Largely fiberoptic, the network would handle data, voice, and video images at 100 megabits per second to the household, with a 3 gigabit national backbone—enough to be called the "everything network of your dreams."

Here are just some of the projected benefits: Students could do research using the National Library of Congress, or any library in the country with full text retrieval possible; medical care would improve because patient records could be transferred anywhere

they were needed; remote diagnosis by faraway specialists would be possible; scientists and engineers around the world could cooperate on the design of new products; video fans could call up any movie and view it; working at home would be common because there would be as much information at home as in the office; business would improve because the network could act as a huge order-entry system, eliminating paper waste and slow response time.

Briefly, the social impact of a national supernetwork is likely to be as great as the building of the transcontinental railway and the interstate highway system combined. The cost: hundreds of billions of dollars.

The national computing network requires rewiring America with fiberoptic cable to the household or neighborhood switch (from which ordinary twisted wire can be used to transmit into individual households); new hardware switches and/or upgrading the existing telephone system; and new software.

Who should build the network (and pay for it)? Owners of existing networks—like AT&T and other long distance companies—want the government to stay out and instead want to evolve the telephone network and existing technologies like ISDN (Integrated Services Digital Network). Critics

charge the phone companies will never invest the money needed, and ISDN is too slow anyway. Moreover, if private enterprise develops the network, they might charge so much that universities, libraries, and homeowners could not afford to use it. The major computer manufacturers like Apple, DEC, IBM and others have formed a group called the Computer Systems Policy Project to lobby for a large government leadership role in building the network.

Source: Computer Systems Policy Project, "Perspectives on the National Information Infrastructure" (January 12, 1993).

To Think About: What impact will the proposed national computing network have on the moral dimensions described above, especially on information rights and obligations, property rights, and accountability and control?
If the network were to become as important as proponents argue, what happens if network service is disrupted, even temporarily?
Who should build the national computing network? What analogies to transcontinental railroads, interstate highways, and telephone utilities seem appropriate? Is it in the interests of U.S. citizens and taxpayers to fund this network?

reduced CRT emissions since the early years of 1980, and European countries like Sweden have adopted very stiff radiation emission standards.

The computer has become a part of our lives—personally as well as socially, culturally, and politically. Like so many technologies that came before, information systems technology can be used to elevate the human spirit and well being. But like other technologies, it often acts as a mirror, reflecting our foibles and even exaggerating them at times. We did not analyze the ethical, social, and political issues of each social impact in this section, but they should be obvious to readers. It is unlikely the issues and our choices will become easier in the near future as information technology continues to transform our world. The development of a national electronic superhighway described in the Window on Technology suggests that all the ethical and social issues we have described will be heightened further as we move into the first digital century.

Management Actions: A Corporate Code of Ethics

Some corporations have developed far reaching corporate IS codes of ethics—Federal Express, IBM, American Express, and Merck and Co.. But most firms have not developed these codes of ethics, which leaves them at the mercy of fate, and their employees in the dark about expected correct behavior. There is some dispute concerning a general code of ethics (about 40 percent of the American Fortune 500 firms have such codes) versus a specific information systems code of ethics (about 40 percent of Fortune 500 firms). As managers, you should strive to develop an IS-specific set of ethical standards for each of the five moral dimensions:

- *Information rights and obligations.* A code should cover topics like employee E-mail privacy, work place monitoring, treatment of corporate information, and policies on customer information.

- *Property rights and obligations.* A code should cover topics like software licenses, ownership of firm data and facilities, ownership of software created by employees on company hardware, and software copyrights. Specific guidelines for contractual relationships with third parties should be covered as well.

- *Accountability and control.* The code should specify a single individual responsible for all information systems, and underneath this individual others who are responsible for individual rights, the protection of property rights, system quality, and quality of life (e.g., job design, ergonomics, employee satisfaction). Responsibilities for control of systems, audits, and management should be clearly defined. The potential liabilities of systems officers, and the corporation, should be detailed in a separate document.

- *System quality.* The code should describe the general levels of data quality and system error that can be tolerated with detailed specifications left to specific projects. The code should require that all systems attempt to estimate data quality and system error probabilities.

- *Quality of life.* The code should state that the purpose of systems is to improve the quality of life for customers and for employees by achieving high levels of product quality, customer service, and employee satisfaction and human dignity through proper ergonomics, job and work flow design, and human resource development.

Management Challenges

1. **Understanding the moral risks of new technology.** Rapid technological change means that the choices facing individuals, the balance of risk and reward, and the probabilities of apprehension for wrongful acts all change as well. In this environment it will be important for management to conduct an ethical and social impact analysis of new technologies. One might take each of the moral dimensions described in this chapter and briefly speculate on how a new technology will impact each dimension. There will be no right answers for how to behave but there should be considered management judgement on the moral risks of new technology.

2. **Establishing corporate ethics policies that include IS issues.** As managers you will be responsible for developing corporate ethics policies and for enforcing them and explaining them to employees. Historically the IS area is the last to be consulted and much more attention has been paid to financial integrity and personnel policies. But from what you now know after reading this chapter, it is clear your corporation should have an ethics policy in the IS area covering such issues as privacy, property, accountability, system quality, and quality of life. The challenge will be in educating non-IS managers to the need for these policies, as well as educating your workforce.

Summary

Understand the relationship among ethical, social, and political issues raised by information systems.

Ethical, social, and political issues are closely related in an information society. Ethical issues confront individuals who must choose a course of action, often in a situation where two or more ethical principles are in conflict (a dilemma). Social issues spring from ethical issues. Societies must develop expectations in individuals about the correct course of action, and social issues then are debates about the kinds of situations and expectations that societies should develop so that individuals behave correctly. Political issues spring from social conflict and have to do largely with laws that prescribe behavior and seek to use the law to create situations where individuals behave correctly.

Identify the main moral dimensions of an information society and apply them to specific situations.

There are five main moral dimensions that tie together ethical, social, and political issues in an information society. These moral dimensions are information rights and obligations, property rights, accountability and control, system quality, and quality of life.

Apply an ethical analysis to difficult situations.

An ethical analysis is a five-step methodology for analyzing a situation. The method involves identifying the facts, values, stakeholders, options, and consequences of actions. Once completed, you can begin to consider what ethical principle you should apply to a situation in order to arrive at a judgment.

Understand specific ethical principles for conduct.

Six ethical principles are available to judge your own conduct (and that of others). These principles are derived independently from several cultural, religious and intellectual traditions. They are not hard and fast rules and may not apply in all situations. The principles are the Golden Rule, Immanuel Kant's Categorical Imperative, Descartes' rule of change, the Utilitarian Principle, the Risk Aversion Principle, and the ethical no free lunch rule.

Develop corporate policies for ethical conduct.

For each of the five moral dimensions, corporations should develop an ethics policy statement to assist individuals and to encourage the correct decisions. The policy areas are as follows. Individual information rights: spell out corporate privacy and due process policies. Property rights: clarify how the corporation will treat property rights of software owners. Accountability and control: clarify who is responsible and accountable for information. System quality: identify methodologies and quality standards to achieve. Quality of life: identify corporate policies on family, computer crime, decision making, vulnerability, job loss, and health risks.

Key Terms

Ethics	Trade secret
Information rights	Copyright
Responsibility	Patent
Accountability	Warranty
Liability	Negligence
Immanuel Kant's Categorial Imperative	Strict liability in tort
Descartes' rule of change	Computer crime
Utilitarian Principle	Computer abuse
Risk Aversion Principle	Repetitive stress injury (RSI)
Ethical no free lunch rule	Carpal tunnel syndrome (CTS)
Privacy	Computer vision syndrome (CVS)
Fair Information Practices	Technostress
Intellectual property	

1. In what ways are ethical, social, and political issues connected? Give some examples.
2. What are the key technological trends that heighten ethical concerns?
3. What are the differences between responsibility, accountability, and liability?
4. What are the five steps in an ethical analysis?
5. Identify six ethical principles.
6. What is a professional code of conduct?
7. What are meant by "privacy" and "fair information practices"?
8. What are the three different regimes that protect intellectual property rights?
9. What are the three categories of liability?
10. Why is it so difficult to hold software services liable for failure or injury?
11. What is the most common cause of system quality problems?
12. Name four "quality of life" impacts of computers and information systems.
13. What is technostress, and how would you measure it?
14. Name three management actions that could reduce RSI injuries.

Discussion Questions

1. Why should anyone care about unemployment caused by re-engineering? Won't these workers be rehired at some point in the future when business gets better?
2. If everyone copied software, there would be no real market for software products, and producers of software would go out of business. Is this really true? What ethical principle is being applied in this statement? Discuss.
3. Should producers of software-based services like ATMs be held liable for economic injuries suffered when their systems fail?

Group Projects

1. With three or four of your classmates, develop a corporate ethics code on privacy. Be sure to consider E-mail privacy, employee monitoring of work sites as well as hallways, entrances, and restrooms. You should also consider corporate use of information about employees concerning their off-job behavior (e.g., lifestyle, marital arrangements, and so forth). Present your ethics code to the class.
2. With three or four of your classmates, interview managers of your university information systems department concerning university ethics policies in the systems area. Does your university have an ethics policy for students and employees? What is it? You could also interview a local firm rather than university officials. Present your findings to the class.

CASE STUDY

Virgin Atlantic: Corporate Hacking by British Airways

In a tough battle for market share, anything goes, right? Maybe, until you're caught, and then you'll be sorry. That's what happened to British Airways, which up until a few years ago was a major state-owned embarrassment. Under Lord King, British Airways moved in a few years to become one of the world's most profitable airlines based largely on its transatlantic service and protection and dominance at Heathrow Airport against other competitors. Not by being nice, but by being toughminded and fiercely competitive on price and service, King was able to turn

British Airways into one of Europe's premiere examples of a success story.

In 1991 an upstart company called Virgin Atlantic began offering cheaper fares between the lucrative New York and London markets. Founded by Richard Branson, a former music entrepreneur, Virgin achieved great success in the United States as the cheap, fashionable way to travel to Europe. The downside was that Virgin had smaller facilities and flew at odd hours at first. As it learned the marketplace, its staff, facilities, and schedule improved. For training, maintenance, and passenger reservations it relied on its big competitor British Airways. In this respect, Virgin Atlantic was quite different from an earlier American phenomenon called Peoples' Express which attempted to perform all its own services and had no reservation alliances.

But when Virgin Atlantic started "cherry picking" a substantial number of British Airway's best first class and repeat business customers, British Airways started to look for new ways to compete. It cancelled cooperation on maintenance and training; it approached Virgin's customers in the media directly and tried to woo them away. This was all fair competition. But then British Airways went too far and successfully devised a corporate hacking scheme to break into Virgin's reservation lists posted on British Airway's own reservation system.

Former British Airways employee Sadig Khalifa explained that he and other British Airways staff were taught how to wiretap into a segment of the British Airways Booking System computer that Virgin rented. Perusing the list of passengers, British Airways was able to identify the home telephone numbers and addresses of first-class passengers, along with the basic flight information. Passengers were then called, according to Virgin's lawyers, by British Airways staff, who enticed them to switch their bookings to British Airways. In a public flurry of comments and charges, Virgin's lawyers charged British Airways with libeling Richard Branson and Virgin Atlantic.

The case was settled out of court in January 1993 before it was even heard in court. British Airways agreed to apologize to Virgin Atlantic and Richard Branson for making false statments, pay $935,000 to Virgin and Branson, and pick up $3 million in court costs.

Observers noted that British Airways' actions were also a violation of England's Data Protection Act, which makes it a crime to interfere with electronic communications and data systems. Critics noted, however, that the kind of wiretapping involved could be accomplished easily with a few hundred dollars in equipment from Radio Shack. Virgin Atlantic had taken no measures to protect its communication link with the Booking System.

Sources: "Tactics and Dirty Tricks," *The Economist* (January 16, 1993), and Elizabeth Heichler, "Airline Hacking Case Reveals CRS' Security Shortcomings," *Computerworld* (January 18, 1993).

Case Study Questions

1. What managerial, technological, and organizational factors allowed the Virgin Airlines–British Airways case to develop?

2. Which of the six ethical principles apply here?

3. We have described five moral dimensions of the information age. Pick one of these dimensions and describe the ethical, social and political aspects of this case. In particular, what would you have done if you were Sadig Khalifa? Or Lord King?

References

Barlow, John Perry, "Electronic Frontier: Private Life in Cyberspace," *Communications of the ACM 34*, no. 8 (August 1991).

Brod, Craig. *Techno Stress—The Human Cost of the Computer Revolution.* Reading MA: Addison-Wesley, 1982.

Brown Bag Software v. Symantec Corp. 960F2D1465 (Ninth Circuit, 1992).

Bulkeley, William M. "Databases Plagued by a Reign of Error." *The Wall Street Journal* (May 26, 1992).

Cafasso, Rosemary. "Rethinking Reengineering." *Computerworld* (March 15, 1993).

Caldwell, Bruce, with John Soat. "The Hidden Persuader." *InformationWEEK* (November 19, 1990).

Carley, William M. "Rigging Computers For Fraud or Malice Is Often an Inside Job." *The Wall Street Journal* (August 27, 1992).

Computer Systems Policy Project, "Perspectives on the National Information Infrastructure." January 12, 1993.

Datamation, December 15, 1992.

Dejoie, Roy, George Fowler, and David Paradice, eds. *Ethical Issues in Information Systems.* Boston: Boyd & Fraser, 1991.

Equifax Report on Consumers in the Information Age, A National Survey. Equifax Inc., 1992.

Feder, Barnaby J. "As Hand Injuries Mount, So Do the Lawsuits." *The New York Times* (June 8, 1992).

Furger, Roberta. "In Search of Relief for Tired, Aching Eyes." *PC World* (February 1993).

Graham, Robert L. "The Legal Protection of Computer Software." *Communications of the ACM* (May 1984).

Joes, Kathryn. "EDS Set to Restore Cash-Machine Network." *The New York Times* (March 26, 1993).

King, Julia. "It's CYA Time." *Computerworld* (March 30, 1992).

Kling, Rob. "When Organizations Are Perpetrators: The Conditions of Computer Abuse and Computer Crime." *Computerization & Controversy: Value Conflicts & Social Choices,* ed. Charles Dunlop and Rob Kling. New York: Academic Press, 1991.

McPartlin, John P. "A Question of Complicity." *InformationWEEK* (June 22, 1992).

McPartlin, John P. "Environmental Agency 'Held Hostage' by Outsourcer." *InformationWEEK* (March 9, 1992).

McPartlin, John P. "Ten Years of Hard Labor." *InformationWEEK* (March 29, 1993).

McPartlin, John P. "The Terrors of Technostress." *InformationWEEK* (July 30, 1990).

Markoff, John. "Computer Viruses: Just Uncommon Colds After All?" *The New York Times* (November 1, 1992).

Markoff, John. "Though Illegal, Copied Software is Now Common." *The New York Times* (July 27, 1992).

Mason, Richard O. "Four Ethical Issues in the Information Age. *MIS Quarterly* 10, no. 1 (March 1986).

Mykytyn, Kathleen, Peter P. Mykytyn, Jr., and Craig W. Slinkman, "Expert Systems: A Question of Liability," *MIS Quarterly* 14, no. 1 (March 1990).

Neumann, Peter G. "Inside RISKS: Computers, Ethics and Values." *Communications of the ACM* 34, no. 87 (July 1991).

Neumann, Peter G. "Inside RISKS: Fraud by Computer." *Communications of the ACM* 35, no. 8 (August 1992).

Office of the Mayor, New York City, "The Trillion Dollar Gamble." 1991.

Oz, Effy, "Ethical Standards for Information Systems Professionals," *MIS Quarterly* 16, no. 4 (December 1992).

Pollack, Andrew. "San Francisco Law on VDTs is Struck Down." *The New York Times* (February 14, 1992).

Ramirez, Anthony. "AT&T to Eliminate Many Operator Jobs." *The New York Times* (March 4, 1992).

Rifkin, Glenn. "The Ethics Gap." *Computerworld* (October 14, 1991).

Rifkin, Jeremy. "Watch Out for Trickle-Down Technology." *The New York Times* (February 24, 1993).

Samuelson, Pamela. "Digital Media and the Law." *Communications of the ACM* 34, no. 10 (October 1991).

Samuelson, Pamela. "Legally Speaking: First Amendment Rights for Information Providers?" *Communications of the ACM* 34, no. 6 (June 1991).

Samuelson, Pamela. "Legally Speaking: Liability for Defective Electronic Information." *Communications of the ACM* 36, no. 1 (January 1993).

Schnorr, Teresa M. "Miscarriage and VDT Exposure." *New England Journal of Medicine* (March 1991).

Sterling, Bruce. *The Hacker Crackdown: Law and Disorder on the Computer Frontier.* New York: Bantam Books, 1992.

Stevens, William K. "Major U.S. Study finds No Miscarriage Risk From Video Terminals," *The New York Times* (March 14, 1991).

Straub, Detmar W. Jr., and William D. Nance. "Discovering and Disciplining Computer Abuse in Organizations: A Field Study." *MIS Quarterly* 14, no. 1 (March 1990).

Straub, Detmar W. Jr., and Rosann Webb Collins. "Key Information Liability Issues Facing Managers: Software Piracy, Proprietary Databases, and Individual Rights to Privacy." *MIS Quarterly* 14, no. 2 (June 1990).

"Supercomputers Manage Holiday Stock," *The Wall Street Journal* (December 23, 1992).

Tabor, Mary W., with Anthony Ramirez. "Computer Savvy, With an Attitude." *The New York Times* (July 23, 1992).

United States Department of Health, Education and Welfare. *Records, Computers and the Rights of Citizens*. Cambridge: MIT Press, 1973.

Wilson, Linda. "Devil in Your Data." *InformationWEEK* (August 31, 1992).

Wolinsky, Carol, and James Sylvester. "Privacy in the Telecommunications Age." *Communications of the ACM* 35, no. 2 (February 1992).

Is The Social Security Administration Ready for the Twenty-First Century?

INTRODUCTION

The Social Security Administration (SSA) consists of approximately 63,000 employees located in 1300 field offices, 10 regional offices, 37 teleservice centers, 7 processing centers, 4 data operations centers, and the Baltimore headquarters. SSA administers the major social insurance programs of the United States and several other related programs, which include:

- Retirement and Survivors Insurance (RSI)
- Disability Insurance (DI)
- Supplemental Security Income (SSI)

In order to administer these programs, SSA maintains 260 million names in its account number file (enumeration file), 240 million earnings records, and 50 million names on its master beneficiary file. In addition to keeping these files current, SSA annually issues 10 million new Social Security cards, pays out $170 billion, posts 380 million wage items reported by employers, receives 7.5 million new claims, and recomputes (because of changes in beneficiary status) 19 million accounts. It also handles 120 million bills and queries from private health insurance companies, carriers, and intermediaries.

Virtually every living American has some relationship with SSA.

In the early 1980s, SSA approached the precipice of financial ruin and administrative collapse. The long-term funding for Social Security payments in the United States was in serious jeopardy, and SSA's computerized administrative systems were nearing collapse.

This was an unusual state of affairs for SSA. As the flagship institution of the New Deal, SSA had developed broad bipartisan support, and there was never any serious question about its long-term financial viability until the late 1970s. In addition, since its inception in 1935, SSA had been one of the leading innovators and implementors of advanced information technology in the United States. SSA was a test site for many of the leading commercial hardware and software innovations of this period.

In 1982 the long-term funding for SSA was secured through a historic compromise between leading Democratic and Republican political figures. However, the administrative information systems of the SSA were still in jeopardy.

In 1982, SSA announced its Systems Modernization Plan (SMP)—a $500 million 5-year effort to completely rebuild its information systems and administrative processes.

Until its termination in 1990, the SMP was one of the largest civilian information system rebuilding efforts in history.

SSA illustrates many central problems of management, information technology, and organization faced by private and public organizations in a period of rapid technical and social change. Although SSA operates in a unique federal government environment, many large private organizations have exhibited similar problems in this time period. The problems and solutions illustrated in this case are generic.

The case is organized into four sections. Section I describes the overall situation at SSA in the period before SMP, roughly 1972–1982. Section II describes the SMP plan and strategy. Section III describes the experience of SMP. Section IV considers the long-term prospects of SSA.

SECTION I: ORGANIZATION, MANAGEMENT, AND SYSTEMS, 1972–1982

The overall system environment at SSA in 1982 could best be described as a hodgepodge of software programs developed over a 20-year period in four different machine environments. In the history of the agency, no one had ever conducted an information system requirements study to understand the overall requirements of the agency or the specific requirements of its subunits. There had been no planning of the information systems function for more than 20 years. Instead, as in many private organizations, systems drifted along from year to year, with only incremental changes.

Software

SSA software resulted from decades of programming techniques. The enumeration system—which supports the issuance of Social Security numbers—was designed in the late 1950s and had never been changed. The earning system was designed in 1975, the claims processing system was unchanged from the early 1960s, and other systems were also inherited from the late 1960s and 1970s. The software was a product of unplanned patchwork, with no mechanisms to prevent its deterioration over time.

From the 1950s to the 1980s, there were four major equipment transitions. However, the software was not improved or redesigned at any of these transitions. All of SSA's files and programs were maintained on over 500,000 reels of magnetic tape, which was susceptible to aging, cracking, and deterioration. Because tape was the storage medium, all data processing was batch sequential.

In summary, there were 76 different software systems making up SSA's basic computer operations. These software systems were themselves congeries of programs that performed the primary business functions of SSA. There were more than 1300 computer programs encompassing over 12 million lines of COBOL and other code.

Most of the 12 million lines of code were undocumented. They worked, but few people in the organization knew how or why. This made maintenance extremely complex. Congress and the president in the 1960s and 1970s made continual changes in the benefit formulas, each of which required extensive maintenance and changes in the underlying software. A change in cost-of-living rates, for instance, required sorting through several large interwoven programs, which took months of work.

Because of the labor-intensive work needed to change undocumented software and the growing operations crisis, software development staff were commonly shifted to manage the operations crisis. The result was little development of new programs.

It did not help matters that few people in Congress, the Office of the President, the Office of Management and Budget, or other responsible parties understood the deleterious impact of program changes on SSA systems capabilities.

What is unusual about SSA is that in the late 1970s it had not begun to make the transition to newer storage technology, file management and database technology, or more modern software techniques. In this respect, SSA was about 5 years behind private industry in making important technological transitions.

Hardware

By 1982, SSA was operating outdated, unreliable, and inadequate hardware, given its mission. Of its 26 large-scale computers, 23 were supporting program-related operations, while the remaining 3 processed administrative workloads. There were no machines dedicated to the development of new systems. Many of the computers had not been manufactured or marketed for 10 years or more. Eleven IBM 360/65 systems were no longer manufactured or supported. Although more modern equipment might have required $1 million annually for maintenance and operations expenses, SSA was spending more than $4 million to keep these antiquated machines in service.

The antiquated hardware forced SSA to rely on third-party maintenance services. Because of frequent breakdowns, over 25% of the production jobs ended before completion (abended jobs) and 30% of the available computer processing power was idle.

As a result of hardware deficiencies, a number of specific program impacts became apparent in 1982:

- Earnings enforcement operations, which help detect overpayments, were more than 3 years behind schedule.

- The computation of benefit amounts to give credit for additional earnings after retirement was 3 years behind schedule.
- SSI claims and posteligibility redeterminations could only be processed three times a week rather than five times a week. This meant delays of several days or weeks for SSI beneficiaries.
- In order to process cost-of-living increases in 1982 for 42 million individuals, SSA had to suspend all other data processing for 1 week.
- In 1982, there was a 3-month backlog of data needed to notify employers about incorrectly reported employee earnings. This created a suspense file with more than 2 million entries of unposted earnings and required additional manual work to handle employer correspondence.

SSA estimated that its gross computing capacity was deficient by more than 2000 CPU hours per month. SSA estimated that it needed 5000 central processing hours per month, but its capacity was only 3000 CPU hour per month.

Telecommunications

SSA depends heavily on telecommunications to perform its mission. Its 1300 field offices need timely access to data stored at the central computer facility in Baltimore. In 1982, however, SSA's telecommunications was the result of an evolving system dating back to 1966. The primary telecommunications system was called the Social Security Administration Data Acquisition and Response System (SSADARS). It was designed to handle 100,000 transactions per day. One year after it was built in 1975, the system was totally saturated. Each year teleprocessing grew by 100%. By 1982 the SSADARS network was frequently breaking down, and was obsolete and highly inefficient.

One result of the saturated communications system was that senior SSA local executives working in field offices were forced to come in on the weekends in order to key in data to the SSADARS system, which was overloaded during the week. The total system downtime in 1982 was 385 hours, or about 11% of the total available hours. By 1982, there was little remaining CPU telecommunications capacity in the off-peak periods to handle the normal growth of current workloads. Entire streams of communications were frequently lost. At peak times, when most people wanted to use the system, it was simply unavailable. The result was telecommunication backlogs ranging from 10,000 to 100,000 messages at a time.

Database

The word *database* can be used only in a very loose sense to refer to SSA's 500,000 reels of magnetic tape on which it stored information on clients in major program areas. Each month SSA performed 30,000 production jobs, requiring more than 150,000 tapes to be loaded onto and off of machines. The tapes themselves were disintegrating, and errors in the tapes, along with their physical breakdown, caused very high error rates and forced a number of reruns. Many of the tapes had no internal labels. More than one third of the operations staff (200 people) was required simply to handle the tapes.

As in many private sector organizations, data were organized at SSA by programs, and many of the data elements were repeated from one program to the next. SSA estimates that there were more than 1300 separate programs, each with its own data set. Because there was no data administration function, it was difficult to determine the total number of data elements, or the level of redundancy within the agency as a whole or even with program areas.

Management Information Systems

Management information systems (MIS) are designed to support middle- and senior-level management by providing routine reports on the operations of the organization, as well as responding to ad hoc inquiries. The data for these reports are generally derived from transaction processing systems at the operational level.

In 1982, SSA had a woefully inadequate capability in the MIS area. Because the data were stored on magnetic tape and were generally not available to end-user managers throughout the organization, all requests for reports had to be funneled through the information systems operations area.

But there was a crisis in operations, and this meant delays of up to several years in the production of reports crucial for management decision making. As long as all of the data were stored in a format that required professional computer and information systems experts to gain access to them, general management always had to deal with the Information Systems Department. This group was preoccupied with programmatic processing to ensure that checks went out on time.

How Could This Happen?

There are two explanations for SSA's fall from a leading-edge systems position to near collapse in the early 1980s. First, there were internal institutional factors involving middle and senior management. Second, a sometimes hostile and rapidly changing environment in the 1970s added to SSA's woes.

The Environment

In the 1970s, Congress had made more than 15 major changes in the RSI program alone. These changes increasingly taxed SSA's systems to the point where systems personnel were working on weekends to make required program changes.

In 1972 Congress passed the Supplemental Security Income (SSI) program, which converted certain state funded and administered income maintenance programs into federal programs. SSA suddenly found itself in the welfare arena, which was far removed from that of a social insurance agency. Unprepared local staffs suddenly faced thousands of angry applicants standing in line. In some cities, riots occurred. Other programs, such as Medicaid and changes in disability insurance, as well as cost-of-living (COLA) escalators, all severely taxed SSA's systems and personnel capacity. The 1978 COLA required changes in over 800 SSA computer programs.

The number of clients served by SSA doubled in the 1970s. But because of a growing economic crisis combining low growth and high inflation (stagflation), Congress was unwilling to expand SSA's work force to meet the demands of new programs. There was growing public and political resistance to expanding federal government employment at the very time when new programs were coming on line and expectations of service were rising.

SSA management in this period overstated its administrative capacity to Congress and did not realize the nature of the growing systems crisis. SSA pleas for additional manpower were consistently turned down or reduced by Congress and the White House. Workloads of employees dramatically increased, and morale and job satisfaction declined. Training was reduced, especially in the systems area, as all resources were diverted to the operations crisis.

Toward the end of the 1970s, the political environment changed as well. A growing conservative movement among Republicans and Democrats interested in reducing the size of all federal programs led to increasing pressure on SSA to reduce employment levels. In the long actuarial funding debate at the beginning of the 1980s, there was talk about "privatizing" Social Security and abolishing the agency altogether.

Complicating SSA's environment was the Brooks Act of 1965, which mandated competitive procurement of computing equipment and services. Up to 1965, SSA had a longstanding and beneficial relationship with IBM. Virtually all of SSA's equipment was manufactured by IBM and purchased on a noncompetitive basis. IBM provided planning, technical support, software support, and consulting services to SSA as part of this relationship.

By the 1970s this close relationship had ended. IBM shifted its support and marketing efforts away from the federal arena because of the Brooks Act. SSA found itself in a new competitive environment, forced to do all of its own planning, development, and procurement work. As the workload rapidly expanded at SSA in the 1970s, the agency needed a well-planned, closely managed transition to new computing equipment and software. This transition took a long time.

Institutional Factors

A challenging environment might have been overcome by a focused and dedicated management group. Perhaps the most critical weakness of all in SSA's operation in the 1970s was its inability to gain management control over the information systems function and over the information resource on which the organization itself was based.

Senior management turnover was a critical problem. In its first 38 years, SSA had six commissioners with an average tenure of 6.5 years. Two men led the agency for 27 of its 38 years. But from 1971 to 1981, SSA had seven commissioners or acting commissioners with an average tenure of 1.1 years. None of these commissioners had any experience at SSA. The senior staff of the agency was also repeatedly shaken up in this period. Compared to earlier senior managers, those of the 1970s failed to realize the critical importance of information systems to SSA's operation. Long-range planning of the agency or systems became impossible. Authority slowly but inevitably devolved to operations-level groups—the only ones that knew what was going on.

With new senior management came four major reorganizations of the agency. Major SSA programs were broken down into functional parts and redistributed to new functional divisions. Program coherence was lost. Performance measures and management control disappeared as managers and employees struggled to adapt to their new functions.

Efforts at Reform

SSA made several efforts in this period to regain control and direction in the systems area on which its entire operation critically depended.

In 1975, SSA created the Office of Advanced Systems (OAS) within the Office of the Commissioner. SSA hoped that this advanced, high-level planning group with direct assess to senior management would develop a strategy for change. OAS developed such a plan called the *Green Book,* which laid out a total reformation of SSA's largely manual and batch processes. From client intake interview to final check dispersal, the Green Book promised virtually total automation at SSA.

Unfortunately, this effort failed. Systems operations management opposed the plan as unworkable, wild-eyed, and lacking any implementation plan. Given the day-to-day crisis at SSA, there were no resources to fund the program. The union was opposed to the plan. There was no White House support for it and no suggestion from Congress or the White House that needed funding would be forthcoming. In 1979 the OAS was abolished by a new management team.

A second effort at reform began in 1979. This time the idea originated with new senior management. Called *partitioning,* the new reform effort sought to break SSA's internal operations into major program lines—like product lines—so that each program could develop its own systems. This plan was quickly rejected. White House and congressional staffs believed that such a strategy was simply an effort by SSA to obtain new hardware without rethinking either the way in which SSA does business or the tremendous software and database problems of the agency. Outside professionals criticized the plan for going in the opposite direction from private industry, which was building integrated databases, distributed systems, and telecommunications networks. The partitioning strategy was never implemented.

A third reform effort also began in 1979. Here SSA sought to replace the aging SSADARS telecommunications network with new, high-speed communications terminals in the district offices and new telecommunications computers in the Baltimore headquarters. After a competitive procurement process, SSA contracted with the Paradyne Corporation for 2000 such terminals.

Unfortunately, the first 16 systems failed all operational tests on delivery in 1981. Investigations produced charges of bidding fraud (selling systems to SSA that did not exist, "black boxes with blinking lights"), securities fraud, bribery, bid rigging, perjury, and inadequate SSA systems requirements definition.

By 1983 SSA took delivery of all of the terminals, and they did perform for their expected life of 8 years. But the procurement scandal further reduced SSA's credibility in Congress and the White House.

Results of Management Chaos

Senior management turnover, lack of concern, and failed efforts at reform took a severe toll in the systems area. Planning of information systems was either not done or was done at such a low operational level that no major changes in operations could be accomplished.

The absence of management planning also meant that the integrity of SSA programs was directly threatened. Privacy protection, physical security, prevention of program abuse, prevention of malicious damage, unauthorized access, program accountability, and systems backup and recovery—all of these areas of systems integrity suffered.

SECTION II: THE SYSTEMS MODERNIZATION PLAN

As the crisis at SSA became increasingly apparent to Congress, the General Accounting Office, and the President's Office, pressure was placed on SSA to develop a new strategy.

In 1981 a new commissioner, John Svahn, a recently appointed former insurance executive with systems experience, began work on a strategic plan to try to move SSA data processing from collapse to a modern system. The result was a 5-year plan called the Systems Modernization Plan (SMP). SMP was intended to bring about long-range, tightly integrated changes in software, hardware, telecommunications, and management systems.

The plan departed from previous SSA plans, which had sought to develop all of their own systems by SSA personnel. The SMP explicitly provided for the use of external experts and contractors.

At $500 million, the original cost estimate in 1982, the SMP was one of the most expensive single information systems projects in history.

SMP Goals

The goals of the SMP were as follows:

- Restore excellence to SSA systems and return the agency to its state-of-the-art position.
- Avoid disruption of service.
- Improve service immediately by purchasing modern hardware.
- Improve staff effectiveness and productivity.
- Restore public confidence by enhancing accountability, auditability, and detection of fraud.

SMP Strategy

As a bold effort to secure a total change at SSA, the SMP adopted a conservative strategy. This strategy called for SSA to do the following:

- Achieve modernization through incremental, evolutionary change, given the unacceptable risks of failure.
- Separate the modernization program from the operations and maintenance programs.
- Use an external system integration contractor to provide continuity to the 5-year project.
- Utilize industry-proven, state-of-the-art systems engineering technology.
- Build on the existing systems, selecting short-term, feasible approaches that minimize risks.
- Establish a single organizational body to plan, manage, and control SMP.
- Elevate systems development and operations to the highest levels of the agency.

SMP Implementation

The original plan foresaw a 5-year effort broken into three stages: survival, transition, and state-of-the-art. In the survival stage (18 months), SSA would focus on new hardware acquisition to solve immediate problems of capacity shortage. In the transition stage (18 months), SSA would begin rebuilding software, data files, and telecommunications systems. In the final state-of-the-art stage, SSA would finalize and integrate projects to achieve a contemporary level of systems.

Specific Projects

The SMP involved six interrelated programs.

1. THE CAPACITY UPGRADE PROGRAM (CUP)

The CUP program was developed to reconfigure and consolidate the physical computing sites around central

headquarters in Baltimore; to acquire much higher-capacity and more modern computers; to eliminate sequentially organized magnetic tape files and switch over to direct access devices; and to develop a local computing network for high-speed data transfers.

2. THE SYSTEM OPERATION AND MANAGEMENT PROGRAM (SOMP)

The SOMP program was intended to provide modern automated tools and procedures for managing and controlling SSA's main computer center operations in Baltimore. Included were automated job scheduling tools, job station monitoring and submission systems, operational job procedures, training, and a central integrated control facility to ensure that SSA would make a smooth transition to a modern data center environment.

3. THE DATA COMMUNICATIONS UTILITY PROGRAM (DCUP)

The DCUP was designed to reengineer SSA's major telecommunications system (SSADARS). What SSA wanted was a transparent conduit for the transmission of data between and among processing units of different manufacture using a single integrated network.

More than 40,000 on-line terminals were to be used in the 1300 field offices.

4. SOFTWARE ENGINEERING PROGRAM (SEP)

SEP was designed to upgrade the existing software and retain as much of it as possible so that an entirely new code did not have to be written.

A critical part of the SEP was a top-down functional analysis (using the enterprise system planning method) of the Social Security process—all of the business and organizational functions of SSA. Hopefully, this top-down planning effort would provide the framework for the redesign of SSA's total system by establishing the requirements for improvements in existing software.

A second key aspect of the software engineering effort was the implementation of new software engineering technology. This involved developing and enforcing programming standards, developing quality controls, and using modern computer-aided software development tools. Special emphasis was placed on the development of modern program documentation, standardization of programs, and conversion to higher-level languages whenever possible.

5. DATABASE INTEGRATION

The database integration project involved four objectives. As a survival tactic, SSA wanted to reduce the current labor-intensive, error-prone magnetic tape operation by converting all records to high-speed disk, direct access storage devices (DASD). A second goal was to establish a data administration function to control the definition of data elements and files. A third goal was to eliminate the data errors by establishing data controls, validating files, and developing modern storage disk technology. A fourth objective was to integrate the variety of databases, making communication among them transparent.

6. ADMINISTRATIVE/MANAGEMENT INFORMATION ENGINEERING PROGRAM (AMIE)

SSA was fundamentally dependent on manual activities to conduct most of its administration. Requests for personnel actions, purchase requisitions, telephone service, travel orders, building modifications, training requests—all of these administrative matters were processed manually.

The AMIE program was designed to integrate MIS with other programmatic modernization activities: to automate and modernize labor-intensive administrative processes and to develop management MIS to improve the planning and administrative process.

SECTION III: THE END OF SMP (1988): SUCCESS AND FAILURE

At the end of 1986 the President appointed a new permanent commissioner, Dorcas Hardy. SMP had become increasingly controversial: critics claimed failure while the agency's leaders claimed success. By 1988 the new Commissioner quietly ended SMP and announced a new plan called the "2000: A Strategic Plan." What had the SMP accomplished in 5 years?

The Critics

For much of the earlier years of SMP the environment was supportive and sympathetic to the modernization program. By 1986, however, criticism was beginning to develop over the rising costs and seemingly endless time frame. In large part the critics drew strength from the fact that the SMP project had been extended by SSA for an additional five years (to 1992) and had doubled in expected cost to $1 billion; no major software breakthroughs were apparent to the public or Congress; and the effort to modernize SSA's "backend" or database appeared to stall.

Turmoil in senior management did not end with SMP. The previous Commissioner was never fully supported by the Reagan White House and remained an acting commissioner, as did the deputy commissioner. The White House increasingly pressed SSA to make plans for reducing its staff by one-quarter, or 20,000 positions. The Commissioner refused and was replaced. The new commissioner, Dorcas Hardy, vigorously pursued the goal of sharp staff reductions. By the end of 1988, the SSA staff had been reduced by 17,000 workers, from 83,000 down to 66,000, mostly by attrition. These reductions were made in anticipation of sharp increases in productivity brought about by the SMP modernization efforts. There was little systematic effort to examine this hope.

Under pressure from the White House, the new commissioner abandoned SSA's pact with the union. The union began a long drawn-out battle with the management for control over the implementation process. This battle frequently resulted in public Congressional testimony challenging management claims of enhanced service, quality, and productivity. In labor's view, SSA management put excessive pressure on employees to work faster in order to "make the modernization program look good." "The Unions and the employees looked forward to system modernization," according to Rose Seaman, an SSA claims representative and SMP oversight person for the American Federation of Government Employees (AFGE), but "systems modernization never delivered. Instead there is great pressure on claims reps to perform clerical functions the system cannot perform, and to alter records so that processing times are reduced."[1]

The General Accounting Office (GAO), responding to requests from the House Government Operations Committee [Rep. Jack Brooks, Democrat of Texas, chairman], issued many highly critical reports of SSA's procurement policies. In one report issued in 1986, GAO charged that SSA failed to redevelop software or to develop a true database architecture. In another 1987 report, GAO claimed that SSA's new Claims Modernization Software would handle only 2% of the workload (merely initial applications for retirement and not the application processing, or post entitlement changes)! The report chided SSA for dropping modernization of the post-entitlement process which accounts for 94% of daily SSA transactions. SSA management heatedly denied GAO's allegations, but backsliding in software became a major weapon of SMP opponents. GAO called for a halt in procurements. Hardy refused and began purchasing 40,000 full color desktop terminals.

A review of SMP by the Office of Technology Assessment (OTA, a congressional research agency), concluded that SSA, Congress, and the White House were all to blame for SSA's failure. The White House was blamed for prematurely seeking huge work force reductions before the new systems were in place. It was also blamed for continuing political interference in the agency and for failure to support senior management. Congress was blamed for not understanding the complexity of SSA programs and for failing to understand the long-term nature of total systems change. In addition, OTA blamed new procurement laws for slowing down and complicating the purchase of new hardware.

OTA pointed to a number of faults at SSA. From the very beginning of SMP, SSA failed to rethink its method of doing business. SMP basically sought to automate an organizational structure and way of doing business established in the 1930s. SSA failed, for instance, to question the role of 1300 field offices—are they really needed in a day of packet-switched networks and PCs? Should SSA's major

---

1. "Union Faults SSA Modernization Plan," *Federal Computer Week*, October 9, 1989.

data files be centralized in Baltimore? SSA failed to re-think its basic architecture of a centralized mainframe operation in Baltimore serving the entire country. Why not a more decentralized structure? Why not minicomputers in every District Office? OTA also pointed to SSA's failure to develop new software on a timely basis and a new database architecture. It was felt these shortcomings, especially in software and database, would ultimately come to haunt SSA in the 90s. In general, SMP lacked a vision for the future around which it could build a powerful new information architecture.[2]

GAO, OTA, and labor critics believed that whatever increases in productivity occurred from 1982–1988 resulted largely from work force reduction, deterioration in service, and asking the remaining employees to work harder, rather than from any technology per se. Although public surveys published by SSA showed the general public thought SSA did a fine job, surveys of field office employees and managers with direct knowledge of the situation showed declining service quality, employee performance, and morale (see Figures V.1 through V.3).

As employee levels dropped, managers complained in interviews that the work load was "oppressive," recalling days in the 1960s when lines of clients surrounded SSA offices. Managers frequently skipped lunch breaks so claims reps and interview clericals could go to lunch. While managers praised the new claims modernization software, teleservice centers, and pre-interviewing techniques which permit clericals to answer questions of clients using on-line queries, the overall reduction in labor force put a "crushing load on District Office personnel." Employees and managers reported many of the most capable managers and claims representatives were leaving SSA for the private sector or other government jobs as working conditions deteriorated.[3]

For the critics SSA had made some improvements in service and processing, but these resulted early in the SMP plan and were largely the result of hardware purchases and running the old software faster. Whatever progress in productivity occurred did so at the expense of employees and service to clients.

The Agency Responds: Progress to 1988

By 1988, SSA management conceded the SMP had indeed doubled in size to a projected $1 billion, but by 1988 the SMP plan had actually spent slightly less ($444 million) than the original estimate of $500 million. Management conceded that the time required to reach state-of-the-art processing had to be extended to 1992; that "there was an excessive emphasis on hardware, that software development was slow, and that the agency carried over large balances of unbudgeted funds

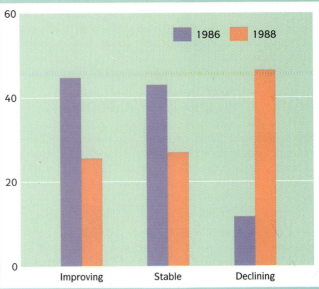

Figure V.1
Field office managers' ratings of office performance, 1986 and 1988. (*Source*: GAO)

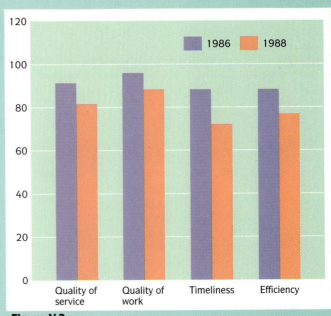

Figure V.2
Field employees' ratings of unit performance as adequate or better, 1986 and 1988. (*Source*: GAO)

from year to year [indicating difficulty in managing projects and allocated funds].[4] In fact, software development was four years behind schedule, and the data-

2. Office of Technology Assessment, "The Social Security Administration and Information Technology, A Case Study," Washington D.C.: U.S. Congress, 1986.
3. Based on interviews in Northeastern U.S. metropolitan area District Offices by the authors and Alan F. Westin.
4. Social Security Administration, "Report on Social Security Administration Computer Modernization and Related Expenditures," Prepared for the Senate Appropriations Committee, February 1989, p. ii.

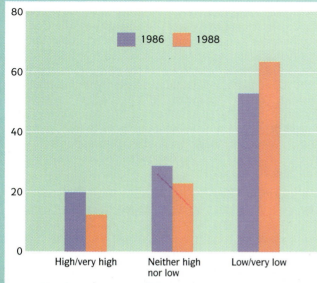

Figure V.3
Field office employees' ratings of employee morale, 1986 and 1988. (*Source*: GAO)

base redesign (the so-called "backend" of the system) was still being considered after five years. Nevertheless, SSA had documented steady improvement in a number of measures of services to beneficiaries, many of which are due to the SMP:

- A 25% decrease in RSI claims processing time.
- A small decrease in DI claims processing time (2.2 days).
- A high and improving rate of RSI claims accuracy (95.7–97.2%).
- A 41% decrease in SSI processing time.
- A 7% decrease in SSI blind/disabled processing time.

Management pointed to the following key changes brought about by the SMP:

1982	Today
6 weeks to receive a Social Security card	Takes 10 working days
4 years to post annual wage reports	Done in 5 months
Over a month to process an RSI claim	Done in about 20 days
4 years to do annual recomputations for those entitled to higher benefits	Done in 6 months
3 weeks of computer processing for annual cost-of-living increases	Done in 25 hours
Payments in emergency situations took 15 days	Received in 5 days

- A 47% decrease in RSDI (Retired Survivors Disability Insurance) change of status processing time.
- Stable administrative costs in RSI since 1980 (1.1% of benefits).

Management reported that overall SMP brought about a 25% increase in productivity. The agency was now doing slightly more "work" in 1988 than it was in 1982 but with 17,000 fewer employees. Progress in specific programs of SMP was impressive according to management.

MANAGEMENT CHANGES

SSA created a new deputy commissioner for systems and raised the status of systems in the organization to the senior management level. Development of the SMP was separated from operations, and both functions were adequately funded.

CAPACITY UPGRADE

Between 1982 and 1988 SSA increased processing capacity twenty-fold, from 20 MIPS to a total of 400 MIPS, replacing outdated computers with hardware supplied by three manufacturers on a competitive basis.

SYSTEMS OPERATION MANAGEMENT PLAN (SOMP)

The central processing facility in Baltimore developed efficient job scheduling standards and procedures for handling tapes and documents so that 95% of its processing is completed on time.

DATA COMMUNICATIONS UTILITY (DCU)

Under SMP a network of more than 50,000 devices was installed nationwide, with the objective of putting a terminal on every claims representative's desktop. Network capacity increased from 1200 characters per second in 1982 to 7000 characters per second in 1988.

DATABASE INTEGRATION

SAA converted 500,000 reels of tape to more modern DASDs. All master files were converted to disk, making it possible to handle more than 2 million inquiries per day directly on-line. SSA developed its own in-house data management system called the Master Data Access Method (MADAM) to handle all on-line and batch access to SSA master files. However, the data are still organized according to major program areas. SSA has yet to develop an integrated database for all or even some of its major programs. In 1989 it settled on a target database architecture that could integrate information from the major program areas.

SOFTWARE ENGINEERING

SSA made major progress redesigning the software for the retirement program. Now millions of retired persons can initiate the claims process or inquire about their accounts using an 800 number teleservice or have a claims representative initiate the claim on-line from a district office. In 1982 this capability was not even dreamed of. Developing such interactive systems to deliver services required entirely new code; the old software could not be salvaged.

SECTION IV: LOOKING AHEAD: A STRATEGIC PLAN AND AN INFORMATION SYSTEMS PLAN

In early 1988 SSA issued a new Agency Strategic Plan that was designed to extend the gains made under SMP and to refocus efforts away from pure hardware solutions towards greater customer service, organizational redesign, software, and office automation (see Figure V.4). When carefully examined, the chart shows processing and case loads growing and administrative costs remaining flat. Identifying long-term areas for improvement, the new plan signalled a greater attention to business design, customer service, software, and the need for repairing relations with SSA employees and field managers.

In August, 1990 Renato A. DiPentima took over as Deputy Commissioner of Systems. Meetings with the General Services Administration, General Accounting Office, and Congressional committees revealed that SSA needed to develop a better plan for its systems and services. Di Pentima then initiated a seven-year Information Systems Plan in September 1991 to support the Agency Strategic Plan. The General Services Administration restored delegated procurement authority to SSA, permitting the agency to buy from $2.5 - 10 million in equipment. This meant that good credible capacity planning was now accepted.

The Information Systems Plan is SSA's long-range plan for managing information systems into the twenty-first century. Its primary goal is to support the Agency Strategic Plan by building a systems environment that improves service to the public and SSA users. Long-term strategic priorities include improving the disability process, the appeals process, and the public's access to SSA by turning SSA into a paperless Agency with electronic claims folders and establishing a cooperative processing architecture.

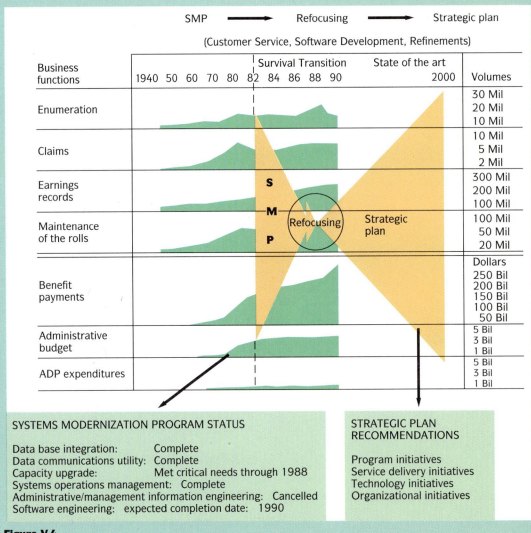

Figure V.4
The business of social security: strategic initiatives

The Information Systems Plan (ISP) was designed to be a continuous plan, that could always be upgraded and this plan was to be driven by SSA's strategic business plan.

Both plans address the challenges faced by SSA as it moves into the twenty-first century. SSA's total workload is expected to increase by 26% between 1990 and 2005. There will be limited funding for new initiatives, coupled with increased demands for a higher level of service to the public. In the past, most SSA clients preferred to visit SSA field offices. Today, they prefer to conduct their business over the telephone and they expect the same fast, efficient service they receive in the private sector. SSA must enhance systems to handle increasing workloads without hiring more employees, keeping costs low because of scarce budgetary resources. The number of field and operational employees has already decreased substantially since the 1980's and the remaining employees require new technologies to handle the increased workload.

The Information Systems Plan calls for moving SSA toward a distributed architecture, ending its total reliance on centralized mainframe computers for its programmatic applications that deliver services to SSA clients. Selected business functions will be distributed between headquarters and local processors. Most SSA employees will use LAN-based intelligent workstations with multiple levels of software running on platforms ranging from mainframes to microcomputers. Databases will be distributed using a multi-level telecommunications system that ranges from LANs to SSANet, the SSA Network (the former Data Communications Utility described earlier). Greater efficiency will result from having processing close to the data source and information user. Figure V.5 illustrates SSA's target systems environment for the 1990s and twenty-first century.

SSA has started to replace "dumb terminals" and stand-alone PCs with intelligent workstations, allowing SSA employees to do some processing at the local level before interfacing with centralized mainframes. By 1992 SSA had set up 13 pilot programs with the objective of installing 95,000 workstations by the year 2000 along with 2000 LANs. Workstations within an office will be connected to LANs, but the SSA's computer center in Baltimore will continue to supply mainframe processing power. All offices and mainframes will be connected to SSANet. By distributing processing and storing data at the level where the work is done, the number of data accesses and network traffic should be minimized, decreasing the response time for many workloads. This arrangement will allow the automation of many functions that are presently not cost-effective to do on a mainframe or practical to do on a standalone PC.

By the end of the 1990s, SSA will have replaced many batch applications with on-line interactive systems, starting with the title II claims process. Eventually the title XVI, disability, and title II postentitlement processes will be handled on-line. By the year 2000, SSA expects to convert most of its major systems to an interactive environment using an "appearance of update" tech-

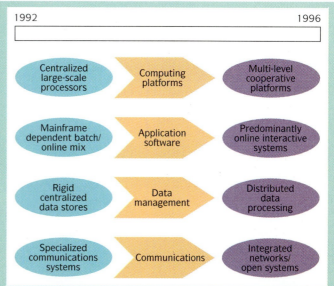

Figure V.5
The 1900s Target Systems Environment

nique which from the user perspective appears to update master records on-line. Expert systems will be used to reduce manual processing.

SSA's total computer capacity loads will increase as workloads grow due to the aging population and the use of automation to increase employee productivity. Some of this capacity will be provided by intelligent workstations at the local level and some will require increased capacity for SSA's central mainframes.

Databases will be more distributed in the future and they will be accessed over SSA's multi-level telecommunication system. However, commercial DBMS are still not capable of handling SSA's specific requirements under a distributed processing environment. SSA plans to monitor the performance improvements of commercial DBMS as they mature for future consideration. The decision to distribute SSA's large databases will be based on cost/benefit and service improvement considerations.

SSA will reduce transmission costs by using telephone switching systems to integrate network access whenever possible, relying on FTS-2000 to provide a common connection to be shared by voice services, video teleconferencing, FAX, LAN interconnections, and SSANet. SSA communications planning will use OSI standards, specifying appropriate protocols, interfaces, and network technologies to obtain required intercommunication and interoperability.

SSA points to many service improvements that resulted from these systems initiatives. An 800 phone number now receives 300,000 calls a day. 70% of babies in the United States are enumerated at birth, eliminating the need to make separate applications for Social Security numbers. Kiosks will be installed in some locations to provide public information.

Much has been learned by SSA about the difficulties of developing software. Management has learned that adding more computers does not automatically translate into fewer employees, especially when transaction volumes are increasing. How successful will SSA be in moving toward a more decentralized architecture? Will SSA's information systems infrastructure be able to provide the level of service the public and Congress expects? These are just some of the difficult questions facing SSA as it moves into the twenty-first century.

Sources: Kenneth C. Laudon (with Alan F. Westin), *Information Technology at SSA, 1935–1990,* forthcoming, 1994; and Office of Technology Assessment, *"The Social Security Administration and Information Technology, A Case Study."* Washington D.C.: U.S. Congress, 1986.

Part Five Case Study Questions

1. What were the major factors in SSA's past that made it a leading innovator in information systems technology? How did these supportive factors change in the 1970s?

2. Describe briefly the problems with SSA's hardware, software, data storage, and telecommunications systems prior to SMP.

3. What were the major environmental and institutional factors that created the crisis at SSA?

4. Why did SSA's reform efforts in the late 1970s fail?

5. What were the major elements of SSA's implementation strategy for SMP? Why was it called a conservative strategy? Compare SMP to an earlier reform plan.

6. Describe briefly the major projects within SMP.

7. What successful changes in management and organizational structure have been brought about by SMP? How secure are these changes (what environmental factors could destroy them)?

8. In what areas did SMP have the greatest success? In what areas did SMP not succeed? Why?

9. What were the liabilities of SSA's system architecture?

10. How successful has SSA been in creating an appropriate information system architecture for the year 2000?

INTERNATIONAL CASE STUDIES

Geelong and District Water Board[1]

Joel B. Barolsky and Peter Weill, University of Melbourne (Australia)

Joe Adamski, the Geelong and District Water Board's (GDWB) Executive Manager Information Systems, clicked his mouse on the phone messages menu option. Two messages had been left. The first was from an IT manager from a large Sydney-based insurance company confirming an appointment to "visit the GDWB and to assess what the insurance company could learn from the GDWB's IT experience." The second was from the general manager of another large water board asking whether Adamski and his team could assist, on a consultancy basis, in their IT strategy formulation and implementation.

The site visit from the insurance company was the 35th such request the Board had received since the completion of the first stage of their IT infrastructure investment strategy in January 1992. These requests were a pleasant diversion but the major focus of the GDWB's IT staff was to nurture and satisfy the increasing demands from the operational areas for building applications utilizing the newly installed IT infrastructure. The Water Board also faced the problem of balancing further in-house developments with external requests for consulting and demands from the GDWB's IT staff for new challenges and additional rewards.

ORGANIZATION BACKGROUND

The GDWB was constituted as a public utility of the Australian State of Victoria in July 1984 following an amalgamation of the Geelong Waterworks and Sewerage Trust and a number of other smaller regional water boards. The Board has the responsibility for the collection and distribution of water and the treatment and disposal of wastewater within a 1,600 square mile region in the southwest part of the State. In 1991, the permanent population serviced by the Board exceeded 200,000 people, this number growing significantly in the holiday periods with an influx of tourists.

The GDWB financed all its capital expenditure and operational expenditure through revenue received from its customers and through additional loan borrowings. Any profits generated were reinvested in the organization or used to pay off long-term debt. For the financial year 1990/91 the Board invested over $35.3 million in capital works and spent over $25 million in operating expenditure. Operating profit for the year 1990–91 exceeded $62.4 million on total assets of $292.5 million.

[1]A summarized version of a case study written by Joel B. Barolsky and Peter Weill of the Graduate School of Management, University of Melbourne, Australia. It was written as the basis of discussion rather than to illustrate either effective or ineffective handling of a managerial situation. Copyright © by Joel B. Barolsky and Peter Weill. Funding for this research was provided by IBM Consulting (USA).

In 1992, the GDWB was headed by a Governing Board with a State Government-appointed chairperson and eight members, elected by the residents of the community, who each sat for a three-year term. Managerial and administrative responsibilities were delegated to the GDWB's Executive Group which consists of the CEO and Executive Managers from each of the five operating divisions, namely Information Systems, Finance, Corporate Services, Engineering Development and Engineering Operations. From 1981 to 1992, the number of GDWB employees across all divisions rose from 304 to 454.

The GDWB's head office, situated in the regional capital city of Geelong, housed most of the Board's customer service, administrative, engineering, IT and other managerial staff. Complementing these activities, the GDWB operated five regional offices and a specialized 24-hour emergency contact service.

Commenting on the Board's competitive environment at the time, the GDWB's CEO, Geoff Vines, stated, "Although the organization operated in a monopolistic situation there still were considerable pressures on us to perform efficiently. Firstly, and most importantly, our objective was to be self funding—our customers wouldn't tolerate indiscriminate rate increases as a result of our inefficiencies and we could not go cap in hand to the State Government. Secondly, the amalgamation trend of water boards was continuing and the stronger the Board was the less likely it would be a target of a takeover. And thirdly, we did in a sense compare ourselves with private sector organizations and in some ways with other water boards. We had limited resources and we have to make the most of them."

KEY PROBLEM AREAS

Relating the situation up until the mid-1980's, Vines said that the Board faced a major problem in collectively identifying its largest assets—the underground pipes, drains, pumps, sewers and other facilities. He explained that most of these facilities were installed at least two or three meters below the surface and therefore it was almost impossible to gain immediate physical access to them. The exact specifications of each particular asset could only be ascertained through a thorough analysis of the original installation documentation and other geophysical surveys and maps of the area.

The limitations on identifying these underground facilities impacted operational performance in a number of key areas:

- most of the maintenance work conducted by the Board was based on reactive responses to leaks and other faults in the systems. It was difficult to introduce a coordinated preventative maintenance program because it was not possible to accurately predict when a particular pipe or piece of equipment was nearing the end of its expected life span.

- only a limited number of hard copies of this facility information could be kept. This significantly reduced the productivity of the engineering and operations' staff, especially in remote areas where they had to request this information from the central record-keeping systems. Backlogs and inaccuracies in filing also impacted efforts to repair, upgrade or install new piping, pumps and other equipment. On numerous occasions changes would be made to one set of plans without the same changes being recorded on the other copies of the same plans. Engineers designing improvements to existing facilities were often confronted with the problem of not being sure whether they were using the most up-to-date information of the facilities currently installed in the area concerned.
- the Board could not place realistic replacement values and depreciation charges on these underground assets.

With over 100,000 rateable properties in its area of responsibility, the GDWB maintained a centralized paper filing system containing more than a billion pages of related property information. The documents, most of which were of different sizes, quality, and age, were divided into 95,000 different files and sorted chronologically within each file. Access to the documents was made difficult as larger documents were cumbersome to copy and older documents were beginning to disintegrate. Having just one physical storage area significantly increased the potential exposure to fire and other risks and limited the wider distribution and sharing of the information. In the early 1980s, it was commonplace for a customer request for a statement of encumbrances placed at one of the GDWB's regional offices to take in excess of four weeks. The delays usually centered on finding the appropriate documents at the Property Services' central files, making the necessary copies, and transferring the documents back to the regional offices.

THE INFORMATION SYSTEMS DIVISION

In 1985, PA Consulting was commissioned to conduct a comprehensive review of the Board's strategy, management, operations structures and systems. One of the recommendations made by the consultants was that the Board should institute a more systematic approach to strategic planning. A major outcome of the planning process that followed was to create a new division for computing services and to recruit a new manager for this new area who reported directly to the CEO. The EDP Division was created with the objectives of "satisfying the Board's Information System needs through the provision of integrated and secure corporate computer systems and communication network." Vines said that the Board needed a stand-alone information services group that could be used as a resource center for all users and that could add value to the work conducted by each functional group within the Board.

In April 1987, Joe Adamski was employed to fill the new position of EDP Manager (later changed to Executive Manager Information Systems). At the time of his arrival, only a small part of the GDWB's work systems were computerized, the main components of which included:

- a 'low-end' IBM System 38, primarily to run financial and other accounting software and some word processing applications. The System ran an in-house developed rate collection system which kept basic information on ratepayers including property details and consumption records;
- 19 "dumb" terminals—none of the Board's regional offices had terminal access to the central computer systems;
- a terminal link to the local university's DEC 20 computer to support the technical and laboratory services; and
- four stand-alone PCs, running some individual word processing packages as well as spreadsheet (Lotus 1−2−3), basic CAD and data base applications.

Computer maintenance, support and development was allocated to the Finance Division and delegated to an EDP supervisor (and three staff) who reported to the Finance Manager. Adamski noted, "The computer set-up when I joined was pretty outdated and inefficient. For example, the secretarial staff at Head Office were using the System 38's word processing facility and had to collect their dot matrix printouts from the computer room situated on the ground floor of the five-story building. In the technical area, some water supply network analysis data was available through the use of the DEC 20 system; however, hard copy output had to be collected from the University which was over five kilometers away. Most of the design engineers were using old drafting tables with rulers, erasers and pencils as their only drafting tools."

Recognizing that some users required immediate solutions to problems they were facing, the Board purchased additional terminals, peripherals and stand-alone microcomputers for the various areas thought to be in greatest need. Adamski said that these additional purchases further compounded some of the Board's computer-related problems. "We had a situation where we had at least four different CAD packages in use in different departments and we couldn't transfer data between them. There was a duplication of peripheral equipment with no sharing of printers, plotters and other output devices. In addition, various managers began to complain that system expertise was too localized and that there was little compatibility between the various applications."

PLANNING THE NEW ROLE FOR IT

In July 1988, Adamski initiated a long-term computing strategy planning process with the establishment of a special planning project team with both IT and user representatives. The team embarked on a major program of interviews and discussion with all user areas within the Board. They investigated other similar public utilities across Australia to assess their IT strategies and infrastructures and made contact with various computer hardware and software vendors to determine the latest available technologies and indicative costs.

The Project Team developed a comprehensive corporate computing strategy that would provide, as Adamski put it, the "quantum leap forward in the Board's IT portfolio." Adamski said that central to the computing strategy that was devised was that there should be as much integration and flexibility as possible in all the Board's technical and administrative systems. "Linked to this strategy was the notion that we should strive for an "open systems" approach with all our applications. This meant that each system had to have publicly specifiable interfaces or "hooks" so that each system could talk to each other. From the users' perspective an open systems approach meant that all the different applications looked pretty much the same and it was simple and easy to cross over from one to the other. It also meant that if we weren't happy with one particular product within the portfolio or we wanted to add a new one we could do it without too much disruption to the whole system."

He continued, "A key decision was made that we should build on our existing IT investments. With this in mind we had to make sure that the new systems were able to use the data and communicate with the System 38. We wanted only one hardware platform using only one operating system and only one relational data base management system (RDBMS). We also wanted only one homogenous network that was able to cater to a number of protocols and interfaces such as the network system for the microcomputers, workstations and the Internet connection. There also had to be a high degree of compatibility and interaction with all the data files and applications that were proposed. In view of this, we chose a UNIX platform with a client/server architecture."

In addition to specifying the software components of the system, the Project Team outlined the hardware that was necessary to run the new systems and the additional staff that needed to be hired. To achieve the stated computing strategies and benefits, the Team also recommended that implementation take place over three key stages, with a formal progress review instituted at the end of each stage.

APPROVAL

In February 1989 the corporate computing strategy planning process was completed and Adamski presented the key recommendations to the Governing Board. In his presentation, Adamski stated that the infrastructure cost of implementing the strategy was estimated to be about $5 million for the entire project (excluding data capture costs) and that the project would take up to the end of 1995 for full commissioning.

Vines stated, "From my perspective, the proposed IT strategy took into account the critical functions in the organization that needed to be supported, such as customer services, asset management and asset creation. These were fundamental components of the Board's corporate objectives and the computer strategy provided a means to realize these objectives and provide both short- and long-term benefits. There were some immediate short-term benefits, such as securing property services data that had no backup, and productivity gains in design and electronic mail. From a long-term perspective, I believe you can never really do an accurate rate-of-return calculation and base your decision solely on that. If you did you probably would never make such a large capital investment in IT. We did try to cost-justify all the new systems as best we could but we stressed that implementing IT strategy should be seen as providing long-term benefits for the entire organization that were not immediately measurable and would come to fruition many years later. Until all the information was captured and loaded on the IT facilities from the manual systems, the full benefits could not be realized."

Following an extensive and rigorous tendering process, it was decided that the Board should follow a multi-vendor solution as no one vendor could provide a total solution. Sun Microsystems was selected as the major hardware vendor and was asked to act as "prime contractors" in implementation. As prime contractors Sun was paid one project fee and then negotiated separate contracts with all other suppliers.

IMPLEMENTATION

In April 1990, the implementation of the IT strategy commenced with the delivery of the Sun file servers and workstations and installation of a homogenous network throughout the Board. Adamski said that the implementation stage went surprisingly smoothly. "We didn't fire anybody as a direct result of the new systems, but jobs were changed. There was some resistance to the new technology—most of it was born out of unfamiliarity and fear of not having the appropriate skills. Some people were very committed in doing things "their way." When some of these people started to perceive tangible productivity benefits, their perspectives started to change. We tried to counsel people as best we could and encourage them to experiment with the new systems. Most people eventually converted but there were still some objectors."

Adamski added that while they were implementing the new systems it was important for the IS Division not to lose sight of its key objectives and role within the organization. "We had to make sure that we didn't get carried away with the new whiz-bang technology and reduce our support and maintenance of the older, more conventional systems. For example, the Board went onto a new tariff system and we had to make significant changes to our rating system to accommodate this. Having an application generator in place significantly improved the systems upgrade time."

In May 1992, the Board's computer facilities included 4 Sun file servers, 80 Sun workstations, 100 microcom-

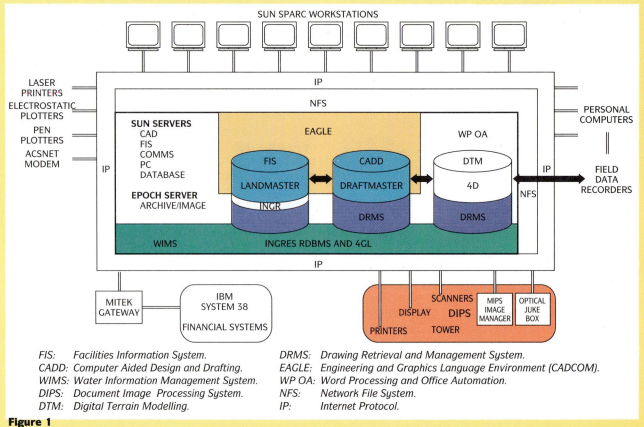

SUN SPARC WORKSTATIONS

LASER PRINTERS
ELECTROSTATIC PLOTTERS
PEN PLOTTERS
ACSNET MODEM

IP
NFS

SUN SERVERS
CAD
FIS
COMMS
PC
DATABASE

EPOCH SERVER
ARCHIVE/IMAGE

EAGLE

FIS
LANDMASTER
INGR

CADD
DRAFTMASTER
DRMS

WP OA

DTM
4D
DRMS

PERSONAL COMPUTERS

IP
NFS

FIELD DATA RECORDERS

WIMS

INGRES RDBMS AND 4GL

IP

IP

MITEK GATEWAY

IBM SYSTEM 38

FINANCIAL SYSTEMS

PRINTERS

DISPLAY

SCANNERS

DIPS

TOWER

MIPS IMAGE MANAGER

OPTICAL JUKE BOX

FIS: Facilities Information System.
CADD: Computer Aided Design and Drafting.
WIMS: Water Information Management System.
DIPS: Document Image Processing System.
DTM: Digital Terrain Modelling.

DRMS: Drawing Retrieval and Management System.
EAGLE: Engineering and Graphics Language Environment (CADCOM).
WP OA: Word Processing and Office Automation.
NFS: Network File System.
IP: Internet Protocol.

Figure 1
GDWB corporate computing system.

puters, 40 terminals, and the IBM System 38 Model 700. By this time, the IS Division had implemented the following components of the systems (see Figure 1 for a schematic of the systems):

(1) **A Document Imaging Processing System (DIPS)** used for scanning, storing and managing all documents on each property within the GDWB region which were being kept in the 95,000 separate paper files. This system was also used for the storage, backup and retrieval of 25,000 engineering plans and drawings. DIPS gave designated Head Office departments and regional offices real-time access to all property documentation and allowed them to print out scanned images when required. The system had a sophisticated indexing system that facilitated easy retrieval of stored images by users and access by other programs. Figure 2 presents a copy of a scanned property plan from DIPS.

(2) A digital mapping **Facilities Information System (FIS)** that provided for the storage, management and on-going maintenance of all graphic (map related) and nongraphic information relating to water and wastewater services, property information, property boundaries, and easements throughout the Board's region. The FIS system provided a computerized "seamless" geographic map covering the entire GDWB region. The system encompassed the storing of all maps in digital form and attaching map coordinates to each digital point. Every point on a digital map was linked to a unique X and Y coordinate, based on the standard Australian Mapping Grid system, and had a specific address linked to it. Once each point on a map was precisely addressed and identified, specific attributes were attached to it. These attributes were then used as methods of recording information or used as indexes for access to/by other programs, for example, sewer pipe details, property details, water consumption, vertical heights above sea level, etc. The selected map area with all the related attributes and information was then displayed graphically in full color on a high resolution workstation monitor (see Figure 3).

The FIS allowed cross referencing to financial, rating and consumption data (through indexing) held on the System 38. It also enabled each underground facility to be numbered, catalogued and identified as an asset with their associated data being integrated into other asset management systems. The FIS enabled data stored on a particular map to be "layered," with water pipes at one layer, sewer pipes at another, property boundaries at a third, future plans at another, and so on. This gave users the ability to recall maps in layers and to select the level and amount of detail they required. The system was centered around a mouse-driven graphic interface where the user zoomed in and out and/or panned around particular areas—at the broadest level, showing the whole of southern Victoria, and at the most detailed, the individual plumbing and

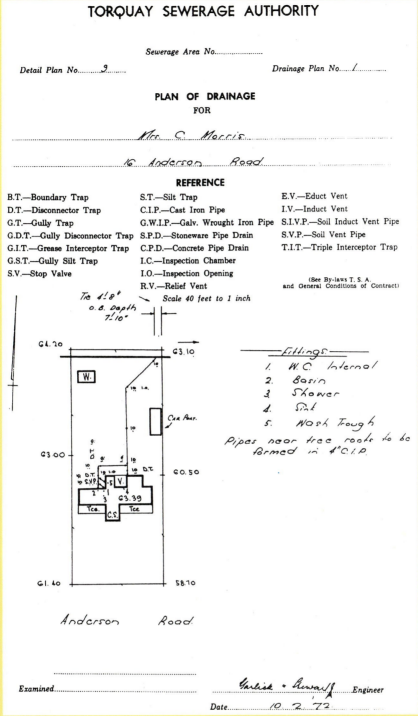

Figure 2
Example of a building plan kept for each rateable property.

drainage plan of one particular property (through cross-referencing to the DIPS system).

(3) A Computer Aided Design and Drafting (CADD) system that provided an integrated programmable 3-D environment for a range of civil, mechanical, electrical, surveying and general engineering design and drafting applications. It offered the following features:

- Display manipulation, including multiple angle views, zooms and pans;

- Geometric analysis, including automatic calculation of areas, perimeters, moments of inertia and centroids; and

- Various customization features such as user-defined menus and prompts and a user-friendly macro language.

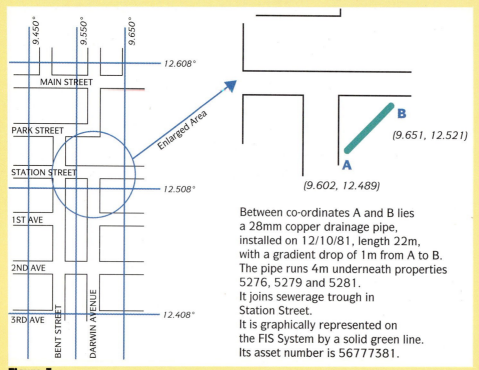

Between co-ordinates A and B lies
a 28mm copper drainage pipe,
installed on 12/10/81, length 22m,
with a gradient drop of 1m from A to B.
The pipe runs 4m underneath properties
5276, 5279 and 5281.
It joins sewerage trough in
Station Street.
It is graphically represented on
the FIS System by a solid green line.
Its asset number is 56777381.

Figure 3
Illustration of the type of information available on the Facilities Information System.

(4) **Word Processing and Office Automation (WP/OA)** systems providing users the ability to prepare quality documentation integrating graphics, spreadsheets, mail merge and data bases, as well as other utilities such as electronic mail and phone message handling.

(5) **A Relational Database Management System and a 4th Generation Language** as a base foundation for the development of new applications. Some of the RDBMS applications included:

- A Drawing and Retrieval Management System (DRMS) to control the development, release and revision of all CADD projects and files; and
- A Water Information Management System (WIMS) used for the storage and management of hydrographic engineering and laboratory data, both current and historical.

OUTCOMES

Vines said that one of the most important strategic outcomes of the changes introduced had been the way in which decision-making at all levels with the organization had been enhanced. "This improvement is largely due to the fact that people have now got ready access to information they have never had before. This information is especially useful in enhancing our ability to forward plan. The flow and reporting of financial information has also speeded up and we now complete our final accounts up to two months earlier than we used to. In the areas that have come on-line there has been a definite improvement in productivity and in customer service. The CADD system, for example, is greatly enhancing our ability to design and plan new facilities. The turnaround time, the accuracy of the plans and the creativity of the designers has been improved dramatically. In many departments there has been a change in work practices—some of the mundane activities are handled by the computer, allowing more productive work to be carried out, like spending more time with customers. Our asset management and control also started to improve. There was greater integrity in the information kept, and having just one central shared record meant that updating with new data or changes to existing data was far more efficient."

Adamski added that the initial reaction by Board staff to the whole corporate computing strategy "ranged from scepticism to outright hostility." He continued, "By the end of 1991, I would say that there had been a general reversal in attitude. Managers started to queue outside my office asking if we could develop specific business applications for them. They had begun to appreciate what the technology could do and most often they suddenly perceived a whole range of opportunities and different ways in which they could operate. One manager asked me, for example, if we could use document imaging technology to eliminate the need for any physical paper flows within his office. Technically this was possible but it was not really cost justifiable and the corporate culture would not really have supported it. Putting together the IS Division budget is now a difficult balancing act with a whole range of options and demands from users. I now ask the users to justify the benefits to be derived from new application proposals and I help out with the cost side. Cost/benefit justification usually drives the decisions as well as the ''fit'' with the existing IT and other corporate objectives. What also must be considered is that these objectives are not written in stone. They are flexible and can and should adjust to changes in both the internal and external environment.''

A number of GDWB staff indicated that the new systems had enhanced their ability to fulfill their work responsibilities:

- A customer service officer at one of the Board's regional offices stated that the DIPS had enabled her to respond to customer requests for encumbrance statements within a matter of minutes instead of weeks. She added that a number of customers had sent letters to their office complimenting them on the improvements in the service they received. She said that new DIPS system had ''flow on'' benefits that weren't fully recognized. She cited the case where local architects were able to charge their clients less because they had more ready access to information from the GDWB.

- A maintenance manager declared that the FIS system had enabled his department to predict when pipes and drains should be replaced before they actually ruptured or broke down, by examining their installation dates and the types of materials used. He said this process over time started to shift the emphasis of his department's maintenance work from being reactive to being more preventative. He added that the system also enabled him to easily identify and contact the residents that would be affected by the work that the Board was going to do in a particular area. He said that the FIS enabled him to plot out with his mouse a particular area of a map on his screen. It would then ''pick up'' all the relevant properties in the area and identify the names and addresses of the current ratepayers residing in those properties.

- A secretary to a senior head office manager said that despite being a little daunted at first by the new wordprocessing system, she felt the system had helped her considerably. She said that besides the obvious benefits in being able to prepare and edit documents

on a WYSIWYG screen, she also had the ability of viewing as well as integrating scanned property plans, correspondence, and other documents from the DIPS System.

Adamski said that one of the flow-on benefits from the FIS system in particular was that the Board had the potential of selling the information stored on the system to authorities such as municipal councils and other public utilities such as Telecom, the State Electricity Commission and the Gas and Fuel Corporation. He added that they had also considered marketing the information to private organizations such as building managers, architects and property developers, and that the return from these sales could significantly reduce the overall costs in developing the FIS system.

THE FUTURE

Commenting on the future prospects for the Board's IS Division, Adamski said, ''There are some very complex applications that we are developing but we now have the skills, the tools, and the infrastructure to develop them cost-effectively and to ensure that they deliver results. I think one of the main reasons why we are in this fortuitous position is that we chose a UNIX platform with client/server processing and a strong networking backbone. It gives us the flexibility and integration that we set out to achieve and we will need in the future to realize both our long- and short-term objectives. It's a lot easier now to cost-justify requests for new applications. The challenges ahead lie in three areas. Firstly, it's going to be difficult to consistently satisfy all our users' needs in that their expectations will be increasing all the time and they will become more demanding. We have to recognize these demands and at the same time keep investing in and maintaining our infrastructure. Secondly, we still have some way to go in developing a total corporate management information system. There are still some ''islands of data'' floating around and the challenge is to get it all integrated. And thirdly, as the most senior IT manager at the Board I have to make sure that we retain our key IT staff and we compensate them adequately, both monetarily and in providing them stimulating and demanding work.''

Case Study Questions

1. Describe the Geelong and District Water Board and the environment in which they operate. What problems did GDWB have before 1988? What were the management, organization, and technology factors that contributed to those problems?

2. Describe the role of information systems at GDWB and the GDWB's information system portfolio before July 1988.

3. Describe and critique the process of upgrading GDWB's information systems portfolio.

4. How did GDWB justify its investments in new information system technology? What were the benefits? How were they justified? What additional information would you need to determine whether these investments were worthwhile?

5. What should Geoff Vines and Joe Adamski do next?

INTERNATIONAL CASE STUDY 2

Vinwood Offshore Petroleum

Alan Underwood, Queensland University of Technology (Australia)

One of Australia's largest petroleum conglomerates, Vinwood Offshore Petroleum, is currently halfway through implementation of its information technology migration plan. The plan is aimed at making better use of organizational data in day-to-day operations and management decision making. The company had reviewed its information technology strategy in 1989 and began looking for new ways to use information technology to enhance its future business development.

Vinwood's plan focuses on creating a cohesive information environment, which it has named Gaze, to facilitate the sharing of communications across the geographically distant locations of its organization (Perth and Karratha in Western Australia, and Melbourne in Victoria), and the integration of the functions performed at these distant locations through a common communications platform.

Vinwood's information resources group convinced the six companies that were business partners involved in Vinwood of the logic and soundness of the proposed IS strategy. "We had a different vision for our computing resources, to help us to manage information. One thing not widely acknowledged is [that] computing is all about automating autonomous manual tasks. Information, as a resource of any organization, needs to be managed, just like every other asset. Up to now many have thought you don't need to manage that resource. Management agreed with our concept of managing the information resource base in the same manner as you manage other assets. Then you are in a position to make strategic use of information to enhance business performance based on what IS is doing and which can tell us where the business is headed."

Gaze is expected to improve Vinwood's business operations by strengthening communications, creating simpler work procedures and making better information analyses available to assist decision making. Ernie Hannan, the manager of information resources at Vinwood, described the history of the project, saying, "A few years back we reviewed our IS strategy. There were some major items in our agenda that were specific to our organization's structure which we needed to look at. We have a large office system within the organization with close to 1650 users. This is an important part of Vinwood's computing platform." He claims the IS changes that had been started are well underway, have been well received by users and will ultimately contribute to Vinwood's future business productivity.

An important component of the plan was the implementation of an integrated office system using a client/server architecture. Vinwood decided to switch to a new hardware platform based on Digital Equipment Corporation technology. Vinwood had developed under the Data General platform for years but, in 1988–89, Data General abandoned development of its comprehensive electronic office (CEO) to start developing in UNIX. This prompted Vinwood to look at its IS strategies and future decisions.

"We decided, because of Data General's technology direction change, we would have to make a significant investment whatever we decided—either to change the platform or, if we stuck with Data General, to upgrade to their new platform so we could develop in a platform that will continue into the future," Hannan said. "We decided that from a networking point of view and where we should head in terms of systems we were much better off moving towards Digital." He added that Vinwood's "computer infrastructure was getting old and maintenance costs were high. As a result of the change we will be able to give updated tools at a lower operating cost."

Digital's integrated office system, along with the use of LANs, will provide a foundation for future Gaze components. For office automation, Vinwood decided it was better to move to Digital's All-In-One with added features and incorporating WordPerfect's word processing system. All-In-One is the simplest way for users to access the new integrated office system. For those using this method, all computing is done on the central computer. Mailing and printing documents will be faster and easier with All-In-One than with Data General's comprehensive electronic office (CEO), Hannan claimed.

Another method of accessing the integrated office system is by using TeamLink. "WordPerfect and Digital produce TeamLink, a Windows-based product that runs on a client/server architecture," says Hannan. "This is a new product, still a test version, but it has unleashed the power of the PCs and central processing. The PC (client) accesses the central computer (server) for services such as electronic mail and document filing. This takes greater advantage of the PC's power. TeamLink runs in the Windows environment. TeamLink can do a lot of processing and information on PCs. It works on the same principle as LANs."

Vinwood started implementing the office system this year. Before moving to the new integrated office system environment, pilots were run in certain departments to ensure the general migration was smooth and painless. The changes implemented to date have already achieved significant productivity gains and relieved many administration headaches.

There are six components to Gaze. Vinwood's integrated office system and All-In-One is just one of those components. The information network, another component, is completed and already implemented. It has the advantage of being upgraded easily. The network, which covers a wide range of the company's activities, has proven easy to use and presents information in a meaningful format. Vinwood's LAN, a high speed, flexible communications network for PC users, provides a range of personal productivity services through printer, application, and file services.

The application service provides access to software that is required occasionally, which means that users no longer have to do without because they cannot justify keeping their own copy. Consequently the application service provides many users with the right tools at a lower cost to Vinwood. The file server gives access to disk space on the central computer. By storing PC files on the central computer, regular backups are performed by the computer center. "You can allow other staff to access your disk space, providing a simple method for sharing PC files among members of your work group, or anyone else on the LAN."

Some applications give line managers information about their people, while others, such as performance information, are focused on small groups. Generally the information is presented in summary form though detailed information is available to the manager with graphical presentation used where possible.

Gaze is presently targeting electronic forms. Vinwood already makes use of some electronic data interchange (EDI) by transferring information to banks and other financial institutions and has started electronic purchasing with firms. With Gaze it is possible to put building blocks in place that will interact and be expandable to monitor business performance and improve productivity, communications, work procedures and work flow.

Source: Janet Rosenberg, "Woodside's IOS Leads to Productivity Advantages." *Pacific Computer Weekly,* October 2, 1992.

Case Study Questions

1. Why did Vinwood need to change its information technology platform? What management, organization, and technology issues had to be addressed before moving from Data General to Digital Equipment Corporation technology?

2. What model of information architecture is illustrated here? Were other alternatives appropriate for Vinwood? Why or why not?

3. Comment on the manager's statement ". . . computing is all about automating autonomous manual tasks" in the context of management decision-making.

4. Identify the management benefits of using proprietary packages such as All-In-One or WordPerfect for office and decision-making applications.

Ginormous Life Insurance Company

Len Fertuck, University of Toronto (Canada)

Ginormous Life is an insurance company with a long tradition. The company has four divisions. Each operates its own computers. The IS group provides analysis, design and programming services to all the divisions. The divisions are actuarial, marketing, operations, and investment, all located at the corporate headquarters building. Marketing also has field offices in twenty cities across the country.

The Actuarial Division is responsible for the design and pricing of new kinds of policies. They use purchased industry data and weekly summaries of data obtained from the Operations Division. They have their own DEC minicomputer, running the UNIX operating system, to store data files. They do most of their analysis on microcomputers and Sun workstations, either on spreadsheets or with a specialized interactive language called APL.

The Marketing Division is responsible for selling policies to new customers and for follow-up of existing customers in case they need changes to their current insurance. All sales orders are sent to the Operations Division for data entry and billing. They use purchased external data for market research and weekly copies of data from operations for follow-ups. They have their own DEC VAX minicomputer with dumb terminals for clerks to enter sales data. There are also many microcomputers used to analyze market data using statistical packages like SAS.

The Operations Division is responsible for processing all mission-critical financial transactions, including payroll. They record all new policies, send regular bills to customers, evaluate and pay all claims, and cancel lapsed policies. They have all their data and programs on a large IBM ES/9000 mainframe. The programs are often large and complex because they must service not only the fifteen products currently being sold, but also the 75 old kinds of policies that are no longer being sold, but still have existing policy holders. Clerks use dumb terminals to enter and update data. Application programs are almost always written in COBOL. Some recent applications have used a SQL relational database to store data, but most use COBOL flat files. The average age of the transaction processing programs is about ten years.

The Investment Division is responsible for investing premiums until they are needed to pay claims. Their data consists primarily of internal portfolio data and research data obtained by direct links to financial data services. They have a DEC minicomputer to store their data. The internal data are received by a weekly download of cash flows from the Operations Division. External data are obtained as needed. They use microcomputers to analyze data obtained from the mini or from commercial data services.

A controlling interest in Ginormous Life has recently been purchased by Financial Behemoth Corp. The management of Financial Behemoth has decided that the firm's efficiency and profitability must be improved. Their first move has been to put Dan D. Mann, a hot-shot information systems specialist from Financial Behemoth, in charge of the Information Systems Division. He has been given the objective of modernizing and streamlining the computer facilities without any increase in budget.

In the first week on the job, Dan discovered that none of the staff of 200 information systems specialists know anything about CASE tools, End-User Computing or LANs. All microcomputer applications have been purchased, so no one has experience in implementing microcomputer systems. There is no evidence of any formal Decision Support Systems or Executive Information Systems in the organization. There have been a few tentative experiments with DB2, a relational database product, purchased from IBM, their mainframe vendor. Most managers say that "they do not need all those fancy Executive Information Systems." They would be happy if Information Systems would just provide basic reports on the financial performance of each product line and customer group.

There have been some problems with these systems. Maintenance is difficult and costly because almost every change to the data structure of applications in operations requires corresponding changes to applications in the other divisions. There has been a growing demand in other divisions for faster access to operations data. For instance, the Investment Division claims that they could make more profitable investments if they had continuous access to the cash position in operations. Marketing complains that they get calls from clients about claims and cannot answer them because they do not have current access to the status of the claim. Management wants current access to a wide variety of data in summary form so they can get a better understanding of the business. The IS group says that it would be difficult to provide access to data in operations because of security considerations. It is difficult to ensure that users do not make unauthorized changes to the COBOL files.

The IS group complains that they cannot deliver all the applications the users want because they are short-staffed. They spend 90 percent of their time maintaining the existing systems, most of which are in the COBOL language. The programmers are mostly old and experienced and employee turnover is unusually low, so there is not likely to be much room for improvement by further training in programming. Morale is generally good despite the perception of overwork. Employees often remark that the company is a very pleasant and benevolent place to work. At least they did until rumors of deregulation and foreign competition started to sweep the industry.

Dan began to look for ways to solve the many problems of the Information Systems Division. He solicited proposals from various vendors and consultants in the computer industry. After a preliminary review of the proposals, Dan was left with three broad options suggested by IBM, Oracle Corp., and Systemotion, a local consulting firm. The proposals are briefly described below.

IBM proposed an integrated solution using IBM hardware and software. The main elements of their proposal are:

- *Data and applications will remain on a mainframe.* The IBM ES/9000 series of hardware running their proprietary operating system will provide mainframe services. Mainframe hardware capacity will have to be approximately doubled. AS/400 microcomputers running under the OS/400 operating system will replace DEC minicomputers. RS/6000 workstations running AIX, a flavor of the UNIX operating system, can be used for actuarial computations. All hardware will be interconnected with IBM's proprietary SNA network architecture. Microcomputers will run under the OS/2 operating system and the IBM LAN Server to support both Microsoft Windows applications and locally designed applications that communicate with mainframe databases.
- *A DB2 relational database will store all data on line.* Users will be able to access any data they need through their terminals or through microcomputers that communicate with the mainframe.
- *Legacy systems will be converted using re-engineering tools,* like Design Recovery and Maintenance Workbench from Intersolve, Inc. These will have the advantage that they will continue to use the COBOL code that the existing programmers are familiar with. New work will be done using CASE tools with code generators that produce COBOL code.
- *Proven technology.* The IBM systems are widely used by many customers and vendors. Many mission-critical application programs are available on the market that address a wide variety of business needs.

Oracle Corp. proposed that all systems be converted to use their Oracle database product and its associated screen and report generators. They said that such a conversion would have the following advantages:

- *Over 75 hardware platforms are supported.* This means that the company is no longer bound to stay with a single vendor. Oracle databases and application programs can be easily moved from one manufacturer's machine to another manufacturer's machine by a relatively simple export and import operation as long as applications are created with Oracle tools. Thus the most economical hardware platform can be used for the application. Oracle will also access data stored in an IBM DB2 database.

- *Integrated CASE tools and application generators.* Oracle has its own CASE tool and its own form and report generators. Databases designed with the Oracle CASE tool can be automatically created in an Oracle database using CASE*Generator. SQL*Forms, one of their application generation tools, can design and generate screens for a wide variety of terminals. The same design can be implemented on dumb terminals, a Macintosh, X-Windows in UNIX, or Systems Application Architecture (SAA) in an IBM environment. Applications are created using graphic tools that eliminate the need for a language like COBOL. In fact, the programmer cannot see the underlying language that is being used for implementation. The designer works entirely with visual prototyping specifications. SQL*ReportWriter can generate reports in the same way.
- *Vertically integrated applications.* Oracle sells a number of common applications, like accounting programs, that can be used as building blocks in developing a complete system. These applications could eliminate the need to redevelop some applications.
- *Distributed network support.* A wide variety of common network protocols like SNA, DecNet, Novell, and TCP/IP are supported. Different parts of the database can be distributed to different machines on the network and accessed or updated by any application. Access can be controlled at the file, record, or field level for each user on the system. All data is stored on line for instant access. The data can be stored on one machine and the applications can be run on a different machine, including a microcomputer or workstation, to provide a client/server environment. The ability to distribute a database allows a large database on an expensive mainframe to be distributed to a number of cheaper minicomputers.

Systemotion proposed a state-of-the-art system using the Sybase Object Oriented Relational Data Base Management System (OORDBMS) with applications implemented in a Microsoft Windows environment. This proposal offers the following advantages:

- *A modern object-oriented database.* Sybase is a relatively new entrant in the database field so it is able to exploit the benefits of an object-oriented approach without having to worry about a large number of legacy applications already coded in an older non-object-oriented version. This means that it is possible to include complex validation rules in the database rather than having to code them in the application code. This reduces application testing and speeds development as well as improving data integrity.
- *Client/server systems.* Since Sybase is object-oriented, it is a natural product for a client/server environment. It becomes particularly easy to install the database on a server (commonly one or more Hewlett-Packard or DEC minicomputers) and place the applications and entry screens on

microcomputers or workstations like those from Sun Microsystems. Object-oriented applications can be easily built using graphic languages like Power Builder or Visual Basic. The database can be easily extended to store graphics like photos or scanned documents. This could allow business re-engineering to reduce the paper burden that is common in insurance firms. The client applications would run on a LAN with Microsoft SQL Server, a networked relational DBMS server.

- **Open UNIX environment.** Many programs have been written for the UNIX operating system. UNIX can be run on many different hardware platforms and network communication systems. This openness will make it possible to integrate applications on a number of platforms while obtaining the cost benefits of downsizing to smaller platforms.

- **Easy integration with purchased Windows applications.** The object-oriented approach meshes well with the Windows environment that has a feature called Object Linking and Embedding (OLE), which permits direct reference from one Windows software product to another. Thus it is quite easy to write a program that obtains data from a central database and brings it into a spreadsheet, like Excel, where it can be analyzed, manipulated, or graphed. The graph, in turn, can be embedded in a word processor report. If new data are downloaded into the spreadsheet, the graph will automatically be updated whenever the report is

opened in the word processor. This makes it easy to satisfy management needs for information within the word-processing or spreadsheet environment they are familiar with. It also makes it relatively easy to create customized management and executive information systems. In addition, many functions can be performed directly by purchased Windows programs to eliminate the need to design, build, and maintain many applications.

Dan is not sure which approach to take for the future of Ginormous Life. He appreciates that whichever route he follows, the technology will have an enormous impact on the kinds of applications his staff will be able to produce in the future and the way in which they will produce them. He is concerned about industry trends toward downsizing and distributions of systems. While this trend may eventually prove to be more efficient, his staff does not have much experience with the new technologies that would be required. He is uncertain about whether there will be a sufficient payoff to justify the organizational turmoil that will result from a major change in direction.

Dan must prepare a strategy for the renewal of the Information Systems Division over the next three years. As his assistant, he has asked you to address the following questions:

Case Study Questions

1. Prepare a list of factors or issues that must be considered in developing a strategy and selecting a technology platform for Ginormous.

2. Analyze how each of the three proposals performs on each factor or issue. If you find issues that a proposal fails to address, advise Dan as to the significance of the omission and how you think the proposal might be modified to address that issue.

3. Advise Dan on special criteria, if any, he might need to apply when evaluating a proposal for a

company-wide information strategy coming from a technology vendor. Explain your reasoning.

4. Assuming Dan were to make his decision without seeking further information from the proposers, recommend to him which proposal he should accept and your reason for selecting that proposal.

5. Based upon your advice in the previous question, state the order in which each component of the new technology should be introduced and the reason for selecting the order.

Kone Elevators

Tapio Reponen, Turku School of Economics and Business Administration (Finland)

Elevators are products that are made according to customer specification. Each building is different, and the products have to fit the building's structure and framework. However, the elevator components can often be selected from a range of standard components either in predefined sets (pre-engineered, standard elevators) or in custom-made combinations (nonstandard elevators). The following description illustrates how information systems can support the process of elevator sales, order, and delivery at Kone Elevators, an international elevator manufacturer with headquarters in Helsinki, Finland.

"Kone Lifts, good morning. Larry Liftagain speaking. How can I help you?"

"Good morning. This is Mr. Beaver from Bayswater Builders. I would like to have a quotation for a lift for our new project, please."

The pre-engineered elevator sale is usually handled by the salesman himself, using tools, materials, and procedures provided by sales support, engineering, and manufacturing. If the salesman needs additional information or if the equipment is outside the pre-engineered range, he contacts the Engineering department for further calculations and specifications.

Larry's sales tool kit consists of his PC with its tendering system, traffic analysis and simulation programs, price and material lists, and his sales guide and technical information binders. He also needs tools to communicate with his own back-up in sales support and in engineering. This is possible either by electronic mail and messaging systems or by conventional phone and fax. Finally, he will enter the order received in the Order book and project management system, where the elevator will be managed and followed up from the specification throughout material order, installation and testing to final hand-over to the customer. After customer hand-over the data is transferred to the maintenance and call-out system for the guarantee period and often beyond.

Tender Enquiry

"Yes, Mr. Beaver, we will be pleased to provide you with a quotation, but I'll need some information from you to specify the type of the lift. What type of building are we dealing with?

"A small office building, with six floors."

"How many occupants will there be on each floor? Have you reserved any space for the lift shaft and the machine room? Is the machine room on top or at the bottom of the building?"

Tender Preparation

Larry has obtained all the data that he needs: the customer details, building drawings, and the specification request from the architect or consultant. He inputs these to the tendering system. The elevator type, load, travel height and number of stops provide the basic range and specification. The further items to be specified are the door type, width, height, control features, elevator car interior, signals and push buttons on car and landings. The specification is made by selecting from a predefined list of items. If the item combinations are restricted or not allowed, a message will be displayed. If the customer requests a feature that does not appear on the standard list, it can either be added as a local item, which will be purchased from a subcontractor, or the salesman can ask for a specification from the Kone factory.

Based on the items selected, the basic tender price is calculated. The price includes the value of materials, which can be partly from a Kone factory and partly from local subcontractors; the installation and labor cost; elevator service during the guarantee period; any adjustable items for market area or building customer type, possibly indexing and discounts included.

The tender documents will be produced by combining the selected values and parameters to predefined letter and text blocks in word-processing. The tender letters and technical description of the items tendered can be modified by the salesman, if required to suit this particular customer and project.

Tender Follow-up and Negotiation

"Good morning, Larry! Nice Monday, the sun is shining and the sky is blue! What's up this week?"

"Good morning, boss! I just printed out my action list for this week. The first thing I'll do is to follow up a tender I sent to Bayswater Builders last week. Then I have another three outstanding tenders which I need to track. The project we tendered in Brighton is due to be decided this week and I'm 90 percent sure we're going to get it."

When the tenders are registered in the salesman's system, the follow-up and updating of data can take place in an organized way. During the negotiations the elevator specifications often change, alternative options are submitted to the customer, the price is negotiated, and the schedules and installation programs are agreed on. All changes and modifications are done by changing parameters in the original tender. Different versions are saved and the full tender history is available for sales managers and salesmen themselves, if required.

Order Booking

"Good afternoon, Mr. Liftagain, this is Mr. Beaver from Bayswater Builders. At our meeting this morning we decided to give the lift order to Kone, for the price and specifications agreed in your revised quotation on Friday. I will send you the letter of instruction confirming this."

When can you give me the detailed schedule and the final drawings?''

The order was received, but this is just the start for the next phase of the job: the implementation. The order is transferred from the tendering system to the order book, job numbers are opened, the customer details, commercial details, cost budget estimate, elevator specification, and project schedule are entered.

Interface to other systems

Information about the new order is sent automatically to the financial department, who will open job numbers in the accounting systems. The new elevators will appear in order book reports for the sales and branch managers and other authorized users.

The factory will be informed about the new order received. This can take place at order booking, or in cases where the drawings and completion of specification is handled locally by the salesman, the complete order is sent to the factory at no-return point—just in time for the manufacture.

Drawings

After the tender and specification have been agreed, the production of layout and design drawings starts. These drawings are produced either by the salesman or by the engineering department when technical expertise and advanced CAD systems are required. The salesman's drawing system can be a parameter driven PC CAD, which fills the building and elevator dimensions into predefined layout sheets. This enables the salesman to submit standard drawings to the architect and builder in a few minutes or hours, sometimes even in their office.

Installation planning and scheduling

"Hi Larry, this is Bob! Listen, I noticed on my capacity plan that you've booked a new order with Bayswater Builders— well done! When you're ready with the specs (= technical specifications), can you arrange the hand-over to Peter, who I've appointed as supervisor. He will also make the detailed installation plan and coordinate the deliveries from the factory, as usual. I can see in his labor plan that he has two men available in September for the installation work. The estimated hours proposed by the computer say we will take 3 weeks to complete, so we can achieve the handover to customer on 1st October, as planned."

Factory Order

When the drawings have been approved, the remaining items of the specification have been agreed on, and the car interior and landing features designed, the salesman fills in the order form and specification for the factory. When the order form is in electronic format, the system checks whether the components, options and the combinations are allowed, the dimensions are within acceptable limits, and all mandatory items have been specified. The completed order is sent electronically to the supplying factory. The order consists of the material list, order header and customer details, contact person, delivery groups and required schedule.

The order confirmation is received, including confirmed transfer price, delivery groups and schedules.

Any items that are purchased locally from subcontractors are specified. Prices and schedules are agreed and monitored.

Site and Installation activities

"Good morning, gentlemen, welcome to our Monday site meeting. The building works are progressing on schedule and the lift installation is due to start next week. We have the Installation Supervisor Peter Jones from Kone Lifts here to agree on the next steps. Peter, can you tell us about your program?''

"Good morning, all. The lift installation is due to start next Monday and to continue for 3 weeks. I have two men working on site and I will be visiting twice a week. The materials will arrive in two shipments. The first one, consisting of the shaft and machine room equipment, will arrive next Monday. The doors, car finishes and signal equipment will arrive the following Monday. I have spoken to your transport manager and he has arranged for your truck driver to assist in moving the equipment from the lorry to the area assigned by the site manager. The installation work will progress in 11 steps—here is the step-by-step plan—starting from unloading and distributing the material, installing the machine room equipment, and ending at commissioning and testing. The time allowed for each activity, you can see in this schedule. My guys will be filling in time sheets and progress reports every week which will be used for the payroll and monitoring of site progress. . . .''

Handover

"Hello Mr. Beaver, how are you? You have a nice group of lifts in here, completed all on time, as planned. Let's take a closer look. . . . So, everything is in order, we have received your interim payments, the final invoice will be sent to you today. I would like to introduce you to out Maintenance Manager Paul Simon. He and his guys will be looking after your lifts for the next 12 months, as per our contract. If you have any further projects, please don't hesitate to contact us."

This is a typical successful elevator order-delivery process, which demonstrates all parts of the process. Selling is not always so easy and becomes more complicated and harder all the time.

KONE ELEVATORS

Kone Elevators is the third largest elevator manufacturer in the world, the market share being around 15 percent, compared to Otis Elevators' (in the U.S.) 25 percent and Shindler's (in Switzerland) 19 percent. The company employs more than 17,000 people worldwide, fewer than one in ten of whom are Finnish. The primary strategic objective, since the late 1960's, has been the creation of a multinational elevator and escalator company via the acquisition of national elevator companies in various countries.

Kone Oy was founded in 1910, and the first elevator was delivered eight years later. In 1968 Kone expanded from the Finnish domestic market into Scandinavia by acquiring the Swedish company ASEA, tripling elevator deliveries in the process. The second step in intensive acquisition took place in 1975 when Kone acquired the Westinghouse elevator and escalator business in Europe, thus doubling sales.

The 1980s saw Kone's breakthrough in North America, and in Europe expansion continued when two leading Italian elevator companies, Sabiem and Fiam, joined the organization in 1985 and 1986 respectively. During 1987, joint-venture operations for elevator production were started in Australia, India and Turkey.

On two occasions the company has absorbed nonprofitable operations as large or even larger than itself and turned them into profitable ones. Profitability has been restored through using the same business concept in all units.

Each acquisition constitutes a separate case. Kone has tried to handle them very flexibly with their own schedules, measures and models. Following acquisition the role of each new unit has been thought over, and some of its operations have been standardized with other units of the corporation. Sometimes the changes have taken several years, and there have been some cultural differences. Although Kone has a similar business concept in each unit, it's been realized in different ways in different countries. On occasions tough measures have had to be used in order to remove obstacles to company reorganization.

Kone has learned several cultural lessons. For instance, in Italy you have to agree on everything with top management. Direct contacts with different functions such as accounting failed to work, if the decisions had not been made first at top level. Implementing new models and systems therefore took more time than expected. In Germany the thinking was quite functional; users thought that it was the task of the systems specialists from Finland to implement new systems without bothering them.

Kone is now a global company whose operations have been organized into five areas: Europe North, Central, and South, Asia-Pacific, and the Americas. Each area is headed by a full-time Area Director. The sales of new elevators and installations are organized by local companies in each country. Within each area, there is one Engineering Center for product engineering and design and tailoring to customer orders. The Engineering Center compiles and delivers market specific elevators from Kone standard components to local customers.

Component manufacturing is organized globally so that in Europe, for example, there are over ten component factories in different countries. The elevator components are transported to the Logistics Center, which is located with the Engineering Center. The Engineering and Logistics Centers are the area service centers of the elevator delivery process. On site elevator installation is carried out in each country by the local organization. A locally competitive product, an elevator that meets customer requirements, is developed in each area, but Kone's standard components are used in all areas.

Kone Elevators is now organized in the following way:

- Sales and Installations, separate companies in each country.
- Engineering and logistics, one unit within each geographical area.
- Components production, a global operation.

COMPETITION IN THE ELEVATOR BUSINESS

The elevator business is a highly competitive one, with overcapacity in production. The demand for new elevators and industrial cranes is on the decline in all markets except the Far East. The downturn in the construction industry seems set to last, since in many countries there is overproduction of both office space and flats. In such a situation the competition for market shares is fierce, and there is a great deal of pressure on price levels.

The business in elevator modernization, maintenance, and repair continues to grow and form an increasingly significant proportion of the sales industry. In this line of business there is a structural, permanent-looking change happening to which companies must adapt. The focus in building new elevators must be shifted toward maintenance. In this competitive situation the maintenance of customer service is extremely important.

Kone Elevators aims at competitive success through a decentralized business concept, the aim of which is to combine economies of scale and local flexibility. The key element in Kone strategy is the global logistics system, which is based on common basic system modules that can be modified and localized to suit local users' needs. The global logistics system informs every person involved in the process of the tasks they need to perform in order to get the elevator delivered and installed on time. The system makes it possible to schedule and record major activities, such as orders to the Engineering Center, component orders released, installations programmed, elevators shipped and installations completed. Each elevator order can be tracked down on screens or reports at the main points of the process. With this system, Kone salesmen can give more reliable and quicker responses to customer requirements.

With this global mode of operation Kone has been successful in a very difficult competitive situation. A combination of good customer service and cost effectiveness has been achieved. However, the structural change in competition offers new challenges to Kone's management, in terms of how to adapt the company to the changing environment.

Director of Information Systems Markku Rajaniemi stated from his Helsinki headquarters that:

''During the 80's many medium-sized elevator companies disappeared from the market, mostly through acquisition. Small companies survived by flexibility and low cost, big companies developed their products and activities and utilized economies of scale, while mid-sized companies were caught in between and got eaten up by the big ones. Kone has also grown by acquiring typically medium-sized companies with small resources for developing activities and low economies of scale. We organized the activities so that local companies can benefit from Kone development activities and scale advantages.

Our competitiveness is very much based on our systems to manage the global logistics where orders, components and products are moving between countries. We try to combine global scale and local flexibility with our three level management (global, area, and country)."

INFORMATION TECHNOLOGY IN KONE ELEVATORS

Kone Elevators has a decentralized data processing set-up, with around 200 medium-size computers (HP9000, AS400) and with around 200 Local Area Networks (NOVEL). The main operating systems are UNIX, OS400, OSF-UX and DOS. In international data transmission different services from multiple network operators are used. The transmission protocols are TCP/IP and SNA Routers.

Kone's information technology strategy is roughly as follows:

The main corporate activities are research and testing of new technologies, updating Elevators Headquarters IT on corporate technical standards, and negotiating and managing frame agreements with corporate-wide hardware and software suppliers. Development, management and support of Kone's international telecommunications network is an important task.

Elevator Headquarters concentrates on developing and updating technical standards and the application architecture, developing the Kone Elevators application portfolio in line with business needs and priorities, and organizing support and maintenance of portfolio applications. Providing Kone units with adequate support in general and specific IT issues is also important.

Company IT activities involve defining business requirements and analyzing business benefits, procuring hardware and software in line with Kone's technical standards, and managing implementation projects. They also include running local computer operations and the development and maintenance of local applications and adaptations. Managing the migration of the local infrastructure towards harmonization constitutes an important task.

Kone Elevators has a common applications architecture, which maps out the main applications in a unit, describes their functionality and defines their interfaces. It also describes the underlying common data structure and how the various applications access data. The applications architecture is a vital communication vehicle in developing, implementing and maintaining systems applications.

The technical standard defines the hardware, software and telecommunications solutions applicable in the units. Deviations from these standards are allowed only after consultation with headquarters' IT function.

Altogether this is a very coordinated decentralized solution. Units have to work within a given frame, but they take care of their own operations. Within the framework there is some flexibility for individual solutions.

In the units, coordination has been experienced as mainly positive, although some complaints have been made about the fact that matters had been defined in too great detail. Personnel in the information systems function are, however, of the opinion that the input of coordination has even been limited, so that the function's resources would just suffice to provide sufficient support to the local unit.

At Kone Elevators there are around one hundred IS professionals who are mainly decentralized in different units. The objective of the IS function is to obtain software that is as complete as possible, in order for its own software production to be as limited as possible. Total IS costs are around 2 percent of sales, an average level in manufacturing.

The applications are divided into three different areas:

- Management systems, e.g. management accounting and budgeting
- Operations support, e.g. logistic systems
- Resource management, e.g. personnel administration, supplier control and customer service.

Kone has concentrated on internal systems. It has not invested much on external links. They have thought that it is enough to have information less frequently, but in a reliable and consistent form. Recently, however, there has been discussion on how to improve the quality of market information, but there are no ongoing projects.

References

Annual Report, Kone 1992.
Hurskainen Jorma, Business Process Approach to Global Logistics Case: Kone Elevators, in Joining the Global Roll, Jahnukainen and Vepsäläinen (eds), Helsinki 1992, pp. 86–102.

Rajaniemi Markku, Process Development in Perspective, ibid, pp. 132–138.
Interviews, Ulla Mäkelä and Markku Rajaniemi, Kone Elevators.

Case Study Questions

1. What kind of global strategy is Kone Elevators pursuing?

2. Evaluate Kone's information systems in light of this strategy. How well do they support it?

3. Evaluate Kone's strategy for managing its international information systems infrastructure.

4. How easy would it have been for Kone to implement the order-delivery system described at the beginning of this case on an international basis? What management, organization, and technology issues had to be addressed?

5. How strategic is the order-delivery system described here for a firm such as Kone? Why?

Festo Pneumatic
Helmut Krcmar and Bettina Schwarzer, University of Hohenheim (Germany)

Festo, a medium-sized German company headquartered in Esslingen, with 3500 employees around the world, is one of the world market leaders in the field of pneumatics and device control. The company was founded in 1925 and opened its first subsidiary, in Italy, in 1956. By now Festo has branches in 187 countries, offering full service for its products around the world (See Figure 4). Festo has four major product groups: Festo Electronic, which offers products and services for electronic device control; Festo Tooltechnic, offering electronic and air-pressure tools for crafts and industry; Festo Didactic, which provides courses for all kinds of device control; and finally Festo Pneumatic, which manufactures valves and cylinders and provides complete solutions for device control.

The major group is Festo Pneumatic, which specializes in the design and manufacturing of valves and cylinders, offering 35,000 components and 4,000 products by catalogue. It also provides custom-made solutions for device control in which cylinders are combined with other Festo components according to specific customer requirements. This combined approach of manufacturing components and offering complete solutions distinguishes Festo from most of its competitors in the pneumatic business. All products are designed and produced in Germany. Only in the case of special made-to-order cylinders does production take place in the subsidiaries to meet customer requirements. Of the products manufactured in Germany, 55% are exported.

Festo Pneumatic has 35 subsidiaries and more than 100 branch offices selling its products. In general, all pneumatic products are designed and manufactured in Germany; therefore the same product is available around the world. As parts are shipped all over the world from the German production site and warehouse, all orders have to be processed centrally. Processing a workload of about 200–300 orders with an average of 4 items per order from each of the major subsidiaries daily, Festo Pneumatic is dependent on a global computer system.

Even though Festo is a fairly small company with only 1000 employees abroad, it is highly internationalized and continuously expanding its international engagements, now turning to Eastern Europe. The subsidiaries are independent companies, but are dependent on the German headquarters because they neither design nor manufacture products. Festo Pneumatic Germany views its subsidiaries as "shops" for selling the company's products in foreign markets. Not only in the business area but also in the field of information systems Festo pursues a centralized approach. Hardware and software are selected in the corporate headquarters, which also provides systems support. The major advantage of this approach is cost savings; detailed knowledge of the sys-

tems can be centralized in one place. Any changes in the system only have to be made in one place and are then taken to all subsidiaries. This not only reduces costs but also guarantees that the system is the same everywhere.

In 1976, confronted with continuing international growth and an increasing workload, Festo Pneumatic decided to implement a common system in the headquarters and the subsidiaries to be able to handle and improve order processing, logistics, and production on an international basis. The goals pursued with the system were "high quality of customer service" and "minimized stock levels." To match the structure of their international operations Festo decided to implement one common system for all subsidiaries, as they had exactly the same information processing requirements in their data exchange with the headquarters. As there was no standardized software package available at that time, a system was developed in-house starting in 1976. Development took place in the headquarters and beginning in 1978 the system was introduced in the subsidiaries.

Due to the lack of standardized software packages at that time and the high costs of in-house development, most competitors did not have sophisticated systems in place when Festo introduced its first integrated system. At that time the rationale for systems development was not strategic advantage—the idea of strategic information systems was not yet known—but simply to make order processing on an international basis more efficient. Still, Festo realized that the new system helped them to gain competitive advantage; the time for order processing was shortened and Festo was able to respond quicker to customer requests.

Over the years the system has been continuously improved to meet changing requirements. Festo's current FIP-2 system, used for order processing, logistics, and manufacturing, was developed based on its experiences with the first system. All components of the old system that worked well are also used in the new system, with new technology replacing the components that were no longer appropriate. The FIP-2 system is based on the Cobol 85, RPG, and High Level RPG programming languages and uses TurboImage for database management.

Before systems development took place, the hardware platform was carefully chosen by experts after a one-year study of different vendors. The main criterion for hardware selection was scalability, to make sure that the same hardware could be used in subsidiaries of different sizes. Festo headquarters always used IBM computers but it selected Hewlett Packard computers for its subsidiaries. Today Festo's 24 subsidiary headquarters run the system on HP 3000 computers with the RISC-technology based operating system MPE/iX. No matter whether four or 2000 people are using the system at

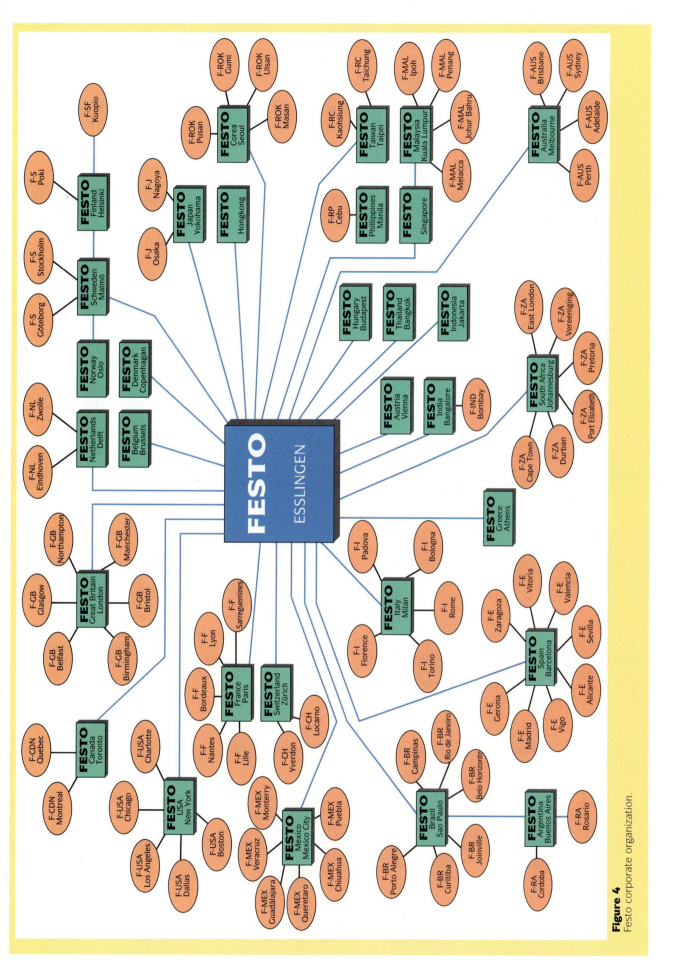

Figure 4
Festo corporate organization.

the same time, all users can work in the same systems environment.

Customers order in the subsidiaries' branches by either telephone or FAX (in some cases there are shops for over-the-counter sales). Festo's branch offices in various countries use microcomputers linked directly to an HP 3000 in each subsidiary's headquarters for order entry. An order is entered into the FIP-2 system on a microcomputer and then transmitted to subsidiary headquarters either immediately or once a day, depending on the type of connection between the branch office and subsidiary headquarters. There the order is checked for availability of components in the country's own warehouse. If the components are available, the order is processed in the country. Otherwise, the orders are collected and transmitted every hour or once a day (depending on the size and importance of the subsidiary) via an X.25 packet-switched network to an HP 3000 in Festo headquarters in Germany. The HP 3000 at German headquarters in turn transforms the data to make processing on an IBM 3090 mainframe possible. The IBM mainframe is linked to Festo's German branches, so German orders are entered directly into this system. The IBM combines orders from abroad with the German orders and processes them. The system checks the stocks in the German warehouse and the production schedule and returns with a confirmation of the order to the subsidiaries, stating the expected date of delivery. Data are then transmitted to an AEG 80−30 computer which is used to manage the warehouse. Festo reports no problems with these linkages on either a national or international level, although some problems may arise when transmitting data to and from technologically underdeveloped countries such as Brazil.

If the components are in stock, the AEG 80-30 in the warehouse handles the request. A warehouse note is printed, giving information on where the components are to be found in the warehouse and how many components are needed for the order. The parts are removed from the warehouse and commissioned. The worker enters the "finished" status into the system and a delivery note, the bill and a confirmation of the order are printed by the system. These papers are put into the packet and sent to the subsidiary either on the road or by air. The subsidiary either puts the components in its own warehouse or puts together the required parts for the individual orders.

Apart from the orders processed together, customer-specific orders can be transmitted to the German headquarters. In this case, all components for the order are packed together and marked in the German warehouse. They are delivered to the subsidiary together with the other parts. After checking them in the subsidiary they can be delivered directly to the customer without putting them into the warehouse.

Designing one common system for use in different countries was not as easy as it sounds and caused a number of problems. Apart from the different languages that are required, for example in printed material for the use of the customer, country-specific features have to be implemented. For example, in Italy the revenue authorities require that bills sent to the same customer have to be numbered in the correct order of issue, whereas in other countries the revenue authorities have their own numbering system and are not interested in the number on the bill. If special features are only needed in one country Festo allows the subsidiary to make the changes itself, providing support for the systems support people in the subsidiaries if needed. If several countries have the same requirements, the changes are made at headquarters and then implemented abroad. In making the changes at headquarters, so far only headquarters systems personnel has been involved. This policy is being changed in order to gain advantage of the knowledge available in the subsidiaries.

Whereas in former times, the system provided Festo with a competitive advantage as the system allowed faster processing of orders, the competitive situation has changed over the years due to the increasing availability of standard software. Today, software is readily available, and in order to be able to compete all companies use integrated systems. Festo has adapted to the new situation and is focusing on improving customer service. One potential area for benefits that has been identified is incorporating expert systems into the system. Expert systems can support the sales people in their meetings by suggesting system configurations. Thereby the ordering process can be speeded up and qualitatively improved.

Case Study Questions

1. What kind of global strategy is Festo Pneumatic pursuing?
2. Evaluate Festo's FIP-2 system in light of this strategy. How well does this system support it?
3. Evaluate Festo Pneumatic's strategy for managing its international information systems infrastructure.
4. How much competitive advantage does Festo's FIP-2 system provide?
5. What problems did Festo have implementing its order processing, logistics and production system? What management, organization, and technology issues had to be addressed?
6. Festo's order processing, logistics, and production system is custom-developed. In this particular instance, is it an advantage or disadvantage to have custom-built software?

Corning Telecommunications Division (A): The Flexible Manufacturing Systems Project

Andrew Boynton, International Institute for Management Development (Switzerland)

Driving across the Gibson Bridge toward his office in July 1990, Bob McAdoo, senior vice president and head of manufacturing for the Telecommunications division of Corning, Inc., thought about the appropriations request he would be discussing with his staff on Friday morning. The division was requesting $5 million for a new planning and scheduling system plus a reconfigured information system to cope with manufacturing changes at its Wilmington, NC, plant, where Corning made optical waveguides. Such a sum was not an incidental capital investment. Moreover, exactly what they would be getting for the money was hard to say. The budget for hardware and packaged software was dwarfed by the costs of design work and consultants. The consultants would be designing a system that had never been built before, and after problems with the last systems-development project, ATLAS, the idea of breaking new ground in software was troubling. (ATLAS, even though it was a well-understood business data system, had been two years late and millions over budget.) In addition, no one could tell McAdoo if the proposed Flexible Manufacturing System (FMS) would work once it was designed, written, and implemented. All they would say is that they "didn't think the plant could continue to work without it."

OPTICAL WAVEGUIDES

Optical waveguides are glass fibers that allow communication by light rather than electricity. One fifth thinner than a human hair, the core of these fibers can carry more than 16,000 simultaneous phone conversations (compared with 24 for copper wire). Unlike copper, optical fiber can also carry information in both directions (sending and receiving) simultaneously. Fibers can transmit light more than 100 miles without regeneration and operate 20,000 feet under water with a 40-year life. Despite their close resemblance to fishing line when coated, fibers can withstand 1 million pounds per square inch of tensile stress. Optical fiber can also carry more information much faster than copper wire. Fiber's carrying capacity of 1.8 billion bits per second could transmit the Encyclopedia Britannica and the Bible around the earth together in less than 2 seconds.

Optical fibers behave like "light pipes." Because of their differences in composition, the refractive index of the core is higher than that of the outer coat (cladding). As a result, light rays traveling through the core will be reflected back into the core if they stray from a straight line and bounce into the core/cladding interface. Consequently, light stays in the core even when the fiber is bent.

The two types of fiber are multimode and single mode. Multimode is primarily used for local building-to-building and intrabuilding wiring, where its comparatively large core size contributes to reduced installation costs. Multimode is available in several glass and coating designs, which when combined with various optical performance levels, results in a wide and increasing variety of stock-keeping units (SKUs).

Single-mode fiber is used primarily by telephone companies. Initial applications were for long-distance telecommunication applications by companies like MCI, AT&T, and Sprint. New types of fiber and coatings, and declining systems costs after 1983, led to many new applications by regional telephone companies (e.g., Bell South), cable television companies, and long-distance communication companies. Given the efforts by telephone companies to emphasize product standardization and compatibility of competing vendors' products, fewer single-mode than multimode fiber SKUs existed. Single-mode fiber represented approximately 90% of the market volume.

Corning sold almost all of its fiber to optical-fiber cablers. A few cablers accounted for approximately 80% of Corning's sales, with 200 customers making up the remaining 20%. Essentially, cablers packaged the optical fiber in a variety of materials to protect it during installation and to limit the effects of its installed environments. From a materials point of view, cablers added little to the value of the fiber, and the fiber itself was a large portion of the cost of fiber cabling. Excess capacity plagued the cabling industry, and barriers to entry were low. Telephone companies' purchases comprised 70% of the optical-cable market, and these companies were adept at creating a level playing field through specification standards and purchasing strategies. Product quality and service were important to the phone companies, but these parameters were viewed largely as requirements for entry. Bidding to attract the phone companies' business was fierce. Overall, profits for optical cablers tended to be low, which was consistent with the financial performance they achieved when these same cablers had been copper-wire cablers.

As the costs of fiber optic systems declined, phone-company fiber-cable installation migrated from long-haul telecommunications trunks (e.g., MCI) through re-

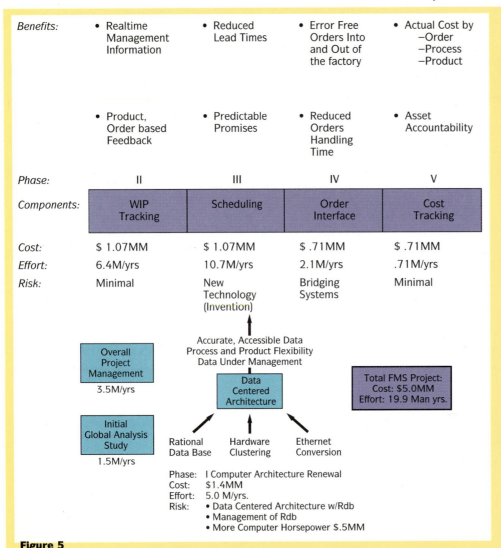

Figure 5
Corning Telecommunications Division (A): flexible manufacturing systems.

gional telecommunications (e.g., Bell South) interoffice trunks joining central-office switching systems to feeder cables connecting central-office switches directly to large businesses or to residential neighborhoods (see Figure 5). Phone companies were betting that optical systems' costs would decline to the degree that they would be no different than the costs of a copper wire system for final telephone line connections to residences (distribution and drop cables). When the fiber could be installed to the home, the phone companies would be able to take advantage of fiber's unlimited capacity to provide a raft of new information services such as video entertainment on demand, home shopping, and home education. This development would allow the phone companies to become the aggressive, high-growth information firms that had been envisioned at the time of divestiture.

The cable television market also used single mode fiber, to improve picture quality and channel capacity and as a defensive posture against the phone companies, who were interested in entering the home entertainment

video market. Cable TV's mass deployment of fiber has lagged the phone companies by five years, but growth since 1988 has been strong.

Beyond the phone companies and cable TV markets, another large and growing segment was premises wiring of banks, corporate offices, universities, hospitals, industrial complexes, and brokerage houses. These customers made up the market for multimode fiber. Standards had not progressed as far in this segment, and several different multimode glass and fiber designs serviced the market. Given the lack of concentrated purchasing observed in the phone company segment, the buying patterns were not as orderly. Many fiber cablers and systems integrators would often bid on the same premises job, and quote turnaround times and cable lead times were key determinants in establishing the winning bidder.

Cablers passed these segment pressures directly to Corning and other suppliers AT&T and Spectran. While Corning and AT&T devoted a large percentage of their fiber capabilities to single mode, Spectran owed its existence to the multimode market. Spectran used attractive pricing, rapid quote turnaround, and competitive lead times to attract business.

Waveguides at Corning Incorporated

Corning, Inc., in 1990 was composed of four primary sectors, Specialty Glass and Ceramics, Communications, Laboratory Services, and Consumer Housewares. Specialty Glass and Ceramics marketed over 40,000 specialty materials, including eyeglass materials and auto-emission filters. The Communications sector produced optical fiber, opto-electrical components for fiber networks, video display glass, and liquid crystal displays. Laboratory Services provided clinical testing, life-science research, and environmental testing services. Consumer Housewares produced such well-known products as Corning Ware, Revere Ware, and Corelle dinnerware.

In 1989–90, the Communications sector contributed approximately 21% to Corning's revenues and 37% to its profits, increases of over 35% in both categories. A significant contribution to corporate profits came from optical waveguides. Corning's quality and delivery had consistently provided a significant profit margin on this product.

Corning developed the first technically feasible optical fiber in 1970. The company then worked for eight years refining the technology and developing a proprietary low-cost manufacturing method. Despite years of only moderate interest from telephone companies and cablers, Corning funded the research and, in 1979, built a manufacturing plant in Wilmington. The plant operated for three years producing only samples and small orders for pilot projects before its first major order was received, which followed the deregulation of the telecommunications industry in 1982.

At that time, MCI announced plans to build a nation-wide fiber-optic network and ordered one hundred thousand kilometers of fiber from Corning. The order, ten times larger than any prior one, was for a new type of single-mode fiber that was still experimental at the company. To meet MCI's requirements, therefore, Corning moved a new generation of fiber technology from the lab to the plant floor, installed new production equipment, and embarked on one of the largest plant expansions in Corning's history. By 1986, sixteen years after proving the commercial feasibility of optical fiber, Corning's fiber-optics operations were running twenty-four hours a day and turning a profit.

The MCI order was quickly followed by others as competition in the telecommunications industry developed. In 1983, Corning funded the largest expenditure request in its history, $100 million, to expand the Wilmington plant to meet rapidly increasing demand and install Corning's fifth generation of fiber-optic manufacturing technology. Corning's dedication to its new technology and its willingness to invest allowed the company to compete with larger rivals such as AT&T and "Japan, Inc.," to become a world leader in waveguide manufacturing. In 1991 Corning Communications, having initiated a "total quality" effort to measure the performance of all business and manufacturing processes to determine competitive capabilities, was pursuing the Baldrige Award.

The initial growth phase, fueled by the needs of long-distance companies, had appeared endless, and to remain an industry's technological leader, Corning had averaged changes in production machinery every 12–24 months. In the second half of 1986, however, as Corning continued to increase its production capacity, the initial growth stopped. The market for long-distance lines was saturated, and increasingly customized fiber-optic, especially multimode, orders from the cable industry changed the demands on Corning's waveguide plant. By 1990, these new demands were not optimally satisfied by the manufacturing and information systems at the plant. By early 1991, construction to again increase the size and capacity of the plant substantially had begun, and this effort required the attention of everyone in the factory to maintain existing production levels.

Mike Jordan, planning and scheduling supervisor, had briefed Bob McAdoo on the complexity of production scheduling at the Wilmington plant: "In making waveguides, the process is different from standard production like making automobiles. With cars, ten Chevy engines and ten Chevy bodies make ten Chevy cars, with some quality reworking. Here, in optical waveguides, we can mix ten batches of the same chemicals under the same conditions with the same computer-controlled processes. Sometimes we'll get seven batches that can be sold; sometimes we'll get ten. Each batch will differ slightly from the other batches. For example, the maximum length of optical fibers will vary as bad sections are cut out. Glass-geometry precision will differ slightly from batch to batch. So we don't know how many saleable end products we'll get because of differences in selection yield. We also don't know how many end products will be Oldsmobiles and how many will be Chevys due to the distribution of characteristics. Luckily, we can substitute Oldsmobiles for Chevys here. Customers will take a higher quality cable for the same price. But this substitution costs us money. Selection, distribution, and substitution complicate the planning process."

Manufacturing waveguides required highly exact, computer-controlled systems, but the early emphasis on standard fiber products with few modifications for the long-distance companies had resulted in a system limited to keeping costs low while maintaining efficiency and high quality. The system was designed to control manufacturing at each step of the production process (Laydown, Consolidation, etc.). The primary function of the information system was to identify equipment and process problems in each individual production stage.

The tight controls coded into the system allowed few modifications in the product or production process. To get around the product and process controls, a small percentage of the plant's production was run as "experimental" products. Each production process had to be individually "tricked" into letting new products move through the system. The products were moved manually through the entire production process with computer overrides at each step. For example, new or customized products with diameters or lengths that were different from standard fibers required engineers to override set specifications in the Draw and Measurement systems. Since all fibers looked essentially identical to the naked eye, special fiber reels were identified with colored dots and batch numbers to flag them as requiring special processing. The manual intervention was not only time-consuming and labor intensive, but also prone to human error.

Computer overrides often conflicted with standard costing information and with constants in production algorithms. Thus costs could not be accumulated on special orders and new products. Inappropriate algorithm constants resulted in incorrect production information, and reported yields exceeded actual process inputs.

Information was captured by the system on each of the individual processes but was used to control only that process. No information was passed along by the system to the next production stage. Operators even keyed in reel identification numbers manually at each stage. This division of production information resulted in a vertically oriented information system that employees called, along with the associated computers, "stovepipes" of information. Each stovepipe was monitored and controlled by a separate staff (the stovepipe's "feudal lord"). Computers stored highly summarized information on products completed and in inventory.

The stovepipe infrastructure of the current system did not allow potentially useful information to be shared across production stages. The different systems had dramatically different field definitions and sizes, which offered little opportunity to integrate the data across the stovepipes. For example, measurement information from the OLS stage could not be used to eliminate later quality checks or to determine sampling strategies in the Measurement stage. The systems provided no means of feeding information forward or backward in the production process. Information on fiber defects discovered in later process steps required manual intervention, communication, and correction. Information gathered in prior stages, such as diameter measurements and usable fiber lengths determined in Draw, were unavailable to Measurement technicians, who might spend hours searching reels for a long usable fiber. Consolidating information from the different systems resulted in unacceptable delays in providing production information. In short, the stovepipe systems did not allow the plant to maximize the use of its capital-intensive equipment.

Designed to meet high demand for a few products, the system did not track work in process. All orders were matched to inventory. However, when a relatively stable supply of a few products had moved through the system, supervisors had been able to coordinate production based on inventory levels.

As the number of products multiplied and became more customized, and as customers demanded shorter lead times, a "Sneaker Patrol," the plant's production and scheduling staff, had become responsible for determining what was in the plant and adjusting production schedules in an attempt to meet customer orders. The 4-week production plan listed the number of blanks of each product type to start. As orders came in or were canceled and as the yields changed in the production process, the Sneaker Patrol made schedule revisions. Currently, numerous daily schedule changes and comprehensive changes are made weekly to the 4-week plan.

Pressure to increase responsiveness can be seen in the fact that, in 1988, Corning fiber salespeople put pressure on Wilmington to respond in less than one day with delivery and cost information for customers; in 1991, they were pressuring Wilmington to respond in less than four hours. In 1991, Wilmington had a several-hour goal and monitored performance to meet that goal.

All changes, which were based on information that was often two days old, were projected by hand. Most information was gathered and transmitted by the production staff, the Sneaker Patrol, walking through the plant with clipboards and changing the colored and numbered dots on different carts of fiber reels. This process was being stretched to the limit as the Wilmington plant continued to add new fiber products and prepared to add additional capacity.

Mike Jordan, who as planning and scheduling supervisor, was also head of the Sneaker Patrol, explained how the process was being stretched: "A customer was buying multimode product of long length. This is not a standard product, so we have to begin a 'yellow-dot experiment,' where the particular yellow dot indicates 'produce long-length multimode.' The customer calls back in a few days and says he doesn't want the long-length. Because we can't waste good in-process fiber, I have to go out and take off the yellow dot from this particular experiment and produce this in-process fiber for stock. The next day, the same customer calls and says he wants a different band-width multimode. I then have to run out again and find some in-process fiber of that band width by looking around the plant and then put a yellow dot on that to indicate the length the customer wants. Can you imagine this happening many times each day? It does!"

The same information gathered for scheduling was used to quote order lead times to customers. Quoting a lead time one or two days longer than a competitor could lose an order. Missing a deadline or shipping incorrect product violated one of Corning's top cultural values. Currently, a significant percentage of customer orders were for shipment in less than 5 days, but the plant took over 6 days to complete most of the orders, even though the production process required significantly less time. All other delays were caused by the logistics of moving between operations (a minimal amount of time) and scheduling conflicts and inefficiencies.

Mike O'Koren, the Wilmington plant manager, described the plant as computer intensive but reliant on "people intervention" and "customized people processes:" "The customers are wanting more one-of-a-kind orders with shorter lead times. Our record of error-free shipments and past turnaround time have made customer service a competitive advantage. Maintaining this advantage is crucial to our success. Right now we don't have a system in place that allows us to shrink lead times. The only way we do it now is with what people do in their heads. We promise orders based on what we think is on the shop floor. We've been stretched pretty thin. As our volume increases and the number of product choices multiplies, the people system is going to break down."

Reliance on customized people processes and mutual production adjustments between feudal lords and the Sneaker Patrol had created a large informal communications network in the plant. Production processes had evolved to conform to this network.

Jordan estimated that the plant could accept orders for 10% more fiber a month if quote times could be reduced through the scheduling of a "made-to-order" manufacturing system. He explained that, in the information environment he envisioned, he could be much more effective: "I want to be able to sit at home or in the office and, on the PC, identify what fiber is in stock or anywhere on the floor. Now I have to check what is in the inventory or on the floor to see what is there. Today we have almost zero visibility about ware in process."

Jordan hoped, however, that any new systems wouldn't be as difficult to implement as the last systems project with which he had been involved: "Although this is my vision for fast response to our customer requests, the last information system project I was involved with, ATLAS, left me with a healthy dose of skepticism. ATLAS has worked out great, but not without some pain. Now we can see all orders, which customers place through the sales force at corporate, in 5 minutes. Before ATLAS, it took over 24 hours for us to get an order. I felt the project was badly undersourced. The system was being designed for multiple uses in multiple divisions. Coordination between all parties was difficult. Senior management in our sector didn't buy in initially, and without that pressure brought to bear, the project stagnated. It didn't work until we at Wilmington held our ground, insisted on getting the resources required, and fought for the project to be completed the right way. After we at Wilmington started kicking, the guys at corporate got involved and insured that corporate IS [Information Systems] put the resources on the project for our sector. We learned a great deal during ATLAS, and it is a real lifesaver now. I just wonder if new systems will be as difficult to implement."

On a recent visit to the Wilmington plant, McAdoo had spoken with O'Koren about the effect of the proposed new information system on the people who composed the informal communications network. O'Koren thought the new system would provide tremendous benefits to customers, but he was less enthusiastic about the effect on plant personnel: "Many people have done nothing but act as information transmitters in this network since the business was started. They feel very threatened. I think they're going to have to learn new jobs."

McAdoo noted that, as O'Koren was speaking, a large fish on his PC's aquarium display had turned and eaten several smaller fish.

THE APPROPRIATIONS REQUEST

The decision to request $5 million to revamp waveguide manufacturing had not been straightforward. On the one hand, the waveguide project had always been a high-risk, high-return project. Historically, large appropriations requests had been granted, and they had paid off. On the other hand, the configuration and timing of the local-loop market appeared as uncertain as the long-distance market had in 1970.

Tom LaGarde, manager of IS at the Wilmington factory, had been heavily involved with the preparation of the request. He discussed with McAdoo how the implementation effort would be managed: "At the highest level, we have a review board consisting of senior managers at corporate that meet twice a year to make sure the project is not out of sync with the company. We have been asked to submit appropriation requests twice a year after the initial request is approved. As we present each request, we have to establish where we've been and where we are going and establish how much money has been spent and what will be needed. We brought in Global Analysis, a Big Five consulting firm, because we felt our corporate IS group, though talented, did not have the experience for this type of project. We're using a computer-based tool to plan, track, test, and manage the project tool that connects each project person. There is a great deal of technical risk beyond the sheer size and complexity of the project. We have no experience with the relational database technology, which has to provide rapid and flexible access to great quantities of information. The other dimension of technical risk is the finite-forward-scheduling component which has never been developed before. We will break the project into seven teams of 5–7 people from about five organizations: contract programming houses, Global Analysis, corporate Engineering and IS, Digital, and the Wilmington factory. As for my organization, I'll have to provide support for the project. At the same time, the plant must have other information needs met. Combine this with a major plant expansion and the plant at capacity, and the difficulties inherent in the implementation become clear."

McAdoo picked up the appropriations request sitting on his desk to read through the body of the proposal. He knew he had to make a case to William Cunningham, manager of the entire Communications sector, to invest this much money on an information system. Furthermore, $5 million would require approval at the chairman level. Would changing the way information was managed at Wilmington convert a factory designed to produce standard products into a flexible manufacturing facility? Were there other, better, alternatives to FMS?

McAdoo and his staff had considered the option that Corning not put any more money into waveguides. They had also looked for, but not found, some other way to fix the current problem. The staff believed in FMS; after all, they had spent the last year in intensive analysis and design. But did they understand the industry forces, and did these forces require the type of strategy suggested by FMS? Finally, would the system work? How, given the ATLAS project delay and cost, could he recommend an information-systems project of this magnitude of this strategic importance?

McAdoo wanted to make sure his staff had thought through the issues carefully before he made a decision. Did his staff have answers to the myriad of important questions? Sighing, McAdoo got up and started the long walk to the meeting with his staff. He would then have the weekend to think things over, but on Monday he had to meet with Cunningham and make a recommendation on FMS.

Case Study Questions

1. Use the competitive forces and value chain models to analyze the Corning Telecommunications Division. What competitive forces did Corning have to deal with? What were the strategic advantages of switching to a flexible manufacturing system for optical waveguides?

2. What were the problems with Corning's existing manufacturing system for optical waveguides? How serious were they? What management, organization, and technology factors contributed to these problems?

3. What management, organization, and technology issues had to be addressed to implement a flexible manufacturing system successfully?

4. What were the dangers and risks of this project?

5. What criteria would you use to determine whether Corning should invest in this project?

6. Should Corning make the $5 million investment in the new flexible manufacturing system? What other alternatives are available?

Glossary

Acceptance testing: Provides the final certification that the system is ready to be used in a production setting. [359]

Accountability: The mechanisms for assessing responsibility for decisions made and actions taken. [704]

Accounting rate of return on investment (ROI): Calculation of the rate of return from an investment by adjusting cash inflows produced by the investment for depreciation. Approximates the accounting income earned by the investment. [367]

Ada: Programming language that is portable across different brands of hardware; is used for both military and nonmilitary applications. [216]

Adhocracy: Task force organization, such as a research organization, designed to respond to a rapidly changing environment and characterized by large groups of specialists organized into short lived multi-disciplinary task forces. [96]

Administrative controls: Formalized standards, rules, procedures, and disciplines to ensure that the organization's controls are properly executed and enforced. [651]

Agency theory: Economic theory that views the firm as a nexus of contracts among self-interested individuals rather than a unified, profit-maximizing entity. [109]

AI shell: The programming environment of an expert system. [596]

Analog signal: A continuous wave form that passes through a communications medium. Used for voice communications. [276]

Anti-virus software: Software designed to detect and often eliminate computer viruses from an information system. [642]

Application controls: Specific controls unique to each computerized application. [647]

Application generator: Software that can generate entire information system

applications; the user needs only to specify what needs to be done and the application generator creates the appropriate program code. [219]

Application software: Programs written for a specific business application in order to perform functions specified by end users. [205]

Application software package: Set of prewritten, precoded, application software programs that are commercially available for sale or lease. [396]

Applications portability: The ability to operate the same software on different hardware platforms. [317]

Applications Portability Profile (APP): Standards for operating systems, database management, data interchange, programming languages, user interfaces, and networking to be enforced by U.S. federal government procurements in order to achieve connectivity. [326]

Arithmetic-logic unit (ALU): Component of the CPU that performs the principal logical and arithmetic operations of the computer. [171]

Artificial intelligence: The effort to develop computer-based systems that can behave like humans, with the ability to learn languages, accomplish physical tasks, use a perceptual apparatus, and emulate human expertise and decision making. [586]

ASCII: American Standard Code for Information Interchange. A 7- or 8-bit binary code used in data transmission, microcomputers, and some large computers. [166]

Assembly language: A programming language developed in the 1950s that resembles machine language but substitutes mnemonics for numeric codes. [215]

Assistant expert system: In the role of an assistant, an expert system that helps a decision maker by doing the routine analysis and tedious work and

pointing out the portions of the work where human expertise is required. [593]

Asynchronous transmission: Low-speed transmission of one character at a time. [280]

Attribute: Piece of information describing a particular entity. [239]

Automated workplace: Vision of the new information architecture that makes desktop microcomputers and workstations the centerpiece of the workplace with mainframes and minicomputers at the periphery. [316]

Backward chaining: Strategy for searching the rule base in an expert system that acts like a problem solver by beginning with a hypothesis and seeking out more information until the hypothesis is either proved or disproved. [597]

Bandwidth: The capacity of a communications channel as measured by the difference between the highest and lowest frequencies that can be transmitted by that channel. [279]

Bar code: Form of OCR technology widely used in supermarkets and retail stores in which identification data are coded into a series of bars. [189]

Baseband: LAN channel technology that provides a single path for transmitting text, graphics, voice, or video data at one time. [286]

BASIC (Beginners All-purpose Symbolic Instruction Code): General-purpose programming language used with microcomputers and for teaching programming. [216]

Batch control totals: A type of input control that requires counting transactions or any quantity field in a batch of transactions prior to processing for comparison and reconciliation after processing. [652]

Batch processing: A method of processing information in which transactions are accumulated and stored until a specified time when it is convenient and/or necessary to process them as a group. [34]

Baud: A change in signal from positive to negative or vice-versa that is used as a measure of transmission speed. [279]

Behavioral models: Descriptions of management based on behavioral scientists' observations of what managers actually do in their jobs. [131]

Bit: A binary digit representing the smallest unit of data in a computer system. It can only have one of two states, representing 0 or 1. [165]

Bit mapping: The technology that allows each pixel on the screen to be addressed and manipulated by the computer. [190]

Bottom-up approach: In the history of artificial intelligence, the effort to build a physical analog to the human brain. [589]

Bounded rationality: Idea that people will avoid new uncertain alternatives and stick with tried-and-true rules and procedures. [141]

Briefing books: On-line data in the form of fixed-format reports for executives; part of early EIS. [569]

Broadband: LAN channel technology that provides several paths for transmitting text, graphics, voice, or video data so that different types of data can be transmitted simultaneously. [287]

Bugs: Program code defects or errors. [432]

Bureaucracy: Formal organization with a clear-cut division of labor, abstract rules and procedures, and impartial decision making that uses technical qualifications and professionalism as a basis for promoting employees. [89]

Bureaucratic models: Models of decision making where decisions are shaped by the organization's standard operating procedures (SOPs). [144]

Bus network: Network topology linking a number of computers by a single circuit with all messages broadcast to the entire network. [281]

Business driver: A force in the environment to which businesses must respond and that influences the direction of business. [671]

Business process: A set of logically related tasks performed to achieve a defined business outcome. [347, 682]

Byte: A string of bits, usually eight, used to represent one number or character stored in a computer system. [165]

C: Powerful programming language with tight control and efficiency of execution; is portable across different

microprocessors and is used primarily with microcomputers. [217]

Cache: High speed storage of frequently used instructions and data. [181]

Capital budgeting: The process of analyzing and selecting various proposals for capital expenditures. [362]

Carpal tunnel syndrome (CTS): Type of RSI in which pressure on the median nerve through the wrist's bony carpal tunnel produces pain. [727]

CD-ROM: Compact disk read-only memory. Read-only optical disk storage used for imaging, reference, and database applications with massive amounts of data and for multimedia. [186]

Cellular telephone: Device that transmits voice or data, using radio waves to communicate with radio antennas placed within geographic areas called cells. [278]

Central processing unit (CPU): Area of the computer system that manipulates symbols, numbers, and letters and controls the other parts of the computer system. [168]

Centralized processing: Processing that is accomplished by one large central computer. [178]

Change agent: In the context of implementation, the individual acting as the catalyst during the change process to ensure successful organizational adaptation to a new system or innovation. [480]

Channels: The links by which data or voice are transmitted between sending and receiving devices in a network. [276]

Choice: Simon's third stage of decision making, when the individual selects among the various solution alternatives. [138]

Class: Feature of object-oriented programming so that all objects belonging to a certain class have all of the features of that class. [224]

Classical model of management: Traditional descriptions of management that focused on its formal functions of planning, organizing, coordinating, deciding, and controlling. [130]

Client/server model: A model for computing that splits the processing between "clients" and "servers" on a network assigning functions to the machine most able to perform the function. [309]

Coaxial cable: Transmission medium consisting of thickly insulated copper wire. Can transmit large volumes of data quickly. [277]

COBOL (COmmon Business Oriented Language): Predominant programming language for business applications because it can process large data files with alphanumeric characters. [215]

Cognitive style: Underlying personality disposition toward the treatment of information, selection of alternatives, and evaluation of consequences. [141]

Colleague expert system: In the role of a colleague, an expert system that permits a decision maker to engage in a discussion of the problem, add information, or even bypass the system entirely, until a joint decision is reached. [593]

Combinatorial explosion: In computer processing, the overload that results when trying to test more rules to reach a solution than the computer is capable of handling. [591]

Competitive forces model: Model used to describe the interaction of external threats and opportunities that affect an organization's strategy and ability to compete. [62]

Compiler: Special system software that translates a higher-level language into machine language for execution by the computer. [208]

Complete expert automaton: An expert system that operates remotely by making decisions without the additional input of human experts or human intervention. [593]

Compound document: Electronic document that consists of differing types of information acquired from separate sources such as graphics, database, spreadsheet, and text-based programs. [524]

Computer abuse: The commission of acts involving a computer which may not be illegal but are considered unethical. [726]

Computer-aided design (CAD): Information system that automates the creation and revision of designs using sophisticated graphics software. [533]

Computer-aided software engineering (CASE): The automation of step-by-step methodologies for software and systems development to reduce the amount of repetitive work the developer needs to do. p. 454]

Computer-based information systems (CBIS): Information systems that rely on computer hardware and software for processing and disseminating information. [9]

Computer crime: The commission of illegal acts through the use of a computer or against a computer system. [724]

Computer generations: Major transitions in computer hardware; each generation is distinguished by a different technology for the components that do the processing. [172]

Computer hardware: Physical equipment used for input, processing, and output work in an information system. [12]

Computer matching: Processing control that matches input data to information held on master files. [653]

Computer mouse: Hand-held input device whose movement on the desktop controls the position of the cursor on the computer display screen. [188]

Computer operations controls: Procedures to ensure the programmed procedures are consistently and correctly applied to data storage and processing. [648]

Computer software: Detailed preprogrammed instructions that coordinate computer hardware components in an information system. [12]

Computer virus: Rogue software programs that are difficult to detect and spread rapidly through computer systems, destroying data or disrupting processing and memory systems. [641]

Computer vision syndrome (CVS): Eye strain condition related to cathode ray tube (CRT) use, with symptoms including headaches, blurred vision, and dry, irritated eyes. [729]

Concentrator: Telecommunications computer that collects and temporarily stores messages from terminals for batch transmission to the host computer. [280]

Connectivity: A measure of how well computers and computer-based devices communicate and share information with one another without human intervention. [316]

Connectivity audit: A method for examining amount of connectivity an organization has by examining five areas of connectivity such as network standards, user interfaces and applications. [329]

Context diagram: Overview data flow diagram depicting an entire system as a single process with its major inputs and outputs. [441]

Control aids: Capabilities that allow the user to control the activities and functions of the DSS. [552]

Control unit: Component of the CPU that controls and coordinates the other parts of the computer system. [171]

Controller: Specialized computer that supervises communications traffic between the CPU and the peripheral devices in a telecommunications system. [280]

Controls: All of the methods, policies, and procedures that ensure protection of the organization's assets, accuracy and reliability of its records, and operational adherence to management standards. [646]

Conversion: The process of changing from the old system to the new system. [359]

Conversion plan: Provides a schedule of all activities required to install a new system. [360]

Cooperative processing: Dividing computing tasks among networked mainframes, minicomputers, microcomputers, or workstations to solve a single common problem. [179, 317]

Cooptation: Bringing the opposition into the process of designing and implementing the solution without giving up control over the direction and nature of the change. [684]

Copyright: A statutory grant which protects creators of intellectual property against copying by others for any purpose for a period of 28 years. [712]

Core systems: Systems that support functions that are absolutely critical to the organization. [682]

Cost-benefit ratio: A method for calculating the returns from a capital expenditure by dividing the total benefits by total costs. [368]

Counterimplementation: A deliberate strategy to thwart the implementation of an information system or an innovation in an organization. [492]

Critical success factors (CSFs): A small number of easily identifiable operational goals shaped by the industry, the firm, the manager, and the broader environment that are believed to assure the success of an organization. Used to determine the information requirements of an organization. [376]

Cultural theory: Behavioral theory stating that information technology must fit into an organization's culture or the technology won't be adopted. [116]

Customization: The modification of a software package to meet an organization's unique requirements without destroying the integrity of the package software. [398]

Cylinder: Represents circular tracks on the same vertical line within a disk pack. [183]

Data administration: A special organizational function for managing the organization's data resources, concerned with data planning, information policy, maintenance of

data dictionaries, and data quality standards. [262]

Data bus width: The number of bits that can be moved at one time between the CPU, primary storage, and the other devices of a computer. [175]

Data conversion: Process of properly transcribing data from one form into another form for computer transactions. [652]

Data definition language: The component of a database management system that defines each data element as it appears in the database. [245]

Data dictionary: An automated or manual tool for storing and organizing information about the data maintained in a database. [246]

Data element: A field. [246]

Data flow diagram (DFD): Primary tool in structured analysis that graphically illustrates the system's component processes and the flow of data between them. [439]

Data flows: The movement of data between processes, external entities, and data stores in a data flow diagram. [439]

Data management software: Software used for creating and manipulating lists, creating files and databases to store data, and combining information for reports. [221]

Data manipulation language: A language associated with a database management system that is employed by end users and programmers to manipulate data in the database. [245]

Data processing vision: Vision of the new information architecture that views microcomputers and workstations as subservient to and closely integrated into the mainframe computing environment. [314]

Data quality audit: Survey of files and samples of files for accuracy and completeness of data in an information system. [657]

Data redundancy: The presence of duplicate data in multiple data files. [242]

Data security controls: Controls to ensure that data files on either disk or tape are not subject to unauthorized access, change, or destruction. [649]

Data stores: Manual or automated inventories of data. [439]

Data workers: People such a secretaries or bookkeepers who process and disseminate the organization's paperwork. [11, 510]

Database: Collection of data organized to service many applications at the same time by organizing data so that they appear to be in one location. [244]

Database administration: Refers to the more technical and operational aspects of managing data, including physical database design and operation. [262]

Database management system (DBMS): Special software to create and maintain a database and enable individual business applications to extract the data they need without having to create separate files or data definitions in their computer programs. [245]

Debugging: The process of discovering and eliminating the errors and defects--the bugs--in program code. [436]

Decision and control theory: Behavioral theory stating that the function of the organization is to make decisions under conditions of uncertainty and risk and that organizations centralize decision making and create a hierarchy of decision making to reduce uncertainty. [110]

Decision support systems (DSS): Computer systems at the management level of an organization that combine data and have sophisticated analytical models to support semistructured and unstructured decision making. [38, 550]

Decision tables: A graphic in the form of a table that portrays the conditions that affect a decision; used for documenting situations in which the decision process is highly structured. [443]

Decision trees: Sequential tree-like diagrams that present the conditions affecting a decision and the actions that can be taken. The branches represent the paths that may be taken in the decision-making process. [444]

Decisional roles: Mintzberg's classification for managerial roles where managers initiate activities, handle disturbances, allocate resources, and negotiate conflicts. [132]

Dedicated lines: Telephone lines that are continuously available for transmission by a lessee. Typically conditioned to transmit data at high speeds for high-volume applications. [287]

Descartes' rule of change: A principle that states that if an action cannot be taken repeatedly, then it is not right to be taken at any time. [706]

Design: Simon's second stage of decision making, when the individual conceives of possible alternative solutions to a problem. [138]

Design: Stage in the systems life cycle that produces the logical and physical design specifications for the systems solution. [389]

Desktop publishing: Technology that produces professional-quality documents combining output from word processors with design, graphics, and special layout features. [38, 517]

Development methodology: A collection of methods, one or more for every activity within every phase of a development project. [434]

Digital image processing: Technology that converts documents and graphic images into computerized form so that they can be stored, processed, and accessed by computer systems. [44]

Digital scanners: Input devices that translate images such as pictures or documents into digital form for processing. [190]

Digital signal: A discrete wave form that transmits data coded into two discrete states as 1-bits and 0-bits, which are represented as on-off electrical impulses. Used for data communications. [276]

Direct access storage device (DASD): Refers to magnetic disk technology which permits the CPU to locate a record directly, in contrast to sequential tape storage that must search the entire file. [185]

Direct cutover: A risky conversion approach where the new system completely replaces the old one on an appointed day. [360]

Direct file access method: Method of accessing records by mathematically transforming the key fields into the specific address for the records. [240]

Direct file organization: Method of storing records so that they can be accessed in any sequence without regard to their actual physical order on storage media. [239]

Distributed database: A database that is stored in more than one physical location. Parts or copies of the database are physically stored in one location and other parts are stored and maintained in other locations. [256]

Distributed processing: The distribution of computer processing work among multiple computers linked by a communication network. [178, 256]

Divisionalized bureaucracy: Combination of many machine bureaucracies, each producing a different product or service, under one central headquarters. [94]

Document imaging systems: Systems that employ digital image processing to store, retrieve, and manipulate a digitized image of a document, allowing the document itself to be discarded. [518]

Documentation: Descriptions of how an information system works from either a technical or end-user standpoint. [360]

Domestic exporter: Global strategy characterized by heavy centralization of corporate activities in the home country of origin. [678]

DOS: Operating system for 16-bit microcomputers based on the IBM Personal Computer standard. [209]

Downsizing: The process of transferring applications from large computers to smaller ones. [179]

Drill down: The ability to move from summary data down to lower and lower levels of detail. [569]

DSS database: A collection of current or historical data from a number of applications or groups. [558]

DSS software system: DSS component that permits easy interaction between the users of the system and the DSS database and model base. [558]

EBCDIC: Extended Binary Coded Decimal Interchange Code. Binary code representing every number, alphabetic character, or special character with 8 bits, used primarily in IBM and other mainframe computers. [166]

Economic feasibility: Determines whether the benefits of the proposed solution outweigh the costs. [353]

Edit checks: Routines performed to verify input data and correct errors prior to processing. [653]

Electronic calendaring: Software that tracks appointments and schedules in an office. [523]

Electronic data interchange (EDI): Direct computer-to-computer exchange between two organizations of standard business transaction documents. [291]

Electronic mail: The computer-to-computer exchange of messages. [290, 523]

Electronic market: A marketplace that is created by computer and communication technologies which link many buyers and sellers via interorganizational systems. [69]

Electronic meeting software: Software designed to enhance the productivity of face-to-face meetings or of meetings among participants in scattered locations. [523]

Electronic meeting system (EMS): Collaborative GDSS that uses information technology to make group meetings more productive by facilitating communication as well as decision making. Supports meetings at the same place and time or in different places and times. [565]

End user: Representative of a department outside of the information systems group for whom information systems applications are developed. [105]

End-user development: The development of information systems by end users with little or no formal assistance from technical specialists. [403]

End-user interface: The part of the information system through which the end user interacts with the system, such as on-line screens and commands. [393]

End-user software: Software tools that permit the development of applications by end users with little or no professional programmer intervention or that enhance the productivity of professional programmers. [205]

Enterprise analysis: An analysis of organization-wide information requirements by looking at the entire organization in terms of organizational units, functions, processes, and data elements; helps identify the key entities and attributes in the organization's data. [373]

Entity: A person, place, or thing about which information must be kept. [239]

Entity-relationship diagram: Methodology for documenting databases illustrating the relationship between various entities in the database. [255]

Entrepreneurial culture: Young, small firm in a fast-changing environment dominated by a single entrepreneur and managed by a single chief executive officer. [93]

Environmental factors: Factors external to the organization that influence the adoption and design of information systems. [106]

EPROM: Erasable programmable read-only memory. Subclass of ROM chip that can be erased and reprogrammed many times. [170]

Ergonomics: The interaction of people and machines in the work environment, including the design of jobs, health issues, and the end-user interface of information systems. [494]

Ethical no free lunch rule: Assumption that all tangible and intangible objects are owned by someone else unless there is a specific declaration otherwise and that the creator wants compensation for this work. [707]

Ethics: Principles of right and wrong that can be used by individual's acting as free moral agents to make choices to guide their behavior. [700]

Executive information systems (EIS): Early ESS that provide senior executives information without the capabilities of ESS for broad-based electronic communications, data analysis, scheduling, and organizing. [569]

Executive support systems (ESS): Information systems at the strategic level of an organization designed to address unstructured decision making through advanced graphics and communications. [39, 568]

Expert system: Knowledge-intensive computer program that captures the expertise of a human in limited domains of knowledge. [593]

External entities: Originators or receivers of information outside the scope of the system portrayed in the data flow diagram. Sometimes called outside interfaces. [440]

External integration tools: Project management technique that links the work of the implementation team to that of users at all organizational levels. [489]

Facsimile (FAX): Machine that digitizes and transmits documents with both text and graphics over telephone lines. [291]

Fair Information Practices (FIP): A set of principles originally set forth in 1973 that governs the collection and use of information about individuals and forms the basis of most U.S. and European privacy law. [710]

Fault-tolerant computer systems: Systems that contain extra hardware, software and power supply components that can back the system up and keep it running to prevent system failure. [643]

Feasibility study: A way to determine whether a solution is achievable, given the organization's resources and constraints. [353]

Feedback: Output that is returned to the appropriate members of the organization to help them evaluate or correct input. [8]

Fiber optic cable: Fast, light, and durable transmission medium consisting of thin strands of clear glass fiber bound into cables. Data are transmitted as light pulses. [277]

Field: A grouping of characters into a word, group of words, or complete number. [239]

File: A group of records of the same type. [239]

File server: Computer in a network that stores various programs and data files for users of the network. Determines access and availability in the network. [286]

Floppy disk: Removable magnetic disk primarily used with microcomputers. The two most common standard sizes are 3.5-inch and 5.25-inch disks that are made up of polyester film with magnetic coating. [184]

Focused differentiation: Competitive strategy for developing new market niches where a business can compete in the target area better than its competitors. [62]

Formal control tools: Project management technique that helps monitor the progress towards completion of a task and fulfillment of goals. [490]

Formal planning tools: Project management technique that structures and sequences tasks, budgeting time, money, and technical resources required to complete the tasks. [489]

FORTRAN (FORmula TRANslator): Programming language developed in 1956 for scientific and mathematical applications. [215]

Forward chaining: Strategy for searching the rule base in an expert system that begins with the information entered by the user and searches the rule base to arrive at a conclusion. [597]

Forward engineering: The final step in re-engineering when the revised specifications are used to generate new, structured program code for a structured and maintainable system. [460]

Fourth-generation language: A programming language that can be employed directly by end users or less skilled programmers to develop computer applications more rapidly than conventional programming languages. [217]

Frame relay: Shared network service technology that packages data into bundles for transmission but does not use error correction routines. Cheaper and faster than packet switching. [289]

Frames: Method of organizing expert system knowledge into chunks, but the relationships are based on shared characteristics determined by the user rather than a hierarchy. [596]

Franchiser: Firm in which the product is created, designed, financed, and initially produced in the home country, but must rely heavily on foreign personnel for further production, marketing, and human resources. [678]

Front-end processor: Small computer managing communications for the host computer in a network. [280]

Function point analysis: Software output metric that measures the number of inputs, outputs, inquiries, files, and external interfaces used in an application. Used to assess developer productivity and software efficiency. [436]

Fuzzy logic: Rule-based AI that tolerates imprecision by using non-specific terms called membership functions to solve problems. [615]

Garbage can model: Model of decision making that states that organizations are not rational and that decisions are solutions that become attached to problems for accidental reasons. [147]

Gateway: Communications processor that connects dissimilar networks by providing the translation from one protocol to another. [286]

General controls: Overall controls that establish a framework for controlling the design, security, and use of computer systems throughout an organization. [647]

Gigabyte: Approximately one billion bytes. Unit of computer storage capacity. [168]

Global culture: The development of common expectations, shared artifacts, and social norms among different cultures and peoples. [672]

Graphical user interface: The part of an operating system that users interact with that uses graphic icons and the computer mouse to issue commands and make selections. [212]

Graphics language: A computer language that displays data from files or databases in graphic format. [218]

Group decision support system (GDSS): An interactive computer-based system to facilitate the solutions to unstructured problems by a set of decision makers working together as a group. [560]

Groupware: Software that recognizes the significance of groups in offices by providing functions and services that support the collaborative activities of work groups. [522]

Hacker: A person who gains unauthorized access to a computer network for profit, criminal mischief, or personal pleasure. [640]

Hard disk: Magnetic disk resembling a thin steel platter with an iron oxide coating; used in large computer systems and in many microcomputers. [183]

Hardware controls: Controls to ensure the physical security and correct performance of computer hardware. [648]

Hierarchical data model: One type of logical database model that organizes data in a treelike structure. A record is subdivided into segments that are connected to each other in one-to-many parent-child relationships. [250]

High-level language: Programming languages where each source code statement generates multiple statements at the machine-language level. [213]

Hypermedia database: Approach to data management that organizes data as a network of nodes linked in any pattern established by the user. [259]

Immanuel Kant's Categorical Imperative: A principle that states that if an action is not right for everyone to take it is not right for anyone. [706]

Implementation: Simon's final stage of decision making, when the individual puts the decision into effect and reports on the progress of the solution. [138]

Implementation: All of the organizational activities working toward the adoption, management, and routinization of an innovation. [479]

Implementation controls: Audit of the systems development process at various points to make sure that it is properly controlled and managed. [648]

Incremental decision making: Choosing policies most like the previous policy. [141]

Index: A table or list that relates record keys to physical locations on direct access files. [240]

Index server: In imaging systems, a device that stores the indexes that allow a user to identify and retrieve a specific document. [519]

Indexed sequential access method (ISAM): File access method to directly access records organized sequentially using an index of key fields. [240]

Inference engine: The strategy used to search through the rule base in an expert system: can be forward or backward chaining. [597]

Information architecture: The particular form that information technology takes in a specific organization to achieve selected goals or functions. [19]

Information center: A special facility within an organization that provides training and support for end-user computing. [406]

Information partnership: Cooperative alliance formed between two corporations for the purpose of sharing information to gain strategic advantage. [72]

Information policy: Formal rules governing the maintenance, distribution, and use of information in an organization. [262]

Information portability: The sharing of computer files among different hardware platforms and software applications. [317]

Information requirements: A detailed statement of the information needs that a new system must satisfy; identifies who needs what information, and when, where, and how the information is needed. [354]

Information rights: The rights that individuals and organizations have with respect to information which pertains to themselves. [702]

Information system: Interrelated components that collect, process, store, and disseminate information to support decision making, control, analysis, and visualization in an organization. [8]

Information systems department: The formal organizational unit that is responsible for the information systems function in the organization. [104]

Information systems managers: Leaders of the various specialists in the information systems department. [105]

Information systems plan: A road map indicating the direction of systems development, the rationale, the current situation, the management strategy, the implementation plan, and the budget. [372]

Information work: Work that primarily consist of creating or processing information. [510]

Information workers: People in the labor force who primarily create, work with, or disseminate information. [510]

Informational roles: Mintzberg's classification for managerial roles where managers act as the nerve centers of their organizations, receiving and disseminating critical information. [132]

Inheritance: Feature of object-oriented programming in which a specific class of objects receives the features of a more general class. [224]

Input: The capture or collection of raw data from within the organization or from its external environment for processing in an information system. [8]

Input authorization: Proper authorization, recording, and monitoring of source documents as they enter the computer system. [652]

Input controls: Procedures to check data for accuracy and completeness when they enter the system, including input authorization, batch control totals, and edits. [652]

Installation: Systems life cycle stage consisting of testing, training, and conversion; the final steps required to put a system into operation. [390]

Institutional factors: Factors internal to the organization that influences the adoption and design of information systems. [106]

Intangible benefits: Benefits that are not easily quantified; they include more efficient customer service or enhanced decision making. [363]

Integrated Services Digital Network (ISDN): International standard for transmitting voice, video, and data to support a wide range of service over the public telephone lines. [323]

Integrated software package: A software package that provides two or more applications, such as spreadsheets and word processing, providing for easy transfer of data between them. [222]

Intellectual property: Intangible property created by individuals or corporations which is subject to protections under trade secret, copyright, and patent law. [712]

Intelligence: The first of Simon's four stages of decision making, when the individual collects information to identify problems occurring in the organization. [138]

Intelligent database search machine: A master machine that can direct the search of a massive database by giving a target pattern to subordinate master machines that search the database simultaneously. [614]

Interaction theory: User-resistance theory stating that resistance is caused by the interaction of people and systems factors. [492]

Internal integration tools: Project management technique that ensures that the implementation team operates as a cohesive unit. [489]

Internal rate of return (IRR): The rate of return or profit that an investment is expected to earn. [367]

International information systems infrastructure: The basic information systems required by organizations to coordinate world-wide trade and other activities. [671]

Interoperability: The ability of a software application to operate on two different machine platforms while maintaining the identical user interface and functionality. [317]

Interorganizational systems: Information systems that automate the flow of information across organizational boundaries and link a company to its customers, distributors, or suppliers. [69]

Interpersonal roles: Mintzberg's classification for managerial roles where managers act as figureheads and leaders for the organization. [132]

Interpreter: A special language translator that translates each source code statement into machine code and executes it one at a time. [208]

Intuitive decision makers: Cognitive style that describes people who approach a problem with multiple methods in an unstructured manner, using trial and error to find a solution. [141]

Iteration structure: The logic pattern in programming where certain actions are repeated while a specified condition occurs or until a certain condition is met. [445]

Iterative: Process of repeating the steps to build a system over and over again. [391]

Joint application design (JAD): A design method which brings users and IS professionals into a room together for an interactive design of the system. [453]

Jukebox: A device for storing and retrieving many optical disks. [519]

Key field: A field in a record that uniquely identifies instances of that record so that it can be retrieved or updated. [239]

Kilobyte: One thousand bytes (actually 1024 storage positions). Used as a measure of microcomputer storage capacity. [168]

Knowledge and information-intense products: Products that require a great deal of learning and knowledge to produce. [508]

Knowledge base: Model of human knowledge that is used by expert systems. [594]

Knowledge engineer: Specialist who elicits information and expertise from other professionals and translates it into a set of rules, frames, or semantic nets for an expert system. [596]

Knowledge work systems (KWS): Information systems that aid knowledge workers in the creation and integration of new knowledge in the organization. [36, 531]

Knowledge workers: People such as engineers, scientists, or architects who design products or services or create new knowledge for the organization. [11, 510]

Knowledge-level decision making: Evaluating new ideas for products and services, ways to communicate new knowledge and distribute information. [136]

Knowledge-level systems: Information systems that support knowledge and data workers in an organization. [14]

Legitimacy: The extent to which one's authority is accepted on grounds of competence, vision, or other qualities. [685]

Liability: The existence of laws that permit individuals to recover the damages done to them by other actors, systems, or organizations. [704]

Local area network (LAN): Telecommunications network that requires its own dedicated channels and that encompasses a limited distance, usually one building or several buildings in close proximity. [285]

Logical design: Lays out the components of the information system and their relationship to each other as they would appear to users. [356]

Logical office: Vision of the new information architecture that focuses on the ability to use portable microcomputers to work in many different physical locations outside the traditional office. [314]

Logical view: Representation of data as they would appear to an application programmer or end user. [248]

Machine bureaucracy: Large bureaucracy organized into functional divisions that centralizes decision making, produces standard products, and exists in a slow-changing environment. [94]

Machine cycle: Series of operations required to process a single machine instruction. [171]

Machine language: Programming language consisting of the 1s and 0s of binary code. [213]

Magnetic disk: A secondary storage medium in which data are stored by means of magnetized spots on a hard or floppy disk. [183]

Magnetic ink character recognition (MICR): Input technology that translates characters written in magnetic ink into digital codes for processing. [189]

Magnetic tape: Inexpensive and relatively stable secondary storage medium in which large volumes of information is stored sequentially by means of magnetized and nonmagnetized spots on tape. [182]

Magneto-optical disk: Optical disk system that is erasable. Data are recorded by a high-powered laser beam that heats tiny spots in the magnetic media. [187]

Mainframe: Largest category of computer, classified as having 50 megabytes to over 1 gigabyte of RAM. [175]

Maintenance: Changes in hardware, software, documentation, or procedures to a production system to correct errors, meet new requirements, or improve processing efficiency. [361]

Man-month: The traditional unit of measurement used by systems designers to estimate the length of time to complete a project. Refers to the amount of work a person can be expected to complete in a month. [485]

Management control: Monitoring how efficiently or effectively resources are utilized and how well operational units are performing. [135]

Management information systems (MIS): Computer systems at the management level of an organization that serve the functions of planning, controlling, and decision making by providing routine summary and exception reports. [38]

Management-level systems: Information systems that support the monitoring, controlling, decision-making, and administrative activities of middle managers. [14]

Managerial roles: Expectations of the activities that managers should perform in an organization. [132]

Master file: Contains all permanent information and is updated during processing by transaction data. [35]

Megabyte: Approximately one million bytes. Unit of computer storage capacity. [168]

Megahertz: A measure of cycle speed, or the pacing of events in a computer; one megahertz equals one million cycles per second. [175]

Memory aids: In DSS, capabilities to update and refresh memory, including databases, views of data, work spaces, and libraries. [552]

Microcomputer: Desktop or portable computer with 640 kilobytes to 64 megabytes of RAM. [175]

Microeconomic model: Model of the firm that views information technology as a factor of production that can be freely substituted for capital and labor. [108]

Microprocessor: Very large-scale integrated circuit technology that integrates the computers memory, logic, and control on a single chip. [172]

Microsecond: One millionth of a second. [168]

Microwave: High-volume, long-distance, point-to-point transmission in which high-frequency radio signals are transmitted through the atmosphere from one terrestrial station to another. [277]

Middle managers: People in the middle of the organizational hierarchy who are responsible for carrying out the plans and goals of senior management. [12]

Migration: The ability to move software from one generation of hardware to another more powerful generation. [317]

Millisecond: One thousandth of a second. [167]

Minicomputer: Middle-range computer with about 10 to 650 megabytes of RAM. [175]

MIS audit: Identifies all the controls that govern individual information systems and assesses their effectiveness. [656]

Model: An abstract representation that illustrates the components or relationships of a phenomenon. [558]

Model base: A collection of mathematical and analytical models that can easily be made accessible to the DSS user. [558]

Modem: Device for translating digital signals into analog signals and vice-versa. [276]

Module: A logical unit of a program that performs one or a small number of functions. [447]

Muddling through: Method of decision making involving successive limited comparisons where the test of a good decision is whether people agree on it. [141]

Multimedia: Technologies that facilitates the integration of two or more types of media such as text, graphics, sound, voice, full-motion video, or animation into a computer-based application. [191]

Multinational: Global strategy that concentrates financial management and control out of a central home base while decentralizing production, sales, and marketing operations to units in other countries. [678]

Multiplexer: Device that enables a single communications channel to carry data transmissions from multiple sources simultaneously. [280]

Multiprocessing: An operating system feature for executing two or more instructions simultaneously in a single computer system by using more than one central processing unit. [208]

Multiprogramming: A method of executing two or more programs concurrently using the same computer. The CPU only executes one program but can service the input/output needs of others at the same time. [206]

Multitasking: The multiprogramming capability of primarily single-user operating systems such as those for microcomputers. [207]

Nanosecond: One billionth of a second. [168]

Negligence: Finding of fault when a product causes physical or economic harm to individuals that could and should have been prevented. [718]

Net present value: The amount of money an investment is worth, taking into account its cost, earnings, and the time value of money. [368]

Network data model: A logical database model that is useful for depicting many-to-many relationships. [252]

Network operating system: Special software that manages the file server in a LAN and routes and manages communications on the network. [286]

Network topology: The shape or arrangement of a network. [281]

Neural network: Hardware or software that attempts to emulate the processing patterns of the biological brain. [609]

New information architecture: An arrangement of the organization's hardware, software, telecommunications, and data resources to put more computing power on the desktop and create a companywide network linking many smaller networks. [305]

Node: Each of the devices in a network. [283]

Normalization: The process of creating small stable data structures from complex groups of data when designing a relational database. [256]

Object code: Program instructions that have been translated into machine language so that they can be executed by the computer. [208]

Object-oriented database: Approach to data management that stores both data and the procedures acting on the data as objects that can be automatically retrieved and shared. [259]

Object-oriented programming: Approach to software development that combines data and procedures into a single object. [223]

Object-oriented software development: Approach to software development that de-emphasizes procedures and shifts the focus from modeling business processes and data to combining data and procedures that create objects. [453]

Office activities: The principal activities performed at offices; these include managing documents, scheduling and communicating with people, managing data, and managing projects. [514]

Office automation systems (OAS): Computer systems, such as word processing, voice-mail systems, and video-conferencing systems, that are designed to increase the productivity of information workers in the office. [36, 516]

On-line processing: A method of processing information in which transactions are entered directly into the computer system and processed immediately. [34]

On-line transaction processing: Transaction processing mode in which transactions entered on-line are immediately processed by the computer. [643]

Open systems: Software systems that can operate on different hardware platforms because they are built on public non-proprietary operating systems, user interfaces, application standards, and networking protocols. [317]

Open Systems Interconnect (OSI): International reference model for linking different types of computers and networks. [319]

Operating system: The system software that manages and controls the activities of the computer. [205]

Operational control: Deciding how to carry out tasks specified by upper and middle management and establishing criteria for completion and resource utilization. [136]

Operational feasibility: Determines whether the proposed solution is desirable within the existing managerial and organizational framework. [353]

Operational-level systems: Information systems that monitor the elementary activities and transactions of the organization. [13]

Operational managers: People who monitor the day-to-day activities of the organization. [12]

Operations: In DSS, logical and mathematical manipulations of data. [552]

Optical character recognition (OCR): Form of source data automation in which optical scanning devices read specially designed data and translate the data into digital form for the computer. [189]

Optical disk: Secondary storage device on which data are recorded and read by laser beams rather than by magnetic means. [185]

Organization (behavioral definition): A collection of rights, privileges, obligations, and responsibilities that are delicately balanced over a period of time through conflict and conflict resolution. [88]

Organization (technical definition): A stable formal social structure that takes resources from the environment and processes them to produce outputs. [87]

Organizational culture: The set of fundamental assumptions about what products the organization should produce, how and where it should produce them, and for whom they should be produced. [92]

Organizational impact analysis: Study of the way a proposed system will affect organizational structure, attitudes, decision making, and operations. [493]

Organizational models: Models of decision making that take into account the structural and political characteristics of an organization. [144]

OS/2: Powerful operating system used with the 32-bit IBM/Personal System/2 microcomputer workstations that supports multitasking, networking, and more memory-intensive applications than DOS. [209]

Output controls: Ensure that the results of computer processing are accurate, complete, and properly distributed. [655]

Outsourcing: The practice of contracting computer center operations, telecommunications networks, or applications development to external vendors. [409]

Packet switching: Technology that breaks blocks of text into small fixed bundles of data and routes them in the most economical way through any available communications channel. [289]

Page: Small section of a program, which can be easily stored in primary storage and quickly accessed from secondary storage. [207]

Parallel processing: Type of processing in which more than one instruction can be processed at a time by breaking down a problem into smaller parts and processing them simultaneously with multiple processors. [181]

Parallel sensor system: A machine consisting of many nodes that each act as a processor feeding information to a hierarchy of higher-level nodes. [612]

Parallel strategy: Conservative conversion approach where both the old system and its replacement are run together until everyone is assured that the new one functions correctly. [360]

Parity: An extra bit built into the EBCDIC and ASCII codes used as a check bit to ensure accuracy. [166]

Particularism: Making judgements and taking actions on the basis of narrow or personal characteristics. [674]

Pascal: Programming language used on microcomputers and to teach sound programming practices in computer science courses. [216]

Patent: A legal document that grants the owner an exclusive monopoly on the ideas behind an invention for 17 years; designed to ensure that the inventors of new machines or methods are rewarded for their labor while making widespread use of their inventions. [713]

Payback method: A measure of the time required to pay back the initial investment of a project. [367]

Pen-based input: Input devices such as tablets, notebooks, and notepads consisting of a flat-screen display tablet and a pen-like stylus that digitizes handwriting. [189]

People-oriented theory: User-resistance theory focusing on factors internal to users. [492]

Personal information manager: Packaged database tool designed to support specific office data management tasks for an information worker. [528]

Phased approach: Introduces the new system in stages either by functions or by organizational units. [360]

Physical design: The process of translating the abstract logical model into the specific technical design for the new system. [356]

Physical view: The representation of data as they would be actually organized on physical storage media. [248]

Pilot study: A strategy to introduce the new system to a limited area of the organization until it is proven to be fully functional. [360]

Pixel: The smallest unit of data for defining an image in the computer. The computer reduces a picture to a grid of pixels. The term pixel comes from picture element. [167]

PL/1 (Programming Language 1): Programming language developed by IBM in 1964 for business and scientific applications. [216]

Pointer: A special type of data element attached to a record that shows the absolute or relative address of another record. [251]

Political models: Models of decision making where decisions result from competition and bargaining among an organization's interest groups and key leaders. [146]

Political theory: Behavioral theory that describes information systems as the outcome of political competition between subgroups for influence over policies, procedures, and resources of the organization. [116]

Portfolio analysis: An analysis of the portfolio of applications within a firm to determine the risks and benefits and select among alternatives for information systems. [370]

Post implementation: Final stage of the systems life cycle in which the system is used and evaluated while in production and is modified to make improvements or meet new requirements. [390]

Post-industrial theory: Behavioral theory stating that the transformation of advanced industrial countries into post-industrial societies creates flatter organizations dominated by knowledge workers where decision making is more decentralized. [112]

Present value: The value, in current dollars, of a payment or stream of payments to be received in the future. [368]

Primary activities: Activities most directly related to the production and distribution of a firm's products or services. [63]

Primary storage: Part of the computer that temporarily stores program instructions and data being used by the instructions for use by the CPU. [169]

Printer: A computer output device that provides paper "hard-copy" output in the form of text or graphics. [190]

Privacy: The claim of individuals to be left alone, free from surveillance or interference from other individuals, organizations, or the state. [710]

Private branch exchange (PBX): Central switching system that handles a firm's voice and digital communications. [283]

Process: Portrays the transformation of input data flows to output data flows in a data flow diagram. [439]

Process specification: Describes the logic of the processes occurring within the lowest-level bubbles of the data flow diagrams. [443]

Processing: The conversion of raw input into a form that is more meaningful to humans. [8]

Processing controls: Routines for establishing that data are complete and accurate during processing. [653]

Product differentiation: Competitive strategy for creating brand loyalty by developing new and unique products and services that are not easily duplicated by competitors. [62]

Production: The stage after the new system is installed and the conversion is complete; during this time the system is reviewed by users and technical specialists to determine how well it has met its original goals. [361]

Production or service workers: People who actually produce the products or services of the organization. [11]

Professional bureaucracy: Knowledge-based organization such as a law firm or hospital that is

dominated by department heads with weak centralized authority; operates in a slowly changing environment. [96]

Profitability index: Used to compare the profitability of alternative investments; it is calculated by dividing the present value of the total cash inflow from an investment by the initial cost of the investment. [369]

Program: A series of statements or instructions to the computer. [204]

Program-data dependence: The close relationship between data stored in files and the software programs that update and maintain those files. Any change in data organization or format requires a change in all the programs associated with those files. [243]

Program security controls: Controls designed to prevent unauthorized changes to programs in systems that are already in production. [648]

Programmers: Highly trained technical specialists who write computer software instructions. [104]

Programming: The process of translating the system specifications prepared during the design stage into program code. [358]

Programming: Stage in the systems life cycle that translates the design specifications produced during the design stage into software program code. [389]

Project definition: Stage in the systems life cycle that determines whether or not the organization has a problem and whether or not the problem can be solved by launching a system project. [389]

Project management software: Software that facilitates the development, scheduling, and management of a project by breaking the complex project into simpler subtasks, each with its own completion time and resource requirements. [528]

PROM: Programmable read-only memory. Subclass of ROM chip used in control devices because it can be programmed once. [170]

Protocol: Set of rules and procedures that govern transmission between the components in a network. [274, 319]

Prototype: Preliminary working version of an information system for demonstration and evaluation purposes. [391]

Prototyping: Process of building an experimental system quickly and inexpensively for demonstration and evaluation so that users can better determine information requirements. [391]

Pseudocode: Method for expressing program logic that uses plain English

statements rather than graphic symbols, trees, tables, or programming languages to describe a procedure. [444]

Query language: A high-level computer language used to retrieve specific information from databases or files. [217]

RAM: Random access memory. Primary storage of data or program instructions that can directly access any randomly chosen location in the same amount of time. [169]

Rational model: Model of human behavior believing that people, organizations, and nations make consistent, value-maximizing calculations within certain constraints. [139]

Rationalization of procedures: Streamlining of standard operating procedures in order to maximize the advantages of computerization and make information systems more efficient. [32]

Record: A group of related fields. [239]

Reduced instruction set computing (RISC): Technology used to enhance the speed of microprocessors by embedding only the most frequently used instructions on a chip. [175]

Reference model: A generic framework for thinking about a problem. [318]

Register: Temporary storage location in the ALU or control unit where small amounts of data and instructions reside for thousandths of a second just before use. [181]

Relational data model: A type of logical database model that treats data as if they were stored in two-dimensional tables. It can relate data stored in one table to data in another as long as the two tables share a common data element. [252]

Repetitive stress injury (RSI): Occupational disease that occurs when muscle groups are forced through the same, repetitive actions often with high impact loads or thousands of repetitions of low impact loads. [727]

Report generator: Software that creates customized reports in a wide range of formats that are not routinely produced by an information system. [218]

Representations: In DSS, conceptualization of information in the form of graphs, charts, lists, reports, and symbols to control operations. [552]

Request for Proposal (RFP): Detailed list of questions submitted to vendors of packaged software or other computer services to determine if the vendor's product can meet the organization's specific requirements. [400]

Resource allocation: Determination of how costs, time, and personnel are assigned to different activities of a systems development project. [434]

Responsibility: Accepting the potential costs, duties, and obligations of one's decisions. [704]

Reverse engineering: The process of taking existing programs, file and database descriptions and converting them into corresponding design-level components that can then be used to create new applications. [460]

Ring network: Network topology in which all computers are linked by a closed loop in a manner that passes data in one direction from one computer to another. [282]

Risk assessment: Determining the potential frequency of occurrence of a problem and the potential damage if the problem were to occur. Used to determine the cost/benefit of a control. [655]

Risk Aversion Principle: Principle that one should take the action which produces the least harm or incurs the least cost. [707]

ROM: Read-only memory. Semiconductor memory chips that contain program instructions. These chips can only be read from; they cannot be written to. [170]

Rule base: The collection of knowledge in an AI system that is represented in the form of IF-THEN rules. [595]

Rule-based expert system: An AI program that has a large number of interconnected and nested IF-THEN statements or "rules" that are the basis for the knowledge in the system. [595]

Run control totals: Procedures for controlling completeness of computer updating by generating control totals that reconcile totals before and after processing. [653]

Satellite: Transmission of data using orbiting satellites to serve as relay stations for transmitting microwave signals over very long distances. [277]

Satisficing: Choosing the first available alternative in order to move closer toward the ultimate goal. [140]

Schema: The logical description of an entire database, listing all the data elements in the database and the relationships among them. [248]

Scoring models: A quick method for deciding among alternative systems based on a system of ratings for selected objectives. [371]

Secondary storage: Relatively long-term, non-volatile storage of data outside the CPU and primary storage. [181]

Sector: Method of storing data on a floppy disk in which the disk is divided into pie-shaped pieces or sectors. Disk storage location can be identified by sector and data record number. [184]

Security: Policies, procedures, and technical measures used to prevent unauthorized access, alteration, theft, or physical damage to information systems. [645]

Segregation of functions: Principle of internal control to divide responsibilities and assign tasks among people so that job functions do not overlap to minimize the risk of errors and fraudulent manipulation of the organization's assets. [651]

Selection structure: The logic pattern in programming where a stated condition determines which of two or more actions can be taken depending on which satisfies the stated condition. [445]

Semantic nets: Expert systems that use the property of inheritance to organize and classify knowledge when the knowledge base is composed of easily identifiable chunks or objects of interrelated characteristics. [595]

Semiconductor: An integrated circuit made by printing thousands and even millions of tiny transistors on a small silicon chip. [170]

Senior managers: People at the highest organizational level who are responsible for making long-range decisions. [12]

Sensitivity analysis: Models that ask "what-if" questions repeatedly to determine the impact of changes in one or more factors on outcomes. [558]

Sequence structure: The sequential single steps or actions in the logic of a program that do not depend on the existence of any condition. [445]

Sequential file organization: A method of storing records in which records must be retrieved in the same physical sequence in which they are stored. [239]

Sociological theory: Behavioral theory stating that organizations develop hierarchical bureaucratic structures and standard operating procedures to cope in unstable environments and that organizations can't change routines when environments change. [111]

Sociotechnical design: Design to produce information systems that blend technical efficiency with sensitivity to organizational and human needs. [494]

Software: The detailed instructions that control the operation of a computer system. [204]

Software controls: Controls to ensure the security and reliability of software. [648]

Software metrics: Objective assessments of the software used in a system in the form of quantified measurements. [435]

Software package: A prewritten, precoded, commercially available set of programs that eliminates the need to write software programs for certain functions. [219]

Software re-engineering: Methodology that addresses the problem of aging software by salvaging and upgrading it so that the users can avoid a long and expensive replacement project. [460]

Source code: Program instructions written in a high-level language before translation into machine language. [208]

Source data automation: Input technology that captures data in computer-readable form at the time and place the data are created. [189]

Spaghetti code: Unstructured, confusing program code with tangled logic that metaphorically resembles a pot of cooked spaghetti. [438]

Spreadsheet: Software displaying data in a grid of columns and rows, with the capability of easily recalculating numerical data. [220]

Standard: Approved reference models and protocols as determined by standard-setting groups for building or developing products or services. [319]

Standard operating procedures (SOPs): Precise, defined rules for accomplishing tasks that have been developed to cope with expected situations. [11, 90]

Standing data: Data that are permanent and affect transactions flowing into and out of a system. [655]

Star network: Network topology in which all computers and other devices are connected to a central host computer. All communications between network devices must pass through the host computer. [281]

Storage technology: Physical media and software governing the storage and organization of data for use in an information system. [12]

Stored program concept: The idea that a program cannot be executed unless it is stored in a computer's primary storage along with required data. [204]

Strategic decision making: Determining the long-term objectives, resources, and policies of an organization. [135]

Strategic information systems: Computer systems at any level of the organization that change the goals, operations, products, services, or environmental relationships to help the organization gain a competitive advantage. [60]

Strategic-level systems: Information systems that support the long-range planning activities of senior management. [15]

Strategic transitions: A movement from one level of sociotechnical system to another. Often required when adopting strategic systems that demand changes in the social and technical elements of an organization. [73]

Strict liability in tort: Class of liability whenever a defective product causes injury and the manufacturer can be held liable regardless of whether or not the defect could have or should have been prevented. [718]

Structure chart: System documentation showing each level of design, the relationship among the levels, and the overall place in the design structure; can document one program, one system, or part of one program. [446]

Structured: Refers to the fact that techniques are instructions that are carefully drawn up, often step-by-step, with each step building upon a previous one. [438]

Structured analysis: Method for defining system inputs, processes, and outputs and for partitioning systems into subsystems or modules that show a logical graphic model of information flow. [438]

Structured decisions: Decisions that are repetitive, routine, and have a definite procedure for handling them. [137]

Structured design: Software design discipline, encompassing a set of design rules and techniques for designing a system from the top down in a hierarchical fashion. [446]

Structured programming: Discipline for organizing and coding programs that simplifies the control paths so that the programs can be easily understood and modified. Uses the basic control structures and modules that have only one entry point and one exit point. [447]

Structured Query Language (SQL): The emerging standard data manipulation language for relational database management systems. [245]

Subschema: The logical description of the part of a database required by a particular function or application program. [248]

Supercomputer: Very sophisticated and powerful computer that can perform very complex computations extremely rapidly. [175]

Support activities: Activities that make the delivery of the primary activities of a firm possible. [63]

Switched lines: Telephone lines that a person can access from his or her terminal to transmit data to another computer, the call being routed or switched through paths to the designated destination. [287]

Switching costs: The expense a customer or company incurs in lost time and resources when changing from one supplier or system to a competing supplier or system. [62]

Synchronous transmission: High-speed simultaneous transmission of large blocks of data. [280]

System failure: An information system that either does not perform as expected, is not operational at a specified time, or cannot be used in the way it was intended. [474]

System flowchart: Graphic design tool that depicts the physical media and sequence of processing steps used in an entire information system. [449]

System-oriented theory: User-resistance theory focusing on factors inherent in the design of the system. [492]

System residence device: The secondary storage device on which a complete operating system is stored. [206]

System 7: Operating system for the Macintosh computer which supports multitasking and has powerful graphics and multimedia capabilities. [211]

System software: Generalized programs that manage the resources of the computer. [204]

System testing: Tests the functioning of the information system as a whole in order to determine if discrete modules will function together as planned. [359]

Systematic decision makers: Cognitive style that describes people who approaches a problem by structuring it in terms of some formal method. [141]

Systems analysis: The analysis of a problem which the organization will try to solve with an information system. [352]

Systems analysts: Specialists who translate business problems and requirements into information requirements and systems. [104]

Systems design: Details how a system will meet the information requirements as determined by the systems analysis. [354]

Systems development: The activities that go into producing an information systems solution to an organizational problem or opportunity. [352]

Systems life cycle: Traditional methodology for developing an information system that partitions the systems development process into six formal stages that must be completed

sequentially with a very formal division of labor between end-users and information systems specialists. [388]

Systems Network Architecture (SNA): Proprietary telecommunications reference model developed by IBM. [322]

Systems study: Stage in the systems life cycle that analyzes the problems of existing systems, defines the objectives to be attained by a solution, and evaluates various solution alternatives. [389]

Tangible benefits: Benefits that can be quantified and assigned monetary value; they include lower operational costs and increased cash flows. [363]

Technical feasibility: Determines whether a proposed solution can be implemented with the available hardware, software, and technical resources. [353]

Technostress: Stress induced by computer use whose symptoms include aggravation, hostility towards humans, impatience, and enervation. [730]

Telecommunications: Communication of information by electronic means, usually over some distance. [272]

Telecommunications software: Special software for controlling and supporting the activities of a telecommunications network. [281]

Telecommunications system: Collection of compatible hardware and software arranged to communicate information from one location to another. [273]

Telecommunications technology: Physical devices and software that link various hardware components and transfer data from one physical location to another. [12]

Teleconferencing: Ability to confer with a group of people simultaneously using the telephone or electronic mail group communication software. [291]

Test plan: Prepared by the development team in conjunction with the users; it includes all of the preparations for the series of tests to be performed on the system. [359]

Testing: The exhaustive and thorough process that determines whether the system produces the desired results under known conditions. [359]

Time-sharing: The sharing of computer resources by many users simultaneously by having the CPU spend a fixed amount of time on each user's program before proceeding to the next. [208]

Top-down: An approach that progresses from the highest most abstract level to the lowest level of detail. [438]

Top-down approach: In the history of artificial intelligence, the effort to develop a logical analog to how the brain works. [590]

Total quality management (TQM): A concept that makes quality control a responsibility to be shared by all people in an organization. [426]

Touch screen: Input technology that permits the entering or selecting of commands and data by touching the surface of a sensitized video display monitor with a finger or pointer. [189]

Track: Concentric circle on the surface area of a disk on which data are stored as magnetized spots; each track can store thousands of bytes. [183]

Trade secret: Any intellectual work or product used for a business purpose that can be classified as belonging to that business provided it is not based on information in the public domain. [712]

Traditional file environment: A way of collecting and maintaining data in an organization that leads to each functional area or division creating and maintaining its own data files and programs. [242]

Transaction cost theory: Economic theory that states that firms exist because they can conduct marketplace transactions internally more cheaply than they can with external firms in the marketplace. [108]

Transaction file: In batch systems, the file in which all transactions are accumulated to await processing. [35]

Transaction processing systems (TPS): Computerized systems that perform and record the daily routine transactions necessary to the conduct of the business; they serve the operational level of the organization. [35]

Transborder data flow: The movement of information across international boundaries in any form. [675]

Transform algorithm: Mathematical formula used to translate a record's key field directly into the record's physical storage location. [240]

Transmission Control Protocol/Internet Protocol (TCP/IP): U.S. Department of Defense reference model for linking different types of computers and networks. [321]

Transnational: Truly globally managed firms which have no national headquarters; value-added activities are managed from a global perspective without reference to national borders, optimizing sources of supply and demand and taking advantage of any local competitive advantage. [679]

Tuple: A row or record in a relational database. [252]

Twisted wire: Transmission medium consisting of pairs of twisted copper wires. Used to transmit analog phone conversations but can be used for data transmission. [277]

Unit testing: The process of testing each program separately in the system. Sometimes called program testing. [359]

UNIX: Operating system for microcomputers, minicomputers, and mainframes that is machine-independent and supports multiuser processing, multitasking, and networking. [210]

Unstructured decisions: Nonroutine decisions in which the decision maker must provide judgement, evaluation, and insights into the problem definition; there is no agreed-upon procedure for making such decisions. [136-137]

User-designer communications gap: The differences in backgrounds, interests, and priorities that impede communication and problem-solving among end users and information systems specialists. [481]

User interface: The part of the information system through which the end user interacts with the system; type of hardware and the series of on-screen commands and responses required for a user to work with the system. [475]

Utilitarian Principle: Principle that one should take the action that achieves the higher or greater value. [707]

Utility program: System software consisting of programs for routine, repetitive tasks, which can be shared by many users. [208]

Value-added network (VAN): Private, multipath, data-only third party managed networks that are used by multiple organizations on a subscription basis. [289]

Value chain model: Model that highlights the activities that add a margin of value to a firm's products or services where information systems can best be applied to achieve a competitive advantage. [63]

Very-high-level programming language: Programming language using fewer instructions than conventional languages. Used primarily as a professional programmer productivity tool. [219]

Video display terminal (VDT): A screen, also referred to as a cathode ray tube (CRT). Provides a visual image of both user input and computer output. [190]

Videoconferencing: Teleconferencing with the capability of participants to see each other over video screens. [291]

Videotex: Multimedia delivery of information to remote terminals typically used for consumer or commercial delivery systems such as electronic shopping, banking, news, and financial database services. [313]

Virtual private networks: Inexpensive telecommunications over public phone lines with computers and software creating an illusion of a private network for a company. [289, 691]

Virtual reality systems: Interactive graphics software and hardware that create computer-generated simulations that provide sensations that emulate real-world activities. [536]

Virtual storage: A way of handling programs more efficiently by the computer by dividing the programs into small fixed or variable-length portions with only a small portion stored in primary memory at one time. [207]

Voice input device: Technology that converts the spoken word into digital form for processing. [190]

Voice mail: System for digitizing a spoken message and transmitting it over a network. [291]

Voice output device: Converts digital output data into spoken words. [191]

Walkthrough: A review of a specification or design document by a small group of people carefully selected based on the skills needed for the particular objectives being tested. [436]

Warranty: A representation expressed by the seller of goods that the goods are fit for purchase and use. [718]

Wide area network (WAN): Telecommunications network that spans a large geographical distance. May consist of a variety of cable, satellite, and microwave technologies. [287]

Windows: A graphical user interface shell that runs in conjunction with the DOS microcomputer operating system. Supports multitasking and some forms of networking. [212]

Windows NT: Powerful operating system developed by Microsoft for use with 32-bit microcomputers and workstations based on Intel and other microprocessors. Supports networking, multitasking, and multiprocessing. [210]

Word length: The number of bits that can be processed at one time by a computer. The larger the word length, the greater the speed of the computer. [175]

Word processing: Office automation technology that facilitates the creation of documents through computerized text editing, formatting, storing, and printing. [37]

Word processing software: Software that handles electronic storage, editing, formatting, and printing of documents. [219]

Workflow management: The process of streamlining business procedures so that documents can be moved easily and efficiently from one location to another. [519]

Workstation: Desktop computer with powerful graphics, mathematical processing, and communications capabilities as well as the ability to perform several complicated tasks at one time. Often used in scientific or design work. [531]

WORM: Write once, read many. Optical disk system that allows users to record data only once; data cannot be erased but can be read indefinitely. [187]

X terminal model: Centrally controlled inexpensive desktop terminal used on a network which can access the operations of several different remote computers simultaneously. [311]

X Windows: Standard for high-level graphics description used for standardized window management and construction of graphical user interfaces. [325]

Name Index

Organizations Index

Stride Rite, 9, 12–13
Sun Microsystems, Inc., 97, 305, 307, 326, 329
Sundstrand Corporation, 73
Sungard Recovery Services, 643
Sybase Inc., 335

T

Taylor Medical, Inc., 337
TDS Healthcare Systems Corporation, 380
Technicron Financial Services, 65
Teknowledge, Inc., 602
Telecom, 288
Telecom Eireann, 275
Telefonica, 288
Telenet, 291
Telmex, 288
Texaco, Inc., 329
Texas Instruments Inc., 254, 286, 408, 467, 483
Thomson Financial Services, 548
Time Life, Inc., 251
Time Warner Inc., 275
Toronto Dominion Securities Inc., 232–233
Toyota Motor Corporation, 22, 90, 91, 156
Toys R Us, 121
Trane's, 554–555
Transaction Technology Inc., 78
Travelers Insurance Company, 46

Trump's Casino, 661
TRW, Inc., 431

U

Ultramar Oil, 518
Unify Corporation, 335
Unilever, 334–335
Unisys Corporation, 162, 163
United Airlines, 69, 71
United Parcel Service (UPS), 4–5, 7, 8–9, 11, 75, 189, 645
United Services Automobile Association, 45, 186, 190, 254
U.S. Aviation Administration Agency, 432
U.S. Department of Agriculture, 179
U.S. Department of Defense, 187, 216, 224, 237, 321
U.S. Department of Energy, 237
U.S. Department of Justice, 273
U.S. Department of Labor, 510
U.S. Foreign Agricultural Service (FAS), 179
U.S. Immigration and Nationalization Services, 186–187
U.S. Pentagon, 532
U.S. Postal Service, 190, 698–699
U.S. West, 275
United Technologies, 288
University Hospital Consortium, 645
University of North Carolina at Chapel Hill, 537

US West Communications, 527
Usability Sciences Corporation, 477

V

Value Health Sciences, Inc., 48
Ventana Corporation, 136
Verifone, 613
Virgin Atlantic, 734–735
Visa USA Inc., 643
Visix Software Inc., 393
Visual Edge Software Ltd., 393
VPL Research, 537

W

Wabco, 409
Wal-Mart Stores, Inc., 121, 122, 151, 195, 270–271, 703
Wang Laboratories, 98, 179, 516
Warnaco, 151
Washington Post, 151
Westpac Banking Corporation, 472–473, 476
Wright-Patterson Air Force Base, 527

X

Xerox Corporation, 115, 286, 288

Z

Zurich Insurance Group, 128–129

International Organizations Index

S

Sanyo Fisher USA, 616
SAP A.G., 417–419, 669
Sealand Transportation, 673
Sendai's subway system, 167
Shell Canada, Ltd., 412
Siemens Nexdorf, 688
Singapore Technologies, 585
Sony, 679
SRI International, 532

T

Telecom, 288
Telecom Eireann, 275
Telefonica, 288
Telmex, 288

Thompson Financial Services, 548
Toronto Dominion Securities, Inc.,
    232–233
Toyota Motor Corporation, 22,
    90–91, 156

U

Unilever, 334–335
United Parcel Service (UPS), 4–5, 7–9,
    11, 75, 189, 645
United Technologies, 288

V

Virgin Atlantic, 734–745
Visual Edge Software Ltd., 393

W

Westpac Banking Corporation,
    472–473, 476

X

Xerox Corporation, 115, 286, 288

Z

Zurich Insurance Group, 128–129

Subject Index

Differentiation
   focused, 62
   product, 62
Digital image processing, 44–45, 518
Digital public switched network,
      323–324, 327
Digital scanners, 190
Digital Services Data Protection
      Directive, 675
Digital signal, telecommunications
      systems and, 276
Direct access storage device (DASD),
      185
Direct cutover, for conversion, 360
Direct file access method, 240, 241
Direct file organization, 240
Disaster, recovery and backups and,
      636–637, 643, 644
Disk pack, 183
Disks
   magnetic, 183–185
   optical, 32, 33, 34, 182, 185–187
Distributed databases, 256–257
Distributed processing, 178, 256, 257,
      258
Divisionalized bureaucracy, 94
Document imaging systems, 517–519,
      520–522
Document management technologies.
      See Office
Documentation, for conversion,
      360–361
Documenting decision
   decision tables for, 443–444
   decision trees for, 444
   pseudocode for, 444–446
Domestic exporter strategy, 678, 680
DOS, 212, 318
   MS-, 209, 210, 212
   PC-, 209, 210, 212
Dot matrix printer, 190
Dow Jones News Retrieval, 312, 313
Downsizing, 179
   to smaller computers, 337–339
Downtime, 638–639
   see also Controls
Drill down, 569
DrillDown, 571
DSS. See Decision-support systems
Due process, privacy and, 710
Duplicated systems, for international
      information systems, 680

E

E-mail. See Electronic mail
EBCDIC (Extended Binary Coded
      Decimal Interchange Code),
      166–167, 317
Echo checks, 648
Economic feasibility, in feasibility study
      for systems analysis, 353
Economic theories. See Organization(s)
EDI. See Electronic data interchange
EDIfact, 324, 687
Edit checks, 653, 654
Egyptian Cabinet, 556–557
EIS. See Executive information systems

Electronic accounting machines
      (EAMs), 60
Electronic banking, 64–65, 71, 75, 78,
      105
Electronic calendaring, 523, 526
Electronic data interchange (EDI),
      291–293, 299–300, 324, 327,
      690
Electronic data processing (EDP), 60
Electronic mail (E-mail), 290–291,
      324, 327, 523, 526, 527, 532
Electronic market, 69
Electronic meeting software, 523
Electronic meeting systems (EMS), 136,
      565–567, 568, 569
Electronic questionnaires, 565
Electronic services, 312–313
Electronic spreadsheet software. See
      Spreadsheets
Employment, information systems and,
      726–727
Empowerment, 722
EMS. See Electronic meeting systems
End-user development, 102, 105,
      403–409, 413
   ideas for new systems from, 351
   management benefits and problems
      of, 404–405
   managing, 406–409
      information centers for, 406–407
      policies and procedures for, 407–409
   as new information architecture
      problem, 327
   strengths and limitations of, 403–404
   system design and, 358
   systems life cycle and, 403
   testing process and, 359
   see also Controls; Fourth-generation
      languages
End-user interface, prototyping and,
      393–395
End-user software, 204, 205
   new information architecture and, 312
   see also Fourth-generation languages
Enterprise analysis, for database
      development, 262
Entity, record and, 239
Entity-relationship diagram, 255
Entrepreneurial structure, 93, 94
Environmental factors, information
      systems development and, 106
Environmental instability, 97–98
Environmental scanning, executive
      support systems needing, 572
Environments, of organizations, 97–98
EPRINET, 630–632
EPROM (erasable programmable
      read-only memory), 170
Ergonomics, 494
   computer terminals and, 328
   of meeting room design, 561, 562,
      563
Error-control software, 281
Errors
   ethical, social and political issues
      related to, 701, 702, 720–722
   likelihood of, 645–646
ESS. See Executive support systems
Ethernet, 286

Ethical analysis, 706
Ethical and social issues, 697–733
   accountability and, 704–705
   automation and jobs and, 698–699
   candidate ethical principles and,
      706–707
   code of ethics and, 732
   codes of conduct and, 707–708
   ethical analysis and, 706
   information leaks and, 705
   liability and, 704–705
   model for thinking about, 700–701
   moral dimensions, 702, 709–731
      accountability and control, 701,
         702, 715–720
      information rights and obligations,
         701, 702, 710–712
      property rights, 701, 702,
         712–715, 716
      quality of life, 701, 702, 722–731
      system quality, 701, 702,
         720–722
   real-world, 708–709, 715–717
   responsibility and, 704–705
   trends raising, 702–704
Ethical no free lunch rule, as candidate
      ethical principle, 707
Ethics, 700
   see also Ethical and social issues
European Commission, 326, 675–676
European Economic Community, 676,
      677, 687
European Free Trade Association, 677
Even parity computer, 167
Excel, 570
Execution cycle, of machine cycle, 171,
      172
Executive information systems (EIS),
      569–570
   see also Executive support systems
Executive support systems (ESS), 35,
      36, 39, 40, 41, 61, 568–575
   benefits, 572–573, 574
   changing role of, 569–570
   developing, 570–572
   examples, 50–51, 573–575
      Fidelity Investments, Inc., 574
      New York State Office of General
         Services, 574–575
      Pratt & Whitney, 573–574
   spreadsheets with, 570, 571, 574
   strategy for, 577–578
Exhaustive searching, in artificial
      intelligence, 592
Existence checks, 654
Expert systems. See Artificial
      intelligence
Extended Binary Coded Decimal
      Interchange Code (EBCDIC),
      166–167, 317
External entity symbol, 439, 440
External integration tools, 488, 489

F

Facsimile (FAX), 291
Factory workers, systems building by,
      348, 349

Failure. *See* Systems failure
Fair Information Practices (FIP), 710
Family, information systems and, 723
Fault-tolerant computer systems, 643
FAX, 291
FDDI. *See* Fiber Distributed Data Interface
Feasibility study, for systems analysis, 351–352
Federal Communications Commission, 275, 720
Federal Copyright Act of 1790, 712–713
Federal Telecommunications System (FTS 2000), 325
Feedback, 8
  origin of, 590
Fiber Distributed Data Interface (FDDI), 324, 327
Fiber optic cable
  for communication channel, 277, 280
  standards for, 324, 327
Fields, in computer file, 238–239
Fifth-generation computers, 195
File server, 286
File-sharing, 193
Files. *See* Computer files
Finance/accounting systems, as transaction processing system, 42
Financial Advisor, 600–601
Financial and Management Information System (FAMIS), 574
Financial institutions, new products and services of, 64–66
Financial Manager, The, 528, 529
Financial models (capital budgeting models). *See* Value, of information systems
Financial workstation, 533, 539–540
First generation computers, 172–173
Flat file organization, 240–242
  see also Computer files
Floating point operation, 195
Floppy disks, 183, 184–185
Flowcharts, 448–450, 451, 452
FOCUS, 218
Focused differentiation, as competitive strategy, 62
Forecasting models, 558
Formal information systems, 135
Formal planning tools, for project management, 489–491
Formal systems, 8–9
Format checks, 654
FORTRAN (FORmula TRANslator), 108, 213, 214, 215, 216, 219, 245
Forward chaining, 597, 598
Forward engineering, 460
Fourth generation computers, 173
Fourth-generation languages, 204, 205, 214, 217–222, 228
  application generators, 218, 219
  application software packages, 218, 219
  graphics languages, 218
  information system misuse and abuse and, 642

LOTUS 1-2-3, 214
  management benefits and problems of, 404–405
  private information systems and, 405
  for prototyping, 391
  query languages, 217–218
  report generators, 218
  strengths and limitations of, 403–404
  very-high-level programming languages, 218, 219
  see also End-user development; Microcomputer tools
Foxbase, 221
FoxBase Plus, 253
Frame relay, 289–290
Frames, for expert system knowledge, 596, 597
Franchisers, for international information systems, 678–679, 680
Freedom, moral dimensions of information society and, 701, 702, 710–712
Front-end CASE tools, 455
Front-end processor, 280
FTS 2000 (Federal Telephone System), 325
Full-duplex transmission, 280
Function point analysis, 436
Future, as management challenge, 51
Fuzzy logic, 615–617

G

GADS (Geodata Analysis and Display System), 555
Gantt chart, 489, 490
"Garbage can" model, of decision making, 144, 147
Gateway, 286, 319
GDSS. *See* Group decision-support systems
GE Information Services, 293
Gemms, 688
General controls. *See* Controls
General cultural factors, as global business drivers, 672–673
General Problem Solver, 591
Generalized computing systems, 135
Geodata Analysis and Display System (GADS), 555
Geographic information system software, 226
Germany, service economy in, 7
Gigabyte, 167, 168
Global coordination, as global business driver, 673–674
Global culture, 672–673
Global economies of scale, as global business driver, 674
Global economy
  emergence and strengthening of, 6–7
  as management challenge, 23
Global European Network (GEN), 287–288
Global knowledge base, as global business driver, 672–673

Global markets, as global business driver, 673
Global networks, 686–689
Global production and operation, as global business driver, 673
Global village, global communications creating, 672
Global world order. *See* International information systems
Goals, of organizations, 99
Golden Rule, as candidate ethical principle, 706
Goods industries, 510
Goods workers, 510, 511
Grand Design systems, 485
Graph Plan, 218
Graphical user interfaces (GUIs), 212, 232–233, 393
  Construction Workstation, 456
  for international information systems, 690
  standards for, 325
  testing, 437
Graphics, bit mapping and, 190
Graphics languages, 218
Group decision making, 560–561
  see also Group decision-support systems
Group decision-support systems (GDSS), 560–568
  characteristics of, 561–563
    hardware, 561–562, 563, 565, 569
    people, 561
    software tools, 561, 563–565
  definition, 560–561
  group decision making enhanced by, 567–568
  meeting, 565–567, 568, 569
Group dictionaries, 565
Groupware. *See* Office
GUIs. *See* Graphical user interfaces

H

Hackers, 640–641, 724, 725
Half-duplex transmission, 280
Hard disk pack, 183
Hard disks, 182, 183, 184
Hardware controls, 647, 651
Hardware. *See* Computer hardware
Harvard Graphics, 218
Health risks, of microcomputer revolution, 727, 729–731
Hertz, 279
Heuristic Dendral, 601
Hewlett-Packard Laserjet 4, 190–191
Hierarchial data model, 250–251, 253–254
Hierarchical work groups, 101
High-density diskette, 182
High Performance Computing Act, 731
Higher-level languages, 213–214
Horizontal organization, 114, 115
Host country systems units, 681
Hub Slashing, 601
Human factors, for office automation planning and implementation, 493–494

Human intelligence, artificial
    intelligence versus, 587–589
Human resources, 42, 63
HyperCard, 259–260
Hypercard database, 596
Hypermedia database, 259–260

I

IBM Enterprise/9000 mainframe, 271
IBM Personal Computer, 97, 175
IBM Personal System/2, 44, 98, 170,
    175, 177, 178, 193, 209, 338
IBM System 36 minicomputer, 337
IDSC. *See* Information and Decision
    Support Center
Ignorance, mismanagement due to, 485
Image processing, CD-ROM for,
    186–187
Impact printers, 190
Implementation, 479–494
    approaches to, 479–480
    counterimplementation and, 492
    for decision support systems,
        559–560
    definition, 479
    management and
        ineffective, 484–486
        organizational impact analysis by,
            493–494
        problem areas and, 486–487
        risk control and, 488–491
        support of, 482
        user resistance overcome and,
            491–492
    outcome of, 480–486
        level of complexity/risk and, 481,
            482–484
        management of implementation
            process and, 481, 484–486
        management support and, 481,
            482
        user involvement and interest and,
            481–482
    problem areas in, 486–487
    as stage of decision making, 138,
        139
Implementation controls, 646–647, 651
IMS (Information Management
    System), 250, 254
Inbound logistics, 63
Incremental decision making, 141
Index, to file, 240
Index server, 519
Indexed sequential access method
    (ISAM), 240
Industrial economies, to service
    economies, 6, 7–8
Inference engine, 597, 598
Infonet, 289
Informal information systems, 9
Information, 60–62
    see also Data
Information and Decision Support
    Center (IDSC), 556–557
Information architecture
    development of, 102–104
    as management challenge, 23

of organization, 18–20
    see also New information
        architecture
Information-based economy, 7–8,
    508–510
Information center, 406–407
Information industries, 510
Information leaks, 705
Information Network, 293
Information partnerships, 72–73
Information policy, 262
Information portability, 317
Information requirements, 354
Information rights and obligations, as
    moral dimension of the
    information age, 701, 702,
    710–712
Information system failure. *See* Systems
    failure
Information systems
    behavioral approach to, 21
    building new, 105–106, 345–352,
        see also Systems development
        groups involved in, 348–349
        as organizational change, 346
        origin of ideas for, 351–352
        redesigning business processes and,
            347–348
    business perspective on, 10–13, *see
        also* Management;
        Organization(s); Technology
    business plan link and. *See*
        Information systems plan
    business value of. *See* Value, of
        information systems
    challenges of for managers, 22–24
    changing applications of, 102
    changing management process and.
        See Management
    computer distinct from, 10
    contemporary approaches to,
        20–22
    definition of, 8–10
    functions of, 9
    journals on, 21
    knowledge-level, 13, 14
    management-level, 13, 14–15
    operational-level, 13–14
    reasons for, 6–8
    relationship between organizations
        and, 16–17
    sociotechnical systems approach to,
        21–22
    strategic-level, 13, 15
    symbols used to describe, 32–34
    technical approach to, 20–21
    two-way relationship with
        organizations, 86–87, *see also*
        Organization(s)
    types, 13–15
    see also Systems design
Information systems department, 104,
    105
    ideas for new systems from,
        351–352
Information systems managers, 105
Information systems plan, 372–377
    information requirements for,
        372–377

critical success factors for,
    376–377
    enterprise analysis for, 373–376
Information systems specialists, 104,
    105
Information systems steering
    committee, 349, 350
Information technology
    growing power and declining cost of,
        17
    in publishing companies, 26
Information work
    definition, 510
    new information architecture and,
        313
    productivity and, 512–513
    see also Office
Information workers
    definition, 510
    number of, 509, 512
    productivity of, 512–513
    see also Data workers; Knowledge
        workers; Office
Informational roles, of managers, 132
Inheritance, 223
Input, 8
    symbols for, 32, 33, 34
Input authorization, 652
Input controls, 652–653, 654
Input devices, 188–190
    computer mouse, 188
    of computer system, 164, 165
    source data automation, 189–190,
        199–200
    touch screens, 188, 189
Input metrics, 436
Installation stage, of systems life cycle,
    388, 389, 390
Institutional factors, information
    systems development and, 106
Instruction, of machine cycle, 171
Intangible benefits, of information
    systems, 363–364
Integrated circuits, 173
Integrated Digital Network (IDN), 323
Integrated Services Digital Network
    (ISDN), 323–324, 327
Integrated software packages, 222
Integration, 40–41, 154–157
    for international information
        systems, 686
    as management challenge, 51
Intel 80386 chip, 215
Intel 80486 chip, 173, 174, 194
Intellectual property, rights to, 701,
    702, 712–715, 716
Intellex Legal Information System
    (ILIS), 366
Intelligence, as stage of decision
    making, 138, 139
    see also Artificial intelligence
Intelligent database search machines,
    614–615
Interaction theory, user resistance
    explained with, 492
Interdepartmental work groups, 101
Internal integration tools, for project
    management, 488, 489
Internal primary storage, *See* RAM

System programmers, 205
System quality, as moral dimension of the information age, 701, 702, 720–722
  see also Quality
System residence device, 206
System 7, 210, 211
System software, 168, 204–213
  examples of. *See* Operating systems
  language translation programs and, 204, 205, 208, 209
  operating system, 204, 205–208
    allocation and assignment by, 205
    functions, 205–206
    graphical use interfaces and, 212
    microcomputer, 209–213
    monitoring by, 205, *see also* Security
    multiprocessing and, 208
    multiprogramming and, 206–208
    multitasking and, 207
    scheduling by, 205
    time sharing and, 208
    virtual storage and, 207–208
  utility programs and, 204, 205, 208
Systematic decision makers, 141
Systems analysis, 352–354, 362, 486–487
  application software packages and, 402
  for decision support systems, 559
  feasibility study for, 353–354
  information requirements for, 354
Systems analyst, 104–105
  as change agent, 480, *see also* Implementation
  systems building by, 348, 349, 351
Systems design, 354–358, 362, 487
  alternatives, 356–358
  application software packages and, 402
  decision making and, 139
    individual models, 142–143
    organizational models, 142
  for decision support systems, 559
  end users and, 358
  logical and physical design for, 356
  managerial roles and, 134–135
  organizational factors and, 118
  specifications, 356
Systems development, 352–362
  management of, 349–351
  problems in with poor implementation, 486–487
  production and maintenance, 361–362
  programming, 358–359, 362, 487
  resource allocation during, 435
  testing, 359, 360, 362, 487
  see also Application software packages; End-user development; Outsourcing; Prototyping; *under* Systems
Systems development process, 402
Systems failure, 474–478
  causes of, 478, *see also* Implementation
  problem areas, 475–476, 477
  success, 476, 478

Systems integration. *See* Integration
Systems life cycle, 388–391, 413
  end-user development and, 403
  limitations of, 390–391
  stages of, 388, 389–390
Systems management, for international information systems, 680
Systems Network Architecture (SNA), 687
  network connectivity and, 322, 327
Systems study stage, of systems life cycle, 388, 389
Systems success, measures of, 476, 478
Systems testing, 359

T

Tangible benefits, of information systems, 363, 364
Task forces, 96, 97, 101, 114
TCP/IP (Transmission Control Protocol/Internet Protocol), 338, 687
TeamWorkStation, 538
Technical approach, to information systems, 20–21
Technical feasibility, in feasibility study for systems analysis, 353
Technical Office Protocol (TOP), 321
Technocratic leadership, 99
Technological discontinuity, 98
Technology, 12–13, 63
  strategic information systems leveraging, 72
  as threat to organizations, 98
  see also Computer hardware; Computer software; Storage technology
Technology platform, international information infrastructure and, 672
Technostress, 730
Telecommunciations systems, communcations channels in, 276–280
  characteristics of, 278–280
  coaxial cable, 277, 280
  fiber optic cable, 277, 280
  transmission direction, 280
  transmission modes, 280
  transmission speed of, 279–280
  twisted wire, 276–277, 280
  wireless transmission, 277–278, 279, 280
Telecommunications, 269–301
  competitive advantage through applications of, 290–293
    electronic data interchange, 291–293, 299–300, 324, 327
    electronic mail, 290–291, 324, 327, 523, 526, 527, 532
    facsimile, 291
    multimedia networks, 292
    teleconferencing, 291, 292
    videoconferencing, 291, 292
    voice mail, 291
  computers tied with communications and, 272–273, 275

  connectivity and. *See* New information architecture
  definition, 272
  ethical issues raised by, 704, 731
  for international information systems, 686–689
  management and, 273, 293–296
    implementation and, 294–296
    telecommunications plan, 294
  security and, 295
  standards for, 276, 323–324, 327
  symbols for, 32, 33, 34
Telecommunications networks
  communications processors in, 280–281
  failure of, 296
  local area networks, 281, 285–287, 323
  new information architecture and, 313
  private branch exchange, 283–285, 323
  protocols in, 274, 276
  telecommunications software for, 281
  topologies, 281–283
    bus network, 281, 282
    ring, 282–283, 284
    star network, 281, 282
  value-added networks, 289–290
  vulnerabilities, 640, 641
  wide area networks, 287–289
Telecommunications plan, 294
  implementing, 294–296
Telecommunications software, 281
Telecommunications systems, 273–281
  analog signals in, 276
  components of, 273–274
  definition, 273
  digital signals in, 276
  functions of, 274, 275
  modem in, 276
Teleconferencing, 291, 292
Telenet, 289
Telerate, 539–540
TEMPEST, 663
Teraflop, 195
Terrabyte, 167, 168
Terrestrial microwave systems, 277, 280
Test plan, 359
Testing
  application software packages and, 402
  in installation stage, 390
  problems, with poor implementation, 487
  quality and, 436, 437
  in systems development process, 359, 360, 362
Third-generation computers, 173, 591
"Third World," 673
THOR satellite recovery system, 236–237
Time
  computers and, 167–168
  man-month projecting, 485
Time-based competition, 722
Time sharing, 208

World Pilot Regions, 685
World trade, 674, 675
    see also International information
        systems
World Trade Center, 724
WORM (write once/read many),
    187

X.12, 324, 327
X.25, 324, 327
X.400, 324, 327
X terminal model, of computing, 309,
    310, 311
X Windows, 311, 325

XCON, 600, 601, 605, 620–626
X.desktop, 393

Yield management system, of airlines,
    70, 71, 72

Photo Credits